Raymond Larson

THE
REPUBLIC OF PLATO

THE REPUBLIC OF PLATO

EDITED
WITH CRITICAL NOTES, COMMENTARY
AND APPENDICES

BY

JAMES ADAM

SOMETIME FELLOW AND SENIOR TUTOR
OF EMMANUEL COLLEGE, CAMBRIDGE

SECOND EDITION
WITH AN INTRODUCTION BY

D. A. REES

FELLOW AND TUTOR OF JESUS COLLEGE, OXFORD

VOLUME I

BOOKS I—V

CAMBRIDGE UNIVERSITY PRESS

CAMBRIDGE

LONDON · NEW YORK · MELBOURNE

Published by the Syndics of the Cambridge University Press
The Pitt Building, Trumpington Street, Cambridge CB2 1RP
Bentley House, 200 Euston Road, London NW1 2DB
32 East 57th Street, New York, NY 10022, USA
296 Beaconsfield Parade, Middle Park, Melbourne 3206, Australia

ISBN: 0 521 05963 1

First published 1902
Second edition 1963
Reprinted 1965, 1969, 1975

First printed in Great Britain at the University Press, Cambridge
Reprinted by offset-lithography by Lowe & Brydone (Printers) Ltd,
Thetford, Norfolk

TO

THE MEMORY OF

ROBERT ALEXANDER NEIL

I GRATEFULLY AND AFFECTIONATELY DEDICATE

THIS BOOK

εἰς ἐκεῖνον τὸν βίον, ὅταν αὖθις γενόμενοι τοῖς τοιούτοις ἐντύχωμεν λόγοις.

ἐν οὐρανῷ ἴσως παράδειγμα ἀνάκειται τῷ βουλομενῳ ὁρᾶν καὶ ὁρῶντι ἑαυτον κατοικίζειν.

PREFACE.

THE *Republic* of Plato touches on so many problems of human life and thought, and appeals to so many diverse types of mind and character, that an editor cannot pretend to have exhausted its significance by means of a commentary. In one sense of the term, indeed, there can never be a definitive or final interpretation of the *Republic*: for the *Republic* is one of those few works of genius which have a perennial interest and value for the human race; and in every successive generation those in whom man's inborn passion for ideals is not quenched, will claim the right to interpret the fountain-head of idealism for themselves, in the light of their own experience and needs. But in another sense of the word, every commentator on the *Republic* believes in the possibility of a final and assured interpretation, and it is this belief which is at once the justification and the solace of his labours. Without desiring in any way to supersede that personal apprehension of Platonism through which alone it has power to cleanse and reanimate the individual soul, we cannot too strongly insist that certain particular images and conceptions, to the exclusion of others, were present in the mind of Plato as he wrote. These images, and these conceptions, it is the duty and province of an editor to elucidate, in the first instance, by a patient and laborious study of Plato's style and diction, divesting himself, as far as may be, of every personal prejudice and predilection. The sentiment should then be expounded and explained, wherever possible, by reference to other passages in the *Republic* and the rest of Plato's writings, and afterwards from other Greek authors, particularly those who wrote before or during the lifetime of Plato. The lines of Goethe,

> Wer den Dichter will verstehen
> Muss in Dichters Lande gehen,

apply with peculiar force to the study of the *Republic*, a dialogue which more than any other work of Plato abounds in allusions both implicit and explicit to the history, poetry, art, religion and philosophy of ancient Greece. By such a method of exegesis, provided it is securely based on a careful analysis of the language, we may hope to disentangle in some degree the different threads which are united in Plato's thought, and thus contribute something towards an objective and impersonal interpretation of the *Republic*, as in itself one of the greatest literary and philosophical monuments of any age, and not merely a treasure-house of arguments in support of any school of thought or dogma.

I have done what in me lies to make an edition of the *Republic* in accordance with these principles. Although it has sometimes appeared necessary, for the better exposition of Plato's meaning, to compare or contrast the doctrine of the *Republic* with the views of later writers on philosophy, any systematic attempt to trace the connexion between Platonism and modern political, religious, or philosophical theory is foreign to the scope of this edition. I am far from underestimating the interest and importance of such an enquiry: no intellectual exercise that I know of is more stimulating or suggestive: but it is unfortunately fraught with danger for anyone whose object is merely to interpret Plato's meaning faithfully and without bias. The history of Platonic criticism from Proclus to the present time has shewn that it is difficult for a commentator who is constantly looking for parallels in contemporary thought to maintain the degree of intellectual detachment which the study of Plato's idealism demands; and although it is true that the genius of Plato outsoars the limits of time and place, the best preparation for following its flight is to make ourselves co-heirs with him in his intellectual heritage, and transport ourselves as far as possible into the atmosphere in which he lived. The influence of Plato on succeeding thinkers from Aristotle down to the present day is a subject of extraordinary range and fascination, but it belongs to the history, rather than to the interpretation, of Platonism. If ever that history is fully told, we shall begin to understand the greatness of the debt we owe to Plato, not only in philosophy, but also in religion. In the meantime we can only rejoice that Platonism is still a living force in both: *ἔτι ἥλιος ἐπὶ τοῖς ὄρεσι καὶ οὔπω δέδυκεν.*

One of the most toilsome duties which an editor of the *Republic* has to face is that of reading and digesting the enormous mass of critical and exegetical literature to which the dialogue, particularly during the last century, has given rise. I have endeavoured to discharge this duty, so far as opportunity allowed; and if the labour has sometimes proved tedious and unremunerative, it is none the less true that in some instances the perusal of obscure and half-forgotten pamphlets and articles has furnished the key to what I believe to be the true interpretation. In many other cases, where the thesis which a writer seeks to prove is demonstrably false, the evidence which he accumulates in its support has served to illustrate and enforce a truer and more temperate view. But in spite of all the learning and ingenuity which have been expended on the *Republic* during recent years, there still remain a large number of passages of which no satisfactory explanation has hitherto been offered, and a still larger number which have been only imperfectly and partially explained. I have submitted all these passages to a fresh examination, partly in the Notes and partly in the Appendices, and although I cannot hope to have placed them all beyond the pale of controversy, I have spared no amount of time and labour to discover the truth, and in many cases I have been able to arrive at views which will, I hope, command the assent of others as well as myself. Wherever I have consciously borrowed anything of importance from previous commentators and writers, I have made acknowledgement in the notes; but a word of special gratitude is due to Schneider, to whom I am more indebted than to any other single commentator on the *Republic*. Since I began my task, the long-expected edition of the *Republic* by Jowett and Campbell has made its appearance, and I have found their scholarly and lucid commentary of service even in those places where it has seemed to me inadequate or inconclusive. Professor Burnet's text of the *Republic* was not available until the larger part of this edition had been printed off, but I have been able to make some use of his work in the later books.

I have to thank a number of friends for assistance rendered in various ways, and above all my former teacher, Dr Henry Jackson, of Trinity College, who has read through all the proofs and contributed many corrections and suggestions. Mr Archer-Hind, of Trinity College, and Mr P. Giles, of Emmanuel College, have also helped me with their criticisms on some portions of the work. To Professor J. Cook Wilson, of New College, Oxford,

I owe a special debt of gratitude for undertaking in response to my appeal an exhaustive discussion of the astronomical difficulties in Book X, and unreservedly placing at my disposal the full results of his investigations. It is due to the kindness of Professor Campbell that I have again been able to use Castellani's collations of the Venetian MSS Π and Ξ, as well as Rostagno's collation of Cesenas M. The late Mr Neil, of Pembroke College, to whose memory I have dedicated the work, read and criticised the notes on the first four books before his untimely death, and often discussed with me many questions connected with the interpretation of Plato in general and the *Republic* in particular. Nor can I refrain from mentioning with affectionate gratitude and veneration the name of my beloved friend and teacher, Sir William Geddes, late Principal of the University of Aberdeen, to whose high enthusiasm and encouragement in early days all that I now know of Plato is ultimately due.

The coin which is figured on the title-page is a silver didrachm of Tarentum, dating from the early part of the third century B.C., and now in the British Museum. It represents a naked boy on horseback, galloping and holding a torch behind him: see the description by Mr A. J. Evans in the *Numismatic Chronicle*, Volume IX (1889), Plate VIII 14. I have to thank Mr Barclay V. Head, of the British Museum, for his kindness in sending me a cast of this appropriate emblem of the scene with which the *Republic* opens.

My best thanks are due to the Managers and staff of the University Press for their unremitting courtesy and care.

It is my hope to be able in course of time to complete this edition by publishing the introductory volume to which occasional reference is made throughout the notes. The introductory volume will deal *inter alia* with the MSS and date of composition of the dialogue, and will also include an essay on the style of Plato, together with essays on various subjects connected with the doctrine of the *Republic*.

EMMANUEL COLLEGE,
CAMBRIDGE.
September 5, 1902.

PREFACE TO THE SECOND EDITION.

MY thanks are due to Mr D. A. Rees for kindly writing an introduction to this reprinted edition of my father's *Republic*; also to the Jowett Copyright Trust, and to a friend who desires to remain anonymous, for generous contributions to the cost; and to the Syndics of the Cambridge University Press for so readily undertaking the work.

N. K. ADAM.

SOUTHAMPTON.
April 1962.

CONTENTS OF VOLUME I.

INTRODUCTION.

I. ADAM'S WORK ON THE 'REPUBLIC'

James Adam died on 30 August 1907 at the age of forty-seven. The major part of his scholarly activity had been devoted to Plato, and, apart from his editions of the *Republic*, he had edited, with introduction and commentary, the *Apology* (1887), *Crito* (1888), *Euthyphro* (1890), and (in conjunction with his wife, Mrs Adela Marion Adam) *Protagoras* (1893). His preliminary publications on the *Republic*, alluded to from time to time in the two-volume *editio maior* of 1902, were almost entirely superseded by the latter; they had comprised a monograph, *The Nuptial Number of Plato: its Solution and Significance* (1891), a number of articles in the *Classical Review*,[1] and a text with apparatus (1897), the second edition of which (1909) Mrs Adam brought into conformity with her husband's later views. His further discussion of textual problems will be mentioned below. In addition, he touched on the *Republic* in his posthumously published Gifford Lectures on *The Religious Teachers of Greece*, delivered at Aberdeen in 1904–6 and published in 1908 with an introductory memoir by Mrs Adam, while the preface to Mrs Adam's own *Plato: Moral and Political Ideals* (1913) states: 'In the earlier

[1] These are as follows: 'On Some Passages in Plato's *Republic*' (sc. VII, 516D, 532B, 533C; VIII, 543B, 547B, 559E, 562B; X, 606C), *C.R.* IV (1890), 356–7; 'Mr Adam and Mr Monro on the Nuptial Number of Plato', *ibid.* VI (1892), 240–4 (Adam on pp. 240–2); 'Note on Plato, *Republic* X, 607C', *ibid.* X (1896), 105; 'Plato, *Republic* II, 368A and *Symposium* 174B', *ibid.* pp. 237–9; 'On Some Difficulties in the Platonic Musical Modes', *ibid.* pp. 378–9; 'Four Conjectures on the *Republic*' (sc. *τῆς ἁπλῆς διηγήσεως* at III, 396E, *γυμναστικ⟨ή⟩, ἧς* at III, 407B, *δημιουργουμένη ἔτι. ἤδη δέ* at III, 414D–E, *λεωργούς* at IV, 421B), *ibid.* pp. 384–6; 'Emendations of Plato, *Republic* IX, 580D and III, 390A' (sc. *δευτέραν δὲ ἴδε τήνδε, ἐάν τι δόξῃ εἶναι* and *παρὰ πλεῖαι* (*πλέαι*) *ὦσι τράπεζαι* | *σίτου καὶ κρειῶν κτλ.*), *ibid.* XI (1897), 349–50; 'Plato, *Republic* VII, 529B, C' (reading *νέων*, and referring to Aristoph. *Nub.* 171–3), *ibid.* XIII (1899), 11–12; 'Plato, *Republic* VI, 507D and 507B' (reading *ἓν αὑτοῖς*), *ibid.* pp. 99–100; 'On Plato, *Republic* X, 616E', *ibid.* XV (1901), 391–3, and *ibid.* p. 466, 'A Correction'; 'The Arithmetical Solution of Plato's Number', *ibid.* XVI (1902), 17–23. Adam also reviewed Wohlrab, *Platons Staat* in *C.R.* VIII (1894), 261–2; T. G. Tucker, *The Proem to the Ideal Republic of Plato*, *ibid.* XV (1901), 317–18; and Burnet's text of the *Republic*, *ibid.* XVI (1902), 215–19.

chapters I have made much use of MS. notes for lectures by my husband.' Two essays in *The Vitality of Platonism and Other Essays* (ed. A. M. Adam, 1911) touch upon Plato and, among other works, upon the *Republic*, 'The Vitality of Platonism' and 'The Doctrine of the Celestial Origin of the Soul from Pindar to Plato'; the latter Adam had delivered as a Praelection in his candidature for the Greek chair at Cambridge in 1906, and it had been published in that year in the volume of *Cambridge Praelections*. While, however, these essays still deserve to be read in their own right, besides giving a vivid insight into Adam's general view of Plato, I doubt if they provide contributions to the detailed interpretation of the *Republic* which are not to be found elsewhere.

As is shown by the preface to the edition of 1902, and also by numerous allusions in the commentary, Adam at one time planned an introductory volume, to deal with the manuscripts, date of composition, dramatic date, characters and similar topics. Of this, however, Mrs Adam writes as follows: 'In the original scheme, Adam had intended to write an introductory volume of essays and a translation; but after he had finished the commentary, he became less and less inclined to attack this remaining part of the work. He became interested in other subjects, particularly in the connexion of the Stoics with Christianity, and he felt that he had said nearly all he had to say about the *Republic* in the notes and Appendixes' (*The Religious Teachers of Greece*, p. xlv). Their son, Professor N. K. Adam, of the University of Southampton, tells me that he knows nothing of any remains relating to these schemes, and inquiries I have made in Cambridge have been similarly fruitless.

2. TEXTUAL PROBLEMS

The text of Plato is one of the best preserved that have come down to us from antiquity.[1,2] Nevertheless, various nineteenth-century scholars (who certainly suffered in some degree from an imperfect knowledge of the manuscripts, though this is far from

[1] For certain points in this survey I am indebted to discussions with Mr T. M. Robinson, of Jesus College, Oxford, formerly of the University of Durham. He is in no way responsible for the errors.

[2] For recent work on all aspects of Plato the reader may, here and now, be referred to the vast bibliography by H. F. Cherniss, in vols. IV and V of *Lustrum* (1959–60, published 1960–1).

being an adequate explanation of their speculative urge) indulged in conjectural restorations which were for the most part uncalled for and either certainly mistaken or highly implausible; large numbers are mentioned, only to be rejected, in Adam's commentary, and the student of the present day, when classical scholarship is no longer afflicted with the *cacoethes emendandi*, may well feel it a pity that he found it necessary to devote so much attention to this task—though even an implausible or erroneous conjecture may not infrequently call attention to a real difficulty in the interpretation of the text.

Adam's treatment of the text, already on the conservative side in his edition of 1897, became more markedly so in that of 1902. His general approach to conjectural emendation was one he shared with the edition of Jowett and Campbell, which had appeared in 1894.[1] He shared it also with Burnet, whose edition of the *Republic* in the series of Oxford Classical Texts appeared almost simultaneously with Adam's *editio maior*. The result is that the text Burnet prints differs on the whole very little from that of Adam, the manuscript tradition being what it is; but in their views on the interrelations of the manuscripts and their relative importance they are somewhat at variance. Burnet set out his views both in the preface to his text and in an article on the MS. Vind. F entitled 'A Neglected MS. of Plato', in which he was critical of Adam.[2] Adam, however, maintained his own position forcibly in a review of Burnet.[3] He thought that Burnet overestimated Vind. F, and that he was mistaken in dismissing Ξ and *q* as unworthy of attention; there was reason, he held, 'for thinking that their readings were selected with some care, and that more than one MS. of Plato went to their formation'. Stuart Jones joined in the discussion, using citations from the *Republic* in Galen and Iamblichus (and also in Eusebius and Stobaeus) as showing that Burnet's view of F could not be upheld,[4] but Burnet continued to defend his position.[5]

[1] But Jowett's own essay in vol. II of that work is excessively sceptical of conjectural emendation in general. On the whole the major nineteenth-century editors of the *Republic* were less free with conjectures than other Platonic scholars.

[2] *C.R.* XVI (1902), 98–101.

[3] *Ibid.* pp. 215–19.

[4] H. Stuart Jones, 'The "Ancient Vulgate" of Plato and Vind. F', *C.R.* XVI (1902), 388–91.

[5] 'Vindobonensis F and the Text of Plato', *C.R.* XVII (1903), 12–14; 'Platonica. I', *C.R.* XVIII (1904), 199–204.

Some years afterwards a full study of the manuscripts of Plato was undertaken by H. Alline, who on the whole followed the views of Burnet.[1] Burnet, Alline argued, had shown that in the *Clitophon* and *Republic* Vind. F represented a tradition independent of A and D (Venetus 185, Bekker's and Adam's Π).[2] D (Π), in the *Clitophon* and *Republic*, is independent of A, and the Malatestianus or Cesenas (M) independent of both.[3] Ξ (Venetus 184, Burnet's E) he rejected, like Burnet, as useless.[4] Discussing the family of manuscripts which includes Parisinus A and Venetus T, he concluded that it went back to the ninth century, and was the product of a careful and scholarly recension originating in the circle of Photius.[5] A. C. Clark[6] studied A, D (Π), T and F, concluding that D (Π) was derived from B, but was not a direct copy.[7] He hesitated to draw conclusions about the origin of F.[8]

Other scholars have attempted to argue from our manuscript evidence to the early history of the text. Among these is Immisch,[9] who used the evidence of Proclus on *Rep.* x, 616 E,[10] while E. Deneke devoted a study to Vind. F,[11] which he thought, while not representing a single tradition, to have as its main source a manuscript of the first century B.C. which belonged to Pomponius Atticus. He argued that its text was not of exactly the same provenience in all the dialogues it contains. G. Pasquali, in his general study of the textual criticism of Greek authors, deals among others with Plato,[12] and maintains the existence already in antiquity of a considerable number of variants, perhaps recorded by Aristophanes of Byzantium.[13] G. Jachmann's study of the text of Plato,[14] in some respects similar to that of Pasquali, argues

[1] H. Alline, *Histoire du texte de Platon* (Paris, 1915; Bibliothèque de l'école des hautes études, 218).

[2] *Ibid.* p. 243. [3] *Ibid.* pp. 288–9. [4] *Ibid.* pp. 313–14. [5] *Ibid.* p. 217.

[6] *The Descent of Manuscripts* (1918), pp. 383–417. [7] *Ibid.* pp. 405 ff.

[8] 'Without further knowledge it is impossible to say whether F is substantially independent, or whether it is of vulgar origin, but corrected by means of marginalia derived from an excellent source', *ibid.* p. 415. F has since been examined more closely (see below).

[9] O. Immisch, *Philologische Studien zu Plato. II. De recensionis Platonicae praesidiis atque rationibus* (Leipzig, 1903).

[10] As did later G. Pasquali, *Storia della tradizione e critica del testo* (Florence, 1934), pp. 268–9.

[11] E. Deneke, *De Platonis Dialogorum Libri Vindobonensis F Memoria* (Göttingen, 1922).

[12] Pasquali, *op. cit.* pp. 247–69. [13] *Ibid.* pp. 258–9.

[14] G. Jachmann, *Der Platontext*. Nachrichten v. d. Akad. d. Wiss. in Göttingen, Phil.-hist. Klasse, 1941 [published 1942], pp. 225–389. See H. Langerbeck's critical notice in *Gnomon*, XXII (1950), 375–80. Jachmann deals most fully with the *Phaedo* and *Laches*.

to an Alexandrian edition with critical marks; it is, however, on the bold side in its suggestion of interpolations.

Burnet's view of F is partially, though not entirely, followed by Chambry in the Budé edition.[1] Burnet had based his text on A, D (Π) (supported by M) and F. Chambry's basis consists of A, F and (as far as III, 389 D) T (Marcianus 4. 1, ignored by Adam and Burnet); but of these the third seems to add very little of importance. He discards D (Π) and M. He mentions also four small papyri, all published in the Oxyrhynchus series: (1) III, 455 (third century A.D.), containing III, 406 A–B; (2) III, 456 (second–third centuries A.D.), containing IV, 422 C–D; (3) XV, 1808 (end of second century A.D.), containing fragments of VIII, 546 B–547 D; (4) I, 24 (third century A.D.), containing X, 607 E–608 A. The fourth of these was already known to Adam. None provides anything of importance for the establishment of the text, except by way of general confirmation of the manuscript tradition. There is a further papyrus, also from Oxyrhynchus, unknown when Chambry was preparing his edition and published by A. Vogliano in *Papiri della Regia Università di Milano*, I (1937), where it is no. 10 (p. 16). Dating from the third century A.D., it gives tiny fragments of VI, 485 C–D, 486 B–C; textually it has little or no importance. No further papyri of the *Republic* are listed in R. A. Pack, *The Greek and Latin Literary Texts from Greco-Roman Egypt* (Ann Arbor, 1952), and none has come to my notice otherwise. Further help in the establishment of Plato's text is provided by the quotations in Stobaeus; for these a proper text was provided for the first time by the Wachsmuth-Hense edition (1884–1912), which was incomplete when Adam and Burnet were preparing their texts but is employed in its complete form by Chambry.[2]

Two recent scholars who have been primarily concerned with other works of Plato, E. R. Dodds with the *Gorgias*[3] and R. S. Bluck with the *Meno*,[4] have discussed T and F. Caution is

Compare also E. Bickel, 'Geschichte und Recensio des Platontextes', *Rhein. Mus.* N.F. XCII (1944), 97–159.

[1] So also by Bickel, *op. cit.* p. 144. See also the edn of J. M. Pabon and M. F. Galiano (3 vols., Madrid, 1949).

[2] On Stobaeus' evidence see E. R. Dodds's edition of the *Gorgias* (1959), p. 65, and R. S. Bluck's edition of the *Meno* (1961), p. 146.

[3] See his edition of 1959, and also his earlier article, 'Notes on Some Manuscripts of Plato', *J. Hell. Stud.* LXXVII (1957), 24–30.

[4] See the introduction to his edition (1961).

necessary in drawing conclusions relative to the text of the *Republic*, since a manuscript may not be based on the same source or sources throughout, but Dodds writes that 'in the eighth tetralogy,[1] where T overlaps with A, there are strong reasons for thinking T a copy of A',[2] and that 'full collation of F tends strongly to confirm Deneke's view that it is a direct or almost direct transcript from an uncial MS.'[3] The date of F is uncertain; it may be of the thirteenth century or of the fourteenth.

L. A. Post, *The Vatican Plato and its Relations*,[4] is primarily concerned with Vat. gr. I (O), which contains the *Laws* and some minor works of Plato, but not the *Republic*. The author gives, however, a full list and description of the surviving manuscripts of Plato.[5]

3. SCHOLIA

A thorough edition of the scholia to Plato was provided for the first time by W. C. Greene,[6] with an introduction and notes. The *scholia vetera* on the *Republic*, which are found in A and W, and also, as far as III, 389 D, in T, occupy pp. 187–276; they are on the whole fairly evenly distributed in bulk over the ten books, though there are fewer on Books IV, X and especially IX than on the other seven, and Greene comments 'Scholia ad doctrinam Platonicam pertinentia in Reipublicae libris I, 2, 4, 5, 7, 10 nulla fere inveniuntur' (p. xxvii). Though of some interest, the scholia are scarcely of great importance; Greene investigates their sources in Hesychius, Proclus, a Neoplatonic 'commentarius recens' and elsewhere. They trace, or attempt to trace, allusions, and provide notes on rare words, but their philosophical interest is only slight, even when (e.g.) they comment on the close of Book VI. One may, however, note the comment on V, 473 C–D, which mentions Marcus Aurelius as an example of a philosopher ruler.

[1] And thus in the *Republic*.

[2] *Gorgias*, introd. p. 37.

[3] *Ibid.* p. 45.

[4] Middletown, Connecticut, 1934; Philological Monographs published by the American Philological Association, no. IV.

[5] The most recent study of the manuscript tradition is in the composite volume, *Geschichte der Textüberlieferung der antiken und mittelalterlichen Literatur* (Zürich, 1961), I, 258–62.

[6] *Scholia Platonica*, ed. W. C. Greene (Haverford, Pa., 1938); Philological Monographs published by the American Philological Association, no. VIII. Cf. also W. C. Greene, 'The Platonic Scholia', *Trans. Amer. Philol. Assoc.* LXVIII (1937), 184–96.

4. PLATO'S LANGUAGE

Adam devotes considerable attention to Plato's use of particles, and to the other niceties of his language.[1] Such minutiae had, in fact, been studied intensively by scholars of the later nineteenth century, such as Lewis Campbell, Lutoslawski and Constantin Ritter, but their principal aim had been to use such linguistic materials for determining the relative chronology of the dialogues, whereas Adam's interest was first and foremost in the shades of meaning themselves.[2] The chief aid to the lexicographical study of Plato is still Ast's *Lexicon Platonicum* (1835–8) which has not been superseded,[3] though we have the ninth edition of Liddell and Scott's *Lexicon*, edited by H. Stuart Jones and R. McKenzie (1940), and also from another angle the work of C. D. Buck and W. Petersen, *A Reverse Index of Greek Nouns and Adjectives* (Chicago, 1944). Plato's use of particles can be studied in the general work of J. D. Denniston, *The Greek Particles* (1934; 2nd ed. 1954), while the same scholar notes aspects of Plato's sentence-construction in his posthumously published *Greek Prose Style* (1952). On the other hand, the use of particles in Plato in particular was the subject of a study by E. des Places.[4] To turn to another field, C. Mugler has collected and sifted material of which a not inconsiderable proportion is relevant to Plato in his large *Dictionnaire historique de la terminologie géométrique des Grecs*,[5] while in the field of philosophical terminology the terms εἶδος and ἰδέα have been studied by various scholars: Constantin Ritter devoted a lengthy essay to them,[6] while their pre-Platonic connexions were studied over a wide range of authors by A. E. Taylor,[7] with whose conclusions, however, C. M. Gillespie expressed a considerable measure of disagreement,[8] rightly

[1] There is an extensive bibliography (to 1926) for the study of Plato's style in Überweg-Praechter, *Grundriss der Geschichte der Philosophie*, I. Teil, Philosophie des Altertums (1926), pp. 71*–73*.

[2] A later addition to the stylometric literature is C. Ritter, *Neue Untersuchungen über Platon* (Munich, 1910), esp. pp. 183–227. See also his *Platon*, I (1910), 232–83. Cf. Adam on Lutoslawski in *C.R.* XII (1898), 218–23.

[3] J. Zürcher added the proper names in his *Lexicon Academicum* (Paderborn, 1954).

[4] *Etudes sur quelques particules de liaison chez Platon* (Paris, 1929).

[5] Paris, 2 vols. 1958–9: Etudes et commentaires, XXVIII–XXIX.

[6] *Neue Untersuchungen über Platon* (Munich, 1910), pp. 228–326.

[7] 'The Words εἶδος, ἰδέα in Pre-Platonic Literature', in *Varia Socratica* (Oxford, 1911), pp. 178–267.

[8] 'The Use of εἶδος and ἰδέα in Hippocrates', *Class. Quart.* VI (1912), 179–203. Gillespie thought Taylor had been misled as to Plato by a mistaken view of Pythagorean conceptions.

finding them unduly speculative; a quarter of a century later Plato's own uses of these terms, as also of neuter adjectives employed substantivally, and of the metaphors used to convey the relation of Forms to particulars, were, together with their pre-Platonic antecedents, the subject of an article by H. C. Baldry.[1] In addition, Plato's use of the word *θεῖος* has been the subject of an exhaustive inquiry by J. van Camp and P. Canart,[2] who go through the dialogues in what they take to be their chronological order, studying the occurrences of *θεῖος* in each. They list twenty-three occurrences in the *Republic*, classifying them (like those elsewhere) as 'religious' ('mythological') or as 'hyperbolic'; one of their principal aims is to show the word as expressive of Plato's attitude to the Forms.[3]

5. THE BACKGROUND TO THE 'REPUBLIC'

We must on the whole count it prudent of Adam that he scarcely committed himself at all on the controversial questions of Platonic chronology: on the one hand there remain matters which are still today in dispute, and on the other the whole range of issues was at the beginning of the century in a more fluid state than it is now. The result is that his exposition, though suffering thereby a certain limitation of scope, nowhere depends for its acceptance on the maintenance of some particular chronological scheme, which would in all probability have appeared, both then and now, open to considerable doubt. It may be noted that he adheres tentatively to the view advanced by Henry Jackson[4] against Zeller that the *Republic* is earlier than the *Philebus*;[5] this, however, would now be universally regarded as certain. But the correctness or incorrectness of Adam's more controversial theses of interpretation, as on the objects of mathematical study and the subject-matter of astronomy, or the astronomy of the myth of Er (let alone the 'nuptial number' of Book VIII), will not, I think, be in any way affected by the maintenance of any chronological ordering among the dialogues that is at all plausible.

1 'Plato's "Technical Terms"', *Class. Quart.* XXXI (1937), 141–50.

2 *Le sens du mot θεῖος chez Platon* (Louvain, 1956).

3 *Op. cit.* p. 164 (on *Republic*); pp. 409–23 (general conclusions).

4 'Plato's Later Theory of Ideas, VII. The Supposed Priority of the *Philebus* to the *Republic*', *J. Philol.* XXV (1897), 65–82.

5 Note on Book IX, 583 B ff.

Similarly we need not concern ourselves here with Plato's relations to earlier thinkers, though (to say the least) a proper discussion of the politics of the *Republic* would require a survey of the sophistic movement; of its metaphysics a discussion of Parmenides (to say nothing of Euclides of Megara); of its mathematics, astronomy and harmonics an extended treatment of Pythagoreanism and not least of Philolaus; and of its dialectic some reference to Zeno. All these are, and are likely to remain, highly controversial topics. Adam, we may note, brought out his edition before the appearance of the first edition of Hermann Diels's *Die Fragmente der Vorsokratiker* (1903), which among other things collects together what little there is to be known of Thrasymachus.[1] But for the rest one may, perhaps, simply allude briefly, from among a multitudinous literature, to G. Milhaud, *Les philosophes-géomètres de la Grèce: Platon et ses prédécesseurs*, of which the first edition came out as long ago as 1900 and the second in 1934; to J. Burnet, *Greek Philosophy: From Thales to Plato* (1914), and to E. Frank, *Plato und die sogenannten Pythagoreer* (Halle, 1923), and on the astronomical side to Sir Thomas Heath, *Aristarchus of Samos: the Ancient Copernicus* (1913). The relevant aspects of the history of Greek mathematics are also covered in the first volume of Sir Thomas Heath's great *Greek Mathematics* (2 vols. 1921). But the history of Greek mathematical and scientific ideas has been prosecuted intensively in recent years, through such work as that of Neugebauer, van der Waerden and Sambursky, and it is impossible here to go into details.

We need to say a little, however, about the relation of Socrates to Plato, which has been a matter of unending dispute throughout the nineteenth and twentieth centuries. Adam himself wrote at some length on Socrates in *The Religious Teachers of Greece*,[2] and he had touched on the issue earlier in the introductions to his editions of the *Apology* and *Crito*, while on pp. xxxii–xxxiii of the introduction to his and Mrs Adam's *Protagoras* the form of hedonism attributed to Socrates in that dialogue is regarded as authentic. This deserves to be noted, although there is, I think, nothing in the edition of the *Republic* that turns upon

[1] See now the 6th and 7th editions, edited by W. Kranz (1951–2 and 1954), and K. Oppenheimer, s.v. 'Thrasymachus', in Pauly, *RE* (1936).

[2] Pp. 320–55.

the historical relations of the two thinkers. However, it is clear from *The Religious Teachers of Greece* that Adam attributed to Socrates the view expressed in *Rep.* I, 335 A ff. that the just man will harm no one;[1] he held (rightly) that the *Apology* expressed no clear belief in immortality,[2] but maintained that Socrates was shown by the *Memorabilia* (over and above anything in Plato) to have argued that the universe exhibited evidence of design.[3] It was a few years after Adam's death that the learned world was startled by the simultaneous presentation by A. E. Taylor and John Burnet of the thesis that Plato had in his dialogues recorded the views of the historical Socrates with a far greater degree of fidelity than had hitherto been thought; this occurred in 1911, with the appearance of Burnet's edition of the *Phaedo* and of Taylor's *Varia Socratica,* followed up by various publications of both scholars, such as the former's *Greek Philosophy: From Thales to Plato* (1914) and his lecture on 'The Socratic Doctrine of the Soul',[4] and the latter's *Socrates* (1932). Burnet, indeed, writes of Plato as follows: 'he seems to have been one of those men whose purely intellectual development was late and continued into old age. At first the artistic interest was paramount; the purely philosophical does not gain the upper hand till his artistic gift declined. It is only in certain parts of the *Republic* and the *Phaedrus* that I can detect anything so far that seems to be Platonic rather than Sokratic, and I attribute that exception to the fact that Plato was about to open the Academy. The higher education of the Guardians seems to be a programme of the studies that were to be pursued there...';[5] the Idea of the Good, on the other hand, he assigns to the influence not of Socrates but of Euclides of Megara.[6] However, the view of these two scholars that a major portion of Plato's positive philosophy (in particular the Theory of Forms and the metaphysics of the soul) can be assigned to Socrates has met with very little acceptance; in fact, some recent writers have gone to extreme limits of scepticism as

[1] Pp. 343–4.

[2] Pp. 344–6. On this, see R. Hackforth, *The Composition of Plato's Apology* (Cambridge, 1933), p. 171. Cf. *Apol.* 29 A–B, 40 C ff.

[3] Esp. Xen. *Mem.* I, 4. For a more recent discussion, see W. Theiler, *Zur Geschichte der teleologischen Naturbetrachtung bis auf Aristoteles* (Zürich and Leipzig, 1925), part I.

[4] *Proc. Brit. Acad.* (1915–16); reprinted in J. Burnet, *Essays and Addresses* (London, 1929), pp. 126–62. Cf. his *Platonism* (1928), chs. 2–3.

[5] *From Thales to Plato*, pp. 212–13.

[6] *Ibid.* pp. 230–3.

to the possibility of our saying anything definite about Socrates as a thinker at all.[1] But in any case it would generally (and, surely, rightly) be held that Adam was almost certainly nearer the truth than were Burnet and Taylor.

6. THE THEORY OF FORMS IN THE 'REPUBLIC'

Adam's commentary on the *Republic* shows that on the nature of the Platonic Forms or Ideas he found himself in sharp disagreement with some of the most influential expositions of his day, and in particular with those of Bernard Bosanquet (*A Companion to Plato's Republic*, 1895)[2] and R. L. Nettleship (*Lectures on the Republic of Plato*, posthumous, 1897).[3] Students and admirers as they were of the critical philosophy—the transcendental idealism—of Kant, and of the absolute idealism which had followed it in Germany, and whose most notable representative had been Hegel, they had been led to interpret Plato sympathetically—all too sympathetically—in the light of this. They were, they held, interpreting him as an exponent, albeit a partially imperfect one, of what was necessarily involved in all sound philosophizing. In particular, they tended to see Plato's Forms, after the fashion of Kantian categories, as modes, although indeed inherently necessary modes, of thinking, rather than as radically independent entities subsisting in their own right. The philosopher, it thus appeared, was not engaged in studying another world than that which we saw around us, the world of sensible appearances; his aim was rather to see that same world in a truer and more comprehensive light.[4] Thus, from another angle, the apprehension of Forms was seen as being essentially the discovery of principles of unity running through, and immanent in, the whole of our experience, and was assimilated in one aspect to the formulation of scientific laws by a modern investigator of nature; and (though here we touch on a passage whose interpretation is almost inevitably controversial) this method of interpretation was applied, in a way with which Adam strongly disagreed, to the conception of astronomy in *Republic* VII. (One consequence, which we may note without pausing to dwell on it, was that

[1] O. Gigon, *Sokrates* (Bern, 1947); V. de Magalhães-Vilhena, *Le problème de Socrate* and *Socrate et la légende platonicienne* (Paris, 1952). Cf. C. J. de Vogel, 'The Present State of the Socratic Problem', *Phronesis*, I (1955–6), 26–35.

[2] Esp. pp. 16–17, 123–4, 206, 274–6, 384–5.

[3] Esp. pp. 133, 195, 252–3, 275–6.

[4] Nettleship, *op. cit.* pp. 195, 275–6.

Aristotle's criticism of the Platonic Ideal Theory, as involving a disastrous χωρισμός of Forms from sensible things, and therewith an unnecessary and unacceptable reduplication of the sensible world,[1] had to be rejected as due simply to a radical misunderstanding.)[2] Again, the Hegelian tradition had tended to minimize, or to reinterpret as (in a Platonic sense) mythical the doctrine of the soul as an immortal substance destined to pass through a series of incarnations; and with this there went naturally a similar reinterpretation of the theory that our knowledge was in reality a matter of recollection from a discarnate prior existence.[3]

Nettleship and Bosanquet were not the only scholars of the period to be associated with this tendency. Among German philosophers of the nineteenth century, we have just seen that Hegel refused to take Plato's theory of immortality as literally intended, while Lotze, a generation or more later, had declared the Ideas to be essentially mental entities.[4] But the most notable product of the German neo-Kantian school of Platonic interpretation was one which appeared in the year after Adam's *Republic*, namely the *Platos Ideenlehre* of Natorp (1903),[5] which in this country was in its turn a major influence on J. A. Stewart's work, *Plato's Doctrine of Ideas* (1909).[6] However, Adam himself rejected this line of interpretation in its entirety, as regards Plato's ideal theory,[7] his astronomy, and his doctrine of the soul, and in the main he was undoubtedly right. So far as concerns his view of Plato's conception of the soul, Adam's position is, quite apart from anything to be found in his *Republic*, set out in a sufficiently striking form in his Cambridge Praelection of 1906, alluded to above. If we turn to the interpretation of the astronomy of *Republic* VII,[8] we encounter a more difficult and controversial matter, and one may perhaps suggest, however tentatively, that Plato had not made his position thoroughly

[1] Arist. *Met.* A. 6, 9, M. 4–5. [2] See below, for references to Stewart and Natorp.

[3] Bosanquet, *op. cit.* pp. 403–4; Hegel, *History of Philosophy*, trans. E. S. Haldane and F. H. Simson, II, 32–43.

[4] Quoted by Adam, II, 169–70. It should be remembered, however, that the greatest of nineteenth-century students of Greek philosophy, Eduard Zeller, gave a 'realist' interpretation of the Forms.

[5] Stress was laid on the treatment of ὑποθέσεις in *Phaedo* 99 D ff., as well as in the *Republic*.

[6] For criticisms, see A. Diès, *Autour de Platon*, II (1927), 352–62.

[7] On V, 476 A. Cf. II, 168–70. [8] 527 C–D, 528 D–530 C.

clear even to himself; but some at least of the evidence points in Adam's favour. On the other issues, however, it would generally be agreed today that he was entirely in the right. The general tendency has been in Adam's direction for half a century and more, and it is difficult to believe that his influence was without importance. To take this country, one may mention the names of Burnet and Taylor (of whom the former at least, to judge by his edition of Aristotle's *Ethics* (1900), seems at no stage to have been influenced by the idealistic school of interpretation), to say nothing of more recent scholars; and no doubt something is due also to the decline in the influence of German idealism, and to the rise of 'realist' tendencies in epistemology which followed, quite apart from the drawing of a sharper distinction between questions of philosophical history and questions of philosophical truth. The Cambridge tradition of interpretation, as represented by Henry Jackson and his pupils, of whom more will be said in a moment, had in any case remained unaffected. But in Germany also there was a movement in some ways parallel, sketched for English readers by D. J. Allan in the introduction to his translation of Stenzel's *Plato's Method of Dialectic* (1940). There the significant point, from the philosophical angle, was the decline of the Neo-Kantian epistemology, and, in part at least, the rise of the phenomenological school of Husserl. As evidence one could point to the *magnum opus* of Constantin Ritter, his *Platon*;[1] or to his much briefer *Kerngedanken der platonischen Philosophie* (1931), written at the close of his life, in which he introduced an explicit discussion of Husserl and Meinong;[2] or to Stenzel's treatment of the Platonic Ideas; or, not least, to the interpretation of Plato given by Jaeger in his *Aristoteles* (1923). This last work has a special significance; whatever the final verdict on the details of its interpretation may be (and we are nowhere in sight of any such finality), it brought together the interpretation of Plato and of Aristotle with a greater wealth of relevant detail, above all from Aristotle's dialogues, than any previous study; it saw Aristotle first as Plato's follower and then as his critic, a critic who went on to reformulate the Platonic Idealism in a manner which jettisoned the χωρισμός of the Ideas. Yet again, that

[1] *Op. cit.* II (1923), 318–20.
[2] English trans. by A. Alles, *The Essence of Plato's Philosophy* (1933), pp. 224–9.

criticism was made to appear by no means as unplausibly wide of the mark as at the hands of Natorp and Stewart.[1]

A further point may be briefly noted about Adam's treatment of the Forms, particularly in view of the general tendencies of Platonic scholarship in the Cambridge of his day. A highly distinctive treatment of Plato had been initiated by Henry Jackson in his famous series of articles in the *Journal of Philology* on 'Plato's Later Theory of Ideas'.[2] Jackson (and, following him, Archer-Hind in his edition of the *Timaeus* (1888)) had maintained, not simply that there was a radical new phase of development in Plato's ideal theory in the period subsequent to the *Republic*, but that this took the form of a 'thorough-going idealism'[3] in a modern sense of that term, such as to involve a mentalistic theory of the universe.[4] Evidence for this was drawn not simply from the *Timaeus* but also from such others among dialogues later than the *Republic* as the *Parmenides* and *Philebus*.[5] Adam seems, however, to have remained in large part unconvinced; at any rate, that seems to be the conclusion to be drawn from his discussion of the *Timaeus* in *The Religious Teachers of Greece*, where he insists that that dialogue is fundamentally dualistic.[6] But in any case the limits, on which I have laid stress above, within which he circumscribed himself in his exposition of the argument of the *Republic*, meant that he need not commit himself on such peripheral points of interpretation.

* * *

Since it would be manifestly impossible, within the compass of this short introductory essay, to cover anything approaching the whole range of the *Republic* as surveyed by Adam, I shall confine myself to a brief survey of a few controversial passages in the light of more recent literature. These are: (1) the argument

[1] P. Natorp, *Platos Ideenlehre* (1903), ch. 12; J. A. Stewart, *Plato's Doctrine of Ideas* (1909), pp. 107–18; Idem, *Notes on the Nicomachean Ethics of Aristotle* (1892), I, 70–89 (on *E.N.* I, 6).

[2] The first appeared in the *J. Philol.* X (1882), 253–98.

[3] Jackson in *J. Philol.* XIII (1885), 20 (with the quotation there from Archer-Hind's edition of the *Phaedo* (1st ed. 1883), p. 131). Cf. *ibid.* p. 40. This article (*J. Philol.* XIII (1885), 1–40) is the third in the series, and is on the *Timaeus*.

[4] Other products of the same tradition were A. B. Cook, *The Metaphysical Basis of Plato's Ethics* (1895), and R. K. Gaye, *The Platonic Conception of Immortality and its Connexion with the Theory of Ideas* (1904).

[5] For the *Philebus*, see the first of Jackson's articles referred to above. For the *Parmenides*, see the second of the series (*J. Philol.* XI (1882), 287–331).

[6] *Op. cit.* pp. 360–74, esp. p. 362.

with Thrasymachus in Book I; (2) the imagery of the sun, line and cave (VI, 506D–VII, 518B, with the passage following); (3) the astronomy of Book VII (527C–D, 528D–530C); (4) the 'nuptial number' of VIII, 546A ff.; (5) the myth of Er, and the astronomy of Book X.[1] The treatment even of these must necessarily be inadequate.

7. THRASYMACHUS IN BOOK I

Much has been written about the argument with Thrasymachus, and in particular one may mention the discussions of Barker[2] and of Joseph.[3] A more recent article which throws considerable light on the passage is that of Professor G. B. Kerferd, 'The Doctrine of Thrasymachus in Plato's "Republic"',[4] which has, in addition to its own contribution, a copious apparatus of bibliographical references. Kerferd distinguishes four views which have been attributed to the Thrasymachus of the dialogue, viz. (1) ethical nihilism (that moral obligation has no real existence, but is an illusion in men's minds); (2) legalism (that moral obligation has no existence apart from legal enactment); (3) a theory of natural right (that moral obligation has real independent existence and arises from the nature of man); (4) psychological egoism (that men always do in fact pursue what they think to be their own interests and must from their nature do so).[5] Of these (4) is clearly not strictly an alternative to the other three. Kerferd presents a careful argument[6] for the view that Thrasy-

[1] My choice of passages has been in large part governed by the space Adam devotes to them. In particular, the so-called nuptial number possessed for him (as it has for many scholars) an interest considerably exceeding its importance; indeed, the attention it has received from Aristotle's day to our own must be one of the major curiosities of the world of learning, and one can only hope that on the mathematical side at least a final solution has now been achieved. Greater interest for the study of Plato's philosophy attaches, for instance, to the treatment of the soul in Book IV, studied by F. M. Cornford ('Psychology and Social Structure in the *Republic* of Plato', *Class. Quart.* VI (1912), 246–65, and 'The Division of the Soul', *Hibbert J.* XXVIII (1929–30), 206–19); R. Hackforth ('The Modification of Plan in Plato's *Republic*', *Class. Quart.* VII (1913), 265–72); J. L. Stocks ('Plato and the Tripartite Soul', *Mind*, XXIV (1915), 207–21, reprinted in *The Limits of Purpose* (1932), pp. 166–88); and H. W. B. Joseph in *Essays in Ancient and Modern Philosophy* (1935). The article of R. D. Archer-Hind, 'On Some Difficulties in the Platonic Psychology' (*J. Philol.* X (1882), 120–31), to which Adam alludes, fails, as he seems to realize, to take adequate account of Plato's development.

[2] *Greek Political Theory: Plato and his Predecessors* (1918; 3rd ed. 1947), pp. 155–9.

[3] 'Plato's *Republic*: The Argument with Thrasymachus' in *Essays in Ancient and Modern Philosophy* (1935), pp. 15–40.

[4] *Durham University J.* XL (n.s. IX) (1947–8), 19–27.

[5] Kerferd makes no mention of Adam, whose position seems to come closest to his (3).

[6] *Loc. cit.* p. 22.

machus maintains a single consistent position, and that this is (3), resting his case principally on two passages, of which the first is the rejection of Cleitophon's suggestion at 340 A–B, and the second is 343 C–344 C. An analysis of this latter passage shows that a consistent interpretation is possible on the following basis: that justice consists in securing another's good, and is thus for the ruler the interest of the weaker, for the ruled the interest of the stronger; and that injustice consists in securing one's own good, and is thus for the ruler the interest of the stronger, for the ruled the interest of the weaker.[1] Kerferd goes on to argue[2] that 'it is only if Thrasymachus is setting up some moral ideal other than and opposed to that of justice that his argument becomes intelligible. This ideal is that of injustice, which consists in seeking one's own interest on all occasions.'

Clearly, if justice consists in securing the interest of the stronger, and this is what all rulers pursue and skilful rulers attain, Thrasymachus cannot consistently praise injustice in them as he does. Kerferd's view is thus attractive in itself, but it may be questioned whether he is right in holding it in a form incompatible with position (1), which many scholars have attributed to Thrasymachus. Position (3) as here exemplified, though advancing an ideal for life, allows properly (despite Kerferd) for no conception of moral obligation, and thus in one sense its ideal may thus reasonably be denied to be a moral one. Again, despite the similarity between Thrasymachus' position and that of Callicles in the *Gorgias*, it must be remembered that the latter is formulated in terms of a 'natural right' or 'natural justice' which the conceptual scheme of the former necessarily excludes.[3]

The most recent discussion is that of A. W. H. Adkins in *Merit and Responsibility: A Study in Greek Values* (1960).[4] He sets out the close connexion between the ideals of the Homeric heroes and those of Callicles and Thrasymachus ('Scratch an Agamemnon, and you will find a Thrasymachus'), and displays the confusion engendered in fifth-century Athens by their survival in a more civilized world. This he sees as the background to the moral elenchus of Socrates. 'Callicles and Thrasymachus',

[1] *Loc. cit.* p. 25. [2] *Ibid.* p. 27.

[3] Pl. *Grg.* 482 E–484 C. See the edition of E. R. Dodds (1959), introduction, pp. 14–15.

[4] Pp. 232–58, 266–81.

he writes, 'are immoralists in a sense, but they are in no sense nihilists.'[1,2]

8. THE SUN, LINE AND CAVE

To turn[3] to VI, 506 D–VII, 518 B, it may be helpful to give some references to the extensive literature which has appeared since 1902. The discussions which have been published have been of very unequal value, but the following may be mentioned: P. Natorp, *Platos Ideenlehre* (1903), pp. 183–96; R. G. Bury, in 'Textual Notes on Plato's *Republic*', *C.R.* XVII (1903), 295–6 (p. 296, on 515 B); F. M. Cornford, 'Plato and Orpheus', *C.R.* XVII (1903), 433–45 (esp. pp. 435–41, on the Cave); J. Cook Wilson, 'On the Platonist Doctrine of the *ἀσύμβλητοι ἀριθμοί*', *C.R.* XVIII (1904), 247–60, esp. pp. 257–60 (on the treatment of mathematics in the simile of the line); J. H. Wright, 'The Origin of Plato's Cave', *Harv. Stud. Class. Phil.* XVII (1906), 131–42 (associating Plato's account with a cave at Vari on Hymettos); J. A. Stewart, *Plato's Doctrine of Ideas* (1909), pp. 48–59; J. L. Stocks, 'The Divided Line of Plato, *Rep.* VI', *Class. Quart.* V (1911), 73–88 (reprinted in *The Limits of Purpose* (1932), pp. 189–218); J. Burnet, *Greek Philosophy: from Thales to Plato* (1914), pp. 228–33; J. Souilhé, *La notion platonicienne d'intermédiaire dans la philosophie des dialogues* (1919), pp. 102 ff.; Sir Thomas Heath, *A History of Greek Mathematics* (2 vols. 1921), I, 289–92; A. S. Ferguson, 'Plato's Simile of Light (I. The Similes of the Sun and the Line. II. The Allegory of the Cave)', *Class. Quart.* XV (1921), 131–52; *ibid.* XVI (1922), 15–28; Idem, 'Plato's Simile of Light again', *Class. Quart.* XXVIII (1934), 190–210; H. J. Paton, 'Plato's Theory of *εἰκασία*', *Proc. Aristotelian Soc.* XXII (1921–2), 69–104 (reprinted in *In Defence of Reason* (1951), pp. 255–82); C.

[1] P. 239. [2] See also K. Vretska in *Wiener Studien*, LXXI (1958), 30–45.

[3] A word may perhaps be interposed on the simile of the ill-steered ship at VI, 488 A–489 A, which was the subject of considerable discussion in the late nineteenth century. Adam's general treatment is certainly correct, but may be supplemented by reference to T. D. Seymour, 'On Plato's Ship of Fools' (*C.R.* XVI (1902), 385–8). This takes the same general standpoint, though hesitating about the reading at 488 E (*οἰόμενοι* MSS., followed by Adam; Seymour tentatively suggests *οἰόμενος*. The basic sense is not affected). The discussion was continued by Lewis Campbell, 'On Plato's *Republic*, p. 488' (*ibid.* XVII (1903), 79–80); R. G. Bury, 'Textual Notes on Plato's *Republic*' (*ibid.* 295–6, esp. p. 296, suggesting *ἀμαθίᾳ τῆς κυβερνητικῆς*); H. W. Garrod, 'Two Passages of the *Republic*' (*ibid.* XX (1906), 209–12, esp. 209–10); and Paul Shorey, 'Note on Plato, *Republic*, 488 D' (*ibid.* pp. 247–8). See also K. Vretska in *Wiener Studien*, LXXI (1958), 45–6.

Ritter, *Platon: sein Leben, seine Schriften, seine Lehre* (1923), II, 13–39; A. E. Taylor, *Plato: the Man and his Work* (1926), pp. 285–94; J. Stenzel, *Platon der Erzieher* (1928), ch. 6; P. Frutiger, *Les Mythes de Platon* (1930), pp. 101–5; E. Hoffmann, 'Der pädagogische Gedanke in Platons Höhlengleichnis', *Arch. f. Gesch. d. Phil.* XL (1931), 47–57; F. M. Cornford, 'Mathematics and Dialectic in the *Republic* VI–VII', *Mind*, XLI (1932), 37–52, 173–90; K. von Fritz, 'Platon, Theaetet und die antike Mathematik', *Philologus*, LXXXVII (N.F., Bd. XLI) (1932), 40–62, 136–78, esp. 149–end; L. Stefanini, *Platone* (1932, 3rd ed. 1949), I, 234–7, 248–60; N. R. Murphy, 'The "Simile of Light" in Plato's *Republic*', *Class. Quart.* XXVI (1932), 93–102; Idem, 'Back to the Cave', *Class. Quart.* XXVIII (1934), 211–13; Idem, *The Interpretation of Plato's Republic* (1951), ch. 8; P. Shorey, *What Plato Said* (1933), pp. 230–5; Idem, Introduction to vol. II of edition of the *Republic* (Loeb series, 1935); J. A. Notopoulos, 'The Meaning of εἰκασία in the Divided Line of Plato's *Republic*', *Harv. Stud. Class. Phil.* XLIV (1933), 193–203; Idem, 'Movement in the Divided Line of Plato's *Republic*', *ibid.* XLVII (1936), 57–83; Idem, 'The Symbolism of the Sun and Light in the *Republic* of Plato', *Class. Phil.* XXXIX (1944), 163–72, 223–40; G. M. A. Grube, *Plato's Thought* (1935), pp. 23–8; L. Robin, *Platon* (1935), pp. 109–13; Idem, *Les rapports de l'être et de la connaissance d'après Platon* (posthumous, ed. P.-M. Schuhl, 1957), pp. 9–27 (on the Cave); A. Diès, Introduction to vol. I of the Budé edition of E. Chambry, pp. lx–lxx (Diès also discusses at some length Plato's relation to the mathematics of his day); H. D. P. Lee, 'Geometrical Method and Aristotle's Account of First Principles', *Class. Quart.* XXIX (1935), 113–24; W. F. R. Hardie, *A Study in Plato* (1936), ch. 6 (on the Line); A.-J. Festugière, *Contemplation et vie contemplative selon Platon* (1936), pp. 167–85, 402–7; Th. Nissen, 'Zur Deutung des platonischen Höhlengleichnisses', *Philologus*, XCI (1936), 270–7; J. Moreau, *La construction de l'idéalisme platonicien* (1939), ch. 7; R. Robinson, *Plato's Earlier Dialectic* (1st ed. Ithaca, New York, 1941; 2nd ed. Oxford, 1953), chs. 10 and 11; R. Hackforth, 'Plato's Divided Line and Dialectic', *Class. Quart.* XXXVI (1942), 1–9; G. Brown, G. C. Field and S. S. Orr, 'The Alleged Metaphysics in the *Republic*', *Proc. Aristotelian Soc.* Supp. XIX (1945), 165–229; M. Croiset, *La*

République de Platon (1946), ch. 7; P.-M. Schuhl, *La fabulation platonicienne* (1947), pp. 45 ff. (on the Cave); H. W. B. Joseph, *Knowledge and the Good in Plato's Republic* (posthumous, 1948); E. Hoffmann, *Platon* (Zürich, 1950), esp. pp. 52–87; H. Leisegang, art. 'Platon', in *RE*, XX, 2 (1950), esp. coll. 2460–7; W. D. Ross, *Plato's Theory of Ideas* (1951), ch. 4; R. S. Brumbaugh, 'Plato's Divided Line', *Rev. Metaphysics*, V (1952), 529–34; J. E. Raven, 'Sun, Divided Line and Cave', *Class. Quart.* XLVII (n.s. III) (1953), 22–32; Dorothy Tarrant, 'The Cave and the Sun', *Hibbert J.* LII (1953–4), 360–7; R. S. Brumbaugh, *Plato's Mathematical Imagination* (Bloomington, Indiana, 1954), pp. 91–104 (on the Line); A. Wedberg, *Plato's Philosophy of Mathematics* (Stockholm, 1955), pp. 99–111; J. P. A. Gould, *The Development of Plato's Ethics* (1955), ch. 12; R. Loriaux, *L'être et la forme selon Platon* (Museum Lessianum, Bruges, 1955), pp. 54–103, 206–10; V. Goldschmidt, 'La ligne de la *République* et la classification des sciences', *Rev. Int. Phil.* IX (1955), 237–55; O. Becker, 'Über eine schwer erklärbare Stelle im platonischen Höhlengleichnis', *Rhein. Mus.* N.F. XCIX (1956), 201–5 (on 514B–515A); D. W. Hamlyn, 'Eikasia in Plato's *Republic*', *Phil. Quart.* VIII (1958), 14–23.

In the face of this mass of divergent material one would be bold to hope for a solution satisfying to everyone. What I propose to do is not to give a detailed exposition, but simply to set out certain lines of interpretation which seem to me reasonably sound, prefacing them with an indication of the points where I think Adam's interpretation open to query. The scholars whose work I have found most helpful are Stocks, Ferguson, Robinson and Ross. But two things must be borne in mind: that this passage cannot be adequately considered in dissociation from the account of mathematics and especially of dialectic in Book VII; and that for at least part of the time Plato was dealing with matters which he had not made, and indeed was not in a position to make, fully intelligible to himself.

I said earlier that Adam's treatment of the Platonic Ideas has, as against that of such earlier interpreters as Nettleship, the immense merit of taking seriously their representation as transcendent entities. But in his treatment of the similes he has, I suspect, failed to liberate himself sufficiently from the influence of expositions which had blurred the edge of that distinction, and so draws a less sharp line than one should between the sensible world and the intelligible. This is likely to be true of any interpretation which, starting from the fact that Plato speaks not of two divided lines but of one, infers that he means its sections to represent a progression through four stages.[1] Consonantly with this there follow both the belief that Plato is giving 'an enumeration of the objects of knowledge and opinion',[2] and the attempt to provide what one might call a 'metaphysic of εἰκόνες',[3] supported by references (of questionable value) to what is said about εἰκαστική in the *Sophist* (233 E–236 C, 264 C).[4] The consequences of the theory of a gradual progression do not, however, end here, for it may be suspected that they provide one of the motives for Adam's adoption of the view (now, I think, almost universally abandoned) that the objects of διάνοια are mathematical 'intermediates' to be located between sensible things and Ideas;[5] while again he seems to minimize the sharp gap for Plato between the sensible and the intelligible when he discusses the applicability of mathematics to the sensible world,[6] and, somewhat similarly, when he appears to suggest that the Idea of the Good provides an explanation and justification of the totality of things, i.e. the framework for a kind of theodicy with an impersonal Good in the place of a personal God.[7] It accords, again, with this that he conceives of a correlation of stages between the line and the cave, since the latter depicts the process whereby the imaginary prisoner is liberated and escapes into the light of day.

It will be apparent from this that, if I am correct, the key to a sound interpretation lies in (1) the maintenance throughout of a sharp division between the sensible and intelligible worlds; (2) a proper interpretation of εἰκασία and πίστις; (3) an appreciation of the difference in function between what is said about the line and what is said about the cave.

[1] Vol. II, pp. 156 ff.

[2] P. 158.

[3] Note on 511 E, and also pp. 157–8.

[4] P. 158. Cornford (*C.R.* XVII (1903), 436) is on surer ground in relating that passage to the Cave.

[5] Notes on 510 D, and esp. pp. 159–62. The view has received what is, so far as the *Republic* is concerned, very hesitant support in A. Wedberg, *Plato's Philosophy of Mathematics* (1955), pp. 99–111.

[6] Pp. 162–3.

[7] *Laws*, X, does not, I think, provide anything of direct value for the present passage. Adam recognizes on pp. 173–4 that the dialectician has no concern with sense-perception.

Bearing the first of these points in mind, let us ask in what sense the simile of the sun provides a teleological picture of the world. The passage has in the first instance to be interpreted by itself, though it is true that outside the *Republic* there are two passages in Plato which help to point to a correct view, one earlier than the *Republic* and one later, viz. *Phaedo* 97 B ff. and *Timaeus* 28 A ff. The former is also relevant to the simile of the line in its use of the notion of hypothesis.[1] But the conception of teleological explanation in the *Phaedo* does not go as far as the *Republic*, and neither there nor in the *Timaeus* do we find the Idea of the Good. The Idea of the Good, we are told, stands in relation to the other Ideas as the sun does in relation to the visible and living things around us; as the sun is the source of their life and visibility, so is the Idea of the Good the source both of the existence and of the intelligibility of the Ideas.[2] They derive from it, and are to be understood by reference to it (a point relevant to the understanding of the line). There is no suggestion here that the Idea of the Good provides an explanation—or, rather, either a direct or a complete explanation—of the entire universe, intelligible and sensible alike. That it provides an indirect and partial explanation can be seen from the *Republic* (in particular the simile of the line); and, so far as is possible for dialogues which do not introduce the Idea of the Good, the *Phaedo* and *Timaeus* afford additional clarification. For whatever exists (in its own degree) and is intelligible (in its own degree) in the phenomenal world is such in virtue of its relation to the world of Ideas, and thus indirectly to the Idea of Good itself. This last does not, therefore, provide a complete explanation of everything, but an explanation of things so far as they partake of or imitate the Forms—so far as they are connected with and derive from that higher level of reality, so far also as they are explicable and intelligible, and so far as they exhibit goodness and strive towards it.[3] The *Phaedo*, for its part, emphasizes the part played by the Forms in all genuine explanation, while the teleological cosmology of the *Timaeus* leaves a special place for the surd element of brute necessity.[4]

[1] 100 A ff. One may note also the use made of the metaphor of reflexion at 99 D–100 A.

[2] 508 B ff.

[3] There is an analogue to this at II, 379 B–C.

[4] 47 E ff.

So far the course of interpretation has been relatively uncontroversial, but the same cannot be said of the simile of the line. Here let it be noticed first that the primary division is that between the two lower sections and the two upper, and that, at whatever point this division is made, if Plato's instructions are followed the second and third of the four sub-sections will always be of equal length. With this in mind, let us turn first to the two lower sub-sections, those representing εἰκασία and πίστις, and ask what Plato intended them to show. This is an important point, since it is significant that those who have built their interpretation on the idea of a progression through four stages have tended to find the first of these an embarrassment, of which they have tried to dispose in various ways, as Adam with his extensive class of εἰκόνες and the theory to cover them, or Paton with his cross-reference to the theory of art in Book X, and its discussion of μίμησις.[1] It is instructive that long ago Jowett and Henry Sidgwick,[2] while maintaining the theory of a progression through stages, made those stages three in number and not four, omitting the first as 'of no metaphysical importance' (Sidgwick, p. 102), while in criticism of Sidgwick Henry Jackson wrote: 'It would seem that the introduction of the first segment is unmeaning, and worse than unmeaning, on the assumption that "the universe is compared to a quadripartite line"; and it may therefore be worth while to inquire whether this assumption is necessary or justifiable.'[3] It could scarcely be maintained that Plato meant that there was an initial stage in our mental history when we were aware simply of shadows and reflexions, and that we progressed from that to the perception of physical objects. Nor does the theory become much more plausible if we substitute the conception of a logical progression for that of a temporal: seeing shadows and reflexions is not logically prior to, or simpler than, seeing physical objects. Nor is there any warrant in the text for treating εἰκόνες as representing sense-data in general.

Let us note further Plato's concentration on a single one of the senses, that of sight, and on the optical phenomena of shadows and reflexions.[4] It was likewise of sight and of the visible

[1] H. J. Paton, 'Plato's Theory of εἰκασία'. See above.
[2] H. Sidgwick, 'On a Passage in Plato, *Republic*, B. VI', *J. Philol.* II (1869), 96–103.
[3] H. Jackson, 'On Plato's Republic VI 509 D sqq.', *J. Philol.* X (1882), 132–50, esp. 134.
[4] Nothing is said of echoes. Contrast VII, 515 B.

that he had written in the simile of the sun. The meaning of *εἰκασία* and of *πίστις* is given within, and delimited by, the context in which they occur, and by their reference to each other: the two terms are correlates. For the rendering of *πίστις* I should be inclined to suggest 'perceptual assurance', but that Professor H. H. Price has used the term in another context, and one whose associations it is important to avoid here.[1] Perhaps one may either set aside this association with sense-datum controversies, or else seek to avoid it by speaking of 'perceptual certainty'. *Εἰκασία*, for its part, has the associations both of *εἰκών* and of *εἰκάζειν*: what one here sees is an *εἰκών*, what one does in consequence is *εἰκάζειν*. Ferguson translates appropriately by the term 'indirect observation',[2] and notes that Greek astronomers used reflexions to facilitate their observation of the sun.[3]

In a simile one frequently uses something which is ordinary and familiar as a key to the understanding of something which is not ordinary and familiar. The relevant features of the present simile are that shadows and reflexions derive both their existence and their intelligibility (on both of which counts we are reminded of the simile of the sun) from the objects of which they are shadows and reflexions; on the one hand they derive from and depend on them, and on the other they point to them and are understood by reference thereto. In addition, *σαφήνεια* is correlated with *ἀλήθεια*, which has the dual sense of 'reality' and 'truth',[4] and it came as naturally to Plato as to us to think of a shadow as less real than a physical object.[5] There is, moreover, a further feature which is not mentioned by Plato, but which is both obvious and congenial to his mode of thinking, namely that a single object may give rise to a multiplicity of shadows or reflexions. We cannot be certain that it was present to his mind, but it is at least likely: however, the present argument does not in any case depend on that supposition.

The simile thus clarifies the nature of those other relations which it exhibits as having the same mathematical proportions as *εἰκασία* to *πίστις*: i.e. the relation of the lower section as a

[1] H. H. Price, *Perception* (1932), ch. VII.

[2] *Phil. Quart.* I (1950–1), 19.

[3] *Ibid.*; also Idem, *Class. Quart.* XXVIII (1934), 200. Cf. *Phd.* 99D–100A and *Rep.* 516A–B (and 532B–C).

[4] 508D–511A, 511E. Cf. V, 478C.

[5] Cf. VII, 515A–D.

whole to the upper section as a whole, and, within the upper section, the relation of the third sub-section to the fourth—in other words, the relation of the sensible world to the intelligible, and, within the intelligible world, the relation of διάνοια and its objects to νόησις and its objects. If we ask what the objects of διάνοια are, there is no passage which points unambiguously and necessarily to the theory, held by many scholars in the nineteenth century and accepted by Adam, of mathematical 'intermediates', and it seems decisively ruled out by the language of 510 D. This makes it certain that διάνοια studies Ideas: it differs from νόησις in employing visual aids (diagrams) and in taking ὑποθέσεις as its starting-points without attempting the ascent to an ἀρχή (an ἀνυπόθετον).[1] The brief indications given at the end of Book VI are amplified, so far as νόησις is concerned, by the account of dialectic in Book VII.[2]

I turn now to two further features of the simile which call for comment, viz. the comparative lengths of the four sub-sections, and the fact that Plato envisages not two lines but one. To take the first, it follows from his instructions that the second sub-section and the third will always be of equal length. But what conclusions, if any, are to be drawn from this? It is fatal to any theory which maintains that Plato was primarily concerned, and damaging to any theory which maintains that he was concerned at all, to establish a progression (whether logical or temporal) of four stages of intelligence; his primary concern is with the ratios $AC:CB::AD:DC::CE:EB$ (see Adam's diagrams, vol. II, 65 and 156). On the other hand, Plato makes no positive use of the equivalence of DC to CE; for him that is not a significant but an irrelevant consequence of the rules of construction, significant indeed only in the fact that he does nothing to avoid it. If his primary concern had been to show a progression through four stages, he could have done so by a different method of division, though at the cost of sacrificing the proportions he had set out to show.

A consideration of Plato's view of the relative σαφήνεια of

[1] 510 B ff.

[2] Esp. 532 A–534 D. There is, however, an asymmetry in the structure of the simile, since that would lead one to think, if Plato had not stated the contrary, that the ἀρχή was alone νοητόν. Certainly it is νοητόν, but those Forms which in themselves are objects of διάνοια are also νοητὰ μετ' ἀρχῆς (VI, 511 D).

each section will reinforce what has been said, and also, perhaps, provide a clue for the answer to our second question. The epistemology of the *Republic* makes it clear that each stage after the first will exhibit σαφήνεια in a higher degree than its predecessors, and it may well be for this reason that he provided one line in his simile and not two. It has already been seen that the comparative lengths of the four sub-sections fail to show this, so far as the second and third are concerned, and the point is confirmed by a consideration of VII, 533 D, where Plato writes of διάνοια as a condition ἐναργεστέρου μὲν ἢ δόξης, ἀμυδροτέρου δὲ ἢ ἐπιστήμης. Since δόξα is represented in the simile by the lower section as a whole, embracing the two sub-sections of εἰκασία and πίστις, it is clear that the length assigned to it will be greater than that assigned to διάνοια, while the length of each relatively to the fourth sub-section is left undetermined. In other words, the proportions do not show the mutual relations of δόξα, διάνοια and νόησις (the ἐπιστήμη of 533 D).

In any case, Plato was not greatly interested in comparing πίστις, taken in itself, with διάνοια. πίστις is not to be equated with δόξα; its illustrative character is the key to its proper comprehension. In discussing πίστις, Plato directs his attention not upon δόξα, nor upon sense-perception in general, but upon a single one of the senses, that of sight, which is sufficient for illustrating the relations he is expounding, including that of δόξα to ἐπιστήμη in general.

The Cave, unlike the Line, does exhibit a temporal movement, and this fact is in itself an indication of the dangers inherent in any attempt at a close correlation of the two. That indication is confirmed by the divergences of interpretation among those who have attempted such a correlation. So far as the Cave looks back, it looks back to the Sun as much as to the Line.[1] Plato begins by saying that his concern is περὶ παιδείας καὶ ἀπαιδευσίας, and ἀπαιδευσία is a term applied not so much to a baby whose mind is as yet an almost total blank as to a youth or man who has not been well brought up.[2] The significance of this can be seen if one approaches the interpretation of the Cave from the conclu-

[1] Cf. 517 A–B.

[2] Ferguson, *Class. Quart.* XVI (1922), 15–16; XXVIII (1934), 206–7. Cf. H. W. B. Joseph, *Knowledge and the Good in Plato's Republic* (1948), p. 26, referring to *Grg.* 527 D–E.

sion towards which it is directed, i.e. by beginning with the philosopher's return to the cave and the reception he meets there. Plato's language leaves no doubt that by this return he means a return to practical life; consonantly with this, the inhabitants of the cave will be those men who are in fact to be found engaged in practical, and above all in public, affairs. If so, the state of mind involved in watching the shadows of the cave and attempting to calculate their sequence will be that of men immersed in the calculations of practical and, above all, political life, knowing and caring for nothing of the moral realities of the world of Forms: in 517 D the shams of which Plato is thinking are exemplified by the semblance of justice as it is found in the law-courts,[1] while the rewards of 516 C are found *par excellence* in the 'glittering prizes' of the politician's world.[2] The best commentary on this passage as a whole is to be found in 172 C–177 C of the *Theaetetus*, a dialogue which was probably written not much later, where Plato sharply contrasts the ideals and life of the philosopher with those of the sharp-witted pleader in the law-courts.[3]

It will follow that the ἀπομαντεύεσθαι of 516 D and the γνωματεύειν of 516 E are not to be equated with the εἰκασία of the Line. There is in both an inference based on an imperfect form of apprehension, and Plato may well have intended his readers to note this, but, if the interpretation of εἰκασία given above is correct, the differences are important: the inference of εἰκασία is from shadows to physical objects, whereas that of the prisoners is first and foremost from present shadows to their successors,[4] and unless their gaze is forcibly redirected backwards and upwards it will continue as it is without any consciousness of the imperfection which clings to it.

The function of the images and of their bearers is to produce the succession of shadows. They are simply part of the mechanism of illusion. To quote Cornford: 'A modern Plato would compare his Cave to an underground cinema, where the audience watch the play of shadows thrown by the film passing before a light at their backs. The film itself is only an image of "real"

[1] Cf. περὶ τῶν τοῦ δικαίου σκιῶν. [2] Cf. 520 C–D.

[3] With *Rep.* 519 A compare *Tht.* 173 A and 175 D. See also 175 B–C.

[4] Note, however, ἀγαλμάτων at 517 D. It is important here that the objects are artificial. See below.

things and events in the world outside the cinema. For the film Plato has to substitute the clumsier apparatus of a procession of artificial objects carried on their heads by persons who are merely part of the machinery, providing for the movement of the objects and the sounds whose echo the prisoners hear. The parapet prevents these persons' shadows from being cast on the wall of the Cave.'[1] The objects are artificial because Plato has in mind a show of puppet-shadows—a galanty-show, to use Ferguson's term.[2] Symbolically, their artificiality underlines the unreality of the life and concerns of the prisoners.

Those who think the Cave to be primarily epistemological, and to express (in particular) an interest in the theory of perception,[3] have doubtless been influenced considerably by the language of 517 A–B. There, however, the sun and the δι' ὄψεως φαινομένη ἕδρα mentioned are those in the simile of the sun; in other words, Plato is alluding to their function in illustrating the relation of the realm of δόξα to that of ἐπιστήμη.

But, over and above this function of the references to sense-perception, there has been present throughout a further interest in it of a negative kind, though not an interest in the relation of 'sense-data' to physical objects. Sense-perception does not provide knowledge, as the philosopher is well aware, and the belief that it does is a disastrous error. It is disastrous because the attainment of knowledge is both to be valued in itself and will bring a moral conversion in its train through the vision of the Good; Plato could not imagine that one might become a genuine philosopher and remain a bad man, and it would almost be true to say that, despite the treatment of virtue and vice in Book IV, he had modified rather than abandoned the Socratic equation of virtue with knowledge and of vice with ignorance.[4] The philosopher will thus not simply have seen, but have attained, the moral virtues in the highest and truest sense: this, perhaps, gives part of their point to the phrases about a μακροτέρα ὁδός (περίοδος) which link IV, 435 D with VI, 504 A–B. But, if enlightenment by the vision of the Forms brings moral virtue, vice is associated with

[1] Cornford, *The Republic of Plato* (1941), p. 223 n.

[2] *Class. Quart.* XVI (1922), 16.

[3] For a good example of such a treatment, see L. Robin, *Les rapports de l'être et de la connaissance d'après Platon* (posthumous, 1957).

[4] Perhaps one might allude to X, 619 C.

the realm of the senses. Plato tended to assimilate the sensory and the sensual; each springs from the body, and it is on such vices as gluttony that he concentrates his attention at 519A–B.[1] The philosopher, so far as possible, has freed himself from the body, though the process will only be fully completed at death.[2] This sort of asceticism is found in its most radical form in the *Phaedo*, where Plato has as yet no tripartition of the soul, thinks of pleasure as purely bodily, and finds no place for virtue in the non-philosopher.[3] He has certainly moved some distance in the *Republic*, but perhaps not as far as might appear if one took Book IV as telling the complete story. The conclusion is that Plato was primarily concerned in the Cave with the sphere of the moral, but that it was natural that he should turn to sense-perception to illustrate what he had to say;[4] not simply did it provide an analogue, but, further, though while we were in this world we were inevitably sensory beings, a neglect of anything beyond the senses would be incompatible with the highest excellence and would, unless we were under the control of those who possessed ἐπιστήμη,[5] be incompatible with virtue altogether. Plato's attitude to sense-perception in his astronomy is a matter we shall have to investigate shortly.

A further question which demands an answer is: 'Is there a cave in Plato's ideal state?' On the one hand, it is stated that the philosophers in that state will be called upon to return to the cave;[6] on the other, the picture of the prisoners suggests the world of actual or historical politics, and it is impossible to suppose that in the ideal state the descending philosopher would receive the treatment described at 516E–517A, which is, as Adam remarks, clearly reminiscent of the death of Socrates.[7] It seems necessary to conclude that the exigencies of Plato's description have involved a certain telescoping process, and the cave as depicted does double duty: since comparatively few of the citizens of Callipolis will be philosophers (though they will be as many as are capable of philosophy), there must of necessity be a cave in that state, a cave from which only a minority will

[1] Cf. IX, 586A–B. [2] With 519A–B cf. X, 611B ff.

[3] Cf. 68B ff.

[4] Cf. his attitude to the φιλοθεάμονες and φιλήκοοι of 475–6, grouped as φιλόδοξοι.

[5] Cf., for example, III, 401B ff. [6] 519B ff.

[7] Plato's advice to philosophers in actual states is to be found at VI, 496C–E, and his radical prescription for a new start at VII, 540E–541B.

ever ascend to the light, but the violent, rebellious and anti-philosophical temper of 516E–517A will be absent.

The connexion of the Cave with the Sun and Line finds symbolic expression in the imagery of light and of the sun which runs all through and which provides the climax to the Cave.[1] The basis for that connexion lies in the indissolubility for Plato, already mentioned, of the link between intellectual enlightenment and morality, especially morality in its highest form, and in the consequent need for an intellectual conversion.[2,3]

9. THE ASTRONOMY OF BOOK VII

Adam examines the astronomy of VII, 528D ff. not only in his commentary but also in the appendix 'On the Propaedeutic Studies of the Republic' (II, 163–8). He writes on pp. 166–7: 'The objects which they [*sc.* astronomy and harmonics] investigate are not sensible phenomena, but intelligible realities occupying an intermediate position between sensibles and Ideas, and resembling Ideas much more than they resemble sensibles. Plato's whole conception of these sciences is idealistic....' Reason has been shown above for rejecting the ascription to the *Republic* of a theory of mathematical 'intermediates';[4] but Plato's treatment of the nature and status of astronomy (I shall say little of harmonics)[5] is difficult, and it is easy to see why Adam found that interpretation attractive here. From among the more recent literature the following may be mentioned in particular: Sir Thomas Heath, *Aristarchus of Samos: the Ancient Copernicus* (1913), pp. 134–41; Idem, *Greek Mathematics* (1921), I, 284–6; J. Burnet, *Greek Philosophy: from Thales to Plato* (1914), pp. 222, 225–7; E. Frank, *Plato und die sogenannten Pythagoreer* (Halle (Saale), 1923), esp. pp. 161 ff.; F. M. Cornford, *The*

[1] 516A–B recurs to the imagery of shadows and reflexions.

[2] The possibility of this conversion enables individual men to break into the otherwise closed circle which, but for that, might appear to make moral and intellectual excellence mutually dependent, thus rendering both impossible without the prior existence of the ideal state, and the ideal state impossible of realization *ab initio*. Cf. VI, 496A ff.

[3] The above is not a full account of the three similes. Attention has been confined to certain aspects only.

[4] Esp. II, 166–7.

[5] But see E. Frank, *Plato und die sogenannten Pythagoreer*, pp. 150 ff. The connexion between astronomy and music is of great importance in the history of Greek cosmology (cf. the music of the spheres: see Adam on X, 617B), and derives, as Plato remarks, (530D), from the Pythagorean tradition, but I venture to hope that what I say will not be falsified by this brevity.

Republic of Plato (1941), p. 241; A. S. Ferguson, 'The Platonic Choice of Lives', *Phil. Quart.* 1 (1950–1), 5–34 (esp. pp. 18–23); B. L. van der Waerden, *Science Awakening* (English translation, with additions by the author, Groningen, 1954), pp. 193–4; and a few scattered observations in A. Wedberg, *Plato's Philosophy of Mathematics* (Stockholm, 1955).

The crucial and controverted question is difficult to formulate in exact terms, but it may be stated provisionally (and provisionally only) as the question whether the study Plato envisaged was one which we should think it more proper to call kinematics or astronomy; or, otherwise, whether the actual heavenly bodies or purely 'ideal' bodies formed its subject-matter. To ask whether his subject-matter was physical is to raise questions of the definition of 'physical', questions which become insistent if one remembers Plato's depreciation of the senses and so of the empirical, if verifiability by means of the senses is (as it would ordinarily be taken to be) an indispensable criterion of the empirical. Students of seventeenth-century thought will be reminded of a somewhat, though not entirely, similar difficulty in Descartes' conception of an *a priori* physics, and a cautious comparison of the two would prove illuminating. (A striking difference lies in the completeness of Descartes' confidence in the applicability of mathematics to the world of material objects—but see below.) Perhaps it may be of some help to reformulate our original question as the question whether the Platonic astronomer's subject-matter is universal or particular; but students of Plato know well that to ask this is to raise a hornet's nest of problems about the Theory of Ideas, problems raised from the time of Aristotle onwards.

With the important qualification that he postulates a set of distinct mathematical entities (μαθηματικά), Adam's interpretation is clearly of the 'ideal' type. In putting it forward he cut loose (as in his treatment of the Forms) from the tradition of Bosanquet and Nettleship. He has been followed by the majority of scholars since, the postulation of 'mathematicals' apart, though Burnet and Ferguson have registered their dissent.

Plato treats astronomy as the fourth in a series whose first three members are arithmetic, plane geometry and solid geometry. It is a natural extension of this series to add kinematics as the study of solids in motion (*φορὰν οὖσαν βάθους*, 528 D–E), and it is stated that the method employed in the Platonic astronomy is to be the same as that of geometry.[1] Moreover, both arithmetic and geometry are praised as lifting the mind from the sensible world to purely intelligible entities,[2] which it has already been seen that Plato identified as Forms.[3] Astronomy in its turn is succeeded by harmonics, which Plato treats as a branch of pure mathematics, condemning both a purely empirical approach and such empirically based musical theory as the Pythagorean.[4] The whole sequence leads on to the systematic study of Forms as undertaken by dialectic.[5] Again, the language used at 529 D—*κάλλιστα μὲν ἡγεῖσθαι καὶ ἀκριβέστατα τῶν τοιούτων ἔχειν, τῶν δὲ ἀληθινῶν πολὺ ἐνδεῖν*, by contrast with *τὸ ὂν τάχος* and *ἡ οὖσα βραδύτης*—is, though Forms are probably not in question here,[6] closely reminiscent of that employed at *Phaedo* 74 A–75 B to indicate the relation of particulars to Forms,[7] and the wording of 530 B (*γίγνεσθαί τε ταῦτα ἀεὶ ὡσαύτως καὶ οὐδαμῇ οὐδὲν παραλλάττειν*) serves to underline this resemblance.[8] Further, Plato's mode of expression at 530 B[9] seems incompatible with any suggestion that his true astronomer studies physical objects, but implies that he studies their real movements as distinct from their apparent, which are all that sight can apprehend: what the true astronomer studies is both intelligible as contrasted with visible,[10] and definitely incorporeal.[11] There is here a contrast with the *a priori* rational physics of Descartes, and a contrast also with Aristotle's cosmology, since there is no suggestion here of the latter's sharp cleavage between the celestial world, changeless

[1] *ὥσπερ γεωμετρίαν οὕτω καὶ ἀστρονομίαν μέτιμεν*, 530 B.

[2] Cf. the language used of arithmetic in 524 D–525 A—*ὁλκὸν ἐπὶ τὴν οὐσίαν*, and *τῶν ἀγωγῶν ἂν εἴη καὶ μεταστρεπτικῶν ἐπὶ τὴν τοῦ ὄντος θέαν*—and also what is said of geometry at 527 B.

[3] Cf. perhaps *αὐτῶν τῶν ἀριθμῶν*, 525 D.

[4] 531 C. Cf. Heath, *Greek Mathematics*, I, 286.

[5] 533 A–B.

[6] On this passage see below. Adam, in accordance with his general view of the mathematical sciences of the *Republic*, denies that Forms are involved, though he translates 'essential speed and essential slowness' (II, 128, 186–7).

[7] *ἐνδεῖν, ἐνδεέστερα, ἐνδεεστέρως ἔχειν, ἐλλείπειν*, etc. Cf. also the language used at *Rep.* 523 E on the deficiencies of sense-perception: *καὶ αἱ ἄλλαι αἰσθήσεις ἆρ' οὐκ ἐνδεῶς τὰ τοιαῦτα δηλοῦσιν; παράδειγμα* is here (529 D) used in the sense of 'instance', 'example'; cf. *Phdr.* 262 C–D, *Plt.* 277 D.

[8] Cf., for example, *ἀεὶ κατὰ ταὐτὰ ὡσαύτως ἔχουσαν*, 479 A.

[9] *σῶμά τε ἔχοντα καὶ ὁρώμενα.*

[10] *λόγῳ μὲν καὶ διανοίᾳ ληπτά, ὄψει δ' οὔ*, 529 D; cf. *νοήσει ἀλλ' οὐκ ὄμμασι*, 529 B.

[11] Cf. *τὰ δ' ἐν τῷ οὐρανῷ ἐάσομεν*, 530 B.

apart from circular locomotion, and the sublunary world of becoming.

What can be safely concluded from the above is that, according to the *Republic*, the visible and corporeal heavens are to serve for the astronomer as a stimulus for the study of an intelligible and non-corporeal heaven in which mathematical relations are perfectly and not imperfectly realized. Is his study, then, to be one of pure kinematics? The arguments in favour of that view have been seen already, but it is necessary to see what validity there is in such objections or problems as have been raised by Burnet and Ferguson. I shall examine five such: (1) the meaning of τὸ ὂν τάχος καὶ ἡ οὖσα βραδύτης at 529 D; (2) the meaning of τὰ ἐνόντα at 529 D; (3) the nature of the προβλήματα envisaged at 530 B; (4) the nature of the rejection of a purely observational astronomy at 527 D; (5) the inferences to be drawn from what is said at 530 A about the 'ratio of day and night'.

(1) This phrase is difficult on Adam's interpretation ('essential speed and essential slowness': see above), whether one envisages Forms or μαθηματικά. Burnet[1] translates 'real velocity' (by contrast with apparent), Cornford 'real relative velocities',[2] and this is surely correct; but, as Cornford realized, the following words show that these are thought of as existing in a purely ideal realm. (2) Adam's translations of τὰ ἐνόντα ('the mathematical realities which are in them'[3] and 'that which is essentially in them')[4] were rejected by Burnet, who went so far as to say that 'Adam's interpretation of this passage is sufficiently refuted by the fantastic account he has to give of τὰ ἐνόντα'.[5] He was surely right to take the term to mean the *contents* of the velocity, i.e. of the orbit taken as moving, and it is significant that on this point of translation Heath, in the main a follower of Adam, changed his view under Burnet's influence between his *Aristarchus of Samos*[6] (1913) and his *History of Greek Mathematics*[7] (1921), though continuing to reject Burnet's type of interpreta-

[1] *Greek Philosophy: from Thales to Plato*, p. 226.

[2] Any definite speed is thought of as a mixture of the two opposites, rapidity and slowness, just as any temperature was thought of as a mixture of heat and cold.

[3] Sc. in the 'true stars', II, 128.

[4] Sc., apparently, in essential speed and essential slowness, *ibid.* Cf. also pp. 186–7.

[5] *Greek Philosophy: from Thales to Plato*, p. 227 n. 1.

[6] P. 136.

[7] Vol. I, p. 285.

tion.[1] But the correction, though perhaps serious for Adam's theory of a distinct class of mathematical entities, does not enable one to decide between kinematics and astronomy. (3) Burnet interprets προβλήμασιν...χρώμενοι at 530B to mean that the astronomer is to treat stellar phenomena as problems, but this is a less natural interpretation of the Greek, and the parallel in the treatment of harmonics at 531C is also against him.[2] (4) At 527D Plato characterizes the astronomy he is rejecting as of the purely observational kind employed by farmers, sailors and military commanders. To this there would appear to be two possible alternatives, namely pure kinematics and a theoretical astronomy, such as one might associate with the Pythagorean tradition; in particular, a mathematical astronomy of the kind developed in the Academy and elsewhere in the decades which followed the *Republic*, and associated with such names as those of Heraclides Ponticus, Eudoxus, Callippus, and Aristotle. The general tenor of the passage, however, is against the latter alternative, and so in particular is the parallel of astronomy with harmonics emphasized at 531B, where Plato rejects both the empirical study of sounds and an empirically based musical theory such as the Pythagorean, and resolves harmonic theory into pure mathematics. As for the Academic astronomers, their work can hardly have influenced the *Republic*, and it is natural enough that Plato should not at this date have envisaged with complete clarity the course which the studies of the Academy were destined to take. (5) Ferguson did good service in emphasizing the astronomical interest displayed in the phrase 'the ratio of day and night',[3] which was used in Greek science to denote the latitude of a place, expressed in terms of the ratio of day to night at the solstices.[4] But one cannot build much on this, for the same passage denies the exactitude of an empirically based astronomy; and if one asks what perfect correlate to this imprecise ratio the *Republic* envisages, a sufficiently elaborated kinematics could provide such.

This does, however, bring into prominence the basic difficulty of our passage, which Adam only partially overcame by his

[1] Cornford translates 'the movements that carry round the bodies involved in them'; but see his footnote *ad loc.*

[2] Cf. Heath, *Aristarchus of Samos*, pp. 138–9.

[3] τὴν νυκτὸς πρὸς ἡμέραν ξυμμετρίαν, 530A.

[4] *Phil. Quart.* I (1950–1), 21.

theory of 'mathematicals'—namely that it is impossible to bring this ideal astronomy comfortably within the framework of the Theory of Forms. Perhaps, however, some degree of illumination can be brought if one bears in mind one of the central problems of that Theory. For, in the interpretation of the astronomy, our central problem has been: 'Given that the heavenly bodies and their movements are imperfect and inexact, falling short of the perfection of their intelligible exemplar, is that exemplar particular or universal?' It is easy to see that this is a puzzling question, none the less puzzling if one mentions kinematics. But it is a familiar point that Plato endeavours to combine in his Forms the features of the universal and of the perfect particular—of the standard or ideal specimen, serving as a goal for imitation. The logical problems of self-predication involved are brought sharply into view in the *Parmenides*.[1] In the *Republic* the same duality can be seen both in 478 E ff. and in what is said of the Idea of the Good in the simile of the sun.[2] Here also the relation of the imperfect to the perfect is not fully clear. Historically it is noteworthy that the *Republic* stands between the otherworldly *Phaedo* and the *Timaeus* and *Laws* with their firm interest in physical astronomy.[3,4]

10. THE NUMBER OF VIII, 546 A FF.

Adam devoted much attention to the interpretation of VIII, 546 A ff. In 1891 he published a monograph entitled 'The Nuptial Number of Plato: its Solution and Significance', but he came to disagree with that in part[5] and treated the subject afresh in his *editio maior*. The following more recent discussions may be mentioned: J. Dupuis, 'Le nombre géométrique de Platon (Post scriptum)', *Rev. Et. Gr.* XV (1902), 288–301; P. Tannery, 'Y a-t-il un nombre géométrique de Platon?', *Rev. Et. Gr.* XVI (1903), 173–9;[6] Sir Thomas Heath, *Aristarchus of Samos* (1913), pp. 171–3; Idem, *Greek Mathematics* (2 vols. 1921), I, 305–8; G. Kafka, 'Zu J. Adam's Erklärung der platonischen Zahl',

[1] Cf. esp. G. Vlastos, 'The Third Man Argument in the *Parmenides*', *Phil. Rev.* LXIII (1954), 319–49, and the ensuing discussion.

[2] At 509 A γνῶσις and ἀλήθεια are relegated to the status of being ἀγαθοειδῆ.

[3] The astronomy of the myth of Er has no parallel in any of the earlier myths.

[4] I have been much indebted to discussions with the late Professor Ferguson and with Professor D. J. Allan of Glasgow University. But neither must be held responsible for my errors.

[5] *Ed. maior*, II, 265.

[6] Neither Dupuis nor Tannery shows acquaintance with Adam's edition.

Philologus, LXXIII (1914), 109–21; A. Diès, 'Le nombre nuptial de Platon (Rép. 546 B/C)', *Comptes rendus de l'Acad. des Inscr. et Belles-Lettres* (1933), pp. 228–35; Idem, 'Le nombre de Platon: Essai d'exégèse et d'histoire' (1936), *Mémoires présentés à l'Acad. des Inscr. et Belles-Lettres*, XIV (1940); Idem, note *ad loc.* in the Budé edition of Chambry, vol. III; A. E. Taylor, 'The Decline and Fall of the State in *Republic, VIII*', *Mind*, XLVIII (1939), 23–38 (esp. pp. 23–6); Ivor Thomas, *Greek Mathematical Works*, vol. I: *Thales to Euclid* (1939) (Loeb series), pp. 398–401; Jula Kerschensteiner, *Platon und der Orient* (Stuttgart, 1945), pp. 179–83 (wisely cautious on Oriental connexions); R. S. Brumbaugh, *Plato's Mathematical Imagination* (Bloomington, Indiana, 1954), pp. 107–50; M. Denkinger, 'L'énigme du nombre de Platon et la loi des dispositifs de M. Diès', *Rev. Et. Gr.* LXVIII (1955), 38–76.[1] I have not seen A. G. Laird, *Plato's Geometrical Number and the Comment of Proclus* (Madison, Wisconsin, 1918), but brief accounts of it are to be found in a review by R. G. Bury in *C.R.* XXXIII (1919), 45–6, and in Heath, *Greek Mathematics*, I, 305–6.[2] Perhaps one should mention also the erroneous by-path followed by H. V. Hilprecht in *The Babylonian Expedition of the University of Pennsylvania. Series A. Cuneiform Texts*, vol. XX, part I: 'Mathematical, Metrological, and Chronological Tablets from the Temple Library of Nippur' (Philadelphia, 1906); this is adversely criticized by O. Neugebauer in *The Exact Sciences of Antiquity* (2nd ed. Providence, Rhode Island, 1957), p. 27 (see below).

By far the most important treatment is that of Diès, who follows Adam in part.[3] Hultsch and Adam both held two numbers to be involved, 12,960,000 and 216, but Diès shows that the passage can be interpreted without introducing 216 (Adam's arguments for which are in fact weak), and that the words down to ἀπέφηναν set out one of the ways in which 12,960,000 can be reached. If he is correct, Adam's discussion of 216 as the number of days of gestation of a seven months' child becomes irrelevant. 12,960,000 is reached by a triple multiplication

[1] See too A. Ahlvers, *Zahl und Klang bei Platon* (Bern, 1952) and O. Becker in *Quell. u. Stud. Gesch. d. Math.* Bd. IV (1937–8).

[2] His work is mentioned also by Thomas and Brumbaugh.

[3] He discusses Adam on pp. 117–23 of his *Mémoire* of 1936, which gives a critical and historical survey of the immense literature on the subject down to that date. Brumbaugh, who misreports Adam (p. 149), makes no mention of Diès.

involving four terms,[1] viz. $(3\times4\times5)^4$; otherwise one can express it as $(3\times4\times3)\times(3\times4\times3)\times(5\times4\times5)\times(5\times4\times5)$ or $(4\times3\times4)\times(5\times4\times5)\times(3\times3\times3)\times(5\times4\times5)$. Here $(3\times3\times3)$ is of the form represented by *ὁμοιούντων*, $(3\times4\times5)$ by *ἀνομοιούντων*, $(3\times4\times3)$ by *αὐξόντων* and $(4\times3\times4)$ and $(5\times4\times5)$ by *φθινόντων*. 48, for its part, is 7^2-1 or $\sqrt{50^2}-2$.[2] However much scope may remain for argument on whatever wider implications Plato may have had in mind, it is difficult to believe that the mathematics have not, at long last, been settled. Some important implications do, however, seem clear. If 12,960,000 is the sole number, and is the number of the *ἀνθρώπειον γεννητόν*, it will follow that Plato does not state the number of the *θεῖον γεννητόν*, but merely alludes to it. In that case discussions, as by Adam, of the length of a Great Year and of the world-cycles of *Politicus* 268 E–274 E[3] will at best be only indirectly relevant.[4] The number is geometrical because geometrically constructed,[5] and it governs the principle of good and bad marriages.[6] Diès holds (as have others) that Plato's motive lies in an elaborate playfulness; if he is correct, the passage has less in the way of cosmic import than has often been held, and this conclusion may not be universally acceptable.

Hilprecht (*loc. cit.*) thought it possible to confirm Adam's arguments for 12,960,000 by means of parallels in tablets from the temple library of Nippur; but according to Neugebauer he misinterpreted the Babylonian mathematics, and if so the question of relevance does not arise.[7]

II. THE MYTH OF ER

The last passage which this introduction undertook to discuss was the myth of Er. Not long after the appearance of Adam's *editio maior*, J. A. Stewart published his general study, *The Myths of*

[1] *τρεῖς ἀποστάσεις, τέτταρας δὲ ὅρους*, 546 B.

[2] $5^2+5^2=50$ or, to the nearest square number, 49; here, as in 3–4–5, the line of thought is set by an interest in right-angled triangles; in such the hypotenuse dominates (*δυνάμεναι*), the other sides are dominated (*δυναστευόμεναι*).

[3] Esp. Adam, II, 295–300.

[4] Diès, introd. to Budé edition of the *Politicus* (1935), p. XXX n.

[5] As against Adam, note *ad loc.* and p. 305.

[6] Hence (against Adam) the correctness of the term *γαμικὸς ἀριθμός* in later tradition (Adam on 546 D; Diès (1933), pp. 234–5). Taylor (*loc. cit.* p. 25), who in the main follows Diès, thinks the *ἀνθρώπειον γεννητόν* is the Platonic state.

[7] See also Diès (*Mémoire* of 1936), pp. 137–8, giving further references for this controversy. G. Sarton (*A History of Science. I. Ancient Science through the Golden Age of Greece* (1953), pp. 435–6) follows Hilprecht.

Plato;[1] consonantly with his neo-Kantian interpretation of the Theory of Forms, this conceived the myths as expressing Plato's approach to a higher truth by way of what, with German idealism in mind, he called transcendental feeling.[2] Since then other general studies have been given to the world, and in particular P. Frutiger, *Les mythes de Platon: Etude philosophique et littéraire* (1930).[3] Frutiger distinguishes sharply between what in Plato is and is not myth,[4] and divides myths proper into three types, allegorical, genetic and parascientific, including the eschatological myths under this last head,[5] and treating the myth of Er with those in the *Gorgias*, *Phaedo* and *Phaedrus*. The general characteristics of a Platonic myth he lists as symbolism, freedom of exposition, and a prudent imprecision of thought.[6] P.-M. Schuhl, *La fabulation platonicienne* (1947) is a collection of essays centred about the general theme of the Platonic myth.[7]

For the myth of Er itself the following publications may be noted which are more recent than Adam's commentary: J. A. Stewart, *The Myths of Plato*, pp. 72–3, 133–72; J. L. E. Dreyer, *History of the Planetary Systems from Thales to Kepler* (1906), pp. 56–61; W. D'Arcy Thompson, 'On Plato's "Theory of the Planets", *Republic* X, 616E', *C.R.* XXIV (1910), 137–42; Sir Thomas Heath, *Aristarchus of Samos* (1913), pp. 148–58; P. Duhem, *Le système du monde. Histoire des doctrines cosmologiques de Platon à Copernic*, I (1913), 59–64, 105–6; E. Frank, *Platon und die sogenannten Pythagoreer* (1923), p. 27; R. B. Onians, 'On the Knees of the Gods', *C.R.* XXXVIII (1924), 2–6; Idem, *The Origins of European Thought* (1951; 2nd ed. 1954), pp. 306–8, 332, 403–4; Hilda Richardson, 'The Myth of Er (Plato, *Republic*, 616B)', *Class. Quart.* XX (1926), 113–33; J. Stenzel, *Platon der Erzieher* (Leipzig, 1928), pp. 179–90 (on the ethical import of the myth); A. Rivaud, 'Etudes platoniciennes. I. Le système astronomique de Platon', *Revue d'histoire de la philosophie*, II (1928), 1–26, esp. 8–20; P.-M. Schuhl, 'Autour du fuseau d'Ananké', *Revue archéologique*,

[1] 1905; 2nd ed. with introd. by G. R. Levy, 1960.

[2] It will be readily understood that this is no place for a general discussion.

[3] This has a good general bibliography to its date of publication.

[4] Among passages falsely considered mythical he includes the allegory of the cave (pp. 101–5). He draws a sharp line between allegory and myth.

[5] *Op. cit.* pp. 212 ff.

[6] *Ibid.* p. 36.

[7] Cf. also L. Edelstein, 'The Function of Myth in Plato's Philosophy', *J. Hist. Ideas*, X (1949), 463–81.

5th ser. XXXII (1930), 58–64 (reprinted in *La fabulation platonicienne* (1947), pp. 82–8); F. M. Cornford, *Plato's Cosmology* (1937), pp. 74–6, 87–9, 106; Idem, *The Republic of Plato* (1941), pp. 340 ff.; J. Bidez, *Eos ou Platon et l'Orient* (Brussels, 1945), pp. 43–51 (also Appendix I, 'Les couleurs des planètes dans le mythe d'Er du Livre X de la République de Platon'); Jula Kerschensteiner, *Platon und der Orient* (Stuttgart, 1945), pp. 137–55; A. S. Ferguson, 'The Platonic Choice of Lives', *Phil. Quart.* I (1950–1), 5–34, esp. 19–20; R. S. Brumbaugh, 'Colors of the Hemispheres in Plato's Myth of Er (*Republic* 616E)', *Class. Phil.* XLVI (1951), 173–6; Idem, 'Plato's *Republic* 616E: The Final "Law of Nines"', *ibid.* XLIX (1954), 33–4; Idem, *Plato's Mathematical Imagination* (1954), 161–203; Plato, *Republic*, trans. H. D. P. Lee (1955), appendix, pp. 402–5; J. S. Morrison, 'Parmenides and Er', *J. Hell. Stud.* LXXV (1955), 59–68. There are also brief passing references in A. B. Cook, *Zeus*, II (1925), 44, 54 and 114, and in A. E. Taylor, *A Commentary on Plato's Timaeus* (1928), pp. 161–71.[1] The note by J. Cook Wilson mentioned by Adam as forthcoming in a note on 616B is referred to in the appendix (p. 473) as already published.[2]

This is another passage containing a complex of problems on which agreement is unlikely to be reached. On the astronomy the contributions of Heath and Rivaud are perhaps the most helpful. Stewart[3] and Heath[4] seem to be on the right lines in taking the river of Lethe to be above ground. The symbolism is difficult, not least over the vexed question of ὑποζώματα; probably Heath is right in suggesting that we should not press the details of the comparison very closely.[5] The most important single contribution comes from Stewart, who argued that Plato was envisaging a mechanical model constructed for explaining the planetary motions.[6] Much scope is left for argument even so, but this seems to be the correct basis for interpretation. It has been most fully worked out by Rivaud, and is also followed by (or receives favourable mention from) Heath, Duhem, Cornford and Schuhl. The other main topic of discussion has lain in the

[1] Cf. also F. M. Cornford in *C.R.* XVII (1903), 442 n. 4, and E. G. Schauroth, 'The ὑποζώματα of Greek Ships', *Harv. Stud. Class. Phil.* XXII (1911), 173–9. On the text of 616E see G. Pasquali in *Studi italiani di filologia classica*, XVI (1908), 447–9.

[2] 'Plato, *Republic*, 616E', *C.R.* XVI (1902), 292–3.

[3] *Op. cit.* pp. 154, 168.

[4] *Op. cit.* p. 151.

[5] *Ibid.* p. 152.

[6] *Op. cit.* p. 165.

sources of the myth, on which various theories have been put forward. Hilda Richardson and J. S. Morrison have drawn detailed comparisons with Parmenides; A. B. Cook (followed by Hilda Richardson) thought of Indo-European legends of a sky-god; Onians, Schuhl, Bidez and Jula Kerschensteiner have explored Babylonian and other Oriental affinities (Bidez thinking of Eudoxus as an intermediary). These last affinities are certainly striking, but an amalgam of influences is clearly present.

The above observations have dealt largely with criticisms of Adam. What they show above all is the vast stimulus he has given to Platonic studies, and to the study of the *Republic* in particular. The debt to him continues to be incalculable.

D. A. REES.

JESUS COLLEGE,
OXFORD.
April 1962.

NOTE ON THE TEXT OF THIS EDITION.

THE materials for the text of the *Republic* will be discussed in the introductory volume to this edition: but it is necessary here to make a brief statement of the rules by which I have been guided in the selection of readings, and in the formation of the *apparatus criticus.*

The fundamental principle to which I have endeavoured to conform in the constitution of the text is as follows:—

"*By reason of its age and excellence, Parisinus A is the primary authority for the text of the Republic, but the other* MSS *are valuable for correcting its errors and supplying its omissions*" (*The Republic of Plato,* 1897, p. x).

The MS which stands next in authority to Parisinus A is admitted by all to be Venetus Π; and in those cases where A is wrong, and the right reading occurs in Π, either alone, or, as happens much more frequently, in common with other MSS, I have been content to cite in the *apparatus criticus* merely the authority of Π, adding, of course, the discarded text of A.

In those cases where neither A nor Π can be held to represent what Plato wrote, I have considered, in the first instance, the reading of all the other available MSS; secondly, the evidence of ancient writers who quote or paraphrase parts of the *Republic*; and, thirdly, emendations; but in the critical notes I have as far as possible restricted myself to Venetus Ξ and Monacensis *q*, partly because I have found by experience that they come to the rescue oftenest when A and Π break down, and partly because they are among the few MSS of the *Republic*, besides A and Π, of which we possess thoroughly trustworthy collations. It is difficult to overestimate the debt which Platonic scholarship owes to Bekker, but the accuracy and completeness of his collations leave much to be desired, and it is safest for the present to cite, as far as may be, only those MSS of Bekker in which his work has been revised and supplemented by subsequent collators.

It sometimes, though comparatively seldom, happens that the reading which appears to be correct occurs only in MSS other than A, Π, Ξ or *q*. In such instances, if the reading which I approve is found in Angelicus *v*, I have sought to lighten the *apparatus criticus* by citing that MS only, even where its testimony is supported by that of other MSS. My experience has been that, next to Π, Ξ and *q*, Angelicus *v* is on the whole the most useful of Bekker's MSS for correcting the errors of A.

In the small number of passages where A, Π, Ξ, *q* and *v* appear all to be in error, I have named the other MSS which give the reading selected, confining myself in the first instance to the MSS collated by Bekker, and quoting the MSS of de Furia and Schneider only where Bekker's afford no help. Cesenas M has seldom been cited in the critical notes unless it appears to be the sole authority for the text adopted, but occasional reference is made to it in the commentary.

If the reading in the text is due to an early citation of Plato, or to an emendator, I mention the authority on which it rests. Considerably fewer emendations have been admitted than in my earlier edition, and in this as in other respects the text will be found to be conservative; but there are still some passages where all the MS and other authorities are unsatisfactory, and in these I have printed the emendations of others or my own, when they appear to me either highly probable or right.

In all cases where I have deserted both A and Π in favour of a reading found in Ξ (or *q*), the readings of A, Π and *q* (or Ξ) have also been recorded in the *apparatus criticus*; and when it has been necessary to desert not only A and Π, but also Ξ and *q*, I have given the readings of each of these four MSS for the information of the student.

The upshot of these rules is that unless the *apparatus criticus* states the contrary, the text of this edition follows Parisinus A, and that the value of the other MSS of Bekker, de Furia, and Schneider has been estimated by the assistance which they give whenever A is at fault. I have tried to give a full account[1] of the readings of the great Paris MS, which I collated in 1891, and afterwards examined again in order to settle the few discrepancies between the results of Professor Campbell's collation and my own. The scale of this edition has permitted me to give a tolerably complete record of the traces of double readings in A, so far at least as they point to variants affecting the sense or interpretation, and in such cases the rules by which the *apparatus criticus* is constructed are analogous to those already explained, as will appear from an inspection of the critical notes on 327 A 3, 328 E 34, 330 E 33, 333 E 28 and elsewhere.

It may be convenient to subjoin a table of the MSS cited in the notes, together with the centuries to which they have been assigned, and the authors of the collations which I have used.

[1] I have however as a rule refrained from chronicling in the notes those cases in which I abandon the punctuation, accentuation, breathings, or spelling of A. Questions of orthography are most conveniently treated in a separate discussion, and something will be said on this subject in the Introduction. In the meantime I may be allowed to borrow from my edition of the text a statement of the rules which I have endeavoured to observe in matters orthographical. "As regards the spelling, A^1 preserves several traces of the true Attic orthography, such as ἀποκτείνυμι (for example in 360 C), ὑός and a few others. These I have sedulously preserved. In general I have silently abandoned the spelling of A wherever the evidence of Inscriptions appeared conclusive against it, and sometimes also (though rarely) on other grounds, as for example in φιλόνικος *versus* φιλόνεικος. Otherwise, in doubtful cases, where no sure guidance comes from Inscriptions, such as the addition or omission of ν ἐφελκυστικόν, εὐπαθία *versus* εὐπάθεια and the like, I have invariably aimed at following the practice of the first hand in A. I have also deferred to Inscriptions so far as to exclude those grammatical forms which have conclusively been shewn to be unattic, such as ἔστωσαν (352 A et al.), ψευδέσθωσαν (381 E), εὑρῆσθαι (for ηὑρῆσθαι), and a few others; but when there seems to be some room for doubt, the reading of A has been retained. In general, the cases where it has seemed necessary to abandon A on these and similar grounds are few and insignificant." The orthography of this edition will be found to be in practical agreement with that adopted by Schanz in his *Platonis opera*.

MS		Century	Collator
Parisinus A	(Schneider's Par. A)	IX	Adam
Venetus Π	(„ Ven. C)	XII	Castellani
„ Ξ	(„ Ven. B)	XV	„
Monacensis *q*	(„ Mon. B)	XV	Schneider
Angelicus *v*	(„ Ang. B)	XVI	Bekker
Vaticanus Θ	(„ Vat. B)	XV	Bekker[1]
„ m[2]	(„ Vat. H)	XIII or XIV	„
„ r	(„ Vat. M)	XV	„
Parisinus D[3]	(„ Par. D)	XII or XIII	„
„ K	(„ Par. K)	XV	„
Vindobonensis Φ	(„ Vind. B)	?	Bekker and Schneider
Florentinus A	(Stallbaum's a)	XIV	de Furia
„ B[4]	(„ b)	XIII[5]	„
„ C	(„ c)	XIV[5]	„
„ R	(„ x)	XV	„
„ T	(„ *α*)	XV	„
„ U	(„ *β*)	XIV	„
„ V	(„ *γ*)	XIII	„
Vindobonensis D[6]		?	Schneider
„ E[7]		?	„
„ F		XIV	„
Monacensis C[8]		XV	„
Lobcovicianus		? XIV or earlier	„
Cesenas M		XII or XIII	Rostagno

I hope to say something on the relationship between these MSS in my introductory volume.

[1] I have also recollated this MS for Books I—III of the *Republic*.

[2] From Book II onwards. I owe my information as to the date of this and the following MS to a communication from Dr Mercati.

[3] IV 429 C—442 D is missing.

[4] Contains only I—II 358 E, followed by the rest of II in a later hand.

[5] Flor. B is usually assigned to the twelfth, and Flor. C to the thirteenth, century. The dates here given are due to Dr Guido Biagi, who has been good enough to re-examine at my request these and the other Florentine MSS.

[6] Contains only I—V.

[7] II 379 B—III 399 B is missing.

[8] Contains only VII and X (up to 604 C).

ΠΛΑΤΩΝΟΣ ΠΟΛΙΤΕΙΑ.

ΤΑ ΤΟΥ ΔΙΑΛΟΓΟΥ ΠΡΟΣΩΠΑ.

ΣΩΚΡΑΤΗΣ ΓΛΑΥΚΩΝ ΠΟΛΕΜΑΡΧΟΣ
ΘΡΑΣΥΜΑΧΟΣ ΑΔΕΙΜΑΝΤΟΣ
ΚΕΦΑΛΟΣ

Α.

St. T. II. p. 327 I. Κατέβην χθὲς εἰς Πειραιᾶ μετὰ Γλαύκωνος τοῦ Ἀρίστωνος, προσευξόμενός τε τῇ θεῷ καὶ ἅμα τὴν ἑορτὴν βουλόμενος θεάσασθαι τίνα τρόπον ποιήσουσιν, ἅτε νῦν πρῶτον ἄγοντες. καλὴ μὲν οὖν

3. ἅτε $A^2Π$: ὥστε A^1.

Πλάτωνος Πολιτεία. On the name, characters, and date of action of the dialogue, see *Introd.* §§ 1, 2, 3.

327 A—**328** B *Socrates describes how he visited the Piraeus in company with Glauco, and was induced by Polemarchus and others to defer his return to Athens.*

327 A 1 **κατέβην κτλ.** Dionys. Hal. *de comp. verb.* p. 208 (Reiske) ὁ δὲ Πλάτων, τοὺς ἑαυτοῦ διαλόγους κτενίζων καὶ βοστρυχίζων, καὶ πάντα τρόπον ἀναπλέκων, οὐ διέλιπεν ὀγδοήκοντα γεγονὼς ἔτη. πᾶσι γὰρ δή που τοῖς φιλολόγοις γνώριμα τὰ περὶ τῆς φιλοπονίας τἀνδρὸς ἱστορούμενα, τά τ' ἄλλα, καὶ δὴ καὶ τὰ περὶ τὴν δέλτον ἣν τελευτήσαντος αὐτοῦ λέγουσιν εὑρεθῆναι ποικίλως μετακειμένην τὴν ἀρχὴν τῆς πολιτείας ἔχουσαν τήνδε "κατέβην χθὲς εἰς Πειραιᾶ μετὰ Γλαύκωνος τοῦ Ἀρίστωνος." See also Quint. VIII 6. 64, and Diog. Laert. III 37. The latter gives as his authorities Euphorion and Panaetius. As Cicero was tolerably familiar with the writings of Panaetius, it is possible that he too has the same story in view in *de Sen.* V 13, where he says of Plato "scribens est mortuus." The anecdote may well be true, but does not of course justify any inference as to the date of composition of the *Republic*. See *Introd.* § 4.

2 **τῇ θεῷ.** What goddess? Bendis or Athena? The festival is the Bendideia (354 A) and it is perhaps safest to acquiesce in the usual view that Bendis is here meant. "Alii Minervam intelligunt, quae vulgo ἡ θεὸς appellabatur; neque mihi videtur Socrates in ista Panathenaeorum propinquitate de Minerva veneranda cogitare non potuisse: sed quod simpliciter τὴν ἑορτὴν dicit, numina diversa statuere non sinit" (Schneider). We hear of a temple of Bendis in the Piraeus in 403 B.C. (τὴν ὁδὸν ἣ φέρει πρός τε τὸ ἱερὸν τῆς Μουνυχίας Ἀρτέμιδος καὶ τὸ Βενδίδειον Xen. *Hell.* II 4. 11). See also *Introd.* § 3 and App. I.

3 **νῦν πρῶτον.** Perhaps 410 B.C. *Introd.* § 3.

μοι καὶ ἡ τῶν ἐπιχωρίων πομπὴ ἔδοξεν εἶναι, οὐ μέντοι ἧττον
ἐφαίνετο πρέπειν ἣν οἱ Θρᾷκες ἔπεμπον. προσευξάμενοι δὲ καὶ
θεωρήσαντες | ἀπῇμεν πρὸς τὸ ἄστυ. κατιδὼν οὖν πόρρωθεν ἡμᾶς **B**
οἴκαδε ὡρμημένους Πολέμαρχος ὁ Κεφάλου ἐκέλευσε δραμόντα
τὸν παῖδα περιμεῖναί ἑ κελεῦσαι. καί μου ὄπισθεν ὁ παῖς λαβό-
μενος τοῦ ἱματίου, Κελεύει ὑμᾶς, ἔφη, Πολέμαρχος περιμεῖναι.
καὶ ἐγὼ μετεστράφην τε καὶ ἠρόμην ὅπου αὐτὸς εἴη. Οὗτος, ἔφη,
ὄπισθεν προσέρχεται· ἀλλὰ περιμένετε. Ἀλλὰ περιμενοῦμεν,
ἦ δ᾽ ὃς ὁ Γλαύκων. καὶ ὀλίγῳ ὕστερον ὅ τε Πολέμαρχος | ἧκε **C**
καὶ Ἀδείμαντος ὁ τοῦ Γλαύκωνος ἀδελφὸς καὶ Νικήρατος ὁ Νικίου
καὶ ἄλλοι τινές, ὡς ἀπὸ τῆς πομπῆς. ὁ οὖν Πολέμαρχος ἔφη
Ὦ Σώκρατες, δοκεῖτέ μοι πρὸς ἄστυ ὡρμῆσθαι ὡς ἀπιόντες.
Οὐ γὰρ κακῶς δοξάζεις, ἦν δ᾽ ἐγώ. Ὁρᾷς οὖν ἡμᾶς, ἔφη, ὅσοι
ἐσμέν; Πῶς γὰρ οὔ; Ἢ τοίνυν τούτων, ἔφη, κρείττους γένεσθε
ἢ μένετ᾽ αὐτοῦ. Οὐκοῦν, ἦν δ᾽ ἐγώ, ἔτι ἓν λείπεται, τὸ ἢν
πείσωμεν ὑμᾶς, ὡς χρὴ ἡμᾶς ἀφεῖναι; Ἦ καὶ δύναισθ᾽ ἄν, ἦ δ᾽
ὅς, πεῖσαι μὴ ἀκούοντας; Οὐδαμῶς, ἔφη ὁ Γλαύκων. Ὡς τοίνυν
μὴ ἀκουσομένων, οὕτω διανοεῖσθε. καὶ ὁ Ἀδείμαντος, Ἆρά γε, |
ἦ δ᾽ ὅς, οὐδ᾽ ἴστε ὅτι λαμπὰς ἔσται πρὸς ἑσπέραν ἀφ᾽ ἵππων τῇ **328**
θεῷ; Ἀφ᾽ ἵππων; ἦν δ᾽ ἐγώ· καινόν γε τοῦτο. λαμπάδια ἔχοντες

4. ἡ τῶν A²Π : ἥττων A¹. 18. ἓν λείπεται Ξq et γρ in mg. A²: ἐλλείπεται A¹Π.

---

5 **οἱ Θρᾷκες.** Probably resident aliens (as opposed to the ἐπιχώριοι or natives), living for commercial purposes in the Piraeus, which at all times contained a large admixture of foreign population. It was part of Athenian policy to encourage commercial settlers by allowing them to exercise their own cults (Foucart *des assoc. relig. chez les Grecs* p. 131). Foucart holds that the worship of the Thracian goddess Bendis was brought to the Piraeus by Thracian merchants (p. 84). Others have supposed that οἱ Θρᾷκες refers to envoys from Thrace, or Thracian mercenaries, the survivors of those who came to Athens in 414 B.C. (Thuc. VII 27); but the other view is more probable.

327 B 6 **τὸ ἄστυ** or **ἄστυ** 327 C is regular for Athens itself as opposed to the Piraeus. Hartman would omit the article (cf. Lys. 13. 88 τοὺς ἐν ἄστει οἱ ἐν τῷ Πειραιεῖ): but it occurs infra 328 C, *Phaedr.* 230 C, Arist. *Pol. Ath.* 38. 1 and elsewhere.

10 **αὐτός**: '*ipse*' '*erus*' '*the master*' as often: cf. e.g. *Prot.* 314 D οὐ σχολὴ αὐτῷ and the Pythagorean αὐτὸς ἔφα. With the deictic **οὗτος** cf. *Symp.* 175 A Σωκράτης οὗτος—ἕστηκεν, 'there goes Socrates—standing.'

327 C 18 **ἓν λείπεται.** See *cr. n.* ἐλλείπεται (which Hermann and others retain) is less pointed, in view of the two alternatives ἢ—κρείττους γένεσθε ἢ μένετ' αὐτοῦ. For λείπεται said of the μεταξύ τι (*Symp.* 202 A) or third alternative, cf. *Theaet.* 188 A ἄλλο γ' οὐδὲν λείπεται περὶ ἕκαστον πλὴν εἰδέναι ἢ μὴ εἰδέναι.

20 **ὡς—διανοεῖσθε**: 'well, you may make up your mind that we shall refuse to listen.' Cf. (with Stallbaum) *Crat.* 439 C διανοηθέντες—ὡς ἰόντων ἁπάντων ἀεὶ καὶ ῥεόντων. **μὴ** is owing to the imperative: cf. Soph. *O. C.* 1154 and Jebb's note.

328 A 1 **λαμπὰς κτλ.** λαμπάς was the official name for a torch-race: see Mommsen *Heortologie* pp. 170 *n.*, 282. **τῇ θεῷ**: see on 327 A and App. I.

διαδώσουσιν ἀλλήλοις ἁμιλλώμενοι τοῖς ἵπποις; ἢ πῶς λέγεις;
Οὕτως, ἔφη ὁ Πολέμαρχος· καὶ πρός γε παννυχίδα ποιήσουσιν,
ἣν ἄξιον θεάσασθαι. ἐξαναστησόμεθα γὰρ μετὰ τὸ δεῖπνον καὶ
τὴν παννυχίδα θεασόμεθα καὶ ξυνεσόμεθά τε πολλοῖς τῶν νέων
B αὐτόθι καὶ διαλεξόμεθα. ἀλλὰ μένετε καὶ μὴ | ἄλλως ποιεῖτε.
καὶ ὁ Γλαύκων, Ἔοικεν, ἔφη, μενετέον εἶναι. Ἀλλ' εἰ δοκεῖ, ἦν
δ' ἐγώ, οὕτω χρὴ ποιεῖν.

II. Ἦιμεν οὖν οἴκαδε εἰς τοῦ Πολεμάρχου, καὶ Λυσίαν τε
αὐτόθι κατελάβομεν καὶ Εὐθύδημον, τοὺς τοῦ Πολεμάρχου ἀδελφούς, καὶ δὴ καὶ Θρασύμαχον τὸν Καλχηδόνιον καὶ Χαρμαντίδην
τὸν Παιανιέα καὶ Κλειτοφῶντα τὸν Ἀριστωνύμου· ἦν δ' ἔνδον
καὶ ὁ πατὴρ ὁ τοῦ Πολεμάρχου Κέφαλος. καὶ μάλα πρεσβύτης
C μοι ἔδοξεν εἶναι· διὰ χρόνου | γὰρ καὶ ἑωράκη αὐτόν. καθῆστο

---

2 **λαμπάδια**: Harpocratio remarks *ἣν νῦν ἡμεῖς λαμπάδα καλοῦμεν, οὕτως ὠνόμαζον*. But λαμπάς was used for 'torch' even in classical Greek. Plato chooses λαμπάδιον because he has just used λαμπάς in a different sense.

3 **διαδωσουσιν κτλ.** shews that—except for the novel substitution of mounted competitors for runners—the torch-race in question was of the kind alluded to in Hdt. VIII 98 and elsewhere as held in honour of Hephaestus. The competition was not between one individual and another, but between different lines of competitors, the torch being passed on from man to man. Victory fell to the chain whose torch, still burning, first reached the goal. The well-known figure in *Laws* 776 B *καθάπερ λαμπάδα τὸν βίον παραδιδόντας ἄλλοις ἐξ ἄλλων* refers to the same form of race. Plato nowhere mentions the simpler form described by Pausanias (I 30. 2), in which individuals contended against each other: see Baumeister *Denkmäler d. kl. Altert.* p. 522.

5 **ἄξιον θεάσασθαι.** Songs and dances were the leading features in a *παννυχίς*. See Soph. *Ant.* 1146—1152 and Eur. *Heracl.* 781—783 *ἀνεμόεντι δὲ γᾶς ἐπ' ὄχθῳ* | (the Acropolis) *ὀλολύγματα παννυχίοις ὑπὸ παρθένων ἰακχεῖ ποδῶν κρότοισιν* (in honour of Athena at the Panathenaea).

ἐξαναστήσομεθα κτλ. The promise is nowhere fulfilled.

328 B 7 **μὴ ἄλλως ποιεῖτε.** Schanz (*Novae Comm. Plat.* p. 25) shews that this phrase, which is tolerably frequent in Plato, always occurs in combination with a positive command (here *μένετε*) except in II 369 B.

328 B—**328** E *The scene at the house of Polemarchus. Socrates begins to interrogate Cephalus on the subject of old age.*

328 B 10 **εἰς τοῦ Πολεμάρχου.** Polemarchus was older than Lysias (infra 331 D), and we are to infer that at this time Cephalus lived with him. There is no reason why we should (with Blass *Att. Ber.* p. 338) reject Plato's statement that Polemarchus had a house in the Piraeus: the words of Lysias (12. 16), which Blass relies upon as shewing that Polemarchus lived not in the Piraeus, but in Athens, refer to 404 B.C. and do not prove it even for that year. Lysias probably lived at this time in a house of his own in the Piraeus, as in 404 B.C. (Lys. 12. 8): it is to be noted that he is mentioned along with the visitors, in contrast with Cephalus (*ἦν δ' ἔνδον κτλ.*—*τεθυκὼς γὰρ ἐτύγχανεν ἐν τῇ αὐλῇ* infra C). Cf. Boeckh *Kl. Schr.* IV p. 475 *n.* 1 and Shuckburgh *Lys. Orat.* ed. 2 p. xii.

15 **διὰ χρόνου—αὐτόν.** *καί* 'indeed' goes with the whole clause: cf. Soph. *Ant.* 1253 *ἀλλ' εἰσόμεσθα μή τι καὶ κατάσχετον* | *κρυφῇ καλύπτει καρδίᾳ θυμουμένη* with Jebb's note. Tucker translates 'for it was some time since I had *so much as* seen him'—throwing, I think, too much emphasis on *καί*.

δὲ ἐστεφανωμένος ἐπί τινος προσκεφαλαίου τε καὶ δίφρου· τεθυκὼς γὰρ ἐτύγχανεν ἐν τῇ αὐλῇ. ἐκαθεζόμεθα οὖν παρ' αὐτόν· ἔκειντο γὰρ δίφροι τινὲς αὐτόθι κύκλῳ. εὐθὺς οὖν με ἰδὼν ὁ Κέφαλος ἠσπάζετό τε καὶ εἶπεν Ὦ Σώκρατες, οὐδὲ θαμίζεις ἡμῖν καταβαίνων εἰς τὸν Πειραιᾶ· χρῆν μέντοι. εἰ μὲν γὰρ ἐγὼ ἔτι ἐν δυνάμει ἦν τοῦ ῥᾳδίως πορεύεσθαι πρὸς τὸ ἄστυ, οὐδὲν ἄν σε ἔδει δεῦρο ἰέναι, | ἀλλ' ἡμεῖς ἂν παρὰ σὲ ᾖμεν· νῦν δέ σε χρὴ πυκνότερον D δεῦρο ἰέναι· ὡς εὖ ἴσθι ὅτι ἔμοιγε, ὅσον αἱ ἄλλαι αἱ κατὰ τὸ σῶμα ἡδοναὶ ἀπομαραίνονται, τοσοῦτον αὔξονται αἱ περὶ τοὺς λόγους ἐπιθυμίαι τε καὶ ἡδοναί. μὴ οὖν ἄλλως ποίει, ἀλλὰ τοῖσδέ τε τοῖς νεανίαις ξύνισθι καὶ δεῦρο παρ' ἡμᾶς **φοίτα ὡς παρὰ φίλους τε καὶ πάνυ οἰκείους.** Καὶ μήν, ἦν δ' ἐγώ, ὦ Κέφαλε, χαίρω

26. ὡς παρὰ φίλους τε Π et in mg. A[2]: om. A[1].

---

328 C 16 **προσκεφαλαίου τε καὶ δίφρου**: virtually a hendiadys, as Hartman remarks, comparing Homer *Il.* IX 200 εἷσεν δ' ἐν κλισμοῖσι τάπησί τε πορφυρέοισιν. It is somewhat fanciful to suppose (with Hartman) that Plato throughout this picture was thinking of the aged Nestor seated among his sons (*Od.* III 32 ff.). τινος adds a touch of vagueness: 'a sort of combination of cushion and chair' (Tucker).

τεθυκὼς γάρ explains ἐστεφανωμένος: "coronati sacrificabant, ut satis constat" Stallbaum. The God to whom Cephalus had been sacrificing was doubtless Ζεὺς ἑρκεῖος, whose altar stood in the αὐλή.

19 **οὐδὲ—Πειραιᾶ.** A negative must be supplied, "ut amice expostulabundus cum Socrate senex hoc dicere videatur: tu neque alia facis, quae debebas, neque nostram domum frequentas. Simili ellipsi nostrates: Du kommst *auch* nicht oft zu uns" (Schneider). οὐδέ is 'also not': for exx. see Riddell *Digest of Platonic Idioms* § 141 and Jebb on Soph. *O. C.* 590 f. οὐδέ in οὐδὲ πάνυ ῥᾴδιον IX 587 C is another instance, in which, as here, the idiom has a kind of colloquial effect. Stallbaum takes οὐδέ with θαμίζεις "ne ventitas quidem ad nos, h. e. raro *sane* domum nostram frequentas"; but his equation hardly holds good, and is not justified by Xen. *Symp.* 4. 23. where οὐδέ coheres closely with the emphatic σοῦ. Others have suspected corruption, proposing οὔ τι (Ast, cf. *Od.* V 88 πάρος γε μὲν οὔ τι θαμίζεις), οὐ δέ (Nitzsch), or οὐ δή (Hartman). οὔ τι is very unlikely; for θαμίζω is not exclusively a poetic word (cf. *Laws* 843 B), and we need not suppose that Plato is thinking of Homer. I agree with Hartman that οὐ δέ is improbable: δέ is not sufficiently explained by saying that it is "adversative to the idea contained in ἠσπάζετο" (J. and C., with Schneider *Additamenta* p. 2). None of the cases quoted by Sauppe *Ep. Crit. ad G. Hermannum* p. 77 (Ar. *Knights* 1302, Hdt. IX 108, Theogn. 659, 887, 1070 and Callinus I 2) seem to me to justify the change of οὐδέ to οὐ δέ. Hartman's correction is better: but I believe the text is sound.

328 D 25 **μὴ οὖν κτλ.** To this sentence *Lach.* 181 B C furnishes a near parallel. νεανίαις refers to Socrates' companions who had come from Athens, as opposed to Cephalus, Polemarchus and the others; the emphasis, as often, being on the καί clause: 'associate with these young men, but come and visit us also.' So also Boeckh *Kl. Schr.* IV p. 475. There is no sufficient reason for reading νεανίσκοις (with Π and other MSS): see *Introd.* § 3.

27 **καὶ μὴν κτλ.**: 'Indeed, Cephalus,' etc. γε need not be added (with Π and other MSS) after χαίρω: cf. *Phaed.* 84 D καὶ μήν, ὦ Σώκρατες, τἀληθῆ σοι ἐρῶ, *Euthyd.* 275 E 304 C al., with Jebb on Soph. *O. T.* 749, 1005.

E διαλεγόμενος τοῖς σφόδρα πρεσβύταις. δοκεῖ γάρ | μοι χρῆναι παρ' αὐτῶν πυνθάνεσθαι, ὥσπερ τινὰ ὁδὸν προεληλυθότων, ἣν καὶ ἡμᾶς ἴσως δεήσει πορεύεσθαι, ποία τίς ἐστιν, τραχεῖα καὶ χαλεπή, ἢ ῥᾳδία καὶ εὔπορος· καὶ δὴ καὶ σοῦ ἡδέως ἂν πυθοίμην, ὅ τί σοι φαίνεται τοῦτο, ἐπειδὴ ἐνταῦθα ἤδη εἶ τῆς ἡλικίας, ὃ δὴ ἐπὶ γήραος οὐδῷ φασὶν εἶναι οἱ ποιηταί, πότερον χαλεπὸν τοῦ βίου ἢ πῶς σὺ αὐτὸ ἐξαγγέλλεις.

329 III. Ἐγώ σοι, ἔφη, νὴ τὸν Δία ἐρῶ, ὦ Σώκρατες, | οἷόν γέ μοι φαίνεται. πολλάκις γὰρ συνερχόμεθά τινες εἰς ταὐτὸ παραπλησίαν ἡλικίαν ἔχοντες, διασῴζοντες τὴν παλαιὰν παροιμίαν. οἱ οὖν πλεῖστοι ἡμῶν ὀλοφύρονται ξυνιόντες, τὰς ἐν τῇ νεότητι ἡδονὰς ποθοῦντες καὶ ἀναμιμνῃσκόμενοι περί τε τἀφροδίσια καὶ περὶ πότους καὶ εὐωχίας καὶ ἄλλ' ἄττα ἃ τῶν τοιούτων ἔχεται, καὶ ἀγανακτοῦσιν ὡς μεγάλων τινῶν ἀπεστερημένοι καὶ τότε μὲν εὖ
B ζῶντες, νῦν δὲ οὐδὲ ζῶντες. ἔνιοι δὲ καὶ τὰς τῶν | οἰκείων προπη-

34. αὐτὸ A[1]Π : αὐτὸς A[2].

---

328 E 30 **τραχεῖα καὶ χαλεπή κτλ.** The language (as Ast observes) is perhaps suggested by Hesiod *OD.* 290 ff. μακρὸς δὲ καὶ ὄρθιος οἶμος ἐς αὐτὴν | καὶ τρηχὺς τὸ πρῶτον· ἐπὴν δ' εἰς ἄκρον ἵκηται, | ῥηιδίη δὴ ἔπειτα πέλει, χαλεπή περ ἐοῦσα. Cf. II 364 D *n.*

33 **ἐπὶ γήραος οὐδῷ.** The phrase occurs first in the *Iliad* (XXII 60, XXIV 487) to denote the natural limit of the life of man. Cephalus is μάλα πρεσβύτης 328 B. The same meaning suits also in *Od.* XV 246 (οὐδ' ἵκετο γήραος οὐδόν) 348 and XXIII 212, *Hymn. Aphr.* 106, Hes. *OD.* 331, Hdt. III 14 and elsewhere. Leaf can hardly (I think) be right in explaining οὐδῷ as = ὁδῷ in *Il.* XXII 60. γήραος is a descriptive genitive (like τέλος γήραος ἀργαλέου Mimn. *Fr.* 2. 6, τοῦ λόγου in δόλιχον—not δολιχὸν—τοῦ λόγου *Prot.* 329 A), old age being itself the threshold by which we leave the House of Life. We enter as it were by one door and pass out by another. The idea underlying the phrase may be compared with Democritus' ὁ κόσμος σκηνή, ὁ βίος πάροδος· ἦλθες, εἶδες, ἀπῆλθες (Mullach *Fr. Phil. Gr.* I p. 356).

χαλεπὸν κτλ. χαλεπόν is neuter on account of τοῦτο in ὅ τί σοι φαίνεται τοῦτο, and τοῦ βίου is a simple partitive genitive: cf. Xen. *Mem.* I 6. 4 ἐπισκεψώμεθα τί χαλεπὸν ᾔσθησαι τοὐμοῦ βίου. I cannot agree with Tucker in rendering 'disagreeable in respect of the sort of life.' Ast takes χαλεπόν as masc. (comparing cases like III 416 B τὴν μεγίστην τῆς εὐλαβείας), but αὐτό shews that he is wrong. Translate simply 'whether it is a painful period of life.' It is needless to insert (with Hartman) τι after χαλεπόν: still worse is Liebhold's addition of τέλος.

34 **ἐξαγγέλλεις**: like the ἐξάγγελος in tragedy, Cephalus is the bearer of news from behind the scenes.

329 A—**329** D *Cephalus delivers his views on old age. It is, or should be, a haven of peace; old men have themselves to blame if they are miserable.*

329 A 3 **παροιμίαν.** ἧλιξ ἥλικα τέρπει (*Phaedr.* 240 C).

4 **ξυνιόντες**: i.q. ὅταν ξυνίωσιν 'whenever they come together.' Such a use of the participle is admissible when the main verb is in the present of habitual action. ξυνόντες is a needless conjecture.

8 **οὐδὲ ζῶντες.** Soph. *Ant.* 1165—1167 τὰς γὰρ ἡδονὰς | ὅταν προδῶσιν ἄνδρες, οὐ τίθημ' ἐγὼ | ζῆν τοῦτον, ἀλλ' ἔμψυχον ἡγοῦμαι νεκρόν. Cf. also Mimn. *Fr.* I. 1 ff.: Sim. *Fr.* 71 τίς γὰρ ἁδονᾶς ἄτερ θνατῶν βίος ποθεινός: Eur. *Fr.* 1065. Similar sentiments are very common throughout Greek literature, especially in poetry.

λακίσεις τοῦ γήρως ὀδύρονται, καὶ ἐπὶ τούτῳ δὴ τὸ γῆρας ὑμνοῦσιν ὅσων κακῶν σφίσιν αἴτιον. ἐμοὶ δὲ δοκοῦσιν, ὦ Σώκρατες, οὗτοι οὐ τὸ αἴτιον αἰτιᾶσθαι. εἰ γὰρ ἦν τοῦτο αἴτιον, κἂν ἐγὼ τὰ αὐτὰ ταῦτα ἐπεπόνθη ἕνεκά γε γήρως καὶ οἱ ἄλλοι πάντες ὅσοι ἐνταῦθα ἦλθον ἡλικίας. νῦν δ' ἔγωγε ἤδη ἐντετύχηκα οὐχ οὕτως ἔχουσιν καὶ ἄλλοις, καὶ δὴ καὶ Σοφοκλεῖ ποτε τῷ ποιητῇ παρεγενόμην ἐρωτωμένῳ ὑπό τινος Πῶς, ἔφη, ὦ | Σοφόκλεις, ἔχεις πρὸς τἀφροδίσια; C ἔτι οἷός τε εἶ γυναικὶ συγγίγνεσθαι; καὶ ὅς, Εὐφήμει, ἔφη, ὦ ἄνθρωπε· ἀσμενέστατα μέντοι αὐτὸ ἀπέφυγον, ὥσπερ λυττῶντά τινα καὶ ἄγριον δεσπότην ἀποφυγών. εὖ οὖν μοι καὶ τότε ἔδοξεν ἐκεῖνος εἰπεῖν καὶ νῦν οὐχ ἧττον. παντάπασι γὰρ τῶν γε τοιούτων ἐν τῷ γήρᾳ πολλὴ εἰρήνη γίγνεται καὶ ἐλευθερία. ἐπειδὰν αἱ ἐπιθυμίαι παύσωνται κατατείνουσαι καὶ χαλάσωσιν, παντάπασιν τὸ τοῦ Σοφοκλέους γίγνεται· | δεσποτῶν πάνυ πολλῶν ἐστι καὶ D μαινομένων ἀπηλλάχθαι. ἀλλὰ καὶ τούτων πέρι καὶ τῶν γε πρὸς τοὺς οἰκείους μία τις αἰτία ἐστίν, οὐ τὸ γῆρας, ὦ Σώκρατες, ἀλλ' ὁ τρόπος τῶν ἀνθρώπων. ἂν μὲν γὰρ κόσμιοι καὶ εὔκολοι ὦσιν, καὶ τὸ γῆρας μετρίως ἐστὶν ἐπίπονον· εἰ δὲ μή, καὶ γῆρας, ὦ Σώκρατες, καὶ νεότης χαλεπὴ τῷ τοιούτῳ ξυμβαίνει.

---

329 C 16 **ἔτι—συγγίγνεσθαι**. These words are rejected by Hirschig, Cobet, and Hartman, but their genuineness is supported by the singular *αὐτό* in *αὐτὸ ἀπέφυγον* and by Plut. *περὶ φιλοπλουτίας* 5. 525 A ὁ Σοφοκλῆς ἐρωτηθεὶς εἰ δύναται γυναικὶ πλησιάζειν, Εὐφήμει, ἄνθρωπε, εἶπεν κτλ. In such matters Greek realism called a spade a spade. In spite of the anecdote here told, few writers have painted sadder pictures of old age than Sophocles: see for example *O. C.* 1235—1238 and *Fr.* 684. More in keeping with the present passage is *Fr.* 688 οὐκ ἔστι γῆρας τῶν σοφῶν, ἐν οἷς ὁ νοῦς | θείᾳ ξύνεστιν ἡμέρᾳ τεθραμμένος.

17 **ἀπέφυγον—ἀποφυγών**. The repetition adds a certain impressiveness to the sentence. Herwerden is in error when he ejects *ἀποφυγών*, which seems to have been read also by Plutarch (referred to in last note).

21 **κατατείνουσαι** is intransitive. If the meaning were (as Ast holds) transitive —man being conceived as the puppet of the desires cf. *Laws* 644 E—we should expect *ἐπι-* or *συν-* rather than *κατατείνουσαι*: see *Phaed.* 94 C and 98 D.

παντάπασιν κτλ. The impressive iteration is in keeping with the age and earnestness of the speaker: cf. 331 A, B.

22 **ἐστι.** Stallbaum and others eject this word, but it is not easy to see why a scribe should have inserted it, particularly in such an idiomatic position. The asyndeton before *δεσποτων* is regular in explanatory clauses. I read *ἐστι* (with A) in preference to *ἔστι*: the meaning 'is possible' does not suit, and would require *ἀπαλλαγῆναι* rather than *ἀπηλλάχθαι*. Translate 'it is the deliverance once and for all from tyrants full many and furious.' The grammatical subject, as in English, remains vague; it is involved in *ἐπειδὰν —χαλάσωσιν*. For the use of *ἐστι* cf. *Euthyphr.* 2 D φαίνεταί μοι—ἄρχεσθαι ὀρθῶς· ὀρθῶς γάρ ἐστι τῶν νέων πρότερον ἐπιμεληθῆναι. The sentence-accent falls on *πολλῶν* and *μαινομένων* and not on *ἐστι*. The view of old age presented here recalls the *μελέτη θανάτου* of the *Phaedo*.

329 D 25 **εὔκολοι.** Like Sophocles himself: ὁ δ' εὔκολος μὲν ἐνθάδ', εὔκολος δ' ἐκεῖ (Ar. *Frogs* 82).

IV. Καὶ ἐγὼ ἀγασθεὶς αὐτοῦ εἰπόντος ταῦτα, βουλόμενος ἔτι
E λέγειν αὐτὸν ἐκίνουν καὶ εἶπον· Ὦ Κέφαλε, οἶμαί σου τοὺς
πολλούς, ὅταν ταῦτα λέγῃς, οὐκ ἀποδέχεσθαι, ἀλλ' ἡγεῖσθαί
σε ῥᾳδίως τὸ γῆρας φέρειν οὐ διὰ τὸν τρόπον, ἀλλὰ διὰ τὸ πολλὴν
οὐσίαν κεκτῆσθαι· τοῖς γὰρ πλουσίοις πολλὰ παραμύθιά φασιν
εἶναι. Ἀληθῆ, ἔφη, λέγεις· οὐ γὰρ ἀποδέχονται. καὶ λέγουσι
μέν τι, οὐ μέντοι γε ὅσον οἴονται, ἀλλὰ τὸ τοῦ Θεμιστοκλέους
330 εὖ ἔχει, ὃς τῷ Σεριφίῳ λοιδορουμένῳ καὶ λέγοντι, ὅτι οὐ δι' αὐτὸν
ἀλλὰ διὰ τὴν πόλιν εὐδοκιμοῖ, ἀπεκρίνατο, ὅτι οὔτ' ἂν αὐτὸς
Σερίφιος ὢν ὀνομαστὸς ἐγένετο οὔτ' ἐκεῖνος Ἀθηναῖος. καὶ τοῖς
δὴ μὴ πλουσίοις, χαλεπῶς δὲ τὸ γῆρας φέρουσιν, εὖ ἔχει ὁ αὐτὸς
λόγος, ὅτι οὔτ' ἂν ὁ ἐπιεικὴς πάνυ τι ῥᾳδίως γῆρας μετὰ πενίας
ἐνέγκοι, οὔθ' ὁ μὴ ἐπιεικὴς πλουτήσας εὔκολός ποτ' ἂν ἑαυτῷ

29. σου A¹Π: σε corr. A².

---

329 D—331 B *Socrates further questions Cephalus. 'Most men will say that it is your riches which make you happy in old age.' C. 'Character has more to do with happiness than wealth.' S. 'What is the chief advantage of money?' C. 'It enables the good man to pay his debts to gods and men before he passes into the other world.'*

29 **ἐκίνουν**. κινεῖν 'rouse' is technical in the Socratic dialect for the stimulating of the intellect by interrogation: cf. (with Stallbaum) *Lys.* 223 A, Xen. *Mem.* IV 2. 2. See also Ar. *Clouds* 745.

329 E 34 **οὐ μέντοι γε.** The collocation μέντοι γε, which rarely occurs in good Greek, is condemned by Porson (on Eur. *Med.* 675) and others. In Plato it is found only here and in *Crat.* 424 C, [*Sisyph.*] 388 A. Here some inferior MSS omit γε. It would be easy (with Hoefer *de particulis Plat.* p. 38, Cobet, and Blaydes) to write οὐ μέντοι ὅσον γε, but "notanda talia potius quam mutanda." The idiom, though exceptional, is (in my judgment) sufficiently supported (see the instances cited by Blaydes on Ar. *Thesm.* 709). It should also perhaps be remembered that the speaker, Cephalus, was not a native Athenian. Cf. 331 B E *nn*.

τὸ τοῦ Θεμιστοκλέους. The story as told by Herodotus VIII 125 is probably more true, if less pointed: ὡς δὲ ἐκ τῆς Λακεδαίμονος ἀπίκετο (sc. Θεμιστοκλῆς) ἐς τὰς Ἀθήνας, ἐνθαῦτα Τιμόδημος Ἀφιδναῖος—φθόνῳ καταμαργέων ἐνείκεε τὸν Θεμιστοκλέα—ὡς διὰ τὰς Ἀθήνας ἔχοι τὰ γέρεα τὰ παρὰ Λακεδαιμονίων, ἀλλ' οὐ δι' ἑωυτόν. ὁ δὲ—εἶπε· οὕτω ἔχει τοι· οὔτ' ἂν ἐγὼ ἐὼν Βελβινίτης (Belbina was a small island about 2 miles south of Sunium) ἐτιμήθην οὕτω πρὸς Σπαρτιητέων, οὔτ' ἂν σὺ ὤνθρωπε ἐὼν Ἀθηναῖος. The changes are not due to Plato: for τῷ in τῷ Σεριφίῳ—for which Heindorf on *Charm.* 155 D wrongly suggests τῳ, like Cicero's *Seriphio cuidam* (*Cato Mai.* 8)—shews that Plato's form of the story was also familiar. The Platonic version, in which Belbina has become Seriphus, and Themistocles' detractor a Seriphian, afterwards held the field.

330 A 3 **καὶ τοῖς δή.** καί is 'also' and δή illative.

6 **εὔκολος—ἑαυτῷ.** The dative is used as with εὐμενής: cf. Ar. *Frogs* 359 μηδ' εὔκολός ἐστι πολίταις (v.l. πολίτης). To suit the application precisely to the story we should require (1) neither would the ἐπιεικής easily endure old age with poverty, (2) nor the μὴ ἐπιεικής easily endure old age with riches. For (2) Plato substitutes 'nor would the bad man ever attain to peace with himself by becoming rich'; thereby conveying the further idea that the bad man is not εὔκολος ἑαυτῷ under any circumstances or at any time. Richards' suggestion ἐν αὑτῷ (i.e. γήρᾳ) for ἑαυτῷ is neat, but loses sight of this additional point. The allusion to old age in the second clause, so far as it is necessary to allude to it, is contained in ποτε.

γένοιτο. Πότερον δέ, ἦν δ' ἐγώ, ὦ Κέφαλε, ὧν κέκτησαι τὰ πλείω
παρέλαβες ἢ ἐπεκτήσω; Ποῖ' ἐπεκτησάμην, | ἔφη, ὦ Σώκρατες; B
μέσος τις γέγονα χρηματιστὴς τοῦ τε πάππου καὶ τοῦ πατρός.
ὁ μὲν γὰρ πάππος τε καὶ ὁμώνυμος ἐμοὶ σχεδόν τι ὅσην ἐγὼ νῦν
οὐσίαν κέκτημαι παραλαβὼν πολλάκις τοσαύτην ἐποίησεν, Λυσανίας δὲ ὁ πατὴρ ἔτι ἐλάττω αὐτὴν ἐποίησε τῆς νῦν οὔσης· ἐγὼ δὲ
ἀγαπῶ, ἐὰν μὴ ἐλάττω καταλίπω τούτοισιν, ἀλλὰ βραχεῖ γέ τινι
πλείω ἢ παρέλαβον. Οὗ τοι ἕνεκα ἠρόμην, ἦν δ' ἐγώ, ὅτι μοι

8. ποῖ' Π²: ποῖ ΑΠ¹Ξq. 14. οὗ τοι unus Flor. B: οὕτοι A: οὗτοι (*sic*) Π: τούτου Ξ: τούτου τοι q.

---

330 A, B 8 **ποῖ' ἐπεκτησάμην κτλ.**: 'do you want to know what I acquired, Socrates?' ποῖα is simply 'what' as in *Men.* 87 E σκεψώμεθα δὴ καθ' ἕκαστον ἀναλαμβάνοντες, ποῖά ἐστιν ἃ ἡμᾶς ὠφελεῖ. ὑγίειά φαμεν καὶ ἰσχὺς καὶ κάλλος καὶ πλοῦτος δή· ταῦτα λέγομεν καὶ τὰ τοιαῦτα ὠφέλιμα, and in the usual τὰ ποῖα ταῦτα; There is no derision implied, as in ποῖος Κτήσιππος (*Euthyd.* 291 A) and the like: had Cephalus desired to pour scorn on the suggestion, he would have said πόθεν ἐπεκτησάμην; (cf. *Crat.* 398 E): and it would be absurd to deride a charge to which you at once plead guilty (γέγονα χρηματιστὴς κτλ.). If Socrates' question had been not πότερον—τὰ πλείω παρέλαβες ἢ ἐπεκτήσω, but ποῖα ἐπεκτήσω, Cephalus would have said ὁποῖα ἐπεκτησάμην: but this idiom is inadmissible, except where the same interrogative occurs in its direct form in the original question. In view of the answer (μέσος τις κτλ.) which Cephalus gives, πόσα for ποῖα would be too precise. Of the various emendations which have been suggested, the only plausible one (in point of sense) is Richards' πότερον for ποῖ' or ποῖ: this would assimilate the original and the repeated question, but is less well adapted to Cephalus' reply. Cephalus in point of fact uses an old man's privilege and accommodates his interrogator's question to his own reply. See also V 465 E *n.*

330 B 11 **Λυσανίας δέ.** Groen van Prinsterer's suggestion (*Platon. Prosopogr.* p. 111) Λυσίας for Λυσανίας is at first sight plausible, since it is in harmony with the well-known Greek custom of calling grandsons after their grandfathers: but the fashion was by no means invariable: see Blümner, *Gr. Privatalterth.* p. 284. [Plut.] *vit. Lys.* 835 C also calls Cephalus son of Lysanias.

13 **τούτοισιν.** Bekker and others read τουτοισί, but there is no reason for deserting the MSS. The archaic dative in -οισι is tolerably often used by Plato. In the *Republic* alone it recurs in 345 E, 388 D, 389 B, 468 D (Homer), 560 E, 564 C, 607 B (-αισι) (poetic): see also Schneider on III 389 B, and for the usage of inscriptions Meisterhans³ p. 126. In this particular passage the archaic ending suits the age of the speaker; but it should be remembered that Plato's style (at least in his more mature dialogues) is not a mere reproduction of the vernacular Attic, but also in no small measure a literary language or 'Kunstsprache,' in which Ionisms and poetic and archaic forms are occasionally employed:' see especially Hirzel *Der Dialog* I pp. 246—250 *nn.* Hirzel (*ib.* p. 34 *n.* 1) gives reasons for holding that a sort of κοινὴ διάλεκτος, resembling the dialect of Herodotus, was actually spoken in certain cultivated circles at Athens in the Periclean age, e.g. by Anaxagoras and his group, by the Ionian sophists and their followers etc., and some of Plato's Ionisms may be inherited from this source. Cf. VII 533 B *n.*

14 **οὗ τοι ἕνεκα—ὅτι.** The reading τούτου for οὗ, though supported by Stobaeus (*Flor.* 94. 22), is a correction made by some one unacquainted with the idiom, which is common enough in conversational style: cf. infra 491 B ὃ μὲν πάντων θαυμαστότατον ἀκοῦσαι, ὅτι κτλ. and Ar. *Frogs* 108. Hartman's τοῦ τοι (interrogative) is ingenious, but unnecessary.

C ἔδοξας οὐ σφόδρα ἀγαπᾶν τὰ | χρήματα. τοῦτο δὲ ποιοῦσιν ὡς τὸ πολὺ οἳ ἂν μὴ αὐτοὶ κτήσωνται· οἱ δὲ κτησάμενοι διπλῇ ἢ οἱ ἄλλοι ἀσπάζονται αὐτά. ὥσπερ γὰρ οἱ ποιηταὶ τὰ αὑτῶν ποιήματα καὶ οἱ πατέρες τοὺς παῖδας ἀγαπῶσιν, ταύτῃ τε δὴ καὶ οἱ χρηματισάμενοι περὶ τὰ χρήματα σπουδάζουσιν ὡς ἔργον ἑαυτῶν, καὶ κατὰ τὴν χρείαν, ᾗπερ οἱ ἄλλοι. χαλεποὶ οὖν καὶ ξυγγενέσθαι εἰσίν, οὐδὲν ἐθέλοντες ἐπαινεῖν ἀλλ' ἢ τὸν πλοῦτον. 'Αληθῆ, ἔφη, λέγεις.

D V. Πάνυ μὲν οὖν, | ἦν δ' ἐγώ. ἀλλά μοι ἔτι τοσόνδε εἰπέ· τί μέγιστον οἴει ἀγαθὸν ἀπολελαυκέναι τοῦ πολλὴν οὐσίαν κεκτῆσθαι; Ὃ, ἦ δ' ὅς, ἴσως οὐκ ἂν πολλοὺς πείσαιμι λέγων. εὖ γὰρ ἴσθι, ἔφη, ὦ Σώκρατες, ὅτι, ἐπειδάν τις ἐγγὺς ᾖ τοῦ οἴεσθαι τελευτήσειν, εἰσέρχεται αὐτῷ δέος καὶ φροντὶς περὶ ὧν ἔμπροσθεν οὐκ εἰσῄει. οἵ τε γὰρ λεγόμενοι μῦθοι περὶ τῶν ἐν Ἅιδου, ὡς τὸν ἐνθάδε ἀδικήσαντα δεῖ ἐκεῖ διδόναι δίκην, καταγελώμενοι τέως, τότε δὴ E στρέφουσιν | αὐτοῦ τὴν ψυχὴν μὴ ἀληθεῖς ὦσιν· καὶ αὐτὸς ἤτοι

20. ᾗπερ Π: ἧπερ A.

---

330 C 16 **διπλῇ ἢ οἱ ἄλλοι.** The meaning is simply 'twice as much as the others': cf. e.g. *Laws* 868 A *διπλῇ τὸ βλάβος ἐκτεισάτω* and 928 B *ζημιούτω—διπλῇ*. The *ἤ* is like *ἤ* after *διπλάσιος*, *πολλαπλάσιος* etc. If *διπλῇ* meant simply 'on two grounds,' it could not be followed by *ἤ*, and we should have to regard *ἢ οἱ ἄλλοι* as an interpolation. Cephalus expresses himself somewhat loosely, as if loving a thing on two grounds, or in two ways, were equivalent to loving it twice as much. *ταύτῃ* below is defined by the *ὥσπερ* clause, and is preferred to *ὥσπερ*, partly in order to correspond to *διπλῇ* but still more to suit *κατὰ τὴν χρείαν*. The present passage is through Aristotle (*Eth. Nic.* IV 2. 1120[b] 14, cf. ib. IX 7. 1168[a] 1—3) the source of the proverb about 'parents and poets.'

21 **ξυγγενέσθαι**: 'to meet' in social intercourse, as in *Ap.* 41 A. *ξυγγίγνεσθαι* (suggested by Richards) would express habitual intercourse, which is not what Plato means to say. With the sentiment cf. *Symp.* 173 C *ὅταν μέν τινας περὶ φιλοσοφίας λόγους ἢ αὐτὸς ποιῶμαι ἢ ἄλλων ἀκούω—ὑπερφυῶς ὡς χαίρω· ὅταν δὲ ἄλλους τινάς, ἄλλως τε καὶ τοὺς ὑμετέρους τοὺς τῶν πλουσίων καὶ χρηματιστικῶν, αὐτός τε ἄχθομαι ὑμᾶς τε τοὺς ἑταίρους ἐλεῶ, ὅτι οἴεσθε τὶ ποιεῖν οὐδὲν ποιοῦντες.*

330 D 26 **ἐπειδὰν—τελευτήσειν**: 'when a man faces the thought that he must die,' not (with Jowett) 'when a man thinks himself to be near death,' which would be *ἐπειδάν τις ἐγγὺς εἶναι οἴηται τοῦ τελευτῆσαι*, as Herwerden proposes to read (cf. *Laws* 922 C *ὅταν ἤδη μέλλειν ἡγώμεθα τελευτᾶν*). "Senum, non iuvenum *τὸ οἴεσθαι τελευτήσειν* est" (Hartman): the weakness of old age convinces us at last that we too must die. Cf. Simon. 85. 7—10 *θνητῶν δ' ὄφρα τις ἄνθος ἔχῃ πολυήρατον ἥβης | κοῦφον ἔχων θυμόν, πόλλ' ἀτέλεστα νοεῖ· | οὔτε γὰρ ἐλπίδ' ἔχει γηρασέμεν οὔτε θανεῖσθαι, | οὐδ' ὑγιὴς ὅταν ᾖ, φροντίδ' ἔχει καμάτου.*

29 **ἀδικήσαντα—διδόναι δίκην.** Plato is fond of this verbal play: cf *Euthyph.* 8 B and 8 E *τῷ γε ἀδικοῦντι δοτέον δίκην*. He who does not render justice in deeds must render justice in punishment: for the tale of justice must be made up. Note that we have here in *ἀδικία* and *δίκη* the first casual allusion to the subject of the *Republic*.

330 E 30 **αὐτὸς κτλ.** *αὐτός* = *ipse* s. *ultro* as opposed to *οἱ λεγόμενοι μῦθοι*. The verb is to be supplied by a kind of

ὑπὸ τῆς τοῦ γήρως ἀσθενείας ἢ καὶ ὥσπερ ἤδη ἐγγυτέρω ὢν τῶν
ἐκεῖ μᾶλλόν τι καθορᾷ αὐτά. ὑποψίας δ' οὖν καὶ δείματος μεστὸς
γίγνεται καὶ ἀναλογίζεται ἤδη καὶ σκοπεῖ, εἴ τινά τι ἠδίκηκεν.
ὁ μὲν οὖν εὑρίσκων ἑαυτοῦ ἐν τῷ βίῳ πολλὰ ἀδικήματα καὶ ἐκ
τῶν ὕπνων, ὥσπερ οἱ παῖδες, θαμὰ ἐγειρόμενος δειμαίνει καὶ ζῇ
μετὰ κακῆς ἐλπίδος· τῷ | δὲ μηδὲν ἑαυτῷ ἄδικον ξυνειδότι ἡδεῖα 331
ἐλπὶς ἀεὶ πάρεστι καὶ ἀγαθή, γηροτρόφος, ὡς καὶ Πίνδαρος
λέγει. χαριέντως γάρ τοι, ὦ Σώκρατες, τοῦτ' ἐκεῖνος εἶπεν, ὅτι
ὃς ἂν δικαίως καὶ ὁσίως τὸν βίον διαγάγῃ, γλυκεῖά οἱ καρδίαν
ἀτάλλοισα γηροτρόφος συναορεῖ ἐλπίς, ἃ μάλιστα θνατῶν
πολύστροφον γνώμαν κυβερνᾷ. εὖ οὖν λέγει θαυμαστῶς
ὡς σφόδρα. πρὸς δὴ τοῦτ' ἔγωγε τίθημι τὴν τῶν χρημάτων
κτῆσιν πλείστου ἀξίαν εἶναι, οὔ τι | παντὶ ἀνδρί, ἀλλὰ τῷ ἐπιεικεῖ. B
τὸ γὰρ μηδὲ ἄκοντά τινα ἐξαπατῆσαι ἢ ψεύσασθαι, μηδ' αὖ
ὀφείλοντα ἢ θεῷ θυσίας τινὰς ἢ ἀνθρώπῳ χρήματα ἔπειτα ἐκεῖσε
ἀπιέναι δεδιότα, μέγα μέρος εἰς τοῦτο ἡ τῶν χρημάτων κτῆσις
συμβάλλεται. ἔχει δὲ καὶ ἄλλας χρείας πολλάς· ἀλλά γε ἓν
ἀνθ' ἑνὸς οὐκ ἐλάχιστον ἔγωγε θείην ἂν εἰς τοῦτο ἀνδρὶ νοῦν

33. ἠδίκηκεν A¹Ξ: ἠδίκησεν Π*q* et corr. A².

---

zeugma from *μᾶλλόν τι καθορᾷ αὐτά* (i.e. *τὰ ἐκεῖ*); or rather the predicate is accommodated to the second alternative. Cf. 344 B infra and VIII 553 C. To regard the bodily weakness of old age as in itself the cause of clearer vision of the world beyond may be in harmony with the doctrine of the *Phaedo*, but Cephalus is not represented as a Platonist. Tucker needlessly doubts the text.

34 **καὶ ἐκ τῶν ὕπνων κτλ.** *καί* is 'both,' not 'and,' and balances *καὶ ζῇ*: 'many a time, like children, awakes out of sleep in terror and lives in the expectation of ill.' For *ὥσπερ οἱ παῖδες* compare *Phaed.* 77 D, E, and for the general sentiment Arist. *Eth. Nic.* I 13. 1102ᵇ 8—11 *ἀργία γάρ ἐστιν ὁ ὕπνος τῆς ψυχῆς ᾗ λέγεται σπουδαία καὶ φαύλη, πλὴν εἴ πῃ κατὰ μικρὸν διικνοῦνταί τινες τῶν κινήσεων, καὶ ταύτῃ βελτίω γίνεται τὰ φαντάσματα τῶν ἐπιεικῶν ἢ τῶν τυχόντων.*

331 A 1 **ἡδεῖα—γηροτρόφος:** *ἡδεῖα* is suggested by Pindar's *γλυκεῖα*, and *καὶ ἀγαθή*, as presently appears, is not part of the quotation, but goes with *ἐλπίς* and is added by Plato in contrast to *μετὰ κακῆς ἐλπίδος.*

γηροτρόφος κτλ.: 'to nurse him in old age, as Pindar also says.' *γηροτρόφος* is best taken by itself and not with *ἀγαθή*.

5 **ἀτάλλοισα κτλ.** *ἀτάλλω* is used of rearing children, and helps out the idea of *γηροτρόφος*: *δὶς παῖδες οἱ γέροντες.* It is not clear how the fragment is to be arranged, nor to what class of Pindar's poems it belongs. See Bergk *Poet. Lyr. Gr.*⁴ I p. 452.

6 **εὖ οὖν—σφόδρα.** The emphasis is quite in keeping with Cephalus' age and character; and Hartman is certainly wrong in condemning the clause: cf. 329 C, 331 B.

331 B 10 **ὀφείλοντα—θεῷ θυσίας τινάς.** *Phaed.* 118 A *εἶπεν, ὃ δὴ τελευταῖον ἐφθέγξατο, ὦ Κρίτων, ἔφη, τῷ Ἀσκληπιῷ ὀφείλομεν ἀλεκτρυόνα· ἀλλὰ ἀπόδοτε καὶ μὴ ἀμελήσητε.* Wealth is in Cephalus' view the indispensable *χορηγία ἀρετῆς.*

12 **ἀλλά γε ἓν ἀνθ' ἑνός.** *ἀλλά γε* is extremely rare in Attic prose: in the

ἔχοντι, ὦ Σώκρατες, πλοῦτον χρησιμώτατον εἶναι. Παγκάλως, ἦν
C δ' ἐγώ, λέγεις, ὦ Κέφαλε. | τοῦτο δ' αὐτό, τὴν δικαιοσύνην, πότερα τὴν ἀλήθειαν αὐτὸ φήσομεν εἶναι ἁπλῶς οὕτως καὶ τὸ ἀποδιδόναι, ἄν τίς τι παρά του λάβῃ, ἢ καὶ αὐτὰ ταῦτα ἔστιν ἐνίοτε μὲν δικαίως, ἐνίοτε δὲ ἀδίκως ποιεῖν; οἷον τοιόνδε λέγω· πᾶς ἄν που εἴποι, εἴ τις λάβοι παρὰ φίλου ἀνδρὸς σωφρονοῦντος ὅπλα, εἰ μανεὶς ἀπαιτοῖ, ὅτι οὔτε χρὴ τὰ τοιαῦτα ἀποδιδόναι, οὔτε δίκαιος ἂν εἴη ὁ ἀποδιδοὺς οὐδ' αὖ πρὸς τὸν οὕτως ἔχοντα πάντα ἐθέλων
D τἀληθῆ λέγειν. | Ὀρθῶς, ἔφη, λέγεις. Οὐκ ἄρα οὗτος ὅρος ἐστὶ δικαιοσύνης, ἀληθῆ τε λέγειν καὶ ἃ ἂν λάβῃ τις ἀποδιδόναι. Πάνυ μὲν οὖν, ἔφη, ὦ Σώκρατες, ὑπολαβὼν ὁ Πολέμαρχος, εἴπερ γέ τι χρὴ Σιμωνίδῃ πείθεσθαι. Καὶ μέντοι, ἔφη ὁ Κέφαλος, καὶ παραδίδωμι ὑμῖν τὸν λόγον· δεῖ γάρ με ἤδη τῶν ἱερῶν ἐπιμεληθῆναι.

Platonic corpus it occurs—according to the best manuscript authority—here and in *Rep.* VIII 543 C, *Phaed.* 86 E, *Hipp. Maior* 287 B, *Phaedr.* 262 A (ἀλλά γε δή), *Phaed.* 116 D (id.). In some of these passages ἀλλ' ἄγε has been conjectured—wrongly, as I think (with Schneider), at all events in the passage from the *Republic*:—but ἀλλ' ἄγε cannot be read in the *Phaedrus* and *Hippias Maior*. There is no *a priori* objection to the collocation, which is also implied in ἀλλὰ γάρ (γ' ἄρα); and in later Greek ἀλλά γε aroused no objection. The meaning is 'but still,' originally 'yes, but': as Schneider says, "γε in his dictionibus concedit aliquatenus praecedentia, sed magis urget sequentia." There is perhaps also a dramatic motive for putting ἀλλά γε into the mouth of Cephalus: see on οὐ μέντοι γε in 329 E. Against the reading of Stobaeus (*Flor.* 94. 22) ἀλλὰ ἕν γε ἀνθ' ἑνός, we may urge the further objection that the idiomatic phrase ἓν ἀνθ' ἑνός ('setting one thing against another,' as Jowett correctly translates it) seems to depend for its peculiar force (like μόνος μόνῳ and the like) on the juxtaposition of its two parts: cf. *Phil.* 63 B (ἓν ἀνθ' ἑνός) and *Laws* 705 B (ἀνθ' ἑνὸς ἕν). The passage quoted by Stallbaum from Euripides *Orest.* 651 ἓν μὲν τόδ' ἡμῖν ἀνθ' ἑνὸς δοῦναί σε χρή is quite different and does not mean 'hoc praecipue,' but 'one thing *in return for* one thing,' as is clear from lines 646 f.

13 **οὐκ ἐλάχιστον** is not adverbial (as Hartman and others suppose), but belongs to τοῦτο: 'setting one thing against another, I should regard this as not the least important object for which wealth is most useful to a man of sense.' The emphasis is characteristic: cf. 329 C, 331 A.

331 C, D *The question 'What is Justice?' is for the first time raised. Is it simply to speak the truth and pay what you owe? Polemarchus succeeds to Cephalus' part in the conversation.*

331 C 16 **τὴν ἀλήθειαν κτλ.** This theory of justice or righteousness is deduced from the words of Cephalus: τὸ γὰρ μηδὲ ἄκοντά τινα ἐξαπατῆσαι ἢ ψεύσασθαι being generalised into ἀλήθειαν (truthfulness, cf. τἀληθῆ λέγειν below), and μηδ' αὖ ὀφείλοντα ἢ θεῷ θυσίας τινὰς ἢ ἀνθρώπῳ χρήματα into ἀποδιδόναι ἄν τίς τι παρά του λάβῃ. Cf. (with Wohlrab) Mimn. *Fr.* 8 ἀληθείη δὲ παρέστω | σοὶ καὶ ἐμοί, πάντων χρῆμα δικαιότατον. It is simply Truth and Honesty, the two chief ingredients in the popular conception of morality.

ἁπλῶς οὕτως: 'quite without qualification.' For this idiomatic οὕτως cf. ῥᾳδίως οὕτω II 377 B *n*.

18 **οἷον τοιόνδε λέγω.** Similar points of casuistry are raised in Socrates' conversation with Euthydemus ap. Xen. *Mem.* IV 2. 12 ff.

21 **οὐδ' αὖ κτλ.** I have removed the comma before οὐδέ, because the ὁ in ὁ ἀποδιδούς covers both participles, the person in both cases being the same.

Οὐκοῦν, ἔφη, ἐγὼ ὁ Πολέμαρχος τῶν γε σῶν κληρονόμος; Πάνυ γε, ἦ δ' ὃς γελάσας· καὶ ἅμα ᾔει πρὸς τὰ ἱερά.

---

331 D 27 **ἔφη**. There is not sufficient reason for changing the best supported reading ἔφη, ἐγώ to ἔφην ἐγώ. Polemarchus is throughout the introduction represented as a vivacious person: e.g. in ὁρᾷς οὖν ἡμᾶς—ὅσοι ἐσμέν (327 C), and in the lively emphasis with which he breaks in just above: πάνυ μὲν οὖν—εἴπερ γέ τι χρὴ Σιμωνίδῃ πείθεσθαι. True to his name, he is first to mingle in the fray. It is this φιλολογία on the part of his son which draws a smile from Cephalus: over-much προθυμία always struck the Greeks as laughable: cf. e.g. Eur. *Ion* 1172 ff. The words in which Socrates addresses Polemarchus σὺ ὁ τοῦ λόγου κληρονόμος are also somewhat more appropriate if the title was self-chosen. Cephalus leaves the argument to be carried on by the assembled company (for ὑμῖν does not mean Polemarchus and Socrates alone): whereupon Polemarchus, seizing hold on the word παραδίδωμι in its sense of 'transmit,' 'bequeath,' playfully claims the right to inherit his λόγος as Cephalus' eldest son and heir. It may be added that ἔφη ἐγώ was much more likely to be changed to ἔφην ἐγώ than *vice versa*. With the Greek compare *Phaed.* 89 C ἀλλὰ καὶ ἐμέ, ἔφη, τὸν Ἰόλεων παρακάλει.

28 **ἅμα ᾔει πρὸς τὰ ἱερά**. Soph. *Fr.* 206 γήρᾳ πρεπόντως σῷζε τὴν εὐφημίαν. The editors quote Cicero *Epp. ad Att.* IV 16. 3 "credo Platonem vix putasse satis consonum fore, si hominem id aetatis in tam longo sermone diutius retinuisset." Cf. the words of Theodorus in *Theaet.* 162 B οἶμαι ὑμᾶς πείσειν ἐμὲ μὲν ἐᾶν θεᾶσθαι καὶ μὴ ἕλκειν πρὸς τὸ γυμνάσιον, σκληρὸν ἤδη ὄντα, τῷ δὲ δὴ νεωτέρῳ τε καὶ ὑγροτέρῳ ὄντι προσπαλαίειν. It is worthy of note that the entrance and exit of Cephalus are alike associated with the services of religion: see 328 C and *Introd.* § 2.

331 E—**332** B *The second half of the definition of Justice which Socrates deduced from Cephalus' remarks is now taken up and discussed in the form in which it was expressed by Simonides—'rendering to each man his due.' In the present section Socrates confines himself to eliciting the meaning of 'due.' As between friends, it is something good; as between enemies, something evil; in general terms it is that which is suitable or appropriate. Simonides in fact meant that Justice consists in doing good to friends and ill to foes.*

331 E ff. By δικαιοσύνη, it should be noted, is here meant man's whole duty to his fellows, as ὁσιότης is right conduct in relation to the gods. In this wide sense the word was commonly understood by the Greeks (cf. Theog. 147 ἐν δὲ δικαιοσύνῃ συλλήβδην πᾶσ' ἀρετὴ ἔνι); and even in the scientific study of ethics, the word still retained the same wider connotation, side by side with its more specific meanings (Arist. *Eth. Nic.* V 3. 1129^b 11 ff.). The view that Justice consists in doing good to friends and harm to enemies, is a faithful reflection of prevalent Greek morality (Luthardt *Die Antike Ethik* p. 19). It is put into the mouth of Simonides as a representative of the poets, on whose writings the young were brought up: cf. *Prot.* 316 D, 325 E, 338 E ff. As typical illustrations we may cite: Hes. *OD.* 707 ff.; Solon 13. 5; Theog. 337 f.; Archilochus *Fr.* 65; Pindar *Pyth.* 2. 83—85; Aesch. *P.V.* 1041 f.; Soph. *Ant.* 643 f.; Eurip. *Med.* 807—810; Meno in Plat. *Men.* 71 E αὕτη ἐστὶν ἀνδρὸς ἀρετή, ἱκανὸν εἶναι τὰ τῆς πόλεως πράττειν, καὶ πράττοντα τοὺς μὲν φίλους εὖ ποιεῖν, τοὺς δ' ἐχθροὺς κακῶς: cf. also *Crito* 49 B, Xen. *Cyr.* I 6. 31 ff. and *Hiero* II 2. Socrates himself in *Mem.* II 3. 14 represents the same principle as generally accepted in Greece: καὶ μὴν πλείστου γε δοκεῖ ἀνὴρ ἐπαίνου ἄξιος εἶναι, ὃς ἂν φθάνῃ τοὺς μὲν πολεμίους κακῶς ποιῶν, τοὺς δὲ φίλους εὐεργετῶν: cf. also ibid. II 6. 35. These references, which might easily be multiplied, shew that Plato is not, as Teichmüller supposes (*Lit. Fehd.* I p. 22 *n.*), specifically refuting Xenophon, but rather criticising an all but universal view. See Nägelsbach *Nachhom. Theol.* pp. 246 ff. It is seldom that a voice is raised in protest, as by Pittacus (according to D. L. I 4. 78) in the memorable words φίλον μὴ λέγειν κακῶς, ἀλλὰ μηδὲ ἐχθρόν. Plato was the first Greek who systematically protested against the doctrine, and supported his protest with arguments drawn from a loftier view of man's nature and work.

E VI. Λέγε δή, | εἶπον ἐγώ, σὺ ὁ τοῦ λόγου κληρονόμος, τί φῂς τὸν Σιμωνίδην λέγοντα ὀρθῶς λέγειν περὶ δικαιοσύνης; Ὅτι, ἦ δ' ὅς, τὸ τὰ ὀφειλόμενα ἑκάστῳ ἀποδιδόναι δίκαιόν ἐστι· τοῦτο λέγων δοκεῖ ἔμοιγε καλῶς λέγειν. Ἀλλὰ μέντοι, ἦν δ' ἐγώ, Σιμωνίδῃ γε οὐ ῥᾴδιον ἀπιστεῖν· σοφὸς γὰρ καὶ θεῖος ἀνήρ· τοῦτο μέντοι ὅ τί ποτε λέγει, σὺ μέν, ὦ Πολέμαρχε, ἴσως γιγνώσκεις, ἐγὼ δὲ ἀγνοῶ. δῆλον γὰρ ὅτι οὐ τοῦτο λέγει, ὅπερ ἄρτι ἐλέγομεν, τό τινος παρακαταθεμένου τι ὁτῳοῦν μὴ σωφρόνως ἀπαιτοῦντι ἀποδιδόναι·
332 καίτοι γε ὀφει|λόμενόν πού ἐστιν τοῦτο, ὃ παρακατέθετο· ἦ γάρ;

---

331 E 29 **ὁ τοῦ λόγου κληρονόμος.** See on παῖδες ἐκείνου τοῦ ἀνδρός II 368 A.

31 **τὰ ὀφειλόμενα—ἐστι.** Probably some current saying attributed to Simonides: there is nothing like it in his fragments. The words do not profess to be a definition of justice: if they did, τό would appear before δίκαιον. It is not likely that Simonides himself explained this particular saying as Polemarchus does, although he would not have disapproved of the explanation. In Xen. *Hier.* II 2 he is represented as saying that tyrants are ἱκανώτατοι—κακῶσαι μὲν ἐχθρούς, ὀνῆσαι δὲ φίλους. The words of Socrates σὺ μέν, ὦ Πολέμαρχε, ἴσως γιγνώσκεις, ἐγὼ δὲ ἀγνοῶ tend to fix the responsibility of the explanation on Polemarchus alone. Probably Simonides (if the saying is his) meant no more than that we should 'render unto Caesar the things which are Caesar's.' Plato virtually confesses in 332 B that his interpretation is forced.

32 **ἔμοιγε**: said with confidence, as Σιμωνίδῃ γε with emphasis and some mockery: with you one might disagree, but not with Simonides.

33 **σοφὸς—θεῖος.** Cf. *Prot.* 315 E. σοφός and θεῖος were fashionable words of praise: in the mouth of Socrates they are generally ironical. Plato's own connotation of the word θεῖος is given in *Men.* 99 C οὐκοῦν, ὦ Μένων, ἄξιον τούτους θείους καλεῖν τοὺς ἄνδρας, οἵτινες νοῦν μὴ ἔχοντες πολλὰ καὶ μεγάλα κατορθοῦσιν ὧν πράττουσι καὶ λέγουσιν; Ὀρθῶς ἂν καλοῖμεν θείους τε, οὓς νῦν δὴ ἐλέγομεν χρησμῳδοὺς καὶ μάντεις καὶ τοὺς ποιητικοὺς ἅπαντας· καὶ τοὺς πολιτικοὺς οὐχ ἥκιστα τούτων φαῖμεν ἂν θείους τε εἶναι καὶ ἐνθουσιάζειν, ἐπίπνους ὄντας καὶ κατεχομένους ἐκ τοῦ θεοῦ, ὅταν κατορθῶσι λέγοντες πολλὰ καὶ μεγάλα πράγματα, μηδὲν εἰδότες ὧν λέγουσι.

ἀνήρ. I formerly read ἀνήρ, but ἀνὴρ (in the predicate) is satisfactory enough: cf. *Men.* 99 D θεῖος ἀνήρ, φασίν, οὗτος.

36 **παρακαταθεμένου κτλ.** Xen. *Cyr.* I 6. 31 ff. καὶ ἔτι προβὰς (sc. ἐπὶ τῶν ἡμετέρων προγόνων γενόμενός ποτε ἀνὴρ διδάσκαλος τῶν παίδων) ταῦτα ἐδίδασκεν ὡς καὶ τοὺς φίλους δίκαιον εἴη ἐξαπατᾶν, ἐπί γε ἀγαθῷ, καὶ κλέπτειν τὰ τῶν φίλων, ἐπί γε ἀγαθῷ: *Mem.* IV 2. 17 ff.

ὁτῳοῦν is to be taken with παρακαταθεμένου and not with ἀπαιτοῦντι.

37 **καίτοι γε ὀφειλόμενον.** There is the same dispute about καίτοι γε as about μέντοι γε and ἀλλά γε (see on 329 E, 331 B). καίτοι γε has the best MS authority in its favour here and in IV 440 D: elsewhere in Plato it is not well-attested except in the νοθευόμενοι, where it occurs *Min.* 318 E, *Axioch.* 364 B, 368 E. καίτοι γε is also found occasionally in Aristophanes, Xenophon, Aristotle, and the orators: see Blaydes on Ar. *Ach.* 611, and the *Lex. Arist.* Many distinguished critics would emend the idiom everywhere; but the instances are far too numerous for such a drastic policy. The difference between καίτοι ὀφειλόμενόν γε που (which Hoefer *de part. Plat.* p. 38 would read) and καίτοι γε ὀφειλόμενον would seem to be that in the former more stress is thrown on the word ὀφειλόμενον, in the latter on τοι. καίτοι γε is 'and *surely*' rather than 'quamquam' (as Kugler holds *de part.* τοι *eiusque comp. ap. Pl. usu* p. 20), cf. IV 440 D *n.* The periphrasis ὀφειλόμενον—ἐστι is used of course to correspond to τὰ ὀφειλόμενα in E above: such periphrases (the principle of which is explained in *Euthyph.* 9 E ff.) are extremely common in Plato. See W. J. Alexander in *A. J. Ph.* IV pp. 299 ff.

Ναί. Ἀποδοτέον δέ γε οὐδ' ὁπωστιοῦν τότε, ὁπότε τις μὴ σωφρόνως ἀπαιτοῖ; Ἀληθῆ, ἦ δ' ὅς. Ἄλλο δή τι ἢ τὸ τοιοῦτον, ὡς ἔοικεν, λέγει Σιμωνίδης τὸ τὰ ὀφειλόμενα δίκαιον εἶναι ἀποδιδόναι. Ἄλλο μέντοι νὴ Δί', ἔφη· τοῖς γὰρ φίλοις οἴεται ὀφείλειν τοὺς φίλους ἀγαθὸν μέν τι δρᾶν, κακὸν δὲ μηδέν. Μανθάνω, ἦν δ' ἐγώ· ὅτι οὐ τὰ ὀφειλόμενα ἀποδίδωσιν, ὃς ἄν τῳ χρυσίον ἀποδῷ παρακαταθεμένῳ, ' ἐάνπερ ἡ ἀπόδοσις καὶ ἡ λῆψις βλαβερὰ B γίγνηται, φίλοι δὲ ὦσιν ὅ τε ἀπολαμβάνων καὶ ὁ ἀποδιδούς· οὐχ οὕτω λέγειν φῂς τὸν Σιμωνίδην; Πάνυ μὲν οὖν. Τί δέ; τοῖς ἐχθροῖς ἀποδοτέον, ὅ τι ἂν τύχῃ ὀφειλόμενον; Παντάπασι μὲν οὖν, ἔφη, ὅ γε ὀφείλεται αὐτοῖς. ὀφείλεται δέ, οἶμαι, παρά γε τοῦ ἐχθροῦ τῷ ἐχθρῷ, ὅπερ καὶ προσήκει, κακόν τι.

12. δὲ Ξ: δέ γε ΑΠq.

---

332 A 2 **ἀποδοτέον—ἀπαιτοῖ**: 'well, but we were not on any account to make restoration at the time when the claimant is'—according to the Greek idiom 'was'—'mad.' Socrates, as in ὅπερ ἄρτι ἐλέγομεν, is appealing to the admissions made by the πατὴρ τοῦ λόγου (in 331 C), as he is justified in doing when addressing his heir. ὁπότε is not—as τότε shews—the particle of 'indefinite frequency,' but stands for ὅτε of the direct: the whole clause τότε ὁπότε τις μὴ σωφρόνως ἀπαιτοῖ is thus in the *oratio obliqua* of self-quotation and exactly corresponds to εἰ μανεὶς ἀπαιτοῖ in 331 C. Madvig's ἀπαιτεῖ for ἀπαιτοῖ is therefore unnecessary. Goodwin *MT.* p. 213 explains the optative otherwise, but not (I think) rightly.

6 **ἀγαθὸν μέν τι δρᾶν** sc. αὐτούς, for τοῖς φίλοις depends on ὀφείλειν, to which τοὺς φίλους is the subject.

μανθάνω—ὅτι. ὅτι is 'because,' not 'that,' as always (I believe) in Plato's use of this phrase: cf. *Euthyph.* 3 B, 9 B and infra III 402 E, VIII 568 E. For the sentiment cf. (with J. and C.) Xen. *Mem.* IV 2 17 ff.

332 B 12 **ὀφείλεται δέ.** See *cr. n.* In explanatory clauses of this kind δέ and not δέ γε is the correct usage: cf. infra 337 D, 344 A. I therefore follow Bekker in reading δέ.

13 **προσήκει.** ὀφειλόμενον has thus been equated with προσῆκον by means of the special cases τὸ τοῖς φίλοις ὀφειλόμενον and τὸ τοῖς ἐχθροῖς ὀφειλόμενον. τὸ προσῆκον is a more general term and is the regular word in classical Greek for 'proper conduct' or 'duty' (as the Greeks conceived it), the Stoic καθῆκον being very rarely used in this sense by good authors.

332 C—**336** A *The definition is further elucidated down to* 333 B: *and thereafter Socrates begins to criticise it.*

In the first place, the definition is made more precise by representing justice as an art, whose business it is to benefit friends and injure foes (332 C, D). *The question is then raised—how does the art of justice do good to friends and harm to foes? By the analogy of other arts Polemarchus is induced to say that Justice benefits friends and harms enemies* (1) *by fighting with them and against them in time of war, and* (2) *in connexion with partnerships concerned with money in time of peace* (332 D—333 B). *The explanation of Simonides' saying is now complete.*

Socrates first directs his attack against (2). *In cases where money has to be used, it is not justice, but some other art, that is useful for the required purpose: in other words justice is* (*in time of peace*) *useful only in dealing with useless or unused money and other unused objects: which is an unworthy view of the art* (333 B—333 E). *Further, the analogy of the other arts shews that the art of justice, if it is the art of keeping money safe, is also the art of stealing money—always provided that it does so for the benefit of friends and the injury of foes* (333 E—334 B). *Polemarchus, in bewilderment, reiterates his*

VII. Ἠινίξατο ἄρα, ἦν δ' ἐγώ, ὡς ἔοικεν, ὁ Σιμωνίδης ποιητι-
C κῶς τὸ δίκαιον ὃ εἴη. διενοεῖτο μὲν γάρ, ὡς | φαίνεται, ὅτι τοῦτ' εἴη δίκαιον, τὸ προσῆκον ἑκάστῳ ἀποδιδόναι, τοῦτο δὲ ὠνόμασεν ὀφειλόμενον. Ἀλλὰ τί οἴει; ἔφη. Ὦ πρὸς Διός, ἦν δ' ἐγώ, εἰ οὖν τις αὐτὸν ἤρετο, ὦ Σιμωνίδη, ἡ τίσιν οὖν τί ἀποδιδοῦσα ὀφειλόμενον καὶ προσῆκον τέχνη ἰατρικὴ καλεῖται; τί ἂν οἴει ἡμῖν αὐτὸν ἀποκρίνασθαι; Δῆλον ὅτι, ἔφη, ἡ σώμασιν φάρμακά

---

definition in the old form, and Socrates thereupon starts a fresh line of argument. By 'friends' and 'foes' Polemarchus means those who seem to us good and bad, not those who are so. But as bad men often seem to us good and good men bad, Justice will often consist in benefiting bad men, and harming good, i.e. in wronging those who do no wrong; or conversely, if we refuse to accept this conclusion, and hold that it is just to benefit the just and hurt the unjust, it will often be just to hurt friends and benefit enemies, viz. when our friends are bad, and our enemies good (334 C—334 E).

Polemarchus hereupon amends his explanation of 'friend' and 'enemy' into 'him who both seems and is good,' and 'him who both seems and is bad': and the definition now becomes, 'It is just to benefit a friend if he is good, and injure an enemy if he is bad (335 A).'

To this amended definition Socrates now addresses himself. He first proves by the analogy of the other arts that to hurt a human being is to make him worse in respect of human excellence, i.e. Justice, in other words to make him more unjust, and afterwards by means of similar analogical reasoning, that no one can be made more unjust by one who is just. Simonides' saying, if Polemarchus has explained it aright, was more worthy of a tyrant than of him (335 A—336 A).

332 B **ff.** The seventh chapter is a good example of Plato's extreme care in composition. A careful study will shew that the structural basis consists of two illustrations followed by an application: this occurs seven times before the conclusion of the argument is reached. Similar, but less elaborate, examples of symmetrical structure are pointed out in my notes on *Crito* 49 B, *Prot.* 325 D.

332 B 14 **ἠνίξατο—ποιητικῶς.** *Theaet.* 194 C τὸ τῆς ψυχῆς κέαρ, ὅ ἔφη Ὅμηρος αἰνιττόμενος τὴν τοῦ κηροῦ ὁμοιότητα. The present passage is no more serious than that in the *Theaetetus*: Plato knew that Simonides merely meant to say 'it is just to render what you owe.'

332 C 17 **ἀλλὰ τί οἴει;** is a rhetorical question, which needs and receives no answer, like τί μήν; and τί μὴν δοκεῖς; (*Theaet.* 162 B). It is equivalent to 'of course.' For the use of τί Stallbaum compares *Gorg.* 480 B τί γὰρ δὴ φῶμεν; to which there is also no reply. This explanation is preferable to that of Madvig, who gives ἀλλὰ τί οἴει to Socrates, and takes ἔφη as equivalent to συνέφη—a harsh usage in a narrated dialogue, and not likely to have been intended by Plato, because sure to be misunderstood. Liebhold's ἄλλο τι οἴει; <οὐκ> ἔφη has everything against it.

ὦ πρὸς Διὸς κτλ. 'In the name of heaven, said I, if any one then had asked him' etc. 'what reply do you think he would have made to us?' ὦ before πρὸς Διός is (as Schanz holds) an interjection, and does not require a vocative to follow it: cf. *Euthyd.* 287 A, 290 E. It is tempting (with Tucker) to take ὦ πρὸς Διός as part of the address to Simonides (cf. *Euthyd.* 294 B ὦ πρὸς τῶν θεῶν, ἦν δ' ἐγώ, ὦ Διονυσόδωρε—αὐτὼ τῷ ὄντι πάντα ἐπίστασθον). But on this view the presence of εἰ οὖν—ἤρετο forms a difficulty, and ὦ πρὸς Διός may very well go with τί ἂν οἴει—ἀποκρίνασθαι.

19 **ὀφειλόμενον καὶ προσῆκον.** It is characteristic of Plato to combine the thing explained and the explanation itself in this way: see my note on *Prot.* 314 A. Here ὀφειλόμενον is necessary to enable Simonides to recognise his own saying.

ἰατρικὴ—μαγειρική. In *Gorg.* 463 A ff. Plato refuses the name of 'art' to ὀψοποιική: it is but an ἐμπειρία or τριβή, a sort of bastard adjunct to ἰατρική, as κομμωτική is to γυμναστική. Here, where less precision is required, both are regarded as τέχναι.

τε καὶ σιτία καὶ ποτά. Ἡ δὲ τίσιν τί ἀποδιδοῦσα ὀφειλόμενον
καὶ προσῆκον τέχνη μαγειρικὴ καλεῖται; Ἡ τοῖς | ὄψοις τὰ D
ἡδύσματα. Εἶεν· ἡ οὖν δὴ τίσιν τί ἀποδιδοῦσα τέχνη δικαιοσύνη
ἂν καλοῖτο; Εἰ μέν τι, ἔφη, δεῖ ἀκολουθεῖν, ὦ Σώκρατες, τοῖς
ἔμπροσθεν εἰρημένοις, ἡ τοῖς φίλοις τε καὶ ἐχθροῖς ὠφελίας τε καὶ
βλάβας ἀποδιδοῦσα. Τὸ τοὺς φίλους ἄρα εὖ ποιεῖν καὶ τοὺς
ἐχθροὺς κακῶς δικαιοσύνην λέγει; Δοκεῖ μοι. Τίς οὖν δυνατώτατος
κάμνοντας φίλους εὖ ποιεῖν καὶ ἐχθροὺς κακῶς πρὸς νόσον καὶ
ὑγίειαν; Ἰατρός. Τίς δὲ πλέοντας | πρὸς τὸν τῆς θαλάττης E
κίνδυνον; Κυβερνήτης. Τί δέ; ὁ δίκαιος ἐν τίνι πράξει καὶ
πρὸς τί ἔργον δυνατώτατος φίλους ὠφελεῖν καὶ ἐχθροὺς βλάπτειν;
Ἐν τῷ προσπολεμεῖν καὶ ἐν τῷ ξυμμαχεῖν, ἔμοιγε δοκεῖ. Εἶεν·
μὴ κάμνουσί γε μήν, ὦ φίλε Πολέμαρχε, ἰατρὸς ἄχρηστος. Ἀληθῆ.
Καὶ μὴ πλέουσι δὴ κυβερνήτης. Ναί. Ἆρα καὶ τοῖς μὴ πολε-
μοῦσιν ὁ δίκαιος ἄχρηστος; Οὐ πάνυ μοι δοκεῖ τοῦτο. Χρήσιμον
ἄρα καὶ ἐν εἰρήνῃ δικαιο|σύνη; Χρήσιμον. Καὶ γὰρ γεωργία· 333
ἢ οὔ; Ναί. Πρός γε καρποῦ κτῆσιν. Ναί. Καὶ μὴν καὶ σκυτο-
τομική; Ναί. Πρός γε ὑποδημάτων ἄν, οἶμαι, φαίης κτῆσιν.
Πάνυ γε. Τί δὲ δή; τὴν δικαιοσύνην πρὸς τίνος χρείαν ἢ κτῆσιν
ἐν εἰρήνῃ φαίης ἂν χρήσιμον εἶναι; Πρὸς τὰ ξυμβόλαια, ὦ
Σώκρατες. Ξυμβόλαια δὲ λέγεις κοινωνήματα, ἤ τι ἄλλο; Κοι-

332 D 23 **εἶεν** according to Timaeus (*Lexicon* s. v.) expresses *συγκατάθεσις μὲν τῶν εἰρημένων, συναφὴ δὲ πρὸς τὰ μέλλοντα*. It rarely expresses *συγκατάθεσις* ('assent') and no more: see on IV 436 C. The word was pronounced *εἷέν* with intervocalic aspiration (Uhlig in *Fl. Jahrb.* 1880 pp. 790 ff.) and may possibly be a compound of *εἶα* and *ἕν* (used as in *ἓν μὲν τόδ' ἤδη τῶν τριῶν παλαισμάτων* Aesch. *Eum.* 589). *εἷέν* is the usual orthography in Paris A, and has left some traces also in the Bodleian MS e.g. *Gorg.* 466 C.

τέχνη δικαιοσύνη. The Socratic view that Justice is an art—a view that dominates the whole of the conversation w. . Polemarchus—is thus introduced quite incidentally.

26 **τὸ—λέγει**. Cf. Xen. *Hiero* II 2 (cited above on 331 E).

332 E 30 **τί δέ; ὁ δίκαιος κτλ.** This punctuation throws more emphasis on *ὁ δίκαιος* than *τί δὲ ὁ δίκαιος;* which appears in some editions. It is therefore to be preferred in introducing the application of the two illustrations. So also below in 333 A *τί δὲ δή; τὴν δικαιοσύνην κτλ.*

32 **προσπολεμεῖν** explains *ἐχθροὺς βλάπτειν* as *ξυμμαχεῖν* explains *φίλους ὠφελεῖν*. Ast's *προπολεμεῖν* (a conjecture of Stephanus) would leave *ἐχθροὺς βλάπτειν* unrepresented. Stephanus' conjecture was natural enough with the wrong reading *καὶ ξυμμαχεῖν*, which Ast also followed. For **ἔμοιγε δοκεῖ** Hartman demands *ἔμοιγε δοκεῖν*; but cf. 333 B, *Crito* 43 D, *Phaed.* 108 D, *Menex.* 236 B. These cases shew that *δοκεῖ* can be used without *ὡς*: and *ἐμοὶ (ἔμοιγε) δοκεῖν* does not occur in the *Republic* (Grünenwald in Schanz's *Beitr. zur hist. Synt. d. gr. Spr.* II 3 p. 12).

333 A 5 **ξυμβόλαια** are contracts where money is involved. Polemarchus (as in *εἰς ἀργυρίου* in B below), in harmony with the natural meaning of Simonides' saying, thinks first of pecuniary dealings as the sphere in which *δικαιοσύνη* acts. Socrates substitutes for *ξυμβόλαια* the more general term *κοινωνήματα*, in order once more to introduce the analogy of the arts.

B νωνήματα δῆτα. Ἆρ' οὖν ὁ δίκαιος | ἀγαθὸς καὶ χρήσιμος κοινωνὸς
εἰς πεττῶν θέσιν, ἢ ὁ πεττευτικός; Ὁ πεττευτικός. Ἀλλ' εἰς
πλίνθων καὶ λίθων θέσιν ὁ δίκαιος χρησιμώτερός τε καὶ ἀμείνων
κοινωνὸς τοῦ οἰκοδομικοῦ; Οὐδαμῶς. Ἀλλ' εἰς τίνα δὴ κοινωνίαν
ὁ δίκαιος ἀμείνων κοινωνὸς τοῦ κιθαριστικοῦ, ὥσπερ ὁ κιθαριστικὸς
τοῦ δικαίου εἰς κρουμάτων; Εἰς ἀργυρίου, ἔμοιγε δοκεῖ. Πλήν γ'
ἴσως, ὦ Πολέμαρχε, πρὸς τὸ χρῆσθαι ἀργυρίῳ, ὅταν δέῃ ἀργυρίου
C κοινῇ πρίασθαι ἢ ἀποδόσθαι | ἵππον· τότε δέ, ὡς ἐγὼ οἶμαι,
ὁ ἱππικός· ἢ γάρ; Φαίνεται. Καὶ μὴν ὅταν γε πλοῖον, ὁ ναυ-
πηγὸς ἢ ὁ κυβερνήτης. Ἔοικεν. Ὅταν οὖν τί δέῃ ἀργυρίῳ
ἢ χρυσίῳ κοινῇ χρῆσθαι, ὁ δίκαιος χρησιμώτερος τῶν ἄλλων;
Ὅταν παρακαταθέσθαι καὶ σῶν εἶναι, ὦ Σώκρατες. Οὐκοῦν
λέγεις, ὅταν μηδὲν δέῃ αὐτῷ χρῆσθαι ἀλλὰ κεῖσθαι; Πάνυ γε.
Ὅταν ἄρα ἄχρηστον ᾖ ἀργύριον, τότε χρήσιμος ἐπ' αὐτῷ ἡ |
D δικαιοσύνη; Κινδυνεύει. Καὶ ὅταν δὴ δρέπανον δέῃ φυλάττειν,
ἡ δικαιοσύνη χρήσιμος καὶ κοινῇ καὶ ἰδίᾳ· ὅταν δὲ χρῆσθαι,
ἡ ἀμπελουργική; Φαίνεται. Φήσεις δὲ καὶ ἀσπίδα καὶ λύραν
ὅταν δέῃ φυλάττειν καὶ μηδὲν χρῆσθαι, χρήσιμον εἶναι τὴν δικαιοσύνην, ὅταν δὲ χρῆσθαι, τὴν ὁπλιτικὴν καὶ τὴν μουσικήν; Ἀνάγκη.
Καὶ περὶ τἆλλα δὴ πάντα ἡ δικαιοσύνη ἑκάστου ἐν μὲν χρήσει
ἄχρηστος, ἐν δὲ ἀχρηστίᾳ χρήσιμος; Κινδυνεύει.
E VIII. | Οὐκ ἂν οὖν, ὦ φίλε, πάνυ γέ τι σπουδαῖον εἴη ἡ

21. *δέῃ q*: δέοι ΑΠΞ. 28. *οὐκ ἂν οὖν* Ξ et corr. in mg. A²: *οὔκουν* A¹q: *οὐκοῦν* Π.

---

333 B 10 εἰς τίνα δὴ κοινωνίαν is idiomatic for *εἰς τίνος δὴ κοινωνίαν*. Compare VIII 556 C *ἢ ἐν ὁδῶν πορείαις ἢ ἐν ἄλλαις τισὶ κοινωνίαις* and *τὴν τιμὴν ταύτην* (where the English idiom would expect *τὴν τιμὴν ταύτης*) in II 371 E. In spite of *εἰς κρουμάτων* and *εἰς ἀργυρίου*, it is not necessary to read (with Richards) *τίνος*.

333 C 18 παρακαταθέσθαι καὶ σῶν εἶναι. The double expression is necessary to explain *κοινῇ χρῆσθαι*: the *κοινωνία* arises because one deposits the money and by the other it is kept safe.

20 **ἄχρηστον—χρήσιμος.** *ἄχρηστος* fluctuates between 'unused' and 'useless': the latter sense is predominant here and gives an epigrammatic tone to the sentence (cf. *ἐν μὲν χρήσει ἄχρηστος, ἐν δὲ ἀχρηστίᾳ χρήσιμος* in D). It is noticeable that Plato does not take into account the possibility of money being deposited at interest: in this case the money could not be said to be useless.

333 D 22 καὶ κοινῇ καὶ ἰδίᾳ: not 'to the individual and to the state,' but 'both in dealings with others, and in personal concerns.' The words *καὶ ἰδίᾳ* are, strictly speaking, irrelevant, for it is with *κοινωνήματα* (in the widest sense) that we are concerned. They are to be regarded merely as a rhetorical amplification for the sake of emphasis: cf. infra 350 A, 351 A *nn.*

333 E 28 οὐκ ἂν οὖν κτλ. See *cr. n.* Some may think that we should read *οὐκοῦν* (with the majority of MSS) and cancel *εἴη* after *σπουδαῖον* (so also Vind.

δικαιοσύνη, εἰ πρὸς τὰ ἄχρηστα χρήσιμον ὂν τυγχάνει. τόδε δὲ
σκεψώμεθα. ἆρ' οὐχ ὁ πατάξαι δεινότατος ἐν μάχῃ εἴτε πυκτικῇ
εἴτε τινὶ καὶ ἄλλῃ, οὗτος καὶ φυλάξασθαι; Πάνυ γε. Ἆρ' οὖν
καὶ νόσον ὅστις δεινὸς φυλάξασθαι, καὶ λαθεῖν οὗτος δεινότατος
ἐμποιήσας; Ἔμοιγε δοκεῖ. Ἀλλὰ μὴν στρατοπέ|δου γε ὁ αὐτὸς **334**
φύλαξ ἀγαθός, ὅσπερ καὶ τὰ τῶν πολεμίων κλέψαι καὶ βουλεύματα
καὶ τὰς ἄλλας πράξεις. Πάνυ γε. Ὅτου τις ἄρα δεινὸς φύλαξ,
τούτου καὶ φὼρ δεινός. Ἔοικεν. Εἰ ἄρα ὁ δίκαιος ἀργύριον
δεινὸς φυλάττειν, καὶ κλέπτειν δεινός. Ὡς γοῦν ὁ λόγος, ἔφη,
σημαίνει. Κλέπτης ἄρα τις ὁ δίκαιος, ὡς ἔοικεν, ἀναπέφανται·
καὶ κινδυνεύεις παρ' Ὁμήρου μεμαθηκέναι αὐτό. καὶ γὰρ ἐκεῖνος
τὸν τοῦ Ὀδυσσέως πρὸς μητρὸς πάππον Αὐτόλυκον | ἀγαπᾷ τε **B**
καί φησιν αὐτὸν πάντας ἀνθρώπους κεκάσθαι κλεπτοσύνῃ θ'
ὅρκῳ τε. ἔοικεν οὖν ἡ δικαιοσύνη καὶ κατὰ σὲ καὶ καθ' Ὅμηρον
καὶ κατὰ Σιμωνίδην κλεπτική τις εἶναι, ἐπ' ὠφελίᾳ μέντοι τῶν
φίλων καὶ ἐπὶ βλάβῃ τῶν ἐχθρῶν. οὐχ οὕτως ἔλεγες; Οὐ μὰ

33. ἐμποιήσας coniecit Schneider: ἐμποιῆσαι ΑΠ^{1}Ξ: καὶ ἐμποιῆσαι Π^2*q*.

D), understanding ἐστι. The accidental omission of ἄν is however not uncommon in Plato's MSS: see on IV 437 B.

31 **οὗτος καὶ φυλάξασθαι**. Because knowledge of anything implies knowledge also of its opposite, according to the usual Socratic view. See *Phaed.* 97 D οὐδὲν ἄλλο σκοπεῖν προσήκειν ἀνθρωπον—ἀλλ' ἢ τὸ ἄριστον καὶ τὸ βέλτιστον· ἀναγκαῖον δὲ εἶναι τὸν αὐτὸν τοῦτον καὶ τὸ χεῖρον εἰδέναι, *Charm.* 166 E, *Hipp. Min.* 367 A ff. See also Stewart's *Notes on the Nicomachean Ethics* Vol. I p. 378.

32 **φυλάξασθαι κτλ.** See *cr. n.* With the emendation in the text, the argument is as follows: (1) he who can πατάξαι, can φυλάξασθαι: (2) he who can φυλάξασθαι (νόσον), can λαθεῖν ἐμποιήσας (νόσον): (3) he who can κλέψαι (τὰ τῶν πολεμίων), is a good φύλαξ of an army. Thus the predicate of each step in the argument corresponds to the subject of the step next following: for λαθεῖν ἐμποιήσας (νόσον) is to be taken as parallel to κλέψαι (τὰ τῶν πολεμίων). The argument is unsound, and not intended to be serious: it is enough that it suffices to bewilder Polemarchus. For a further discussion on this passage see App. II.

334 A 1 **στρατοπέδου γε κτλ.** The στρατηγός must be both φυλακτικός τε καὶ κλέπτης according to Socrates in Xen. *Mem.* III 1. 6.

2 **κλέπτειν** and **κλέμμα** were used (especially by Spartans) with reference to military operations involving surprise and stealth (Classen on Thuc. V 9. 5).

6 **κλέπτης—ἀναπέφανται.** Cf. *Hipp. Min.* 365 C ff., where this view is worked out at length, *ib.* 369 B ἀναπέφανται ὁ αὐτὸς ὢν ψευδής τε καὶ ἀληθής and Xen. *Mem.* IV 2. 20 ff. ἀναπέφανται, as J. and C. remark, expresses an unexpected result—here a paradox. Like ὁ ἑκὼν ἁμαρτάνων ἀμείνων, the conclusion is a logical inference from the Socratic identification of virtue and knowledge, made without regard to experience.

334 B 8 **ἀγαπᾷ**, 'esteems,' is said with reference to ἐσθλόν in Hom. *Od.* XIX 395 f. μητρὸς ἑῆς πατέρ' ἐσθλόν, ὃς ἀνθρώπους ἐκέκαστο | κλεπτοσύνῃ θ' ὅρκῳ τε. The suggested ἄγαται for ἀγαπᾷ τε would be too strong: see *Symp.* 180 B μᾶλλον—θαυμάζουσιν καὶ ἄγανται—ὅταν ὁ ἐρώμενος τὸν ἐραστὴν ἀγαπᾷ, where the meaning of ἀγαπᾷ is shewn by οὕτω περὶ πολλοῦ ἐποιεῖτο in 180 A.

τὸν Δί', ἔφη, ἀλλ' οὐκέτι οἶδα ἔγωγε ὅ τι ἔλεγον· τοῦτο μέντοι
ἔμοιγε δοκεῖ ἔτι, ὠφελεῖν μὲν τοὺς φίλους ἡ δικαιοσύνη, βλάπτειν
C δὲ τοὺς ἐχθρούς. Φίλους δὲ λέγεις | εἶναι πότερον τοὺς δοκοῦντας
ἑκάστῳ χρηστοὺς εἶναι, ἢ τοὺς ὄντας, κἂν μὴ δοκῶσι, καὶ ἐχθροὺς
ὡσαύτως; Εἰκὸς μέν, ἔφη, οὓς ἄν τις ἡγῆται χρηστούς, φιλεῖν,
οὓς δ' ἂν πονηρούς, μισεῖν. Ἆρ' οὖν οὐχ ἁμαρτάνουσιν οἱ ἄνθρωποι περὶ τοῦτο, ὥστε δοκεῖν αὐτοῖς πολλοὺς μὲν χρηστοὺς εἶναι
μὴ ὄντας, πολλοὺς δὲ τοὐναντίον; Ἁμαρτάνουσιν. Τούτοις ἄρα
οἱ μὲν ἀγαθοὶ ἐχθροί, οἱ δὲ κακοὶ φίλοι; Πάνυ γε. Ἀλλ' ὅμως
D δίκαιον τότε τούτοις, τοὺς μὲν πονηροὺς ὠφελεῖν, | τοὺς δὲ ἀγαθοὺς
βλάπτειν; Φαίνεται. Ἀλλὰ μὴν οἵ γε ἀγαθοὶ δίκαιοί τε καὶ
οἷοι μὴ ἀδικεῖν. Ἀληθῆ. Κατὰ δὴ τὸν σὸν λόγον τοὺς μηδὲν
ἀδικοῦντας δίκαιον κακῶς ποιεῖν. Μηδαμῶς, ἔφη, ὦ Σώκρατες·
πονηρὸς γὰρ ἔοικεν εἶναι ὁ λόγος. Τοὺς ἀδίκους ἄρα, ἦν δ' ἐγώ,
δίκαιον βλάπτειν, τοὺς δὲ δικαίους ὠφελεῖν. Οὗτος ἐκείνου καλλίων φαίνεται. Πολλοῖς ἄρα, ὦ Πολέμαρχε, ξυμβήσεται, ὅσοι
E διημαρτήκασιν τῶν ἀνθρώπων, δίκαιον εἶναι | τοὺς μὲν φίλους
βλάπτειν· πονηροὶ γὰρ αὐτοῖς εἰσίν· τοὺς δ' ἐχθροὺς ὠφελεῖν·
ἀγαθοὶ γάρ· καὶ οὕτως ἐροῦμεν αὐτὸ τοὐναντίον ἢ τὸν Σιμωνίδην
ἔφαμεν λέγειν. Καὶ μάλα, ἔφη, οὕτω ξυμβαίνει. ἀλλὰ μεταθώ-
μεθα· κινδυνεύομεν γὰρ οὐκ ὀρθῶς τὸν φίλον καὶ ἐχθρὸν θέσθαι.

---

13 **τοῦτο—ἔτι.** So Euthyphro (15 B) harks back to his first definition of piety (6 E) after he has been refuted by Socrates. Cf. also VII 515 E *n*.

14 **δοκεῖ** does double duty, first with *τοῦτο* and then with *δικαιοσύνη*: cf. VI 493 A, VII 517 B, 525 B, 530 B and (with Stallbaum) *Ap.* 25 B. Hartman needlessly doubts the text.

15 **φίλους δὲ λέγεις κτλ.** The same mode of argument recurs in 339 B ff. Cf. also *Hipp. Maior* 284 D.

334 C 21 **φίλοι κτλ.** Schneider rightly observes that *κατὰ δὴ τὸν σὸν λόγον* below tends to shew that *ἀλλ' ὅμως —βλάπτειν* is interrogative. The argument is in the form of a dilemma: either (*a*) it is just to injure those who do us no injustice (and benefit those who do), or (*b*) it is just to injure friends and benefit foes. The first alternative is immoral (*πονηρός*), and the second directly opposed to Simonides' view. Socrates suppresses the words which I have put in brackets, because they lessen rather than increase the immorality of the conclusion: the second alternative is expressed in full as the *αὐτὸ τοὐναντίον ἢ τὸν Σιμωνίδην ἔφαμεν λέγειν*.

334 D 28 **ὅσοι κτλ.**: not 'those of mankind who are in error' (J. and C.) but 'those who have mistaken their men': cf. *Phaedr.* 257 D *τοῦ ἑταίρου συχνὸν διαμαρτάνεις*. So also Schneider, and Davies and Vaughan.

334 E 30 **πονηροὶ γὰρ κτλ.** Stallbaum (followed by D. and V.) wrongly takes *αὐτοῖς* as 'in their eyes.' The reasoning is difficult only from its brevity. If it is *δίκαιον βλάπτειν ἀδίκους*, and men sometimes suppose that a man is good *when he is bad* (*πονηροὶ γὰρ αὐτοῖς εἰσιν* 'for they have bad friends'), then since friend has been defined as one whom we suppose to be good (334 C), it is sometimes *δίκαιον βλάπτειν φίλους*. Stallbaum's view is quite inconsistent with the definition of friends in 334 C as *οὓς ἄν τις ἡγῆται χρηστούς*.

33 **τὸν φίλον καὶ ἐχθρόν.** Hartman (with some inferior MSS) wishes to insert *τόν* before *ἐχθρόν*; but cf. infra III 400 D and

Πῶς θέμενοι, ὦ Πολέμαρχε; Τὸν δοκοῦντα χρηστόν, τοῦτον φίλον
εἶναι. Νῦν δὲ πῶς, ἦν δ' ἐγώ, μεταθώμεθα; Τὸν δοκοῦντά τε,
ἦ δ' ὅς, καὶ τὸν ὄντα χρηστὸν φίλον· τὸν δὲ δοκοῦντα | μέν, ὄντα 335
δὲ μή, δοκεῖν ἀλλὰ μὴ εἶναι φίλον· καὶ περὶ τοῦ ἐχθροῦ δὲ ἡ αὐτὴ
θέσις. Φίλος μὲν δή, ὡς ἔοικε, τούτῳ τῷ λόγῳ ὁ ἀγαθὸς ἔσται,
ἐχθρὸς δὲ ὁ πονηρός. Ναί. Κελεύεις δὴ ἡμᾶς προσθεῖναι τῷ
δικαίῳ, ἤ, ὡς τὸ πρῶτον ἐλέγομεν, λέγοντες δίκαιον εἶναι τὸν μὲν
φίλον εὖ ποιεῖν, τὸν δ' ἐχθρὸν κακῶς, νῦν πρὸς τούτῳ ὧδε λέγειν,
ὅτι ἔστιν δίκαιον τὸν μὲν φίλον ἀγαθὸν ὄντα εὖ ποιεῖν, τὸν δ'
ἐχθρὸν κακὸν ὄντα βλάπτειν; Πάνυ μὲν οὖν, ἔφη, | οὕτως ἄν μοι B
δοκεῖ καλῶς λέγεσθαι.

IX. Ἔστιν ἄρα, ἦν δ' ἐγώ, δικαίου ἀνδρὸς βλάπτειν καὶ

---

many other examples cited by himself. To pronounce them all corrupt is to destroy the basis on which our knowledge of Platonic idiom rests.

35 **τὸν δοκοῦντά τε—καὶ τὸν ὄντα.** The meaning required—'he who both seems and is good'—would be more correctly expressed by *τὸν δοκοῦντά τε—καὶ ὄντα* (so Ast and others), but "aliquid tribuendum interpositis *ἦ δ' ὅς*, quae negligentiam repetendi, si est negligentia, saltem excusant" (Schneider, who compares also infra 341 B *ποτέρως λέγεις τὸν ἄρχοντά τε καὶ τὸν κρείττονα*). In *τὸν δὲ δοκοῦντα μέν, ὄντα δὲ μή* Polemarchus expresses himself more accurately.

335 A 3 **ὁ ἀγαθός—ὁ πονηρός.** Socrates unfairly neglects the *δοκῶν*, although according to Polemarchus' amended definition the *ἀγαθός* who seemed *πονηρός* would not be a friend, nor the *πονηρός* who seemed *ἀγαθός* an enemy. Polemarchus' theory indeed points to a division of men into three classes: friends, enemies, and those who are neither (viz. those who seem good and are bad, and those who seem bad and are good). The somewhat ideal view that the *ἀγαθός* is *φίλος* and the *πονηρὸς ἐχθρός* is genuinely Socratic (cf. *Mem.* II 6. 14 ff.): it is part of the wider view that all men desire the good (*Symp.* 206 A, *Gorg.* 467 C ff.).

4 **προσθεῖναι—βλάπτειν.** *ἤ* after *τῷ δικαίῳ* must mean 'or in other words': cf. infra 349 E *πλεονεκτεῖν ἢ ἀξιοῦν πλέον ἔχειν* and *Phaed.* 85 D *ἐπὶ βεβαιοτέρου ὀχήματος, ἢ λόγου θείου τινός* (so the Bodleian, but *ἤ* is cancelled by many editors). The late expression *Φαίδων ἢ περὶ ψυχῆς* involves essentially the same use of *ἤ*. The clause *ὡς—κακῶς* is summed up in *τούτῳ*, and the whole sentence means: 'do you wish us to make an addition to our account of justice, or in other words to say now—in addition to our original definition where we said it was just to do good to friends and harm to enemies—that it is just to do good to friends *if they are good* etc.' This explanation is (I think) the least vulnerable one, if the text is to be retained. With *προσθεῖναι* used absolutely cf. 339 B. For other views see App. III.

335 B 10 **ἔστιν ἄρα κτλ.** Cf. *Crito* 49 A ff., *Gorg.* 469 B, [*περὶ ἀρετῆς*] 376 E. This chapter contains the only element of permanent ethical interest and value in the discussion with Polemarchus—the only element, moreover, which reappears in a later book of the *Republic* (II 379 B). The underlying principle—that *κακῶς ποιεῖν* = *κακὸν ποιεῖν*—is in accordance with the traditional Greek view of life. For illustrations we may cite *Od.* XVIII 136 f. *τοῖος γὰρ νόος ἐστὶν ἐπιχθονίων ἀνθρώπων | οἷον ἐπ' ἦμαρ ἄγησι πατὴρ ἀνδρῶν τε θεῶν τε*, Arch. *Fr.* 70 (Bergk), and Simon. *Fr.* 5. 10—14 *ἄνδρα δ' οὐκ ἔστι μὴ οὐ κακὸν ἔμμεναι | ὃν ἀμάχανος συμφορὰ καθέλοι· | πράξας μὲν εὖ πᾶς ἀνὴρ ἀγαθός,| κακὸς δ' εἰ κακῶς < τις >, | κἀπὶ πλεῖστον ἄριστοι, τούς κε θεοὶ φιλῶσιν.* The same point of view is manifest in the transition of meaning in *μοχθηρός* and *πονηρός* from 'laborious,' 'afflicted' (e.g. Hesiod *Fr.* 95. 1 Göttling) to 'depraved.' Conversely, prosperity makes one morally better, as in Solon 13. 69 f. *τῷ δὲ κακῶς ἔρδοντι θεὸς περὶ πάντα τίθησιν | συντυχίην ἀγαθήν, ἔκλυσιν ἀφροσύνης*, and in the frequent identification of *εὐπραγία* or *εὐδαιμονία*

ὁντινοῦν ἀνθρώπων; Καὶ πάνυ γε, ἔφη, τούς γε πονηρούς τε καὶ
ἐχθροὺς δεῖ βλάπτειν. Βλαπτόμενοι δ' ἵπποι βελτίους ἢ χείρους
γίγνονται; Χείρους. Ἆρα εἰς τὴν τῶν κυνῶν ἀρετήν, ἢ εἰς τὴν
τῶν ἵππων; Εἰς τὴν τῶν ἵππων. Ἆρ' οὖν καὶ κύνες βλαπτόμενοι
χείρους γίγνονται εἰς τὴν τῶν κυνῶν, ἀλλ' οὐκ εἰς τὴν τῶν ἵππων
C ἀρετήν; Ἀνάγκη. Ἀνθρώπους δέ, ὦ ἑταῖρε, μὴ | οὕτω φῶμεν,
βλαπτομένους εἰς τὴν ἀνθρωπείαν ἀρετὴν χείρους γίγνεσθαι;
Πάνυ μὲν οὖν. Ἀλλ' ἡ δικαιοσύνη οὐκ ἀνθρωπεία ἀρετή; Καὶ
τοῦτ' ἀνάγκη. Καὶ τοὺς βλαπτομένους ἄρα, ὦ φίλε, τῶν ἀνθρώπων
ἀνάγκη ἀδικωτέρους γίγνεσθαι. Ἔοικεν. Ἆρ' οὖν τῇ μουσικῇ
οἱ μουσικοὶ ἀμούσους δύνανται ποιεῖν; Ἀδύνατον. Ἀλλὰ τῇ
ἱππικῇ οἱ ἱππικοὶ ἀφίππους; Οὐκ ἔστιν. Ἀλλὰ τῇ δικαιοσύνῃ
D δὴ οἱ δίκαιοι ἀδίκους; ἢ καὶ ξυλλήβδην | ἀρετῇ οἱ ἀγαθοὶ κακούς;
Ἀλλὰ ἀδύνατον. Οὐ γὰρ θερμότητος, οἶμαι, ἔργον ψύχειν, ἀλλὰ
τοῦ ἐναντίου. Ναί. Οὐδὲ ξηρότητος ὑγραίνειν, ἀλλὰ τοῦ ἐναντίου.
Πάνυ γε. Οὐδὲ δὴ τοῦ ἀγαθοῦ βλάπτειν, ἀλλὰ τοῦ ἐναντίου.
Φαίνεται. Ὁ δέ γε δίκαιος ἀγαθός; Πάνυ γε. Οὐκ ἄρα τοῦ
δικαίου βλάπτειν ἔργον, ὦ Πολέμαρχε, οὔτε φίλον οὔτ' ἄλλον
οὐδένα, ἀλλὰ τοῦ ἐναντίου, τοῦ ἀδίκου. Παντάπασί μοι δοκεῖς
E ἀληθῆ λέγειν, ἔφη, ὦ | Σώκρατες. Εἰ ἄρα τὰ ὀφειλόμενα ἑκάστῳ
ἀποδιδόναι φησίν τις δίκαιον εἶναι, τοῦτο δὲ δὴ νοεῖ αὐτῷ, τοῖς
μὲν ἐχθροῖς βλάβην ὀφείλεσθαι παρὰ τοῦ δικαίου ἀνδρός, τοῖς
δὲ φίλοις ὠφελίαν, οὐκ ἦν σοφὸς ὁ ταῦτα εἰπών· οὐ γὰρ ἀληθῆ
ἔλεγεν· οὐδαμοῦ γὰρ δίκαιον οὐδένα ἡμῖν ἐφάνη ὂν βλάπτειν.
Συγχωρῶ, ἦ δ' ὅς. Μαχούμεθα ἄρα, ἦν δ' ἐγώ, κοινῇ ἐγώ τε καὶ

---

with εὖ πράττειν e.g. *Charm.* 172 A, 173 D, *Alc.* I 116 B, Arist. *Eth. Nic.* I 8. 1098b 20. It is by the analogy of the arts that Socrates in this chapter seeks to prove, first the identification κακῶς ποιεῖν = κακὸν ποιεῖν, and second that the good man cannot harm others: the Socratic conception of right conduct as an art is still predominant. It is important to observe that it was by means of this Socratic weapon that Plato achieved this noble anticipation of Christian ethical theory (St Matth. 5. 44 al.). Cf. also *Gorg.* 472 D ff.

16 **ἀνθρώπους δὲ κτλ.** Cf. 352 E—353 E.

335 E 33 **οὐκ ἦν σοφὸς—εἰπών.** Teichmüller (*Lit. Fehd.* I p. 22 *n.*) finds in this an allusion to Xenophon, who puts into the mouth of Socrates (addressing Critobulus in *Mem.* II 6. 35) the words ἔγνωκας ἀνδρὸς ἀρετὴν εἶναι, νικᾶν τοὺς μὲν φίλους εὖ ποιοῦντα, τοὺς δὲ ἐχθροὺς κακῶς: but the reference is only to 331 E σοφὸς γὰρ καὶ θεῖος ἀνήρ. The presents φησίν and νοεῖ are used in a general way, because such a theory and such an interpretation of it might be held by any one at any time: in οὐκ ἦν σοφὸς ὁ ταῦτα εἰπών the time is changed to the past to suggest οὐκ ἦν Σιμωνίδης ὁ ταῦτα εἰπών (Simonides being σοφός 331 E). But for ὁ ταῦτα εἰπών, ἦν would be ἐστι. It is a mistake to take ἦν as 'is after all': ἦν is hardly so used in Plato without ἄρα, nor is *Phaedr.* 230 A (cited by Goodwin *MT.* p. 13) an example of that idiom.

σύ, ἐάν τις αὐτὸ φῇ ἢ Σιμωνίδην ἢ Βίαντα ἢ Πιττακὸν εἰρηκέναι ἤ τιν' ἄλλον τῶν σοφῶν τε καὶ μακαρίων ἀνδρῶν; Ἐγὼ γοῦν, ἔφη, ἕτοιμός εἰμι κοινωνεῖν τῆς μάχης. Ἀλλ' οἶσθα, ἦν δ' ἐγώ, | οὗ 336
μοι δοκεῖ εἶναι τὸ ῥῆμα, τὸ φάναι δίκαιον εἶναι τοὺς μὲν φίλους ὠφελεῖν, τοὺς δ' ἐχθροὺς βλάπτειν; Τίνος; ἔφη. Οἶμαι αὐτὸ Περιάνδρου εἶναι ἢ Περδίκκου ἢ Ξέρξου ἢ Ἰσμηνίου τοῦ Θηβαίου ἤ τινος ἄλλου μέγα οἰομένου δύνασθαι πλουσίου ἀνδρός. Ἀληθέσ-

37. ἐγὼ γοῦν Π: ἔγωγ' οὖν A.

---

36 **ἐάν τις αὐτὸ φῇ—Σιμωνίδην**: as Xenophon virtually does in *Hier.* II 2: see 331 E *n.*

37 **τῶν σοφῶν τε καὶ μακαρίων ἀνδρῶν.** *μακάριος* is somewhat stronger than *θεῖος*, which it suggests, *μάκαρες* being a usual epithet of gods. The whole phrase is intended to carry us back to 331 E *σοφὸς γὰρ καὶ θεῖος ἀνήρ.* Ast's view that *μακαρίων* means "qui ante nostram aetatem floruerunt," as if 'sainted,' misses the allusion to 331 E, and is a little far-fetched: it is enough that *μακάριος* conveys the same ironical commendation as *θεῖος*: cf. (with Stallbaum) *Men.* 71 A.

ἐγὼ γοῦν. See *cr. n.* With Hartman, I adopt Bekker's restoration: cf. VII 527 D. For *γοῦν* A everywhere writes *γ' οὖν*.

336 A 4 **Περιάνδρου κτλ.** Periander, Xerxes and Perdiccas are taken as types of tyrants, and no tyrant is *σοφός* (*Rep.* IX 587 D). It is noticeable that Periander does not appear in the list of the seven wise men in *Prot.* 343 A. The expedition of Xerxes against Greece is cited by Callicles in *Gorg.* 483 D in connexion with the doctrine that might is right. In *Περδίκκου* the allusion is to Perdiccas II, father of Archelaus (*Gorg.* 471 B): he died late in 414 or early in 413, three years before the probable date of action of the *Republic* (*Introd.* § 3), after proving himself a fickle friend and foe to the Athenians during the Peloponnesian war. Ismenias is mentioned again in *Men.* 90 A as having become rich *δόντος τινός—ὁ νῦν νεωστὶ εἰληφὼς τὰ Πολυκράτους χρήματα.* There can be no doubt that he is to be identified with the Ismenias who (see Xen. *Hell.* III 5. 1) in 395 took money from Timocrates the Rhodian, envoy of the Persian King, in order to stir up war against Sparta, and who in 382, when the Spartans had seized the Cadmea, was condemned on this charge among others (Xen. *Hell.* V 2. 35; Plut. *Pelop.* 5. 2). Plato implies that Ismenias kept enough Persian gold to enrich himself. he was no true Greek if he did not. But what is meant by saying that he had received the money of *Polycrates*? This question has been much discussed. Possibly 'the money of Polycrates' (with allusion, of course, to the riches of the Samian tyrant) was a sarcastic expression current in Athens for 'the money of Timocrates': this is perhaps the more likely as we are informed that the Athenians got no share of it themselves (*Hell.* III 5. 2). Plato would naturally avail himself of such a political gibe to express his dislike of a man who took gold from the natural enemy of Greece (*Rep.* V 470 C) to stir up not war, but sedition (ib. 470 B), and withdraw Agesilaus from fighting with the barbarian: for his political ideal in foreign policy was that of Cimon. See also on V 471 B. It is not however likely, I think, that the present passage was written after Ismenias' death, for Plato is not given to reviling his contemporaries after their death. That the other three persons cited by Plato were already dead would only make his reproof of the living more marked and scathing. The present passage—so far as it goes—is on the whole in favour of Teichmüller's view (*Lit. Fehd.* I p. 25) that the first book of the *Republic* was written soon after 395, when the disgraceful affair was still fresh in men's minds. See *Introd.* § 4.

5 **οἰομένου** is to be pressed (as in III 395 D, 409 C: cf. IV 431 C): their power is fancied, not real: they cannot even do the thing they want: cf. *Gorg.* 467 A ff. *πῶς ἂν οὖν οἱ ῥήτορες μέγα δύναιντο ἢ οἱ τύραννοι ἐν ταῖς πόλεσιν, ἐὰν μὴ Σωκράτης*

ταῦτα, ἔφη, λέγεις. Εἶεν, ἦν δ' ἐγώ· ἐπειδὴ δὲ οὐδὲ τοῦτο ἐφάνη ἡ δικαιοσύνη ὂν οὐδὲ τὸ δίκαιον, τί ἂν ἄλλο τις αὐτὸ φαίη εἶναι;

B X. Καὶ ὁ Θρασύμαχος πολλάκις μὲν καὶ διαλεγομένων ἡμῶν μεταξὺ ὥρμα ἀντιλαμβάνεσθαι τοῦ λόγου, ἔπειτα ὑπὸ τῶν παρακαθημένων διεκωλύετο βουλομένων διακοῦσαι τὸν λόγον· ὡς δὲ διεπαυσάμεθα καὶ ἐγὼ ταῦτ' εἶπον, οὐκέτι ἡσυχίαν ἦγεν, ἀλλὰ συστρέψας ἑαυτὸν ὥσπερ θηρίον ἧκεν ἐφ' ἡμᾶς ὡς διαρπασόμενος. καὶ ἐγώ τε καὶ ὁ Πολέμαρχος δείσαντες διεπτοήθημεν·
C ὁ δ' εἰς τὸ μέσον φθεγξάμενος Τίς, ἔφη, ὑμᾶς πάλαι φλυαρία ἔχει, ὦ Σώκρατες; καὶ τί εὐηθίζεσθε πρὸς ἀλλήλους ὑποκατακλινόμενοι ὑμῖν αὐτοῖς; ἀλλ' εἴπερ ὡς ἀληθῶς βούλει εἰδέναι τὸ δίκαιον ὅ τι ἐστί, μὴ μόνον ἐρώτα μηδὲ φιλοτιμοῦ ἐλέγχων, ἐπειδάν τίς τι ἀποκρίνηται, ἐγνωκὼς τοῦτο, ὅτι ῥᾷον ἐρωτᾶν ἢ ἀποκρίνεσθαι, ἀλλὰ καὶ αὐτὸς ἀπόκριναι καὶ εἰπέ, τί φῂς εἶναι

ἐξελεγχθῇ—ὅτι ποιοῦσιν ἃ βούλονται;—οὔ φημι ποιεῖν αὐτοὺς ἃ βούλονται. He alone (says Plato) is truly powerful who wills what is good and has the power to obtain it.

336 A—**337** B *Introduction of Thrasymachus.*

On Plato's representation of Thrasymachus in the *Republic*, see *Introd.* § 2.

336 B 11 **ὡς δὲ διεπαυσάμεθα.** Cobet's suggestion *ὡς δὲ δὴ ἐπαυσάμεθα* misses the point. No doubt *διαπαύομαι* is (as he says) "intermitto orationem post aliquam moram denuo dicturus" (cf. *Tim.* 78 E, *Symp.* 191 C), but this is precisely the sense required, for the question with which Socrates concludes (*τί ἂν ἄλλο κτλ.*) shews that he desires to resume the discussion.

ταῦτ' εἶπον refers to *εἶεν—φαίη εἶναι.*

12 **συστρέψας—διαρπασόμενος**: 'gathering himself up he sprang at us like a wild beast as though he would seize and carry us off.' Thrasymachus comes down like a wolf on the fold. *ἧκεν* is not from *ἥκω*, but from *ἵημι*: this is also Ast's view (in his *Lex. Plat.*). The expression *ἥκειν ἐφ' ἡμᾶς* would be too weak after *συστρέψας ἑαυτὸν ὥσπερ θηρίον.* The object to *ἧκεν* is *ἑαυτόν*, easily supplied from *συστρέψας ἑαυτόν*: lit. 'he let himself go at us.' Cf. Ar. *Frogs* 133. It should be noted also that compounds of *ἵημι* occasionally drop *ἑαυτόν* altogether and become intransitive (e.g. VIII 563 A, *Prot.* 336 A). Hartman's *ἧττεν* for *ἧκεν* is not likely to find favour. For *διαρπασόμενος* Cobet would read *διασπασόμενος.* Plato however does not use *διασπᾶν* of harrying by wild beasts, but in the sense of *disiungere, seiungere* (VI 503 B, *Laws* 669 D): and even Cobet does not propose to change *Pol.* 274 B *διηρπάζοντο ὑπ' αὐτῶν* (i.e. *θηρίων*). J. and C.'s citation of *Il.* XVI 355 *αἶψα διαρπάζουσιν* (i.e. *οἱ λύκοι τὰς ἄρνας*) seems to me (in spite of Hartman's wonder) strictly relevant, if only we take *διαρπάζειν* as 'harry,' and not (with J. and C.) as 'tear in pieces.'

336 C 15 **τί εὐηθίζεσθε κτλ.** *εὐηθίζεσθε* refers to the readiness of the interlocutors to assent to one another's questions: cf. *Charm.* 175 C *οὕτως ἡμῶν εὐηθικῶν τυχοῦσα ἡ σκέψις καὶ οὐ σκληρῶν.*

ὑποκατακλινόμενοι: a metaphor, not from the wrestling schools, but from taking a lower or inferior seat at table or the like: cf. *Symp.* 222 E *ἐὰν οὖν ὑπὸ σοὶ κατακλινῇ Ἀγαθών* and Plut. *quomodo adul. ab amico internoscatur* 58 D *τὰς τοιαύτας ὑποκατακλίσεις* (alluding to men who take the front seats at theatres etc., in order to flatter the rich by giving up their seats to them). Thrasymachus' brutal frankness is not intended by Plato to be altogether wide of the mark: see App. II and 335 A *n.*

17 **μὴ—φιλοτιμοῦ ἐλέγχων.** A common reproach against Socrates: cf. *Theaet.* 150 C.

τὸ δίκαιον· καὶ ὅπως μοι | μὴ ἐρεῖς, ὅτι τὸ δέον ἐστὶν μηδ' ὅτι D
τὸ ὠφέλιμον μηδ' ὅτι τὸ λυσιτελοῦν μηδ' ὅτι τὸ κερδαλέον μηδ'
ὅτι τὸ ξυμφέρον, ἀλλὰ σαφῶς μοι καὶ ἀκριβῶς λέγε ὅ τι ἂν λέγῃς·
ὡς ἐγὼ οὐκ ἀποδέξομαι, ἐὰν ὕθλους τοιούτους λέγῃς. καὶ ἐγὼ
ἀκούσας ἐξεπλάγην καὶ προσβλέπων αὐτὸν ἐφοβούμην, καί μοι
δοκῶ, εἰ μὴ πρότερος ἑωράκη αὐτὸν ἢ ἐκεῖνος ἐμέ, ἄφωνος ἂν
γενέσθαι. νῦν δὲ ἡνίκα ὑπὸ τοῦ λόγου ἤρχετο ἐξαγριαίνεσθαι,
προσέβλεψα | αὐτὸν πρότερος, ὥστε αὐτῷ οἷός τ' ἐγενόμην ἀπο- E
κρίνασθαι, καὶ εἶπον ὑποτρέμων Ὦ Θρασύμαχε, μὴ χαλεπὸς ἡμῖν
ἴσθι· εἰ γὰρ ἐξαμαρτάνομεν ἐν τῇ τῶν λόγων σκέψει ἐγώ τε καὶ
ὅδε, εὖ ἴσθι ὅτι ἄκοντες ἁμαρτάνομεν. μὴ γὰρ δὴ οἴου, εἰ μὲν
χρυσίον ἐζητοῦμεν, οὐκ ἄν ποτε ἡμᾶς ἑκόντας εἶναι ὑποκατακλίνεσθαι ἀλλήλοις ἐν τῇ ζητήσει καὶ διαφθείρειν τὴν εὕρεσιν αὐτοῦ,
δικαιοσύνην δὲ ζητοῦντας, πρᾶγμα πολλῶν χρυσίων τιμιώτερον,
ἔπειθ' οὕτως ἀνοήτως ὑπείκειν ἀλλήλοις καὶ οὐ σπουδάζειν ὅ τι
μάλιστα φανῆναι αὐτό. οἴου γε σύ, ὦ φίλε· ἀλλ', οἶμαι, οὐ
δυνάμεθα· ἐλεεῖσθαι οὖν ἡμᾶς πολὺ μᾶλλον εἰκός ἐστίν | που 337
ὑπὸ ὑμῶν τῶν δεινῶν ἢ χαλεπαίνεσθαι.

35. γε Θ^2 et (antecedente οἷον) Φ: τε AΠ: pro οἴου γε σύ praebent οἷόν γε ἐστὶν Ξ, μὴ οἴου σύ *q*.

---

336 D 20 **ὅπως μοι κτλ.** This idiom is colloquial and abrupt, almost rude: cf. 337 B and the examples cited in Goodwin *MT.* p. 94. Thrasymachus will not tolerate the stale and barren platitudes—note ὕθλους below—of ordinary disputation: cf. [*Clitoph.*] 409 C οὗτος μὲν—τὸ συμφέρον ἀπεκρίνατο, ἄλλος δὲ τὸ δέον, ἕτερος δὲ τὸ ὠφέλιμον, ὁ δὲ τὸ λυσιτελοῦν and Stewart's *Nicomachean Ethics* Vol. I p. 16, with the references there quoted.

25 **εἰ μὴ πρότερος—γενέσθαι.** The θηρίον of 336 B has become a wolf. This is the earliest allusion in Greek literature to the belief that if a wolf sees you first you become dumb. Like Virgil *Ecl.* IX 53 the present passage favours Schaefer's emendation Λύκος εἶδέ σ'; for Λύκον εἶδες in Theocr. XIV 22.

336 E 28 **μὴ χαλεπὸς ἡμῖν ἴσθι:** ἀεὶ θρασύμαχος εἶ, said Herodicus on one occasion to the sophist (Arist. *Rhet.* II 23. 1400ᵇ 20).

29 **ἐξαμαρτάνομεν—ἁμαρτάνομεν**: the preposition is often dropped in repeating a compound verb: cf. V 452 A, VII 533 A, X 608 A and my note on *Prot.* 311 A. I can see no sufficient reason for inserting τι before ἐξαμαρτάνομεν (with Π and some other MSS), although Stallbaum and others approve of the addition.

30 **μὴ γὰρ δὴ οἴου κτλ.** Cf. *Laws* 931 C, where there is a similar *a fortiori* sentence couched in the imperatival form.

31 **ἑκόντας εἶναι.** This phrase is used sixteen times by Plato, always in negative clauses, and generally in the nominative or accusative (Grünenwald in Schanz's *Beiträge zur hist. Synt. d. gr. Spr.* II 3. 1 ff.).

35 **οἴου γε σύ, ὦ φίλε**: i.e. ἡμᾶς σπουδάζειν ὅ τι μάλιστα φανῆναι αὐτό. For the justification of this view see App. IV.

36 **εἰκός ἐστιν.** There is no reason for omitting ἐστίν (with Hartman and apparently also Usener *Unser Platotext* p. 40).

337 A 2 **χαλεπαίνεσθαι.** This strained use of the passive of χαλεπαίνω in order to make the antithesis to ἐλεεῖσθαι formal as well as real is not found elsewhere in Plato. For parallels see Cope's *Rhetoric of Aristotle* Vol. I p. 299.

XI. Καὶ ὃς ἀκούσας ἀνεκάγχασέ τε μάλα σαρδάνιον καὶ εἶπεν Ὦ Ἡράκλεις, ἔφη, αὕτη 'κείνη ἡ εἰωθυῖα εἰρωνεία Σωκράτους, καὶ

4. αὕτη Π: αὐτὴ A.

---

337 A—**339** B *After some wrangling, Thrasymachus finally declares justice to be 'the interest of the stronger.' Rulers are stronger than those whom they rule: and in every state they pass laws in their own interest: and what is done in their own interest they call just.*

337 A ff. The natural history definition of justice (ὁ φύσει ὅρος τοῦ δικαίου *Laws* IV 714 C) is here for the first time mentioned in the *Republic*. It is to be noticed that the theory is presented by Thrasymachus not—in the first instance—as a rule of conduct for the individual, but as a political theory: his object is to describe the actual practice of Greek states (338 D ff.). We are thus for the first time introduced to the *political* aspect of δικαιοσύνη. The same view of the definition is taken in *Laws* 714 C ff., and it is the same theory which is afterwards (in II 358 E ff.) represented by Glauco as an hypothesis on which not Thrasymachus only but many others (Θρασυμάχου καὶ μυρίων ἄλλων 358 C) explained the origin and constitution of existing states: cf. also *Gorg.* 483 A ff. We are therefore justified in supposing that the definition which Plato puts into the mouth of Thrasymachus represents a theory current in the politics of the day. The conduct of Athens towards her allies furnished many examples of the practical application of this rule of government; and, if we may trust Thucydides, similar principles were frankly laid down by Athenian statesmen in their speeches: see for example I 76. 2 ἀεὶ καθεστῶτος τὸν ἥσσω ὑπὸ τοῦ δυνατωτέρου κατείργεσθαι, and cf. I 77. 4, V 89 and 105. 2 τὸ ἀνθρώπειον σαφῶς διὰ παντὸς ὑπὸ φύσεως ἀναγκαίας οὗ ἂν κρατῇ ἄρχειν. It is indeed not too much to say that 'Might is Right' was the only argument by which the existence of the Athenian empire could be defended before the tribunal of Greek public opinion, which regarded the independent πόλις as the only legitimate form of civic life. Hence the dominion of Athens is often in Thucydides called a τυραννίς, from which the Spartans claimed to be liberating their countrymen: see III 37. 2 τυραννίδα ἔχετε τὴν ἀρχήν, 62. 5 ff., IV 85. 6, and cf. Henkel *Studien zur Gesch. d. gr. Lehre vom Staat* pp. 126—128. The most conspicuous assertion of the principle before Plato's time was found in Pindar's much-quoted fragment (Bergk 169 and ap. Pl. *Gorg* 484 B) νόμος ὁ πάντων βασιλεὺς | θνατῶν τε καὶ ἀθανάτων | ἄγει δικαιῶν τὸ βιαιότατον | ὑπερτάτᾳ χειρί κτλ., though it may well be doubted (with Dümmler *Prolegomena zu Platon's Staat* p. 34) whether Pindar intended to suggest any such view. It is in order to refute this theory, as expounded by Glauco and Adimantus, Thrasymachus' successors in the argument (see on παῖδες ἐκείνου τοῦ ἀνδρός II 368 A) that Socrates finds it necessary to draw a picture of an Ideal State (ib. 368 D ff.), so that the *political* theory of Plato's *Republic* may truly be said to commence here. For more on this subject see Chiappelli *Per la storia della Sofistica Greca* in *Archiv f. Gesch. d. Philos.* III pp. 263 ff.

3 **σαρδάνιον.** Plato uses this expression as Homer does, of a sinister smile which bodes pain to others: *Od.* XX 301 f. μείδησε δὲ θυμῷ | σαρδάνιον μάλα τοῖον (of Odysseus among the suitors). Among later authors it more frequently denotes the forced smile which disguises the sufferer's own pain; and so apparently Simonides used the phrase (*Fr.* 202 A Bergk). The explanations volunteered by the ancients apply only to the non-Homeric usage: the Scholiast, however, at the end of his note on this passage correctly remarks, μήποτε οὖν τὸ Ὁμηρικόν, ὅθεν καὶ ἡ παροιμία ἴσως ἐρρύη, "μείδησε δὲ κτλ.," τὸν ἀπ' αὐτῶν τῶν χειλῶν γέλωτα καὶ μέχρι τοῦ σεσηρέναι γιγνόμενον σημαίνει. The spelling σαρδόνιον came into vogue through the popular etymology from the bitter Sardinian herb, ἧς οἱ γευσάμενοι δοκοῦσι μὲν γελῶντες, σπασμῷ δὲ ἀποθνήσκουσιν (Schol.). The Scholiast's suggested derivation from σαίρειν (*ringi*, as of an angry dog) suits the meaning which the phrase bears in Homer and Plato, and is probably right. Photius' σαρδάζων· μετὰ πικρίας γελῶν preserves the δ.

ταῦτ' ἐγὼ ᾔδη τε καὶ τούτοις προὔλεγον, ὅτι σὺ ἀποκρίνασθαι
μὲν οὐκ ἐθελήσοις, εἰρωνεύσοιο δὲ καὶ πάντα μᾶλλον ποιήσοις
ἢ ἀποκρινοῖο, εἴ τίς τί σ' ἐρωτᾷ. Σοφὸς γὰρ εἶ, ἦν δ' ἐγώ, ὦ
Θρασύμαχε· εὖ οὖν ᾔδησθα ὅτι, εἴ τινα ἔροιο ὁπόσα ἐστὶ τὰ
δώδεκα, καὶ ἐρόμενος | προείποις αὐτῷ· ὅπως μοι, ὦ ἄνθρωπε, B
μὴ ἐρεῖς, ὅτι ἔστιν τὰ δώδεκα δὶς ἓξ μηδ' ὅτι τρὶς τέτταρα μηδ'
ὅτι ἑξάκις δύο μηδ' ὅτι τετράκις τρία· ὡς οὐκ ἀποδέξομαί σου,
ἐὰν τοιαῦτα φλυαρῇς· δῆλον, οἶμαι, σοὶ ἦν ὅτι οὐδεὶς ἀποκρινοῖτο
τῷ οὕτως πυνθανομένῳ. ἀλλ' εἴ σοι εἶπεν· ὦ Θρασύμαχε, πῶς
λέγεις; μὴ ἀποκρίνωμαι ὧν προεῖπες μηδέν; πότερον, ὦ θαυμάσιε,
μηδ' εἰ τούτων τι τυγχάνει ὄν, ἀλλ' ἕτερον εἴπω τι τοῦ ἀληθοῦς;
ἢ πῶς λέγεις; | τί ἂν αὐτῷ εἶπες πρὸς ταῦτα; Εἶεν, ἔφη· ὡς δὴ C
ὅμοιον τοῦτο ἐκείνῳ. Οὐδέν γε κωλύει, ἦν δ' ἐγώ· εἰ δ' οὖν καὶ
μὴ ἔστιν ὅμοιον, φαίνεται δὲ τῷ ἐρωτηθέντι τοιοῦτον, ἧττόν τι
αὐτὸν οἴει ἀποκρινεῖσθαι τὸ φαινόμενον ἑαυτῷ, ἐάν τε ἡμεῖς
ἀπαγορεύωμεν ἐάν τε μή; Ἄλλο τι οὖν, ἔφη, καὶ σὺ οὕτω ποιήσεις;
ὧν ἐγὼ ἀπεῖπον, τούτων τι ἀποκρινεῖ; Οὐκ ἂν θαυμάσαιμι, ἦν
δ' ἐγώ, εἴ μοι σκεψαμένῳ οὕτω δόξειεν. Τί οὖν, ἔφη, ἂν ἐγὼ δείξω
ἑτέραν | ἀπόκρισιν παρὰ πάσας ταύτας περὶ δικαιοσύνης βελτίω D

7. ἀποκρινοῖο *q*: ἀποκρίνοιο ΑΞ: ἀποκρίναιο Π. 12. ἀποκρινοῖτο *q*: ἀποκρίνοιτο ΑΠΞ. 19. ἀποκρινεῖσθαι Π: ἀποκρίνεσθαι Α.

---

6 **ποιήσοις** is rejected by Cobet and Herwerden. "Post *οὐδὲν ἄλλο ἤ, τί ἄλλο ἤ, πάντα μᾶλλον ἤ* verbum omittunt" (says Cobet, quoting Theophr. *Char.* c. 25). *ποιήσοις* is not however otiose, but suggests the phrase *πάντα ποιεῖν*, 'leave nothing undone,' as in *Euthyph.* 8 C *πάντα ποιοῦσι καὶ λέγουσι φεύγοντες τὴν δίκην*: cf. *Ap.* 39 A.

7 **ἐρωτᾷ**. I formerly read *ἐρωτῴ* (with Goodwin *MT.* p. 277). A few inferior MSS have *ἔροιτο*. The optative is certainly the regular periodic construction in clauses of this kind: but the indicative may perhaps be allowed in loose conversational style.

337 B 15 **τυγχάνει ὄν**. Stallbaum explains *ὄν* as 'being *true*,' and *τι* as the subject to *τυγχάνει*. This view is perhaps less natural than to make *ὄν* the copula and *τι* the predicate: for the pronoun 'it' i.e. *τὸ ἐρωτώμενον* (Schneider) can be quite easily understood. For the use of *τυγχάνει ὄν* ('really is') cf. II 379 A, VII 518 E, *Euthyph.* 4 E with my note ad loc.

337 C 16 **ὡς δή**. The force of *ὡς* in this common ironical expression (*quasi vero*, cf. *Gorg.* 468 E, 499 B) is referred by Jebb (Soph. *O. C.* 809) to an ellipse: '(do you mean) forsooth that.' An objection to this theory is that it will not explain *ὡς δή τοι* in cases like II 366 C, *Phaedr.* 242 C, *Tim.* 26 B. It seems better to explain these usages on the same principle. The view that *ὡς* is exclamatory will not account for II 366 C, and is not specially appropriate in the other places. Neither is it easy to make *ὡς*=*ἐπεί* ('your illustration is excellent, *seeing that* the cases are so very similar!' Tucker). Schneider (on II 366 C) regards *ὡς* as nearly equivalent to *ὥστε* (cf. note on II 365 D). Probably *ὡς* is in reality consequential (like the English 'so'), the relative retaining its original demonstrative sense. This explanation will, I believe, suit all the passages in question.

337 D 23 **περὶ δικαιοσύνης κτλ.**

τούτων; τί ἀξιοῖς παθεῖν; Τί ἄλλο, ἦν δ' ἐγώ, ἢ ὅπερ προσήκει πάσχειν τῷ μὴ εἰδότι; προσήκει δέ που μαθεῖν παρὰ τοῦ εἰδότος· καὶ ἐγὼ οὖν τοῦτο ἀξιῶ παθεῖν. Ἡδὺς γὰρ εἶ, ἔφη. ἀλλὰ πρὸς τῷ μαθεῖν καὶ ἀπότεισον ἀργύριον. Οὐκοῦν ἐπειδάν μοι γένηται, εἶπον. Ἀλλ' ἔστιν, ἔφη ὁ Γλαύκων· ἀλλ' ἕνεκα ἀργυρίου, ὦ Θρασύμαχε, λέγε· πάντες γὰρ ἡμεῖς Σωκράτει εἰσοίσομεν. Πάνυ
E γε, οἶμαι, | ἦ δ' ὅς, ἵνα Σωκράτης τὸ εἰωθὸς διαπράξηται, αὐτὸς μὲν μὴ ἀποκρίνηται, ἄλλου δ' ἀποκρινομένου λαμβάνῃ λόγον καὶ ἐλέγχῃ. Πῶς γὰρ ἄν, ἔφην ἐγώ, ὦ βέλτιστε, τὶς ἀποκρίναιτο πρῶτον μὲν μὴ εἰδὼς μηδὲ φάσκων εἰδέναι, ἔπειτα, εἴ τι καὶ οἴεται περὶ τούτων, ἀπειρημένον αὐτῷ [εἴη], ὅπως μηδὲν ἐρεῖ ὧν ἡγεῖται, ὑπ' ἀνδρὸς οὐ φαύλου; ἀλλὰ σὲ δὴ μᾶλλον εἰκὸς λέγειν· σὺ γὰρ δὴ |
338 φῂς εἰδέναι καὶ ἔχειν εἰπεῖν. μὴ οὖν ἄλλως ποίει, ἀλλ' ἐμοί τε χαρίζου ἀποκρινόμενος καὶ μὴ φθονήσῃς καὶ Γλαύκωνα τόνδε διδάξαι καὶ τοὺς ἄλλους.

34. αὐτῷ Bremius: αὐτῷ εἴη codd.

περὶ δικαιοσύνης and τούτων are rejected by Herwerden, but the fulness of expression suits the arrogant tone of Thrasymachus.

24 **τί ἀξιοῖς παθεῖν;** Here and in what follows there is a play on the judicial formula παθεῖν ἢ ἀποτεῖσαι, where παθεῖν refers to δεσμός φυγή θάνατος ἀτιμία, and ἀποτεῖσαι to fines. In a δίκη τιμητός, the defendant if found guilty would be asked in the words τί ἀξιοῖς παθεῖν καὶ ἀποτεῖσαι to propose an alternative penalty to that demanded by the accuser; after which it was the duty of the judges finally to assess (τιμᾶν) the penalty: cf. *Ap.* 36 B and *Laws* 933 D. It is partly the paronomasia in the words παθεῖν μαθεῖν (cf. the ancient text πάθος μάθος Aesch. *Ag.* 176) which draws from Thrasymachus the mock compliment ἡδὺς γὰρ εἶ ('you are vastly entertaining') although (cf. ὦ ἥδιστε 348 C) Thrasymachus is also jeering at the simplicity of Socrates.

26 **πρὸς τῷ μαθεῖν καὶ ἀπότεισον.** Hertz and Herwerden conjecture παθεῖν for μαθεῖν: but this would make Thrasymachus ignore Socrates' identification of παθεῖν with μαθεῖν. In ἀπότεισον ἀργύριον Plato no doubt satirizes (somewhat crudely, it must be allowed) the avarice of Thrasymachus and his class, in contrast with whom Socrates has no money, because his conversations are gratis.

29 **εἰσοίσομεν.** The metaphor is from a banquet to which each contributes his share: cf. *Symp.* 177 C ἐγὼ οὖν ἐπιθυμῶ ἅμα μὲν τούτῳ ἔρανον εἰσενεγκεῖν κτλ.

337 E 34 **ἀπειρημένον αὐτῷ.** See *cr. n.* The retention of εἴη after αὐτῷ can only be defended by regarding μὴ εἰδὼς μηδὲ φάσκων as equivalent to εἰ μὴ εἰδείη μηδὲ φάσκοι and carrying on the εἰ; but this is excessively harsh and no parallel has yet been adduced. Of the two alternatives, to insert an εἰ before ἀπειρημένον or εἴη, and to drop εἴη (with Bremius), I prefer the latter as simpler in itself and accounting more easily for the corruption. The accusative absolute may have been misunderstood and εἴη inserted by a negligent reader owing to εἰ in the previous line. Richter (in *Fl. Jahrb.* 1867 p. 137) inserts δ' before αὐτῷ and retains εἴη, regarding εἴ τι καὶ οἴεται and ἀπειρημένον δ' αὐτῷ εἴη as coordinate clauses under the rule of the same εἰ; but to this there are many objections. Tucker's suggestion εἰ, ὅ τι καὶ οἴεται περὶ τούτων, ἀπειρημένον αὐτῷ εἴη κτλ. ('if, in regard to whatever he *thinks* about them, it were forbidden' etc.) strikes me as heavy and cumbrous.

338 A 1 **μὴ οὖν ἄλλως ποίει**: 328 B *n.*

XII. Εἰπόντος δέ μου ταῦτα ὅ τε Γλαύκων καὶ οἱ ἄλλοι ἐδέοντο αὐτοῦ μὴ ἄλλως ποιεῖν. καὶ ὁ Θρασύμαχος φανερὸς μὲν ἦν ἐπιθυμῶν εἰπεῖν, ἵν' εὐδοκιμήσειεν, ἡγούμενος ἔχειν ἀπόκρισιν παγκάλην· προσεποιεῖτο δὲ φιλονικεῖν πρὸς τὸ ἐμὲ εἶναι τὸν ἀποκρινόμενον. τελευτῶν δὲ ξυνεχώρησεν, κἄπειτα | Αὕτη δή, B ἔφη, ἡ Σωκράτους σοφία, αὐτὸν μὲν μὴ ἐθέλειν διδάσκειν, παρὰ δὲ τῶν ἄλλων περιιόντα μανθάνειν καὶ τούτων μηδὲ χάριν ἀποδιδόναι. Ὅτι μέν, ἦν δ' ἐγώ, μανθάνω παρὰ τῶν ἄλλων, ἀληθῆ εἶπες, ὦ Θρασύμαχε· ὅτι δὲ οὔ με φῂς χάριν ἐκτίνειν, ψεύδει· ἐκτίνω γὰρ ὅσην δύναμαι· δύναμαι δὲ ἐπαινεῖν μόνον· χρήματα γὰρ οὐκ ἔχω· ὡς δὲ προθύμως τοῦτο δρῶ, ἐάν τίς μοι δοκῇ εὖ λέγειν, εὖ εἴσει αὐτίκα δὴ μάλα, ἐπειδὰν ἀποκρίνῃ· οἶμαι γάρ | σε εὖ ἐρεῖν. Ἄκουε δή, ἦ δ' ὅς. φημὶ γὰρ ἐγὼ εἶναι τὸ δίκαιον C οὐκ ἄλλο τι ἢ τὸ τοῦ κρείττονος ξυμφέρον. ἀλλὰ τί οὐκ ἐπαινεῖς; ἀλλ' οὐκ ἐθελήσεις. Ἐὰν μάθω γε πρῶτον, ἔφην, τί λέγεις· νῦν γὰρ οὔπω οἶδα. τὸ τοῦ κρείττονος φῂς ξυμφέρον δίκαιον εἶναι. καὶ τοῦτο, ὦ Θρασύμαχε, τί ποτε λέγεις; οὐ γάρ που τό γε τοιόνδε φῄς· εἰ Πουλυδάμας ἡμῶν κρείττων ὁ παγκρατιαστὴς καὶ αὐτῷ ξυμφέρει τὰ βόεια κρέα πρὸς τὸ σῶμα, τοῦτο τὸ σιτίον εἶναι | καὶ ἡμῖν τοῖς ἥττοσιν ἐκείνου ξυμφέρον ἅμα καὶ δίκαιον. D Βδελυρὸς γὰρ εἶ, ἔφη, ὦ Σώκρατες, καὶ ταύτῃ ὑπολαμβάνεις, ᾗ ἂν κακουργήσαις μάλιστα τὸν λόγον. Οὐδαμῶς, ὦ ἄριστε, ἦν δ' ἐγώ·

---

338 C 16 **ἄκουε δή** calls for attention, ostentatiously, like a herald: cf. X 595 C, *Ap.* 20 D, *Prot.* 353 C.

21 **Πουλυδάμας—ὁ παγκρατιαστής.** *οὗτος ὁ Πουλυδάμας ἀπὸ Σκοτούσσης ἦν, πόλεως Θεσσαλίας, διασημότατος παγκρατιαστής, ὑπερμεγέθης*, says the Scholiast. He was victor in the ninety-third Olympian games 408 B.C. Stallbaum refers to Pausanias (VI 5) and others for the wonderful stories of his prowess. His statue at Olympia by Lysippus was very famous. Cf. Boeckh *Kl. Schr.* IV p. 446.

22 **τοῦτο τὸ σιτίον κτλ.** Teichmüller (*Lit. Fehd.* II p. 196) finds in this a confirmation of his belief that Plato was a vegetarian: but it is implied merely that a beef diet was not considered wholesome for persons out of training. Aristotle may have had this passage in view in *Eth. Nic.* II 5. 1106ᵃ 36 ff., though his illustration is there taken from quantity, and not from quality, of food. Cf. also *Gorg.* 490 C.

338 D 23 **ξυμφέρον ἅμα καὶ δίκαιον.** The sophistry is undisguised. If *βόεια κρέα* is Polydamas' *συμφέρον* and *δίκαιον*, and *δίκαιον* is assumed to be everywhere identical with itself, it follows that *βόεια κρέα* is our *δίκαιον*, but not our *ξυμφέρον*, otherwise we are also *κρείττονες*. To avoid this, Wohlrab ingeniously takes *ἐκείνου* not with *ἥττοσιν* but with *ξυμφέρον ἅμα καὶ δίκαιον*, as if the meaning were 'Polydamas' *συμφέρον καὶ δίκαιον* is also *δίκαιον* for us.' This explanation is however linguistically harsh and comparatively pointless. On *βδελυρὸς γὰρ εἶ* Tucker aptly reminds us that the prevailing feature in Theophrastus' description of the *βδελυρός* (*Char.* c. 11) is *παιδιὰ ἐπιφανὴς καὶ ἐπονείδιστος* ('obtrusive and objectionable pleasantry' Jebb).

25 **κακουργήσαις.** Cope observes that the word is used "of the knavish tricks

ἀλλὰ σαφέστερον εἰπὲ τί λέγεις. Εἶτ' οὐκ οἶσθ', ἔφη, ὅτι τῶν
πόλεων αἱ μὲν τυραννοῦνται, αἱ δὲ δημοκρατοῦνται, αἱ δὲ ἀριστοκρατοῦνται; Πῶς γὰρ οὔ; Οὐκοῦν τοῦτο κρατεῖ ἐν ἑκάστῃ πόλει,
E τὸ ἄρχον; Πάνυ γε. Τίθεται δέ γε τοὺς | νόμους ἑκάστη ἡ ἀρχὴ
πρὸς τὸ αὑτῇ ξυμφέρον, δημοκρατία μὲν δημοκρατικούς, τυραννὶς
δὲ τυραννικούς, καὶ αἱ ἄλλαι οὕτως· θέμεναι δὲ ἀπέφηναν τοῦτο
δίκαιον τοῖς ἀρχομένοις εἶναι, τὸ σφίσι ξυμφέρον, καὶ τὸν τούτου
ἐκβαίνοντα κολάζουσιν ὡς παρανομοῦντά τε καὶ ἀδικοῦντα. τοῦτ'
339 οὖν ἐστίν, ὦ βέλτιστε, ὃ λέγω, ἐν ἁπάσαις ταῖς | πόλεσιν ταὐτὸν
εἶναι δίκαιον, τὸ τῆς καθεστηκυίας ἀρχῆς ξυμφέρον· αὕτη δέ που
κρατεῖ, ὥστε ξυμβαίνει τῷ ὀρθῶς λογιζομένῳ πανταχοῦ εἶναι τὸ
αὐτὸ δίκαιον, τὸ τοῦ κρείττονος ξυμφέρον. Νῦν, ἦν δ' ἐγώ, ἔμαθον
ὃ λέγεις· εἰ δὲ ἀληθὲς ἢ μή, πειράσομαι μαθεῖν. τὸ ξυμφέρον μὲν
οὖν, ὦ Θρασύμαχε, καὶ σὺ ἀπεκρίνω δίκαιον εἶναι· καίτοι ἔμοιγε
ἀπηγόρευες ὅπως μὴ τοῦτο ἀποκρινοίμην· πρόσεστι δὲ δὴ αὐτόθι |
B τὸ τοῦ κρείττονος. Σμικρά γε ἴσως, ἔφη, προσθήκη. Οὔπω δῆλον
οὐδ' εἰ μεγάλη· ἀλλ' ὅτι μὲν τοῦτο σκεπτέον εἰ ἀληθῆ λέγεις,
δῆλον. ἐπειδὴ γὰρ ξυμφέρον γέ τι εἶναι καὶ ἐγὼ ὁμολογῶ τὸ

29. ἑκάστη Π: ἑκάστῃ A.

---

and fallacies which may be employed in rhētorical and dialectical reasoning" (*Aristotle's Rhetoric* Vol. I p. 17). Cf. *Gorg.* 483 A (cited by Tucker).

26 **εἶτ' οὐκ οἶσθα κτλ.** 'Do you mean to say you don't know' etc. The division of constitutions into Monarchy, Oligarchy (for which Aristocracy is here substituted) and Democracy was familiar to everybody: see Aeschin. *Ctes.* 6, *Tim.* 4 ὁμολογοῦνται γὰρ τρεῖς εἶναι πολιτεῖαι παρὰ πᾶσιν ἀνθρώποις, τυραννὶς καὶ ὀλιγαρχία καὶ δημοκρατία. Cf. Whibley *Greek Oligarchies* pp. 17, 24. Thrasymachus proceeds to define κρείττων as ὁ κρατῶν (not ὁ ἰσχυρότερος, as Socrates had insinuated): -κρατοῦνται in δημοκρατοῦνται and ἀριστοκρατοῦνται well brings out his meaning. Cf. *Laws* 714 B νόμων εἴδη τινές φασιν εἶναι τοσαῦτα ὅσαπερ πολιτειῶν, and C οὔτε γὰρ πρὸς τὸν πόλεμον οὔτε πρὸς ἀρετὴν ὅλην βλέπειν δεῖν φασι τοὺς νόμους, ἀλλ' ἥτις ἂν καθεστηκυῖα ᾖ πολιτεία, ταύτῃ δεῖν τὸ ξυμφέρον ὅπως ἄρξει τε ἀεὶ καὶ μὴ καταλυθήσεται, καὶ τὸν φύσει ὅρον τοῦ δικαίου λέγεσθαι κάλλισθ' οὕτως. Πῶς; Ὅτι τὸ τοῦ κρείττονος ξυμφέρον ἐστί.

29 **τίθεται δέ γε**: *Laws* l. c. τίθεται δήπου, φασί, τοὺς νόμους ἐν τῇ πόλει ἑκάστοτε τὸ κρατοῦν. ἢ γάρ; Ἀληθῆ λέγεις. Ἆρ' οὖν οἴει, φασί, ποτὲ δῆμον νικήσαντα ἤ τινα πολιτείαν ἄλλην ἢ καὶ τύραννον θήσεσθαι ἑκόντα πρὸς ἄλλο τι πρῶτον νόμους ἢ τὸ συμφέρον ἑαυτῷ τῆς ἀρχῆς τοῦ μένειν; Πῶς γὰρ ἄν; Aristotle makes it the distinguishing mark of his three perverted forms (παρεκβάσεις) of constitution (τυραννίς, ὀλιγαρχία, δημοκρατία) that they seek their own and not τὸ κοινῇ συμφέρον: *Pol.* Γ 7. 1279^b 4 ff.

338 E 32 **τὸν τούτου ἐκβαίνοντα κτλ.** *Laws* 714 D οὐκοῦν καὶ ὃς ἂν ταῦτα τὰ τεθέντα παραβαίνῃ, κολάσει ὁ θέμενος ὡς ἀδικοῦντα, δίκαια ταῦτ' εἶναι ἐπονομάζων; Ἔοικε γοῦν. Ταῦτ' ἄρ' ἀεὶ καὶ οὕτω καὶ ταύτῃ τὸ δίκαιον ἂν ἔχοι. Φησὶ γοῦν οὗτος ὁ λόγος. νόμος and δίκαιον are identified by this theory.

339 A 1 **ταὐτὸν εἶναι δίκαιον.** Herwerden would expunge ταὐτόν, but ταὐτὸν is not more otiose here than τὸ αὐτὸ below.

339 B 10 **ξυμφέρον γέ τι.** There

δίκαιον, σὺ δὲ προστίθης καὶ αὐτὸ φῂς εἶναι τὸ τοῦ κρείττονος,
ἐγὼ δὲ ἀγνοῶ, σκεπτέον δή. Σκόπει, ἔφη.

XIII. Ταῦτ' ἔσται, ἦν δ' ἐγώ. καί μοι εἰπέ· οὐ καὶ πείθεσθαι
μέντοι τοῖς ἄρχουσιν δίκαιον φῂς εἶναι; Ἔγωγε. Πότερον δὲ
ἀναμάρτητοί εἰσιν οἱ ἄρχοντες ἐν ταῖς πόλεσιν ἑκάσταις ἢ οἷοί C
τι καὶ ἁμαρτεῖν; Πάντως που, ἔφη, οἷοί τι καὶ ἁμαρτεῖν. Οὐκοῦν
ἐπιχειροῦντες νόμους τιθέναι τοὺς μὲν ὀρθῶς τιθέασιν, τοὺς δέ
τινας οὐκ ὀρθῶς; Οἶμαι ἔγωγε. Τὸ δὲ ὀρθῶς ἄρα τὸ τὰ ξυμφέ-
ροντά ἐστι τίθεσθαι ἑαυτοῖς, τὸ δὲ μὴ ὀρθῶς ἀξύμφορα; ἢ πῶς
λέγεις; Οὕτως. Ἃ δ' ἂν θῶνται, ποιητέον τοῖς ἀρχομένοις, καὶ
τοῦτό ἐστι τὸ δίκαιον; Πῶς γὰρ οὔ; Οὐ μόνον ἄρα δίκαιόν ἐστι
κατὰ τὸν σὸν λόγον τὸ τοῦ κρείττονος ξυμφέρον ποιεῖν, ἀλλὰ καὶ D
τοὐναντίον, τὸ μὴ ξυμφέρον. Τί λέγεις σύ; ἔφη. Ἃ σὺ λέγεις,
ἔμοιγε δοκῶ· σκοπῶμεν δὲ βέλτιον. οὐχ ὡμολόγηται τοὺς ἄρχοντας τοῖς ἀρχομένοις προστάττοντας ποιεῖν ἄττα ἐνίοτε διαμαρ-
τάνειν τοῦ ἑαυτοῖς βελτίστου, ἃ δ' ἂν προστάττωσιν οἱ ἄρχοντες

11. αὐτὸ A²Π: αὐτὸς A¹. 14. δίκαιον Π: καὶ δίκαιον A. 24. δὲ Ξq: δὴ AΠ.

---

is here a hint of the main purpose of the *Republic*, which is to prove that δίκαιον is ξυμφέρον in the truest sense for the individual and the state.

339 B—**341** A *Now that the meaning of the definition has been explained, Socrates proceeds to attack it. Even if we assume that rulers seek their own advantage, yet they often err, and enact laws to their own disadvantage: therefore, as it is just for subjects to obey their rulers, Justice will sometimes consist in doing what is not the interest of the stronger. Socrates reiterates this objection and is supported by Polemarchus. It is urged by Clitophon that Thrasymachus meant by 'the interest of the stronger' what was thought—whether rightly or wrongly—by the stronger to be to their interest. Thrasymachus declines to avail himself of this suggestion, and explains that, strictly speaking, rulers,* qua *rulers, cannot err. This statement he supports by arguing from the analogy of medical practitioners and others, pleading that his earlier concession was but a popular way of expressing the fact that rulers seem to err. Therefore the original definition was strictly correct. Justice is the interest of the stronger, since rulers make laws in their own interest, and,* qua *rulers, are infallible.*

On the reasoning of Thrasymachus in these two chapters see 341 A *n.*

339 B 13 **οὐ—μέντοι.** "In interrogationibus haec particula" (μέντοι) "ita cum οὐ negatione coniungitur, ut gravissima sententiae vox intercedat, quo modo aliquis eis quae ex altero quaerit summam veritatis ingerit speciem" (Hoefer *de part. Plat.* p. 34). μέντοι is simply 'of course,' 'surely': 'surely you regard it as just to obey the rulers, do you not?' The idiom is frequent in Plato. The other examples of it (cited by Stallbaum) in the *Republic* are infra 346 A, VII 521 D, IX 581 A, 584 A, X 596 E.

14 **πότερον δὲ ἀναμάρτητοι κτλ.** The reasoning echoes that of 334 C above.

339 C 17 **τιθέναι—τίθεσθαι**: we should expect τιθέναι in both cases, as the ἄρχοντες according to the theory we are discussing are κρείττονες and supreme as legislators: but the middle of personal interest is naturally used in combination with τὰ ξυμφέροντα ἑαυτοῖς: cf. infra 341 A.

339 D 23 **τί λέγεις σύ;** a favourite eristic formula: see Ar. *Clouds* 1174 τοῦτο τοὐπιχώριον | ἀτεχνῶς ἐπανθεῖ, τὸ τί λέγεις σύ;

δίκαιον εἶναι τοῖς ἀρχομένοις ποιεῖν; ταῦτ' οὐχ ὡμολόγηται;
E Οἶμαι ἔγωγε, ἔφη. Οἴου τοίνυν, ἦν δ' ἐγώ, καὶ τὸ ἀξύμφορα
ποιεῖν τοῖς ἄρχουσί τε καὶ κρείττοσι δίκαιον εἶναι ὡμολογῆσθαί
σοι, ὅταν οἱ μὲν ἄρχοντες ἄκοντες κακὰ αὑτοῖς προστάττωσιν, τοῖς
δὲ δίκαιον εἶναι φῇς ταῦτα ποιεῖν ἃ ἐκεῖνοι προσέταξαν· ἆρα τότε,
ὦ σοφώτατε Θρασύμαχε, οὐκ ἀναγκαῖον συμβαίνειν αὐτὸ οὑτωσὶ
δίκαιον εἶναι ποιεῖν τοὐναντίον ἢ ὃ σὺ λέγεις; τὸ γὰρ τοῦ κρείττονος ἀξύμφορον δήπου προστάττεται τοῖς ἥττοσιν ποιεῖν. Ναὶ
340 μὰ Δί', ἔφη, ὦ Σώκρατες, ὁ Πολέμαρχος, σαφέστατά γε. Ἐὰν σύ
γ', ἔφη, αὐτῷ μαρτυρήσῃς, ὁ Κλειτοφῶν ὑπολαβών. Καὶ τί,
ἔφη, δεῖται μάρτυρος; αὐτὸς γὰρ Θρασύμαχος ὁμολογεῖ τοὺς μὲν
ἄρχοντας ἐνίοτε ἑαυτοῖς κακὰ προστάττειν, τοῖς δὲ ἀρχομένοις
δίκαιον εἶναι ταῦτα ποιεῖν. Τὸ γὰρ τὰ κελευόμενα ποιεῖν, ὦ
Πολέμαρχε, ὑπὸ τῶν ἀρχόντων δίκαιον εἶναι ἔθετο Θρασύμαχος.
Καὶ γὰρ τὸ τοῦ κρείττονος, ὦ Κλειτοφῶν, συμφέρον δίκαιον εἶναι
B ἔθετο. ταῦτα δὲ ἀμφότερα θέμενος ὡμολόγησεν αὖ ἐνίοτε τοὺς
κρείττους τὰ αὑτοῖς ἀξύμφορα κελεύειν τοὺς ἥττους τε καὶ ἀρχομένους ποιεῖν. ἐκ δὲ τούτων τῶν ὁμολογιῶν οὐδὲν μᾶλλον τὸ τοῦ
κρείττονος ξυμφέρον δίκαιον ἂν εἴη ἢ τὸ μὴ ξυμφέρον. Ἀλλ', ἔφη
ὁ Κλειτοφῶν, τὸ τοῦ κρείττονος ξυμφέρον ἔλεγεν ὃ ἡγοῖτο ὁ
κρείττων αὑτῷ ξυμφέρειν· τοῦτο ποιητέον εἶναι τῷ ἥττονι, καὶ

---

28 **τοίνυν**: not 'therefore,' but 'also,' a frequent use in Plato. In the *Republic* it occurs 29 times, according to Kugler *de particulae* τοι *eiusque comp. ap. Pl. usu* p. 34.

339 E 30 **ὅταν οἱ μὲν—τοῖς δέ** (i.e. *τοῖς ἀρχομένοις*). These two clauses depend, not on *ὡμολογῆσθαι*, but on *ποιεῖν*: it is just to do *τὰ ἀξύμφορα τοῖς ἄρχουσιν* as often as the rulers unwillingly prescribe what is evil for themselves and so long as Thrasymachus says it is just for subjects to do what the rulers have prescribed. Desire for brevity and balance leads Plato to put both clauses under the government of *ὅταν*, although 'since' rather than 'whenever' is the more appropriate conjunction for introducing the second: for Thrasymachus does not sometimes but always assert that it is just to obey the rulers. The suggested reading *φῄς* for *φῇς* would require us to take *τοῖς δέ κτλ.* as an independent sentence, and leave *μέν* in *οἱ μέν* without a corresponding *δέ*.

32 **αὐτό** is 'the matter,' 'the case before us': cf. IV 428 A (*αὐτῷ*), VII 518 B (*αὐτῶν*), 524 E (*αὐτῷ*), *Theaet.* 172 E al. The text has been needlessly suspected by Madvig and other critics.

οὑτωσί: not 'in that case' (Campbell), but (with Jowett) simply 'thus,' as explained in *δίκαιον—λέγεις*: cf. *Ap.* 26 E *οὑτωσί σοι δοκῶ; οὐδένα νομίζω θεὸν εἶναι;*

34 **ναὶ μὰ Δία κτλ.** The interlude is intended to mark that the first stage has been reached in the refutation of Thrasymachus.

340 A 1 **ἐάν σύ γε** is of course ironical. The disciples of the rival disputants now enter the fray.

5 **τὸ γὰρ τὰ κελευόμενα κτλ.** If this, and no more, had been Thrasymachus' definition, it would remain unrefuted; commands would be commands, whether expedient for the rulers or not.

340 B 12 **ὃ ἡγοῖτο—ξυμφέρειν.** This explanation is involved in Clitophon's earlier statement *τὸ τὰ κελευόμενα ποιεῖν*

τὸ δίκαιον τοῦτο ἐτίθετο. Ἀλλ' οὐχ οὕτως, ἦ δ' ὃς ὁ Πολέμαρχος,
ἐλέγετο. Οὐδέν, ἦν | δ' ἐγώ, ὦ Πολέμαρχε, διαφέρει, ἀλλ' εἰ νῦν C
οὕτω λέγει Θρασύμαχος, οὕτως αὐτοῦ ἀποδεχώμεθα.

XIV. Καί μοι εἰπέ, ὦ Θρασύμαχε· τοῦτο ἦν ὃ ἐβούλου
λέγειν τὸ δίκαιον, τὸ τοῦ κρείττονος ξυμφέρον δοκοῦν εἶναι τῷ
κρείττονι, ἐάν τε ξυμφέρῃ ἐάν τε μή; οὕτως σε φῶμεν λέγειν;
Ἥκιστά γ', ἔφη· ἀλλὰ κρείττω με οἴει καλεῖν τὸν ἐξαμαρτάνοντα,
ὅταν ἐξαμαρτάνῃ; Ἔγωγε, εἶπον, ᾤμην σε τοῦτο λέγειν, ὅτε τοὺς
ἄρχοντας ὡμολόγεις οὐκ ἀναμαρτήτους | εἶναι, ἀλλά τι καὶ ἐξαμαρ- D
τάνειν. Συκοφάντης γὰρ εἶ, ἔφη, ὦ Σώκρατες, ἐν τοῖς λόγοις· ἐπεὶ
αὐτίκα ἰατρὸν καλεῖς σὺ τὸν ἐξαμαρτάνοντα περὶ τοὺς κάμνοντας
κατ' αὐτὸ τοῦτο ὃ ἐξαμαρτάνει; ἢ λογιστικόν, ὃς ἂν ἐν λογισμῷ
ἁμαρτάνῃ, τότε ὅταν ἁμαρτάνῃ, κατὰ ταύτην τὴν ἁμαρτίαν; ἀλλ',
οἶμαι, λέγομεν τῷ ῥήματι οὕτως, ὅτι ὁ ἰατρὸς ἐξήμαρτεν καὶ ὁ
λογιστὴς ἐξήμαρτεν καὶ ὁ γραμματιστής· τὸ δ', οἶμαι, ἕκαστος
τούτων, καθ' ὅσον τοῦτ' ἔστιν ὃ προσαγορεύομεν | αὐτόν, οὐδέποτε E
ἁμαρτάνει· ὥστε κατὰ τὸν ἀκριβῆ λόγον, ἐπειδὴ καὶ σὺ ἀκριβο-
λογεῖ, οὐδεὶς τῶν δημιουργῶν ἁμαρτάνει. ἐπιλιπούσης γὰρ ἐπιστήμης ὁ ἁμαρτάνων ἁμαρτάνει, ἐν ᾧ οὐκ ἔστι δημιουργός· ὥστε
δημιουργὸς ἢ σοφὸς ἢ ἄρχων οὐδεὶς ἁμαρτάνει τότε ὅταν ἄρχων ᾖ,

31. ἐπιλιπούσης A¹Π: ἐπιλειπούσης A².

ὑπὸ τῶν ἀρχόντων: that which the rulers κελεύουσι is what they believe to be in their interests. Clitophon's defence finds no justification in the terms of Thrasymachus' definition; but it was the most obvious way of attempting to reconcile that definition with the admission that rulers are capable of erring.

340 C 18 **τὸ τοῦ κρείττονος ξυμφέρον κτλ.** Bonitz (*Zeitschr. f. öst. Gymn.* 1865 p. 648), followed by Wohlrab, proposes to add the words τὸ ξυμφέρον after ξυμφέρον, "parum venuste," as Hartman thinks. Neither is it well (with Hartman) to omit τοῦ κρείττονος. The apparent harshness of the construction ('that which seems to be the stronger's interest to the stronger') is justified by its brevity and precision, and by the desire to introduce the exact words of the original definition into its amended form.

340 D 23 **συκοφάντης.** Cf. (with Tucker) Arist. *Soph. El.* 15. 174ᵇ 9 σοφιστικὸν συκοφάντημα τῶν ἐρωτώντων and *Rhet.* II 24. 1402ᵃ 14 ἐπὶ τῶν ἐριστικῶν τὸ κατὰ τί καὶ πρός τι καὶ πῇ οὐ προστιθέμενα ποιεῖ τὴν συκοφαντίαν.

27 **λέγομεν τῷ ῥήματι οὕτως.** Bekker (with whom Shilleto on Dem. *F. L.* § 91 agrees) would insert μέν after λέγομεν: but (as Schneider remarks) the emphasis on τῷ ῥήματι does duty instead of the particle, and even otherwise, μέν is not essential: cf. III 398 A (where Shilleto would also add μέν), infra 343 C, II 363 E, X 605 C al.

28 **τὸ δέ** = 'whereas in point of fact' is a favourite Platonic idiom: cf. IV 443 C, VII 527 A, 527 D al.

340 E 31 **ἐπιλιπούσης.** See *cr. n.* The present, which Stallbaum and others adopt, may be right, but the older reading is at least as good. The failure in knowledge must precede the actual error. For the mistake see *Introd.* § 5.

ἀλλὰ πᾶς γ' ἂν εἴποι, ὅτι ὁ ἰατρὸς ἥμαρτεν καὶ ὁ ἄρχων ἥμαρτεν.
τοιοῦτον οὖν δή σοι καὶ ἐμὲ ὑπόλαβε νῦν δὴ ἀποκρίνεσθαι· τὸ δὲ
341 ἀκριβέστατον ἐκεῖνο τυγχάνει ὄν, τὸν ἄρχοντα, καθ' ὅσον | ἄρχων
ἐστί, μὴ ἁμαρτάνειν, μὴ ἁμαρτάνοντα δὲ τὸ αὑτῷ βέλτιστον
τίθεσθαι, τοῦτο δὲ τῷ ἀρχομένῳ ποιητέον. ὥστε, ὅπερ ἐξ ἀρχῆς
ἔλεγον, δίκαιον λέγω τὸ τοῦ κρείττονος ποιεῖν συμφέρον.

XV. Εἶεν, ἦν δ' ἐγώ, ὦ Θρασύμαχε· δοκῶ σοι συκοφαντεῖν;
Πάνυ μὲν οὖν, ἔφη. Οἴει γάρ με ἐξ ἐπιβουλῆς ἐν τοῖς λόγοις
κακουργοῦντά σε ἐρέσθαι ὡς ἠρόμην; Εὖ μὲν οὖν οἶδα, ἔφη· καὶ
οὐδέν γέ σοι πλέον ἔσται· οὔτε γὰρ ἄν με λάθοις κακουργῶν,
B οὔτε | μὴ λαθὼν βιάσασθαι τῷ λόγῳ δύναιο. Οὐδέ γ' ἂν ἐπι-
χειρήσαιμι, ἦν δ' ἐγώ, ὦ μακάριε. ἀλλ' ἵνα μὴ αὖθις ἡμῖν
τοιοῦτον ἐγγένηται, διόρισαι, ποτέρως λέγεις τὸν ἄρχοντά τε καὶ

---

35 **ἀποκρίνεσθαι.** The imperfect infinitive, as Schneider remarks (*Addit.* p. 6).

341 A—**342** E *Socrates now meets Thrasymachus on his own ground, and attacks his definition according tp the 'strictest form' of argument. He shews by analogy that every ruler* qua *ruler seeks the good of those whom he rules, since every art aims at the good of its own peculiar charge or object, and not at its own, for* qua *art there is nothing lacking to it.*

341 A ff. It is to be noted that the discussion is now transferred from the region of facts into an atmosphere of idealism. For this, Thrasymachus is primarily responsible. The theory that the ruler *qua* ruler makes no mistakes, is no doubt true ideally, but practically it is of little moment, since he will suffer *qua* ruler for the errors which he commits in moments of aberration. The strength of Thrasymachus' theory lay in its correspondence with the facts (real or apparent) of experience; it is the temptation to defend his theory against the criticism of Socrates which leads him to abandon facts for ideas; and as soon as he is refuted on the idealistic plane, he descends to facts again (343 A ff.). The vein of idealism struck by Thrasymachus is worked to some purpose by Socrates. To assert that rulers *qua* rulers always seek the good of their subjects is in reality to set before us a political ideal, and Plato's Ideal Commonwealth is intended to be its embodiment in a state. Plato was probably the first to develope and elaborate this principle of political science, but the legislations of Solon and other early lawgivers furnish examples of its application to practical politics (see especially Arist. *Rep. Ath.* ch. 12 and Solon's verses there cited), and it is formulated by the historical Socrates in Xen. *Mem.* III 2, with which compare *Cyrop.* VIII 2. 14. See also Henkel *Studien zur Gesch. d. gr. Lehre vom Staat* pp. 44, 145, and Whibley *Greek Oligarchies* p. 11 *n.* 29.

5 **συκοφαντεῖν** is explained in ἐξ ἐπιβουλῆς—κακουργοῦντά σε, where κακουργοῦντα (as Schneider observes) is not used as in 338 D of putting an evil or sophistical interpretation on a theory, but of damaging a man's personal reputation and credit: "scilicet existimationis et pecuniae detrimentum facturus sibi videbatur sophista ideoque Socratem se, quamquam frustra, impugnare in sequentibus quoque criminatur."

341 B 9 **μὴ λαθών**: "si non latueris" (Schneider). Stephanus conjectured μήν and Ast με for μή: but either change would destroy the antithesis between λανθάνειν and βιάζεσθαι—secret guile and open fraud: cf. II 365 D ἀλλὰ δὴ θεοὺς οὔτε λανθάνειν, οὔτε βιάσασθαι δυνατόν. Hirschig's excision of μὴ λαθών greatly impairs the emphasis.

τὸν κρείττονα, τὸν ὡς ἔπος εἰπεῖν ἢ τὸν ἀκριβεῖ λόγῳ, ὃ νῦν δὴ ἔλεγες, οὗ τὸ ξυμφέρον κρείττονος ὄντος δίκαιον ἔσται τῷ ἥττονι ποιεῖν. Τὸν τῷ ἀκριβεστάτῳ, ἔφη, λόγῳ ἄρχοντα ὄντα. πρὸς ταῦτα κακούργει καὶ συκοφάντει, εἴ τι δύνασαι· οὐδέν σου παρίεμαι· ἀλλ' οὐ μὴ | οἷός τ' ᾖς. Οἴει γὰρ ἄν με, εἶπον, οὕτω C μανῆναι, ὥστε ξυρεῖν ἐπιχειρεῖν λέοντα καὶ συκοφαντεῖν Θρασύμαχον; Νῦν γοῦν, ἔφη, ἐπεχείρησας, οὐδὲν ὢν καὶ ταῦτα. Ἅδην, ἦν δ' ἐγώ, τῶν τοιούτων. ἀλλ' εἰπέ μοι· ὁ τῷ ἀκριβεῖ λόγῳ ἰατρός, ὃν ἄρτι ἔλεγες, πότερον χρηματιστής ἐστιν ἢ τῶν καμνόντων θεραπευτής; καὶ λέγε τὸν τῷ ὄντι ἰατρὸν ὄντα. Τῶν καμνόντων, ἔφη, θεραπευτής. Τί δὲ κυβερνήτης; ὁ ὀρθῶς κυβερνήτης ναυτῶν ἄρχων ἐστὶν ἢ ναύτης; Ναυτῶν | ἄρχων. Οὐδέν, D οἶμαι, τοῦτο ὑπολογιστέον, ὅτι πλεῖ ἐν τῇ νηΐ, οὐδ' ἐστὶν κλητέος ναύτης· οὐ γὰρ κατὰ τὸ πλεῖν κυβερνήτης καλεῖται, ἀλλὰ κατὰ τὴν τέχνην καὶ τὴν τῶν ναυτῶν ἀρχήν. Ἀληθῆ, ἔφη. Οὐκοῦν ἑκάστῳ τούτων ἔστιν τι ξυμφέρον; Πάνυ γε. Οὐ καὶ ἡ τέχνη,

12. ὃ A[2]Π: om. A[1]. 18. γοῦν Π: γε οὖν A.

---

12 **τὸν ὡς ἔπος εἰπεῖν.** The only exact parallel to this use of ὡς ἔπος εἰπεῖν in Plato is *Laws* 656 E σκοπῶν δ' εὑρήσεις αὐτόθι τὰ μυριοστὸν ἔτος γεγραμμένα ἢ τετυπωμένα οὐχ ὡς ἔπος εἰπεῖν μυριοστὸν ἀλλ' ὄντως. This idiomatic phrase is rare before Plato, who uses it 77 times with the meaning 'to put the matter in a word,' implying that other and possibly more exact means of describing the thing in question might be found. In 52 of these cases the phrase is combined with πᾶς or οὐδείς and their family of words, in the sense of *fere*, *propemodum*: its use in other connexions is in part a return to old poetic usage; cf. Aesch. *Pers.* 714, Eur. *Hipp.* 1162, *Heracl.* 167. See Grünenwald in Schanz's *Beiträge zur hist. Synt. d. gr. Spr.* II 3, pp. 21 ff. The other examples in the *Republic* are V 464 D, VIII 551 B, IX 577 C.

ὃ νῦν δὴ ἔλεγες: viz. in 340 E κατὰ τὸν ἀκριβῆ λόγον. The antecedent is the phrase ἀκριβεῖ λόγῳ. The conjecture of Benedictus, ὅν for ὅ, though adopted by several editors, would (as Schneider remarks) leave it uncertain whether λόγῳ or τόν was referred to by the relative. There is no MS authority for ὅν.

341 C 17 **ξυρεῖν—λέοντα.** παροιμία ἐπὶ τῶν καθ' ἑαυτῶν τι ἢ ἀδύνατα ποιεῖν ἐπιχειρούντων λεγομένη (Schol.). The proverb is very rare, and does not seem to occur elsewhere in classical Greek.

18 **οὐδὲν ὢν καὶ ταῦτα**: 'though you were a nonentity at that too': i.e. at bluffing me, as well as in other respects. So (I think) Schneider, rightly ("aber auch darin ist's nichts mit dir"). Others (e.g. Shorey in *A. J. Ph.* XVI p. 234) explain 'and that too though you are a thing of naught.' But in that case καὶ ταῦτα would surely precede οὐδὲν ὤν. Tucker can hardly be right in making καὶ ταῦτα simply 'moreover' 'too,' 'and proved a failure, too.' Nor (in spite of J. B. Mayor in *Cl. Rev.* X p. 110) is it quite enough to translate (with Campbell) 'though here again you are nobody,' i.e. 'with as little effect as ever.'

21 **καὶ λέγε—ὄντα** is expunged by Herwerden, but the emphatic reiteration is in keeping with the whole tone of the passage. For the sense we may recall the words of the so-called oath of Hippocrates εἰς οἰκίας δὲ ὁκόσας ἂν ἐσίω, ἐσελεύσομαι ἐπ' ὠφελείῃ τῶν καμνόντων (Vol. I. p. 2 ed. Kühn).

341 D 27 **ἑκάστῳ τούτων**: viz. τοῖς κάμνουσι, τοῖς ναύταις, and in general the sub-

ἦν δ' ἐγώ, ἐπὶ τούτῳ πέφυκεν, ἐπὶ τῷ τὸ ξυμφέρον ἑκάστῳ ζητεῖν
τε καὶ ἐκπορίζειν; Ἐπὶ τούτῳ, ἔφη. Ἆρ' οὖν καὶ ἑκάστη τῶν
τεχνῶν ἔστιν τι ξυμφέρον ἄλλο ἢ ὅ τι μάλιστα τελέαν εἶναι; |
E Πῶς τοῦτο ἐρωτᾷς; Ὥσπερ, ἔφην ἐγώ, εἴ με ἔροιο, εἰ ἐξαρκεῖ
σώματι εἶναι σώματι ἢ προσδεῖταί τινος, εἴποιμ' ἂν ὅτι Παντάπασι
μὲν οὖν προσδεῖται. διὰ ταῦτα καὶ ἡ τέχνη ἐστὶν ἡ ἰατρικὴ νῦν
ηὑρημένη, ὅτι σῶμά ἐστι πονηρὸν καὶ οὐκ ἐξαρκεῖ αὐτῷ τοιούτῳ
εἶναι. τούτῳ οὖν ὅπως ἐκπορίζῃ τὰ συμφέροντα, ἐπὶ τούτῳ
παρεσκευάσθη ἡ τέχνη. ἦ ὀρθῶς σοι δοκῶ, ἔφην, ἂν εἰπεῖν οὕτω
342 λέγων, ἢ οὔ; Ὀρθῶς, | ἔφη. Τί δὲ δή; αὐτὴ ἡ ἰατρική ἐστιν
πονηρά, ἢ ἄλλη τις τέχνη ἔσθ' ὅ τι προσδεῖταί τινος ἀρετῆς,
ὥσπερ ὀφθαλμοὶ ὄψεως καὶ ὦτα ἀκοῆς καὶ διὰ ταῦτα ἐπ' αὐτοῖς
δεῖ τινὸς τέχνης τῆς τὸ ξυμφέρον εἰς ταῦτα σκεψομένης τε καὶ

1. *αὐτὴ* A²Π: *αὕτη* A¹.

---

jects upon whom the art is exercised. The expression is a little vague (cf. VIII 543 C *n.*) but it is rash and unnecessary to insert *εἴδει* or write *ἑκάστῳ* <*τῶν εἰδῶν*> *τούτων*, as Tucker recommends.

29 **ἆρ' οὖν—τελέαν εἶναι.** I have retained this reading, in deference to the MSS, but it is open to grave objection. As the sentence stands, the meaning is that every art (as well as every object of an art—this is implied by *καί*) has *one συμφέρον*, viz. to be as perfect as it can, but no other. In the sequel this is interpreted to mean that no art needs any additional *ἀρετή*; since it is (*qua* art) perfect already: *οὔτε γὰρ πονηρία οὔτε ἁμαρτία οὐδεμία οὐδεμιᾷ τέχνῃ πάρεστιν κτλ.* (342 B). But the words of the sentence *ἆρ' οὖν—τελέαν εἶναι* have to be taken very loosely in order to admit of this interpretation. We must suppose them equivalent to 'No art has a *συμφέρον* of its own, unless you are to call the fact that it is perfect its *συμφέρον*.' If Plato had written the passage as it stands in *q* and in the margin of Flor. U (both MSS probably of the fifteenth century), it would be open to no objection: *ἆρ' οὖν καὶ ἑκάστη τῶν τεχνῶν ἔστι τι ξυμφέρον ἄλλο* <*οὗ προσδεῖται*>, *ἢ* <*ἐξαρκεῖ ἑκάστη αὐτὴ αὑτῇ, ὥστε*> *ὅ τι μάλιστα τελέαν εἶναι;* This reading was adopted by Bekker, and by Stallbaum in his first edition; and a careful study of the whole passage confirms the judgment of Schneider, "Platonem non solum potuisse, sed etiam debuisse vel haec ipsa vel consimilia scribere." The same sense, expressed more briefly, may be obtained by the insertion of *δεῖ* before *εἶναι*: 'has every art also a *ξυμφέρον* besides (i.e. besides the *ξυμφέρον* of its object), or must it be as perfect as possible?' *ἑκάστην* does not require to be repeated any more than in 346 A below. The alteration is very slight; for *δεῖ εἶναι*, *δεῖναι* may have been written by mistake and *δ* afterwards ejected.

341 E 33 **νῦν κτλ.**: 'has now been invented.' The art of medicine is not coeval with body. I can see no reason for thinking (with Campbell) that *νῦν* is corrupt for *ἡμῖν*.

34 **σῶμά ἐστι πονηρὸν κτλ.** *Lys.* 217 B *ἀναγκάζεται δέ γε σῶμα διὰ νόσον ἰατρικὴν ἀσπάζεσθαι καὶ φιλεῖν.*

35 **ὅπως ἐκπορίζῃ.** This is said by Weber (Schanz's *Beiträge* II 2, p. 67) to be the only example in Plato of *ὅπως* with the subjunctive after a preterite tense.

342 A 3 **ἐπ' αὐτοῖς.** Hartman proposes *ἔτ' αὐτοῖς*. *αὐτοῖς* (sc. *ὀφθαλμοῖς, ὠσίν*) may be emphatic (ipsis), and *ἐπί*, 'over and above,' 'besides': 'we require in addition to the organs themselves, an art' etc. But it is perhaps simpler to make *ἐπί* = 'to preside over': cf. *ἐφ' οἷς ἔστιν* VI 511 E *n.*

4 **εἰς ταῦτα** means *εἰς ὄψιν καὶ ἀκοήν*. The art in question considers what is advantageous *with respect to* (*εἰς*) seeing and hearing.

ἐκποριούσης; ἆρα καὶ ἐν αὐτῇ τῇ τέχνῃ ἔνι τις πονηρία, καὶ δεῖ ἑκάστῃ τέχνῃ ἄλλης τέχνης, ἥτις αὐτῇ τὸ ξυμφέρον σκέψεται, καὶ τῇ σκοπουμένῃ ἑτέρας αὖ τοιαύτης, καὶ τοῦτ' ἔστιν ἀπέραντον; ἢ αὐτὴ αὑτῇ τὸ ξυμφέρον | σκέψεται; ἢ οὔτε αὑτῆς οὔτε ἄλλης **B** προσδεῖται ἐπὶ τὴν αὑτῆς πονηρίαν τὸ ξυμφέρον σκοπεῖν· οὔτε γὰρ πονηρία οὔτε ἁμαρτία οὐδεμία οὐδεμιᾷ τέχνῃ πάρεστιν, οὐδὲ προσήκει τέχνῃ ἄλλῳ τὸ ξυμφέρον ζητεῖν ἢ ἐκείνῳ οὗ τέχνη ἐστίν, αὐτὴ δὲ ἀβλαβὴς καὶ ἀκέραιός ἐστιν ὀρθὴ οὖσα, ἕωσπερ ἂν ᾖ ἑκάστη ἀκριβὴς ὅλη ἥπερ ἐστί; καὶ σκόπει ἐκείνῳ τῷ ἀκριβεῖ λόγῳ· οὕτως ἢ ἄλλως ἔχει; Οὕτως, ἔφη, φαίνεται. Οὐκ ἄρα, ἦν δ' ἐγώ, ἰατρικὴ ἰατρικῇ | τὸ ξυμφέρον σκοπεῖ ἀλλὰ σώματι. **C** Ναί, ἔφη. Οὐδὲ ἱππικὴ ἱππικῇ ἀλλ' ἵπποις· οὐδὲ ἄλλη τέχνη οὐδεμία ἑαυτῇ, οὐδὲ γὰρ προσδεῖται, ἀλλ' ἐκείνῳ οὗ τέχνη ἐστίν. Φαίνεται, ἔφη, οὕτως. Ἀλλὰ μήν, ὦ Θρασύμαχε, ἄρχουσί γε αἱ τέχναι καὶ κρατοῦσιν ἐκείνου, οὗπέρ εἰσιν τέχναι. Συνεχώρησεν ἐνταῦθα καὶ μάλα μόγις. Οὐκ ἄρα ἐπιστήμη γε οὐδεμία τὸ τοῦ κρείττονος ξυμφέρον σκοπεῖ οὐδ' ἐπιτάττει, ἀλλὰ τὸ τοῦ ἥττονός | τε καὶ ἀρχομένου ὑπὸ ἑαυτῆς. Ξυνωμολόγησε μὲν καὶ ταῦτα **D** τελευτῶν, ἐπεχείρει δὲ περὶ αὐτὰ μάχεσθαι· ἐπειδὴ δὲ ὡμολόγησεν, Ἄλλο τι οὖν, ἦν δ' ἐγώ, οὐδὲ ἰατρὸς οὐδείς, καθ' ὅσον ἰατρός, τὸ τῷ ἰατρῷ ξυμφέρον σκοπεῖ οὐδ' ἐπιτάττει, ἀλλὰ τὸ τῷ κάμνοντι; ὡμολόγηται γὰρ ὁ ἀκριβὴς ἰατρὸς σωμάτων εἶναι ἄρχων ἀλλ' οὐ χρηματιστής. ἢ οὐχ ὡμολόγηται; Ξυνέφη. Οὐκοῦν καὶ ὁ κυβερνήτης ὁ ἀκριβὴς ναυτῶν εἶναι ἄρχων ἀλλ' | οὐ ναύτης; **E**

5. ἐκποριούσης *q* : ἐκποριζούσης ΑΠΞ. δεῖ Π : δεῖ ἀεὶ A[1] : δεῖ αἰεὶ A[2].
12. αὐτὴ Ξq^2 : αὔτη ΑΠq^1.

---

5 **ἐκποριούσης.** See *cr. n.* ἐκποριούσης appears in three Florentine MSS. The present is difficult, if not impossible, in so close a union with the future: cf. X 604 A and VI 494 D. See *Introd.* § 5.

8 **ἢ αὐτὴ—σκέψεται;** This question (which is of course to be answered in the negative) shews the awkwardness of the reading of A in ἆρ' οὖν—τελέαν εἶναι (341 D), which might almost be construed to mean that each art *does* seek its own συμφέρον, viz. the perfection of itself.

342 B 12 **ἕωσπερ κτλ.**: 'that is, so long as an art, taken in its strict sense' ("streng genommen" Schneider) 'preserves its essence entire and unimpaired.' The predicate is ὅλη ἥπερ ἐστί, and ἀκριβής =ἀκριβὴς οὖσα in the sense which ἀκριβής bears throughout this passage (341 B al.). Hartman's insertion of ἡ before ἀκριβής is unsatisfactory; his alternative proposal to change ἀκριβής to ἀκριβῶς spoils the emphasis, and gives a wrong sense.

342 C 20 **ἐπιστήμη** is here a synonym for τέχνη. All arts rule: and ruling is itself an art or science, not a happy inspiration (cf. *Mem.* III 6). Like other arts, ruling seeks only the good of that which it rules.

342 D 26 **ὡμολόγηται γὰρ—χρηματιστής.** Ast compares Arist. *Pol.* A 9. 1258a 10 ff. ἀνδρίας γὰρ οὐ χρήματα ποιεῖν ἐστιν ἀλλὰ θάρσος, οὐδὲ στρατηγικῆς καὶ ἰατρικῆς, ἀλλὰ τῆς μὲν νίκην, τῆς δ' ὑγίειαν.

Ὡμολόγηται. Οὐκ ἄρα ὅ γε τοιοῦτος κυβερνήτης τε καὶ ἄρχων τὸ τῷ κυβερνήτῃ ξυμφέρον σκέψεταί τε καὶ προστάξει, ἀλλὰ τὸ τῷ ναύτῃ τε καὶ ἀρχομένῳ. Ξυνέφησε μόγις. Οὐκοῦν, ἦν δ' ἐγώ, ὦ Θρασύμαχε, οὐδὲ ἄλλος οὐδεὶς ἐν οὐδεμιᾷ ἀρχῇ, καθ' ὅσον ἄρχων ἐστίν, τὸ αὑτῷ ξυμφέρον σκοπεῖ οὐδ' ἐπιτάττει, ἀλλὰ τὸ τῷ ἀρχομένῳ καὶ ᾧ ἂν αὐτὸς δημιουργῇ, καὶ πρὸς ἐκεῖνο βλέπων καὶ τὸ ἐκείνῳ ξυμφέρον καὶ πρέπον καὶ λέγει ἃ λέγει καὶ ποιεῖ ἃ ποιεῖ ἅπαντα.

343 XVI. | Ἐπειδὴ οὖν ἐνταῦθα ἦμεν τοῦ λόγου καὶ πᾶσι καταφανὲς ἦν, ὅτι ὁ τοῦ δικαίου λόγος εἰς τοὐναντίον περιειστήκει, ὁ Θρασύμαχος ἀντὶ τοῦ ἀποκρίνεσθαι, Εἰπέ μοι, ἔφη, ὦ Σώκρατες, τίτθη σοι ἔστιν; Τί δέ; ἦν δ' ἐγώ· οὐκ ἀποκρίνεσθαι χρῆν μᾶλλον ἢ τοιαῦτα ἐρωτᾶν; Ὅτι τοί σε, ἔφη, κορυζῶντα περιορᾷ καὶ οὐκ ἀπομύττει δεόμενον, ὅς γε αὐτῇ οὐδὲ πρόβατα οὐδὲ ποιμένα

---

342 E 34 **ᾧ ἂν—βλέπων.** ᾧ is of course (τῷ) ὅ, and τῷ ἀρχομένῳ is also neuter (not masculine), like ἀρχομένου in D. Bremius took τῷ ἀρχομένῳ as masculine, and consequently changed (with inferior MS authority) πρὸς ἐκεῖνο into πρὸς ἐκεῖνον: he has been followed by Stallbaum and others. But as ᾧ must be neuter, it would be intolerable to make ἀρχομένῳ masculine, since both words (as denoting the same object) are covered by the same article, viz. τῷ before ἀρχομένῳ. ἐκείνῳ is of course neuter also.

343 A—**344** C *Thrasymachus with much insolence of tone now abandons the idealistic point of view, and takes an example from experience. The shepherd does not, as a matter of fact, seek the good of his flock, but fattens them for his own or his master's advantage. In like manner it is their own advantage that is aimed at by rulers who deserve the name. Justice is 'other men's good'* (ἀλλότριον ἀγαθόν), *whereas Injustice is one's own: the just man comes off second best everywhere, alike in commercial and in political transactions. That it is far more to one's interest to be unjust than to be just, we may see from the case of tyrants, who represent Injustice in its most perfect form. All men envy them. Finally, Thrasymachus reiterates his original theory with the remark that Injustice on a sufficiently large scale is at once stronger, more worthy of a freeman, and more masterly and commanding than Justice.*

343 A ff. It should be noted that Thrasymachus has in no way changed his theory, but only reverts to his original standpoint, that of experience. In the panegyric on Injustice in the present chapter, the new and important point is the appeal to the evidence of tyranny and the emotions which it roused in the mind of the Greeks. See on 344 B.

2 **εἰς τοὐναντίον.** Justice has now become τὸ τοῦ ἥττονος (rather than κρείττονος) συμφέρον.

5 **κορυζῶντα**: 'snivelling,' μωραίνοντα, μυξάζοντα· κόρυζα γὰρ ἡ μύξα, ἣν οἱ Ἀττικοὶ κατάρρουν φασίν (Schol.). Ruhnken on Timaeus *Lex.* s.v. quotes among other passages Lucian *Alex.* § 20 ἦν δὲ τὸ μηχάνημα τοῦτο ἀνδρὶ μὲν οἵῳ σοι, εἰ δὲ μὴ φορτικὸν εἰπεῖν, καὶ οἵῳ ἐμοί, πρόδηλον καὶ γνῶναι ῥᾴδιον, τοῖς δὲ ἰδιώταις καὶ κορύζης μεστοῖς τὴν ῥῖνα τεράστιον καὶ πάνυ ἀπίστῳ ὅμοιον, and Horace *Sat.* I 4. 8 (of Lucilius) emunctae naris.

6 **ὅς γε αὐτῇ κτλ.** "Apte αὐτῇ interpositum; nam ipsi nutrici Socratis insipientiam opprobrio esse, Thrasymachus vult significare" Ast. Richter (*Fl. Jahrb.* for 1867 p. 140) ought not to have suggested ὅς γε αὐτός. The sense is 'for she cannot teach you to recognise even sheep or shepherd,' not 'you do not know either sheep or shepherd' (J. and C.), which would require οὔτε—οὔτε. The phrase is clearly a half-proverbial expression borrowed from the nursery.

γιγνώσκεις. Ὅτι δὴ τί μάλιστα; ἦν δ' ἐγώ. Ὅτι οἴει τοὺς
ποιμένας ǀ ἢ τοὺς βουκόλους τὸ τῶν προβάτων ἢ τὸ τῶν βοῶν B
ἀγαθὸν σκοπεῖν καὶ παχύνειν αὐτοὺς καὶ θεραπεύειν πρὸς ἄλλο
τι βλέποντας ἢ τὸ τῶν δεσποτῶν ἀγαθὸν καὶ τὸ αὐτῶν, καὶ δὴ
καὶ τοὺς ἐν ταῖς πόλεσιν ἄρχοντας, οἳ ὡς ἀληθῶς ἄρχουσιν,
ἄλλως πως ἡγεῖ διανοεῖσθαι πρὸς τοὺς ἀρχομένους ἢ ὥσπερ ἄν
τις πρὸς πρόβατα διατεθείη, καὶ ἄλλο τι σκοπεῖν αὐτοὺς διὰ
νυκτὸς καὶ ἡμέρας ἢ τοῦτο ὅθεν αὐτοὶ ὠφελήσονται. καὶ οὕτω
πόρρω εἶ ǀ περί τε τοῦ δικαίου καὶ δικαιοσύνης καὶ ἀδίκου τε καὶ C
ἀδικίας, ὥστε ἀγνοεῖς, ὅτι ἡ μὲν δικαιοσύνη καὶ τὸ δίκαιον ἀλλότριον
ἀγαθὸν τῷ ὄντι, τοῦ κρείττονός τε καὶ ἄρχοντος ξυμφέρον, οἰκεία
δὲ τοῦ πειθομένου τε καὶ ὑπηρετοῦντος βλάβη, ἡ δὲ ἀδικία τοὐναντίον, καὶ ἄρχει τῶν ὡς ἀληθῶς εὐηθικῶν τε καὶ δικαίων, οἱ δ'

---

7 **ὅτι οἴει τοὺς ποιμένας κτλ.** Thrasymachus gives a new turn to the nursery saying. The illustration from the shepherd and his sheep (which is now for the first time introduced) was used by the historical Socrates to justify the opposite conclusion (Xen. *Mem.* III 2. 1) ἐντυχὼν δέ ποτε στρατηγεῖν ᾑρημένῳ τῳ, Τοῦ ἕνεκεν, ἔφη, Ὅμηρον οἴει τὸν Ἀγαμέμνονα προσαγορεῦσαι ποιμένα λαῶν; ἆρά γε ὅτι, ὥσπερ τὸν ποιμένα ἐπιμελεῖσθαι δεῖ, ὅπως σῶαί τε ἔσονται αἱ ὄϊες, καὶ τὰ ἐπιτήδεια ἕξουσιν, οὕτω καὶ τὸν στρατηγὸν ἐπιμελεῖσθαι δεῖ, ὅπως σῶοί τε οἱ στρατιῶται ἔσονται, καὶ τὰ ἐπιτήδεια ἕξουσι, καὶ οὗ ἕνεκα στρατεύονται τοῦτο ἔσται; So also Arist. *Eth. Nic.* VIII 13. 1161ᵃ 12 ff. εὖ γὰρ ποιεῖ τοὺς βασιλευομένους, εἴπερ ἀγαθὸς ὢν ἐπιμελεῖται αὐτῶν, ἵν' εὖ πράττωσιν, ὥσπερ νομεὺς προβάτων· ὅθεν καὶ Ὅμηρος τὸν Ἀγαμέμνονα ποιμένα λαῶν εἶπεν. In Plato *Pol.* 271 D ff. the deities of the golden age are compared to shepherds, and the comparison of a good ruler to a shepherd is very frequent in Plato: see Ast's *Lex. Plat.* s. v. νομεύς. In Socrates' view 'the shepherd careth for his sheep.' With Thrasymachus' attitude should be compared the picture of the tyrant in *Theaet.* 174 D as a συβώτην ἢ ποιμένα ἤ τινα βουκόλον—πολὺ βδάλλοντα (he squeezes as much milk as he can out of his flock): also Solon ap. Arist. *Rep. Ath.* ch. 12 εἰ γάρ τις ἄλλος ταύτης τῆς τιμῆς ἔτυχεν, οὐκ ἂν κατέσχε δῆμον οὐδ' ἐπαύσατο, | πρὶν ἀνταράξας πῖαρ ἐξεῖλεν γάλα. In the word ἀμοργοί or ἀμολγοί used by Cratinus in the sense of πόλεως ὄλεθροι (Meineke *Fr. Com. Graec.* II 1, p. 140) the image is the same. Compare the eloquent words of Ruskin in *Sesame and Lilies* § 43 and Milton's *Lycidas* 113—129.

343 B 12 **ἡγεῖ διανοεῖσθαι.** The conjecture διακεῖσθαι for διανοεῖσθαι is tempting in view of διατεθείη which follows, but διανοεῖσθαι is better suited to σκοπεῖν and βλέποντας just above. For the somewhat rare construction Schneider compares *Laws* 626 D αὐτῷ δὲ πρὸς αὐτὸν πότερον ὡς πολεμίῳ πρὸς πολέμιον διανοητέον, ἢ πῶς ἔτι λέγομεν; and 628 D.

15 **πόρρω εἶ περί.** πόρρω can hardly (I think) mean 'far from' (sc. knowing): this would require πόρρω εἶ <τοῦ τι εἰδέναι> περί, as Herwerden suggests: cf. *Lys.* 212 A οὕτω πόρρω εἰμὶ τοῦ κτήματος ὥστε κτλ. The meaning is (I believe) 'so far on'; 'so profoundly versed are you in justice' etc.: cf. πόρρω ἤδη ἐστὶ τοῦ βίου *Ap.* 38 C and phrases like πόρρω σοφίας ἐλαύνειν: see also Blaydes on Ar. *Wasps* 192. Such biting sarcasm is appropriate in the mouth of Thrasymachus.

343 C 16 **ἀλλότριον ἀγαθόν.** Arist. *Eth. Nic.* V 3. 1130ᵃ 3 f. διὰ δὲ τὸ αὐτὸ τοῦτο καὶ ἀλλότριον ἀγαθὸν δοκεῖ εἶναι ἡ δικαιοσύνη μόνη τῶν ἀρετῶν, ὅτι πρὸς ἕτερόν ἐστιν· ἄλλῳ γὰρ τὰ συμφέροντα πράττει, ἢ ἄρχοντι ἢ κοινωνῷ (with Stewart's note) and ib. 10. 1134ᵇ 5.

17 **τῷ ὄντι** is not τῷ ὄντι δικαίῳ, but *revera* (as Stallbaum observes).

19 **ὡς ἀληθῶς** as well as ἀληθῶς, τῷ

ἀρχόμενοι ποιοῦσιν τὸ ἐκείνου ξυμφέρον κρείττονος ὄντος, καὶ
D εὐδαίμονα ἐκεῖνον ποιοῦσιν ὑπηρετοῦντες αὐτῷ, ἑαυτοὺς δὲ | οὐδ'
ὁπωστιοῦν. σκοπεῖσθαι δέ, ὦ εὐηθέστατε Σώκρατες, οὑτωσὶ χρή,
ὅτι δίκαιος ἀνὴρ ἀδίκου πανταχοῦ ἔλαττον ἔχει. πρῶτον μὲν
ἐν τοῖς πρὸς ἀλλήλους ξυμβολαίοις, ὅπου ἂν ὁ τοιοῦτος τῷ τοιούτῳ
κοινωνήσῃ, οὐδαμοῦ ἂν εὕροις ἐν τῇ διαλύσει τῆς κοινωνίας πλέον
ἔχοντα τὸν δίκαιον τοῦ ἀδίκου ἀλλ' ἔλαττον· ἔπειτα ἐν τοῖς πρὸς
τὴν πόλιν, ὅταν τέ τινες εἰσφοραὶ ὦσιν, ὁ μὲν δίκαιος ἀπὸ τῶν
E ἴσων πλέον εἰσφέρει, ὁ δ' ἔλαττον, ὅταν τε λήψεις, | ὁ μὲν οὐδέν,
ὁ δὲ πολλὰ κερδαίνει. καὶ γὰρ ὅταν ἀρχήν τινα ἄρχῃ ἑκάτερος,
τῷ μὲν δικαίῳ ὑπάρχει, καὶ εἰ μηδεμία ἄλλη ζημία, τά γε οἰκεῖα
δι' ἀμέλειαν μοχθηροτέρως ἔχειν, ἐκ δὲ τοῦ δημοσίου μηδὲν
ὠφελεῖσθαι διὰ τὸ δίκαιον εἶναι, πρὸς δὲ τούτοις ἀπεχθέσθαι τοῖς
τε οἰκείοις καὶ τοῖς γνωρίμοις, ὅταν μηδὲν ἐθέλῃ αὐτοῖς ὑπηρετεῖν
παρὰ τὸ δίκαιον· τῷ δὲ ἀδίκῳ πάντα τούτων τἀναντία ὑπάρχει.
344 λέγω γὰρ ὅνπερ νῦν δὴ ἔλεγον, τὸν μεγά|λα δυνάμενον πλεονεκτεῖν.
τοῦτον οὖν σκόπει, εἴπερ βούλει κρίνειν, ὅσῳ μᾶλλον ξυμφέρει
ἰδίᾳ αὐτῷ ἄδικον εἶναι ἢ τὸ δίκαιον. πάντων δὲ ῥᾷστα μαθήσει,
ἐὰν ἐπὶ τὴν τελεωτάτην ἀδικίαν ἔλθῃς, ἣ τὸν μὲν ἀδικήσαντα
εὐδαιμονέστατον ποιεῖ, τοὺς δὲ ἀδικηθέντας καὶ ἀδικῆσαι οὐκ ἂν
ἐθέλοντας ἀθλιωτάτους. ἔστιν δὲ τοῦτο τυραννίς, ἣ οὐ κατὰ

ὄντι, and the like, is used to indicate that a word is to be taken in its strict and full etymological sense (εὐ-ηθικῶν): cf. *Phaed.* 80 D εἰς Ἅιδου ὡς ἀληθῶς, and infra II 376 B, V 474 A, VI 511 B, VIII 551 E *nn.*

343 E 30 **τά γε οἰκεῖα—μοχθηροτέρως.** Wells aptly cites the refusal of Deioces in Herod. I 97 to continue as an arbiter: *οὐ γάρ οἱ λυσιτελέειν τῶν ἑαυτοῦ ἐξημεληκότα τοῖσι πέλας δι' ἡμέρης δικάζειν.* Cf. also *Ap.* 23 B, 31 B. In like manner Aristotle mentions it as one of the safeguards of a democracy engaged in agriculture that the necessity of looking after their private interests will prevent the citizens from often attending the assembly (*Pol.* Z 4. 1318[b] 11). Plato is fond of the comparative ending in -ως (affected, says Cobet, by those "qui nitidissime scribunt"): see Kühner-Blass *Gr. Gramm.* I p. 577.

32 **ἀπεχθέσθαι.** *ἀπέχθομαι* as a present is not well attested in Plato's time; and the aorist 'to incur the enmity of' is at least as suitable in point of meaning here.

35 **λέγω γὰρ ὅνπερ νῦν δὴ ἔλεγον.** Ast points out that nothing in what has been already said corresponds to the words *τὸν μεγάλα δυνάμενον πλεονεκτεῖν*, and reads *ὅπερ* on slight MS authority. But no special reference is intended: the words mean simply 'I mean the man I meant just now.' Thrasymachus asserts that he has all along been referring to *τὸν μεγάλα κτλ.*

344 A 3 **ἢ τὸ δίκαιον**: i.e. *ἢ τὸ δίκαιον εἶναι τῷ δικαίῳ.* The reading *αὐτῷ* (found in A, but no dependence can be put on this MS in such matters) would require the omission of the article before *δίκαιον* (so Stallbaum and others). Tucker inclines to render 'how much more he is personally benefited by being unjust than by justice,' but the ordinary view is preferable.

6 **ἢ οὐ κτλ.** This laboured sentence is perhaps intended as a parody of some sophistic style: cf. *Gorg.* 448 C.

σμικρὸν τἀλλότρια καὶ λάθρᾳ καὶ βίᾳ ἀφαιρεῖται, καὶ ἱερὰ καὶ ὅσια καὶ ἴδια καὶ δημόσια, ἀλλὰ ξυλλήβδην, | ὧν ἐφ' ἑκάστῳ B μέρει ὅταν τις ἀδικήσας μὴ λάθῃ, ζημιοῦταί τε καὶ ὀνείδη ἔχει τὰ μέγιστα· καὶ γὰρ ἱερόσυλοι καὶ ἀνδραποδισταὶ καὶ τοιχωρύχοι καὶ ἀποστερηταὶ καὶ κλέπται οἱ κατὰ μέρη ἀδικοῦντες τῶν τοιούτων κακουργημάτων καλοῦνται· ἐπειδὰν δέ τις πρὸς τοῖς τῶν πολιτῶν χρήμασιν καὶ αὐτοὺς ἀνδραποδισάμενος δουλώσηται, ἀντὶ τούτων τῶν αἰσχρῶν ὀνομάτων εὐδαίμονες καὶ μακάριοι κέκληνται, οὐ μόνον ὑπὸ τῶν πολιτῶν | ἀλλὰ καὶ ὑπὸ τῶν ἄλλων, C ὅσοι ἂν πύθωνται αὐτὸν τὴν ὅλην ἀδικίαν ἠδικηκότα· οὐ γὰρ τὸ ποιεῖν τὰ ἄδικα ἀλλὰ τὸ πάσχειν φοβούμενοι ὀνειδίζουσιν οἱ ὀνειδίζοντες τὴν ἀδικίαν. οὕτως, ὦ Σώκρατες, καὶ ἰσχυρότερον καὶ ἐλευθεριώτερον καὶ δεσποτικώτερον ἀδικία δικαιοσύνης ἐστὶν ἱκανῶς γιγνομένη, καὶ ὅπερ ἐξ ἀρχῆς ἔλεγον, τὸ μὲν τοῦ κρείττονος ξυμφέρον τὸ δίκαιον τυγχάνει ὄν, τὸ δ' ἄδικον ἑαυτῷ λυσιτελοῦν τε καὶ ξυμφέρον.

7. βίᾳ Π: βία A.

---

344 B 8 **ὧν** depends on **μέρει.**

10 **ἀνδραποδισταί**: 'kidnappers.' The word is defined by Pollux III 78 as ὁ τὸν ἐλεύθερον καταδουλωσάμενος ἢ τὸν ἀλλότριον οἰκέτην ἀπαγόμενος. Thessaly had an evil name for this kind of crime (Blaydes on Ar. *Plut.* 521); but the frequent references to it in Attic literature shew that Greece itself was not exempt. See on IX 575 B and the article in Stephanus-Hase *Thes.* s.v.

11 **τῶν τοιούτων κακουργημάτων** is usually explained as depending on κατὰ μέρη, but as κατὰ μέρη is adverbial, this is somewhat awkward. It is perhaps better to regard the genitive as partitive, τι being omitted as in κινήσειεν ἂν τῶν ἀξίων λόγου νόμων IV 445 E, where see note.

12 **πρὸς τοῖς—χρήμασιν** is virtually equivalent to πρὸς τῷ τὰ τῶν πολιτῶν ἀφελέσθαι, and combined by zeugma with δουλώσηται. Cf. I 330 E *n.*

14 **εὐδαίμονες—κέκληνται.** The generic singular τις has become a plural, as in *Phaed.* 109 D, infra VII 536 A. Envy of tyranny and tyrants was common in the Athens of Plato's younger days: compare *Gorg.* 484 A, 470 D (where it is maintained by Polus that Archelaus of Macedon is εὐδαίμων, and Socrates says ὀλίγου σοι πάντες συμφήσουσι ταῦτα Ἀθηναῖοι καὶ οἱ ξένοι 472 A) and *Alc.* II 141 A ff. The plays of Euripides in particular (see VIII 568 A) often eulogised the tyrant: e.g. *Troad.* 1169 ff., *Fr.* 252, *Phoen.* 524 ff. In earlier days Solon's friends had blamed him for not making himself tyrant of Athens: see the dramatic fragment (33 ed. Bergk), where the prevalent passion for tyranny is forcibly expressed in the lines ἤθελον γάρ κεν κρατήσας, πλοῦτον ἄφθονον λαβὼν | καὶ τυραννεύσας Ἀθηνῶν μοῦνον ἡμέραν μίαν, | ἀσκὸς ὕστερον δεδάρθαι κἀπιτετρῖφθαι γένος (4—6). See also Newman's *Politics of Aristotle* I pp. 388—392.

344 C 16 **οὐ γὰρ—τὴν ἀδικίαν.** Cf. *Gorg.* 483 A φύσει μὲν γὰρ πᾶν αἴσχιόν ἐστιν, ὅπερ καὶ κάκιον, τὸ ἀδικεῖσθαι, νόμῳ δὲ τὸ ἀδικεῖν.

20 **ἱκανῶς γιγνομένη**: 'realised on an adequate scale' (D. and V.). For the construction of γίγνεσθαι with an adverb cf. (with Ast) *Soph.* 230 C and infra VI 504 C. After τὸ δ' ἄδικον below, Herwerden would insert τό to go with ἑαυτῷ λυσιτελοῦν τε καὶ ξυμφέρον, but only τυγχάνει (and not τυγχάνει ὄν) is to be understood after ἄδικον; nor is the last clause intended as a strict and formal definition of injustice.

D XVII. Ταῦτα εἰπὼν ὁ | Θρασύμαχος ἐν νῷ εἶχεν ἀπιέναι, ὥσπερ βαλανεὺς ἡμῶν καταντλήσας κατὰ τῶν ὤτων ἀθρόον καὶ πολὺν τὸν λόγον. οὐ μὴν εἴασάν γε αὐτὸν οἱ παρόντες, ἀλλ᾽ ἠνάγκασαν ὑπομεῖναί τε καὶ παρασχεῖν τῶν εἰρημένων λόγον. καὶ δὴ ἔγωγε καὶ αὐτὸς πάνυ ἐδεόμην τε καὶ εἶπον Ὦ δαιμόνιε Θρασύμαχε, οἷον ἐμβαλὼν λόγον ἐν νῷ ἔχεις ἀπιέναι, πρὶν διδάξαι ἱκανῶς ἢ μαθεῖν εἴτε οὕτως εἴτε ἄλλως ἔχει; ἢ σμικρὸν οἴει
E ἐπιχειρεῖν πρᾶγμα | διορίζεσθαι, ἀλλ᾽ οὐ βίου διαγωγήν, ᾗ ἂν διαγόμενος ἕκαστος ἡμῶν λυσιτελεστάτην ζωὴν ζῴη; Ἐγὼ γὰρ

31. ζῴη $A^2\Pi$: ζῶν A^1.

---

344 D—**347** E *The reply of Socrates falls into two parts. In the first* (344 D—347 E), *after emphatically expressing his dissent from Thrasymachus' views, and protesting against the Sophist's retractation* (*in the example of the shepherd and his sheep*) *of the doctrine that every ruler seeks the good of his subjects, Socrates reverts to the stricter form of reasoning to which Thrasymachus had formerly challenged him, and points out that no rulers, properly so called, rule willingly: they require wages. When any kind of rule, e.g. an art, is attended with advantage to the ruler, the advantage comes from the concomitant operation of the 'art of wage-earning,' and not from the rule itself. Medicine produces health; the art of wages, wages; the doctor takes his fee, not* qua *doctor, but* qua *wage-earner. Thus it is not the ruler,* qua *ruler, but the subjects, as was already said, who reap the advantage. The wages which induce a man to rule, may be money, or honour, or the prospect of a penalty if he should refuse. The most efficacious penalty, in the case of the best natures, is the prospect of being ruled by worse men than themselves. In a city of good men, freedom from office would be as eagerly sought for as office itself is now. Herewith ends for the present the refutation of the theory that Justice is the interest of the stronger. Socrates promises to resume the subject on another occasion.*

344 D ff. The ensuing discussion is not a new argument (see 345 C ἔτι γὰρ τὰ ἔμπροσθεν ἐπισκεψώμεθα) in support of Socrates' view, but a restatement of his theory, with an addition necessitated by Thrasymachus' example of the shepherd. The shepherd (says Socrates) is no shepherd, when he fattens his sheep for his own gain, nor the ruler a ruler, when he enriches himself at the expense of his subjects. On such occasions both shepherd and ruler are in reality μισθωτικοί—professors of μισθωτική, an art which is distinct from that of ruling, though usually associated with it. This analysis is new and valuable in itself; it also enables Socrates (in 347 D) to make the first explicit allusion in the *Republic* to an ideal state, and to formulate what afterwards becomes a leading principle of the Platonic commonwealth—the reluctance of the ruling class to accept office.

344 D 24 **καταντλήσας.** For the metaphor cf. infra VII 536 B, *Lys.* 204 D, Lucian *Dem. Enc.* 16 (imitated from this passage) and other examples in Blaydes on Ar. *Wasps* 483.

28 **ἐμβαλών**: cf. *Theaet.* 165 D, *Prot.* 342 E. The whole expression recalls the Latin proverb *scrupulum abeunti* (Cic. *de Fin.* IV 80).

344 E 31 **διαγόμενος.** The use of this verb in Soph. *El.* 782 χρόνος διῆγέ με, Dem. 18. 89 πόλεμος—διῆγεν ὑμᾶς, Xen. *Rep. Lac.* I 3 and elsewhere is in favour of regarding διαγόμενος ('living') as grammatically passive and not middle both here and in *Laws* 758 A. Cf. Stephanus-Hase *Thes.* s.v. διάγω.

ἐγὼ γὰρ κτλ. I agree with Stallbaum and others in taking this sentence as interrogative: 'do you mean that *I* think otherwise about this matter?' i.e. think that it is *not* a question of βίου διαγωγή. J. and C. complain that this interpretation is "wanting in point." It is surely much to the point to make Thrasymachus repudiate the imputation of trifling. His doctrine appears all the more dangerous when he confesses that it is no

οἶμαι, ἔφη ὁ Θρασύμαχος, τουτὶ ἄλλως ἔχειν; Ἔοικας, ἦν δ' ἐγώ,
ἤτοι ἡμῶν γε οὐδὲν κήδεσθαι, οὐδέ τι φροντίζειν εἴτε χεῖρον εἴτε
βέλτιον βιωσόμεθα ἀγνοοῦντες ὃ σὺ φῂς εἰδέναι. ἀλλ', ὦ 'γαθέ,
προθυμοῦ καὶ ἡμῖν ἐνδείξασθαι· οὔτοι κα|κῶς σοι κείσεται, ὅ τι 345
ἂν ἡμᾶς τοσούσδε ὄντας εὐεργετήσῃς. ἐγὼ γὰρ δή σοι λέγω
τό γ' ἐμόν, ὅτι οὐ πείθομαι οὐδ' οἶμαι ἀδικίαν δικαιοσύνης κερδα-
λεώτερον εἶναι, οὐδ' ἐὰν ἐᾷ τις αὐτὴν καὶ μὴ διακωλύῃ πράττειν
ἃ βούλεται. ἀλλ', ὦ 'γαθέ, ἔστω μὲν ἄδικος, δυνάσθω δὲ ἀδικεῖν
ἢ τῷ λανθάνειν ἢ τῷ διαμάχεσθαι· ὅμως ἐμέ γε οὐ πείθει ὡς ἔστι
τῆς δικαιοσύνης κερδαλεώτερον. ταῦτ' οὖν καὶ | ἕτερος ἴσως τις B
ἡμῶν πέπονθεν, οὐ μόνος ἐγώ. πεῖσον οὖν, ὦ μακάριε, ἱκανῶς
ἡμᾶς, ὅτι οὐκ ὀρθῶς βουλευόμεθα δικαιοσύνην ἀδικίας περὶ
πλείονος ποιούμενοι. Καὶ πῶς, ἔφη, σὲ πείσω; εἰ γὰρ οἷς νῦν
δὴ ἔλεγον μὴ πέπεισαι, τί σοι ἔτι ποιήσω; ἢ εἰς τὴν ψυχὴν φέρων
ἐνθῶ τὸν λόγον; Μὰ Δί', ἦν δ' ἐγώ, μὴ σύ γε· ἀλλὰ πρῶτον μέν,
ἃ ἂν εἴπῃς, ἔμμενε τούτοις, ἢ ἐὰν μετατιθῇ, φανερῶς μετατίθεσο
καὶ ἡμᾶς μὴ ἐξαπάτα. νῦν δὲ ὁρᾷς, ὦ | Θρασύμαχε, ἔτι γὰρ τὰ C
ἔμπροσθεν ἐπισκεψώμεθα, ὅτι τὸν ὡς ἀληθῶς ἰατρὸν τὸ πρῶτον
ὁριζόμενος τὸν ὡς ἀληθῶς ποιμένα οὐκέτι ᾤου δεῖν ὕστερον ἀκριβῶς
φυλάξαι, ἀλλὰ ποιμαίνειν οἴει αὐτὸν τὰ πρόβατα, καθ' ὅσον

17. ποιμαίνειν Π et γρ in marg. A^2: πιαίνειν A.

---

sophistic paradox, but a rule of life. I can see nothing to justify Apelt's conjecture ἔγωγ' ἄρ' for ἐγὼ γὰρ (*Observ. Crit.* p. 11).

33 **ἤτοι ἡμῶν γε.** ἤτοι or ἤτοι—γε = 'or else' (not 'or rather' as J. and C.). The regular construction is ἤτοι—ἤ, and ἤ—ἤτοι was condemned by the grammarians as a solecism, though it occurs in Pind. *Nem.* 6. 5. With the use of ἤτοι in this passage cf. III 400 C, IV 433 A τοῦτό ἐστιν—ἤτοι τούτου τι εἶδος ἡ δικαιοσύνη. Emendations have been suggested on all these passages of Plato: here ἤ τοι (van Prinsterer, Hartman) and in the other two passages ἤ: but we are not justified in altering the text. Cf. Kugler *de partic.* τοι *eiusque comp. ap. Pl. usu* p. 14.

345 A 5 **ἔστω μὲν ἄδικος κτλ.** The subject is ὁ ἄδικος, supplied from ἀδικίαν. To πείθει also ὁ ἄδικος is the subject; but ἡ ἀδικία or τὸ ἀδικεῖν is the subject of ἔστι. The effect is exactly as in the English 'let him be unjust' etc., 'nevertheless he cannot convince *me* that it is really more profitable than justice.' J. and C. understand τις before ἔστω, needlessly, as I think, and suppose that the "supposed impunity of injustice" is the subject to πείθει, but πείθει is much better with a personal subject. Although the sentence is a trifle loose, it is clear enough, and there is no occasion for reading πείθεις (with Vind. D and Ficinus).

345 B 12 **ἐνθῶ.** ἐντιθέναι (as Wohlrab points out) was used of nurses feeding children: cf. Ar. *Knights* 716 f., supra 343 A, and (for the general idea) Theognis 435 and Pl. *Symp.* 175 D. In μὰ Δία, μὴ σύ γε Socrates shudders at the prospect of having Thrasymachus for his intellectual nurse.

345 C 17 **ποιμαίνειν.** See *cr. n.* Cobet (*Mnem.* IX p. 355) calls for πιαίνειν, but the "addita verba καθ' ὅσον ποιμήν ἐστιν

ποιμήν ἐστιν, οὐ πρὸς τὸ τῶν προβάτων βέλτιστον βλέποντα,
ἀλλ' ὥσπερ δαιτυμόνα τινὰ καὶ μέλλοντα ἑστιάσεσθαι, πρὸς τὴν
D εὐωχίαν, ἢ αὖ πρὸς τὸ ἀποδόσθαι, ὥσπερ χρηματιστὴν ¦ ἀλλ' οὐ
ποιμένα. τῇ δὲ ποιμενικῇ οὐ δήπου ἄλλου του μέλει ἤ, ἐφ' ᾧ
τέτακται, ὅπως τούτῳ τὸ βέλτιστον ἐκποριεῖ· ἐπεὶ τά γε αὑτῆς,
ὥστ' εἶναι βελτίστη, ἱκανῶς δήπου ἐκπεπόρισται, ἕως γ' ἂν μηδὲν
ἐνδέῃ τοῦ ποιμενικὴ εἶναι· οὕτω δὲ ᾤμην ἔγωγε νῦν δὴ ἀναγκαῖον
εἶναι ἡμῖν ὁμολογεῖν, πᾶσαν ἀρχήν, καθ' ὅσον ἀρχή, μηδενὶ ἄλλῳ
τὸ βέλτιστον σκοπεῖσθαι ἢ ἐκείνῳ τῷ ἀρχομένῳ τε καὶ θεραπευο-
E μένῳ, ¦ ἔν τε πολιτικῇ καὶ ἰδιωτικῇ ἀρχῇ. σὺ δὲ τοὺς ἄρχοντας
ἐν ταῖς πόλεσιν, τοὺς ἀληθῶς ἄρχοντας, ἑκόντας οἴει ἄρχειν;
Μὰ Δί' οὔκ, ἔφη, ἀλλ' εὖ οἶδα.

XVIII. Τί δέ; ἦν δ' ἐγώ, ὦ Θρασύμαχε, τὰς ἄλλας ἀρχὰς
οὐκ ἐννοεῖς ὅτι οὐδεὶς ἐθέλει ἄρχειν ἑκών, ἀλλὰ μισθὸν αἰτοῦσιν,
ὡς οὐχὶ αὐτοῖσιν ὠφελίαν ἐσομένην ἐκ τοῦ ἄρχειν ἀλλὰ τοῖς
346 ἀρχο|μένοις; ἐπεὶ τοσόνδε εἰπέ· οὐχὶ ἑκάστην μέντοι φαμὲν
ἑκάστοτε τῶν τεχνῶν τούτῳ ἑτέραν εἶναι, τῷ ἑτέραν τὴν δύναμιν
ἔχειν; καί, ὦ μακάριε, μὴ παρὰ δόξαν ἀποκρίνου, ἵνα τι καὶ
περαίνωμεν. Ἀλλὰ τούτῳ, ἔφη, ἑτέρα. Οὐκοῦν καὶ ὠφελίαν
ἑκάστη ἰδίαν τινὰ ἡμῖν παρέχεται, ἀλλ' οὐ κοινήν, οἷον ἰατρικὴ
μὲν ὑγίειαν, κυβερνητικὴ δὲ σωτηρίαν ἐν τῷ πλεῖν, καὶ αἱ ἄλλαι

5. οἷον A^2Π: οἷοι A^1.

---

circa *universum* pastoris negotium errantem a Socrate Thrasymachum notari docent" (Schneider). How Thrasymachus errs is explained in οὐ πρὸς τὸ κτλ. πιαίνειν might perhaps be read, if the ἀλλά clause is taken closely with what precedes: you did not think it necessary (says Socrates) to adhere rigidly to the genuine shepherd, but think he *fattens* his sheep *qua* shepherd. In that case, however, we should expect ἀλλ' οὐ—βλέπειν in place of οὐ—βλέποντα, to form the antithesis to πιαίνειν.

345 D 24 **οὕτω δὲ ᾤμην**. Some inferior MSS (with Eusebius *Praep. Ev.* XII 44. 2) read δή for δέ, and so Ast and Stallbaum. The connecting particle is better than the illative here, where Socrates is merely recalling his former train of reasoning: 'and it was thus that I came to think' etc.

345 E 31 **οὐδεὶς—μισθόν**. Cf. Arist. *Eth. Nic.* V 10. 1134^b 5 ff. καὶ διὰ τοῦτο ἀλλότριον εἶναί φασιν ἀγαθὸν τὴν δικαιοσύνην—μισθὸς ἄρα τις δοτέος.

32 **αὐτοῖσιν**: see 330 B *n.*

346 A 1 **οὐχὶ—μέντοι**: 339 B *n.*

3 **παρὰ δόξαν** is simply 'contrary to your opinion' ("gegen deine Ueberzeugung" Schneider) as in *Prot.* 337 B, cf. 349 A ἕως ἂν σε ὑπολαμβάνω λέγειν ἅπερ διανοεῖ and 350 E. The words could hardly mean an 'unexpected or paradoxical' reply (as Tucker construes). Socrates is appealing—note ὦ μακάριε—to Thrasymachus not to obstruct the discovery of the truth by want of candour and sincerity.

4 **ἀλλὰ — ἑτέρα** sc. ἐστίν. The reading ἑτέραν is in itself equally good, but has inferior MS authority. Herwerden needlessly recommends the omission of ἑτέρα, or (as alternatives) ἀλλὰ τούτῳ, ἔφη, τῷ ἑτέραν, or ἀλλὰ τούτῳ, ἔφη, ἑτέραν, τῷ ἑτέραν.

οὕτω; Πάνυ γε. Οὐκοῦν καὶ μισθωτικὴ μισθόν; αὕτη γὰρ
αὐτῆς | ἡ δύναμις. ἢ τὴν ἰατρικὴν σὺ καὶ τὴν κυβερνητικὴν B
τὴν αὐτὴν καλεῖς; ἢ ἐάνπερ βούλῃ ἀκριβῶς διορίζειν, ὥσπερ
ὑπέθου, οὐδέν τι μᾶλλον, ἐάν τις κυβερνῶν ὑγιὴς γίγνηται διὰ
τὸ ξυμφέρειν αὐτῷ πλεῖν ἐν τῇ θαλάττῃ, ἕνεκα τούτου καλεῖς
μᾶλλον αὐτὴν ἰατρικήν; Οὐ δῆτα, ἔφη. Οὐδέ γ', οἶμαι, τὴν
μισθωτικήν, ἐὰν ὑγιαίνῃ τις μισθαρνῶν. Οὐ δῆτα. Τί δέ; τὴν
ἰατρικὴν μισθαρνητικήν, ἐὰν ἰώμενός τις μισθαρνῇ; | Οὐκ ἔφη. C
Οὐκοῦν τήν γε ὠφελίαν ἑκάστης τῆς τέχνης ἰδίαν ὡμολογήσαμεν
εἶναι; Ἔστω, ἔφη. Ἥντινα ἄρα ὠφελίαν κοινῇ ὠφελοῦνται
πάντες οἱ δημιουργοί, δῆλον ὅτι κοινῇ τινὶ τῷ αὐτῷ προσχρώμενοι
ἀπ' ἐκείνου ὠφελοῦνται. Ἔοικεν, ἔφη. Φαμὲν δέ γε τὸ μισθὸν
ἀρνυμένους ὠφελεῖσθαι τοὺς δημιουργοὺς ἀπὸ τοῦ προσχρῆσθαι
τῇ μισθωτικῇ τέχνῃ γίγνεσθαι αὐτοῖς. Ξυνέφη μόγις. Οὐκ ἄρα
ἀπὸ τῆς αὑτοῦ τέχνης ἑκάστῳ | αὕτη ἡ ὠφελία ἐστίν, ἡ τοῦ μισθοῦ D
λῆψις, ἀλλ', εἰ δεῖ ἀκριβῶς σκοπεῖσθαι, ἡ μὲν ἰατρικὴ ὑγίειαν
ποιεῖ, ἡ δὲ μισθαρνητικὴ μισθόν, καὶ ἡ μὲν οἰκοδομικὴ οἰκίαν,
ἡ δὲ μισθαρνητικὴ αὐτῇ ἑπομένη μισθόν, καὶ αἱ ἄλλαι πᾶσαι
οὕτως· τὸ αὑτῆς ἑκάστη ἔργον ἐργάζεται καὶ ὠφελεῖ ἐκεῖνο, ἐφ'
ᾧ τέτακται. ἐὰν δὲ μὴ μισθὸς αὐτῇ προσγίγνηται, ἔσθ' ὅ τι
ὠφελεῖται ὁ δημιουργὸς ἀπὸ τῆς τέχνης; Οὐ φαίνεται, ἔφη. Ἆρ'
οὖν οὐδ' ὠφελεῖ τότε, ὅταν | προῖκα ἐργάζηται; Οἶμαι ἔγωγε. E
Οὐκοῦν, ὦ Θρασύμαχε, τοῦτο ἤδη δῆλον, ὅτι οὐδεμία τέχνη οὐδὲ

11. *ξυμφέρειν* Ξ²*q*: *ξυμφέρον* ΑΠΞ¹. 21. *αὕτη* Ξ*q*: *αὐτὴ* Α: *αὐτῇ* (*sic*) Π.

---

7 **οὐκοῦν κτλ.** Aristotle agrees with this analysis: see *Pol.* A 3. 1258ᵃ 10 ff. It should be noted that the antecedent to *αὕτη* is not *μισθόν*, but *τὸ παρέχεσθαι μισθόν*.

346 B 10 **διὰ τὸ ξυμφέρειν.** See *cr. n.* To *ξυμφέρον* there are two objections: first that *διά* with the participle used like *διά* with the infinitive is rare and dubious; second that *ξυμφέρον* is more naturally to be taken as a virtual adjective than as a participle. The last objection might be surmounted by reading *ξυμφέρον* < *ὄν* >, but the more serious flaw would still remain, and *ξυμφέρειν* is in itself so much superior, that (like most editors) I feel bound to adopt it.

12 **οὐδέ γ' οἶμαι τὴν μισθωτικήν** sc. *καλεῖς ἰατρικήν*. The reasoning is somewhat subtle. *ἰατρική*, *κυβερνητική*, *μισθωτική* (*μισθαρνητική*), says Socrates, are three distinct arts. *κυβερνητική* is not to be called *ἰατρική*, even if *ἰατρική* should accompany its operation, nor is *μισθωτική* to be called *ἰατρική* in a similar case. Nor is *ἰατρική* to be called *μισθωτική*, even if *ἰατρική* should be accompanied by *μισθωτική*.

346 C 17 **κοινῇ—προσχρώμενοι**: 'from the common use of some additional element which is the same in all.'

18 **τὸ μισθὸν ἀρνυμένους.** *δέ γε* as usual introduces the minor premise. The semi-poetic word *ἀρνυμένους* is used to suggest *μισθαρνεῖν* and *μισθαρνητική*, the word *μισθόν* at the same time bringing the product of the art well into view. As *τὸ—δημιουργούς* is the subject to *γίγνεσθαι*, the masculine *τόν*—so most MSS—for *τό* is impossible.

ἀρχὴ τὸ αὑτῇ ὠφέλιμον παρασκευάζει, ἀλλ', ὅπερ πάλαι ἐλέγομεν,
τὸ τῷ ἀρχομένῳ καὶ παρασκευάζει καὶ ἐπιτάττει, τὸ ἐκείνου
ξυμφέρον ἥττονος ὄντος σκοποῦσα, ἀλλ' οὐ τὸ τοῦ κρείττονος.
διὰ δὴ ταῦτα ἔγωγε, ὦ φίλε Θρασύμαχε, καὶ ἄρτι ἔλεγον μηδένα
ἐθέλειν ἑκόντα ἄρχειν καὶ τὰ ἀλλότρια κακὰ μεταχειρίζεσθαι
ἀνορθοῦντα, ἀλλὰ μισθὸν αἰτεῖν, ὅτι ὁ μέλλων καλῶς τῇ τέχνῃ |
347 πράξειν οὐδέποτε αὑτῷ τὸ βέλτιστον πράττει οὐδ' ἐπιτάττει κατὰ
τὴν τέχνην ἐπιτάττων, ἀλλὰ τῷ ἀρχομένῳ· ὧν δὴ ἕνεκα, ὡς ἔοικε,
μισθὸν δεῖν ὑπάρχειν τοῖς μέλλουσιν ἐθελήσειν ἄρχειν, ἢ ἀργύριον
ἢ τιμήν, ἢ ζημίαν, ἐὰν μὴ ἄρχῃ.

XIX. Πῶς τοῦτο λέγεις, ὦ Σώκρατες; ἔφη ὁ Γλαύκων. τοὺς
μὲν γὰρ δύο μισθοὺς γιγνώσκω· τὴν δὲ ζημίαν ἥντινα λέγεις καὶ
ὡς ἐν μισθοῦ μέρει εἴρηκας, οὐ ξυνῆκα. Τὸν τῶν βελτίστων
B ἄρα μισθόν, ἔφην, οὐ ξυνιεῖς, δι' | ὃν ἄρχουσιν οἱ ἐπιεικέστατοι,
ὅταν ἐθέλωσιν ἄρχειν. ἢ οὐκ οἶσθα, ὅτι τὸ φιλότιμόν τε καὶ
φιλάργυρον εἶναι ὄνειδος λέγεταί τε καὶ ἔστιν; Ἔγωγε, ἔφη.
Διὰ ταῦτα τοίνυν, ἦν δ' ἐγώ, οὔτε χρημάτων ἕνεκα ἐθέλουσιν
ἄρχειν οἱ ἀγαθοὶ οὔτε τιμῆς· οὔτε γὰρ φανερῶς πραττόμενοι τῆς
ἀρχῆς ἕνεκα μισθὸν μισθωτοὶ βούλονται κεκλῆσθαι, οὔτε λάθρᾳ
αὐτοὶ ἐκ τῆς ἀρχῆς λαμβάνοντες κλέπται· οὐδ' αὖ τιμῆς ἕνεκα·
C οὐ γάρ εἰσι φιλότιμοι. δεῖ δὴ | αὐτοῖς ἀνάγκην προσεῖναι καὶ

2. ὧν Ξ, superscripto οὗ: ᾧ A: οὗ Π*q*. 15. δὴ Π: δὲ A.

---

346 E 33 **ἔλεγον μηδένα ἐθέλειν.** *μή* with the infinitive after verbs of saying, thinking and the like "carries with it the emphasis of the witness on oath, so to speak the emphasis of desire" (Gildersleeve in *A. J. Ph.* I 50). Cf. *Theaet.* 155 A, *Euthyph.* 6 B, *Phaed.* 94 C al., and infr. III 407 E, IV 419 A.

347 A 2 **ὡς ἔοικε** belongs to **ὧν ἕνεκα,** and *δεῖν* is in indirect narration after *ἔλεγον* above. There would be no object in qualifying the force of *δεῖν*; it is not disputed that rulers *must* have their reward. Hence Stallbaum is wrong in regarding *δεῖν* as under the influence of *ἔοικε*, an illogical idiom which is common in Herodotus (Stein on I 65), and found occasionally in Tragedy (Jebb on *Trach.* 1238) and in Plato (*Phil.* 20 D, *Soph.* 263 D, *Euthyd.* 280 D). That *ὡς ἔοικε* has no influence on *δεῖν* in this passage may also be seen from the fact that *δεῖν* (not *δεῖ*) would still be used if *ὡς ἔοικε* were removed. *δεῖν* is not for *δέον*; the late participial form *δεῖν* is not found in Plato: see my note on *Euthyph.* 4 D.

4 **ἄρχῃ.** The transition from plural to singular and conversely is common: see for examples III 408 B, 411 C, 413 D, E, IV 426 A, C, V 463 D, VI 496 C, 500 C, VIII 554 A, C, 558 A, IX 591 A, X 601 D, E, 604 D, and cf. Heindorf on *Gorg.* 478 C, *Prot.* 319 D.

7 **ὡς ἐν μισθοῦ μέρει.** *ὡς* is not (with Wohlrab) to be taken with *ἐν μισθοῦ μέρει*, but stands for the indirect interrogative *ὅπως*.

347 B 14 **αὐτοί** = 'by themselves,' 'ultro,' should be construed with *λαμβάνοντες*. The conjecture *αὐτόν* for *αὐτοί* is very tame.

ζημίαν, εἰ μέλλουσιν ἐθέλειν ἄρχειν· ὅθεν κινδυνεύει τὸ ἑκόντα ἐπὶ τὸ ἄρχειν ἰέναι ἀλλὰ μὴ ἀνάγκην περιμένειν αἰσχρὸν νενομίσθαι. τῆς δὲ ζημίας μεγίστη τὸ ὑπὸ πονηροτέρου ἄρχεσθαι, ἐὰν μὴ αὐτὸς ἐθέλῃ ἄρχειν· ἣν δείσαντές μοι φαίνονται ἄρχειν, ὅταν ἄρχωσιν, οἱ ἐπιεικεῖς, καὶ τότε ἔρχονται ἐπὶ τὸ ἄρχειν, οὐχ ὡς ἐπ' ἀγαθόν τι ἰόντες οὐδ' ὡς εὐπαθήσοντες ἐν αὐτῷ, ἀλλ' ὡς ἐπ' ἀναγκαῖον καὶ οὐκ ἔχοντες ἑαυτῶν βελτίοσιν | ἐπιτρέψαι οὐδὲ D ὁμοίοις. ἐπεὶ κινδυνεύει, πόλις ἀνδρῶν ἀγαθῶν εἰ γένοιτο, περιμάχητον ἂν εἶναι τὸ μὴ ἄρχειν, ὥσπερ νυνὶ τὸ ἄρχειν, καὶ ἐνταῦθ' ἂν καταφανὲς γενέσθαι, ὅτι τῷ ὄντι ἀληθινὸς ἄρχων οὐ πέφυκε τὸ αὑτῷ ξυμφέρον σκοπεῖσθαι, ἀλλὰ τὸ τῷ ἀρχομένῳ· ὥστε πᾶς ἂν ὁ γιγνώσκων τὸ ὠφελεῖσθαι μᾶλλον ἕλοιτο ὑπ' ἄλλου ἢ ἄλλον ὠφελῶν πράγματα ἔχειν. τοῦτο μὲν οὖν ἔγωγε οὐδαμῇ συγχωρῶ | Θρασυμάχῳ, ὡς τὸ δίκαιόν ἐστιν τὸ τοῦ κρείττονος ξυμφέρον. E ἀλλὰ τοῦτο μὲν δὴ καὶ εἰσαῦθις σκεψόμεθα· πολὺ δέ μοι δοκεῖ

---

347 C 16 **ὅθεν κινδυνεύει—νενομίσθαι.** These words are intended to indicate parenthetically that Socrates' thesis finds support in the common judgment of men. Good men, he says, require to be compelled to rule. This may be why (*ὅθεν*) it is accounted a disgrace to enter on office willingly: that is to say, if you do so, you may be inferred to be, not *ἀγαθός*, but *φιλότιμος* or *φιλάργυρος*, which *ὄνειδος λέγεταί τε καὶ ἔστιν* 347 B. There is no good reason for rejecting the clause, as some have proposed to do.

347 D 23 **πόλις ἀνδρῶν ἀγαθῶν** is the first express allusion to an Ideal City in the *Republic*. The principle here laid down—the reluctance of the best men to undertake the task of government—is fully recognised in Plato's commonwealth, where the *ἄρχοντες* are represented as unwilling to desert the life of contemplation for the cares of office. 'Nolo episcopari' is in fact one of the leading guarantees which Plato gives against the abuse of political power (Nohle *Die Staatslehre Plato's in ihr. gesch. Entwick.* p. 119). See VI 520 E, 521 A, where this topic is resumed. Cf. also *Sesame and Lilies* § 43 "The true kings—rule quietly, if at all, and hate ruling; too many of them make 'il gran rifiuto.'"

25 **τῷ ὄντι κτλ.** *τῷ ὄντι* belongs to *οὐ πέφυκε*, not to *ἀληθινός* (as Ast supposes). Richter suggests **ἀληθινός** for *ἀληθινός*, but what is said of a single ruler applies to all: cf. (with Schneider) *Laws* 733 E *λέγωμεν δὴ σώφρονα βίον ἕνα εἶναι καὶ φρόνιμον ἕνα καὶ ἕνα τὸν ἀνδρεῖον.*

26 **πᾶς ἂν κτλ.** The articular infinitive with *αἱρεῖσθαι* is hard to parallel, and on this ground Richards would cancel *τό*. I once thought that *τὸ ὠφελεῖσθαι* might be taken as the object after *γιγνώσκων* ('he who knows what being benefited is,' i.e. virtually 'who knows his own interests'); but this is harsh, and I now acquiesce in the usual interpretation. With *γιγνώσκων* (*intellegens*) used absolutely cf. (with Schneider) *Laws* 733 E *σώφρονα μὲν οὖν βίον ὁ γιγνώσκων θήσει πρᾶον ἐπὶ πάντα.* For the sentiment cf. Soph. *O. T.* 584—598, Eur. *Ion* 621—632, *Hipp.* 1016—1020.

347 E 30 **εἰσαῦθις σκεψόμεθα.** The reference has been much discussed. Pfleiderer's idea (*Zur Lösung d. Pl. Fr.* p. 72) that the words were introduced by Plato "bei der Gesammtredaktion des Werkes" to prepare us for the second half of Book X is most unlikely, because (among other reasons) Book X does not expressly revert to this topic at all. Siebeck (*Zur Chron. d. Pl. Dialoge* pp. 121 ff.) holds that phrases of this sort always refer either to some future dialogue contemplated by Plato, or to a later part of the same dialogue. It is difficult to establish either alternative in the present case; nor

μεῖζον εἶναι, ὃ νῦν λέγει Θρασύμαχος, τὸν τοῦ ἀδίκου βίον φάσκων
εἶναι κρείττω ἢ τὸν τοῦ δικαίου. σὺ οὖν ποτέρως, ἦν δ' ἐγώ,
ὦ Γλαύκων, αἱρεῖ καὶ πότερον ἀληθεστέρως δοκεῖ σοι λέγεσθαι;
Τὸν τοῦ δικαίου ἔγωγε, ἔφη, λυσιτελέστερον βίον εἶναι. Ἤκουσας,
348 ἦν δ' ἐγώ, | ὅσα ἄρτι Θρασύμαχος ἀγαθὰ διῆλθε τῷ τοῦ ἀδίκου;
Ἤκουσα, ἔφη, ἀλλ' οὐ πείθομαι. Βούλει οὖν αὐτὸν πείθωμεν, ἂν
δυνώμεθά πῃ ἐξευρεῖν, ὡς οὐκ ἀληθῆ λέγει; Πῶς γὰρ οὐ βούλομαι;
ἦ δ' ὅς. Ἂν μὲν τοίνυν, ἦν δ' ἐγώ, ἀντικατατείναντες λέγωμεν

33. ἀληθεστέρως *v*: ὡς ἀληθεστέρως ΑΠΞ*q*. 34. ἔφη A^{2}Π: om. A^1.

---

has Siebeck, I think, succeeded in proving his point even elsewhere. It is simplest to suppose that such formulae (like εἰσαῦθις ἐπισκεπτέον in Arist. *Eth. Nic.* I 5. 1097^b 14) are in general only a convenient way of dropping the subject, although there may occasionally be a specific reference. Here there is none. So also Hirmer *Entst. u. Komp. d. Pl. Polit.* in *Fl. Jahrb. Supplementband* XXIII p. 607 *n.* 2.

347 E—**348** B *Introduction to the second part of Socrates' reply to Thrasymachus.* See 344 D, 348 B *nn.*

347 E 31 **τὸν τοῦ ἀδίκου βίον—δικαίου.** In these words Socrates sums up the remarks of Thrasymachus from 343 B (καὶ οὕτω πόρρω κτλ.) to 344 C (λυσιτελοῦν τε καὶ ξυμφέρον).

32 **ποτέρως — λέγεσθαι.** Ast's suggestion πότερον, ἦν δ' ἐγώ, ὦ Γλαύκων, αἱρεῖ; καὶ ποτέρως ἀληθεστέρως δοκεῖ σοι λέγεσθαι; is now generally adopted, but (apart from its considerable divergence from the MS reading) the juxtaposition of ποτέρως and ἀληθεστέρως is unpleasing. The ποτέρως αἱρεῖ of A is quite unobjectionable: cf. VII 528 A οὕτως—αἱροῦμαι; and it is (I think) an objection to πότερον αἱρεῖ that it would represent Socrates as asking Glauco not which *view* he elected to take, but which *life*—the just or the unjust—he chose for himself. Schneider (after Bekker) retains the reading of the best MSS in πότερον ὡς ἀληθεστέρως, and explains the last two words as equivalent to ὥσπερ ὃ ἀληθεστέρως λέγεται: but ὡς ἀληθεστέρως could not (if written by Plato) be anything but the comparative of ὡς ἀληθῶς, and that is quite different in sense from ἀληθεστέρως. I have omitted ὡς (with Bremius and a few MSS of inferior authority), "ut ortum ex varia lectione πότερον et ποτέρως in ποτερόνως conflata" (Schneider). I am glad to find that Tucker adopts the same solution.

348 A 1 **διῆλθε**: i.q. διῆλθεν ὄντα or διελθὼν ἔλεξεν εἶναι (Schneider). Cf. II 363 A ἄφθονα ἔχουσι λέγειν ἀγαθὰ τοῖς ὁσίοις with *n.* ad loc. In view of ἐν ἑκατέρῳ λέγομεν in B below, it is easy to suggest διῆλθεν <ἐν>; but the text is probably sound.

4 **ἂν μὲν τοίνυν κτλ.** The alternatives are between continuous speech and dialectic. By λόγον in παρὰ λόγον Thrasymachus' speech in 343 A ff. is meant: to this Socrates would reply, after which Thrasymachus would speak again, and finally Socrates. Thus each party would have delivered two speeches. In Athenian lawsuits there were often two speeches delivered by the accuser and two by the defendant (Meier und Schömann *Attische Process* p. 924), so that Plato's imagery is borrowed from the law-court, whence δικαστῶν τινῶν τῶν διακρινούντων just below. This point escaped Ast, who reads καὶ αὖθις οὗτος ἄλλον ἡμῖν (after Ficinus and Stephanus).

ἀντικατατείναντες is intransitive: cf. II 358 D κατατείνας ἐρῶ τὸν ἄδικον βίον ἐπαινῶν and 367 B: the notion (as in ξυντείνω, ξυντεταμένως and the like) is of nervous tension. The word cannot mean 'replying to one another in set speeches' (J. and C.). "Setting out alternative lists of advantages" (remarks Bosanquet) "was the well-known method of fable or poetry. See Book II" 361 D—362 C and 362 E—365 A: "and compare Prodicus' *Choice of Heracles* (Xen. *Mem.* II 1) and the discussion between the Just and Unjust arguments in the *Clouds* of Aristophanes."

αὐτῷ λόγον παρὰ λόγον, ὅσα αὖ ἀγαθὰ ἔχει τὸ δίκαιον εἶναι, καὶ αὖθις οὗτος, καὶ ἄλλον ἡμεῖς, ἀριθμεῖν δεήσει τἀγαθὰ καὶ μετρεῖν ὅσα ἑκάτεροι ἐν ἑκατέρῳ λέγομεν, καὶ ἤδη δικαστῶν **B** τινῶν τῶν διακρινούντων δεησόμεθα· ἂν δὲ ὥσπερ ἄρτι ἀνομολογούμενοι πρὸς ἀλλήλους σκοπῶμεν, ἅμα αὐτοί τε δικασταὶ καὶ ῥήτορες ἐσόμεθα. Πάνυ μὲν οὖν, ἔφη. Ὁποτέρως οὖν σοι, ἦν δ' ἐγώ, ἀρέσκει. Οὕτως, ἔφη.

XX. Ἴθι δή, ἦν δ' ἐγώ, ὦ Θρασύμαχε, ἀπόκριναι ἡμῖν ἐξ ἀρχῆς· τὴν τελέαν ἀδικίαν τελέας οὔσης δικαιοσύνης λυσιτελεστέραν φῂς εἶναι; Πάνυ μὲν οὖν καὶ φημί, ἔφη, καὶ δι' ἅ, εἴρηκα. **C** Φέρε δὴ τὸ τοιόνδε περὶ αὐτῶν πῶς λέγεις; τὸ μέν που ἀρετὴν αὐτοῖν καλεῖς, τὸ δὲ κακίαν; Πῶς γὰρ οὔ; Οὐκοῦν τὴν μὲν

5. αὖ A^2Π : ἂν A^1.

---

348 B 10 **ὁποτέρως** is virtually indirect: translate 'whichever you please, then.' Hermann reads ποτέρως, but the text ought not to be changed either here or in *Euthyd.* 271 A τίς ἦν, ὦ Σώκρατες, ᾧ χθὲς ἐν Λυκείῳ διελέγου;—τίς ἦν; Ὁπότερον καὶ ἐρωτᾷς, ὦ Κρίτων· οὐ γὰρ εἷς, ἀλλὰ δύ' ἤστην, i.e. (it depends on) which of these you are asking about etc. Cf. also ἥτις—αὐτῶν ἡ ἀρετή 353 C. In *Rep.* IX 578 E ἐν ποίῳ ἄν τινι καὶ ὁπόσῳ φόβῳ οἴει γενέσθαι αὐτόν and *Gorg.* 522 A, the ὁπόσῳ is perhaps due to the proximity of οἴει, which gives the question a certain semblance of indirectness; ὁποίῳ in *Alc.* I 110 C and ὁποίου infra 400 A may be similarly explained; while in *Meno* 74 D ἀλλὰ μή μοι οὕτως—ἀλλ' ὅ τι ἐστὶν τοῦτο, it is easy to supply a verb of saying. Possibly (as Heindorf thinks) ὅτι (B ὅ τί) in *Euthyd.* 287 B is corrupt for τί, as ὅπως for πῶς in *Charm.* 170 C. In *Lys.* 212 C ὁπότερος οὖν αὐτῶν ποτέρου φίλος ἐστιν; ὁ φιλῶν τοῦ φιλουμένου—ἢ ὁ φιλούμενος τοῦ φιλοῦντος; we ought no doubt to read ὁ πότερος (with Hermann).

348 B—**350** C *Thrasymachus now identifies Justice with Simplicity, Injustice with Discretion. Injustice he assigns to Virtue and Wisdom, Justice to their opposites. He further declares that Injustice is strong and beautiful, and is ready to predicate of it all that is usually predicated of Justice* (348 B—349 B).

Socrates then commences a very subtle refutation, addressing himself to the assertion that Injustice is Virtue and Wisdom (349 B—350 C). (1) *The just man endeavours to overreach the unjust, but not the just: the unjust man to overreach both the just and the unjust. Therefore, generally, the just man endeavours to overreach the unlike; the unjust man to overreach both the like and the unlike. Further, the unjust man, being wise and good, resembles the wise and good, while the just man, being foolish and evil, resembles the foolish and evil; in brief, each is as those whom he resembles.* (2) *Again, from the analogy of the arts it is seen that the man who knows tries to overreach the unlike, while the ignorant man tries to overreach both the like and the unlike. But the man who knows is wise, and the wise man good; we may therefore in the last sentence substitute 'wise and good man' for 'the man who knows,' and 'foolish and evil' for 'ignorant.' Comparing, then, conclusions* (1) *and* (2), *we see that the just are like the wise and good, that is, are wise and good* (*since they are such as those whom they resemble*), *while the unjust in like manner are foolish and evil. Thus is refuted the thesis that Injustice is Virtue and Wisdom.*

348 B ff. The second division of Socrates' reply begins here. Though professedly attacking the section of Thrasymachus' speech contained in 343 C—344 C, and summed up in the theory that the life of the Unjust is better than that of the Just (347 E), it is not till 352 D that Socrates directly grapples with this theory. In the meantime, certain further deliver-

δικαιοσύνην ἀρετήν, τὴν δὲ ἀδικίαν κακίαν; Εἰκός γ', ἔφη, ὦ
ἥδιστε, ἐπειδὴ καὶ λέγω ἀδικίαν μὲν λυσιτελεῖν, δικαιοσύνην δ' οὔ.
Ἀλλὰ τί μήν; Τοὐναντίον, ἦ δ' ὅς. Ἦ τὴν δικαιοσύνην κακίαν; |
D Οὔκ, ἀλλὰ πάνυ γενναίαν εὐήθειαν. Τὴν ἀδικίαν ἄρα κακοήθειαν
καλεῖς; Οὔκ, ἀλλ' εὐβουλίαν, ἔφη. Ἦ καὶ φρόνιμοί σοι, ὦ
Θρασύμαχε, δοκοῦσιν εἶναι καὶ ἀγαθοὶ οἱ ἄδικοι; Οἵ γε τελέως,
ἔφη, οἷοί τε ἀδικεῖν, πόλεις τε καὶ ἔθνη δυνάμενοι ἀνθρώπων ὑφ'
ἑαυτοὺς ποιεῖσθαι. σὺ δὲ οἴει με ἴσως τοὺς τὰ βαλλάντια ἀπο-
τέμνοντας λέγειν. λυσιτελεῖ μὲν οὖν, ἦ δ' ὅς, καὶ τὰ τοιαῦτα,
ἐάνπερ λανθάνῃ· ἔστι δὲ οὐκ ἄξια λόγου, ἀλλ' ἃ νῦν δὴ ἔλεγον. |
E Τοῦτο μέντοι, ἔφην, οὐκ ἀγνοῶ ὅ τι βούλει λέγειν· ἀλλὰ τόδε
ἐθαύμασα, εἰ ἐν ἀρετῆς καὶ σοφίας τίθης μέρει τὴν ἀδικίαν, τὴν
δὲ δικαιοσύνην ἐν τοῖς ἐναντίοις. Ἀλλὰ πάνυ οὕτω τίθημι.
Τοῦτο, ἦν δ' ἐγώ, ἤδη στερεώτερον, ὦ ἑταῖρε, καὶ οὐκέτι ῥᾴδιον

19. ἦ Π: ἡ A. 30. ῥᾴδιον *v*: ῥᾷον ΑΠΞ*q*.

---

ances of Thrasymachus on the nature of Injustice are refuted by means of arguments which have an indirect bearing on the question at issue (see 352 D *φαίνονται μὲν οὖν καὶ νῦν, ὡς ἐμοὶ δοκεῖ, ἐξ ὧν εἰρήκαμεν· ὅμως δ' ἔτι βέλτιον σκεπτέον*). This part of Socrates' reply may therefore be regarded as itself subdivided into two parts—the first being an indirect, the second a direct refutation of Thrasymachus. Cf. 352 D *n.*

348 C 17 **εἰκός γε—τοὐναντίον.** Thrasymachus' view of *δικαιοσύνη* is like Callicles' theory of *ἀρετή* in *Gorg.* 491 E ff. esp. 492 B *τρυφὴ καὶ ἀκολασία καὶ ἐλευθερία, ἐὰν ἐπικουρίαν ἔχῃ, τοῦτ' ἐστὶν ἀρετή τε καὶ εὐδαιμονία.* The irony is clearly marked by *ὦ ἥδιστε*, and Hartman should not have revived Hirschig's proposal to read <*οὔκουν*> *εἰκός γε.*

19 **ἀλλὰ τί μήν;** 'Well, what else?' Cf. (with J. and C.) *Symp.* 206 E.

348 D 20 **πάνυ γενναίαν εὐήθειαν**: 'sublime simplicity.' Such contempt for *εὐήθεια* recalls Thucydides' description of contemporary morals: cf. especially III 83. 1 *καὶ τὸ εὔηθες, οὗ τὸ γενναῖον πλεῖστον μετέχει, καταγελασθὲν ἠφανίσθη.*

21 **εὐβουλία** was preeminently a political virtue: cf. *Alc.* I 125 E *πολιτείας κοινωνούντων τίνα καλεῖς ἐπιστήμην; Εὐβουλίαν ἔγωγε*, *Prot.* 318 E, and infra IV 428 B. It is therefore fitly used by Thrasymachus to describe his theory, which is a theory of political rather than of private morality: cf. *πόλεις τε—ποιεῖσθαι* below.

23 **ὑφ' ἑαυτοὺς ποιεῖσθαι.** *ἑαυτοῖς* is found in some inferior MSS, but the accusative is also admissible. Cf. Thuc. IV 60 (cited by Schneider) *εἰκὸς—αὐτοὺς τάδε πάντα πειράσασθαι ὑπὸ σφᾶς ποιεῖσθαι.* In *τελέως* Thrasymachus recalls the *τελέαν ἀδικίαν* of 348 B.

24 **σὺ δὲ οἴει—λέγειν.** Baiter (with Paris A) assigns these words to Socrates; but they come much more naturally from Thrasymachus: cf. 344 B. *βαλλάντια* and not *βαλάντια* is the spelling of A here and in VIII 552 D (*βαλλαντιοτόμοι*): in IX 575 B (*βαλλαντιοτομοῦσι*) the second λ is due to an early corrector. The double -λλ- has also the best MS authority in *Gorg.* 508 E, *Symp.* 190 E. See also Blaydes on Ar. *Frogs* 772. For **ἦ δ' ὅς** below after *ἔφη* cf. *Phaed.* 78 A and VII 522 A.

348 E 30 **ἤδη στερεώτερον**: 'still more stubborn.' *στερέος* is like *σκληρός* in *Theaet.* 155 E *σκληροὺς—καὶ ἀντιτύπους ἀνθρώπους*, but stronger, suggesting castiron hardness and inflexibility.

ῥᾴδιον. See *cr. n.* Schneider refers to *Laws* 757 B *τὴν δὲ ἀληθεστάτην καὶ ἀρίστην ἰσότητα οὐκέτι ῥᾴδιον παντὶ ἰδεῖν.* *ῥᾷον* is not (I think) possible here: and a scribe might easily omit ΙΔ in ΡΑΙΔΙΟΝ. Cf. *Introd.* § 5.

ἔχειν ὅ τί τις εἴπῃ. εἰ γὰρ λυσιτελεῖν μὲν τὴν ἀδικίαν ἐτίθεσο,
κακίαν μέντοι ἢ αἰσχρὸν αὐτὸ ὡμολόγεις εἶναι, ὥσπερ ἄλλοι τινές,
εἴχομεν ἄν τι λέγειν κατὰ τὰ νομιζόμενα λέγοντες· νῦν δὲ δῆλος
εἶ ὅτι φήσεις αὐτὸ καὶ καλὸν καὶ ἰσχυρὸν εἶναι καὶ τἄλλα αὐτῷ
πάντα προσθήσεις, | ἃ ἡμεῖς τῷ δικαίῳ προσετίθεμεν, ἐπειδή 349
γε καὶ ἐν ἀρετῇ αὐτὸ καὶ σοφίᾳ ἐτόλμησας θεῖναι. Ἀληθέστατα,
ἔφη, μαντεύει. Ἀλλ' οὐ μέντοι, ἦν δ' ἐγώ, ἀποκνητέον γε τῷ
λόγῳ ἐπεξελθεῖν σκοπούμενον, ἕως ἄν σε ὑπολαμβάνω λέγειν
ἅπερ διανοεῖ. ἐμοὶ γὰρ δοκεῖς σύ, ὦ Θρασύμαχε, ἀτεχνῶς νῦν
οὐ σκώπτειν, ἀλλὰ τὰ δοκοῦντα περὶ τῆς ἀληθείας λέγειν. Τί δέ
σοι, ἔφη, τοῦτο διαφέρει, εἴτε μοι δοκεῖ εἴτε μή, ἀλλ' οὐ τὸν λόγον
ἐλέγχεις; | Οὐδέν, ἦν δ' ἐγώ. ἀλλὰ τόδε μοι πειρῶ ἔτι πρὸς B
τούτοις ἀποκρίνασθαι· ὁ δίκαιος τοῦ δικαίου δοκεῖ τί σοι ἂν
ἐθέλειν πλέον ἔχειν; Οὐδαμῶς, ἔφη· οὐ γὰρ ἂν ἦν ἀστεῖος, ὥσπερ
νῦν, καὶ εὐήθης. Τί δέ; τῆς δικαίας πράξεως; Οὐδὲ τῆς <πράξεως

11. πράξεως τῆς nos: om. codd.

---

31 **εἰ γὰρ κτλ.** *Gorg.* 483 C νόμῳ μὲν τοῦτο ἄδικον καὶ αἰσχρὸν λέγεται, τὸ πλέον ζητεῖν ἔχειν τῶν πολλῶν, καὶ ἀδικεῖν αὐτὸ καλοῦσιν. Dümmler (*Zur Comp. d. Pl. St.* p. 13) goes so far as to assert that ὥσπερ ἄλλοι τινές is an express reference to Polus in the *Gorgias*; but nothing is gained by so hazardous a conjecture.

349 A 1 **προσετίθεμεν**: 'used to attribute to,' sc. before you announced your view—with ironical deference, like ἐλέγομεν in *Prot.* 353 C τί οὖν φατε τοῦτο εἶναι, ὃ ἡμεῖς ἧττω εἶναι τῶν ἡδονῶν ἐλέγομεν; Stallbaum takes the imperfect as referring to 345 C, but neither there nor in 348 C (cited by Schneider) is there anything to justify a particular reference.

5 **ἐμοὶ γὰρ—λέγειν.** A similar remark is made after Callicles has expounded kindred views in *Gorg.* 492 D σαφῶς γὰρ σὺ νῦν λέγεις ἃ οἱ ἄλλοι διανοοῦνται μέν, λέγειν δὲ οὐκ ἐθέλουσι.

6 **τὰ δοκοῦντα κτλ.** can only mean 'what you think about the truth,' not 'what you think to be the truth' (D. and V.) or 'your real mind' (Schneider and Jowett). We should expect ἀδικίας for ἀληθείας, as H. Wolf proposed to read, for it is Injustice, not Truth, which is the subject of dispute. But as ἀδικίας has not a vestige of support from the MSS, I have not ventured to make the change. The truth in question must be understood as the truth about justice and injustice. Herwerden's ἐπὶ τῆς ἀληθείας (for which he compares Dem. *de Cor.* 17, 226, and 294) will hardly command assent.

τί δέ—ἐλέγχεις; Cf. *Charm.* 161 C πάντως γὰρ οὐ τοῦτο σκεπτέον ὅστις αὐτὸ εἶπεν, ἀλλὰ πότερον ἀληθὲς λέγεται ἢ οὔ.

349 B 10 **πλέον ἔχειν.** The literal and derived significations of this phrase are treated as identical throughout the curious reasoning which follows. Primarily, πλέον ἔχειν refers to quantitative superiority; in its derived sense, it is used (together with πλεονεκτεῖν) more generally of 'overreaching.'

11 **τῆς δικαίας πράξεως.** 'To have more than the just action' means 'to do more than is just' (cf. πλείω—αἱρεῖσθαι—πράττειν 350 A), outdo, overreach what is just in action. The notion of virtue as a μεσότης is implied.

οὐδὲ τῆς κτλ. See *cr. n.* I do not think that οὐδὲ τῆς δικαίας can be right. The whole emphasis (as οὐδὲ shews) must be on πράξεως, and the emphatic word should be expressed. οὐδὲ τῆς πράξεως τῆς δικαίας (sc. any more than the ἀνδρὸς δικαίου) gives exactly the emphasis required. In the cases quoted by Schneider

τῆς> δικαίας, ἔφη. Τοῦ δὲ ἀδίκου πότερον ἀξιοῖ ἂν πλεονεκτεῖν καὶ ἡγοῖτο δίκαιον εἶναι, ἢ οὐκ ἂν ἡγοῖτο δίκαιον; Ἡγοῖτ' ἄν, ἦ δ' ὅς, καὶ ἀξιοῖ, ἀλλ' οὐκ ἂν δύναιτο. Ἀλλ' οὐ τοῦτο, ἦν C δ' ἐγώ, ἐρωτῶ, ἀλλ' εἰ τοῦ μὲν δικαίου | μὴ ἀξιοῖ πλέον ἔχειν μηδὲ βούλεται ὁ δίκαιος, τοῦ δὲ ἀδίκου; Ἀλλ' οὕτως, ἔφη, ἔχει. Τί δὲ δὴ ὁ ἄδικος; ἆρα ἀξιοῖ τοῦ δικαίου πλεονεκτεῖν καὶ τῆς δικαίας πράξεως; Πῶς γὰρ οὔκ; ἔφη, ὅς γε πάντων πλέον ἔχειν ἀξιοῖ. Οὐκοῦν καὶ ἀδίκου ἀνθρώπου τε καὶ πράξεως ὁ ἄδικος πλεονεκτήσει καὶ ἁμιλλήσεται ὡς ἁπάντων πλεῖστον αὐτὸς λάβῃ; Ἔστι ταῦτα.

XXI. Ὧδε δὴ λέγωμεν, ἔφην· ὁ δίκαιος τοῦ μὲν ὁμοίου οὐ D πλεονεκτεῖ, τοῦ δὲ ἀνομοίου, ὁ δὲ ἄδικος τοῦ τε | ὁμοίου καὶ τοῦ ἀνομοίου. Ἄριστα, ἔφη, εἴρηκας. Ἔστιν δέ γε, ἔφην, φρόνιμός τε καὶ ἀγαθὸς ὁ ἄδικος, ὁ δὲ δίκαιος οὐδέτερα. Καὶ τοῦτ', ἔφη, εὖ. Οὐκοῦν, ἦν δ' ἐγώ, καὶ ἔοικε τῷ φρονίμῳ καὶ τῷ ἀγαθῷ ὁ ἄδικος, ὁ δὲ δίκαιος οὐκ ἔοικεν; Πῶς γὰρ οὐ μέλλει, ἔφη, ὁ τοιοῦτος ὢν καὶ ἐοικέναι τοῖς τοιούτοις, ὁ δὲ μὴ ἐοικέναι; Καλῶς. τοιοῦτος ἄρα ἐστὶν ἑκάτερος αὐτῶν οἷσπερ ἔοικεν. Ἀλλὰ τί μέλλει; ἔφη.

(*Laws* 754 B, 916 B, infra VII 516 B) the omitted word is unemphatic and easily supplied. For the error cf. *Crito* 50 B where the first hand of the Bodleian MS reads *τὰς δικασθείσας* by mistake for *τὰς <δίκας τὰς> δικασθείσας*. See also *Introd.* § 5.

349 C 19 **οὐκοῦν καὶ—λάβῃ**. The *ἄδικος πρᾶξις* which the unjust man overreaches is to be regarded as *ἄδικος* because it has itself overreached (not fallen short of) the mean. *ὡς* with the subjunctive after verbs of striving does not seem to occur elsewhere in Plato: like its use in a pure final clause (of which there is only one example in Plato, viz. *Tim.* 92 A) it is almost exclusively confined (among Attic writers) to Xenophon and the tragedians. See Weber's tables in Goodwin *MT.* p. 398, and cf. Gildersleeve in *A. J. Ph.* IV p. 419.

22 **τοῦ μὲν ὁμοίου—τοῦ δὲ ἀνομοίου.** This generalisation of 'like' and 'unlike' into abstract notions, without regard to their relativity, is suggestive of (but does not of course presuppose) the Ideas of *τὰ πρός τι* which we meet with in *Phaed.* 74 A.

349 D 26 **οὐκοῦν κτλ.** A proviso which is made use of in 350 C (*ἀλλὰ μὴν —ἑκάτερον εἶναι*).

28 **ὁ δὲ μὴ ἐοικέναι.** *ὁ δέ* is simply 'the other' (as is marked in A by a pause after *δέ*), i.e. *ὁ μὴ τοιοῦτος*: cf. 339 E (*τοῖς δέ* for *τοῖς δὲ ἀρχομένοις*), 343 D *ὁ μὲν δίκαιος ἀπὸ τῶν ἴσων πλέον εἰσφέρει, ὁ δ' ἔλαττον* and IX 587 B. J. and C., with most of the editors, adopt the reading of Stephanus (*ὁ δὲ μὴ μὴ ἐοικέναι*), which has the support of some inferior MSS; but the idiom is sufficiently well authenticated, and the collocation of the two negatives would be unpleasing. I am glad to see that Tucker takes the same view.

29 **οἷσπερ ἔοικεν.** Madvig's *οἷοισπερ ἔοικεν* is refuted by 350 C *ὡμολογοῦμεν ᾧ γε* (i.e. *οἷος ᾧ γε*) *ὅμοιος ἑκάτερος εἴη, τοιοῦτον καὶ ἑκάτερον εἶναι.* Cf. also Arist. *Pol.* H 13. 1332ª 22. The construction was supported by Schneider from *Phaed.* 92 B, but *ὅ* and not *ᾧ* is now read there on the authority of the best MS.

ἀλλὰ τί μέλλει (sc. *εἶναι*); A rare formula, occurring also in *Hipp. Min.* 377 D: cf. *τί δ' οὐ μέλλει;* VIII 566 D, X 605 C. With the force of *τί* ('what else') cf. *ἀλλὰ τί οἴει* supra 332 C.

Εἶεν, ὦ Θρασύμαχε· μουσικὸν δέ τινα λέγεις, ἕτερον | δὲ ἄμουσον; E
Ἔγωγε. Πότερον φρόνιμον καὶ πότερον ἄφρονα; Τὸν μὲν μουσικὸν
δήπου φρόνιμον, τὸν δὲ ἄμουσον ἄφρονα. Οὐκοῦν καὶ ἅπερ
φρόνιμον, ἀγαθόν, ἃ δὲ ἄφρονα, κακόν; Ναί. Τί δὲ ἰατρικόν; οὐχ
οὕτως; Οὕτως. Δοκεῖ ἂν οὖν τίς σοι, ὦ ἄριστε, μουσικὸς ἀνὴρ
ἁρμοττόμενος λύραν ἐθέλειν μουσικοῦ ἀνδρὸς ἐν τῇ ἐπιτάσει
καὶ ἀνέσει τῶν χορδῶν πλεονεκτεῖν ἢ ἀξιοῦν πλέον ἔχειν; Οὐκ
ἔμοιγε. Τί δέ; ἀμούσου; Ἀνάγκη, ἔφη. Τί δὲ ἰατρικός; | ἐν 350
τῇ ἐδωδῇ ἢ πόσει ἐθέλειν ἄν τι ἰατρικοῦ πλεονεκτεῖν ἢ ἀνδρὸς
ἢ πράγματος; Οὐ δῆτα. Μὴ ἰατρικοῦ δέ; Ναί. Περὶ πάσης
δὲ ὅρα ἐπιστήμης τε καὶ ἀνεπιστημοσύνης, εἴ τίς σοι δοκεῖ ἐπιστήμων ὁστισοῦν πλείω ἂν ἐθέλειν αἱρεῖσθαι ἢ ὅσα ἄλλος ἐπιστήμων
ἢ πράττειν ἢ λέγειν, καὶ οὐ ταὐτὰ τῷ ὁμοίῳ ἑαυτῷ εἰς τὴν αὐτὴν
πρᾶξιν. Ἀλλ' ἴσως, ἔφη, ἀνάγκη τοῦτό γε οὕτως ἔχειν. Τί δὲ
ὁ ἀνεπιστήμων; οὐχὶ ὁμοίως μὲν ἐπιστήμονος πλεονεκτήσειεν | ἄν, B
ὁμοίως δὲ ἀνεπιστήμονος; Ἴσως. Ὁ δὲ ἐπιστήμων σοφός; Φημί.
Ὁ δὲ σοφὸς ἀγαθός; Φημί. Ὁ ἄρα ἀγαθός τε καὶ σοφὸς τοῦ μὲν
ὁμοίου οὐκ ἐθελήσει πλεονεκτεῖν, τοῦ δὲ ἀνομοίου τε καὶ ἐναντίου.
Ἔοικεν, ἔφη. Ὁ δὲ κακός τε καὶ ἀμαθὴς τοῦ τε ὁμοίου καὶ τοῦ

---

30 **μουσικὸν δέ τινα κτλ.** Here begin the usual Socratic illustrations from the arts, with the concomitant identification of virtue and knowledge (ὁ δὲ σοφὸς ἀγαθός; Φημί 350 B).

349 E 34 **δοκεῖ ἂν οὖν—ἀξιοῦν πλέον ἔχειν.** Socrates ignores the proverb καὶ κεραμεὺς κεραμεῖ κοτέει καὶ ἀοιδὸς ἀοιδῷ. Strictly speaking, however, it is not *qua* κεραμεύς, but *qua* moneymaker (or the like) that the κεραμεὺς κοτέει. J. and C. cite an admirable parallel from Shakespeare (*King John* IV 2) "When workmen strive to do better than well, They do confound their skill in covetousness." The words ἢ ἀξιοῦν πλέον ἔχειν have a suspicious look, and are rejected by Heller (*Fl. Jahrb.* 1875 p. 171) and others, but such duplicate expressions are common in Plato, and as the illustration from the harp introduces a new and important stage in the argument, Plato may have wished to remind us that after all πλεονεκτεῖν is only the πλέον ἔχειν with which we started (349 B). It should be noted, too, that ἀξιοῦν is a little more than ἐθέλειν.

350 A 1 **ἐν τῇ ἐδωδῇ ἢ πόσει** refers of course to the patient's diet. Plato carefully writes πλεονεκτεῖν here in preference to πλέον ἔχειν. The 'overreaching' in such a case might well consist in giving the patient less.

6 **ἢ πράττειν ἢ λέγειν.** The idea of πλεονεκτεῖν in speaking has not been introduced before, nor is it made use of in the sequel. We must regard the addition of ἢ λέγειν as merely a rhetorical device to increase the emphasis: see on 333 D and 351 A.

7 **τί δὲ ὁ ἀνεπιστήμων; κτλ.** Proclus' commentary on these words is interesting, though he probably reads more into them than Plato intended here: καὶ ὅλως τῷ μὲν ἀγαθῷ τὸ κακὸν ἠναντίωται μόνον, τῷ δὲ κακῷ καὶ τὸ καλὸν (leg. κακὸν) καὶ τὸ ἀγαθόν· ἀναιρετικὸν οὖν ἐστι τοῦ ἀγαθοῦ καὶ τοῦ πρὸς αὐτὸ ἐναντίου κακοῦ (*in Alc.* I p. 323 ed. Creuzer). The identifications in ὁ δὲ ἐπιστήμων σοφός and ὁ δὲ σοφὸς ἀγαθός below have been allowed before in the special cases of the μουσικός and the ἰατρικός (349 E).

ἐναντίου. Φαίνεται. Οὐκοῦν, ὦ Θρασύμαχε, ἦν δ' ἐγώ, ὁ ἄδικος
ἡμῖν τοῦ ἀνομοίου τε καὶ ὁμοίου πλεονεκτεῖ; ἢ οὐχ οὕτως ἔλεγες;
C Ἔγωγε, ἔφη. Ὁ δέ γε δίκαιος τοῦ μὲν ὁμοίου οὐ πλεονεκτήσει,
τοῦ δὲ ἀνομοίου; Ναί. Ἔοικεν ἄρα, ἦν δ' ἐγώ, ὁ μὲν δίκαιος τῷ
σοφῷ καὶ ἀγαθῷ, ὁ δὲ ἄδικος τῷ κακῷ καὶ ἀμαθεῖ. Κινδυνεύει.
Ἀλλὰ μὴν ὡμολογοῦμεν, ᾧ γε ὅμοιος ἑκάτερος εἴη, τοιοῦτον καὶ
ἑκάτερον εἶναι. Ὡμολογοῦμεν γάρ. Ὁ μὲν ἄρα δίκαιος ἡμῖν
ἀναπέφανται ὢν ἀγαθός τε καὶ σοφός, ὁ δὲ ἄδικος ἀμαθής τε καὶ
κακός.

XXII. Ὁ δὲ Θρασύμαχος ὡμολόγησε μὲν πάντα ταῦτα, οὐχ
D ὡς ἐγὼ νῦν ῥᾳδίως λέγω, ἀλλ' ἑλκόμενος καὶ μόγις, μετὰ ἱδρῶτος
θαυμαστοῦ ὅσου, ἅτε καὶ θέρους ὄντος. τότε καὶ εἶδον ἐγώ,

---

350 C 20 **ἀναπέφανται.** Stallbaum naïvely reminds us that *ἀναπέφανται* is often used of a conclusion which "praeter exspectationem emergit et elucet." The pervading fallacy in the discussion is akin to the *a dicto secundum quid ad dictum simpliciter*. Thus 'like' and 'unlike' are used absolutely, and each of them is equated with itself. The wise man is held to be good, because one is good in that in which one is wise (this might however be justified on the "stricter mode of reasoning"). Finally, the just man is inferred to be wise and good, on the principle that one is what one resembles: but whether the resemblance be in essence or in accident, we are not told. The argument should be regarded as a dialectical *tour de force*,—*φιλόνικον μᾶλλον ἢ φιλάληθες*. The reasoning in the next section of the argument strikes a deeper note.

350 C—**352** D *Socrates now attacks the second assertion made by Thrasymachus in* 349 A, *viz. that Injustice is strong. Justice* (*he argues*) *is stronger than Injustice, both because it is* (*as we have seen*) *virtue and wisdom, and because in its effects it is the antithesis of Injustice, which infuses hatred and sedition, both into aggregates of individuals, and into the individual himself. Injustice weakens by preventing community of action; it makes men collectively and individually hateful to themselves and to the just, among whom are the gods. When Injustice seems to be strong, it is in virtue of some latent Justice which it still retains.*

350 C ff. The argument in this section has a deeper ethical import than any which has preceded, and foreshadows some of the central doctrines of the *Republic*. See notes on 351 D, E, and (for the importance of the whole discussion in the general history of philosophy) Bosanquet's *Companion*, p. 63, where it is justly observed that the argument "marks an era in philosophy. It is a first reading of the central facts of society, morality, and nature. In social analysis it founds the idea of organization and division of labour....In morality it gives the conception of a distinctively human life which is the content or positive end of the distinctively human will. And for natural knowledge it suggests the connection between function and definition, and consequently between purpose and reality, which is profoundly developed in the sixth and seventh books. These conceptions become corner-stones of Aristotle's Philosophy, and still, when seen in their connection, form the very core of the best thought."

22 **ὁ δὲ Θρασύμαχος κτλ.** 'Now Thrasymachus' etc. *δέ* is not "flat" (Tucker), but at least as good as *δή*, and much better supported by the MSS.

οὐχ ὡς ἐγὼ νῦν ῥᾳδίως λέγω. "Expectabam certe: *οὐχ ὡς ἐγὼ νῦν λέγω ῥᾳδίως*," says Herwerden; but the antecedent in Greek is idiomatically attracted into the relative clause (Kühner *Gr. Gramm.* II p. 922). Translate 'not in the easy way in which I now repeat them.'

350 D 24 **ἅτε καὶ θέρους ὄντος.** The action is probably laid in Hecatombaeon (roughly our July): see *Introd.* § 3.

πρότερον δὲ οὔπω, Θρασύμαχον ἐρυθριῶντα. ἐπειδὴ δὲ οὖν διωμολογησάμεθα τὴν δικαιοσύνην ἀρετὴν εἶναι καὶ σοφίαν, τὴν δὲ ἀδικίαν κακίαν τε καὶ ἀμαθίαν, Εἶεν, ἦν δ' ἐγώ, τοῦτο μὲν ἡμῖν οὕτω κείσθω, ἔφαμεν δὲ δὴ καὶ ἰσχυρὸν εἶναι τὴν ἀδικίαν· ἢ οὐ μέμνησαι, ὦ Θρασύμαχε; Μέμνημαι, ἔφη· ἀλλ' ἔμοιγε οὐδὲ ἃ νῦν λέγεις ἀρέσκει, καὶ ἔχω περὶ αὐτῶν λέγειν. εἰ οὖν λέγοιμι, | εὖ **E**
οἶδ' ὅτι δημηγορεῖν ἄν με φαίης· ἢ οὖν ἔα με εἰπεῖν ὅσα βούλομαι, ἤ, εἰ βούλει ἐρωτᾶν, ἐρώτα· ἐγὼ δέ σοι, ὥσπερ ταῖς γραυσὶν ταῖς τοὺς μύθους λεγούσαις, εἶεν ἐρῶ καὶ κατανεύσομαι καὶ ἀνανεύσομαι. Μηδαμῶς, ἦν δ' ἐγώ, παρά γε τὴν σαυτοῦ δόξαν. Ὥστε σοι, ἔφη, ἀρέσκειν, ἐπειδήπερ οὐκ ἐᾷς λέγειν. καίτοι τί ἄλλο βούλει; Οὐδὲν μὰ Δία, ἦν δ' ἐγώ, ἀλλ' εἴπερ τοῦτο ποιήσεις, ποίει· ἐγὼ δὲ ἐρωτήσω. Ἐρώτα δή. Τοῦτο τοίνυν ἐρωτῶ, ὅπερ ἄρτι, ἵνα καὶ ἑξῆς διασκεψώμεθα | τὸν λόγον, ὁποῖόν τι τυγχάνει ὂν δικαιοσύνη **351**
πρὸς ἀδικίαν. ἐλέχθη γάρ που, ὅτι καὶ δυνατώτερον καὶ ἰσχυρότερον εἴη ἀδικία δικαιοσύνης· νῦν δέ γ', ἔφην, εἴπερ σοφία τε καὶ ἀρετή ἐστιν δικαιοσύνη, ῥᾳδίως, οἶμαι, φανήσεται καὶ ἰσχυρότερον ἀδικίας, ἐπειδήπερ ἐστὶν ἀμαθία ἡ ἀδικία· οὐδεὶς ἂν ἔτι τοῦτο ἀγνοήσειεν. ἀλλ' οὔ τι οὕτως ἁπλῶς, ὦ Θρασύμαχε, ἔγωγε ἐπιθυμῶ, ἀλλὰ τῇδέ πῃ σκέψασθαι· πόλιν φαίης ἂν ἄδικον εἶναι

3. ἔφην *q* et fortasse A^1: ἔφη A^2ΠΞ.

Bekker (following the punctuation of A) takes τότε with ὄντος, but πρότερον δὲ οὔπω shews that it belongs to καὶ εἶδον.

τότε καὶ is simply 'then too'; I cannot see anything "mock-heroic" in the expression, as J. and C. do.

30 **εἰ οὖν λέγοιμι κτλ.** εἰ δ' οὖν is read by Ast: "sed sufficit externum, ut ita dicam, vinculum οὖν (Schneider)." δημηγορεῖν and εἰπεῖν ὅσα βούλομαι are the opposites of διαλέγεσθαι and βραχυλογία (*Prot.* 336 B, 335 A).

350 E 32 **ὥσπερ ταῖς γραυσί.** Cf. *Gorg.* 527 A τάχα δ' οὖν ταῦτα μῦθός σοι δοκεῖ λέγεσθαι, ὥσπερ γραός, καὶ καταφρονεῖς αὐτῶν: *Pol.* 268 E ἀλλὰ δὴ τῷ μύθῳ μου πάνυ πρόσεχε τὸν νοῦν, καθάπερ οἱ παῖδες. παῖς for ταῖς was read before Ast on the authority of one MS; but ταῖς is quite satisfactory.

37 **ὅπερ ἄρτι.** The words ἔφαμεν δὲ δὴ καὶ ἰσχυρὸν εἶναι τὴν ἀδικίαν· ἢ οὐ μέμνησαι; (350 D), which are referred to in ἄρτι, involve the general question of the relation between justice and injustice; whence we have ὁποῖόν τι τυγχάνει ὂν δικαιοσύνη πρὸς ἀδικίαν. ὁποῖον depends on ἐρωτῶ, not on λόγον.

351 A 2 **ἐλέχθη γάρ που**: 344 C, 348 E. It has nowhere been expressly said that Injustice is δυνατώτερον than Justice, but καὶ δυνατώτερον is added for emphasis (see on ἢ λέγειν in 350 A); and indeed according to the theory of Thrasymachus δύναμις (power in a general sense) rests solely on ἰσχύς (physical strength). δύναμις and ἰσχύς are clearly distinguished in *Prot.* 351 A.

6 **ἁπλῶς.** The Platonic use of ἁπλοῦν has been investigated by Bonitz in *Hermes* II (1867) pp. 307 ff. Its antitheses are διπλοῦν, διάφορον, σύνθετον, πεπλεγμένον, ποικίλον, and the like, and it denotes that which is uniform, or single and simple, or true without any difference or qualifications. ἁπλῶς οὕτως means merely 'in this simple or general way' ("im Allgemeinen" Schneider): a more elaborate and profounder proof (thinks Socrates) is necessary.

B καὶ | ἄλλας πόλεις ἐπιχειρεῖν δουλοῦσθαι ἀδίκως καὶ καταδεδου-
λῶσθαι, πολλὰς δὲ καὶ ὑφ' ἑαυτῇ ἔχειν δουλωσαμένην; Πῶς γὰρ
οὔκ; ἔφη· καὶ τοῦτό γε ἡ ἀρίστη μάλιστα ποιήσει καὶ τελεώτατα
οὖσα ἄδικος. Μανθάνω, ἔφην· ὅτι σὸς οὗτος ἦν ὁ λόγος. ἀλλὰ
τόδε περὶ αὐτοῦ σκοπῶ· πότερον ἡ κρείττων γιγνομένη πόλις
πόλεως ἄνευ δικαιοσύνης τὴν δύναμιν ταύτην ἕξει, ἢ ἀνάγκη αὐτῇ
C μετὰ δικαιοσύνης; Εἰ μέν, ἔφη, ὡς σὺ ἄρτι | ἔλεγες ἔχει, ἡ δικαιο-
σύνη σοφία, μετὰ δικαιοσύνης· εἰ δ' ὡς ἐγὼ ἔλεγον, μετὰ ἀδικίας.
Πάνυ ἄγαμαι, ἦν δ' ἐγώ, ὦ Θρασύμαχε, ὅτι οὐκ ἐπινεύεις μόνον
καὶ ἀνανεύεις, ἀλλὰ καὶ ἀποκρίνει πάνυ καλῶς. Σοὶ γάρ, ἔφη,
χαρίζομαι.

XXIII. Εὖ γε σὺ ποιῶν· ἀλλὰ δὴ καὶ τόδε μοι χάρισαι καὶ
λέγε· δοκεῖς ἂν ἢ πόλιν ἢ στρατόπεδον ἢ λῃστὰς ἢ κλέπτας ἢ
ἄλλο τι ἔθνος, ὅσα κοινῇ ἐπί τι ἔρχεται ἀδίκως, πρᾶξαι ἄν τι
D δύνασθαι, εἰ ἀδικοῖεν ἀλλήλους; | Οὐ δῆτα, ἦ δ' ὅς. Τί δ' εἰ μὴ
ἀδικοῖεν; οὐ μᾶλλον; Πάνυ γε. Στάσεις γάρ που, ὦ Θρασύμαχε,
ἥ γε ἀδικία καὶ μίση καὶ μάχας ἐν ἀλλήλοις παρέχει, ἡ δὲ δικαιοσύνη ὁμόνοιαν καὶ φιλίαν· ἦ γάρ; Ἔστω, ἦ δ' ὅς, ἵνα σοι μὴ

14. ἡ A²Π: fortasse εἰ ἡ A¹.
19. Ita Π et corr. in mg. A²: σοὶ γὰρ ἔφη χαρίζομαι· εὖ γέ σοι ποιῶν A¹.

---

351 B 8 **καὶ καταδεδουλῶσθαι** is rejected by Cobet, but successfully defended by Heller (*Fl. Jahrb.* 1875 p. 172). There is in reality no pleonasm: we have first an attempt (ἐπιχειρεῖν), then a successful attempt (καταδεδουλῶσθαι), then the results of success (πολλὰς δὲ καὶ ὑφ' ἑαυτῇ ἔχειν δουλωσαμένην). A powerful city like Athens might, and often did, display her energy in all three directions simultaneously. For the collocation of δουλοῦσθαι and καταδουλοῦσθαι (middle) Heller compares infra IX 589 D, E and *Menex.* 240 A.

10 **ἡ ἀρίστη.** Thrasymachus refuses to withdraw from the position that ἀδικία is ἀρετή, in spite of Socrates' refutation. This is why Socrates says μανθάνω κτλ. 'I understand: (you say so) because this was *your* theory.' ὅτι is not 'that': see above on 332 A. Richter suggested κρατίστη for ἀρίστη on account of κρείττων just below; but κρείττων is said not by Thrasymachus, but by Socrates.

14 **εἰ—ἔχει.** After ἔχει, εἰ is inserted by Stallbaum, following a suggestion of Baiter's. Cf. also J. B. Mayor in *Cl. Rev.* X p. 111. It so happens that ἡ is written in A over an erasure large enough to have contained εἰ ἡ, but there is no trace of εἰ, and mere erasures in A are seldom useful in determining the text. For ἡ Richter suggests ᾗ, which would however give a wrong meaning. Tucker also offers a variety of conjectures, but the text is perfectly sound: cf. II 359 B μάλιστ' ἂν αἰσθοίμεθα, εἰ τοιόνδε ποιήσαιμεν τῇ διανοίᾳ· δόντες (i.e. εἰ δόντες) ἐξουσίαν —εἶτ' ἐπακολουθήσαιμεν κτλ. and IX 589 D εἴπερ τοιόνδε τι γίγνεται, λαμβάνων (i.e. εἰ λαμβάνων)—καταδουλοῦται.

351 C 20 **ἢ λῃστὰς κτλ.** Cf. (with Ast) Isocrates *Panath.* 226 οὐδεὶς ἂν αὐτοὺς (τοὺς Σπαρτιάτας) διά γε τὴν ὁμόνοιαν δικαίως ἐπαινέσειεν, οὐδὲν μᾶλλον ἢ τοὺς καταποντιστὰς καὶ λῃστὰς καὶ τοὺς περὶ τὰς ἄλλας ἀδικίας ὄντας· καὶ γὰρ ἐκεῖνοι σφίσιν αὐτοῖς ὁμονοοῦντες τοὺς ἄλλους ἀπολλύουσιν. There must be some honour even among thieves.

351 D 25 **ὁμόνοιαν καὶ φιλίαν.** The conception of δικαιοσύνη which meets us in Book IV 433 A—434 E is dimly outlined here.

διαφέρωμαι. Ἀλλ' εὖ γε σὺ ποιῶν, ὦ ἄριστε. τόδε δέ μοι λέγε·
ἆρα εἰ τοῦτο ἔργον ἀδικίας, μῖσος ἐμποιεῖν ὅπου ἂν ἐνῇ, οὐ καὶ ἐν
ἐλευθέροις τε καὶ δούλοις ἐγγιγνομένη μισεῖν ποιήσει ἀλλήλους
καὶ στασιάζειν καὶ ἀδυνάτους εἶναι κοινῇ | μετ' ἀλλήλων πράττειν; E
Πάνυ γε. Τί δέ; ἂν ἐν δυοῖν ἐγγένηται, οὐ διοίσονται καὶ μισή-
σουσιν καὶ ἐχθροὶ ἔσονται ἀλλήλοις τε καὶ τοῖς δικαίοις; Ἔσονται,
ἔφη. Ἐὰν δὲ δή, ὦ θαυμάσιε, ἐν ἑνὶ ἐγγένηται ἀδικία, μῶν μὴ
ἀπολεῖ τὴν αὑτῆς δύναμιν, ἢ οὐδὲν ἧττον ἕξει; Μηδὲν ἧττον
ἐχέτω, ἔφη. Οὐκοῦν τοιάνδε τινὰ φαίνεται ἔχουσα τὴν δύναμιν,
οἵαν, ᾧ ἂν ἐγγένηται, εἴτε πόλει τινὶ εἴτε γένει εἴτε στρατοπέδῳ
εἴτε ἄλλῳ ὁτῳοῦν, πρῶτον μὲν ἀδύνατον | αὐτὸ ποιεῖν πράττειν 352
μεθ' αὑτοῦ διὰ τὸ στασιάζειν καὶ διαφέρεσθαι, ἔτι δ' ἐχθρὸν εἶναι
ἑαυτῷ τε καὶ τῷ ἐναντίῳ παντὶ καὶ τῷ δικαίῳ; οὐχ οὕτως;
Πάνυ γε. Καὶ ἐν ἑνὶ δή, οἶμαι, ἐνοῦσα ταὐτα πάντα ποιήσει,
ἅπερ πέφυκεν ἐργάζεσθαι· πρῶτον μὲν ἀδύνατον αὐτὸν πράττειν
ποιήσει στασιάζοντα καὶ οὐχ ὁμονοοῦντα αὐτὸν ἑαυτῷ, ἔπειτα
ἐχθρὸν καὶ ἑαυτῷ καὶ τοῖς δικαίοις· ἦ γάρ; Ναί. Δίκαιοι δέ
γ' εἰσίν, ὦ φίλε, καὶ οἱ θεοί; Ἔστων, | ἔφη. Καὶ θεοῖς ἄρα B

26. διαφέρωμαι Π: διαφέρωμεν A. 33. ἧττον Π et in mg. A²: om. A¹.
1. ποιεῖν Π: ποιεῖ A.

27 **ἐν ἐλευθέροις κτλ.**: 'whether it makes its appearance among freemen or among slaves.' Plato wishes to emphasize the universality of the rule, and that is why he specifies the two classes into which society is divided. Cf. *Gorg.* 514 D, 515 A. It is less natural and easy to construe (with Tucker) 'in a society where there are both freemen and slaves.'

351 E 31 **ἀλλήλοις τε καὶ τοῖς δικαίοις**. So in 349 C above it is said that the unjust try to overreach both one another and the just.

32 **ἐν ἑνὶ κτλ.** The results of Book IV are foreshadowed more clearly in what follows. The notion that justice present in the individual keeps the individual at peace with himself is more fully developed in 441 D, and implicitly assumes a psychological theory like that in Book IV, where soul is shewn to have 'parts' (435 C ff.). Further, in Book IV, Plato first describes justice in the State, and afterwards justice in the individual, using the larger aggregate to assist him to find it in the smaller. The same method is observed here in the description of injustice, and afterwards in Books VIII and IX, where the varieties of ἀδικία in states and individuals are described. The present passage (351 A—352 A), in fact, contains the undeveloped germ of the whole method and doctrine of the *Republic* (with the exception of Books V—VII). Cf. Hirmer *Entst. u. Kompos. d. Pl. Pol.* p. 608.

μῶν μὴ (a strengthened *num*) occurs only twice in the *Republic*, here and in VI 505 C. In the later dialogues μῶν is especially frequent (Frederking in *Fl. Jahrb.* 1882 p. 539). A classified list of examples is given by Kugler *de part. τοι eiusque comp. ap. Pl. usu* p. 40.

35 **οἵαν—ποιεῖν.** See *cr. n.* ποιεῖ would involve (as even Schneider admits) "durissimum et haud scio an vitiosum anacoluthon." Cf. οἷοι μὴ ἀδικεῖν in 334 D. Tucker proposes to eject οἵαν and retain ποιεῖ, but the reading of Π is preferable in every way. For the error see *Introd.* § 5.

352 A 3 **παντὶ**: i.e. whether just or unjust: cf. 351 E ἐχθροὶ ἔσονται (viz. οἱ ἄδικοι) ἀλλήλοις τε καὶ τοῖς δικαίοις.

8 **ἔστων.** On the form see *Introd.* § 5.

ἐχθρὸς ἔσται ὁ ἄδικος, ὦ Θρασύμαχε, ὁ δὲ δίκαιος φίλος. Εὐωχοῦ τοῦ λόγου, ἔφη, θαρρῶν· οὐ γὰρ ἔγωγέ σοι ἐναντιώσομαι, ἵνα μὴ τοῖσδε ἀπέχθωμαι. Ἴθι δή, ἦν δ' ἐγώ, καὶ τὰ λοιπά μοι τῆς ἑστιάσεως ἀποπλήρωσον ἀποκρινόμενος ὥσπερ καὶ νῦν. ὅτι μὲν γὰρ καὶ σοφώτεροι καὶ ἀμείνους καὶ δυνατώτεροι πράττειν οἱ δίκαιοι φαίνονται, οἱ δὲ ἄδικοι οὐδὲν πράττειν μετ' ἀλλήλων οἷοί
C τε, ἀλλὰ δὴ καὶ οὕς | φαμεν ἐρρωμένως πώποτέ τι μετ' ἀλλήλων κοινῇ πρᾶξαι ἀδίκους ὄντας, τοῦτο οὐ παντάπασιν ἀληθὲς λέγομεν· οὐ γὰρ ἂν ἀπείχοντο ἀλλήλων κομιδῇ ὄντες ἄδικοι, ἀλλὰ δῆλον ὅτι ἐνῆν τις αὐτοῖς δικαιοσύνη, ἣ αὐτοὺς ἐποίει μήτοι καὶ ἀλλήλους γε καὶ ἐφ' οὓς ᾖσαν ἅμα ἀδικεῖν, δι' ἣν ἔπραξαν ἃ ἔπραξαν, ὥρμησαν δὲ ἐπὶ τὰ ἄδικα ἀδικίᾳ ἡμιμόχθηροι ὄντες, ἐπεὶ οἵ γε παμπόνηροι καὶ τελέως ἄδικοι τελέως εἰσὶν καὶ πράττειν ἀδύνατοι·
D ταῦτα | μὲν οὖν ὅτι οὕτως ἔχει, μανθάνω, ἀλλ' οὐχ ὡς σὺ τὸ

15. δὴ καὶ οὓς A²Ξ: δικαίους A¹: καὶ οὓς Π*q*.

---

352 B 11 **τὰ λοιπά κτλ.**: viz. the discussion which begins in D below.

12 **ὅτι μὲν γὰρ κτλ.** The whole sentence is summed up in *ταῦτα μὲν οὖν ὅτι οὕτως ἔχει* (352 D) and placed in this recapitulated form under the government of *μανθάνω*. The introduction of the antithesis (ἀλλὰ δὴ κτλ.) to οἱ δὲ ἄδικοι οὐδὲν πράττειν μετ' ἀλλήλων οἷοί τε, and of the explanations required by that antithesis, complicates the sentence, without, however, rendering it obscure. For similar anacolutha with ὅτι see V 465 A, VI 493 D *nn*. and cf. Engelhardt *Anac. Plat. Spec.* III pp. 38, 40. The whole sentence forms a kind of transition to "the rest of the feast" by summing up what has been so far proved; viz. that Justice is wisdom and virtue (καὶ σοφώτεροι καὶ ἀμείνους), and more capable of action than Injustice (δυνατώτεροι πράττειν); even the difficulty raised in ἀλλὰ δὴ—ἀδύνατοι is not new, having been briefly explained in 351 C. Liebhold's ἔτι for ὅτι is an unhappy suggestion; nor should ὅτι be rendered 'quoniam,' as Hartman proposes.

352 C 18 **μήτοι—γε**: a strong negative somewhat rarely used by Plato: cf. *Phil.* 67 A and infra III 388 B, C. See Kugler *de part.* τοι *eiusque comp. ap. Pl. usu* p. 11.

352 D—**354** C *The argument here reverts to 347 E, and the rest of the book offers a direct refutation of the view that Injustice is more advantageous than Justice, in other words, that the life of the unjust man is better than that of the just. An indirect refutation, says Socrates, is afforded by the recent discussion (from 348 B to 352 D); the direct is as follows. Everything has its peculiar work or product* (ἔργον)*—that, namely, which it alone produces, or which it produces better than aught else. Everything moreover has its own peculiar excellence, without which it will not do its work well. Now the work of soul is to deliberate, to rule, to live: its excellence is Justice. Therefore the just soul will live well, and to live well is to be blest and happy. And as this is more advantageous than to be miserable, Injustice can never be more advantageous than Justice. In conclusion, Socrates sums up regretfully: until we know what Justice is, we are not likely to discover whether it is a virtue or a vice, and whether its possessor is happy or unhappy.*

352 D ff. The view that everything has its own peculiar function, which it can perform better than anything else, afterwards becomes one of the cardinal principles of the Ideal State (II 369 E ff.); and the statement that everything has an excellence or virtue of its own is reaffirmed

πρῶτον ἐτίθεσο. εἰ δὲ καὶ ἄμεινον ζῶσιν οἱ δίκαιοι τῶν ἀδίκων
καὶ εὐδαιμονέστεροί εἰσιν, ὅπερ τὸ ὕστερον προὐθέμεθα σκέψασθαι,
σκεπτέον. φαίνονται μὲν οὖν καὶ νῦν, ὥς γέ μοι δοκεῖ, ἐξ ὧν
εἰρήκαμεν· ὅμως δ' ἔτι βέλτιον σκεπτέον. οὐ γὰρ περὶ τοῦ
ἐπιτυχόντος ὁ λόγος, ἀλλὰ περὶ τοῦ ὅντινα τρόπον χρὴ ζῆν.
Σκόπει δή, ἔφη. Σκοπῶ, ἦν δ' ἐγώ. καί μοι λέγε· δοκεῖ τί σοι
εἶναι ἵππου ἔργον; | Ἔμοιγε. Ἆρ' οὖν τοῦτο ἂν θείης καὶ ἵππου E
καὶ ἄλλου ὁτουοῦν ἔργον, ὃ ἂν ᾗ μόνῳ ἐκείνῳ ποιῇ τις ἢ ἄριστα;
Οὐ μανθάνω, ἔφη. Ἀλλ' ὧδε· ἔσθ' ὅτῳ ἂν ἄλλῳ ἴδοις ἢ
ὀφθαλμοῖς; Οὐ δῆτα. Τί δέ; ἀκούσαις ἄλλῳ ἢ ὠσίν; Οὐδαμῶς.
Οὐκοῦν δικαίως ἂν ταῦτα τούτων φαῖμεν ἔργα εἶναι; Πάνυ γε.
Τί δέ; | μαχαίρᾳ ἂν ἀμπέλου κλῆμα ἀποτέμοις καὶ σμίλῃ καὶ 353
ἄλλοις πολλοῖς; Πῶς γὰρ οὔ; Ἀλλ' οὐδενί γ' ἄν, οἶμαι, οὕτω
καλῶς, ὡς δρεπάνῳ τῷ ἐπὶ τοῦτο ἐργασθέντι. Ἀληθῆ. Ἆρ' οὖν
οὐ τοῦτο τούτου ἔργον θήσομεν; Θήσομεν μὲν οὖν.

XXIV. Νῦν δή, οἶμαι, ἄμεινον ἂν μάθοις ὃ ἄρτι ἠρώτων,
πυνθανόμενος εἰ οὐ τοῦτο ἑκάστου εἴη ἔργον, ὃ ἂν ἢ μόνον τι ἢ
κάλλιστα τῶν ἄλλων ἀπεργάζηται. Ἀλλ', ἔφη, μανθάνω τε καί
μοι δοκεῖ τοῦτο ἑκάστου | πράγματος ἔργον εἶναι. Εἶεν, ἦν δ' ἐγώ· B
οὐκοῦν καὶ ἀρετὴ δοκεῖ σοι εἶναι ἑκάστῳ, ᾧπερ καὶ ἔργον τι
προστέτακται; ἴωμεν δὲ ἐπὶ τὰ αὐτὰ πάλιν. ὀφθαλμῶν, φαμέν,

25. ὥς γε μοι (sic) Π: ὥστέ μοι A[1]: ὥς γ' ἐμοὶ corr. A[2]. 26. δ' ἔτι Ξq: δέ τι ΑΠ. 33. φαῖμεν Stephanus: φαμὲν codd. 1. ἂν v cum Stobaeo (*Flor.* 9. 63): om. ΑΠΞq.

---

in Book X, where we are also told that everything has its own peculiar vice, that of soul being ἀδικία (608 E ff.).

27 **ὅντινα τρόπον χρὴ ζῆν.** A reminiscence of the πῶς βιωτέον of Socrates: cf. 344 E.

352 E 30 **ὃ ἂν—ἄριστα.** The political applications of this principle are developed from II 369 E onwards: cf. IV 433 A ff.

32 **ἀκούσαις κτλ.** The rapid succession of questions makes it possible to dispense with ἂν in the second: cf. II 382 E.

33 **φαῖμεν.** See *cr. n.* If φαμέν is retained, ἂν will belong to εἶναι (cf. VI 493 C), but it is inappropriate here to make εἶναι future or hypothetical. Schneider, while retaining φαμέν, refers ἂν to δικαίως, "ut sensus sit: οὐκοῦν, εἰ ταῦτα τούτων φαμὲν ἔργα εἶναι, δικαίως ἂν φαῖμεν"—a harsh and unnatural view. We may either drop ἂν and keep φαμέν, as (with one of Stobaeus' MSS *Flor.* 9. 63) I formerly did: or change φαμέν to φαῖμεν. The latter solution is easier and better. Similarly in φαῖμεν below (353 D) the ι is due to A[2]. See also *Introd.* § 5.

353 A 1 **ἀποτέμοις**—see *cr. n.*—can hardly, I think, dispense with the particle ἄν. It should be noted that the illustrations are of two kinds—the first to illustrate ᾗ μόνῳ ἐκείνῳ, the second to illustrate ἄριστα; after each division the conclusion is stated, in the second case more diffidently (ἆρ' οὖν οὐ—θήσομεν), perhaps because it is less obvious.

6 **μόνον τι.** Cornarius unhappily suggested τις for τι and Stephanus μόνῳ τις for μόνον τι (cf. 352 E). μόνον τι is of course the subject to ἀπεργάζηται.

353 B 9 **οὐκοῦν—προστέτακται.** Cf.

ἔστιν ἔργον; Ἔστιν. Ἆρ' οὖν καὶ ἀρετὴ ὀφθαλμῶν ἔστιν; Καὶ
ἀρετή. Τί δέ; ὤτων ἦν τι ἔργον; Ναί. Οὐκοῦν καὶ ἀρετή;
Καὶ ἀρετή. Τί δὲ πάντων πέρι τῶν ἄλλων; οὐχ οὕτω; Οὕτω.
Ἔχε δή· ἆρ' ἄν ποτε ὄμματα τὸ αὑτῶν ἔργον καλῶς ἀπεργάσαιντο
C μὴ ἔχοντα τὴν αὑτῶν | οἰκείαν ἀρετήν, ἀλλ' ἀντὶ τῆς ἀρετῆς
κακίαν; Καὶ πῶς ἄν; ἔφη· τυφλότητα γὰρ ἴσως λέγεις ἀντὶ
τῆς ὄψεως. Ἥτις, ἦν δ' ἐγώ, αὐτῶν ἡ ἀρετή· οὐ γάρ πω τοῦτο
ἐρωτῶ, ἀλλ' εἰ τῇ οἰκείᾳ μὲν ἀρετῇ τὸ αὑτῶν ἔργον εὖ ἐργάσεται
τὰ ἐργαζόμενα, κακίᾳ δὲ κακῶς. Ἀληθές, ἔφη, τοῦτό γε λέγεις.
Οὐκοῦν καὶ ὦτα στερόμενα τῆς αὑτῶν ἀρετῆς κακῶς τὸ αὑτῶν
ἔργον ἀπεργάσεται; Πάνυ γε. Τίθεμεν οὖν καὶ τἆλλα πάντα
D εἰς | τὸν αὐτὸν λόγον; Ἔμοιγε δοκεῖ. Ἴθι δή, μετὰ ταῦτα τόδε
σκέψαι· ψυχῆς ἔστιν τι ἔργον, ὃ ἄλλῳ τῶν ὄντων οὐδ' ἂν ἑνὶ
πράξαις; οἷον τὸ τοιόνδε· τὸ ἐπιμελεῖσθαι καὶ ἄρχειν καὶ βουλεύεσθαι καὶ τὰ τοιαῦτα πάντα, ἔσθ' ὅτῳ ἄλλῳ ἢ ψυχῇ δικαίως

24. πράξαις A[1]Π: πράξαιο corr. A[2].

Men. 72 A οὐκ ἀπορία εἰπεῖν ἀρετῆς πέρι ὅ τι ἔστιν. καθ' ἑκάστην γὰρ τῶν πράξεων καὶ τῶν ἡλικιῶν πρὸς ἕκαστον ἔργον ἑκάστῳ ἡμῶν ἡ ἀρετή ἐστιν. ὡσαύτως δὲ—καὶ ἡ κακία: also infra X 608 E with Arist. *Eth. Nic.* II 5. 1106[a] 15 ff.

12 **ἦν**: 'is, as we saw,' viz. at 352 E: cf. infra IV 441 D, VI 490 A, VII 522 A.

14 **ἀπεργάσαιντο**. Heindorf (on *Crat.* 424 E) would read ἀπεργάσαιτο, and Baiter adopts his suggestion; but (as Stallbaum observes) the use of ὀφθαλμοί just above may affect the construction. In the same way, perhaps, the occurrence of γυναῖκες καὶ τἆλλα θηρία immediately before causes Plato to write δεήσοιντο (the reading of A) rather than δεήσοιτο in *Tim.* 76 E. Of the other alleged cases of a plural verb after a neuter plural in Plato, some (e.g. *Laws* 634 E, 683 B) are not supported by the best MSS; one—ἐξ ὧν τά τε ὀνόματα καὶ τὰ ῥήματα συντίθενται (so AT) *Crat.* 424 E—is distributive; some refer to living objects, e.g. *Laws* 658 C (with which contrast κρίνοι just before) and *Lach.* 180 E; at least one (*Phil.* 24 E) is perhaps corrupt. See also on *Rep.* II 365 B.

353 C 16 **τυφλότητα κτλ.** τυφλότης is also said to be the disease or vice of the eyes in *Alc.* I 126 B, a passage probably imitated from this. In the stricter discussion of X 608 E it is not τυφλότης but ὀφθαλμία which is the vice to which the eyes are subject.

17 **οὐ γάρ πω—ἐρωτῶ** is 'I do not, at this stage, enquire'; but the words do not, I think, contain an express promise that the subject will be afterwards resumed. Although the peculiar vice of the eyes is specified in Book X (l.c.), their virtue is not; and τοῦτο refers to ἥτις αὐτῶν ἡ ἀρετή. Cf. 347 E *n.*

353 D 23 **ψυχῆς ἔστιν τι ἔργον**: cf. III 407 A and Arist. *Eth. Nic.* I 6. 1097[b] 22—1098[a] 17, where this discussion is closely imitated. That it is the ἔργον of soul (and in particular of νοῦς) to rule (ἄρχειν, ἐπιμελεῖσθαι, and the like), is continually asserted in Plato: see for example *Phaedr.* 246 B πᾶσα ἡ ψυχὴ παντὸς ἐπιμελεῖται τοῦ ἀψύχου, *Crat.* 400 A, *Phil.* 30 C, *Laws* 896 A. The same doctrine is made the ground of the subjection of body to soul which is inculcated in the *Phaedo* (80 A, 94 B), and in *Alc.* I 130 A. Cf. also Isocrates περὶ ἀντιδόσεως 180 ὁμολογεῖται μὲν γὰρ τὴν φύσιν ἡμῶν ἔκ τε τοῦ σώματος συγκεῖσθαι καὶ τῆς ψυχῆς· αὐτοῖν δὲ τούτοιν οὐδεὶς ἔστιν ὅστις οὐκ ἂν φήσειεν ἡγεμονικωτέραν πεφυκέναι τὴν ψυχὴν καὶ πλείονος ἀξίαν· τῆς μὲν γὰρ ἔργον εἶναι βουλεύσασθαι καὶ περὶ τῶν ἰδίων καὶ περὶ τῶν κοινῶν, τοῦ δὲ σώματος ὑπηρετῆσαι τοῖς ὑπὸ τῆς ψυχῆς γνωσθεῖσιν.

ἂν αὐτὰ ἀποδοῖμεν καὶ φαῖμεν ἴδια ἐκείνου εἶναι; Οὐδενὶ ἄλλῳ. Τί δ' αὖ τὸ ζῆν; ψυχῆς φήσομεν ἔργον εἶναι; Μάλιστά γ', ἔφη. Οὐκοῦν καὶ ἀρετήν φαμέν τινα ψυχῆς εἶναι; Φαμέν. | Ἆρ' οὖν **E**
ποτέ, ὦ Θρασύμαχε, ψυχὴ τὰ αὑτῆς ἔργα εὖ ἀπεργάσεται στερομένη τῆς οἰκείας ἀρετῆς, ἢ ἀδύνατον; Ἀδύνατον. Ἀνάγκη ἄρα κακῇ ψυχῇ κακῶς ἄρχειν καὶ ἐπιμελεῖσθαι, τῇ δὲ ἀγαθῇ πάντα ταῦτα εὖ πράττειν. Ἀνάγκη. Οὐκοῦν ἀρετήν γε συνεχωρήσαμεν ψυχῆς εἶναι δικαιοσύνην, κακίαν δὲ ἀδικίαν; Συνεχωρήσαμεν γάρ. Ἡ μὲν ἄρα δικαία ψυχὴ καὶ ὁ δίκαιος ἀνὴρ εὖ βιώσεται, κακῶς δὲ ὁ ἄδικος. Φαίνεται, ἔφη, κατὰ τὸν σὸν λόγον. | Ἀλλὰ μὴν **354**
ὅ γε εὖ ζῶν μακάριός τε καὶ εὐδαίμων, ὁ δὲ μὴ τἀναντία. Πῶς γὰρ οὔ; Ὁ μὲν δίκαιος ἄρα εὐδαίμων, ὁ δ' ἄδικος ἄθλιος. Ἔστων, ἔφη. Ἀλλὰ μὴν ἄθλιόν γε εἶναι οὐ λυσιτελεῖ, εὐδαίμονα δέ. Πῶς γὰρ οὔ; Οὐδέποτ' ἄρα, ὦ μακάριε Θρασύμαχε, λυσιτελέστερον ἀδικία δικαιοσύνης. Ταῦτα δή σοι, ἔφη, ὦ Σώκρατες, εἱστιάσθω ἐν τοῖς Βενδιδείοις. Ὑπὸ σοῦ γε, ἦν δ' ἐγώ, ὦ Θρασύμαχε, ἐπειδή

26. *φαῖμεν* $A^2Π$: *φαμὲν* A^1. *ἐκείνου* $Ξq^2$: *ἐκείνης* $AΠq^1$.

---

26 **ἐκείνου.** The reading *ἐκείνης*—see *cr. n.*—can only be defended by supposing that Plato was guilty of a strange confusion, unless we make a pause at *ἄλλῳ*, and take *ἤ* as 'or,' not 'than'; but *ἤ* after *ἄλλῳ* would certainly here be understood as 'than,' and an alternative question should be less ambiguously expressed. After *ψυχῇ* the corruption to *ἐκείνης* was natural enough. Madvig would eject the word.

27 **τὸ ζῆν** is *κατ' ἐξοχήν* the *ἔργον* of *ψυχή* in Plato: cf. *Crat.* 399 D, E *τοῦτο ἄρα* (sc. *ψυχή*), *ὅταν παρῇ τῷ σώματι, αἴτιόν ἐστι τοῦ ζῆν αὐτῷ, τὴν τοῦ ἀναπνεῖν δύναμιν παρέχον καὶ ἀναψῦχον, ἅμα δὲ ἐκλείποντος τοῦ ἀναψύχοντος τὸ σῶμα ἀπόλλυταί τε καὶ τελευτᾷ· ὅθεν δή μοι δοκοῦσιν αὐτὸ ψυχὴν καλέσαι*, and *Phaed.* 105 D. The influence of this idea makes itself felt in all the proofs of immortality in Plato, and not least in X 608 E ff. See *nn.* ad loc.

353 E 32 **συνεχωρήσαμεν κτλ.** The reference is to 350 C, D: cf. also 348 C. In these passages Justice has been identified with Virtue, but not expressly with virtue *of soul.* For this reason Hartman would eject *ψυχῆς*. But as Plato has just been using *ἀρετή* 'excellence' in connexion with things other than soul (ears and eyes), it is important that he should now make it clear that in identifying *δικαιοσύνη* and *ἀρετή*, he meant soul's *ἀρετή*. Otherwise a soul may possess its *ἀρετή* without being just; in which case the conclusion which he is aiming at will not follow.

354 A 2 **ὅ γε εὖ ζῶν κτλ.** The ambiguity (as it appears to us) of *εὖ ζῆν* and *εὖ πράττειν* is frequently used by Plato to suggest that the virtuous life is the happy one, e.g. *Charm.* 172 A, 173 D: see note on 335 B. Aristotle says that Plato was the first to establish this identification: see the third fragment of his elegies *vv.* 4—6 ed. Bergk *ὃς μόνος ἢ πρῶτος θνητῶν κατέδειξεν ἐναργῶς | οἰκείῳ τε βίῳ καὶ μεθόδοισι λόγων | ὡς ἀγαθός τε καὶ εὐδαίμων ἅμα γίνεται ἀνήρ.*

6 **εἱστιάσθω.** The metaphor occurs again in 352 B, V 458 A, IX 571 D. It is one of the formal links connecting the *Timaeus* with the *Republic*: see *Tim.* 17 A. Cf. Shakespeare *Macbeth* Act I Scene 4 "In his commendations I am fed: It is a banquet to me."

7 **Βενδιδείοις.** See *Introd.* § 3.

In **ὑπὸ σοῦ γε κτλ.** Plato seems to be making the *amende honorable* to Thrasymachus: cf. VI 498 C, D *μὴ διάβαλλε—ἐμὲ καὶ Θρασύμαχον ἄρτι φίλους γεγονότας, οὐδὲ πρὸ τοῦ ἐχθροὺς γεγονότας.*

μοι πρᾶος ἐγένου καὶ χαλεπαίνων ἐπαύσω. οὐ μέντοι καλῶς γε
B εἱστίαμαι, δι' | ἐμαυτόν, ἀλλ' οὐ διὰ σέ· ἀλλ' ὥσπερ οἱ λίχνοι τοῦ
ἀεὶ παραφερομένου ἀπογεύονται ἁρπάζοντες, πρὶν τοῦ προτέρου
μετρίως ἀπολαῦσαι, καὶ ἐγώ μοι δοκῶ οὕτω, πρὶν ὃ τὸ πρῶτον
ἐσκοποῦμεν εὑρεῖν, τὸ δίκαιον ὅ τί ποτ' ἐστίν, ἀφέμενος ἐκείνου
ὁρμῆσαι ἐπὶ τὸ σκέψασθαι περὶ αὐτοῦ, εἴτε κακία ἐστὶν καὶ
ἀμαθία εἴτε σοφία καὶ ἀρετή, καὶ ἐμπεσόντος αὖ ὕστερον λόγου,
ὅτι λυσιτελέστερον ἡ ἀδικία τῆς δικαιοσύνης, οὐκ ἀπεσχόμην
C τὸ μὴ οὐκ ἐπὶ τοῦτο ἐλθεῖν ἀπ' ἐκείνου, ὥστε μοι | νυνὶ γέγονεν
ἐκ τοῦ διαλόγου μηδὲν εἰδέναι· ὁπότε γὰρ τὸ δίκαιον μὴ οἶδα
ὅ ἐστιν, σχολῇ εἴσομαι εἴτε ἀρετή τις οὖσα τυγχάνει εἴτε καὶ οὔ,
καὶ πότερον ὁ ἔχων αὐτὸ οὐκ εὐδαίμων ἐστὶν ἢ εὐδαίμων.

ΤΕΛΟΣ ΠΟΛΙΤΕΙΑΣ Α'.

11. *ἐγώ μοι* Θ𝔯: *ἐγῷμαι* ΑΞ: *ἐγὼ οἶμαι* Π*q*.

---

354 B 10 **παραφερομένου.** Casaubon's conjecture *περιφερομένου* is neat, but inappropriate, the reference being to the successive courses at a feast, which were not usually carried round among the Greeks. In Athen. IV 33 the carrying round of viands is mentioned as an Egyptian custom: *τρίτη δ' ἐστὶν ἰδέα δείπνων αἰγυπτιακή, τραπεζῶν μὲν οὐ παρατιθεμένων, πινάκων δὲ περιφερομένων.*

11 **ἐγώ μοι δοκῶ κτλ.** *Lys.* 222 E *δέομαι οὖν ὥσπερ οἱ σοφοὶ ἐν τοῖς δικαστηρίοις, τὰ εἰρημένα ἅπαντα ἀναπεμπάσασθαι.*

The tone of the concluding summary recalls the usual finish of the earlier and professedly negative Socratic dialogues, like the *Charmides* (175 B—176 A). The only section of the dialogue which Socrates passes over in silence is the refutation of the statement that Injustice is strong (350 D—352 C). The original question—the *quid sit* of Justice—is abandoned at 347 E: the *quale sit* occupies the rest of the dialogue, and Socrates enquires first whether Justice is vicious and ignorant, or wise and good (347 E—350 C), next whether it is strong or weak (350 D—352 C), and lastly whether it is more or less advantageous than Injustice (352 D—354 A). To speculate on the *quale sit* of a thing before determining its *quid sit* is condemned by Plato in *Men.* 71 B *ὃ δὲ μὴ οἶδα τί ἐστι, πῶς ἂν ὁποῖόν γε τι εἰδείην;* cf. *ibid.* 86 D and 100 B. The words with which the first book concludes lead us to expect that in the remaining books the problem will be discussed in proper logical order—the essence first, and afterwards the quality, of Justice. The expectation is duly fulfilled; and Book I is therefore in the full sense of the term a *προοίμιον* to the whole work.

APPENDICES TO BOOK I.

I.

I **327** A. *προσευξόμενός τε τῇ θεῷ καὶ ἅμα τὴν ἑορτὴν βουλόμενος θεάσασθαι τίνα τρόπον ποιήσουσιν, ἅτε νῦν πρῶτον ἄγοντες.*

The question whether *τῇ θεῷ* here and in 328 A is Bendis or Athena is not so simple as it appears.

In favour of Athena it may be urged (1) that *ἡ θεός* regularly means Athena in Attic literature (see for example Ar. *Eq.* 656, 903 al., and Plato *Laws* 806 B): (2) that in view of the relation between the *Republic* and the *Timaeus* it is difficult to separate *τῇ θεῷ* here from *τὴν θεόν* and *τῆς θεοῦ* in *Tim.* 21 A and 26 E, where the goddess is certainly Athena, (3) that it is dramatically appropriate for an Athenian to dedicate his ideal city to the patron goddess of Athens. Plato's perfect city would thus become in a certain sense a *βασιλεία τῆς θεοῦ*.

On the other hand, the goddess and the festival are mentioned so closely together that (if we have regard to the *Republic* by itself) we are scarcely justified in interpreting *τῇ θεῷ* without reference to *τὴν ἑορτήν*, and it is quite in harmony with Socrates' principles that he should be among the first to pay his vows at the shrine of the new goddess as soon as the *νόμος πόλεως* received her. See Xen. *Mem.* I 3. 1, IV 3. 16. It is therefore safer to accept the usual view that Plato is thinking of Bendis.

II.

I **333** E—**334** A. *ἆρ' οὐχ ὁ πατάξαι δεινότατος ἐν μάχῃ εἴτε πυκτικῇ εἴτε τινὶ καὶ ἄλλῃ, οὗτος καὶ φυλάξασθαι; Πάνυ γε. Ἆρ' οὖν καὶ νόσον ὅστις δεινὸς φυλάξασθαι,* **καὶ λαθεῖν** *οὗτος δεινότατος* **ἐμποιήσας**; *Ἔμοιγε δοκεῖ. Ἀλλὰ μὴν στρατοπέδου γε ὁ αὐτὸς φύλαξ ἀγαθός, ὅσπερ καὶ τὰ τῶν πολεμίων κλέψαι καὶ βουλεύματα καὶ τὰς ἄλλας πράξεις. Πάνυ γε. Ὅτου τις ἄρα δεινὸς φύλαξ, τούτου καὶ φὼρ δεινός. Ἔοικεν.*

The reading *φυλάξασθαι καὶ λαθεῖν, οὗτος δεινότατος καὶ ἐμποιῆσαι*, which has slight MS authority, is defended by Boeckh (*Kl. Schr.* IV pp. 326 ff.), with whom Zahlfleisch (*Zeitschr. f. öst. Gymn.* Vol. XXVIII 1877, pp. 603 ff.) and others agree. Boeckh points out that *καὶ λαθεῖν* (sc. *νόσον*, according to his view) suggests (from its notion of clandestine cunning) the idea of stealing. This may be admitted, but the idea of stealing is much more forcibly suggested (as Stallbaum points out), if *καὶ λαθεῖν* is construed with *οὗτος δεινότατος κτλ.*, and this involves the necessity of changing (with Schneider) *ἐμποιῆσαι* of the MSS to *ἐμποιήσας*, for the construction *λαθεῖν ἐμποιῆσαι*, though retained by Campbell, is destitute of authority.

Even if Schneider's emendation be adopted, the argument is (as stated in the notes) fantastical and inconclusive. In order that the conclusion ὅτου τις ἄρα δεινὸς φύλαξ, τούτου καὶ φὼρ δεινός should be valid, φυλάξασθαι should be φυλάξαι, and the objects of the two verbs in proposition (1) should be identical, as well as those in propositions (2) and (3). As it is, if we express φυλάξασθαι in terms of φυλάξαι, they are not identical: for in (1) it is the enemy whom you smite, but yourself whom you guard: in (2) it is yourself (or your patient) whom you guard, but the disease which you secretly implant: in (3) you guard your own army, but steal the enemy's plans, etc. Nevertheless Schneider's emendation is preferable to the traditional reading, which not only contains all the same fallacies as the other, but leaves the three stages of the argument in comparative isolation, attaches the first hint of 'stealing' (λαθεῖν) to the wrong member of the clause, and involves the use of the somewhat strained expression λαθεῖν νόσον. It should be added that the change from ἐμποιῆσαι to ἐμποιήσας is not greater than the insertion of καί before ἐμποιῆσαι, and that ἐμποιήσας was very likely to be corrupted under the influence of δεινὸς φυλάξασθαι just before. The emphatic position of καὶ λαθεῖν is necessary to call attention to the first suggestion of the idea contained in κλέψαι; nor can I agree with J. and C. that in Schneider's emendation "the emphasis falls on the wrong word." In λαθεῖν ἐμποιήσας, which is virtually a single expression, λαθεῖν is more important, in view of the conclusion καὶ κλέπτειν δεινός, than ἐμποιήσας.

Hartman condemns the words καὶ λαθεῖν, and thinks ὅστις and οὗτος have changed places: "cum enim ubique τὸ φυλάξασθαι urgeatur (ὁ πατάξαι δεινότατος, οὗτος καὶ φυλάξασθαι—ὅσπερ κλέψαι..., ὁ αὐτὸς φύλαξ ἀγαθός), requiritur οὗτος δεινὸς φυλάξασθαι, ὅστις δεινότατος κτλ.; quibus tribus exemplis praemissis inversa ratione concludit ὅτου τις ἄρα δεινὸς φύλαξ, τούτου καὶ φὼρ δεινός." Tucker revives the old conjecture καὶ ἀλθεῖν ('heal') instead of καὶ λαθεῖν, and suggests (as an alternative) that λαθεῖν should be μαθεῖν (i.e. καὶ μαθεῖν οὗτος δεινότατος ἐμποιῆσαι 'clever at learning how to implant'). None of these conjectures appears to me so probable as that of Schneider.

III.

I 335 A. Κελεύεις δὴ ἡμᾶς προσθεῖναι τῷ δικαίῳ, ἤ, ὡς τὸ πρῶτον ἐλέγομεν, λέγοντες δίκαιον εἶναι τὸν μὲν φίλον εὖ ποιεῖν, τὸν δ' ἐχθρὸν κακῶς, νῦν πρὸς τούτῳ ὧδε λέγειν, ὅτι ἔστιν δίκαιον τὸν μὲν φίλον ἀγαθὸν ὄντα εὖ ποιεῖν, τὸν δ' ἐχθρὸν κακὸν ὄντα βλάπτειν;

In this difficult passage Schneider takes ἤ as 'than,' and προσθεῖναι as equivalent to a comparative with a verb; but no exact parallel has hitherto been adduced, and the idiom even if admissible is exceedingly harsh. Neither the suggestion of Stephanus (προσθεῖναι τῷ δικαίῳ ἄλλως ἤ) nor that of Richards (to insert πλέον after ἤ) carries conviction. It should also be remarked that the words νῦν πρὸς τούτῳ ὧδε λέγειν follow somewhat awkwardly as an explanation of προσθεῖναι τῷ δικαίῳ if ἢ ὡς is interpreted in Schneider's way. Stallbaum's ἢ ὡς—τὸν δὲ ἐχθρὸν κακῶς; νῦν πρὸς τούτῳ ὧδε λέγειν, is very unpleasing, not so much from the necessity of understanding λέγειν after ἤ ('or to say, as we said at first' etc.) as because it is extremely violent to separate ἤ from νῦν πρὸς τούτῳ ὧδε λέγειν. Faesius' proposal (in which he is followed by Ast, Madvig, and several editors) to eject ἤ gives the required sense ('do you bid us add to the view of justice which etc.,' προσθεῖναι being explained by πρὸς τούτῳ ὧδε λέγειν), but it fails to account for the presence of ἤ in the MSS. It may seem an objection to the view which I take that ἤ in a sentence of this kind would naturally introduce an alternative, whereas πρὸς τούτῳ ὧδε λέγειν only explains προσθεῖναι. This objection, such as it is, applies with still greater force to the view that ἤ is 'than.' Some will probably regard the whole clause from ἤ—λέγειν as a marginal commentary on προσθεῖναι; but this is much too drastic. Possibly ἤ should be replaced by καί—the corruption is said to be common (Bast *Comment. Palaeogr.* p. 815); but I am not convinced that ἤ does not sometimes mean 'or in other words' even in classical Greek.

IV.

I **336** E. *μὴ γὰρ δὴ οἴου, εἰ μὲν χρυσίον ἐζητοῦμεν, οὐκ ἄν ποτε ἡμᾶς ἑκόντας εἶναι ὑποκατακλίνεσθαι ἀλλήλοις ἐν τῇ ζητήσει καὶ διαφθείρειν τὴν εὕρεσιν αὐτοῦ, δικαιοσύνην δὲ ζητοῦντας, πρᾶγμα πολλῶν χρυσίων τιμιώτερον, ἔπειθ' οὕτως ἀνοήτως ὑπείκειν ἀλλήλοις καὶ οὐ σπουδάζειν ὅ τι μάλιστα φανῆναι αὐτό.* **οἴου γε σύ,** *ὦ φίλε· ἀλλ', οἶμαι, οὐ δυνάμεθα.*

Schneider's explanation of the words οἴου γε σύ (sc. ἡμᾶς σπουδάζειν ὅ τι μάλιστα φανῆναι αὐτό) would probably have met with wider acceptance if he had taken more pains to justify his view. The key to the meaning is to be found in the affirmative οἴεσθαί γε χρή which sometimes follows *a fortiori* reasoning of this kind in Plato. Two examples will suffice: *Prot.* 325 B, C τὰ μὲν ἄλλα ἄρα τοὺς υἱεῖς διδάσκονται, ἐφ' οἷς οὐκ ἔστι θάνατος ἡ ζημία ἐὰν μὴ ἐπίστωνται, ἐφ' ᾧ δὲ ἥ τε ζημία θάνατος αὐτῶν τοῖς παισί—ταῦτα δ' ἄρα οὐ διδάσκονται οὐδ' ἐπιμελοῦνται πᾶσαν ἐπιμέλειαν; οἴεσθαί γε χρή, and *Phaed.* 68 A ἢ ἀνθρωπίνων μὲν παιδικῶν—ἀποθανόντων πολλοὶ δὴ ἑκόντες ἠθέλησαν εἰς ἅδου ἰέναι—φρονήσεως δὲ ἄρα τις τῷ ὄντι ἐρῶν—ἀγανακτήσει τε ἀποθνήσκων καὶ οὐκ ἄσμενος εἶσιν αὐτόσε; οἴεσθαί γε χρή. If in place of the imperative μὴ γὰρ δὴ οἴου, Plato had used an interrogation (as he generally does in sentences of this kind), writing let us say ἢ οἴει instead of μὴ γὰρ δὴ οἴου, he would have added οἴεσθαί γε χρή. The same way of writing, dictated of course by the desire to emphasize the δέ clause, causes him to say οἴου γε when the sentence is in the imperatival form. σύ is of course necessary on account of ὦ φίλε. For the affirmative sense of οἴου cf. infra 346 E ἆρ' οὖν οὐδ' ὠφελεῖ τότε, ὅταν προῖκα ἐργάζηται; Οἶμαι ἔγωγε, and X 608 D. Of the various suggestions made on this passage that of O. Apelt ἰού, ἰού, ὦ φίλε "aber wehe, o Freund, unsere Kraft, glaube ich, reicht nicht aus dazu" (*Fl. Jahrb.* 1891, p. 557) deserves mention for its ingenuity; but except for the corruption of γε to τε (see *cr. n.*), the text is sound. There is certainly no occasion to follow *q* and Stallbaum in writing μὴ οἴου σύ for οἴου γε σύ.

B.

357 I. Ἐγὼ μὲν οὖν ταῦτα εἰπὼν ᾤμην λόγου ἀπηλλάχθαι· τὸ δ'
ἦν ἄρα, ὡς ἔοικε, προοίμιον. ὁ γὰρ Γλαύκων ἀεί τε ἀνδρειότατος
ὢν τυγχάνει πρὸς ἅπαντα, καὶ δὴ καὶ τότε τοῦ Θρασυμάχου τὴν
ἀπόρρησιν οὐκ ἀπεδέξατο, ἀλλ' ἔφη Ὦ Σώκρατες, πότερον ἡμᾶς
B βούλει δοκεῖν πεπεικέναι, ἢ ὡς ἀληθῶς | πεῖσαι ὅτι παντὶ τρόπῳ
ἄμεινόν ἐστιν δίκαιον εἶναι ἢ ἄδικον; Ὡς ἀληθῶς, εἶπον, ἔγωγ' ἂν
ἑλοίμην, εἰ ἐπ' ἐμοὶ εἴη. Οὐ τοίνυν, ἔφη, ποιεῖς ὃ βούλει. λέγε
γάρ μοι· ἆρά σοι δοκεῖ τοιόνδε τι εἶναι ἀγαθόν, ὃ δεξαίμεθ' ἂν
ἔχειν οὐ τῶν ἀποβαινόντων ἐφιέμενοι, ἀλλ' αὐτὸ αὑτοῦ ἕνεκα

---

357 A—**358** E *Socrates had thought the conversation at an end, but Glauco revives the theory of Thrasymachus. A threefold classification of goods is first agreed upon. Goods are desirable either* (1) *for their own sakes, or* (2) *both for their own sakes and for their consequences, or* (3) *for their consequences alone. Justice is placed by Socrates in the second and noblest of these three classes. Glauco on the other hand asserts that the Many place it in the third, and proposes to advocate the belief of the Many, not as holding it himself, but in order to compel Socrates to defend Justice and condemn Injustice solely on their merits. Thrasymachus, he thinks, has cried off too soon.*

357 A 1 **ἐγὼ κτλ.** λόγου is abstract = *τοῦ λέγειν*, not 'the discussion' (Jowett), which would be *τοῦ λόγου*. For *τὸ δέ* see on I 340 D.

2 **ἦν ἄρα**: 'was after all,' as in IV 443 C *τὸ δέ γε ἦν ἄρα—εἴδωλόν τι τῆς δικαιοσύνης* and Soph. *Tr.* 1172 *τὸ δ' ἦν ἄρ' οὐδὲν ἄλλο πλὴν θανεῖν ἐμέ*. With *προοίμιον* cf. infra VII 531 D, Aesch. *P. V.* 740 f. *οὓς γὰρ νῦν ἀκήκοας λόγους | εἶναι δοκεῖ σοι μηδέπω 'ν προοιμίοις*, and Shakespeare *Macbeth* I 3 "As happy prologues to the swelling act Of the imperial theme." For the sense see the last note on Book I. There is no good ground for supposing (with von Sybel *De Platonis Proemiis Academicis*) that either Book I of the *Republic* or the rest of Plato's dialogues were intended merely as *προοίμια* or 'Programs' to attract pupils to his lectures.

5 **βούλει κτλ.** The antithesis is between *δοκεῖν πεπεικέναι* and *πεῖσαι*, and *βούλει* is used in its natural sense, not (as Ast thinks) with the force of *μᾶλλον βούλει*.

357 B 7 **λέγε γάρ μοι.** Other classifications of 'goods' in Plato will be found in *Laws* 631 B ff. and 697 B ff. (with which compare Arist. *Eth. Nic.* I 8. 1098^b 12 ff.). See also *Euthyd.* 279 A ff., *Gorg.* 467 E, *Phil.* 66 A ff. The nearest parallels to the present classification are furnished by Stoicism, in which goods were classified as (*a*) *τελικά*, (*b*) *ποιητικά*, (*c*) both *τελικά* and *ποιητικά*, and the *προηγμένα* as (*a*) *δι' αὑτά*, (*b*) *δι' ἕτερα*, (*c*) *καὶ δι' αὑτὰ καὶ δι' ἕτερα* see D. L. VII 96, 107.

ἀσπαζόμενοι; οἷον τὸ χαίρειν καὶ αἱ ἡδοναὶ ὅσαι ἀβλαβεῖς καὶ
μηδὲν εἰς τὸν ἔπειτα χρόνον διὰ ταύτας γίγνεται ἄλλο ἢ χαίρειν
ἔχοντα. Ἔμοιγε, ἦν δ' ἐγώ, δοκεῖ τι εἶναι τοιοῦτον. | Τί δέ; ὃ αὐτό C
τε αὑτοῦ χάριν ἀγαπῶμεν καὶ τῶν ἀπ' αὐτοῦ γιγνομένων; οἷον αὖ
τὸ φρονεῖν καὶ τὸ ὁρᾶν καὶ τὸ ὑγιαίνειν· τὰ γὰρ τοιαῦτά που δι'
ἀμφότερα ἀσπαζόμεθα. Ναί, εἶπον. Τρίτον δὲ ὁρᾷς τι, ἔφη,
εἶδος ἀγαθοῦ, ἐν ᾧ τὸ γυμνάζεσθαι καὶ τὸ κάμνοντα ἰατρεύεσθαι
καὶ ἰάτρευσίς τε καὶ ὁ ἄλλος χρηματισμός; ταῦτα γὰρ ἐπίπονα
φαῖμεν ἄν, ὠφελεῖν δὲ ἡμᾶς, καὶ αὐτὰ μὲν ἑαυτῶν | ἕνεκα οὐκ ἂν D
δεξαίμεθα ἔχειν, τῶν δὲ μισθῶν τε χάριν καὶ τῶν ἄλλων ὅσα
γίγνεται ἀπ' αὐτῶν. Ἔστιν γὰρ οὖν, ἔφην, καὶ τοῦτο τρίτον.
ἀλλὰ τί δή; Ἐν ποίῳ, ἔφη, τούτων τὴν δικαιοσύνην τίθης; Ἐγὼ
μὲν οἶμαι, ἦν δ' ἐ|γώ, ἐν τῷ καλλίστῳ, ὃ καὶ δι' αὑτὸ καὶ διὰ τὰ 358
γιγνόμενα ἀπ' αὐτοῦ ἀγαπητέον τῷ μέλλοντι μακαρίῳ ἔσεσθαι.
Οὐ τοίνυν δοκεῖ, ἔφη, τοῖς πολλοῖς, ἀλλὰ τοῦ ἐπιπόνου εἴδους,

---

10 **χαίρειν—ἀβλαβεῖς.** These 'innocent pleasures' are defined in *Laws* 667 E as those which bring no consequences in their train, good, bad, or otherwise (cf. καὶ μηδὲν εἰς τὸν ἔπειτα χρόνον διὰ ταύτας γίγνεται ἄλλο ἢ χαίρειν ἔχοντα). They are not quite identical with the 'pure pleasures' of *Phil.* 51 B, which are not necessarily devoid of all results, but only of pain. The same conception recurs in Aristotle, who regards the ἀβλαβεῖς ἡδοναί both as conducive to the ethical end and as useful for purposes of recreation (*Pol.* Θ 5. 1339ᵇ 25).

καὶ μηδὲν κτλ. The relative passes into a demonstrative (ταύτας) in the second half of the sentence, as in III 412 D, VI 505 D, E, VII 521 B, and elsewhere. The idiom is regular in Greek, but the second pronoun is more usually some case of αὐτός than of οὗτος, e.g. III 395 D, VI 511 C, *Gorg.* 452 D, *Theaet.* 192 A. Cobet however (*Mnem.* XI p. 167) goes too far in maintaining that αὐτός is alone permissible in this idiom. Cf. Engelhardt *Anac. Plat. Spec.* III pp. 41—43. μηδέν is used in preference to οὐδέν: for "cogitatione circumscriptum genus significatur" (Schneider). With the sentiment Muretus compared Arist. *Eth. Nic.* X 2. 1172ᵇ 22 οὐδένα γὰρ ἐπερωτᾶν τίνος ἕνεκα ἥδεται, ὡς καθ' αὑτὴν οὖσαν αἱρετὴν τὴν ἡδονήν.

12 **ἔχοντα**: sc. αὐτάς (so also Schneider), not the idiomatic 'to continue rejoicing' (as Campbell suggests). The essential mark of these pleasures, viz. that they give pleasure only while they last, is brought out by ἔχοντα, which recalls δεξαίμεθ' ἂν ἔχειν just above, and is used without an expressed object as in 366 E.

357 C 14 **τὸ φρονεῖν—ὑγιαίνειν.** ἀκούειν is added in 367 C. Cf. Arist. *Eth. Nic.* I 4. 1096ᵇ 16 καθ' αὑτὰ δὲ ποῖα θείη τις ἄν; ἢ ὅσα καὶ μονούμενα διώκεται, οἷον τὸ φρονεῖν καὶ ὁρᾶν καὶ ἡδοναί τινες καὶ τιμαί; ταῦτα γὰρ εἰ καὶ δι' ἄλλο τι διώκομεν, ὅμως τῶν καθ' αὑτὰ ἀγαθῶν θείη τις ἄν: also *Met.* A 1. 980ᵃ 2 ff. Aristotle himself does not suggest that a special class should be made of things desirable both in themselves and for their results; but *integri sensus* and *bona valetudo* are included in the Stoic category of προηγμένα καὶ δι' αὑτὰ καὶ δι' ἕτερα (Cic. *De Fin.* III 56: cf. D. L. VII 107).

16 **γυμνάζεσθαι κτλ.** Cf. *Prot.* 354 A and *Gorg.* 467 C, D (where χρηματισμός is again said to belong to this class). ἰάτρευσις as an example of χρηματισμός (in spite of the ἀκριβὴς λόγος of I 342 B ff.) is suggested by ἰατρεύεσθαι. ὁ ἄλλος is 'the rest of,' and should not be taken (with Stallbaum) as *praeterea*: cf. *Gorg.* l.c. οἱ πλέοντές τε καὶ τὸν ἄλλον χρηματισμὸν χρηματιζόμενοι and *Crito* 53 E.

ὃ μισθῶν θ' ἕνεκα καὶ εὐδοκιμήσεων διὰ δόξαν ἐπιτηδευτέον, αὐτὸ
δὲ δι' αὐτὸ φευκτέον ὡς ὂν χαλεπόν.
II. Οἶδα, ἦν δ' ἐγώ, ὅτι δοκεῖ οὕτω, καὶ πάλαι ὑπὸ Θρασυμάχου ὡς τοιοῦτον ὂν ψέγεται, ἀδικία δ' ἐπαινεῖται· ἀλλ' ἐγώ τις,
B ὡς ἔοικε, δυσμαθής. Ἴθι | δή, ἔφη, ἄκουσον καὶ ἐμοῦ, ἐάν σοι
ταὐτὰ δοκῇ. Θρασύμαχος γάρ μοι φαίνεται πρῳαίτερον τοῦ
δέοντος ὑπὸ σοῦ ὥσπερ ὄφις κηληθῆναι, ἐμοὶ δὲ οὔπω κατὰ νοῦν
ἡ ἀπόδειξις γέγονεν περὶ ἑκατέρου· ἐπιθυμῶ γὰρ ἀκοῦσαι τί τ'
ἔστιν ἑκάτερον καὶ τίνα ἔχει δύναμιν αὐτὸ καθ' αὑτὸ ἐνὸν ἐν τῇ
ψυχῇ, τοὺς δὲ μισθοὺς καὶ τὰ γιγνόμενα ἀπ' αὐτῶν ἐᾶσαι χαίρειν.
οὑτωσὶ οὖν ποιήσω, ἐὰν καὶ σοὶ δοκῇ· ἐπαναν εώσομαι τὸν Θρασυ-
C μάχου λόγον, καὶ | πρῶτον μὲν ἐρῶ δικαιοσύνην οἷον εἶναί φασιν
καὶ ὅθεν γεγονέναι· δεύτερον δὲ ὅτι πάντες αὐτὸ οἱ ἐπιτηδεύοντες
ἄκοντες ἐπιτηδεύουσιν ὡς ἀναγκαῖον ἀλλ' οὐχ ὡς ἀγαθόν· τρίτον
δὲ ὅτι εἰκότως αὐτὸ δρῶσι· πολὺ γὰρ ἀμείνων ἄρα ὁ τοῦ ἀδίκου
ἢ ὁ τοῦ δικαίου βίος, ὡς λέγουσιν. ἐπεὶ ἔμοιγε, ὦ Σώκρατες, οὔτι
δοκεῖ οὕτως· ἀπορῶ μέντοι διατεθρυλημένος τὰ ὦτα, ἀκούων
Θρασυμάχου καὶ μυρίων ἄλλων, τὸν δὲ ὑπὲρ τῆς δικαιοσύνης
D λόγον, | ὡς ἄμεινον ἀδικίας, οὐδενός πω ἀκήκοα ὡς βούλομαι·
βούλομαι δὲ αὐτὸ καθ' αὑτὸ ἐγκωμιαζόμενον ἀκοῦσαι. μάλιστα
δ' οἶμαι ἂν σοῦ πυθέσθαι· διὸ κατατείνας ἐρῶ τὸν ἄδικον βίον
ἐπαινῶν, εἰπὼν δὲ ἐνδείξομαί σοι, ὃν τρόπον αὖ βούλομαι καὶ

7. ἀδικία δ' ἐπαινεῖται Π: om. A.

---

358 A 4 **μισθῶν θ' ἕνεκα κτλ.** Herwerden would read *μισθῶν τε μὲν ἕνεκα*, but for *δέ* without *μέν* preceding see I 340 D *n*. The words *διὰ δόξαν*, which are condemned by the same critic, may no doubt be a gloss on *εὐδοκιμήσεων ἕνεκα*. I incline however to think them genuine. Plato is not averse to duplicate expressions of this kind (see Schanz *Nov. Comm. Plat.* pp. 12—15), and the emphatic addition of *διὰ δόξαν* helps in the absence of *μέν* to prepare us for the antithesis *αὐτὸ δὲ δι' αὐτὸ κτλ.* Cf. 363 A below.

7 **ψέγεται.** See *cr. n.* The words *ἀδικία δ' ἐπαινεῖται* are probably genuine: for the mention of *ἀδικία* seems to be necessary to justify the pronoun *ἑκατέρου* just below: cf. also in D *βούλομαι καὶ σοῦ ἀκούειν ἀδικίαν μὲν ψέγοντος, δικαιοσύνην δὲ ἐπαινοῦντος.* For the omission see *Introd.* § 5.

358 C 17 **ὡς ἀναγκαῖον ἀλλ' οὐχ ὡς ἀγαθόν.** Cf. infra 360 C and VI 493 C *τὴν δὲ τοῦ ἀναγκαίου καὶ ἀγαθοῦ φύσιν ὅσον διαφέρει τῷ ὄντι κτλ.*

18 **ἀμείνων ἄρα.** *ἄρα* disclaims responsibility for the theory: cf. 362 A, 364 B, E al.

21 **Θρασυμάχου—ἄλλων.** See on I 337 A ff.

358 D 24 **κατατείνας κτλ.**: 'I will speak vehemently in praise of the unjust life.' The explanation of Photius and Suidas (*κατατείνας ἐρῶ· ἀντὶ τοῦ μακρὸν λόγον διεξελεύσομαι*) does not suit II 367 B *ὡς δύναμαι μάλιστα κατατείνας λέγω.* For this intransitive use of *κατατείνω* cf. I 348 A and Boeckh's emendation of Eur. *Iph. Aul.* 336 *οὔτε κατατενῶ* (*καταινῶ* MSS) *λίαν ἐγώ.*

σοῦ ἀκούειν ἀδικίαν μὲν ψέγοντος, δικαιοσύνην δὲ ἐπαινοῦντος.
ἀλλ' ὅρα, εἴ σοι βουλομένῳ ἃ λέγω. Πάντων μάλιστα, ἦν δ' ἐγώ·
περὶ γὰρ τίνος | ἂν μᾶλλον πολλάκις τις νοῦν ἔχων χαίροι λέγων E
καὶ ἀκούων; Κάλλιστα, ἔφη, λέγεις· καὶ ὃ πρῶτον ἔφην ἐρεῖν, περὶ
τούτου ἄκουε, οἷόν τέ τι καὶ ὅθεν γέγονε δικαιοσύνη.

30. *οἷόν τέ τι* nos: *τί ὄν τε* ΑΞ: *τί οἷόν τε* Π: *τί οἴονται* q.

---

27 **εἴ σοι βουλομένῳ.** In *Crat.* 384 A *ἐστί* is again omitted in this phrase. A still bolder example is cited by Stallbaum from Antipho 6. 8 *ἐὰν ὑμῖν ἡδομένοις.* See Schanz *Novae Comm. Plat.* pp. 31—35.

358 E 30 **οἷόν τέ τι.** The reading of A *τί ὄν τε καὶ ὅθεν γέγονε* involves the separation of *ὅθεν* from *γέγονε*, and is otherwise much too harsh to be right. There is something to be said in favour of Schneider's *περὶ τούτου ἄκουε τί οἴονται, καὶ ὅθεν γέγονε δικαιοσύνη* (see *cr. n.*), especially as the confusion between *οἷόν τε* and *οἴονται* occurs rather frequently in Platonic MSS (see Schneider on I 329 E), but the specific reference in *ὃ ἔφην πρῶτον ἐρεῖν* to 358 C *πρῶτον μὲν ἐρῶ δικαιοσύνην οἷον εἶναί φασι καὶ ὅθεν γεγονέναι* points to the presence of *οἷον* here. The reading *οἷόν τε*, adopted by Stallbaum, as well as by Jowett and Campbell, on the authority of three MSS (Vind. F, Flor. RT), is unexceptionable in point of sense, but fails to account for the presence of *τί* in the best MSS. I have ventured to read *οἷόν τέ τι* (sc. *ἐστί*), supposing that the confusion arose from the accidental omission of *τι*, which was afterwards (as *τί*) wrongly inserted before *οἷόν* (where it remained in Π), *οἷον* itself being afterwards changed to *ὄν* in order to provide a kind of construction ('being what, and whence, it arises,' J. and C.). This *ὄν* was itself fortified by *τυγχάνει* in Flor. B and the Aldine edition. Campbell's suggestion that "*τί ὄν τε* may be a corruption of *τί ἐστί*" is improbable: still less can Herwerden and Hartman induce us to reject the whole clause. Few will approve of Tucker's conjecture *τί τῷ ὄντι καὶ ὅθεν κτλ.* Dr Jackson suggests *ἄκουέ τι, οἷόν τε καὶ κτλ.*, and a reviewer of my *Text of the Republic* in *Lit. Centralblatt* 1898 p. 296 *οἷόν τ' ἐστί κτλ.*

358 E—**359** B *Glauco will first describe the origin and nature of Justice according to the theory which he has undertaken to maintain. According to nature, to commit injustice is a good, to suffer injustice an evil. But as there is more evil in suffering than good in committing injustice, experience causes men to enter into a compact neither to commit nor suffer wrong. The collective prescriptions of this compact are called Law and Justice. Justice is accordingly a compromise between the best policy, i.e. doing wrong without incurring any penalty, and the worst, i.e. suffering wrong without being able to exact vengeance. No one will accept the compromise who is strong enough to do wrong successfully.*

358 E ff. In thus resuscitating the theory of Thrasymachus, Glauco removes a serious stumbling-block by introducing the distinction between *φύσις* and *νόμος.* Civilisation revolts against the anti-social doctrines of Thrasymachus in their application to itself, but receives them more favourably when its own existence is safeguarded by relegating them to an age anterior to society. The view maintained by Glauco is allied to that of Callicles in *Gorg.* 482 E ff.; and it has already been pointed out (on I 337 A, 344 B) that similar views were tolerably widely entertained in Plato's time. To the evidence previously adduced may be added *Laws* 690 B, 889 E, Eur. *Phoen.* 509 and *Frag.* 912 *ἡ φύσις ἐβούλεθ' ᾗ νόμων οὐδὲν μέλει.* But whereas the doctrine of Callicles breaks down in explaining the *origin* of Law (*Gorg.* 483 C, cf. 488 D—489 D), Glauco's theory endeavours to solve this difficulty by postulating a social contract. A kindred solution is ascribed by Aristotle to the Sophist Lycophron: *Pol.* Γ 1280[b] 10 *ὁ νόμος συνθήκη, καὶ καθάπερ ἔφη Λυκόφρων ὁ σοφιστής, ἐγγυητὴς ἀλλήλοις τῶν δικαίων.* The theory of a Social Contract was revived by Epicurus: see D. L. X 150. The views of the "incomplete Protagoreans" in *Theaet.* 172 B (with which cf. *Laws* 889 E), though they do not offer an explanation of the origin of

Πεφυκέναι γὰρ δή φασιν τὸ μὲν ἀδικεῖν ἀγαθόν, τὸ δὲ ἀδικεῖσθαι κακόν, πλέονι δὲ κακῷ ὑπερβάλλειν τὸ ἀδικεῖσθαι ἢ ἀγαθῷ τὸ ἀδικεῖν, ὥστ' ἐπειδὰν ἀλλήλους ἀδικῶσί τε καὶ ἀδικῶνται καὶ
359 ἀμφοτέρων γεύωνται, τοῖς μὴ δυναμένοις τὸ μὲν ἐκφεύγειν | τὸ δὲ αἱρεῖν, δοκεῖν λυσιτελεῖν ξυνθέσθαι ἀλλήλοις μήτ' ἀδικεῖν μήτ' ἀδικεῖσθαι· καὶ ἐντεῦθεν δὴ ἄρξασθαι νόμους τίθεσθαι καὶ ξυνθήκας αὐτῶν, καὶ ὀνομάσαι τὸ ὑπὸ τοῦ νόμου ἐπίταγμα νόμιμόν τε καὶ δίκαιον· καὶ εἶναι δὴ ταύτην γένεσίν τε καὶ οὐσίαν δικαιοσύνης, μεταξὺ οὖσαν τοῦ μὲν ἀρίστου ὄντος, ἐὰν ἀδικῶν μὴ διδῷ δίκην, τοῦ δὲ κακίστου, ἐὰν ἀδικούμενος τιμωρεῖσθαι ἀδύνατος ᾖ· τὸ δὲ
B δίκαιον ἐν μέσῳ ὂν τούτων ἀμφοτέρων ἀγαπᾶσθαι οὐχ | ὡς ἀγαθόν, ἀλλ' ὡς ἀρρωστίᾳ τοῦ ἀδικεῖν τιμώμενον· ἐπεὶ τὸν δυνάμενον

2. δοκεῖν Ast: δοκεῖ codd.

Law, are parallel in so far as they regard it as depending for its binding force solely upon the sanction of society.

31 **πεφυκέναι γὰρ—κακόν.** Cf. *Gorg.* 483 A φύσει μὲν γὰρ πᾶν αἴσχιόν ἐστιν ὅπερ καὶ κάκιον, τὸ ἀδικεῖσθαι, νόμῳ δὲ τὸ ἀδικεῖν. That the natural relation between man and man is one of war is a view expressed in *Laws* 626 A ἣν γὰρ καλοῦσιν οἱ πλεῖστοι τῶν ἀνθρώπων εἰρήνην, τοῦτ' εἶναι μόνον ὄνομα, τῷ δ' ἔργῳ πάσαις πρὸς πάσας τὰς πόλεις ἀεὶ πόλεμον ἀκήρυκτον κατὰ φύσιν εἶναι. A similar theory is contained in the myth of Protagoras (*Prot.* 322 B ff.).

34 **τοῖς μὴ δυναμένοις κτλ.**: i.e. (according to the theory of Callicles) τοῖς ἀσθενέσι ἀνθρώποις καὶ τοῖς πολλοῖς (*Gorg.* 483 B). In place of δοκεῖ in 359 A I have adopted Ast's conjecture δοκεῖν. Throughout this paragraph Glauco consistently presents his view at second hand. For the collocation of infinitives cf. ἀδικεῖν, ἀδικεῖν 360 D, and for the error itself *Introd.* § 5.

359 A 3 **ξυνθήκας αὐτῶν**: 'covenants between one another,' 'mutual covenants.' Reading αὐτῶν, Tucker suggests that the meaning is, 'they established laws and covenants concerning them,' i.e. concerning matters connected with ἀδικεῖν and ἀδικεῖσθαι—a very improbable view.

4 **νόμιμόν τε καὶ δίκαιον**: φημὶ γὰρ ἐγὼ τὸ νόμιμον δίκαιον εἶναι, said Socrates (*Mem.* IV 4. 12).

6 **τοῦ μὲν ἀρίστου κτλ.** Cf. the reasoning of Philus (whose position in Cicero's work corresponds to that of Glauco here) in Cic. *de Rep.* III 23 "nam cum de tribus unum esset optandum, aut facere iniuriam nec accipere, aut et facere et accipere, aut neutrum, optimum est facere, impune si possis, secundum nec facere nec pati, miserrimum digladiari semper tum faciendis tum accipiendis iniuriis." Cicero is following Carneades (*ibid.* 8), who may have been thinking of the present passage. ἀγαπᾶσθαι below (as J. and C. observe) "implies acquiescence rather than decided preference."

359 B 9 **ἐπεὶ τὸν δυνάμενον κτλ.** is further elaborated with much vigour in *Gorg.* 484 A. With ὡς ἀληθῶς ἄνδρα should be compared the emphatic ἀνήρ in that passage (ἐὰν δέ γε, οἶμαι, φύσιν ἱκανὴν γένηται ἔχων ἀνήρ), and Eur. *Phoen.* 509 ἀνανδρία γάρ, τὸ πλέον ὅστις ἀπολέσας | τοὔλασσον ἔλαβε.

359 B—**360** D *Secondly* (*urges Glauco*), *no one is willingly just. Give the just and the unjust the fullest power to work their will, by ensuring them against all evil consequences—give them the faculty of becoming invisible, such as Gyges possessed through his ring, and the just man will shew himself no better than the unjust. If, with this power to screen himself, the just man still refused to do wrong, no doubt men would praise him openly, but in secret they would judge him wholly miserable and foolish.*

αὐτὸ ποιεῖν καὶ ὡς ἀληθῶς ἄνδρα οὐδ' ἂν ἐνί ποτε ξυνθέσθαι τὸ μήτε ἀδικεῖν μήτε ἀδικεῖσθαι· μαίνεσθαι γὰρ ἄν. ἡ μὲν οὖν δὴ φύσις δικαιοσύνης, ὦ Σώκρατες, αὕτη τε καὶ τοιαύτη, καὶ ἐξ ὧν πέφυκε, τοιαῦτα, ὡς ὁ λόγος.

III. Ὡς δὲ καὶ οἱ ἐπιτηδεύοντες ἀδυναμίᾳ τοῦ ἀδικεῖν ἄκοντες αὐτὸ ἐπιτηδεύουσι, μάλιστ' ἂν αἰσθοίμεθα, εἰ τοιόνδε ποιήσαιμεν τῇ διανοίᾳ· | δόντες ἐξουσίαν ἑκατέρῳ ποιεῖν ὅ τι ἂν βούληται, τῷ C τε δικαίῳ καὶ τῷ ἀδίκῳ, εἶτ' ἐπακολουθήσαιμεν θεώμενοι, ποῖ ἡ ἐπιθυμία ἑκάτερον ἄξει. ἐπ' αὐτοφώρῳ οὖν λάβοιμεν ἂν τὸν δίκαιον τῷ ἀδίκῳ εἰς ταὐτὸν ἰόντα διὰ τὴν πλεονεξίαν, ὃ πᾶσα φύσις διώκειν πέφυκεν ὡς ἀγαθόν, νόμῳ δὲ βίᾳ παράγεται ἐπὶ τὴν τοῦ ἴσου τιμήν. εἴη δ' ἂν ἡ ἐξουσία ἣν λέγω τοιάδε μάλιστα, εἰ αὐτοῖς γένοιτο οἵαν ποτέ φασιν δύναμιν τῷ Γύγου | τοῦ Λυδοῦ D προγόνῳ γενέσθαι. εἶναι μὲν γὰρ αὐτὸν ποιμένα θητεύοντα παρὰ τῷ τότε Λυδίας ἄρχοντι, ὄμβρου δὲ πολλοῦ γενομένου καὶ σεισμοῦ ῥαγῆναί τι τῆς γῆς καὶ γενέσθαι χάσμα κατὰ τὸν τόπον ᾗ ἔνεμεν· ἰδόντα δὲ καὶ θαυμάσαντα καταβῆναι· καὶ ἰδεῖν ἄλλα τε δὴ μυθολογοῦσιν θαυμαστὰ καὶ ἵππον χαλκοῦν κοῖλον,

25. τι A²Π: om. A¹.

---

359 B 15 **εἰ τοιόνδε—δόντες.** δόντες κτλ. explains τοιόνδε. εἰ need not be twice expressed: cf. I 351 C *n.*

359 C 20 **νόμῳ—παράγεται.** The language is perhaps suggested by the lines of Pindar cited in *Gorg.* 484 B νόμος ὁ πάντων βασιλεὺς θνατῶν τε καὶ ἀθανάτων— ἄγει δικαιῶν τὸ βιαιότατον ὑπερτάτᾳ χειρί κτλ. (cf. *Prot.* 337 D). but the preposition in παράγεται adds the further notion that equality is not Nature's highway. For βίᾳ i.q. βιαίως in conjunction with another dative Schneider cites VIII 552 E οὓς ἐπιμελείᾳ βίᾳ κατέχουσιν αἱ ἀρχαί. In the next line it is better to regard τοιάδε as explained by εἰ—γενέσθαι, than as balancing οἵαν, in which case εἰ αὐτοῖς γένοιτο would be superfluous. The opportunity (ἐξουσία) of working their will comes from the possession (εἰ αὐτοῖς γένοιτο) of a certain active faculty (δύναμις) like that of Gyges.

22 **τῷ Γύγου κτλ.** Cf. X 612 B τὸν Γύγου δακτύλιον. In Appendix I I have given reasons for believing that the Gyges of the proverbial 'Gyges' ring' was not "Gyges the Lydian"—the hero of Herodotus' story (I 7), but a homonymous ancestor of his. If so, we must (on the hypothesis that the text is sound) suppose that Plato here omits the name of the original Gyges either because he wishes tacitly to contradict a prevalent misconception, or (more probably) because his readers might be presumed to know or to be capable of inferring that the ancestor of Gyges the Lydian was also called Gyges. The MS reading is supported by Proclus (τῷ κατὰ τὸν Γύγου πρόγονον διηγήματι in Schöll *Procli Comm. in Remp. Pl. part. ined.* p. 60. 30). For other views of this passage see App. I.

359 D 28 **ὡς φαίνεσθαι**: with νεκρόν, as Schneider saw: "utrum vere mortuus fuerit, an specie, fabula incertum reliquit." Stallbaum wrongly interprets 'nimirum *videbatur* Gyges cernere' etc.: this would be expressed by δοκεῖν. Ast connects the phrase with μείζω ἢ κατ' ἄνθρωπον: but this is very weak in point of sense. The words are omitted by Cicero (*De Off.* III 38).

29 **ἔχειν.** See *cr. n.* and (for the omission in A) *Introd.* § 5. ἔχειν in the sense of

θυρίδας ἔχοντα, καθ' ἃς ἐγκύψαντα ἰδεῖν ἐνόντα νεκρόν, ὡς φαί-
νεσθαι, μείζω ἢ κατ' ἄνθρωπον· τοῦτον δὲ ἄλλο μὲν ἔχειν οὐδέν, |
E περὶ δὲ τῇ χειρὶ χρυσοῦν δακτύλιον, ὃν περιελόμενον ἐκβῆναι.
συλλόγου δὲ γενομένου τοῖς ποιμέσιν εἰωθότος, ἵν' ἐξαγγέλλοιεν
κατὰ μῆνα τῷ βασιλεῖ τὰ περὶ τὰ ποίμνια, ἀφικέσθαι καὶ ἐκεῖνον
ἔχοντα τὸν δακτύλιον. καθήμενον οὖν μετὰ τῶν ἄλλων τυχεῖν
τὴν σφενδόνην τοῦ δακτυλίου περιαγαγόντα πρὸς ἑαυτὸν εἰς τὸ
360 εἴσω τῆς χειρός. τούτου δὲ γενομένου ἀφανῆ αὐτὸν γενέ|σθαι τοῖς
παρακαθημένοις, καὶ διαλέγεσθαι ὡς περὶ οἰχομένου. καὶ τὸν
θαυμάζειν τε καὶ πάλιν ἐπιψηλαφῶντα τὸν δακτύλιον στρέψαι
ἔξω τὴν σφενδόνην, καὶ στρέψαντα φανερὸν γενέσθαι. καὶ τοῦτο
ἐννοήσαντα ἀποπειρᾶσθαι τοῦ δακτυλίου, εἰ ταύτην ἔχοι τὴν
δύναμιν, καὶ αὐτῷ οὕτω ξυμβαίνειν, στρέφοντι μὲν εἴσω τὴν
σφενδόνην ἀδήλῳ γίγνεσθαι, ἔξω δὲ δήλῳ. αἰσθόμενον δὲ εὐθὺς
διαπράξασθαι τῶν ἀγγέλων γενέσθαι τῶν παρὰ τὸν βασιλέα·
B ἐλθόντα δὲ καὶ τὴν γυναῖκα αὐτοῦ μοιχεύσαντα, μετ' ἐκείνης
ἐπιθέμενον τῷ βασιλεῖ ἀποκτεῖναι καὶ τὴν ἀρχὴν κατασχεῖν.
εἰ οὖν δύο τοιούτω δακτυλίω γενοίσθην, καὶ τὸν μὲν ὁ δίκαιος
περιθεῖτο, τὸν δὲ ὁ ἄδικος, οὐδεὶς ἂν γένοιτο, ὡς δόξειεν, οὕτως
ἀδαμάντινος, ὃς ἂν μείνειεν ἐν τῇ δικαιοσύνῃ καὶ τολμήσειεν
ἀπέχεσθαι τῶν ἀλλοτρίων καὶ μὴ ἅπτεσθαι, ἐξὸν αὐτῷ καὶ ἐκ τῆς

29. ἔχειν Π: om. A. 8. τῶν—βασιλέα q et in mg. A²: om. A¹: τὸν—βασιλέα Π: τῶν περὶ τὸν βασιλέα Ξ.

'have on' 'wear,' i.q. φορεῖν, is tolerably frequent in Homer, though rarer in Attic: see Stephanus-Hase *Thes.* s.v. For the change of subject in ἔχειν—ἐκβῆναι cf. III 414 D *n.* Other views on the text and interpretation of this passage are discussed in App. II.

359 E 30 **χειρί.** Herwerden's δακτύλῳ is unnecessary, and even unpleasant with δακτύλιον so near. Cf. χρυσόχειρες in Luc. *Tim.* 20. "Etiamnunc homines ita loquuntur" (Hartman).

31 **ἵν' ἐξαγγέλλοιεν κτλ.**: 'to report, as was done every month.' The present expresses the habit (J. and C.).

360 A 4 **σφενδόνην**: the 'collet' or 'bezel' (Lat. *funda* or *pala annuli*)—which is as it were the sling in which the stone is set.

360 B 12 **ὡς δόξειεν.** "Optativus eandem vim habet, quam solet in oratione obliqua habere, efficitque, ut verba οὐδεὶς ἂν γένοιτο οὕτως etc. ex aliorum ore missa videantur" (Schneider). This explanation appears to me better than any other, although I can discover no exact parallel in Greek. Glauco is most careful throughout the whole of this section to disclaim responsibility for the views he advocates: cf. ὡς ὁ λόγος 359 B, ἐπεὶ—ἀδικεῖν in C, ὡς φήσει κτλ. in D below: also 361 E al. Tucker would translate 'as it might seem,' defending the optative by Ar. *Birds* 180 ὥσπερ εἴποι τις and Eur. *Andr.* 929 ὡς εἴποι τις. Others erroneously hold that ἂν may be supplied from ἂν γένοιτο, while Ast is desirous of inserting the particle on conjecture. I do not think that the optative can be explained as an instance of irregular assimilation or attraction.

13 **ἂν μείνειεν.** For ἂν cf. *Symp.* 179 A and other examples in Kühner *Gr. Gr.* II p. 934.

ἀγορᾶς ἀδεῶς ὅ τι βούλοιτο λαμβάνειν, καὶ εἰσιόντι εἰς | τὰς C
οἰκίας συγγίγνεσθαι ὅτῳ βούλοιτο, καὶ ἀποκτεινύναι καὶ ἐκ δεσμῶν
λύειν οὕστινας βούλοιτο, καὶ τἆλλα πράττειν ἐν τοῖς ἀνθρώποις
ἰσόθεον ὄντα. οὕτω δὲ δρῶν οὐδὲν ἂν διάφορον τοῦ ἑτέρου ποιοῖ,
ἀλλ' ἐπὶ ταὐτὸν ἴοιεν ἀμφότεροι. καίτοι μέγα τοῦτο τεκμήριον
ἂν φαίη τις, ὅτι οὐδεὶς ἑκὼν δίκαιος ἀλλ' ἀναγκαζόμενος, ὡς οὐκ
ἀγαθοῦ ἰδίᾳ ὄντος, ἐπεὶ ὅπου γ' ἂν οἴηται ἕκαστος οἷός τε ἔσεσθαι
ἀδικεῖν, ἀδικεῖν. λυσιτελεῖν γὰρ δὴ οἴεται | πᾶς ἀνὴρ πολὺ μᾶλλον D
ἰδίᾳ τὴν ἀδικίαν τῆς δικαιοσύνης, ἀληθῆ οἰόμενος, ὡς φήσει ὁ περὶ
τοῦ τοιούτου λόγου λέγων· ἐπεὶ εἴ τις τοιαύτης ἐξουσίας ἐπιλαβό-
μενος μηδέν ποτε ἐθέλοι ἀδικῆσαι μηδὲ ἅψαιτο τῶν ἀλλοτρίων,
ἀθλιώτατος μὲν ἂν δόξειεν εἶναι τοῖς αἰσθανομένοις καὶ ἀνοητότατος, ἐπαινοῖεν δ' ἂν αὐτὸν ἀλλήλων ἐναντίον ἐξαπατῶντες
ἀλλήλους διὰ τὸν τοῦ ἀδικεῖσθαι φόβον. ταῦτα μὲν οὖν δὴ οὕτω.

IV. Τὴν δὲ κρίσιν αὐτὴν τοῦ βίου πέρι ὧν λέγομεν, ἐὰν E

26. ἀνοητότατος $A^1\Pi$: ἀνοητοτάτοις corr. A^2.

---

360 C 18 **ἰσόθεον ὄντα.** The half-conscious irony of ἰσόθεος foreshadows Plato's attack on the popular theology.

20 **οὐδεὶς ἑκὼν δίκαιος** here and in 366 D sums up the Thrasymachean theory in a phrase which suggests the Socratic and Platonic antithesis οὐδεὶς ἑκὼν πονηρός.

360 D 23 **περὶ—λέγων.** περί can hardly be for ὑπέρ, nor dare we write ὑπέρ for περί (as Badham suggests). The words mean simply 'qui de hoc argumento verba facit,' 'the exponent of such a theory.' Cf. 362 D ἱκανῶς εἰρῆσθαι περὶ τοῦ λόγου. Muretus seems to have desiderated πατήρ for περί: cf. expressions like *Phaedr.* 275 E (λόγος) τοῦ πατρὸς ἀεὶ δεῖται βοηθοῦ. On the strength of this Herwerden would read ὁ πατὴρ τοῦ τοιούτου λόγου, rejecting λέγων ("posteaquam ex πῆρ factum est περί, corrector addidit λέγων"). The 'father of the theory' would mean Thrasymachus: see on ὦ παῖδες in 368 A. It is just possible that πατήρ was read by Ficinus ("ut sermonis huius perhibent auctores"), and if so, the variant may have some ancient authority now lost; but Herwerden's proposal is too drastic, and the text is probably sound.

26 **ἀθλιώτατος.** Apelt conjectures ἠλιθιώτατος, but cf. (with Hartman) I 344 A τοὺς δὲ—ἀδικῆσαι οὐκ ἂν ἐθέλοντας ἀθλιωτάτους.

360 D—**362** C *In the third place, the life of the unjust man (according to our theory) is far better than that of the just. Let us suppose that each is the perfect embodiment of his character—the one a consummate artist in iniquity, able to coerce where needful, and so apt at concealment that he enjoys the highest reputation for justice, while guilty of the worst acts of injustice; the other wishful not to be esteemed, but to be, good, and labouring until he dies under the imputation of the worst injustice, although he remains just. Only by means of this supposition can we make sure that the just man has not been attracted by the rewards of justice, but by justice itself. What will be the result? The just will be wholly miserable and unsuccessful, the unjust wholly prosperous and happy, doing good to their friends and evil to their foes; nay more, the unjust will be dearer to the gods than the just, because they have wherewith to win their favour.*

360 D 29 **τὴν δὲ κρίσιν κτλ.** αὐτήν opposes the third division of Glauco's speech to the other two (see 358 C), and marks it as the most important. A kindred use of αὐτός recurs at 370 E ἀλλὰ μήν,—κατοικίσαι γε αὐτὴν τὴν πόλιν —ἀδύνατον. I formerly read αὖ τήν for αὐτήν, but the MS reading is quite de-

διαστησώμεθα τόν τε δικαιότατον καὶ τὸν ἀδικώτατον, οἷοί τ' ἐσόμεθα κρῖναι ὀρθῶς· εἰ δὲ μή, οὔ. τίς οὖν δὴ ἡ διάστασις; ἥδε· μηδὲν ἀφαιρῶμεν μήτε τοῦ ἀδίκου ἀπὸ τῆς ἀδικίας, μήτε τοῦ δικαίου ἀπὸ τῆς δικαιοσύνης, ἀλλὰ τέλεον ἑκάτερον εἰς τὸ ἑαυτοῦ ἐπιτήδευμα τιθῶμεν. πρῶτον μὲν οὖν ὁ ἄδικος ὥσπερ οἱ δεινοὶ δημιουργοὶ ποιείτω· οἷον κυβερνήτης ἄκρος ἢ ἰατρὸς τά τε ἀδύνατα ἐν τῇ
361 τέχνῃ καὶ τὰ δυνατὰ διαισθάνεται, καὶ | τοῖς μὲν ἐπιχειρεῖ, τὰ δὲ ἐᾷ· ἔτι δὲ ἐὰν ἄρα πῃ σφαλῇ, ἱκανὸς ἐπανορθοῦσθαι· οὕτω καὶ ὁ ἄδικος ἐπιχειρῶν ὀρθῶς τοῖς ἀδικήμασιν λανθανέτω, εἰ μέλλει σφόδρα ἄδικος εἶναι· τὸν ἁλισκόμενον δὲ φαῦλον ἡγητέον· ἐσχάτη γὰρ ἀδικία δοκεῖν δίκαιον εἶναι μὴ ὄντα. δοτέον οὖν τῷ τελέως ἀδίκῳ τὴν τελεωτάτην ἀδικίαν, καὶ οὐκ ἀφαιρετέον, ἀλλ' ἐατέον τὰ μέγιστα ἀδικοῦντα τὴν μεγίστην δόξαν αὑτῷ παρεσκευακέναι
B εἰς δικαιοσύνην, | καὶ ἐὰν ἄρα σφάλληταί τι, ἐπανορθοῦσθαι δυνατῷ εἶναι, λέγειν τε ἱκανῷ ὄντι πρὸς τὸ πείθειν, ἐάν τι μηνύηται τῶν ἀδικημάτων, καὶ βιάσασθαι, ὅσα ἂν βίας δέηται, διά τε ἀνδρείαν καὶ ῥώμην καὶ διὰ παρασκευὴν φίλων καὶ οὐσίας. τοῦτον δὲ τοιοῦτον θέντες τὸν δίκαιον παρ' αὐτὸν ἱστῶμεν τῷ λόγῳ, ἄνδρα ἁπλοῦν καὶ γενναῖον, κατ' Αἰσχύλον οὐ δοκεῖν ἀλλ' εἶναι ἀγαθὸν ἐθέλοντα. ἀφαιρετέον δὴ τὸ δοκεῖν. εἰ γὰρ δόξει δίκαιος εἶναι, |
C ἔσονται αὐτῷ τιμαὶ καὶ δωρεαὶ δοκοῦντι τοιούτῳ εἶναι· ἄδηλον

31. τίς Π: τί A. 33. ἑαυτοῦ Π: ἑαυτῷ A.

---

fensible. It should be noticed that *κρίσιν* is at first a kind of pendent accusative, afterwards "resumed as a cognate accusative with *κρῖναι*" (J. and C.). Tucker strangely makes *κρίσιν* = 'choice.' The word means of course (our) 'judgment' concerning etc. Cf. 361 D *ἵν' ἀμφότεροι —κρίνωνται* and *εἰς τὴν κρίσιν ἐκκαθαίρεις*.

360 E 33 **εἰς** goes with *τέλεον*: cf. *δόξαν εἰς* 361 A.

361 A 2 **οὕτω—λανθανέτω.** *ἐπιχειρῶν ὀρθῶς* means of course attempting possible, and abstaining from impossible, *ἀδικήματα*. But as an *ἀδίκημα* is possible only if the *ἀδικῶν* is able to conceal it (the alternative of open violence is recognised later 361 B), it is necessary that the unjust man should escape detection. Hence *λανθανέτω*, although *λανθάνειν* was not attributed (because not essential) to the pilot and doctor (360 E).

4 **φαῦλον** means a 'bungler' (D. and V.). With the sentiment cf. *Prot.* 317 A *τὸ οὖν ἀποδιδράσκοντα μὴ δύνασθαι ἀποδρᾶναι, ἀλλὰ καταφανῆ εἶναι, πολλὴ μωρία καὶ τοῦ ἐπιχειρήματος*: also *Laws* 845 B, and the Spartan practice of punishing boys not for stealing, but for being caught (Xen. *Rep. Lac.* 2. 8). With *ἐσχάτη γὰρ ἀδικία κτλ.* the editors compare Cicero *de Off.* I 41 "totius autem iniustitiae nulla capitalior est, quam eorum, qui, cum maxime fallunt, id agunt, ut viri boni esse videantur."

361 B 13 **κατ' Αἰσχύλον—ἀγαθόν.** *Sept.* 592—594 (of Amphiaraus) *οὐ γὰρ δοκεῖν ἄριστος, ἀλλ' εἶναι θέλει | βαθεῖαν ἄλοκα διὰ φρενὸς καρπούμενος, | ἐξ ἧς τὰ κεδνὰ βλαστάνει βουλεύματα.* Herwerden would expunge *ἀγαθόν* ("mente repetatur *ἁπλοῦν καὶ γενναῖον*"), on the ground that if Plato had added any adjective, it would have been **δίκαιον**. (The Scholiast substitutes **δίκαιος** for *ἄριστος* in Aeschylus.) *ἀγαθόν* gives excellent sense, and is nearer to the poet's words.

οὖν εἴτε τοῦ δικαίου εἴτε τῶν δωρεῶν τε καὶ τιμῶν ἕνεκα τοιοῦτος εἴη. γυμνωτέος δὴ πάντων πλὴν δικαιοσύνης, καὶ ποιητέος ἐναντίως διακείμενος τῷ προτέρῳ· μηδὲν γὰρ ἀδικῶν δόξαν ἐχέτω τὴν μεγίστην ἀδικίας, ἵνα ᾖ βεβασανισμένος εἰς δικαιοσύνην τῷ μὴ τέγγεσθαι ὑπὸ κακοδοξίας καὶ τῶν ἀπ' αὐτῆς γιγνομένων· ἀλλὰ ἔστω ἀμετάστατος μέχρι θανάτου, | δοκῶν μὲν εἶναι ἄδικος διὰ **D** βίου, ὢν δὲ δίκαιος, ἵνα ἀμφότεροι εἰς τὸ ἔσχατον ἐληλυθότες, ὁ μὲν δικαιοσύνης, ὁ δὲ ἀδικίας, κρίνωνται ὁπότερος αὐτοῖν εὐδαιμονέστερος.

V. Βαβαί, ἦν δ' ἐγώ, ὦ φίλε Γλαύκων, ὡς ἐρρωμένως ἑκάτερον ὥσπερ ἀνδριάντα εἰς τὴν κρίσιν ἐκκαθαίρεις τοῖν ἀνδροῖν. Ὡς μάλιστ', ἔφη, δύναμαι. ὄντοιν δὲ τοιούτοιν, οὐδὲν ἔτι, ὡς ἐγᾦμαι, χαλεπὸν ἐπεξελθεῖν τῷ λόγῳ, οἷος ἑκάτερον βίος ἐπιμένει. λεκτέον | οὖν· καὶ δὴ κἂν ἀγροικοτέρως λέγηται, μὴ ἐμὲ οἴου λέγειν, **E** ὦ Σώκρατες, ἀλλὰ τοὺς ἐπαινοῦντας πρὸ δικαιοσύνης ἀδικίαν.

20. ἀπ' Eusebius (*Præp. Ev.* XII 10. 3) et Theodoretus (*Gr. Affect. Curat.* XII p. 1021 ed. Schulze): ὑπ' codd. 21. ἔστω Vind. D Flor. V cum Eusebio et Theodoreto: ἴτω A[1]: ἤτω A[2]Π[2]Ξ*q*: ἠτῶ (*sic*) Π[1].

---

361 C 17 **εἴη** is explained by Stallbaum as an optative of wish (though in a subordinate clause): 'it is not clear therefore whether he is fain to be just,' etc. This gives a fair sense, but the idiom is obscure, and unsupported by other examples. J. and C. remark that "the optative accords with the conditional nature of the case in an imagined future," taking ἄδηλον as for ἄδηλον ἂν εἴη. But an omitted ἂν εἴη cannot be responsible for the mood of τοιοῦτος εἴη, nor could ἂν εἴη easily be omitted (see Schanz *Nov. Comm. Pl.* p. 33). Still less should we accept Hartman's ἄδηλον <ἂν> οὖν, sc. εἴη. Madvig ejects εἴη altogether, understanding ἐστι after τοιοῦτος. This may be right, but its intrusion is not easy to explain. I think the word is genuine, and means 'was': 'it is not clear then, say they, whether he was just,' etc. Glauco again disclaims responsibility: cf. 360 B *n.* εἴη would in direct speech be ἦν: and the idiom is like that in III 406 E, where see note. For the sequence of moods and tenses cf. VI 490 A *n.* Failing this interpretation, the word must (I think) be spurious. Herwerden's proposal—τοιούτῳ εἶναι, ἄδηλον ὄν (retaining εἴη)—does not surmount the difficulty and is also wrong in point of sense.

20 **ἀπ' αὐτῆς.** See *cr. n.* The sense required is not 'what is produced by' (ὑπό) 'it,' but 'what results from it': cf. γίγνεσθαι ἀπό (in a similar connexion) 357 C and 358 B. The scribe no doubt assimilated the preposition to the preceding ὑπό.

21 **ἔστω.** See *cr. n.* I formerly read ἴτω with A[1] and the majority of editors, but I now agree with Schneider that ἔστω is right. ἴτω cannot be used by itself as a synonym for 'live,' or as a copula: we should require ἴτω διὰ βίου, instead of ἴτω μέχρι θανάτου (to transpose the two phrases would of course be too violent a change). The sole authority for ἴτω is the first hand in A: and this is certainly insufficient to outweigh the inherent superiority of ἔστω. Most MSS have ἤτω, a late form for ἔστω.

361 D 26 **ἐκκαθαίρεις**: not 'polish up' (J. and C.) but rather 'scour clean' (D. and V.), 'purge' from all extraneous matter: see 361 C γυμνωτέος δὴ πάντων πλὴν δικαιοσύνης.

361 E 29 **ἀγροικοτέρως** is said with reference to the exaggeration and coarseness of the description: cf. *Ap.* 32 D, *Gorg.* 509 A.

ἐροῦσι δὲ τάδε, ὅτι οὕτω διακείμενος ὁ δίκαιος μαστιγώσεται,
στρεβλώσεται, δεδήσεται, ἐκκαυθήσεται τὠφθαλμώ, τελευτῶν |
362 πάντα κακὰ παθὼν ἀνασχινδυλευθήσεται καὶ γνώσεται, ὅτι οὐκ
εἶναι δίκαιον ἀλλὰ δοκεῖν δεῖ ἐθέλειν· τὸ δὲ τοῦ Αἰσχύλου πολὺ
ἦν ἄρα ὀρθότερον λέγειν κατὰ τοῦ ἀδίκου. τῷ ὄντι γὰρ φήσουσι
τὸν ἄδικον, ἅτε ἐπιτηδεύοντα πρᾶγμα ἀληθείας ἐχόμενον καὶ οὐ
πρὸς δόξαν ζῶντα, οὐ δοκεῖν ἄδικον ἀλλ' εἶναι ἐθέλειν,

βαθεῖαν ἄλοκα διὰ φρενὸς καρπούμενον,
B | ἐξ ἧς τὰ κεδνὰ βλαστάνει βουλεύματα,

πρῶτον μὲν ἄρχειν ἐν τῇ πόλει δοκοῦντι δικαίῳ εἶναι, ἔπειτα
γαμεῖν ὁπόθεν ἂν βούληται, ἐκδιδόναι εἰς οὓς ἂν βούληται, ξυμβάλλειν, κοινωνεῖν οἷς ἂν ἐθέλῃ, καὶ παρὰ ταῦτα πάντα ὠφελεῖσθαι
κερδαίνοντα τῷ μὴ δυσχεραίνειν τὸ ἀδικεῖν· εἰς ἀγῶνας τοίνυν
ἰόντα καὶ ἰδίᾳ καὶ δημοσίᾳ περιγίγνεσθαι καὶ πλεονεκτεῖν τῶν
ἐχθρῶν, πλεονεκτοῦντα δὲ πλουτεῖν καὶ τούς τε φίλους εὖ ποιεῖν
C καὶ τοὺς ἐχθροὺς | βλάπτειν, καὶ θεοῖς θυσίας καὶ ἀναθήματα
ἱκανῶς καὶ μεγαλοπρεπῶς θύειν τε καὶ ἀνατιθέναι, καὶ θεραπεύειν
τοῦ δικαίου πολὺ ἄμεινον τοὺς θεοὺς καὶ τῶν ἀνθρώπων οὓς ἂν

---

32 **δεδήσεται**: 'will be kept in chains.' *δεθήσεται* (so *v* and some other MSS) is required by Herwerden, and may be right. But in Xen. *Cyr.* IV 3. 18 *δεδήσομαι* is similarly combined with several first futures.

ἐκκαυθήσεται κτλ. Schneider refers to Hdt. VII 18 *θερμοῖσι σιδηρίοισι ἐκκαίειν—τοὺς ὀφθαλμούς*, and *Gorg.* 473 C *ἐὰν—στρεβλῶται καὶ ἐκτέμνηται καὶ τοὺς ὀφθαλμοὺς ἐκκάηται.* That *ἐκκαυθήσεται* (and not *ἐκκοπήσεται*, the reading of some inferior MSS, and of the ancient authorities who cite this passage) is right here, is probable also from X 613 E *ἃ ἄγροικα ἔφησθα σὺ εἶναι ἀληθῆ λέγων, εἶτα στρεβλώσονται καὶ ἐκκαυθήσονται*, whether the last clause is genuine or not. It is not clear that Cicero (*de Rep.* III 27) did not find *ἐκκαυθήσεται* in his text; for though he has *effodiantur oculi*, he adds afterwards *vinciatur*, *uratur*. Herwerden recasts the words of Plato to suit Cicero's translation, but Cicero is a much less trustworthy witness than Paris A.

362 A 3 **ἄρα**: see on 358 C. *τῷ ὄντι* in the same line belongs not to *φήσουσι*, but to *τὸν ἄδικον—ἐθέλειν.*

6 **βαθεῖαν κτλ.**: "reaping in his thoughts the fruit of the deep furrow, from which good counsel grows" (Verrall). Plato takes *τὰ κεδνὰ βουλεύματα* more concretely, and places in apposition thereto **ἄρχειν** and the other infinitives down to *ὠφελεῖσθαι*, *δοκοῦντι* being the dative of interest after *βλαστάνει*. For the change from the dative *δοκοῦντι* to the accusative *κερδαίνοντα* cf. *Euthyph.* 5 A and infra IV 422 B, C.

362 B 10 **κοινωνεῖν**. Cobet deletes this word, as well as *καὶ κοινωνήματα* in *Laws* 738 A *πρὸς ἅπαντα τὰ ξυμβόλαια καὶ κοινωνήματα.* In view of the same passage Platt (*Cl. Rev.* III p. 72) would read *καὶ κοινωνεῖν*. No change is necessary, for *κοινωνεῖν* is a term of wider connotation than *ξυμβάλλειν* (see I 333 A *n.*), and the asyndeton has a rhetorical effect: cf. III 407 B, V 465 C, VI 488 C, IX 590 A *nn.*

12 **πλεονεκτεῖν** recalls I 343 D, E, 349 B ff., as *τούς τε φίλους εὖ ποιεῖν κτλ.* recalls the theory attributed to Simonides in I 334 B. Here however it is not Justice, but Injustice masquerading as Justice, which is said to benefit friends and injure enemies.

βούληται, ὥστε καὶ θεοφιλέστερον αὐτὸν εἶναι μᾶλλον προσήκειν ἐκ τῶν εἰκότων ἢ τὸν δίκαιον. οὕτω φασίν, ὦ Σώκρατες, παρὰ θεῶν καὶ παρ' ἀνθρώπων τῷ ἀδίκῳ παρεσκευάσθαι τὸν βίον ἄμεινον ἢ τῷ δικαίῳ.

VI. Ταῦτ' εἰπόντος τοῦ Γλαύκωνος, ἐγὼ μὲν | ἐν νῷ εἶχόν τι D
λέγειν πρὸς ταῦτα, ὁ δὲ ἀδελφὸς αὐτοῦ Ἀδείμαντος, Οὔ τί που οἴει, ἔφη, ὦ Σώκρατες, ἱκανῶς εἰρῆσθαι περὶ τοῦ λόγου; Ἀλλὰ τί μήν; εἶπον. Αὐτό, ἦ δ' ὅς, οὐκ εἴρηται ὃ μάλιστα ἔδει ῥηθῆναι. Οὐκοῦν, ἦν δ' ἐγώ, τὸ λεγόμενον, ἀδελφὸς ἀνδρὶ παρείη· ὥστε καὶ σύ, εἴ τι ὅδε ἐλλείπει, ἐπάμυνε. καίτοι ἐμέ γε ἱκανὰ καὶ τὰ ὑπὸ τούτου ῥηθέντα καταπαλαῖσαι καὶ ἀδύνατον ποιῆσαι βοηθεῖν δικαιοσύνῃ. | Καὶ ὅς, Οὐδέν, ἔφη, λέγεις, ἀλλ' ἔτι καὶ τάδε ἄκουε· E

23. ἔφη Π: om. A.

---

362 C 17 **μᾶλλον προσήκειν.** The comparative is attached to the verb as well as to the adjective, so as to combine the force of two expressions, viz. (1) ὥστε καὶ θεοφιλῆ αὐτὸν εἶναι μᾶλλον προσήκειν and (2) ὥστε καὶ θεοφιλέστερον αὐτὸν εἶναι προσήκειν. In cases like λαθραιότερον μᾶλλον *Laws* 781 A, μᾶλλον is quite redundant: in *Hipp. Mai.* 285 A ἔστι δέ γε—ὠφελιμώτερον—παιδεύεσθαι μᾶλλον ἢ κτλ. it is resumptive. See on the whole subject Kühner *Gr. Gr.* II p. 25.

19 **παρεσκευάσθαι—ἄμεινον.** For ἄμεινον Richards would read ἀμείνον' or ἀμείνονα: cf. 358 C πολὺ γὰρ ἀμείνων ἄρα ὁ τοῦ ἀδίκου ἢ ὁ τοῦ δικαίου βίος. The change is tempting at first sight; but Plato generally uses ἀμείνω and not ἀμείνονα, and the adverb expresses what is virtually the same meaning, since a βίος ἄμεινον παρεσκευασμένος (cf. πόλιν εὖ παρεσκευασμένην *Laws* 751 B) is (according to the views here described) a βίος ἀμείνων. Hermann's χεῖρον' for χεῖρον in *Phaed.* 85 B, though adopted by Schanz, is also unnecessary, for ἔχειν may be intransitive.

362 C—**363** E *At this point Glauco gives way to Adimantus. Glauco had maintained the superiority of Injustice over Justice by directly praising Injustice: Adimantus will uphold the same thesis by describing the arguments usually advanced in favour of Justice. In the first place, when parents and friends exhort the young to follow Justice, they do not praise Justice herself, but the rewards which Justice earns from men and gods. Homer and Hesiod describe the benefits derived from Justice in this present life, while Musaeus and his son guarantee to her votaries sensual bliss hereafter, and others promise to the pious a long line of descendants, but relegate the wicked to punishment after death and unpopularity during life.*

362 D 23 **ἔφη.** See *cr. n.* ἔφη is present in the majority of MSS, and cannot be dispensed with, where the interlocutor is specified, as here. See *Introd.* § 5.

25 **ἀδελφὸς ἀνδρὶ παρείη**: *frater adsit fratri.* Ast proposed to insert ἂν before ἀνδρί, making the sentence interrogative. The rhythm would thus approximate to the usual paroemiac rhythm of proverbs: but the brevity and force of the proverb would suffer. If change were needed it would be better to adopt Shilleto's elegant suggestion ἀδελφεὸς ἀνδρὶ παρείη (note on Dem. *F. L.* § 262), but even if this was the original expression, it would be quite in Plato's manner to substitute the modern for the archaic word, in defiance of rhythm. The source of the proverb (with which compare συγγνώμη ἀδελφῷ βοηθεῖν *F. L.* § 264) is found by the Scholiast in *Od.* XVI 97 f. ἤ τι κασιγνήτοις ἐπιμέμφεαι, οἷσί περ ἀνὴρ | μαρναμένοισι πέποιθε, καὶ εἰ μέγα νεῖκος ὄρηται. Cf. also *Il.* XXI 308 f. and Xen. *Mem.* II 3. 19.

δεῖ γὰρ διελθεῖν ἡμᾶς καὶ τοὺς ἐναντίους λόγους ὧν ὅδε εἶπεν,
οἳ δικαιοσύνην μὲν ἐπαινοῦσιν, ἀδικίαν δὲ ψέγουσιν, ἵν' ᾖ σαφέστερον ὅ μοι δοκεῖ βούλεσθαι Γλαύκων. λέγουσι δέ που καὶ
παρακελεύονται πατέρες τε ὑέσιν καὶ πάντες οἱ τινῶν κηδόμενοι
363 ὡς χρὴ δίκαιον | εἶναι, οὐκ αὐτὸ δικαιοσύνην ἐπαινοῦντες, ἀλλὰ
τὰς ἀπ' αὐτῆς εὐδοκιμήσεις, ἵνα δοκοῦντι δικαίῳ εἶναι γίγνηται
ἀπὸ τῆς δόξης ἀρχαί τε καὶ γάμοι καὶ ὅσαπερ Γλαύκων διῆλθεν
ἄρτι, ἀπὸ τοῦ εὐδοκιμεῖν ὄντα τῷ δικαίῳ. ἐπὶ πλέον δὲ οὗτοι
τὰ τῶν δοξῶν λέγουσιν· τὰς γὰρ παρὰ θεῶν εὐδοκιμήσεις ἐμβάλ-
λοντες ἄφθονα ἔχουσι λέγειν ἀγαθὰ τοῖς ὁσίοις, ἅ φασι θεοὺς

2. ἀπ' A^2Π: ὑπ' A.

---

362 E 29 **ἐναντίους.** Adimantus' λόγοι are ἐναντίοι, because they praise Justice, and censure Injustice: whereas Glauco had done the reverse: κατατείνας ἐρῶ τὸν ἄδικον βίον ἐπαινῶν (358 D).

363 A 1 **αὐτὸ δικαιοσύνην.** Not αὐτοδικαιοσύνην (with the second hand in A), which would be the (chiefly post-Platonic) expression for the Idea of Justice (cf. αὐτοάνθρωπος and the like). αὐτό is *ipsum*, 'by itself,' as in αὐτοὶ γάρ ἐσμεν: cf. *Theaet.* 146 E γνῶναι ἐπιστήμην αὐτὸ ὅ τι ποτ' ἐστιν, and infra V 472 C, X 612 B (cited by J. and C.). αὐτό may be thus used even when the feminine of the article is present, e.g. *Prot.* 361 A αὐτὸ ἡ ἀρετή: cf. also *Crat.* 411 D.

2 **γίγνηται.** The nominatives are treated as equivalent to a neuter plural, whence the singular verb. Cf. *Symp.* 188 B, *Laws* 925 E, Andocides I 145. γίγνεσθαι is the verb in each of these examples. See also infra V 462 E.

4 **τῷ δικαίῳ.** Schneider is right in refusing to change the δικαίῳ of A, Π and most MSS to ἀδίκῳ, which has the authority of a few inferior MSS. The reference in διῆλθεν ἄρτι is no doubt to 362 B, where the benefits accrue to the man who *seems* to be just, although in reality he is unjust. But ὄντα etc. should be taken, not with διῆλθεν, but as part of the parents' exhortation. This yields a better rhythm, and much better sense. The parents exhort their children to be just, in order that (ἵνα depends on χρὴ δίκαιον εἶναι) they may obtain the rewards ἀπὸ τοῦ εὐδοκιμεῖν ὄντα τῷ δικαίῳ. They very properly assume that the surest way to *seem* to be just (and so to obtain the rewards of justice) is to *be* just: cf. Xen. *Mem.* II 6. 39 συντομωτάτη τε καὶ ἀσφαλεστάτη καὶ καλλίστη ὁδὸς—ὅ τι ἂν βούλῃ δοκεῖν ἀγαθὸς εἶναι, τοῦτο καὶ γενέσθαι ἀγαθὸν πειρᾶσθαι and *ib.* I 7. 1 with Heracl. *Fr.* 137 ed. Bywater συντομωτάτην ὁδὸν—εἰς εὐδοξίαν τὸ γενέσθαι ἀγαθόν. Glauco's picture of the just man as one who seems to be unjust is untrue to the facts of experience, as Socrates points out in X 612 D: nor did even Glauco go so far as to say that the unjust man, *qua* unjust, ηὐδοκίμει, but only ὁ δοκῶν δίκαιος εἶναι (who may, of course, be unjust). The divorce between appearance and reality is purely argumentative, and out of place in parental exhortations. Further, in order to make ἀπὸ τοῦ εὐδοκιμεῖν ὄντα etc. represent what Glauco said, we should have to read τῷ ἀδίκῳ μὲν δοκοῦντι δὲ δικαίῳ: otherwise the words δοξαζομένων δὲ ἀδίκων in the corresponding phrase (363 E) might just as well be omitted. If ὄντα is construed with διῆλθεν, the words τῷ δικαίῳ must (with Ast) be expunged: but that the clause represents what the parents say is further proved by the exact correspondence of ἀπὸ τοῦ εὐδοκιμεῖν ὄντα τῷ δικαίῳ with τὰς ἀπ' αὐτῆς (sc. δικαιοσύνης) εὐδοκιμήσεις, which is what the parents praise. I have dwelt on this point at some length because recent English editors (except Tucker) have wrongly deserted Paris A.

6 **τοῖς ὁσίοις** depends on ἀγαθά ('good things for the pious'): cf. ἀγαθὰ διῆλθε τῷ τοῦ ἀδίκου I 348 A *n.* This is much simpler than to punctuate ἀγαθά, τοῖς ὁσίοις ἅ as the other editors do. Such a postponement of the relative is rare, and

διδόναι, ὥσπερ ὁ γενναῖος Ἡσίοδός τε καὶ Ὅμηρός φασιν, ὁ μὲν τὰς δρῦς | τοῖς δικαίοις τοὺς θεοὺς ποιεῖν B

ἄκρας μέν τε φέρειν βαλάνους, μέσσας δὲ μελίσσας.
εἰροπόκοι δ' ὄϊες, φησίν, μαλλοῖς καταβεβρίθασι,

καὶ ἄλλα δὴ πολλὰ ἀγαθὰ τούτων ἐχόμενα· παραπλήσια δὲ καὶ ὁ ἕτερος· ὥστε τευ γάρ φησιν

ἤ βασιλῆος ἀμύμονος, ὅστε θεουδὴς
εὐδικίας ἀνέχῃσι, φέρῃσι δὲ γαῖα μέλαινα
| πυροὺς καὶ κριθάς, βρίθῃσι δὲ δένδρεα καρπῷ, C
τίκτῃ δ' ἔμπεδα μῆλα, θάλασσα δὲ παρέχῃ ἰχθῦς.

Μουσαῖος δὲ τούτων νεανικώτερα τἀγαθὰ καὶ ὁ ὑὸς αὐτοῦ παρὰ θεῶν διδόασιν τοῖς δικαίοις· εἰς Ἅιδου γὰρ ἀγαγόντες τῷ λόγῳ καὶ κατακλίναντες καὶ συμπόσιον τῶν ὁσίων κατασκευάσαντες ἐστεφανωμένους ποιοῦσιν | τὸν ἅπαντα χρόνον ἤδη διάγειν μεθύοντας, D
ἡγησάμενοι κάλλιστον ἀρετῆς μισθὸν μέθην αἰώνιον· οἱ δ' ἔτι

---

here, I think, unduly harsh, in spite of the analogy of III 390 B and IV 425 C. Cobet felt the difficulty when in an unhappy moment he suggested ἀγαθά, ἃ τοῖς ὁσίοις κτλ.

7 **Ἡσίοδός τε κτλ.** Hesiod and Homer are appealed to as recognised theological authorities: see Hdt. II 53.

363 B 9 **ἄκρας — καταβεβρίθασι.** *OD.* 232 f. τοῖσι (i.e. ἰθυδίκῃσιν ἀνδράσι) φέρει μὲν γαῖα πολὺν βίον, οὔρεσι δὲ δρῦς | ἄκρη μέν τε φέρει βαλάνους, μέσση δὲ μελίσσας· | εἰροπόκοι δ' ὄϊες μαλλοῖς καταβεβρίθασι. Further rewards of justice (ἄλλα δὴ πολλὰ ἀγαθά) are enumerated in *vv.* 227—231, and 235—237. Many other illustrations in support of Plato's attack on Greek religion throughout this passage will be found in Nägelsbach's *Hom. Theol.* and *Nachhom. Theol.* passim.

12 **ὥστε τευ—ἰχθῦς.** *Od.* XIX 109 ff. The ἤ before βασιλῆος is difficult: apparently the author intended to give two comparisons, but dropped the second. We are hardly justified, I think, in abolishing the anacoluthon by reading (with Platt) ὥστέ τεο βασιλῆος or (with Ameis) ὥστε τευ ἤ.

363 C 17 **Μουσαῖος κτλ.** By Musaeus' son Plato probably means Eumolpus (cf. Suidas s.vv. Εὔμολπος and Μουσαῖος). In this section of the argument Plato directs his attack against certain forms of the Orphic conception of a future life: see Lobeck *Aglaophamus* p. 807 with Rohde *Psyche*[2] II pp. 127, 129 *nn.*, and Dieterich *Nekyia* pp. 72 ff. 77 ff. *nn.* Lobeck refers to Plut. *Comp. Cim. et Lucull.* 2 Πλάτων ἐπισκώπτει τοὺς περὶ τὸν Ὀρφέα τοῖς εὖ βεβιωκόσι φάσκοντας ἀποκεῖσθαι γέρας ἐν ᾅδου μέθην αἰώνιον and id. *Ne suav. quidem vivi posse sec. Epic.* 1105 B, where the allusion to Plato is less clear: also D. L. VI 4.

19 **συμπόσιον τῶν ὁσίων.** ὅσιοι was the regular appellation of the μύσται (ὁσίους μύστας *hymn. Orph.* 84. 3 ed. Abel). For the συμπόσιον cf. [*Axioch.*] 371 D συμπόσιά τε εὐμελῆ καὶ εἰλαπίναι αὐτοχορήγητοι καὶ ἀκήρατος ἀλυπία καὶ ἡδεῖα δίαιτα. The stock example in antiquity of earthly virtue rewarded by the delights of a sensuous paradise is Heracles: see e.g. Pind. *Nem.* I 71, Theocr. XVII 28 f. and Horace *Od.* III 3. 9 f., IV 8. 29 f. A somewhat higher note is struck in Pind. *Ol.* II 61 ff. and *Fr.* 129 f. Several of these passages shew traces of Orphic influence, but the special instance of Heracles is traceable to Homer (*Od.* XI 602 f.).

363 D 21 **μέθην αἰώνιον** may be illustrated from the fragment of Pherecrates ap. Athen. VI 268 E ff.

τούτων μακροτέρους ἀποτίνουσιν μισθοὺς παρὰ θεῶν· παῖδας γὰρ
παίδων φασὶ καὶ γένος κατόπισθεν λείπεσθαι τοῦ ὁσίου καὶ
εὐόρκου. ταῦτα δὴ καὶ ἄλλα τοιαῦτα ἐγκωμιάζουσιν δικαιοσύνην·
τοὺς δὲ ἀνοσίους αὖ καὶ ἀδίκους εἰς πηλόν τινα κατορύττουσιν ἐν
E Ἅιδου καὶ κοσκίνῳ ὕδωρ ἀναγκάζουσι φέρειν, ἔτι τε ζῶντας εἰς
κακὰς δόξας ἄγοντες, ἅπερ Γλαύκων περὶ τῶν δικαίων δοξαζομένων
δὲ ἀδίκων διῆλθε τιμωρήματα, ταῦτα περὶ τῶν ἀδίκων λέγουσιν,
ἄλλα δὲ οὐκ ἔχουσιν. ὁ μὲν οὖν ἔπαινος καὶ ὁ ψόγος οὗτος
ἑκατέρων.

22. ἀποτίνουσιν *q*: ἀποτείνουσιν ΑΠΞ.

---

22 **ἀποτίνουσιν.** See *cr. n.* The reading of A is defended by Stallbaum as an abbreviation for μακροτέρους λόγους ἀποτείνουσι περὶ μισθῶν παρὰ θεῶν; but no other example of this harsh condensation has been adduced, and the sense is far from satisfactory. A better meaning is conveyed by Schneider's translation, "Andere aber lassen die Belohnungen der Götter *noch weiter reichen als diese*": for it is clear from the next clause that μακροτέρους ('more extensive,' not, of course, 'greater,' which would be μείζους) refers to the extension of the rewards of virtue beyond the personality of the individual concerned. But μακροτέρους ἀποτείνουσιν μισθούς is (to say the least) an obscure and difficult expression; and ἀποτίνουσιν (i.q. λέγουσιν ἀποτίνεσθαι) receives strong support from the parallel use of διδόασιν in C above, and κατορύττουσιν, ἀναγκάζουσι, and ἄγοντες below. The collocation of μακροτέρους with ἀποτίνουσι may easily have led to the corruption ἀποτείνουσι, owing to the frequency of such expressions as μακροὺς λόγους ἀποτείνειν. For the error see *Introd.* § 5.

παῖδας—κατόπισθεν. The Scholiast remarks ἐξ Ἡροδότου (VI 86) ἀπὸ τοῦ δοθέντος χρησμοῦ Γλαύκῳ τῷ Λάκωνι ὡς Ἀνδρὸς δ' εὐόρκου γενεὴ μετόπισθεν ἀμείνων. The story of Glaucus admirably illustrates the view herein expressed; but Plato is more probably thinking of Hesiod *OD.* 285 (a line which is identical with that quoted from the oracle), and also perhaps of some such lines as those of Tyrtaeus 12. 29 f. καὶ τύμβος καὶ παῖδες ἐν ἀνθρώποις ἀρίσημοι | καὶ παίδων παῖδες καὶ γένος ἐξοπίσω.

25 **εἰς πηλόν τινα κατορύττουσιν.** τινα is contemptuous: 'something which they call mud': cf. 372 B infra and *Symp.* 210 D (ἀνθρώπου τινός). The 'mud' is Orphic: see Abel *Orphic.* p. 247 and cf. *Phaed.* 69 C, *Rep.* VII 533 D, and the σκῶρ ἀείνων of Ar. *Frogs* 146, with Blaydes' note. See also Rohde *Psyche*[2] I p. 313 *n.* and Dieterich *Nekyia* pp. 82 f. The employment of the Danaid legend in Orphic teaching is illustrated by *Gorg.* 493 B: cf. also Dieterich *Nekyia* pp. 69 f., 75.

363 E 27 **δοξαζομένων δέ.** For δέ without μέν see I 340 D *n.*

29 **ἄλλα δὲ οὐκ ἔχουσιν**: sc. λέγειν τιμωρήματα. Adimantus means that they dissuade men from injustice merely on account of its results, ignoring τίνα ἔχει δύναμιν αὐτὸ καθ' αὐτὸ ἐνὸν ἐν τῇ ψυχῇ (358 B). J. and C. aptly cite *Theaet.* 176 D, E ἀγνοοῦσι γὰρ ζημίαν ἀδικίας, ὃ δεῖ ἥκιστα ἀγνοεῖν· οὐ γάρ ἐστιν ἣν δοκοῦσιν, πληγαί τε καὶ θάνατοι, ὧν ἐνίοτε πάσχουσιν οὐδὲν ἀδικοῦντες, ἀλλ' ἣν ἀδύνατον ἐκφυγεῖν, viz. "that by their wicked acts they become like the pattern of evil."

363 E—**365** A *Secondly* (*continues Adimantus*), *both by poets and in private life virtue is called honourable but difficult, vice easy, and disgraceful only by convention. Injustice, men say, is in general the best policy: they admire the vicious rich, and despise the virtuous poor. Strangest of all, the gods themselves are said to be sometimes kind to the wicked, and unkind to the good; and seers profess to have power from the gods to atone for unjust dealing by pleasurable rites, and undertake to damage enemies for a trifling expenditure of money. In support of such teaching they quote the poets, Hesiod for example, and Homer. There are likewise books containing sacrificial formulae, by*

VII. Πρὸς δὲ τούτοις σκέψαι, ὦ Σώκρατες, ἄλλο αὖ εἶδος
λόγων περὶ δικαιοσύνης τε καὶ ἀδικίας ἰδίᾳ τε λεγόμενον καὶ ὑπὸ
ποιητῶν. | πάντες γὰρ ἐξ ἑνὸς στόματος ὑμνοῦσιν, ὡς καλὸν μὲν 364
ἡ σωφροσύνη τε καὶ δικαιοσύνη, χαλεπὸν μέντοι καὶ ἐπίπονον·
ἀκολασία δὲ καὶ ἀδικία ἡδὺ μὲν καὶ εὐπετὲς κτήσασθαι, δόξῃ δὲ
μόνον καὶ νόμῳ αἰσχρόν. λυσιτελέστερα δὲ τῶν δικαίων τὰ ἄδικα
ὡς ἐπὶ τὸ πλῆθος λέγουσι, καὶ πονηροὺς πλουσίους καὶ ἄλλας
δυνάμεις ἔχοντας εὐδαιμονίζειν καὶ τιμᾶν εὐχερῶς ἐθέλουσιν δημοσίᾳ τε καὶ ἰδίᾳ, τοὺς δὲ ἀτιμάζειν καὶ ὑπερορᾶν, οἳ ἄν πῃ
ἀσθενεῖς τε καὶ πένητες ὦσιν, ὁμολογοῦντες αὐτοὺς ἀμείνους εἶναι B
τῶν ἑτέρων. τούτων δὲ πάντων οἱ περὶ θεῶν τε λόγοι καὶ ἀρετῆς
θαυμασιώτατοι λέγονται, ὡς ἄρα καὶ θεοὶ πολλοῖς μὲν ἀγαθοῖς
δυστυχίας τε καὶ βίον κακὸν ἔνειμαν, τοῖς δ' ἐναντίοις ἐναντίαν
μοῖραν. ἀγύρται δὲ καὶ μάντεις ἐπὶ πλουσίων θύρας ἰόντες πεί-

2. τε καὶ δικαιοσύνη Π: om. A.

---

the use of which men are persuaded that their sins may be pardoned both in life and after death.

363 E ff. The phase of Greek religious life here censured is illustrated by Dieterich *Nek.* pp. 81 f. and Rohde *Psyche*² II 74 ff.: cf. also Lobeck *Aglaoph.* pp. 643 ff.

32 **ἰδίᾳ** has been understood of writing in prose, but the reference is only to the representations of private persons, e.g. parents, etc.)(to poets, who were in a sense the professional teachers of Hellas: cf. X 606 C, *Laws* 890 A ἰδιωτῶν τε καὶ ποιητῶν, and 366 E below.

364 A 1 **καλὸν μὲν—ἐπίπονον.** See *cr. n.* For the omission of τε καὶ δικαιοσύνη see *Introd.* § 5. The sentiment may be illustrated by Hesiod *OD.* 289—292 and Simon. ap. Pl. *Prot.* 339 B ff. ἄνδρ' ἀγαθὸν μὲν ἀλαθέως γενέσθαι χαλεπὸν κτλ.; cf. also Simonides' imitation of Hesiod (*Fr.* 58 ed. Bergk).

5 **ὡς ἐπὶ τὸ πλῆθος**: i.q. ὡς ἐπὶ τὸ πολύ. So also *Phaedr.* 275 B. The sentiment recurs in Isocr. *de Pace* § 31.

πονηρούς is the substantive, and ἄλλας δυνάμεις ἔχοντας balances πλουσίους. πλούτους, parallel to ἄλλας δυνάμεις, and also dependent on ἔχοντας, might appear neater. But there is no reason for deserting the MSS, although Plato is fond of the plural of πλοῦτος (cf. e.g. VI 495 A, X 618 B, 619 A). The sentiment is best illustrated from Polus's description of the happiness of Archelaus in *Gorg.* 471 A ff.

364 B 10 **ὡς ἄρα—μοῖραν.** ἄρα hints dissent: cf. 358 C *n.* The gnomic poets often express themselves in this vein: e.g. Solon 15. 1 πολλοὶ γὰρ πλουτεῦσι κακοί, ἀγαθοὶ δὲ πένονται, Theogn. 373—380. A kindred sentiment occurs in Sophocles *Phil.* 447—452. For the most part however it is held that Justice asserts herself in the end: see for example Solon 4. 15 f., 13. 7—32. Euripides expresses the general teaching of Greek tragedy on this subject when he writes (*Ion* 1621 f.) ἐς τέλος γὰρ οἱ μὲν ἐσθλοὶ τυγχάνουσιν ἀξίων, | οἱ κακοὶ δ', ὥσπερ πεφύκασ', οὔποτ' εὖ πράξειαν ἄν. There is no occasion to write (with Richards) πολλάκις τοῖς for πολλοῖς.

12 **ἐπὶ πλουσίων θύρας ἰόντες.** This semi-proverbial expression (cf. VI 489 B, C) stigmatises the avarice of seers and mendicant priests (ἀγύρται from ἀγείρω, cf. infra 381 D). Plato's contempt for μαντική in general is expressed in the *Euthyphro* and sporadically in various dialogues (see e.g. *Tim.* 71 E, with Archer-Hind's note); but his attack is here particularly directed (cf. infra 364 E) against such Ὀρφεοτελεσταί or Orphic friars as Theophrastus speaks of in his description of the δεισι-

θουσιν ὡς ἔστι παρὰ σφίσι δύναμις ἐκ θεῶν ποριζομένη θυσίαις
C *τε καὶ ἐπῳδαῖς, εἴτε τι ἀδίκημά του ¦ γέγονεν αὐτοῦ ἢ προγόνων,*
ἀκεῖσθαι μεθ' ἡδονῶν τε καὶ ἑορτῶν· ἐάν τέ τινα ἐχθρὸν πημῆναι
ἐθέλῃ, μετὰ σμικρῶν δαπανῶν ὁμοίως δίκαιον ἀδίκῳ βλάψειν
ἐπαγωγαῖς τισὶν καὶ καταδέσμοις, τοὺς θεούς, ὥς φασιν, πείθοντές
σφισιν ὑπηρετεῖν. τούτοις δὲ πᾶσιν τοῖς λόγοις μάρτυρας ποιητὰς
ἐπάγονται, οἱ μὲν κακίας περὶ εὐπετείας ᾄδοντες

16. *βλάψειν* q: *βλάψει* ΑΠΞ. 19. *περὶ* Madvig: *πέρι* ΑΠΞq. *ᾄδοντες* Muretus: *διδόντες* codd.

δαίμων (*Charact.* 16) *καὶ τελεσθησόμενος πρὸς τοὺς Ὀρφεοτελεστὰς κατὰ μῆνα πορεύεσθαι μετὰ τῆς γυναικός, ἐὰν δὲ μὴ σχολάζῃ ἡ γυνή, μετὰ τῆς τίτθης καὶ τῶν παιδίων.* The kind of ceremonies which they practised may be seen from Dem. *de Cor.* §§ 258 ff. Plato agreed with the more enlightened section of his countrymen in condemning such degrading cults and superstitions on the ground of their immoral tendency: see especially Foucart *des Assoc. religieuses chez les Grecs* pp. 153—157, where the opinions of ancient writers on this subject are collected. On *ἀγύρται* in general reference may be made to J. H. Wright in *Harvard Studies in Cl. Philol.* VI p. 66 *n.*

364 C 15 **ἐάν τε — βλάψειν** is in *oratio obliqua*: 'et si quis inimicum laedere velit, nocituros se parvo sumptu iusto pariter et iniusto' (Schneider *Addit.* p. 11). This explanation (which Tucker also proposes without knowing that Schneider had forestalled him) is by far the best and simplest. For other views see App. III.

17 **ἐπαγωγαῖς—καταδέσμοις.** *ἐπαγωγαί* are *ἀγωγαὶ δαίμονος φαύλου ἐπί τινα γενόμεναι* (Timaeus *Lex.* s.v.). The datives are usually construed with *πείθοντες*, and *καταδέσμοις* understood as the binding formulae "by which the seer compels the invisible powers to work his will" (Rohde *Psyche*[2] II p. 88 *n.*). But in the *κατάδεσμοι* which have been discovered it is the victim and not the god who is bound down; see e.g. CIG 538 (an Athenian inscription of about 380 B.C.)—*καταδῶ Κτησίαν—καὶ Κλεοφράδην καταδῶ—καὶ τοὺς μετὰ Κτησίου ἅπαντας καταδῶ.* This and other instances from leaden tablets found in graves are given by Wachsmuth *Rhein. Mus.* XVIII (1863) pp. 560 ff.: cf. also Marquardt *Röm. Staatsverwaltung* III p. 109 *n.* 6. On this account I think it better to connect *ἐπαγωγαῖς τισὶν καὶ καταδέσμοις* with *βλάψειν*, exactly as in *Laws* 933 D *ἐὰν δὲ καταδέσεσιν ἢ ἐπαγωγαῖς ἤ τισιν ἐπῳδαῖς ἢ τῶν τοιούτων φαρμακειῶν ὡντινωνοῦν δόξῃ ὅμοιος εἶναι βλάπτοντι—τεθνάτω.* Plato is still alluding to the debasing forms of oriental superstition which had gained a footing in Greece in his day: see Foucart l. c. p. 172.

θεοὺς — σφισιν ὑπηρετεῖν: whereas true religion consists in man's *ὑπηρεσία τοῖς θεοῖς* *Euthyph.* 13 D ff.

19 **οἱ μὲν κτλ.**: 'some declaiming about the easiness of vice, how that' etc. *οἱ μὲν—ᾄδοντες* recalls 364 A, while *οἱ δέ* refers to the *ἀγύρται καὶ μάντεις* of 364 B. The reference in the first case is as precise as possible: *πάντες γὰρ ἐξ ἑνὸς στόματος ὑμνοῦσιν ὡς καλὸν μὲν ἡ σωφροσύνη τε καὶ δικαιοσύνη, χαλεπὸν μέντοι καὶ ἐπίπονον· ἀκολασία δὲ καὶ ἀδικία ἡδὺ μὲν καὶ εὐπετὲς κτήσασθαι, δόξῃ δὲ μόνον καὶ νόμῳ αἰσχρόν* (364 A). Those who *ὑμνοῦσιν ὡς—ἀκολασία—καὶ ἀδικία—εὐπετὲς κτήσασθαι* can be accurately described as *κακίας περὶ εὐπετείας ᾄδοντες*, but scarcely by *οἱ κακίας πέρι εὐπετείας διδόντες*, because 'to offer facilities for vice' is not the same thing as to say that vice is easy. Stallbaum attempts to evade this difficulty by taking *διδόντες* as equivalent to *διδόσθαι λέγοντες*, but neither is 'saying that facilities are offered for vice' quite the same as 'saying that vice is easy.' It is also difficult to find another instance of the plural of *εὐπέτεια*. The verbal echoes seem to me very strongly in favour of *περὶ—ᾄδοντες*. For *ᾄδοντες* = 'harping on' (like the *ὑμνοῦσιν* to which it refers) cf. *Lys.* 205 C *ἃ δὲ ἡ πόλις ὅλη ᾄδει* and 205 D *ἅπερ αἱ γραῖαι ᾄδουσι* (with reference to the proverbial *γραῶν ὕθλος*): the use of *ᾄδειν* in

ὡς τὴν μὲν κακότητα καὶ ἰλαδὸν ἔστιν ἑλέσθαι
ῥηϊδίως· λείη μὲν ὁδός, μάλα δ' ἐγγύθι ναίει· D
τῆς δ' ἀρετῆς ἱδρῶτα θεοὶ προπάροιθεν ἔθηκαν

καί τινα ὁδὸν μακράν τε καὶ ἀνάντη· οἱ δὲ τῆς τῶν θεῶν ὑπ' ἀνθρώπων παραγωγῆς τὸν Ὅμηρον μαρτύρονται, ὅτι καὶ ἐκεῖνος εἶπεν

λιστοὶ δέ τε καὶ θεοὶ αὐτοί,
καὶ τοὺς μὲν θυσίαισι καὶ εὐχωλαῖς ἀγαναῖσιν
λοιβῇ τε κνίσῃ τε παρατρωπῶσ' ἄνθρωποι E
λισσόμενοι, ὅτε κέν τις ὑπερβήῃ καὶ ἁμάρτῃ.

βίβλων δὲ ὅμαδον παρέχονται Μουσαίου καὶ Ὀρφέως, Σελήνης τε καὶ Μουσῶν ἐγγόνων, ὥς φασι, καθ' ἃς θυηπολοῦσιν, πείθοντες

23. ἀνάντη $A^1\Pi$: καὶ τραχεῖαν addidit in mg. A^2. 26. λιστοὶ δέ τε a manu rec. Π: λιστοὶ δὲ στρεπτοὶ τε A^1: λιστοὶ δὲ στρεπτοὶ δέ τε A^2: στρεπτοὶ δέ τε $\Pi^1\Xi q$: λιστοὶ στρεπτοὶ δέ τε Π^2.

Laws 854 C is different, but akin. For the corruption of ᾄδοντες to διδόντες see *Introd.* § 5. The conjectures of Liebhold (*Fl. Jahrb.* 1888 p. 107) and Zeller (*Arch. f. Gesch. d. Phil.* II p. 694) κακίας πέρι εὐπετείας διελθόντες and κακίας πέρι εὐπέτειαν διδόντας have little in their favour.

364 C, D 20 **ὡς τὴν—ἔθηκαν.** Hesiod *OD.* 287—289. ὡς is due to Plato: Hesiod has τὴν μέν τοι κτλ. For λείη the MSS of Hesiod read ὀλίγη: λείη (also in *Laws* 718 E, Xen. *Mem.* II 1. 20 and elsewhere) proves the existence of a different recension. Cf. G. E. Howes *Harvard Studies in Cl. Philol.* VI p. 165. The verses are partially quoted or referred to again in *Laws* 718 E, *Prot.* 340 D; their influence is also seen in *Phaedr.* 272 C.

364 D 23 **καί τινα ὁδὸν κτλ.**: Hesiod *OD.* 290 μακρὸς δὲ καὶ ὄρθιος οἶμος ἐς αὐτὴν | καὶ τρηχὺς κτλ. The last two words account for the marginal addition καὶ τραχεῖαν in A.

364 D, E 26 **λιστοὶ—ἁμάρτῃ.** See *cr. n.* The words are spoken by Phoenix to Achilles in *Il.* IX 497—501. Plato edits the lines to suit his own purposes. For λιστοί our text of Homer has στρεπτοί. The word λιστοί (though implied in ἄλλιστος, τρίλλιστος) does not occur elsewhere, a fact which is strongly in favour of its genuineness here. We must suppose that the recension which Plato used had λιστοί. The theology contained in these lines meets us continually in ancient literature: cf. also the words of the king in *Hamlet* III 3 "And what's in prayer but this twofold force To be forestalled ere we come to fall Or pardoned being down?" Plato expresses his dissent in *Laws* 716 E ff., 905 D: in *Alc.* II 149 E we read οὐ γὰρ οἶμαι τοιοῦτόν ἐστι, τὸ τῶν θεῶν ὥστε ὑπὸ δώρων παράγεσθαι οἷον κακὸν τοκιστήν.

364 E 30 **βίβλων—ἐγγόνων.** The allusion is to Orphic liturgies. Musaeus was the son of Selene, according to Philochorus quoted by the Scholiast on Ar. *Frogs* 1033: cf. φαεσφόρου ἔκγονε Μήνης | Μουσαῖε in Abel *Orphic. Fr.* 4. Orpheus' mother was the Muse Calliope (Suidas s.v. Ὀρφεύς). There is no solid basis for the old view that ἔκγονος means 'son,' and ἔγγονος 'grandson.' The etymological form is ἔκγονος, but ἐκ- was often assimilated to ἐγ- before γ during the 4th century B.C., particularly in this word: cf. also ἐγγειτόνων etc. on Inscriptions. See Meisterhans[3] p. 107. Elsewhere in the *Republic* ἔκγονος is the regular spelling.

31 **καθ' ἃς θυηπολοῦσιν**: sacrificial liturgies. A θυηπολικόν is mentioned by Suidas (s.v. Ὀρφεύς) as one of the 'works' of Orpheus: see also Lobeck *Aglaoph.* p. 371 and Rohde *Psyche*[2] II pp. 112, 113 *nn.*

οὐ μόνον ἰδιώτας ἀλλὰ καὶ πόλεις, ὡς ἄρα λύσεις τε καὶ καθαρμοὶ
365 ἀδικημάτων διὰ θυσιῶν καὶ παιδιᾶς ἡδονῶν εἰσὶ μὲν ἔτι | ζῶσιν,
εἰσὶ δὲ καὶ τελευτήσασιν, ἃς δὴ τελετὰς καλοῦσιν, αἳ τῶν ἐκεῖ
κακῶν ἀπολύουσιν ἡμᾶς, μὴ θύσαντας δὲ δεινὰ περιμένει.

VIII. Ταῦτα πάντα, ἔφη, ὦ φίλε Σώκρατες, τοιαῦτα καὶ τοσαῦτα λεγόμενα ἀρετῆς πέρι καὶ κακίας, ὡς ἄνθρωποι καὶ θεοὶ περὶ αὐτὰ ἔχουσι τιμῆς, τί οἰόμεθα ἀκουούσας νέων ψυχὰς ποιεῖν,

---

32 **πόλεις**: as for instance when Epimenides the Cretan purified Athens (see Grote III 85—89). Plato may be thinking of this event, which in defiance of chronology he placed ten years before the Persian wars (*Laws* 642 D, E). Cf. also infra 366 A and *Laws* 909 B.

λύσεις — καθαρμοί. λύσεις means 'modes of absolution' (Lobeck *Aglaoph.* p. 810): cf. 366 A οἱ λύσιοι θεοί and Arist. *Pol.* B 4 1262ª 32 τὰς νομιζομένας λύσεις. The Scholium on Ar. *Frogs* 1033 contains the remark: οὗτος (i.e. Musaeus) δὲ παραλύσεις καὶ τελετὰς καὶ καθαρμοὺς συντέθεικεν. For παραλύσεις Blaydes proposes λύσεις, while Rutherford reads περὶ λύσεις (apparently with the Ravenna Codex), inserting also on his own conjecture ποιήματα after συντέθεικεν. I have no doubt that the Scholiast wrote παρὰ λύσεις: 'besides Absolutions, he has composed also τελεταί and καθαρμοί.' καθαρμοί formed a distinct class of religious literature, and were written by Epimenides, Empedocles, and others: see Grote I p. 27 *n.* 3.

33 **παιδιᾶς ἡδονῶν**: 'pleasures of play.' παιδιᾶς depends on ἡδονῶν, and is here used abstractly: cf. Thuc. III 38. 7 ἀκοῆς ἡδονῇ and (with Schneider) Paus. I 21. 7 θέας ἡδονήν. Madvig would eject ἡδονῶν, but without ἡδονῶν Plato would probably have written παιδιῶν (cf. *Laws* 829 B): other suggestions, such as καὶ παιδιᾶς καὶ ἡδονῶν, or καὶ παιδιᾶς διὰ ἡδονῶν, or καὶ παιδιῶν καὶ ἡδονῶν are open to graver objection. For παίζειν and the like in connexion with religious celebrations Stallbaum cites Hdt. IX 11 Ὑακίνθιά τε ἄγετε καὶ παίζετε and VIII 99 ἐν θυσίῃσί τε καὶ εὐπαθείῃσι: add *Phaedr.* 276 B, *Laws* 666 B. Plato's point is that atonement if it is made a pleasure and not a penance sets a premium on sin.

365 A 2 **τελευτήσασιν — τελετάς.** The Orpheotelestae connected τελεταί with τελευτᾶν, sometimes on the ground assigned by Plato here, sometimes because they alleged that the sensations of dying resembled those of initiation into the great mysteries (Plut. *Frag. de An.* 725). This and other ancient derivations are given by Lobeck *Aglaoph.* pp. 124, 126, 172. For περιμένει Cobet needlessly conjectures περιμένειν.

365 A—**367** E *Finally, what is the effect on the souls of the young? Young men of ability are encouraged to practise Injustice, while outwardly pretending to be just. To escape detection by their fellow-men, they form political clubs, and employ persuasion and force. The gods they can afford to ignore; for either there are no gods, or they regard not man, or—according to those who are the sole authorities for their existence—they can be propitiated out of the proceeds of Injustice. There are special rites and gods who can deliver us from punishment after death: so the gods' own children say. So strong are the arguments in favour of Injustice that even those who can refute them make allowances, recognising that no one is voluntarily just except from innate goodness of disposition or scientific knowledge.*

It rests with you, Socrates (*says Adimantus*), *now for the first time to praise Justice and censure Injustice in and by themselves, apart from their accessories. Nay more; you must assign to each the reputation which is enjoyed by the other. Do not merely shew us that Justice is better than Injustice; tell us what effect they severally produce on their possessors, in consequence of which the one is good, and the other evil.*

365 A 6 **τιμῆς** i. q. τοῦ τιμᾶν. Cf. (with J. and C.) 359 C above.

τί—ποιεῖν. The subject to ποιεῖν is ταῦτα πάντα—λεγόμενα: ψυχάς is its secondary object. Cf. infra 367 B τί ποιοῦσα ἑκατέρα τὸν ἔχοντα κτλ. and 367 E. This view, which Schneider also holds, is better than to make ψυχάς subject to ποιεῖν and ταῦτα πάντα κτλ. dependent on ἀκουούσας.

ὅσοι εὐφυεῖς καὶ ἱκανοὶ ἐπὶ πάντα τὰ λεγόμενα ὥσπερ ἐπιπτόμενοι
συλλογίσασθαι ἐξ αὐτῶν, ποῖός | τις ἂν ὢν καὶ πῇ πορευθεὶς τὸν B
βίον ὡς ἄριστα διέλθοι; λέγοι γὰρ ἂν ἐκ τῶν εἰκότων πρὸς αὑτὸν
κατὰ Πίνδαρον ἐκεῖνο τὸ Πότερον δίκᾳ τεῖχος ὕψιον ἢ σκο-
λιαῖς ἀπάταις ἀναβὰς καὶ ἐμαυτὸν οὕτω περιφράξας διαβιῶ;
τὰ μὲν γὰρ λεγόμενα δικαίῳ μὲν ὄντι μοι, ἐὰν καὶ μὴ δοκῶ, ὄφελος
οὐδέν φασιν εἶναι, πόνους δὲ καὶ ζημίας φανεράς· ἀδίκῳ δὲ δόξαν
δικαιοσύνης παρασκευασαμένῳ θεσπέσιος βίος λέγεται. οὐκοῦν, |
ἐπειδὴ τὸ δοκεῖν, ὡς δηλοῦσί μοι οἱ σοφοί, καὶ τὰν ἀλάθειαν C
βιᾶται καὶ κύριον εὐδαιμονίας, ἐπὶ τοῦτο δὴ τρεπτέον ὅλως·
πρόθυρα μὲν καὶ σχῆμα κύκλῳ περὶ ἐμαυτὸν σκιαγραφίαν ἀρετῆς
περιγραπτέον, τὴν δὲ τοῦ σοφωτάτου Ἀρχιλόχου ἀλώπεκα ἑλκτέον

---

7 **ἐπιπτόμενοι.** The image, as Jowett remarks, suggests a bee gathering honey: cf. *Ion* 534 B λέγουσι γὰρ—οἱ ποιηταὶ ὅτι ἀπὸ κρηνῶν μελιρρύτων ἐκ Μουσῶν κήπων τινῶν καὶ ναπῶν δρεπόμενοι τὰ μέλη ἡμῖν φέρουσιν ὥσπερ αἱ μέλιτται, Simon. *Fr.* 47 ὁμιλεῖ δ' ἄνθεσιν (viz. the poet) ὥτε μέλισσα ξανθὸν μέλι κηδομένα and Pind. *Pyth.* X 53 f.

365 B 10 **πότερον δίκᾳ—ἀναβάς.** The fragment (which appears tolerably often in ancient citations) is restored as follows by Bergk (*Fr.* 213) Πότερον δίκᾳ τεῖχος ὕψιον | ἢ σκολίαις ἀπάταις ἀναβαίνῃ | ἐπιχθονίων γένος ἀνδρῶν | δίχα μοι νόος ἀτρέκειαν εἰπεῖν. It is, I think, unlikely that θεσπέσιος βίος and κύριον εὐδαιμονίας below "si non a Pindaro, certe ex poetis petita sunt" (Bergk).

12 **ἐὰν καὶ μὴ δοκῶ** has been commonly altered to ἐὰν μὴ καὶ δοκῶ on the suggestion of Dobree and Boeckh (with a few inferior MSS): but the text is sound. We are dealing with ταῦτα πάντα—λεγόμενα κτλ.; and it has not been said that it is useless to be just, unless one is also believed to be just (ἐὰν μὴ καὶ δοκῶ). This would imply that it *is* useful to be just, if one is also considered just; but what has been urged is that Justice is in itself never advantageous, although its εὐδοκιμήσεις (363 A) are: see 358 C, E, 360 C (οὐδεὶς ἑκὼν δίκαιος, ἀλλ' ἀναγκαζόμενος, ὡς οὐκ ἀγαθοῦ ἰδίᾳ ὄντος), 362 A (οὐκ εἶναι δίκαιον, ἀλλὰ δοκεῖν δεῖ ἐθέλειν). The words ἐὰν καὶ μὴ δοκῶ mean 'if I also seem unjust,' for οὐ δοκῶ δίκαιος εἶναι, not δοκῶ οὐ δίκαιος εἶναι, is the Greek idiom. This meaning suits exactly. What has to be established is that δοκεῖν prevails over εἶναι in human life (οὐκοῦν—βιᾶται). The proof is as follows. To *be* just and *seem* unjust is misery (see 361 E): to *be* unjust, and *seem* just is bliss (see 362 A, C): therefore δοκεῖν is everything, and ἐπὶ τοῦτο τρεπτέον ὅλως.

13 **φασιν.** Is τὰ λεγόμενα the subject? or is the sentence an anacoluthon? ("nam quo modo res ipsa comparata sit, nescio: quae quidem vulgo dicuntur, talia sunt, ut iusto mihi commodi quicquam fore negetur" Schneider). The latter view is the more likely. Similar anacolutha are cited by Engelhardt *Anac. Pl. Spec.* III p. 40.

365 C 15 **οἱ σοφοί.** Simonides (σοφὸς γὰρ καὶ θεῖος ἀνήρ I 331 E) *Fr.* 76 Bergk. Plato himself sets no small store by a good name (coupled with virtue) in *Laws* 950 C.

17 **πρόθυρα—σχῆμα**: 'as my porch and trappings.' The mixture of metaphors is thoroughly Platonic: cf. VII 527 D *n.* With σχῆμα (any kind of external or adventitious means of impressing others or hiding one's own deficiencies) cf. *Gorg.* 511 E περιπατεῖ ἐν μετρίῳ σχήματι.

σκιαγραφίαν ('perspective drawing' VII 523 B, X 602 D) with its cognate words is continually used by Plato of things unreal, counterfeit, illusory: cf. infra IX 583 B *n.*, 586 B al., and Wohlrab on *Theaet.* 208 E.

18 **τοῦ σοφωτάτου κτλ.** Archilochus seems to have canonized the fox as the embodiment of cunning in Greek literature: fragments are preserved of at least two fables of his in which the fox appears (86—88 and 89 ed. Bergk). In the second (89. 5, 6) occur the lines τῷ δ' (sc. πιθήκῳ)

ἐξόπισθεν κερδαλέαν καὶ ποικίλην. ἀλλὰ γάρ, φησί τις, οὐ ῥᾴδιον ἀεὶ λανθάνειν κακὸν ὄντα. οὐδὲ γὰρ ἄλλο οὐδὲν εὐπετές,
D φήσομεν, τῶν μεγάλων· ἀλλ' ὅμως, εἰ μέλλομεν εὐδαιμονήσειν, ταύτῃ ἰτέον, ὡς τὰ ἴχνη τῶν λόγων φέρει. ἐπὶ γὰρ τὸ λανθάνειν ξυνωμοσίας τε καὶ ἑταιρίας συνάξομεν, εἰσίν τε πειθοῦς διδάσκαλοι σοφίαν δημηγορικήν τε καὶ δικανικὴν διδόντες, ἐξ ὧν τὰ μὲν πείσομεν, τὰ δὲ βιασόμεθα, ὡς πλεονεκτοῦντες δίκην μὴ διδόναι. ἀλλὰ δὴ θεοὺς οὔτε λανθάνειν οὔτε βιάσασθαι δυνατόν. οὐκοῦν,

---

ἆρ' ἀλώπηξ κερδαλέη συνήντετο | πυκνὸν ἔχουσα νόον. The κερδαλέαν καὶ ποικίλην of Plato corresponds in meaning to κερδαλέη—πυκνὸν ἔχουσα νόον, and may have ended one of the iambics in this or another Archilochean fable: it is at all events clear that they are from Archilochus. 'The crafty and subtle fox of Archilochus' means simply 'the crafty and subtle fox of which Archilochus speaks': the rest of the imagery is due to Plato. With the general sentiment cf. St Matth. vii 15 ἔρχονται πρὸς ὑμᾶς ἐν ἐνδύμασι προβάτων (this is the σκιαγραφία ἀρετῆς), ἔσωθεν δέ εἰσιν λύκοι ἅρπαγες: with ἑλκτέον ἐξόπισθεν (opposed to πρόθυρα μὲν καὶ σχῆμα) Milton *Samson Agonistes* 358—360 "Why are his gifts desirable, to tempt Our earnest prayers, then, given with solemn hand As graces, draw a scorpion's tail behind?" Unnecessary difficulty has been caused by an erroneous gloss of Timaeus (τὴν ἀλωπεκῆν· τὴν πανουργίαν), which seems to imply that he read ἀλωπεκῆν 'fox's skin' for ἀλώπεκα in this passage. Ruhnken (followed by Ast and Stallbaum) while retaining ἀλώπεκα explained it of the fox's skin; but it would be pointless to 'drag behind a fox's skin.' With ἀλώπεκα—'fox' for 'foxiness'—cf. infra 382 D ποιητὴς—ψευδὴς ἐν θεῷ οὐκ ἔνι, *Phaed.* 77 E, and the well-known "astutam vapido servas sub pectore vulpem" Persius V 117.

19 **ἀλλὰ γάρ** 'at enim,' like ἀλλὰ δή (infra D, X 600 A al.), introduces an objection: cf. infra 366 A al.

20 **οὐδὲ γὰρ—μεγάλων**: an audacious application of the proverb χαλεπὰ τὰ καλά.

22 **ὡς—φέρει.** For ὡς we might expect ᾗ (Ficinus has *qua*). ταύτῃ must be taken as referring to what precedes, though further explained by ὡς—φέρει. ἴχνη and φέρει shew that the metaphor is still the ὁδὸς βίου. The words ἴχνη φέρει may be from Archilochus. For the sentiment cf. III 394 D.

365 D 23 **ξυνωμοσίας—ἑταιρίας.** An allusion to the political life of Athens: cf. *Ap.* 36 B, *Theaet.* 173 D, Thuc. VIII 54 ξυνωμοσίας, αἵπερ ἐτύγχανον πρότερον ἐν τῇ πόλει οὖσαι ἐπὶ δίκαις καὶ ἀρχαῖς. In the *Laws*, Plato would suppress all such secret clubs and cabals with a strong hand: see 856 B ff. The πειθοῦς διδάσκαλοι mentioned presently are the Sophists.

25 **ὡς** for ὥστε (except in idiomatic phrases like ὡς ἔπος εἰπεῖν, ὥς γε ἐντεῦθεν ἰδεῖν) is a curious archaism, tolerably frequent in Xenophon (e.g. *Cyrop.* I 2. 8, V 2. 5, VI 4. 16, VIII 5. 1 and 7. 27), but almost unexampled in Plato. The *Protagoras* (330 E) furnishes an instance with οὕτως preceding (cf. Xen. *Cyr.* IV 2. 13). ὡς in *Phaed.* 108 E is perhaps to be explained in the same way: cf. also *Alc.* II 141 B and *Symp.* 213 B παραχωρῆσαι γὰρ τὸν Σωκράτη ὡς ἐκεῖνον καθίζειν. See also on ὡς δή in I 337 C. As βιάζομαι can be followed by the simple infinitive, it might seem preferable to connect ὡς πλεονεκτοῦντες as a participial explanatory clause either with βιασόμεθα or with δίκην μὴ διδόναι ('not to be punished for aggrandisement'); but the first alternative gives a wrong sense to πλεονεκτοῦντες, and the second involves too harsh an inversion.

26 **οὐκοῦν κτλ.** Cf. *Laws* 885 B θεοὺς ἡγούμενος εἶναι κατὰ νόμους οὐδεὶς πώποτε οὔτε ἔργον ἀσεβὲς εἰργάσατο ἑκὼν οὔτε λόγον ἀφῆκεν ἄνομον, ἀλλὰ ἓν δή τι τῶν τριῶν πάσχων, ἢ τοῦτο ὅπερ εἶπον οὐχ ἡγούμενος, ἢ τὸ δεύτερον ὄντας οὐ φροντίζειν ἀνθρώπων, ἢ τρίτον εὐπαραμυθήτους εἶναι θυσίαις τε καὶ εὐχαῖς παραγομένους. These three classes of heretics are severally refuted in 886 A—899 D, 899 D—905 D, 905 D—907 B. It is clear both from this passage and from the *Laws* that

εἰ μὲν μὴ εἰσὶν ἢ μηδὲν αὐτοῖς τῶν ἀνθρωπίνων μέλει, τί καὶ ἡμῖν
μελητέον τοῦ λανθάνειν; εἰ δὲ εἰσί τε καὶ ἐπιμελοῦνται, οὐκ E
ἄλλοθέν τοι αὐτοὺς ἴσμεν ἢ ἀκηκόαμεν ἢ ἔκ τε τῶν λόγων καὶ
τῶν γενεαλογησάντων ποιητῶν· οἱ δὲ αὐτοὶ οὗτοι λέγουσιν, ὡς
εἰσὶν οἷοι θυσίαις τε καὶ εὐχωλαῖς ἀγανῇσιν καὶ ἀναθήμασιν
παράγεσθαι ἀναπειθόμενοι· οἷς ἢ ἀμφότερα ἢ οὐδέτερα πειστέον·
εἰ δ' οὖν πειστέον, ἀδικητέον καὶ θυτέον ἀπὸ τῶν ἀδικημάτων.
δίκαιοι μὲν γὰρ ὄντες ἀζήμιοι ὑπὸ θεῶν ἐσόμεθα, τὰ δ' ἐξ ἀδικίας 366
κέρδη ἀπωσόμεθα· ἄδικοι δὲ κερδανοῦμέν τε καὶ λισσόμενοι ὑπερβαίνοντες καὶ ἁμαρτάνοντες πείθοντες αὐτοὺς ἀζήμιοι ἀπαλλάξομεν.
ἀλλὰ γὰρ ἐν Ἅιδου δίκην δώσομεν ὧν ἂν ἐνθάδε ἀδικήσωμεν,
ἢ αὐτοὶ ἢ παῖδες παίδων. ἀλλ' ὦ φίλε, φήσει λογιζόμενος, αἱ

27. τί καὶ *v*: καὶ ΑΠΞ: οὐδ' *q*.

---

the air was full of such heresies in Plato's day. The first was doubtless fostered by the sceptical attitude of Protagoras—περὶ μὲν θεῶν οὐκ ἔχω εἰδέναι οὔθ' ὡς εἰσὶν οὔθ' ὡς οὐκ εἰσίν (ap. D. L. IX 51): for the second cf. Aesch. *Ag.* 369—372 οὐκ ἔφα τις | θεοὺς βροτῶν ἀξιοῦσθαι μέλειν | ὅσοις ἀθίκτων χάρις | πατοῖθ'· ὁ δ' οὐκ εὐσεβής: the third—the most pernicious of all, according to Plato *Laws* 948 C—furnished the *raison d'être* of a degenerate priesthood.

27 **τί καὶ ἡμῖν κτλ.** 'If the gods do not care for us, why should we in our turn (καί) care' etc. For the text see *cr. n.* and App. III.

365 E 29 **ἀκηκόαμεν—ποιητῶν.** The first ἤ is 'or' and the second 'than.' In λόγων Plato may be thinking *inter alia* of the works of early λογογράφοι like Pherecydes, who wrote genealogies of gods and heroes in prose; but there is no occasion to change λόγων into λογίων with Muretus. γενεαλογησάντων ποιητῶν refers to Homer and the Hesiodic and Orphic theogonies.

31 **θυσίαις—ἀγανῇσιν**: see 364 D.

33 **ἀπό**: 'from the proceeds of.' Cf. *Laws* 906 C, D τοῦτον δὴ τὸν λόγον ἀναγκαῖον λέγειν τὸν λέγοντα ὡς εἰσὶ συγγνώμονες ἀεὶ θεοὶ τοῖς τῶν ἀνθρώπων ἀδίκοις καὶ ἀδικοῦσιν, ἂν αὐτοῖς τῶν ἀδικημάτων τις ἀπονέμῃ, καθάπερ κυσὶ λύκοι τῶν ἁρπασμάτων σμικρὰ ἀπονέμοιεν, οἱ δὲ ἡμερούμενοι τοῖς δώροις συγχωροῖεν τὰ ποίμνια διαρπάζειν.

366 A 2 **ὑπερβαίνοντες καὶ ἁμαρτάνοντες** are subordinate to λισσόμενοι: "by praying when we transgress and sin, we shall persuade them," etc. There is again a reference to λισσόμενοι ὅτε κέν τις ὑπερβήῃ καὶ ἁμάρτῃ quoted in 364 E. The position of the participles is justified by the allusion to this line.

5 **ἢ—ἤ.** It was a common Greek belief that the sins of the fathers are visited upon the children: see the passages cited by Nägelsbach *Nachhom. Theol.* pp. 34 ff. If we take Plato at his word, Adimantus represents this vicarious punishment as extending even to the other world.

ἢ παῖδες παίδων. Baiter conjectures <ἢ παῖδες> ἢ παῖδες παίδων, and so I formerly printed. But παῖδες παίδων means little more than 'descendants' (cf. *Laws* 927 B), and the text may stand. Similarly in Ruskin *Modern Painters* Ch. I "all those labours which men have given their lives and their sons' sons' lives to complete."

ὦ φίλε—λογιζόμενος. ὦ φίλε is the objector who urges ἀλλὰ γὰρ—παίδων. In φήσει Plato recurs to the singular of 365 B λέγοι γὰρ ἂν κτλ. λογιζόμενος is not 'reasoning,' but 'making his calculation,' 'calculos subducens': such a man's morality is nothing but a balancing of profit and loss. Hermann's devotion to Paris A led him to conjecture ἀλλ' ὠφελήσουσιν ἁγνιζομένους αἱ τελεταί rather than admit a simple case of omission

B τελεταὶ αὖ μέγα δύνανται καὶ οἱ λύσιοι θεοί, ὡς αἱ μέγισται | πόλεις
λέγουσι καὶ οἱ θεῶν παῖδες, ποιηταὶ καὶ προφῆται τῶν θεῶν
γενόμενοι, οἳ ταῦτα οὕτως ἔχειν μηνύουσιν.

IX. Κατὰ τίνα οὖν ἔτι λόγον δικαιοσύνην ἂν πρὸ μεγίστης
ἀδικίας αἱροίμεθ' ἄν; ἣν ἐὰν μετ' εὐσχημοσύνης κιβδήλου κτησώ-
μεθα, καὶ παρὰ θεοῖς καὶ παρ' ἀνθρώποις πράξομεν κατὰ νοῦν
ζῶντές τε καὶ τελευτήσαντες, ὡς ὁ τῶν πολλῶν τε καὶ ἄκρων
λεγόμενος λόγος. ἐκ δὴ πάντων τῶν εἰρημένων τίς μηχανή, ὦ
C Σώκρατες, δικαιοσύνην | τιμᾶν ἐθέλειν, ᾧ τις δύναμις ὑπάρχει
ψυχῆς ἢ χρημάτων ἢ σώματος ἢ γένους, ἀλλὰ μὴ γελᾶν ἐπαινου-
μένης ἀκούοντα; ὡς δή τοι εἴ τις ἔχει ψευδῆ μὲν ἀποφῆναι ἃ
εἰρήκαμεν, ἱκανῶς δὲ ἔγνωκεν ὅτι ἄριστον δικαιοσύνη, πολλήν
που συγγνώμην ἔχει καὶ οὐκ ὀργίζεται τοῖς ἀδίκοις, ἀλλ' οἶδεν,
ὅτι πλὴν εἴ τις θείᾳ φύσει δυσχεραίνων τὸ ἀδικεῖν ἢ ἐπιστήμην
D λαβὼν ἀπέχεται αὐτοῦ, τῶν γε ἄλλων | οὐδεὶς ἑκὼν δίκαιος, ἀλλὰ
ὑπὸ ἀνανδρίας ἢ γήρως ἤ τινος ἄλλης ἀσθενείας ψέγει τὸ ἀδικεῖν,
ἀδυνατῶν αὐτὸ δρᾶν. ὡς δέ, δῆλον· ὁ γὰρ πρῶτος τῶν τοιούτων
εἰς δύναμιν ἐλθὼν πρῶτος ἀδικεῖ, καθ' ὅσον ἂν οἷός τ' ᾖ. καὶ
τούτων ἁπάντων οὐδὲν ἄλλο αἴτιον ἢ ἐκεῖνο, ὅθενπερ ἅπας ὁ λόγος
οὗτος ὥρμησεν καὶ τῷδε καὶ ἐμοὶ πρὸς σέ, ὦ Σώκρατες, εἰπεῖν, ὅτι
E Ὦ θαυμάσιε, πάντων ὑμῶν, ὅσοι ἐπαινέται | φατὲ δικαιοσύνης

6. αὖ μέγα δύνανται Π: om. A. 22. ὡς δὲ $A^2Π^1$: ὧδε $A^1Π^2$.

---

arising from homoioteleuton: see *cr. n.* Vermehren proposes ἀλλ' ὠφελήσουσιν αἱ νομιζόμεναι τελεταί (*Plat. Stud.* p. 90), but we should certainly follow Π here. See also *Introd.* § 5.

6 **λύσιοι**: 'givers of absolution': cf. 364 E. Certain Chthonian deities of the Orphic theology are meant, such as Hecate, Demeter, Dionysus λύσιος or λυσεύς, and above all Ζεὺς μειλίχιος. See Lobeck *Aglaoph.* p. 303.

366 B 7 **θεῶν παῖδες**: e.g. Musaeus and Orpheus (Σελήνης τε καὶ Μουσῶν ἔγγονοι 364 E). Madvig's rejection of οἳ (so also Ficinus) before ταῦτα in the last clause seriously impairs the rhythm of the sentence.

12 **ἄκρων**. ἄκρος was a fashionable expression to apply to the *élite* of any profession or art: cf. *Theaet.* 152 E τῶν ποιητῶν οἱ ἄκροι τῆς ποιήσεως ἑκατέρας, *Pol.* 292 E, supra 360 E, infra III 405 A, V 459 B.

366 C 16 **ὡς δή τοι**: see on I 337 C.

19 **θείᾳ φύσει—ἐπιστήμην.** θείᾳ φύσει means a disposition which is good by divine grace or nature, not as the result of knowledge or compulsion. The virtue of such men is θείᾳ μοίρᾳ παραγιγνομένη ἄνευ νοῦ (*Men.* 99 E): they are ἄνευ ἀνάγκης, αὐτοφυῶς, θείᾳ μοίρᾳ ἀγαθοί (*Laws* 642 C), resembling Wordsworth's "Glad Hearts! without reproach or blot, Who do thy work and know it not." Cf. VI 493 A *n.* ἐπιστήμην is scientific knowledge of the good in the Socratic, not yet in the Platonic, sense.

366 D 20 **οὐδεὶς ἑκὼν δίκαιος** gives the lie to the Socratic οὐδεὶς ἑκὼν ἄδικος: cf. 360 C. For ἀνανδρίας below see on 359 B.

εἶναι, ἀπὸ τῶν ἐξ ἀρχῆς ἡρώων ἀρξάμενοι, ὅσων λόγοι λελειμμένοι,
μέχρι τῶν νῦν ἀνθρώπων οὐδεὶς πώποτε ἔψεξεν ἀδικίαν οὐδ'
ἐπῄνεσεν δικαιοσύνην ἄλλως ἢ δόξας τε καὶ τιμὰς καὶ δωρεὰς τὰς
ἀπ' αὐτῶν γιγνομένας· αὐτὸ δ' ἑκάτερον τῇ αὑτοῦ δυνάμει ἐν τῇ
τοῦ ἔχοντος ψυχῇ ἐνὸν καὶ λανθάνον θεούς τε καὶ ἀνθρώπους
οὐδεὶς πώποτε οὔτ' ἐν ποιήσει οὔτ' ἐν ἰδίοις λόγοις ἐπεξῆλθεν
ἱκανῶς τῷ λόγῳ, ὡς τὸ μὲν μέγιστον κακῶν ὅσα ἴσχει ψυχὴ ἐν
αὑτῇ, δικαιοσύνη δὲ μέγιστον ἀγαθόν. εἰ | γὰρ οὕτως ἐλέγετο ἐξ 367
ἀρχῆς ὑπὸ πάντων ὑμῶν καὶ ἐκ νέων ἡμᾶς ἐπείθετε, οὐκ ἂν
ἀλλήλους ἐφυλάττομεν μὴ ἀδικεῖν, ἀλλ' αὐτὸς αὑτοῦ ἦν ἕκαστος
φύλαξ, δεδιὼς μὴ ἀδικῶν τῷ μεγίστῳ κακῷ ξύνοικος ᾖ. ταῦτα,
ὦ Σώκρατες, ἴσως δὲ καὶ ἔτι τούτων πλείω Θρασύμαχός τε καὶ
ἄλλος πού τις ὑπὲρ δικαιοσύνης τε καὶ ἀδικίας λέγοιεν ἂν μετα-
στρέφοντες αὐτοῖν τὴν δύναμιν, φορτικῶς, ὥς γέ μοι δοκεῖ· ἀλλ'
ἐγώ, οὐδὲν γάρ σε δέομαι | ἀποκρύπτεσθαι, σοῦ ἐπιθυμῶν ἀκοῦσαι B
τἀναντία, ὡς δύναμαι μάλιστα κατατείνας λέγω. μὴ οὖν ἡμῖν
μόνον ἐνδείξῃ τῷ λόγῳ, ὅτι δικαιοσύνη ἀδικίας κρεῖττον, ἀλλὰ
τί ποιοῦσα ἑκατέρα τὸν ἔχοντα αὐτὴ δι' αὑτὴν ἡ μὲν κακόν, ἡ δὲ
ἀγαθόν ἐστιν· τὰς δὲ δόξας ἀφαίρει, ὥσπερ Γλαύκων διεκελεύσατο.
εἰ γὰρ μὴ ἀφαιρήσεις ἑκατέρωθεν τὰς ἀληθεῖς, τὰς δὲ ψευδεῖς
προσθήσεις, οὐ τὸ δίκαιον φήσομεν ἐπαινεῖν σε, ἀλλὰ τὸ δοκεῖν,
οὐδὲ τὸ ἄδικον | εἶναι ψέγειν, ἀλλὰ τὸ δοκεῖν, καὶ παρακελεύεσθαι C
ἄδικον ὄντα λανθάνειν, καὶ ὁμολογεῖν Θρασυμάχῳ, ὅτι τὸ μὲν

27. *εἶναι* Π: om. A. 15. *ἀλλὰ τὸ δοκεῖν* Π et in mg. A^2: om. A^1.

---

366 E 27 **ἡρώων.** J. and C. think "Plato is referring to well-known tales and maxims, which the poets and logographers had put into the mouths of ancient heroes." It is simpler to understand the expression of Orpheus, Musaeus, and other *θεῶν παῖδες, ποιηταὶ καὶ προφῆται τῶν θεῶν γενόμενοι*: see 366 B *n*. So also Dreinhöfer *Plato's Schrift üb. d. Staat nach Disposition u. Inhalt* p. 2 *n*. 16.

29 **ἄλλως ἤ.** Praise of the *δόξαι* of Justice is somewhat inaccurately spoken of as praise of justice itself: but it is unnecessary to insert *διά* (with Richards) before *δόξας*. Cf. 367 D *τῶν μὲν ἄλλων ἀποδεχοίμην ἂν οὕτως ἐπαινούντων δικαιοσύνην καὶ ψεγόντων ἀδικίαν, δόξας τε περὶ αὐτῶν καὶ μισθοὺς ἐγκωμιαζόντων καὶ λοιδορούντων.*

32 **ἰδίοις**: see on 363 E.

367 A 3 **ἀλλ' αὐτὸς—ξύνοικος ᾖ.** This thesis is developed and elaborated in *Gorg.* 472 D—481 B.

6 **ὑπέρ** is here little if anything more than *περί*, cf. *Laws* 777 A *ὑπὲρ τοῦ Διὸς ἀγορεύων*. This usage, which appears on Inscriptions after 300 B.C. (Meisterhans^3 p. 222), is very rare in Plato. It occurs occasionally in the Attic orators, especially with *λέγειν*, and is tolerably common in Polybius and later Greek: see Stephanus-Hase *Thes.* s. v. *ὑπέρ* and Jannaris *Hist. Gr. Gr.* § 1685. I do not think we are justified in translating (with Tucker) 'on behalf of their view of the relations of justice and injustice.'

367 B 9 **κατατείνας**: 358 D *n*.

δίκαιον ἀλλότριον ἀγαθόν, ξυμφέρον τοῦ κρείττονος, τὸ δὲ ἄδικον
αὑτῷ μὲν ξυμφέρον καὶ λυσιτελοῦν, τῷ δὲ ἥττονι ἀξύμφορον.
ἐπειδὴ οὖν ὡμολόγησας τῶν μεγίστων ἀγαθῶν εἶναι δικαιοσύνην,
ἃ τῶν τε ἀποβαινόντων ἀπ' αὐτῶν ἕνεκα ἄξια κεκτῆσθαι, πολὺ δὲ
μᾶλλον αὐτὰ αὑτῶν, οἷον ὁρᾶν, ἀκούειν, φρονεῖν, καὶ ὑγιαίνειν δή,
D καὶ ὅσ' ἄλλα ἀγαθὰ γόνιμα τῇ αὑτῶν φύσει ἀλλ' οὐ δόξῃ ἐστίν,—
τοῦτ' οὖν αὐτὸ ἐπαίνεσον δικαιοσύνης, ὃ αὐτὴ δι' αὑτὴν τὸν ἔχοντα
ὀνίνησιν καὶ ἀδικία βλάπτει· μισθοὺς δὲ καὶ δόξας πάρες ἄλλοις
ἐπαινεῖν. ὡς ἐγὼ τῶν μὲν ἄλλων ἀποδεχοίμην ἂν οὕτως ἐπαινούντων δικαιοσύνην καὶ ψεγόντων ἀδικίαν, δόξας τε περὶ αὐτῶν
καὶ μισθοὺς ἐγκωμιαζόντων καὶ λοιδορούντων, σοῦ δὲ οὐκ ἄν, εἰ
E μὴ σὺ κελεύοις, διότι πάντα τὸν βίον οὐδὲν ἄλλο σκοπῶν διελή-
λυθας ἢ τοῦτο. μὴ οὖν ἡμῖν ἐνδείξῃ μόνον τῷ λόγῳ, ὅτι δικαιοσύνη ἀδικίας κρεῖττον, ἀλλὰ τί ποιοῦσα ἑκατέρα τὸν ἔχοντα αὐτὴ
δι' αὑτήν, ἐάν τε λανθάνῃ ἐάν τε μὴ θεούς τε καὶ ἀνθρώπους,
ἣ μὲν ἀγαθόν, ἣ δὲ κακόν ἐστι.

X. Καὶ ἐγὼ ἀκούσας ἀεὶ μὲν δὴ τὴν φύσιν τοῦ τε Γλαύκωνος

18. μὲν A²Π: om. A¹. 25. ἀποδεχοίμην Π et in mg. A²: ἀποσχοίμην in contextu A.

---

367 C 17 **ἀλλότριον ἀγαθόν**: I 343 C *n*.

19 **ὡμολόγησας**: 358 A.

20 **πολὺ δὲ μᾶλλον**. The sequence of δέ after τε is frequent in Plato with δὲ καί, εἰ δὲ βούλει, τί δέ, ἔτι δέ, μέγιστον δέ, τὸ δὲ κεφάλαιον and the like. For a classified list of examples see Hoefer *de part. Plat.* pp. 15—17.

21 **ἀκούειν** is added to Glauco's list (357 C) by Adimantus, who is also responsible for the exaggeration πολὺ μᾶλλον.

καὶ—δή with ὑγιαίνειν marks it as different in kind from the other examples: cf. (with J. and C.) *Men.* 87 E καὶ πλοῦτος δή and infra 373 A.

367 D 22 **γόνιμα**: i.q. γνήσια, but more forcible: cf. *Theaet.* 151 E, Ar. *Frogs* 96.

24 **καὶ ἀδικία βλάπτει.** The sense is: καὶ ψέγε τοῦτ' αὐτὸ ἀδικίας ὃ αὐτὴ δι' αὑτὴν τὸν ἔχοντα βλάπτει. Hartman would cancel the words, needlessly, although the zeugma is bolder than usual. For the stylistic effect cf. ἀδικία δ' ἐπαινεῖται 358 A above.

25 **ἀποδεχοίμην** and ἀνασχοίμην are equally good Greek (cf. *Prot.* 339 D, *Phaed.* 92 A, E al.), but as ἀπο- is supported by both A and Π, it is more probable that the error lies in -σχοίμην than in ἀπο-, especially as ἀποδεχοίμην is found also in the margin of A. The ἀπο- is at least as old as the Scholium, which mentions the two readings ἀποσχοίμην and ἀνασχοίμην. The latter is an obvious correction of ἀποσχοίμην, and has survived in Ξ and a few inferior MSS besides.

367 E—**369** B *In a short interlude Socrates, after complimenting Glauco and Adimantus, remarks on the magnitude of the task before him—none other than the defence of Justice against her slanderers. As the weak-sighted are better able to recognise small letters at a distance if they have previously studied the same letters on a larger scale and on an ampler ground, so (says Socrates) let us first study Justice* in magno, *that is, in a state, and afterwards look for her lineaments* in parvo, *in other words, in the Individual. The contemplation of a State in process of creation will shew us Justice and Injustice coming into existence.*

καὶ τοῦ Ἀδειμάντου ἠγάμην, ἀτὰρ οὖν καὶ τότε πάνυ γε ἥσθην |
καὶ εἶπον· Οὐ κακῶς εἰς ὑμᾶς, ὦ παῖδες ἐκείνου τοῦ ἀνδρός, τὴν 368
ἀρχὴν τῶν ἐλεγείων ἐποίησεν ὁ Γλαύκωνος ἐραστής, εὐδοκιμή-
σαντας περὶ τὴν Μεγαροῖ μάχην, εἰπών·

παῖδες Ἀρίστωνος, κλεινοῦ θεῖον γένος ἀνδρός.

τοῦτό μοι, ὦ φίλοι, εὖ δοκεῖ ἔχειν· πάνυ γὰρ θεῖον πεπόνθατε,
εἰ μὴ πέπεισθε ἀδικίαν δικαιοσύνης ἄμεινον εἶναι, οὕτω δυνάμενοι
εἰπεῖν ὑπὲρ αὐτοῦ. δοκεῖτε δή μοι ὡς ἀληθῶς οὐ πεπεῖσθαι· |
τεκμαίρομαι δὲ ἐκ τοῦ ἄλλου τοῦ ὑμετέρου τρόπου, ἐπεὶ κατά γε B
αὐτοὺς τοὺς λόγους ἠπίστουν ἂν ὑμῖν· ὅσῳ δὲ μᾶλλον πιστεύω,
τοσούτῳ μᾶλλον ἀπορῶ ὅ τι χρήσωμαι· οὔτε γὰρ ὅπως βοηθῶ

10. χρήσωμαι $A^1Π$: χρήσομαι A^2.

---

368 A 1 **ὦ παῖδες ἐκείνου τοῦ ἀνδρός.** This curious phrase occurs once again in Plato viz. *Phil.* 36 D, where Protarchus is addressed in the words ὦ παῖ ἐκείνου τἀνδρός. Philebus has withdrawn from the discussion, his part in which he has bequeathed to Protarchus, who is therefore playfully called his son. That this is the meaning appears from *Phil.* 11 A, B, 11 C δέχει δὴ τοῦτον τὸν νῦν διδόμενον, ὦ Πρώταρχε, λόγον; Ἀνάγκη δέχεσθαι· Φίληβος γὰρ ἡμῖν ὁ καλὸς ἀπείρηκεν, 12 A, 16 B, 19 A: cf. also 15 C and 28 B. In precisely the same way Glauco and Adimantus are the 'children of Thrasymachus.' They are διάδοχοι τοῦ λόγου as appears from 357 A, 358 B (ἐπανανεώσομαι τὸν Θρασυμάχου λόγον), 367 A and 367 C, as well as from the substance of their arguments. This image is in fact one of the links by means of which Plato binds the dialogue together: as Polemarchus is heir to Cephalus (331 E), so Glauco and Adimantus are heirs to Thrasymachus. In explaining ἐκείνου τοῦ ἀνδρός of Thrasymachus, Stallbaum is therefore not "ridiculous" (as J. and C. assert) but right. See my article in *Cl. Rev.* X p. 237.

2 **ὁ Γλαύκωνος ἐραστής** may be Critias, as Schleiermacher supposed; but there is no evidence in support of the conjecture: see Bergk *Poet. Lyr. Gr.*[4] II p. 283.

3 **τὴν Μεγαροῖ μάχην**: perhaps in 409 B.C.: see Diod. Sic. XIII 65. If so, Plato is guilty of a slight anachronism, supposing that the scene of the dialogue is laid in 410. See *Introd.* § 3.

4 **παῖδες—ἀνδρός.** By Ἀρίστωνος, the author of the line of course meant Aristo, father of Glauco and Adimantus; but Ἀρίστων suggests ἄριστος (cf. IX 580 B) and the pun conveys a friendly, if half-ironical, compliment to 'his excellency' Thrasymachus, whose παῖδες (so far as the argument is concerned) Glauco and his brother are: see on ὦ παῖδες above. In *Symp.* 174 B, when inviting Aristodemus to come as an uninvited guest to sup with Agathon, Socrates indulges in a similarly playful pun: ἕπου τοίνυν, ἔφη, ἵνα καὶ τὴν παροιμίαν διαφθείρωμεν μεταβάλλοντες, ὡς ἄρα καὶ ἀγαθῶν ἐπὶ δαῖτας ἴασιν αὐτόματοι ἀγαθοί. (The διαφθορά consists in the substitution of ἀγαθῶν for δειλῶν, the form of the proverb which Plato had in view being αὐτόματοι δ' ἀγαθοὶ δειλῶν ἐπὶ δαῖτας ἴασιν, as the Scholiast remarks. Arnold Hug is ill-advised in adopting Lachmann's suggestion to read Ἀγάθων' i.e. Ἀγάθωνι for ἀγαθῶν: see *Cl. Rev.* X p. 238.) Other plays on proper names in Plato are collected by Riddell *Digest* pp. 250 f. In κλεινοῦ Stallbaum finds a 'lusus facetus' on ἐκείνου; but this particular *lusus* (if it exists) is accidental and unmeaning.

5 **θεῖον.** The addition of τι (proposed by Herwerden) is unnecessary: cf. III 388 D *n.* θεῖος is here used, like ἔνθεος, of inspiration: if the speaker does not understand or believe what he says, he is, like a rhapsodist or poet, nothing but the mouthpiece of the inspiring deity: cf. *Phaedr.* 245 A, *Ion* 533 E, 535 E—536 D.

ἔχω· δοκῶ γάρ μοι ἀδύνατος εἶναι· σημεῖον δέ μοι, ὅτι ἃ πρὸς
Θρασύμαχον λέγων ᾤμην ἀποφαίνειν, ὡς ἄμεινον δικαιοσύνη
ἀδικίας, οὐκ ἀπεδέξασθέ μου· οὔτ' αὖ ὅπως μὴ βοηθήσω ἔχω·
C δέδοικα γάρ, μὴ οὐδ' ὅσιον ᾖ παραγενόμενον δικαιοσύνῃ | κακη-
γορουμένῃ ἀπαγορεύειν καὶ μὴ βοηθεῖν ἔτι ἐμπνέοντα καὶ δυνάμενον
φθέγγεσθαι. κράτιστον οὖν οὕτως ὅπως δύναμαι ἐπικουρεῖν αὐτῇ.
ὅ τε οὖν Γλαύκων καὶ οἱ ἄλλοι ἐδέοντο παντὶ τρόπῳ βοηθῆσαι καὶ
μὴ ἀνεῖναι τὸν λόγον, ἀλλὰ διερευνήσασθαι τί τέ ἐστιν ἑκάτερον
καὶ περὶ τῆς ὠφελίας αὐτοῖν τἀληθὲς ποτέρως ἔχει. εἶπον οὖν
ὅπερ ἐμοὶ ἔδοξεν, ὅτι Τὸ ζήτημα ᾧ ἐπιχειροῦμεν οὐ φαῦλον ἀλλ'
D ὀξὺ βλέποντος, ὡς ἐμοὶ φαίνεται. | ἐπειδὴ οὖν ἡμεῖς οὐ δεινοί,
δοκεῖ μοι, ἦν δ' ἐγώ, τοιαύτην ποιήσασθαι ζήτησιν αὐτοῦ, οἵανπερ
ἂν εἰ προσέταξέ τις γράμματα σμικρὰ πόρρωθεν ἀναγνῶναι μὴ
πάνυ ὀξὺ βλέπουσιν, ἔπειτά τις ἐνενόησεν, ὅτι τὰ αὐτὰ γράμματα
ἔστι που καὶ ἄλλοθι μείζω τε καὶ ἐν μείζονι· ἕρμαιον ἂν ἐφάνη,
οἶμαι, ἐκεῖνα πρῶτον ἀναγνόντας οὕτως ἐπισκοπεῖν τὰ ἐλάττω,
εἰ τὰ αὐτὰ ὄντα τυγχάνει. Πάνυ μὲν οὖν, ἔφη ὁ Ἀδείμαντος·
E ἀλλὰ τί τοιοῦτον, ὦ Σώκρατες, | ἐν τῇ περὶ τὸ δίκαιον ζητήσει
καθορᾷς; Ἐγώ σοι, ἔφην, ἐρῶ. δικαιοσύνη, φαμέν, ἔστι μὲν
ἀνδρὸς ἑνός, ἔστι δέ που καὶ ὅλης πόλεως; Πάνυ γε, ἦ δ' ὅς.
Οὐκοῦν μεῖζον πόλις ἑνὸς ἀνδρός; Μεῖζον, ἔφη. Ἴσως τοίνυν
πλείων ἂν δικαιοσύνη ἐν τῷ μείζονι ἐνείη καὶ ῥᾴων καταμαθεῖν.
369 εἰ οὖν βούλεσθε, πρῶτον ἐν | ταῖς πόλεσι ζητήσωμεν ποῖόν τι

31. μεῖζον (bis) $A^1\Pi$: μείζων (bis) A^2.

---

368 C 18 **τί τέ ἐστιν—ἔχει** recalls the conclusion of Book I (354 B, C).

368 D 22 **οἵανπερ ἂν** sc. *ἐποιησάμεθα*, the verb being omitted as it frequently is with *ὥσπερ ἂν εἰ*.

25 **ἕρμαιον—τυγχάνει.** I have followed Schneider in printing a colon before *ἕρμαιον*: for the sentence *ἕρμαιον—τυγχάνει* is not the grammatical apodosis to the *εἰ* clause, but a further result. The asyndeton with *ἕρμαιον* is the usual asyndeton of ampliative clauses. For the principle underlying the method of inquiry here enunciated, see *Soph.* 218 C *ὅσα δ' αὖ τῶν μεγάλων δεῖ διαπονεῖσθαι καλῶς, περὶ τῶν τοιούτων δέδοκται πᾶσι καὶ πάλαι τὸ πρότερον ἐν σμικροῖς καὶ ῥᾴοσιν αὐτὰ δεῖν μελετᾶν, πρὶν ἐν αὐτοῖς τοῖς μεγίστοις* and *Pol.* 286 A. (Contrast *Phil.* 48 B, where the opposite course is recommended.) In the special case of the State versus the Individual, the words *ἐν σμικροῖς, ἐν ἐλάττοσιν* are not applicable, but *ἐν ῥᾴοσιν πρότερον δεῖ μελετᾶν* is the essential part of the principle, and Justice in the State is *ῥᾴων καταμαθεῖν* (368 E) than in the Individual. Cf. also infra 377 C *ἐν τοῖς μείζοσιν—μύθοις ὀψόμεθα καὶ τοὺς ἐλάττους.* Illustrations from letters are tolerably frequent in Plato: cf. e.g. IV 402 A f., *Theaet.* 205 D—206 A, *Pol.* 277 E ff.

368 E 33—**369** A 3 **πρῶτον—ἐπισκοποῦντες** lays down the method to be pursued in the rest of the treatise, except in books V—VII, which are professedly a 'digression,' and X, which is of the nature of an epilogue. At each suc-

ἐστιν· ἔπειτα οὕτως ἐπισκεψώμεθα καὶ ἐν ἑνὶ ἑκάστῳ, τὴν τοῦ
μείζονος ὁμοιότητα ἐν τῇ τοῦ ἐλάττονος ἰδέᾳ ἐπισκοποῦντες. Ἀλλά
μοι δοκεῖς, ἔφη, καλῶς λέγειν. Ἆρ' οὖν, ἦν δ' ἐγώ, εἰ γιγνομένην
πόλιν θεασαίμεθα λόγῳ, καὶ τὴν δικαιοσύνην αὐτῆς ἴδοιμεν ἂν
γιγνομένην καὶ τὴν ἀδικίαν; Τάχ' ἄν, ἦ δ' ὅς. Οὐκοῦν γενομένου
αὐτοῦ ἐλπὶς εὐπετέστερον ἰδεῖν ὃ ζητοῦμεν; | Πολύ γε. Δοκεῖ οὖν B
χρῆναι ἐπιχειρῆσαι περαίνειν; οἶμαι μὲν γὰρ οὐκ ὀλίγον ἔργον
αὐτὸ εἶναι· σκοπεῖτε οὖν. Ἔσκεπται, ἔφη ὁ Ἀδείμαντος· ἀλλὰ
μὴ ἄλλως ποίει.

---

cessive stage in the exposition of his subject, Plato reminds us more or less explicitly of the method which he here proposes to follow:—at the end of the first sketch of a State 371 E; in connexion with the φλεγμαίνουσα πόλις 372 E; before entering on the theory of education 376 C, D and again in III 392 C, when he has finished the treatment of λόγοι; at Adimantus' objection IV 420 B, C; at the end of the picture of the just state IV 427 D ff.; in passing to Justice in the Individual IV 434 D ff.; at V 472 B ff., where the question is raised 'Is this State possible?'; on beginning the account of the degenerate commonwealths and men in VIII 545 B; and finally when the whole argument draws to a head at IX 577 C.

369 A 2 **τὴν τοῦ μείζονος ὁμοιότητα.** Justice in the State is in fact to be used as a means of explaining Justice in the Individual, which is after all the real Justice: cf. IV 443 B ff. *nn.* The relation between the two is that of a παράδειγμα and that which the παράδειγμα is intended to explain: see *Pol.* 278 C οὐκοῦν τοῦτο μὲν ἱκανῶς συνειλήφαμεν, ὅτι παραδείγματός γ' ἐστὶ τότε γένεσις, ὁπόταν ὂν ταὐτὸν ἐν ἑτέρῳ διεσπασμένῳ, δοξαζόμενον ὀρθῶς καὶ συναχθὲν περὶ ἑκάτερον ὡς συνάμφω μίαν ἀληθῆ δόξαν ἀποτελῇ; Φαίνεται. Plato has been severely blamed (as e.g. by Grote *Plato* III pp. 123 ff.) for representing the Commonwealth as the Individual "writ large." Plato, however, laid stress upon this view, as tending to cement the union between the citizen and the State, which was rapidly dissolving in his day. This is well brought out by Krohn *Plat. Frag.* p. 5. Cf. also Pöhlmann *Gesch. d. antik. Kommunismus* etc. pp. 146 ff.

4 **εἰ γιγνομένην—ἀδικίαν.** This would lead us to expect that we are to discover Justice and Injustice in the same State. In the sequel we find Justice only in the Ideal City: it is the degenerate Cities of VIII and IX that furnish the picture of Injustice. Plato does not expressly announce his change of plan till IV 420 B, C: ᾠήθημεν γὰρ ἐν τῇ τοιαύτῃ μάλιστα ἂν εὑρεῖν δικαιοσύνην καὶ αὖ ἐν τῇ κάκιστα οἰκουμένῃ ἀδικίαν—νῦν μὲν οὖν—τὴν εὐδαίμονα πλάττομεν—αὐτίκα δὲ τὴν ἐναντίαν σκεψόμεθα. The discrepancy must, I think, be admitted (see Krohn *Pl. St.* p. 32, and Kunert *die doppelte Recens. d. Pl. St.* pp. 10 ff.), but such corrections and developments of plan are characteristic of the dialogue as a form of literature, and do not establish the theory of a double recension of the *Republic*. Cf. Grimmelt *de reip. Pl. comp. et unit.* p. 19, and Westerwick *de Rep. Pl.* pp. 43—45.

369 B—**372** D *The First Sketch of a City-state.*

A city is called into being by the fact that the individual is not self-sufficient. We may regard it as the union of many men mutually helping one another in one place. The individual gives and takes because he thinks it better for himself to do so.

Now man's first need is food, his second housing, his third clothing and the like. The smallest possible State will therefore consist of a farmer, a builder, a weaver and a shoemaker etc.—four or five men in all. Each of these must work for all, because Nature has adapted different men for different kinds of work, and because every kind of work has its critical moment when it must be done and cannot be neglected. Our principle is—One man, one work. We shall accordingly require carpenters and smiths to make instruments for the farmer, weaver, and shoemaker, as well as various kinds of herdsmen, to furnish cattle for ploughing and carrying, together with hides and fleeces for the makers of clothing. Since it is almost impossible to

XI. Γίγνεται τοίνυν, ἦν δ' ἐγώ, πόλις, ὡς ἐγᾦμαι, ἐπειδὴ
τυγχάνει ἡμῶν ἕκαστος οὐκ αὐτάρκης, ἀλλὰ πολλῶν ἐνδεής· ἢ τίν'
οἴει ἀρχὴν ἄλλην πόλιν οἰκίζειν; Οὐδεμίαν, ἦ δ' ὅς. Οὕτω δὴ
C ἄρα παραλαμβάνων ἄλλος ἄλλον ἐπ' ἄλλου, τὸν δ' ἐπ' ἄλλου
χρείᾳ, πολλῶν δεόμενοι, πολλοὺς εἰς μίαν οἴκησιν ἀγείραντες
κοινωνούς τε καὶ βοηθούς—ταύτῃ τῇ ξυνοικίᾳ ἐθέμεθα πόλιν

---

make the city self-supporting, we shall require middlemen to introduce imports; and as imports necessarily imply exports, the number of farmers and manufacturers in our city will increase, and we shall need travelling merchants to dispose of their produce. Owners of transport-ships will also be necessary, if there is traffic by sea.

Moreover, to facilitate exchange within the city, there must be a market, and coined money, and retail traders to act as middlemen between the producer and the consumer. The retail traders should be those who are physically unfit to engage in any other pursuit. There will also be hired labourers in our city.

Where then in such a commonwealth are Justice and Injustice? Along with which of the component parts of the State do they make their appearance? Adimantus suggests that we should look for them in the reciprocal intercourse of the various classes in the city. Let us see, says Socrates. The citizens will live the simple easy-going life of vegetarians, satisfying only the modest demands of their natural appetites. On a hint from Glauco, a few additional vegetarian luxuries are conceded.

369 B 11 **γίγνεται—πόλις κτλ.** The present episode is ostensibly an historical account of the genesis of society, and from this point of view should be compared with *Laws* III 676 A ff. Some of the features are derived from an analysis of the industrial basis of society as it exists in civilised times: others (see 372 B—D), are semi-mythical and idyllic, recalling pictures of the golden age such as we find in *Pol.* 269 C ff., and in the caricatures of the comedians (e.g. ap. Athen. VI 267 E ff.). But the prevailing atmosphere is not historical or legendary, but idealistic (note δεῖ in 369 E and elsewhere), and Plato's πρώτη πόλις (Arist. *Pol.* Δ 4. 1291ᵃ 17) should primarily be regarded as—in its essential features—a preliminary and provisional description of the industrial foundation on which the higher parts of his own ideal city are to rest. Cf. also on 372 B, D, Rettig *Proleg. in Plat. remp.* p. 42 and Steinhart *Einleitung* p. 156.

12 **τυγχάνει** as a mere copula is very rare in Attic prose, and it would be easy here to insert ὤν after πολλῶν: see Porson on Eur. *Hec.* 782. In the Platonic dialogues this usage recurs in *Phaedr.* 263 C, *Gorg.* 502 B, *Alc.* I 129 A, 133 A, *Hipp. Mai.* 300 A, *Laws* 918 C, *Tim.* 61 C, nor is it possible in the last three examples to account for its omission by lipography. The idiom occurs in Sophocles and Euripides, once in Aristophanes (*Eccl.* 1141), and (though condemned by Phrynichus) must also be admitted (though rarely) in prose: see the instances cited by Blaydes on Ar. (l.c.) and cf. Rutherford's *New Phrynichus* p. 342.

πολλῶν ἐνδεής. In the account of the genesis of society given in the *Laws* (676 A—680 E), more stress is laid on the social instinct of man: in *Prot.* 322 B ff the operating cause is man's defencelessness against wild beasts. Grote (*Plato* III p. 139 *n.*) censures Plato for not mentioning the "reciprocal liability of injury" among the generative causes of civic life; but this (as well as assistance against external aggression) is hinted at in βοηθούς.

14 **ἄλλος—χρείᾳ.** The words are short for ἄλλος ἄλλον, τὸν μὲν ἐπ' ἄλλου, τὸν δ' ἐπ' ἄλλου χρείᾳ (for the omission of τὸν μέν cf. *Prot.* 330 A, *Theaet.* 181 D al.): 'one taking to himself one man, another another—the one man for one, the other for another purpose.' Essentially the same meaning would no doubt be conveyed without τὸν δ' ἐπ' ἄλλου, which Herwerden following two inferior MSS would omit; but the fuller form of expression is chosen in order, I think, to prepare us for the principle of 'One man, one work' to be presently enunciated.

16 **ταύτῃ τῇ ξυνοικίᾳ.** Stallbaum rightly regards the sentence as an anaco-

ὄνομα. ἦ γάρ; Πάνυ μὲν οὖν. Μεταδίδωσι δὴ ἄλλος ἄλλῳ,
εἴ τι μεταδίδωσιν, ἢ μεταλαμβάνει, οἰόμενος αὑτῷ ἄμεινον εἶναι;
Πάνυ γε. Ἴθι δή, ἦν δ' ἐγώ, τῷ λόγῳ ἐξ ἀρχῆς ποιῶμεν πόλιν.
ποιήσει δὲ αὐτήν, ὡς ἔοικεν, ἡ ἡμετέρα χρεία. Πῶς δ' οὔ; Ἀλλὰ
μὴν πρώτη γε καὶ μεγίστη | τῶν χρειῶν ἡ τῆς τροφῆς παρασκευὴ D
τοῦ εἶναί τε καὶ ζῆν ἕνεκα. Παντάπασί γε. Δευτέρα δὴ οἰκήσεως,
τρίτη δὲ ἐσθῆτος καὶ τῶν τοιούτων. Ἔστι ταῦτα. Φέρε δή, ἦν δ'
ἐγώ, πῶς ἡ πόλις ἀρκέσει ἐπὶ τοσαύτην παρασκευήν; ἄλλο τι
γεωργὸς μὲν εἷς, ὁ δὲ οἰκοδόμος, ἄλλος δέ τις ὑφάντης; ἢ καὶ
σκυτοτόμον αὐτόσε προσθήσομεν, ἤ τιν' ἄλλον τῶν περὶ τὸ σῶμα
θεραπευτήν; Πάνυ γε. Εἴη δ' ἂν ἥ γε ἀναγκαιοτάτη πόλις ἐκ
τεττάρων ἢ πέντε ἀνδρῶν. | Φαίνεται. Τί δὴ οὖν; ἕνα ἕκαστον E
τούτων δεῖ τὸ αὑτοῦ ἔργον ἅπασι κοινὸν κατατιθέναι, οἷον τὸν
γεωργὸν ἕνα ὄντα παρασκευάζειν σιτία τέτταρσιν καὶ τετραπλάσιον
χρόνον τε καὶ πόνον ἀναλίσκειν ἐπὶ σίτου παρασκευῇ, καὶ ἄλλοις
κοινωνεῖν, ἢ ἀμελήσαντα ἑαυτῷ μόνον τέταρτον μέρος ποιεῖν τούτου
τοῦ | σιτίου ἐν τετάρτῳ μέρει τοῦ χρόνου, τὰ δὲ τρία, τὸ μὲν ἐπὶ 370
τῇ τῆς οἰκίας παρασκευῇ διατρίβειν, τὸ δὲ ἱματίου, τὸ δὲ ὑποδημάτων, καὶ μὴ ἄλλοις κοινωνοῦντα πράγματα ἔχειν, ἀλλ' αὐτὸν
δι' αὑτὸν τὰ αὑτοῦ πράττειν; καὶ ὁ Ἀδείμαντος ἔφη, Ἀλλ' ἴσως,
ὦ Σώκρατες, οὕτω ῥᾷον ἢ 'κείνως. Οὐδέν, ἦν δ' ἐγώ, μὰ Δία

1. σιτίου A²Π: σίτου A¹. 5. ῥᾷον q: ῥᾴδιον ΑΠΞ.

---

luthon, the antecedent to ταύτῃ being the words from παραλαμβάνων to βοηθούς. If the subject to ἐθέμεθα (a gnomic aorist) were ἄλλος—δεόμενοι—ἀγείραντες, we should probably have had παραλαμβάνοντες for παραλαμβάνων: and besides, Plato is not yet describing the particular city which we are ποιεῖν λόγῳ (infra line 19), but laying down the law as to the γένεσις of cities in general. For the anacoluthon see Engelhardt *Anac. Pl. Spec.* III p. 40.

369 D 26 **τῶν περὶ τὸ σῶμα**: neuter, not masculine; otherwise Plato would have written θεραπευτῶν (as in *q* and some other MSS).

27 **ἀναγκαιοτάτη πόλις.** Referring to this passage, Aristotle (*Pol.* Δ 4. 1291ᵃ 10—19) attacks Plato for making the end of his city not τὸ καλόν, but τὰ ἀναγκαῖα. No doubt, the end of this 'first city'—so Aristotle calls it—is primarily τὰ ἀναγκαῖα; but Plato would reply that the cities of the farmers, the auxiliaries, and the rulers, are in reality *one* city, γινομένη μὲν τοῦ ζῆν ἕνεκεν, οὖσα δὲ τοῦ εὖ ζῆν (Arist. *Pol.* A 2. 1252ᵇ 29. Cf. *Laws* 828 D δεῖ δὲ αὐτὴν καθάπερ ἕνα ἄνθρωπον ζῆν εὖ).

369 E 28 **ἕνα ἕκαστον κτλ.** Cf. *Charm.* 161 E δοκεῖ ἄν σοι πόλις εὖ οἰκεῖσθαι ὑπὸ τούτου τοῦ νόμου τοῦ κελεύοντος τὸ ἑαυτοῦ ἱμάτιον ἕκαστον ὑφαίνειν καὶ πλύνειν, καὶ ὑποδήματα σκυτοτομεῖν, καὶ λήκυθον καὶ στλεγγίδα καὶ τἆλλα πάντα κατὰ τὸν αὐτὸν λόγον κτλ.;

370 A 5 **οὕτω ῥᾷον ἢ 'κείνως.** οὕτω refers to the alternative which is more familiar, although mentioned first: cf. (with Ast) Xen. *Mem.* I 3. 13 τοῦτο τὸ θηρίον—τοσούτῳ δεινότερόν ἐστι τῶν φαλαγγίων ὅσῳ ἐκεῖνα μὲν ἁψάμενα, τοῦτο δὲ οὐδ' ἁπτόμενον—ἐνίησί τι. On the corruption ῥᾴδιον for ῥᾷον (also in *Men.* 94 E) see *Introd.* § 5.

ἄτοπον. ἐννοῶ γὰρ καὶ αὐτὸς εἰπόντος σοῦ, ὅτι πρῶτον μὲν
B φύεται ἕκαστος οὐ πάνυ | ὅμοιος ἑκάστῳ, ἀλλὰ διαφέρων τὴν
φύσιν, ἄλλος ἐπ' ἄλλου ἔργου πρᾶξιν. ἢ οὐ δοκεῖ σοι; Ἔμοιγε.
Τί δέ; πότερον κάλλιον πράττοι ἄν τις εἷς ὢν πολλὰς τέχνας
ἐργαζόμενος, ἢ ὅταν μίαν εἷς; Ὅταν, ἦ δ' ὅς, εἷς μίαν. Ἀλλὰ
μήν, οἶμαι, καὶ τόδε δῆλον, ὡς, ἐάν τίς τινος παρῇ ἔργου καιρόν,
διόλλυται. Δῆλον γάρ. Οὐ γάρ, οἶμαι, ἐθέλει τὸ πραττόμενον
τὴν τοῦ πράττοντος σχολὴν περιμένειν, ἀλλ' ἀνάγκη τὸν πράτ-
C τοντα τῷ πραττομένῳ | ἐπακολουθεῖν μὴ ἐν παρέργου μέρει.
Ἀνάγκη. Ἐκ δὴ τούτων πλείω τε ἕκαστα γίγνεται καὶ κάλλιον
καὶ ῥᾷον, ὅταν εἷς ἓν κατὰ φύσιν καὶ ἐν καιρῷ, σχολὴν τῶν ἄλλων
ἄγων, πράττῃ. Παντάπασι μὲν οὖν. Πλειόνων δή, ὦ Ἀδείμαντε,
δεῖ πολιτῶν ἢ τεττάρων ἐπὶ τὰς παρασκευὰς ὧν ἐλέγομεν. ὁ γὰρ
γεωργός, ὡς ἔοικεν, οὐκ αὐτὸς ποιήσεται ἑαυτῷ τὸ ἄροτρον, εἰ
D μέλλει καλὸν εἶναι, | οὐδὲ σμινύην οὐδὲ τἆλλα ὄργανα ὅσα περὶ
γεωργίαν. οὐδ' αὖ ὁ οἰκοδόμος· πολλῶν δὲ καὶ τούτῳ δεῖ. ὡσαύ-

9. τις A^2Π : τι A^1.

7 **φύεται** strikes the keynote of the City of Books II—IV. The first critic to lay sufficient stress on this point was Krohn: see *Pl. St.* pp. 59—62, where he collects the references to *φύσις* throughout Books I—IV. The City of II—IV is a *κατὰ φύσιν οἰκισθεῖσα πόλις*. What is meant by *φύσις*? Not inorganic Nature, but the 'nature' of a *πόλις* or aggregate of *πολῖται*, i.e. (as the unit in a city is the man) human nature, in other words, the nature of the human soul, which, according to Plato and Socrates, constitutes a man's true and proper individuality. It is not however human nature as it is, but as it ought to be, which is the foundation on which the Platonic State is built; so that, although the doctrine of transcendent Ideas is excluded from the first four books (see on III 402 C), Idealism at all events is present. See also Krohn *Plat. Frage* pp. 8—11, and (for the connotation of *φύσις*) Benn's article on 'The Idea of Nature in Plato' in *Archiv f. Gesch. d. Phil.* IX pp. 24—49 and Pöhlmann l.c. pp. 110 ff.

370 B 10 **ὅταν—εἷς μίαν.** This principle—the cardinal principle of the *Republic*, reiterated also with great emphasis in *Laws* 846 D—847 B—is deduced by Plato from *φύσις*, whose rule is specialization: cf. 370 C *ὅταν εἷς ἓν κατὰ φύσιν—πράττῃ*. Plato (as usual in the *Republic*) is thinking of *Man's* nature, one man being naturally fitted for one pursuit, another for another: cf. III 395 B, IV 433 A, 434 A, B. The principle of specialization had already been enunciated by Socrates: see e.g. Xen. *Mem.* III 9. 3, 15, *Cyrop.* VIII 2. 5, 6. Aristotle widens it into a general law of Nature: *οὐθὲν γὰρ ἡ φύσις ποιεῖ τοιοῦτον οἷον οἱ χαλκοτύποι τὴν Δελφικὴν μάχαιραν πενιχρῶς, ἀλλ' ἓν πρὸς ἕν* (*Pol.* A 2. 1252^b^ 1 ff.). In its application to politics, the principle becomes in Plato's hands a weapon for attacking the foundations of Athenian democracy (see *Gorg.* 455 A—C), to which, in this respect, his own Ideal City was a kind of counterblast.

370 C 15 **κάλλιον.** Did Plato write *καλλίω*? *κάλλιον γίγνεται* may no doubt mean 'are better made,' which is fairly satisfactory in point of sense, but *καλλίω* forms a better balance to *πλείω τε*, and is more suited to *καλόν* just below. With *ῥᾷον* immediately following, the corruption would be easy. On the other hand the collocation *καλλίω καὶ ῥᾷον* is unpleasing, and it is probably safer to adhere to the MSS.

τως δ' ὁ ὑφάντης τε καὶ ὁ σκυτοτόμος. Ἀληθῆ. Τέκτονες δὴ καὶ χαλκῆς καὶ τοιοῦτοί τινες πολλοὶ δημιουργοί, κοινωνοὶ ἡμῖν τοῦ πολιχνίου γιγνόμενοι, συχνὸν αὐτὸ ποιοῦσιν. Πάνυ μὲν οὖν. Ἀλλ' οὐκ ἄν πω πάνυ γε μέγα τι εἴη, εἰ αὐτοῖς βουκόλους τε καὶ ποιμένας τούς τε ἄλλους νομέας προσθεῖμεν, | ἵνα οἵ τε γεωργοὶ **E** ἐπὶ τὸ ἀροῦν ἔχοιεν βοῦς, οἵ τε οἰκοδόμοι πρὸς τὰς ἀγωγὰς μετὰ τῶν γεωργῶν χρῆσθαι ὑποζυγίοις, ὑφάνται δὲ καὶ σκυτοτόμοι δέρμασίν τε καὶ ἐρίοις. Οὐδέ γε, ἦ δ' ὅς, σμικρὰ πόλις ἂν εἴη ἔχουσα πάντα ταῦτα. Ἀλλὰ μήν, ἦν δ' ἐγώ, κατοικίσαι γε αὐτὴν τὴν πόλιν εἰς τοιοῦτον τόπον, οὗ ἐπεισαγωγίμων μὴ δεήσεται, σχεδόν τι ἀδύνατον. Ἀδύνατον γάρ. Προσδεήσει ἄρα ἔτι καὶ ἄλλων, οἳ ἐξ ἄλλης πόλεως αὐτῇ κομιοῦσιν ὧν δεῖται. Δεήσει. Καὶ μὴν κενὸς ἂν ἴῃ ὁ διάκονος, μηδὲν ἄγων ὧν ἐκεῖνοι δέονται, παρ' ὧν ἂν κομίζωνται ὧν ἂν αὐτοῖς | χρεία, κενὸς ἄπεισιν. ἦ γάρ; **371** Δοκεῖ μοι. Δεῖ δὴ τὰ οἴκοι μὴ μόνον ἑαυτοῖς ποιεῖν ἱκανά, ἀλλὰ καὶ οἷα καὶ ὅσα ἐκείνοις ὧν ἂν δέωνται. Δεῖ γάρ. Πλειόνων δὴ γεωργῶν τε καὶ τῶν ἄλλων δημιουργῶν δεῖ ἡμῖν τῇ πόλει. Πλειόνων γάρ. Καὶ δὴ καὶ τῶν ἄλλων διακόνων που τῶν τε εἰσαξόντων καὶ ἐξαξόντων ἕκαστα. οὗτοι δέ εἰσιν ἔμποροι· ἦ γάρ; Ναί. Καὶ ἐμπόρων δὴ δεησόμεθα. Πάνυ γε. Καὶ ἐὰν μέν γε κατὰ θάλατταν ἡ ἐμπορία γίγνηται, συχνῶν | καὶ ἄλλων προσδεή- **B** σεται τῶν ἐπιστημόνων τῆς περὶ τὴν θάλατταν ἐργασίας. Συχνῶν μέντοι.

34. κενὸς A²Π: ἐκεῖνος A¹. ἴῃ q: εἴη ΑΠΞ.

---

370 E 27 **ἐπὶ τὸ ἀροῦν.** See on 372 B.

30 **αὐτὴν τὴν πόλιν**: *ipsam urbem*: the city as opposed to the inhabitants (τέκτονες, χαλκῆς etc.). Cf. 360 D *n.* It is not necessary to adopt Hermann's conjecture αὖ for αὐτήν, or (with Hartman) to eject τὴν πόλιν.

32 **σχεδόν τι ἀδύνατον.** Plato nevertheless endeavours to secure this advantage in the *Laws*: see 704 A—705 B. Cf. Arist. *Pol.* H 5. 1326ᵇ 26 ff.

34 **ὧν ἐκεῖνοι δέονται.** All exchange with foreign cities is to be in kind: money is used only for transactions within the city: see infra 371 C ff. Here again Plato is constructing his city κατὰ φύσιν: cf. Arist. *Pol.* A 9. 1257ᵃ 28 ἡ μὲν οὖν τοιαύτη μεταβλητικὴ οὔτε παρὰ φύσιν οὔτε χρηματιστικῆς ἐστὶν εἶδος οὐδέν.

35 **ὧν ἂν αὐτοῖς χρεία.** αὐτοῖς is of course emphatic (*ipsis*). For the rare omission of ᾖ cf. III 416 D and Schanz *Nov. Comm. Pl.* p. 33 with Cope's *Rhetoric of Aristotle* Vol. II p. 328.

371 A 3 **ὧν ἂν δέωνται.** ὧν is masculine in spite of ὧν ἐκεῖνοι δέονται just above. The reading of q ἐκείνοις ἄξουσιν, οἳ μεταδώσουσιν ὧν ἂν δέωνται is a free correction (after 371 B) intended to make ὧν neuter.

371 B 9 **τῆς—ἐργασίας** is not the work of a seaman (as Jowett seems to suppose), but a special department of ἐμπορία, viz. ναυκληρία: see Arist. *Pol.* A 11. 1258ᵇ 21 ff. The ναύκληρος owned a ship and conveyed passengers and cargo for payment (cf. *Gorg.* 511 D, E): he is frequently mentioned along with the ἔμπορος, e.g. *Pol.* 290 A ἐμπόρους καὶ

XII. Τί δὲ δή; ἐν αὐτῇ τῇ πόλει πῶς ἀλλήλοις μεταδώσουσιν ὧν ἂν ἕκαστοι ἐργάζωνται; ὧν δὴ ἕνεκα καὶ κοινωνίαν ποιησάμενοι πόλιν ᾠκίσαμεν. Δῆλον δή, ἦ δ' ὅς, ὅτι πωλοῦντες καὶ ὠνούμενοι. Ἀγορὰ δὴ ἡμῖν καὶ νόμισμα ξύμβολον τῆς ἀλλαγῆς ἕνεκα γενή- **C** σεται ἐκ τούτου. Πάνυ μὲν οὖν. Ἂν οὖν κομίσας ὁ γεωργὸς εἰς τὴν ἀγοράν τι ὧν ποιεῖ, ἤ τις ἄλλος τῶν δημιουργῶν, μὴ εἰς τὸν αὐτὸν χρόνον ἥκῃ τοῖς δεομένοις τὰ παρ' αὐτοῦ ἀλλάξασθαι, ἀργήσει τῆς αὑτοῦ δημιουργίας καθήμενος ἐν ἀγορᾷ; Οὐδαμῶς, ἦ δ' ὅς, ἀλλὰ εἰσὶν οἳ τοῦτο ὁρῶντες ἑαυτοὺς ἐπὶ τὴν διακονίαν τάττουσιν ταύτην, ἐν μὲν ταῖς ὀρθῶς οἰκουμέναις πόλεσι σχεδόν τι οἱ ἀσθενέστατοι τὰ σώματα καὶ ἀχρεῖοί τι ἄλλο ἔργον πράττειν. **D** αὐτοῦ γὰρ δεῖ μένοντας αὐτοὺς περὶ τὴν ἀγορὰν τὰ μὲν ἀντ' ἀργυρίου ἀλλάξασθαι τοῖς τι δεομένοις ἀποδόσθαι, τοῖς δὲ ἀντὶ αὖ ἀργυρίου διαλλάττειν, ὅσοι τι δέονται πρίασθαι. Αὕτη ἄρα, ἦν δ' ἐγώ, ἡ χρεία καπήλων ἡμῖν γένεσιν ἐμποιεῖ τῇ πόλει. ἢ οὐ καπήλους καλοῦμεν τοὺς πρὸς ὠνήν τε καὶ πρᾶσιν διακονοῦντας ἱδρυμένους ἐν ἀγορᾷ, τοὺς δὲ πλάνητας ἐπὶ τὰς πόλεις ἐμπόρους; Πάνυ μὲν οὖν. Ἔτι δή τινες, ὡς ἐγᾦμαι, εἰσὶ καὶ ἄλλοι διάκονοι, **E** οἳ ἂν τὰ μὲν τῆς διανοίας μὴ πάνυ ἀξιοκοινώνητοι ὦσιν, τὴν δὲ τοῦ σώματος ἰσχὺν ἱκανὴν ἐπὶ τοὺς πόνους ἔχωσιν· οἳ δὴ πωλοῦντες τὴν τῆς ἰσχύος χρείαν, τὴν τιμὴν ταύτην μισθὸν καλοῦντες, κέκληνται, ὡς ἐγᾦμαι, μισθωτοί· ἦ γάρ; Πάνυ μὲν οὖν. Πλήρωμα

ναυκλήρους καὶ καπήλους, *Laws* 831 E, Xen. *Vect.* 3. 4, 5. 3.

12 **ὧν δὴ ἕνεκα.** *ὧν* can hardly (as J. and C. suppose) refer to *μεταδώσουσιν*: it must denote the same objects as the previous *ὧν*. The meaning is 'for the sake of which things we established the principle of community and founded a city.' Cf. 369 C *κοινωνοὺς—μεταδίδωσι δὴ ἄλλος ἄλλῳ κτλ.*

14 **νόμισμα—ἕνεκα.** Cf. *Laws* 742 A *νόμισμα δ' ἕνεκα ἀλλαγῆς τῆς καθ' ἡμέραν.* See also 370 E *n.* Plato regards coined money as a necessary evil—the offspring, not of *φύσις*, but of *νόμος* (cf. Arist. *Eth. Nic.* V 8. 1133^a 30 ff. *διὰ τοῦτο τοὔνομα ἔχει νόμισμα, ὅτι οὐ φύσει ἀλλὰ νόμῳ ἐστί* and *Pol.* A 9. 1257^b 10 ff.), a mere conventional symbol, the private possession of which is denied to the highest classes of the State (III 416 D ff.).

371 C 21 **οἱ ἀσθενέστατοι κτλ.** Cf. *Laws* 918 A—920 C, where *καπηλεία* is confined by Plato to those *ὧν διαφθειρομένων οὐκ ἂν γίγνοιτο μεγάλη λύμη τῇ πόλει* (919 C).

371 D 26 **καπήλους—ἐμπόρους.** *Soph.* 223 D *τῆς μεταβλητικῆς οὐχ ἡ μὲν κατὰ πόλιν ἀλλαγή, σχεδὸν αὐτῆς ἥμισυ μέρος ὄν, καπηλικὴ προσαγορεύεται; Ναί. Τὸ δέ γε ἐξ ἄλλης εἰς ἄλλην πόλιν διαλλαττόμενον ὠνῇ καὶ πράσει ἐμπορική; Τί δ' οὔ;*

371 E 29 **ἀξιοκοινώνητοι**: worthy of being admitted into the *κοινωνία* of our city. This explanation (Schneider's) is better than 'worthy of one's society' (L. and S.).

31 **τὴν τιμὴν ταύτην.** *ταύτην* is idiomatic for *ταύτης*: see I 333 B *n.*

32 **μισθωτοί.** Plato does not admit slave labour in his city, unless perhaps in the persons of barbarians. The exclusion of slaves is also a touch of 'Nature': cf. Arist. *Pol.* A 3. 1253^b 20 *τοῖς δὲ παρὰ φύσιν* (sc. *δοκεῖ*) *τὸ δεσπόζειν* with Suse-

δὴ πόλεώς εἰσιν, ὡς ἔοικε, καὶ μισθωτοί. Δοκεῖ μοι. Ἆρ' οὖν, ὦ Ἀδείμαντε, ἤδη ἡμῖν ηὔξηται ἡ πόλις, ὥστ' εἶναι τελέα; Ἴσως. Ποῦ οὖν ἄν ποτε ἐν αὐτῇ εἴη ἥ τε δικαιοσύνη καὶ ἡ ἀδικία; καὶ τίνι ἅμα ἐγγενομένη ὧν ἐσκέμμεθα; Ἐγὼ μέν, ἔφη, | **372** οὐκ ἐννοῶ, ὦ Σώκρατες, εἰ μή που ἐν αὐτῶν τούτων χρείᾳ τινὶ τῇ πρὸς ἀλλήλους. Ἀλλ' ἴσως, ἦν δ' ἐγώ, καλῶς λέγεις· καὶ σκεπτέον γε καὶ οὐκ ἀποκνητέον.

πρῶτον οὖν σκεψώμεθα, τίνα τρόπον διαιτήσονται οἱ οὕτω παρεσκευασμένοι. ἄλλο τι ἢ σῖτόν τε ποιοῦντες καὶ οἶνον καὶ ἱμάτια καὶ ὑποδήματα; καὶ οἰκοδομησάμενοι οἰκίας θέρους μὲν τὰ πολλὰ γυμνοί τε καὶ ἀνυπόδητοι ἐργάσονται, τοῦ δὲ χειμῶνος ἠμφιεσμένοι τε καὶ | **B** ὑποδεδεμένοι ἱκανῶς· θρέψονται δὲ ἐκ μὲν

34. ἡ A^2Π : om. A^1.

---

mihl and Hicks *ad loc.* If barbarians may be enslaved, it is because they are φύσει δοῦλοι: cf. V 469 B ff., with 470 C and Arist. *Pol.* A 2. 1252^b 9 ταὐτὸ φύσει βάρβαρον καὶ δοῦλον.

372 A 2 **ἐν αὐτῶν—ἀλλήλους.** The reply is to the first question, not to the second: see on V 465 E. In so far as δικαιοσύνη can be said to exist in so elementary a state, Plato would have identified it with the performance by each class (farmers, artisans, etc.) of their own work and no more. This is the *first* view of δικαιοσύνη in the *Republic*: for the *second* see IV 432 ff., 441 D ff., and for the *third* or metaphysical VI 504 B *n.*

7 **ὑποδήματα.** I have placed the mark of interrogation after ὑποδήματα, as it is only the present participles which belong to διαιτήσονται. 'And when they have built themselves houses' marks a fresh start, no longer interrogative, for which reason I have also departed from the usual punctuation after ἱκανῶς (in B) and πόλεμον (in C).

372 B 9 **θρέψονται κτλ.** The picture which Plato proceeds to draw represents the working of well-regulated ἐπιθυμία or appetite—the psychological groundwork of the third or lowest order in Plato's city. τὰ μέν is the wheaten meal (ἄλευρα), τὰ δέ the barley-meal (ἄλφιτα). Only the wheaten meal was (as a rule) baked (πέσσειν or ὀπτᾶν) into loaves (ἄρτοι): the barley-meal was "kneaded into a simple dough (μάσσειν, whence μᾶζα), dried in a mould, and afterwards moistened with water and eaten" (Blümner, *Gr. Privatalt.* p. 218). μᾶζαι made of barley meal was the staple food of the common Greek: the wheaten loaf was a luxury. The double chiasmus ἄλφιτα, μάξαντες, μάζας)(ἄλευρα, πέψαντες, ἄρτους is noticeable: cf. *Crito* 47 C.

It will be observed that the inhabitants of this 'First City' subsist upon a vegetable diet. Cattle are used for ploughing and carrying, and supply wool and skins to make clothing and shoes (370 D, E), but animal food is unknown. It is improbable that Plato deliberately borrowed this trait from the current legends about the golden age (cf. *Pol.* 271 D ff.): for he allows the slaughter of cattle for skins, whereas in the golden age animal life was held sacred (see Empedocles ap. Arist. *Rhet.* I 13. 1373^b 14 ff. and Robertson Smith *Religion of the Semites* pp. 282 ff.). But he no doubt regarded vegetarianism as characteristic of the primitive innocence of a pastoral community (*Laws* 782 A—D). In Plato's days, as now, the Greek peasant was almost a vegetarian. To argue from this and kindred passages (esp. *Tim.* 77 A—C and 80 E) as Teichmüller does (*Lit. Fehd.* II pp. 187—202), that Plato was himself a vegetarian, is somewhat hazardous. Whether Plato wished his farmers to be vegetarians or not, he permits the soldiers to eat flesh: cf. III 404 B ff.

τῶν κριθῶν ἄλφιτα σκευαζόμενοι, ἐκ δὲ τῶν πυρῶν ἄλευρα· τὰ
μὲν πέψαντες, τὰ δὲ μάξαντες μάζας γενναίας καὶ ἄρτους ἐπὶ
κάλαμόν τινα παραβαλλόμενοι ἢ φύλλα καθαρά, κατακλινέντες
ἐπὶ στιβάδων ἐστρωμένων μίλακί τε καὶ μυρρίναις, εὐωχήσονται
αὐτοί τε καὶ τὰ παιδία, ἐπιπίνοντες τοῦ οἴνου, ἐστεφανωμένοι καὶ
ὑμνοῦντες τοὺς θεούς, ἡδέως ξυνόντες ἀλλήλοις, οὐχ ὑπὲρ τὴν
C οὐσίαν ποιούμενοι τοὺς παῖδας, εὐλαβούμενοι πενίαν ἢ πόλεμον.

XIII. Καὶ ὁ Γλαύκων ὑπολαβών, Ἄνευ ὄψου, ἔφη, ὡς ἔοικας, ποιεῖς τοὺς ἄνδρας ἑστιωμένους. Ἀληθῆ, ἦν δ' ἐγώ, λέγεις. ἐπελαθόμην ὅτι καὶ ὄψον ἕξουσιν. ἅλας τε δῆλον ὅτι καὶ ἐλάας καὶ τυρὸν καὶ βολβοὺς καὶ λάχανα οἷα δὴ ἐν ἀγροῖς ἑψήματα ἑψήσονται. καὶ τραγήματά που παραθήσομεν αὐτοῖς τῶν τε σύκων καὶ ἐρεβίνθων καὶ κυάμων, καὶ μύρτα καὶ φηγοὺς σπο-

---

10 **τὰ μὲν πέψαντες κτλ.** The asyndeton (as usual) is ampliative. The punctuation in the text avoids the difficulty of the two verbs *θρέψονται* and *εὐωχήσονται*. Schneider places the colon before *μάζας*, but this is much less natural. For *μάζας γενναίας*, 'noble bannocks' (J. and C.), cf. (with Stallbaum) *Laws* 844 E *τὰ γενναῖα σῦκα ἐπονομαζόμενα*. *κάλαμον* is not 'a mat of reeds' (Jowett, with L. and S.), which would be much too artistic, but 'reeds,' *κάλαμον* being collective as in Arist. *Hist. An.* IX 36. 620ᵃ 35; and *τινα* is contemptuous (cf. II 363 D *n.*).

12 **παραβαλλόμενοι** is also contemptuous for the *παρατιθέμενοι* of civilised society: it suggests throwing food before animals (cf. 372 D).

13 **στιβάδων**: not 'mattresses' (L. and S.): why should they 'strew' mattresses? The whole point of the passage is that instead of reclining on manufactured couches they lie on natural ones of bryony and myrtle boughs: contrast 372 D. *στρωννύναι στιβάδας* is simply 'to make couches of leaves': cf. *στορέσαι λέχος*. The word *μῖλαξ* means bryony (as Schneider saw): cf. Sandys on Eur. *Bacch.* 107 *χλοήρει μίλακι καλλικάρπῳ*. The 'yew' of the English translators would make a sombre and lugubrious couch.

14 **ἐπιπίνοντες**. *ἐπί* means 'after': cf. Xen. *Cyr.* VI 2 28 *μετὰ δὲ τὸν σῖτον εἰ οἶνον ἐπιπίνοιμεν*. In Greek banquets there was little or no drinking during dinner. The conjecture *ὑποπίνοντες* (Stephanus-Hase *Thes.* s. v. *ἐπιπίνω*) is unnecessary.

372 C 16 **ἢ πόλεμον**. The origin of war is over-population (373 D).

17 **ἄνευ ὄψου κτλ.** *ὄψον* is meant by Glauco in its narrower sense of animal food (whether fish or flesh); Socrates on the other hand uses the word in its wider sense of anything eaten in addition to, or along with, bread, e.g. vegetables (see Blümner *Gr. Privatalt.* p. 223). A spirited and athletic Athenian like Glauco cannot tolerate a vegetarian diet: cf. 372 D.

18 **ἑστιωμένους**: sarcastic, with reference to *εὐωχήσονται*: 'you call it feasting when they have nothing but dry bread!' (J. and C.).

19 **ἅλας—ἑψήσονται**. 'Of course they will make salt and olives and cheese and vegetables whether wild' (*βολβούς*) 'or cultivated' (*λάχανα*) 'into such boiled dishes as can be prepared in the country.' *ἕψημα* is not 'something for boiling,' but something boiled; and *ἑψήσονται* is used with two accusatives, one external (*ἅλας*, &c.) and the other internal (*ἑψήματα*). Plato hints that cookery in the country (*ἐν ἀγροῖς*, cf. *κατ' ἀγρούς* III 399 D) is inferior to that in the town. For the kind of dishes in question cf. Ath. II 64 E *περὶ δὲ τῆς τῶν βολβῶν σκευασίας Φιλήμων φησὶ τὸν βολβόν, εἰ βούλει, σκόπει | ὅσα δαπανήσας εὐδοκιμεῖ, τυρὸν μέλι | σήσαμον ἔλαιον κρόμμυον ὄξος σίλφιον· | αὐτὸς δ' ἐφ' αὑτοῦ 'στὶν πονηρὸς καὶ πικρός*.

22 **φηγούς**: 'acorns,' not 'beech-nuts' (D. and V.): see Blaydes on Ar. *Peace* 1137.

διοῦσιν | πρὸς τὸ πῦρ, μετρίως ὑποπίνοντες· καὶ οὕτω διάγοντες D
τὸν βίον ἐν εἰρήνῃ μετὰ ὑγιείας, ὡς εἰκός, γηραιοὶ τελευτῶντες
ἄλλον τοιοῦτον βίον τοῖς ἐκγόνοις παραδώσουσιν. καὶ ὅς, Εἰ δὲ
ὑῶν πόλιν, ὦ Σώκρατες, ἔφη, κατεσκεύαζες, τί ἂν αὐτὰς ἄλλο ἢ
ταῦτα ἐχόρταζες; Ἀλλὰ πῶς χρή, ἦν δ' ἐγώ, ὦ Γλαύκων; Ἅπερ
νομίζεται, ἔφη· ἐπί τε κλινῶν κατακεῖσθαι, οἶμαι, τοὺς μέλλοντας
μὴ ταλαιπωρεῖσθαι, καὶ ἀπὸ τραπεζῶν | δειπνεῖν, καὶ ὄψα ἅπερ E
καὶ οἱ νῦν ἔχουσι καὶ τραγήματα. Εἶεν, ἦν δ' ἐγώ, μανθάνω· οὐ

---

372 D 23 **ὑποπίνοντες.** Wine was sipped during dessert. ὑπο- in ὑποπίνοντες emphasizes the moderation already expressed in μετρίως: cf. *Lys.* 223 B ὑποπεπωκότες ἐν τοῖς Ἑρμαίοις. Dr Jackson connects πρὸς τὸ πῦρ with ὑποπίνοντες, comparing IV 420 E, Ar. *Ach.* 751 al. This may be right, but the ordinary view seems to me somewhat more natural.

372 D—**373** C *Glauco protests against the swinish character of such a life: more comfort, he thinks, should be allowed. While expressing his opinion that the healthy State is that which he has already described, Socrates is willing to describe the 'inflamed'* (φλεγμαίνουσα) *City, in case Justice and Injustice should be discovered in it* (372 D—372 E).

The Second Sketch of a City now begins (372 E ff.).

Some will not be satisfied with the provisions of our first city, but will demand a variety of physical comforts and delicacies, and artistic delights. A crowd of hunters and imitative artists of different kinds will accordingly spring up, and the race of middlemen will be largely increased. As a flesh diet will come into fashion, swineherds will be in demand, and cattle will multiply. The new style of living will bring doctors to the front.

372 D ff. The provisions of the πρώτη πόλις are insufficient for the satisfaction of human needs: for there is θυμός as well as ἐπιθυμία in the soul of man. Hence we must advance a stage further. Plato's method is as follows. He begins by enumerating many of the features of ordinary Greek life, as he found it, without distinguishing the good from the bad. The resulting picture he calls a τρυφῶσα or φλεγμαίνουσα πόλις. The next step is to purge this τρυφῶσα πόλις (cf. III 399 E λελήθαμέν γε διακαθαίροντες πάλιν ἣν ἄρτι τρυφᾶν ἔφαμεν πόλιν) by excluding some of the features, and correcting and regulating others, both by prescriptive enactments and still more by the influence of education. It is this κεκαθαρμένη πόλις which forms what we may call Plato's δευτέρα πόλις (II 372 E—IV): his third and crowning effort, the City of the Rulers, is contained in Books V—VII. Cf. VIII 543 E *n.* and Hirzel *der Dialog* I pp. 235 ff.

372 D 26 **ὑῶν.** The city of Pigs is supposed by Zeller[4] II 1 pp. 325, 893, and Dümmler *Antisthenica* pp. 5 ff., *Proleg. zur Pl. Staat* p. 61, to be a contemptuous allusion to Antisthenes' ideal commonwealth (on which see Susemihl in *Fl. Jahrb.* 1887 pp. 207—214). This conjecture requires us to interpret Plato's first sketch of a State as wholly ironical and intended 'to warn us against the false ideal of a Nature-City' (Zeller l. c.). I agree with Henkel (*Stud. zur Gesch. d. Gr. Lehre vom Staat* pp. 8 f.) in thinking that there is no solid ground for Zeller's theory. The πρώτη πόλις is not of course Plato's ideal republic, and his description of it is plentifully bestrewn with irony, but it is nevertheless the foundation on which his city is built, and, in point of fact, although some of its features are implicitly corrected or superseded in the sequel, it still remains on the whole, and as far as it goes, a not unpleasing picture of the life of the lowest stratum in Plato's city, and it is nowhere expressly cancelled or abolished. See also on 369 B and 372 E. The εὐχερὴς βίος (*Pol.* 266 C) of the πρώτη πόλις is fitly compared to that of pigs, the εὐχερέστατον γένος τῶν ὄντων (*ib.*); and it is appropriate that Glauco, who is nothing if not θυμοειδής (*Introd.* § 2), should thus express his contempt for a life which hardly if at all rises above the level of ἐπιθυμία.

372 E 30 **καὶ οἱ νῦν ἔχουσι:** e.g.

πόλιν, ὡς ἔοικε, σκοποῦμεν μόνον ὅπως γίγνεται, ἀλλὰ καὶ τρυφῶσαν πόλιν. ἴσως οὖν οὐδὲ κακῶς ἔχει· σκοποῦντες γὰρ καὶ
τοιαύτην τάχ' ἂν κατίδοιμεν τήν τε δικαιοσύνην καὶ ἀδικίαν ὅπῃ
ποτὲ ταῖς πόλεσιν ἐμφύονται. ἡ μὲν οὖν ἀληθινὴ πόλις δοκεῖ μοι
εἶναι ἣν διεληλύθαμεν, ὥσπερ ὑγιής τις· εἰ δ' αὖ βούλεσθε, καὶ
φλεγμαίνουσαν πόλιν θεωρήσωμεν· οὐδὲν ἀποκωλύει. ταῦτα γὰρ
373 δή τισιν, ὡς δοκεῖ, | οὐκ ἐξαρκέσει, οὐδὲ αὕτη ἡ δίαιτα, ἀλλὰ κλῖναί
τε προσέσονται καὶ τράπεζαι καὶ τἆλλα σκεύη, καὶ ὄψα δὴ καὶ
μύρα καὶ θυμιάματα καὶ ἑταῖραι καὶ πέμματα, ἕκαστα τούτων
παντοδαπά. καὶ δὴ καὶ ἃ τὸ πρῶτον ἐλέγομεν οὐκέτι τἀναγκαῖα

36. *θεωρήσωμεν* A²Π: *θεωρήσομεν* A¹.

---

fish, flesh, fowl: see on 372 C. The words *ἅπερ—ἔχουσι* are to be taken with *τραγήματα* as well as with *ὄψα*. Glauco is thinking of delicacies like the preserved sorb-apples (*ὄα τεταριχευμένα*) alluded to in *Symp.* 190 D. See Blümner *Gr. Privatalt.* p. 222 *n.* 2.

31 **τρυφῶσαν πόλιν.** Krohn (*Pl. St.* pp. 34, 72) thinks that Plato originally meant to look for *ἀδικία* in this *τρυφῶσα πόλις*: but see on 369 A.

34 **ἀληθινὴ—φλεγμαίνουσαν.** There is a vein of irony in *ἀληθινή*: for the *πρώτη πόλις* is not the final form of Plato's city. The epithets *τρυφῶσαν*, *φλεγμαίνουσαν* are not however ironical (as Dümmler seems to hold *Proleg.* p. 62): see III 399 E.

35 **εἰ δ' αὖ—ἀποκωλύει.** I have adopted Richards' suggestion, and printed a comma after *βούλεσθε*, a colon before *οὐδέν*. The meaning is: 'but if you wish it, let us contemplate also' etc. The scribe in Paris A must have understood *καὶ θεωρήσωμεν* in the same way, for he assigns the words *οὐδὲν ἀποκωλύει* to Glauco. We are hardly justified in making *θεωρήσωμεν* the subjunctive after *βούλεσθε*, in the absence of other examples in which the subjunctive follows a dependent *βούλει* (*βούλεσθε*). A possible view would be to take *θεωρήσωμεν* as = *δεῖ θεωρῆσαι* and construe 'but if you wish it and we are to contemplate' etc., cf. *Crat.* 425 D *εἰ μὴ ἄρα δὴ* (MSS *δεῖ*)—*καὶ ἡμεῖς*—*ἀπαλλαγῶμεν* ('unless we too are to get quit'), and Postgate in *Transactions of the Camb. Philol. Soc.* III Pt. I pp. 50—55. But Richards' proposal is a better one.

36 **ταῦτα—τισιν.** *γάρ* is introductory and means not 'for' but 'well.' *τισιν* contains a sly allusion to Glauco: cf. V 465 E, VI 504 C.

373 A 2 **καὶ ὄψα δή.** For *δή* see 367 C *n.*

3 **ἑταῖραι.** G. W. Nitzsch (*Rhein. Mus.* 1857, pp. 471 f.), Richter (*Fl. Jahrb.* 1867, p. 141), Madvig, and Stallbaum take offence at the juxtaposition of *ἑταῖραι* and *πέμματα* and suggest respectively *ἀθῆραι* (apparently an error for *ἀθάραι*, cf. Ar. *Plut.* 673), *ἐραῖα* (= *ἑψήματα* in Schol. on 445 C), *ἐσχαρῖται* 'panes delicati,' and *ἕτερα* (with the following *καί* deleted),—conjectures which are altogether needless and refute one another. The text is successfully defended by Hug (*Hermes* 1876, p. 254), who cites an exact parallel in Ar. *Ach.* 1090—1092 *κλῖναι, τράπεζαι, προσκεφάλαια, στρώματα, | στέφανοι, μύρον, τραγήμαθ', αἱ πόρναι πάρα, | ἄμυλοι πλακοῦντες, σησαμοῦντες, ἴτρια |* (varieties of *πέμματα*). Cf. also Amphis ap. Ath. XIV 642 A *οἶνος ἡδύς, ᾠά, σησαμαῖ, | μύρον, στέφανος, αὐλητρίς* and infra III 404 D, IX 573 D *n.* From these passages it may fairly be doubted whether Plato's mention of *ἑταῖραι* is in any way even *παρὰ προσδοκίαν* (as the Oxford editors suggest): for *αὐλητρίδες* were almost as common a feature at dessert as the cakes (*πέμματα*) etc. which accompany them here: see e.g. Xen. *Mem.* I 5. 4, *Symp.* 2. 1, Pl. *Symp.* 176 E, *Prot.* 347 D. Vahlen (*Index Lect. per sem. hib.* 1875—6 Berol.) quotes also Catullus' "cenabis bene—si tecum attuleris bonam atque magnam | cenam non sine candida puella | et vino et sale et omnibus cachinnis" (13. 1 ff.).

θετέον, οἰκίας τε καὶ ἱμάτια καὶ ὑποδήματα, ἀλλὰ τήν τε ζῳγραφίαν κινητέον καὶ τὴν ποικιλίαν καὶ χρυσὸν καὶ ἐλέφαντα καὶ πάντα τὰ τοιαῦτα κτητέον. ἦ γάρ; Ναί, | ἔφη. Οὐκοῦν μείζονά τε αὖ τὴν B πόλιν δεῖ ποιεῖν, ἐκείνη γὰρ ἡ ὑγιεινὴ οὐκέτι ἱκανή, ἀλλ' ἤδη ὄγκου ἐμπληστέα καὶ πλήθους, ἃ οὐκέτι τοῦ ἀναγκαίου ἕνεκά ἐστιν ἐν ταῖς πόλεσιν, οἷον οἵ τε θηρευταὶ πάντες οἵ τε μιμηταί, πολλοὶ μὲν οἱ περὶ τὰ σχήματά τε καὶ χρώματα, πολλοὶ δὲ οἱ περὶ μουσικήν, ποιηταί τε καὶ τούτων ὑπηρέται, ῥαψῳδοί, ὑποκριταί, χορευταί, ἐργολάβοι, σκευῶν τε παντοδαπῶν δημιουργοί, τῶν τε | ἄλλων καὶ C τῶν περὶ τὸν γυναικεῖον κόσμον. καὶ δὴ καὶ διακόνων πλειόνων δεησόμεθα. ἢ οὐ δοκεῖ δεήσειν παιδαγωγῶν, τιτθῶν, τροφῶν, κομμωτριῶν, κουρέων, καὶ αὖ ὀψοποιῶν τε καὶ μαγείρων; ἔτι δὲ καὶ συβωτῶν προσδεησόμεθα· τοῦτο γὰρ ἡμῖν ἐν τῇ προτέρᾳ πόλει οὐκ ἐνῆν· ἔδει γὰρ οὐδέν· ἐν δὲ ταύτῃ καὶ τούτου προσδεήσει,

6. καὶ τὴν ποικιλίαν Π: om. A. 7. αὖ τὴν Π: αὐτὴν A.

---

6 **καὶ τὴν ποικιλίαν.** *ποικιλία* means variety of colour as e.g. in embroidery: cf. 378 C, III 401 A, *Euthyph.* 6 C. On the omission in A see *Introd.* § 5.

χρυσὸν καὶ ἐλέφαντα: with reference to chryselephantine statuary. Note that (according to Plato) the demand for decorative arts does not arise till the physical necessities of man are satisfied. Cf. Nettleship *Lectures and Remains*, II p. 73.

373 B 7 **μείζονά τε αὖ τήν.** *τέ* is *ἀνακόλουθον* (Hoefer *de part. Pl.* p. 14): for other instances in the *Republic* see V 463 D, VII 522 B, IX 575 A. In this passage Richter would change *τε αὖ τήν* into *τοιαύτην*, comparing 372 E; but the text is sound, and *τοιαύτην* would be quite wrong. *αὐτὴν τὴν πόλιν* (cf. 370 E), conjectured by Heller instead of *αὖ τὴν πόλιν*, is neat but needless.

9 **πλήθους ἅ**: i.e. *πλήθους τούτων ἅ*, as Ficinus understood the words. Stallbaum's alternative suggestion (that *ἅ* refers directly to *ὄγκου* and *πλήθους*) gives a poor sense. Cf. infra 373 E *n*.

10 **θηρευταὶ πάντες.** The addition of *πάντες* shews that *θηρευταί* is used in a wide sense, including every variety of fishing as well as hunting: *Laws* 823 B *θήρα γὰρ πάμπολύ τι πρᾶγμά ἐστι, περιειλημμένον ὀνόματι νῦν σχεδὸν ἑνί. πολλὴ μὲν γὰρ ἡ τῶν ἐνύδρων, πολλὴ δὲ ἡ τῶν πτηνῶν, πάμπολυ δὲ καὶ τὸ περὶ τὰ πεζὰ θηρεύματα.* In *Euthyd.* 290 B—D, *Soph.* 219 E ff., and *Laws* (l.c.), Plato makes *θηρευτική* include 'fishing for men' e.g. in war, or by Sophists etc. This wider meaning clearly rests upon a Platonic—or rather Socratic (see Xen. *Mem.* II 6. 29, quoted by J. and C.)—metaphor, and is not intended here. Cf. Benseler in *Fl. Jahrb.* 1881, pp. 236 ff. Aristotle on the other hand regards hunting as characteristic of the most primitive society (*Pol.* A 8. 1256ª 35 ff.), and so too Plato himself in *Laws* 679 A.

12 **ῥαψῳδοί—ἐργολάβοι** are the poet's servants. In Athens and elsewhere they formed regular guilds or *σύνοδοι τῶν περὶ τὸν Διόνυσον τεχνιτῶν*: cf. Arist. *Probl.* XXX 10. 956ᵇ 11 *οἱ Διονυσιακοὶ τεχνῖται.* The *ἐργολάβος* contracted with the poet for the performance of his play, acting as a kind of financial agent or middleman between him and the *σύνοδος* to which he belonged. See Müller *Bühnenalterthümer*, pp. 392—414.

373 C 15 **παιδαγωγῶν—κουρέων.** We infer that in the 'healthy' State fathers were *παιδαγωγοί*, mothers suckled (*τιτθῶν*) and nursed (*τροφῶν*) their own children, and the professional hair-dresser was unknown.

17 **συβωτῶν.** See on 372 B.

δεήσει δὲ καὶ τῶν ἄλλων βοσκημάτων παμπόλλων, εἴ τις αὐτὰ
D ἔδεται. ἦ γάρ; Πῶς γὰρ οὔ; | Οὐκοῦν καὶ ἰατρῶν ἐν χρείαις ἐσόμεθα πολὺ μᾶλλον οὕτω διαιτώμενοι ἢ ὡς τὸ πρότερον; Πολύ γε.

XIV. Καὶ ἡ χώρα που ἡ τότε ἱκανὴ τρέφειν τοὺς τότε σμικρὰ δὴ ἐξ ἱκανῆς ἔσται· ἢ πῶς λέγομεν; Οὕτως, ἔφη. Οὐκοῦν τῆς τῶν πλησίον χώρας ἡμῖν ἀποτμητέον, εἰ μέλλομεν ἱκανὴν ἕξειν νέμειν τε καὶ ἀροῦν, καὶ ἐκείνοις αὖ τῆς ἡμετέρας, ἐὰν καὶ ἐκεῖνοι ἀφῶσιν αὑτοὺς ἐπὶ χρημάτων κτῆσιν ἄπειρον, ὑπερβάντες
E τὸν τῶν ἀναγκαίων | ὅρον; Πολλὴ ἀνάγκη, ἔφη, ὦ Σώκρατες. Πολεμήσομεν τὸ μετὰ τοῦτο, ὦ Γλαύκων; ἢ πῶς ἔσται; Οὕτως, ἔφη. Καὶ μηδέν γέ πω λέγωμεν, ἦν δ' ἐγώ, μήτ' εἴ τι κακὸν μήτ' εἰ ἀγαθὸν ὁ πόλεμος ἐργάζεται, ἀλλὰ τοσοῦτον μόνον, ὅτι πολέμου αὖ γένεσιν ηὑρήκαμεν, ἐξ ὧν μάλιστα ταῖς πόλεσιν καὶ ἰδίᾳ καὶ δημοσίᾳ κακὰ γίγνεται ὅταν γίγνηται. Πάνυ μὲν οὖν. Ἔτι δή,

23. λέγομεν A^2Π: λέγωμεν A^1. 31, 32. καὶ ἰδίᾳ καὶ δημοσίᾳ Π et in mg. A^2: om. A^1.

---

373 D 20 **χρείαις.** Cobet's χρείᾳ is not, I think, necessary. The plural (for which cf. 369 D al.) refers to the different occasions when we may require the help of doctors.

373 D—**376** C *In consequence of the increase of population we shall require more land. We must accordingly appropriate some of our neighbours' territory, just as under similar conditions they will lay hands upon ours. Herein we have the genesis of War. The duties of War—according to our principle of the subdivision of labour—will involve us in a standing army of professional soldiers or 'Guardians.' Now as War demands not only concentration and application, but also a certain natural aptitude, our Guardians must be qualified by Nature for their duties: that is to say, like generous dogs, they must be quick to perceive, swift to pursue, and strong in actual fight. They should also be brave and spirited, but gentle to their fellow-citizens and one another. The union of gentleness with spirit in the same nature is rare, but not unknown among men, any more than it is among dogs. Our Guardians must in fact be 'philosophic'* (φιλόσοφοι), *like the dog, who is a true philosopher when he defines friend and foe respectively by knowledge and by ignorance, hating the unknown, and welcoming the known. In brief, we shall require a guardian to be naturally philosophic, spirited, swift, and strong.*

373 D 23 **λέγομεν.** λέγωμεν may be right, but the first hand of A was apt to err in these subjunctive forms (*Introd.* § 5), and the Indicative is somewhat more natural here: cf. (with Schneider) 377 E ἀλλὰ πῶς δὴ λέγομεν καὶ ποῖα;

373 E 28 **πολεμήσομεν.** Stallbaum adds δή after πολεμήσομεν with some inferior MSS. The effect of its omission is to lay special stress on the first mention of πόλεμος in πολεμήσομεν, which should be pronounced with emphasis. Cf. IV 432 C, IX 583 C.

30 **πολέμου — γένεσιν.** War then arises from the acquisition of territory and wealth: cf. *Phaed.* 66 C διὰ γὰρ τὴν τῶν χρημάτων κτῆσιν πάντες οἱ πόλεμοι ἡμῖν γίγνονται, where war is farther traced to the body and its desires, to satisfy which we seek to multiply our possessions. Cf. Arist. *Pol.* A 8. 1256^b^ 23 ἡ πολεμικὴ φύσει κτητική πως ἔσται.

31 **ἐξ ὧν—γίγνηται** defines γένεσιν. War comes ἐξ ὧν i.e. ἐκ τούτων ὧν κτλ. (ὧν for ἐξ ὧν, according to the usual Greek idiom, cf. *Euthyph.* 10 C, and III 402 A ἐν ἅπασιν οἷς ἔστι al.), from that which involves both cities and individuals in calamities, viz. from the desire of money. Cf. 373 B *n.* and (for the sentiment

ὦ φίλε, μείζονος τῆς πόλεως δεῖ οὔτι σμικρῷ, ἀλλ' ὅλῳ στρατο|πέδῳ, 374
ὃ ἐξελθὸν ὑπὲρ τῆς οὐσίας ἁπάσης καὶ ὑπὲρ ὧν νῦν δὴ ἐλέγομεν διαμαχεῖται τοῖς ἐπιοῦσιν. Τί δέ; ἦ δ' ὅς· αὐτοὶ οὐχ ἱκανοί; Οὔκ, εἰ σύ γε, ἦν δ' ἐγώ, καὶ ἡμεῖς ἅπαντες ὡμολογήσαμεν καλῶς, ἡνίκα ἐπλάττομεν τὴν πόλιν· ὡμολογοῦμεν δέ που, εἰ μέμνησαι, ἀδύνατον ἕνα πολλὰς καλῶς ἐργάζεσθαι τέχνας. Ἀληθῆ λέγεις, ἔφη. Τί οὖν; ἦν δ' ἐγώ· ἡ περὶ τὸν πόλεμον | ἀγωνία οὐ τεχνικὴ B
δοκεῖ εἶναι; Καὶ μάλα, ἔφη. Ἦ οὖν τι σκυτικῆς δεῖ μᾶλλον κήδεσθαι ἢ πολεμικῆς; Οὐδαμῶς. Ἀλλ' ἄρα τὸν μὲν σκυτοτόμον διεκωλύομεν μήτε γεωργὸν ἐπιχειρεῖν εἶναι ἅμα μήτε ὑφάντην μήτε οἰκοδόμον, ἀλλὰ σκυτοτόμον, ἵνα δὴ ἡμῖν τὸ τῆς σκυτικῆς ἔργον καλῶς γίγνοιτο, καὶ τῶν ἄλλων ἑνὶ ἑκάστῳ ὡσαύτως ἓν ἀπεδίδομεν,

11. ἀλλὰ σκυτοτόμον Π: om. A.

Laws 870 A ff. ἡ τῶν χρημάτων τῆς ἀπλήστου καὶ ἀπείρου κτήσεως ἔρωτας μυρίους ἐντίκτουσα δύναμις διὰ φύσιν τε καὶ ἀπαιδευσίαν τὴν κακὴν κτλ. The love of money—so Plato held—is the root of all evil. This explanation is due to Schleiermacher; others (Schneider, Stallbaum, J. and C. as an alternative) refer ἐξ ὧν to war and the like='ex cuiusmodi rebus' (Stallbaum). It is an objection to such a view that it makes Plato say that evils come from War (and the like), directly after he has declined to say anything of the sort (μηδέν γέ πω — ἐργάζεται). Further, if ὧν referred to war, the sentiment would in itself be a platitude and almost deserve to be expunged from the text, as it is by Herwerden. On the other hand ἐξ ὧν—γίγνηται is on Schleiermacher's view quite consistent with μηδέν γέ πω— ἐργάζεται, for although war arises from that which harms a State, in itself it may (and does) actually do good. Good in other words may come out of evil; which is exactly the principle on which Plato evolves his ideal city out of the τρυφῶσα πόλις. ὅταν γίγνηται (sc. κακά) is equivalent (as J. and C. remark) to ἑκάστοτε: cf. *Phaed.* 68 D φόβῳ μειζόνων κακῶν ὑπομένουσιν αὐτῶν οἱ ἀνδρεῖοι τὸν θάνατον ὅταν ὑπομένωσιν.

33 **ὅλῳ.** Herwerden's conjecture μεγάλῳ seems to shew that he connected σμικρῷ with στρατοπέδῳ, but the meaning is 'not by a small amount, but by a whole army.' For the datives cf. IX 579 C *n.*

374 A 3 **αὐτοὶ οὐχ ἱκανοί;** Glauco speaks as an Athenian citizen-soldier. In making war a profession, and citizens synonymous with soldiers, Plato is laconizing. The language which Isocrates (*Archid.* 81) applies to Sparta might in point of fact be used of Plato's State: τῶν Ἑλλήνων διενηνόχαμεν οὐ τῷ μεγέθει τῆς πόλεως, οὐδὲ τῷ πλήθει τῶν ἀνθρώπων, ἀλλ' ὅτι τὴν πολιτείαν ὁμοίαν κατεστησάμεθα στρατοπέδῳ καλῶς διοικουμένῳ καὶ πειθαρχεῖν ἐθέλοντι τοῖς ἄρχουσιν. Cf. Grote *Plato* III pp. 176, 209.

5 **ὡμολογοῦμεν**: without εἶναι as in X 610 C ἀθανάτους τὰς ψυχὰς ὁμολογεῖν, and *Soph.* 246 E. The analogy of these cases shews that ἀδύνατον here is not neuter but masculine, agreeing with ἕνα. The reference is to 370 B.

374 B 9 **ἀλλ' ἄρα.** As διεκωλύομεν is certainly interrogative, Ast conjectured ἆρα for ἄρα, but ἄρα (*nimirum*) is regularly present in *a fortiori* arguments of this kind, either in the δέ clause (*Ap.* 34 C, 37 C, D, *Crito* 46 D) or in both (*Crito* 50 E, *Prot.* 325 B, C). In place of the second ἄρα is here written δή (τὰ δὲ δὴ περὶ τὸν πόλεμον κτλ.). For the combination ἀλλ' ἄρα cf. *Soph.* 243 E ἀλλ' ἄρα τὰ ἄμφω βούλεσθε καλεῖν ὄν; Ἴσως.

11 **ἀλλὰ σκυτοτόμον**. See *cr. n.* and *Introd.* § 5. The homoioteleuton as well as the presence of the clause ἵνα—γίγνοιτο is in favour of the genuineness of these words: and the construction itself, which requires ἐκελεύομεν or the like to be supplied out of διεκωλύομεν (see Heindorf on *Gorg.* 457 C and Kühner *Gr. Gr.* II p. 1072), is too idiomatic to have been readily invented by a scribe.

πρὸς ὃ ἐπεφύκει ἕκαστος καὶ ἐφ' ᾧ ἔμελλε τῶν ἄλλων σχολὴν
C ἄγων διὰ βίου αὐτὸ ἐργαζόμενος οὐ παριεὶς τοὺς καιροὺς καλῶς
ἀπεργάζεσθαι· τὰ δὲ δὴ περὶ τὸν πόλεμον πότερον οὐ περὶ
πλείστου ἐστὶν εὖ ἀπεργασθέντα; ἢ οὕτω ῥᾴδιον, ὥστε καὶ
γεωργῶν τις ἅμα πολεμικὸς ἔσται καὶ σκυτοτομῶν καὶ ἄλλην
τέχνην ἡντινοῦν ἐργαζόμενος, πεττευτικὸς δὲ ἢ κυβευτικὸς ἱκανῶς
οὐδ' ἂν εἷς γένοιτο μὴ αὐτὸ τοῦτο ἐκ παιδὸς ἐπιτηδεύων, ἀλλὰ
D παρέργῳ χρώμενος; καὶ ἀσπίδα μὲν λαβὼν ἤ τι ἄλλο τῶν
πολεμικῶν ὅπλων τε καὶ ὀργάνων αὐθημερὸν ὁπλιτικῆς ἤ τινος
ἄλλης μάχης τῶν κατὰ πόλεμον ἱκανὸς ἔσται ἀγωνιστής, τῶν δὲ
ἄλλων ὀργάνων οὐδὲν οὐδένα δημιουργὸν οὐδὲ ἀθλητὴν ληφθὲν
ποιήσει, οὐδ' ἔσται χρήσιμον τῷ μήτε τὴν ἐπιστήμην ἑκάστου
λαβόντι μήτε τὴν μελέτην ἱκανὴν παρασχομένῳ; Πολλοῦ γὰρ ἄν,
ἦ δ' ὅς, τὰ ὄργανα ἦν ἄξια.
E XV. Οὐκοῦν, ἦν δ' ἐγώ, ὅσῳ μέγιστον τὸ τῶν φυλάκων ἔργον,
τοσούτῳ σχολῆς τε τῶν ἄλλων πλείστης ἂν εἴη καὶ αὖ τέχνης τε
καὶ ἐπιμελείας μεγίστης δεόμενον. Οἶμαι ἔγωγε, ἦ δ' ὅς. Ἆρ' οὖν
οὐ καὶ φύσεως ἐπιτηδείας εἰς αὐτὸ τὸ ἐπιτήδευμα; Πῶς δ' οὔ;
Ἡμέτερον δὴ ἔργον ἂν εἴη, ὡς ἔοικεν, εἴπερ οἷοί τ' ἐσμέν, ἐκλέξασθαι,
τίνες τε καὶ ποῖαι φύσεις ἐπιτήδειαι εἰς πόλεως φυλακήν. Ἡμέτερον
μέντοι. Μὰ Δία, ἦν δ' ἐγώ, οὐκ ἄρα φαῦλον πρᾶγμα ἠράμεθα·
375 ὅμως δὲ οὐκ ἀποδειλιατέον, ὅσον γ' ἂν δύναμις παρείκῃ. | Οὐ γὰρ

17. σκυτοτομῶν Π: σκυτοτόμων A.

---

13 **ἐφ' ᾧ**: with σχολὴν ἄγων (Schneider): cf. *Ap.* 36 D. The phraseology here recalls 370 B and C.

374 C 16 **ἢ οὕτω ῥᾴδιον**: singular in spite of the plural τὰ περί. Cf. (with Schneider) *Hipp. Maior* 299 A, *Laws* 708 D.

374 D 21 **τε καὶ ὀργάνων** is ejected by Herwerden, who is also inclined to denounce τὰ ὄργανα below. But it is just these words which "point the analogy: the weapons of the warrior are his tools." (J. and C.) On similarly inadequate grounds τῶν νέων has been condemned in *Euthyph.* 3 A τοὺς τῶν νέων τὰς βλάστας διαφθείροντας: see my note ad loc. τινος ἄλλης μάχης below refers for example to ψιλοί or πελτασταί; the ἀσπίς (it should be remembered) was worn by the ὁπλίτης (whence ἀσπίδα μὲν λαβὼν—ὁπλιτικῆς). The necessity of special knowledge and training for success in war is insisted on by the historical Socrates in Xen. *Mem.* III 1.

27 **φυλάκων**. This is the first occurrence of φύλακες in the technical sense which it bears throughout the *Republic*. It is important to remember that the name includes not only the soldiers, but also—after they have been introduced—the rulers; when it becomes necessary to distinguish between the two classes, the former are called ἐπίκουροι (first named in III 414 B), the latter φύλακες παντελεῖς (III 414 B), τέλεοι φύλακες (IV 428 D) or the like, or more commonly ἄρχοντες (first alluded to in III 389 B, but not expressly separated off until 412 B ff., and finally and fully described only in Books VI and VII).

374 E 34 **ὅσον γ' ἂν δύναμις παρείκῃ**. The phrase is not found elsewhere

οὖν, ἔφη. Οἴει οὖν τι, ἦν δ' ἐγώ, διαφέρειν φύσιν γενναίου σκύλακος εἰς φυλακὴν νεανίσκου εὐγενοῦς; Τὸ ποῖον λέγεις; Οἷον ὀξύν τέ που δεῖ αὐτοῖν ἑκάτερον εἶναι πρὸς αἴσθησιν καὶ ἐλαφρὸν πρὸς τὸ αἰσθανόμενον διωκαθεῖν, καὶ ἰσχυρὸν αὖ, ἐὰν δέῃ ἑλόντα διαμάχεσθαι. Δεῖ γὰρ οὖν, ἔφη, πάντων τούτων. Καὶ μὴν ἀνδρεῖόν γε, εἴπερ εὖ μαχεῖται. Πῶς δ' οὔ; Ἀνδρεῖος δὲ εἶναι ἆρα ἐθελήσει ὁ μὴ θυμοειδὴς εἴτε ἵππος εἴτε κύων ἢ ἄλλο ὁτιοῦν ζῷον; ἢ | οὐκ B ἐννενόηκας, ὡς ἄμαχόν τε καὶ ἀνίκητον θυμός, οὗ παρόντος ψυχὴ πᾶσα πρὸς πάντα ἄφοβός τέ ἐστι καὶ ἀήττητος; Ἐννενόηκα. Τὰ μὲν τοίνυν τοῦ σώματος οἷον δεῖ τὸν φύλακα εἶναι, δῆλα. Ναί. Καὶ μὴν καὶ τὰ τῆς ψυχῆς, ὅτι γε θυμοειδῆ. Καὶ τοῦτο. Πῶς οὖν, ἦν δ' ἐγώ, ὦ Γλαύκων, οὐκ ἄγριοι ἀλλήλοις ἔσονται καὶ τοῖς ἄλλοις πολίταις, ὄντες τοιοῦτοι τὰς φύσεις; Μὰ Δία, ἦ δ' ὅς, οὐ ῥᾳδίως. Ἀλλὰ μέντοι δεῖ γε πρὸς μὲν | τοὺς οἰκείους πράους C

14. ἄλλοις *q*: ἀλλοτρίοις ΑΠΞ.

---

in Plato, although παρείκει is found with a personal subject (ὁ θεός, θεοί) again in *Theaet.* 150 D, *Laws* 934 C. Herwerden would eject δύναμις (cf. *Symp.* 187 E καθ' ὅσον παρείκει), but such a word is very unlikely to have been interpolated. δύναμις is simply 'our powers': the article is omitted as in the idiomatic κατὰ δύναμιν, εἰς δύναμιν.

375 A 2 **σκύλακος**. A play on σκύλαξ and φύλαξ is intended. Analogies from the animal kingdom were freely employed by the historical Socrates: for the dog in particular cf. Xen. *Mem.* IV 1. 3 καὶ τῶν κυνῶν τῶν εὐφυεστάτων, φιλοπόνων τε οὐσῶν καὶ ἐπιθετικῶν τοῖς θηρίοις, τὰς μὲν καλῶς ἀχθείσας ἀρίστας γίγνεσθαι—, ἀναγώγους δὲ γιγνομένας ματαίους τε καὶ μανιώδεις καὶ δυσπειθεστάτας. Cf. *n.* on φύεται 370 A.

5 **αἰσθανόμενον**: 'the moment he perceives.' The present (where one might expect the aorist) emphasizes the rapidity with which pursuit follows upon sight.

7 **ἀνδρεῖος**. For ἀνδρεῖος applied to beasts cf. Isocr. 15. 211 εἰ περὶ τοὺς ἵππους καὶ τοὺς κύνας καὶ τὰ πλεῖστα τῶν ζῴων ὁρῶντες τέχνας ἔχοντάς τινας, αἷς τὰ μὲν ἀνδρειότερα, τὰ δὲ πραότερα, τὰ δὲ φρονιμώτερα ποιοῦσι, περὶ τὴν τῶν ἀνθρώπων φύσιν μηδεμίαν οἴονται τοιαύτην ηὑρῆσθαι παιδείαν κτλ. See also *Lach.* 196 D—197 B and Arist. *Eth. Nic.* III 11. 1116^{b} 33 ff.

8 **θυμοειδής**. The technical term θυμοειδής is here for the first time used in the *Republic.* Plato probably inherited the word from Socrates (see Xen. *Mem.* IV 1. 3 τῶν τε ἵππων τοὺς εὐφυεστάτους, θυμοειδεῖς τε καὶ σφοδροὺς ὄντας κτλ.): in practice he employs it as the adjective corresponding to θυμός (see e.g. III 411 A, B), as ἐπιθυμητικός corresponds to ἐπιθυμία. The usual translation 'spirited' probably expresses the meaning as nearly as can be done by a single word. For a full discussion of the word reference may be made to P. Meyer ὁ θυμὸς *ap. Arist. Platonemque* (1876), whose conclusion (p. 65) is "τὸν θυμὸν esse eam naturalem vim, qua ductus suam quisque propriam naturam explere studeat, quaque incitatus, quaecunque hanc naturam ipsi propriam tollere vel laedere conentur, fugiat, quae contra perfectiorem reddere possint, adpetat." See also on IV 439 E.

375 B 9 **ἄμαχόν—ἀνίκητον**. Ast may be right in supposing that Plato has in view the words of Heraclitus, often referred to in antiquity, θυμῷ μάχεσθαι χαλεπόν· ὅ τι γὰρ ἂν χρηίζῃ γίνεσθαι, ψυχῆς ὠνέεται (*Fr.* 105 Bywater).

οὗ παρόντος—ἀήττητος. Cf. Arist. *Eth. Nic.* III 11. 1116^{b} 26 ἰτητικώτατον γὰρ ὁ θυμὸς πρὸς τοὺς κινδύνους.

αὐτοὺς εἶναι, πρὸς δὲ τοὺς πολεμίους χαλεπούς· εἰ δὲ μή, οὐ
περιμενοῦσιν ἄλλους σφᾶς διολέσαι, ἀλλ' αὐτοὶ φθήσονται αὐτὸ
δράσαντες. Ἀληθῆ, ἔφη. Τί οὖν, ἦν δ' ἐγώ, ποιήσομεν; πόθεν
ἅμα πρᾶον καὶ μεγαλόθυμον ἦθος εὑρήσομεν; ἐναντία γάρ που
θυμοειδεῖ πραεῖα φύσις. Φαίνεται. Ἀλλὰ μέντοι τούτων ὁποτέρου
ἂν στέρηται, φύλαξ ἀγαθὸς οὐ μὴ γένηται· ταῦτα δὲ ἀδυνάτοις
D ἔοικεν, καὶ οὕτω δὴ | ξυμβαίνει ἀγαθὸν φύλακα ἀδύνατον γενέσθαι.
Κινδυνεύει, ἔφη. καὶ ἐγὼ ἀπορήσας τε καὶ ἐπισκεψάμενος τὰ
ἔμπροσθεν, Δικαίως γε, ἦν δ' ἐγώ, ὦ φίλε, ἀποροῦμεν· ἧς γὰρ
προὐθέμεθα εἰκόνος ἀπελείφθημεν. Πῶς λέγεις; Οὐκ ἐνοήσαμεν,
ὅτι εἰσὶν ἄρα φύσεις, οἵας ἡμεῖς οὐκ ᾠήθημεν, ἔχουσαι τἀναντία
ταῦτα. Ποῦ δή; Ἴδοι μὲν ἄν τις καὶ ἐν ἄλλοις ζῴοις, οὐ μέντ' ἂν
E ἥκιστα ἐν ᾧ ἡμεῖς παρεβάλλομεν τῷ φύλακι. | οἶσθα γάρ που τῶν
γενναίων κυνῶν, ὅτι τοῦτο φύσει αὐτῶν τὸ ἦθος, πρὸς μὲν τοὺς
συνήθεις τε καὶ γνωρίμους ὡς οἷόν τε πραοτάτους εἶναι, πρὸς δὲ
τοὺς ἀγνῶτας τοὐναντίον. Οἶδα μέντοι. Τοῦτο μὲν ἄρα, ἦν δ' ἐγώ,
δυνατόν, καὶ οὐ παρὰ φύσιν ζητοῦμεν τοιοῦτον εἶναι τὸν φύλακα.
Οὐκ ἔοικεν.

XVI. Ἆρ' οὖν σοι δοκεῖ ἔτι τοῦδε προσδεῖσθαι ὁ φυλακικὸς ἐσόμενος, πρὸς τῷ θυμοειδεῖ ἔτι προσγενέσθαι φιλόσοφος τὴν

---

375 C 19 **ἐναντία γὰρ—φύσις.** Plato regarded this opposition as the fundamental antithesis of human character, and thought it a statesman's foremost duty to blend the *θυμοειδές* and *πρᾶον* harmoniously together: see *Pol.* 306 C—311 C, infra III 410 B ff., VI 503 C, *Theaet.* 144 A, B.

21 **ταῦτα—ἔοικεν.** Van Heusde (*Initia Phil. Plat.* p. 471 *n.* 1) somewhat hastily declares these words to be corrupt, and supplies *ἀμφότερα ἔχειν* after *ταῦτα δέ*. *ταῦτα* refers like *τούτων* simply to the two qualities *πρᾶον* and *μεγαλόθυμον*: 'these'—meaning the combination of these as opposed to one of them—'are apparently unattainable': cf. VI 499 D *οὐ γὰρ ἀδύνατος γενέσθαι, οὐδ' ἡμεῖς ἀδύνατα λέγομεν.*

375 D 25 **ἐνοήσαμεν—φύσεις.** *ἐνενοήσαμεν* (with *q*) is read by most of the editors, quite unnecessarily, as Schneider shews. *νοεῖν* is not 'putare,' nor—I think—'perpendere,' but simply 'animadvertere,' 'notice,' as often. Such a meaning is peculiarly appropriate with *ἴδοι* following. Presently *ἄρα* is not 'then' (J. and C.), but 'after all.'

28 **τῷ φύλακι**: not *τῷ σκύλακι*, as Groen van Prinsterer conjectured (*Plat. Prosop.* p. 209). *τῷ φύλακι* of course depends on *παρεβάλλομεν*, and *ἐν ᾧ* is for *ἐν τούτῳ ὅ*.

375 E 29 **αὐτῶν τὸ ἦθος.** With *αὐτῶν* (unnecessary, but welcome, after *τῶν γενναίων κυνῶν*) cf. IV 428 A *n.*

πρὸς μὲν—τοὐναντίον. In *Od.* XVI 4—10 the dogs of Eumaeus do not bark at Telemachus, and Odysseus remarks (8, 9) *Εὔμαι', ἦ μάλα τίς τοι ἐλεύσεται ἐνθάδ' ἑταῖρος | ἢ καὶ γνώριμος ἄλλος, ἐπεὶ κύνες οὐχ ὑλάουσιν | ἀλλὰ περισσαίνουσι.* See also *Od.* XIV 30, where they bark at the stranger Odysseus, and cf. Heracl. 115 (Bywater) *κύνες καὶ βαΰζουσι ὃν ἂν μὴ γινώσκωσι.* In Aristotle similar characteristics are attributed to the lion: see *Physiogn.* 5. 809^b 34—36 *μεγαλόψυχον καὶ φιλόνικον, καὶ πραῢ καὶ δίκαιον καὶ φιλόστοργον πρὸς ἃ ἂν ὁμιλήσῃ*, and *Hist. An.* IX 44. 629^b 10—12.

35 **πρὸς τῷ θυμοειδεῖ κτλ.** There

φύσιν; Πῶς δή; ἔφη· οὐ γὰρ | ἐννοῶ. Καὶ τοῦτο, ἦν δ' ἐγώ, 376
ἐν τοῖς κυσὶν κατόψει, ὃ καὶ ἄξιον θαυμάσαι τοῦ θηρίου. Τὸ ποῖον;
῞Οτι ὃν μὲν ἂν ἴδῃ ἀγνῶτα, χαλεπαίνει, οὐδὲν δὴ κακὸν προπε-
πονθώς· ὃν δ' ἂν γνώριμον, ἀσπάζεται, κἂν μηδὲν πώποτε ὑπ'
αὐτοῦ ἀγαθὸν πεπόνθῃ. ἢ οὔπω τοῦτο ἐθαύμασας; Οὐ πάνυ,
ἔφη, μέχρι τούτου προσέσχον τὸν νοῦν· ὅτι δέ που δρᾷ ταῦτα,
δῆλον. Ἀλλὰ μὴν κομψόν γε φαίνεται τὸ πάθος αὐτοῦ τῆς
φύσεως | καὶ ὡς ἀληθῶς φιλόσοφον. Πῇ δή; Ἧι, ἦν δ' ἐγώ, ὄψιν B
οὐδενὶ ἄλλῳ φίλην καὶ ἐχθρὰν διακρίνει, ἢ τῷ τὴν μὲν καταμαθεῖν,
τὴν δὲ ἀγνοῆσαι. καίτοι πῶς οὐκ ἂν φιλομαθὲς εἴη, συνέσει τε

3. ὅτι ὃν Π: ὃν A. δὴ *q*: δὲ ΑΠ: γε Ξ. 3, 4. προπεπονθὼς Π: προσπεπονθὼς A¹: προπεπονθὸς A². 4. μηδὲν A²Π: μηδὲ (ut videtur) A¹.

---

seems to be no other example in good Greek of προσγενέσθαι meaning 'to become in addition': but we may compare προσέσονται II 373 A, προσέχειν VII 521 D, προσείπωμεν X 607 B, and similar instances with other verbs. I formerly wrote φιλόσοφον for φιλόσοφος ('that to the element of spirit nature should have added'—προσγενέσθαι, i.q. accessisse, cf. I 346 D—'a philosophical temperament'). The accusative with infinitive has however a harsh effect. Herwerden cuts the knot by deleting the προσ- of προσγενέσθαι.

376 A 3 **ὅτι—προπεπονθώς.** Schneider justly observes that ὅτι is not likely to be an interpolation, and might easily have disappeared before ὅν, as it has in A (see *cr. n.*). In itself the presence of ὅτι is an improvement. For οὐδὲν δή *v* (supported also by Stobaeus *Flor.* 43. 149) reads οὐδέν, which may be right. Cobet's οὐδὲ ἕν is too emphatic.

5 **οὐ πάνυ—τὸν νοῦν**: 'I have hardly thought of the matter till now.' μέχρι δεῦρο is more idiomatic than μέχρι τούτου in this sense, but Xen. *Cyr.* VIII 8. 9 and Dem. *de Cor.* 48 are closely analogous instances. The alternative rendering 'my observation has hardly extended so far' is (in view of οὔπω τοῦτο ἐθαύμασας;) less suitable.

376 B 8 **ὡς ἀληθῶς φιλόσοφον.** ὡς ἀληθῶς indicates that φιλόσοφον is to be taken in its etymological sense: cf. I 343 C *n.* The dog shews 'a love of knowledge' because he loves the known, and hates the unknown. Brandt (*Zur Entwick. d. Pl. Lehr. v. d. Seelentheilen* p. 10) ingeniously takes φιλόσοφον as = σοφὸν τοὺς φίλους: but the other interpretation is more natural and relevant. There is perhaps an allusion to the Cynics: see Schol. in Arist. ed. Brandis (Berlin 1836) 23ᵇ 16 ff. τετάρτη δὲ (sc. αἰτία τοῦ κληθῆναι Κυνικοὺς) ὅτι διακριτικὸν ζῷον ὁ κύων γνώσει καὶ ἀγνοίᾳ τὸν φίλον καὶ τὸν ἀλλότριον ὁρίζον· ὃν γὰρ γιγνώσκει, νομίζει φίλον εἶναι καὶ εἰ ῥόπαλον ἐπιφέροιτο, ὃν δὲ ἀγνοεῖ ἐχθρόν, καὶ εἰ δέλεαρ ἐπιφερόμενος εἴη. οὕτως οὖν καὶ οὗτοι τοὺς μὲν ἐπιτηδείους πρὸς φιλοσοφίαν φίλους ἐνόμιζον καὶ εὐμενεῖς ἐδέχοντο, τοὺς δὲ ἀνεπιτηδείους ἀπήλαυνον δίκην κυνῶν κατ' αὐτῶν ὑλακτοῦντες, and Philoponus *ib.* 35ᵃ 5—12. The Cynics were themselves very fond of pointing the moral from the lower animals to man (Dümmler *Proleg.* p. 58 *n.* 2), and Plato here paints them not unkindly in colours of their own. It should be noted that throughout II—IV Plato uses φιλόσοφος and φιλοσοφία with less of an intellectual than of a moral connotation. In the earlier books the word is for the most part connected with a gentle considerate disposition or character, whether naturally implanted or the result of culture (cf III 410 E, 411 C, 411 E): in 407 C the sense is somewhat different. See Nettleship in *Hellenica* pp. 77—79, and Krohn *Pl. St.* p. 71. It is not until the latter part of Book V (473 B ff.) where Plato is proposing to enter on the third and final stage of his ideal city, viz. the κατάστασις τῶν ἀρχόντων, that the intellectual aspect of the word begins to predominate over the moral. Cf. IV 439 D *n.*

καὶ ἀγνοίᾳ ὁριζόμενον τό τε οἰκεῖον καὶ τὸ ἀλλότριον; Οὐδαμῶς, ἦ δ᾽ ὅς, ὅπως οὔ. Ἀλλὰ μέντοι, εἶπον ἐγώ, τό γε φιλομαθὲς καὶ φιλόσοφον ταὐτόν; Ταὐτὸν γάρ, ἔφη. Οὐκοῦν θαρροῦντες τιθῶμεν καὶ ἐν ἀνθρώπῳ, εἰ μέλλει πρὸς τοὺς οἰκείους καὶ γνωρίμους | C πρᾶός τις ἔσεσθαι, φύσει φιλόσοφον καὶ φιλομαθῆ αὐτὸν δεῖν εἶναι; Τιθῶμεν, ἔφη. Φιλόσοφος δὴ καὶ θυμοειδὴς καὶ ταχὺς καὶ ἰσχυρὸς ἡμῖν τὴν φύσιν ἔσται ὁ μέλλων καλὸς κἀγαθὸς ἔσεσθαι φύλαξ πόλεως; Παντάπασι μὲν οὖν, ἔφη. Οὗτος μὲν δὴ ἂν οὕτως ὑπάρχοι. θρέψονται δὲ δὴ ἡμῖν οὗτοι καὶ παιδευθήσονται τίνα D τρόπον; καὶ ἆρά τι προὔργου ἡμῖν ἐστὶν αὐτὸ σκοποῦσι | πρὸς τὸ κατιδεῖν, οὗπερ ἕνεκα πάντα σκοποῦμεν, δικαιοσύνην τε καὶ ἀδικίαν τίνα τρόπον ἐν πόλει γίγνεται, ἵνα μὴ ἐῶμεν ἱκανὸν λόγον ἢ συχνὸν διεξίωμεν; καὶ ὁ τοῦ Γλαύκωνος ἀδελφὸς Πάνυ μὲν οὖν, ἔφη, ἔγωγε προσδοκῶ προὔργου εἶναι εἰς τοῦτο ταύτην τὴν σκέψιν. Μὰ Δία, ἦν δ᾽ ἐγώ, ὦ φίλε Ἀδείμαντε, οὐκ ἄρα ἀφετέον, οὐδ᾽ εἰ μακροτέρα τυγχάνει οὖσα. Οὐ γὰρ οὖν. Ἴθι οὖν, ὥσπερ ἐν μύθῳ μυθολογοῦντές τε καὶ σχολὴν ἄγοντες λόγῳ E παιδεύωμεν | τοὺς ἄνδρας. Ἀλλὰ χρή.

15. φιλόσοφον Π et in mg. A[2]: om. A[1]. 22, 23. ἵνα—διεξίωμεν Π et in mg. A[2]: om. A[1].

---

376 C 15 **φύσει** is better taken with φιλόσοφον than with πρᾶος. Cf. 375 B.

20 **ἆρά τι προὔργου κτλ.** See on 368 E.

376 D 22 **ἵνα μὴ—διεξίωμεν.** See *cr. n.* The omission in the text of A may be accidental (see *Introd.* § 5), but the sentence is certainly a difficult one. If the MSS are right, the meaning must be "For we do not want to be tedious,"—but συχνός is rather 'lengthy'—"and we do not want to leave unsaid what is required for completeness" (J. and C., comparing for συχνός *Theaet.* 185 E, *Phil.* 23 B al.). The conjectures of Teuffel (*Rhein. Mus.* 1850 p. 469) and Herwerden (*Mnem.* N. S. XI p. 339)—ἵνα ἢ (so *q*) ἐῶμεν συχνὸν (so *v*) λόγον ἢ ἱκανὸν (so *v*) διεξίωμεν and ἵνα μὴ ἢ ἐῶμεν συχνὸν λόγον ἢ οὐχ ἱκανὸν διεξίωμεν—improve the antithesis, but are much too violent. It is safest to retain the MS reading until a thoroughly satisfactory emendation appears. Dr Jackson suggests ἵνα μὴ ἐῶμεν ἱκανὸν λόγον ἢ οὐχ ἱκανὸν διεξίωμεν.

376 C—**378** E *Let us next consider how to educate our future Guardians: the enquiry may help us to discover the origin of Justice and Injustice.*

We may accept the traditional view that Education consists in 'Music,' or culture of the soul, and Gymnastic, or culture of the body. 'Music' must be begun before Gymnastic. Now 'Music' includes literature (λόγοι), *and literature is either true or false* (μῦθοι). *We shall educate our children by false literature before we teach them true; but we shall eschew all legends that inculcate views inconsistent with those which we desire our Guardians to entertain when they are men. Makers of legend or fable must be submitted to a censorship, and most of our present legends rejected. Caricatures of the gods, like the stories about Cronus and Uranus, Zeus and Cronus, are not only false in themselves, but ought not, even if they were true, to be told to children, lest they breed inhumanity and filial impiety; nor should children be persuaded by Poetry or other imitative arts to believe that the gods*

XVII. Τίς οὖν ἡ παιδεία; ἢ χαλεπὸν εὑρεῖν βελτίω τῆς ὑπὸ τοῦ πολλοῦ χρόνου ηὑρημένης; ἔστιν δέ που ἡ μὲν ἐπὶ σώμασι γυμναστική, ἡ δ' ἐπὶ ψυχῇ μουσική. Ἔστιν γάρ. Ἆρ' οὖν οὐ μουσικῇ πρότερον ἀρξόμεθα παιδεύοντες ἢ γυμναστικῇ; Πῶς δ' οὔ; Μουσικῆς δ', εἶπον, τίθης λόγους, ἢ οὔ; Ἔγωγε. Λόγων δὲ διττὸν εἶδος, τὸ μὲν ἀληθές, ψεῦδος δ' ἕτερον; Ναί. Παιδευτέον δ' | ἐν ἀμφοτέροις, πρότερον δ' ἐν τοῖς ψεύδεσιν; Οὐ μανθάνω, **377** ἔφη, πῶς λέγεις. Οὐ μανθάνεις, ἦν δ' ἐγώ, ὅτι πρῶτον τοῖς παιδίοις μύθους λέγομεν; τοῦτο δέ που ὡς τὸ ὅλον εἰπεῖν ψεῦδος, ἔνι δὲ καὶ ἀληθῆ. πρότερον δὲ μύθοις πρὸς τὰ παιδία ἢ γυμνασίοις χρώμεθα. Ἔστι ταῦτα. Τοῦτο δὴ ἔλεγον, ὅτι μουσικῆς πρότερον ἁπτέον ἢ γυμναστικῆς. Ὀρθῶς, ἔφη. Οὐκοῦν οἶσθ' ὅτι ἀρχὴ

33. εἶπον v: εἰπὼν ΑΠΞ q[1]: εἶπεν q[2]. 1. ψεύδεσιν Π: ψευδέσιν Α.

quarrel and fight among themselves. No plea of a 'deeper meaning' (ὑπόνοια) can justify the telling of such tales to children; for children cannot distinguish the spirit from the letter, and impressions made thus early are difficult to efface.

376 E ff. **τίς οὖν ἡ παιδεία; κτλ.** The educational scheme contained in Books II and III contributes to the purgation of the τρυφῶσα πόλις, and thereby helps to complete Plato's second picture of an ideal city: see on 372 D ff. For the correct understanding of these regulations it is well to bear in mind (1) that Plato's object in this preliminary discipline is to train the character rather than the intellect (cf. IV 430 C *n.*), and (2) that all the guardians have to pass through this curriculum. The higher scheme of education (in Book VII), on the other hand, is confined to those guardians who are to be made Rulers in the State, and its express aim is to educate the intellect rather than the will. See especially VI 502 E, VII 521 D—522 A *nn.* The best discussion on Plato's theory of education in its broader aspects is still, I think, Nettleship's Essay in *Hellenica* pp. 67—180. *Platon's Erziehungstheorie n. s. Schrift. dargestellt* von Dr A. Drygas Schneidemühl 1880 is a useful summary. For Plato's criticism of poetry, we may refer in particular to Heine's excellent dissertation *De rat. quae Platoni c. poet. Gr. intercedit* &c. Vratislaviae 1880, and to Reber's *Plato und die Poesie* Leipzig, 1864.

376 E 30 **ἔστιν δέ που—μουσική.** The usual Greek view (see for example Isocr. 15. 180—185), corrected by Plato in III 410 C ff.

33 **εἶπον.** Richter (*Fl. Jahrb.* 1867 p. 141) revives Muretus' conjecture εἶδος: but εἶπον is alone satisfactory. The confusion of ο and ω occurs in Inscriptions from the third century B.C. onwards (Meisterhans[3] p. 24 *n.* 128). See also *Introd.* § 5.

λόγων δὲ—ἕτερον. The word 'lies' is here used by Plato in its popular sense of that which is false in fact: his own definition of the 'veritable lie' is different: see 382 B *n.* 'Lies' are necessary—so Plato holds—in education: only they must be moral lies. Under 'lies' he includes stories (μῦθοι) about the gods, about the daemons and heroes long since dead, about a future life—all of them subjects where the alleged facts cannot be verified. The ἀληθεῖς λόγοι are concerned with men, and are passed over by Plato, because he could not state his view without anticipating the conclusion which the *Republic* is intended to prove (see III 392 A—C). This point is missed by Krohn (*Pl. St.* p. 12).

377 A 4 **ἀληθῆ**: i.e. truths of fact or history, not yet with reference to moral truth, for nothing has been said to change the connotation of ψευδής or its opposite ἀληθής. In Plato's view legend contains some elements of historical truth.

6 **ἀρχὴ—μέγιστον**: semi-proverbial, with reference to ἀρχὴ ἥμισυ παντός: cf.

B παντὸς ἔργου μέγιστον, ἄλλως τε καὶ νέῳ καὶ ἁπαλῷ | ὁτῳοῦν;
μάλιστα γὰρ δὴ τότε πλάττεται καὶ ἐνδύεται τύπον, ὃν ἄν τις
βούληται ἐνσημήνασθαι ἑκάστῳ. Κομιδῇ μὲν οὖν. Ἆρ' οὖν
ῥᾳδίως οὕτω παρήσομεν τοὺς ἐπιτυχόντας ὑπὸ τῶν ἐπιτυχόντων
μύθους πλασθέντας ἀκούειν τοὺς παῖδας καὶ λαμβάνειν ἐν ταῖς
ψυχαῖς ὡς ἐπὶ τὸ πολὺ ἐναντίας δόξας ἐκείναις, ἅς, ἐπειδὰν
τελεωθῶσιν, ἔχειν οἰησόμεθα δεῖν αὐτούς; Οὐδ' ὁπωστιοῦν παρή-
σομεν. Πρῶτον δὴ ἡμῖν, ὡς ἔοικεν, ἐπιστατητέον τοῖς μυθοποιοῖς, |
C καὶ ὃν μὲν ἂν καλὸν ποιήσωσιν, ἐγκριτέον, ὃν δ' ἂν μή, ἀποκριτέον·
τοὺς δ' ἐγκριθέντας πείσομεν τὰς τροφούς τε καὶ μητέρας λέγειν
τοῖς παισὶν καὶ πλάττειν τὰς ψυχὰς αὐτῶν τοῖς μύθοις πολὺ
μᾶλλον ἢ τὰ σώματα ταῖς χερσίν· ὧν δὲ νῦν λέγουσι τοὺς πολλοὺς
ἐκβλητέον. Ποίους δή; ἔφη. Ἐν τοῖς μείζοσιν, ἦν δ' ἐγώ, μύθοις
ὀψόμεθα καὶ τοὺς ἐλάττους. δεῖ γὰρ δὴ τὸν αὐτὸν τύπον εἶναι
D καὶ ταὐτὸν δύνασθαι τούς τε μείζους καὶ | τοὺς ἐλάττους. ἢ οὐκ
οἴει; Ἔγωγ', ἔφη· ἀλλ' οὐκ ἐννοῶ οὐδὲ τοὺς μείζους τίνας λέγεις.
Οὓς Ἡσίοδός τε, εἶπον, καὶ Ὅμηρος ἡμῖν ἐλεγέτην καὶ οἱ ἄλλοι

8. τύπον Richards: τύπος codd.

Laws 753 E, and (for the application of the sentiment) *ib.* 765 E.

377 B 8 **μάλιστα — τύπον.** See *cr. n.* To τύπος there are two objections: (1) the subject of πλάττεται and ἐνδύεται should be the same; but the subject of πλάττεται is not τύπος, but the νέῳ καὶ ἁπαλῷ ὁτῳοῦν, cf. πλάττειν τὰς ψυχὰς in C below: (2) it is more natural and correct to say that an object which 'is being moulded' 'puts on' a τύπος, than to say that the τύπος sinks into it. Reading τύπον we obtain the proper contrast between ἐνδύεται and ἐνσημήνασθαι: the youth puts on whatever impression or type the educator desires to stamp him with. The metaphor becomes more explicit in Plutarch *De lib. educ.* 3 F καθάπερ γὰρ σφραγῖδες τοῖς ἁπαλοῖς ἐναπομάττονται κηροῖς, οὕτως αἱ μαθήσεις ταῖς τῶν ἔτι παιδίων ψυχαῖς ἐναποτυποῦνται. Cf. also *Theaet.* 191 D and Hor. *Epp.* II 2. 8 argilla quidvis imitaberis uda.

10 **ῥᾳδίως οὕτω**: 'carelessly, without more ado': cf. 378 A and I 331 C. This idiomatic οὕτω is common with adverbs like ῥᾳδίως, εἰκῇ, ἁπλῶς, νῦν, ἐξαίφνης: for examples see Blaydes on Ar. *Wasps* 461.

377 C 15 **καλὸν**: sc. μῦθον, which some MSS (including Π) insert. For μῦθον understood from μυθοποιοῖς cf. III 399 D, where τοῦτο i.e. αὐλός is understood from αὐλοποιούς, 410 A, where αὐτοί (i.e. ἰατροί) follows ἰατρική, IV 421 E, and (with Schneider) *Laws* 886 C θεογονίαν διεξέρχονται, γενόμενοί τε (sc. οἱ θεοί) ὡς πρὸς ἀλλήλους ὡμίλησαν.

17 **πλάττειν κτλ.** Mothers and nurses practised massage on the bodies of infants: cf. *Laws* 789 E τιθέντες νόμους τὴν μὲν κύουσαν περιπατεῖν, τὸ γενόμενον δὲ πλάττειν τε οἷον κήρινον ἕως ὑγρόν, καὶ μέχρι δυοῖν ἐτοῖν σπαργανᾶν, and *Alc.* I 121 D. A trace of massage practised for medical purposes appears in Zeno *Fr.* 180 (ed. Pearson).

377 D 23 **ἐλεγέτην.** The dual links together Homer and Hesiod as jointly responsible for Greek theology: see on 363 A. Among the first to rebel against their authority were Pythagoras, Xenophanes, and Heraclitus (D. L. VIII 21, IX 18, IX 1). Xenophanes' protest was particularly famous in antiquity: see Sext. Emp. *adv. Math.* I 289 and IX 193 ap. Ritter and Preller *Hist. Philos. Gr.*[7] pp. 76, 77. Plato's attack on the Olympian

ποιηταί. οὗτοι γάρ που μύθους τοῖς ἀνθρώποις ψευδεῖς συντι-
θέντες ἔλεγόν τε καὶ λέγουσι. Ποίους δή, ἦ δ᾽ ὅς, καὶ τί αὐτῶν
μεμφόμενος λέγεις; Ὅπερ, ἦν δ᾽ ἐγώ, χρὴ καὶ πρῶτον καὶ μάλιστα
μέμφεσθαι, ἄλλως τε καὶ ἐάν τις μὴ καλῶς ψεύδηται. Τί τοῦτο; E
Ὅταν εἰκάζῃ τις κακῶς τῷ λόγῳ περὶ θεῶν τε καὶ ἡρώων οἷοί
εἰσιν, ὥσπερ γραφεὺς μηδὲν ἐοικότα γράφων οἷς ἂν ὅμοια βουληθῇ
γράψαι. Καὶ γάρ, ἔφη, ὀρθῶς ἔχει τά γε τοιαῦτα μέμφεσθαι.
ἀλλὰ πῶς δὴ λέγομεν καὶ ποῖα; Πρῶτον μέν, ἦν δ᾽ ἐγώ, τὸ μέγιστον
καὶ περὶ τῶν μεγίστων ψεῦδος ὁ εἰπὼν οὐ καλῶς ἐψεύσατο, ὡς
Οὐρανός τε εἰργάσατο ἅ φησι δρᾶσαι αὐτὸν Ἡσίοδος, ὅ τε αὖ
Κρόνος ὡς ἐτιμωρήσατο αὐτόν· τὰ δὲ δὴ | τοῦ Κρόνου ἔργα καὶ 378
πάθη ὑπὸ τοῦ ὑέος, οὐδ᾽ ἂν εἰ ἦν ἀληθῆ, ᾤμην δεῖν ῥᾳδίως οὕτω
λέγεσθαι πρὸς ἄφρονάς τε καὶ νέους, ἀλλὰ μάλιστα μὲν σιγᾶσθαι,
εἰ δὲ ἀνάγκη τις ἦν λέγειν, δι᾽ ἀπορρήτων ἀκούειν ὡς ὀλιγίστους,
θυσαμένους οὐ χοῖρον, ἀλλά τι μέγα καὶ ἄπορον θῦμα, ὅπως ὅ τι
ἐλαχίστοις συνέβη ἀκοῦσαι. Καὶ γάρ, ἦ δ᾽ ὅς, οὗτοί γε οἱ λόγοι
χαλεποί. Καὶ οὐ λεκτέοι γ᾽, ἔφην, ὦ Ἀδείμαντε, ἐν τῇ ἡμετέρᾳ B
πόλει, οὐδὲ λεκτέον νέῳ ἀκούοντι, ὡς ἀδικῶν τὰ ἔσχατα οὐδὲν ἂν

---

theology in this and the succeeding book was perhaps the severest blow that Paganism received before the Christian era, and pointed the way for those exaggerated diatribes against the heathen gods in which it afterwards became the fashion of early Christian apologists to indulge, beginning with the *Apology* of Aristides (cc. 8—11). Cf. X 607 B *n.*

26 **ὅπερ—ψεύδηται.** *ὅπερ* is *τὸ εἰκάζειν κακῶς περὶ θεῶν* etc. A distinction is drawn between mere lies and the lie which is in itself *οὐ καλόν*, unbeautiful and immoral in tendency, e.g. the story of Uranus and Cronus (*ὁ εἰπὼν οὐ καλῶς ἐψεύσατο* in E below). Such legends not merely misrepresent the gods, but also corrupt mankind.

377 E 28 **εἰκάζῃ.** It is taken for granted that Poetry is a species of imitation: cf. *Laws* 668 A—C.

32 **τῶν μεγίστων**: masculine, not neuter: cf. 378 B.

33 **Ἡσίοδος.** *Theog.* 154—181.

34 **τὰ δὲ δὴ κτλ.** *δή* emphasizes the case of Cronus as the most important (cf. *Prot.* 311 D, 312 E): it is so because the delinquent is Zeus, the reigning king of gods and men. The example set by Zeus on this occasion was no doubt sometimes used to justify wrong-doing: see for example Aesch. *Eum.* 640, 641, Ar. *Clouds* 904—906 *πῶς δῆτα δίκης οὔσης ὁ Ζεὺς | οὐκ ἀπόλωλεν τὸν πατέρ᾽ αὑτοῦ | δήσας; ib.* 1079 ff., Eur. *H. F.* 1317—1319, and especially Pl. *Euthyph.* 5 E—6 A, where Euthyphro urges the analogy in all seriousness to justify his vexatious prosecution of his own father. The pernicious effect of such legends on human conduct is again pointed out in *Laws* 886 C, 941 B: cf. also Isocr. *Bus.* 38—43, Luc. *Men.* 3, and Grote *Plato* III p. 194 *n.*

378 A 2 **ῥᾳδίως οὕτω**: 377 B *n.*

5 **θυσαμένους—ἀκοῦσαι.** *ἀπορρήτων* suggests the mysteries, whence the allusion to the 'mystic pig' (Ar. *Ach.* 764). For *ἄπορον*, 'unprocurable' (Jowett), *ἄπυρον* has been suggested, absurdly enough. *ἄπορον* is further explained by *ὅπως—ἀκοῦσαι.* It should be noted that *ὅπως* with a past tense of the indicative in clauses of this kind is rare in Plato: it occurs again only in *Laws* 830 B, 959 C (where *ἄν* should be expunged). Cf. Weber in Schanz's *Beiträge zur hist. Synt. d. Gr. Sprache* II 2, p. 64.

θαυμαστὸν ποιοῖ, οὐδ' αὖ ἀδικοῦντα πατέρα κολάζων παντὶ τρόπῳ, ἀλλὰ δρῴη ἂν ὅπερ θεῶν οἱ πρῶτοί τε καὶ μέγιστοι. Οὐ μὰ τὸν Δία, ἦ δ' ὅς, οὐδὲ αὐτῷ μοι δοκεῖ ἐπιτήδεια εἶναι λέγειν. Οὐδέ γε, ἦν δ' ἐγώ, τὸ παράπαν, ὡς θεοὶ θεοῖς πολεμοῦσί τε καὶ ἐπιβου-
C λεύουσι καὶ μάχονται· οὐδὲ γὰρ ἀληθῆ· | εἴ γε δεῖ ἡμῖν τοὺς μέλλοντας τὴν πόλιν φυλάξειν αἴσχιστον νομίζειν τὸ ῥᾳδίως ἀλλήλοις ἀπεχθάνεσθαι· πολλοῦ δεῖ γιγαντομαχίας τε μυθολογητέον αὐτοῖς καὶ ποικιλτέον, καὶ ἄλλας ἔχθρας πολλὰς καὶ παντοδαπὰς θεῶν τε καὶ ἡρώων πρὸς συγγενεῖς τε καὶ οἰκείους αὐτῶν. ἀλλ' εἴ πως μέλλομεν πείσειν, ὡς οὐδεὶς πώποτε πολίτης ἕτερος ἑτέρῳ ἀπήχθετο οὐδ' ἔστιν τοῦτο ὅσιον, τοιαῦτα λεκτέα μᾶλλον πρὸς
D τὰ παιδία εὐθὺς | καὶ γέρουσι καὶ γραυσί, καὶ πρεσβυτέροις γιγνομένοις καὶ τοὺς ποιητὰς ἐγγὺς τούτων ἀναγκαστέον λογο-

11. δοκεῖ *v*: δοκῶ ΑΠΞ *q*. 19. λεκτέα Π: om. Α.

---

378 B 9 **οὐδ' αὖ** has been needlessly doubted by Richter (*Fl. Jahrb.* 1867 p. 142), who suggests οὐδέν. The words ἀδικῶν—ποιοῖ correspond to the conduct of Uranus and Cronus towards their children: οὐδ' αὖ—τρόπῳ to Cronus' treatment of Uranus, and Zeus' of Cronus. Cf *Euthyph.* 5 E—6 A. The *Euthyphro* presents so many parallels to § 378 that some have—erroneously, no doubt—supposed it to be a spurious elaboration of that section: see my edition of the dialogue p. xxix.

378 C 15 **πολλοῦ δεῖ—ποικιλτέον.** πολλοῦ δεῖ is not adverbial (like ἥκιστα), as J. and C assert: otherwise δεῖ would be δεῖν (so Herwerden would read *Mnem.* N. S. XI p. 339). The asyndeton is justified by emphasis and the ampliative character of the sentence. The verbals are best explained (with Stallbaum) by supposing an ellipse of εἶναι: cf. Schanz *Nov. Comm. Pl.* p. 33.

16 **ποικιλτέον.** ποικίλλειν is used of depicting in a variety of colours (VIII 557 C), not necessarily by embroidery. Cf. 373 A *n.* There is probably a special reference here to the πέπλος. At the greater, if not also at the lesser, Panathenaic festival, a robe woven by Athenian maidens and representing the triumph of Athena and the Olympians over the giants, together with other celestial fights, was carried in procession to the Acropolis, and presented to the statue of the goddess in the Erechtheum: cf. *Euthyph.* 6 B, C and Mommsen *Feste d. Stadt Athen* pp. 107 ff. The subject was depicted on the Parthenon frieze: see Baumeister *Denkm. d. kl. Alterth.* II p. 1185. The allusion to the ceremony is the more appropriate in this connexion, if, as appears to be probable, the action of the dialogue takes place just before the great Panathenaea of 410 B.C. See *Introd.* § 3.

18 **ὡς οὐδεὶς κτλ.** Plato desires to obtain a religious sanction for his institutions, as in the myth III 414 B ff. The best δημηγόρος, according to Socrates, is ὁ στάσεις τε παύων καὶ ὁμόνοιαν ἐμποιῶν (Xen. *Mem.* IV 6. 14): and the Platonic State may from this point of view be regarded as "an attempt to determine the ways and means of securing political ὁμόνοια" (Krohn *Pl. St.* p. 369).

19 **λεκτέα**—see *cr. n.*—cannot be dispensed with. Madvig's suggestion, that μᾶλλον is corrupt for φατέον or ᾀστέον or the like, and Liebhold's μελητέον for μᾶλλον, are much less probable than the accidental omission of λεκτέα in A. See *Introd.* § 5. Vermehren (*Pl. Stud.* p. 92), rejecting λεκτέα, would carry on μυθολογητέον or the like; but this solution is much too difficult.

378 D 20 **καὶ πρεσβυτέροις γιγνομένοις.** The dative goes with λογοποιεῖν ('to make tales for them as they grow older'), and καί before τοὺς ποιητάς means

ποιεῖν. Ἥρας δὲ δεσμοὺς ὑπὸ ὑέος καὶ Ἡφαίστου ῥίψεις ὑπὸ
πατρός, μέλλοντος τῇ μητρὶ τυπτομένῃ ἀμύνειν, καὶ θεομαχίας
ὅσας Ὅμηρος πεποίηκεν οὐ παραδεκτέον εἰς τὴν πόλιν, οὔτ' ἐν
ὑπονοίαις πεποιημένας οὔτε ἄνευ ὑπονοιῶν. ὁ γὰρ νέος οὐχ οἷός
τε κρίνειν ὅ τί τε ὑπόνοια καὶ ὃ μή, ἀλλ' ἃ ἂν τηλικοῦτος ὢν λάβῃ
ἐν ταῖς δόξαις, δυσέκνιπτά | τε καὶ ἀμετάστατα φιλεῖ γίγνεσθαι. **E**
ὧν δὴ ἴσως ἕνεκα περὶ παντὸς ποιητέον, ἃ πρῶτα ἀκούουσιν, ὅ τι
κάλλιστα μεμυθολογημένα πρὸς ἀρετὴν ἀκούειν.

XVIII. Ἔχει γάρ, ἔφη, λόγον. ἀλλ' εἴ τις αὖ καὶ ταῦτα
ἐρωτῴη ἡμᾶς, ταῦτα ἅττα ἐστὶν καὶ τίνες οἱ μῦθοι, τίνας ἂν
φαῖμεν; καὶ ἐγὼ εἶπον Ὦ Ἀδείμαντε, οὐκ ἐσμὲν ποιηταὶ ἐγώ τε
καὶ σὺ ἐν τῷ παρόντι, | ἀλλ' οἰκισταὶ πόλεως. οἰκισταῖς δὲ τοὺς **379**
μὲν τύπους προσήκει εἰδέναι, ἐν οἷς δεῖ μυθολογεῖν τοὺς ποιητάς,
παρ' οὓς ἐὰν ποιῶσιν οὐκ ἐπιτρεπτέον, οὐ μὴν αὐτοῖς γε ποιητέον
μύθους. Ὀρθῶς, ἔφη· ἀλλ' αὐτὸ δὴ τοῦτο, οἱ τύποι περὶ θεολογίας,

---

etiam. This explanation was proposed by Richter (*Fl. Jahrb.* 1867 p. 138) and Vermehren (l. c. p. 91), and is probably right. Cf. Ar. *Frogs* 1054 f. Others connect the words with καὶ γέρουσι καὶ γραυσί: old men, old women, and the boys themselves as they grow older, must tell such stories πρὸς τὰ παιδία εὐθύς. But it is difficult to understand τοῖς παιδίοις with γιγνομένοις unless πρεσβυτέροις γιγνομένοις is construed with λογοποιεῖν.

22 **ὑέος**. Hephaestus. Διός is a false reading derived from a mistaken reference to *Il.* XV 18 ff. The story (according to Clement ap. Suid. s. vv. Ἥρας δὲ δεσμοὺς ὑπὸ υἱέος) was in Pindar: παρὰ Πινδάρῳ γὰρ ὑπὸ Ἡφαίστου δεσμεύεται ἐν τῷ ὑπ' αὐτοῦ κατασκευασθέντι θρόνῳ—καί φασι δεθῆναι αὐτὴν ἐπιβουλεύσασαν Ἡρακλεῖ. Cf. Paus. I 20. 3.

Ἡφαίστου ῥίψεις. *Il.* I 586—594.

23 **θεομαχίας—οὐ παραδεκτέον**. Homer *Il.* XX 1—74, XXI 385—513. Cf. Xenophanes *Fr.* 1. 19—22 (Bergk) and Pind. *Ol.* IX 43, 44 μή νυν λαλάγει τὰ τοιαῦτ'· ἔα πόλεμον μάχαν τε πᾶσαν χωρὶς ἀθανάτων.

24 **ἐν ὑπονοίαις**: adverbial, like ἐν φαρμάκου εἴδει III 389 B (J. and C.). The allegorical interpretation of Homer probably originated in the desire to save his character for piety and morality: πάντῃ γὰρ ἠσέβησεν (says Heraclides *Alleg. Hom.* ad init.), εἰ μηδὲν ἠλληγόρησεν. Before the time of Plato it was practised by Theagenes of Rhegium, Anaxagoras, Metrodorus of Lampsacus, Stesimbrotos of Thasos and others: see Wolf *Proleg. ad Homerum* pp. 161—166 and Jebb's *Homer* p. 89. In Plato's day the Cynics were the chief exponents of this school of criticism, especially Antisthenes: examples may be found in Winckelmann's *Antisth. Frag.* pp. 16, 23—28: cf. also Dümmler *Antisthenica* pp. 16 ff. Dümmler, many of whose combinations are highly speculative, regards the present passage as directed against Antisthenes, whose rivalry with Plato is well known: but there is nothing to suggest any personal reference. The historical Socrates occasionally played with the same weapons, as appears from Xen. *Symp.* 3. 6, and *Mem.* I 3. 7: so also does Plato, but seldom, if ever, without irony, e.g. *Rep.* I 332 B ἠνίξατο—ὁ Σιμωνίδης ποιητικῶς: cf. also *Theaet.* 194 C, *Alc.* II 147 B—D al. Plato's attacks upon Homer lent a great impetus to this method of exegesis—the only method, as it was thought, by which his animadversions could be met: cf. Schow's *Heraclides* pp. 223—234.

378 E—**380** C *What then are the moulds in which our legends must be cast? God should always be represented as He really is. Now God is good, and as good cannot be the cause of evil, He*

τίνες ἂν εἶεν; Τοιοίδε πού τινες, ἦν δ' ἐγώ· οἷος τυγχάνει ὁ θεὸς
ὤν, ἀεὶ δήπου ἀποδοτέον, ἐάν τέ τις αὐτὸν ἐν ἔπεσιν ποιῇ, ἐάν τε
ἐν μέλεσιν, ἐάν τε ἐν τραγῳδίᾳ. Δεῖ γάρ. Οὐκοῦν ἀγαθὸς ὅ γε
B θεὸς τῷ ὄντι | τε καὶ λεκτέον οὕτω; Τί μήν; Ἀλλὰ μὴν οὐδέν
γε τῶν ἀγαθῶν βλαβερόν. ἢ γάρ; Οὔ μοι δοκεῖ. Ἆρ' οὖν ὃ μὴ
βλαβερόν, βλάπτει; Οὐδαμῶς. Ὃ δὲ μὴ βλάπτει, κακόν τι ποιεῖ;
Οὐδὲ τοῦτο. Ὃ δέ γε μηδὲν κακὸν ποιεῖ, οὐδ' ἄν τινος εἴη κακοῦ
αἴτιον; Πῶς γάρ; Τί δέ; ὠφέλιμον τὸ ἀγαθόν; Ναί. Αἴτιον
ἄρα εὐπραγίας; Ναί. Οὐκ ἄρα πάντων γε αἴτιον τὸ ἀγαθόν,
ἀλλὰ τῶν μὲν εὖ ἐχόντων αἴτιον, τῶν δὲ κακῶν ἀναίτιον. Παν-
C τελῶς | γ', ἔφη. Οὐδ' ἄρα, ἦν δ' ἐγώ, ὁ θεός, ἐπειδὴ ἀγαθός,
πάντων ἂν εἴη αἴτιος, ὡς οἱ πολλοὶ λέγουσιν, ἀλλὰ ὀλίγων μὲν
τοῖς ἀνθρώποις αἴτιος, πολλῶν δὲ ἀναίτιος· πολὺ γὰρ ἐλάττω
τἀγαθὰ τῶν κακῶν ἡμῖν· καὶ τῶν μὲν ἀγαθῶν οὐδένα ἄλλον

6, 7. ἐάν τε ἐν μέλεσιν Π: om. A. 10. μὴ βλάπτει—Ὃ δέ γε Π et in mg. A²: om. A¹.

---

is the cause of little to the human race, for evil is far more common in the world than good. This is one of the canons which our poets are to observe; but it is constantly violated by Homer and others. Evil must never be attributed to the gods; or, if it is, it must be represented as a chastening visitation for the sufferer's good.

379 A 5 **οἷος τυγχάνει—ἐν μέλεσιν.** τυγχάνει ὤν = 'really is': cf. I 337 B *n.* On the omission of ἐάν τε ἐν μέλεσιν in A see *Introd.* § 5.

379 B 8 **ἀλλὰ μὴν κτλ.** It is first proved that good is not the cause of evil (ἀλλὰ μὴν—πῶς γάρ;), and next that good is the cause of εὐπραγία (τί δέ;—ναί): the conclusions are then stated in the reverse order. The step by which each conclusion is reached—the identification of ἀγαθόν and ὠφέλιμον—is Socratic (cf. Xen. *Mem.* IV 6. 8); but it is doubtful if the historical Socrates ever went so far as to deny that God is sometimes the cause of real evil or adversity to man, in spite of his belief in Providence (*Mem.* I 4 and IV 3; yet I 4. 16 οἴει δ' ἂν τοὺς θεοὺς τοῖς ἀνθρώποις δόξαν ἐμφῦσαι, ὡς ἱκανοί εἰσιν εὖ καὶ κακῶς ποιεῖν, εἰ μὴ δυνατοὶ ἦσαν;). The moral goodness of the Deity himself was proclaimed before Socrates and Plato by Xenophanes, Pindar, and the dramatists, but the inference, that God, because He is good, is never the cause of evil, is probably due to Plato. Bacchylides expresses a kindred sentiment in *Fr.* 29 (Bergk) Ζεὺς ὑψιμέδων, ὃς ἅπαντα δέρκεται, | οὐκ αἴτιος θνατοῖς μεγάλων ἀχέων. Read in the light of Book VI, the theology of this and the succeeding chapters gains, no doubt, in significance and depth; yet it is illegitimate to argue on this account (as Susemihl does *Genet. Entwick.* II p. 121) that the existence of the Idea of Good is already presupposed, unless it is shewn that Plato could not have purified his theology except by metaphysics. In point of fact, Plato might have written the end of Book III even if he had never thought of the Ideas at all.

379 C 15 **οὐδ' ἄρα—πάντων.** Contrast Aesch. *Ag.* 1485, 1486 Διὸς παναιτίου πανεργέτα. | τί γὰρ βροτοῖς ἄνευ Διὸς τελεῖται; *Suppl.* 822—824 and many other examples in Nägelsbach *Hom. Theol.* pp. 26, 51 ff., and *Nachhom. Theol.* pp. 16, 18, 60 ff., 73 ff.

17 **πολὺ γὰρ—ἡμῖν.** An old saying, as appears from Pind. *Pyth.* 3. 81 ff. μανθάνων οἶσθα προτέρων· | ἓν παρ' ἐσλὸν πήματα σύνδυο δαίονται βροτοῖς | ἀθάνατοι, and Eur. *Suppl.* 196, 7: cf. also Hom. *Il.* XXIV 527 ff., Philem. *Fr. Inc.* 65 (ed. Meineke). Plato and Aristotle

αἰτιατέον, τῶν δὲ κακῶν ἄλλ' ἄττα δεῖ ζητεῖν τὰ αἴτια, ἀλλ' οὐ
τὸν θεόν. Ἀληθέστατα, ἔφη, δοκεῖς μοι λέγειν. Οὐκ ἄρα, ἦν δ'
ἐγώ, ἀποδεκτέον οὔτε Ὁμήρου οὔτ' ἄλλου ποιητοῦ ταύτην | τὴν D
ἁμαρτίαν περὶ τοὺς θεοὺς ἀνοήτως ἁμαρτάνοντος καὶ λέγοντος,
ὡς δοιοὶ πίθοι

κατακείαται ἐν Διὸς οὔδει
κηρῶν ἔμπλειοι, ὁ μὲν ἐσθλῶν, αὐτὰρ ὃ δειλῶν·

καὶ ᾧ μὲν ἂν μείξας ὁ Ζεὺς δῷ ἀμφοτέρων,

ἄλλοτε μέν τε κακῷ ὅ γε κύρεται, ἄλλοτε δ' ἐσθλῷ,

ᾧ δ' ἂν μή, ἀλλ' ἄκρατα τὰ ἕτερα,

τὸν δὲ κακὴ βούβρωστις ἐπὶ χθόνα δῖαν ἐλαύνει·

| οὐδ' ὡς ταμίας ἡμῖν Ζεὺς E

ἀγαθῶν τε κακῶν τε τέτυκται.

XIX. Τὴν δὲ τῶν ὅρκων καὶ σπονδῶν σύγχυσιν, ἣν ὁ Πάνδαρος συνέχεεν, ἐάν τις φῇ δι' Ἀθηνᾶς τε καὶ Διὸς γεγονέναι, οὐκ
ἐπαινεσόμεθα, οὐδὲ θεῶν ἔριν τε καὶ κρί|σιν διὰ Θέμιτός τε καὶ 380
Διός· οὐδ' αὖ, ὡς Αἰσχύλος λέγει, ἐατέον ἀκούειν τοὺς νέους, ὅτι

---

make room for it in their philosophies: see e.g. *Pol.* 273 D, *Laws* 906 A, and Arist. *Probl.* X 45. 895ᵇ 39 ff. ἡ φύσις φαῦλα μὲν πάντα ποιεῖ, καὶ πλείους καὶ πλείω, σπουδαῖα δ' ἐλάττω, καὶ οὐ πάντα δύναται. The counterpart in the sphere of morals is Bias's οἱ πολλοὶ κακοί: with which may be compared *Rep.* IV 428 E, 431 A, 442 A, C, IX 588 D. It is a melancholy cry born of the age of iron: in the golden age—so Plato tells us *Pol.* 273 C—the balance was the other way.

19 **ἀλλ' ἄττα—τὰ αἴτια.** The dualism should not be taken too seriously, in spite of the good and evil souls in *Laws* 896 E. Plato is not now constructing a philosophy, but casting moulds for theology and poetry.

379 D 23 **δοιοὶ πίθοι.** See *Il.* XXIV 527—532 δοιοὶ γάρ τε πίθοι κατακείαται ἐν Διὸς οὔδει | δώρων οἷα δίδωσι κακῶν, ἕτερος δὲ ἑάων· | ᾧ μέν κ' ἀμμίξας δώῃ Ζεὺς τερπικέραυνος, | ἄλλοτε μέν τε κακῷ ὅ γε κύρεται, ἄλλοτε δ' ἐσθλῷ· | ᾧ δέ κε τῶν λυγρῶν δώῃ, λωβητὸν ἔθηκεν | καί ἑ κακὴ βούβρωστις ἐπὶ χθόνα δῖαν ἐλαύνει. In our Homer there is apparently only one jar of good to two of evil (see Leaf ad loc. and cf. 379 C *n.*): in Plato there is one of each. So great a difference is not likely to be due to Plato: it is easier to believe that he used a different recension from the Alexandrian. The use of κῆρες unpersonified was apparently not admitted by the Alexandrian critics. Cf. Wolf *Proleg.* p. 37, and Howes in *Harvard Studies in Cl. Phil.* VI p. 204.

379 E 31 **ἀγαθῶν—τέτυκται** is either from a lost line of Homer, or from some other poet (as Schneider inclines to think): note οὔτ' ἄλλου ποιητοῦ just above. There can hardly be any reference to *Il.* IV 84 Ζεύς, ὅς τ' ἀνθρώπων ταμίης πολέμοιο τέτυκται, as Howes imagines (l. c. p. 196). The sentiment is common: cf. e.g. Hes. *O. D.* 669 and Pind. *Isthm.* IV 52, 53 Ζεὺς τά τε καὶ τὰ νέμει, Ζεὺς ὁ πάντων κύριος.

32 **σπονδῶν σύγχυσιν.** *Il.* IV 69 ff.

34 **θεῶν ἔριν τε καὶ κρίσιν.** This is usually explained as referring to the Theomachy (*Il.* XX 1—74), which was caused by Zeus and Themis in the sense that Zeus sent Themis to summon the gods to the council at which it was

θεὸς μὲν αἰτίαν φύει βροτοῖς,
ὅταν κακῶσαι δῶμα παμπήδην θέλῃ.

ἀλλ' ἐάν τις ποιῇ, ἐν οἷς ταῦτα τὰ ἰαμβεῖα ἔνεστιν, τὰ τῆς Νιόβης πάθη ἢ τὰ Πελοπιδῶν ἢ τὰ Τρωϊκὰ ἤ τι ἄλλο τῶν τοιούτων, ἢ οὐ θεοῦ ἔργα ἐατέον αὐτὰ λέγειν, ἢ εἰ θεοῦ, ἐξευρετέον αὐτοῖς σχεδὸν ὃν νῦν ἡμεῖς λόγον ζητοῦμεν, καὶ λεκτέον, ὡς ὁ μὲν θεὸς δίκαιά τε
B καὶ ἀγαθὰ | εἰργάζετο, οἱ δὲ ὠνίναντο κολαζόμενοι· ὡς δὲ ἄθλιοι

---

sanctioned (*v.* 4). But (1) Themis' part in causing the Theomachy is very small, (2) the simplest and most natural meaning of *κρίσις* is not 'contention,' but 'judgment' or 'decision,' and (3) the Theomachy in Homer is not productive of evil to men, but only to the gods themselves: its citation here would therefore be quite irrelevant. W. R. Hardie (in *Cl. Rev.* IV p. 182) is, I believe, right in supposing that the strife of the goddesses three and Paris' judgment is meant. *ἔρις* and *κρίσις* are regularly thus used: e.g. Eur. *I. A.* 1307 *κρίσιν—στυγνὰν ἔριν τε καλλονᾶς*; cf. *ib.* 581, *Hel.* 708, *Troad.* 924, *Hec.* 644 f. Κρίσις was the name of Sophocles' play on the judgment of Paris (*Fr.* 330). The poem referred to by Plato is the Cypria (so also Wilamowitz *Hom. Unters.* p. 367 *n.* 46), which traced the war of Troy to the judgment of Paris, and that to Zeus' deliberations with Themis (Ζεὺς βουλεύεται μετὰ τῆς Θέμιδος περὶ τοῦ Τρωικοῦ πολέμου Kinkel *Epic. Graec. Fr.* p. 17. **Θέμιδος** is Heyne's emendation for **Θέτιδος**: but it is scarcely open to doubt: for the marriage of Peleus and Thetis, at which the three goddesses quarrelled, was an episode of the poem, and Thetis could hardly therefore have been privy to the plot. See Kinkel l. c. pp. 20, 22 and Jebb's *Homer* p. 153). Themis was Zeus' ἀρχαία ἄλοχος (Pind. *Fr.* 30 Bergk), and still appears as one of the Olympians in *Il.* XV 87. The Cypria is quoted again by Plato in *Euthyph.* 12 A. We may fairly suppose that *θεῶν ἔρις τε καὶ κρίσις* was the heading of one of the introductory episodes in the poem: to this also the omission of the article with *ἔριν τε καὶ κρίσιν* seems to point. Mr Hardie thinks Plato may have attributed the poem to Homer; but *Euthyph.* l. c. (ὁ ποιητὴς ὁ ποιήσας) does not favour this view.

380 A 3 **θεὸς μὲν—θέλῃ**: Aesch. *Fr.* 160. For other examples of this familiar Greek idea see Nägelsbach *Hom. Theol.* p. 321 and *Nachhom. Theol.* pp. 54 ff.

5 **ἐν οἷς—ἔνεστιν.** I have left these words in the text, although they are certainly open to suspicion, and have been condemned by Platt (*Cl. Rev.* III p. 72). The antecedent to *οἷς* is apparently *τὰ τῆς Νιόβης πάθη*; but the play was not called 'The sufferings of Niobe' but 'Niobe,' and the relative can hardly precede its antecedent in sentences of this kind. If *οἷς* is referred to *ταῦτα* understood after *ποιῇ*, then *ἐν* is difficult: 'if any one puts into poetry topics in which these iambics occur' gives no good sense. Unless Plato is writing very inaccurately, we must pronounce the clause a marginal gloss on *τὰ—πάθη*.

380 B 9 **ὠνίναντο κολαζόμενοι.** An earlier generation looked upon punishment as retributory—*δράσαντι παθεῖν*. This view appears in Hes. *Fr.* 217, ed. Goettling, and especially in Aeschylus, e.g. *Ag.* 1563 f., *Choeph.* 309—314, 400—404, 886, 927: in Sophocles and Euripides it is rarer (*Ant.* 1074—1076, *El.* 1411 f., 1495 f., *Andr.* 438, *Suppl.* 614—616), and Euripides expressly argues against it in *Or.* 508 ff. Traces of a milder theory were however contained in the doctrine *πάθος μάθος* (*Ag.* 176 ff.), as well as in the use of words like *σωφρονίζειν, δικαιοῦν, εὐθύνειν*, for 'punish.' In Plato punishment is remedial. Ignorance or vice is in the soul what disease is in the body (IV 444 C, cf. IX 591 A, B), and the judge is the soul's physician (III 409 E ff., *Gorg.* 478 D): hence (*Gorg.* 480 B ff.) the sinner should go before the judge as a patient visits his doctor, and we should even prosecute our guilty friends and relations. See also *Laws* 854 D, 862 E, 934 A, 944 D *τὸν γὰρ κακὸν ἀεὶ δεῖ κολάζειν, ἵν' ἀμείνων ᾖ.* The punishment, again, which awaits the wicked after death is intended to cure

μὲν οἱ δίκην διδόντες, ἦν δὲ δὴ ὁ δρῶν ταῦτα θεός, οὐκ ἐατέον λέγειν τὸν ποιητήν. ἀλλ' εἰ μὲν ὅτι ἐδεήθησαν κολάσεως λέγοιεν ὡς ἄθλιοι οἱ κακοί, διδόντες δὲ δίκην ὠφελοῦντο ὑπὸ τοῦ θεοῦ, ἐατέον· κακῶν δὲ αἴτιον φάναι θεόν τινι γίγνεσθαι ἀγαθὸν ὄντα, διαμαχετέον παντὶ τρόπῳ μήτε τινὰ λέγειν ταῦτα ἐν τῇ αὑτοῦ πόλει, εἰ μέλλει εὐνομήσεσθαι, μήτε τινὰ ἀκούειν, μήτε νεώτερον | μήτε πρεσβύτερον, C μήτε ἐν μέτρῳ μήτε ἄνευ μέτρου μυθολογοῦντα, ὡς οὔτε ὅσια ἂν λεγόμενα, εἰ λέγοιτο, οὔτε ξύμφορα ἡμῖν οὔτε σύμφωνα αὐτὰ αὑτοῖς. Σύμψηφός σοί εἰμι, ἔφη, τούτου τοῦ νόμου, καί μοι ἀρέσκει. Οὗτος μὲν τοίνυν, ἦν δ' ἐγώ, εἷς ἂν εἴη τῶν περὶ θεοὺς νόμων τε καὶ τύπων, ἐν ᾧ δεήσει τοὺς λέγοντας λέγειν καὶ τοὺς ποιοῦντας ποιεῖν, μὴ πάντων αἴτιον τὸν θεόν, ἀλλὰ τῶν ἀγαθῶν. Καὶ μάλ', ἔφη, ἀπόχρη.

Τί δὲ δὴ | ὁ δεύτερος ὅδε; ἆρα γόητα τὸν θεὸν οἴει εἶναι καὶ D οἷον ἐξ ἐπιβουλῆς φαντάζεσθαι ἄλλοτε ἐν ἄλλαις ἰδέαις, τοτὲ μὲν

16. μήτε ἐν Π: μὴ ἐν A.

---

their souls, unless they are incurable: and such as are themselves incurable, help to cure others by their deterrent example (X 616 A): so that in its deepest relations this doctrine reaches to the very roots of Plato's philosophy, with all due deference to Mr W. S. Lilly, who with much intemperance of language denounces those who attribute such a view to Plato (*Fortnightly Review* N.S. XLVI p. 116).

14 **ἐν τῇ αὑτοῦ πόλει**: 'in one's own city,' with reference to the subject of διαμαχετέον, not to τινα. Plato implies that the preachers of such theology must be suppressed in his ideal city. In all this Teichmüller (*Lit. Fehd.* I p. 114) detects an assault upon Isocrates, but his evidence is of the slightest.

380 C 16 **μυθολογοῦντα** is rejected by Herwerden: Ast suggested *μυθολογούμενα*. The choice of the participle is determined by λέγειν, which is more important than ἀκούειν: for without saying hearing is impossible. *μήτε νεώτερον μήτε πρεσβύτερον* belongs both to λέγειν and to ἀκούειν.

20 **νόμων τε καὶ τύπων**. All laws are in Plato's view only moulds or outlines, within which our actions should fall. Cf. infra 383 C and especially *Pol.* 294 A ff.

380 D—**383** C *In the second place, God is changeless, and incapable of deceiving. He is changeless, since He is the best. That which is the best cannot be changed by others, and will not change itself, for it can only change to what is worse. Homer and the other poets err in attributing changefulness to the gods. Neither can God deceive, for while the true or veritable lie, that is to say, ignorance of truth within the soul, is hateful alike to gods and men, the spoken lie, which is but an image of the other, is admissible only when used against enemies, or on behalf of friends, or to invest the ancient and unknown with a semblance of reality. God has no need of lying for any of these ends: he is therefore wholly true. In this respect also Homer and Aeschylus misrepresent the divine nature.*

380 D 23 **ἆρα γόητα κτλ.** Although the gods are constantly represented as deceivers in Greek poetry and legend, Plato was by no means the first to uphold the opposite view. In Pindar (*Ol.* 10. 4) Truth is the daughter of Zeus, and the dramatists often teach a similar doctrine: see Nägelsbach *Nachhom. Theol.* p. 46. There is a close imitation of Plato's argument throughout this passage in Arist. *Fr.* 15. 1476ᵇ 14 ff. ed. Rose.

αὐτὸν γιγνόμενον καὶ ἀλλάττοντα τὸ αὑτοῦ εἶδος εἰς πολλὰς
μορφάς, τοτὲ δὲ ἡμᾶς ἀπατῶντα καὶ ποιοῦντα περὶ αὑτοῦ τοιαῦτα
δοκεῖν, ἢ ἁπλοῦν τε εἶναι καὶ πάντων ἥκιστα τῆς ἑαυτοῦ ἰδέας
ἐκβαίνειν; Οὐκ ἔχω, ἔφη, νῦν γε οὕτως εἰπεῖν. Τί δὲ τόδε; οὐκ
ἀνάγκη, εἴπερ τι ἐξίσταιτο τῆς αὑτοῦ ἰδέας, ἢ αὐτὸ ὑφ' ἑαυτοῦ
E μεθίστασθαι | ἢ ὑπ' ἄλλου; Ἀνάγκη. Οὐκοῦν ὑπὸ μὲν ἄλλου
τὰ ἄριστα ἔχοντα ἥκιστα ἀλλοιοῦταί τε καὶ κινεῖται; οἷον σῶμα
ὑπὸ σιτίων τε καὶ ποτῶν καὶ πόνων, καὶ πᾶν φυτὸν ὑπὸ εἱλήσεών
τε καὶ ἀνέμων καὶ τῶν τοιούτων παθημάτων, οὐ τὸ ὑγιέστατον καὶ
381 ἰσχυρότατον ἥκιστα | ἀλλοιοῦται; Πῶς δ' οὔ; Ψυχὴν δὲ οὐ τὴν
ἀνδρειοτάτην καὶ φρονιμωτάτην ἥκιστ' ἄν τι ἔξωθεν πάθος ταρά-
ξειέν τε καὶ ἀλλοιώσειεν; Ναί. Καὶ μήν που καὶ τά γε ξύνθετα
πάντα σκεύη τε καὶ οἰκοδομήματα καὶ ἀμφιέσματα κατὰ τὸν αὐτὸν
λόγον τὰ εὖ εἰργασμένα καὶ εὖ ἔχοντα ὑπὸ χρόνου τε καὶ τῶν
ἄλλων παθημάτων ἥκιστα ἀλλοιοῦται. Ἔστι δὴ ταῦτα. Πᾶν
B δὴ τὸ καλῶς ἔχον, ἢ φύσει ἢ | τέχνῃ ἢ ἀμφοτέροις, ἐλαχίστην

31. καὶ κινεῖται—σιτίων τε Π et in mg. A[2]: om. A[1]. 33. οὐ Π: οὗ A.
4. καὶ ἀμφιέσματα Π: om. A.

---

25 **αὐτόν** is emphatic: the contrast is between actual and apparent transformations of the Deity. After *αὐτόν*, Herwerden would insert *παντοδαπόν*, comparing 381 E; before it, Richards adds *ἄλλον*, by which Benedictus and Ast replace *αὐτόν*. Hartman proposes <*τι*> *γιγνόμενον*. It has apparently escaped notice that *γιγνόμενον*, as well as *ἀλλάττοντα τὸ αὑτοῦ εἶδος*, belongs to *εἰς πολλὰς μορφάς* in the sense of 'passing into': cf. *Tim.* 57 A *εἰς ἄλλο τι γιγνόμενον*, infra III 400 B *εἰς βραχύ τε καὶ μακρὸν γιγνόμενον*, IX 588 C, and the frequent idiom *γένεσις εἰς* e.g. *Phaed.* 71 B, 71 E, *Phil.* 26 D, *Tim.* 49 C, 54 B.

27 **ἁπλοῦν**: one of the watchwords of Plato's State (370 B, C, 374 A—D al.): his citizens are to be nothing if not *ἁπλοῖ*. In making the gods a reflection of the type of human character which he desired to foster, Plato is acting strictly in accordance with the method of Greek theology, whose Olympus is an image of human society. The end of human action is *ὁμοίωσις θεῷ κατὰ τὸ δυνατόν* (*Theaet.* 176 B); and Plato's God, changeless and with 'no shadow of turning,' furnished the citizens of his ideal city with an abiding standard of human conduct. Cf. 383 C.

28 **τί δὲ τόδε;** Steinhart (*Platon's Werke* V p. 680) justly observes that the method of reasoning employed here—the disproof of each of the two members of the opposite alternative—recalls the arguments by which Parmenides established the attributes of Being (see RP.[7] §§ 95, 98); but the resemblance is not close enough to suggest that Plato was thinking of Parmenides when he wrote this chapter. Although the unchangeableness of God was taught by Xenophanes and the Eleatics, there are few if any traces of such a doctrine outside the philosophers before Plato.

380 E 30 **ὑπὸ μὲν ἄλλου κτλ.** *μέν* has its counterpart in *ἀλλ' ἆρα αὐτὸς αὑτὸν κτλ.* 381 B.

31 **κινεῖται**: a more general word for change than *ἀλλοιοῦται*: cf. *Theaet.* 181 D *δύο δὴ—εἴδη κινήσεως, ἀλλοίωσιν, τὴν δὲ περιφοράν*. The doctrine of the permanence and immutability of good enunciated here foreshadows, but does not presuppose, the metaphysical predominance of the Good in Book VI.

381 A 4 **καὶ ἀμφιέσματα**. See *cr. n.* and *Introd.* § 5.

μεταβολὴν ὑπ' ἄλλου ἐνδέχεται. Ἔοικεν. Ἀλλὰ *μὴν ὁ θεός γε καὶ τὰ τοῦ θεοῦ πάντῃ ἄριστα ἔχει.* Πῶς δ' οὔ; Ταύτῃ *μὲν δὴ ἥκιστα ἂν πολλὰς μορφὰς ἴσχοι ὁ θεός.* Ἥκιστα δῆτα.

XX. Ἀλλ' *ἆρα αὐτὸς αὑτὸν μεταβάλλοι ἂν καὶ ἀλλοιοῖ;* Δῆλον, *ἔφη, ὅτι, εἴπερ ἀλλοιοῦται.* Πότερον *οὖν ἐπὶ τὸ βέλτιόν τε καὶ κάλλιον μεταβάλλει ἑαυτόν, ἢ ἐπὶ τὸ χεῖρον καὶ τὸ αἴσχιον ἑαυτοῦ;* Ἀνάγκη, *ἔφη, ἐπὶ τὸ χεῖρον, εἴπερ ἀλλοιοῦται.* | *οὐ γάρ* C *που ἐνδεᾶ γε φήσομεν τὸν θεὸν κάλλους ἢ ἀρετῆς εἶναι.* Ὀρθότατα, *ἦν δ' ἐγώ, λέγεις· καὶ οὕτως ἔχοντος δοκεῖ ἄν τίς σοι, ὦ* Ἀδείμαντε, *ἑκὼν αὑτὸν χείρω ποιεῖν ὁπῃοῦν ἢ θεῶν ἢ ἀνθρώπων;* Ἀδύνατον, *ἔφη.* Ἀδύνατον *ἄρα, ἔφην, καὶ θεῷ ἐθέλειν αὑτὸν ἀλλοιοῦν· ἀλλ', ὡς ἔοικε, κάλλιστος καὶ ἄριστος ὢν εἰς τὸ δυνατὸν ἕκαστος αὐτῶν μένει ἀεὶ ἁπλῶς ἐν τῇ αὑτοῦ μορφῇ.* Ἅπασα, *ἔφη, ἀνάγκη, ἔμοιγε δοκεῖ.* Μηδεὶς *ἄρα,* | *ἦν δ' ἐγώ, ὦ ἄριστε, λεγέτω ἡμῖν τῶν ποιητῶν,* D *ὡς*

θεοὶ ξείνοισιν ἐοικότες ἀλλοδαποῖσι
παντοῖοι τελέθοντες ἐπιστρωφῶσι πόληας·

μηδὲ Πρωτέως *καὶ* Θέτιδος *καταψευδέσθω μηδείς, μηδ' ἐν τραγῳδίαις μηδ' ἐν τοῖς ἄλλοις ποιήμασιν εἰσαγέτω* Ἥραν *ἠλλοιωμένην ὡς ἱέρειαν ἀγείρουσαν*

Ἰνάχου Ἀργείου ποταμοῦ παισὶν βιοδώροις·

9. *γε* Π: *τε* A.

---

381 C 20 **ἀνάγκη**: sc. *ἐστίν*. For *ἔμοιγε δοκεῖ* without *ὡς* see on I 332 E. Hartman needlessly suggests *ἔμοιγε δοκεῖν*.

381 D 23 **θεοὶ—πόληας**. *Od.* XVII 485 f. Cf. Nägelsbach *Hom. Theol.* pp. 166—168.

25 **Πρωτέως καὶ Θέτιδος**. For Proteus see *Od.* IV 456—458. Aeschylus also wrote a satyric drama called Proteus: *Fragg.* 208—213. The transformations of Thetis to escape marrying Peleus had been celebrated by Pindar (*Nem.* IV 62 ff.), Sophocles (*Fr.* 548), perhaps also (as Stallbaum thinks) by Hesiod in his *ἐπιθαλάμιον εἰς Πηλέα καὶ Θέτιν* (see Goettling's Hesiod pp. XLIX and 304).

27 **ὡς ἱέρειαν—βιοδώροις**: from Aesch. *Ξαντρίαι* (Schol. on Ar. *Frogs* 1344). Dindorf (Aesch. *Fr.* 170) restores as follows: *ὀρεσσιγόνοισι* | *Νύμφαις κρηνιάσιν κυδραῖσι θεαῖσιν ἀγείρω,* | *Ἰνάχου Ἀργείου ποταμοῦ παισὶν βιοδώροις.* Herwerden's *βιοδώρου* is a wanton change: the sons of the river-god are his tributaries, and life-giving like himself. It is not clear why Hera was disguised as a priestess. The incident in Inachus' history most suited to dramatic treatment was the persecution of his daughter Io by Hera in consequence of her intrigue with Zeus. As Io was a priestess of Hera, Hera may have disguised herself as another priestess in order to discover her husband's unfaithfulness: see Apollod. *Bibl.* II 1. 3 *φωραθεὶς δὲ* (sc. *ὁ Ζεὺς*) *ὑφ' Ἥρας, τῆς μὲν κόρης ἁψάμενος εἰς βοῦν μετεμόρφωσε λευκήν, αὐτὴν δὲ ἀπωμόσατο μὴ συνελθεῖν.* The subject seems to have been treated by Sophocles in his satyric drama *Inachus* (*Fragg.* 255—278). With *ὡς ἱέρειαν ἀγείρουσαν* cf. *ἀγύρται* in 364 B and note ad loc.

E καὶ ἄλλα | τοιαῦτα πολλὰ μὴ ἡμῖν ψευδέσθων· μηδ' αὖ ὑπὸ
τούτων ἀναπειθόμεναι αἱ μητέρες τὰ παιδία ἐκδειματούντων, λέ-
γουσαι τοὺς μύθους κακῶς, ὡς ἄρα θεοί τινες περιέρχονται νύκτωρ
πολλοῖς ξένοις καὶ παντοδαποῖς ἰνδαλλόμενοι, ἵνα μὴ ἅμα μὲν εἰς
θεοὺς βλασφημῶσιν, ἅμα δὲ τοὺς παῖδας ἀπεργάζωνται δειλοτέρους.
Μὴ γάρ, ἔφη. Ἀλλ' ἆρα, ἦν δ' ἐγώ, αὐτοὶ μὲν οἱ θεοί εἰσιν οἷοι
μὴ μεταβάλλειν, ἡμῖν δὲ ποιοῦσιν δοκεῖν σφᾶς παντοδαποὺς
φαίνεσθαι, ἐξαπατῶντες καὶ γοητεύοντες; Ἴσως, ἔφη. Τί δέ; ἦν
382 δ' ἐγώ· ψεύδεσθαι | θεὸς ἐθέλοι ἂν ἢ λόγῳ ἢ ἔργῳ φάντασμα
προτείνων; Οὐκ οἶδα, ἦ δ' ὅς. Οὐκ οἶσθα, ἦν δ' ἐγώ, ὅτι τό γε
ὡς ἀληθῶς ψεῦδος, εἰ οἷόν τε τοῦτο εἰπεῖν, πάντες θεοί τε καὶ
ἄνθρωποι μισοῦσιν; Πῶς, ἔφη, λέγεις; Οὕτως, ἦν δ' ἐγώ, ὅτι τῷ
κυριωτάτῳ που ἑαυτῶν ψεύδεσθαι καὶ περὶ τὰ κυριώτατα οὐδεὶς
ἑκὼν ἐθέλει, ἀλλὰ πάντων μάλιστα φοβεῖται ἐκεῖ αὐτὸ κεκτῆσθαι.
B Οὐδὲ νῦν πω, ἦ δ' ὅς, μανθάνω. Οἴει γάρ τί με, ἔφην, | σεμνὸν
λέγειν· ἐγὼ δὲ λέγω, ὅτι τῇ ψυχῇ περὶ τὰ ὄντα ψεύδεσθαί τε καὶ

---

381 E 29 **τοιαῦτα πολλά.** For examples see Heyne's Virgil II pp. 146—152 (cited by Ast on 381 D). πολλὰ ψεύδονται ἀοιδοί, said the proverb.

31 **κακῶς**: like οὐ καλῶς 377 E.

ὡς—ἰνδαλλόμενοι. ἄρα expresses incredulity (358 C *n.*) and τινες contempt. Plato is thinking, *inter alia*, of the bugbears of the nursery—Lamia, Mormo, and Empusa, whose power of self-transformation was unlimited: see Blaydes on Ar. *Frogs* 293. ξένοις need not here be limited to the masculine gender. Cf. Strab. I 19 παισὶ προσφέρομεν—εἰς ἀποτροπὴν—τοὺς φοβεροὺς (μύθους). ἥ τε γὰρ Λαμία μῦθός ἐστι καὶ ἡ Γοργὼ καὶ ὁ Ἐφιάλτης καὶ ἡ Μορμολύκη.

382 A 1 **φάντασμα** is said with reference to φαίνεσθαι just above, and should be taken both with λόγῳ and ἔργῳ. The φάντασμα λόγῳ is the *spoken* lie: an example of the φάντασμα ἔργῳ is a φαντασία or unreal appearance (382 E). The words ἔργῳ φάντασμα προτείνων must not be understood of actual self-transformations of the gods.

2 **τό γε ὡς ἀληθῶς ψεῦδος κτλ.** Cf. τοῦ ἀληθῶς ψεύδους *Theaet.* 189 C, and (for the sentiment) *Laws* 730 C.

5 **οὐδεὶς ἑκὼν κτλ.** With Plato, as with Socrates, vice is ignorance, and involuntary. The doctrine reappears below in III 413 A, IX 589 C: it is further implied by the entire scheme of education in Books VI and VII. For other assertions of this view in Plato see Simson *der Begriff d. Seele bei Pl.* p. 125 *n.* 359. Cf. also Soph. *Fr.* 663 ἡ δὲ μωρία | μάλιστ' ἀδελφὴ τῆς πονηρίας ἔφυ. The identification of ignorance and vice is in harmony with popular Greek psychology, in which the intellect was not clearly distinguished from the will; it can be traced in the moral connotation of words like ἀμαθής, ἀπαίδευτος, ἀγνώμων. In close connexion with this conception of vice is Plato's view of punishment as remedial: see 380 B *n.*

382 B 8 **τὰ ὄντα κτλ.** τὰ ὄντα = 'the truth.' The contrast between the act and state in ψεύδεσθαί τε καὶ ἐψεῦσθαι resembles I 351 B: ἐψεῦσθαι, moreover, suitably bridges the distance between ψεύδεσθαι and ἀμαθῆ εἶναι. ἔχειν τὸ ψεῦδος corresponds to ψεύδεσθαι, κεκτῆσθαι τὸ ψεῦδος to ἐψεῦσθαι: the contrast is between 'holding, ready for use, that which is already possessed,' and permanent possession: cf. Soph. *Ant.* 1278 and Jebb ad loc. The words ἐν τῷ τοιούτῳ, 'in such a case' (i.e. ἐν τῷ ἐψεῦσθαι τῇ ψυχῇ περὶ τὰ ὄντα), are quite satisfactory (cf. III 393 C), and ought not to have caused Herwerden difficulty.

ἐψεῦσθαι καὶ ἀμαθῆ εἶναι καὶ ἐνταῦθα ἔχειν τε καὶ κεκτῆσθαι τὸ ψεῦδος πάντες ἥκιστα ἂν δέξαιντο καὶ μισοῦσι μάλιστα αὐτὸ ἐν τῷ τοιούτῳ. Πολύ γε, ἔφη. Ἀλλὰ μὴν ὀρθότατά γ' ἄν, ὃ νῦν δὴ ἔλεγον, τοῦτο ὡς ἀληθῶς ψεῦδος καλοῖτο, ἡ ἐν τῇ ψυχῇ ἄγνοια, ἡ τοῦ ἐψευσμένου· ἐπεὶ τό γε ἐν τοῖς λόγοις μίμημά τι τοῦ ἐν τῇ ψυχῇ ἐστὶν παθήματος, καὶ ὕστερον γεγονός, | εἴδωλον, οὐ πάνυ C ἄκρατον ψεῦδος. ἢ οὐχ οὕτω; Πάνυ μὲν οὖν.

XXI. Τὸ μὲν δὴ τῷ ὄντι ψεῦδος οὐ μόνον ὑπὸ θεῶν ἀλλὰ καὶ ὑπ' ἀνθρώπων μισεῖται. Δοκεῖ μοι. Τί δὲ δή; τὸ ἐν τοῖς λόγοις ψεῦδος πότε καὶ τῷ χρήσιμον, ὥστε μὴ ἄξιον εἶναι μίσους; ἆρ' οὐ πρός τε τοὺς πολεμίους, καὶ τῶν καλουμένων φίλων, ὅταν διὰ

9. ἐψεῦσθαι καὶ Π et in mg. A[2]: om. A[1].

---

13 **μίμημά τι—ψεῦδος.** *τοῦ ἐν τῇ ψυχῇ παθήματος* must not be explained (with Bosanquet *Companion* p. 93) as the state of mind of him who *tells* a lie: for that is knowledge, and the spoken lie certainly is not an imitation of knowledge. They refer to the 'true lie,' which is a certain *πάθημα* in the soul of the 'true liar,' viz. ignorance, and of which the spoken lie is an imitation. It is a tolerably accurate definition of a lie to call it 'an imitation of ignorance in the soul': cf. IV 443 C *n*. The spoken lie is 'not a wholly unmixed lie,' because it implies that the speaker *knows* the truth: in a certain sense therefore it is mixed with truth. It is *ὕστερον γεγονός*, because the spoken lie cannot be uttered until the truth is known. Inasmuch as the spoken lie is mixed with truth, it is better than the 'veritable lie.' We have here nothing but a special application of the old Socratic paradox *ὁ ἑκὼν ἁμαρτάνων ἀμείνων* (see on I 334 A). I have placed a comma after *γεγονός*, to mark the antithesis between *εἴδωλον* and *ἄκρατον ψεῦδος*, and because *εἴδωλον* is not so much to be taken with *τοῦ ἐν τῇ ψυχῇ παθήματος*: rather it stands for *εἴδωλον ψεύδους*, as *οὐ πάνυ ἄκρατον ψεῦδος* shews. The distinction between veritable and spoken lies savours, no doubt, of idealism: but it enables Plato to call his ideal archons ideally truthful, even when practically they tell lies, and it is with this object in view that the distinction is introduced. See III 389 B.

382 C 18 **πότε—μίσους;** *τῷ* is masculine: it is presently shewn that the spoken lie is useless to God. Plato does not permit a man to lie in his own interest. Ordinary Greek morality, in spite of Achilles' *ἐχθρὸς γάρ μοι κεῖνος ὁμῶς Ἀΐδαο πύλῃσιν* etc., probably did. The saying of Democritus *ἀληθομυθεύειν χρεών, ὅπου λώιον* (Stob. *Flor.* 12. 13) leaves us to infer that we may also lie *ὅπου λώιον*. Cf. Soph. *Fr.* 323 *καλὸν μὲν οὖν οὐκ ἔστι τὰ ψεύδη λέγειν· | ὅτῳ δ' ὄλεθρον δεινὸν ἀλήθει' ἄγει, | συγγνωστὸν εἰπεῖν ἐστὶ καὶ τὸ μὴ καλόν*. The cynical immorality of Hdt. III 72 exceeds what Greek public opinion would have tolerated: cf. Arist. *Eth. Nic.* IV ch. 13. See also on III 389 B and Nägelsbach *Nachhom. Theol.* pp. 240 ff.

ἆρ' οὐ—πολεμίους κτλ. Cf. I 331 E—332 B.

19 **τῶν καλουμένων φίλων** depends on *ἀποτροπῆς*. If *ὅταν διὰ μανίαν—τότε* had been omitted, the construction would be quite clear: as it is, some difficulty has been felt. Schneider understands *τινες* as subject to *ἐπιχειρῶσι*: by Hermann *ὅταν* is changed to *οἳ ἂν*: by Herwerden *ὅταν* to *οἳ ἂν* and *τότε* to *τοῦτο*: while Stallbaum resorts to an anacoluthon, as if Plato had intended to say *τῶν καλουμένων φίλων ἕνεκα*. None of these expedients is so simple as to connect *ἀποτροπῆς* with *φίλων*. The clause *ὅταν—πράττειν* cancels out with *τότε* and does not affect the construction. *καλουμένων*, 'so-called,' involves a theory of friendship, viz. that no one who is *ἀνόητος καὶ μαινόμενος* can be a friend to man (any more than to God: cf. 382 E).

μανίαν ἤ τινα ἄνοιαν κακόν τι ἐπιχειρῶσιν πράττειν, τότε ἀποτρο-
D πῆς ἕνεκα ὡς φάρμακον χρήσιμον γίγνεται; καὶ ἐν αἷς νῦν | δὴ
ἐλέγομεν ταῖς μυθολογίαις, διὰ τὸ μὴ εἰδέναι ὅπῃ τἀληθὲς ἔχει
περὶ τῶν παλαιῶν, ἀφομοιοῦντες τῷ ἀληθεῖ τὸ ψεῦδος ὅ τι μάλιστα,
οὕτω χρήσιμον ποιοῦμεν; Καὶ μάλα, ἦ δ' ὅς, οὕτως ἔχει. Κατὰ
τί δὴ οὖν τούτων τῷ θεῷ τὸ ψεῦδος χρήσιμον; πότερον διὰ τὸ μὴ
εἰδέναι τὰ παλαιὰ ἀφομοιῶν ἂν ψεύδοιτο; Γελοῖον μέντ' ἂν εἴη,
ἔφη. Ποιητὴς μὲν ἄρα ψευδὴς ἐν θεῷ οὐκ ἔνι. Οὔ μοι δοκεῖ.
E Ἀλλὰ δεδιὼς τοὺς ἐχθροὺς | ψεύδοιτο; Πολλοῦ γε δεῖ. Ἀλλὰ
δι' οἰκείων ἄνοιαν ἢ μανίαν; Ἀλλ' οὐδείς, ἔφη, τῶν ἀνοήτων καὶ
μαινομένων θεοφιλής. Οὐκ ἄρα ἔστιν οὗ ἕνεκα ἂν θεὸς ψεύδοιτο.
Οὐκ ἔστιν. Πάντῃ ἄρα ἀψευδὲς τὸ δαιμόνιόν τε καὶ τὸ θεῖον.
Παντάπασι μὲν οὖν, ἔφη. Κομιδῇ ἄρα ὁ θεὸς ἁπλοῦν καὶ ἀληθὲς
ἔν τε ἔργῳ καὶ ἐν λόγῳ, καὶ οὔτε αὐτὸς μεθίσταται οὔτε ἄλλους
ἐξαπατᾷ, οὔτε κατὰ φαντασίας οὔτε κατὰ λόγους οὔτε κατὰ
383 σημείων πομπὰς ὕπαρ οὐδ' ὄναρ. | Οὕτως, ἔφη, ἔμοιγε καὶ αὐτῷ
φαίνεται σοῦ λέγοντος. Συγχωρεῖς ἄρα, ἔφην, τοῦτον δεύτερον
τύπον εἶναι, ἐν ᾧ δεῖ περὶ θεῶν καὶ λέγειν καὶ ποιεῖν, ὡς μήτε
αὐτοὺς γόητας ὄντας τῷ μεταβάλλειν ἑαυτοὺς μήτε ἡμᾶς ψεύδεσι
παράγειν ἐν λόγῳ ἢ ἐν ἔργῳ; Συγχωρῶ. Πολλὰ ἄρα Ὁμήρου

34. *οὔτε κατὰ φαντασίας* Π: om. A. 35. *ὕπαρ οὐδ' ὄναρ* A^1: *οὐθ' ὕπαρ οὐδ' ὄναρ* A^2ΠΞq^1: *οὐθ' ὕπαρ οὐθ' ὄναρ* q^2.

---

382 D 22 **μυθολογίαις κτλ.** Plato seems to have supposed that ancient history and mythology could be manufactured to order. Cf. Arist. *Pol.* B 9. 1269^b 28 and Susemihl ad loc. He attempts the task himself in III 414 B ff., *Prot.* 320 C—322 D (unless this is really an extract from one of Protagoras' own works), *Pol.* 269 A—274 E, *Tim.* 21 A—25 D, *Critias*, and *Laws* 676 B—682 D.

26 **εἰδέναι.** The omniscience of the gods was no new doctrine: see Nägelsbach *Hom. Theol.* p. 23, *Nachhom. Theol.* pp. 23 ff.

27 **ποιητὴς—ἔνι.** 'There is nothing of the lying poet in God.' Cf. 365 C *n.* I can see no point in Stallbaum's notion that there is a play on the two senses of *ποιητής*—'poet' and 'creator.'

382 E 28 **ψεύδοιτο.** *ἄν* is carried on: cf. I 352 E *n.*

30 **μαινομένων.** *Phaedr.* 265 A *μανίας δέ γε εἴδη δύο, τὴν μὲν ὑπὸ νοσημάτων ἀνθρωπίνων, τὴν δὲ ὑπὸ θείας ἐξαλλαγῆς τῶν εἰωθότων νομίμων γιγνομένην.* Plato refers here only to the first variety: the second is discussed in *Phaedr.* 265 B ff.

32 **κομιδῇ ἄρα κτλ.** The words *ἁπλοῦν, οὔτε αὐτὸς μεθίσταται* sum up 380 D—381 E (see on *ἁπλοῦν* in 380 D), the rest 382 A—D.

34 **οὔτε κατὰ φαντασίας.** See *cr. n.* and *Introd.* § 5. *φαίνεσθαι* and *ἔργῳ φάντασμα προτείνων* in 381 E, 382 A favour the view that these words are genuine.

35 **ὕπαρ οὐδ' ὄναρ.** See *cr. n.* *ὕπαρ οὐδ' ὄναρ* is not co-ordinate with *οὔτε κατὰ φαντασίας* etc., but subordinate to them: for *φαντασίαι, λόγοι*, and especially *σημείων πομπαί* might be vouchsafed either in waking moments or in dreams: see Stengel and Oehmichen in Iwan Müller's *Handbuch* V 3 pp. 37—47. For the doctrine cf. Xen. *Mem.* I 3. 4.

383 A 5 **παράγειν.** *παράγοντας*

ἐπαινοῦντες ἄλλα τοῦτο οὐκ ἐπαινεσόμεθα, τὴν τοῦ ἐνυπνίου πομπὴν ὑπὸ Διὸς τῷ Ἀγαμέμνονι, οὐδὲ Αἰσχύλου, ὅταν φῇ ἡ Θέτις τὸν Ἀπόλλω ἐν τοῖς αὑτῆς | γάμοις ᾄδοντα B

ἐνδατεῖσθαι τὰς ἑὰς εὐπαιδίας,
νόσων τ' ἀπείρους καὶ μακραίωνας βίους.
ξύμπαντά τ' εἰπών, θεοφιλεῖς ἐμὰς τύχας
παιῶν' ἐπηυφήμησεν, εὐθυμῶν ἐμέ.
κἀγὼ τὸ Φοίβου θεῖον ἀψευδὲς στόμα
ἤλπιζον εἶναι, μαντικῇ βρύον τέχνῃ.
ὁ δ', αὐτὸς ὑμνῶν, αὐτὸς ἐν θοίνῃ παρών,
αὐτὸς τάδ' εἰπών, αὐτός ἐστιν ὁ κτανὼν
τὸν παῖδα τὸν ἐμόν.

| ὅταν τις τοιαῦτα λέγῃ περὶ θεῶν, χαλεπανοῦμέν τε καὶ χορὸν οὐ C δώσομεν, οὐδὲ τοὺς διδασκάλους ἐάσομεν ἐπὶ παιδείᾳ χρῆσθαι τῶν

8. Ἀπόλλω A^{2}Π: Ἀπόλλων vel Ἀπόλλων' ut videtur A^1. αὑτῆς A^{2}Π: αὑτοῖς A^1.

(conjectured by Richards) would be easier, but the slip, if such it be, is excusable. ὡς—ὄντας is not the accusative absolute: if it were, ὡς would express the reason, and here it does not. We are defining the τύπος: and the construction is (they must ποιεῖν) ὡς μήτε αὐτοὺς γόητας ὄντας, 'represent the gods as neither themselves being sorcerers,' etc. In παράγειν the construction is changed, but the change is natural, for our rule applies both to λόγος and ποίησις (καὶ λέγειν καὶ ποιεῖν), and λέγειν takes the accusative and infinitive. Both λέγειν and ποιεῖν affect the construction, which involves a sort of chiasmus. Cf. III 390 B *n*.

6 **τοῦ ἐνυπνίου πομπήν**. *Il.* II 1—34.

8 **ἡ Θέτις κτλ**. The verses are perhaps, as Schneider conjectures, from Aeschylus' Ὅπλων κρίσις, in which Thetis was one of the characters (Schol. on Ar. *Ach.* 883). Apollo with his harp (ἔχων φόρμιγγα) appears as present at the marriage of Thetis also in Homer (*Il.* XXIV 62, 63). Plato accommodates the beginning of the quotation to his own sentence: in Aeschylus perhaps it ran ὁ δ' ἐνεδατεῖτο τὰς ἐμὰς εὐπαιδίας (so Butler, quoted by Schneider). ἐνδατεῖσθαι, 'to dwell upon or emphasize,' is elsewhere always used in an ominous sense (see Jebb on Soph. *O. T.* 205): and here too, perhaps, it strikes a foreboding note. The words μακραίωνας βίους were doubted by Stephanus, who suggested μακραίωνος βίου (so Euseb. *Praep. Ev.* XIII 3. 35) or μακραίωνας βίου: but Apollo's prophecies did not refer to Achilles only, so that the plural is justified. ἀπείρους should be taken not with εὐπαιδίας, but with βίους, which is in apposition to εὐπαιδίας. In the next line θεοφιλεῖς ἐμὰς τύχας depends on the compound expression παιῶν' ἐπηυφήμησεν—a construction frequent in Aeschylus, especially with verbs which denote singing, celebrating, etc. (*Ag.* 174, 175 al.): after enumerating all the blessings in store for Thetis (ξύμπαντά τ' εἰπών) Apollo raised a paean over her θεοφιλεῖς τύχας. This explanation—Schneider's—is much better than to connect ξύμπαντα adverbially with θεοφιλεῖς.

383 B 13 **κἀγὼ—εἶναι**. Contrast Aesch. *P. V.* 1032 ψευδηγορεῖν γὰρ οὐκ ἐπίσταται στόμα | τὸ Δῖον, ἀλλὰ πᾶν ἔπος τελεῖ: see on 380 D above.

14 **ἤλπιζον**: 'fancied,' not 'hoped': cf. V 451 A, IX 573 C, and ἐλπίς in VII 517 B. This idiomatic usage is illustrated by Rutherford on Babrius 9. 2.

νέων, εἰ μέλλουσιν ἡμῖν οἱ φύλακες θεοσεβεῖς τε καὶ θεῖοι γίγνεσθαι, καθ' ὅσον ἀνθρώπῳ ἐπὶ πλεῖστον οἷόν τε. Παντάπασιν, ἔφη, ἔγωγε τοὺς τύπους τούτους συγχωρῶ καὶ ὡς νόμοις ἂν χρῴμην.

ΤΕΛΟΣ ΠΟΛΙΤΕΙΑΣ Β'.

---

383 C 20 **θεῖοι—οἷόν τε.** The object of all worship and all religion, as of human action in general, is assimilation to God: cf. X 613 A *n*.

APPENDICES TO BOOK II.

I.

II 359 D. τῷ **Γύγου** τοῦ Λυδοῦ προγόνῳ.

Most of the emendations (e.g. Γύγῃ τῷ τοῦ Λυδοῦ προγόνῳ) which have been suggested in order to bring the present passage into harmony with the allusion in Book X 612 B, assume that the Gyges of 'Gyges' ring' is identical with the famous Gyges (who reigned about 687—654 B.C.), founder of the third or Mermnad dynasty of Lydian kings (Hdt. I 8—13). On this assumption τοῦ Λυδοῦ cannot mean 'Lydus' (the eponymous ruler of Lydia: see Hdt. I 7), but must mean 'the Lydian' i.e. (according to the usual interpretation) Croesus, who was the πέμπτος ἀπόγονος Γύγεω (Hdt. I 13). There is however no proof to shew that ὁ Λυδός could without further specification denote Croesus; and on this ground alone Wiegand's proposal (adopted by Hermann, Baiter, and Hartman) τῷ [Γύγου] τοῦ Λυδοῦ προγόνῳ breaks down: while Jowett and Campbell's alternative suggestions τῷ Κροίσου τοῦ Λυδοῦ προγόνῳ, and Γύγῃ τῷ Κροίσου τοῦ Λυδοῦ προγόνῳ, although satisfactory in point of sense, fail to account for the disappearance of Κροίσου. The proposals of Ast—τῷ Γύγῃ τοῦ Λυδοῦ (or Λυδῶν) προγόνῳ, and [τῷ] Γύγου τοῦ Λυδοῦ [προγόνῳ]—will hardly win favour, while Stallbaum's τῷ Γύγῃ [τοῦ Λυδοῦ προγόνῳ] merely cuts the knot.

There is however no solid reason for connecting the Gyges of the proverb with the historical Gyges. In narrating the adventures of the latter, Herodotus makes no mention of a magic ring; but if such a legend had been told of the founder of the Mermnadae, Herodotus is hardly likely to have ignored it. In Plato's narrative, on the other hand, everything hangs on the ring. Nor is the magic ring known to Nicolaus Damascenus, whose account of Gyges seems to follow a different tradition from that of Herodotus: see Müller's *Frag. Hist. Graec.* III pp. 382—386. It is therefore possible that Plato's story refers not to Herodotus' Gyges, but to some homonymous ancestor of his, perhaps (as Stein suggests on Hdt. I 13) the mythical founder of the family, whose name may have survived in the λίμνη Γυγαίη (Hdt. I 93). The Gyges of history was not the first member of his family to bear that name: his great-grandfather at least was also called Gyges (Nic. Dam. l.c.). The resemblance between the two stories—that of Herodotus and that of Plato—is confined to two incidents, viz. the joint murder of the reigning sovereign by the queen and her paramour, and their succession to the throne. In these two features the history of the later Gyges may well have been embellished from the legends about his mythical namesake, or he may actually have copied his ancestor's example. It is noticeable that Cicero says nothing to shew that he identified the Gyges of Plato's story with the Gyges of history; and in a poem by Nizámí (as Mr J. G. Frazer has pointed out to me), where Plato tells the story of the ring, the name of Gyges is not even mentioned. (See Prof. Cowell's article in the *Journal of the Asiatic Society of Bengal*, Vol. 30 pp. 151—157. Prof. Cowell thinks Nizámí became acquainted with the legend through Arabic translations of the *Republic.*) Thinking it probable, therefore, that the proverbial ring of Gyges belonged not to Herodotus' Gyges, but to one of his ancestors bearing the same name, I have retained the MS reading. I do not think that the suppression of the name is a difficulty, though it would be easy to write (as I formerly did) <τῷ Γύγῃ>, τῷ Γύγου τοῦ Λυδοῦ προγόνῳ. See *Introd.* § 5. Such a solution would bring the text into strict verbal harmony with x 612 B, with Cicero *De off.* III 38 (where the story is related, not of an ancestor of Gyges, but of Gyges himself—*hinc ille Gyges inducitur a Platone*), with Lucian *Nav.* 41 and *Bis Acc.* 21, and with Philostratus *Vit. Apoll.* 101. In each of these places we hear of 'Gyges' ring,' not of 'Gyges' ancestor's ring.' But it is better to adhere to the almost unanimous testimony of the MSS, especially as in this particular passage they are reinforced by Proclus. Schneider can hardly be right in supposing that the older Gyges is an invention of Plato's, although in other respects his note is deserving of attention: "Platoni vero licebat alterum Gygen fingere, ingenio et fortuna similem interfectori Candaulae, quem ideo genus ab illo ducentem facit, prioris nomen, quippe quod commune ei cum posteriori esset, reticens."

II.

II 359 E. τοῦτον δὲ ἄλλο μὲν ἔχειν οὐδέν, περὶ δὲ τῇ χειρὶ χρυσοῦν δακτύλιον, ὃν περιελόμενον ἐκβῆναι.

If (with A) we omit ἔχειν, the meaning must still be: 'the corpse (τοῦτον) <had> nothing else upon it, only on its hand a gold ring, which he (Gyges) took off and went out.' But it is impossible in Greek, as in English, to dispense with 'had.'

Dr Jackson proposes to read τούτου for τοῦτον, and omit ἔχειν and ὅν, understanding the sentence to mean 'he took nothing from the corpse except a gold ring on its hand, and then went out' (*Proceedings of the Cambridge Philol. Soc.* Vol. II 1882, p. 12). In favour of this view he urges that 'the nudity of the corpse is not mentioned, either in Cicero's paraphrase *de Officiis* III 9 § 38, or in that of Nizámí' (see *App.* I). Philostratus is also silent on the subject (*Heroic.* 28). If the principle of this solution is correct, I should prefer to retain τοῦτον: for there seems to be no reason why περιαιρεῖσθαι should not take two accusatives like ἀφαιρεῖσθαι, περικρούειν, περικόπτειν, and the like; or, as Dr Verrall remarks (*Proceedings*, etc. l.c.)—I think with less probability—τοῦτον might be 'regarded as a second accusative after ποιήσαντα understood with ἄλλο μὲν οὐδέν.' The reading τοῦτον δὲ ἄλλο μὲν οὐδέν, περὶ δὲ τῇ χειρὶ χρυσοῦν δακτύλιον περιελόμενον ἐκβῆναι is adopted also by the Zurich editors (1839) on the suggestion of Winckelmann.

Dr Jackson's view of the passage, in which I formerly concurred, gives excellent sense, and may be right. But it is to be noticed (1) that our chief authority for ἔχειν is Ven. Π, a MS which is quite independent of Paris A and constantly enables us to restore lacunae in that MS, and (2) that there are other examples in Paris A of the omission of a single word without the excuse of homoioteleuton. See *Introd.* § 5. Ξ and Flor. B omit ἔχειν, but add φέρειν after δακτύλιον—an obvious attempt to amend the error which survives in A.

Madvig conjectures **πλούτου** δὲ οὐδέν and Liebhold (*Fl. Jahrb.* 1888, p. 107) **κόσμου** δὲ ἄλλο μὲν <ἔχοντ'> οὐδέν for τοῦτον δὲ ἄλλο μὲν οὐδέν. Neither of these proposals has any plausibility, and it is best to regard this as one of the places where we owe the right reading to Π.

III.

II **364** C. ἐάν τέ τινα ἐχθρὸν πημῆναι ἐθέλῃ, μετὰ σμικρῶν δαπανῶν ὁμοίως δίκαιον ἀδίκῳ **βλάψειν** κτλ.

Instead of βλάψειν, the best MSS read βλάψει. If βλάψει is retained, the subject must be either (1) τις or ὁ ἐθέλων πημαίνειν supplied out of πημῆναι ἐθέλῃ, or (2) the prophet consulted. The latter alternative gives the right sense, but the change from the singular to the plural (in πείθοντες) is very harsh. If we adopt the first alternative (to which J. and C. incline), we must regard the clause ἐάν τέ τινα—βλάψει as semi-parenthetical, and connect πείθοντες with ἀγύρται δὲ καὶ μάντεις at the beginning of the sentence. Such a solution is not less harsh than (2). βλάψει must, I think, be pronounced corrupt. Muretus read βλάψαι, depending, like ἀκεῖσθαι, on δύναμις; but βλάψαι is not likely to have been corrupted into βλάψει, nor is it clear why the aorist should take the place of the present (as in ἀκεῖσθαι). Reading βλάψειν, we might perhaps regard the construction as one of the rare cases in which δύναμις and the like are followed by a future infinitive: see Jebb's Soph. *Phil.* p. 252, Kühner *Gr. Gr.* II p. 164, and cf. *Phaed.* 73 A οὐκ ἂν οἷοί τ' ἦσαν τοῦτο ποιήσειν (so the Bodleian MS). There is still however a serious difficulty in the collocation of the present ἀκεῖσθαι with the future βλάψειν. The explanation given by Schneider in his *Additamenta* is linguistically unassailable and gives an excellent sense. For the common confusion of -ει and -ειν see *Introd.* § 5.

IV.

II **365** D, E. οὐκοῦν, εἰ μὲν μὴ εἰσίν, ἢ μηδὲν αὐτοῖς τῶν ἀνθρωπίνων μέλει, **τί καὶ** ἡμῖν μελητέον τοῦ λανθάνειν;

The reading of the best MSS, καὶ ἡμῖν μελητέον τοῦ λανθάνειν, is defended by Shorey (*A. J. Ph.* XVI p. 231), but (as I think) unsuccessfully, and even the most conservative editors abandon it.

We have to choose between (1) <*τί*> *καὶ ἡμῖν μελητέον τοῦ λανθάνειν;* (found in several inferior MSS besides *v*), (2) *οὐδ' ἡμῖν μελητέον κτλ.* (*q* Flor. U), (3) *καὶ ἡμῖν* < *οὐ* > *μελητέον κτλ.* (Paris D in margin), (4) *καὶ ἡμῖν ἀμελητέον* (a conjecture of Baiter's). It is possible that each of these readings is due to conjecture, and we can scarcely hope to restore the hand of Plato with certainty in this passage.

I formerly (with Bekker and others) printed *οὐδ' ἡμῖν*. The meaning is satisfactory, but the correction does not seem probable in itself. The same may be said of (3) and (4). I have now followed Stallbaum in supposing that *τί* was accidentally omitted after the -*ει* of *μέλει*. Such a slip is easy enough, and would be most likely to be corrected by the introduction of a negative, as in (2) and (3). Moreover, as Stallbaum says, *τί καὶ ἡμῖν* "huius sermonis alacritati plane est accommodatum," and *καί* is, I think, sufficiently justified by the obvious contrast between the gods and ourselves. Tucker objects that '"If the gods do *not* care, why should we *also* care?" is as bad in Greek as in English': but *καί* is hardly so much as 'also': it merely points the contrast. Cf. III 414 E *n*. There is no difficulty in *οὐκοῦν* followed by a question, so long as the question is merely rhetorical. Hermann proposes *οὔκουν—καὶ ἡμῖν μελητέον*, but the negative would require to be reinforced before *ἡμῖν*. I can see no probability in Tucker's conjecture, viz. *οὐκοῦν*—< *οὐδὲν* > *καὶ ἡμῖν μελητέον*.

Γ.

I. Τὰ μὲν δὴ περὶ θεούς, ἦν δ' ἐγώ, τοιαῦτ' ἄττα, ὡς ἔοικεν, 386
ἀκουστέον τε καὶ οὐκ ἀκουστέον εὐθὺς ἐκ παίδων τοῖς θεούς τε
τιμήσουσιν καὶ γονέας τήν τε ἀλλήλων φιλίαν μὴ περὶ σμικροῦ
ποιησομένοις. Καὶ οἶμαί γ', ἔφη, ὀρθῶς ἡμῖν φαίνεσθαι. Τί δὲ
δή; εἰ μέλλουσιν εἶναι ἀνδρεῖοι, ἆρα οὐ ταῦτά τε λεκτέον καὶ οἷα
αὐτοὺς ποιῆσαι ἥκιστα τὸν θάνατον δεδιέναι; ἢ ἡγεῖ | τινά ποτ' B
ἂν γενέσθαι ἀνδρεῖον, ἔχοντα ἐν αὑτῷ τοῦτο τὸ δεῖμα; Μὰ Δία,
ἦ δ' ὅς, οὐκ ἔγωγε. Τί δέ; τἀν Ἅιδου ἡγούμενον εἶναί τε καὶ δεινὰ
εἶναι οἴει τινὰ θανάτου ἀδεῆ ἔσεσθαι καὶ ἐν ταῖς μάχαις αἱρήσεσθαι
πρὸ ἥττης τε καὶ δουλείας θάνατον; Οὐδαμῶς. Δεῖ δή, ὡς ἔοικεν,
ἡμᾶς ἐπιστατεῖν καὶ περὶ τούτων τῶν μύθων τοῖς ἐπιχειροῦσιν

---

386 A—**389** A *So much for the doctrines by means of which we are to foster the sentiments of piety towards gods and parents and mutual friendship among the citizens.*

In order to encourage Bravery, we shall require our poets to extol and not to decry the life which awaits us after death: otherwise their poetry will be not merely untrue, but detrimental to our future soldiers. Here again Homer deserves censure. Fear-inspiring names like Cocytus must be discarded, as well as lamentations put into the mouths of famous men: for the good man has no cause to bewail the death of a good comrade, either for his comrade's sake or for his own. Homer offends against this canon when he represents Achilles and Priam as indulging in lamentations over their dead; and still more when he makes the gods, and even the greatest of the gods, give way to grief. Moreover, as excessive mirth is apt to rebound into the opposite extreme, our youths must not be laughter-loving. Homer errs in depicting good men and gods as overcome with laughter.

386 A 1 **τὰ μὲν δὴ περὶ θεοὺς κτλ.** Rettig (*Proleg.* pp. 61 ff.) and others suppose that the virtue of ὁσιότης is alluded to here—a virtue which in the earlier dialogues is sometimes placed by the side of the four cardinal virtues (*Prot.* 329 C, *Men.* 78 D, *Gorg.* 507 B). But ὁσιότης is not specifically named (in spite of II 380 C), and it is clear from the words καὶ γονέας—ποιησομένοις that Plato is thinking at least as much of duty to man as of duty to gods: cf. II 378 B C, 381 E, 383 C. See also App. I.

5 **ἀνδρεῖοι.** Plato has in view chiefly courage in war: hence the importance which he attaches to removing the fear of death. Cf. Tyrtaeus 10 (τεθνάμεναι γὰρ καλὸν κτλ.) and 12. 23—32. The poems of Tyrtaeus are not open to Plato's censure in this connexion. Pfleiderer (*Zur Lösung der Pl. Fr.* p. 23) wrongly represents the present passage as tantamount (or nearly so) to a denial of the immortality of the soul, which is affirmed in Book X. It is possible to criticise the popular conception of immortality without disbelieving in a higher form of the same doctrine, and this is just what Plato does here.

11 **καὶ περὶ τούτων τῶν μύθων** should

λέγειν, καὶ δεῖσθαι μὴ λοιδορεῖν ἁπλῶς οὕτως τὰ ἐν Ἅιδου, ἀλλὰ C μᾶλλον ἐπαινεῖν, ὡς οὔτε ἀληθῆ λέγοντας οὔτε ὠφέλιμα τοῖς μέλλουσιν μαχίμοις ἔσεσθαι. Δεῖ μέντοι, ἔφη. Ἐξαλείψομεν ἄρα, ἦν δ' ἐγώ, ἀπὸ τοῦδε τοῦ ἔπους ἀρξάμενοι πάντα τὰ τοιαῦτα,

> βουλοίμην κ' ἐπάρουρος ἐὼν θητευέμεν ἄλλῳ,
> ἀνδρὶ παρ' ἀκλήρῳ, ᾧ μὴ βίοτος πολὺς εἴη,
> ἢ πᾶσιν νεκύεσσι καταφθιμένοισιν ἀνάσσειν·

καὶ τὸ

> D οἰκία δὲ θνητοῖσι καὶ ἀθανάτοισι φανείη
> σμερδαλέ' εὐρώεντα, τά τε στυγέουσι θεοί περ·

καὶ

> ὢ πόποι, ἦ ῥά τις ἔστι καὶ εἰν Ἀΐδαο δόμοισιν
> ψυχὴ καὶ εἴδωλον, ἀτὰρ φρένες οὐκ ἔνι πάμπαν·

καὶ τὸ

> οἴῳ πεπνῦσθαι, ταὶ δὲ σκιαὶ ἀΐσσουσι·

καὶ

> ψυχὴ δ' ἐκ ῥεθέων πταμένη Ἄϊδόσδε βεβήκει,
> ὃν πότμον γοόωσα, λιποῦσ' ἀνδροτῆτα καὶ ἥβην·

17. ᾧ—εἴη Π: om. A. 20. θνητοῖσι Π: θνητοῖς A.

---

be taken with ἐπιστατεῖν rather than with λέγειν (sc. αὐτούς, i.e. τοὺς μύθους). Hartman, connecting the words with λέγειν, would expunge τῶν μύθων "cum poetae non *de* fabulis τὰ ἐν Ἅιδου describentibus λέγειν soleant, sed ipsi Orci territamenta narrent"—a just criticism, and conclusive in favour of the construction which Hartman rejects.

12 **λοιδορεῖν.** The traditional literary picture of the Greek Hades deserves what Plato says of it (see the quotations in Nägelsbach *Hom. Theol.* pp. 397 ff., *Nachh. Theol.* pp. 396—398), although a brighter prospect was held out in the Eleusinian mysteries and the Orphic theology (*Nachh. Theol.* pp. 398—407).

ἁπλῶς οὕτως. II 377 B *n.*

386 C 13 **λέγοντας.** For the accusative after the dative ἐπιχειροῦσι cf. *Euthyph.* 5 A, *Crito* 51 D. Before λέγοντας Ξ[1] (with a few other MSS) adds ἄν, as if εἰ λοιδοροῖεν should be understood (cf. II 380 C); but we should supply not λοιδοροῖεν, but εἰ λοιδοροῦσι (Schneider).

15 **τοῦδε τοῦ ἔπους κτλ.** The singular ἔπος is sometimes used of more than one verse, e.g. Hdt. VII 143. The lines are addressed by the shade of Achilles to Odysseus: *Od.* XI 489—491. On the omission of ᾧ μὴ βίοτος πολὺς εἴη see *Introd.* § 5.

386 D 20 **οἰκία—θεοί περ.** *Il.* XX 64, 65. The words in Homer are under the construction of δείσας—μή.

23 **ὢ πόποι.** The exclamation of Achilles when the ghost of Patroclus eludes his embrace: *Il.* XXIII 103, 104. On φρένες as the "physical basis of life" in Homer see Leaf ad loc.

26 **οἴῳ—ἀΐσσουσι.** Tiresias retained in the other world something of the physical reality of his earthly existence: *Od.* X 493—495 τοῦ τε φρένες ἔμπεδοί εἰσιν· | τῷ καὶ τεθνηῶτι νόον πόρε Περσεφόνεια | οἴῳ πεπνῦσθαι· τοὶ δὲ σκιαὶ ἀΐσσουσιν. Plato allows the force of attraction to alter τοί to ταί: cf. *Men.* 100 A οἷος πέπνυται τῶν ἐν Ἅιδου, αἱ δὲ σκιαὶ ἀΐσσουσι.

28 **ψυχὴ—ἥβην.** *Il.* XVI 856, 857. ῥεθέων, explained by the ancients as μέλη

| καὶ τὸ 387

ψυχὴ δὲ κατὰ χθονός, ἠΰτε καπνός,
ᾤχετο τετριγυῖα·

καὶ

ὡς δ' ὅτε νυκτερίδες μυχῷ ἄντρου θεσπεσίοιο
τρίζουσαι ποτέονται, ἐπεί κέ τις ἀποπέσῃσιν
ὁρμαθοῦ ἐκ πέτρης, ἀνά τ' ἀλλήλῃσιν ἔχονται,
ὣς αἱ τετριγυῖαι ἅμ' ᾔεσαν.

| ταῦτα καὶ τὰ τοιαῦτα πάντα παραιτησόμεθα Ὅμηρόν τε καὶ τοὺς B ἄλλους ποιητὰς μὴ χαλεπαίνειν ἂν διαγράφωμεν, οὐχ ὡς οὐ ποιητικὰ καὶ ἡδέα τοῖς πολλοῖς ἀκούειν, ἀλλ' ὅσῳ ποιητικώτερα, τοσούτῳ ἧττον ἀκουστέον παισὶ καὶ ἀνδράσιν, οὓς δεῖ ἐλευθέρους εἶναι, δουλείαν θανάτου μᾶλλον πεφοβημένους. Παντάπασι μὲν οὖν.

II. Οὐκοῦν ἔτι καὶ τὰ περὶ ταῦτα ὀνόματα πάντα τὰ δεινά τε καὶ φοβερὰ ἀποβλητέα, κωκυτούς τε καὶ στύγας | καὶ ἐνέρους καὶ C ἀλίβαντας, καὶ ἄλλα ὅσα τούτου τοῦ τύπου ὀνομαζόμενα φρίττειν

13. πεφοβημένους A²Π: πεφοβημένοις A¹.

τοῦ σώματος (Hesych. s.v.), more probably denotes the mouth (as part of the face): cf. Leaf ad loc. and *Il.* IX 409. Leaf plausibly suggests that ἀν in ἀνδροτῆτα, 'manhood'—found in all but two MSS of the *Iliad*—was only the written sign of the *nasalis sonans*, and counted as a short vowel.

387 A 2 **ψυχὴ δὲ—τετριγυῖα.** *Il.* XXIII 100. "The voice," says Leaf, "is as weak a copy of the living voice as is the εἴδωλον of the αὐτός": whence τετριγυῖα and τετριγυῖαι again just below.

5 **ὡς δ' ὅτε—ᾔεσαν.** Said of the souls of the suitors following Hermes down to Hades: *Od.* XXIV 6—9. Possibly we should read ἤισαν for ᾔεσαν (with Howes, *Harvard Studies in Cl. Philol.* VI p. 190).

387 C 16 **ἐνέρους καὶ ἀλίβαντας.** The Scholiast writes: ἐνέρους τοὺς νεκρούς, ἀπὸ τοῦ ἐν τῇ ἔρᾳ (ὅ ἐστι γῇ) κεῖσθαι. Cf. ἔραζε. Early psychology scarcely separated the dead body from the surviving spirit: the latter still lived where the body lay 'within the ground.' Hence 'those within the ground' (opposed to the ἐπιχθόνιοι or living) became an expression for the spirits of the departed, and the denizens of the lower world in general: see *Il.* XV 188, XX 61. The Scholiast's derivation is more probable than that of Brugmann, who (*Grundriss* II p. 180) derives the word from ἐν and a nominal suffix -ερο. Plato at any rate would have preferred the Scholiast. On ἀλίβαντας (not found in Homer or Hesiod) see Plut. *Quaest. Symp.* VIII 736 A (cited by Ast) ὁ δὲ ἀλίβας καὶ ὁ σκελετὸς ἐπὶ τοῖς νεκροῖς γέγονε, λοιδορουμένης ὀνόματα ξηρότητος. The ancients derived the word from ἀ and the root of λείβω λιψ etc., calling the dead 'sapless' διὰ τὴν τῆς λιβάδος ἀμεθεξίαν (Schol.). L. and S. object that the ἀ is long, relying perhaps on the line of Callimachus in *Et. M.* 63, 51 ἔβηξαν οἷον ἀλίβαντα πίνοντες (where ἀλίβαντᾳ = ὄξος). There, however, the right reading may be ἀλίβαντα, i.e. οἱ ἀλίβαντα. But in Sophocles *Fr.* 751 ed. Dindorf the α is certainly long, unless the text is corrupt. Possibly the word is connected with ἠλίβατος; cf. Hesych. s. v. ἠλίβατον, where we are told that Στησίχορος Τάρταρον ἠλίβατον τὸν βαθὺν λέγει.

17 **τούτου τοῦ τύπου.** Instead of writing ἄλλα ὀνόματα ὅσα τούτου τοῦ

δὴ ποιεῖ πάντας τοὺς ἀκούοντας. καὶ ἴσως εὖ ἔχει πρὸς ἄλλο τι· ἡμεῖς δὲ ὑπὲρ τῶν φυλάκων φοβούμεθα, μὴ ἐκ τῆς τοιαύτης φρίκης θερμότεροι καὶ μαλακώτεροι τοῦ δέοντος γένωνται ἡμῖν. Καὶ ὀρθῶς γ', ἔφη, φοβούμεθα. Ἀφαιρετέα ἄρα; Ναί. Τὸν δὲ ἐναντίον τύπον τούτοις λεκτέον καὶ ποιητέον; Δῆλα δή. Καὶ τοὺς
D ὀδυρμοὺς ἄρα ἐξαιρήσομεν | καὶ τοὺς οἴκτους τοὺς τῶν ἐλλογίμων ἀνδρῶν. Ἀνάγκη, ἔφη, εἴπερ καὶ τὰ πρότερα. Σκόπει δή, ἦν δ' ἐγώ, εἰ ὀρθῶς ἐξαιρήσομεν ἢ οὔ. φαμὲν δὲ δή, ὅτι ὁ ἐπιεικὴς ἀνὴρ τῷ ἐπιεικεῖ, οὗπερ καὶ ἑταῖρός ἐστιν, τὸ τεθνάναι οὐ δεινὸν ἡγήσεται. Φαμὲν γάρ. Οὐκ ἄρα ὑπέρ γ' ἐκείνου ὡς δεινόν τι πεπονθότος ὀδύροιτ' ἄν. Οὐ δῆτα. Ἀλλὰ μὴν καὶ τόδε λέγομεν,

18. ποιεῖ Hertz: ποιεῖ ὡς οἴεται ΑΠΞ: ποιεῖ ὡς οἷόν τε *q*. 19. ὑπὲρ Π: ὑπὸ A. 26. ἑταῖρός Ξ*q* et idem (vel potius ἕταιρός) A^2: ἕτερος A^1Π.

τύπου ὄντα Plato writes ἄλλα ὅσα τούτου τοῦ τύπου ὀνομαζόμενα, with precisely the same meaning: τούτου τοῦ τύπου therefore depends on the copula involved in ὀνομαζόμενα. Stallbaum takes ὀνομαζόμενα as "quum pronuntiantur"; but this is pointless. The words mean simply 'other names of this type which make all who hear them shudder' etc.

φρίττειν δὴ ποιεῖ. The remark ὡς οἴεται, which appears in the best MSS—see *cr. n.*—after ποιεῖ gives no sense, and is admittedly corrupt. ὡς οἷόν τε, found in four inferior MSS besides *q*, is a rare phrase, occurring, I believe, nowhere else in Plato (except of course in combination with superlatives, e.g. III 412 B, VI 484 C), though found in Aristotle (*Pol.* E 11. 1313ª 39, where Bekker conjectured οἴονται); but 'to shiver as much as possible' is painfully frigid. No emendation at all satisfactory has yet been proposed—neither Winckelmann's οἰκέτας, nor Hermann's ὅσα ἔτη (with reference to recitations of the rhapsodists!), nor Madvig's ὡς οἰητέα, nor Campbell's ὡς ἐτεά. Hertz (*Fl. Jahrb.* 1872 p. 852) supposes the words to be a gloss by some Christian reader, meaning 'as he' (i.e Plato) 'imagines.' The author of the gloss wished to indicate that he at least could hear such tales without shivering. After ὡς οἴεται found its way into the text, it was probably altered to οἴονται (to suit the plural ἀκούοντας), from which οἷόν τε is a corruption: cf. II 358 E, where *q* has οἴονται as against οἷόν τε of the best MSS. See also on VI 504 E.

18 **καὶ ἴσως—ἄλλο τι**: "videlicet ad suavitatem et delectationem: v. p. 387 B, 390 A, 397 D, 398 A al." (Stallbaum).

19 **μὴ ἐκ—ἡμῖν.** φρίκη is a cold shiver, sometimes followed by sweat, whence ἐκ τῆς τοιαύτης φρίκης θερμότεροι. Cf. (with Hartman) *Phaedr.* 251 A ἰδόντα δὲ αὐτόν, οἷον ἐκ τῆς φρίκης, μεταβολή τε καὶ ἱδρὼς καὶ θερμότης ἀήθης λαμβάνει, where Thompson remarks that φρίκη is used by Hippocrates of the 'cold fit of a fever.' In θερμότεροι καὶ μαλακώτεροι Plato is thinking of the softening effect of heat upon iron: cf. (with J. and C.) infra 411 B ὥσπερ σίδηρον ἐμάλαξε, *Laws* 666 C, 671 B καθάπερ τινὰ σίδηρον τὰς ψυχὰς τῶν πινόντων διαπύρους γιγνομένας μαλθακωτέρας γίγνεσθαι; see also *Il.* XVIII 468—477 and Whitelaw on Soph. *Ajax* 651 in *Cl. Rev.* V pp. 66, 230. In so far as it associates heat with cowardice, the comparison breaks down, for heat meant courage to the Greeks. For this reason Stephanus conjectured ἀθερμότεροι and Ast ἀθυμότεροι, a reading afterwards found in *v*. Ast's conjecture is thus refuted by Hartman (l.c.): "Astii coniectura inepta est, quum ἀθυμία vitium sit, non vero iusta ac temperata μαλακία (dixit enim μαλακώτεροι τοῦ δέοντος)." In the next sentence Hartman expunges φοβούμεθα without sufficient cause.

387 D 23 **τῶν ἐλλογίμων ἀνδρῶν**: a subjective, not an objective genitive: see E below, and 388 E, 390 D εἴ πού τινες—καρτερίαι—καὶ λέγονται καὶ πράττονται ὑπὸ ἐλλογίμων ἀνδρῶν with X 605 D.

25 **ὁ ἐπιεικὴς ἀνὴρ—προσδεῖται.** This

ὡς ὁ τοιοῦτος μάλιστα αὐτὸς αὑτῷ αὐτάρκης πρὸς τὸ εὖ ζῆν, καὶ διαφερόντως | τῶν ἄλλων ἥκιστα ἑτέρου προσδεῖται. Ἀληθῆ, ἔφη. E
Ἥκιστα ἄρ' αὐτῷ δεινὸν στερηθῆναι ὑέος ἢ ἀδελφοῦ ἢ χρημάτων ἢ ἄλλου του τῶν τοιούτων. Ἥκιστα μέντοι. Ἥκιστ' ἄρα καὶ ὀδύρεται, φέρει δὲ ὡς πραότατα, ὅταν τις αὐτὸν τοιαύτη ξυμφορὰ καταλάβῃ. Πολύ γε. Ὀρθῶς ἄρ' ἂν ἐξαιροῖμεν τοὺς θρήνους τῶν ὀνομαστῶν ἀνδρῶν, γυναιξὶ δὲ ἀποδιδοῖμεν, καὶ οὐδὲ ταύταις σπουδαίαις, καὶ | ὅσοι κακοὶ τῶν ἀνδρῶν, ἵνα ἡμῖν δυσχεραίνωσιν 38
ὅμοια τούτοις ποιεῖν οὓς δή φαμεν ἐπὶ φυλακῇ τῆς χώρας τρέφειν. Ὀρθῶς, ἔφη. Πάλιν δὴ Ὁμήρου τε δεησόμεθα καὶ τῶν ἄλλων ποιητῶν μὴ ποιεῖν Ἀχιλλέα, θεᾶς παῖδα,

ἄλλοτ' ἐπὶ πλευρᾶς κατακείμενον, ἄλλοτε δ' αὖτε
ὕπτιον, ἄλλοτε δὲ πρηνῆ,
τοτὲ δ' ὀρθὸν ἀναστάντα
πλωΐζοντ' ἀλύοντ' ἐπὶ θῖν' ἁλὸς ἀτρυγέτοιο,

33. ὀδύρεται, φέρει coniecit Stallbaum: ὀδύρεσθαι, φέρειν ΑΠΞq^1: χρὴ pro καὶ q^2.
34. ἄρ' ἂν Π: ἄρα A.

passage is full of Socratic colouring. οὗπερ καὶ ἑταῖρός ἐστι contains a suggestion that only good men can be comrades: cf. Xen. *Mem.* II 6. 19, 20 and Pl. *Lys.* 214 C. That death has no terrors for the good man is laid down in *Ap.* 41 C ff. The self-sufficiency of virtue was illustrated in the person of Socrates himself (*Mem.* I 2. 14, IV 8. 11), and continually preached by him (*Mem.* II 6. 2, cf. IV 7. 1). Steinhart appears to me to exaggerate the force of αὐτάρκης when he characterises the doctrine of this passage as anti-christian (*Einleitung* p. 160).

387 E 31 **ὑέος.** The fortitude of Pericles on receiving the news of the death of his two sons was a case in point, and may have been known to Plato. It is commemorated in a fine fragment of Protagoras preserved by Plut. *Consol. ad Apoll.* 33. 118 E, F.

33 **ὀδύρεται, φέρει.** See *cr. n.* The infinitives ὀδύρεσθαι and φέρειν are explained by Stallbaum as dependent on λέγομεν, but this is too harsh. The rhetorical repetition of ἥκιστ' ἄρα proves that like στερηθῆναι they should be under the government either of δεινόν itself, or of some notion supplied out of δεινόν. As the former alternative gives the wrong sense we must, if the text is sound, take refuge in the latter. Hartman by a *tour de force* resolves ἥκιστα δεινόν into ἥκιστα εἰκὸς αὐτὸν δεδιέναι, and carries on the εἰκός. It would be somewhat easier, I think, though still very harsh, to supply δεινός out of δεινόν, δεινός being used as in δεινὸς καταράσασθαι τῷ λίθῳ (Theophr. *Char.* 15, cf. infra 395 C): but it is difficult not to believe that the text is corrupt. In *q*, καί has been corrected to χρή, and the insertion of δεῖ before καί is suggested by Hartman. The question however is not what the good man ought to do, but what he actually does, and for this reason Richards' ἔοικε after ὀδύρεσθαι is better, although otherwise unlikely. Stallbaum's alternative proposal to read ὀδύρεται, φέρει δέ seems to me far the best both in point of sense, and because it might easily pass into ὀδύρεσθαι, φέρειν δέ under the influence of στερηθῆναι. For these reasons I have printed it in the text. Cf. *Introd.* § 5.

388 A 5 **ἄλλοτ'—ἀτρυγέτοιο.** The picture of Achilles sorrowing for Patroclus in *Iliad* XXIV 10—12. Plato accommodates the Homeric narrative to his own ποιεῖν, and reads πλωΐζοντ'—ἀτρυγέτοιο instead of δινεύεσκ' ἀλύων παρὰ θῖν' ἁλός, which appears in our Homer. πλωΐζω elsewhere is always used of sail-

B | μηδὲ ἀμφοτέραισιν χερσὶν ἑλόντα κόνιν αἰθαλόεσσαν χευάμενον κὰκ κεφαλῆς, μηδὲ ἄλλα κλαίοντά τε καὶ ὀδυρόμενον, ὅσα καὶ οἷα ἐκεῖνος ἐποιησε· μηδὲ Πρίαμον, ἐγγὺς θεῶν γεγονότα, λιτανεύοντά τε καὶ

κυλινδόμενον κατὰ κόπρον,
ἐξονομακλήδην ὀνομάζοντ' ἄνδρα ἕκαστον.

πολὺ δ' ἔτι τούτων μᾶλλον δεησόμεθα μήτοι θεούς γε ποιεῖν ὀδυρομένους καὶ λέγοντας

C | ὤμοι ἐγὼ δειλή, ὤμοι δυσαριστοτόκεια·

εἰ δ' οὖν θεούς, μήτοι τόν γε μέγιστον τῶν θεῶν τολμῆσαι οὕτως ἀνομοίως μιμήσασθαι, ὥστε, ὢ πόποι, φάναι,

ἦ φίλον ἄνδρα διωκόμενον περὶ ἄστυ
ὀφθαλμοῖσιν ὁρῶμαι, ἐμὸν δ' ὀλοφύρεται ἦτορ·

καὶ

αἲ αἲ ἐγών, ὅ τέ μοι Σαρπηδόνα φίλτατον ἀνδρῶν
D | μοῖρ' ὑπὸ Πατρόκλοιο Μενοιτιάδαο δαμῆναι.

23. ὅ τέ Leaf ad *Il.* XVI 433: ὅτε codd.

---

ing in the literal sense (yet ἐκ τοῦ νοῦ ἐκπλώειν in Hdt. VI 12), but it cannot bear such a meaning here. If the MSS are right, πλωΐζοντ' must be regarded (with Schneider) as a metaphor, the agitated movements of Achilles being compared to the unsteady motion of a ship upon the sea. Achilles is so to speak 'at sea' and shews it in his gait; cf. the metaphorical sense of χειμάζομαι. The picture savours of the burlesque, and Howes suggests that πλωίζων may be a deliberate parody on Plato's part (*Harvard Studies* etc. VI p. 202). As no other example of such a use of πλωίζω has been adduced, the word is perhaps corrupt. Heyne's πρωΐζοντ' "matutinum se agentem" (οὐδέ μιν ἠὼς | φαινομένη λήθεσκεν ὑπεὶρ ἅλα, says Homer) will never command a wide assent: still less πλώϊσοντ' (Benedictus), πρῴ ἰόντ' (Ast), whose quantity is not above suspicion, or πρῴ ἰύζοντ' (Liebhold *Fl. Jahrb.* 1888, p. 108). αἰάζοντ' (Herwerden and Naber) is better in point of sense, but the alteration is too great. I have thought of πόλλ' ᾠζοντ' (ᾤζεις 'cry ὤ' and not ὤζεις is the spelling of the Codex Mediceus in Aesch. *Eum.* 124), or ἀφλοίζοντ' (cf. ἀφλοισμός in *Il.* XV 607). Perhaps, however, πλωΐζοντ' conceals some word meaning 'to rush wildly from his tent,' ἐπὶ θῖν' being probably for ἐπὶ θῖνα, not for ἐπὶ θινί. There is apparently a contrast between Achilles' anguish within his tent and without, and some word is needed to mark his exit. Nothing can be made of the variant πλάζοντ' (in a few inferior MSS). In default of anything better we must (I suppose) provisionally acquiesce in Schneider's interpretation.

388 B 9 **μηδὲ—κεφαλῆς.** *Il.* XVIII 23, 24.

11 **ἐκεῖνος.** Homer.

ἐγγὺς θεῶν. Zeus was Priam's seventh ancestor (Apollod. III 12). The phrase has a dash of old-world romance about it: cf. 391 E infra and Stallbaum on *Phil.* 16 C οἱ μὲν παλαιοί, κρείττονες ἡμῶν καὶ ἐγγυτέρω θεῶν οἰκοῦντες.

12 **λιτανεύοντά τε—ἕκαστον.** *Il.* XXII 414, 415.

388 C 17 **ὤμοι κτλ.** Said by Thetis in *Il.* XVIII 54.

19 **ὢ πόποι.** *Il.* XXII 168, 169. The words are uttered by Zeus with reference to Hector. For ἄστυ our Homer has τεῖχος.

23 **αἲ αἲ—δαμῆναι.** *Il.* XVI 433, 434. The only variant is ὤμοι for αἲ αἲ.

III. Εἰ γάρ, ὦ φίλε Ἀδείμαντε, τὰ τοιαῦτα ἡμῖν οἱ νέοι
σπουδῇ ἀκούοιεν καὶ μὴ καταγελῷεν ὡς ἀναξίως λεγομένων, σχολῇ
ἂν ἑαυτόν γέ τις ἄνθρωπον ὄντα ἀνάξιον ἡγήσαιτο τούτων καὶ
ἐπιπλήξειεν, εἰ καὶ ἐπίοι αὐτῷ τοιοῦτον ἢ λέγειν ἢ ποιεῖν, ἀλλ'
οὐδὲν αἰσχυνόμενος οὐδὲ καρτερῶν πολλοὺς ἐπὶ σμικροῖσιν παθή-
μασιν θρήνους ἂν ᾄδοι καὶ ὀδυρμούς. Ἀληθέστατα, ἔφη, λέγεις. E
Δεῖ δέ γε οὔχ, ὡς ἄρτι ἡμῖν ὁ λόγος ἐσήμαινεν· ᾧ πειστέον, ἕως ἄν
τις ἡμᾶς ἄλλῳ καλλίονι πείσῃ. Οὐ γὰρ οὖν δεῖ. Ἀλλὰ μὴν οὐδὲ
φιλογέλωτάς γε δεῖ εἶναι. σχεδὸν γὰρ ὅταν τις ἐφιῇ ἰσχυρῷ
γέλωτι, ἰσχυρὰν καὶ μεταβολὴν ζητεῖ τὸ τοιοῦτον. Δοκεῖ μοι,
ἔφη. Οὔτε ἄρα ἀνθρώπους ἀξίους λόγου κρατουμένους ὑπὸ γέλωτος
ἄν τις ποιῇ, ἀποδεκτέον, πολὺ δὲ ἧττον, ἐὰν θεούς. Πολὺ μέντοι, 389
ἦ δ' ὅς. Οὐκοῦν Ὁμήρου οὐδὲ τὰ τοιαῦτα ἀποδεξόμεθα περὶ
θεῶν·

ἄσβεστος δ' ἄρ' ἐνῶρτο γέλως μακάρεσσι θεοῖσιν,
ὡς ἴδον Ἥφαιστον διὰ δώματα ποιπνύοντα

οὐκ ἀποδεκτέον κατὰ τὸν σὸν λόγον. Εἰ σύ, ἔφη, βούλει ἐμὸν
τιθέναι· οὐ γὰρ οὖν δὴ ἀποδεκτέον. B

33. ἐφιῇ (vel potius ἐφίῃ) Ξ: ἔφην Aq: ἔφη Π.

---

388 D 28 **εἰ καὶ ἐπίοι αὐτῷ.** *καί* is not 'even' (J. and C.), otherwise there would be too much emphasis on *ἐπίοι*, but 'also': 'if it should also occur to himself' (sc. as Homer says it occurs to gods). The emphatic word is *αὐτῷ*. For *τοιοῦτον* Hartman requires either *τοιοῦτόν τι* or *τὸ τοιοῦτον*; but cf. 416 B, IV 426 B, 429 E, IX 590 E and II 368 A *n.*

29 **σμικροῖσιν.** See on I 330 B. *ἐπὶ σμικροῖσι παθήμασι* has a poetical rhythm, and may possibly be from a hexameter.

388 E 31 **ἕως ἄν τις—πείσῃ.** Cf. *Phaed.* 85 C, D, *Gorg.* 527 A.

33 **ἐφιῇ—τοιοῦτον.** See *cr. n.* The present *ἐφιῇ* is slightly better than *ἐφῇ*: for *τὸ τοιοῦτον* denotes the state or condition rather than the act. *ἐφῇ* comes rather nearer to the reading of A and Π, and is preferred by Baiter and Hartman. For *ζητεῖ* H. Wolf conjectured *ποιεῖ*, Herwerden *τίκτει* or *ἐντίκτει*, in both cases needlessly: cf. with J. and C. *ἐθέλει* in II 370 B. The sentiment is generalised in VIII 563 E.

35 **οὔτε ἄρα.** *οὔτε* followed by *δέ* is rare (examples in Kühner *Gr. Gr.* II p. 832) but *δέ* follows *τε* very often, especially in *πολὺ δέ*, *μέγιστον δέ* etc.: see II 367 C *n.* Cobet's *οὔτἄρα* i.q. *οὔτοι ἄρα*, though approved by Hartman, is therefore unnecessary.

389 A 2 **οὐκοῦν—λόγον.** The lines are *Il.* I 599, 600. Hermann wished to read *οὔκουν* and reject *ἀποδεξόμεθα περὶ θεῶν*, placing *τὰ τοιαῦτα* under the government of *ἀποδεκτέον*. *οὔκουν* may be right, but the change is not necessary. *τὰ τοιαῦτα* does not refer specifically to the verses, but means *τὸ κρατεῖσθαι ὑπὸ γέλωτος* and the like; while the two verses are themselves the object of *ἀποδεκτέον*. I have accordingly placed a colon after *θεῶν* and removed the pause after *ποιπνύοντα*; a remedy which removes, I think, the objections felt by Hermann to *ἀποδεξόμεθα περὶ θεῶν*, and by Herwerden to *περὶ θεῶν*. The asyndeton in *ἄσβεστος δ' ἄρ'* etc. is common in ampliative and illustrative sentences.

389 B—**392** A *A high value should also be placed upon truth. The medicinal lie may indeed be permitted to our rulers, in the interests of the State: but any others*

Ἀλλὰ μὴν καὶ ἀλήθειάν γε περὶ πολλοῦ ποιητέον. εἰ γὰρ ὀρθῶς ἐλέγομεν ἄρτι, καὶ τῷ ὄντι θεοῖσι μὲν ἄχρηστον ψεῦδος, ἀνθρώποις δὲ χρήσιμον ὡς ἐν φαρμάκου εἴδει, δῆλον, ὅτι τό γε τοιοῦτον ἰατροῖς δοτέον, ἰδιώταις δὲ οὐχ ἁπτέον. Δῆλον, ἔφη. Τοῖς ἄρχουσιν δὴ τῆς πόλεως, εἴπερ τισὶν ἄλλοις, προσήκει ψεύδεσθαι ἢ πολεμίων ἢ πολιτῶν ἕνεκα ἐπ' ὠφελίᾳ τῆς πόλεως, τοῖς
C δὲ ἄλλοις πᾶσιν οὐχ ἁπτέον τοῦ τοιούτου, ἀλλὰ | πρός γε δὴ τοὺς τοιούτους ἄρχοντας ἰδιώτῃ ψεύσασθαι ταὐτὸν καὶ μεῖζον ἁμάρτημα φήσομεν ἢ κάμνοντι πρὸς ἰατρὸν ἢ ἀσκοῦντι πρὸς παιδοτρίβην περὶ τῶν τοῦ αὑτοῦ σώματος παθημάτων μὴ τἀληθῆ λέγειν, ἢ πρὸς κυβερνήτην περὶ τῆς νεώς τε καὶ τῶν ναυτῶν μὴ τὰ ὄντα λέγοντι ὅπως ἢ αὐτὸς ἢ τις τῶν ξυνναυτῶν πράξεως ἔχει. Ἀληθέσ-
D τατα, ἔφη. Ἂν ἄρ' ἄλλον τινὰ λαμβάνῃ ψευδόμενον | ἐν τῇ πόλει τῶν οἳ δημιουργοὶ ἔασι,

μάντιν ἢ ἰητῆρα κακῶν ἢ τέκτονα δούρων,

15. τοιούτους Π et in mg. A²: om. A¹.

---

who lie are to be punished. To lie to the rulers is worse than lying to a physician about one's illness.

Not less necessary is self-control, which will enable our citizens to obey the rulers, and to rule their own appetites. Homer frequently represents heroes and gods as lacking in this virtue—as insubordinate, gluttonous, lustful, avaricious, prone to revenge, and mean. The effect is to discourage in the young the virtue which we desiderate, and all such representations must therefore be forbidden: they are both impious and untrue.

389 B 8 **ἀλλὰ μὴν καὶ ἀλήθειαν** ff. On the place of this section in the general plan of the *Republic* see App. I.

9 **θεοῖσι μὲν—εἴδει.** For the dative θεοῖσι see I 330 B *n.* ἐν φαρμάκου εἴδει (cf. II 382 C, D) implies the usual Socratic analogy between body and soul: see on II 380 B.

11 **οὐχ ἁπτέον κτλ.** Cf. *Laws* 916 E ff.

389 C 15 **τοιούτους** is omitted by Hartman, and is certainly open to doubt. The balance of MS evidence is in its favour, although a few inferior MSS and one MS of Stobaeus (*Flor.* 46. 95), agree with A¹ in omitting it. It must either mean rulers who act ἐπ' ὠφελίᾳ τῆς πόλεως, or else such rulers as Plato's. The former alternative is not altogether satisfactory, and it is difficult not to believe that Plato was in reality referring to his own rulers. The serious objection to this view is that we have not yet heard anything of Plato's rulers: they are not described till 412 B. I think the solution may be that the present section on truth is a later addition made by Plato after he had written his first account of the rulers in Book III. See also App. I.

19 **λέγοντι** has caused difficulty, and Madvig would expunge the word. The explanation is simple enough. μὴ τἀληθῆ λέγειν should be repeated between ἢ and πρός, and μὴ τὰ ὄντα λέγοντι ὅπως taken closely together, 'or to lie' (μὴ τἀληθῆ λέγειν understood) 'to a pilot about the ship and its crew by misrepresenting the facts about one's own condition etc.' One MS of Stobaeus (l.c.) has λέγοντα, which is also possible, and could only be explained in this way. I have removed the comma usually printed after λέγοντι.

20 **λαμβάνῃ**: sc. ὁ ἄρχων. Cf. I 347 A *n.* λαμβάνῃς (Ficinus and Benedictus) gives a wrong sense.

389 D 21 **τῶν οἳ—δούρων.** *Od.* XVII 383, 384. κακῶν is of course neuter. If Schneider could shew that this quotation refers to a case in which a chieftain in Homer did or did not punish a δημιουργός for lying, he would make out a

κολάσει ὡς ἐπιτήδευμα εἰσάγοντα πόλεως ὥσπερ νεὼς ἀνατρεπτικόν τε καὶ ὀλέθριον. Ἐάν γε, ἦ δ᾽ ὅς, ἐπί γε λόγῳ ἔργα τελῆται.

Τί δέ; σωφροσύνης ἆρα οὐ δεήσει ἡμῖν τοῖς νεανίαις; Πῶς δ᾽ οὔ; Σωφροσύνης δὲ ὡς πλήθει οὐ τὰ τοιάδε μέγιστα, ἀρχόντων μὲν ὑπηκόους εἶναι, αὐτοὺς δὲ ἄρχοντας τῶν | περὶ πότους καὶ E ἀφροδίσια καὶ περὶ ἐδωδὰς ἡδονῶν; Ἔμοιγε δοκεῖ. Τὰ δὴ τοιάδε φήσομεν, οἶμαι, καλῶς λέγεσθαι, οἷα καὶ Ὁμήρῳ Διομήδης λέγει,

τέττα, σιωπῇ ἧσο, ἐμῷ δ᾽ ἐπιπείθεο μύθῳ,

καὶ τὰ τούτων ἐχόμενα, τὰ

ἴσαν μένεα πνείοντες Ἀχαιοί,
σιγῇ, δειδιότες σημάντορας,

καὶ ὅσα ἄλλα τοιαῦτα. Καλῶς. Τί δέ; τὰ τοιάδε

οἰνοβαρές, κυνὸς ὄμματ᾽ ἔχων, κραδίην δ᾽ ἐλάφοιο

23. κολάσει ὡς Π: κολάσεως A.

---

prima facie case for his view that Plato is here prescribing canons for poetical representations, but there is nothing of this in Homer; and we must suppose that Plato is speaking here of his own citizens. See App. I.

24 **ἐάν γε—τελῆται** does not mean 'if our theory is carried out' (J. and C.) or 'if our ideal city is ever realised' (Rettig). Such a remark would be frigid and superfluous. The meaning is merely that the ruler will first use words, but, if these fail, he will afterwards proceed to deeds i.e. κολάσει. The first γε assents: the second enters a caveat. ἔργα τελῆται = ἔργων τέλος γίγνηται.

27 **σωφροσύνης δὲ—μέγιστα**: 'for the mass of men, are not the cardinal points of temperance such as these?' (Jebb on Soph. *O. C.* 20 μακρὰν γὰρ ὡς γέροντι προὐστάλης ὁδόν—a precise parallel). There is no authority for interpreting these words (with Stallbaum, Hartman etc.) as 'plerumque' 'in universum.' Plato is warning us not to regard his account of σωφροσύνη here as scientifically accurate and complete. It is the most obvious and conspicuous aspects of self-control which poets should chiefly impress upon the multitude, and to these Plato confines his attention. On the Greek conception of σωφροσύνη see the passages collected by Nägelsbach, *Nachhom. Theol.* pp. 227 ff.

389 E 30 **Ὁμήρῳ**. For this Ξ and a few other MSS read παρ᾽ Ὁμήρῳ. Schneider successfully defends Ὁμήρῳ by Arist. *Pol.* Θ 5. 1339ᵇ 7 οὐ γὰρ ὁ Ζεὺς αὐτὸς ᾄδει καὶ κιθαρίζει τοῖς ποιηταῖς. The line is addressed by Diomede to Sthenelus in *Il.* IV 412.

32 **τὰ τούτων ἐχόμενα.** The two verses which Plato here quotes do not follow τέττα, σιωπῇ κτλ., and do not even occur together in our Homer. ἴσαν—Ἀχαιοί is from *Il.* III 8 (οἱ δ᾽ ἄρ᾽ ἴσαν σιγῇ μένεα πνείοντες Ἀχαιοί), σιγῇ—σημάντορας from IV 431. Some editors bracket the first verse, but (as Hartman points out) it is not likely that a scribe should have interpolated a line from *Il.* III before one from *Il.* IV. Plato may be guilty of 'contamination,' or the lines may really have occurred together in his text of Homer. J. and C. suggest that Plato perhaps did not mean the lines to be connected. The objection to this view is that σιγῇ (as in our text of Homer, though there it is in a different place) goes best with ἴσαν, and that ἴσαν μένεα πνείοντες Ἀχαιοί is not *by itself* an illustration of obedience to rulers, and therefore would not be relevant here. See on the whole subject of Platonic quotations from Homer, Howes in *Harvard Studies* etc. VI pp. 153—237, with whose conclusions (p. 210) I heartily agree.

36 **οἰνοβαρὲς κτλ.** Achilles to Aga-

390 | καὶ τὰ τούτων ἑξῆς, ἆρα καλῶς, καὶ ὅσα ἄλλα τις ἐν λόγῳ ἢ ἐν ποιήσει εἴρηκε νεανιεύματα ἰδιωτῶν εἰς ἄρχοντας; Οὐ καλῶς. Οὐ γάρ, οἶμαι, εἴς γε σωφροσύνην νέοις ἐπιτήδεια ἀκούειν. εἰ δέ τινα ἄλλην ἡδονὴν παρέχεται, θαυμαστὸν οὐδέν. ἢ πῶς σοι φαίνεται; Οὕτως, ἔφη.

IV. Τί δέ; ποιεῖν ἄνδρα τὸν σοφώτατον λέγοντα, ὡς δοκεῖ αὐτῷ κάλλιστον εἶναι πάντων, ὅταν

παρὰ πλέαι ὦσι τράπεζαι
B | σίτου καὶ κρειῶν, μέθυ δ' ἐκ κρητῆρος ἀφύσσων
οἰνοχόος φορέῃσι καὶ ἐγχείῃ δεπάεσσι,

δοκεῖ σοι ἐπιτήδειον εἶναι πρὸς ἐγκράτειαν ἑαυτοῦ ἀκούειν νέῳ; ἢ τὸ

λιμῷ δ' οἴκτιστον θανέειν καὶ πότμον ἐπισπεῖν;

ἢ Δία, καθευδόντων τῶν ἄλλων θεῶν τε καὶ ἀνθρώπων, ὡς, μόνος ἐγρηγορὼς ἃ ἐβουλεύσατο, τούτων πάντων ῥᾳδίως ἐπιλανθανόμενον
C | διὰ τὴν τῶν ἀφροδισίων ἐπιθυμίαν, καὶ οὕτως ἐκπλαγέντα ἰδόντα τὴν Ἥραν, ὥστε μηδ' εἰς τὸ δωμάτιον ἐθέλειν ἐλθεῖν, ἀλλ' αὐτοῦ

2. νεανιεύματα $\Pi^2 q$: νεανικεύματα A: νεανισκεύματα Ξ et fortasse Π^1. 8. παρὰ πλέαι nos: παραπλεῖαι vel παράπλειαι ΑΠΞ*q*.

---

memnon in *Il.* I 225. The point of this illustration is not in the abusive epithets, but in the insubordination which they and the rest of the speech (τὰ τούτων ἑξῆς) express.

390 A 2 **νεανιεύματα**. See *cr. n.* The spelling seems established by the verb νεανιεύεσθαι: e.g. *Gorg.* 482 C. νεανισκεύματα has however some authority, for νεανισκεύομαι was used (Photius s.v.). νεανικεύματα, to say the least, is doubtful, nor is νεανικοῦν (Photius s.v.) enough to justify such a form, in spite of Schneider (*Addit.* p. 19).

8 **παρὰ πλέαι—δεπάεσσι**. Odysseus in *Od.* IX 8—10. Our text of Homer has παρὰ δὲ πλήθωσι. I have written παρὰ πλέαι for παράπλειαι or παραπλεῖαι of nearly all the MSS. Vat. r and Vind. B have περιπλεῖαι, Cesenas M παράπλειαι (sic). παράπλειαι (which Howes l.c. p. 205 thinks Plato found in his text of Homer) is in reality a *vox nihili*; even if it did occur, it could not mean 'almost full,' as L. and S. say: and such a meaning would be ludicrously inappropriate here. With παρὰ δὲ πλέαι cf. Anacr. 94. 1 ed. Bergk κρητῆρι παρὰ πλέῳ οἰνοποτάζων. See my article in *Cl. Rev.* XI p. 349.

390 B 13 **λιμῷ δ'—ἐπισπεῖν**. *Od.* XII 342.

14 **ἢ Δία—ἐπιλανθανόμενον**. μόνος ἐγρηγορώς refers to *Il.* II 1—4: the incident itself is narrated in *Il.* XIV 294 ff. For the postponement of the relative ἃ cf. IV 425 C. The effect is to throw emphasis on μόνος ἐγρηγορώς—that Zeus should forget what he had purposely kept awake to devise makes the scandal all the worse—and brings it into sharper contrast with καθευδόντων—ἀνθρώπων. ὡς must be taken with ἐπιλανθανόμενον, the construction being ἢ ποιεῖν Δία ὡς ἐπιλανθανόμενον: cf. II 383 A. Stallbaum explains ὡς μόνος ἐγρηγορώς as "ut solus vigil": while J. and C. supply ἀκούειν after ἤ. Neither view seems to me at all satisfactory. The text has been often called in question. Instead of ὡς Hermann reads καί: Herwerden and Richards suggest ὅσα (dropping ἃ before ἐβουλεύσατο). The best emendation is perhaps Jackson's εἷς for ὡς (*Journal of Phil.* IV p. 147), but I see no good reason why ὡς cannot be

βουλόμενον χαμαὶ ξυγγίγνεσθαι, καὶ λέγοντα ὡς οὕτως ὑπὸ ἐπιθυμίας ἔχεται, ὡς οὐδ' ὅτε τὸ πρῶτον ἐφοίτων πρὸς ἀλλήλους φίλους λήθοντε τοκῆας; οὐδὲ Ἄρεώς τε καὶ Ἀφροδίτης ὑπὸ Ἡφαίστου δεσμὸν δι' ἕτερα τοιαῦτα. Οὐ μὰ τὸν Δία, ἦ δ' ὅς, οὔ μοι φαίνεται ἐπιτήδειον. Ἀλλ' | εἴ πού τινες, ἦν δ' ἐγώ, D
καρτερίαι πρὸς ἅπαντα καὶ λέγονται καὶ πράττονται ὑπὸ ἐλλογίμων ἀνδρῶν, θεατέον τε καὶ ἀκουστέον, οἷον καὶ τὸ

στῆθος δὲ πλήξας κραδίην ἠνίπαπε μύθῳ·
τέτλαθι δή, κραδίη· καὶ κύντερον ἄλλο ποτ' ἔτλης.

Παντάπασι μὲν οὖν, ἔφη. Οὐ μὲν δὴ δωροδόκους γε ἐατέον εἶναι τοὺς ἄνδρας οὐδὲ φιλοχρημάτους. | Οὐδαμῶς. Οὐδ' ᾀστέον αὐτοῖς E
ὅτι

δῶρα θεοὺς πείθει, δῶρ' αἰδοίους βασιλῆας·

οὐδὲ τὸν τοῦ Ἀχιλλέως παιδαγωγὸν Φοίνικα ἐπαινετέον, ὡς μετρίως ἔλεγε συμβουλεύων αὐτῷ δῶρα μὲν λαβόντι ἐπαμύνειν τοῖς Ἀχαιοῖς, ἄνευ δὲ δώρων, μὴ ἀπαλλάττεσθαι τῆς μήνιος. οὐδ' αὐτὸν τὸν Ἀχιλλέα ἀξιώσομεν οὐδ' ὁμολογήσομεν οὕτω φιλο-

---

construed with ἐπιλανθανόμενον. The pause which on this view is necessary after ὡς helps still further to increase the stress on μόνος ἐγρηγορώς, which Plato certainly intended to emphasize.

390 C 18 **βουλόμενον—τοκῆας.** βουλόμενον is not otiose after ἐθέλειν (as Hartman alleges): 'to wish' (βούλεσθαι) and 'to be willing' (ἐθέλειν) are different ideas. The same critic also rejects καί before λέγοντα "quia ea verba excusationem τοῦ ἐθέλειν humi consuescere continent"; but it is more effective to represent so gross an utterance as an additional part of the picture. For φοιτᾶν πρός cf. Lys. I 15, 19, where the meaning is the same. Herwerden should not have wished to replace the preposition by παρά. In Homer the line εἰς εὐνὴν φοιτῶντε φίλους λήθοντε τοκῆας (*Il.* XIV 296) is not said by Zeus, as Plato—doubtless intentionally, to increase the effect—makes it appear to be.

20 **Ἄρεως—δεσμόν.** *Od.* VIII 266 ff. δεσμόν is still under the government of ποιεῖν.

390 D 23 **καὶ λέγονται καὶ πράττονται κτλ.**: 'are either described or done by famous men' etc.: described e.g. in poetry by Homer's heroes, or done in actual life before our eyes. θεατέον refers to πράττονται, ἀκουστέον to λέγονται by the usual chiasmus. J. and C. translate "performed by famous men or told concerning them," understanding περὶ ἐλλογίμων ἀνδρῶν with λέγονται, but this cannot be right.

25 **στῆθος δὲ—ἔτλης.** Odysseus in *Od.* XX 17, 18.

27 **δωροδόκους κτλ.** The excessive love of money is a sign of ἀκράτεια: so that its mention here is relevant enough, although the vice was not specifically named in 389 D.

390 E 30 **δῶρα—βασιλῆας**: an old saying attributed by some to Hesiod (οἱ μὲν Ἡσιόδειον οἴονται τὸν στίχον Suidas s. vv. δῶρα κτλ.). It is referred to by Eur. *Med.* 964 πείθειν δῶρα καὶ θεοὺς λόγος. Cf. Nägelsbach *Nachhom. Theol.* II p. 64.

32 **συμβουλεύων.** *Il.* IX 515 ff. The genitive μήνιος, for which a few MSS read μήνιδος, is natural in paraphrasing Homer. Cf. the form Θάλεω in X 600 A.

34 **οὐδ' ὁμολογήσομεν.** "Dele futile interpretamentum" exclaims Hartman. The words are genuine, and add a new point: cf. 391 A φάναι καὶ ἄλλων λεγόντων πείθεσθαι.

χρήματον εἶναι, ὥστε παρὰ τοῦ Ἀγαμέμνονος δῶρα λαβεῖν, καὶ
391 τιμὴν αὖ λαβόντα νεκροῦ ἀπολύειν, | ἄλλως δὲ μὴ 'θέλειν.
Οὔκουν δίκαιόν γε, ἔφη, ἐπαινεῖν τὰ τοιαῦτα. Ὀκνῶ δέ γε, ἦν
δ' ἐγώ, δι' Ὅμηρον λέγειν, ὅτι οὐδ' ὅσιον ταῦτά γε κατὰ Ἀχιλλέως
φάναι καὶ ἄλλων λεγόντων πείθεσθαι, καὶ αὖ ὡς πρὸς τὸν Ἀπόλλω
εἶπεν

ἔβλαψάς μ' ἑκάεργε, θεῶν ὀλοώτατε πάντων·
ἦ σ' ἂν τεισαίμην, εἴ μοι δύναμίς γε παρείη,

B | καὶ ὡς πρὸς τὸν ποταμόν, θεὸν ὄντα, ἀπειθῶς εἶχεν καὶ μάχεσθαι
ἕτοιμος ἦν, καὶ αὖ τὰς τοῦ ἑτέρου ποταμοῦ Σπερχειοῦ ἱερὰς τρίχας

Πατρόκλῳ ἥρωϊ, ἔφη, κόμην ὀπάσαιμι φέρεσθαι,

νεκρῷ ὄντι, καὶ ὡς ἔδρασεν τοῦτο, οὐ πειστέον. τάς τε αὖ Ἕκτορος
ἕλξεις περὶ τὸ σῆμα τὸ Πατρόκλου καὶ τὰς τῶν ζωγρηθέντων
σφαγὰς εἰς τὴν πυράν, ξύμπαντα ταῦτα οὐ φήσομεν ἀληθῆ εἰρῆσθαι,
C οὐδ' ἐάσομεν πείθεσθαι τοὺς | ἡμετέρους, ὡς Ἀχιλλεύς, θεᾶς ὢν
παῖς καὶ Πηλέως, σωφρονεστάτου τε καὶ τρίτου ἀπὸ Διός, καὶ ὑπὸ
τῷ σοφωτάτῳ Χείρωνι τεθραμμένος, τοσαύτης ἦν ταραχῆς πλέως,
ὥστ' ἔχειν ἐν αὑτῷ νοσήματε δύο ἐναντίω ἀλλήλοιν, ἀνελευθερίαν
μετὰ φιλοχρηματίας καὶ αὖ ὑπερηφανίαν θεῶν τε καὶ ἀνθρώπων.
Ὀρθῶς, ἔφη, λέγεις.

V. Μὴ τοίνυν, ἦν δ' ἐγώ, μηδὲ τάδε πειθώμεθα μηδ' ἐῶμεν
D λέγειν, ὡς Θησεὺς Ποσειδῶνος ὑὸς Πειρίθους τε | Διὸς ὥρμησαν
οὕτως ἐπὶ δεινὰς ἁρπαγάς, μηδέ τιν' ἄλλον θεοῦ παῖδά τε καὶ ἥρω

22. ἄλλον Π: ἄλλου A, sed υ puncto notavit A².

---

35 **δῶρα λαβεῖν.** *Il.* XIX 278 ff. Plato is unjust to Achilles: see ib. 147 ff. (J. and C.).

36 **τιμὴν κτλ.** *Il.* XXIV 502, 555, 594.

391 A 1 **ἄλλως—ἐθέλειν** is again unfair: see *Il.* l.c. 560.

6 **ἔβλαψας—παρείη.** *Il.* XXII 15, 20.

391 B 8 **ποταμόν.** Scamander: *Il.* XXI 130—132, 212—226, 233 ff.

9 **καὶ αὖ κτλ.** ὡς should be repeated with ἔφη (J. and C.). Herwerden rejects both τοῦ and Σπερχειοῦ, the former because he thinks the article would suggest the Simois. Why should it not specify the other river towards which Achilles (according to Plato) shewed insubordination? Plato (as Hartman remarks) has just as much right to mention the river's name as that of Achilles' tutor (390 E). The reference is to *Il.* XXIII 140—151. Although the locks were 'sacred to Spercheius,' the vow was nevertheless conditional on Achilles' safe return, which he knew was hopeless. This is the reason which Achilles gives for offering his locks to the shade of Patroclus rather than to Spercheius: ib. 150. ὀπάσαιμι—'suffer me to give'—is in reality a prayer to the Spercheius.

11 **Ἕκτορος ἕλξεις.** *Il.* XXIV 14 ff.

13 **σφαγάς** *Il.* XXIII 175 ff.

391 C 15 **τρίτου ἀπὸ Διός.** Peleus' father, Aeacus, was son of Zeus.

20 **μηδὲ—μηδέ.** Bekker read μήτε—μήτε; but μηδὲ τάδε is of course *ne haec quidem*.

391 D 21 **ὥρμησαν—ἁρπαγάς.** Pi-

τολμῆσαι ἂν δεινὰ καὶ ἀσεβῆ ἐργάσασθαι, οἷα νῦν καταψεύδονται αὐτῶν· ἀλλὰ προσαναγκάζωμεν τοὺς ποιητὰς ἢ μὴ τούτων αὐτὰ ἔργα φάναι, ἢ τούτους μὴ εἶναι θεῶν παῖδας, ἀμφότερα δὲ μὴ λέγειν, μηδὲ ἡμῖν ἐπιχειρεῖν πείθειν τοὺς νέους, ὡς οἱ θεοὶ κακὰ γεννῶσιν, καὶ ἥρωες ἀνθρώπων οὐδὲν βελτίους. ὅπερ γὰρ ἐν τοῖς E
πρόσθεν ἐλέγομεν, οὔθ' ὅσια ταῦτα οὔτε ἀληθῆ. ἐπεδείξαμεν γάρ που, ὅτι ἐκ θεῶν κακὰ γίγνεσθαι ἀδύνατον. Πῶς γὰρ οὔ; Καὶ μὴν τοῖς γε ἀκούουσιν βλαβερά. πᾶς γὰρ ἑαυτῷ ξυγγνώμην ἕξει κακῷ ὄντι, πεισθεὶς ὡς ἄρα τοιαῦτα πράττουσίν τε καὶ ἔπραττον καὶ

οἱ θεῶν ἀγχίσποροι,
<οἱ> Ζηνὸς ἐγγύς, ὧν κατ' Ἰδαῖον πάγον
Διὸς πατρῴου βωμός ἐστ' ἐν αἰθέρι,
καὶ οὔ πώ σφιν ἐξίτηλον αἷμα δαιμόνων.

ὧν ἕνεκα παυστέον τοὺς τοιούτους μύθους, μὴ ἡμῖν πολλὴν εὐχέρειαν | ἐντίκτωσι τοῖς νέοις πονηρίας. Κομιδῇ μὲν οὖν, ἔφη. 392

34. οἱ Bekker: om. codd. ὧν Ξq: ὢν AΠ.

---

rithous assisted Theseus to abduct Helen: and Theseus Pirithous in his attempt to carry off Persephone from the lower world. οὕτως belongs to δεινάς: the order is regular and idiomatic: cf. *Ap.* 36 A, *Symp.* 192 C al. Sophocles and Euripides each wrote a play called 'Theseus': but Plato is probably alluding to some epic Theseis. Cf. Kinkel *Epic. Gr. Frag.* p. 217.

24 **αὐτά** is censured by Heller, who conjectures τοιαῦτα, while Hartman keeps αὐτά but rejects ἔργα. Stallbaum says we should expect ταῦτα for αὐτά: but ταῦτα would be too precise. αὐτά means simply 'the actions in question.' Cf. I 339 E *n.* The turn of the sentence recalls II 380 A ἢ οὐ θεοῦ ἔργα ἐατέον αὐτὰ λέγειν ἢ κτλ. Cf. also infra 408 C.

26 **κακά**. Hartman approves Cobet's conjecture κακούς, "cum γεννᾶν hic translaticiam vim non obtineat." Why not? Cf. κακὰ γίγνεσθαι just below. κακούς would be extremely tame and commonplace.

391 E 27 **ἐν τοῖς πρόσθεν**. II 378 B, 380 C.

31 **ἄρα**: II 358 C *n.*

32 **οἱ—δαιμόνων**. From Aeschylus' *Niobe*: see Dindorf *Fr.* 155. The passage is also quoted in part by Strabo (XII 8. 21), from whom it appears that Niobe is the speaker, and that οἱ θεῶν ἀγχίσποροι are her father Tantalus and his kindred (οἱ περὶ Τάνταλον). ὧν—αἰθέρι means 'whose is the altar to ancestral Zeus on Mount Ida high in heaven,' i.e. their θεὸς πατρῷος is Zeus (who was Tantalus' father), and they worship him on the heights of Ida. Tantalus' territory extended to Ida: see Strabo l.c. ὁ Τάνταλος λέγει σπείρω δ' ἄρουραν δώδεχ' ἡμερῶν ὁδόν, | Βερέκυντα χῶρον, ἔνθ' Ἀδραστείας ἕδος | Ἴδη τε μυκηθμοῖσι καὶ βρυχήμασιν | πρέπουσι μήλων. For ὧν κατ' Ἰδαῖον πάγον Strabo has οἷς ἐν Ἰδαίῳ πάγῳ, a much inferior reading. καί before οὔπω may be Plato's (so Stallbaum and others),—in which case the last line is from a different part of the play,—but is much more likely to come from Aeschylus, the resolution of κοὔπω being due to Plato. The line follows naturally on the others, and is not sufficiently important to have been selected from a different context. The verses are complete in themselves, and present a stately picture of the sons of the gods, which is the only reason why they are cited here.

392 A—C *So much for legends about gods, heroes, daemons, and the unseen world: it remains to determine what shall*

Τί οὖν, ἦν δ᾽ ἐγώ, ἡμῖν ἔτι λοιπὸν εἶδος λόγων πέρι ὁριζομένοις
οἵους τε λεκτέον καὶ μή; περὶ γὰρ θεῶν ὡς δεῖ λέγεσθαι εἴρηται,
καὶ περὶ δαιμόνων τε καὶ ἡρώων καὶ τῶν ἐν Ἅιδου. Πάνυ μὲν
οὖν. Οὐκοῦν καὶ περὶ ἀνθρώπων τὸ λοιπὸν εἴη ἄν; Δῆλα δή.
Ἀδύνατον δή, ὦ φίλε, ἡμῖν τοῦτό γε ἐν τῷ παρόντι τάξαι. Πῶς;
Ὅτι οἶμαι ἡμᾶς ἐρεῖν, ὡς ἄρα καὶ ποιηταὶ καὶ λογοποιοὶ κακῶς
B λέγουσιν περὶ ἀνθρώπων τὰ μέγιστα, ὅτι εἰσὶν ἄδικοι μέν,
εὐδαίμονες δὲ πολλοί, δίκαιοι δὲ ἄθλιοι, καὶ ὡς λυσιτελεῖ τὸ
ἀδικεῖν, ἐὰν λανθάνῃ, ἡ δὲ δικαιοσύνη ἀλλότριον μὲν ἀγαθόν,
οἰκεία δὲ ζημία· καὶ τὰ μὲν τοιαῦτα ἀπερεῖν λέγειν, τὰ δ᾽ ἐναντία
τούτων προστάξειν ᾄδειν τε καὶ μυθολογεῖν· ἢ οὐκ οἴει; Εὖ μὲν
οὖν, ἔφη, οἶδα. Οὐκοῦν ἐὰν ὁμολογῇς ὀρθῶς με λέγειν, φήσω
σε ὡμολογηκέναι ἃ πάλαι ζητοῦμεν; Ὀρθῶς, ἔφη, ὑπέλαβες.
C Οὐκοῦν περὶ ἀνθρώπων ὅτι τοιούτους δεῖ λόγους λέγεσθαι, τότε
διομολογησόμεθα, ὅταν εὕρωμεν, οἷόν ἐστιν δικαιοσύνη, καὶ ὡς

2. ἡμῖν Π: om. A. πέρι ὁριζομένοις *q*: περιορίζομεν οἷς A: περιοριζομένοις ΠΞ. 14. ζητοῦμεν Stallbaum (cum Ficino): ἐζητοῦμεν codd.

---

be said about men. But on this subject we cannot lay down rules until we have discovered the nature of Justice, and proved that Justice benefits the just, apart from all appearances.

392 A 2 **τί οὖν κτλ.** This is the ἀληθὲς εἶδος λόγων. Plato has prescribed canons for the ψευδεῖς λόγοι or legends about gods etc.; but rules for ἀληθεῖς λόγοι, i.e. λόγοι relating to men and human affairs, cannot be drawn up without begging the conclusion which the *Republic* seeks to establish. See also on II 376 E.

ἡμῖν. See *cr. n.* Without ἡμῖν, we should have τοῖς λόγων πέρι ὁριζομένοις. I agree with Hartman and the majority of editors in retaining the word. See *Introd.* § 5.

6 **ἀδύνατον δή.** For δή Stallbaum approves Ast's conjecture δέ. δέ would be too weak, if the meaning were adversative, but it is not. δή is only 'well': cf. II 368 A (Schneider).

7 **καὶ ποιηταὶ καὶ λογοποιοί.** On λογοποιοί see II 365 E *n.*; and for the statement itself *Laws* 660 E ff., 662 B.

392 B 10 **ἀλλότριον—ἀγαθόν.** I 343 C *n.*

14 **ζητοῦμεν.** Stallbaum's conjecture —see *cr. n.*—is now generally accepted. ἐζητοῦμεν would imply that the discussion had changed, but it has not. Cf. IV 420 C ὃ πάλαι ζητοῦμεν.

392 C 15 **τότε διομολογησόμεθα κτλ.** This is not "an ironical or fanciful excuse for varying the order of the subject" (J. and C.), for if Socrates declared at this stage that justice is a good for its possessor he would in point of fact be presupposing the results of the whole investigation. See IX 588 B—592 B. Others (e.g. Hirzel *der Dialog* p. 237 *n.*) have taken τότε διομολογησόμεθα as a hint of the additional discussion on Poetry in Book X: but there is nothing either here or in that book to justify any such interpretation. Cf. X 595 A *n.* What Plato's regulations about λόγοι περὶ ἀνθρώπων would have been may be easily gathered from the end of Book IX and X 608 C ff., although the subject is nowhere specifically and expressly resumed in the *Republic*. Cf. I 347 E *n.*

392 C—**394** D *We have now finished our treatment of the subject-matter of poetry, and have next to discuss its form. All composition is in a certain sense narrative, narrating things past, present or future. Narration in this sense may be either* (1) *simple and unmixed,* (2) *imitative,* (3) *both simple and imitative. Homer furnishes*

φύσει λυσιτελοῦν τῷ ἔχοντι, ἐάν τε δοκῇ ἐάν τε μὴ τοιοῦτος εἶναι;
Ἀληθέστατα, ἔφη.
VI. Τὰ μὲν δὴ λόγων πέρι ἐχέτω τέλος, τὸ δὲ λέξεως, ὡς ἐγὼ
οἶμαι, μετὰ τοῦτο σκεπτέον, καὶ ἡμῖν ἅ τε λεκτέον καὶ ὡς λεκτέον
παντελῶς ἐσκέψεται. καὶ ὁ Ἀδείμαντος, Τοῦτο, ἦ δ' ὅς, οὐ
μανθάνω ὅ τι λέγεις. Ἀλλὰ μέντοι, | ἦν δ' ἐγώ, δεῖ γε. ἴσως D
οὖν τῇδε μᾶλλον εἴσει. ἆρ' οὐ πάντα, ὅσα ὑπὸ μυθολόγων ἢ
ποιητῶν λέγεται, διήγησις οὖσα τυγχάνει ἢ γεγονότων ἢ ὄντων
ἢ μελλόντων; Τί γάρ, ἔφη, ἄλλο; Ἆρ' οὖν οὐχὶ ἤτοι ἁπλῇ
διηγήσει, ἢ διὰ μιμήσεως γιγνομένῃ, ἢ δι' ἀμφοτέρων περαίνουσιν;
Καὶ τοῦτο, ἦ δ' ὅς, ἔτι δέομαι σαφέστερον μαθεῖν. Γελοῖος, ἦν
δ' ἐγώ, ἔοικα διδάσκαλος εἶναι καὶ ἀσαφής. ὥσπερ οὖν οἱ ἀδύνατοι
λέγειν, οὐ κατὰ ὅλον | ἀλλ' ἀπολαβὼν μέρος τι πειράσομαί σοι E
ἐν τούτῳ δηλῶσαι ὃ βούλομαι. καί μοι εἰπέ· ἐπίστασαι τῆς
Ἰλιάδος τὰ πρῶτα, ἐν οἷς ὁ ποιητής φησι τὸν μὲν Χρύσην δεῖσθαι
τοῦ Ἀγαμέμνονος ἀπολῦσαι τὴν θυγατέρα, τὸν δὲ χαλεπαίνειν,
τὸν δέ, ἐπειδὴ οὐκ ἐτύγχανεν, | κατεύχεσθαι τῶν Ἀχαιῶν πρὸς τὸν 393
θεόν; Ἔγωγε. Οἶσθ' οὖν, ὅτι μέχρι μὲν τούτων τῶν ἐπῶν,

καὶ ἐλίσσετο πάντας Ἀχαιούς,
Ἀτρείδα δὲ μάλιστα δύω, κοσμήτορε λαῶν,

---

an example of the third kind: his poetry is purely narrative, when he is speaking in propria persona, *it is imitative, when he puts his words into the mouth of any of his characters. Tragedy and Comedy exemplify the imitative style. The best example of the purely narrative is the Dithyramb, of the third or mixed variety, the Epic. Which of these forms shall we admit, and on what occasions?*

392 C ff. That Poetry and Art are a species of *μίμησις*, was an accepted canon in Greece even before the time of Plato: see Butcher *Aristotle's Theory of Poetry and Fine Art*[2] p. 121. Starting from this principle, Plato gradually deepens and intensifies the connotation of *μίμησις* as the dialogue advances. At first, the word denotes a specific variety of style—the dramatic as opposed to the narrative (392 D—394 D). But as according to Plato style is at once the expression of, and also exercises a reflex influence on, the soul (400 D *n.*), *μίμησις* begins to assume an ethical import and is used to express imitation or assimilation in matters appertaining to or bearing upon character and conduct (394 E, 395 C *nn.*: cf. also 401 B—404 C). Finally, in Book X, after the psychological point of view has been superseded by the metaphysical, the word acquires an ontological or metaphysical significance: see on X 595 C. On the subject generally, reference may be made to the dissertation of Abeken *de μιμήσεως apud Platonem et Aristotelem notione*.

19 **τὸ δὲ λέξεως.** Hartman approves the variant *τὰ δὲ λέξεως*: but the subject of *λέξις* is better treated as a unity until it has been subdivided.

392 D 23 **μυθολόγων ἢ ποιητῶν.** *μυθολόγων* is said so as to include writers of *μῦθοι* in prose: cf. 394 B and II 365 E *n.*

28 **ὥσπερ οὖν κτλ.** Plato means that poor speakers cannot grapple with an abstract notion, but use a part of it, i.e. a concrete example. *οὐ κατὰ ὅλον κτλ.* may be illustrated from *Symp.* 205 B, C.

393 A 3 **καὶ ἐλίσσετο—λαῶν.** *Il.* I 15, 16. Leaf reads *λίσσετο* because

λέγει τε αὐτὸς ὁ ποιητὴς καὶ οὐδὲ ἐπιχειρεῖ ἡμῶν τὴν διάνοιαν ἄλλοσε τρέπειν, ὡς ἄλλος τις ὁ λέγων ἢ αὐτός· τὰ δὲ μετὰ ταῦτα
B | ὥσπερ αὐτὸς ὢν ὁ Χρύσης λέγει καὶ πειρᾶται ἡμᾶς ὅ τι μάλιστα ποιῆσαι μὴ Ὅμηρον δοκεῖν εἶναι τὸν λέγοντα, ἀλλὰ τὸν ἱερέα, πρεσβύτην ὄντα. καὶ τὴν ἄλλην δὴ πᾶσαν σχεδόν τι οὕτω πεποίηται διήγησιν περί τε τῶν ἐν Ἰλίῳ καὶ περὶ τῶν ἐν Ἰθάκῃ καὶ ὅλῃ Ὀδυσσείᾳ παθημάτων. Πάνυ μὲν οὖν, ἔφη. Οὐκοῦν διήγησις μέν ἐστιν καὶ ὅταν τὰς ῥήσεις ἑκάστοτε λέγῃ καὶ ὅταν τὰ μεταξὺ τῶν ῥήσεων; Πῶς γὰρ οὔ; Ἀλλ᾽ ὅταν γέ τινα λέγῃ
C ῥῆσιν ὥς τις | ἄλλος ὤν, ἆρ᾽ οὐ τότε ὁμοιοῦν αὐτὸν φήσομεν ὅ τι μάλιστα τὴν αὑτοῦ λέξιν ἑκάστῳ, ὃν ἂν προείπῃ ὡς ἐροῦντα; Φήσομεν· τί γάρ; Οὐκοῦν τό γε ὁμοιοῦν ἑαυτὸν ἄλλῳ ἢ κατὰ φωνὴν ἢ κατὰ σχῆμα μιμεῖσθαί ἐστιν ἐκεῖνον ᾧ ἄν τις ὁμοιοῖ; Τί μήν; Ἐν δὴ τῷ τοιούτῳ, ὡς ἔοικεν, οὗτός τε καὶ οἱ ἄλλοι ποιηταὶ διὰ μιμήσεως τὴν διήγησιν ποιοῦνται. Πάνυ μὲν οὖν. Εἰ δέ γε μηδαμοῦ ἑαυτὸν ἀποκρύπτοιτο ὁ ποιητής, πᾶσα ἂν αὐτῷ
D ἄνευ μιμήσεως ἡ ποίησίς τε καὶ διήγησις γεγονυῖα εἴη. | ἵνα δὲ μὴ εἴπῃς, ὅτι οὐκ αὖ μανθάνεις, ὅπως ἂν τοῦτο γένοιτο, ἐγὼ φράσω. εἰ γὰρ Ὅμηρος εἰπών, ὅτι ἦλθεν ὁ Χρύσης τῆς τε θυγατρὸς λύτρα φέρων καὶ ἱκέτης τῶν Ἀχαιῶν, μάλιστα δὲ τῶν βασιλέων, μετὰ τοῦτο μὴ ὡς Χρύσης γενόμενος ἔλεγεν, ἀλλ᾽ ἔτι ὡς Ὅμηρος, οἶσθ᾽ ὅτι οὐκ ἂν μίμησις ἦν ἀλλ᾽ ἁπλῆ διήγησις. εἶχε δ᾽ ἂν ὧδέ πως· φράσω δὲ ἄνευ μέτρου· οὐ γάρ εἰμι ποιητικός· ἐλθὼν ὁ ἱερεὺς
E ηὔχετο | ἐκείνοις μὲν τοὺς θεοὺς δοῦναι ἑλόντας τὴν Τροίαν αὐτοὺς σωθῆναι, τὴν δὲ θυγατέρα οἱ λῦσαι δεξαμένους ἄποινα καὶ τὸν θεὸν αἰδεσθέντας. ταῦτα δὲ εἰπόντος αὐτοῦ οἱ μὲν ἄλλοι ἐσέβοντο

"λίσσομαι apparently had a second initial consonant, and is never preceded by a short vowel." The word had probably been Atticised by Plato's time.

393 B 8 **δοκεῖν—ὄντα.** *δοκεῖν* is here 'to fancy' not 'to seem.' Contrast II 381 E *ἡμῖν δὲ ποιοῦσι δοκεῖν σφᾶς παντοδαποὺς φαίνεσθαι*—a passage which is cited by Hartman to justify *ποιῆσαι* as against the variant *πεῖσαι*.

10 **περί· τε τῶν—παθημάτων.** This clause is rejected by Herwerden. The difficulty—which lies in the collocation of Ἰθάκῃ the place and Ὀδυσσείᾳ the poem—is no doubt lessened by reading (with Richards) *καὶ ἐν* or *κἀν* before *ὅλῃ*, but does not wholly disappear. Possibly the last twelve books of the *Odyssey*, in which the scene is Ithaca, were sometimes known collectively as Ἰθάκη.

393 D, E 23 **ὅτι ἦλθεν—βασιλέων** paraphrases *Il.* I 12—16.

25 **ὡς Χρύσης γενόμενος**: 'as if he had been transformed into Chryses,' not merely 'in the person of Chryses' (Jowett). In 'simple narrative' he *is* Homer: when Chryses begins to speak, he *becomes* Chryses. Cf. 393 B *ὥσπερ αὐτὸς ὢν ὁ Χρύσης* ('as if he himself were Chryses').

27 **ἐλθὼν—αἰδεσθέντας.** *Il.* I 17—21. The emphatic *αὐτοὺς* accurately represents Homer's *ὑμῖν μέν*. For λῦσαι H. Wolf conjectured *ἀπολῦσαι*; but Plato is closely following Homer, who has λύσαιτε. *τὸν θεόν* is Apollo.

30 **ταῦτα δὲ—βέλεσιν.** *Il.* I 22—

*καὶ συνῄνουν, ὁ δὲ Ἀγαμέμνων ἠγρίαινεν ἐντελλόμενος νῦν τε
ἀπιέναι καὶ αὖθις μὴ ἐλθεῖν, μὴ αὐτῷ τό τε σκῆπτρον καὶ τὰ τοῦ
θεοῦ στέμματα οὐκ ἐπαρκέσοι· πρὶν δὲ λυθῆναι αὐτοῦ τὴν θυγατέρα,
ἐν Ἄργει ἔφη γηράσειν μετὰ οὗ· ἀπιέναι δ' ἐκέλευεν καὶ μὴ
ἐρεθίζειν, ἵνα σῶς οἴκαδε ἔλθοι. | ὁ δὲ πρεσβύτης ἀκούσας ἔδεισέν* **394**
*τε καὶ ἀπῄει σιγῇ, ἀποχωρήσας δὲ ἐκ τοῦ στρατοπέδου πολλὰ
τῷ Ἀπόλλωνι ηὔχετο, τάς τε ἐπωνυμίας τοῦ θεοῦ ἀνακαλῶν καὶ
ὑπομιμνῄσκων καὶ ἀπαιτῶν, εἴ τι πώποτε ἢ ἐν ναῶν οἰκοδομήσεσιν
ἢ ἐν ἱερῶν θυσίαις κεχαρισμένον δωρήσαιτο· ὧν δὴ χάριν κατηύχετο
τεῖσαι τοὺς Ἀχαιοὺς τὰ ἃ δάκρυα τοῖς ἐκείνου βέλεσιν. οὕτως,
ἦν δ' ἐγώ, ὦ ἑταῖρε, ἄνευ | μιμήσεως ἁπλῆ διήγησις γίγνεται.* **B**
Μανθάνω, ἔφη.

VII. *Μάνθανε τοίνυν, ἦν δ' ἐγώ, ὅτι ταύτης αὖ ἐναντία γίγνεται, ὅταν τις τὰ τοῦ ποιητοῦ τὰ μεταξὺ τῶν ῥήσεων ἐξαιρῶν τὰ ἀμοιβαῖα καταλείπῃ. Καὶ τοῦτο, ἔφη, μανθάνω, ὅτι ἔστιν τὸ περὶ τὰς τραγῳδίας τοιοῦτον. Ὀρθότατα, ἔφην, ὑπέλαβες,*

---

42. The paraphrasis is accurate, and Plato leaves nothing essential out. There is no sign that his text differed from ours in this passage.

32 **μὴ—οὐκ ἐπαρκέσοι.** *ἐπαρκέσοι* presupposes *ἐπαρκέσει* in the *narratio recta*: Homer has *μή νύ τοι οὐ χραίσμῃ σκῆπτρον καὶ στέμμα θεοῖο.* It is usual to regard this sentence as final: if so, it is the solitary instance in Plato where the future after a final *μή* must be admitted. See Weber in Schanz's *Beiträge* II 2, p. 60 and Goodwin *MT.* pp. 45, 91. The nearest parallel is *Euthyph.* 15 D *ἀλλὰ καὶ τοὺς θεοὺς ἂν ἔδεισας παρακινδυνεύειν, μὴ οὐκ ὀρθῶς αὐτὸ ποιήσοις*, where *μή* depends on a verb of fearing. It is better, both in point of grammar and of sense, to regard this sentence also as expressing apprehension ('for fear lest'), although no verb of fearing is present. It is not final in any proper sense of the word. Bekker read *ἐπαρκέσειε*, saying that Θ has *ἐπαρκέσειεν*.

34 **μὴ ἐρεθίζειν.** Valckenaer's conjecture *μή ἑ ἐρεθίζειν* (*μή μ' ἐρέθιζε* in Homer) is attractive in view of *τὰ ἃ δάκρυα* in 394 A for Homer's *ἐμὰ δάκρυα*, and because it provides an object for *ἐρεθίζειν*. Plato uses the pronoun tolerably often (e.g. in I 327 B, X 617 E, *Symp.* 175 C, 223 B): other Attic writers seldom, if ever (Kühner-Blass *Gr. d. Gr. Spr.* I p. 592). It is not however clear that *ἐρεθίζειν* could not be used without an object expressed, and I therefore revert to the MS reading.

394 A 4 **ἐν ναῶν οἰκοδομήσεσιν** shews that Plato understood Homer's *ἔρεψα* (*εἴ ποτέ τοι χαρίεντ' ἐπὶ νηὸν ἔρεψα*) of building. According to Leaf, *ἔρεψα* seems to denote the most primitive form of temple —"a mere roof to protect the image of a god standing in a grove."

6 **τεῖσαι—βέλεσιν.** *Ἀχαιούς* is of course the subject to *τεῖσαι* ('pay for,' 'expiate'): in Homer it is *τίσειαν Δαναοὶ ἐμὰ δάκρυα σοῖσι βέλεσσιν*. The translation 'that he would avenge his tears upon the Achaeans' (D. and V.) is wrong. *ἅ* is apparently a solitary instance of *ὅς* = 'suus' in Attic prose (Kühner-Blass l.c. I 1, p. 602). Plato chooses the word because it expresses Homer's *ἐμά* briefly and neatly, rather than from any conscious desire to make the paraphrase archaic.

394 B 12 **τραγῳδίας.** Adimantus quotes a single concrete instance—'tragedies'—to shew that he now apprehends the meaning of *μίμησις*. Socrates, out of politeness and because he wishes to make progress, interprets this as a recognition of the imitative character of Tragedy and Comedy in general (*ὥσπερ σὺ λέγεις τραγῳδία τε καὶ κωμῳδία*), as in point of fact it virtually is. *ὥσπερ σὺ λέγεις* is not

καὶ οἶμαί σοι ἤδη δηλοῦν ὃ ἔμπροσθεν οὐχ οἷός τ' ἦ, ὅτι τῆς
C ποιήσεώς τε καὶ μυθολογίας ἡ μὲν διὰ μιμήσεως ¦ ὅλη ἐστίν,
ὥσπερ σὺ λέγεις, τραγῳδία τε καὶ κωμῳδία, ἡ δὲ δι' ἀπαγγελίας
αὐτοῦ τοῦ ποιητοῦ· εὕροις δ' ἂν αὐτὴν μάλιστά που ἐν διθυράμβοις·
ἡ δ' αὖ δι' ἀμφοτέρων ἔν τε τῇ τῶν ἐπῶν ποιήσει, πολλαχοῦ δὲ καὶ
ἄλλοθι, εἴ μοι μανθάνεις. Ἀλλὰ ξυνίημι, ἔφη, ὃ τότε ἐβούλου
λέγειν. Καὶ τὸ πρὸ τούτου δὴ ἀναμνήσθητι, ὅτι ἔφαμεν, ἃ μὲν
λεκτέον, ἤδη εἰρῆσθαι, ὡς δὲ λεκτέον, ἔτι σκεπτέον εἶναι. Ἀλλὰ
D μέμνημαι. Τοῦτο τοίνυν αὐτὸ ἦν ὃ ἔλεγον, ¦ ὅτι χρείη διομολογή-
σασθαι, πότερον ἐάσομεν τοὺς ποιητὰς μιμουμένους ἡμῖν τὰς
διηγήσεις ποιεῖσθαι, ἢ τὰ μὲν μιμουμένους, τὰ δὲ μή, καὶ ὁποῖα
ἑκάτερα, ἢ οὐδὲ μιμεῖσθαι. Μαντεύομαι, ἔφη, σκοπεῖσθαί σε, εἴτε
παραδεξόμεθα τραγῳδίαν τε καὶ κωμῳδίαν εἰς τὴν πόλιν, εἴτε καὶ
οὔ. Ἴσως, ἦν δ' ἐγώ· ἴσως δὲ καὶ πλείω ἔτι τούτων· οὐ γὰρ δὴ
ἔγωγέ πω οἶδα, ἀλλ' ὅπῃ ἂν ὁ λόγος ὥσπερ πνεῦμα φέρῃ, ταύτῃ
E ἰτέον. Καὶ καλῶς γ', ἔφη, λέγεις. ¦ Τόδε τοίνυν, ὦ Ἀδείμαντε,

---

true in the beggarly literal sense of *λέγειν*, but it is sufficiently so for polite conversation. To insert—with Herwerden and Hartman—*τε καὶ κωμῳδίας* after *τραγῳδίας* seems to me unnecessary and pedantic.

394 C 16 **εὕροις δ' ἂν—διθυράμβοις.** The dithyramb was at first purely narrative or nearly so; it afterwards became mimetic (Arist. *Probl.* XIX 15. 918^b 19). Only one of Pindar's dithyrambic fragments appears to be 'mimetic' (*Frag.* 74). On the growth and decline of the Dithyramb see Smyth *Greek Melic Poets* pp. xliii—lviii.

17 **τε—δὲ καί.** II 367 C *n.*

18 **εἴ μοι μανθάνεις**: 'if I can make you understand,' with reference to *μανθάνω* in 392 C, 394 B, C. Heindorf's *εἴ μου μανθάνεις* (as in *Phil.* 51 C) is attractive, but the corruption is not easy to explain, and the MS reading is sufficiently defended by I 343 A *ὅς γε αὐτῇ οὐδὲ πρόβατα—γιγνώσκεις* (so also Hartman).

21 **τοῦτο—αὐτό** refers to *ὅτι χρείη—μιμεῖσθαι*, and *ἔλεγον* is 'was saying' i.e. 'was trying to say,' viz. when I digressed.

394 D 24 **εἴτε παραδεξόμεθα κτλ.** Krohn (*Pl. St.* p. 13) declares this passage to be inconsistent with II 373 B, where *ὑποκριταί, χορευταί, ἐργολάβοι* are admitted. He forgets or ignores the fact that in § 373 Plato is describing the *τρυφῶσα πόλις*, which he is now engaged in 'purging' (399 E). See II 372 D *n.*

26 **ἴσως δὲ—τούτων.** In this remark J. and C. find "an anticipation of the condemnation of epic poetry in Book X." I cannot see that it does more than prepare the way for *ἀλλ' ὅπῃ ἂν—ἰτέον*. See on X 595 A.

394 E—**397** D *Our guardians must not be prone to imitation. We have agreed that one man can do but one thing well, and it is impossible for one man even to imitate two things aright, as we may see from the special instances of poetical composition and acting. The sole duty of our guardians is to make and keep the city free; if they practise imitation at all, their models must be such as are appropriate to the free—that is to say, men of brave and virtuous character, for imitation means assimilation. Dramatic poetry continually offends against this canon. In general, the good man will not make use of imitation except when he is narrating the sayings or deeds of the virtuous, or some lapse of the vicious into virtue, or sometimes in mere play. His style of speech will combine plain narrative and imitation, but he will use the latter sparingly; whereas the bad man will imitate more often than narrate, and no kind of imitation will come amiss to him. In respect of mode and time, the language of Virtue will be nearly uniform, that of Vice varied.*

ἄθρει, πότερον μιμητικοὺς ἡμῖν δεῖ εἶναι τοὺς φύλακας ἢ οὔ. ἢ καὶ τοῦτο τοῖς ἔμπροσθεν ἕπεται, ὅτι εἷς ἕκαστος ἓν μὲν ἂν ἐπιτήδευμα καλῶς ἐπιτηδεύοι, πολλὰ δ' οὔ, ἀλλ' εἰ τοῦτο ἐπιχειροῖ, πολλῶν ἐφαπτόμενος πάντων ἀποτυγχάνοι ἄν, ὥστ' εἶναί που ἐλλόγιμος; Τί δ' οὐ μέλλει; Οὐκοῦν καὶ περὶ μιμήσεως ὁ αὐτὸς λόγος, ὅτι πολλὰ ὁ αὐτὸς μιμεῖσθαι εὖ ὥσπερ ἓν οὐ δυνατός; Οὐ γὰρ οὖν. Σχολῇ ἄρα ἐ|πιτηδεύσει γέ τι ἅμα τῶν ἀξίων λόγου 395 ἐπιτηδευμάτων καὶ πολλὰ μιμήσεται καὶ ἔσται μιμητικός, ἐπεί που οὐδὲ τὰ δοκοῦντα ἐγγὺς ἀλλήλων εἶναι δύο μιμήματα δύνανται οἱ αὐτοὶ ἅμα εὖ μιμεῖσθαι, οἷον κωμῳδίαν καὶ τραγῳδίαν ποιοῦντες. ἢ οὐ μιμήματα ἄρτι τούτω ἐκάλεις; Ἔγωγε· καὶ ἀληθῆ γε λέγεις, ὅτι οὐ δύνανται οἱ αὐτοί. Οὐδὲ μὴν ῥαψῳδοί γε καὶ ὑποκριταὶ

5. μιμήματά Ξ: μιμήματά τε A (sed τά in litura) Π: μίμημά τι q^1: μιμήματε q^2.

---

394 E 29 **πότερον μιμητικοὺς κτλ.** The question is not 'Are our guardians to become dramatic poets?' but 'Are they to have the imitative habit of mind?' The answer is in the negative, and the drama is banished because it fosters this habit in spectators. Cf. 395 D *n*.

30 **ὅτι—πολλὰ δ' οὔ** explains *τοῖς ἔμπροσθεν*, as Hartman points out, and not *τοῦτο*, as D. and V. translate. *ἔμπροσθεν* refers to II 370 B.

32 **πολλῶν κτλ.** suggests, perhaps intentionally, *πόλλ' ἠπίστατο ἔργα, κακῶς δ' ἠπίστατο πάντα*. The words *ὥστ'—ἐλλόγιμος*—equivalent to a neuter accusative—are undeservedly cancelled by Herwerden and Hartman. Translate 'he will fail in all of them to attain creditable distinction': cf. the adverb *κακῶς* in *κακῶς δ' ἠπίστατο πάντα*.

33 **οὐκοῦν κτλ.** The reasoning is *a fortiori*: if two or more departments of merely imitative art cannot be represented by the same person, still less can imitation be combined with any serious pursuit (*σχολῇ ἄρα κτλ.*).

395 A 3 **οὐδὲ τὰ δοκοῦντα—ποιοῦντες.** The reverse is affirmed by Socrates in *Symp.* 223 D *τοῦ αὐτοῦ ἀνδρὸς εἶναι κωμῳδίαν καὶ τραγῳδίαν ἐπίστασθαι ποιεῖν, καὶ τὸν τέχνῃ τραγῳδοποιὸν ὄντα καὶ κωμῳδοποιὸν εἶναι.* The solution is that in the *Symposium* Socrates is applying to the drama the Socratic principle *μία ἐπιστήμη* s. *δύναμις τῶν ἐναντίων*: theoretically, therefore, and ideally, the tragedian is also capable of writing a comedy. In the *Republic*, on the other hand, he is describing Greek dramatic art as he found it: for which reason he writes *δύνανται* and not *δύναιντ' ἄν* (a corruption in *v*, wrongly adopted by Stallbaum). Cf. *Ion* 534 C. Aristophanes did not write tragedy, nor the tragedians comedy. The passage in the *Symposium* is interesting as an unconscious prophecy of the Shakespearian drama. Cf. Reber *Plato u. d. Poesie* p. 11.

5 **μιμήματα.** See *cr. n.* Former editors variously read *μιμήματα* or *μιμήματε*. Either is admissible, so far as concerns the Greek, but the plural was perhaps—owing to the proximity of *τούτω*—somewhat more likely to be corrupted to the dual in this instance than *vice versâ*. Cf. X 614 C *δύο—χάσματα ἐχομένω ἀλλήλοιν* with *n.* ad loc. The reading *μιμήματά τε* represents the correction *μιμήματα* with *τε* written above. This is, I think, a somewhat simpler view than to suppose that an original *μιμήματε* became *μιμήματέ τε* by dittography, and *τέ* was afterwards changed to *τά*. Roeper, however, pronounces in favour of the dual (*de dual. usu Pl.* p. 14), and it must be admitted that duals are peculiarly liable to corruption in the MSS of the *Republic*. See *Introd.* § 5.

6 **ῥαψῳδοί—ὑποκριταί.** Even *ῥαψῳδοί* seem to have generally confined themselves to a particular poet: see *Ion* 531 C, 536 B.

ἅμα. Ἀληθῆ. Ἀλλ' οὐδέ τοι ὑποκριταὶ κωμῳδοῖς τε καὶ τραγῳ-
B δοῖς οἱ αὐτοί· πάντα δὲ ταῦτα μιμήματα. ἢ οὔ; Μιμήματα.
Καὶ ἔτι γε τούτων, ὦ Ἀδείμαντε, φαίνεταί μοι εἰς σμικρότερα
κατακεκερματίσθαι ἡ τοῦ ἀνθρώπου φύσις, ὥστε ἀδύνατος εἶναι
πολλὰ καλῶς μιμεῖσθαι, ἢ αὐτὰ ἐκεῖνα πράττειν, ὧν δὴ καὶ τὰ
μιμήματά ἐστιν ἀφομοιώματα. Ἀληθέστατα, ἦ δ' ὅς.

VIII. Εἰ ἄρα τὸν πρῶτον λόγον διασώσομεν, τοὺς φύλακας
ἡμῖν τῶν ἄλλων πασῶν δημιουργιῶν ἀφειμένους δεῖν εἶναι δημιουρ-
C γοὺς ἐλευθερίας τῆς πόλεως πάνυ ἀκριβεῖς καὶ μηδὲν ἄλλο ἐπιτηδεύειν, ὅ τι μὴ εἰς τοῦτο φέρει, οὐδὲν δὴ δέοι ἂν αὐτοὺς ἄλλο
πράττειν οὐδὲ μιμεῖσθαι· ἐὰν δὲ μιμῶνται, μιμεῖσθαι τὰ τούτοις
προσήκοντα εὐθὺς ἐκ παίδων, ἀνδρείους, σώφρονας, ὁσίους, ἐλευθέρους, καὶ τὰ τοιαῦτα πάντα, τὰ δὲ ἀνελεύθερα μήτε ποιεῖν μήτε
δεινοὺς εἶναι μιμήσασθαι, μηδὲ ἄλλο μηδὲν τῶν αἰσχρῶν, ἵνα μὴ
D ἐκ τῆς μιμήσεως τοῦ εἶναι ἀπολαύσωσιν. ἢ οὐκ ᾔσθησαι, ὅτι αἱ
μιμήσεις, ἐὰν ἐκ νέων πόρρω διατελέσωσιν, εἰς ἔθη τε καὶ φύσιν

20. μὴ Π: om. A.

---

7 **ἀλλ' οὐδὲ—οἱ αὐτοί.** This was true without exception till comparatively late times: see Müller *Gr. Bühnenalt.* pp. 185—188. κωμῳδοῖς and τραγῳδοῖς (literally 'at the tragedians' etc.) are local—almost adverbial—datives, regularly used to denote the exhibitions of comedies and tragedies: see e.g. Arist. *Eth. Nic.* IV 6. 1123ᵃ23, Aesch. *in Ctes.* 36, and cf. the Latin use of 'gladiatoribus' for 'at a gladiatorial show.'

395 B, C 11 **ἢ αὐτὰ ἐκεῖνα πράττειν.** καλῶς should be repeated with πράττειν, and ἤ is simply 'or,' not 'or else.' The alternative rendering given by J. and C. 'or else—if able to imitate—is not able to do the things themselves,' does violence to both grammar and sense.

14 **δημιουργοὺς ἐλευθερίας.** An artificial and somewhat strained expression, selected in order at once to compare and contrast the guardians with other artists. They too are artists, and their ἔργον is Freedom. To ἐλευθερία Plato attaches his own meaning: true freedom lies in the subordination of the lower to the higher, both in private conduct and in political life: cf. Xen. *Mem.* I 2. 5, 6 and infra IX 577 D, E, X 617 E *nn.* It is in this sense that ἐλευθέρους is used below.

17 **τούτοις**: viz. τοῖς δημιουργοῖς ἐλευθερίας τῆς πόλεως.

20 **ἵνα μὴ—ἀπολαύσωσιν** reveals the object of this attack upon the drama: cf. II 383 C and infra 401 B. An admirable illustration of the sentiment is quoted by Susemihl from Plut. *Sol.* 29. 6 μετὰ δὲ τὴν θέαν προσαγορεύσας (sc. ὁ Σόλων) αὐτὸν (viz. τὸν Θέσπιν) ἠρώτησεν, εἰ τοσούτων ἐναντίον οὐκ αἰσχύνεται τηλικαῦτα ψευδόμενος. φήσαντος δὲ τοῦ Θέσπιδος μὴ δεινὸν εἶναι τὸ μετὰ παιδιᾶς λέγειν τοιαῦτα καὶ πράσσειν, σφόδρα τῇ βακτηρίᾳ τὴν γῆν ὁ Σόλων πατάξας Ταχὺ μέντοι τὴν παιδιάν, ἔφη, ταύτην ἐπαινοῦντες καὶ τιμῶντες εὑρήσομεν ἐν τοῖς συμβολαίοις. To omit μή (with A and a few other MSS), and govern ἵνα by μιμεῖσθαι above is grammatically difficult, and gives an unsatisfactory sense. The genitive τοῦ εἶναι has been called in question by Hartman (following Ast) on the ground that "qui τοῦ εἶναι (sc. αἰσχροὶ) ἀπολαύσωσιν iam *sunt* turpitudine infecti." This would be true, if Plato had written the present ἀπολαύωσιν, but the aorist is ingressive, and τοῦ εἶναι ἀπολαύσωσιν is virtually equivalent to γένωνται τοῦθ' ὃ μιμοῦνται. Few will acquiesce in Ast's conjecture τὸ εἶναι, or in Stallbaum's view that τοῦ εἶναι is a partitive genitive.

καθίστανται καὶ κατὰ σῶμα καὶ φωνὰς καὶ κατὰ τὴν διάνοιαν; Καὶ μάλα, ἦ δ' ὅς. Οὐ δὴ ἐπιτρέψομεν, ἦν δ' ἐγώ, ὧν φαμὲν κήδεσθαι καὶ δεῖν αὐτοὺς ἄνδρας ἀγαθοὺς γενέσθαι, γυναῖκα μιμεῖσθαι ἄνδρας ὄντας, ἢ νέαν ἢ πρεσβυτέραν, ἢ ἀνδρὶ λοιδορουμένην ἢ πρὸς θεοὺς ἐρίζουσάν τε καὶ μεγαλαυχουμένην, οἰομένην εὐδαίμονα εἶναι, ἢ ἐν ξυμφοραῖς τε καὶ πένθεσιν | καὶ θρήνοις **E** ἐχομένην· κάμνουσαν δὲ ἢ ἐρῶσαν ἢ ὠδίνουσαν πολλοῦ καὶ δεήσομεν. Παντάπασι μὲν οὖν, ἦ δ' ὅς. Οὐδέ γε δούλας τε καὶ δούλους πράττοντας ὅσα δούλων. Οὐδὲ τοῦτο. Οὐδέ γε ἄνδρας κακούς, ὡς ἔοικεν, δειλούς τε καὶ τὰ ἐναντία πράττοντας ὧν νῦν δὴ εἴπομεν, κακηγοροῦντάς τε καὶ κωμῳδοῦντας ἀλλήλους καὶ αἰσχρολογοῦντας, μεθύοντας ἢ καὶ | νήφοντας, ἢ καὶ ἄλλα ὅσα **396** οἱ τοιοῦτοι καὶ ἐν λόγοις καὶ ἐν ἔργοις ἁμαρτάνουσιν εἰς αὑτούς τε καὶ εἰς ἄλλους. οἶμαι δὲ οὐδὲ μαινομένοις ἐθιστέον ἀφομοιοῦν αὑτοὺς ἐν λόγοις οὐδὲ ἐν ἔργοις. γνωστέον μὲν γὰρ καὶ μαινομένους καὶ πονηροὺς ἄνδρας τε καὶ γυναῖκας, ποιητέον δὲ οὐδὲν τούτων οὐδὲ μιμητέον. Ἀληθέστατα, ἔφη. Τί δέ; ἦν δ' ἐγώ· χαλκεύοντας ἤ τι ἄλλο δημιουργοῦντας, ἢ ἐλαύνοντας τριήρεις ἢ κελεύοντας

---

395 D 23 **καὶ κατὰ σῶμα—διάνοιαν.** For σῶμα Stallbaum conjectured σχῆμα, but Plato would surely have said σχήματα, as in 397 B. Hartman boldly ejects κατὰ φωνάς and reads καὶ κατὰ <τὸ> σῶμα καὶ κατὰ τὴν διάνοιαν, remarking that κατὰ τὸ σῶμα by itself includes "gestus, habitus, *vocem*, vultum, similia." This is in a sense true, but there is no reason why one particular instance of physical resemblance should not be selected for special remark. Plato differentiates the external from the internal characteristics by combining σῶμα and φωνάς under a single preposition, and repeating κατά before τὴν διάνοιαν.

25 **αὐτούς.** For αὐτούς following ὧν see on II 357 B. The rule against the repetition of the relative in such cases is sometimes dispensed with for the sake of rhetorical emphasis, e.g. in II 374 B and perhaps *Theaet.* 192 B.

26 **μιμεῖσθαι.** In what sense can the guardians be said to 'imitate' in such a case, or in those specified in 396 A, B? Not as actors, but as spectators. Acting involves three elements—the character, the actor, and the spectator. In good acting the spectator identifies himself with the actor through sympathy; and as the actor 'imitates,' so does he. Such is Plato's theory, though merely glanced at here. Cf. X 605 C ff., *Ion* 533 D ff., and see the excellent remarks of Nettleship *Lectures and Remains* II pp. 100—104.

ἢ ἀνδρὶ κτλ. ἀνδρί is of course 'husband,' not simply 'a man' (D. and V.). Contemporary comedy doubtless furnished abundant illustrations. In πρὸς θεοὺς ἐρίζουσαν κτλ. Plato may be thinking of Aeschylus' *Niobe* (see on II 380 A). The emphasis on οἰομένην should be noted: cf. I 336 A *n.*

395 E 29 **κάμνουσαν—ὠδίνουσαν** glances at Euripides and his school: cf. Ar. *Frogs* 1043, 1044 and 1080, with the Scholiast's remark on 1080 ἔγραψε γὰρ (ὁ Εὐριπίδης) τὴν Αὔγην ὠδίνουσαν ἐν ἱερῷ. Plato's strictures throughout this passage tell much more heavily against Euripides than against the other two dramatists.

396 A 1 **ἢ καὶ ἄλλα.** ἄλλα must be coordinated with αἰσχρολογοῦντας, not with νήφοντας, so that Hartman's correction (καί for ἢ καί), though scarcely necessary, is an improvement, and may be right.

3 **μαινομένοις.** As in the *Eumenides*, *Ajax*, *Hercules Furens*.

4 **γνωστέον κτλ.** cf. 409 A.

B τούτοις, ἢ τι ἄλλο τῶν περὶ | ταῦτα μιμητέον; Καὶ πῶς, ἔφη, οἷς γε οὐδὲ προσέχειν τὸν νοῦν τούτων οὐδενὶ ἐξέσται; Τί δέ; ἵππους χρεμετίζοντας καὶ ταύρους μυκωμένους καὶ ποταμοὺς ψοφοῦντας καὶ θάλατταν κτυποῦσαν καὶ βροντὰς καὶ πάντα αὖ τὰ τοιαῦτα ἦ μιμήσονται; Ἀλλ' ἀπείρηται αὐτοῖς, ἔφη, μήτε μαίνεσθαι μήτε μαινομένοις ἀφομοιοῦσθαι. Εἰ ἄρα, ἦν δ' ἐγώ, μανθάνω ἃ σὺ λέγεις, ἔστιν τι εἶδος λέξεώς τε καὶ διηγήσεως, ἐν ᾧ ἂν διηγοῖτο **C** ὁ τῷ ὄντι καλὸς | κἀγαθός, ὁπότε τι δέοι αὐτὸν λέγειν, καὶ ἕτερον αὖ ἀνόμοιον τούτῳ εἶδος, οὗ ἂν ἔχοιτο ἀεὶ καὶ ἐν ᾧ διηγοῖτο ὁ ἐναντίως ἐκείνῳ φὺς τε καὶ τραφείς. Ποῖα δή, ἔφη, ταῦτα; Ὁ μέν μοι δοκεῖ, ἦν δ' ἐγώ, μέτριος ἀνήρ, ἐπειδὰν ἀφίκηται ἐν τῇ διηγήσει ἐπὶ λέξιν τινὰ ἢ πρᾶξιν ἀνδρὸς ἀγαθοῦ, ἐθελήσειν ὡς αὐτὸς ὢν ἐκεῖνος ἀπαγγέλλειν καὶ οὐκ αἰσχυνεῖσθαι ἐπὶ τῇ τοιαύτῃ μιμήσει, μάλιστα μὲν μιμούμενος τὸν ἀγαθὸν ἀσφαλῶς τε καὶ ἐμφρόνως **D** | πράττοντα, ἐλάττω δὲ καὶ ἧττον ἢ ὑπὸ νόσων ἢ ὑπὸ ἐρώτων ἐσφαλμένον ἢ καὶ ὑπὸ μέθης ἤ τινος ἄλλης ξυμφορᾶς· ὅταν δὲ γίγνηται κατά τινα ἑαυτοῦ ἀνάξιον, οὐκ ἐθελήσειν σπουδῇ ἀπεικάζειν ἑαυτὸν τῷ χείρονι, εἰ μὴ ἄρα κατὰ βραχύ, ὅταν τι χρηστὸν ποιῇ, ἀλλ' αἰσχυνεῖσθαι, ἅμα μὲν ἀγύμναστος ὢν τοῦ μιμεῖσθαι

25. ἑαυτὸν Π: ἑαυτοῦ A.

---

396 B 8 **μιμητέον**. See on *μιμεῖσθαι* 395 D.

9 **ἵππους—βροντάς**. The reference is probably to stage machinery and musical effects etc. in dramatic poetry generally, as well as in the later and degenerate form of the dithyramb (see on 394 C). Cf. (with Nettleship *Lect. and Rem.* II p. 105) *Laws* 669 C ff. and Ar. *Plut.* 290 ff. The *βροντεῖον* and *κεραυνοσκοπεῖον* for producing thunder and lightning were familiar enough (Müller *Gr. Bühnenalt.* p. 157 *n.* 2). It is clear, as Nettleship remarks, that "Plato felt strongly that Greek literature and music were declining" in his days: see *Laws* 659 A ff., 700 A ff., 797 A ff.

396 C 17 **ὁ μὲν—ἀνήρ**. It seems difficult (as Schneider remarked) either to connect *ὁ μέν* with *μέτριος ἀνήρ*, or to understand *ὁ μέν* as 'the one' and suppose that *μέτριος ἀνήρ* is in apposition to it. If the latter alternative is right, we should expect *μέτριος* < *ὢν* > *ἀνήρ*, or < *ὁ* > *μέτριος ἀνήρ*, and in view of other cases in which the article is placed at some distance from its noun (e.g. *ὁ δέ γε, οἶμαι, ἦν δ' ἐγώ, καταληφθεὶς θανάτῳ δίδοται* VIII 566 C), I still prefer the former view. Some may be inclined to regard *μέτριος ἀνήρ* as a gloss. I have sometimes been tempted to make *μοι δοκεῖ* parenthetical (exactly = 'methinks'), in which case *ὁ μέν* can easily be connected with *μέτριος*. The idiom occurs in *Phaed.* 108 D *ὁ βίος μοι δοκεῖ ὁ ἐμός—τῷ μήκει τοῦ λόγου οὐκ ἐξαρκεῖ* and *Menex.* 236 B: cf. also *Crito* 43 D, 50 B, and I 332 E *n.* This solution would involve the change of *ἐθελήσειν* to *ἐθελήσει*—so *v*—and of *αἰσχυνεῖσθαι* to *αἰσχυνεῖται* just below, as well as again in D. Such a corruption, once started, *ἔρχεται*—as Plato might say—*ὡς κύκλος αὐξανομένη*; but I do not venture to change the text.

396 D 22 **καὶ ἧττον** is not superfluous with *ἐλάττω*. *ἐλάττω* means 'in fewer respects,' and *ἧττον* 'to a less degree.'

24 **σπουδῇ**. Cf. *ὅ τι μὴ παιδιᾶς χάριν* in E and *σπουδῇ* 397 A.

τοὺς τοιούτους, ἅμα δὲ καὶ δυσχεραίνων αὐτὸν ἐκμάττειν τε καὶ ἐνιστάναι εἰς τοὺς τῶν κακιόνων τύπους, | ἀτιμάζων τῇ διανοίᾳ, **E** ὅ τι μὴ παιδιᾶς χάριν. Εἰκός, ἔφη.

IX. Οὐκοῦν διηγήσει χρήσεται οἵᾳ ἡμεῖς ὀλίγον πρότερον διήλθομεν περὶ τὰ τοῦ Ὁμήρου ἔπη, καὶ ἔσται αὐτοῦ ἡ λέξις μετέχουσα μὲν ἀμφοτέρων, μιμήσεώς τε καὶ τῆς ἁπλῆς διηγήσεως, σμικρὸν δέ τι μέρος ἐν πολλῷ λόγῳ τῆς μιμήσεως· ἢ οὐδὲν λέγω; Καὶ μάλα, ἔφη, οἷόν γε ἀνάγκη τὸν τύπον εἶναι τοῦ τοιούτου ῥήτορος. Οὐκοῦν, ἦν δ' ἐγώ, ὁ μὴ | τοιοῦτος αὖ, ὅσῳ ἂν φαυλότερος **397** ᾖ, πάντα τε μᾶλλον μιμήσεται καὶ οὐδὲν ἑαυτοῦ ἀνάξιον οἰήσεται εἶναι, ὥστε πάντα ἐπιχειρήσει μιμεῖσθαι σπουδῇ τε καὶ ἐναντίον πολλῶν, καὶ ἃ νῦν δὴ ἐλέγομεν, βροντάς τε καὶ ψόφους ἀνέμων τε καὶ χαλαζῶν καὶ ἀξόνων καὶ τροχιλιῶν, καὶ σαλπίγγων καὶ αὐλῶν καὶ συρίγγων καὶ πάντων ὀργάνων φωνάς, καὶ ἔτι κυνῶν καὶ προβάτων καὶ ὀρνέων φθόγγους· καὶ ἔσται δὴ ἡ τούτου λέξις ἅπασα διὰ | μιμήσεως φωναῖς τε καὶ σχήμασιν, ἢ σμικρόν τι **B** διηγήσεως ἔχουσα; Ἀνάγκη, ἔφη, καὶ τοῦτο. Ταῦτα τοίνυν, ἦν δ' ἐγώ, ἔλεγον τὰ δύο εἴδη τῆς λέξεως. Καὶ γὰρ ἔστιν, ἔφη.

32. ἁπλῆς nos: ἄλλης codd. 2. μιμήσεται *q*: διηγήσεται ΑΠΞ. 4. δὴ ἐλέγομεν Α²Π: διελέγομεν Α¹. τε Π: γε Α.

---

396 E 29 **ὅ τι μὴ παιδιᾶς χάριν.** Cf. VII 518 B.

30 **οἵᾳ.** According to Van Cleef (*de Attract. usu Plat.* p. 36), οἷος is not elsewhere attracted in Plato.

32 **τῆς ἁπλῆς.** See *cr. n.* The reading of the MSS τῆς ἄλλης ought strictly speaking to mean 'the rest of διήγησις,' i.e. besides μίμησις. A reference to 392 D will shew that the rest of διήγησις includes (1) simple διήγησις, (2) the mixed style. If the text is sound, Plato therefore says that the good man's λέξις will resemble Homer's in partaking of all three varieties. This is a cumbrous and unnecessary elaboration: for if style partakes both in μίμησις and in simple διήγησις, it is already *ipso facto* 'mixed.' To take ἄλλης as 'besides' may be admissible, but in any case it is desirable to define the kind of διήγησις meant. I believe that Plato wrote ἁπλῆς. The good man's style will resemble Homer's, which has already been said to partake of μίμησις (393 C) and of ἁπλῆ διήγησις (394 B). The corruption—common in uncial MSS—is illustrated by Bast *Comment. Palaeogr.* p. 730. Cf. my article in *Cl. Rev.* X pp. 384 f.

33 **μέρος** (as Schneider points out) depends on μετέχουσα: cf. *Euthyd.* 306 A ὧν ἀμφοτέρων μέρος μετέχουσι.

397 A 2 **μιμήσεται.** See *cr. n.* The choice of reading lies between this and Madvig's emendation <μιμήσεται ἢ> διηγήσεται. In favour of μιμήσεται is μᾶλλον, which correlates with ὅσῳ ἂν φαυλότερος ᾖ. The corruption doubtless arose from a misinterpretation of μᾶλλον. Thinking that an ἤ clause was needed to explain it, a scribe added ἢ διηγήσεται in the margin, and διηγήσεται was afterwards taken as a variant and ousted μιμήσεται. These arguments, which are Hartman's, seem to me conclusive in favour of μιμήσεται, which Schneider first restored.

3 **σπουδῇ τε καὶ ἐναντίον πολλῶν:** like the professional dramatist or actor.

5 **τροχιλιῶν κτλ.** Cf. supra 396 B *n.*

397 B 8 **σχήμασιν** 'gestures.'

10 **ἔλεγον.** 396 B, C.

Οὐκοῦν αὐτοῖν τὸ μὲν σμικρὰς τὰς μεταβολὰς ἔχει, καὶ ἐάν τις
ἀποδιδῷ πρέπουσαν ἁρμονίαν καὶ ῥυθμὸν τῇ λέξει, ὀλίγου πρὸς
τὴν αὐτὴν γίγνεται λέγειν τῷ ὀρθῶς λέγοντι καὶ ἐν μιᾷ ἁρμονίᾳ·
C σμικραὶ γὰρ αἱ μεταβολαί· καὶ δὴ ἐν ῥυθμῷ ὡσαύτως | παρα-
πλησίῳ τινί; Κομιδῇ μὲν οὖν, ἔφη, οὕτως ἔχει. Τί δέ; τὸ τοῦ
ἑτέρου εἶδος οὐ τῶν ἐναντίων δεῖται, πασῶν μὲν ἁρμονιῶν, πάντων
δὲ ῥυθμῶν, εἰ μέλλει αὖ οἰκείως λέγεσθαι, διὰ τὸ παντοδαπὰς
μορφὰς τῶν μεταβολῶν ἔχειν; Καὶ σφόδρα γε οὕτως ἔχει. Ἆρ'
οὖν πάντες οἱ ποιηταὶ καὶ οἵ τι λέγοντες ἢ τῷ ἑτέρῳ τούτων
ἐπιτυγχάνουσιν τύπῳ τῆς λέξεως, ἢ τῷ ἑτέρῳ, ἢ ἐξ ἀμφοτέρων
D τινὶ ξυγκεραννύντες; Ἀνάγκη, ἔφη. | Τί οὖν ποιήσομεν; ἦν δ' ἐγώ·
πότερον εἰς τὴν πόλιν πάντας τούτους παραδεξόμεθα ἢ τῶν ἀκράτων
τὸν ἕτερον ἢ τὸν κεκραμένον; Ἐὰν ἡ ἐμή, ἔφη, νικᾷ, τὸν τοῦ
ἐπιεικοῦς μιμητὴν ἄκρατον. Ἀλλὰ μήν, ὦ Ἀδείμαντε, ἡδύς γε
καὶ ὁ κεκραμένος, πολὺ δὲ ἥδιστος παισί τε καὶ παιδαγωγοῖς ὁ
ἐναντίος οὗ σὺ αἱρεῖ, καὶ τῷ πλείστῳ ὄχλῳ. Ἥδιστος γάρ. Ἀλλ'

---

13 **πρὸς τὴν αὐτήν**: sc. ἁρμονίαν, as Schneider saw. To supply λέξιν with Stallbaum, Hartman, and others is not satisfactory, nor is it easy to understand χορδήν (with Campbell). On the other hand ἁρμονίαν may be readily supplied in view of ἐν μιᾷ ἁρμονίᾳ following. ὁ λόγος qualifies τὴν αὐτήν. The somewhat vague expression πρὸς τὴν αὐτήν, where the musical sense of πρός may be illustrated by πρὸς Λίβυν λακεῖν | αὐλόν (Eur. *Alc.* 346), is afterwards made more explicit and precise by ἐν μιᾷ ἁρμονίᾳ i.e. 'in one musical mode' (see on 398 E), as opposed to πασῶν—ἁρμονιῶν in C. μεταβολή was technically used of passing from one ἁρμονία to another: see Cleonid. *Isag. Harm.* 13 and Bacchius *Isag.* 53 ed. von Jan. We shall best apprehend the full meaning of the whole passage if we read it in connexion with 399 A, B. The general sentiment may be illustrated from Arist. *Eth. Nic.* IV 8. 1125a 12 ff. καὶ κίνησις δὲ βραδεῖα τοῦ μεγαλοψύχου δοκεῖ εἶναι, καὶ φωνὴ βαρεῖα, καὶ λέξις στάσιμος, Pl. *Charm.* 159 B, Dem. 37. 52 and elsewhere.

397 C 17 **διὰ τὸ παντοδαπὰς—ἔχειν.** As the λέξις itself is full of variety, it requires for its proper or appropriate (οἰκείως) expression every variety of mode and rhythm or musical time. μορφὰς τῶν μεταβολῶν is surely good enough Greek: I cannot see the point of Richards' μορφὰς ἐκ τῶν μεταβολῶν, still less why Hartman should eject τῶν μεταβολῶν or—as an alternative—μορφάς.

20 **ἐπιτυγχάνουσιν** = 'hit upon,' 'stumble upon,' as if by accident and ἄνευ νοῦ, not 'succeed,' as J. B. Mayor is disposed to construe (*Cl. Rev.* X p. 109). The same scholar proposes to change ξυγκεραννύντες into ξυγκεκραμένῳ, but the text is much more idiomatic as it stands.

397 D—**398** B *We shall therefore admit that style only which imitates the good man's way of speaking. The mixed and mimetic varieties do not suit us, for the character of our citizens is simple and uniform. Those poets who refuse to comply we will dismiss with compliments into another city.*

397 D 23 **τὸν ἕτερον**: 'one or other.' Presently τοῦ ἐπιεικοῦς 'the good man' is said for 'the good man's style of speaking'; see 398 B and cf. 399 B *n.* Before ἄκρατον, many editors add τόν (with Ξ²): but the position of ἄκρατον is normal: cf. τὰ ἐν ὕδασι φαντάσματα θεῖα VII 532 C and note ad loc.

25 **παισί—τῷ πλείστῳ ὄχλῳ.** The expression recurs in *Laws* 700 C (quoted by J. and C.).

ἴσως, ἦν δ' ἐγώ, οὐκ ἂν αὐτὸν ἁρμόττειν φαίης τῇ ἡμετέρᾳ πολιτείᾳ,
ὅτι | οὐκ ἔστιν διπλοῦς ἀνὴρ παρ' ἡμῖν οὐδὲ πολλαπλοῦς, ἐπειδὴ E
ἕκαστος ἓν πράττει. Οὐ γὰρ οὖν ἁρμόττει. Οὐκοῦν διὰ ταῦτα
ἐν μόνῃ τῇ τοιαύτῃ πόλει τόν τε σκυτοτόμον σκυτοτόμον εὑρήσομεν
καὶ οὐ κυβερνήτην πρὸς τῇ σκυτοτομίᾳ, καὶ τὸν γεωργὸν γεωργὸν
καὶ οὐ δικαστὴν πρὸς τῇ γεωργίᾳ, καὶ τὸν πολεμικὸν πολεμικὸν
καὶ οὐ χρηματιστὴν πρὸς τῇ πολεμικῇ, καὶ πάντας οὕτω; Ἀληθῆ,
ἔφη. Ἄνδρα δή, ὡς ἔοικε, δυνάμενον | ὑπὸ σοφίας παντοδαπὸν 398
γίγνεσθαι καὶ μιμεῖσθαι πάντα χρήματα, εἰ ἡμῖν ἀφίκοιτο εἰς τὴν
πόλιν αὐτός τε καὶ τὰ ποιήματα βουλόμενος ἐπιδείξασθαι, προσκυνοῖμεν ἂν αὐτὸν ὡς ἱερὸν καὶ θαυμαστὸν καὶ ἡδύν, εἴποιμεν δ' ἄν,
ὅτι οὔτ' ἔστιν τοιοῦτος ἀνὴρ ἐν τῇ πόλει παρ' ἡμῖν οὔτε θέμις
ἐγγενέσθαι, ἀποπέμποιμέν τε εἰς ἄλλην πόλιν μύρον κατὰ τῆς
κεφαλῆς καταχέαντες καὶ ἐρίῳ στέψαντες, αὐτοὶ δ' ἂν τῷ αὐστη-

5. *οὔτ'* nos: *οὐκ* codd.

---

397 E 29 **οὐκοῦν διὰ ταῦτα κτλ.** There is probably a satirical reference to Athenian democracy: see *Prot.* 319 D.

398 A 3 **αὐτός—ἐπιδείξασθαι**: 'anxious to shew himself off together with his poems.' *ἐπιδείξασθαι* is intransitive—i.q. *ἐπίδειξιν ποιήσασθαι*, cf. *Lach.* 179 E—with *αὐτός*, but transitive with *ποιήματα*. This explanation, which is due to Schneider, gives a much better sense than if we regard *αὐτός τε καὶ τὰ ποιήματα* as subject to *ἀφίκοιτο*, or translate 'himself, and wanting to shew his poems' (J. and C.). A reference to *αὐτός τε καὶ τὸν ἀδελφὸν παρακάλει* in IV 427 D is therefore hardly to the point.

προσκυνοῖμεν. The insertion of *μέν*, recommended by Shilleto (Dem. *F. L.* § 91) and Richards, is unnecessary: cf. I 340 D *n.* For *προσκυνεῖν* 'to kiss the hand' (adorare), as to the image or shrine of a god, see Cope's *Rhetoric of Aristotle* Vol. I p. 86.

5 **οὔτ' ἔστιν—οὔτε θέμις.** It is perhaps better to correct *οὐκ* into *οὔτ'*—see *cr. n.*—than the second *οὔτε* into *οὐδέ* (with Bekker and the other editors).

6 **μύρον—στέψαντες.** The idea suggested by *προσκυνοῖμεν* and *ἱερόν*, that the poet is a sort of *θεός* or *θεῖος ἀνήρ*, is now elaborated with ironical politeness. The images of the gods were anointed, and crowned with garlands, not only on great occasions (cf. Cic. *Verr.* IV 77), but also at other times, according to Proclus, who remarks on this passage *μύρον αὐτῆς* (sc. *τῆς ποιητικῆς*) *καταχέας, ὡς τῶν ἐν τοῖς ἁγιωτάτοις ἱεροῖς ἀγαλμάτων θέμις, καὶ ὡς ἱερὰν στέψας αὐτήν, ὥσπερ καὶ ἐκεῖνα στέφειν ἦν νόμος* (*in remp.* p. 42 ed. Kroll). Schneider aptly compares Paus. X 24. 6 *τούτου* (a sacred stone) *καὶ ἔλαιον ὁσημέραι καταχέουσι καὶ κατὰ ἑορτὴν ἑκάστην ἔρια ἐπιτιθέασι τὰ ἀργά.* For other illustrations see Frazer on Paus. l.c., and Munro on Lucr. V 1199. Apropos of the present passage, Dio Chrysostom and other ancient writers cited by Ast refer to the anointing of swallows by Greek women: *καὶ κελεύει μάλα εἰρωνικῶς* (so Ast: MSS *εἰρηνικῶς*) *στέψαντας αὐτὸν ἐρίῳ καὶ μύρῳ καταχέαντας ἀφιέναι παρ' ἄλλους· τοῦτο δὲ αἱ γυναῖκες ἐπὶ τῶν χελιδόνων ποιοῦσι* (Dio Chr. *Or.* 53 p. 276 ed. Reiske). To this custom Ast supposes that Plato is alluding, the poets being as it were faithless and garrulous swallows (cf. *χελιδόνων μουσεῖα*), as well as to the Pythagorean precept 'not to admit swallows into the house' (Plut. *Symp.* VIII 727 B ff.), on which see Frazer in *Cl. Rev.* V pp. 1—3. This explanation lends an additional point to *ἀποπέμποιμεν*: and *προσκυνοῖμεν* might fairly be interpreted of the joyful salutations with which the Greeks hailed the advent of the swallow in the spring (see e.g. Baumeister *Denk. d. Kl. Alterth.* p. 1985). G. B. Hussey

B ροτέρῳ καὶ ἀηδεστέρῳ ποιητῇ χρῴμεθα | καὶ μυθολόγῳ ὠφελίας ἕνεκα, ὃς ἡμῖν τὴν τοῦ ἐπιεικοῦς λέξιν μιμοῖτο καὶ τὰ λεγόμενα λέγοι ἐν ἐκείνοις τοῖς τύποις, οἷς κατ' ἀρχὰς ἐνομοθετησάμεθα, ὅτε τοὺς στρατιώτας ἐπεχειροῦμεν παιδεύειν. Καὶ μάλ', ἔφη, οὕτως ἂν ποιοῖμεν, εἰ ἐφ' ἡμῖν εἴη. Νῦν δή, εἶπον ἐγώ, ὦ φίλε, κινδυνεύει ἡμῖν τῆς μουσικῆς τὸ περὶ λόγους τε καὶ μύθους παντελῶς διαπεπεράνθαι· ἅ τε γὰρ λεκτέον καὶ ὡς λεκτέον, εἴρηται. Καὶ αὐτῷ μοι δοκεῖ, ἔφη.

C X. Οὐκοῦν | μετὰ τοῦτο, ἦν δ' ἐγώ, τὸ περὶ ᾠδῆς τρόπου καὶ

8. χρῴμεθα Π: χρώμεθα A.

(*Proceedings of the American Philol. Association* Vol. XXII pp. xliii ff.) thinks that Plato has in his mind the well-known χελιδονισμός of which we read in Athenaeus (VIII 360 B ff.), remarking that in the swallow song 'the custom seems to have been to carry some sort of symbolic swallow from house to house.' It is perhaps more probable (as Mr J. G. Frazer suggests to me) that "the ceremony of anointing the swallows and crowning them with wool was performed on the children who went from door to door in spring, singing the swallow song and apparently personating the swallow." But the tone of the whole passage, with its air of studiously exaggerated politeness and compliment, as well as the particular expressions προσκυνοῖμεν, ἱερόν, and θαυμαστόν, are strongly in favour of Proclus' interpretation, although Plato's thoughts may have dwelt for a moment on the practices connected with the χελιδονισμός when he wrote the words ἀποπέμποιμεν—στέψαντες.

398 B 10 **κατ' ἀρχάς.** II 379 A ff.

398 C—**399** E *We have now to treat of lyric poetry. Song involves three factors, viz. words, a certain musical mode, and a certain movement or time. Our regulations about words when unaccompanied by music apply equally to words when sung, and the musical mode and time must conform to the words. Now we proscribed all lamentation in our city, so that we must exclude the lugubrious modes; and those which are relaxing in their effects must be rejected on similar grounds. In short, we shall retain two modes and no more, one to imitate the brave man's utterances in times of stress and strain, the other to imitate his accents in seasons of peace and calm. We shall deal similarly with instruments of music, forbidding all those which lend themselves to a variety of modes. It is thus that we purge our 'luxurious city.'*

398 C 16 **τὸ περὶ ᾠδῆς κτλ.** The discussion has hitherto confined itself chiefly to tragedy and comedy. It remains to discuss lyrical poetry also on its formal side. Now the chief formal characteristic of lyric poetry is its invariable association with music. It is therefore necessary to lay down canons for musical composition. This is the justification for the sections on 'harmony' and rhythm, which are wrongly pronounced to be irrelevant by Krohn (*Pl. St.* p. 15).

The present section, and its ancient commentators (Arist. *Pol.* Θ 7. 1342ª 28—1342ᵇ 34, Plut. *de Mus.* cc. 15—17, Aristid. Quint. I pp. 21, 22 ed. Meibom), have been fully discussed by Westphal (*Gr. Harmonik* pp. 187–234). Westphal's views have been combatted by C. von Jan (see especially his article *Die Tonarten bei Platon im dritten Buche der Republik* in *Fl. Jahrb.* 1867 pp. 815 ff. and 1883, pp. 1354—1362 and 1568—1579), and more recently (in other respects) by Monro in his 'Modes of ancient Greek Music.' The last edition of the *Harmonik* (1886) contains Westphal's reply to von Jan's criticism (pp. 209—215). See also von Jan in Baumeister's *Denkmäler d. Kl. Alt.* pp. 976 ff., Susemihl and Hicks *The Politics of Aristotle* Vol. I pp. 595 ff. and 624—631, and H. S. Jones and Monro in the *Cl. Rev.* VIII pp. 448—454 and IX pp. 79—81. The writers in Meibom's *Antiquae Musicae auctores septem* have

μελῶν λοιπόν; Δῆλα δή. Ἆρ' οὖν οὐ πᾶς ἤδη ἂν εὕροι, ἃ ἡμῖν
λεκτέον περὶ αὐτῶν, οἷα δεῖ εἶναι, εἴπερ μέλλομεν τοῖς προειρημένοις
συμφωνήσειν; καὶ ὁ Γλαύκων ἐπιγελάσας, Ἐγὼ τοίνυν, ἔφη, ὦ
Σώκρατες, κινδυνεύω ἐκτὸς τῶν πάντων εἶναι· οὔκουν ἱκανῶς γε
ἔχω ἐν τῷ παρόντι ξυμβαλέσθαι, ποῖα ἄττα δεῖ ἡμᾶς λέγειν,
ὑποπτεύω μέντοι. Πάντως δήπου, ἦν δ' ἐγώ, πρῶτον μὲν τόδε
ἱκανῶς ἔχεις λέγειν, | ὅτι τὸ μέλος ἐκ τριῶν ἐστὶν συγκείμενον, D
λόγου τε καὶ ἁρμονίας καὶ ῥυθμοῦ. Ναί, ἔφη, τοῦτό γε. Οὐκοῦν
ὅσον γε αὐτοῦ λόγος ἐστίν, οὐδὲν δήπου διαφέρει τοῦ μὴ ᾀδομένου
λόγου πρὸς τὸ ἐν τοῖς αὐτοῖς δεῖν τύποις λέγεσθαι οἷς ἄρτι
προείπομεν, καὶ ὡσαύτως; Ἀληθῆ, ἔφη. Καὶ μὴν τήν γε ἁρμονίαν
καὶ ῥυθμὸν ἀκολουθεῖν δεῖ τῷ λόγῳ. Πῶς δ' οὔ; Ἀλλὰ μέντοι
θρήνων τε καὶ ὀδυρμῶν ἔφαμεν ἐν λόγοις οὐδὲν προσδεῖσθαι.
Οὐ γὰρ οὖν. Τίνες οὖν θρηνώδεις | ἁρμονίαι; λέγε μοι· σὺ γὰρ E

---

now been re-edited—Aristoxenus by Marquard (Berlin 1868), Aristides Quintilianus by A. Jahn (Berlin 1882), Alypius and others by von Jan in his *Musici Scriptores Graeci* (Lipsiae 1895), where also the passages of Aristotle bearing on the subject are carefully collected, together with all the extant remains of Greek Music. The account of *Die Musik der Griechen* by Gleditsch in Iwan Müller's *Handbuch* will be found a useful and compendious introduction to the study of this part of the *Republic*. Von Kralik's recent monograph *Altgriechische Musik* (Stuttgart und Wien) is interesting, but too slight to be of much service. Taken by itself, the language of Plato in this chapter seems to me to point to the existence of four leading or simple modes, viz. Dorian, Phrygian, Lydian and Ionian (the last two having each two varieties, a *σύντονος* and a *χαλαρά*), and one composite mode, the Mixolydian. See App. II.

16 **τρόπου**. Hartman suggests *τρόπον*, in view of *τὸ περὶ ῥυθμούς* 399 E; but cf. 392 C. *τρόπος* is not here used in its technical sense, for which see Monro l. c. p. 63.

19 **συμφωνήσειν**. The metaphor may be suggested by the subject under discussion: cf. *Phaed.* 92 C.

398 D 24 **λόγου—ῥυθμοῦ**. In the best period of Greek music, lyric poetry was written only for music, and music only for poetry, the separation of the two being condemned as illegitimate: see Monro l.c. pp. 119, 120. The elements of music are *ῥυθμός* and *ἁρμονία*. The former 'reconciles' *ταχύ* and *βραδύ* by arranging a proper sequence of short and long notes and syllables, the latter *ὀξύ* and *βαρύ* by a proper arrangement of notes of higher and lower pitch (*Symp.* 187 A—C). In the wider sense, therefore, any *ὁμολογία* of *ὀξύ* and *βαρύ* is a *ἁρμονία*, but in practice the word was used specifically of certain scales or modes, and it is in this sense (according to Westphal) that Plato uses it here and in 398 E, where see note.

27 **ὡσαύτως**: i.e. *ἐν τῇ αὐτῇ λέξει* as defined in 396 E, 397 D.

καὶ μὴν κτλ. The poet should be his own musician, and write the music to suit the words, not *vice versâ*. This was another characteristic feature of classical Greek music, although a change set in during the fourth century B.C. See Westphal *Gr. Rhythmik* p. 1 and *Laws* 669 D, E, 812 D.

398 E 30 **ἁρμονίαι** (according to the orthodox view) are 'musical modes' and not simply 'keys.' They differed from each other both in the arrangement of the intervals (like our major and minor modes) and also in pitch. It must have been the former difference which chiefly—though not perhaps exclusively—accounted for the different effects of different modes upon the character and emotions, just as we are ourselves affected in different ways by music written in major and in minor keys. See H. S. Jones in *Cl. Rev.* VIII p. 449.

μουσικός. Μιξολυδιστί, ἔφη, καὶ συντονολυδιστὶ καὶ τοιαῦταί τινες. Οὐκοῦν αὗται, ἦν δ' ἐγώ, ἀφαιρετέαι; ἄχρηστοι γὰρ καὶ γυναιξὶν ἃς δεῖ ἐπιεικεῖς εἶναι, μὴ ὅτι ἀνδράσι. Πάνυ γε. Ἀλλὰ μὴν μέθη γε φύλαξιν ἀπρεπέστατον καὶ μαλακία καὶ ἀργία. Πῶς γὰρ οὔ; Τίνες οὖν μαλακαί τε καὶ συμποτικαὶ τῶν ἁρμονιῶν;
399 Ἰαστί, ἦ δ' ὅς, καὶ λυδιστὶ αὖ τινες χαλαραὶ καλοῦνται. | Ταύταις οὖν, ὦ φίλε, ἐπὶ πολεμικῶν ἀνδρῶν ἔσθ' ὅ τι χρήσει; Οὐδαμῶς, ἔφη· ἀλλὰ κινδυνεύει σοι δωριστὶ λείπεσθαι καὶ φρυγιστί. Οὐκ οἶδα, ἔφην ἐγώ, τὰς ἁρμονίας, ἀλλὰ κατάλειπε ἐκείνην τὴν ἁρμονίαν, ἣ ἔν τε πολεμικῇ πράξει ὄντος ἀνδρείου καὶ ἐν πάσῃ βιαίῳ ἐργασίᾳ πρεπόντως ἂν μιμήσαιτο φθόγγους τε καὶ προσῳδίας, καὶ ἀποτυχόντος ἢ εἰς τραύματα ἢ εἰς θανάτους ἰόντος ἢ εἴς τινα ἄλλην
B ξυμφορὰν πεσόντος, ἐν πᾶσι τούτοις παρατεταγμένως καὶ καρτε-

31. συντονολυδιστὶ A^2Ξ: συντονοιλυδιστὶ A^1: σύντονοι λυδιστὶ Π *q*. 36. αὖ τινες A^1 $Π^1$: αἵτινες A^2Ξ: καὶ τοιαῦταί τινες $Π^2$ *q*.

---

31 **μιξολυδιστὶ κτλ.** The omission of the article has been questioned, but in merely naming the scales it can be dispensed with: cf. (with Stallbaum) Arist. *Pol.* Θ 5. 1340^b 1 (τὴν μιξολυδιστὶ καλουμένην). On the ἁρμονίαι recognized by Plato see App. II.

36 **Ἰαστὶ—καλοῦνται**: 'there are also varieties of Lydian and Ionian which are called 'slack'.' Jowett and Campbell, reading αἵτινες (see *cr. n.*), remark that the "indefinite relative suits with Plato's affected ignorance"; but the speaker is Glauco, not Socrates, and Glauco is μουσικός. See note on 399 C. Richards condemns αἵτινες χαλαραὶ καλοῦνται as spurious because αἵτινες "cannot be used in this way in good Attic prose of Plato's date." With the older and better attested reading αὖ τινες, which I have ventured to restore, everything is plain. The words αὖ τινες establish once for all what Westphal (l.c. p. 198) and von Jan (l.c. p. 816) detected even when αἵτινες was read, viz. that Plato is referring not to Ionian and Lydian, but to *slack* Ionian and *slack* Lydian, a point which escaped Monro (l.c. p. 7) but not his reviewer (*Cl. Rev.* VIII p. 449). See also my article in *Cl. Rev.* X pp. 378 f. We learn from Aristotle that certain musical critics censured Plato for rejecting τὰς ἀνειμένας ἁρμονίας and for characterising them as μεθυστικαί, βακχευτικὸν γὰρ ἥ γε μέθη ποιεῖ μᾶλλον (*Pol.* Θ 7. 1342^b 23—27). It was partly perhaps in deference to these criticisms that Plato altered his view of μέθη in *Laws* 666 A ff.: see also Grote *Plato* III p. 328 *n.*

399 A 3 **δωριστὶ καὶ φρυγιστί.** The absence of the Aeolian mode is remarkable, for it must certainly have been known to Plato (see Pratinas quoted in App. II). Westphal agrees with Bellermann in supposing (l.c. p. 195) that αἰολιστί is included under δωριστί. Aristotle also ignores αἰολιστί, unless indeed (as Westphal holds ib. p. 196) it was identical with ὑποδωριστί. In *Lach.* 188 D φρυγιστί is excluded (perhaps because the speaker is Laches, whose ideal of courage is military rather than pacific), and Dorian, 'the only national Greek mode,' alone recognized.

4 **ἐκείνην τὴν ἁρμονίαν**: viz. Dorian, not Phrygian, as Ast seems to have thought.

6 **μιμήσαιτο.** Cf. *Laws* 798 D τὰ περὶ τοὺς ῥυθμοὺς καὶ πᾶσαν μουσικήν ἐστι τρόπων μιμήματα βελτιόνων καὶ χειρόνων ἀνθρώπων and 397 B above.

καὶ ἀποτυχόντος. καί connects ὄντος and ἀμυνομένου. ἀποτυχόντος (which is itself logically subordinate to ἀμυνομένου) has three subordinate alternatives (ἢ—πεσόντος), all of which are summarised in ἐν πᾶσι τούτοις.

ρούντως ἀμυνομένου τὴν τύχην· καὶ ἄλλην αὖ ἐν εἰρηνικῇ τε καὶ μὴ βιαίῳ ἀλλ' ἐν ἑκουσίῳ πράξει ὄντος, ἤ τινά τι πείθοντός τε καὶ δεομένου, ἢ εὐχῇ θεὸν ἢ διδαχῇ καὶ νουθετήσει ἄνθρωπον, ἢ τοὐναντίον ἄλλῳ δεομένῳ ἢ διδάσκοντι ἢ μεταπείθοντι ἑαυτὸν ὑπέχοντα, καὶ ἐκ τούτων πράξαντα κατὰ νοῦν, καὶ μὴ ὑπερηφάνως ἔχοντα, ἀλλὰ σωφρόνως τε καὶ μετρίως ἐν πᾶσι τούτοις πράττοντά τε καὶ τὰ | ἀποβαίνοντα ἀγαπῶντα. ταύτας δύο ἁρμονίας, βίαιον, C *ἑκούσιον, δυστυχούντων, εὐτυχούντων, σωφρόνων, ἀνδρείων αἵτινες*

13. *ὑπέχοντα* unus Ξ: *ἐπέχοντα* AΠ: *παρέχοντα* *q*. 15. *τὰ* Π: om. A. 16. *ἀνδρείων* Ξ: *ἀνδρείων ἁρμονίας* AΠ *q*.

---

399 B 9 **ἄλλην**: viz. Phrygian. Aristotle blames Plato for retaining the Phrygian mode, while rejecting the *αὐλός*, with which it was usually associated: *ἄμφω γὰρ ὀργιαστικὰ καὶ παθητικά* (*Pol.* Θ 7. 1342^b 3). Plato, however, rejects the flute, not because it is orgiastic, but because it is *πολυαρμόνιον* (399 D). In Plato's opinion the Phrygian mode expressed sobriety and resignation: Aristotle thought it ecstatic and purgative (l.c. 1341^a 23). The difference of view is interesting and important as shewing that the ethical effect of different modes was a disputed point even among the ancients.

11 **ἢ εὐχῇ—ἄνθρωπον** is subordinate to *πείθοντός τε καὶ δεομένου*.

13 **ὑπέχοντα**. *ἐπέχοντα*—see *cr. n.*—cannot, I think, be right. *ἐπέχειν τὴν διάνοιαν* (*Laws* 926 B) certainly does not justify *ἐπέχειν ἑαυτόν*, and even if it did, 'submitting to' and not merely 'attending to' is the sense required. With *ὑπέχοντα* cf. *Gorg.* 497 B *ὑπόσχες Σωκράτει ἐξελέγξαι ὅπως ἂν βούληται*, where the reflexive pronoun is omitted, as often with *παρέχειν*. Here it is better to take *ἑαυτόν* with *ὑπέχοντα* than with *μεταπείθοντι*. By changing the construction and writing accusatives instead of genitives, Plato makes the man himself rather than his *φθόγγοι* appear the object of imitation (cf. 397 D *n.*). This is natural enough, because the situations described in *ἢ τοὐναντίον—ἀγαπῶντα* give less scope for *φθόγγοι*. Stephanus wished to read the genitive throughout (*ὑπέχοντος, πράξαντος* etc.: so also *v* and two Florentine MSS), but there is also inscriptional evidence for a genitive or dative participle followed by an accusative in the course of a long sentence: see Meisterhans[3] p. 205.

κατὰ νοῦν: 'to his liking': cf. *εὐτυχούντων* below.

399 C 15 **ταύτας—λεῖπε**. The style is intentionally weighty and formal, as befits a solemn pronouncement: cf. X 617 D, E. After *ταύτας* there is a slight pause: 'Just these, two modes and none other.' The insertion of *τάς* would impair the effect, besides suggesting that Socrates had in view two of the current modes, which, not being himself *μουσικός*, he professedly had not. It is Glauco's business to fit the cap (398 E, 399 A); Socrates only makes it. The indefinite *αἵτινες* (before *φθόγγους*) is therefore strictly appropriate in the mouth of Socrates, although it would not be in Glauco's. *ἁρμονίας* is rejected by Herwerden in both places (see *cr. n.*), but it is almost as indispensable here as it is wrong after *ἀνδρείων*, although Stallbaum rejects the word here and retains it there. The genitives *δυστυχούντων* etc. must depend on *φθόγγους*. For *βίαιον, ἑκούσιον* ('one involuntary, one voluntary'), Ast suggests *βιαίου, ἑκουσίου*, Hartman *βιαίων ἑκουσίων*. A human being cannot however be called *βίαιος* because he is engaged *ἐν βιαίῳ πράξει*, although the mode which imitates his accents may be so described with propriety and even elegance: cf. (with Schneider) such expressions as *φόνος ξυγγενής* for the slaughter of kindred. The words *δυστυχούντων—κάλλιστα* simply define the meaning of *βίαιον* and *ἑκούσιον* ('whatever musical modes they be that shall best imitate the accents of' etc.): the relative is postponed in order to keep the essential marks of the *ἁρμονίαι* together, but the careful reader will note that Plato begins a chiasmus with *δυστυχούντων*, as if to separate the genitives from what precedes and prepare us to

φθόγγους μιμήσονται κάλλιστα, ταύτας λεῖπε. Ἀλλ', ἦ δ' ὅς, οὐκ
ἄλλας αἰτεῖς λείπειν, ἢ ἃς νῦν δὴ ἐγὼ ἔλεγον. Οὐκ ἄρα, ἦν δ'
ἐγώ, πολυχορδίας γε οὐδὲ παναρμονίου ἡμῖν δεήσει ἐν ταῖς ᾠδαῖς
τε καὶ μέλεσιν. Οὔ μοι, ἔφη, φαίνεται. Τριγώνων ἄρα καὶ
D πηκτίδων καὶ πάντων ὀργάνων, ὅσα | πολύχορδα καὶ πολυαρμόνια,
δημιουργοὺς οὐ θρέψομεν. Οὐ φαινόμεθα. Τί δέ; αὐλοποιοὺς ἢ
αὐλητὰς παραδέξει εἰς τὴν πόλιν; ἢ οὐ τοῦτο πολυχορδότατον,

---

find their construction in the sequel. Had he written *εὐτυχούντων, δυστυχούντων, ἀνδρείων, σωφρόνων* the double chiasmus would have compelled us to connect the genitives with *δύο ἁρμονίας*.

17 **οὐκ ἄλλας—ἔλεγον**. The Dorian to express *ἀνδρεία*, the Phrygian *σωφροσύνη*. These are the two contrasting virtues which Plato's *μουσική* endeavours to combine (410 E).

19 **παναρμονίου**. In Plato the noun *παναρμόνιον* occurs only here and in 404 D *ᾠδῇ τῇ ἐν τῷ παναρμονίῳ καὶ ἐν πᾶσι ῥυθμοῖς πεποιημένῃ*. In the latter passage it certainly does not denote a musical instrument of any kind. Here the word is sometimes understood of a particular and definite musical instrument, but a careful study of the context shews that it does not bear this meaning even here. Plato has decided to admit only two modes, the Dorian and the Phrygian. 'Consequently,' he continues, 'we shall have no need in our songs and melodies of *πολυχορδία* or *παναρμόνιον*, and *therefore* (*ἄρα*) we shall dispense with *τρίγωνοι, πηκτίδες* etc., with all instruments, in short, which are *πολύχορδα* and *πολυαρμόνια*.' The prohibition of certain musical instruments is an inference from the general principle that *πολυχορδία* and *παναρμόνιον* are unnecessary, so that *παναρμόνιον* cannot itself be a particular musical instrument. Probably, as Mr Archer-Hind has suggested to me, the *παναρμόνιον* was "not a mode or modes, but a style of composition, in which the 'Tondichter' passed freely from *δωριστί* to *φρυγιστί* and *λυδιστί* and as many others as he chose. The name may even have been given to well-known compositions in this style—cf. *νόμος πολυκέφαλος*—the fantasia with many subjects. The effect, I should think, may have been analogous to a series of bold and sudden modulations in modern music." See also on *αὐτὰ τὰ παναρμονία* in 399 D.

20 **τριγώνων—πηκτίδων**. These were foreign instruments of high pitch, and many strings. The *τρίγωνον* in particular was associated with loose and voluptuous melodies. For an exhaustive account of both see Susemihl and Hicks' *Politics of Arist.* vol. I pp. 632—636 or von Jan's *de fidibus Graecorum* pp. 29 ff., 33 ff.

399 D 23 **αὐλητάς**. The *αὐλός* resembled the clarinet. It had a "mouthpiece (*ζεῦγος*) in which a vibrating reed (*γλῶττα*) was fitted," and was sometimes played in pairs. See *Dict. Ant.* s.v. *tibia*. Plato banishes the 'flute' and retains the Dorian mode, although Dorian melodies were often played on it, as Milton well knew: see the noble description of the "Dorian mood of flutes and soft recorders" in *Par. Lost* I 550 ff. In Boeotia, where the *αὐλός* was highly esteemed, it was supposed rather to calm than to excite the feelings. See Rhys Roberts *The Ancient Boeotians* pp. 33—35.

ἢ οὐ τοῦτο πολυχορδότατον; *τοῦτο* is that with which *αὐλοποιοί* and *αὐληταί* are concerned, viz. the 'flute': cf. II 377 C *n.* *οὗτος* instead of *τοῦτο* would have been a trifle harsh. *πολυχορδότατον* has been repeatedly called in question, and there is the usual crop of emendations, intended to obliterate the metaphor. Schneider has however shewn that the MS reading is sound, by citing Pollux IV 67 *Πλάτων δὲ καὶ πολύχορδον εἴρηκε τὸν αὐλόν*, and Simon. *Fr.* 46 *ὁ καλλιβόας πολύχορδος αὐλός*, and comparing expressions like *αὐλὸν κρέκειν, ἁρμόζειν, κρούειν*. Many other illustrations are given by Smyth, *Greek Melic Poets* p. 326. Here the metaphor is intended to arrest attention by its boldness and prepare us for the theory of the origin of *παναρμόνια* in the next clause; but *πολυχορδότατον* in itself, like *πάμφωνος* in Pindar (*Pyth.* 12. 19 al.), refers only to the number of different notes which the flute, thanks to various contrivances, such as plugs, wax, etc., was capable of producing.

καὶ αὐτὰ τὰ παναρμόνια αὐλοῦ τυγχάνει ὄντα μίμημα; Δῆλα δή, ἦ δ' ὅς. Λύρα δή σοι, ἦν δ' ἐγώ, καὶ κιθάρα λείπεται, καὶ κατὰ πόλιν χρήσιμα· καὶ αὖ κατ' ἀγροὺς τοῖς νομεῦσι σύριγξ ἄν τις εἴη. Ὡς γοῦν, ἔφη, ὁ λόγος ἡμῖν σημαίνει. Οὐδέν γε, ἦν δ' ἐγώ, E
καινὸν ποιοῦμεν, ὦ φίλε, κρίνοντες τὸν Ἀπόλλω καὶ τὰ τοῦ Ἀπόλλωνος ὄργανα πρὸ Μαρσύου τε καὶ τῶν ἐκείνου ὀργάνων.

See Abdy Williams in *Proceedings of the Musical Association* 1897—8 p. 135. Plato objects to the multiplicity of strings and notes as admitting and even inviting change and fusion of modes. We are told by Paus. IX 12. 5 (cited by Monro l.c. p. 38: cf. Ath. XIV 631 E) that it was one Pronomus of Thebes who πρῶτος ἐπενόησεν αὐλοὺς ἐς ἅπαν ἁρμονίας εἶδος ἔχοντας ἐπιτηδείως. Down to his day there were three forms of 'flutes,' intended for the Dorian, Phrygian and Lydian modes respectively. On the means by which this change was effected see *Dict. Ant.* s.v. *tibia*.

24 **αὐτὰ τὰ παναρμόνια**: sc. ὄργανα, such as πηκτίδες and τρίγωνοι. Plato means those instruments on which panharmonic melodies could be played (cf. Proclus *in remp.* p. 63 ed. Kroll): but we must beware of translating (with D. and V.) 'the panharmonium itself,' for no single specific instrument is here intended, as some later lexicographers appear to have supposed. The gloss in Hesychius παναρμόνιον· εἶδος ὀργάνου, ἐξ ὅλου τεταγμένον is not quite clear, and may conceivably refer to a whole class of instruments, but Photius apparently thought that there was a special instrument called παναρμόνιον. His note (p. 388, 26 ed. Porson) is as follows: παναρμόνιον· ὄργανον μουσικόν· Ἄλεξις, ἐν ᾧ τὸ παναρμόνιον τὸ καινὸν ἔντεινον τεχνῶν (Τέχνων Meineke). Photius may of course be right in his interpretation of Alexis' line: but παναρμόνιον in Plato never, I believe, refers to one particular instrument: and even Alexis may mean no more than 'perform the new panharmonic melody,' ἐντείνω being used as in τὸ κάλλιστον ἐντείνας μέλος, Dionys. Hal. *de admir. vi dicendi in Dem.* c. 48.

25 **λύρα—κιθάρα**. The λύρα was the stringed instrument in common use; the κιθάρα was employed chiefly by professional musicians or κιθαρῳδοί. See Monro in *Dict. Ant.* s.v. *Lyra*, where illustrations of the two instruments are given, and von Jan *de fid. Gr.* pp. 5—26. By admitting the professional κιθάρα, Plato perhaps lends his sanction to musical festivals or contests in the approved modes.

καὶ κατὰ κτλ. After χρήσιμα supply ἐστίν. This is better than to eject καί (with Ast and—according to Bekker—Vat. Θ). Demetrius (περὶ ἑρμ. § 185, cited by Schneider) finds in the words καὶ αὖ κατ' ἀγροὺς τοῖς ποιμέσι (sic, not νομεῦσι) σύριγξ ἄν τις εἴη an imitation of the sound of the σύριγξ. "Ceterum Demetrii rationem me non perspicere fateor," says Schneider. Demetrius' remark is, I believe, correct, and has reference to the sigmatismus in the words of Plato: cf. *Laws* 700 C τὸ δὲ κῦρος τούτων—οὐ σύριγξ (used for συριγμός) ἦν οὐδέ τινες ἄμουσοι βοαὶ πλήθους, καθάπερ τὰ νῦν. The σύριγξ was either μονοκάλαμος, resembling our flute, or πολυκάλαμος (like Pan's pipe): see *Dict. Ant.* s.v. The indefinite τις shews that Plato did not wish to specify which variety he intended.

399 E 27 **οὐδέν γε—ὀργάνων**. Plato puts himself in the position of the Muses, who preferred Apollo's performance on the κιθάρα to that of Marsyas on the flute (Apollod. I 4. 2). This is the force of οὐδέν γε καινὸν ποιοῦμεν. The words τὰ τοῦ Ἀπόλλωνος ὄργανα must not be pressed; for although Apollo invented the cithara, the lyre was ascribed to Hermes (Paus. V 14. 8: cf. the Homeric *Hymn to Hermes*), and the syrinx to Pan. The discovery of the flute was also ascribed to Athena, especially by the Boeotians. A third account represents Marsyas as picking up the instrument after Athena had discovered and discarded it. This legend may be an attempt to reconcile the two conflicting stories, and probably dates from the decline of the flute as an instrument of education in Athens during the fourth century (Arist. *Pol.* Θ 6. 1341ᵃ 32 ff. Cf. Preller *Gr. Myth.* p. 223). In making Marsyas its discoverer, Plato declares the flute a

Μὰ Δία, ἦ δ' ὅς, οὔ μοι φαινόμεθα. Καὶ νὴ τὸν κύνα, εἶπον,
λελήθαμέν γε διακαθαίροντες πάλιν ἣν ἄρτι τρυφᾶν ἔφαμεν πόλιν.
Σωφρονοῦντές γε ἡμεῖς, ἦ δ' ὅς.
XI. Ἴθι δή, ἔφην, καὶ τὰ λοιπὰ καθαίρωμεν. ἑπόμενον γὰρ
δὴ ταῖς ἁρμονίαις ἂν ἡμῖν εἴη τὸ περὶ ῥυθμούς, μὴ ποικίλους
αὐτοὺς διώκειν μηδὲ παντοδαπὰς βάσεις, ἀλλὰ βίου ῥυθμοὺς ἰδεῖν
400 κοσμίου τε καὶ ἀνδρείου τίνες εἰσίν· οὓς ἰδόντα | τὸν πόδα τῷ
τοιούτου λόγῳ ἀναγκάζειν ἕπεσθαι καὶ τὸ μέλος, ἀλλὰ μὴ λόγον
ποδί τε καὶ μέλει. οἵτινες δ' ἂν εἶεν οὗτοι οἱ ῥυθμοί, σὸν ἔργον,
ὥσπερ τὰς ἁρμονίας, φράσαι. Ἀλλὰ μὰ Δί', ἔφη, οὐκ ἔχω λέγειν.
ὅτι μὲν γὰρ τρί' ἄττα ἐστὶν εἴδη, ἐξ ὧν αἱ βάσεις πλέκονται,
ὥσπερ ἐν τοῖς φθόγγοις τέτταρα, ὅθεν αἱ πᾶσαι ἁρμονίαι, τεθεα-

---

foreign instrument, and appropriately excludes it from his 'Greek city' (V 470 E).

30 **νὴ τὸν κύνα.** This peculiarly Socratic oath occurs only once again in the *Republic* (IX 592 A). In both passages it marks the highest degree of emphasis. On the oath itself see my note on *Ap.* 21 E and Blaydes on Ar. *Wasps* 83.

31 **ἄρτι**: II 372 E *n*.

399 E—**401** A *Let us now continue the purgation of our city by laying down rules for rhythm and time. Our rhythm must not be varied or manifold; for time as well as tune should conform to words, and not conversely. It is agreed that there are certain rhythms expressive of sobriety and courage. These and these only will be admitted into our city. For particulars, we shall apply to Damon; but we can enunciate the general principle ourselves. Rhythm and Mode reflect style, and style expresses character. It is to promote the growth of character that we shall require the young to pursue the beautiful throughout the realms alike of Art and Nature.*

The section on Rhythms is hardly less difficult than that on Modes. Westphal translates it with a short commentary in his *Gr. Rhythmik* pp. 237—239, but without shedding any light upon the darkest places. Schneider and Stallbaum give little help. I have found Gleditsch's summary account of *die Metrik der Griechen* (in Iwan Müller's *Handbuch*) a most useful guide in dealing with the subject.

35 **βάσεις.** The word βάσις in the technical writers on Rhythm generally means a dipody or combination of two feet under one main ictus: cf. Schol. in Heph. I 3. I p. 124 ed. Westphal βάσις δέ ἐστι τὸ ἐκ δύο ποδῶν συνεστηκός, τοῦ μὲν ἄρσει, τοῦ δὲ θέσει παραλαμβανομένου. Such a technical use of the word would be out of place here, especially in the mouth of Socrates; and the word is employed throughout as equivalent simply to 'step' or 'foot.' Even technical writers sometimes so use it: cf. the Scholiast already cited δέξεται δὲ (sc. the Iambic metre) ἐν μὲν τῇ πρώτῃ βάσει ἴαμβον καὶ σπονδεῖον II 5. p. 151 and Gleditsch l.c. p. 702.

36 **κοσμίου τε καὶ ἀνδρείου** recalls 399 C σωφρόνων ἀνδρείων, and would seem to point to the necessity of two kinds of rhythm, one to go with the Phrygian mode and express sobriety and self-control, the other to join the Dorian mode in expressing courage. On the ethical qualities of Greek rhythm in general, consult Westphal *Gr. Rhythmik* pp. 226—239 and Arist. *Rhet.* III 8, with Cope's notes.

400 A 2 **μὴ λόγον—μέλει.** See 398 D *n*.

5 **τρί' ἄττα εἴδη.** Arist. Quint. I 34 ed. Meibom γένη τοίνυν ἐστὶ ῥυθμικὰ τρία· τὸ ἴσον ($\frac{2}{2}$), τὸ ἡμιόλιον ($\frac{3}{2}$), τὸ διπλάσιον ($\frac{2}{1}$). To the first belong dactyls, spondees, anapaests: the second includes paeons, cretics, and bacchei: under the third fall trochees, iambics, ionics. See Gleditsch l.c. p. 694.

6 **ὥσπερ—ἁρμονίαι.** What are the τέτταρα εἴδη? The following answers (among others) have been given: 1° the ervals of the fourth, fifth, octave, and

μένος ἂν εἴποιμι· ποῖα δ' ὁποίου βίου μιμήματα, λέγειν οὐκ ἔχω.
'Αλλὰ | ταῦτα μέν, ἦν δ' ἐγώ, καὶ μετὰ Δάμωνος βουλευσόμεθα, B
τίνες τε ἀνελευθερίας καὶ ὕβρεως ἢ μανίας καὶ ἄλλης κακίας
πρέπουσαι βάσεις, καὶ τίνας τοῖς ἐναντίοις λειπτέον ῥυθμούς.
οἶμαι δέ με ἀκηκοέναι οὐ σαφῶς ἐνόπλιόν τέ τινα ὀνομάζοντος
αὐτοῦ ξύνθετον καὶ δάκτυλον καὶ ἡρῷόν γε, οὐκ οἶδα ὅπως διακο-

7. εἴποιμι *v*: εἴποι A: ἐπίοιμι ΠΞ*q*. ποῖα δ' ὁποίου βίου Π: om. A.

---

double octave (Ast): 2° the four notes of the tetrachord, which was probably the historical and at all events the 'theoretical unit of the scale' (Stallbaum, Jowett and Campbell): 3° "the four ratios which give the primary musical intervals—viz. the ratios 2 : 1, 3 : 2, 4 : 3 and 9 : 8, which give the octave, fifth, fourth, and tone" (Monro l.c. p. 106 *n.*; cf. also *Dict. Ant.* II p. 193): 4° the four ἁρμονίαι Φρυγιστί, Λυδιστί, Δωριστί, Λοκριστί (Westphal *Rhythmik* p. 238). Ast's view cannot be right, unless we suppose that ἁρμονίαι here includes scales of double compass, which is most unlikely. Westphal's explanation is improbable, for Plato has said nothing of Λοκριστί, and (though perhaps no great stress should be laid on this) it is awkward to derive the ἁρμονίαι (ὅθεν αἱ πᾶσαι ἁρμονίαι) from themselves. If the principle of Westphal's interpretation is right, I should be inclined to substitute 'Ιαστί for Λοκριστί, having regard to 398 E, where see *n.* Cf. *Cl. Rev.* X p. 379. (I have since found that Prantl also took this view: see *n.* 116 in his translation.) I do not think that Stallbaum has hit the truth, for Plato's language is not suggestive of any allusion to the origin of the octave from the combination of two tetrachords, and a single tetrachord cannot produce a ἁρμονία (ὅθεν αἱ πᾶσαι ἁρμονίαι). Possibly the τέτταρα εἴδη ἐν τοῖς φθόγγοις denote simply the keynote, its octave, and the intervals of a tone and a semitone: for these are as it were the threads out of which all modes 'are woven' (πλέκονται should be repeated with ἁρμονίαι), the difference between the modes depending on the difference in position of the tones and semitones. But Euclid lays the greatest stress upon the ratios 3 : 2 and 4 : 3 as the component elements of the octave: see for example *Sect. Can.* 6 τὸ διπλάσιον διάστημα ἐκ δύο τῶν μεγίστων ἐπιμορίων συνέστηκεν, ἔκ τε τοῦ ἡμιολίου καὶ ἐκ τοῦ ἐπιτρίτου and cf. ib. 8, 12, and for this reason I now believe that Monro's view has most in its favour.

7 **ποῖα δ' ὁποίου κτλ.** On ὁποίου see I 348 B *n.*, and for the error in Paris A *Introd.* § 5.

400 B 8 **Δάμωνος**. μετὰ Δάμωνος is almost a formula with Plato: cf. infra C, 424 C, and *Lach.* 200 B. Susemihl (on Arist. *Pol.* Θ 5. 1340^{b} 5) thinks that Plato is alluding to a special work by Damon on the ἦθος and πάθος of modes and rhythms. The word ἀκηκοέναι and the general tone of the passage seem rather to refer to an oral demonstration.

10 **τίνας—ῥυθμούς.** In general, πόδες ἀπὸ ἄρσεως, or feet in which the θέσις (i.e. the syllable bearing the ictus) followed the ἄρσις, were believed to express more energy and life, than πόδες ἀπὸ θέσεως. See Gleditsch p. 694, and for details as to the ἦθος of the different rhythms ib. pp. 713, 721, 725, 730, 739, 744, 766.

11 **οἶμαι δέ με κτλ.** Schneider's δέ γε (found in some inferior MSS) is not appropriate here. The superfluous pronoun after οἶμαι is a well-established colloquialism: cf. *Charm.* 173 A, *Symp.* 175 E. οἶμαι, ἀκηκοέναι, and οὐ σαφῶς ὀνομάζοντος are just the words one might employ in giving one's recollections of an abstruse and half-understood lecture, and this is just what Plato is either doing or, more probably, affecting to do. A few technical terms and a vague idea (οὐκ οἶδ' ὅπως) of some of the processes are all that he remembers.

ἐνόπλιον—ἡρῷόν γε. ἐνόπλιος ξύνθετος, δάκτυλος, ἡρῷος are expressions from the lecture: in English they would be in inverted commas. The ἐνόπλιος is not ⏑ – – – ⏑ ⏑ ⏑ ⏑ (Proclus *in remp.* p. 61, if, as appears probable, by παριαμβίς he means the παρίαμβος or pyrrich), nor the cretic (J. and C.), nor, strictly speaking, the anapaestic foot (Hartman), but ⏒ ⏑́ ⏑ ⏑ ⏑́ ⏑ ⏑ ⏑́, a common processional

σμοῦντος καὶ ἴσον ἄνω καὶ κάτω τιθέντος, εἰς βραχύ τε καὶ μακρὸν
γιγνόμενον, καί, ὥς ἐγὼ οἶμαι, ἴαμβον, καί τιν' ἄλλον τροχαῖον
C ὠνόμαζε, μήκη δὲ καὶ βραχύτητας | προσῆπτε. καὶ τούτων τισὶν

14. τιν' A^2Ξ: fortasse τὸν A^1: τι Π *q*, qui sequentia ἄλλον—βραχύτητας omittunt.

(προσοδιακός) or marching rhythm, consisting of an ἰωνικὸς ἀπὸ μείζονος and a choriambus (Hephaestion c. 15), or (as the Scholiast on Ar. *Clouds* 651 measures it) a spondee, pyrrich, trochee and iambus. For examples we may cite Sappho's αὖτα δὲ σὺ Καλλιόπη (*Fr.* 82) and Tyrtaeus' ἄγετ' ὦ Σπάρτας ἔνοπλοι (*Fr.* 16). See Gleditsch l.c. pp. 717, 722, and Bacchius *Isag.* 101 ed. von Jan, whose example is ὁ τὸν πίτυος στέφανον. ξύνθετος probably refers to the composite character of the rhythm, as described, for example, by the Scholiast on the *Clouds*. The later technical expression for this peculiarity was ἐπισύνθετος (Gleditsch p. 746). δάκτυλον must be understood as a foot, not as a rhythm, although the ἐνόπλιος ξύνθετος certainly, and probably also the ἡρῷος, are rhythms. There is no difficulty about this, provided we remember that Plato is quoting (or pretending to quote) isolated technical expressions from Damon's lecture. The ingenious, though hazardous, proposal of Blaydes, to read καὶ < κατὰ > δάκτυλον (cf. *Clouds* 651), would confine the instances to rhythms until we reach ἴαμβον. Dr Jackson suggests δακτυλικόν in place of δάκτυλον. It is tempting (with J. and C.) to take ἡρῷος as 'spondee,' but there seems to be no authority for such a use of the word. The ἡρῷος πούς is apparently a dactyl; although the ἡρῷος ῥυθμός admits of the spondee. Unless, therefore, we take ἡρῷος as a rhythm, the spondee seems to be altogether excluded. It is unnecessary to do more than allude to Hartman's excision of ξύνθετον καὶ δάκτυλον.

13 **ἴσον—τιθέντος.** ἄνω and κάτω *refer* of course to the position of the arsis and thesis (cf. ὁ ἄνω, ὁ κάτω χρόνος said of the notes at which the foot or bâton is raised and brought down respectively), but Westphal's remark that Plato uses τὸ ἄνω and τὸ κάτω is misleading (*Rhythmik* p. 104). The words must be taken as adverbs, and can only be explained by supposing that when Damon was demonstrating the equality of arsis and thesis he 'placed'—τιθέντος is not 'assuming' as διακοσμοῦντος shews—the former in a diagram above the latter, in some such way as ¯ ⏑́⏑. The position of the ictus—ἄνω καὶ κάτω, not κάτω καὶ ἄνω—shews that Plato is speaking of the dactyl and spondee which replace the anapaest in the anapaestic rhythm: for in the dactylic rhythm proper the ictus falls on the first syllable (see Gleditsch p. 693). Now the ἐνόπλιος is also anapaestic, so that it looks as if Damon had taken as the subject of his demonstration some passage like *Persae* 9, 10 ἤδη | κακόμαντις ἄγαν ὀρσολοπεῖται, and analysed it into an ἐνόπλιος ξύνθετος, a dactyl, and a spondee (included, as stated above, under the ἡρῷος ῥυθμός).

εἰς βραχύ—γιγνόμενον. These words can only mean 'passing into a short and a long,' "mit kurzem und langen Ausgang" (Schneider), "so dass er sowohl in eine kurze als auch in eine lange Silbe auslief" (Prantl): see on II 380 D. The slight inaccuracy involved in saying γιγνόμενον, where τελευτῶντα (cf. VI 511 C) would have been more precise, is perhaps in keeping with the airy nonchalance of Socrates' description. The construction is missed by Westphal (*Rhythmik* p. 237) and the English translators and editors. γιγνόμενον agrees with ἡρῷον: the ἡρῷος ῥυθμὸς γίγνεται εἰς βραχύ when it uses a dactyl, εἰς μακρόν when it uses a spondee (or anapaest), the two alternatives being denoted by τε καί. I have sometimes felt disposed to take the words as referring to the iambus, and place them just before ὡς ἐγὼ οἶμαι, translating 'and when it' (the rhythm) 'changed to a short and a long, I think he called it an iambus': but although this interpretation gives a somewhat better sense to γιγνόμενον, I am not convinced that the MSS are wrong. Hartman also suggests the transposition of καί, but he might have spared his "minime audax coniectura" ἐκ βραχέων τε καὶ μακρῶν γιγνόμενον. See also the next note.

15 **μήκη—προσῆπτε.** Hartman takes these words as explaining the trochee only, laying emphasis on the precedence given to μήκη; but the use of the plural shews that the iambus is also included.

οἶμαι τὰς ἀγωγὰς τοῦ ποδὸς αὐτὸν οὐχ ἧττον ψέγειν τε καὶ ἐπαινεῖν ἢ τοὺς ῥυθμοὺς αὐτούς, ἤτοι ξυναμφότερόν τι· οὐ γὰρ ἔχω λέγειν. ἀλλὰ ταῦτα μέν, ὥσπερ εἶπον, εἰς Δάμωνα ἀναβεβλήσθω· διελέσθαι γὰρ οὐ σμικροῦ λόγου. ἢ σὺ οἴει; Μὰ Δί', οὐκ ἔγωγε. Ἀλλὰ τόδε γε, ὅτι τὸ τῆς εὐσχημοσύνης τε καὶ ἀσχημοσύνης τῷ εὐρύθμῳ τε καὶ ἀρρύθμῳ ἀκολουθεῖ, δύνασαι διελέσθαι; Πῶς δ' οὔ; Ἀλλὰ μὴν τὸ εὔρυθμόν γε **D** καὶ τὸ ἄρρυθμον, τὸ μὲν τῇ καλῇ λέξει ἕπεται ὁμοιούμενον, τὸ δὲ τῇ ἐναντίᾳ, καὶ τὸ εὐάρμοστον καὶ ἀνάρμοστον ὡσαύτως, εἴπερ ῥυθμός γε καὶ ἁρμονία λόγῳ, ὥσπερ ἄρτι ἐλέγετο, ἀλλὰ μὴ λόγος τούτοις. Ἀλλὰ μήν, ἦ δ' ὅς, ταῦτά γε λόγῳ ἀκολουθητέον. Τί δ' ὁ τρόπος τῆς λέξεως, ἦν δ' ἐγώ, καὶ ὁ λόγος; οὐ τῷ τῆς ψυχῆς ἤθει ἕπεται; Πῶς γὰρ οὔ; Τῇ δὲ λέξει τὰ ἄλλα; Ναί. Εὐλογία ἄρα καὶ εὐαρμοστία καὶ εὐσχημοσύνη καὶ εὐρυθμία **E** εὐηθείᾳ ἀκολουθεῖ, οὐχ ἣν ἄνοιαν οὖσαν ὑποκοριζόμενοι καλοῦμεν ὡς εὐήθειαν, ἀλλὰ τὴν ὡς ἀληθῶς

24. καὶ ἀνάρμοστον Π: om. A.

The meaning is simply 'and he assigned them longs and shorts,' i.e. to each one long, and one short. This clause is in favour of keeping *εἰς βραχύ—γιγνόμενον* in its place; if we transpose (as suggested in the last note), the short and long of the iambus will be alluded to twice.

400 C 16 **ἀγωγάς**. *ἀγωγή* is *tempo* (Gleditsch p. 688). The unit of measurement was the *χρόνος πρῶτος* or ⏑: and hence the dactyl, for example, has usually a *τετράσημος ἀγωγή*, the iambus a *τρίσημος*, and so on. See *Excerpta Neapol.* in von Jan's *Mus. Script. Gr.* § 14. The duration of the *χρόνος πρῶτος* was of course relative, and not absolute, so that the time occupied in singing or declaiming a foot often varied, and we are told that *ἔστιν ὅτε καὶ ἐν δισήμῳ* (sc. *ἀγωγῇ*) *γίνεται δακτυλικὸς πούς* (*Exc. Neap.* l. c.). But it is clear that in general the *ἀγωγαί* of the different kinds of feet were different from one another. Hartman ejects *τοῦ ποδός*, "cum apud Platonem *πούς* et *ῥυθμός* non discrepent." The distinction between *πούς* and *ῥυθμός* is not always preserved by writers on metre (e.g. Bacchius *Isag.* 100 ff. ed. von Jan), but Plato seems to make the *πούς* differ from the *ῥυθμός* as the unit from the whole.

17 **ἤτοι**. See on I 344 E.

20 **εὐσχημοσύνης**: grace or beauty of form in the widest sense. The word is introduced in view of the application of these principles to objects appealing to the eye: see 401 A.

400 D 24 **ἀνάρμοστον**. The article (which Baiter and Hartman require) is unnecessary. See on I 334 E.

26 **ἀκολουθητέον** (i.q. *δεῖ ἀκολουθεῖν*) has *ταῦτα* for its subject, as Stallbaum points out: cf. *Laws* 803 D *τί παίζοντα ἐστὶ διαβιωτέον*; and infra V 467 C.

27 **τῷ τῆς ψυχῆς ἤθει ἕπεται**. Le style c'est l'homme. Conversely, thought is the dialogue of the soul with itself: see *Theaet.* 189 E (with Wohlrab's note) and *Soph.* 263 E. Cf. also IV 437 C *n.* and Homer's *διελέξατο θυμός*.

400 E 30 **ὡς εὐήθειαν** is expunged by Herwerden; Baiter would omit *ὡς*. If *ὡς* belonged to *εὐήθειαν* (as these critics apparently supposed), it would deserve expulsion; but it goes with *οὖσαν* understood. The antithesis is between *ἄνοιαν* and *εὐήθειαν*: and if the sentence is read so as to lay stress on these two words, it will be seen how easily *οὖσαν* can be repeated after *εὐήθειαν*. The sense is: not the *εὐήθεια* which is really *ἄνοια*, but which we euphemistically designate as if it were *εὐ-ήθεια* (i.e., as before, in the good sense of the word), but *εὐήθεια* in

εὖ τε καὶ καλῶς τὸ ἦθος κατεσκευασμένην διάνοιαν. Παντάπασι
μὲν οὖν, ἔφη. Ἆρ' οὖν οὐ πανταχοῦ ταῦτα διωκτέα τοῖς νέοις,
εἰ μέλλουσι τὸ αὑτῶν πράττειν; Διωκτέα μὲν οὖν. Ἔστιν δέ
401 γέ που πλήρης μὲν γρα|φικὴ αὐτῶν καὶ πᾶσα ἡ τοιαύτη δημιουργία,
πλήρης δὲ ὑφαντικὴ καὶ ποικιλία καὶ οἰκοδομία καὶ πᾶσα αὖ ἡ
τῶν ἄλλων σκευῶν ἐργασία, ἔτι δὲ ἡ τῶν σωμάτων φύσις καὶ ἡ
τῶν ἄλλων φυτῶν· ἐν πᾶσι γὰρ τούτοις ἔνεστιν εὐσχημοσύνη ἢ
ἀσχημοσύνη. καὶ ἡ μὲν ἀσχημοσύνη καὶ ἀρρυθμία καὶ ἀναρμοστία
κακολογίας καὶ κακοηθείας ἀδελφά, τὰ δ' ἐναντία τοῦ ἐναντίου,
σώφρονός τε καὶ ἀγαθοῦ ἤθους, ἀδελφά τε καὶ μιμήματα. Παντελῶς μὲν οὖν, ἔφη.
B XII. Ἆρ' οὖν τοῖς ποιηταῖς ἡμῖν μόνον | ἐπιστατητέον καὶ
προσαναγκαστέον τὴν τοῦ ἀγαθοῦ εἰκόνα ἤθους ἐμποιεῖν τοῖς

---

its true and etymological sense (ὡς ἀληθῶς)—the εὖ τὸ ἦθος κατεσκευασμένην διάνοιαν. This explanation seems to me better than to regard ὡς εὐήθειαν as attracted for ὡς εὐήθεια (sc. ἐστίν), a construction for which we may compare *Prot.* 357 D: see my note ad loc. For ὡς ἀληθῶς cf. I 343 C *n.*

33 **τὸ αὑτῶν πράττειν.** The principle of ἁπλότης, which is the corner-stone of Plato's city, presents itself in the education of the young, as the pursuit of εὐήθεια.

ἔστιν δέ γέ που κτλ. This lofty conception of ἁρμονία and ῥυθμός—for αὐτῶν shews that these are included no less than εὐσχημοσύνη—stretching throughout the whole domain of art and nature, may have been suggested by Pythagorean teaching: but the view of education as the pursuit and assimilation of all this beauty is due to Plato himself. Cf. 403 C *n.*

401 A 2 **ποικιλία.** II 378 C *n.*

401 A—**403** C *To these canons not only poets but all other artists must conform. We shall admit no artists save only those who are able to track out the nature of the beautiful, and beguile our children even in their earliest years into unconscious harmony with the beauty of reason. The value of a musical training lies in its peculiar power of imparting grace and beauty to the soul. It enables the learner to discriminate between the fair and the foul in other spheres, admitting only that which is beautiful and fair, at first instinctively, but afterwards, when reason comes, with fullest consciousness, and joyful recognition of the beauty to which he is himself akin. No one is truly imbued with musical culture until he can recognise the originals of virtue wherever they are found, as well as their copies everywhere. Such an one will love supremely the union of a beautiful soul with physical beauty, but will let inner beauty atone in part for outward defect, and his passion will be pure from sensual taint. Our account of Music is now ended: for the end of Music is the love of Beauty.*

401 B 10 **τὴν τοῦ ἀγαθοῦ κτλ.** This famous section describes in glowing language, like that of the *Symposium*, Plato's ideal of art. He does not desire to banish art, as is sometimes asserted, but rather idealises it by effecting—as he believed—its reconciliation with beauty and truth. Art aspired to be καλόν in his day: Plato wished it to be so in the fullest sense of the word: and his idea of beauty is sufficiently comprehensive to include moral and spiritual beauty as well as physical. Plato was doubtless unfair in the application of his principle to some of the Greek artists and poets, but in itself his ideal—the love of spiritual beauty—is one to which the best and most enduring art—which alone can find a place in an ideal city—consciously or unconsciously ever seeks to conform. See Nettleship *Lect. and Rem.* II pp. 112—116.

τοῖς ποιήμασιν κτλ. Cf. *Laws* 656 D, E. Nettleship (*Hell.* pp. 117 f.) remarks on the fact that "Plato in his criticism of

ποιήμασιν ἢ μὴ παρ' ἡμῖν ποιεῖν, ἢ καὶ τοῖς ἄλλοις δημιουργοῖς
ἐπιστατητέον καὶ διακωλυτέον τὸ κακόηθες τοῦτο καὶ ἀκόλαστον
καὶ ἀνελεύθερον καὶ ἄσχημον μήτε ἐν εἰκόσι ζῴων μήτε ἐν οἰκοδο-
μήμασι μήτε ἐν ἄλλῳ μηδενὶ δημιουργουμένῳ ἐμποιεῖν, ἢ ὁ μὴ οἷός
τε ὢν οὐκ ἐατέος παρ' ἡμῖν δημιουργεῖν, ἵνα μὴ ἐν κακίας εἰκόσι
τρεφόμενοι ἡμῖν οἱ φύλακες ὥσπερ ἐν κακῇ βοτάνῃ, | πολλὰ C
ἑκάστης ἡμέρας κατὰ σμικρὸν ἀπὸ πολλῶν δρεπόμενοί τε καὶ
νεμόμενοι, ἕν τι ξυνιστάντες λανθάνωσιν κακὸν μέγα ἐν τῇ αὑτῶν
ψυχῇ, ἀλλ' ἐκείνους ζητητέον τοὺς δημιουργοὺς τοὺς εὐφυῶς δυναμένους ἰχνεύειν τὴν τοῦ καλοῦ τε καὶ εὐσχήμονος φύσιν, ἵνα ὥσπερ
ἐν ὑγιεινῷ τόπῳ οἰκοῦντες οἱ νέοι ἀπὸ παντὸς ὠφελῶνται, ὁπόθεν
ἂν αὐτοῖς ἀπὸ τῶν καλῶν ἔργων ἢ πρὸς ὄψιν ἢ πρὸς ἀκοήν τις
προσβάλῃ ὥσπερ αὔρα φέρουσα ἀπὸ χρηστῶν τόπων ὑγίειαν,
καὶ εὐθὺς | ἐκ παίδων λανθάνῃ εἰς ὁμοιότητά τε καὶ φιλίαν καὶ D
ξυμφωνίαν τῷ καλῷ λόγῳ ἄγουσα; Πολὺ γὰρ ἄν, ἔφη, κάλλιστα
οὕτω τραφεῖεν. Ἆρ' οὖν, ἦν δ' ἐγώ, ὦ Γλαύκων, τούτων ἕνεκα
κυριωτάτη ἐν μουσικῇ τροφή, ὅτι μάλιστα καταδύεται εἰς τὸ ἐντὸς
τῆς ψυχῆς ὅ τε ῥυθμὸς καὶ ἁρμονία, καὶ ἐρρωμενέστατα ἅπτεται

18. νεμόμενοι Π: ἀνεμόμενοι A et in mg. ἀνιμώμενοι A^2. 22. τις nos: τι codd.

Greek art has almost ignored the painters and sculptors, and confined his assaults to the musicians and still more to the poets." This is true, although the present passage shews that his canons were intended to regulate painting, sculpture, architecture, and the minor arts as well as music and poetry. Among other reasons, Nettleship plausibly suggests that Plato "did not see in the sculptors and architects of his time the signs of degeneracy which drew his attention to the poets and musicians." Cf. 401 C.

401 C 21 **ὁπόθεν ἂν κτλ.** No Greek could read these words without thinking of Olympia; no Athenian without recalling the glories of the Acropolis. It was probably in the spirit of this ideal that Epaminondas—himself a man of Platonic sympathies, if not a Platonist—hinted to his countrymen that their city could not be truly great until the Propylaea crowned their citadel (Aesch. *περὶ παραπρεσβείας* 105. See also Nettleship *Hell.* pp. 115—123). Partly on grounds of style, and partly for grammatical reasons, I believe that Plato wrote τις and not τι (see *cr. n.*). 'Whenever *anything* strikes on their eyes or ears from fair works of art' sounds material and gross in a passage so full of poetic feeling; and in the second place ἄγουσα agrees with αὔρα, whereas it should be ἄγον and agree with τι if τι is right. Translate 'Whensoever from beautiful works of art there smites upon their eyes or ears as it were a salubrious breath from healthful regions.' In the same way a sort of ἵμερος flows into the soul from beauty, awakening love and admiration (*Phaedr.* 251 C). The melodious current of Plato's rhythmic utterance flows onward like the steady though gentle breeze which it describes. With αὔρα—ὑγίειαν cf. Arist. *Probl.* I 52. 865^b 19 πόλις ὑγιεινὴ καὶ τόπος εὔπνους (διὸ καὶ ἡ θάλασσα ὑγιεινή). For the syntax of τις—ὥσπερ αὔρα · φέρουσα cf. τὰς τῆς γενέσεως ξυγγενεῖς ὥσπερ μολυβδίδας VII 519 B, where a similar corruption occurs in some of the MSS: see *n.* ad loc. Paris A has τί for τὶς again in II 360 E.

401 D 27 **ἐν μουσικῇ τροφή.** The insertion of ἡ before ἐν (suggested by Rückert) is needless: cf. 404 B.

αὐτῆς, φέροντα τὴν εὐσχημοσύνην, καὶ ποιεῖ εὐσχήμονα, ἐάν τις
E ὀρθῶς τραφῇ, εἰ δὲ μή, τοὐναντίον; καὶ ὅτι αὖ τῶν παραλειπομένων καὶ μὴ καλῶς δημιουργηθέντων ἢ μὴ καλῶς φύντων ὀξύτατ᾽
ἂν αἰσθάνοιτο ὁ ἐκεῖ τραφεὶς ὡς ἔδει, καὶ ὀρθῶς δὴ δυσχεραίνων
τὰ μὲν καλὰ ἐπαινοῖ καὶ χαίρων καὶ καταδεχόμενος εἰς τὴν ψυχὴν
402 τρέφοιτ᾽ ἂν ἀπ᾽ αὐτῶν καὶ γίγνοιτο καλός τε κἀγαθός, | τὰ δ᾽
αἰσχρὰ ψέγοι τ᾽ ἂν ὀρθῶς καὶ μισοῖ ἔτι νέος ὤν, πρὶν λόγον
δυνατὸς εἶναι λαβεῖν, ἐλθόντος δὲ τοῦ λόγου ἀσπάζοιτ᾽ ἂν αὐτὸν
γνωρίζων δι᾽ οἰκειότητα μάλιστα ὁ οὕτω τραφείς; Ἐμοὶ γοῦν
δοκεῖ, ἔφη, τῶν τοιούτων ἕνεκα ἐν μουσικῇ εἶναι ἡ τροφή. Ὥσπερ
ἄρα, ἦν δ᾽ ἐγώ, γραμμάτων πέρι τότε ἱκανῶς εἴχομεν, ὅτε τὰ
στοιχεῖα μὴ λανθάνοι ἡμᾶς ὀλίγα ὄντα ἐν ἅπασιν οἷς ἔστιν
περιφερόμενα, καὶ οὔτ᾽ ἐν σμικρῷ οὔτ᾽ ἐν μεγάλῳ ἠτιμάζομεν
B αὐτά, ὡς οὐ δέοι αἰσθάνεσθαι, ἀλλὰ πανταχοῦ προὐθυμούμεθα
διαγιγνώσκειν, ὡς οὐ πρότερον ἐσόμενοι γραμματικοὶ πρὶν οὕτως
ἔχοιμεν—Ἀληθῆ. Οὐκοῦν καὶ εἰκόνας γραμμάτων, εἴ που ἢ ἐν

30. αὖ τῶν Π: αὐτῶν A. 4. ἐμοὶ γοῦν A¹Π: ἔμοιγ᾽ οὖν A². 11. εἰκόνας Ξ*q*: εἰ εἰκόνας AΠ.

---

29 **φέροντα**: not 'imparting' (Jowett), but 'bearing,' 'carrying,' like *φέρουσα* in the simile: cf. *Symp.* 188 A *ἥκει φέροντα εὐετηρίαν*.

401 E 31 **καὶ μὴ καλῶς**. Herwerden's conjecture *ἢ* for *καί* misses the precise force of *παραλειπομένων* 'falling short': cf. *Critias* 107 D *ὀξέως αἰσθανόμενοι τὸ παραλειπόμενον*. The word is explained in *καὶ μὴ—φύντων*, where the contrast is between imperfections of art and imperfections of nature.

32 **ἐκεῖ**: i.e. *ἐν μουσικῇ*.

ὀρθῶς δὴ κτλ. I formerly (with Baiter and others) adopted Vermehren's proposal (*Pl. Stud.* p. 94) to read *ὀρθῶς δὴ* <*χαίρων καὶ*> *δυσχεραίνων τὰ μὲν καλὰ ἐπαινοῖ καὶ* [*χαίρων καὶ*] *καταδεχόμενος κτλ.* The correction is certainly an attractive one, in view especially of *Laws* 653 B, C, where education is defined as *μισεῖν μὲν ἃ χρὴ μισεῖν—στέργειν δὲ ἃ χρὴ στέργειν*, and 654 D *τὰ μὲν ἀσπαζόμενος ὅσα καλά, τὰ δὲ δυσχεραίνων ὁπόσα μὴ καλά*, and Arist. *Eth. Nic.* II 2. 1104ᵇ 11 ff. But the MS reading, though less pointed and pregnant, is in itself satisfactory enough, if *δυσχεραίνων* be understood with reference to what precedes (*τῶν παραλειπομένων*), and we are therefore hardly justified in altering the text. (The omission of *χαίρων καί* in *q* should not be used as evidence of dislocation.) Hartman (after Stallbaum) excises *καί* between *χαίρων* and *καταδεχόμενος*, but this too is unnecessary. We may translate (with Jowett) 'and rejoicing in them' (as opposed to *δυσχεραίνων* just before) 'and receiving them into his soul.' The preposition *κατα-* in *καταδεχόμενος* suggests that beauty is an exile coming home again: the return of exiled truth and beauty is indeed with Plato the aim of education and of life. Cf. *Phaedr.* 250 A—252 A.

34 **τρέφοιτο**. For the metaphor cf. *Phaedr.* 248 B ff.

402 A 6 **γραμμάτων**. See on II 368 D. The reference in *εἴχομεν*, however, is not to that passage, but to the actual experience of the speakers.

7 **ἐν ἅπασιν οἷς ἔστιν**: i.q. *ἐν ἅπασιν ἐν οἷς ἔστι*, by a common idiom: see on II 373 E and cf. VII 520 D, IX 590 C.

402 B 9 **ὡς οὐ δέοι** depends on the idea of thinking involved in *ἀτιμάζομεν*. Richards suggested *δέον*, "sine causa," as Hartman observes.

11 **εἰκόνας γραμμάτων**. The reference to letters throughout this part of the

ὕδασιν ἢ ἐν κατόπτροις ἐμφαίνοιντο, οὐ πρότερον γνωσόμεθα,
πρὶν ἂν αὐτὰ γνῶμεν, ἀλλ' ἔστιν τῆς αὐτῆς τέχνης τε καὶ μελέτης;
Παντάπασι μὲν οὖν. Ἆρ' οὖν, ὃ λέγω, πρὸς θεῶν, οὕτως οὐδὲ
μουσικοὶ πρότερον ἐσόμεθα, οὔτε αὐτοὶ οὔτε οὓς φαμεν ἡμῖν C
παιδευτέον εἶναι τοὺς φύλακας, πρὶν ἂν τὰ τῆς σωφροσύνης εἴδη
καὶ ἀνδρείας καὶ ἐλευθεριότητος καὶ μεγαλοπρεπείας καὶ ὅσα
τούτων ἀδελφὰ καὶ τὰ τούτων αὖ ἐναντία πανταχοῦ περιφερόμενα

Republic is only by way of illustration, and we must beware of reading more into Plato's words than they are capable of meaning in the context where they occur. No doubt it is true, as Dr Jackson remarks, that "this passage makes us acquainted with the relation of copy and model which is to become important later," but Bosanquet goes too far when he asserts that "the expression 'images of letters' *points forward* to the classification of grades of knowledge, at the end of Book VI, the allegory of the cave at the beginning of Book VII, and the argument of Book X."

13 **αὐτά** is emphatic: 'the letters themselves' as opposed to their εἰκόνες. There is of course no allusion to 'Ideas' of letters.

402 C 16 **τὰ τῆς σωφροσύνης εἴδη κτλ.** Are the εἴδη Plato's Ideas? So Zeller (II[4] I p. 560 *n.*), and many other critics, understand the word; nor can it be denied that the language of Plato, *if interpreted in the light of Book VII*, can bear this meaning. Nevertheless we are bound in the first instance to interpret this passage by itself, and not by Book VII, the more so as the doctrine of transcendent or separate (χωρισταί) Ideas appears nowhere else in I—IV, and seems to be expressly reserved by Plato for his philosophical, as distinct from his musical education (see IV 435 D and VI 504 B *n.*). What is meant by the words εἰκόνας αὐτῶν? The context shews conclusively that εἰκόνες refers to copies (sc. of the virtues σωφροσύνη etc.) represented in poetry and the fine arts (so also Krohn *Pl. Frage* p. 47). On any other interpretation the introduction of these εἰκόνες is irrelevant in a discussion on the rules which imitative art must obey. This being so, if εἴδη means the Ideas, Poetry will be a direct imitation of the Ideas, which is inconsistent with X 595 C—598 D. Or does Plato mean to suggest that Poetry and Art in his ideal city are really to imitate the Ideas directly? This is a bold and attractive solution, and there are several hints elsewhere to the same or nearly the same effect, but Plato expressly speaks of the εἴδη here only as immanent, and not transcendent (ἐνόντα ἐν οἷς ἔνεστιν), and we must therefore suppose that the artist copies from the life (cf. ἐν τῇ ψυχῇ καλὰ ἤθη ἐνόντα D). The word εἴδη is repeatedly used by Plato without reference to transcendent Ideas, as has been amply proved by Krohn (*Pl. St.* pp. 65, 66), Pfleiderer (*Zur Lösung* etc. p. 17), and Campbell (II pp. 296 ff.). Here it does not mean 'varieties' (as if there were more than one variety of σωφροσύνη), but simply 'forms' or 'kinds,' in the sense in which the immanent reality which every general notion attempts to express is a 'form' or 'kind'—a genus or species—of the totality of things. Cf. IV 435 B *n.* The genitives are genitives of definition. The use of εἴδη in the sense of "immanente Seinsformen" (Krohn) is interesting as a harbinger of the Ideal theory of VI and VII—a sort of half-way house between the Socratic λόγοι and Plato's ideas. It recurs in IV 434 D, 435 B, 437 D. See further Krohn *Pl. Frage* pp. 54—58, and cf. VI 504 D *n.* But although the separatists have (as I think) made out their claim that transcendent Ideas do not appear in Books I—IV, I agree with Hirmer (*Entst. u. Komp. d. Pl. Pol.* p. 645) in thinking their deductions from this fact unwarrantable.

17 **μεγαλοπρεπείας**. μεγαλοπρέπεια in Plato is 'highmindedness,' not, as in Aristotle, 'magnificence': cf. VI 486 A *n.* In like manner Plato's ἐλευθεριότης denotes the virtue proper to an ἐλεύθερος, and is not restricted to liberality in spending money. Contrast Arist. *Eth. Nic.* IV cc. 2—6.

γνωρίζωμεν καὶ ἐνόντα ἐν οἷς ἔνεστιν αἰσθανώμεθα καὶ αὐτὰ καὶ
εἰκόνας αὐτῶν, καὶ μήτε ἐν σμικροῖς μήτε ἐν μεγάλοις ἀτιμάζωμεν,
ἀλλὰ τῆς αὐτῆς οἰώμεθα τέχνης εἶναι καὶ μελέτης; Πολλὴ ἀνάγκη,
D ἔφη. Οὐκοῦν, ἦν δ' ἐγώ, | ὅτου ἂν ξυμπίπτῃ ἔν τε τῇ ψυχῇ καλὰ
ἤθη ἐνόντα καὶ ἐν τῷ εἴδει ὁμολογοῦντα ἐκείνοις καὶ ξυμφωνοῦντα,
τοῦ αὐτοῦ μετέχοντα τύπου, τοῦτ' ἂν εἴη κάλλιστον θέαμα τῷ
δυναμένῳ θεᾶσθαι; Πολύ γε. Καὶ μὴν τό γε κάλλιστον ἐρασμιώτατον. Πῶς δ' οὔ; Τῶν δὴ ὅ τι μάλιστα τοιούτων ἀνθρώπων ὅ γε
μουσικὸς ἐρῴη ἄν· εἰ δὲ ἀξύμφωνος εἴη, οὐκ ἂν ἐρῴη. Οὐκ ἄν,
εἴ γέ τι, ἔφη, κατὰ τὴν ψυχὴν ἐλλείποι· εἰ μέντοι τι κατὰ τὸ σῶμα,
E ὑπομείνειεν ἄν, ὥστε ἐθέλειν ἀσπάζεσθαι. Μανθάνω, ἦν | δ' ἐγώ·
ὅτι ἔστιν σοι ἢ γέγονεν παιδικὰ τοιαῦτα· καὶ συγχωρῶ. ἀλλὰ
τόδε μοι εἰπέ· σωφροσύνῃ καὶ ἡδονῇ ὑπερβαλλούσῃ ἔστι τις
κοινωνία; Καὶ πῶς, ἔφη, ἥ γε ἔκφρονα ποιεῖ οὐχ ἧττον ἢ λύπη;
403 Ἀλλὰ τῇ ἄλλῃ ἀρετῇ; | Οὐδαμῶς. Τί δέ; ὕβρει τε καὶ ἀκολασίᾳ;
Πάντων μάλιστα. Μείζω δέ τινα καὶ ὀξυτέραν ἔχεις εἰπεῖν
ἡδονὴν τῆς περὶ τὰ ἀφροδίσια; Οὐκ ἔχω, ἦ δ' ὅς, οὐδέ γε μανικω-
τέραν. Ὁ δὲ ὀρθὸς ἔρως πέφυκε κοσμίου τε καὶ καλοῦ σωφρόνως
τε καὶ μουσικῶς ἐρᾶν; Καὶ μάλα, ἦ δ' ὅς. Οὐδὲν ἄρα προσοιστέον
μανικὸν οὐδὲ ξυγγενὲς ἀκολασίας τῷ ὀρθῷ ἔρωτι; **Οὐ προσοιστέον.**
B **Οὐ προσοιστέον ἄρα** | αὕτη ἡ ἡδονή, οὐδὲ κοινωνητέον **αὐτῆς**
ἐραστῇ τε καὶ παιδικοῖς ὀρθῶς ἐρῶσί τε καὶ ἐρωμένοις; **Οὐ μέντοι,**
μὰ Δί', ἔφη, ὦ Σώκρατες, προσοιστέον. Οὕτω δή, ὡς ἔοικε,
νομοθετήσεις ἐν τῇ οἰκιζομένῃ πόλει, **φιλεῖν** μὲν καὶ ξυνεῖναι καὶ

19, 20. γνωρίζωμεν—αἰσθανώμεθα—ἀτιμάζωμεν A^{1}Π: γνωρίζομεν—αἰσθανόμεθα—ἀτιμάζομεν A^{2}. 21. οἰώμεθα Π: οἰόμεθα A. 26. δὴ ὅ τι Π: διότι A. 10. νομοθετήσεις Π: ὁ νομοθετὴς (sic) εἷς A, sed ὁ addidit A^{2}.

402 D 26 **τῶν δὴ—ἀσπάζεσθαι.** Cf. *Symp.* 209 B and 210 B, C. The whole of Diotima's wonderful speech (210 D—212 A) should be compared with the closing sections of this chapter. In point of language the words κάλλιστον θέαμα—ἐρασμιώτατον closely resemble *Tim.* 87 D.

27 **ἀξύμφωνος**: i.e. (as Glauco's answer shews) strictly speaking one whose soul and body do not harmonise in point of beauty, but the word also suggests "the man who has no music in his soul." Cf. *Symp.* 206 C τὰ δὲ (κύησις καὶ γέννησις) ἐν τῷ ἀναρμόστῳ ἀδύνατον γενέσθαι. With the sentiment in general cf. *Tim.* 87 D ff.

402 E 29 **μανθάνω—ὅτι**: 'I understand: (you say so) because' etc.: see I 332 A *n.*

403 A 7 **οὐ προσοιστέον ἄρα.** This somewhat extreme example of a common liberty in concord serves to increase the rhetorical emphasis by the energetic repetition of Glauco's *ipsissima verba.* The emphasis becomes still greater in Glauco's reply **οὐ μέντοι, μὰ Δία, προσοιστέον.** The particle **μέντοι** is especially used in replies when the words of a previous speaker are repeated (Hoefer *de part. Plat.* p. 32). *q* and Flor. U have προσοιστέα.

403 B 10 **φιλεῖν** is 'kiss' (as Schneider rightly translates the word): cf.

ἅπτεσθαι ὥσπερ ὑέος παιδικῶν ἐραστήν, τῶν καλῶν χάριν, ἐὰν
πείθῃ· τὰ δ' ἄλλα οὕτως ὁμιλεῖν πρὸς ὅν τις σπουδάζοι, ὅπως
μηδέποτε δόξει μακρότερα τούτων ξυγγίγνεσθαι· εἰ δὲ μή, ψόγον C
ἀμουσίας καὶ ἀπειροκαλίας ὑφέξοντα. Οὕτως, ἔφη. Ἆρ' οὖν,
ἦν δ' ἐγώ, καὶ σοὶ φαίνεται τέλος ἡμῖν ἔχειν ὁ περὶ μουσικῆς λόγος;
οἷ γοῦν δεῖ τελευτᾶν, τετελεύτηκεν· δεῖ δέ που τελευτᾶν τὰ
μουσικὰ εἰς τὰ τοῦ καλοῦ ἐρωτικά. Ξύμφημι, ἦ δ' ὅς.

XIII. Μετὰ δὴ μουσικὴν γυμναστικῇ θρεπτέοι οἱ νεανίαι.

---

v 468 B and Arist. *Pol.* B 4. 1262ᵃ 32 ff., where χρήσεις (as Hicks observes) means 'endearments.'

11 **ἅπτεσθαι κτλ.** We think of Socrates and the 'disciple whom he loved' in the *Phaedo*: εἰώθει γάρ, ὁπότε τύχοι, παίζειν μου εἰς τὰς τρίχας (89 B).

ὥσπερ ὑέος. Herwerden's conjecture ὡς πατὴρ ὑέος (or ὥσπερ πατὴρ ὑέος) deserves the praise of ingenuity, but Plato's text is better and more expressive, because it represents the object of affection almost as the lover's very son. It should be noted that in Plato's ἔρως it is the elder who loves, and the younger who is loved; and that the aim and purpose of Platonic love is τόκος ἐν καλῷ (*Symp.* 206 B)—the bringing to birth of noble thoughts and aspirations from the beautiful soul of youth. Socrates was the embodiment of Plato's ideal in this respect (*Symp.* 216 D ff.). Some true and excellent observations on the subject will be found in Dugas *L'Amitié Antique* pp. 50—53 al.

τῶν καλῶν χάριν. Plato is resolved that Love, as well as Art, shall serve Virtue and not Vice.

12 **τὰ δ' ἄλλα—ξυγγίγνεσθαι.** σπουδάζειν πρός τινα occurs with the same sense in *Gorg.* 510 C. Madvig's περὶ ὧν for πρὸς ὅν would give quite a wrong meaning. σπουδάζει has been suggested for σπουδάζοι (Ast, Richards, Hartman), but the optative puts the case more generally: any one in whom one may be interested. Cf. Soph. *Ant.* 666 ἀλλ' ὃν πόλις στήσειε, τοῦδε χρὴ κλύειν, with Jebb's note. The previous sentence has told us what the actual relations of the pair of friends must be; and Plato now forbids all conduct likely in any way to occasion scandal or misapprehension: hence δόξει ('be supposed to'). Such conduct is in bad taste (ψόγον ἀμουσίας), rather than positively αἰσχρόν or immoral, like actual vice. μαργότερα τούτῳ (Herwerden) instead of μακρότερα τούτων is a singularly gross conjecture.

403 C 14 **ὑφέξοντα.** "Si ὑφέξοντα non sanum, corrige ὑφέξειν" (Hartman). This catches the point, but, as Hartman admits, the text can be defended as it stands. The participle agrees with the subject of ὁμιλεῖν, εἰ δὲ μή being all but adverbial, and therefore not followed by a main clause. Cf. *Prot.* 311 D.

16 **δεῖ δέ που κτλ.** The love of Beauty is φιλοσοφία (*Symp.* 204 B); so that the famous saying of the *Phaedo* (61 A) φιλοσοφία μεγίστη μουσική resembles this. I agree with Krohn (*Pl. St.* p. 71) in holding that τοῦ καλοῦ is still beauty as it is revealed in Nature and in Art (see on 402 C), the πολὺ πέλαγος τοῦ καλοῦ of *Symp.* 210 D, and not yet the transcendent Idea of the Beautiful, the contemplation of which demands a still higher flight (ib. 210 D—212 A). But Plato leaves his μουσικός already knocking at the gates 'of the blest promised Land.'

403 C—**405** A *Let us now discuss the subject of physical training. We may safely entrust the duty of making specific rules to the intelligences which we train, and content ourselves with tracing outlines. Every kind of excess or self-indulgence in eating, drinking, and the other appetites, must be forbidden. Gymnastic must be 'simple' like her sister Music. Complexity in the one case breeds disease, in the other vice; so that doctors and judges rise in public estimation, and chicanery and medicine give themselves airs.*

403 C 18 **γυμναστικῇ κτλ.** Plato's statements on γυμναστική have been carefully collected and expounded by Kanter *Platos Anschauungen über Gymnastik*, Graudenz 1886. Admirable remarks on the whole subject will be found in Nettleship *Hell.* pp. 132—134: cf. also his *Lectures and Remains* II pp.

D Τί μήν; Δεῖ μὲν δὴ καὶ ταύτῃ ἀκριβῶς τρέφεσθαι ἐκ παίδων | διὰ
βίου, ἔχει δέ πως, ὡς ἐγᾦμαι, ὧδε· σκόπει δὲ καὶ σύ· ἐμοὶ μὲν γὰρ
οὐ φαίνεται, ὃ ἂν χρηστὸν ᾖ σῶμα, τοῦτο τῇ αὑτοῦ ἀρετῇ ψυχὴν
ἀγαθὴν ποιεῖν, ἀλλὰ τοὐναντίον ψυχὴ ἀγαθὴ τῇ αὑτῆς ἀρετῇ σῶμα
παρέχειν ὡς οἷόν τε βέλτιστον· σοὶ δὲ πῶς φαίνεται; Καὶ ἐμοί,
ἔφη, οὕτως. Οὐκοῦν εἰ τὴν διάνοιαν ἱκανῶς θεραπεύσαντες παρα-
E δοῖμεν αὐτῇ τὰ περὶ τὸ σῶμα ἀκριβολογεῖσθαι, ἡμεῖς δὲ | ὅσον τοὺς
τύπους ὑφηγησαίμεθα, ἵνα μὴ μακρολογῶμεν, ὀρθῶς ἂν ποιοῖμεν;
Πάνυ μὲν οὖν. Μέθης μὲν δὴ εἴπομεν ὅτι ἀφεκτέον αὐτοῖς· παντὶ
γάρ που μᾶλλον ἐγχωρεῖ, ἢ φύλακι, μεθυσθέντι μὴ εἰδέναι, ὅπου
γῆς ἐστίν. Γελοῖον γάρ, ἦ δ' ὅς, τόν γε φύλακα φύλακος δεῖσθαι.
Τί δὲ δὴ σίτων πέρι; ἀθληταὶ μὲν γὰρ οἱ ἄνδρες τοῦ μεγίστου
ἀγῶνος. ἢ οὐχί; Ναί. Ἆρ' οὖν ἡ τῶνδε τῶν ἀσκητῶν ἕξις
404 προσήκουσ' | ἂν εἴη τούτοις; Ἴσως. Ἀλλ', ἦν δ' ἐγώ, ὑπνώδης
αὕτη γέ τις καὶ σφαλερὰ πρὸς ὑγίειαν· ἢ οὐχ ὁρᾷς ὅτι καθεύδουσί
τε τὸν βίον καί, ἐὰν σμικρὰ ἐκβῶσιν τῆς τεταγμένης διαίτης,
μεγάλα καὶ σφόδρα νοσοῦσιν οὗτοι οἱ ἀσκηταί; Ὁρῶ. Κομψοτέρας
δή τινος, ἦν δ' ἐγώ, ἀσκήσεως δεῖ τοῖς πολεμικοῖς ἀθληταῖς, οὓς

26. *μακρολογῶμεν* A²Π: *μακρολογοῖμεν* A¹.

123—126. Plato deals here chiefly with the hygienic aspect of gymnastic—a subject which was much discussed in his day: see *Dict. Ant.* I p. 929, where we are reminded that gymnasia were dedicated to Apollo, father of Asclepius, and himself a god of healing. In his interesting treatise *Die Platonischen Dialoge in ihrem Verhältnisse zu den Hippokratischen Schriften* (Landshut 1882) Poschenrieder has shewn that Plato was strongly influenced throughout this passage by the views of Hippocrates and his school. See also Häser *Lehrb. d. Gesch. d. Med.* etc. I pp. 94 ff. The athletics of Gymnastic are treated of in *Laws* 795 D ff., 833 ff.

403 D 22 **ψυχὴ ἀγαθὴ—βέλτιστον.** No very recondite theory of the relation of body and soul is here involved. Plato simply means that the soul has more power over the body than the body over the soul. (The restriction in *ὡς οἷόν τε* should be noted.) On this principle some doctors held that to cure the body one should minister to the mind diseased: see the curious passage in *Charm.* 156 B—157 C. The general sentiment is well illustrated by J. and C. from Democr. *Fr. Mor.* 128 (Müllach) *ἀνθρώποισι ἁρμόδιον ψυχῆς μᾶλλον ἢ σώματος ποιέεσθαι λόγον· ψυχὴ μὲν γὰρ τελεωτάτη σκήνεος μοχθηρίην ὀρθοῖ, σκήνεος δὲ ἰσχὺς ἄνευ λογισμοῦ ψυχὴν οὐδέν τι ἀμείνω ποιεῖ.*

403 E 27 **εἴπομεν.** 398 E.

30 **ἀθληταὶ — ἀγῶνος.** Cf. *Laws* 829 E *ἀθλητὰς τῶν μεγίστων ἀγώνων*, and *Lach.* 182 A.

31 **τῶνδε** means contemporary athletes: cf. IV 425 C *n.* With Plato's strictures on Greek athletics cf. Arist. *Pol.* Θ. 4. 1338ᵇ 10 (with Susemihl and Hicks' note) and especially Eur. *Fr.* 284: for his attack on the diet and training of athletes cf. *Dict. Ant.* I pp. 98, 928 and the authorities there cited.

404 A 3 **ἐὰν σμικρὰ ἐκβῶσιν κτλ.** Poschenrieder (l.c.) cites the Hippocratean *Praedictiones* II c. I Littré *τοὺς ἀθλητὰς γινώσκειν...ἤν τι τοῦ σιτίου ἀπολίπωσιν, ἢ ἑτεροῖόν τι φάγωσιν, ἢ ποτῷ πλέονι χρήσωνται, ἢ τοῦ περιπάτου ἀπολίπωσιν ἢ ἀφροδισίων τι πράξωσι· τούτων πάντων οὐδὲν λανθάνει, οὐδ' εἰ σμικρόν τι εἴη ἀπειθήσας ὥνθρωπος.*

γε ὥσπερ κύνας ἀγρύπνους τε ἀνάγκη εἶναι καὶ ὅ τι μάλιστα ὀξὺ ὁρᾶν καὶ ἀκούειν καὶ πολλὰς μεταβολὰς ἐν ταῖς στρατείαις μεταβάλλοντας ὑδάτων τε καὶ τῶν ἄλλων σίτων καὶ εἱλήσεων **B** καὶ χειμώνων μὴ ἀκροσφαλεῖς εἶναι πρὸς ὑγίειαν. Φαίνεταί μοι. Ἆρ' οὖν ἡ βελτίστη γυμναστικὴ ἀδελφή τις ἂν εἴη τῆς μουσικῆς, ἣν ὀλίγον πρότερον διῇμεν; Πῶς λέγεις; Ἁπλῆ που καὶ ἐπιεικὴς γυμναστική, καὶ μάλιστα ἡ τῶν περὶ τὸν πόλεμον. Πῇ δή; Καὶ παρ' Ὁμήρου, ἦν δ' ἐγώ, τά γε τοιαῦτα μάθοι ἄν τις. οἶσθα γὰρ ὅτι ἐπὶ στρατείας ἐν ταῖς τῶν ἡρώων ἑστιάσεσιν οὔτε ἰχθύσιν αὐτοὺς ἑστιᾷ, καὶ ταῦτα ἐπὶ θαλάττῃ ἐν Ἑλλησπόντῳ **C** ὄντας, οὔτε ἑφθοῖς κρέασιν, ἀλλὰ μόνον ὀπτοῖς, ἃ δὴ μάλιστ' ἂν εἴη στρατιώταις εὔπορα· πανταχοῦ γάρ, ὡς ἔπος εἰπεῖν, αὐτῷ τῷ πυρὶ χρῆσθαι εὐπορώτερον, ἢ ἀγγεῖα ξυμπεριφέρειν. Καὶ μάλα.

6. τε Π: τε καὶ A. 7. στρατείαις Θr: στρατιαῖς AΞ*q*: στρατίαις (sic) Π. 14. στρατείας Π[2]*q*: στρατιᾶς AΞ: στατιᾶς (sic) Π[1].

---

6 **ὥσπερ κύνας**. II 375 A.

7 **πολλὰς μεταβολὰς κτλ.** Cf. [Hippocr.] *de umoribus* V p. 496 c. 15 Littré αἱ μεταβολαὶ μάλιστα τίκτουσι νοσήματα καὶ αἱ μέγισται μάλιστα καὶ ἐν τῇσιν ὥρῃσιν αἱ μεγάλαι μεταλλαγαὶ καὶ ἐν τοῖσι ἄλλοισιν: cf. also *Aphorism.* IV p. 486 § 1 al. and Pl. *Laws* 797 D ff. (Poschenrieder l.c. pp. 31 ff.)

404 B 11 **ἁπλῆ—πόλεμον**. The sentence is usually explained by carrying on ἡ βελτίστη γυμναστικὴ ἂν εἴη and regarding ἁπλῆ—γυμναστική as the predicate both to ἡ βελτίστη γυμναστική and to ἡ τῶν περὶ τὸν πόλεμον. Besides its extreme cumbrousness, this view makes Plato say that the *best* gymnastic is *good* (ἐπιεικής is practically synonymous with ἀγαθή), which is, to say the least, unnecessary. It seems to me much simpler and better to make ἐπιεικὴς γυμναστική the subject to ἁπλῆ. The meaning is: will the best course of training be sister to the music we described? How so? ἐπιεικὴς γυμναστική, like ἐπιεικὴς μουσική (this is the force of καί), is (ἐστὶ understood) ἁπλῆ, and so above all is that of soldiers. Hartman, who saw that the passage must be taken in this way, would write ἡ for καί, and I once preferred καὶ <ἡ>, but the article can be dispensed with (cf. 401 D *n.*), and καί is necessary. As the emphasis is primarily on γυμναστική, some may prefer to read γυμναστικὴ ἐπιεικής or γυμναστικὴ ἡ ἐπιεικής; but if the stress of the voice is laid on γυμναστική, and ἐπιεικὴς γυμναστική treated as a single expression (cf. V 453 A *n.*), I think the text may stand.

14 **οὔτε ἰχθύσιν κτλ.** Cf. Eubulus ap. Athen. I 25 C (Jackson).

404 C 15 **ἐν Ἑλλησπόντῳ** is rejected by Cobet and Hartman; if the Homeric heroes were ἐν Ἑλλησπόντῳ, the fish forsooth would more easily have eaten them than they the fish! This is however so obvious that even Cobet's "scriba sciolus" would have seen it, and avoided the preposition ἐν. The fact is that Ἑλλήσποντος was constantly used to denote the whole coast stretching from the Pontus to the Aegean, including Bosporos and Propontis. See Stein on Hdt. IV 38 and cf. Thuc. II 9. The usage is also found in Inscriptions (Meisterhans[3] p. 226. 16). An Athenian of Plato's day was much more likely to employ the name Ἑλλήσποντος in this idiomatic sense than a later copyist; and for this reason I have no doubt that the expression is genuine, although the words of Hartman "nihil refert utrum ἐν Ἑλλησπόντῳ an ἐν Αἰγύπτῳ sint" are nearly, if not quite, true. Plato may however intend to remind us that fish were plentiful in the region of the Hellespont: cf. *Il.* IX 360 and Athen. IV 157 B.

17 **ὡς ἔπος εἰπεῖν**. I 341 B *n.*

Οὐδὲ μὴν ἡδυσμάτων, ὡς ἐγᾦμαι, Ὅμηρος πώποτε ἐμνήσθη.
ἢ τοῦτο μὲν καὶ οἱ ἄλλοι ἀσκηταὶ ἴσασιν, ὅτι τῷ μέλλοντι σώματι
εὖ ἕξειν ἀφεκτέον τῶν τοιούτων ἁπάντων; Καὶ ὀρθῶς γε, ἔφη,
D ἴσασί τε καὶ ἀπέχονται. | Συρακοσίαν δέ, ὦ φίλε, τράπεζαν καὶ
Σικελικὴν ποικιλίαν ὄψου, ὡς ἔοικας, οὐκ αἰνεῖς, εἴπερ σοι ταῦτα
δοκεῖ ὀρθῶς ἔχειν. Οὔ μοι δοκῶ. Ψέγεις ἄρα καὶ Κορινθίαν
κόρην φίλην εἶναι ἀνδράσιν μέλλουσιν εὖ σώματος ἕξειν. Παντάπασι μὲν οὖν. Οὐκοῦν καὶ Ἀττικῶν πεμμάτων τὰς δοκούσας
εἶναι εὐπαθείας; Ἀνάγκη. Ὅλην γάρ, οἶμαι, τὴν τοιαύτην σίτησιν
καὶ δίαιταν τῇ μελοποιίᾳ τε καὶ ᾠδῇ τῇ ἐν τῷ παναρμονίῳ καὶ ἐν
E πᾶσι ῥυθμοῖς | πεποιημένῃ ἀπεικάζοντες ὀρθῶς ἂν ἀπεικάζοιμεν.
Πῶς γὰρ οὔ; Οὐκοῦν ἐκεῖ μὲν ἀκολασίαν ἡ ποικιλία ἐνέτικτεν,
ἐνταῦθα δὲ νόσον, ἡ δὲ ἁπλότης κατὰ μὲν μουσικὴν ἐν ψυχαῖς
σωφροσύνην, κατὰ δὲ γυμναστικὴν ἐν σώμασιν ὑγίειαν; Ἀληθέ-
405 στατα, ἔφη. Ἀκολασίας δὲ καὶ νόσων | πληθυουσῶν ἐν πόλει ἆρ'
οὐ δικαστήριά τε καὶ ἰατρεῖα πολλὰ ἀνοίγεται, καὶ δικανική τε καὶ

---

21 **καὶ ὀρθῶς γε—ἀπέχονται.** ὀρθῶς must be taken with both verbs: 'Yes, and they do well in knowing it and in abstaining.'

404 D 22 **Συρακοσίαν—ὄψου.** For δέ ('autem') Stallbaum unnecessarily reads δή. The Συρακοσία τράπεζα was proverbial: see Blaydes on Ar. *Fr.* 206 and the curious account of Syracusan gluttony in Pl. *Epp.* VII 326 B ff. There is no sufficient basis for Cobet's idea that Plato is here borrowing from some comic poet. Later scandal insinuated that it was the delights of Syracusan living that drew Plato thrice to Sicily (Hermann *Gesch. u. System* p. 116 *n.* 133, where the authorities are cited).

24 **Κορινθίαν κόρην.** Cf. II 373 A *n.* Κορινθία κόρη is a grisette: see the commentators on Ar. *Plut.* 149, and on the general subject Blümner *Privatalt.* pp. 254—256. φίλην is more refined for 'mistress' (ἑταῖρα). The word κόρην has been doubted: "innocentem puellam eicere ex Platonis republica voluerunt triumviri praestantissimi Buttmannus, Morgensternius, et nuperrime Astius." So says Stallbaum, her successful champion.

26 **Ἀττικῶν πεμμάτων.** The fame of Athenian pastry was as great as its variety: see Athen. XIV cc. 51—58 and other references in Blümner l.c. p. 220.

28 **παναρμονίῳ.** See on 399 C.

405 A 2 **ἰατρεῖα** were both dispensaries and consulting-rooms etc. See *Laws* 646 C and other references in Blümner l.c. p. 359. In some ἰατρεῖα patients were also housed and treated by doctors (Häser *Lehrbuch d. Gesch. d. Med.* etc. I pp. 86 ff.), so that in certain cases they resembled a sort of private hospital. For the remedial conception of punishment prevailing in the whole of this section see II 380 B *n.*

δικανική. Cobet calls for δικαστική, and at first sight δικαστῶν just below seems to favour his view. But Plato deliberately selects the less reputable word, meaning by it the arts by which men try to lead the true δικαστής (cf. *Ap.* 40 A) astray: see infra B, C. In his own city there is no δικανική, but only δικαστική (409 E, 410 A). It appears from *Laws* IV 720 C ff. that a doctor's assistants were usually slaves, and that slaves for the most part treated slaves, and freemen freemen, but the rule was not universal (see Blümner l. c. p. 359 *n.* 1). Plato holds that the increase of citizen doctors points to the spread of self-indulgence among the free-born population.

405 A—**410** A *It is a sign of bad education when we require first-rate physicians and judges; still more shameful is it to pride oneself on escaping the*

ἰατρικὴ σεμνύνονται, ὅταν δὴ καὶ ἐλεύθεροι πολλοὶ καὶ σφόδρα περὶ αὐτὰ σπουδάζωσιν; Τί γὰρ οὐ μέλλει;

XIV. Τῆς δὲ κακῆς τε καὶ αἰσχρᾶς παιδείας ἐν πόλει ἆρα μή τι μεῖζον ἕξεις λαβεῖν τεκμήριον, ἢ τὸ δεῖσθαι ἰατρῶν καὶ δικαστῶν ἄκρων μὴ μόνον τοὺς φαύλους τε καὶ χειροτέχνας, ἀλλὰ καὶ τοὺς ἐν ἐλευθέρῳ σχήματι προσποιουμένους τεθράφθαι; ἢ οὐκ | αἰσχρὸν **B** δοκεῖ καὶ ἀπαιδευσίας μέγα τεκμήριον τὸ ἐπακτῷ παρ' ἄλλων, ὡς δεσποτῶν τε καὶ κριτῶν, τῷ δικαίῳ ἀναγκάζεσθαι χρῆσθαι καὶ ἀπορίᾳ οἰκείων; Πάντων μὲν οὖν, ἔφη, αἴσχιστον. Ἦ δοκεῖ σοι, ἦν δ' ἐγώ, τούτου αἴσχιον εἶναι τοῦτο, ὅταν τις μὴ μόνον τὸ πολὺ τοῦ βίου ἐν δικαστηρίοις φεύγων τε καὶ διώκων κατατρίβηται, ἀλλὰ καὶ ὑπὸ ἀπειροκαλίας ἐπ' αὐτῷ δὴ τούτῳ πεισθῇ καλλωπίζεσθαι, ὡς δεινὸς ὢν περὶ τὸ ἀδικεῖν | καὶ ἱκανὸς πάσας μὲν στροφὰς **C** στρέφεσθαι, πάσας δὲ διεξόδους διεξελθὼν ἀποστραφῆναι λυγιζό-

15. ἱκανὸς A²Π: ἱκανῶς A¹. 16. διεξελθὼν A²Π: διεξελθεῖν A¹.

---

punishment of wrong-doing by the aid of legal subterfuges. We should also be ashamed to enlarge the terminology of medicine by our self-indulgence. It was otherwise with medical science in the time of Homer, although Herodicus has now invented a new sort of treatment, whose only result is to prolong the process of dying. Asclepius knew better; for he saw that work was more than life. We recognise this fact in the case of artisans and mechanics; but Asclepius knew that rich men also have a work to do, and in the interests both of his patients and their country, declined to treat incurable diseases. Legends to the contrary effect are false. Yet we cannot dispense with doctors and judges: only they must be good doctors and good judges. The most skilled physicians are those who, besides having learnt their art, have had the largest experience of disease in their own persons; but no one can be a good judge whose soul is not unstained. Our judges must be old, and gain their knowledge of crime by science, not by personal experience. The vicious judge cannot recognise innocence when he sees it. Vice will never know Virtue, but Virtue may be taught to know Vice as well as herself. Our doctors will permit the physically incurable to die; the morally incurable our judges will put to death.

405 B 11 **καὶ ἀπορίᾳ οἰκείων** has suffered severely at the hands of critics, who have bracketed *καί* (Ast and others), or read *καὶ ἀπορία οἰκείων* (Hermann), or *δικαίων ἀπορίᾳ οἰκείων* (Madvig), or finally denounced the words as a 'futile interpretamentum.' Schneider explains *καί* as "idque" ("und zwar" in his translation), and so also Prantl, and Shilleto (on Dem. *F. L.* § 101). This interpretation appears to me forced and unnatural. It is simplest to make *ἀπορίᾳ* as well as *τῷ δικαίῳ* depend on *χρῆσθαι*, and regard *χρῆσθαι ἀπορίᾳ* as equivalent to *εἶναι ἄποροι*, just as *χρῆσθαι ἀμαθίᾳ* (for example) means no more than *εἶναι ἀμαθεῖς*. The plural *οἰκείων* does not refer to *δεσποτῶν*, but is the genitive of *οἰκεία*, which means 'resources of one's own,' 'personal resources')(*ἐπακτῷ παρ' ἄλλων*. Cf. the use of *τὰ οἰκεῖα* in the literal sense for *res familiaris* I 343 E al.

ἦ δοκεῖ κτλ. Glauco has said that *χρῆσθαι ἐπακτῷ τῷ δικαίῳ* is the *most* disgraceful thing of all. Socrates asks him whether it (*τοῦτο*) is more disgraceful than the other case (*τούτου*) which he is about to mention; and Glauco's reply is 'no: this other case is even more disgraceful than the first' (infra C). The meaning was missed by the critic who (see *Rev. de Philol.* XV p. 83) ingeniously suggested the insertion of *ἢ οὔ;* after *δικαστοῦ* just before Glauco's reply. In what follows the litigiousness of the Athenian nature is satirised.

405 C 16 **ἀποστραφῆναι**: an expressive and epigrammatic condensation

μενος, ὥστε μὴ παρασχεῖν δίκην, καὶ ταῦτα σμικρῶν τε καὶ οὐδενὸς ἀξίων ἕνεκα, ἀγνοῶν, ὅσῳ κάλλιον καὶ ἄμεινον τὸ παρασκευάζειν τὸν βίον αὑτῷ μηδὲν δεῖσθαι νυστάζοντος δικαστοῦ; Οὔκ, ἀλλὰ τοῦτ', ἔφη, ἐκείνου ἔτι αἴσχιον. Τὸ δὲ ἰατρικῆς, ἦν δ' ἐγώ, δεῖσθαι, ὅ τι μὴ τραυμάτων ἕνεκα ἤ τινων ἐπετείων νοσημάτων ἐπιπεσόντων,
D ἀλλὰ | δι' ἀργίαν τε καὶ δίαιταν οἵαν διήλθομεν ῥευμάτων τε καὶ πνευμάτων ὥσπερ λίμνας ἐμπιμπλαμένους φύσας τε καὶ κατάρρους νοσήμασιν ὀνόματα τίθεσθαι ἀναγκάζειν τοὺς κομψοὺς Ἀσκληπιάδας, οὐκ αἰσχρὸν δοκεῖ; Καὶ μάλ', ἔφη, ὡς ἀληθῶς καινὰ ταῦτα καὶ ἄτοπα νοσημάτων ὀνόματα. Οἷα, ἦν δ' ἐγώ, ὡς οἶμαι, οὐκ ἦν ἐπ' Ἀσκληπιοῦ· τεκμαίρομαι δέ, ὅτι αὐτοῦ οἱ ὑεῖς ἐν Τροίᾳ |

---

for *ἀπολυθῆναι στρεφόμενος*. *λυγιζόμενος* is rightly explained by the Scholiast as *στρεφόμενος, καμπτόμενος, ἀπὸ τῶν λύγων· λύγος δέ ἐστι φυτὸν ἱμαντῶδες*. The corruption *λογιζόμενος* (found in all MSS except A and—according to Rostagno —M) was easy and almost inevitable.

17 **παρασχεῖν δίκην**. The same phrase appears in Eur. *Hipp.* 49, 50, and Herwerden should not have proposed *ὑποσχεῖν*. Plato's view in the *Gorgias* is that the guilty should denounce themselves to the judge and be cured by suffering punishment: see II 380 B *n.*

405 D 23 **φύσας τε καὶ κατάρρους.** The order is chiastic, *φύσας* referring to *πνευμάτων*, and *κατάρρους* to *ῥευμάτων*. Plato clearly indicates that the medical use of these words was only beginning in his day, and it is the application of these words to diseases which he derides, not the words themselves when used of bellows, blasts, and torrents (see the *Lexica*). The experiment in language is better preserved by rendering 'blasts and torrents' than 'flatulence and catarrh.' For *φῦσα* cf. (with Poschenrieder l. c. p. 47) [Hippocr.] *de flatibus* VI p. 94 c. 3 Littré *πνεύματα δὲ τὰ μὲν ἐν τοῖσι σώμασι φῦσαι καλέονται, τὰ δὲ ἔξω τῶν σωμάτων ἀήρ*, and ib. c. 7 *ὅταν οὖν τὸ σῶμα σιτίων πλησθῇ, καὶ πνεύματος πλησμονὴ ἐπὶ πλέον γίγνεται τῶν σιτίων χρονιζομένων· χρονίζεται δὲ τὰ σιτία διὰ τὸ πλῆθος οὐ δυνάμενα διελθεῖν· ἐμφραχθείσης δὲ τῆς κάτω κοιλίης, ἐς ὅλον τὸ σῶμα διέδραμον αἱ φῦσαι*. Other examples of the use of the term in the Hippocratean corpus are cited by Stephanus-Hase *Thes.* s.v. With *κατάρρους* cf. *Crat.* 440 C *ἀτεχνῶς ὥσπερ οἱ κατάρρῳ νοσοῦντες ἄνθρωποι*. The word is found in the Hippocratean writings, and denotes "defluxionem aut omnem humoris ex capite ad os et asperam arteriam, atque per eam ad pulmonem, delationem ac descensum" (Stephanus-Hase s. v., where examples are quoted).

24 **τοὺς κομψοὺς Ἀσκληπιάδας.** The epithets *κομψοί* and *χαρίεντες* were often applied to the more advanced and scientific sort of physicians (Blümner *Privatalt.* p. 358 *n.* 2). The *Ἀσκληπιάδαι* were a well-recognised sect or college of physicians, with schools in Cyrene, Rhodes, Cos and Cnidos. See Günther in Iwan Müller's *Handbuch* V I p. 103, and Hug on *Symp.* 186 E.

25 **καὶ μάλ'—ὀνόματα**: 'Yes, indeed, these are truly' etc. Glauco does not reply to *οὐκ αἰσχρὸν δοκεῖ*, but simply corroborates what Socrates has said about the new medical terminology. This is simpler than to place (with Schneider) a colon after *ἔφη*, and take *καὶ μάλα* with *αἰσχρόν*. The asyndeton on Schneider's view is too harsh, and would almost require the insertion of *καί* before *ὡς*, or (if *ὡς ἀληθῶς* were taken as *ὡς ἀληθῶς αἰσχρόν*) before *καινά*; neither of which alternatives is satisfying. For similar inexactness in replies see V 465 E *n.*

405 DE 27 **οἱ ὑεῖς—ἐπετίμησαν.** In themselves these words can only mean that Machaon and Podalirius (the two chief army doctors to the Greek host, *Il.* XI 833) found no fault with the damsel who gave the wounded Eurypylus an inflammatory potion, or with Patroclus, who was curing him, for directing or permitting her to do so. In our Homer, however, the potion is given, not to Eurypylus but to the wounded Machaon, by

Εὐρυπύλῳ τετρωμένῳ ἐπ' οἶνον Πράμνειον ἄλφιτα πολλὰ ἐπιπασ- E
θέντα καὶ τυρὸν ἐπιξυσθέντα, ἃ δὴ δοκεῖ φλεγματώδη εἶναι, οὐκ 406
ἐμέμψαντο τῇ δούσῃ πιεῖν, οὐδὲ Πατρόκλῳ τῷ ἰωμένῳ ἐπετίμησαν.
Καὶ μὲν δή, ἔφη, ἄτοπόν γε τὸ πῶμα οὕτως ἔχοντι. Οὔκ, εἴ γ'
ἐννοεῖς, εἶπον, ὅτι τῇ παιδαγωγικῇ τῶν νοσημάτων ταύτῃ τῇ νῦν
ἰατρικῇ πρὸ τοῦ Ἀσκληπιάδαι οὐκ ἐχρῶντο, ὥς φασι, πρὶν Ἡρόδικον
γενέσθαι· Ἡρόδικος δὲ παιδοτρίβης ὢν καὶ νοσώδης γενόμενος,
μείξας γυμναστικὴν ἰατρικῇ, ἀπέκναισε πρῶτον μὲν καὶ μάλιστα B
ἑαυτόν, ἔπειτ' ἄλλους ὕστερον πολλούς. Πῇ δή; ἔφη. Μακρόν,
ἦν δ' ἐγώ, τὸν θάνατον αὑτῷ ποιήσας. παρακολουθῶν γὰρ τῷ
νοσήματι θανασίμῳ ὄντι οὔτε ἰάσασθαι, οἶμαι, οἷός τ' ἦν ἑαυτόν,
ἐν ἀσχολίᾳ τε πάντων ἰατρευόμενος διὰ βίου ἔζη ἀποκναιόμενος,
εἴ τι τῆς εἰωθυίας διαίτης ἐκβαίη, δυσθανατῶν δὲ ὑπὸ σοφίας εἰς

Hecamede, Nestor's slave (*Il.* XI 624); and this is correctly related in *Ion* 538 B. The inconsistency led Ast to suspect the genuineness both of *Εὐρυπύλῳ*—see however 408 A—and of *οὐδὲ Πατρόκλῳ τῷ ἰωμένῳ*; but there can be little doubt that the text is sound. We must suppose either that Plato is confused, or else that in his text of Homer such a potion was administered, not only to the wounded Machaon (as in the *Ion* l.c.), but also to the wounded Eurupylus, with Patroclus' sanction. The first alternative is possible, and approved by Howes (*Harvard Studies* etc. VI p. 198): but as it is clear from the *Ion*—if the *Ion* is genuine—that Plato was familiar with the story of Machaon's treatment, I think it more likely that Plato's Homer related a similar incident in connexion with the treatment of Eurypylus also. For the healing of Eurypylus see *Il.* XI 844 ff., XV 394.

405 E 28 **οἶνον Πράμνειον**. Athenaeus, alluding to this passage, informs us that Pramneian wine was *παχὺς καὶ πολυτρόφος* (I 10 B).

406 A 1 **φλεγματώδη**: 'inflammatory.' Cf. [Hippocr.] *περὶ νούσων* IV c. 35 (VII p. 548 Littré) *ἐπήν τις φάγῃ τυρὸν ἢ ὅ τι ἐστὶ δριμύ, ἢ ἄλλο τι φάγῃ ἢ πίῃ ὅ τι ἐστὶ φλεγματῶδες, αὐτίκα οἱ ἐπιθέει ἐπὶ τὸ στόμα καὶ τὰς ῥῖνας* (Poschenrieder l.c. p. 49).

4 **τῇ παιδαγωγικῇ—ἰατρικῇ**. Cf. *Tim.* 89 C *παιδαγωγεῖν δεῖ διαίταις πάντα τὰ τοιαῦτα—ἀλλ' οὐ φαρμακεύοντα κακὸν δύσκολον ἐρεθιστέον*.

5 **Ἡρόδικον**. Herodicus, a native of Megara, and afterwards a citizen of Selymbria, is mentioned by Plato again in *Prot.* 316 E and *Phaedr.* 227 D. He was one of the earliest to study scientifically the therapeutics of exercise and diet, and particularly recommended long walks, according to Plato (*Phaedr.* l.c. *τὸν περίπατον Μέγαράδε*. Cf. Häser *Lehrb. d. Gesch. d. Med.* etc. I p. 94). The description of his health given here is confirmed by Aristotle *Rhet.* I 5. 1361b 4—6 *πολλοὶ—ὑγιαίνουσιν ὥσπερ Ἡρόδικος λέγεται, οὓς οὐδεὶς ἂν εὐδαιμονίσειε τῆς ὑγιείας διὰ τὸ πάντων ἀπέχεσθαι τῶν ἀνθρωπίνων ἢ τῶν πλείστων* (a passage curiously misunderstood by J. and C., who seem to take *λέγεται* for *λέγει*). Plato himself thoroughly appreciates the connexion between *γυμναστική* and *ἰατρική*: see for example *Gorg.* 452 A ff., 464 B ff., *Soph.* 228 E, *Pol.* 295 C.

6 **νοσώδης γενόμενος**. *εἰς φθίσιν ἀνήκεστον πάθος ἐμπεσών*, says Plutarch (*de his qui sero* etc. 554 C).

406 B 8 **μακρὸν—τὸν θάνατον κτλ.** Cf. Eur. *Suppl.* 1109—1113 *μισῶ δ' ὅσοι χρῄζουσιν ἐκτείνειν βίον | βρωτοῖσι καὶ ποτοῖσι καὶ μαγεύμασι | παρεκτρέποντες ὀχετὸν ὥστε μὴ θανεῖν· | οὓς χρῆν, ἐπειδὰν μηδὲν ὠφελῶσι γῆν, | θανόντας ἔρρειν κἀκποδὼν εἶναι νέοις*, and Aesch. *Fr.* 395, Soph. *Fr.* 689.

12 **δυσθανατῶν**: not "dum malam obit mortem" (Stallbaum), but 'dying hard' like *δυσθνῄσκων*.

γῆρας ἀφίκετο. Καλὸν ἄρα τὸ γέρας, ἔφη, τῆς τέχνης ἠνέγκατο.
C Οἶον εἰκός, ἦν δ' ἐγώ, τὸν μὴ εἰδότα, ὅτι Ἀσκληπιὸς οὐκ ἀγνοίᾳ οὐδὲ ἀπειρίᾳ τούτου τοῦ εἴδους τῆς ἰατρικῆς τοῖς ἐκγόνοις οὐ κατέδειξεν αὐτό, ἀλλ' εἰδὼς ὅτι πᾶσι τοῖς εὐνομουμένοις ἔργον τι ἑκάστῳ ἐν τῇ πόλει προστέτακται, ὃ ἀναγκαῖον ἐργάζεσθαι, καὶ οὐδενὶ σχολὴ διὰ βίου κάμνειν ἰατρευομένῳ. ὃ ἡμεῖς γελοίως ἐπὶ μὲν τῶν δημιουργῶν αἰσθανόμεθα, ἐπὶ δὲ τῶν πλουσίων τε καὶ εὐδαιμόνων δοκούντων εἶναι οὐκ αἰσθανόμεθα. Πῶς; ἔφη.

D XV. Τέκτων μέν, ἦν δ' ἐγώ, κάμνων ἀξιοῖ παρὰ τοῦ ἰατροῦ φάρμακον πιὼν ἐξεμέσαι τὸ νόσημα, ἢ κάτω καθαρθεὶς ἢ καύσει ἢ τομῇ χρησάμενος ἀπηλλάχθαι· ἐὰν δέ τις αὐτῷ μακρὰν δίαιταν προστάττῃ, πιλίδιά τε περὶ τὴν κεφαλὴν περιτιθεὶς καὶ τὰ τούτοις ἑπόμενα, ταχὺ εἶπεν, ὅτι οὐ σχολὴ κάμνειν, οὐδὲ λυσιτελεῖ οὕτω ζῆν, νοσήματι τὸν νοῦν προσέχοντα, τῆς δὲ προκειμένης ἐργασίας
E ἀμελοῦντα. καὶ μετὰ ταῦτα χαίρειν εἰπὼν τῷ τοιούτῳ ἰατρῷ, εἰς τὴν εἰωθυῖαν δίαιταν ἐμβάς, ὑγιὴς γενόμενος ζῇ τὰ ἑαυτοῦ πράττων· ἐὰν δὲ μὴ ἱκανὸν ᾖ τὸ σῶμα ὑπενεγκεῖν, τελευτήσας πραγμάτων ἀπηλλάγη. Καὶ τῷ τοιούτῳ μέν γ', ἔφη, δοκεῖ πρέπειν οὕτω

23. *μακρὰν* Ξ: *μικρὰν* AΠ: *σμικρὰν* *q*.

---

13 **καλόν.** Because he was the first to profit by his own invention. The assonance *γῆρας—γέρας* is quite in Plato's manner: cf. IV 439 C, VI 487 C, VIII 557 C *nn.*

406 C 18 **οὐδενὶ σχολὴ κτλ.** Steinhart (*Platon's Werke* V p. 172) thinks it strange that so idealistic a thinker as Plato should not recognise the power of spiritual strength to rise superior to bodily weakness. This truth was not ignored by Plato (see infra 408 E and VI 496 B), although here, perhaps, he forgets that conspicuous examples of fortitude and resignation have a political as well as a private value: "they also serve who only stand and wait."

406 D 22 **καύσει ἢ τομῇ.** The two methods of ancient surgery: see Blümner *Privatalt.* p. 353 *n.*

23 **μακρὰν** has less authority than *μικράν* (see *cr. n.*), but is probably right. The contrast with the immediate remedies just described seems to require an allusion to the duration of the regimen: cf. also *μακρὸν—τὸν θάνατον* in B above. *μικράν* is not sufficiently defended by a reference to *κατὰ σμικρόν* in 407 D, nor by the allusion to *πιλίδια καὶ τὰ τούτοις ἑπόμενα.* Moreover *σμικρός*, and not *μικρός*, is the prevailing form throughout the *Republic.* *μικρός* appears to occur only in V 453 D and VI 498 D. On the inscriptional usage see Meisterhans[3] p. 89.

24 **πιλίδια.** Felt caps were worn by the sick and delicate (see the references in Blümner l.c. p. 180 *n.* 5); but as artisans and sailors usually wore felt caps too (*Dict. Ant.* II p. 427), Plato perhaps alludes to some special coverings for the head prescribed by doctors from time to time in a course of medical treatment. The plural also points to this. If not, he uses the expression quite generally, as an example of the treatment he condemns. Well-to-do Greeks generally went bareheaded.

25 **εἶπεν.** The 'momentary' aorist well expresses the carpenter's decided businesslike tone. His view of life resembles that of the 'meditative skipper' in *Gorg.* 511 D ff.

406 E 28 **ὑγιὴς—ἀπηλλάγη.** He regains his health on losing his doctor, or if he dies, dies without help. Cf. Plut. *Apophth. Lac.* 231 A τοῦ δὲ ἰατροῦ εἰπόντος

ἰατρικῇ χρῆσθαι. Ἆρα, ἦν δ' ἐγώ, ὅτι ἦν τι αὐτῷ ἔργον, | ὃ εἰ 407
μὴ πράττοι, οὐκ ἐλυσιτέλει ζῆν; Δῆλον, ἔφη. Ὁ δὲ δὴ πλούσιος, ὥς φαμεν, οὐδὲν ἔχει τοιοῦτον ἔργον προκείμενον, οὗ ἀναγκαζομένῳ ἀπέχεσθαι ἀβίωτον. Οὔκουν δὴ λέγεταί γε. Φωκυλίδου γάρ, ἦν δ' ἐγώ, οὐκ ἀκούεις, πῶς φησὶ δεῖν, ὅταν τῳ ἤδη βίος ᾖ, ἀρετὴν ἀσκεῖν; Οἶμαι δέ γε, ἔφη, καὶ πρότερον. Μηδέν, εἶπον, περὶ τούτου αὐτῷ μαχώμεθα, ἀλλ' ἡμᾶς αὐτοὺς διδάξωμεν, πότερον μελετητέον τοῦτο τῷ πλουσίῳ καὶ ἀβίωτον τῷ μὴ | μελετῶντι B
ἦ νοσοτροφία τεκτονικῇ μὲν καὶ ταῖς ἄλλαις τέχναις ἐμπόδιον τῇ προσέξει τοῦ νοῦ, τὸ δὲ Φωκυλίδου παρακέλευμα οὐδὲν ἐμποδίζει. Ναὶ μὰ τὸν Δία, ἦ δ' ὅς, σχεδόν γέ τι πάντων μάλιστα ἥ γε

9. ἦ Π: ἡ A.

αὐτῷ, Γέρων γέγονας, Διότι, εἶπεν, οὐκ ἐχρησάμην σοι ἰατρῷ. (The anecdote is told of Pausanias the Spartan king.)

31 **ἦν**. The carpenter is now dismissed: hence the imperfect ἦν, which should be retained in translating. Stallbaum (followed by J. and C.) explains ἦν as the 'philosophic' imperfect = ἐστίν, ὡς ἄρτι ἐλέγομεν (in 406 C). This is much less simple and lively. "Wohl weil er ein Geschäft hatte, bei dessen Unterlassung es ihm nicht erspriesslich war zu leben?" Schneider, rightly. Cf. II 361 C *n*.

407 A 3 **ἔργον προκείμενον**. The view of work and duty here presented recalls I 352 E—353 E.

5 **ἀκούεις**. Phocylides, being dead, yet speaketh. The present ἀκούεις is just as legitimate as φησί, and well expresses the living voice of poetry in oral circulation. Heindorf (on *Gorg*. 503 C) misses the point of the idiom when he says that ἀκούεις is for ἀκήκοας; while Stallbaum's explanation 'probas' is positively wrong. The line, as restored by Bergk Phoc. *Fr*. 10, is δίζησθαι βιοτήν, ἀρετὴν δ' ὅταν ᾖ βίος ἤδη. The Horatian 'quaerenda pecunia primum, | virtus post nummos' gives the meaning, if *primum* and *post* are understood in a strictly temporal sense. Phocylides' maxim is one of the earliest expressions of the all but universal cry χρήματα χρήματ' ἀνήρ (first in Alcaeus *Fr*. 49 Bergk), which Socrates and Plato continually preached against. It will be noticed that Plato for his own purposes represents Phocylides as laying the stress on ἀρετὴν ἀσκεῖν rather than on δίζησθαι βιοτήν, where it really falls.

8 **τοῦτο**: viz. τὸ ἀρετὴν ἀσκεῖν, as explained in the margin of A.

407 B 9 **τῇ προσέξει τοῦ νοῦ** is added as a kind of afterthought or additional specification, precisely like the infinitives in *Gorg*. 513 E ἐπιχειρητέον ἐστι τῇ πόλει καὶ τοῖς πολίταις θεραπεύειν, infra 407 C, IV 437 B, 443 B, V 450 B, X 598 B, *Crito* 52 B. The datives τεκτονικῇ etc. depend grammatically on ἐμπόδιον only, and have nothing to do with προσέξει. παρακέλευμα presently is of course the accusative, the subject to ἐμποδίζει being νοσοτροφία, and οὐδέν adverbial. Richter (in *Fl. Jahrb*. 1867 p. 140) should not have revived the reading of Bekker μελετῶντι ἢ νοσοτροφία· τεκτονικῇ μὲν γὰρ κτλ., which is lacking both in authority and point.

11 **ναὶ μὰ τὸν Δία—εἰκός γε, ἔφην** (in C). See *cr. n*. With the MS reading εἰκός γ' ἔφη, the distribution of the speeches causes difficulty. It will be enough to mention three alternatives, for no one has adopted or is likely to adopt the punctuation of A, where σχεδόν γέ τι—περὶ τοῦ σώματος is assigned to Socrates. We may give either (1) the whole speech ναὶ μὰ—περὶ τοῦ σώματος to Glauco, excising εἰκός γε, ἔφη with Π *q* and some other MSS (so Schneider 1830); or (2) ναὶ μὰ—ἐπιμέλεια τοῦ σώματος to Glauco, and καὶ γὰρ—περὶ τοῦ σώματος to Socrates (Stallbaum); or (3) ναὶ μὰ—δύσκολος to Glauco, and τὸ δὲ δὴ—περὶ τοῦ σώματος to Socrates (Baiter and others, including Schneider 1842). The first view fails to account for the appearance of εἰκός γε ἔφη in A, but is right, I think, in assigning the whole speech to Glauco. Neither

περαιτέρω γυμναστικῆς, ἡ περιττὴ αὕτη ἐπιμέλεια τοῦ σώματος·
καὶ γὰρ πρὸς οἰκονομίας καὶ πρὸς στρατείας καὶ πρὸς ἑδραίους
ἐν πόλει ἀρχὰς δύσκολος. τὸ δὲ δὴ μέγιστον, ὅτι καὶ πρὸς
C μαθήσεις ἁστινασοῦν καὶ ἐννοήσεις τε καὶ μελέτας | πρὸς ἑαυτὸν
χαλεπή, κεφαλῆς τινὰς αἰεὶ διατάσεις καὶ ἰλίγγους ὑποπτεύουσα
καὶ αἰτιωμένη ἐκ φιλοσοφίας ἐγγίγνεσθαι, ὥστε, ὅπῃ αὕτη, ἀρετῇ
ἀσκεῖσθαι καὶ δοκιμάζεσθαι πάντῃ ἐμπόδιος· κάμνειν γὰρ οἴεσθαι
ποιεῖ ἀεὶ καὶ ὠδίνοντα μήποτε λήγειν περὶ τοῦ σώματος. Εἰκός
γε, ἔφην. οὐκοῦν ταῦτα γιγνώσκοντα φῶμεν καὶ Ἀσκληπιὸν τοὺς
μὲν φύσει τε καὶ διαίτῃ ὑγιεινῶς ἔχοντας τὰ σώματα, νόσημα δέ
D τι ἀποκεκριμένον | ἴσχοντας ἐν αὐτοῖς, τούτοις μὲν καὶ ταύτῃ τῇ

16. τινὰς Ξ*q*: τινος (sic) ΑΠ. διατάσεις *v* cum Galeno (v p. 874 Kühn): διαστάσεις ΑΠΞ*q*. 17. αὕτη Ξ: ταύτῃ ΑΠ. In *q* legitur ὅπῃ ἀρετὴ ἀσκεῖται καὶ δοκιμάζεται, αὕτη πάντῃ ἐμπόδιος. 18. ἀσκεῖσθαι καὶ δοκιμάζεσθαι Ξ: ἀσκεῖται καὶ δοκιμάζεται ΑΠ*q*. 20. ἔφην nos: ἔφη ΑΞ: εἰκός γ' ἔφη om. Π*q*.

---

at καὶ γὰρ πρὸς οἰκονομίας nor at τὸ δὲ δὴ μέγιστον is it easy and natural to change the speakers. The simple expedient of writing ἔφην for ἔφη appears to me to set matters straight. For the corruption see *Introd.* § 5. οὐκοῦν ταῦτα etc. is also said by Socrates.

ἥ γε περαιτέρω κτλ. 'This excessive care of the body, which goes beyond what sound bodily regimen permits.' The Greek has a rhetorical effect like τὸ δεινόν, τὸ μέγα ἐκεῖνο—θρέμμα IX 590 A. With περαιτέρω and the genitive cf. *Gorg.* 484 C περαιτέρω τοῦ δέοντος. I once conjectured ἥ γε περαιτέρω γυμναστική, ἧς ('cuius est') etc. (*Cl. Rev.* X p. 385), but Plato seems to mean that treatment of this kind has no claim to the name γυμναστική at all, and not that it is γυμναστική run mad. The MS reading is defended also by a reviewer of my *Text of the Republic* in *Hermathena* XX p. 252.

407 C 15 **πρὸς ἑαυτόν**: with μελέτας, as in μελετᾶν, φροντίζειν πρὸς ἑαυτόν etc.

16 **διατάσεις**, though its MS authority (see *cr. n.*) is slight, can hardly fail to be what Plato wrote. Similarly in 546 C A[1] has ἕκαστον twice for ἑκατόν. See *Introd.* § 5.

17 **ὅπῃ—ἐμπόδιος.** The reading of Ξ (followed by Stallbaum and the older editors) is certainly right. αὕτη (sc. ἐστιν) is νοσοτροφία; and ἐμπόδιος ἀρετῇ ἀσκεῖσθαι is exactly like ἐπιχειρεῖν τῇ πόλει θεραπεύειν (see 407 B *n.*). The presence of νοσοτροφία makes it impossible for virtue to be practised or tested, as when, for example, to take a pedant's illustration, a boy evades both lectures and examinations by cherishing a nervous headache. Recent English editors have followed Baiter, and read ὅπῃ ταύτῃ ἀρετὴ ἀσκεῖται καὶ δοκιμάζεται, taking ταύτῃ as ἐν φιλοσοφίᾳ, but this gives a much less satisfactory meaning. After αὕτη had been changed to ταύτῃ, the rest of the corruption was easy; but a trace of the original reading may survive in the ἀρετῇ (not ἀρετή) of A.

22 **ἀποκεκριμένον**: an isolated, local malady; "morbum separatum, non totum corpus afficientem" (Ast). Unnecessary difficulty has been raised. The word is in no sense technical, and ἀποκρίνω in the sense of 'separate' is common enough. The corruption ἀποκεκρυμμένον might have been foretold.

407 D **τούτοις μὲν κτλ.** The words τοὺς μὲν ὑγιεινῶς ἔχοντας led us to expect ἰᾶσθαι, but the construction changes in order to introduce the invention of medicine, and the 'healing' reappears in a different form in φαρμάκοις τε—δίαιταν. The sentence is bad grammar, but good conversational style of the looser kind. It is not easy to say whether τε after φαρμάκοις connects the clauses, or only φαρμάκοις with τομαῖς. The former use is comparatively rare in Plato (Hoefer, *de part. Plat.* p. 7). Partly on this ground, and partly because the union of the aorist

ἕξει καταδεῖξαι ἰατρικήν, φαρμάκοις τε καὶ τομαῖς τὰ νοσήματα ἐκβάλλοντα αὐτῶν τὴν εἰωθυῖαν προστάττειν δίαιταν ἵνα μὴ τὰ πολιτικὰ βλάπτοι, τὰ δ' εἴσω διὰ παντὸς νενοσηκότα σώματα οὐκ ἐπιχειρεῖν διαίταις κατὰ σμικρὸν ἀπαντλοῦντα καὶ ἐπιχέοντα μακρὸν καὶ κακὸν βίον ἀνθρώπῳ ποιεῖν, καὶ ἔκγονα αὐτῶν, ὡς τὸ εἰκός, ἕτερα τοιαῦτα φυτεύειν, ἀλλὰ τὸν μὴ δυνάμενον ἐν τῇ **E** καθεστηκυίᾳ περιόδῳ ζῆν μὴ οἴεσθαι δεῖν θεραπεύειν, ὡς οὔτε αὐτῷ οὔτε πόλει λυσιτελῆ; Πολιτικόν, ἔφη, λέγεις Ἀσκληπιόν. Δῆλον, ἦν δ' ἐγώ, ὅτι τοιοῦτος ἦν· καὶ οἱ παῖδες αὐτοῦ οὐχ ὁρᾷς ὡς καὶ ἐν Τροίᾳ ἀγαθοὶ πρὸς τὸν πόλεμον ἐφάνησαν, καὶ τῇ **408** ἰατρικῇ, ὡς ἐγὼ λέγω, ἐχρῶντο; ἢ οὐ μέμνησαι, ὅτι καὶ τῷ Μενέλεῳ ἐκ τοῦ τραύματος, οὗ ὁ Πάνδαρος ἔβαλεν,

αἷμ' ἐκμυζήσαντ' ἐπί τ' ἤπια φάρμακ' ἔπασσον,

31. ὅτι—ἦν, quae ante οὐχ ὁρᾷς praebent AΠ, e Schneideri coniectura huc transtulimus.

καταδεῖξαι with προστάττειν is a little awkward, I prefer the second alternative. The asyndeton, which is of the usual explanatory or ampliative kind, is in keeping with the loose structure of the whole sentence, and seems to me to add a certain didactic impressiveness here: cf. 409 B. τὰ δ' εἴσω—σώματα depends not so much on ἀπαντλοῦντα directly as on the composite notion ἀπαντλοῦντα καὶ ἐπιχέοντα, which expresses a certain mode of treatment, and is as it were a species of the general idiom ποιεῖν τινά τι. φυτεύειν must depend on ποιεῖν. Plato's sentences are seldom so disjointed as this: cf. however VI 488 B ff., VIII 558 A.

407 E 29 **μὴ οἴεσθαι**: for the negative (which is the more natural here, as it belongs logically to δεῖν, though grammatically to οἴεσθαι) see I 346 E *n.* οἴεσθαι, like ἐπιχειρεῖν, depends on φῶμεν.

30 **λυσιτελῆ** is taken by Schneider as the accusative neuter in apposition to the idea in θεραπεύειν. If so, αὑτῷ for αὐτῷ must be written (with A). It is however so natural to take λυσιτελῆ as masculine that Plato would surely have expressed the other meaning in a less ambiguous way. The usual view yields a satisfactory sense, and should be preferred.

31 **δῆλον κτλ.** See *cr. n.* The awkwardness of taking ὅτι as 'because' was early felt and led to the insertion of δεικνύοιεν ἄν in several MSS (καὶ οἱ παῖδες αὐτοῦ δεικνύοιεν ἂν ὅτι τοιοῦτος ἦν)—a reading adopted by the older editors. Few will now dispute that δεικνύοιεν ἄν is a gloss. Besides Schneider's suggestion, which I adopt, two other proposals merit consideration: (1) δῆλοι, ἦν δ' ἐγώ, καὶ οἱ παῖδες αὐτοῦ ὅτι τοιοῦτος ἦν (Sauppe, comparing *Crito* 44 D), (2) δῆλον, ἦν δ' ἐγώ, καὶ οἱ παῖδες αὐτοῦ ὅτι τοιοῦτοι. ἢ οὐχ ὁρᾷς κτλ. (Madvig). The first, though regarded as possible by Schneider (*Addit.* p. 25), involves what is, to say the least, a very exceptional use of δῆλος, with which "subiectum sententiae verbo ὅτι incipientis idem esse solet quod sententiae primariae" (Hartman). Sauppe's parallel from the *Crito* is a doubtful exception to Hartman's rule. Moreover οὐχ ὁρᾷς κτλ. is too lively: we should expect ἢ (so Π[2] Ξ[2] and other MSS) οὐχ ὁρᾷς κτλ. Madvig's correction already involves two changes (τοιοῦτοι and ἢ), but would be improved by making a third, viz. δῆλοι for δῆλον. The minimum of dislocation which yields a satisfactory sense is the reading which suggested itself to Schneider, although he did not himself adopt it. Some may be inclined to pronounce ὅτι τοιοῦτος ἦν a marginal gloss on δῆλον, as once occurred to Hartman.

408 A 2 **ὡς ἐγὼ λέγω.** ὡς is emphatic, 'in the way I describe.'

4 **αἷμ'—ἔπασσον.** *Il.* IV 218 αἷμ' ἐκμυζήσας ἐπ' ἄρ' ἤπια φάρμακα εἰδὼς | πάσσε, said of Machaon only. Plato

ὅ τι δ' ἐχρῆν μετὰ τοῦτο ἢ πιεῖν ἢ φαγεῖν οὐδὲν μᾶλλον ἢ τῷ
Εὐρυπύλῳ προσέταττον, ὡς ἱκανῶν ὄντων τῶν φαρμάκων ἰάσασθαι
ἄνδρας πρὸ τῶν τραυμάτων ὑγιεινούς τε καὶ κοσμίους ἐν διαίτῃ,
B κἂν εἰ τύχοιεν ἐν τῷ παραχρῆμα κυκεῶνα πιόντες, νοσώδη δὲ φύσει
τε καὶ ἀκόλαστον οὔτε αὑτοῖς οὔτε τοῖς ἄλλοις ᾤοντο λυσιτελεῖν
ζῆν, οὐδ' ἐπὶ τούτοις τὴν τέχνην δεῖν εἶναι, οὐδὲ θεραπευτέον
αὐτούς, οὐδ' εἰ Μίδου πλουσιώτεροι εἶεν. Πάνυ κομψούς, ἔφη,
λέγεις Ἀσκληπιοῦ παῖδας.

XVI. Πρέπει, ἦν δ' ἐγώ. καίτοι ἀπειθοῦντές γε ἡμῖν οἱ
τραγῳδοποιοί τε καὶ Πίνδαρος Ἀπόλλωνος μέν φασιν Ἀσκληπιὸν
C εἶναι, ὑπὸ δὲ χρυσοῦ πεισθῆναι πλούσιον ἄνδρα θανάσιμον ἤδη
ὄντα ἰάσασθαι, ὅθεν δὴ καὶ κεραυνωθῆναι αὐτόν. ἡμεῖς δὲ κατὰ
τὰ προειρημένα οὐ πειθόμεθα αὐτοῖς ἀμφότερα, ἀλλ' εἰ μὲν θεοῦ
ἦν, οὐκ ἦν, φήσομεν, αἰσχροκερδής, εἰ δὲ αἰσχροκερδής, οὐκ ἦν θεοῦ.
Ὀρθότατα, ἦ δ' ὅς, ταῦτά γε. ἀλλὰ περὶ τοῦδε τί λέγεις, ὦ
Σώκρατες; ἆρ' οὐκ ἀγαθοὺς δεῖ ἐν τῇ πόλει κεκτῆσθαι ἰατρούς;
εἶεν δ' ἂν που μάλιστα τοιοῦτοι ὅσοι πλείστους μὲν ὑγιεινούς,
D πλείστους δὲ νοσώδεις μετεχειρίσαντο, καὶ δικασταὶ αὖ ὡσαύτως
οἱ παντοδαπαῖς φύσεσιν ὡμιληκότες. Καὶ μάλα, εἶπον, ἀγαθοὺς
λέγω. ἀλλ' οἶσθα οὓς ἡγοῦμαι τοιούτους; Ἂν εἴπῃς, ἔφη. Ἀλλὰ

---

ingeniously accommodates the line to his own purposes. ἐκμυζήσαντ' is of course the aorist indicative ἐκμυζήσαντο, not the dual participle as J. and C. hold. This was pointed out by Schneider. Verbs denoting any kind of organic action are apt to be middle in Attic (Rutherford *New Phrynichus* pp. 138 ff.). It would be easy to write ἐκμύζησάν τ' (as I once did) and retain Homer's active, but it is not worth while.

408 B 8 **κἂν εἰ** has come to mean no more than καὶ εἰ: cf. infra V 477 A, IX 579 D, X 612 C and Jebb on Soph. *El.* pp. 224 f. The change from the plural πιόντες to the singular νοσώδη has been doubted by Herwerden; but see I 347 A *n.* In illustration of κυκεῶνα πιόντες Schneider (*Addit.* p. 25) refers to Hippocr. περὶ διαίτης ὀξέων II p. 304 f. Littré οἱ γὰρ ἀρχόμενοι τῶν ὀξέων νουσημάτων ἔστιν ὅτε οἱ μὲν σιτία ἔφαγον—οἱ δὲ καὶ κυκεῶνα ἐρρόφεον· ἅπαντα δὲ ταῦτα κακίω μέν ἐστιν ἢ εἰ ἑτεροίως τις διαιτηθείη κτλ.

11 **Μίδου πλουσιώτεροι**: with reference (as Stallbaum observes) to Tyrt. 12. 6 (Bergk): cf. *Laws* 660 E.

14 **τραγῳδοποιοί τε καὶ Πίνδαρος.** Aesch. *Ag.* 1022 f., Eur. *Alc.* 3, Pind. *Pyth.* 3. 55—58 (αἴθων δὲ κεραυνὸς ἐνέσκιμψεν μόρον).

408 C 17 **πειθόμεθα** was much more likely to be corrupted to πεισόμεθα (so *q*, with Stallbaum and others) than *vice versâ*, on account of φήσομεν. The present is more pointed and expressive; our rule has been laid down (391 D), and we abide by it now and always.

21 **ὅσοι κτλ.** Glauco's conception of the medical art resembles that of the later ἐμπειρικοί: see Celsus *de med.* Proem. pp. 5—9 ed. Daremberg, and infra 408 D *n.*

408 D 23 **καὶ μάλα—λέγω.** Socrates replies to ἆρ' οὐκ—ἰατρούς; ignoring, or nearly ignoring, εἶεν δ' ἂν—ὡμιληκότες: cf. V 465 E *n.* καὶ μάλα is simply 'certainly,' and ἀγαθοὺς λέγω lays stress on ἀγαθούς: 'that is, if they are really good,' '*good* ones, I mean.' There is perhaps a hint that the good physician and the good judge must also be good men: cf. 409 C. To substitute with Hartman μάλιστα for μάλα (as in many MSS) is to mistake the force of λέγω.

πειράσομαι, ἦν δ' ἐγώ. σὺ μέντοι οὐχ ὅμοιον πρᾶγμα τῷ αὐτῷ λόγῳ ἤρου. Πῶς; ἔφη. Ἰατροὶ μέν, εἶπον, δεινότατοι ἂν γένοιντο, εἰ ἐκ παίδων ἀρξάμενοι πρὸς τῷ μανθάνειν τὴν τέχνην ὡς πλείστοις τε καὶ πονηροτάτοις σώμασιν ὁμιλήσειαν καὶ αὐτοὶ πάσας νόσους **E** κάμοιεν καὶ εἶεν μὴ πάνυ ὑγιεινοὶ φύσει. οὐ γάρ, οἶμαι, σώματι σῶμα θεραπεύουσιν· οὐ γὰρ ἂν αὐτὰ ἐνεχώρει κακὰ εἶναί ποτε καὶ γενέσθαι· ἀλλὰ ψυχῇ σῶμα, ᾗ οὐκ ἐγχωρεῖ κακὴν γενομένην τε καὶ οὖσαν εὖ τι θεραπεύειν. Ὀρθῶς, ἔφη. Δικαστὴς δέ γε, ὦ φίλε, ψυχῇ ψυχῆς ἄρχει, ᾗ | οὐκ ἐγχωρεῖ ἐκ νέας ἐν πονηραῖς ψυχαῖς **409** τεθράφθαι τε καὶ ὡμιληκέναι καὶ πάντα ἀδικήματα αὐτὴν ἠδικηκυῖαν διεξεληλυθέναι, ὥστε ὀξέως ἀφ' αὐτῆς τεκμαίρεσθαι τὰ τῶν ἄλλων ἀδικήματα, οἷον κατὰ σῶμα νόσους· ἀλλ' ἄπειρον αὐτὴν καὶ ἀκέραιον δεῖ κακῶν ἠθῶν νέαν οὖσαν γεγονέναι, εἰ μέλλει καλὴ κἀγαθὴ οὖσα κρίνειν ὑγιῶς τὰ δίκαια. διὸ δὴ καὶ εὐήθεις νέοι ὄντες οἱ ἐπιεικεῖς φαίνονται καὶ εὐεξαπάτητοι ὑπὸ τῶν ἀδίκων, ἅτε οὐκ ἔχοντες ἐν ἑαυτοῖς παραδείγματα ὁμοιοπαθῆ τοῖς πονηροῖς. **B** Καὶ μὲν δή, ἔφη, σφόδρα γε αὐτὸ πάσχουσι. Τοιγάρτοι, ἦν δ' ἐγώ, οὐ νέον ἀλλὰ γέροντα δεῖ τὸν ἀγαθὸν δικαστὴν εἶναι, ὀψιμαθῆ γεγονότα τῆς ἀδικίας οἷόν ἐστιν, οὐκ οἰκείαν ἐν τῇ αὑτοῦ ψυχῇ ἐνοῦσαν ᾐσθημένον, ἀλλ' ἀλλοτρίαν ἐν ἀλλοτρίαις μεμελετηκότα ἐν πολλῷ χρόνῳ διαισθάνεσθαι, οἷον πέφυκε κακόν, ἐπιστήμῃ, οὐκ ἐμπειρίᾳ οἰκείᾳ κεχρημένον. Γενναιότατος γοῦν, ἔφη, ἔοικεν εἶναι **C**

31. ᾗ Π: ᾖ A. 33. ᾗ Π: η A^1: ᾖ A^2.

---

26 **ἰατροὶ κτλ.** The combination of scientific knowledge (*πρὸς τῷ μανθάνειν τὴν τέχνην*) and medical experience which Plato desiderates reminds us of the standpoint of the *μεθοδικοί*, whose principles were in some respects a compromise between those of the *δογματικοί* or Theorists, and those of the Empirics: see Celsus l.c. pp. 9—13 and Häser *Lehrb. d. Gesch. d. Med.* etc. pp. 245 ff., 268 ff.

408 E 33 **ψυχῇ ψυχῆς.** Cf. *Gorg.* 523 C—E.

409 A, B 2 **αὐτήν**: *ipsam*, not *eam*, as Jowett apparently translates it.

6 **διὸ δὴ καὶ εὐήθεις.** "For unstained thoughts do seldom dream on evil: Birds never limed no secret bushes fear" (*Rape of Lucrece*). Cf. infra VII 517 D ff., *Theaet.* 174 C ff. The use of *παραδείγματα* recalls *Theaet.* 176 E, though the idea is somewhat different here. The word means 'models,' 'standards,' not 'samples of experience' (J. and C.), and *τοῖς πονηροῖς* is equivalent to *τοῖς τῶν πονηρῶν παραδείγμασι*. Cf. infra C, D, where *παράδειγμα τοῦ τοιούτου* is 'a model' (not 'a sample') 'of such a character.' So also Schneider, who translates by 'Vorbild.'

10 **ὀψιμαθῆ κτλ.** The common taunt *ὀψιμαθής* is in such a case an epithet of praise.

11 **οὐκ οἰκείαν κτλ.** For the asyndeton see 407 D *n.* *δεῖ αἰσθάνεσθαι* for *διαισθάνεσθαι* (Stob. *Flor.* 45. 96) is ingenious, but weak. As Steinhart remarks (*Einleitung* p. 173), the scientific knowledge of virtue, according to Socrates and Plato, implies a knowledge of its opposite, viz. vice: see on I 334 A, and cf. infra 409 D.

ὁ τοιοῦτος δικαστής. Καὶ ἀγαθός γε, ἦν δ' ἐγώ, ὃ σὺ ἠρώτας· ὁ γὰρ ἔχων ψυχὴν ἀγαθὴν ἀγαθός· ὁ δὲ δεινὸς ἐκεῖνος καὶ καχύποπτος, ὁ πολλὰ αὐτὸς ἠδικηκὼς καὶ πανοῦργός τε καὶ σοφὸς οἰόμενος εἶναι, ὅταν μὲν ὁμοίοις ὁμιλῇ, δεινὸς φαίνεται ἐξευλαβούμενος, πρὸς τὰ ἐν αὑτῷ παραδείγματα ἀποσκοπῶν· ὅταν δὲ ἀγαθοῖς
D καὶ πρεσβυτέροις ἤδη πλησιάσῃ, ἀβέλτερος αὖ φαίνεται, ἀπιστῶν παρὰ καιρὸν καὶ ἀγνοῶν ὑγιὲς ἦθος, ἅτε οὐκ ἔχων παράδειγμα τοῦ τοιούτου. πλεονάκις δὲ πονηροῖς ἢ χρηστοῖς ἐντυγχάνων σοφώτερος ἢ ἀμαθέστερος δοκεῖ εἶναι αὑτῷ τε καὶ ἄλλοις. Παντάπασι μὲν οὖν, ἔφη, ἀληθῆ.

XVII. Οὐ τοίνυν, ἦν δ' ἐγώ, τοιοῦτον χρὴ τὸν δικαστὴν ζητεῖν τὸν ἀγαθόν τε καὶ σοφόν, ἀλλὰ τὸν πρότερον. πονηρία μὲν γὰρ ἀρετήν τε καὶ αὑτὴν οὔποτ' ἂν γνοίη, ἀρετὴ δὲ φύσεως παιδευο-
E μένης χρόνῳ ἅμα αὑτῆς τε καὶ πονηρίας ἐπιστήμην λήψεται. σοφὸς οὖν οὗτος, ὥς μοι δοκεῖ, ἀλλ' οὐχ ὁ κακὸς γίγνεται. Καὶ ἐμοί, ἔφη, ξυνδοκεῖ. Οὐκοῦν καὶ ἰατρικὴν οἵαν εἴπομεν μετὰ τῆς τοιαύτης δικαστικῆς κατὰ πόλιν νομοθετήσεις, αἳ τῶν πολιτῶν σοι
410 τοὺς μὲν εὐφυεῖς τὰ σώματα καὶ | τὰς ψυχὰς θεραπεύσουσι, τοὺς δὲ μή, ὅσοι μὲν κατὰ σῶμα τοιοῦτοι, ἀποθνῄσκειν ἐάσουσιν, τοὺς

23. σοφώτερος A²Ξq: ἀσοφώτερος A¹Π²: ἀσαφώτερος (sic) Π¹.

---

409 C 18 **οἰόμενος.** Cf. *Theaet.* 173 B δεινοί τε καὶ σοφοὶ γεγονότες, ὡς οἴονται, and I 336 A *n.*

20 **καὶ πρεσβυτέροις κτλ.** The touching allusion to Socrates' condemnation will not escape the sympathetic reader. Plato seldom talks in this vein without thinking of his master: cf. *Theaet.* 174 C and the still more affecting words in VII 517 A. It is from incidental references such as these that we can best appreciate the profound influence which the death of Socrates exercised upon Plato. See also VIII 560 D *n.*

409 D 26 **πονηρία μὲν γὰρ—λήψεται.** See on 409 B and the suggestive remarks of Stewart on Aristotle's *Eth. Nic.* V I. 1129ᵃ 17. Strictly speaking, Vice cannot have *scientific* knowledge (ἐπιστήμη) even of herself, since Vice is ignorance (and scientific knowledge of Vice would imply a scientific knowledge of Virtue); but she recognises herself by ἐμπειρία οἰκεία: cf. 409 B.

27 **ἀρετὴ δὲ κτλ.**: 'whereas Virtue will in course of time, if natural endowments are improved by education, attain to scientific knowledge at once of herself and Vice.' The contrast between πονηρία μέν and ἀρετὴ δέ is much impaired if we connect ἀρετή with φύσεως (in the sense of 'a virtuous nature'): and for this reason I now agree with Schneider in thinking φύσεως παιδευομένης a genitive absolute. I formerly accepted Richards' emendation παιδευομένη, which is decidedly more logical, if φύσεως depends on ἀρετή: but Schneider's view is better. χρόνῳ belongs to λήψεται, and not to παιδευομένης (as if 'educated by time,' Jowett): mere lapse of time will never give ἐπιστήμη. Cf. ὀψιμαθῆ and ἐν πολλῷ χρόνῳ διαισθάνεσθαι in 409 B.

410 A 2 **ἀποθνῄσκειν ἐάσουσιν.** Cf. Plut. *Apophth. Lac.* 231 A κράτιστον δὲ ἔλεγε (sc. Παυσανίας) τοῦτον ἰατρὸν εἶναι τὸν μὴ κατασήποντα τοὺς ἀρρωστοῦντας, ἀλλὰ τάχιστα θάπτοντα. In laying down this law, Plato speaks from the standpoint of the Regal or Political Art, prescribing for the subordinate arts of Medicine and Justice the conditions under

δὲ κατὰ τὴν ψυχὴν κακοφυεῖς καὶ ἀνιάτους αὐτοὶ ἀποκτενοῦσιν; Τὸ γοῦν ἄριστον, ἔφη, αὐτοῖς τε τοῖς πάσχουσιν καὶ τῇ πόλει οὕτω πέφανται. Οἱ δὲ δὴ νέοι, ἦν δ' ἐγώ, δῆλον ὅτι εὐλαβήσονταί σοι δικαστικῆς εἰς χρείαν ἰέναι, τῇ ἁπλῇ ἐκείνῃ μουσικῇ χρώμενοι, ἣν δὴ ἔφαμεν σωφροσύνην ἐντίκτειν. Τί μήν; ἔφη. Ἆρ' οὖν οὐ κατὰ ταὐτὰ | ἴχνη ταῦτα ὁ μουσικὸς γυμναστικὴν διώκων, ἐὰν B ἐθέλῃ, αἱρήσει, ὥστε μηδὲν ἰατρικῆς δεῖσθαι ὅ τι μὴ ἀνάγκη; Ἔμοιγε δοκεῖ. Αὐτὰ μὴν τὰ γυμνάσια καὶ τοὺς πόνους πρὸς τὸ θυμοειδὲς τῆς φύσεως βλέπων κἀκεῖνο ἐγείρων πονήσει μᾶλλον ἢ πρὸς ἰσχύν, οὐχ ὥσπερ οἱ ἄλλοι ἀθληταὶ ῥώμης ἕνεκα σιτία καὶ πόνους μεταχειρίζονται. Ὀρθότατα, ἦ δ' ὅς. Ἆρ' οὖν, ἦν δ' ἐγώ, ὦ Γλαύκων, καὶ οἱ καθιστάντες μουσικῇ καὶ γυμναστικῇ | παιδεύειν οὐχ οὗ ἕνεκά τινες οἴονται καθιστᾶσιν, ἵνα τῇ μὲν τὸ C

13. *μεταχειρίζονται* Galenus (v p. 875 Kühn): *μεταχειριεῖται* codd.

---

which it is good to live and good to die. See Grote *Plato* I p. 362.

3 **αὐτοί** = *ipsi* is said in opposition to the mere 'permission to die' which bodily disease requires. *αὐταί* (suggested by Richards) is unnecessary: see II 377 C *n.*

410 A—**412** B *Our young men will seldom need the help of judges and doctors, thanks to their education in Music and Gymnastic. They will pursue both arts with a view to the cultivation of the soul rather than of the body. Exclusive devotion to one of the two makes men in the one case hard and fierce, in the other, effeminate and mild. The psychological elements of Spirit and the Love of Knowledge must be attuned to one another. Music and Gymnastic are intended to effect this harmony: and excess or deficiency in either of these educative instruments reflects itself in morbid and degenerate phases of character. He who can best blend Music with Gymnastic is the true musician; and such an one we must provide in our city, if it is to last.*

410 A 7 **ἆρ' οὖν κτλ.** This epilogue describes concisely the aim and underlying principle of Plato's earlier scheme of education. Its object is to produce citizens who shall combine gentleness and strength—sensibility and courage—intellectual activity and moral stedfastness. It is an ideal in which the distinctive virtues of Athens and Sparta—of Greece and Rome—are united and transfigured. See II 375 C and the passages referred to there. The ideal of Pericles (*φιλοσοφεῖν ἄνευ μαλακίας*) in many ways resembles Plato's (Thuc. II 40). Cf. also Nettleship *Hell.* pp. 88—90 and Bosanquet *Companion* pp. 115—117. It is noteworthy that the doctrine of this section is best explained by a comparison with one of the dialogues often held to be late (*Pol.* 306 C—311 C): see also *Laws* 773 C, D. This is not pointed out by Krohn in his otherwise acute analysis (*Pl. St.* pp. 24—28).

410 B 8 **ὁ μουσικὸς—αἱρήσει.** *ὁ μουσικός* is *ὁ τῇ ἁπλῇ μουσικῇ χρώμενος*, as defined in the last sentence. *ἴχνη διώκων* and *αἱρήσει* are metaphors from the chase: see II 375 A.

10 **αὐτὰ μὴν—ἰσχύν.** The theory of gymnastic propounded here was apparently new in Plato's time (see on II 376 E), although the practice of athletics as an educative discipline, especially at Sparta, conformed to it in no small measure (see Plut. *Lyc.* 17 ff., Xen. *Rep. Lac.* 2 ff.).

13 **μεταχειρίζονται.** See *cr. n.* I have followed Hermann in adopting Galen's text. With *οὐχ* (*μή*) *ὡς* or *ὥσπερ* the verb should have for its subject the nominative contained in the *ὡς* clause: cf. VII 539 D, X 610 D. *Symp.* 179 E is in reality no exception to this rule.

410 C 15 **τινες.** It has been supposed that *τινες* refers to Isocrates, who in his *Antidosis* (180—185) expounds at

σῶμα θεραπεύοιντο, τῇ δὲ τὴν ψυχήν; Ἀλλὰ τί μήν; ἔφη. Κινδυνεύουσιν, ἦν δ' ἐγώ, ἀμφότερα τῆς ψυχῆς ἕνεκα τὸ μέγιστον καθιστάναι. Πῶς δή; Οὐκ ἐννοεῖς, εἶπον, ὡς διατίθενται αὐτὴν τὴν διάνοιαν οἳ ἂν γυμναστικῇ μὲν διὰ βίου ὁμιλήσωσιν, μουσικῆς δὲ μὴ ἅψωνται; ἢ ὅσοι ἂν τοὐναντίον διατεθῶσιν; Τίνος δέ, ἦ
D δ' ὅς, | πέρι λέγεις; Ἀγριότητός τε καὶ σκληρότητος, καὶ αὖ μαλακίας τε καὶ ἡμερότητος, ἦν δ' ἐγώ. Ἔγωγε, ἔφη, ὅτι οἱ μὲν γυμναστικῇ ἀκράτῳ χρησάμενοι ἀγριώτεροι τοῦ δέοντος ἀποβαίνουσιν, οἱ δὲ μουσικῇ μαλακώτεροι αὖ γίγνονται ἢ ὡς κάλλιον αὐτοῖς. Καὶ μήν, ἦν δ' ἐγώ, τό γε ἄγριον τὸ θυμοειδὲς ἂν τῆς φύσεως παρέχοιτο, καὶ ὀρθῶς μὲν τραφὲν ἀνδρεῖον ἂν εἴη, μᾶλλον δ' ἐπιταθὲν τοῦ δέοντος σκληρόν τε καὶ χαλεπὸν γίγνοιτ' ἄν, ὡς
E τὸ εἰκός. Δοκεῖ μοι, ἔφη. Τί δέ; τὸ ἥμερον | οὐχ ἡ φιλόσοφος ἂν ἔχοι φύσις; καὶ μᾶλλον μὲν ἀνεθέντος αὐτοῦ μαλακώτερον εἴη

---

length the usual Greek view of gymnastic. This is possible only if the present section was added within the last four years or so of Plato's life, which is most improbable. See Hirmer *Entst. u. Komp. d. pl. Pol.* p. 663, and *Introd.* § 4. In other passages the *Antidosis* has been held to presuppose the *Republic*: see Dümmler *Chronologische Beitr.* etc. pp. 12, 13.

καθιστᾶσιν. Cf. Dem. 24. 145 οὗτος γὰρ (sc. ὁ νόμος)—οὐκ ἐπὶ τοῖς κεκριμένοις—κεῖται, ἀλλ' ἐπὶ τοῖς ἀκρίτοις, ἵνα μὴ—ἀναγκάζοιντο ἀγωνίζεσθαι, and *Phil.* 34 C (where however it is easy to write λάβωμεν). In the first of these cases the reference is, as here, to the establishment of laws or ordinances. καθιστᾶσιν is used somewhat like φησί 407 A. Madvig's emendation καθίστασαν commends itself to Weber (*Entwick. d. Absichtssätze* in Schanz's *Beiträge* II 2 p. 58) and others, but has not yet been proved to be necessary, and καθιστάναι below tells rather against it. For other examples of the idiom see Kühner *Gr. Gr.* II pp. 897, 898. Cases like Soph. *O. C.* 11 and *El.* 57, 760 are different, and have been justly emended. As regards the sentiment, it is characteristic of Plato to invent a historical sanction for his theories (cf. 414 B ff.); but he doubtless sincerely believed that the spirit of Greek gymnastics had degenerated.

410 D 22 **ἦν δ' ἐγώ.** There seems to be no other case in which ἦν δ' ἐγώ is so long deferred. Stallbaum and Bekker insert the words after σκληρότητος without any MS authority. If change is needed, ἦν δ' ἐγώ had better be omitted (so *q*, whose reading is very different here). But it is better to note than to obliterate such peculiarities.

24 **ἢ ὡς** is not 'pro simplici ἤ vel ὡς positum' (Stallbaum), but = 'quam quomodo.'

410 E 29 **αὐτοῦ.** Does the pronoun mean τοῦ ἡμέρου or τοῦ φιλοσόφου? Four qualities are first distinguished: viz. the wild, the hard, the soft and the tame. The source of wildness is the spirited element, which if rightly cultivated becomes brave, if unduly strained, hard. So far, all is clear; but difficulties now begin. We should expect Plato to continue: τὸ ἥμερον is an attribute of τὸ φιλόσοφον, and τὸ φιλόσοφον—not τὸ ἥμερον—when relaxed becomes too soft, when rightly educated becomes κόσμιον (the virtue which contrasts with τὸ ἀνδρεῖον). At first sight, then, it looks as if αὐτοῦ meant 'the philosophic temperament' (so Stallbaum and J. and C.); but this is grammatically impossible, unless we make τὸ ἥμερον the subject to μαλακώτερον εἴη and therefore to ἥμερόν τε καὶ κόσμιον, which is hardly tolerable. We must therefore acquiesce in taking αὐτοῦ as τοῦ ἡμέρου, unless there is corruption somewhere. If Plato had written καὶ μᾶλλον μὲν ἀνεθὲν μαλακώτερον εἴη τοῦ δέοντος, καλῶς δὲ τραφὲν σῶφρόν τε καὶ κόσμιον, everything would be clear,

τοῦ δέοντος, καλῶς δὲ τραφέντος ἥμερόν τε καὶ κόσμιον; Ἔστι
ταῦτα. Δεῖν δέ γέ φαμεν τοὺς φύλακας ἀμφοτέρα ἔχειν τούτω τὼ
φύσει. Δεῖ γάρ. Οὐκοῦν ἡρμόσθαι δεῖ αὐτὰς πρὸς ἀλλήλας;
Πῶς δ' οὔ; Καὶ τοῦ μὲν ἡρμοσμένου σώφρων τε καὶ ἀνδρεία ἡ |
ψυχή; Πάνυ γε. Τοῦ δὲ ἀναρμόστου δειλὴ καὶ ἄγροικος; Καὶ 411
μάλα.

XVIII. Οὐκοῦν ὅταν μέν τις μουσικῇ παρέχῃ καταυλεῖν καὶ
καταχεῖν τῆς ψυχῆς διὰ τῶν ὤτων ὥσπερ διὰ χώνης ἃς νῦν δὴ
ἡμεῖς ἐλέγομεν τὰς γλυκείας τε καὶ μαλακὰς καὶ θρηνώδεις ἁρμονίας,
καὶ μινυρίζων τε καὶ γεγανωμένος ὑπὸ τῆς ᾠδῆς διατελῇ τὸν βίον
ὅλον, οὗτος τὸ μὲν πρῶτον, εἴ τι θυμοειδὲς εἶχεν, ὥσπερ σίδηρον B
ἐμάλαξεν καὶ χρήσιμον ἐξ ἀχρήστου καὶ σκληροῦ ἐποίησεν· ὅταν

31. ἀμφοτέρα Schneider: ἀμφότερα codd.

but I do not venture to change the text. σῶφρον for ἥμερον is suggested also by Krohn (*Pl. St.* p. 26). Apelt proposes ἔμμετρον (*Berl. Philol. Wochenschr.* 1895 p. 969).

31 **ἀμφοτέρα—φύσει**: viz. τὸ θυμοειδές and τὸ φιλόσοφον.

33 **σώφρων τε καὶ ἀνδρεία**. σωφροσύνη is the virtue of τὸ φιλόσοφον, ἀνδρεία of τὸ θυμοειδές: cf. 399 C and *Pol.* 307 C. The meaning would be caught more easily if Plato had written—as perhaps he did—σῶφρόν τε καὶ κόσμιον for ἥμερόν τε καὶ κόσμιον above, just as he wrote ἀνδρεῖον (410 D). ἄγροικος (implying, like ἀνελεύθερος, ἀνδραποδώδης, with which it is coupled in *Laws* 880 A, lack of power to control the feelings) is properly opposed to σώφρων here.

411 A 3 **καταυλεῖν—ἁρμονίας**. καταυλεῖν (as Ast observes) does not govern ἁρμονίας, but is used absolutely: cf. *Laws* 790 E (of mothers singing and rocking their children to sleep) ἀτεχνῶς οἷον καταυλοῦσι τῶν παιδίων, καθάπερ αἱ τῶν ἐκφρόνων βακχειῶν ἰάσεις, ταύτῃ τῇ τῆς κινήσεως ἅμα χορείᾳ καὶ μούσῃ χρώμεναι. So expressive a word could ill be spared, although van Heusde's καταντλεῖν is ingenious enough. Cobet would read καταντλεῖν and cut out καὶ καταχεῖν, while Hartman inclines to eject καταυλεῖν καί, but the text is sound. ἁρμονίας depends on καταχεῖν. With χώνης cf. (with Hiller *Fl. Jahrb.* 1874 p. 174) Ar. *Thesm.* 18 δίκην δὲ χοάνης ὦτα: see Blaydes ad loc. The context in Aristophanes lends some colour to Hiller's notion that the comparison was taken from some earlier philosopher: cf. Theophr. *de sensu* § 9.

411 B 7 **σίδηρον ἐμάλαξε κτλ.** See on 387 C. Apparently then the first effect even of the μαλακαὶ ἁρμονίαι is good. This apparent inconsistency with 398 E ff. is emphasized by Krohn (*Pl. St.* p. 25), but Krohn fails to observe that Plato is here describing the facts of common experience, whereas before he was making laws of his own. It is quite possible to admit that the relaxing modes are beneficial in moderation, and yet forbid them, because moderation in them is difficult to maintain.

8 **ὅταν—τήκει.** The object of κηλῇ, τήκει and λείβει is τὸ θυμοειδές: that of ποιήσῃ is τὴν ψυχήν. So much is, I think, certain; but ἐπέχων is less easy. The word has been interpreted as (1) 'listening to' (Schneider, comparing 399 B, where, however, ὑπέχοντα should probably be read), (2) 'pressing on,' 'persevering,' 'continuing': cf. *Theaet.* 165 D ἐπέχων καὶ οὐκ ἀνιείς (J. and C.). The sense which Schneider gives to ἐπέχων is ill-supported: and we must accept the second alternative. Morgenstern's emendation ἐπιχέων (accepted by Herwerden and Hartman) is attractive but not quite convincing ("when he ceases not to pour the music in" etc.). ἐπιχέων would preserve the metaphor, which is clearly intended (in καταχεῖν, χώνης, and σίδηρον ἐμάλαξε) to suggest the process of smelting, and of which an echo still survives in τήκει, λείβει and ἐκτήξῃ. See

δ' ἐπέχων μὴ ἀνιῇ ἀλλὰ κηλῇ, τὸ μετὰ τοῦτο ἤδη τήκει καὶ λείβει, ἕως ἂν ἐκτήξῃ τὸν θυμὸν καὶ ἐκτέμῃ ὥσπερ νεῦρα ἐκ τῆς ψυχῆς καὶ ποιήσῃ μαλθακὸν αἰχμητήν. Πάνυ μὲν οὖν, ἔφη. Καὶ ἐὰν μέν γε, ἦν δ' ἐγώ, ἐξ ἀρχῆς φύσει ἄθυμον λάβῃ, ταχὺ τοῦτο διεπράξατο· ἐὰν δὲ θυμοειδῆ, ἀσθενῆ ποιήσας τὸν θυμὸν ὀξύρροπον C ἀπειργάσατο, ἀπὸ σμικρῶν | ταχὺ ἐρεθιζόμενόν τε καὶ κατασβεννύμενον. ἀκράχολοι οὖν καὶ ὀργίλοι ἀντὶ θυμοειδοῦς γεγένηνται, δυσκολίας ἔμπλεοι. Κομιδῇ μὲν οὖν. Τί δέ; ἂν αὖ γυμναστικῇ πολλὰ πονῇ καὶ εὐωχῆται εὖ μάλα, μουσικῆς δὲ καὶ φιλοσοφίας μὴ ἅπτηται, οὐ πρῶτον μὲν εὖ ἴσχων τὸ σῶμα φρονήματός τε καὶ θυμοῦ ἐμπίμπλαται καὶ ἀνδρειότερος γίγνεται αὐτὸς αὑτοῦ; Καὶ μάλα γε. Τί δέ; ἐπειδὰν ἄλλο μηδὲν πράττῃ μηδὲ κοινωνῇ D Μούσης μηδαμῇ, | οὐκ εἴ τι καὶ ἐνῆν αὐτοῦ φιλομαθὲς ἐν τῇ ψυχῇ, ἅτε οὔτε μαθήματος γευόμενον οὐδενὸς οὔτε ζητήματος, οὔτε λόγου μετίσχον οὔτε τῆς ἄλλης μουσικῆς, ἀσθενές τε καὶ κωφὸν καὶ τυφλὸν γίγνεται, ἅτε οὐκ ἐγειρόμενον οὐδὲ τρεφόμενον οὐδὲ διακαθαιρομένων τῶν αἰσθήσεων αὐτοῦ; Οὕτως, ἔφη. Μισόλογος δή,

15. ἀκράχολοι Π: ἀκρόχολοι A. Cf. Lobeck *Phryn.* p. 664. γεγένηνται $A^2Π^2Ξ$ *q*: γεγένηται $A^1Π^1$. 16. γυμναστικῇ $A^1Π$: γυμναστικὸς corr. A^2. 22. γευόμενον *q*: γενομένου A: γευομένου Π. 24, 25. διακαθαιρομένων $A^2Ξ$ *q*: διακαθαιρόμενον $A^1Π$.

Blümner *Technologie* etc. IV pp. 108 ff. *nn.* The θυμοειδές is the iron which music softens and may even dissolve: farther than this the comparison is not to be pressed.

9 **κηλῇ**: as one might charm or fascinate a snake: *Euthyd.* 290 A, *Phaedr.* 259 A.

καὶ λείβει—αἰχμητήν. For λείβει thus used cf. Ar. *Knights* 327. μαλθακὸς αἰχμητής is said of Menelaus in *Il.* XVII 588.

12 **ἐὰν—λάβῃ**: 'if he has received,' not 'if he act upon' (J. and C.). Plato means that if the individual in question received at the beginning a soul—ψυχήν is understood—naturally spiritless, he soon makes it a 'feeble warrior.' "Wenn er gleich eine von Natur zornlose Seele bekommen hat" (Schneider). The subject throughout is the τις with which the sentence began. For the usual Greek idiom, by which the person concerned is represented as acting on himself (ἐκτήξῃ τὸν θυμόν etc.) instead of being acted on, cf. Eur. *I. A.* 187 φοινίσσουσα παρῆδ' ἐμὰν | αἰσχύνᾳ νεοθαλεῖ with Headlam's note: also V 462 C, D *nn.* and IX 572 A *n.*

411 C 14 **ἐρεθιζόμενον.** ῥιπιζόμενον, suggested by Herwerden, is picturesque enough: but 'provoked and extinguished' is even more natural in Greek than in English, for ἐρεθίζω could readily be used of fanning a fire: see the *lexica* s.v.

15 **ἀντὶ θυμοειδοῦς—ἔμπλεοι.** θυμοειδοῦς is of course masculine and not neuter (as J. and C. suggest). Even if we allow that the dative is neuter in cases like *Symp.* 195 C νέος—ἐστι, πρὸς δὲ τῷ νέῳ ἁπαλός, and *Theaet.* 185 E, the presence of the article makes all the difference. Ast (with Ξ) reads θυμοειδῶν. So harsh a change from plural to singular (ὀργίλοι but θυμοειδοῦς) is remarkable, but hardly more so than ἀποθανουμένους ὅς in IV 426 C. Cf. also I 347 A *n.* Krohn points out that ἀνδρεῖον is here represented as a μεσότης between σκληρόν and ὀργίλον (*Pl. St.* p. 27).

17 **εὐωχῆται**: should be understood literally, of good living.

οἶμαι, ὁ τοιοῦτος γίγνεται καὶ ἄμουσος, καὶ πειθοῖ μὲν διὰ λόγων
οὐδὲν ἔτι χρῆται, βίᾳ δὲ καὶ ἀγριότητι ὥσπερ θηρίον | πρὸς πάντα **E**
διαπράττεται, καὶ ἐν ἀμαθίᾳ καὶ σκαιότητι μετὰ ἀρρυθμίας τε καὶ
ἀχαριστίας ζῇ. Παντάπασιν, ἦ δ' ὅς, οὕτως ἔχει. Ἐπὶ δὴ δύ'
ὄντε τούτω, ὡς ἔοικε, δύο τέχνα θεὸν ἔγωγ' ἄν τινα φαίην δεδωκέναι
τοῖς ἀνθρώποις, μουσικήν τε καὶ γυμναστικὴν ἐπὶ τὸ θυμοειδὲς καὶ
τὸ φιλόσοφον, οὐκ ἐπὶ ψυχὴν καὶ σῶμα, εἰ μὴ εἴη πάρεργον, ἀλλ'
ἐπ' ἐκείνω, ὅπως ἂν ἀλλήλοιν ξυναρμοσθῆτον | ἐπιτεινομένω καὶ **412**
ἀνιεμένω μέχρι τοῦ προσήκοντος. Καὶ γὰρ ἔοικεν, ἔφη. Τὸν
κάλλιστ' ἄρα μουσικῇ γυμναστικὴν κεραννύντα καὶ μετριώτατα
τῇ ψυχῇ προσφέροντα, τοῦτον ὀρθότατ' ἂν φαῖμεν εἶναι τελέως
μουσικώτατον καὶ εὐαρμοστότατον, πολὺ μᾶλλον ἢ τὸν τὰς χορδὰς
ἀλλήλαις ξυνιστάντα. Εἰκότως γ', ἔφη, ὦ Σώκρατες. Οὐκοῦν
καὶ ἐν τῇ πόλει ἡμῖν, ὦ Γλαύκων, δεήσει τοῦ τοιούτου τινὸς ἀεὶ

29. ἀχαριστίας $A^1\Pi$: ἀχαρισίας corr. A^2. ἐπὶ δὴ *q* : ἐπειδὴ A : ἐπεὶ δὴ ΠΞ. 32. εἴη πάρεργον Π^2 *q* : εἶπερ εργον (sic) A^1 : ᾗ πάρεργον A^2 : εἰ πάρεργον Π^1 : ᾗ (i.e. ᾖ) πάρεργον Ξ. 3. μετριώτατα Ξ q^2 : μετριότατα AΠ q^1.

---

411 D 27 **ὥσπερ θήριον—διαπράττεται.** If the MSS are right, πάντα is masculine. But although διαπράττεσθαι by itself can be used without an expressed object (*Prot.* 319 C al.), it is strange to find διαπράττεσθαι πρός τινα so used: see *Crat.* 395 B, *Alc.* II 143 C. On this account διαπράττεται has been by some ejected (Hermann), by others emended into διαράττεται (Morgenstern), διατάττεται (Madvig and one Florentine MS); while others read θηρίον τὰ πάντα διαπράττεται (Lambrechts), or προσδιαπράττεται πάντα (Chandler), or expunge πρός (Bywater). Perhaps we should read ὥσπερ θηρίον πρὸς <θηρίον> κτλ. ('attains all his ends by violence and ferocity, like one wild beast with another'). Cf. Shakespeare *Rape of Lucrece* "The rough beast that knows no gentle right."

411 E 28 **σκαιότητι.** 'Ineptitude.' Cf. Soph. *Ant.* 1028 with Jebb's note.

29 **ἀχαριστίας** is 'ungraciousness.'

32 **εἰ μὴ εἴη πάρεργον** occurs also in *Phaed.* 91 A (according to the Bodleian MS). Phrases of this kind seldom admit of variation; for which reason we should hesitate to admit the εἰ μὴ εἰ πάρεργον of Π^1.

33 **ὅπως ἂν κτλ.** The soul has, so to speak, two strings, the φιλόσοφον and the θυμοειδές, which make a kind of ἁρμονία when they are tuned to the proper pitch by Music and Gymnastic. The θυμοειδές is slackened (ἀνίεται) by μουσική, tightened or braced (ἐπιτείνεται) by γυμναστική (410 D, 411 A—E); conversely, we must suppose that the φιλόσοφον is slackened by γυμναστική, and tightened by μουσική. Music and Gymnastic are therefore both of them necessary for each of the two strings (cf. IV 441 E *n.*), although the slackening of the θυμοειδές of itself also tightens the φιλόσοφον, which is likewise slackened when the tension of the other is increased. Cf. *Tim.* 88 B, C. The effect of all this musical imagery is to suggest that Character is the Music of the Soul: cf. *Lach.* 188 D.

412 A 7 **τοῦ—ἐπιστάτου.** Some MSS (including Ξ and *q*) omit τοῦ, and no precise parallel has yet been adduced for ὁ τοιοῦτός τις used in this way. In IX 581 E, cited by Schneider (*Addit.* p. 27), Paris A has ἐν τοιούτῳ τινί, not ἐν τῷ τοιούτῳ τινί. The article may perhaps be justified by the description of the ἐπιστάτης in the last sentence, and τινὸς taken closely with τοιούτου ('some such superintendent as we have described'); but there is certainly some ground for suspecting interpolation (with Bekker and others). The ἐπιστάτης, as Jowett observes, is a sort of minister of education,

B ἐπιστάτου, εἰ μέλλει ἡ πολιτεία σῴζεσθαι; Δεήσει μέντοι, ὡς οἷόν τέ γε μάλιστα.

XIX. Οἱ μὲν δὴ τύποι τῆς παιδείας τε καὶ τροφῆς οὗτοι ἂν εἶεν. χορείας γὰρ τί ἄν τις διεξίοι τῶν τοιούτων καὶ θήρας τε καὶ κυνηγέσια καὶ γυμνικοὺς ἀγῶνας καὶ ἱππικούς; σχεδὸν γάρ τι δῆλα δή, ὅτι τούτοις ἑπόμενα δεῖ αὐτὰ εἶναι, καὶ οὐκέτι χαλεπὰ εὑρεῖν. Ἴσως, ἦ δ᾽ ὅς, οὐ χαλεπά. Εἶεν, ἦν δ᾽ ἐγώ· τὸ δὴ μετὰ τοῦτο τί ἂν ἡμῖν διαιρετέον εἴη; ἆρ᾽ οὐκ αὐτῶν τούτων οἵτινες
C ἄρξουσί τε καὶ ἄρξονται; Τί μήν; Ὅτι μὲν πρεσβυτέρους τοὺς ἄρχοντας δεῖ εἶναι, νεωτέρους δὲ τοὺς ἀρχομένους, δῆλον; Δῆλον. Καὶ ὅτι γε τοὺς ἀρίστους αὐτῶν; Καὶ τοῦτο. Οἱ δὲ γεωργῶν ἄριστοι ἆρ᾽ οὐ γεωργικώτατοι γίγνονται; Ναί. Νῦν δ᾽, ἐπειδὴ φυλάκων αὐτοὺς ἀρίστους δεῖ εἶναι, ἆρ᾽ οὐ φυλακικωτάτους πόλεως; Ναί. Οὐκοῦν φρονίμους τε εἰς τοῦτο δεῖ ὑπάρχειν καὶ δυνατοὺς

---

such as we find in *Laws* 765 D ff. The same function is in *Pol.* 308 D ff. assigned to the Regal or Political Art.

412 B 8 **ὡς οἷόν τέ γε μάλιστα.** I have placed a comma before ὡς; cf. *Phaed.* 74 B φῶμεν μέντοι νὴ Δί᾽, ἔφη ὁ Σιμμίας, θαυμαστῶς γε (Hoefer *Part. Plat.* p. 33).

412 B—**414** B *So much for Education. It remains to ask 'Which of the guardians are to be our rulers?' The elder shall rule the younger, and the better the worse. Now the best guardians are those who care most for their country and her interests. We shall make our selection on this principle; and we must further try those whom we select and see whether their patriotism is proof against all seductive influences. Every true opinion or belief—and the belief on which patriotism rests is true,—like everything else which we call good, is unwillingly discarded, but may be forcibly expelled by persuasion or forgetfulness, by pain, pleasure and the like. We shall apply these tests to prove our guardians. Those who emerge unscathed will become our rulers. They are the true Guardians; the others should be called Auxiliaries.*

412 B ff. This is the first appearance of the Rulers in Plato's State, if we except the passing allusion in 389 C. Their presence is necessary to take the place of the original νομοθέτης when the State has once been founded (VI 497 D); they represent in fact the Royal or Kingly art, whose business it is to prescribe to others their specific good or end. See on 410 A and Nohle *die Statslehre Platos* pp. 47 f., 85 ff., 113 ff. Such is their duty according to the later books; but here it is not so described, and the whole subject is treated in an exoteric way. The full and esoteric discussion of this subject is reserved for VI and VII. To this later treatment reference is made in 414 A and 416 B. The advocates of the original unity of the *Republic* justly lay stress upon the tentative and provisional nature of the regulations here laid down (e.g. Susemihl *Gen. Entw.* p. 143, Zeller[4] II 1. p. 560 *n.*); whereas the separatists hold that Plato's wider conception of the Ruling class is chronologically later than the account now given (Krohn *Pl. St.* pp. 28—31). An excellent defence of the conservative view will be found in Hirmer *Entst. u. Komp. d. pl. Pol.* pp. 613 ff. See also *Introd.* § 4.

11 **χορείας—ἱππικούς.** See *Laws* 814 D ff., 822 D ff., 830 C ff., 832 D ff.

13 **οὐκέτι**: 'not now,' sc. when we have trained our Guardians. On such idiomatic uses of οὐκέτι and its opposite ἤδη see Cope's *Rhetoric of Aristotle*, Vol. I p. 13.

412 C 16 **πρεσβυτέρους κτλ.** The different principles on which rulers may be appointed are fully discussed in *Laws* 690 A ff.

21 **φρονίμους κτλ.** Intellectual ability and accomplishments, authority, and pa-

καὶ ἔτι κηδεμόνας τῆς πόλεως; | *Ἔστι ταῦτα. Κήδοιτο δέ γ' ἄν* D
τις μάλιστα τούτου ὃ τυγχάνοι φιλῶν. Ἀνάγκη. Καὶ μὴν τοῦτό
γ' ἂν μάλιστα φιλοῖ, ᾧ ξυμφέρειν ἡγοῖτο τὰ αὐτὰ καὶ ἑαυτῷ καὶ
ἐκείνου μὲν εὖ πράττοντος οἴοιτο ξυμβαίνειν καὶ ἑαυτῷ εὖ πράττειν,
μὴ δέ, τοὐναντίον. Οὕτως, ἔφη. Ἐκλεκτέον ἄρ' ἐκ τῶν ἄλλων
φυλάκων τοιούτους ἄνδρας, οἳ ἂν σκοποῦσιν ἡμῖν μάλιστα φαίνωνται
παρὰ πάντα τὸν βίον, ὃ μὲν ἂν τῇ πόλει ἡγήσωνται | *ξυμφέρειν,* E
πάσῃ προθυμίᾳ ποιεῖν, ὃ δ' ἂν μή, μηδενὶ τρόπῳ πρᾶξαι ἂν ἐθέλειν.
Ἐπιτήδειοι γάρ, ἔφη. Δοκεῖ δή μοι τηρητέον αὐτοὺς εἶναι ἐν
ἁπάσαις ταῖς ἡλικίαις, εἰ φυλακικοί εἰσι τούτου τοῦ δόγματος
καὶ μήτε γοητευόμενοι μήτε βιαζόμενοι ἐκβάλλουσιν ἐπιλανθανό-
μενοι δόξαν τὴν τοῦ ποιεῖν δεῖν ἃ τῇ πόλει βέλτιστα. Τίνα, ἔφη,
λέγεις τὴν ἐκβολήν; Ἐγώ σοι, ἔφην, ἐρῶ. φαίνεταί μοι δόξα
ἐξιέναι ἐκ διανοίας ἢ ἑκουσίως ἢ ἀκουσίως, ἑκουσίως μὲν ἡ ψευ|δὴς 413
τοῦ μεταμανθάνοντος, ἀκουσίως δὲ πᾶσα ἡ ἀληθής. Τὸ μὲν τῆς
ἑκουσίου, ἔφη, μανθάνω, τὸ δὲ τῆς ἀκουσίου δέομαι μαθεῖν. Τί δαί;
οὐ καὶ σὺ ἡγεῖ, ἔφην ἐγώ, τῶν μὲν ἀγαθῶν ἀκουσίως στέρεσθαι

24. *καὶ ἐκείνου* Hermann: *καὶ ὅταν μάλιστα ἐκείνου* codd.

---

triotic sentiment are the three requisites of the Rulers as laid down here. In VI and VII it is the first which is emphasized, here it is the last. This is in harmony with the whole spirit of I—IV, in which, as Krohn remarks (*Pl. St.* p. 29), "the intellect is subordinated to the moral powers, and with the education of the character in richly-endowed natures the fruits of insight ripen of themselves."

412 D 24 **καὶ ἐκείνου.** See *cr. n.* Stobaeus (*Flor.* 43. 152) reads *καὶ ὅτι* (or *ὅ τι*) *μάλιστα ἐκείνου κτλ.*, which is good enough Greek, and would mean 'whatever policy he thinks by bringing prosperity to the other brings prosperity also to himself,' *ὅ τι* being an accusative of respect belonging to *εὖ πράττοντος*. If the principle of this interpretation is right, I should read *ὅ τι ἂν* for *ὅταν*, taking *ἂν* with *ξυμβαίνειν*. *ἂν* loves the shelter of a relative, particularly *ὅ τι*, and the corruption is the easier because *ὅταν* in A and other MSS is written *ὅτ' ἄν*. But *φιλεῖν* cannot well be said of one's attitude to a policy or course of action; and Hermann's proposal gives a more satisfactory sense. The occurrence of (*τοῦτ*)*ό γ' ἂν μάλιστα* just before may be responsible for the slip. It is to be understood—though Plato has not expressly said so—that the guardians believe their own interests to be best consulted by promoting those of their country. *μὴ δέ* is *μὴ δὲ εὖ πράττοντος*, and *τοὐναντίον* is *ξυμβαίνειν καὶ ἑαυτῷ κακῶς πράττειν*.

412 E 32 **ἐπιλανθανόμενοι** helps out the idea in *ἐκβάλλουσιν* and forms a natural antithesis to *φυλακικοί* which, while playing upon *φύλακες*, also implies the notion of remembering: cf. *φύλαξ μουσικῆς* 413 E. The word has been undeservedly attacked, chiefly because in 413 B it receives a more special and precise signification. But each of the three temptations to be presently enumerated, *κλοπή*, *βία* and *γοητεία*, may be correctly described as varieties of forgetting; nor is it in Plato's manner to introduce a classification prematurely, as he would have done by writing *μήτε γοητευόμενοι μήτε βιαζόμενοι* — < *μήτε* > *ἐπιλανθανόμενοι* (with Heller), or adding *μήτε κλεπτόμενοι* before *ἐκβάλλουσιν* (with Hartman). Cobet, *more suo*, expunges the word.

35 **ἑκουσίως ἢ ἀκουσίως**: with reference to the usual Socratic theory that Knowledge or Virtue is voluntary, Ignorance or Vice involuntary: see on II 382 A.

τοὺς ἀνθρώπους, τῶν δὲ κακῶν ἑκουσίως; ἢ οὐ τὸ μὲν ἐψεῦσθαι
τῆς ἀληθείας κακόν, τὸ δὲ ἀληθεύειν ἀγαθόν; ἢ οὐ τὸ τὰ ὄντα
δοξάζειν ἀληθεύειν δοκεῖ σοι εἶναι; Ἀλλ', ἦ δ' ὅς, ὀρθῶς λέγεις,
καί μοι δοκοῦσιν ἄκοντες ἀληθοῦς δόξης στερίσκεσθαι. Οὐκοῦν
B | κλαπέντες ἢ γοητευθέντες ἢ βιασθέντες τοῦτο πάσχουσιν; Οὐδὲ
νῦν, ἔφη, μανθάνω. Τραγικῶς, ἦν δ' ἐγώ, κινδυνεύω λέγειν.
κλαπέντας μὲν γὰρ τοὺς μεταπεισθέντας λέγω καὶ τοὺς ἐπιλανθα-
νομένους, ὅτι τῶν μὲν χρόνος, τῶν δὲ λόγος ἐξαιρούμενος λανθάνει.
νῦν γάρ που μανθάνεις; Ναί. Τοὺς τοίνυν βιασθέντας λέγω οὓς
ἂν ὀδύνη τις ἢ ἀλγηδὼν μεταδοξάσαι ποιήσῃ. Καὶ τοῦτ', ἔφη,
C ἔμαθον, καὶ ὀρθῶς λέγεις. Τοὺς μὴν γοητευθέντας, | ὡς ἐγᾦμαι,
κἂν σὺ φαίης εἶναι οἳ ἂν μεταδοξάσωσιν ἢ ὑφ' ἡδονῆς κηληθέντες
ἢ ὑπὸ φόβου τι δείσαντες. Ἔοικε γάρ, ἦ δ' ὅς, γοητεύειν πάντα
ὅσα ἀπατᾷ.

XX. Ὃ τοίνυν ἄρτι ἔλεγον, ζητητέον, τίνες ἄριστοι φύλακες τοῦ παρ' αὑτοῖς δόγματος, τοῦτο ὡς ποιητέον, ὃ ἂν τῇ πόλει ἀεὶ δοκῶσι βέλτιστον εἶναι αὑτοῖς ποιεῖν. τηρητέον δὴ εὐθὺς ἐκ παίδων, προθεμένοις ἔργα, ἐν οἷς ἄν τις τὸ τοιοῦτον μάλιστα

---

413 A 4 **τῶν μὲν ἀγαθῶν—ἑκουσίως.** See IV 438 A *n.*

6 **ἢ οὐ—εἶναι.** It is necessary expressly to equate ἀληθεύειν with ἀληθὴς δόξα, because ordinarily it means to speak rather than to think what is true. Cf. II 382 A. Hartman approves of Ast for bracketing the words "quod argumentationem turbant," but the contrary is true. Men unwillingly relinquish what is good. ἀληθεύειν is good; and ἀληθὴς δόξα is ἀληθεύειν; therefore we unwillingly relinquish ἀληθὴς δόξα—which is just what we wished to prove.

413 B 10 **τραγικῶς**: i.e. ὑψηλολογούμενος, in lofty high-flown metaphorical language such as may well become obscure: cf. VIII 545 E. κλέπτειν thus used is tragic: cf. (with J. and C.) Soph. *Ant.* 681 εἰ μὴ τῷ χρόνῳ κεκλέμμεθα.

13 **τοίνυν** = 'praeterea' here, not 'igitur': I 339 D *n.*

413 C 17 **τι δείσαντες** = 'having some fear' (J. and C.).

20 **τοῦτο ὡς ποιητέον κτλ.**: 'that it is their duty to do that which on each occasion they think it is best for them to do in the interests of the State.' I have provisionally retained the reading of the best MSS, although it is open to suspicion on several grounds. The position of τοῦτο is unusual, and αὑτοῖς ποιεῖν is, to say the least, superfluous. Gaisford (with whom Cobet agrees) wished to expunge the entire clause as a gloss on δόγματος. This solution, though drastic, may be right: for an explanation of δόγματος is hardly needed after 412 D, E, and τοῦτο looks like the commencement of an explanatory note 'this, viz. that' etc. A simpler alternative, adopted by most editors, is to cancel αὑτοῖς ποιεῖν, but it is difficult to see why a scribe should have introduced the words. The sentence, if genuine, seems to want the finishing touch. Cf. 407 D *n.*

22 **προθεμένοις ἔργα.** It is clear that Plato is referring to specific tests, and not (as Bosanquet seems to think) to the duties of war and the public service generally. So also Susemihl (*Gen. Entw.* II p. 143), and Steinhart (*Einleitung* p. 173), the latter of whom compares, not very aptly, the tests of the Pythagorean brotherhood and the appalling spectacles displayed in the mysteries. Three kinds of tests are required: (1) κλοπή, (2) βία, (3) γοητεία. Examples of the second kind are furnished by the severer discipline of gymnastic, the chase etc.: cf.

ἐπιλανθάνοιτο καὶ ἐξαπατῷτο, καὶ τὸν μὲν μνήμονα καὶ δυσεξα-
πάτητον ἐγκριτέον, τὸν δὲ μὴ ἀποκριτέον. ἦ γάρ; Ναί. Καὶ **D**
πόνους γε αὖ καὶ ἀλγηδόνας καὶ ἀγῶνας αὐτοῖς θετέον, ἐν οἷς ταὐτὰ
ταῦτα τηρητέον. Ὀρθῶς, ἔφη. Οὐκοῦν, ἦν δ' ἐγώ, καὶ τρίτου
εἴδους τοῦ τῆς γοητείας ἅμιλλαν ποιητέον, καὶ θεατέον—ὥσπερ
τοὺς πώλους ἐπὶ τοὺς ψόφους τε καὶ θορύβους ἄγοντες σκοποῦσιν
εἰ φοβεροί, οὕτω νέους ὄντας εἰς δείματ' ἄττα κομιστέον καὶ εἰς
ἡδονὰς αὖ μεταβλητέον, βασανίζοντας πολὺ μᾶλλον ἢ χρυσὸν ἐν **E**
πυρί,—εἰ δυσγοήτευτος καὶ εὐσχήμων ἐν πᾶσι φαίνεται, φύλαξ
αὑτοῦ ὢν ἀγαθὸς καὶ μουσικῆς ἧς ἐμάνθανεν, εὔρυθμόν τε καὶ
εὐάρμοστον ἑαυτὸν ἐν πᾶσι τούτοις παρέχων, οἷος δὴ ἂν ὢν καὶ
ἑαυτῷ καὶ πόλει χρησιμώτατος εἴη. καὶ τὸν ἀεὶ ἔν τε παισὶ καὶ
νεανίσκοις καὶ ἐν ἀνδράσι βασανιζόμενον καὶ ἀκήρατον ἐκβαίνοντα
καταστατέον ἄρχοντα τῆς πόλεως καὶ φύλακα, καὶ τιμὰς δοτέον **414**
καὶ ζῶντι καὶ τελευτήσαντι, τάφων τε καὶ τῶν ἄλλων μνημείων
μέγιστα γέρα λαγχάνοντα· τὸν δὲ μὴ τοιοῦτον ἀποκριτέον. τοιαύτη
τις, ἦν δ' ἐγώ, δοκεῖ μοι, ὦ Γλαύκων, ἡ ἐκλογὴ εἶναι καὶ κατάστασις
τῶν ἀρχόντων τε καὶ φυλάκων, ὡς ἐν τύπῳ, μὴ δι' ἀκριβείας,
εἰρῆσθαι. Καὶ ἐμοί, ἦ δ' ὅς, οὕτως πῃ φαίνεται. Ἆρ' οὖν ὡς
ἀληθῶς ὀρθότατον καλεῖν τούτους μὲν φύλακας παντελεῖς τῶν **B**

27. τοῦ τῆς Ξ: τούτοις Aq: τούτους Π.

Laws 633 B ff., where the probationary value of these and similar exercises is appropriately insisted on by the Spartan stranger. It was fully recognised in the Spartan ἀγωγή (Plut. *Lyc.* 17. 4 ff.). The third order of tests may be illustrated from *Laws* 634 A, B, 635 C, 647 D ff., 649 A, 673 E ff. ἡ ἐν οἴνῳ βάσανος (649 D) consists in giving wine to test men's self-control (τοῦ σωφρονεῖν ἕνεκα μελέτης 673 E). Plato gives no account of the first variety; but a good illustration of one species of it (cf. τοὺς μεταπεισθέντας 413 B) is provided by the speeches of self-seeking statesmen and unpatriotic sophists and poets. It is a curious fact that Plato's κλοπή still leaves a loophole by which vicious poetry may creep in again. On the general question, Plato does well to insist on the educational value of temptation; the theory and practice of modern times recognises it in connexion with βία, but experience too often shews that κλοπή and γοητεία mean playing with fire. Cf. Grote *Plato* III p. 328.

413 D 27 **τοῦ τῆς—θεατέον**. Two εἴδη of tests have been described, κλοπή and βία: the third is γοητεία. I incline to think that Stallbaum is right in restoring τοῦ τῆς: see *cr. n.* and *Introd.* § 5. τούτοις 'misere languet,' and if a dative were needed, it should rather be αὐτοῖς. Herwerden expunges θεατέον; but asyndeton before ὥσπερ is frequent in sentences of this kind.

413 E 31 **δυσγοήτευτος**. For the change from plural to singular cf. I 347 A *n*.

414 A 3 **λαγχάνοντα**. The accusative recurs to φύλακα, and is all the easier because τιμὰς δοτέον is little more than τιμητέον. Plato's usage is lax in such matters, and it is better not to emend: cf. (with Schneider) *Laws* 760 E, 877 A and Engelhardt *Anac. Pl. Spec.* III p. 45.

5 **ὡς ἐν τύπῳ—εἰρῆσθαι.** Cf. VI 502 D *n*.

τε ἔξωθεν πολεμίων τῶν τε ἐντὸς φιλίων, ὅπως οἱ μὲν μὴ βουλήσονται, οἱ δὲ μὴ δυνήσονται κακουργεῖν, τοὺς δὲ νέους, οὓς νῦν δὴ φύλακας ἐκαλοῦμεν, ἐπικούρους τε καὶ βοηθοὺς τοῖς τῶν ἀρχόντων δόγμασιν; Ἔμοιγε δοκεῖ, ἔφη.

XXI. Τίς ἂν οὖν ἡμῖν, ἦν δ' ἐγώ, μηχανὴ γένοιτο τῶν ψευδῶν τῶν ἐν δέοντι γιγνομένων, ὧν νῦν δὴ ἐλέγομεν, γενναῖόν τι ἓν
C ψευδομένους πεῖσαι μάλιστα μὲν καὶ αὐτοὺς τοὺς ἄρχοντας, εἰ δὲ μή, τὴν ἄλλην πόλιν; Ποῖόν τι; ἔφη. Μηδὲν καινόν, ἦν δ'

9. νῦν δὴ Π: δὴ νῦν A.   13. νῦν δὴ v: δὴ νῦν ΑΠΞq.

---

414 B 10 **ἐπικούρους.** Plato henceforward uses this expression when he wishes specifically to allude to the second class of his citizens. φύλακες remains the general term including both ἄρχοντες and ἐπίκουροι. See on II 374 D.

414 B—**415** D *In order to establish all these regulations in the city, we must have recourse to a heroic falsehood. We shall tell the citizens that they were only dreaming when they believed themselves to be trained by us. In reality, they were being moulded and fashioned in the womb of Earth, they and all their equipments; so that it is their duty to defend their country like a mother, and regard their fellow-citizens as brothers born of Earth. We shall add that in creating some to be rulers, God mingled in their substance gold; silver he put in the auxiliaries; iron and copper in the farmers and artisans. The citizens will for the most part produce children like themselves; but silver offspring will sometimes come from gold, or gold from silver and the like. It is the first and foremost duty of the Rulers to lift and degrade children into their proper classes, alleging an oracle that the city shall perish when iron or copper becomes its guardian. It may be impossible to convince the first generation of our citizens that the lie is true; but their posterity may credit it.*

414 B ff. After discrediting the current mythological and religious views, Plato now proceeds to replace them by something more in harmony with his own principles. Throughout this episode he is making legend in accordance with II 382 D διὰ τὸ μὴ εἰδέναι ὅπῃ τἀληθὲς ἔχει περὶ τῶν παλαιῶν, ἀφομοιοῦντες τῷ ἀληθεῖ τὸ ψεῦδος ὅ τι μάλιστα οὕτω χρήσιμον ποιοῦμεν. His particular object is to give a religious and quasi-historical sanction to the sentiment of patriotism and the institution of caste. With this aim in view he frames a μῦθος in which the belief of many Greek communities (especially the Athenians: cf. Isocr. *Paneg.* 24 f., Eur. *Fr.* 362) in an autochthonous ancestry is skilfully combined with the popular association of different metals with different degrees of merit, as in the Hesiodic ages of man. Cf. Hirzel *Der Dialog* pp. 263 f. The episode should not be understood as ironical: without it, the present sketch of a State would be incomplete. We require some guarantee for the permanence of the city and its institutions; and nothing could be more in keeping with the prevailingly moral and religious spirit of Plato's 'musical' education than that he should find that guarantee in faith rather than in reason. The case is different when the Platonic city attains its full maturity, and it is equally appropriate that Reason, embodied in the Rulers, should then become the final guarantee.

414 B 13 **ὧν νῦν δή.** See *cr. n.* Although νῦν occasionally refers to the immediate past (e.g. I 341 C, IX 592 A, X 611 B: see also Jebb on Soph. *Ant.* 151), neither here nor in οὓς νῦν δή just before can δὴ νῦν be retained: for δή "neque per se intelligi neque ad ὧν referri potest" (Schneider). The reference is to II 382 D, III 389 B.

414 C 14 **μάλιστα μέν.** See on 415 D.

15 **μηδὲν καινὸν κτλ.** We want no novelty, but something with which the Greeks are already familiar, for our city is a Greek city (V 470 E).

ἐγώ, ἀλλὰ Φοινικικόν τι, πρότερον μὲν ἤδη πολλαχοῦ γεγονός, ὥς φασιν οἱ ποιηταὶ καὶ πεπείκασιν, ἐφ' ἡμῶν δὲ οὐ γεγονὸς οὐδ' οἶδα εἰ γενόμενον ἄν, πεῖσαι δὲ συχνῆς πειθοῦς. Ὡς ἔοικας, ἔφη, ὀκνοῦντι λέγειν. Δόξω δέ σοι, ἦν δ' ἐγώ, καὶ μάλ' εἰκότως ὀκνεῖν, ἐπειδὰν εἴπω. Λέγ', ἔφη, καὶ μὴ φοβοῦ. Λέγω δή· | D καίτοι οὐκ οἶδα ὁποίᾳ τόλμῃ ἢ ποίοις λόγοις χρώμενος ἐρῶ καὶ ἐπιχειρήσω πρῶτον μὲν αὐτοὺς τοὺς ἄρχοντας πείθειν καὶ τοὺς στρατιώτας, ἔπειτα δὲ καὶ τὴν ἄλλην πόλιν, ὡς ἄρ' ἃ ἡμεῖς αὐτοὺς ἐτρέφομέν τε καὶ ἐπαιδεύομεν, ὥσπερ ὀνείρατα ἐδόκουν ταῦτα πάντα πάσχειν τε καὶ γίγνεσθαι περὶ αὐτούς, ἦσαν δὲ τότε τῇ ἀληθείᾳ ὑπὸ γῆς ἐντὸς πλαττόμενοι καὶ τρεφόμενοι καὶ αὐτοὶ καὶ τὰ ὅπλα αὐτῶν καὶ ἡ ἄλλη σκευὴ δημιουργουμένη. | E ἐπειδὴ δὲ παντελῶς ἐξειργασμένοι ἦσαν, καὶ ἡ γῆ αὐτοὺς μήτηρ οὖσα ἀνῆκεν, καὶ νῦν δεῖ ὡς

28. δεῖ *q*: δὴ ΑΠΞ.

---

16 **Φοινικικόν τι**: because the story of the Σπαρτοί was Phoenician, Cadmus the Phoenician having sown the dragon's teeth from which they sprang (Apollod. III 4. 1). Cf. *Laws* 663 E. Steinhart (*Einleit.* p. 177) and Susemihl (*Gen. Entw.* II p. 144) find in Φοινικικόν a further hint that the institution of caste was something foreign and non-Hellenic: but the words cannot be thus interpreted. The Egyptian system of caste (see Hdt. II 164 ff.) differed from Plato's in essential points, and there is no real evidence to shew that he was influenced by it in any way: nor is 'Phoenician' ('Sidonian' in *Laws* l.c.) equivalent to 'Egyptian.' Cf. Hermann *Gesch. u. Syst.* p. 55 and *nn.* Ψεῦσμα Φοινικικόν afterwards became a proverb, perhaps owing to this passage.

πολλαχοῦ γεγονός means simply 'which has happened in many places.' γεγονός and γενόμενον in themselves refer to the actual occurrences, which ὥς φασιν—πεπείκασιν reduces again to legend and matter of faith. πολλαχοῦ is plentifully illustrated in Preller *Gr. Myth.* pp. 79 ff. Presently οὐδ' οἶδα εἰ γενόμενον ἄν (for which Herwerden neatly but needlessly suggests οὐδ' οἶδ' ἂν εἰ γενόμενον) hints that the age of miracles is past.

414 D 21 **ὁποίᾳ—ἢ ποίοις.** Cf. 400 A *n.* It is very exceptional to find the indirect interrogative preceding the direct: cf. Soph. *O. T.* 71 with Jebb's note.

ἐρῶ. I have removed the colon after ἐρῶ on Richards' suggestion.

24 **ὥσπερ ὀνείρατα—αὐτούς**: lit. 'all these things which they fancied themselves suffering and happening to them were so to speak dreams.' ἐδόκουν is 'imagined' as in Aesch. *Pers.* 188 (also of a dream) and elsewhere. The object of πάσχειν, viz. ταῦτα πάντα, becomes the subject of γίγνεσθαι: cf. (for the change of subject) *Ap.* 40 A, *Symp.* 200 D and supra I 333 C, II 359 D, E, 360 A. It must be allowed that the effect of this idiom is here unusually harsh. I once conjectured ὑπάρχειν for πάσχειν, taking ἐδόκουν still as 'fancied': but the text is probably sound.

25 **ὑπὸ γῆς κτλ.** Herwerden bids us bracket either ὑπό or ἐντός: but Plato rarely if ever lets the preposition ἐντός follow its noun. ὑπό is 'under,' not 'by' (it is ὁ θεός, not ἡ γῆ, who πλάττει, infra 415 A), and ἐντός is adverbial; "drinnen unter der Erde" (Schneider). Mortal creatures are similarly moulded within the earth in Protagoras' prehistoric myth (τυποῦσιν αὐτὰ θεοὶ γῆς ἔνδον 320 D): cf. also *Symp.* 191 C, *Pol.* 272 A, *Tim.* 42 D. The myth of the *Politicus* (269 A ff.) connects the autochthonous origin of man with the golden age, in agreement with a wide-spread tradition, which gave rise to a considerable literature (Dümmler *Proleg. zu Platons Staat* p. 46). It is in the spirit of this tradition that Plato here represents the first generation of his ideal city as autochthonous.

414 E 28 **καί—καί.** The double καί marks "the correspondence of the

περὶ μητρὸς καὶ τροφοῦ τῆς χώρας ἐν ᾗ εἰσὶ βουλεύεσθαί τε καὶ
ἀμύνειν αὐτούς, ἐάν τις ἐπ' αὐτὴν ἴῃ, καὶ ὑπὲρ τῶν ἄλλων πολιτῶν
ὡς ἀδελφῶν ὄντων καὶ γηγενῶν διανοεῖσθαι. Οὐκ ἐτός, ἔφη,
415 πάλαι ᾐσχύνου τὸ ψεῦδος λέγειν. Πάνυ, ἦν δ' ἐγώ, | εἰκότως·
ἀλλ' ὅμως ἄκουε καὶ τὸ λοιπὸν τοῦ μύθου. ἐστὲ μὲν γὰρ δὴ
πάντες οἱ ἐν τῇ πόλει ἀδελφοί, ὡς φήσομεν πρὸς αὐτοὺς μυθολο-
γοῦντες, ἀλλ' ὁ θεὸς πλάττων, ὅσοι μὲν ὑμῶν ἱκανοὶ ἄρχειν,
χρυσὸν ἐν τῇ γενέσει συνέμειξεν αὐτοῖς, διὸ τιμιώτατοί εἰσιν·
ὅσοι δ' ἐπίκουροι, ἄργυρον· σίδηρον δὲ καὶ χαλκὸν τοῖς τε γεωργοῖς
καὶ τοῖς ἄλλοις δημιουργοῖς. ἅτε οὖν ξυγγενεῖς ὄντες πάντες τὸ
B μὲν πολὺ ὁμοίους ἂν ὑμῖν αὐτοῖς γεννῷτε, ἔστι δ' ὅτε ἐκ | χρυσοῦ
γεννηθείη ἂν ἀργυροῦν καὶ ἐξ ἀργυροῦ χρυσοῦν ἔκγονον καὶ τἆλλα
πάντα οὕτως ἐξ ἀλλήλων. τοῖς οὖν ἄρχουσι καὶ πρῶτον καὶ

---

two clauses" (J. and C.). As the Earth proved herself their mother, so they must shew themselves her sons. If the text is sound, it must be explained in this way; but exact parallels are rare. Thuc. IV 8. 9 (cited by Schneider *Addit.* p. 27) is different: see Classen ad loc. and on VIII 27. 5. More to the point is Soph. *Ant.* 1192 f. καὶ παρὼν ἐρῶ, | κοὐδὲν παρήσω τῆς ἀληθείας ἔπος: see Jebb ad loc. Ast expunges καί before ἡ γῆ, while Hermann alters it to ὡς (carrying on the ὡς of ὡς ἄρα). Neither change can be called satisfactory. I formerly suggested δημιουργουμένη ἔτι. ἤδη δὲ κτλ. (*Cl. Rev.* X p. 385): cf. *Symp.* 220 C ἤδη ἦν μεσημβρία, καὶ ἄνθρωποι ᾐσθάνοντο. The change is slight, but ἔτι 'languet,' and it is better to retain the MS reading.

ὡς περὶ μητρὸς — διανοεῖσθαι. Cf. (with J. and C.) Aesch. *Sept.* 10—20, 412—416, and infra V 470 D. For the omission of the preposition before τῆς χώρας cf. VIII 553 B *n.* ὑπέρ with τῶν ἄλλων is scarcely more than περί: see II 367 A *n.*

415 A 3 **ὡς φήσομεν.** The sense (as Schneider observes) is ὡς ὁ μῦθος λέγει, ὃν πρὸς αὐτοὺς ἐροῦμεν. Hartman cancels ὡς, but it was more likely to have been wrongly omitted here than inserted.

5 **χρυσὸν κτλ.** The metals are borrowed from Hesiod (*O. D.* 109—201), as Plato indicates in VIII 546 E. Hesiod enumerates five ages of men (interposing the age of heroes between those of copper and iron), but the older legend probably recognised four only: see Rohde *Psyche*^{2} I p. 87. Plato makes the golden and the other classes coexist—a truer and profounder view than Hesiod's. In other respects, the myth (as Jackson has pointed out in Susemihl and Hicks *Politics of Aristotle* p. 244) is not to be pressed: for "it does not recognise the promotion of ἐπίκουροι" to be ἄρχοντες. We should expect the φύλακες to contain admixtures, both of gold and silver, such as are to be Rulers receiving more gold than silver, and conversely; but the Greek does not favour this idea. Iron again seems to be exclusively (though less emphatically) reserved for the farmers, and copper for the artisans: cf. infra B, C, VIII 547 A, B, and Arist. *Pol.* B 5. 1264^b 14. It makes the ψεῦδος all the more γενναῖον and effective to tell the citizens that the classes are even more distinct than they really are.

7 **ἅτε οὖν ξυγγενεῖς ὄντες** is said with reference to the δέ clause, on which the stress falls. The fundamental kinship of the different classes will occasionally reassert itself in their offspring. So J. and C., rightly.

415 B 9 **ἐξ ἀργυροῦ**: sc. ἐκγόνου, which should also be supplied with χρυσοῦ. Plato sees in fancy the onward march of generations καθάπερ λαμπάδα τὸν βίον παραδιδόντες: cf. IV 424 A. Ast's proposal ἀργύρου should not have received the approval of Hartman; and D. and V. miss a characteristic touch by translating ἀργυροῦ "a silver parent."

μάλιστα παραγγέλλει ὁ θεός, ὅπως μηδενὸς οὕτω φύλακες ἀγαθοὶ
ἔσονται μηδ' οὕτω σφόδρα φυλάξουσι μηδὲν ὡς τοὺς ἐκγόνους,
ὅ τι αὐτοῖς τούτων ἐν ταῖς ψυχαῖς παραμέμικται, καὶ ἐάν τε
σφέτερος ἔκγονος ὑπόχαλκος ἢ ὑποσίδηρος γένηται, μηδενὶ τρόπῳ C
κατελεήσουσιν, ἀλλὰ τὴν τῇ φύσει προσήκουσαν τιμὴν ἀποδόντες
ὤσουσιν εἰς δημιουργοὺς ἢ εἰς γεωργούς, καὶ ἂν αὖ ἐκ τούτων τις
ὑπόχρυσος ἢ ὑπάργυρος φυῇ, τιμήσαντες ἀνάξουσι τοὺς μὲν εἰς
φυλακήν, τοὺς δὲ εἰς ἐπικουρίαν, ὡς χρησμοῦ ὄντος τότε τὴν πόλιν
διαφθαρῆναι, ὅταν αὐτὴν ὁ σίδηρος ἢ ὁ χαλκὸς φυλάξῃ. τοῦτον
οὖν τὸν μῦθον ὅπως ἂν πεισθεῖεν, ἔχεις τινὰ μηχανήν; Οὐδαμῶς,
ἔφη, ὅπως γ' ἂν αὐτοὶ οὗτοι· ὅπως μέντ' ἂν οἱ τούτων ὑεῖς καὶ οἱ D
ἔπειτα οἵ τ' ἄλλοι ἄνθρωποι οἱ ὕστερον. Ἀλλὰ καὶ τοῦτο, ἦν δ'
ἐγώ, εὖ ἂν ἔχοι πρὸς τὸ μᾶλλον αὐτοὺς τῆς πόλεώς τε καὶ ἀλλήλων
κήδεσθαι· σχεδὸν γάρ τι μανθάνω ὃ λέγεις.

19. ὁ σίδηρος ἢ ὁ χαλκὸς q: ὁ σίδηρος φύλαξ ἢ ὁ χαλκοῦς A^1Π: ὁ σιδηροῦς φύλαξ ἢ ὁ χαλκοῦς A^2: ὁ σιδηροῦς ἢ ὁ χαλκοῦς Ξ.

---

13 **ἐάν τε κτλ.** This provision is the corner-stone of Plato's State, and as soon as it gives way, the edifice is doomed (VIII 546 E—547 A). It is only by the elevation of the worthy and the degradation of the unfit that class-distinctions can be made to coincide with those of Nature (cf. IV 423 D); and unless they do, the foundation of the city, which is τὸ ἑαυτοῦ πράττειν, is sapped. Hence the emphasis with which Plato introduces this subject. His theory, it should be noted, conforms at least as much to the interest of the individual as to that of the State; for it provides congenial work for all according to their natural capacities, and uncongenial labour, whether above or below one's powers, is a fertile source of misery and crime. Aristotle (*Pol.* B 4. 1262^b 27) seems to doubt if Plato's scheme was feasible. Granted rulers who are φρόνιμοι εἰς τοῦτο, δυνατοί, and κηδεμόνες τῆς πόλεως (412 C), in a small city—a thousand warriors, says Plato, will suffice (IV 423 A, cf. Grote *Plato* III p. 206 *n.*)—it could probably be worked without much difficulty. See also IV 423 E ff. We are not of course to suppose that the child was once for all assigned to his class at birth; he would be watched and tested again and again, before being finally disposed of, so that the likelihood of mistakes on the part of the Rulers is greatly lessened. Cf. *Tim.* 19 A.

415 C 17 **τιμήσαντες**: not "having estimated their values" (J. and C.): but simply 'they will do him honour and' etc. The suggestions ἀντιτιμήσαντες or τιμήσαντες κατ' ἀξίαν will hardly command assent. τιμήν in τιμὴν ἀποδόντες above may also be translated 'honour' if τὴν τῇ φύσει προσήκουσαν is taken in its full force: the honour appropriate to his nature and no more.

415 D 21 **ὅπως μέντ' ἂν κτλ.** Cf. *Laws* 663 E—664 A. Grote justly observes that "Plato has fair reason for his confident assertion that if such legends could once be imprinted on the minds of his citizens, as portions of an established creed, they would maintain themselves for a long time in unimpaired force and credit" (l. c. III p. 188). The first generation of citizens would remain incredulous, but the γενναῖον ψεῦδος would be impressed upon their children, and soon be universally believed. It would require but little effort for a Greek city like Plato's (V 470 E) to entertain in course of time a view which has so many points of contact with Greek tradition. Here Plato seems to hint that even his Rulers (for οἱ τούτων ὑεῖς must include these also) will in time believe; the Rulers of VI—VII might teach the legend as an ἐν δέοντι ψεῦδος, but would themselves refuse their assent.

24 **σχεδὸν—λέγεις**: viz. that the story

XXII. Καὶ τοῦτο μὲν δὴ ἕξει ὅπῃ ἂν αὐτὸ ἡ φήμη ἀγάγῃ·
ἡμεῖς δὲ τούτους τοὺς γηγενεῖς ὁπλίσαντες προάγωμεν ἡγουμένων
τῶν ἀρχόντων. ἐλθόντες δὲ θεασάσθων τῆς πόλεως ὅπου κάλλι-
E στον στρατοπεδεύσασθαι, ὅθεν τούς τε ἔνδον | μάλιστ' ἂν κατέχοιεν,
εἴ τις μὴ ἐθέλοι τοῖς νόμοις πείθεσθαι, τούς τε ἔξωθεν ἀπαμύνοιεν,
εἰ πολέμιος ὥσπερ λύκος ἐπὶ ποίμνην τις ἴοι, στρατοπεδευσάμενοι
δέ, θύσαντες οἷς χρή, εὐνὰς ποιησάσθων. ἢ πῶς; Οὕτως, ἔφη.
Οὐκοῦν τοιαύτας, οἵας χειμῶνός τε στέγειν καὶ θέρους ἱκανὰς
εἶναι; Πῶς γὰρ οὐχί; οἰκήσεις γάρ, ἔφη, δοκεῖς μοι λέγειν. Ναί,
416 ἦν δ' ἐγώ, στρατιωτικάς γε, ἀλλ' οὐ χρηματιστικάς. | Πῶς, ἔφη,
αὖ τοῦτο λέγεις διαφέρειν ἐκείνου; Ἐγώ σοι, ἦν δ' ἐγώ, πειράσομαι
εἰπεῖν. δεινότατον γάρ που πάντων καὶ αἴσχιστον ποιμέσι τοιούτους γε καὶ οὕτω τρέφειν κύνας ἐπικούρους ποιμνίων, ὥστε ὑπὸ
ἀκολασίας ἢ λιμοῦ ἤ τινος ἄλλου κακοῦ ἔθους αὐτοὺς τοὺς κύνας

3. αἴσχιστον Ξ q: αἴσχιστόν που A: αἴσχιόν που Π.

---

is intended to form part of the city's permanent religious creed, and so encourage patriotism and fraternity.

415 D—**417** B *Our Rulers and Auxiliaries shall have a camp within the city, so as to check lawless citizens and ward off foreign foes. Their education will prevent them from preying on the others, provided we arrange their circumstances rightly. We shall assign them common property and houses, as well as common meals, to be furnished by the other citizens in return for the protection they enjoy. The use of gold and silver must be forbidden to our Guardians.*

415 D ff. The communism of the *Republic* is, next to its educational curriculum, the principal guarantee which Plato provides against the abuse of political power on the part of his Guardians (Nohle *die Statslehre Platos* pp. 129 ff.). At the present stage Socrates gives only a brief and exoteric account of the system, reserving the full and final exposition for Book V. Plato may have been thinking of certain Spartan and Pythagorean institutions when he framed some of the regulations in this section: but his communism is much more thorough-going than anything of the kind before his day. See Steinhart *Einleitung* pp. 179—181, and especially Grote l.c. III pp. 207—216. Aristotle's criticisms (*Pol.* B 5. 1262^b 37—1263^b 29) are interesting and acute, although he ignores some essential points, and is unable throughout to rise to the level of Plato's idealism. See also Jowett *Introd.* pp. 175—179 and Nettleship *Lect. and Rem.* II pp. 136 f.

25 **τοῦτο—ἀγάγῃ**: 'this will be as the *vox populi* shall determine': i.e. it will depend upon φήμη whether our fable is believed or not. φήμη is not of course an oracle (as Ficinus supposed), but the half-personified voice of popular belief. Cf. *Laws* 838 C, D.

28 **τούς τε ἔνδον κτλ.** Henkel (*Studien zur Gesch. d. Gr. Lehre vom Staat* p. 52 *n.* 13) remarks that the prevention of faction inside the city is characteristically put in the foreground. The greatest danger to a Greek city was from internal dissension: cf. V 470 C ff. *nn.*

415 E 30 **στρατοπεδευσάμενοι.** The Spartan government was compared to that of a στρατόπεδον (Isocr. 6. 81: cf. Gilbert *Gr. Const. Ant.* E. T. pp. 61 ff.). Plato's city is literally a camp. His proposals would probably strike the average Athenian as a dangerous and tyrannical exaggeration of Spartan usages. See Jowett *Introd.* p. 176.

416 A 2 **διαφέρειν ἐκείνου** is rejected by Herwerden; but Schneider's explanation hits the mark: "αὖ alterum hoc de discrimine insolentius dictum notat: prius fuerat quod domos εὐνάς dixerat."

ἐπιχειρῆσαι τοῖς προβάτοις κακουργεῖν καὶ ἀντὶ κυνῶν λύκοις
ὁμοιωθῆναι. Δεινόν, ἦ δ' ὅς· πῶς δ' οὔ; Οὐκοῦν φυλακτέον |
παντὶ τρόπῳ, μὴ τοιοῦτον ἡμῖν οἱ ἐπίκουροι ποιήσωσι πρὸς τοὺς B
πολίτας, ἐπειδὴ αὐτῶν κρείττους εἰσίν, ἀντὶ ξυμμάχων εὐμενῶν
δεσπόταις ἀγρίοις ἀφομοιωθῶσιν; Φυλακτέον, ἔφη. Οὐκοῦν τὴν
μεγίστην τῆς εὐλαβείας παρεσκευασμένοι ἂν εἶεν, εἰ τῷ ὄντι καλῶς
πεπαιδευμένοι εἰσίν; Ἀλλὰ μὴν εἰσίν γ', ἔφη. καὶ ἐγὼ εἶπον,
Τοῦτο μὲν οὐκ ἄξιον διισχυρίζεσθαι, ὦ φίλε Γλαύκων· ὃ μέντοι
ἄρτι ἐλέγομεν, ἄξιον, ὅτι δεῖ αὐτοὺς τῆς ὀρθῆς | τυχεῖν παιδείας, C
ἥτις ποτέ ἐστιν, εἰ μέλλουσι τὸ μέγιστον ἔχειν πρὸς τὸ ἥμεροι
εἶναι αὐτοῖς τε καὶ τοῖς φυλαττομένοις ὑπ' αὐτῶν. Καὶ ὀρθῶς
γε, ἦ δ' ὅς. Πρὸς τοίνυν τῇ παιδείᾳ ταύτῃ φαίη ἄν τις νοῦν ἔχων
δεῖν καὶ τὰς οἰκήσεις καὶ τὴν ἄλλην οὐσίαν τοιαύτην αὐτοῖς
παρεσκευάσθαι, ἥτις μήτε τοὺς φύλακας ὡς ἀρίστους εἶναι παύσοι
αὐτούς, κακουργεῖν τε μὴ ἐπαροῖ περὶ τοὺς ἄλλους | πολίτας. D
Καὶ ἀληθῶς γε φήσει. Ὅρα δή, εἶπον ἐγώ, εἰ τοιόνδε τινὰ τρόπον

12. ἐγὼ *v*: ἔγωγ' ΑΠΞ*q*. 19. παρεσκευάσθαι Π: παρασκευάσασθαι Α. 20. ἐπαροῖ Θ: ἐπάρῃ ΑΠΞ*q*.

---

6 **κακουργεῖν**. See 407 B *n*. The idiom is abundantly attested, both in Plato and in other Greek authors, although Madvig and Cobet have done their best to expel it from Plato's text here and wherever else it occurs.

416 B 8 **μὴ τοιοῦτον—ποιήσωσι.** For *τοιοῦτον* cf. 388 D *n*. Richter conjectured *μὴ τοιοῦτοι—ποιηθῶσι*, "parum venuste," as Hartman mercifully says.

9 **ἀντὶ ξυμμάχων — ἀφομοιωθῶσιν.** For the usual ampliative or explanatory asyndeton cf. 409 B. Aristotle objects that Plato's regulations would virtually divide his city into two hostile camps (*Pol.* B 5. 1264[a] 24), and Grote does not see "what reply the Platonic *Republic* furnishes to this objection" (l.c. III p. 213). In reply to Aristotle, Plato might have pointed to his regulations about the interchange of classes (415 B ff.), which would have the effect of binding them together more securely. Moreover, where each individual has the work to do for which he is best qualified, one fruitful cause of discontent and sedition is removed. The wives and families of the lower class would also tend to keep them quiet. Nor does Aristotle's objection allow sufficient weight to the training by which Plato tries to protect his guardians from such 'spiritual pride' as would alienate their subjects.

12 **καὶ ἐγὼ εἶπον.** See *cr. n.* *καὶ ἔγωγ' εἶπον*, though generally retained, is surely wrong: it could only mean 'I too, said I.' No editor cites any other instance of *ἔγωγε* in this formula.

13 **τοῦτο μὲν κτλ.** prepares us for the second scheme of education in Book VII: cf. 412 B, 414 A *nn.*

416 C 19 **ἥτις—ἐπαροῖ.** *αὐτούς* is emphatic: "ipsos per se" (Schneider). The contrast is between the guardians in themselves, and in their dealings with the others. It is difficult to decide between *παύσει—ἐπαρεῖ* (Bekker and others) and *παύσοι—ἐπαροῖ*. The latter is *exquisitius*, and better supported on the whole. For the confusion between -*ῃ* (subjunctive) and -*οι* (optative) in A see *Introd.* § 5. Cobet calls for *τοῦ* instead of *τούς* before *φύλακας*, but *φύλακας* requires the article. *παύειν* with the infinitive is rare, and means 'prevent,' not 'make to cease': cf. Hdt. V 67 (with Stein's note) and Ar. *Ach.* 634, where Reiske's conjecture *πείσας* should not be accepted.

δεῖ αὐτοὺς ζῆν τε καὶ οἰκεῖν, εἰ μέλλουσι τοιοῦτοι ἔσεσθαι· πρῶτον
μὲν οὐσίαν κεκτημένον μηδεμίαν μηδένα ἰδίαν, ἂν μὴ πᾶσα ἀνάγκη·
ἔπειτα οἴκησιν καὶ ταμιεῖον μηδενὶ εἶναι μηδὲν τοιοῦτον, εἰς ὃ οὐ
πᾶς ὁ βουλόμενος εἴσεισι· τὰ δ' ἐπιτήδεια, ὅσων δέονται ἄνδρες
E ἀθληταὶ πολέμου σώφρονές τε καὶ ἀνδρεῖοι, ταξαμένους | παρὰ
τῶν ἄλλων πολιτῶν δέχεσθαι μισθὸν τῆς φυλακῆς τοσοῦτον, ὅσον
μήτε περιεῖναι αὐτοῖς εἰς τὸν ἐνιαυτὸν μήτε ἐνδεῖν· φοιτῶντας δὲ
εἰς ξυσσίτια ὥσπερ ἐστρατοπεδευμένους κοινῇ ζῆν· χρυσίον δὲ
καὶ ἀργύριον εἰπεῖν αὐτοῖς ὅτι θεῖον παρὰ θεῶν αἰεὶ ἐν τῇ ψυχῇ
ἔχουσι καὶ οὐδὲν προσδέονται τοῦ ἀνθρωπείου, οὐδὲ ὅσια τὴν
ἐκείνου κτῆσιν τῇ τοῦ θνητοῦ χρυσοῦ κτήσει ξυμμιγνύντας μιαίνειν,
417 διότι πολλὰ καὶ ἀνόσια περὶ τὸ τῶν | πολλῶν νόμισμα γέγονεν,
τὸ παρ' ἐκείνοις δὲ ἀκήρατον· ἀλλὰ μόνοις αὐτοῖς τῶν ἐν τῇ πόλει
μεταχειρίζεσθαι καὶ ἅπτεσθαι χρυσοῦ καὶ ἀργύρου οὐ θέμις, οὐδ'
ὑπὸ τὸν αὐτὸν ὄροφον ἰέναι οὐδὲ περιάψασθαι οὐδὲ πίνειν ἐξ
ἀργύρου ἢ χρυσοῦ. καὶ οὕτω μὲν σῴζοιντό τ' ἂν καὶ σῴζοιεν τὴν

4. τὸν αὐτὸν $A^2\Pi^2\Xi q^1$: τῶν αὐτῶν A^1 : τῶν αὐτὸν Π^1 : τὸν αὐτῶν corr. in mg. q^2.

---

416 D 22 **πρῶτον μὲν κτλ.** A certain measure of communism in property seems to have existed among the Pythagoreans (RP.[7] p. 43); but there is no reason to suppose that Plato is deliberately borrowing from them here: cf. Steinhart *Einleitung* p. 179. The main object of Plato is of course to prevent the formation of private interests likely to compete with the claims of public duty. We remark that there has been no hint so far of common wives and children, although Blaschke (*der Zusammenhang d. Fam. u. Gütergemeinschaft d. pl. St. m. d. pol. u. phil. Syst. Platos* p. 7) thinks he finds one in 415 A. Cf. 415 D *n.*

23 **ἂν μὴ πᾶσα ἀνάγκη.** For ᾖ omitted see II 371 A *n.* The conjecture ἦν for ἄν (Herwerden) is elegant, but superfluous.

25 **τὰ δ' ἐπιτήδεια—μισθόν.** It is fair that the lower classes should provide the others with the means of leisure, for it is they who 'reap all the benefit of the laborious training bestowed on the guardians.' They are the 'ultimate and capital objects' of Plato's solicitude. Grote justly adds that "this is a larger and more generous view of the purpose of political institutions than we find either in Aristotle or in Xenophon" (l.c. III p. 213).

26 **ταξαμένους** is strangely represented in Schneider's translation by "zu bestimmten Zeiten." It refers to the fixing of fees or payments in return for services rendered. Cf. *Men.* 91 B.

416 E 29 **ξυσσίτια.** A Spartan feature: see Gilbert *Gk. Const. Ant.* E. T. p. 65. Cf. *Laws* 762 B ff.

χρυσίον κτλ. So also in Sparta, according to Xen. *Rep. Lac.* 7. 6; with which cf. Plut. *Lys.* 19. 6, where the ephors are said to have put to death a friend of Lysander λαβόντες ἀργύριον ἰδίᾳ κεκτημένον. Plato is keenly conscious of the corrupting influence of wealth: see *Gorg.* 525 D ff., and cf. II 373 E, IV 421 D *nn.* His guardians are φύσει πλουσίω τὰς ψυχάς (VIII 547 B) and need no other riches.

417 A 4 **ὑπὸ—ἰέναι**: as though Wealth communicated a taint, like a murderer *sub isdem trabibus* (ὁμωρόφιος). The Greek is much more expressive and picturesque than Apelt's conjecture ὑπὸ τὸν αὐτῶν ὄροφον προσιέναι (*Observ. Cr.* p. 11).

5 **σῴζοιντό τ' ἂν καὶ σῴζοιεν.** Cf.

πόλιν· ὁπότε δ' αὐτοὶ γῆν τε ἰδίαν καὶ οἰκίας καὶ νομίσματα κτήσονται, οἰκονόμοι μὲν καὶ γεωργοὶ ἀντὶ φυλάκων ἔσονται, δεσπόται δ' ἐχθροὶ ἀντὶ ξυμμάχων | τῶν ἄλλων πολιτῶν γενήσονται, B μισοῦντες δὲ δὴ καὶ μισούμενοι καὶ ἐπιβουλεύοντες καὶ ἐπιβουλευόμενοι διάξουσι πάντα τὸν βίον, πολὺ πλείω καὶ μᾶλλον δεδιότες τοὺς ἔνδον ἢ τοὺς ἔξωθεν πολεμίους, θέοντες ἤδη τότε ἐγγύτατα ὀλέθρου αὐτοί τε καὶ ἡ ἄλλη πόλις. τούτων οὖν πάντων ἕνεκα, ἦν δ' ἐγώ, φῶμεν οὕτω δεῖν κατεσκευάσθαι τοὺς φύλακας οἰκήσεώς τε πέρι καὶ τῶν ἄλλων, καὶ ταῦτα νομοθετήσωμεν, ἢ μή; Πάνυ γε, ἦ δ' ὃς ὁ Γλαύκων.

ΤΕΛΟΣ ΠΟΛΙΤΕΙΑΣ Γ'.

---

621 B μῦθος ἐσώθη—καὶ ἡμᾶς ἂν σώσειεν. σῴζεσθαι of moral salvation is common in Plato: cf. e.g. VI 492 E, 502 B.

6 **ὁπότε δ' αὐτοὶ—ἔσονται.** From this sentence it seems clear that the community of goods does not extend to the lower classes, although Aristotle complains that Plato has not said anything precise upon the matter (*Pol.* B 5. 1264ᵃ 15). Aristotle seems, however, to have understood that they were not to have common wives, for he cynically observes that it would have been better if they had, as then they would have been more divided and less likely to combine against the guardians (ib. 4. 1262ᵃ 40 ff.).

APPENDICES TO BOOK III.

I.

III **389** B—D. The section on truth offers some serious difficulties. Throughout the whole of this division of the *Republic* (377 A—392 A) Plato is laying down precepts to which the μῦθοι of poets are to conform (cf. 377 B and 392 A), and in each case it is pointed out how the precept in question has been violated by Homer and other poets. Here, however, nothing is said to shew that we are prescribing for the poets, and no illustrations, either of our precept or of its violation, are cited from them. Schneider, indeed, attempts to extort this meaning from the section; but his theory, strictly understood, would require us to suppose that ἰατροῖς δοτέον, ἰδιώταις οὐχ ἁπτέον, προσήκει ψεύδεσθαι, οὐχ ἁπτέον τοῦ τοιούτου in B, ψεύσασθαι, ψευδόμενον in C, and κολάσει in D refer not to Plato's own city, but to poetical representations; that τῆς πόλεως in B is not Plato's city, but any city figuring in poetry; and that τοὺς τοιούτους ἄρχοντας in C are not Plato's rulers, but others. Such a supposition is hardly possible, if τοιούτους in C is genuine (see note ad loc.), and in any case it is neither natural nor obvious. It may with safety be asserted that if the section had occurred in any other context no one would have supposed it to contain rules for poetical fables: in itself it merely lays down the duty of the lower classes to speak the truth, with the conditions under which the rulers may lie. Cf. Rettig *Proleg.* pp. 62, 63 and notes on 389 D. Rettig, following up a hint of Schleiermacher's, thinks the section was introduced to prepare the way for the rulers' 'lie' about the origin of the State; while Susemihl (*Genet. Entw.* II p. 120) in some mysterious way appears to connect it with the theory of Ideas "as the true and higher Measure of the correct representation of Gods, Daemons, Heroes and the lower world." The latter view is altogether fanciful; and neither of these explanations justifies Plato for having inserted the passage in this particular connexion, where he is discussing poetical legend, however much Rettig may extol the "art" with which he has concealed his art. The following seems to me a more probable explanation. We are professedly dealing with poetical representations of the gods and heroes, and we should expect Plato to require the poets to represent them as truthful and to enforce his remarks by poetical illustrations. He does not do so, because it has already been done in II 382—383. Instead of this, he reverts to 382 C (τότε ἀποτροπῆς ἕνεκα ὡς φάρμακον χρήσιμον γίγνεται sc. τὸ ἐν τοῖς λόγοις ψεῦδος), and emphasizes, more than he has hitherto done, the reason why truthfulness must be ascribed to the gods, viz. in order to encourage the virtue among men. That Plato laid the greatest stress upon the virtue of Truth appears from the fine passage in *Laws* 730 B, C, beginning Ἀλήθεια δὴ πάντων μὲν ἀγαθῶν θεοῖς ἡγεῖται, πάντων δὲ ἀνθρώποις: thus it is not unnatural that he should recur to the subject here. The section should be taken as a kind of afterthought to 382—383, which it is intended partly to explain and partly to supplement. The whole section on Truth is for this and other reasons possibly later than the context in which it appears: see also on τοὺς τοιούτους ἄρχοντας, 389 C.

A further question has been raised as to what Plato intended by the virtue of ἀλήθεια. Rettig (l.c. pp. 61 and 65 ff.) and Stallbaum, anxious to find in all this a preliminary sketch of the cardinal virtues, interpret it as a sort of wisdom; but in that case, why did not Plato call it by its name? He is content to use the names of two other cardinal virtues, ἀνδρεία and σωφροσύνη, although they have not yet been defined. Nor does this account of ἀλήθεια contain any of the distinctive features of Wisdom, either in its popular sense or in the sense which it bears in Book IV. There is no reason to suppose that Plato means anything but what he says, and he himself describes the virtue as 'speaking the truth.' The whole attempt to see in this division of the dialogue a foreshadowing of the psychological theory of the virtues is, I believe, a mistake: only two of the virtues are named at all, ἀνδρεία and σωφροσύνη, and these quite without any ulterior meaning or motive. Plato is simply describing in a somewhat desultory way (ὅπῃ ἂν ὁ λόγος ὥσπερ πνεῦμα φέρῃ)—since a rigid plan is not necessary here—the kind of character which Poetry should endeavour to foster: a character which shall honour gods and parents, set value on reciprocal friendship (386 A), be courageous, truthful, and distinguished for self-control. To force this description into the strait-jacket of the cardinal virtues would be pedantic. As it is, no essential feature of the καλὸς κἀγαθός is omitted.

II.

On Plato's ἁρμονίαι.

III 398 E—399 B. Plato enumerates in all six scales in three groups. The first group is θρηνώδες, and includes Mixo-Lydian, Syntono-Lydian, and such like; the second is μαλακόν, and embraces Chalaro-Ionian and Chalaro-Lydian; to the third, which occupies a middle position between the other two, belong Dorian and Phrygian. Chalaro-Ionian seems further to imply the existence of Syntono-Ionian, and we read of both in Pratinas *Fr.* 5 Bergk, μήτε σύντονον δίωκε μήτε τὰν ἀνειμέναν Ἰαστὶ μοῦσαν, | ἀλλὰ τὰν μέσαν...νεῶν ἄρουραν αἰόλιζε τῷ μέλει, if Westphal's interpretation is (as I believe) right (*Harmonik* p. 186. See also Monro *Modes of Greek Music* pp. 5, 6). It has been supposed that Plato's μιξολυδιστί is only συντονοιαστί under another name; but the name Mixo-Lydian seems rather to point to a compromise between two distinct modes, one of which was the Lydian. Possibly the συντονοιαστί is included under τοιαῦταί τινες, as von Jan holds *Fl. Jahrb.* 1867 p. 823.

According to Westphal (l.c. pp. 215 ff.), whose theory is partly based upon what must, I fear, be regarded as a speculative deduction from Aristides Quintil. I pp. 21, 22 ed. Meibom, Plato's ἁρμονίαι were as follows:—

(1)	Mixo-Lydian	B C D E F G A B,
(2)	Syntono-Lydian	A B C′ D′ E′ F′ G′ A′,
(3)	Chalaro-Ionian	G A B C′ D′ E′ F′ G′,
(4)	Chalaro-Lydian	F G A B C′ D′ E′ F′,
(5)	Dorian	E F G A B C′ D′ E′,
(6)	Phrygian	D E F G A B C′ D′.

It will be observed that Westphal's scales are all of them ἁρμονίαι in the strict sense of the term, i.e. they differ in the order of their intervals; and that the Syntono-Lydian begins a major third higher than the Chalaro-Lydian.

An entirely different theory has been propounded by von Jan (*Fl. Jahrb.* 1867 pp. 815 ff.), who gives the following series of scales:—

(1)	Mixo-Lydian	E♯ F♯ G♯ A♯ B C′♯ D′♯ E′♯,
(2)	Syntono-Lydian	E F♯ G♯ A B C′♯ D′♯ E′,
(3)	Chalaro-Ionian	E♭ F G A♭ B♭ C′ D′♭ E′♭,
(4)	Chalaro-Lydian	E♭ F G A♭ B♭ C′ D′ E′♭,
(5)	Dorian	E F G A B C′ D′ E′,
(6)	Phrygian	E F♯ G A B C′♯ D′ E′.

According to this view, the Syntono-Lydian and the Chalaro-Lydian are in reality the same mode, differing from one another only in pitch. Plato's language appears to me to point to such a conclusion (see on 398 C, E), but it is not altogether easy for us to believe that the difference of a semitone in pitch could have converted τὸ θρηνῶδες into τὸ συμποτικόν. It will further be remarked that if we take the Dorian as the original and fundamental ἁρμονία (*Lach.* 188 D), the θρηνώδεις ἁρμονίαι, according to von Jan's theory, can be made from it by tuning different strings a semitone higher, and the χαλαραί by tuning different strings a semitone lower.

Von Jan's hypothesis is severely censured by Westphal (l.c. pp. 209—215), and strong arguments can be urged against it from the standpoint of modern music. I have quoted it in this Appendix because of its symmetry, and also because, so far as it goes, it seems to me to be more in harmony with the scanty indications furnished by Plato's language than the theory of Westphal. It is true, as Westphal urges, that Plato applies the term ἁρμονία to Syntono-Lydian and Chalaro-Lydian as well as to Dorian, Phrygian etc.; but I do not think it follows that Syntono-Lydian and Chalaro-Lydian differed in the arrangement of intervals: for σύντονος and χαλαρά ought to refer to pitch alone: and συντονολυδιστί or χαλαραλυδιστί may have been called a ἁρμονία not *qua* σύντονος or χαλαρά, but *qua* λυδιστί. The references to Plato's ἁρμονίαι in Arist. *Pol.* Θ 5. 1340[a] 40 ff. may be explained in the same way. Wherever Aristotle speaks of ἀνειμέναι and σύντονοι ἁρμονίαι, he is referring, as the editors hold, to Chalaro-Lydian, Chalaro-Ionian, and Syntono-Lydian, Syntono-Ionian; and these are properly called ἁρμονίαι as being varieties of λυδιστί and ἰαστί. See my article in *Cl. Rev.* x pp. 378 f. The passage on the modes or (as he calls them) τρόποι in Bacchius' *Isagoge* § 46 ff. seems—as far as concerns the relative pitch of the scales—to point to a solution with which neither Westphal nor von Jan agrees, but Bacchius gives us no information about the order of intervals in Plato's ἁρμονίαι.

Δ.

419 I. Καὶ ὁ Ἀδείμαντος ὑπολαβὼν Τί οὖν, ἔφη, ὦ Σώκρατες, ἀπολογήσει, ἐάν τίς σε φῇ μὴ πάνυ τι εὐδαίμονας ποιεῖν τούτους τοὺς ἄνδρας, καὶ ταῦτα δι' ἑαυτούς, ὧν ἔστι μὲν ἡ πόλις τῇ ἀληθείᾳ, οἱ δὲ μηδὲν ἀπολαύουσιν ἀγαθὸν τῆς πόλεως, οἷον ἄλλοι ἀγρούς τε

---

419 A—**423** B *Adimantus now interposes with the objection that the Guardians will be far from happy. Although they are in reality masters of the city, they have nothing which they can call their own—none of the contributing factors of individual or personal gratification. In reply, it is not admitted that the Guardians will be unhappy, but even supposing that they are, our purpose was, not to make happy Guardians, but to found a happy City, in order to discover Justice within its borders. Our Guardians must not be made happy at the cost of efficiency in their peculiar duty. Wealth is hardly less unpropitious to the exercise of arts and professions than Poverty. When our city is at war with two communities, she will not lack resources; for she will make alliance with one of the two by promising to it the other's wealth. Nor will she be in danger from her ally afterwards. Other States are each of them not one but manifold, and our city, if she have but a thousand defenders, is the greatest single state in Greece or Barbary.*

419 A ff. 1 **καὶ ὁ Ἀδείμαντος κτλ.** Adimantus' objection is the dying echo of the view already advocated by Thrasymachus, that a ruler should rule for his own profit: cf. I 343 A, 344 B *nn.* Socrates declines to discuss the question now, because it is irrelevant. In the further account of the communism of the ruling class, the difficulty solves itself. A higher happiness—so we are told—comes from self-victory than from indulgence (V 465 D ff.: cf. IX 583 C *n.*). Compare the conversation of Socrates with Aristippus in *Mem.* II 1. 17 ff.

2 **μή.** On *μή* with the infinitive after verbs of saying see I 346 E *n.*

3 **δι' ἑαυτούς**: i.e. they have themselves to thank for not being *εὐδαίμονες.* Cf. V 465 E *οὐκ οἶδα ὅτου λόγος ἡμῖν ἐπέπληξεν ὅτι τοὺς φύλακας οὐκ εὐδαίμονας ποιοῖμεν, οἷς ἐξὸν πάντα ἔχειν τὰ τῶν πολιτῶν οὐδὲν ἔχοιεν;* and Solon 33 1 f. *οὐκ ἔφυ Σόλων βαθύφρων οὐδὲ βουλήεις ἀνήρ· | ἐσθλὰ γὰρ θεοῦ διδόντος αὐτὸς οὐκ ἐδέξατο* (he of his own initiative refused). *διά* is used exactly as in I 354 B. This view, which is Ast's, gives an excellent meaning, and Schneider, who at first proposed a subtler explanation, adopts it in his translation ("durch ihre eigene Schuld"). The various conjectures *δή, αὐτοῖς ὧν* (Stephanus), *δὴ αὐτοὺς ὧν* (Buttmann), *αὐτοὺς δι' ὧν* (Herwerden) need no refutation.

4 **ἄλλοι**: not *οἱ ἄλλοι* (Bekker, Stallbaum, etc.), which might be taken as referring to the lower classes in Plato's State. Plato would not be likely to permit these to have *οἰκίαι καλαὶ καὶ μεγάλαι.* *ἄλλοι* means 'other rulers,' i.e. rulers in other cities; and *κεκτημένοι* belongs to *οἱ δέ*: 'possessing, like other rulers, lands,' etc. So Schneider, rightly. For the idiomatic position of *οἷον ἄλλοι* cf. VII 515 A, 528 B, IX 589 B al.

κεκτημένοι καὶ οἰκίας οἰκοδομούμενοι καλὰς καὶ μεγάλας καὶ
ταύταις πρέπουσαν κατασκευὴν κτώμενοι καὶ θυσίας θεοῖς ἰδίας
θύοντες καὶ ξενοδοκοῦντες καὶ δὴ καί, ἃ νῦν δὴ σὺ ἔλεγες, χρυσόν
τε καὶ ἄργυρον κεκτημένοι καὶ πάντα ὅσα νομίζεται τοῖς μέλλουσιν
μακαρίοις εἶναι; ἀλλ' ἀτεχνῶς, φαίη ἄν, ὥσπερ ἐπίκουροι μισθω-
τοὶ ἐν τῇ πόλει φαίνονται | καθῆσθαι οὐδὲν ἄλλο ἢ φρουροῦντες. 420
Ναί, ἦν δ' ἐγώ, καὶ ταῦτά γε ἐπισίτιοι καὶ οὐδὲ μισθὸν πρὸς τοῖς
σιτίοις λαμβάνοντες ὥσπερ οἱ ἄλλοι, ὥστε οὐδ' ἂν ἀποδημῆσαι
βούλωνται ἰδίᾳ, ἐξέσται αὐτοῖς, οὐδ' ἑταίραις διδόναι οὐδ' ἀναλίσκειν ἄν ποι βούλωνται ἄλλοσε, οἷα δὴ οἱ εὐδαίμονες δοκοῦντες
εἶναι ἀναλίσκουσι. ταῦτα καὶ ἄλλα τοιαῦτα συχνὰ τῆς κατη-
γορίας ἀπολείπεις. Ἀλλ', ἦ δ' ὅς, ἔστω καὶ ταῦτα κατηγορημένα.
Τί οὖν δὴ | ἀπολογησόμεθα, φῄς; Ναί. Τὸν αὐτὸν οἶμον, ἦν δ' B
ἐγώ, πορευόμενοι εὑρήσομεν, ὡς ἐγᾦμαι, ἃ λεκτέα. ἐροῦμεν γάρ,
ὅτι θαυμαστὸν μὲν ἂν οὐδὲν εἴη, εἰ καὶ οὗτοι οὕτως εὐδαιμονέστατοί
εἰσιν, οὐ μὴν πρὸς τοῦτο βλέποντες τὴν πόλιν οἰκίζομεν, ὅπως ἕν
τι ἡμῖν ἔθνος ἔσται διαφερόντως εὔδαιμον, ἀλλ' ὅπως ὅ τι μάλιστα
ὅλη ἡ πόλις. ᾠήθημεν γὰρ ἐν τῇ τοιαύτῃ μάλιστα ἂν εὑρεῖν
δικαιοσύνην καὶ αὖ ἐν τῇ κάκιστα οἰκουμένῃ ἀδικίαν, κατιδόντες

13. ἂν εὑρεῖν Π: ἀνευρεῖν A.

---

9 **μισθωτοί** is not otiose as Badham supposes. We should translate 'just like paid auxiliaries.' The emphasis on *μισθωτοί* prepares us for Socrates' correction when he says they do not, strictly speaking, even get *μισθός*.

420 A 2 **ἐπισίτιοι.** *ἐπίσιτοι* (which Cobet and Hartman call for) would be more in accordance with the analogy of *παράσιτος* etc.; but the longer form is established by fragments of comic poets (ap. Ath. VI 246 F—247 A, where *ἐπισιτίων* in the fragment of Timocles defies emendation).

3 **οἱ ἄλλοι**: sc. *ἐπίκουροι* or mercenaries.

ἀποδημῆσαι. Regulations about *ἀποδημία* are laid down in *Laws* 949 E ff.

5 **οἷα δὴ κτλ.** For *οἷα* Hermann once conjectured *οἷ*: neatly, but *οἷ* is too precise. *οἷα δή*=*οἷα δὴ ἀναλώματα*. With *οἱ εὐδαίμονες δοκοῦντες εἶναι* cf. III 406 C. It is *εὐδαιμονία* in the popular sense of 'having a good time' which Adimantus complains is denied to the guardians.

420 B 8 **οἶμον.** A poetic word. Plato is perhaps thinking of some such phrase as Pindar's *ἐπέων οἶμος* (*Ol.* IX 47). The 'way' is simply that each class must do its own appointed work, if the city is to be a happy and harmonious whole: cf. 423 D.

10 **εἰ καὶ οὗτοι κτλ.** *καί* means 'as well as the rest of the city.' Aristotle misrepresents Plato when, in spite of this sentence and V 465 D ff., he says that the guardians are deprived of *εὐδαιμονία* (*Pol.* B 5. 1264^b 15 ff., with Susemihl's note). They are happy not only because they triumph over self (465 D), but—like the others—because they do the work to which Nature has called them: cf. I 352 D—354 A.

11 **ὅπως ἕν τι κτλ.** Cf. *Laws* 715 B and Thuc. II 60. 2, where Pericles says *ἐγὼ γὰρ ἡγοῦμαι πόλιν πλείω ξύμπασαν ὀρθουμένην ὠφελεῖν τοὺς ἰδιώτας ἢ καθ' ἕκαστον τῶν πολιτῶν εὐπραγοῦσαν, ἀθρόαν δὲ σφαλλομένην.*

13 **ᾠήθημεν—σκεψόμεθα.** See on II 369 A.

C δὲ | κρῖναι ἄν, ὃ πάλαι ζητοῦμεν. νῦν μὲν οὖν, ὡς οἰόμεθα, τὴν εὐδαίμονα πλάττομεν οὐκ ἀπολαβόντες ὀλίγους ἐν αὐτῇ τοιούτους τινὰς τιθέντες, ἀλλ' ὅλην· αὐτίκα δὲ τὴν ἐναντίαν σκεψόμεθα. ὥσπερ οὖν ἂν εἰ ἡμᾶς ἀνδριάντας γράφοντας προσελθών τις ἔψεγε λέγων, ὅτι οὐ τοῖς καλλίστοις τοῦ ζῴου τὰ κάλλιστα φάρμακα προστίθεμεν· οἱ γὰρ ὀφθαλμοί, κάλλιστον ὄν, οὐκ ὀστρείῳ ἐναληλιμμένοι εἶεν, ἀλλὰ μέλανι· μετρίως ἂν ἐδοκοῦμεν |
D πρὸς αὐτὸν ἀπολογεῖσθαι λέγοντες· Ὦ θαυμάσιε, μὴ οἴου δεῖν ἡμᾶς οὕτω καλοὺς ὀφθαλμοὺς γράφειν, ὥστε μηδὲ ὀφθαλμοὺς φαίνεσθαι, μηδ' αὖ τἆλλα μέρη, ἀλλ' ἄθρει εἰ τὰ προσήκοντα ἑκάστοις ἀποδιδόντες τὸ ὅλον καλὸν ποιοῦμεν· καὶ δὴ καὶ νῦν μὴ ἀνάγκαζε ἡμᾶς τοιαύτην εὐδαιμονίαν τοῖς φύλαξι προσάπτειν,
E ἣ ἐκείνους πᾶν μᾶλλον ἀπεργάσεται ἢ φύλακας. ἐπιστάμεθα | γὰρ καὶ τοὺς γεωργοὺς ξυστίδας ἀμφιέσαντες καὶ χρυσὸν περιθέντες πρὸς ἡδονὴν ἐργάζεσθαι κελεύειν τὴν γῆν, καὶ τοὺς κεραμέας κατακλίναντες ἐπὶ δεξιὰ πρὸς τὸ πῦρ διαπίνοντάς τε καὶ εὐωχου-

30. ἐπὶ δεξιὰ Ξ*q*: ἐπιδέξια A: ἐπὶ δεξιᾶ (sic) Π.

---

420 C 16 **οὐκ ἀπολαβόντες—τιθέντες.** ἀπολαβόντες is absolute, almost adverbial (cf. *Gorg.* 495 E); and ὀλίγους goes with τιθέντες. So Schneider and others rightly explain the construction.

17 **αὐτίκα δὲ τὴν ἐναντίαν κτλ.** Here we have the first express promise of Books VIII and IX, although the promise is afterwards fulfilled in an ampler manner than is indicated here. See also 427 D.

18 **ὥσπερ οὖν ἂν—μέλανι.** Cf. (with J. and C.) *Hipp. Maior* 290 B. ἀνδριάντας γράφοντας means 'painting statues of men.' Cf. Euripides *Fr.* 764. 2 γραπτοὺς ἐν αἐτοῖσι προσβλέπων τύπους. The question whether statues were ever painted in the best period is an old controversy, the echoes of which have hardly yet died away. Schubart (*Fl. Jahr.* 1874, pp. 20 ff.) and others prefer to take ἀνδριάντας merely as 'likenesses of men,' but the word was regularly, if not indeed always, used of statues. That the surface of archaic statues was regularly painted is now no longer doubtful: see Gardner *Handbook of Greek Sculpture* pp. 28 ff. During the best period, in the case of marble or other polished surfaces, the painting was regularly confined to the eyes, eyelids, eyebrows, hair and the like. See on the whole subject Sittl's *Arch. der Kunst* (in Iwan Müller's *Handbuch*) pp. 413, 414. μέλανι does not necessarily mean jet black, but only some dark and quiet colour. In point of fact, the eyes of the early marble statues on the Acropolis "are painted with a dark pigment, almost black" (Gardner l.c. p. 30). The use—regular in Greek—of γράφειν for painting is an interesting survival of the time when decorative art was little beyond carving in relief (Sittl l.c. p. 416). The present passage is strangely ignored by Sertorius in his interesting article "Plato und die Malerei" in *Arch. f. Gesch. d. Phil.* IX pp. 123—148.

420 E 28 **ξυστίδας.** The name ξυστίς was given to various kinds of purple robes or mantles—among them those worn by kings upon the stage, and by riders in festal processions. The authorities are cited in Müller *Gr. Bühnenalt.* p. 234 *n.* 1. If the Scholiasts on Ar. *Clouds* 70 and Theocr. II 74 are to be trusted, we should write ξύστιδας, not ξυστίδας.

30 **ἐπὶ δεξιά.** Whether we read ἐπιδέξια or ἐπὶ δεξιά the word should be understood as 'from left to right.' At a Greek banquet, the guests were always placed ἐπὶ δεξιά, i.e. so that the guest on your right hand occupied a lower place

μένους, τὸν τροχὸν παραθεμένους, ὅσον ἂν ἐπιθυμῶσι κεραμεύειν,
καὶ τοὺς ἄλλους πάντας τοιούτῳ τρόπῳ μακαρίους ποιεῖν, ἵνα δὴ
ὅλη ἡ πόλις εὐδαιμονῇ. ἀλλ' ἡμᾶς μὴ οὕτω νουθέτει· ὡς, ἂν σοὶ
πειθώμεθα, οὔτε ὁ γεωργὸς γεωργὸς ἔσται, οὔτε | ὁ κεραμεὺς κερα- **421**
μεύς, οὔτε ἄλλος οὐδεὶς οὐδὲν ἔχων σχῆμα ἐξ ὧν πόλις γίγνεται.
ἀλλὰ τῶν μὲν ἄλλων ἐλάττων λόγος· νευρορράφοι γὰρ φαῦλοι
γενόμενοι καὶ διαφθαρέντες καὶ προσποιησάμενοι εἶναι μὴ ὄντες
πόλει οὐδὲν δεινόν· φύλακες δὲ νόμων τε καὶ πόλεως μὴ ὄντες
ἀλλὰ δοκοῦντες ὁρᾷς δὴ ὅτι πᾶσαν ἄρδην πόλιν ἀπολλύασιν καὶ
αὖ τοῦ εὖ οἰκεῖν καὶ εὐδαιμονεῖν μόνοι τὸν καιρὸν ἔχουσιν. εἰ μὲν
οὖν ἡμεῖς μὲν φύλακας ὡς ἀληθῶς ποιοῦμεν, ἥκιστα | κακούργους **B**
τῆς πόλεως, ὁ δ' ἐκεῖνο λέγων γεωργούς τινας καὶ ὥσπερ ἐν
πανηγύρει ἀλλ' οὐκ ἐν πόλει ἑστιάτορας εὐδαίμονας, ἄλλο ἄν τι
ἢ πόλιν λέγοι. σκεπτέον οὖν, πότερον πρὸς τοῦτο βλέποντες τοὺς
φύλακας καθιστῶμεν, ὅπως ὅ τι πλείστη αὐτοῖς εὐδαιμονία ἐγγενή-
σεται, ἢ τοῦτο μὲν εἰς τὴν πόλιν ὅλην βλέποντας θεατέον εἰ ἐκείνῃ

(ὑποκατακεκλιμένος) than you, and the wine circulated from left to right of the banqueters. See Blümner *Privatalt.* p. 237 *n.* 7 and Darbishire *Relliq. Philol.* p. 78. The word suggests a banquet with all the formalities, and heightens the incongruity of the situation, like the purple robes and golden crowns of the farmers. Schneider's exhaustive discussion seems to me conclusive in favour of writing ἐπὶ δεξιά as two words. Casaubon has been followed by most of the editors (except Schneider) in taking ἐπιδέξια as an adverb = 'commode' (Ast), 'commode et eleganter' (Stallbaum etc.), or 'dexterously,' 'cleverly' (J. and C.); but it may well be doubted if the word could mean 'commode,' and 'dexterously' is inappropriate. Cf. Darbishire l.c. p. 78 *n.* 1. ἐπὶ δεξιά goes with κατακλίναντες and πρὸς τὸ πῦρ (cf. Blaydes on Ar. *Ach.* 751) with διαπίνοντας. The fire is that by which the potters bake their pottery; their workshop has for the nonce become a hall of banqueting.

421 A 2 **ἐξ ὧν**: i.e. *τούτων τῶν σχημάτων ἐξ ὧν*. Cf. II 373 E *n.*

6 **καὶ αὖ**: *rursusque* (Ficinus), i.e. *sicuti et contra*, as Ast observes.

7 **εἰ μὲν οὖν—λέγοι.** This difficult passage has suffered severely at the hands of critics, but the text is probably nearly, if not quite, sound. If we take the words as they stand in A, they mean, broadly speaking, that if *we* are making true guardians, and *he* (ὁ ἐκεῖνο λέγων means the τις in 419 A) is making something different, he cannot, like ourselves, be speaking of a πόλις, but of something else. This is logical and gives an excellent sense: cf. 422 E εὐδαίμων εἶ—ὅτι οἴει ἄξιον εἶναι ἄλλην τινὰ προσειπεῖν πόλιν ἢ τὴν τοιαύτην οἵαν ἡμεῖς κατεσκευάζομεν. Now *we* are making guardians in the true sense of the term, such as are least likely to harm the city; whereas the author of the other proposals is making (not guardians, but since he gives them ἀγροί 419 A) a sort of farmers (cf. III 417 B οἰκονόμοι μὲν καὶ γεωργοὶ ἀντὶ φυλάκων ἔσονται) and men who *do* harm their city, because they "for their bellies' sake, Creep, and intrude and climb into the fold." The advocates of such a theory must mean something different from a city—something like the "shearers' feast" in Lycidas: cf. I 343 A *n.* γεωργούς is possibly corrupt; if so, I think we should read λεωργούς to contrast with ἥκιστα κακουργούς. The word occurs in the *Memorabilia*, if not in Plato. See *Cl. Rev.* X p. 385. Other emendations are enumerated in App. I.

ἐγγίγνεται, τοὺς δ' ἐπικούρους τούτους καὶ τοὺς φύλακας ἐκεῖνο |
C ἀναγκαστέον ποιεῖν καὶ πειστέον, ὅπως ὅ τι ἄριστοι δημιουργοὶ
τοῦ ἑαυτῶν ἔργου ἔσονται, καὶ τοὺς ἄλλους ἅπαντας ὡσαύτως, καὶ
οὕτω ξυμπάσης τῆς πόλεως αὐξανομένης καὶ καλῶς οἰκιζομένης
ἐατέον ὅπως ἑκάστοις τοῖς ἔθνεσιν ἡ φύσις ἀποδίδωσι τοῦ μεταλαμβάνειν εὐδαιμονίας.

II. Ἀλλ', ἦ δ' ὅς, καλῶς μοι δοκεῖς λέγειν. Ἆρ' οὖν, ἦν δ'
ἐγώ, καὶ τὸ τούτου ἀδελφὸν δόξω σοι μετρίως λέγειν; Τί μάλιστα;
D Τοὺς ἄλλους αὖ δημιουργοὺς σκόπει εἰ τάδε | διαφθείρει, ὥστε καὶ
κακοὺς γίγνεσθαι. Τὰ ποῖα δὴ ταῦτα; Πλοῦτος, ἦν δ' ἐγώ, καὶ
πενία. Πῶς δή; Ὧδε. πλουτήσας χυτρεὺς δοκεῖ σοι ἔτι
ἐθελήσειν ἐπιμελεῖσθαι τῆς τέχνης; Οὐδαμῶς, ἔφη. Ἀργὸς δὲ
καὶ ἀμελὴς γενήσεται μᾶλλον αὐτὸς αὑτοῦ; Πολύ γε. Οὐκοῦν
κακίων χυτρεὺς γίγνεται; Καὶ τοῦτο, ἔφη, πολύ. Καὶ μὴν καὶ
ὄργανά γε μὴ ἔχων παρέχεσθαι ὑπὸ πενίας ἤ τι ἄλλο τῶν εἰς
E τὴν τέχνην τά τε ἔργα πονηρότερα | ἐργάσεται καὶ τοὺς ὑεῖς ἢ
ἄλλους, οὓς ἂν διδάσκῃ, χείρους δημιουργοὺς διδάξεται. Πῶς δ'

22. διαφθείρει Π: διαφέρει A.

---

14 **ἐκεῖνο κτλ.**: i.e. to pursue the *other* policy, which *we* enjoin. ἐκεῖνο does more than merely anticipate ὅπως—ἔσονται.

421 C 18 **ἐατέον**. The infinitive, which would naturally follow ἐατέον, is 'drawn into construction' with ὅπως—ἀποδίδωσι. I once thought of ἐκτέον (i.q. δεῖ ἔχειν, cf. V 468 A), taking the genitive as in πῶς ἔχεις τοῦ μεταλαμβάνειν εὐδαιμονίας; But the MS reading is satisfactory enough.

421 D 22 **ὥστε—γίγνεσθαι**: 'so that they also become bad.' These words, though expunged by Hartman, are welcome, if not necessary, in view of κακίων χυτρεὺς γίγνεται and χείρους δὲ αὐτοί in D and E. καί indicates that κακοὺς γίγνεσθαι is more than διαφθείρει; and so it is represented in the sequel. The reading of A (see *cr. n.*) perhaps points to a variant διαφθερεῖ.

24 **πλουτήσας—τέχνης**. Ar. *Plut.* 510—534 (cited by Ast) furnishes an excellent commentary on this text. See also on III 416 E.

28 **παρέχεσθαι** is 'to provide out of his own resources' (de suo praebere): cf. VIII 554 A. Cobet cancels the word; Herwerden and Hartman prefer πορίζεσθαι, for which there is no MS authority. πορίζεσθαι would imply that the χυτρεύς buys his ὄργανα ready-made from others, whereas παρέχεσθαι expresses no opinion on this point.

421 E 30 **διδάξεται**. Thompson, Cobet, and others peremptorily call for διδάξει. See however Riddell *Digest of Idioms* § 87. Riddell conclusively shews (1) that in *Men.* 93 D ἐδιδάξατο as well as ἐπαιδεύσατο is said of a parent teaching his own son (a passage misunderstood—I think—by Jebb on Soph. *Ant.* 356: cf. *Men.* 93 C), (2) that ἐδίδαξε is used of a parent getting his sons taught by others in *Men.* 94 B and 94 D (bis). Another example of the second usage is *Prot.* 324 D. The fact is that "the Active Voice is quite as susceptible as the Middle of the meaning 'to get a thing done by another'; neither Voice, however, by any proper inherent force, but in virtue solely of the common principle, that *qui facit per alium facit per se*," Riddell. Jebb (l.c.) observes that "once or twice ἐδιδαξάμην is merely ἐδίδαξα with the idea of

οὔ; Ὑπ' ἀμφοτέρων δή, πενίας τε καὶ πλούτου, χείρω μὲν τὰ τῶν
τεχνῶν ἔργα, χείρους δὲ αὐτοί. Φαίνεται. Ἕτερα δή, ὡς ἔοικε,
τοῖς φύλαξιν ηὑρήκαμεν, ἃ παντὶ τρόπῳ φυλακτέον ὅπως μήποτε
αὐτοὺς λήσει εἰς τὴν πόλιν παραδύντα. Ποῖα ταῦτα; Πλοῦτός
τε, ἦν δ' ἐγώ, καὶ πενία· | ὡς τοῦ μὲν τρυφὴν καὶ ἀργίαν καὶ 422
νεωτερισμὸν ποιοῦντος, τοῦ δὲ ἀνελευθερίαν καὶ κακοεργίαν πρὸς
τῷ νεωτερισμῷ. Πάνυ μὲν οὖν, ἔφη. τόδε μέντοι, ὦ Σώκρατες,
σκόπει, πῶς ἡμῖν ἡ πόλις οἵα τ' ἔσται πολεμεῖν, ἐπειδὰν χρήματα
μὴ κεκτημένη ᾖ, ἄλλως τε κἂν πρὸς μεγάλην τε καὶ πλουσίαν
ἀναγκασθῇ πολεμεῖν. Δῆλον, ἦν δ' ἐγώ, ὅτι πρὸς μὲν μίαν χαλε-
πώτερον, πρὸς δὲ δύο τοιαύτας | ῥᾷον. Πῶς εἶπες; ἦ δ' ὅς. B
Πρῶτον μέν που, εἶπον, ἐὰν δέῃ μάχεσθαι, ἆρα οὐ πλουσίοις
ἀνδράσι μαχοῦνται αὐτοὶ ὄντες πολέμου ἀθληταί; Ναὶ τοῦτό γε,
ἔφη. Τί οὖν, ἦν δ' ἐγώ, ὦ Ἀδείμαντε; εἷς πύκτης ὡς οἷόν τε
κάλλιστα ἐπὶ τοῦτο παρεσκευασμένος δυοῖν μὴ πύκταιν, πλουσίοιν
δὲ καὶ πιόνοιν, οὐκ ἂν δοκεῖ σοι ῥᾳδίως μάχεσθαι; Οὐκ ἂν ἴσως,
ἔφη, ἅμα γε. Οὐδ' εἰ ἐξείη, ἦν δ' ἐγώ, ὑποφεύγοντι τὸν πρότερον
ἀεὶ προσφερόμενον | ἀναστρέφοντα κρούειν, καὶ τοῦτο ποιοῖ πολλά- C
κις ἐν ἡλίῳ τε καὶ πνίγει; ἆρά γε οὐ καὶ πλείους χειρώσαιτ' ἂν
τοιούτους ὁ τοιοῦτος; Ἀμέλει, ἔφη, οὐδὲν ἂν γένοιτο θαυμαστόν.
Ἀλλ' οὐκ οἴει πυκτικῆς πλέον μετέχειν τοὺς πλουσίους ἐπιστήμῃ
τε καὶ ἐμπειρίᾳ ἢ πολεμικῆς; Ἔγωγ', ἔφη. Ῥᾳδίως ἄρα ἡμῖν

---

the teacher's interest superadded": it may be doubted if "once or twice" is strong enough, but at all events this is the usage here, and in V 467 E. The active *διδάσκῃ* is appropriately used of teaching others (*ἄλλους κτλ.*); in *διδάξεται* the personal interest reappears, for it is the sons who are the prominent pupils (whence *ἢ ἄλλους* and not *καὶ ἄλλους*). Richter's view (*Fl. Jahrb.* 1867 p. 147) that *διδάξεται* denotes the result of the action rather than the action itself is partly true, but it is not the middle which gives it this force. In Ar. *Clouds* 783, as Socrates is not Strepsiades' father, we may accept Elmsley's emendation *διδάξαιμ' ἂν* for *διδαξαίμην* without prejudice to the present case.

32 **αὐτοί**: viz. *οἱ τεχνῖται*: see II 377 C *n.* We need not change *τεχνῶν* to *τεχνιτῶν*.

422 A 2 **ποιοῦντος** = 'producing' gives a satisfactory sense. Wealth and Poverty are not to be allowed *παραδῦναι εἰς τὴν πόλιν*, because—we have here the statement of a general law—they are the authors of luxury etc. *ἐμποιοῦντος* (in Ξ and other MSS) is an obvious 'emendation,' though adopted by Stallbaum and others: cf. 444 D.

κακοεργίαν. If the form is right, Plato must intend to draw attention to the etymology of the word. *κακουργίαν* appears in two or three inferior MSS, and (as *ε* seems to be written over an erasure) was perhaps the original reading in Paris A.

422 C 14 **πολλάκις**: not 'perhaps' (one of J. and C.'s alternative suggestions) but 'frequently,' 'repeatedly.' *πολλάκις* does not mean 'perhaps,' except after *εἰ*, *ἐάν*, *ἵνα*, *μή* and the like: see Ast's *lex. Plat.* III p. 144 and Heindorf on *Phaed.* 60 E.

οἱ ἀθληταὶ ἐκ τῶν εἰκότων διπλασίοις τε καὶ τριπλασίοις αὑτῶν
μαχοῦνται. Συγχωρήσομαί σοι, ἔφη· δοκεῖς γάρ μοι ὀρθῶς λέγειν.
D Τί δ'; ἂν πρεσβείαν πέμψαντες εἰς τὴν ἑτέραν πόλιν τἀληθῆ
εἴπωσιν, ὅτι ἡμεῖς μὲν οὐδὲν χρυσίῳ οὐδ' ἀργυρίῳ χρώμεθα, οὐδ'
ἡμῖν θέμις, ὑμῖν δέ· συμπολεμήσαντες οὖν μεθ' ἡμῶν ἔχετε τὰ τῶν
ἑτέρων· οἴει τινὰς ἀκούσαντας ταῦτα αἱρήσεσθαι κυσὶ πολεμεῖν
στερεοῖς τε καὶ ἰσχνοῖς μᾶλλον ἢ μετὰ κυνῶν προβάτοις πίοσί τε
καὶ ἁπαλοῖς; Οὔ μοι δοκεῖ. ἀλλ' ἐὰν εἰς μίαν, ἔφη, πόλιν συνα-
E θροισθῇ τὰ τῶν ἄλλων χρήματα, ὅρα μὴ κίνδυνον φέρῃ τῇ μὴ
πλουτούσῃ. Εὐδαίμων εἶ, ἦν δ' ἐγώ, ὅτι οἴει ἄξιον εἶναι ἄλλην
τινὰ προσειπεῖν πόλιν ἢ τὴν τοιαύτην οἵαν ἡμεῖς κατεσκευάζομεν.
'Αλλὰ τί μήν; ἔφη. Μειζόνως, ἦν δ' ἐγώ, χρὴ προσαγορεύειν τὰς
ἄλλας· ἑκάστη γὰρ αὐτῶν πόλεις εἰσὶ πάμπολλαι, ἀλλ' οὐ πόλις,

31. πάμπολλαι $A^2\Pi$: πάμπολαι A^1.

---

422 D 21 **τί δέ; κτλ.** ἂν πρεσβείαν κτλ. has for its apodosis οἴει τινὰς κτλ. I have placed a mark of interrogation after τί δέ. The alternatives are to place it after τῶν ἑτέρων, or else to suppose with Ast that the construction is suddenly changed at οἴει. Neither solution is so simple as to write τί δ'; Cf. 425 C, 426 A, and (for the elision before a pause) 428 C.

24 **κυσί.** In the game of πόλεις, the counters were called 'Dogs' (Pollux IX 98). The comparison of our auxiliaries to dogs prepares the way for the allusion in 422 E: where see note. This has been pointed out by Ridgeway (*Journal of Hell. Studies* XVI p. 288), who gives illustrations of three 'dogs' of this description found in Egypt and now in the British Museum.

422 E 28 **εὐδαίμων εἶ κτλ.**: 'you are fortunate to be able to think etc.': cf. V 450 C. εὐδαίμων is less common in this ironical sense than μακάριος.

31 **ἑκάστη γὰρ κτλ.**: 'for each of them is, as the saying goes, no city, but a-many cities.' The phrase τὸ τῶν παιζόντων in Plato seems always to mean 'as they say in the proverb' or 'proverbial saying': see IX 573 C, *Laws* 780 C, and cf. ib. 723 D. Now it is probable from the position of τὸ τῶν παιζόντων that ἀλλ' οὐ πόλις forms part of the proverb: so that the whole saying may have run πόλεις μέν εἰσι παμπόλεις, ἀλλ' οὐ πόλις. (Herwerden, *more suo*, cancels ἀλλ' οὐ πόλις, but we have of course no right to take this step.) The form παμπόλεις for πάμπολλαι may be allowed in a pun on πόλεις, especially as the Epic plural of πολύς is sometimes found with feminine nouns. It should be remarked also that the first hand in Paris A wrote πάμπολαι (see *cr. n.*), though this may be merely accidental. What the ordinary application of the proverb was, we cannot say: presumably it was generally employed, as here by Plato, in speaking of a city divided against itself. The origin of the saying is to be sought in the variety of πεττεία known as πόλεις παίζειν, an expression which, according to the Scholiast on this passage of Plato, as well as Suidas s.v. πόλις, and Hesychius s.v. πόλεις παίζειν, had itself also a proverbial signification. In this game the abacus was divided into 60 spaces, each of which was called πόλις in ancient times (Photius s.v. πόλεις παίζειν ed. Porson. Porson's alteration of ξ' i.e. 60 into ζ' is a gratuitous change, as Schneider hints. See also Eustathius on *Od.* I p. 29. 13 ff., ed. Lips., quoted by Schneider). The name πόλις was moreover sometimes applied to the game itself (Cratinus Δραπετίδες *Fr.* 3 ed. Meineke καὶ κύνα καὶ πόλιν ἣν παίζουσιν), as well as to the πλινθίον or *abacus* on which it was played (Pollux IX 98). There is also, I think, some reason

τὸ τῶν παιζόντων. δύο μέν, κἂν ὁτιοῦν ᾖ, πολεμία ἀλλήλαις,
ἡ μὲν πενήτων, ἡ δὲ πλουσίων· τούτων δ' | ἐν ἑκατέρᾳ πάνυ 423
πολλαί, αἷς ἐὰν μὲν ὡς μιᾷ προσφέρῃ, παντὸς ἂν ἁμάρτοις, ἐὰν
δὲ ὡς πολλαῖς, διδοὺς τὰ τῶν ἑτέρων τοῖς ἑτέροις χρήματά τε καὶ
δυνάμεις ἢ καὶ αὐτούς, ξυμμάχοις μὲν ἀεὶ πολλοῖς χρήσει, πολεμίοις δ' ὀλίγοις. καὶ ἕως ἂν ἡ πόλις σοι οἰκῇ σωφρόνως ὡς ἄρτι
ἐτάχθη, μεγίστη ἔσται, οὐ τῷ εὐδοκιμεῖν λέγω, ἀλλ' ὡς ἀληθῶς
μεγίστη, καὶ ἐὰν μόνον ᾖ χιλίων τῶν προπολεμούντων. οὕτω γὰρ
μεγάλην πόλιν μίαν οὐ ῥᾳδίως οὔτε ἐν | Ἕλλησιν οὔτε ἐν βαρ- B
βάροις εὑρήσεις, δοκούσας δὲ πολλὰς καὶ πολλαπλασίας τῆς
τηλικαύτης. ἢ ἄλλως οἴει; Οὐ μὰ τὸν Δί', ἔφη.

32. πολεμία Π: πολέμια A. 2. πολλαὶ A²Π : πολαὶ A¹. 5. ἕως v: ὡς ΑΠΞ: οὕτω q.

for believing that each of the players' sides was called collectively his πόλις. In Susemihl and Hicks *Politics of Aristotle* p. 148 *n.*, Dr Jackson remarks that the words πάμπολλαι πόλεις, ἀλλ' οὐ πόλις make it likely "that a compact body of pieces was called πόλις." If we may go further, and suppose that the *whole* of a player's side was called his πόλις, the words of Plato δύο μὲν—πολεμία ἀλλήλαις, ἡ μὲν πενήτων, ἡ δὲ πλουσίων· τούτων δ' ἐν ἑκατέρᾳ πάνυ πολλαί receive additional point by becoming an exact counterpart of the game. A defeated player, gazing ruefully at his depopulated squares, each of which, as well as the whole of his side, is a 'city,' might therefore well exclaim, 'Cities upon cities, but no city!' for there can be no city without men (ἔρημος ἀνδρῶν μὴ ξυνοικούντων ἔσω Soph. *O. T.* 57). I have thought of other possibilities, but this hypothesis as to the origin of the proverb suits the words of Plato better than any other which I can devise. For a different view see Hoffmann in *Fl. Jahrb.* 1863 pp. 240 ff. Cf. also Meineke *Fr. Com. Gr.* II pp. 44 f. It should be mentioned that Stewart (*Cl. Rev.* VII p. 359) thinks there need be no allusion to the game of πόλεις in this passage, but only a jest about making one into many (cf. *Men.* 77 A παῦσαι πολλὰ ποιῶν ἐκ τοῦ ἑνός, ὅπερ φασὶ τοὺς συντρίβοντάς τι ἑκάστοτε οἱ σκώπτοντες), while Schneider finds only a "lusus in verbis atque in consociatione singularis et pluralis." Neither of these suggestions meets the situation.

32 **δύο—κἂν ὁτιοῦν ᾖ**: 'two, in any case,' lit. 'if there be even anything at all,' i.e. 'whatever there be.' So also Schneider. The subject to ὁτιοῦν ᾖ is impersonal, and not the city, as Jowett seems to suppose.

πολεμία. On this—comparatively rare—termination of the dual feminine in Plato see Roeper *de dual. usu Pl.* pp. 3 ff. Cf. IX 587 B *n.*

423 A 6 **εὐδοκιμεῖν**. Stallbaum and others read δοκεῖν with one inferior MS. But εὐδοκιμεῖν is at least equally good: 'great, I do not say in fame, but great in the true sense of the word "great."' σωφροσύνη is a city's truest greatness, not aggression, and "the applauding thunder at its heels, Which men call Fame."

7 **χιλίων**. Aristotle takes this seriously as fixing the number of Plato's ἐπίκουροι (*Pol.* B 6. 1265ᵃ 9), but it is only the minimum: see 423 B *n.* We hear of constitutions of a thousand very frequently throughout Greek political history, especially in the Greek colonies of Italy; and Plato may have had some of these precedents in his mind, both here and in *Pol.* 292 E ἐν χιλιάνδρῳ πόλει. See Whibley *Gk. Oligarchies* pp. 134 ff. By Aristotle's time the ruling Spartans, it is interesting to notice, numbered under 1000 (*Pol.* B 9. 1270ᵃ 29—31). See Grote *Plato* III p. 206 *n.*

423 B 9 **καὶ πολλαπλασίας** is the predicate to δοκούσας, and καί means 'even.' So J. and C. rightly.

III. Οὐκοῦν, ἦν δ' ἐγώ, οὗτος ἂν εἴη καὶ κάλλιστος ὅρος τοῖς ἡμετέροις ἄρχουσιν, ὅσην δεῖ τὸ μέγεθος τὴν πόλιν ποιεῖσθαι καὶ ἡλίκῃ οὔσῃ ὅσην χώραν ἀφορισαμένους τὴν ἄλλην χαίρειν ἐᾶν. Τίς, ἔφη, ὅρος; Οἶμαι μέν, ἦν δ' ἐγώ, τόνδε· μέχρι οὗ ἂν ἐθέλῃ αὐξομένη εἶναι μία, μέχρι τούτου αὔξειν, πέρα δὲ μή. Καὶ καλῶς | γ', ἔφη. Οὐκοῦν καὶ τοῦτο αὖ ἄλλο πρόσταγμα τοῖς φύλαξι προστάξομεν, φυλάττειν παντὶ τρόπῳ, ὅπως μήτε σμικρὰ ἡ πόλις ἔσται μήτε μεγάλη δοκοῦσα, ἀλλά τις ἱκανὴ καὶ μία. Καὶ φαῦλόν γ', ἔφη, ἴσως αὐτοῖς προστάξομεν. Καὶ τούτου γε, ἦν δ' ἐγώ, ἔτι φαυλότερον τόδε, οὗ καὶ ἐν τῷ πρόσθεν ἐπεμνήσθημεν λέγοντες, ὡς δέοι, ἐάν τε τῶν φυλάκων τις φαῦλος ἔκγονος γένηται, εἰς τοὺς ἄλλους αὐτὸν ἀποπέμπεσθαι, ἐάν τ' | ἐκ τῶν ἄλλων σπουδαῖος, εἰς τοὺς φύλακας. τοῦτο δ' ἐβούλετο δηλοῦν, ὅτι καὶ τοὺς ἄλλους πολίτας, πρὸς ὅ τις πέφυκεν, πρὸς τοῦτο ἕνα πρὸς ἓν ἕκαστον ἔργον δεῖ κομίζειν, ὅπως ἂν ἓν τὸ αὑτοῦ ἐπιτηδεύων ἕκαστος μὴ πολλοί, ἀλλ' εἷς γίγνηται, καὶ οὕτω δὴ ξύμπασα ἡ πόλις μία φύηται, ἀλλὰ μὴ πολλαί. Ἔστι γάρ, ἔφη, τοῦτο ἐκείνου σμικρότερον.

22. αὐτὸν Π: αὐτῶν A.

---

423 B—**424** C *Our city must not be increased beyond the limits essential to its unity. It will be the duty of the Guardians to see to this, as well as to assign the children to their proper classes in the State. These and similar duties will be easy, if our educational curriculum is stedfastly upheld; and it will readily appear that the principle of community should also be applied to matrimony and procreation. Our citizens will thus improve as one generation succeeds another. We must forbid all innovations in music and gymnastic because they are productive of political change.*

423 B 14 **μέχρι—πέρα δὲ μή.** The extent to which the city may safely increase beyond 1000 προπολεμοῦντες (and the necessary farmers etc.) is therefore left to the judgment of the guardians. Like every natural organism, it should grow to the limits prescribed for it by nature (cf. 424 A *n.*); but Plato probably conceived of it even in its maturity as relatively small. The regulations about marriage and the interchange between the different classes would be easier to work if the State was not too large. See also on χιλίων in 423 A, and on the general subject Newman's *Politics of Aristotle* I pp. 313—315.

423 C 18 **μεγάλη δοκοῦσα**: 'seeming-great': see 422 E.

19 **ἴσως** points the irony, which is continued in φαυλότερον.

20 **πρόσθεν.** III 415 B, C *nn.*

423 D 24 **ἕκαστον**: with ἕνα, not of course with ἔργον, as Hartman seems to suppose. With what follows cf. *Laws* 847 B ἀναγκαζόντων ἕνα μόνον ἀλλὰ μὴ πολλοὺς εἶναι and infra 443 E.

26 **μία—ἀλλὰ μὴ πολλαί.** Aristotle's criticism (*Pol.* B 2. 1261^a 17—^{b} 15) is interesting, but captious. Plato would entirely agree with him that τὸ ἴσον τὸ ἀντιπεπονθὸς σῴζει τὰς πολιτείας. 'The reciprocity of services and functions' between the three classes is the very foundation of Plato's city, which is far from being an undifferentiated unity. It is rather a ἓν ἐκ πολλῶν, the πολλά being the three divisions of the State. See Susemihl and Hicks l.c. I p. 215. φύηται should be noted; unity of this kind is κατὰ φύσιν.

27 **σμικρότερον** is still ironical. In what follows Plato speaks his real mind: cf. *Laws* 813 D.

Οὗτοι, ἦν δ' ἐγώ, ὦ ἀγαθὲ Ἀδείμαντε, ὡς δόξειεν ἄν τις, ταῦτα
πολλὰ καὶ μεγάλα αὐτοῖς προστάττομεν, ¦ ἀλλὰ πάντα φαῦλα, E
ἐὰν τὸ λεγόμενον ἓν μέγα φυλάττωσι, μᾶλλον δ' ἀντὶ μεγάλου
ἱκανόν. Τί τοῦτο; ἔφη. Τὴν παιδείαν, ἦν δ' ἐγώ, καὶ τροφήν.
ἐὰν γὰρ εὖ παιδευόμενοι μέτριοι ἄνδρες γίγνωνται, πάντα ταῦτα
ῥᾳδίως διόψονται καὶ ἄλλα γε, ὅσα νῦν ἡμεῖς παραλείπομεν, τήν
τε τῶν γυναικῶν κτῆσιν καὶ γάμων καὶ παιδοποιίας, ὅτι | δεῖ ταῦτα 424
κατὰ τὴν παροιμίαν πάντα ὅ τι μάλιστα κοινὰ τὰ φίλων ποιεῖσθαι.
Ὀρθότατα γάρ, ἔφη, γίγνοιτ' ἄν. Καὶ μήν, εἶπον, πολιτεία, ἐάνπερ
ἅπαξ ὁρμήσῃ εὖ, ἔρχεται ὥσπερ κύκλος αὐξανομένη. τροφὴ γὰρ

---

423 E 30 **ἓν μέγα.** ἓν balances πολλά: we need but one regulation, 'the proverbial one great thing, or rather not great, but adequate.' J. and C. err in translating ἱκανόν "to a sufficient extent"; and Stallbaum in making λεγόμενον "quod dicebamus." ἓν μέγα is illustrated by J. and C. from *Pol.* 297 A.

32 **εὖ παιδευόμενοι.** Does this refer to the scheme of education already given, or is it a promise of the philosopher's training in Books VI and VII? Krohn takes the former view (*Pl. St.* p. 127), and (if we have regard only to the preceding discussion) it must be allowed that this is the natural interpretation of Plato's words. At the same time, it is not easy to see how the musical education of II and III would enable the guardians to grasp such a conception as the community of wives and children. And in the later books Plato expressly declares that the training necessary for the Rulers was inadequately discussed before: see VI 497 C ff., 502 D. For these reasons we must, I think, suppose that Plato when he wrote these words was thinking of the education still to be provided. Cf. also III 414 A.

33 **τήν τε τῶν γυναικῶν κτλ.** is the first mention of communism in wives and children. According to an ingenious chorizontic theory, it was this sentence which inspired the *Ecclesiazusae* of Aristophanes, to whose caricature Plato replies in Book V (Stein *de Ar. Eccles. arg.* etc. and Brandt *Zur Entwick. d. Pl. Lehre v. d. Seelentheilen*, p. 6). See on the whole subject App. I to Book V. In γάμων and παιδοποιίας there is a kind of zeugma: for κτῆσιν suits only γυναικῶν. Plato marks the difference by placing τε after τήν and not after τῶν. γάμους (conjectured by Richards) would depend on διόψονται; but διόψονται γάμους καὶ παιδοποιίας is surely an impossible expression.

424 A 2 **κοινὰ τὰ φίλων.** "Locus brevitatem loquendi paullo insolentiorem habet, quam sic explico: δεῖ πάντα ταῦτα ὅ τι μάλιστα ποιεῖσθαι κοινά, ὥστε κατὰ τὴν παροιμίαν κοινὰ τὰ φίλων εἶναι" (Schneider). Hartman's proposal to omit τὰ φίλων has much in its favour. It is more elegant to suggest than quote so familiar a proverb; and the note τὰ φίλων might well have been added by a scribe upon the margin. In V 449 C on the other hand the addition of τὰ φίλων is appropriate and right.

3 **ὀρθότατα κτλ.** Adimantus accepts the principle, both here and in V 449 C. The doubts which he expresses later concern not the principle, but the τρόπος τῆς κοινωνίας (ib.). It is obvious that the principle κοινὰ τὰ φίλων might be applied to marriage etc. in a sentimental kind of way, without involving such a kind of community as is afterwards described. As Rettig points out (*Proleg.* p. 95 *n.*), Adimantus takes ὅ τι μάλιστα as "in quantum fieri posset maxime."

4 **ἔρχεται κτλ.**: 'goes on growing like a circle.' So Schneider, rightly. Others take κύκλος (1) as a hoop or wheel—"goes on with accumulating force like a wheel" (J. and C.), or (2) as an ever-widening circle in ruffled water (Krohn, Herwerden etc.). As to (2), κύκλος cannot mean a circle in water, unless we insert ἐν ὕδατι, which Herwerden has the audacity to do. If we adopt the first solution, we make

καὶ παίδευσις χρηστὴ σῳζομένη φύσεις ἀγαθὰς ἐμποιεῖ, καὶ αὖ φύσεις χρησταὶ τοιαύτης παιδείας ἀντιλαμβανόμεναι ἔτι βελτίους B *τῶν προτέρων φύονται εἴς τε τἆλλα καὶ εἰς τὸ γεννᾶν,* | *ὥσπερ καὶ ἐν τοῖς ἄλλοις ζῴοις. Εἰκός γ', ἔφη. Ὡς τοίνυν διὰ βραχέων εἰπεῖν, τούτου ἀνθεκτέον τοῖς ἐπιμεληταῖς τῆς πόλεως, ὅπως ἂν αὐτοὺς μὴ λάθῃ διαφθαρέν, ἀλλὰ παρὰ πάντα αὐτὸ φυλάττωσι, τὸ μὴ νεωτερίζειν περὶ γυμναστικήν τε καὶ μουσικὴν παρὰ τὴν τάξιν, ἀλλ' ὡς οἷόν τε μάλιστα φυλάττειν, φοβουμένους ὅταν τις λέγῃ, ὡς τὴν ἀοιδὴν*

μᾶλλον ἐπιφρονέουσ' ἄνθρωποι,
ἥτις ἀειδόντεσσι νεωτάτη ἀμφιπέληται,

C | *μὴ πολλάκις τὸν ποιητήν τις οἴηται λέγειν οὐκ ᾄσματα νέα, ἀλλὰ τρόπον ᾠδῆς νέον, καὶ τοῦτο ἐπαινῇ. δεῖ δ' οὔτ' ἐπαινεῖν τὸ τοιοῦτον οὔτε ὑπολαμβάνειν· εἶδος γὰρ καινὸν μουσικῆς μεταβάλλειν εὐλαβητέον ὡς ἐν ὅλῳ κινδυνεύοντα· οὐδαμοῦ γὰρ κινοῦνται*

κύκλος a specific kind of circle: but nothing in the context warrants this. It is also very doubtful if *αὐξανομένη* can = 'with accumulating force': certainly *κύκλος αὐξάνεται* could not bear this meaning; and to exclude *αὐξανομένη* from the comparison (as J. and C. also suggest) renders *ὥσπερ κύκλος* practically otiose. The fact is that the growth of a natural (*κατὰ φύσιν*) city is just like the drawing of a circle in Plato's way of thinking. Like a circle it grows and expands, like a circle too, when its zenith is passed, it narrows to the inevitable end. Here it is only the growth which is dwelt upon; but *ὥσπερ κύκλος* seems to warn us of impending decay and foreshadow Books VIII—IX. For more on this point see my *Number of Plato* pp. 58—62. *αὐξανομένη* is 'growing' in the widest sense i.e. reaching its full maturity of size and strength and beauty; but in what follows Plato characteristically confines himself to what he conceived to be a city's truest growth, the improvement of the citizens.

τροφὴ γὰρ κτλ. Plato seems therefore to hold that acquired characters can be transmitted to posterity. The general sentiment may be illustrated by the quaint catches sung by choirs of old men, men in their prime, and boys at Sparta: (1) *Ἀμὲς πόκ' ἦμες ἄλκιμοι νεανίαι*, (2) *Ἀμὲς δέ γ' εἰμές· εἰ δὲ λῇς, πεῖραν λάβε*, (3) *Ἀμὲς δέ γ' ἐσσόμεσθα πολλῷ κάρρονες* (ap. Plut. *Lyc.* 21. 3). Cf. V 461 A.

7 **εἰς τὸ γεννᾶν—ζῴοις.** Cf. V 459 A ff.

424 B 9 **τούτου** is not intended to anticipate the *ὅπως* clause, but means—like *αὐτό* below—our system of education. This is clear from *διαφθαρέν*, which is the antithesis to *σῳζομένη* above, and like it, is said of the *παιδεία*. *τὸ μὴ νεωτερίζειν* is in loose apposition to **αὐτό.**

13 **τὴν—ἀμφιπέληται.** *Od.* I 351 f. *τὴν γὰρ ἀοιδὴν μᾶλλον ἐπικλείουσ' ἄνθρωποι κτλ.* Plato's variant probably points to a different recension; for *ἐπιφρονεύουσιν* (sic)· *ἐπακούουσιν* in Hesychius seems to refer to the same passage (Schneider). For the sentiment cf. Pind. *Ol.* 9. 48 *αἴνει δὲ παλαιὸν μὲν οἶνον, ἄνθεα δ' ὕμνων | νεωτέρων*, Xen. *Cyr.* I 6. 38 and many other illustrations in Smyth *Greek Melic Poets* p. 174.

424 C 16 **πολλάκις.** 422 C *n.*

17 **τρόπον ᾠδῆς νέον.** Pind. *Ol.* 3. 4 *Μοῖσα δ' οὕτω μοι παρεστάκοι νεοσίγαλον εὑρόντι τρόπον.* Pindar would incur Plato's censure for these words.

18 **ὑπολαμβάνειν:** i.e. understand such to be the poet's meaning.

μουσικῆς τρόποι ἄνευ πολιτικῶν νόμων τῶν μεγίστων, ὥς φησί τε Δάμων καὶ ἐγὼ πείθομαι. Καὶ ἐμὲ τοίνυν, ἔφη ὁ Ἀδείμαντος, θὲς τῶν πεπεισμένων.

IV. | Τὸ δὴ φυλακτήριον, ἦν δ᾽ ἐγώ, ὡς ἔοικεν, ἐνταῦθά που D οἰκοδομητέον τοῖς φύλαξιν, ἐν μουσικῇ. Ἡ γοῦν παρανομία, ἔφη,

---

20 **μουσικῆς τρόποι.** In later musical theory *τρόποι* was technically used to denote the three varieties of musical composition—*νομικός, διθυραμβικός, τραγικός*. They were called *τρόποι* (according to Aristid. Quint. p. 30 Meib.) because they expressed different psychical characters (*διὰ τὸ συνεμφαίνειν πως τὸ ἦθος κατὰ τὰ μέλη τῆς διανοίας*), because, in short, they were *μιμήματα τρόπων*. Plato's *μουσικῆς τρόποι* need not however be confined to Aristides' three varieties. On the connexion between musical and political changes see *Laws* 700 A—701 D. The connexion was recognised universally throughout Greece, and particularly at Sparta, where—as Pausanias (III 12. 10) tells us—Timotheus had his lyre confiscated for adding to it four new strings: cf. also Cic. *de Leg.* II 39. Wherever in the ancient Greek *πόλις* the conception of the individual is hardly separated from that of the citizen, moral and political changes are believed to go hand in hand; and the effect of music on morality is explained in III 400 D—401 A: cf. *Laws* 673 A *τὰ μὲν τοίνυν τῆς φωνῆς μέχρι τῆς ψυχῆς πρὸς ἀρετῆς παιδείαν οὐκ οἶδ᾽ ὅντινα τρόπον ὠνομάσαμεν μουσικήν*. Bosanquet raises the question whether musical innovations are the cause or only the symptoms of political. Plato, I think, regarded them primarily as the cause (*Laws* ll.cc.). We can better understand their effect if we remember that they were accompanied by changes not only in rhythm, but also in the quality, ethical and otherwise, of the words sung; and if we also bear in mind the enormous influence of the theatre in Greek life. The latter point is emphasized in this connexion by Plato (ll.cc.) and Aristoxenus (ap. Ath. XIV 31). See on the whole subject Newman's *Politics of Aristotle* I pp. 359—369 and Nettleship *Hellenica* pp. 123—130.

φησί—Δάμων. III 400 B *n.*

21 **τοίνυν**='also': see I 339 D *n.*

424 D—**427** A *Our Guardians must above all things guard against changes in musical education. Musical innovations even if sanctioned only in play soon make themselves felt in every quarter of the State. The spirit of law and virtue must be infused into children even through their pastimes. For this reason, we should not neglect details of dress and manners, although they call for no special enactments, but will readily conform to the spirit of our rules about education. Many other individual points may safely be left to our guardians, if only God vouchsafes to them the preservation of our laws; otherwise it is in vain for them to pass law upon law, acting like those who hope to cure their diseases by continually changing their medicines. As nothing but a complete change in their habits will benefit such men, so only a revolution will cure a state which is similarly situated. Such cities honour and make proud the men who minister to their desires; but the true statesman does not care to cut the Hydra. In a bad city, petty legislation is useless; in a good, superfluous.*

424 D ff. This section has a certain historical interest from its scarcely-veiled impeachment of Athenian politics and manners: see on 425 A, 425 C, 426 C.

23 **φυλακτήριον—μουσικῇ.** *μουσική* is at once the vital and the most vulnerable —see next note—part of our State; hence the guard-house must be built in Music. *ἐν* is quasi-local, as *ἐνταῦθά που* shews; we shall confuse the metaphor if we suppose (as some have done) that Music is itself the guard-house.

24 **ἡ γοῦν—αὕτη.** *αὕτη* is *ἡ ἐν μουσικῇ*. Madvig's suggestion *ταύτῃ* should not be accepted; it would make *παρανομία* 'lawlessness' in general, whereas Socrates' reply and Adimantus' next remark shew that only *ἡ ἄμουσος παρανομία* (*Laws* 700 D) is meant. *παρανομία* is aptly used of heterodoxy in music, thanks to the musical sense of *νόμος*. Cf. infra 424 E and Shorey in *Chicago Studies in Cl. Phil.* I p. 222 *n.* 4. The position of *αὕτη* increases its emphasis.

ῥᾳδίως αὕτη λανθάνει παραδυομένη. Ναί, ἔφην, ὡς ἐν παιδιᾶς γε μέρει καὶ ὡς κακὸν οὐδὲν ἐργαζομένη. Οὐδὲ γὰρ ἐργάζεται, ἔφη, ἄλλο γε ἢ κατὰ σμικρὸν εἰσοικισαμένη ἠρέμα ὑπορρεῖ πρὸς τὰ ἤθη τε καὶ τὰ ἐπιτηδεύματα· ἐκ δὲ τούτων εἰς τὰ πρὸς ἀλλήλους ξυμβόλαια μείζων ἐκβαίνει· ἐκ δὲ δὴ τῶν ξυμβολαίων ἔρχεται
E ἐπὶ | τοὺς νόμους καὶ πολιτείας σὺν πολλῇ, ὦ Σώκρατες, ἀσελγείᾳ, ἕως ἂν τελευτῶσα πάντα ἰδίᾳ καὶ δημοσίᾳ ἀνατρέψῃ. Εἶεν, ἦν δ' ἐγώ· οὕτω τοῦτ' ἔχει; Δοκεῖ μοι, ἔφη. Οὐκοῦν, ὃ ἐξ ἀρχῆς ἐλέγομεν, τοῖς ἡμετέροις παισὶν ἐννομωτέρου εὐθὺς παιδιᾶς μεθεκτέον, ὡς παρανόμου γιγνομένης αὐτῆς καὶ παίδων τοιούτων ἐννό-
425 μους τε καὶ σπουδαίους ἐξ | αὐτῶν ἄνδρας αὐξάνεσθαι ἀδύνατον ὄν; Πῶς δ' οὐχί; ἔφη. Ὅταν δὴ ἄρα καλῶς ἀρξάμενοι παῖδες παίζειν εὐνομίαν διὰ τῆς μουσικῆς εἰσδέξωνται, πάλιν τοὐναντίον ἢ 'κείνοις εἰς πάντα ξυνέπεταί τε καὶ αὔξει, ἐπανορθοῦσα εἴ τι καὶ πρότερον τῆς πόλεως ἔκειτο. Ἀληθῆ μέντοι, ἔφη. Καὶ τὰ σμικρὰ ἄρα, εἶπον, δοκοῦντα εἶναι νόμιμα ἐξευρίσκουσιν οὗτοι, ἃ οἱ πρότερον ἀπώλλυσαν πάντα. Ποῖα; Τὰ τοιάδε· σιγάς τε τῶν

---

25 **ἐν παιδιᾶς γε μέρει.** Plato is animadverting on the common view that music should be cultivated πρὸς παιδιάν rather than πρὸς παιδείαν. Aristotle allows a threefold use of music—for pastime (παιδιά), education, and the rational employment of leisure: *Pol.* Θ 5. 1339ª 16 and ᵇ 14 ff.

27 **ὑπορρεῖ κτλ.**: as a gentle river may become a destructive torrent before its course is ended. The sentence eloquently describes the decay of Athenian music, character, and politics from the simplicity of earlier times, as appears from *Laws* 700 A—701 D. See also on οἱ πρότερον 425 A. For πολιτείας Hartman would read the singular; but the plural is more forcible. Laws and constitutions are overthrown by the devouring flood. σύν in Plato (as in good Attic generally) is rare; one of its recognised uses is in modal phrases of this kind, especially where (as here and in VI 492 B, VIII 564 C, X 619 B) the style seeks elevation: cf. Lina *De praep. usu. Plat.* pp. 32—34 and Mommsen *Beiträge z. d. Lehre v. d. Gr. Praep.* pp. 376 ff.

424 E 32 **ὃ—ἐλέγομεν**: 'as we were trying to say at the outset,' i.e. of this discussion 424 A. No *specific* reference to an earlier part of the dialogue is intended: at all events II 377 B is not in point. According to Plato παιδιά should—(to borrow a saying of Aristotle's) —παιδεύειν πρὸς τὴν πολιτείαν—educate children in the spirit of their commonwealth: *Laws* 798 B ff. Conversely, Aristotle reminds us, education is itself the older boys' rattle (*Pol.* Θ 6. 1340ᵇ 30). It should be noted that παιδιᾶς (cf. παίζειν in 425 A) refers like παιδιᾶς in D above to music; if music is to be a pastime, it must be one which is ἔννομος. In ἐννομωτέρου and παρανόμου there may also be a play on the musical sense of νόμος: cf. 424 D *n.*

34 **τοιούτων**: viz. παρανόμων.

425 A 4 **'κείνοις**: those whom Adimantus in effect described in 424 D. See also next note.

6 **οἱ πρότερον**: 'their predecessors' (Jowett), i.e. the predecessors of our citizens. The expression betrays the fact that Plato is now censuring the decay of Athenian manners, as of Athenian music and character in 424 D. In ἐξευρίσκουσιν—πάντα Plato speaks as if his regulations were a programme for the reform of his native city. Cf. Krohn *Pl. St.* pp. 32, 33.

νεωτέρων | B *παρὰ πρεσβυτέροις, ἃς πρέπει, καὶ κατακλίσεις καὶ ὑπαναστάσεις καὶ γονέων θεραπείας, καὶ κουράς γε καὶ ἀμπεχόνας καὶ ὑποδέσεις καὶ ὅλον τὸν τοῦ σώματος σχηματισμὸν καὶ τἆλλα ὅσα τοιαῦτα. ἢ οὐκ οἴει;* Ἔγωγε. *Νομοθετεῖν δ' αὐτὰ οἶμαι εὔηθες· οὔτε γάρ που γίγνεται οὔτ' ἂν μείνειεν λόγῳ τε καὶ γράμμασιν νομοθετηθέντα.* Πῶς γάρ; *Κινδυνεύει γοῦν, ἦν δ' ἐγώ, ὦ Ἀδείμαντε, ἐκ τῆς παιδείας ὅποι ἄν τις ὁρμήσῃ, τοιαῦτα* | C *καὶ τὰ ἑπόμενα εἶναι. ἢ οὐκ ἀεὶ τὸ ὅμοιον ὂν ὅμοιον παρακαλεῖ;* Τί μήν; *Καὶ τελευτῶν δή, οἶμαι, φαῖμεν ἂν εἰς ἕν τι τέλεον καὶ νεανικὸν ἀποβαίνειν αὐτὸ ἢ ἀγαθὸν ἢ καὶ τοὐναντίον.* Τί γὰρ οὔκ; ἦ δ' ὅς. *Ἐγὼ μὲν τοίνυν, εἶπον, διὰ ταῦτα οὐκ ἂν ἔτι τὰ τοιαῦτα ἐπιχειρήσαιμι νομοθετεῖν.* Εἰκότως γ', ἔφη. *Τί δέ; ὦ πρὸς θεῶν,*

---

425 A, B 7 **σιγάς τε—τοιαῦτα.** Cf. Ar. *Clouds* 961—1023. Aristophanes mentions the *σιγαὶ τῶν νεωτέρων* (963), the *ὑπαναστάσεις* (993), the *γονέων θεραπεῖαι* (994, 998), and various details of *τοῦ σώματος σχηματισμός* (973, 983).

8 **κατακλίσεις** means literally 'settings down,' i.e. causing or permitting others to sit down, as when the Spartans, for example, in the well-known story, made way for the aged stranger at the Panathenaea (Plut. *Apophth. Lac.* 52. 235 D). Cf. *κατακλίναντες* in 420 E and II 363 C. The word—which has been curiously misunderstood—is coupled with *ὑπανάστασις* also in Arist. *Eth. Nic.* IX 2. 1165ᵃ 28. See also Xen. *Mem.* II 3. 16. After *πρέπει* supply *σιγᾶν* out of *σιγάς*. The older editors read *ὡς* for *ἃς* with several *deterioris notae* MSS.

9 **καὶ—γέ** with *κουράς* marks the transition to a new class of particulars: cf. *Crit.* 47 B, *Gorg.* 450 D al. Hartman should not have suggested *καὶ—τε*. It was the Spartans who laid greatest stress upon the points enumerated here: cf. Xen. *Rep. Lac.* 3. 5, Plut. *Cleom.* 9. 1 (*κείρεσθαι τὸν μύστακα καὶ προσέχειν τοῖς νόμοις*). See also Xen. *Cyr.* VIII 7. 10.

425 B 12 **οὔτε γάρ—νομοθετηθέντα.** Plato means that specific enactments are powerless either to produce or to maintain civilities and proprieties of this kind. The flowers of civilisation must bloom naturally, or not at all. With the general sentiment of this passage cf. Isocr. *Areop.* 41 *δεῖν δὲ τοὺς ὀρθῶς πολιτευομένους οὐ τὰς στοὰς ἐμπιμπλάναι γραμμάτων ἀλλ' ἐν ταῖς ψυχαῖς ἔχειν τὸ δίκαιον· οὐ γὰρ τοῖς ψηφίσμασιν ἀλλὰ τοῖς ἤθεσι καλῶς οἰκεῖσθαι τὰς πόλεις.*

14 **ὅποι—εἶναι**: "the bent given by education will determine all that follows" (D. and V.): "wohin einer die Richtung durch die Erziehung bekommen hat, dem auch das folgende entspricht" (Schneider). The sense is satisfactory, nor is the apparent correlation of *ὅποι* and *τοιαῦτα* a sufficient reason for impugning the text, as (in common with Dobree and others) I formerly did. *ὅπῃ* (so Ast with *q*) would convey the idea of direction more precisely than *ὅποι*, but as the route is determined by the goal, we may be satisfied. Of the various emendations—*ὁποῖ'* (Heller), *ὁποῖος* (Stallbaum, who afterwards recanted), *ὁποίας* (Dobree)—that of Dobree deserves high praise for elegance and point. The meaning would be 'as is the education from which one starts, so is the sequel'; and for *ὁποίας* = *ἐξ ὁποίας* we might compare III 402 A, VII 520 D. I once thought of *ὁποία ἄν τις ὁρμὴ ᾖ*, but am now content with the text as it stands.

425 C 16 **τελευτῶν—ἀγαθόν.** Cf. 424 A *ἐάνπερ ἅπαξ ὁρμήσῃ εὖ, ἔρχεται ὥσπερ κύκλος αὐξανομένη.*

18 **οὐκ ἂν ἔτι.** On *ἔτι* see III 412 B *n.*

19 **τί δέ; κτλ.** 'Once more: in heaven's name, said I, these market-troubles about contracts which the different classes of citizens make with one another in the market-place etc.—shall we condescend to make laws about any of *them*?' I have placed a mark of interrogation after *τί δέ* (quid vero?): cf. 422 D *n.* and 426 A. This increases the

ἔφην, τάδε τὰ ἀγοραῖα ξυμβολαίων τε πέρι κατ' ἀγορὰν ἕκαστοι
D ἃ πρὸς ἀλλήλους ξυμβάλλουσιν, εἰ δὲ | βούλει, καὶ χειροτεχνικῶν
περὶ ξυμβολαίων καὶ λοιδοριῶν καὶ αἰκείας καὶ δικῶν λήξεως καὶ
δικαστῶν καταστάσεως, καὶ εἴ που τελῶν τινὲς ἢ πράξεις ἢ θέσεις
ἀναγκαῖοί εἰσιν ἢ κατ' ἀγορὰς ἢ λιμένας, ἢ καὶ τὸ παράπαν
ἀγορανομικὰ ἄττα ἢ ἀστυνομικὰ ἢ ἐλλιμενικὰ ἢ ὅσα ἄλλα τοιαῦτα,
τούτων τολμήσομέν τι νομοθετεῖν; Ἀλλ' οὐκ ἄξιον, ἔφη, ἀνδράσι
καλοῖς κἀγαθοῖς ἐπιτάττειν· τὰ πολλὰ γὰρ αὐτῶν, ὅσα δεῖ νομο-
E θετήσασθαι, | ῥᾳδίως που εὑρήσουσιν. Ναί, ὦ φίλε, εἶπον, ἐάν γε
θεὸς αὐτοῖς διδῷ σωτηρίαν τῶν νόμων ὧν ἔμπροσθεν διήλθομεν.
Εἰ δὲ μή γε, ἦ δ' ὅς, πολλὰ τοιαῦτα τιθέμενοι ἀεὶ καὶ ἐπανορθού-
μενοι τὸν βίον διατελοῦσιν, οἰόμενοι ἐπιλήψεσθαι τοῦ βελτίστου.
Λέγεις, ἔφην ἐγώ, βιώσεσθαι τοὺς τοιούτους ὥσπερ τοὺς κάμνοντάς
τε καὶ οὐκ ἐθέλοντας ὑπὸ ἀκολασίας ἐκβῆναι πονηρᾶς διαίτης.

20. τάδε Π: om. A. 22. λήξεως *q*: λήξεις ΑΠΞ. 24. παράπαν Ξ: πάμπαν ΑΠ *q*. 29. διήλθομεν A²Ξ *q*: ἤλθομεν A¹Π.

---

emphasis on ὦ πρὸς θεῶν: cf. I 332 C ὦ πρὸς Διός, ἦν δ' ἐγώ, εἰ οὖν κτλ. Herwerden puts the pause after τάδε, where it is less suitable; others wrongly omit the word. τάδε (see *cr. n.*) cannot well be dispensed with: it means 'these familiar': cf. III 403 E, and for the omission in A *Introd.* § 5. Herwerden also cuts out ἀγοραῖα on account of κατ' ἀγοράν, but the reduplication is quite in Plato's way. The postponement of ἃ throws emphasis on κατ' ἀγοράν, and thereby helps to contrast ἀγοραῖα ξυμβόλαια with χειροτεχνικά etc.: cf. III 390 B. It is natural to see in this sentence a reference to the judicial and mercantile arrangements of Athens and her empire: see 424 D *n.*

425 D 21 **χειροτεχνικῶν κτλ.** χειροτεχνικὰ ξυμβόλαια are contracts with builders and the like (*Laws* 920 D).

22 **δικῶν λήξεως** means simply 'the bringing of lawsuits': originally 'obtaining (by lot) one's rights,' hence 'obtaining leave to claim one's rights' (Meier and Schömann *Att. Process* pp. 790—794). The reading λήξεις (see *cr. n.*) cannot be defended.

23 **θέσεις**: not 'the imposition of taxes' (L. and S.), but 'the payments,' as πράξεις is 'the exactions.'

24 **τὸ παράπαν** means 'in general,' 'generally.' τὸ πάμπαν (see *cr. n.*) is never (I believe) so used, not even in *Tim.* 64 E cited by Baiter. Regulations on nearly all the points here specified are laid down in the *Laws*: on ξυμβόλαια 913 A ff., 920 D ff., on λοιδορία 934 E ff., on αἰκεία (unprovoked assault) 879 B ff., on δικῶν λῆξις 949 C, on δικαστῶν κατάστασις 767 A ff., 956 B ff., on ἀστυνόμοι and ἀγορανόμοι 763 C ff. There is no taxation in the city of the *Laws* (847 B).

27 **καλοῖς κἀγαθοῖς.** Cf. VI 489 E *n.* **ὅσα δεῖ νομοθετήσασθαι** shews that Plato does not wish to leave all these matters undefined by legislation; but the legislation is to come from the guardians he has educated. One reason is that laws on matters of this kind can never be final: cf. *Laws* 769 D. If the guardians are true to the spirit of Plato's commonwealth, they will easily frame such minor regulations, and re-adjust them—should it prove necessary—from time to time. The effort to obtain finality (οἰόμενοι ἐπιλήψεσθαι τοῦ βελτίστου) in such matters is foredoomed to failure (cf. 426 E), and no one makes it, until he has forgotten the real foundation of a nation's greatness, and lost his sense of the proportion of things. This is Plato's meaning.

Πάνυ μὲν οὖν. Καὶ μὴν | οὗτοί γε χαριέντως διατελοῦσιν. 426
ἰατρευόμενοι γὰρ οὐδὲν περαίνουσιν, πλήν γε ποικιλώτερα καὶ
μείζω ποιοῦσι τὰ νοσήματα, καὶ ἀεὶ ἐλπίζοντες, ἐάν τις φάρμακον
συμβουλεύσῃ, ὑπὸ τούτου ἔσεσθαι ὑγιεῖς. Πάνυ γάρ, ἔφη, τῶν
οὕτω καμνόντων τὰ τοιαῦτα πάθη. Τί δέ; ἦν δ' ἐγώ· τόδε αὐτῶν
οὐ χαρίεν, τὸ πάντων ἔχθιστον ἡγεῖσθαι τὸν τἀληθῆ λέγοντα, ὅτι,
πρὶν ἂν μεθύων καὶ ἐμπιμπλάμενος καὶ ἀφροδισιάζων καὶ ἀργῶν
παύσηται, | οὔτε φάρμακα οὔτε καύσεις οὔτε τομαὶ οὐδ' αὖ ἐπῳδαὶ B
αὐτὸν οὐδὲ περίαπτα οὐδὲ ἄλλο τῶν τοιούτων οὐδὲν ὀνήσει; Οὐ
πάνυ χαρίεν, ἔφη· τὸ γὰρ τῷ εὖ λέγοντι χαλεπαίνειν οὐκ ἔχει
χάριν. Οὐκ ἐπαινέτης εἶ, ἔφην ἐγώ, ὡς ἔοικας, τῶν τοιούτων
ἀνδρῶν. Οὐ μέντοι μὰ Δία.

V. Οὐδ' ἂν ἡ πόλις ἄρα, ὅπερ ἄρτι ἐλέγομεν, ὅλη τοιοῦτον
ποιῇ, οὐκ ἐπαινέσει. ἢ οὐ φαίνονταί σοι ταὐτὸν ἐργάζεσθαι
τούτοις τῶν πόλεων ὅσαι κακῶς πολιτευόμεναι | προαγορεύουσι C
τοῖς πολίταις τὴν μὲν κατάστασιν τῆς πόλεως ὅλην μὴ κινεῖν,
ὡς ἀποθανουμένους, ὃς ἂν τοῦτο δρᾷ· ὃς δ' ἂν σφᾶς οὕτω

4. ὑγιεῖς Ξ *q*: ὑγιής AΠ. 9. αὐτὸν A¹Π: αὐτῶν A².

---

426 A 2 **πλήν γε κτλ.** If the text is sound we must take πλήν γε as πλήν γε ὅτι (which H. Wolf was wishful to restore) and καί before ἀεὶ ἐλπίζοντες as = *idque* (with Stallbaum), unless we supply διάγουσι or the like by a sort of zeugma after ἐλπίζοντες. As regards καὶ ἀεὶ ἐλπίζοντες, J. and C. hold that the participle is resumed from ἰατρευόμενοι; but the effect of this interpretation is very harsh, because ἰατρευόμενοι goes so closely with οὐδὲν περαίνουσι as almost to form a single expression. It is not 'they make no advance, submitting to a cure and always hoping,' but 'they make no advance under treatment.' The troublesome καί before ἐλπίζοντες is omitted by some inferior MSS, is dotted in *q*, and apparently erased in Ξ. I once conjectured ποιοῦντες, comparing *Critias* 109 B πλὴν οὐ—βιαζόμενοι, but it is perhaps safer to acquiesce in the MS reading. Dümmler (*Chron. Beitr.* pp. 9—11) believes that Isocrates *Antid.* 62 expressly alludes to this passage. Isocrates at all events censures τοὺς ἐπιπλήττοντας τοῖς νῦν ἁμαρτανομένοις in words that might easily refer to Plato. See also on 426 C.

5 **αὐτῶν—μεθύων.** On the plural passing into the singular see I 347 A *n.*

426 B 13 **τοιοῦτον.** Cf. III 388 D *n.*

426 C 15 **προαγορεύουσι κτλ.** Athens is plainly in Plato's mind. The Athenians carefully guarded their constitution by means of the γραφὴ παρανόμων and the εἰσαγγελία (see Gilbert's *Gk. Const. Ant.* E.T. pp. 299, 304 ff.); but nowhere were ψηφίσματα so common, and in these the demagogue found a wide field for exercising the arts of flattery and insinuation. Cf. Gilbert *Beiträge zur innern Gesch. Athens* pp. 73—93. With ἀποθανουμένους ὃς cf. III 411 C *n.*, VIII 566 D (πάντας ᾧ ἂν περιτυγχάνῃ).

17 **ὃς δ' ἂν σφᾶς κτλ.** Dümmler (l.c.) takes this to be Isocrates, who is also—so he thinks—satirised in the similar passage VI 493 A ff., and elsewhere. If so, σοφὸς τὰ μεγάλα, οἴονται τῇ ἀληθείᾳ πολιτικοὶ εἶναι, and ἢ οἴει—περὶ αὐτοῦ (D, E) are sufficiently true and scathing. We must however observe that Plato is describing a type, and the type is that of the demagogue rather than the merely academic and sophistical rhetorician, as appears from δεινὸς ᾖ ἀποπληροῦν and

πολιτευομένους ἥδιστα θεραπεύῃ καὶ χαρίζηται ὑποτρέχων καὶ προγιγνώσκων τὰς σφετέρας βουλήσεις καὶ ταύτας δεινὸς ᾖ ἀποπληροῦν, οὗτος ἄρα ἀγαθός τε ἔσται ἀνὴρ καὶ σοφὸς τὰ μεγάλα καὶ τιμήσεται ὑπὸ σφῶν; Ταὐτὸν μὲν οὖν, ἔφη, ἔμοιγε δοκοῦσι
D δρᾶν, καὶ οὐδ' ὁπωστιοῦν ἐπαινῶ. | Τί δ' αὖ; τοὺς ἐθέλοντας θεραπεύειν τὰς τοιαύτας πόλεις καὶ προθυμουμένους οὐκ ἄγασαι τῆς ἀνδρείας τε καὶ εὐχερείας; Ἔγωγ', ἔφη, πλήν γ' ὅσοι ἐξηπάτηνται ὑπ' αὐτῶν καὶ οἴονται τῇ ἀληθείᾳ πολιτικοὶ εἶναι, ὅτι ἐπαινοῦνται ὑπὸ τῶν πολλῶν. Πῶς λέγεις; οὐ συγγιγνώσκεις, ἦν δ' ἐγώ, τοῖς ἀνδράσιν; ἢ οἴει οἷόν τ' εἶναι ἀνδρὶ μὴ ἐπισταμένῳ μετρεῖν, ἑτέρων τοιούτων πολλῶν λεγόντων ὅτι τετράπηχύς ἐστιν,
E αὐτὸν ταῦτα | μὴ ἡγεῖσθαι περὶ αὑτοῦ; Οὐκ αὖ, ἔφη, τοῦτό γε. Μὴ τοίνυν χαλέπαινε· καὶ γάρ πού εἰσι πάντων χαριέστατοι οἱ τοιοῦτοι, νομοθετοῦντές τε οἷα ἄρτι διήλθομεν καὶ ἐπανορθοῦντες, ἀεὶ οἰόμενοί τι πέρας εὑρήσειν περὶ τὰ ἐν τοῖς ξυμβολαίοις κακουργήματα καὶ περὶ ἃ νῦν δὴ ἐγὼ ἔλεγον, ἀγνοοῦντες ὅτι τῷ ὄντι
27 ὥσπερ Ὕδραν τέμνουσιν. Καὶ μήν, | ἔφη, οὐκ ἄλλο τί γε ποιοῦσιν. Ἐγὼ μὲν τοίνυν, ἦν δ' ἐγώ, τὸ τοιοῦτον εἶδος νόμων πέρι καὶ πολιτείας οὔτ' ἐν κακῶς οὔτ' ἐν εὖ πολιτευομένῃ πόλει ᾤμην ἂν

---

426 E. These two types are cast in similar moulds; and Dümmler may be right in supposing that Plato thought of Isocrates as he wrote this satire, and pointed his shafts accordingly. If so, they hit the mark, and rankled, as it was natural they should. Isocrates apparently attempts a reply in his *Antidosis* (Dümmler l.c. p. 9).

20 **οὗτος ἄρα—ἔσται.** To insert *ὡς* after *οὗτος* (as Richards proposes) would spoil the effect, and be grammatically awkward. Plato wishes to suggest the language of a proclamation 'he shall be a good man and true,' etc. *ἄρα* is enough (as Hartman notes) to mark the indirect: cf. II 358 C *n*.

426 D 24 **ἀνδρείας—εὐχερείας**: 'courage and complaisance.' *εὐχέρεια* is not 'dexterity (L. and S., with the English translators), a meaning which the word never bears in Plato; but 'facilitas,' 'humanitas,' kind, obliging behaviour. "Herzhaftigkeit und Gutmüthigkeit," Schneider, rightly.

28 **τετράπηχυς**: 'a six-footer.' Dümmler (l.c.) questions this word, without saying why. It is more appropriate than a word expressing greater height; especially if any personal allusion is intended. Isocrates was not an intellectual giant, nor would even his applauding contemporaries (I think) have called him so.

426 E 29 **οὐκ αὖ—τοῦτό γε**: sc. *οἴομαι*. The point of *αὖ* is that Adimantus returned an affirmative answer last time (426 D). *οὐκ ἄν*, which is generally read, has not sufficient authority, and is difficult to justify. For *οὐκ αὖ* cf. III 393 D and infra 442 A.

30 **πάντων χαριέστατοι.** To this perhaps Isocrates replies in *Antid.* 62 *χαριέντως μὲν εἰρῆσθαι ταῦτα φήσουσι, τὸ γὰρ εὖ φθονήσουσιν εἰπεῖν* (Dümmler l.c.).

31 **νομοθετοῦντες κτλ.** It improves the rhetorical effect to treat all the participles as coordinate, instead of making the first two dependent on the third, or the third subordinate to them. For this reason I have placed a comma after *ἐπανορθοῦντες*.

427 A 3 **οὔτ'—ᾤμην ἄν**: 'I should not have thought so' were it not for these

δεῖν τὸν ἀληθινὸν νομοθέτην πραγματεύεσθαι· ἐν τῇ μὲν ὅτι ἀνωφελῆ καὶ πλέον οὐδέν, ἐν δὲ τῇ, ὅτι τὰ μὲν αὐτῶν κἂν ὁστισοῦν εὕροι, τὰ δὲ ὅτι αὐτόματα ἔπεισιν ἐκ τῶν ἔμπροσθεν ἐπιτηδευμάτων.

| Τί οὖν, ἔφη, ἔτι ἂν ἡμῖν λοιπὸν τῆς νομοθεσίας εἴη; καὶ ἐγὼ **B** εἶπον ὅτι Ἡμῖν μὲν οὐδέν, τῷ μέντοι Ἀπόλλωνι τῷ ἐν Δελφοῖς τά τε μέγιστα καὶ κάλλιστα καὶ πρῶτα τῶν νομοθετημάτων. Τὰ ποῖα; ἦ δ' ὅς. Ἱερῶν τε ἱδρύσεις καὶ θυσίαι καὶ ἄλλαι θεῶν τε καὶ δαιμόνων καὶ ἡρώων θεραπεῖαι, τελευτησάντων τε αὖ θῆκαι καὶ ὅσα τοῖς ἐκεῖ δεῖ ὑπηρετοῦντας ἵλεως αὐτοὺς ἔχειν. τὰ γὰρ δὴ τοιαῦτα οὔτ' ἐπιστάμεθα ἡμεῖς οἰκίζοντές τε πόλιν | οὐδενὶ **C** ἄλλῳ πεισόμεθα, ἐὰν νοῦν ἔχωμεν, οὐδὲ χρησόμεθα ἐξηγητῇ, ἀλλ'

12. *τελευτησάντων τε* Ξ: *τελευτησάντων* ΑΠ *q*.

---

great authorities. Jowett misses the irony by neglecting the tense ('I conceive that the true legislator will not trouble himself,' etc.). *τὸν ἀληθινὸν νομοθέτην* and *κἂν ὁστισοῦν εὕροι* would strike home, if Isocrates is meant.

5 **ἀνωφελῆ — ἐπιτηδευμάτων.** For *ἀνωφελῆ* Ξ has *ἀνωφελές*, an obvious 'correction.' The plural, as Schneider observes, is supported by *τὰ μὲν αὐτῶν* (where *αὐτῶν* is also neuter). *ὅτι* after *τὰ δέ* has been called in question by Stallbaum and Hartman. Taken strictly, it must depend on a verbal notion supplied out of *πραγματεύεσθαι* (Stallbaum) or *κἂν ὁστισοῦν εὕροι*; but in a half-adverbial phrase like *τὰ δέ*, we should not pry too closely into the grammatical construction. The effect is exactly like the English 'because some of them, etc., in other cases, because,' etc.

427 B, C *In all that appertains to temples and religious worship, as well as services paid to the dead, Apollo, the guide of our fathers, and indeed of all mankind, shall direct us.*

427 B **τί οὖν κτλ.** With this section of the *Republic* we should compare V 461 E, 469 A, VII 540 C, and *Laws* 738 B ff. Plato would fain be no iconoclast: his object is to purify, rather than to abolish, the old religion. He tries, in short, to put new wine into old bottles. In particular, when he makes Apollo preside at the foundation of his city (*οἰκίζοντές τε πόλιν οὐδενὶ ἄλλῳ πεισόμεθα*), he is acting in accordance with the universal custom of the Greeks, who consulted the oracle at Delphi before planting colonies, and revered him as the universal *ἀρχηγέτης* and *οἰκιστής* (Preller *Gr. Myth.* p. 269). It is equally in harmony with Hellenic, and especially Athenian, usage to refer all matters of public worship to Apollo: see on 427 C. Delphi was the abiding centre of Greek religious and political unity; and it is therefore right that a Greek city (V 470 E), one of whose objects is to promote unity and comity among Greeks (ib. 469 B ff.), should attach itself to Apollo.

9 **τῷ μέντοι Ἀπόλλωνι κτλ.** Cf. *Mem.* I 3. 1 (of Socrates) *φανερὸς ἦν καὶ ποιῶν καὶ λέγων, ᾗπερ ἡ Πυθία ἀποκρίνεται τοῖς ἐρωτῶσι, πῶς δεῖ ποιεῖν ἢ περὶ θυσίας ἢ περὶ προγόνων θεραπείας ἢ περὶ ἄλλου τινὸς τῶν τοιούτων.* The answer of the priestess was 'Serve the gods *νόμῳ πόλεως*' (l.c. and IV 3. 16). The spirit in which we worship matters, rather than whom or how we worship. So large and tolerant a sentiment is worthy of the Delphic priesthood and of Plato.

12 **τελευτησάντων τε.** See *cr. n.* Asyndeton is indefensible here. We must either with all the editors (except J. and C.) read *τε*, or add *καί* after *θεραπεῖαι*.

427 C 15 **ἐξηγητῇ—πατρίῳ.** *πατρῴῳ* instead of *πατρίῳ* is called for by Ast on slight MS authority. *Ἀπόλλων* was ancestor of the Ionians, being father of Ion

ἢ τῷ πατρίῳ· οὗτος γὰρ δήπου ὁ θεὸς περὶ τὰ τοιαῦτα πᾶσιν ἀνθρώποις πάτριος ἐξηγητὴς ἐν μέσῳ τῆς γῆς ἐπὶ τοῦ ὀμφαλοῦ καθήμενος ἐξηγεῖται. Καὶ καλῶς γ', ἔφη, λέγεις· καὶ ποιητέον οὕτω.

D VI. Ὠικισμένη μὲν τοίνυν, ἦν δ' ἐγώ, | ἤδη ἂν σοι εἴη, ὦ παῖ

(*Euthyd.* 302 D), and was worshipped by them as Ἀπόλλων πατρῷος (Preller *Gr. Myth.* p. 272). But (as Schneider observes) "Socrates hic non magis quam alibi in his libris tanquam Atheniensis loquitur, sed tanquam Graecus. Graecis autem omnibus πάτριος, hoc est, a maioribus traditus harum rerum arbiter et interpres erat Delphicus Apollo." An allusion to the special connexion of Ionians with Apollo would be out of place, particularly as πᾶσιν ἀνθρώποις follows. In Athens the ἐξηγηταί formed a college of three members, charged with religious duties. According to Schöll (in *Hermes* VI pp. 36 ff.) the members were partly chosen by Apollo in his capacity of πάτριος ἐξηγητής; apparently the Athenians chose nine, out of whom three were selected—one from each triad—by the representatives of the god: whence their designation πυθόχρηστοι. It is on this model that Plato perhaps frames his regulations in *Laws* 759 D.

16 **πᾶσιν ἀνθρώποις.** Delphi is then a religious centre, not for Greeks only, but for all mankind. It was certainly the nearest approach to such a centre that antiquity provided, for it commanded the homage of barbarians as well as Greeks. See Middleton *Journ. of Hell. Studies* IX p. 308. Middleton cites Livy XXXVIII 48. 2 "commune humani generis oraculum," Cicero *pro Font.* 30 "oraculum orbis terrae," and gives examples of the offerings paid by foreigners at Apollo's shrine. Even now, perhaps, Plato would deny that the oracle is dumb, though—true to its own principle of worshipping νόμῳ πόλεως—it speaks through other voices, and of other gods. See also on V 470 C.

17 **ἐν μέσῳ—ἐξηγεῖται.** Cf. Eur. *Ion* 5, 6 ὀμφαλὸν | μέσον καθίζων Φοῖβος ὑμνῳδεῖ βροτοῖς. The ὀμφαλός was "a conical mass of 'white marble or stone'" (Paus. X 16) in the sanctuary of Apollo at Delphi, "said to mark the centre of the earth." Two gold eagles stood at its sides, representing the eagles which, according to the legend, met there, having been despatched simultaneously by Zeus from the extreme East and West of the world (Strabo IX 3. 6). The ὀμφαλός is frequently represented as the seat of Apollo (ἐπὶ τοῦ ὀμφαλοῦ καθήμενος), "especially upon coins, when he is represented in the character of the giver of oracles": see for example Imhoof-Blumner and P. Gardner in *J. H. S.* VIII p. 18, and Plate LXXIV vii. Middleton, on whose article "The Temple of Apollo at Delphi" (cited above) this note is chiefly based, thinks "the word ὀμφαλός was probably derived from ὀμφή, a voice, because the divine voice was heard there." If this is true, the legends associating the shrine with the 'navel' or centre of the earth may be due to popular etymology. ὀμφαλός, 'navel,' is an Indo-Germanic word (Brugmann *Grundriss* II p. 187). Herwerden's excision of the words ἐν μέσῳ betrays ignorance of what the ὀμφαλός really was. See also Frazer on Paus. l.c.

427 D—**429** A *Our city is now founded. Where then is Justice, where Injustice? How do they differ, and which is essential to happiness? Let us approach the question thus. Our city is perfectly virtuous, and must therefore be wise, brave, temperate and just. If we discover three of these elements in the city, the residue will be the fourth.*

Let us take Wisdom first. It is not the technical knowledge or skill of the lower classes which renders our city wise, but rather the knowledge which deliberates for the whole city's interests. Now this knowledge is embodied in the Rulers. They form the smallest section of the State, but it is none the less in virtue of their presence that we call the whole city wise.

427 D ff. The process of purgation has now been ended, and Plato's δευτέρα πόλις is complete (see II 372 E ff.). We are therefore ready to look for the second view of Justice. See on II 372 A. It

Ἀρίστωνος, ἡ πόλις· τὸ δὲ δὴ μετὰ τοῦτο σκόπει ἐν αὐτῇ φῶς ποθὲν πορισάμενος ἱκανὸν αὐτός τε καὶ τὸν ἀδελφὸν παρακάλει καὶ Πολέμαρχον καὶ τοὺς ἄλλους, ἐάν πως ἴδωμεν, ποῦ ποτ' ἂν εἴη ἡ δικαιοσύνη καὶ ποῦ ἡ ἀδικία, καὶ τί ἀλλήλοιν διαφέρετον, καὶ πότερον δεῖ κεκτῆσθαι τὸν μέλλοντα εὐδαίμονα εἶναι, ἐάν τε λανθάνῃ ἐάν τε μὴ πάντας θεούς τε καὶ ἀνθρώπους. Οὐδὲν λέγεις,
ἔφη ὁ Γλαύκων· σὺ γὰρ ὑπέσχου ζητήσειν, | ὡς οὐχ ὅσιόν σοι ὂν **E**
μὴ οὐ βοηθεῖν δικαιοσύνῃ εἰς δύναμιν παντὶ τρόπῳ. Ἀληθῆ, ἔφην ἐγώ, ὑπομιμνῄσκεις, καὶ ποιητέον μέν γε οὕτως, χρὴ δὲ καὶ ὑμᾶς ξυλλαμβάνειν. Ἀλλ', ἔφη, ποιήσομεν οὕτω. Ἐλπίζω τοίνυν, ἦν δ' ἐγώ, εὑρήσειν αὐτὸ ὧδε. οἶμαι ἡμῖν τὴν πόλιν, εἴπερ ὀρθῶς γε ᾤκισται, τελέως ἀγαθὴν εἶναι. Ἀνάγκη, ἔφη. Δῆλον δὴ ὅτι σοφή τ' ἐστὶ καὶ ἀνδρεία καὶ σώφρων καὶ δικαία. Δῆλον. Οὐκοῦν

22. ποθὲν Ξ*q*: πόθεν ΑΠ.

---

should be observed that this part of the *Republic* has an independent value in the history of Ethics as the first explicit assertion of the doctrine of four cardinal virtues (427 E *n.*). For an account of Plato's teaching on the Virtues we may refer to Michaelis *die Entwicklungsstufen in Plato's Tugendlehre*, and especially to Hammond *On the Notion of Virtue in the Dialogues of Plato* Boston 1892.

427 D 22 **αὐτός τε καὶ—παρακάλει.** For the idiom cf. (with Schneider) *Phaedr.* 253 B μιμούμενοι αὐτοί τε καὶ τὰ παιδικὰ πείθοντες.

24 **ποῦ ἡ ἀδικία.** If our city is τελέως ἀγαθή (427 E), it is useless to look for ἀδικία in it. On this difficulty see II 369 A *n.*

25 **πότερον.** Herwerden's ποτέραν is quite unnecessary, as Hartman shews; cf. 428 A, 433 D, 434 C, 445 B, V 449 D.

ἐάν τε λανθάνῃ κτλ. recalls II 367 E.

427 E 27 **ὡς οὐχ ὅσιον—τρόπῳ:** II 368 B, C.

33 **σοφή—δικαία.** This is apparently the earliest passage in Greek literature where the doctrine of four cardinal virtues (if by cardinal virtues we mean those which make up the sum of perfect goodness) is expressly enunciated. The doctrine may of course be Pythagorean, but evidence is wanting, and it is doubtful whether Pindar's τέσσαρες ἀρεταί *Nem.* III 74 are to be interpreted as the cardinal virtues: see Bury ad loc. The nearest approach to the doctrine before Plato is in Xen. *Mem.* III 9. 1—5 (as Krohn has pointed out *Pl. St.* p. 372), with which compare IV 6. 1—12, where Justice, Wisdom, and Courage are named, as well as other virtues, including εὐσέβεια. Cf. also Aesch. *Sept.* 610 σώφρων δίκαιος ἀγαθὸς εὐσεβὴς ἀνήρ. From other passages in Plato, none of which are so precise and technical as this, it would seem that ὁσιότης made a good fight for a fifth place: *Prot.* 329 C, *Lach.* 199 D, *Men.* 78 D, *Gorg.* 507 B. In *Phaed.* 69 C and *Laws* 631 C σωφροσύνη, δικαιοσύνη, ἀνδρεία and φρόνησις (not σοφία) are named together, without ὁσιότης, which in the *Euthyphro* (12 D ff.) is a subdivision of δικαιοσύνη. From Adimantus' ready assent (cf. V 476 A *n.*), we may reasonably infer that the doctrine of four cardinal virtues was already a familiar tenet of the Platonic school. Schleiermacher thinks it may have been taken over "aus dem allgemeinen Gebrauch" (*Einleitung* p. 26). There is however no evidence to shew that these four virtues *and no others* were regarded as the essential elements of a perfect character before Plato. If the theory was originated by Plato himself, it is possible enough that in restricting the number to four, Plato was not uninfluenced by the sacred character of the number four in Pythagoreanism, just as Aristotle has been supposed to have limited his categories to ten on similar grounds. An interesting conjecture is

ὅ τι ἂν αὐτῶν εὕρωμεν ἐν αὐτῇ, τὸ ὑπόλοιπον ἔσται τὸ οὐχ
428 ηὑ|ρημένον; Τί μήν; Ὥσπερ τοίνυν ἄλλων τινῶν τεττάρων, εἰ
ἕν τι ἐζητοῦμεν αὐτῶν ἐν ὁτῳοῦν, ὁπότε πρῶτον ἐκεῖνο ἔγνωμεν,
ἱκανῶς ἂν εἶχεν ἡμῖν, εἰ δὲ τὰ τρία πρότερον ἐγνωρίσαμεν, αὐτῷ
ἂν τούτῳ ἐγνώριστο τὸ ζητούμενον· δῆλον γὰρ ὅτι οὐκ ἄλλο ἔτι
ἦν ἢ τὸ ὑπολειφθέν. Ὀρθῶς, ἔφη, λέγεις. Οὐκοῦν καὶ περὶ τούτων,
ἐπειδὴ τέτταρα ὄντα τυγχάνει, ὡσαύτως ζητητέον; Δῆλα δή.
B Καὶ μὲν δὴ πρῶτόν γέ μοι δοκεῖ ἐν αὐτῷ κατάδηλον | εἶναι ἡ
σοφία· καί τι ἄτοπον περὶ αὐτὴν φαίνεται. Τί; ἦ δ' ὅς. Σοφὴ

---

suggested by the remarks of Schleiermacher (l.c. p. 21). Our city is *ex hypothesi* perfectly virtuous. Its constituent elements are Rulers, Auxiliaries, Farmers and Artisans. Now the virtues which are exhibited in the lives and mutual relationship of these classes are, as Plato holds, Wisdom, Courage, Temperance, and Justice. Consequently these virtues are the component factors of moral perfection; in other words they are the cardinal virtues. We may admit that there is no *petitio principii* in such a method of investigation, which is, in fact, akin to the perfectly legitimate method described in *Men.* 86 E: cf. also V 458 A. If this suggestion is correct, the doctrine of four cardinal virtues will be directly descended from the arrangements of Plato's ideal city. But it is clear from what Plato himself says, both here and in 429 A, 430 D, 432 B, 433 B f., that the doctrine is already an accepted part of his ethical system, and not merely a provisional hypothesis which is intended to be confirmed by what follows. For the relative value and importance of the four cardinal virtues in Plato's way of thinking see *Laws* 630 D ff.

οὐκοῦν — ηὑρημένον. Essentially the same method is used by Aristotle to reach his conclusion that virtue is a *ἕξις* (*Eth. Nic.* II 4). Cf. also (with J. and C.) *Lys.* 216 D, E. Jowett observes that the true function of "this half-logical, half-mathematical method of residues" is in dealing with "abstract quantity" and "the laws of Nature." It is undeniable that this method is much more likely to lead us astray in ethics than in mathematics or the natural sciences, owing to the nature of the subject; but it is valid if our analysis of the phenomena is exhaustive and exact. A similar method was frequently employed in the Eleatic school: see II 380 D *n.* Plato not unfrequently extends the methods of mathematical reasoning beyond what we should consider their proper sphere: the whole of the preliminary studies, for example, in Book VII are to be pursued according to the methods of pure mathematics. See on VII 528 E ff. and the Appendix to Book VII "On the propaedeutic studies of the *Republic*."

428 A 1 **ὥσπερ τοίνυν—αὐτῶν.** For the logically superfluous (though welcome) *αὐτῶν* cf. II 375 E, infra 439 B, VIII 558 A, and Heindorf on *Gorg.* 482 D. *Theaet.* 155 E is a much harsher example, and has often been emended. The apodosis to the *ὥσπερ* clause is contained in *οὐκοῦν—ζητητέον*.

4 **οὐκ ἄλλο ἔτι ἦν.** On *ἔτι* (i.e. "after the other three were found" J. and C.) see III 412 B *n.*

7 **αὐτῷ.** A corrector in *q* wrote *αὐτῇ*, which Schleiermacher preferred. Hartman suggests *αὐτοῖς*. *αὐτῷ* is, however, not the city, but simply 'the matter,' 'the subject under discussion'; an idiomatic usage for which cf. I 339 E *n.* For the neuter *κατάδηλον* cf. 427 D *n.* Hartman's *κατάδηλος* is unnecessary.

428 B 8 **σοφία** as here described means *φρόνησις*—so it is called in 433 B, C—in its application to politics, not metaphysical knowledge of the Idea of Good. It deliberates for the good of the whole city (428 D), but the good is not yet elevated to the rank of an Idea. This point has been rightly emphasized by Krohn (*Pl. St.* pp. 40, 362), who points out the essentially Socratic character of this virtue, comparing Xen. *Mem.* I 2. 64 and IV 1. 2 (a sentiment of which Books II—IV of the *Republic* are an amplification and exposition in detail).

μὲν τῷ ὄντι δοκεῖ μοι ἡ πόλις εἶναι ἣν διήλθομεν· εὔβουλος γάρ. οὐχί; Ναί. Καὶ μὴν τοῦτό γε αὐτό, ἡ εὐβουλία, δῆλον ὅτι ἐπιστήμη τίς ἐστιν· οὐ γάρ που ἀμαθίᾳ γε ἀλλ' ἐπιστήμῃ εὖ βουλεύονται. Δῆλον. Πολλαὶ δέ γε καὶ παντοδαπαὶ ἐπιστῆμαι ἐν τῇ πόλει εἰσίν. Πῶς γὰρ οὔ; Ἆρ' οὖν διὰ τὴν τῶν τεκτόνων ἐπιστήμην σοφὴ καὶ εὔβουλος ἡ πόλις προσρητέα; Οὐδαμῶς, C ἔφη, διά γε ταύτην, ἀλλὰ τεκτονική. Οὐκ ἄρα διὰ τὴν ὑπὲρ τῶν ξυλίνων σκευῶν ἐπιστήμην βουλευομένην ὡς ἂν ἔχοι βέλτιστα, σοφὴ κλητέα πόλις. Οὐ μέντοι. Τί δέ; τὴν ὑπὲρ τῶν ἐκ τοῦ χαλκοῦ ἤ τινα ἄλλην τῶν τοιούτων; Οὐδ' ἡντινοῦν, ἔφη. Οὐδὲ τὴν ὑπὲρ τοῦ καρποῦ τῆς γενέσεως ἐκ τῆς γῆς, ἀλλὰ γεωργική. Δοκεῖ μοι. Τί δ'; ἦν δ' ἐγώ· ἔστι τις ἐπιστήμη ἐν τῇ ἄρτι ὑφ' ἡμῶν οἰκισθείσῃ παρά τισι τῶν πολιτῶν, ᾗ οὐχ ὑπὲρ τῶν ἐν τῇ D πόλει τινὸς βουλεύεται, ἀλλ' ὑπὲρ αὐτῆς ὅλης, ὅντιν' ἂν τρόπον αὐτή τε πρὸς αὑτὴν καὶ πρὸς τὰς ἄλλας πόλεις ἄριστα ὁμιλοῖ; Ἔστι μέντοι. Τίς, ἔφην ἐγώ, καὶ ἐν τίσιν; Αὕτη, ἦ δ' ὅς, ἡ φυλακικὴ καὶ ἐν τούτοις τοῖς ἄρχουσιν, οὓς νῦν δὴ τελέους φύλακας

16. βουλευομένην Heindorf: βουλευομένη codd. 22. ὅντιν' ἂν Ast: ὅντινα codd.

See also *Prot.* 352 B and *Laws* III 689 B. Commentators before Krohn (Steinhart for example *Einleit.* p. 185, and Susemihl *Gen. Entw.* II p. 153) did not sufficiently grasp the almost exclusively political character of σοφία here, although it is expressly dwelt upon by Plato throughout, and particularly in 429 A. I say 'almost,' because here, as elsewhere, Plato, as his manner is, contrives to drop some hints preparing us for a still higher conception of the virtue of the guardians. See on 429 C and 442 C.

ἄτοπον: because it is its smallest section which makes the whole city wise (428 E).

9 **εὔβουλος**. εὐβουλία was primarily a political virtue: see on I 348 D.

428 C 16 **βουλευομένην**. Heindorf's emendation (see *cr. n.*), which is accepted by Ast, Stallbaum, Baiter and Hartman, appears to me certain for these reasons. First, in τὴν ὑπὲρ τῶν ἐκ τοῦ χαλκοῦ ἤ τινα ἄλλην τῶν τοιούτων below we must understand ἐπιστήμην βουλευομένην, so that βουλευομένην and not βουλευομένη must have been written before. Secondly, if we read βουλευομένη, we must write (with Hermann etc. and a few inferior MSS) ᾗ for ἡ before οὐχ ὑπὲρ τῶν below. Schneider retains βουλευομένη, but understands βουλευομένην before ἐπιστήμην—an indefensible construction, which *Laws* 807 C (to which he appeals in *Addit.* p. 31) in no way justifies.

17 **τὴν ὑπὲρ—τοιούτων**. For the carrying on of the preposition (here διά) cf. (with Schneider) *Phaed.* 64 D ἐσπουδακέναι περὶ τὰς ἡδονὰς καλουμένας τὰς τοιάσδε, οἷον σιτίων κτλ. Ἥκιστά γε κτλ. Τί δέ; τὰς τῶν ἀφροδισίων;

428 D 22 **ὅντιν' ἂν—ὁμιλοῖ**. ἂν cannot, I think, be dispensed with here. It is better to insert it after ὅντινα than (with Baiter) after ἄριστα, for (as Schneider shews by many examples) ἂν likes to attach itself to the relative in sentences of this kind. The political wisdom here described is akin to the βασιλικὴ τέχνη of *Euthyd.* 291 C ff. and elsewhere, as well as to Aristotle's view of πολιτική as the architectonic art (*Eth. Nic.* I 1. 1094^b 27 with Stewart's note). It knows what is good and evil, and legislates for the other arts, but the good which it knows is a political and moral conception, not (as yet) the metaphysical Idea of Book VI.

25 **νῦν δή**. III 414 B (φύλακας παντελεῖς).

ὠνομάζομεν. Διὰ ταύτην οὖν τὴν ἐπιστήμην τί τὴν πόλιν προσαγορεύεις; Εὔβουλον, ἔφη, καὶ τῷ ὄντι σοφήν. Πότερον οὖν, ἦν δ'
E ἐγώ, ἐν τῇ πόλει οἴει ἡμῖν χαλκέας | πλείους ἐνέσεσθαι ἢ τοὺς
ἀληθινοὺς φύλακας τούτους; Πολύ, ἔφη, χαλκέας. Οὐκοῦν, ἔφην,
καὶ τῶν ἄλλων, ὅσοι ἐπιστήμας ἔχοντες ὀνομάζονταί τινες εἶναι,
πάντων τούτων οὗτοι ἂν εἶεν ὀλίγιστοι; Πολύ γε. Τῷ σμικροτάτῳ
ἄρα ἔθνει καὶ μέρει ἑαυτῆς καὶ τῇ ἐν τούτῳ ἐπιστήμῃ, τῷ προεστῶτι
καὶ ἄρχοντι, ὅλη σοφὴ ἂν εἴη κατὰ φύσιν οἰκισθεῖσα πόλις· καὶ
429 τοῦτο, ὡς ἔοικε, φύσει ὀλίγιστον γίγνεται | γένος, ᾧ προσήκει
ταύτης τῆς ἐπιστήμης μεταλαγχάνειν, ἣν μόνην δεῖ τῶν ἄλλων
ἐπιστημῶν σοφίαν καλεῖσθαι. Ἀληθέστατα, ἔφη, λέγεις. Τοῦτο
μὲν δὴ ἓν τῶν τεττάρων οὐκ οἶδα ὅντινα τρόπον ηὑρήκαμεν αὐτό
τε καὶ ὅπου τῆς πόλεως ἵδρυται. Ἐμοὶ γοῦν δοκεῖ, ἔφη, ἀπο-
χρώντως ηὑρῆσθαι.

27. οὖν Ξ: om. ΑΠ *q*. 5. ἐμοὶ γοῦν Π: ἔμοιγ' οὖν A.

---

26 **τί τὴν πόλιν προσαγορεύεις.** It should be noted that 'wise' (to confine ourselves for the present to the virtue of wisdom) is used (1) of the rulers in the State and the λογιστικόν in man, (2) of the city and the individual as wholes: cf. 441 D ff. Which of these two meanings is intended to be original and primary? This subject is admirably discussed by Hirzel *Hermes* VIII pp. 379 ff., who shews that the wisdom of the rulers and the λογιστικόν is the fundamental one: cf. Arist. *Top.* V 8. 138[b] 1 ff., where τὸ πρῶτον φρόνιμον is said to be ἴδιον λογιστικοῦ. The same, *mutatis mutandis*, holds good of Courage; and also, though with a difference, of Temperance and Justice. In calling the whole city wise because the rulers are wise, Plato is influenced by its analogy with the individual man, whom we readily and easily call wise, although strictly speaking he is wise only by reason of the λογιστικόν within him. Comparing 443 C ff., we observe that the city is wise because its rulers are wise, and its rulers are wise because their λογιστικόν is wise. In other words the wisdom of the λογιστικόν is the unit out of which the wisdom of the whole city is constructed. See on 443 B ff.

27 **πότερον οὖν.** See *cr. n.* We have still to explain τι ἄτοπον in 428 B, for Adimantus' τί has not yet been answered. For this reason οὖν after πότερον is welcome, if not (as Schneider thinks) indispensable.

428 E 29 **πολὺ—χαλκέας.** Cf. II 379 C *n.*

33 **ὅλη σοφὴ κτλ.** The subject is πόλις κατὰ φύσιν οἰκισθεῖσα, 'a city founded in accordance with Nature.' On κατὰ φύσιν see II 370 A *n.*

429 A 2 **ἣν μόνην—σοφίαν καλεῖσθαι.** Pfleiderer (*Zur Lösung d. Pl. Frage* pp. 46 ff.) compares *Symp.* 209 A ff. πολὺ δὲ μεγίστη—καὶ καλλίστη τῆς φρονήσεως ἡ περὶ τὰς τῶν πόλεών τε καὶ οἰκήσεων διακοσμήσεις, ᾗ δὴ ὄνομά ἐστι σωφροσύνη τε καὶ δικαιοσύνη. The difference in phraseology does not obscure the essential kinship of the two passages.

429 A—**430** C *The virtue of Courage will reside in the Warrior-class. It is owing to their bravery that we call the city brave, for the general character of the city as a whole cannot be determined by any courage or cowardice present among the others. The Soldiers will in spite of every temptation continue true to the principles laid down by law concerning what should, and what should not, be feared; and they will do so the more stedfastly, because their musical and gymnastic training has already prepared them for the legislation in question. It is in the*

VII. Ἀλλὰ μὴν ἀνδρεία γε αὐτή τε καὶ ἐν ᾧ κεῖται τῆς πόλεως, δι' ὃ τοιαύτη κλητέα ἡ πόλις, οὐ πάνυ χαλεπὸν ἰδεῖν. Πῶς δή; Τίς ἄν, ἦν δ' ἐγώ, | εἰς ἄλλο τι ἀποβλέψας ἢ δειλὴν B ἢ ἀνδρείαν πόλιν εἴποι, ἀλλ' ἢ εἰς τοῦτο τὸ μέρος, ὃ προπολεμεῖ τε καὶ στρατεύεται ὑπὲρ αὐτῆς; Οὐδ' ἂν εἷς, ἔφη, εἰς ἄλλο τι. Οὐ γὰρ οἶμαι, εἶπον, οἵ γε ἄλλοι ἐν αὐτῇ ἢ δειλοὶ ἢ ἀνδρεῖοι ὄντες κύριοι ἂν εἶεν ἢ τοίαν αὐτὴν εἶναι ἢ τοίαν. Οὐ γάρ. Καὶ ἀνδρεία ἄρα πόλις μέρει τινὶ ἑαυτῆς ἐστί, διὰ τὸ ἐν ἐκείνῳ ἔχειν δύναμιν τοιαύτην, ἣ διὰ παντὸς σώσει τὴν | περὶ τῶν δεινῶν δόξαν, ταῦτά C τε αὐτὰ εἶναι καὶ τοιαῦτα, ἅ τε καὶ οἷα ὁ νομοθέτης παρήγγειλεν ἐν τῇ παιδείᾳ. ἢ οὐ τοῦτο ἀνδρείαν καλεῖς; Οὐ πάνυ, ἔφη, ἔμαθον ὃ εἶπες, ἀλλ' αὖθις εἰπέ. Σωτηρίαν ἔγωγ', εἶπον, λέγω τινὰ εἶναι τὴν ἀνδρείαν. Ποίαν δὴ σωτηρίαν; Τὴν τῆς δόξης τῆς ὑπὸ νόμου διὰ τῆς παιδείας γεγονυίας περὶ τῶν δεινῶν, ἅ τέ ἐστι καὶ οἷα· διὰ παντὸς δὲ ἔλεγον αὐτῆς σωτηρίαν τὸ ἔν τε λύπαις ὄντα

16. παρήγγειλεν *v*: παρήγγειλλεν (sic) A[1]: παρήγγελλεν A[2]Π *q*: παρήγγελεν (sic) Ξ. 20. γεγονυίας *q*: γεγονυῖαν ΑΠΞ. 21. αὐτῆς nos: αὐτὴν codd.

---

preservation of these principles that the courage of a city consists, a kind of courage which is distinct from the corresponding virtue in lower animals and slaves, because its basis is education. Another time we may discuss the virtue of Courage more fully, but for our present purpose this suffices.

429 C 16 **ὁ νομοθέτης—παιδείᾳ.** The δόξα is then prescribed by the legislator (i.e. in Plato's city, by Plato, cf. ὑπὸ νόμου below, νομίμου in 430 B, and σὺ ὁ νομοθέτης in VI 497 D), not by the rulers from time to time. It is important to notice this point, because it shews that the rulers are not here, as in a certain sense they are in VI—VII, in the position of the original legislator: see VI 497 C *n.* Cf. however III 414 A *n.* and infra 442 C *n.*

19 **ποίαν δὴ σωτηρίαν;** ποίαν expresses incredulity and wonder, which δή saves from falling into contempt. See I 330 A *n.* On the definition of courage given here see 430 C *n.*

20 **γεγονυίας.** Cf. γεγονυῖαν in 430 B.

21 **αὐτῆς σωτηρίαν.** See *cr. n.* αὐτήν of the MSS must mean either (1) the σωτηρία or (2) ἀνδρεία (so Hartman). In either case the αὐτήν which follows has a different antecedent viz. τὴν περὶ τῶν δεινῶν δόξαν, so that the sentence becomes both awkward and obscure. Moreover, in whichever way we understand αὐτήν, the MSS leave us with three accusatives (αὐτήν, σωτηρίαν and the clause introduced by τό), the precise relationship of which is far from clear. Various suggestions have been made to escape these difficulties. Instead of αὐτήν Jackson suggests αὖ τήν (*J. Ph.* IV p. 148); while Stallbaum and others read τῷ (eo quod) for τό, before which Hartman for his part wishes to insert διά. Hermann and Baiter cut the knot by expunging both αὐτήν and σωτηρίαν. Jackson's remedy is the simplest, but αὖ creates a difficulty. The new point in the explanation which he supposes it to mark is, I think, emphasized too much by αὖ; nor indeed is it quite easy to separate αὖ from ἔλεγον. I believe Plato wrote αὐτῆς. The words διὰ παντὸς αὐτῆς σωτηρίαν recall and correspond exactly to ἣ διὰ παντὸς σώσει τὴν περὶ τῶν δεινῶν δόξαν, and to 430 B σωτηρίαν διὰ παντὸς δόξης κτλ., and the meaning is 'by preserving it perpetually I meant preserving it throughout when one is in pains and in pleasures' etc. Grammatically, the infinitives are the direct object of ἔλεγον ('I called'), and διὰ παντὸς αὐτῆς σωτηρίαν is its secondary object. The presence of αὐτῆς σωτηρίαν

D διασῴζεσθαι αὐτὴν καὶ ἐν | ἡδοναῖς καὶ ἐν ἐπιθυμίαις καὶ ἐν φόβοις καὶ μὴ ἐκβάλλειν. ᾧ δέ μοι δοκεῖ ὅμοιον εἶναι, ἐθέλω ἀπεικάσαι, εἰ βούλει. Ἀλλὰ βούλομαι. Οὐκοῦν οἶσθα, ἦν δ' ἐγώ, ὅτι οἱ βαφεῖς, ἐπειδὰν βουληθῶσι βάψαι ἔρια ὥστ' εἶναι ἁλουργά, πρῶτον μὲν ἐκλέγονται ἐκ τοσούτων χρωμάτων μίαν φύσιν τὴν τῶν λευκῶν, ἔπειτα προπαρασκευάζουσιν οὐκ ὀλίγῃ παρασκευῇ θεραπεύσαντες, ὅπως δέξεται ὅ τι μάλιστα τὸ ἄνθος, καὶ οὕτω δὴ

---

is necessary to correspond to *διασῴζεσθαι αὐτήν*, but *διὰ παντὸς* takes the first place, because it is the phrase requiring elucidation. The corruption of *αὐτῆς* to *αὐτήν* is of a piece with that of *γεγονυίας* to *γεγονυῖαν* (see *cr. n.*) and its all but inevitable consequence. The correction printed above is accepted by a reviewer of my *Text of the Republic* in *Hermathena* XXIV p. 252.

λύπαις—φόβοις. III 412 E ff.

429 D 25 **ἁλουργά** = 'purple': see *Tim.* 68 B, with Archer-Hind's note. Herwerden cuts out *ὥστ' εἶναι*, but without these words the wool which we are dyeing would be purple, whereas it is white, and we are making it purple. See on *ἐάν τε καὶ ταῦτα* in E.

26 **πρῶτον μὲν κτλ.** As far as concerns the language and grammatical construction of this passage it is clear that the object of *ἐκλέγονται* should be the same as that of *προπαρασκευάζουσιν*, *θεραπεύσαντες*, and *βάπτουσι*, and identical with the subject of *δέξεται*. Now the object of *βάπτουσι* is the wool selected to be dyed; it is therefore the wool which is subjected to *προπαρασκευή*, and consequently white substances of wool are meant by *μίαν φύσιν τὴν τῶν λευκῶν* (so also Blümner *Technologie* etc. I pp. 221 ff.). That this interpretation is right, appears also from the application of the simile. The guardians are the white woollen substances specially selected (note *ἐξελεγόμεθα* 429 E), their education is the *προπαρασκευή*; and the *δόξα περὶ δεινῶν κτλ.* is the dye. This is expressly pointed out in 429 E—430 A. *τοσούτων* is strictly in point, for woollen substances may be of any colour, since they may have been already dyed. Plato informs us that dyers selected white woollen substances when they wished to impart a lasting purple hue. Cf. *Tim.* 50 D, E. The *προπαρασκευή* included the process called *στύψις*, i.e. steeping the wool in an astringent solution (*πρόστυμμα*) to make it take the dye better (Arist. *de Col.* 4. 794^a 29 and *Probl.* XXII 11. 931^a 13 ff. *προβρέχουσιν ἐν τοῖς στρυφνοῖς τῷ διεργασθὲν μᾶλλον δέχεσθαι τὴν βαφήν*: cf. also Theoph. *de Odor.* 17 *ὑποστύφουσι γὰρ πᾶν εἰς τὸ δέξασθαι μᾶλλον τὴν ὀσμὴν ὥσπερ τὰ ἔρια εἰς τὴν βαφήν*). Aristotle uses a metaphor from dyeing in a similar way in *Eth. Nic.* II 2. 1105^a 3. Cf. also Cicero Hortens. *Fr.* 62 ed. Nobbe "ut ei qui combibi purpuream volunt, sufficiunt prius lanam medicamentis quibusdam, sic litteris talibusque doctrinis ante excoli animos et ad sapientiam concipiendam imbui et praeparari decet," and see on the whole subject Blümner l. c. I pp. 221 ff., 238 ff.

28 **θεραπεύσαντες.** If the text is sound, we must suppose either that two processes of preparation are alluded to, viz. *θεραπεία* and *προπαρασκευή*; or else that *θεραπεύσαντες* is used for *θεραπεύοντες*. The first alternative is inadmissible: for *προθεραπεύσας* in E shews that the *θεραπεία* and *προπαρασκευή* are identical. As for the second, Schneider remarks "aoristum ipsum pro praesenti positum vix credo." There are some instances in which "an aorist participle denoting that in which the action of a verb of *past* time consists may express time coincident with that of the verb, when the actions of the verb and the participle are practically one" (Goodwin *MT.* p. 52: cf. Kühner *Gr. Gr.* II pp. 161 ff.), but as *προπαρασκευάζουσιν* is a verb of present or universal time, Goodwin's rule is inapplicable here. Hartman ejects the participle, and Schneider is anxious to read *θεραπεύοντες*. In my edition of the Text, I had recourse to transposition, and placed *θεραπεύσαντες* before *οὕτω δή* ('and they do not dip the wool till they have finished dressing it'). It is, however, safer to adhere to the MSS and regard *θεραπεύσαντες* as one of those 'timeless aorists,' of which many examples are quoted by F. Carter in *Cl. Rev.* V pp. 4 ff. The MS reading is supported not only by Stobaeus (*Flor.* 43.

βάπτουσι. καὶ | ὃ μὲν ἂν τούτῳ τῷ τρόπῳ βαφῇ, δευσοποιὸν E
γίγνεται τὸ βαφέν, καὶ ἡ πλύσις οὔτ' ἄνευ ῥυμμάτων οὔτε μετὰ ῥυμμάτων δύναται αὐτῶν τὸ ἄνθος ἀφαιρεῖσθαι· ἃ δ' ἂν μή, οἶσθα οἷα δὴ γίγνεται, ἐάν τέ τις ἄλλα χρώματα βάπτῃ ἐάν τε καὶ ταῦτα μὴ προθεραπεύσας. Οἶδα, ἔφη, ὅτι ἔκπλυτα καὶ γελοῖα. Τοιοῦτον τοίνυν, ἦν δ' ἐγώ, ὑπόλαβε κατὰ δύναμιν ἐργάζεσθαι καὶ ἡμᾶς, ὅτε ἐξελεγόμεθα τοὺς στρατιώτας καὶ ἐπαιδεύομεν | μουσικῇ καὶ 430
γυμναστικῇ· μηδὲν οἴου ἄλλο μηχανᾶσθαι, ἢ ὅπως ἡμῖν ὅ τι κάλλιστα τοὺς νόμους πεισθέντες δέξοιντο ὥσπερ βαφήν, ἵνα δευσοποιὸς αὐτῶν ἡ δόξα γίγνοιτο καὶ περὶ δεινῶν καὶ περὶ τῶν ἄλλων διὰ τὸ τήν τε φύσιν καὶ τὴν τροφὴν ἐπιτηδείαν ἐσχηκέναι, καὶ μὴ αὐτῶν ἐκπλῦναι τὴν βαφὴν τὰ ῥύμματα ταῦτα, δεινὰ ὄντα ἐκκλύζειν, ἥ τε ἡδονή, παντὸς χαλεστραιου δεινοτέρα οὖσα τοῦτο | δρᾶν καὶ κονίας, λύπη τε καὶ φόβος καὶ ἐπιθυμία, παντὸς ἄλλου B
ῥύμματος. τὴν δὴ τοιαύτην δύναμιν καὶ σωτηρίαν διὰ παντὸς

---

97), but also (as Jackson has pointed out to me) by Theo Smyrnaeus *de utilit. math.* p. 13 ed. Hiller.

28 **τὸ ἄνθος**: the colour, as appears from Arist. *de Col.* l. c. 794ᵃ 34 et al. Though it is used of purple here, it was not confined to purple: see on VIII 557 C.

429 E 29 **δευσοποιὸν—βαφέν**. *δευσοποιόν· ἔμμονον καὶ δυσαπόπλυτον* (Timaeus *Lex.* s.v. *δευσοποιόν*, where Ruhnken illustrates the word very fully). The point of course is that such *προπαρασκευή* rendered the colour proof against washing. *δευσοποιός*, *ἀνέκπλυτος*, and *μόνιμος* were constantly used in connexion with dyeing: see Blümner l. c. I p. 221 *nn*. The words *τὸ βαφέν* are bracketed by Herwerden; but *ὃ ἂν* is not 'quod,' but 'si quid' (Schneider).

30 **ῥυμμάτων**. *ῥύμματα* is the generic word for detergents of any kind (Blümner *Privatalt.* p. 214 *n.* 1): cf. *παντὸς ἄλλου ῥύμματος* 430 B.

32 **ἐάν τε καὶ ταῦτα**. *ταῦτα* is *τὰ λευκά* i.e. white substances: cf. *τῶν λευκῶν* in D above. Even white wool, unless specially prepared, will not retain the dye when it is dipped: much less other colours. This is the force of *καί* in *καὶ ταῦτα*. The words *ἄλλα χρώματα* refer to the colour of the wool which is dipped, not to the colour of the dye, as Herwerden supposes when he calls for *τοῦτο*: cf. *n.* on *ὥστ' εἶναι* in D above.

33 **ἔκπλυτα καὶ γελοῖα**: a sort of hendiadys: cf. VIII 558 A *θεσπεσία καὶ ἡδεῖα*. Stallbaum's suggestion *ἀγελαῖα* for *γελοῖα* is itself *γελοιότερον*. For *τοιοῦτον* cf. III 388 D *n*.

430 A 6 **ἐκπλῦναι**. Not *ἐκπλύνοι* (with Herwerden); for the action of *ἐκπλῦναι* is more rapid than that of *γίγνοιτο*.

7 **χαλεστραίου κτλ**. *χαλεστραῖον λίτρον* (or *νίτρον*, but *λίτρον* is the Attic form) came from *Χαλέστρα*, a lake and city in Macedonia. *λίτρον* is supposed to be 'native carbonate of soda': see Blaydes on Ar. *Frogs* 712. The spelling *χαλεστραῖον* is established (as against *χαλαστραῖον* in Tim. *Lex.* s. v. and the Scholiast) by Hdt. VII 123 (*χαλέστρα*) and other authorities quoted by Schneider. *κονία* as appears from *ψευδολίτρου κονίας* in Ar. l. c. was a preparation of *λίτρον*, whence Plato couples them here. See on the subject generally *Dict. Ant.* I p. 881.

430 B 8 **παντὸς ἄλλου ῥύμματος** is cancelled by Badham and others. It is difficult however not to feel that something is wanted to balance *χαλεστραίου* and *κονίας*, especially as these are two specific detergents of the same class. Further, without *παντὸς ἄλλου ῥύμματος* Plato would probably have written *καὶ λύπη κτλ*. The sentence as it stands rings Platonic; nor was *παντὸς ἄλλου ῥύμματος* at all likely to be added by a scribe. The words were also in the text

δόξης ὀρθῆς τε καὶ νομίμου δεινῶν πέρι καὶ μὴ ἀνδρείαν ἔγωγε
καλῶ καὶ τίθεμαι, εἰ μή τι σὺ ἄλλο λέγεις. Ἀλλ' οὐδέν, ἦ δ' ὅς,
λέγω· δοκεῖς γάρ μοι τὴν ὀρθὴν δόξαν περὶ τῶν αὐτῶν τούτων
ἄνευ παιδείας γεγονυῖαν, τήν τε θηριώδη καὶ ἀνδραποδώδη, οὔτε
C πάνυ μόνιμον ἡγεῖσθαι ἄλλο τέ τι ἢ ἀνδρείαν καλεῖν. Ἀληθέστατα,
ἦν δ' ἐγώ, λέγεις. Ἀποδέχομαι τοίνυν τοῦτο ἀνδρείαν εἶναι.
Καὶ γὰρ ἀποδέχου, ἦν δ' ἐγώ, πολιτικήν γε, καὶ ὀρθῶς ἀποδέξει.

14. μόνιμον Stobaeus (*Flor.* 43. 97): νόμιμον codd.

---

used by Stobaeus and Theo Smyrnaeus: see *Flor.* 43. 97 and *de utilit. math.* p. 14. I suggest the following interpretation. The action of pleasure differs from that of pain, fear, and desire, in being more gentle, and less violent (*βίαιος*). Pleasure in short relaxes (*χαλᾷ*) while pain (of which fear and desire as such are both varieties) contracts: cf. III 411 A on the effect of *γλυκεῖαι ἁρμονίαι*, *Tim.* 66 C and Stallbaum on *Phil.* 46 D. Now *χαλεστραίου* suggests *χαλᾶν*, and it is probably for this reason that Plato compares pleasure to it. Such a play on words is quite in Plato's manner: cf. *Prot.* 361 D. If we suppose that other *ῥύμματα* were harder, and less agreeable in their action, the point of comparing pain etc. with 'every other detergent' will appear.

12 **τὴν ὀρθὴν δόξαν** has been questioned, on the ground that beasts cannot have *ὀρθὴ δόξα*. It was no doubt a feeling of this kind which gave birth to the reading *αὐτήν* for *ὀρθήν* in some inferior MSS. Herwerden employs his favourite remedy of excision; and other equally unsatisfactory remedies will be found in Hartman. The text is quite sound. True opinion is in Plato the basis of action done in ignorance of what is right but in obedience to an authority which knows. A dog and a slave act from true opinion as often as they obey a master who orders them to do what is right. So also (among others) Rettig (*Proleg.* p. 109) and Krohn (*Pl. St.* p. 42) rightly understand the passage. Cf. *n.* on *πολιτικήν* in C below.

13 **οὔτε—τε** = 'not only not—but also' lays stress on the second clause: cf. 427 C, VIII 566 D, E, IX 587 A al.

14 **μόνιμον.** See *cr. n.* The reading of some of Stobaeus' MSS (*Flor.* 43. 97) (which Dobree and others approved) appears to me almost certainly right, although it has been adopted by no recent editor. *νόμιμον*, as Rettig shews (*Proleg.* p. 110), must be used in precisely the same sense as in *δόξης ὀρθῆς τε καὶ νομίμου* just before. If so, Plato flatly (except for the *οὔτε πάνυ*) contradicts himself. For the only reason why a *δόξα* is *ὀρθή* is that it is *νόμιμος* 'in accordance with the law': nor is it possible for even a dog to possess an *ὀρθὴ δόξα* which is not *νόμιμος*. In obeying a just command, the *δόξα* of a dog is therefore not *οὐ πάνυ νόμιμος*, but wholly *νόμιμος*. On the other hand *μόνιμον* is not only appropriate but necessary in what is practically a résumé of Socrates' whole account of courage (*δοκεῖς γάρ μοι —καλεῖν*). The only difference between the *ὀρθὴ δόξα* of a guardian and a dog lies in this, that the former has received *παιδεία*, while the latter has not. And it is precisely this difference which makes the guardian's *δόξα* lasting, as the whole of the simile from dyeing was intended to shew (*ἵνα δευσοποιὸς κτλ.* 430 A). Finally, the soldier's *ὀρθὴ δόξα* has just been defined (in 430 B) as *σωτηρίαν διὰ παντός κτλ.* To *διὰ παντός* the words *οὐ πάνυ μόνιμον* are the necessary contrast: the *δόξα* is in both cases *ὀρθή τε καὶ νόμιμος*, only you can depend on the guardian always, *ἔν τε λύπαις καὶ ἐν ἡδοναῖς καὶ ἐν ἐπιθυμίαις καὶ ἐν φόβοις* (429 D), but not always on your dog and slave. Cf. *Men.* 97 E f.

ἄλλο τε—ἀνδρείαν. With the sentiment cf. *Lach.* 197 A ff., where however it is because they are destitute of knowledge that courage is denied to the lower animals. Isocrates *Antid.* 211 speaks of dogs etc. as brave.

430 C 16 **πολιτικήν γε—δίιμεν.** In this passage *πολιτικὴν ἀνδρείαν* means, I think, primarily the virtue of a *πόλις* as opposed to that of an *ἰδιώτης*: cf. 442 D αὖθις δὲ περὶ αὐτοῦ, ἐὰν βούλῃ, ἔτι κάλλιον δίιμεν· νῦν γὰρ οὐ τοῦτο ἐζητοῦμεν, ἀλλὰ δικαιοσύνην· πρὸς οὖν τὴν ἐκείνου ζήτησιν, ὡς ἐγᾦμαι, ἱκανῶς ἔχει. Ἀλλὰ καλῶς, ἔφη, λέγεις.

VIII. Δύο μήν, ἦν δ' ἐγώ, ἔτι λοιπά, ἃ δεῖ κατιδεῖν ἐν τῇ D
πόλει, ἥ τε σωφροσύνη καὶ οὗ δὴ ἕνεκα πάντα ζητοῦμεν, δικαιοσύνη. Πάνυ μὲν οὖν. Πῶς οὖν ἂν τὴν δικαιοσύνην εὕροιμεν, ἵνα μηκέτι πραγματευώμεθα περὶ σωφροσύνης; Ἐγὼ μὲν τοίνυν, ἔφη, οὔτε

πόλεώς τε καὶ ἰδιώτου. Our πόλις is brave because her soldiers are brave (429 B); so that in describing the courage of the soldiers we have really and truly been describing that of our city. But the ἀνδρεία with which we are now concerned is πολιτική in another, and more important sense, being based on 'correct opinion' (cf. *Phaed.* 82 A, B), i.e. in this instance on opinion which is in conformity with the law of the πόλις (cf. Aristotle's πολιτικὴ ἀνδρεία *Eth. Nic.* III 11. 1116ª 16 ff.), and not on 'knowledge,' like the scientific or philosophic virtue to which we are introduced in Books VI and VII. In this Platonic connotation of the term, δημοτική or πολιτικὴ ἀνδρεία is inferior both to the courage which rests upon knowledge in the Socratic sense (*Lach.* 195 A, 196 E ff., *Prot.* 349 D ff.) and to that which rests on knowledge of the Idea of the Good (cf. VI 506 A), although it is nevertheless on a much higher plane than the so-called courage of slaves and brute beasts, because it is μετὰ παιδείας γεγονυῖα. In αὖθις—δίιμεν Siebeck (*Zur Chron. d. Pl. Dial.* pp. 126 ff.) finds a promise of the *Laches*. To this view it seems to me a serious objection that the *Laches* has nothing to say of the characteristically Platonic distinction between ἐπιστήμη and ὀρθὴ δόξα: for that very reason it is probably earlier than this passage. Courage in the *Laches* is little more than Socratic courage (cf. *Mem.* IV 6. 10 ff.), for the knowledge of the good into which it is finally resolved is not knowledge of the Idea. Others have found in αὖθις a reference to the account of Courage in the individual (442 B), or to V 467 A ff., or to VI 486 B. None of these references are in point; and it is simplest to take Plato at his word. He drops the subject because further discussion of it would be irrelevant; he will resume it on another occasion if Adimantus wishes, but Adimantus is content. Cf. VII 532 D *n.* and see also on I 347 E. The whole of this section of the dialogue is important because it emphatically reaffirms the principle that courage as well as the other virtues enumerated here rests on ὀρθὴ δόξα and not on ἐπιστήμη. We have already seen that Plato's earlier scheme of education aims at implanting only ὀρθὴ δόξα. Cf. II 376 E *n.*

17 **νῦν γὰρ—ἐζητοῦμεν.** νῦν = 'as it is': so that Cobet's ζητοῦμεν (found also in one or two MSS) is unnecessary.

430 D—**432** A *Thirdly, we consider Temperance. This virtue resembles a kind of 'harmony' or mutual accord. It is often explained as self-control. Self-control means that the better self rules the worse; and this is surely true of our city, for in it the higher controls the lower, and the irrational desires of the inferior many are subject to the rational desires of the virtuous few. Further, our citizens are in accord with one another as to who shall rule and who shall be ruled, so that Temperance is present in both ruled and rulers, pervading the whole city through and through and rendering it accordant with itself. We may define Temperance as accord between the naturally better and the naturally worse, on the question which of them should rule.*

430 D ff. The difficulties connected with Plato's view of Temperance and Justice and their mutual relationship have been to a large extent cleared up by Hirzel (*Hermes* VIII pp. 379—411). Hirzel's conclusions, some of which have been attacked by W. A. Hammond in his instructive dissertation "On the notion of Virtue in the Dialogues of Plato," but not, I think, successfully, are now accepted in the main by Zeller[4] II 1, pp. 884 ff. Till Hirzel wrote, the tendency was to regard the two virtues as nearly, if not quite, identical—in which case one of the two would be practically superfluous. In that case, Plato's search for Justice is little better than a fiasco, and

οἶδα οὔτ' ἂν βουλοίμην αὐτὸ πρότερον φανῆναι, εἴπερ μηκέτι ἐπισκεψόμεθα σωφροσύνην· ἀλλ' εἰ ἔμοιγε βούλει χαρίζεσθαι, σκόπει πρότερον τοῦτο ἐκείνου. Ἀλλὰ μέντοι, ἦν δ' ἐγώ, βούλομαί
E | γε, εἰ μὴ ἀδικῶ. Σκόπει δή, ἔφη. Σκεπτέον, εἶπον· καὶ ὥς γε ἐντεῦθεν ἰδεῖν, ξυμφωνίᾳ τινὶ καὶ ἁρμονίᾳ προσέοικεν μᾶλλον ἢ τὰ πρότερον. Πῶς; Κόσμος πού τις, ἦν δ' ἐγώ, ἡ σωφροσύνη ἐστὶν καὶ ἡδονῶν τινῶν καὶ ἐπιθυμιῶν ἐγκράτεια, ὥς φασι, κρείττω δὴ αὑτοῦ λέγοντες οὐκ οἶδ' ὅντινα τρόπον. καὶ ἄλλα ἄττα τοιαῦτα ὥσπερ ἴχνη αὐτῆς λέγεται. ἦ γάρ; Πάντων μάλιστα, ἔφη. Οὐκοῦν τὸ μὲν κρείττω αὑτοῦ γελοῖον; ὁ γὰρ ἑαυτοῦ κρείττων
431 καὶ ἥττων δήπου ἂν αὑτοῦ εἴη καὶ ὁ ἥττων κρείττων· | ὁ αὐτὸς γὰρ ἐν ἅπασιν τούτοις προσαγορεύεται. Τί δ' οὔ; Ἀλλ', ἦν δ'

31. λέγοντες in mg. A^2: φαίνονται ΠΞ*q* et (punctis notatum) A.

---

his ideal city falls to pieces. Cf. Rettig *Proleg.* p. 137. Hirzel succeeds in shewing that Justice and Temperance are different, and both of them necessary to Plato's perfect city; nor does he employ any other method than a strict interpretation of Plato's own words as they occur. See on 432 A.

430 D 24 **πρότερον** is omitted by Richards as illogical. So slight a flaw is easy to forgive; and ἔτι in μηκέτι suggests that πρότερον is genuine. Nor could Adimantus well have said that in any event he did not wish Justice—οὗ δὴ ἕνεκα πάντα ζητοῦμεν—to be discovered.

430 E 27 **εἰ μὴ ἀδικῶ.** Cf. X 608 D, 612 D, *Charm.* 156 A, *Menex.* 236 B. The translation "as I am an honest man" (D. and V.) is inaccurate; but Schneider's "ich thäte ja sonst nichts recht" hits the mark. In English we require an independent clause, 'I have no right to refuse.'

ὥς γε ἐντεῦθεν ἰδεῖν: 'seen from where we stand,' i.e. on a first view: cf. ὡς ἐνθένδε ἰδεῖν *Pol.* 289 D, infra 432 B, X 595 B, and see Grünenwald in Schanz's *Beiträge* etc. II 3 pp. 1—37.

28 **ξυμφωνίᾳ—ἁρμονίᾳ.** On ἁρμονία see III 398 E *n.* In its musical application συμφωνία is used both of consonance as in the octave or double octave and also of other musical intervals: cf. VII 531 A and von Jan's *Mus. Script. Gr.* p. 102 and *passim.* The ξυμφωνία in which σωφροσύνη consists is apparently of the former kind: cf. 432 A *n.*

30 **ἡδονῶν—ἐγκράτεια.** It is chiefly this which is insisted on in the popular view of σωφροσύνη taken in III 389 D ff. Cf. Xen. *Cyr.* VIII 1. 32, Isocr. 3. 44, and other passages cited by Nägelsbach *Nachhom. Theol.* II p. 233. Here the essential mark of σωφροσύνη is ξυμφωνία as to who shall be rulers, and who subjects; a point which is not mentioned in III. In other fundamental respects, also, the two descriptions differ; and Hirzel rightly insists that the σωφροσύνη of Book IV must be examined independently and by itself (l.c. p. 409).

κρείττω—αὑτοῦ: a common formula in the popular acceptation of σωφροσύνη: see Nägelsbach l.c.

31 **λέγοντες.** See *cr. n.* λέγοντες is found also in Flor. A, in some MSS of Stobaeus (*Flor.* 43, 97) and in Cesenas M. λέγοντες should (with Stallbaum) be taken as agreeing with the nominative of φασι, 'as men say, calling one lord of oneself in some mysterious way.' δή, 'forsooth,' helps out οὐκ οἶδ' ὅντινα τρόπον. For other views on this passage see App. II.

33 **κρείττω αὑτοῦ.** Stallbaum reads κρείττων αὑτοῦ, and wishes to do so also in 431 A below. The accusative is more natural in both places, partly because it suggests τὸ κρείττω αὑτοῦ εἶναι (cf. ὁ γὰρ ἑαυτοῦ κρείττων καὶ ἥττων—ἂν αὑτοῦ εἴη), partly because of κρείττω αὑτοῦ just before.

ἐγώ, φαίνεταί μοι βούλεσθαι λέγειν οὗτος ὁ λόγος, ὥς τι ἐν αὐτῷ τῷ ἀνθρώπῳ περὶ τὴν ψυχὴν τὸ μὲν βέλτιον ἔνι, τὸ δὲ χεῖρον, καὶ ὅταν μὲν τὸ βέλτιον φύσει τοῦ χείρονος ἐγκρατὲς ᾖ, τοῦτο λέγειν τὸ κρείττω αὑτοῦ· ἐπαινεῖ γοῦν· ὅταν δὲ ὑπὸ τροφῆς κακῆς ἤ τινος ὁμιλίας κρατηθῇ ὑπὸ πλήθους τοῦ χείρονος σμικρότερον τὸ βέλτιον ὄν, τοῦτο δὲ ὡς ἐν ὀνείδει ψέγειν | τε καὶ καλεῖν ἥττω B ἑαυτοῦ καὶ ἀκόλαστον τὸν οὕτω διακείμενον. Καὶ γὰρ ἔοικεν, ἔφη. Ἀπόβλεπε τοίνυν, ἦν δ' ἐγώ, πρὸς τὴν νέαν ἡμῖν πόλιν, καὶ εὑρήσεις ἐν αὐτῇ τὸ ἕτερον τούτων ἐνόν· κρείττω γὰρ αὐτὴν αὑτῆς δικαίως φήσεις προσαγορεύεσθαι, εἴπερ, οὗ τὸ ἄμεινον τοῦ χείρονος ἄρχει, σῶφρον κλητέον καὶ κρεῖττον αὑτοῦ. Ἀλλ' ἀποβλέπω, ἔφη, καὶ ἀληθῆ λέγεις. Καὶ μὴν καὶ τάς γε πολλὰς καὶ παντοδαπὰς ἐπιθυμίας καὶ ἡδονάς τε | καὶ λύπας ἐν παισὶ μάλιστα C ἄν τις εὕροι καὶ γυναιξὶ καὶ οἰκέταις καὶ τῶν ἐλευθέρων λεγομένων ἐν τοῖς πολλοῖς τε καὶ φαύλοις. Πάνυ μὲν οὖν. Τὰς δέ γε ἁπλᾶς

6. τὸ Π: τὸν A. 12. οὗ Ξ *q*: οὖν AΠ. 15. παισὶ H. Wolf: πᾶσι codd.

---

431 A 3 **τι—τὸ μὲν—τὸ δέ.** For the subdivision of τις cf. V 463 B, VIII 560 A, *Gorg.* 499 C. Other examples of 'partitive apposition' are V 461 D, 477 C, VIII 552 C: cf. also VIII 556 B, IX 592 A, X 618 E.

6 **τὸ κρείττω αὑτοῦ**: sc. φαίνεταί μοι τοῦτο λέγειν. The expression κρείττω αὑτοῦ is the subject, and τοῦτο the object. τόν for τό (see *cr. n.*) is indefensible. See also on τοῦτο δέ below.

7 **πλήθους τοῦ χείρονος.** II 379 C *n.*

8 **τοῦτο δὲ—διακείμενον.** τοῦτο is the object of ψέγειν, whose subject is still strictly speaking τὸ κρείττω αὑτοῦ or (which is the same thing) οὗτος ὁ λόγος. In ψέγειν and καλεῖν the λόγος is half-personified: 'this the phrase censures as something disgraceful, and calls the man who is in this condition a slave to himself and intemperate.' For the recapitulatory τοῦτο δέ cf. *Ap.* 28 E with my note ad loc. Hartman's τοῦτο δή is an unhappy suggestion.

431 B 9 **ἔοικεν**: sc. ὁ λόγος τοῦτο βούλεσθαι λέγειν: not (as J. and C.) "it seems a natural way of speaking."

11 **κρείττω—αὑτῆς.** Cf. *Laws* 626 E ff., where κρείττων αὑτῆς is similarly applied to a city and explained in the same way.

12 **οὗ**: not the adverb, as Stallbaum supposed, but a partitive genitive: 'that whereof the better part rules the worse' etc.

431 C 15 **παισί.** See *cr. n.* The corruption—an easy one in minuscule MSS—recurs in VI 494 B. See *Introd.* § 5 and Bast *Comm. Pal.* p. 705. The object of this part of the argument is to shew that our city is σώφρων not only as being κρείττων αὑτῆς but as being κρείττων ἡδονῶν τε καὶ ἐπιθυμιῶν—a kindred, but not quite identical, notion: cf. 431 D. In adding γυναιξί Plato speaks from the ordinary Greek standpoint; in permitting some women to be guardians, he tacitly allows that in some cases their desires (unlike those of οἰκέται etc.) are μετὰ νοῦ. Cf. *Laws* 780 E ff.

16 **λεγομένων** is emphatic. No one is free who is a slave to his desires. Cf. I 336 A *n.*

17 **τὰς δέ γε κτλ.** I have returned to the MS reading. The accusative with τυγχάνω and its congeners is—except with neuter pronouns (Jebb on Soph. *O. T.* 1298)—almost unexampled (ἐπιτόσσαις with accusative in Pind. *Pyth.* 10. 33), and Herwerden reads the dative, an easy correction; but it is perhaps safer to take the accusative as a sort of anacoluthon "occasioned by the parallel of the previous sentence" τάς γε πολλὰς—εὕροι (J. and C.). Baiter brackets the verb ἐπιτεύξει.

τε καὶ μετρίας, αἳ δὴ μετὰ νοῦ τε καὶ δόξης ὀρθῆς λογισμῷ ἄγονται, ἐν ὀλίγοις τε ἐπιτεύξει καὶ τοῖς βέλτιστα μὲν φῦσιν, βέλτιστα δὲ παιδευθεῖσιν. Ἀληθῆ, ἔφη. Οὐκοῦν καὶ ταῦτα ὁρᾷς ἐνόντα σοι ἐν τῇ πόλει, καὶ κρατουμένας αὐτόθι τὰς ἐπιθυμίας τὰς ἐν τοῖς
D πολλοῖς τε καὶ | φαύλοις ὑπό τε τῶν ἐπιθυμιῶν καὶ τῆς φρονήσεως τῆς ἐν τοῖς ἐλάττοσί τε καὶ ἐπιεικεστέροις; Ἔγωγ᾽, ἔφη.

IX. Εἰ ἄρα δεῖ τινὰ πόλιν προσαγορεύειν κρείττω ἡδονῶν τε καὶ ἐπιθυμιῶν καὶ αὐτὴν αὑτῆς, καὶ ταύτην προσρητέον. Παντάπασιν μὲν οὖν, ἔφη. Ἆρ᾽ οὖν οὐ καὶ σώφρονα κατὰ πάντα ταῦτα; Καὶ μάλα, ἔφη. Καὶ μὴν εἴπερ αὖ ἐν ἄλλῃ πόλει ἡ αὐτὴ δόξα
E ἔνεστι τοῖς τε ἄρχουσι καὶ ἀρχομένοις | περὶ τοῦ οὕστινας δεῖ ἄρχειν, καὶ ἐν ταύτῃ ἂν εἴη τοῦτο ἐνόν. ἢ οὐ δοκεῖ; Καὶ μάλα, ἔφη, σφόδρα. Ἐν ποτέροις οὖν φήσεις τῶν πολιτῶν τὸ σωφρονεῖν ἐνεῖναι, ὅταν οὕτως ἔχωσιν; ἐν τοῖς ἄρχουσιν ἢ ἐν τοῖς ἀρχομένοις; Ἐν ἀμφοτέροις που, ἔφη. Ὁρᾷς οὖν, ἦν δ᾽ ἐγώ, ὅτι ἐπιεικῶς ἐμαντευόμεθα ἄρτι, ὡς ἁρμονίᾳ τινὶ ἡ σωφροσύνη ὡμοίωται; Τί δή; Ὅτι οὐχ ὥσπερ ἡ ἀνδρεία καὶ ἡ σοφία ἐν μέρει τινὶ
432 ἑκατέρα ἐνοῦσα ἡ μὲν | σοφήν, ἡ δὲ ἀνδρείαν τὴν πόλιν παρείχετο, οὐχ οὕτω ποιεῖ αὕτη, ἀλλὰ δι᾽ ὅλης ἀτεχνῶς τέταται, διὰ πασῶν

1. παρείχετο A^2Π: παρέσχετο A^1.

431 D 27 **καὶ μὴν—σφόδρα** gives a third feature of the *σωφροσύνη* of a city. We have shewn our city to be (1) *κρείττων αὑτῆς*. (2) *κρείττων ἡδονῶν τε καὶ ἐπιθυμιῶν*. It is also (3) *ὁμονοητικὴ περὶ τοῦ οὕστινας δεῖ ἄρχειν*. (3) corresponds to *κόσμος*, (2) to *ἐγκράτεια*, (1) to *κρείττω αὑτοῦ* in 430 E. Thus the discussion in this chapter follows a chiastic order.

431 E 32 **ἐν ἀμφοτέροις**. Cf. 442 C, D. Aristotle and others seem to have supposed that *σωφροσύνη* was the special virtue of the lowest class in the State and the lowest element in the soul: see *Top.* V 6. 136[b] 10 ff. and 8. 138[b] 1 ff. and [Arist.] *περὶ ἀρετῶν καὶ κακιῶν* 1. 1249[a] 30 ff. *ἐν ἀμφοτέροις* proves this view erroneous. The error arose partly perhaps from a desire to make the theory superficially symmetrical, partly perhaps from a notion that Plato's rulers would not be likely to dispute their own right to rule. But *σωφροσύνη* in Plato's sense is necessary for his Rulers as well as for their subjects; without it, they might *nolle episcopari*: cf. I 346 D *n.*

432 A 2 **δι᾽ ὅλης—διὰ πασῶν**. *δι᾽ ὅλης* sc. *τῆς πόλεως*, not *λύρας*, as J. and C. strangely suppose. *διὰ πασῶν* sc. *τῶν χορδῶν* should be taken with *ξυνᾴδοντας* (so also Schneider). *ἡ διὰ πασῶν συμφωνία* is the octave (Arist. *Probl.* XIX 35. 920[a] 27 ff.), the *καλλίστη συμφωνία*, according to the Greeks (Arist. l.c.), readily sounding to the ear as absolute unison; hence the point of *ταὐτόν*, which is an accusative depending directly on *ξυνᾴδοντας*. See Arist. l.c. 14. 918[b] 7 ff. *διὰ τί λανθάνει τὸ διὰ πασῶν καὶ δοκεῖ ὁμόφωνον εἶναι, οἷον ἐν τῷ φοινικίῳ καὶ ἐν τῷ ἀνθρώπῳ;* The whole expression *διὰ πασῶν ξυνᾴδοντας ταὐτόν* therefore means that the concord of the citizens on the matter in question is absolute and complete. Further than this I do not think the comparison is to be pressed. If we seek to find analogies between *ἀσθενεστάτους*, *ἰσχυροτάτους*, *μέσους* and the *ὑπάτη*, *νήτη* and *μέση* of the scale, we are met by the difficulty that the *μέση* cannot be said to produce the same (*ταὐτόν*) note as the *ὑπάτη* and *νήτη*, and we are not at liberty

παρεχομένη ξυνᾴδοντας τούς τε ἀσθενεστάτους ταὐτὸν καὶ τοὺς ἰσχυροτάτους καὶ τοὺς μέσους, εἰ μὲν βούλει, φρονήσει, εἰ δὲ βούλει, ἰσχύϊ, εἰ δέ, καὶ πλήθει ἢ χρήμασιν ἢ ἄλλῳ ὁτῳοῦν τῶν τοιούτων· ὥστε ὀρθότατ' ἂν φαῖμεν ταύτην τὴν ὁμόνοιαν σωφροσύνην εἶναι, χείρονός τε καὶ ἀμείνονος κατὰ φύσιν ξυμφωνίαν, ὁπότερον δεῖ ἄρχειν, καὶ ἐν πόλει | καὶ ἐν ἑνὶ ἑκάστῳ. Πάνυ μοι, **B** ἔφη, ξυνδοκεῖ. Εἶεν, ἦν δ' ἐγώ· τὰ μὲν τρία ἡμῖν ἐν τῇ πόλει

---

to suppose that Plato is thinking of ἡ δὶς διὰ πασῶν in the face of his own words, which refer only to a single octave (διὰ πασῶν παρεχομένη κτλ.). In talking of σωφροσύνη Plato usually distinguishes only between two classes—rulers and ruled: 431 D, E and infra χείρονός τε καὶ ἀμείνονος. See also on 443 D.

4 **φρονήσει—ἰσχύϊ—πλήθει** define ἀσθενεστάτους, ἰσχυροτάτους, μέσους. The equipoise and measured cadence of this stately sentence may well suggest a chorus of voices singing in unison. Cf. III 401 C. Cobet's excision of the second βούλει is sadly out of tune.

6 **ταύτην τὴν ὁμόνοιαν** prepares us for the definition about to follow. There are various ὁμόνοιαι: this one is agreement ὁπότερον δεῖ ἄρχειν etc.

7 **χείρονος κτλ.**: 'concord between the naturally better and the naturally worse, on the question which should rule, whether in a city or in an individual.' ἐν ἑνὶ ἑκάστῳ anticipates 442 C f.; but is justified here by 431 A, B.

We may now sum up Plato's account of σωφροσύνη so far as it is a virtue of the State. It involves three elements: (1) the rule of the better over the worse, (2) the rule of φρόνησις over the desires, (3) the agreement of better and worse as to which shall rule. (1) and (2) are different ways of expressing the same thing; neither is fundamental, for (granted the presence of σοφία and ἀνδρεία) both of them follow from (3), whereas (3) does not follow from either. Plato accordingly admits (3) only into his final definition. It follows from (3) that σωφροσύνη, unlike σοφία and ἀνδρεία, is a virtue possessed by all the three classes of the City. Krohn (*Pl. St.* p. 372) pronounces σωφροσύνη otiose and "ornamental." The charge is best refuted by considering whether the City is complete without it. (The part played by Justice will be discussed later.) Apart from σωφροσύνη, what virtue remains for the third class of citizens? and what guarantee is there that σοφία will consent to rule? (see on ἐν ἀμφοτέροις 431 E). Whereas σωφροσύνη not only provides for the third class, but furnishes a point of union in which all the classes may meet, and the City, so far, become μία ἐκ πολλῶν (cf. 443 E). If we bear in mind that the Rulers are only select Guardians, and that φύλακες includes both Rulers and Auxiliaries, we may tabulate the virtues of the three classes thus:—

Virtues of Rulers, σοφία + ἀνδρεία + σωφροσύνη.
Virtues of Soldiers, ἀνδρεία + σωφροσύνη.
Virtues of Farmers, etc., σωφροσύνη.

Hirzel is, I think, mistaken in holding that σωφροσύνη is a virtue of the whole and not of the parts; the fact is that it is a virtue both of the whole and of each of the parts. Strictly speaking, of course, ὁμόνοια or ξυμφωνία implies more parts than one, and *con*cord is impossible to a unit; but the essence of the virtue consists in the view that the best shall rule, and this view is present in each of the three classes. For δικαιοσύνη see 434 C *n*.

Plato's account of σωφροσύνη in other dialogues differs in many respects from this, and is rather a hindrance than a help in elucidating the present passage. Cf. Hirzel l.c. p. 409. The σωφροσύνη of the *Charmides* is fully discussed by Knuth *Quaestiones de not.* τῆς σωφροσύνης *Plat. criticae* (1874): cf. also Hammond l.c. pp. 138 f., 157 f.

432 B—**434** C *Where then is Justice? We must beware lest she escape us. Socrates presently exclaims that he has found the trail. Justice is the principle, or else one form of the principle, which we laid down at the beginning, viz. that each individual shall fulfil that function only for which he is naturally best fitted. In other words,*

κατῶπται, ὥς γε οὑτωσὶ δόξαι· τὸ δὲ δὴ λοιπὸν εἶδος, δι᾽ ὃ ἂν ἔτι ἀρετῆς μετέχοι πόλις, τί ποτ᾽ ἂν εἴη; δῆλον γάρ, ὅτι τοῦτ᾽ ἔστιν ἡ δικαιοσύνη. Δῆλον. Οὐκοῦν, ὦ Γλαύκων, νῦν δὴ ἡμᾶς δεῖ ὥσπερ κυνηγέτας τινὰς θάμνον κύκλῳ περιίστασθαι προσέχοντας τὸν νοῦν, μή πῃ διαφύγῃ ἡ δικαιοσύνη καὶ ἀφανισθεῖσα ἄδηλος
C γένηται· φανερὸν γὰρ | δὴ ὅτι ταύτῃ πῃ ἔστιν. ὅρα οὖν καὶ προθυμοῦ κατιδεῖν, ἐάν πως πρότερος ἐμοῦ ἴδῃς καὶ ἐμοὶ φράσῃς. Εἰ γὰρ ὤφελον, ἔφη· ἀλλὰ μᾶλλον, ἐάν μοι ἑπομένῳ χρῇ καὶ τὰ δεικνύμενα δυναμένῳ καθορᾶν, πάνυ μοι μετρίῳ χρήσει. Ἕπου, ἦν δ᾽ ἐγώ, εὐξάμενος μετ᾽ ἐμοῦ. Ποιήσω ταῦτα· ἀλλὰ μόνον, ἦ δ᾽ ὅς, ἡγοῦ. Καὶ μήν, εἶπον ἐγώ, δύσβατός γέ τις ὁ τόπος φαίνεται καὶ ἐπίσκιος· ἔστι γοῦν σκοτεινὸς καὶ δυσδιερεύνητος·

13. θάμνον Π: θάμνων A. 16. φράσῃς Π: φράσεις A. 17. ὤφελον Π: ὄφελον A. 18. μετρίῳ H. Richards: μετρίως codd.

Justice is, in a certain sense, 'minding one's own business.' Four considerations point to this conclusion. In the first place, it is in order to make the other three take root that we require a fourth virtue; and it is just the division of duty according to natural capacity which renders the other three virtues possible. Secondly, this is the only principle which can be compared with the other three virtues in respect of benefit conferred upon the State: and Justice must be comparable with them in this respect. Thirdly, it is by this principle that the Rulers will direct their judicial decisions, and Justice is the principle by which our Rulers judge. Lastly, the violation of this principle works the greatest mischief in the City. So does Injustice; so that the principle itself is identical with Justice.

For Plato's view of Civic Justice see on 434 C.

432 B 10 **ὥς γε—δόξαι.** This phrase is apparently quite unique in Plato: see Grünenwald cited on 430 E.

13 **ὥσπερ κυνηγέτας.** The image is a favourite one with Plato: cf. *Laws* 654 E, *Parm.* 128 C, *Lys.* 218 C. Other examples may be found in Stallbaum's note on this passage. The particular kind of hunting from which Plato takes his illustration is clearly described in Xen. *de Ven.* 8. 4—8. A net was drawn round the bush where the hare was, and the hunters stood round, ready μεταθεῖν κατὰ τὰ ἴχνη, ἐὰν ἐκκυλισθῇ ἐκ τῶν δικτύων.

432 C 16 **φράσῃς**: 'point out.' There is no occasion to read (with Ast and *q*) καί μοι φράσεις.

18 **μετρίῳ.** See *cr. n.* μετρίως χρῆσθαι could only mean 'to *treat* fairly,' but this is not to the point. The only relevant meaning is 'you will find me very tolerable,' and μετρίῳ μοι χρήσει conveys this sense exactly. Cf. ἑπομένῳ χρῇ—καὶ δυναμένῳ and Xen. *Cyr.* III 2. 4 ὀλίγοις τε καὶ ἀσθενέσι χρησαίμεθ᾽ ἂν πολεμίοις, *Symp.* 2. 9, 10. On the error see *Introd.* § 5.

19 **εὐξάμενος**: like a pious huntsman: cf. Xen. *de Ven.* 6. 13 εὐξάμενον τῷ Ἀπόλλωνι καὶ τῇ Ἀρτέμιδι τῇ Ἀγροτέρᾳ μεταδοῦναι τῆς θήρας. Cf. also (with Stallbaum) *Phil.* 25 B εὔχου δὴ καὶ σκόπει and *Tim.* 27 C. ἕπου οὖν (suggested by Richards) seems to me much less spirited and picturesque than ἕπου; and the cacophony is also unpleasing. For the asyndeton cf. II 373 E *n.*

21 **ἔστι γοῦν—δυσδιερεύνητος** has been objected to as adding little or nothing to δύσβατος—ἐπίσκιος. But δυσδιερεύνητος, 'difficult to beat,' said of beating or scouring the brake to rouse (κινεῖν Xen. *de Ven.* 8. 7) the game and drive it out into the net, could ill be spared; so apt a word is much too good for a copyist. Cf. *Menex.* 240 B, where διερευνᾶσθαι is used of the famous 'beating' of Euboea by Datis' soldiers: and see also *Laws* 698 D.

ἀλλὰ γὰρ ὅμως ἰτέον. | Ἰτέον γάρ, ἔφη. καὶ ἐγὼ κατιδὼν Ἰοῦ ἰοῦ, D
εἶπον, ὦ Γλαύκων· κινδυνεύομέν τι ἔχειν ἴχνος, καί μοι δοκεῖ οὐ
πάνυ τι ἐκφευξεῖσθαι ἡμᾶς. Εὖ ἀγγέλλεις, ἦ δ' ὅς. Ἦ μήν, ἦν
δ' ἐγώ, βλακικόν γε ἡμῶν τὸ πάθος. Τὸ ποῖον; Πάλαι, ὦ μακάριε,
φαίνεται πρὸ ποδῶν ἡμῖν ἐξ ἀρχῆς κυλινδεῖσθαι, καὶ οὐχ ἑωρῶμεν
ἄρ' αὐτό, ἀλλ' ἦμεν καταγελαστότατοι· ὥσπερ οἱ ἐν ταῖς χερσὶν
ἔχοντες ζητοῦσιν | ἐνίοτε ὃ ἔχουσιν, καὶ ἡμεῖς εἰς αὐτὸ μὲν οὐκ E
ἀπεβλέπομεν, πόρρω δέ ποι ἀπεσκοποῦμεν, ᾗ δὴ καὶ ἐλάνθανεν
ἴσως ἡμᾶς. Πῶς, ἔφη, λέγεις; Οὕτως, εἶπον, ὡς δοκοῦμέν μοι
καὶ λέγοντες αὐτὸ καὶ ἀκούοντες πάλαι οὐ μανθάνειν ἡμῶν αὐτῶν,
ὅτι ἐλέγομεν τρόπον τινὰ αὐτό. Μακρόν, ἔφη, τὸ προοίμιον τῷ
ἐπιθυμοῦντι ἀκοῦσαι.

X. Ἀλλ', ἦν δ' ἐγώ, ἄκουε, | εἴ τι ἄρα λέγω. ὃ γὰρ ἐξ ἀρχῆς 433
ἐθέμεθα δεῖν ποιεῖν διὰ παντός, ὅτε τὴν πόλιν κατῳκίζομεν, τοῦτό
ἐστιν, ὥς ἐμοὶ δοκεῖ, ἤτοι τούτου τι εἶδος ἡ δικαιοσύνη. ἐθέμεθα
δὲ δήπου καὶ πολλάκις ἐλέγομεν, εἰ μέμνησαι, ὅτι ἕνα ἕκαστον
ἓν δέοι ἐπιτηδεύειν τῶν περὶ τὴν πόλιν, εἰς ὃ αὐτοῦ ἡ φύσις
ἐπιτηδειοτάτη πεφυκυῖα εἴη. Ἐλέγομεν γάρ. Καὶ μὴν ὅτι γε
τὸ τὰ αὐτοῦ πράττειν καὶ μὴ πολυπραγμονεῖν δικαιοσύνη ἐστί,

22. *ἰοῦ ἰοῦ* nos: *ἰοὺ ἰοὺ* codd. 4. *δὲ* A²Π: om. A¹.

---

432 D 22 **ἰοῦ, ἰοῦ**: 'Joy! Joy!' *ἰού* dolentis, *ἰοῦ* gaudentis, according to the Scholiast on Ar. *Peace* 318: cf. Suidas s.v. Ancient authorities differed on the point (see Blaydes' critical note l.c.), but modern scholars for the most part agree with Suidas.

24 **ἐκφευξεῖσθαι—εὖ ἀγγέλλεις**. The contracted form of the future of *φεύγω* is established by the authority both of the Paris MS, and also of Aristophanes and Euripides, as Schanz has proved (Vol. XII p. xvi). Schanz may be right in supposing that it is borrowed "ex ore populi." For *εὖ ἀγγέλλεις* Phrynichus (s.v. *εὐαγγελίζομαί σε*) apparently read *εὐαγγελεῖς*, on which see Lobeck *Phryn.* p. 632 and Cobet *N. L.* p. 163. *εὐαγγελῶ* does not seem to be used in Attic prose. In *Theaet.* 144 B *εὖ ἀγγέλλεις* is read by B, *εὖ ἀγγελεῖς* by T.

433 A 3 **ἤτοι**. See I 344 E *n*.

τι εἶδος, like *τρόπον τινά* in 432 E and 433 B, hints, I think, that Civic Justice is not, after all, the true and original form of Justice. Hence, in 434 D, Plato is careful to warn us that the subject of Justice is not exhausted till individual Justice has been discussed. See on *τοιοῦτο* in 443 C.

6 **ἐπιτηδειοτάτη**. *ἐπιτηδειότατα* (Herwerden) is not good: cf. II 374 E and supra 430 A. A few MSS omit *πεφυκυῖα*, not unnaturally; but the reduplication in *φύσις—πεφυκυῖα* adds to the emphasis. Plato never tires of emphasizing the 'natural' features of his city in Books II—IV.

7 **δικαιοσύνη** has been questioned by Richards, on the ground that "the inference announced in *τοῦτο τοίνυν κτλ.* is already stated in *καὶ μὴν ὅτι κτλ.*, which from its form (*καὶ μήν*) is yet evidently only a step in the reasoning." Richards suggests *δίκαιον*, and Hartman *δικαιοσύνης*, neatly but needlessly. *τοίνυν* in B does not express an inference, but is simply 'well,' as in II 369 B, III 413 C, IV 436 B and a host of other passages collected by Kugler (*de part. τοι* etc. p. 35). Plato first states a popular view, and then proceeds to shew that it is mainly right on grounds presently to be stated (whence *οἶσθ' ὅθεν τεκμαίρομαι;*).

B καὶ τοῦτο ἄλλων τε πολλῶν ἀκηκόαμεν καὶ αὐτοὶ πολλάκις εἰρήκαμεν. Εἰρήκαμεν γάρ. Τοῦτο τοίνυν, ἦν δ' ἐγώ, ὦ φίλε, κινδυνεύει τρόπον τινὰ γιγνόμενον ἡ δικαιοσύνη εἶναι, τὸ τὰ αὑτοῦ πράττειν· οἶσθα ὅθεν τεκμαίρομαι; Οὔκ, ἀλλὰ λέγ', ἔφη. Δοκεῖ μοι, ἦν δ' ἐγώ, τὸ ὑπόλοιπον ἐν τῇ πόλει ὧν ἐσκέμμεθα, σωφροσύνης καὶ ἀνδρείας καὶ φρονήσεως, τοῦτο εἶναι, ὃ πᾶσιν ἐκείνοις τὴν δύναμιν παρέσχεν, ὥστε ἐγγενέσθαι, καὶ ἐγγενομένοις γε σωτηρίαν παρέχει, ἕωσπερ ἂν ἐνῇ. καίτοι ἔφαμεν δικαιοσύνην

15. παρέχει Vind. DF: παρέχειν ΑΠΞ *q*.

No stress should be laid on the fact that δικαιοσύνη is in one case the predicate, and in the other the subject: complete identity is predicated in both cases, as the abstract δικαιοσύνη shews. It might be different if we read δίκαιον, but for this there is no occasion. There is still however a difficulty in δικαιοσύνη: see next note.

433 B 9 **εἰρήκαμεν γάρ.** This has not been said in the *Republic*, nor (so far as I know) in any of Plato's earlier dialogues (if we except *Alc.* I 127 C), so that εἰρήκαμεν refers to ordinary conversation. Such a view has affinities with the legal view of Justice as the virtue which respects the rights of others (cf. 433 E and I 331 A ff.), and is natural enough, especially with the loose connotation which δικαιοσύνη had in popular language. It is however curious that in *Charm.* 161 B ff. precisely the same account is given of Temperance: ἄρτι γὰρ ἀνεμνήσθην ὃ ἤδη του ἤκουσα λέγοντος, ὅτι σωφροσύνη ἂν εἴη τὸ τὰ ἑαυτοῦ πράττειν: cf. *Tim.* 72 A εὖ καὶ πάλαι λέγεται τὸ πράττειν καὶ γνῶναι τά τε αὑτοῦ καὶ ἑαυτὸν σώφρονι μόνῳ προσήκειν. In its popular connotation, σωφροσύνη was not always distinguished from δικαιοσύνη, and even the philosophers (as Strabo VII 3. 4 observes) sometimes used the words in nearly an identical sense. See Nägelsbach *Nachhom. Theol.* p. 238. Steinhart and others find in the difference between this passage and the *Charmides* l.c. an indication of the Socratic and Platonic doctrine of the unity of Virtue. No doubt there is a certain sense in which virtue is one (see below on 434 C), but we must insist that the specific virtues are represented by Plato in the *Republic* as distinct; on any other hypothesis, the perfect City falls to pieces. Perhaps δικαιοσύνη after πολυπραγμονεῖν is an error for σωφροσύνη, and Plato is here deliberately *correcting* the popular view. If so, καὶ μὴν—γε means 'and yet,' i.e. in spite of what we now say that *Justice* is εἷς ἓν κατὰ φύσιν, 'we and others have also said that *Temperance* is τὰ αὑτοῦ πράττειν.' Adimantus assents. 'Well,' continues Socrates, 'it is apparently (not Temperance, but) *Justice* which is τὰ αὑτοῦ πράττειν.' This view gives a much better sense to καί in καὶ τοῦτο, and ἡ δικαιοσύνη receives the proper emphasis.

11 **δοκεῖ—εὕροιμεν.** Things which are equal to the same thing are equal to one another. Now (1) the Virtue which enables the others to take root, and (2) Justice, each = τὸ ὑπόλοιπον. Therefore Justice enables the other Virtues to take root. <But that which does so is τὰ αὑτοῦ πράττειν. Consequently Justice is τὰ αὑτοῦ πράττειν.> Plato seldom leaves so much to be mentally supplied in his reasoning.

15 **παρέχει.** See *cr. n.* Former editors (except Ast) retain παρέχειν and explain it as depending directly on δοκεῖ. If this is right, καί before ἐγγενομένοις joins τοῦτο εἶναι and παρέχειν; but καὶ ἐγγενομένοις γε, following immediately on ἐγγενέσθαι, naturally suggests that παρέχειν and ἐγγενέσθαι are coordinate and both under the government of ὥστε. That this was felt in antiquity is proved by the variant ἐγγενόμενα for ἐγγενομένοις, preserved in Stobaeus (*Flor.* 43. 98) and in Ξ. The author of the reading ἐγγενόμενα must have understood Plato to mean 'which enabled them all to make their appearance in the city, and having done so, to keep it safe, so long as they are there,' and this, I think, is the natural meaning of Plato's words, if παρέχειν is retained. But the sentiment is compara-

| ἔσεσθαι τὸ ὑπολειφθὲν ἐκείνων, εἰ τὰ τρία εὕροιμεν. Καὶ γὰρ C
ἀνάγκη, ἔφη. Ἀλλὰ μέντοι, ἦν δ' ἐγώ, εἰ δέοι γε κρῖναι, τί τὴν
πόλιν ἡμῖν τούτων μάλιστα ἀγαθὴν ἀπεργάσεται ἐγγενόμενον,
δύσκριτον ἂν εἴη, πότερον ἡ ὁμοδοξία τῶν ἀρχόντων τε καὶ
ἀρχομένων, ἢ ἡ περὶ δεινῶν τε καὶ μή, ἅττα ἐστί, δόξης ἐννόμου
σωτηρία ἐν τοῖς στρατιώταις ἐγγενομένη, ἢ ἡ ἐν τοῖς ἄρχουσι
φρόνησίς τε καὶ φυλακὴ ἐνοῦσα, ἢ | τοῦτο μάλιστα ἀγαθὴν αὐτὴν D
ποιεῖ ἐνὸν καὶ ἐν παιδὶ καὶ ἐν γυναικὶ καὶ δούλῳ καὶ ἐλευθέρῳ καὶ
δημιουργῷ καὶ ἄρχοντι καὶ ἀρχομένῳ, ὅτι τὸ αὑτοῦ ἕκαστος εἷς
ὢν ἔπραττεν καὶ οὐκ ἐπολυπραγμόνει. Δύσκριτον, ἔφη· πῶς δ'
οὔ; Ἐνάμιλλον ἄρα, ὡς ἔοικε, πρὸς ἀρετὴν πόλεως τῇ τε σοφίᾳ
αὐτῆς καὶ τῇ σωφροσύνῃ καὶ τῇ ἀνδρείᾳ ἡ τοῦ ἕκαστον ἐν αὐτῇ τὰ
αὑτοῦ πράττειν δύναμις. Καὶ μάλα, ἔφη. Οὐκοῦν δικαιοσύνην
τό γε τούτοις ἐνάμιλλον ἂν εἰς | ἀρετὴν πόλεως θείης; Παντάπασι E
μὲν οὖν. Σκόπει δὴ καὶ τῇδε, εἰ οὕτω δόξει. ἆρα τοῖς ἄρχουσιν
ἐν τῇ πόλει τὰς δίκας προστάξεις δικάζειν; Τί μήν; Ἦ ἄλλου
οὑτινοσοῦν μᾶλλον ἐφιέμενοι δικάσουσιν ἢ τούτου, ὅπως ἂν ἕκαστοι
μήτ' ἔχωσι τἀλλότρια μήτε τῶν αὑτῶν στέρωνται; Οὔκ, ἀλλὰ
τούτου. Ὡς δικαίου ὄντος; Ναί. Καὶ ταύτῃ ἄρα πῃ ἡ τοῦ
οἰκείου τε καὶ ἑαυτοῦ ἕξις τε καὶ πρᾶξις δικαιοσύνη ἂν | ὁμολογοῖτο. 434

21. ἢ ἡ $Ξ^2$q: ἢ Α$Ξ^1$: ἡ Π. 30. οὕτω ΑΠ: in mg. γρ. σαυτῷ A^2. 32. οὑτινοσοῦν Ξ: τινὸς οὖν ΑΠq. τούτου Π: τοῦτο Α. 34. τούτου A^2Π: τοῦτο A^1.

tively weak; and consequently Ast and Hartman wish to cancel *παρέχειν*, making *σωτηρίαν* depend upon *παρέσχεν*; but a present tense is necessary. *παρέχει* seems to me what Plato wrote, 'aye, and after they have appeared it preserves them, so long as it is present in the city.' A relative clause often passes into an independent sentence (see on II 357 B); and the idiom is appropriate here because it responds to the emphatic *καὶ—γέ*. For *καὶ—γε* cf. 425 B *n*.

433 D 23 **δούλῳ—ἀρχομένῳ**. On *δούλῳ* see V 469 C *n*. Richards would insert *καὶ γεωργῷ* after *δημιουργῷ*, pointing out that the other words go in pairs; but the difference between *δημιουργῷ* and *γεωργῷ* is insignificant, since both artisan and farmer belong to the same class in the city.

24 **εἷς ὤν**. Most of Stobaeus' MSS (*Flor.* l.c.) read *εἷς ὢν ἕν*. *ἕν* is unnecessary with *καὶ οὐκ ἐπολυπραγμόνει* following (Schneider).

433 E 30 **σκόπει κτλ.** This *τεκμήριον* turns on the judicial sense of *δικαιοσύνη*: cf. I 331 E ff. The judicial functions of the rulers follow naturally from 428 D, where it is said that *σοφία βουλεύεται—ὅντιν' ἂν τρόπον αὐτή τε* (sc. *ἡ πόλις*) *πρὸς αὑτὴν—ἄριστα ὁμιλοῖ κτλ.* It is clear that no class except the rulers can be judges in the State, and judges are necessary: see III 408 D ff.

35 **ἑαυτοῦ κτλ.** *ἑαυτοῦ* is a possessive genitive depending on *τοῦ*. It should be noted that although *ἕξις τοῦ οἰκείου* is not the same thing as *πρᾶξις τοῦ οἰκείου*, the latter involves the former. Plato is looking for a point of contact between his own view of Justice and the popular judicial meaning of the word, and finds it in *ἕξις τοῦ οἰκείου*. Krohn (*Pl. St.* p. 49) appears to me to attach too much weight to *ἕξις τοῦ οἰκείου* when he calls it a new "Begriffselement," and complains that it is "weder sachlich erläutert, noch logisch streng abgeleitet."

Ἔστι ταῦτα. Ἰδὲ δή, ἐὰν σοὶ ὅπερ ἐμοὶ ξυνδοκῇ. τέκτων σκυτο-
τόμου ἐπιχειρῶν ἔργα ἐργάζεσθαι ἢ σκυτοτόμος τέκτονος, ἢ τὰ
ὄργανα μεταλαμβάνοντες τἀλλήλων ἢ τιμάς, ἢ καὶ ὁ αὐτὸς ἐπιχειρῶν ἀμφότερα πράττειν, πάντα τἆλλα μεταλλαττόμενα ἆρά
σοι ἄν τι δοκεῖ μέγα βλάψαι πόλιν; Οὐ πάνυ, ἔφη. Ἀλλ' ὅταν
γε, οἶμαι, δημιουργὸς ὢν ἤ τις ἄλλος χρηματιστὴς φύσει ἔπειτα
B ἐπαιρόμενος | ἢ πλούτῳ ἢ πλήθει ἢ ἰσχύϊ ἢ ἄλλῳ τῳ τοιούτῳ εἰς
τὸ τοῦ πολεμικοῦ εἶδος ἐπιχειρῇ ἰέναι, ἢ τῶν πολεμικῶν τις εἰς τὸ
τοῦ βουλευτικοῦ καὶ φύλακος ἀνάξιος ὤν, καὶ τὰ ἀλλήλων οὗτοι
ὄργανα μεταλαμβάνωσι καὶ τὰς τιμάς, ἢ ὅταν ὁ αὐτὸς πάντα
ταῦτα ἅμα ἐπιχειρῇ πράττειν, τότε οἶμαι καὶ σοὶ δοκεῖν ταύτην
τὴν τούτων μεταβολὴν καὶ πολυπραγμοσύνην ὄλεθρον εἶναι τῇ
πόλει. Παντάπασι μὲν οὖν. Ἡ τριῶν ἄρα ὄντων γενῶν πολυπραγ-
C μοσύνη καὶ μεταβολὴ | εἰς ἄλληλα μεγίστη τε βλάβη τῇ πόλει
καὶ ὀρθότατ' ἂν προσαγορεύοιτο μάλιστα κακουργία. Κομιδῇ
μὲν οὖν. Κακουργίαν δὲ τὴν μεγίστην τῆς ἑαυτοῦ πόλεως οὐκ
ἀδικίαν φήσεις εἶναι; Πῶς δ' οὔ; Τοῦτο μὲν ἄρα ἀδικία.

XI. Πάλιν δὲ ὧδε λέγωμεν· χρηματιστικοῦ, ἐπικουρικοῦ,

8. τῳ Π: τῷ A.

Cf. 442 E. It should be mentioned that the poet Gray (with less than his usual critical acumen) conjectured τοῦ <ποιεῖν> τὸ οἰκεῖόν τε καὶ <τὸ> ἑαυτοῦ, comparing οἰκειοπραγία in 434 C.

434 A 5 **πάντα τἆλλα** means everything except what Socrates is about to mention, that is everything except the interchange of rulers and ruled. So J. and C., rightly, I think: cf. 421 A, VII 518 D and *Laws* 798 D. Other editors explain τἆλλα as "reliquorum opificum opera"; and so also *q*, reading ἢ πάντα τἆλλα τά γε τοιαῦτα; but it is difficult to extract this meaning out of τἆλλα without τά γε τοιαῦτα, and the asyndeton is also very harsh. Madvig's conjecture ταῦτα is improbable, though adopted by Baiter. Adimantus would catch the meaning all the more easily on account of the similar statement in 421 A, and because πάντα would be pronounced with emphasis, as the asyndeton also indicates. I have removed the comma usually printed after μεταλλαττόμενα; for πάντα τἆλλα includes within its scope all the cases mentioned, and is directly the subject of δοκεῖ.

6 **ἀλλ' ὅταν κτλ.** Plato is probably thinking of Athens again: cf. supra 424 D *n.* and Krohn *Pl. St.* p. 46. φύσει belongs to ὤν. Hartman needlessly expunges ὤν and reads φύς for φύσει. The subject to ὤν is simply the pronoun 'he,' used loosely, as often in English.

434 B 10 **βουλευτικοῦ—ὤν.** "Valde miror editt. verba βουλευτικοῦ καὶ φύλακος ἀνάξιος ὤν concoxisse" cries Hartman. The genitives of course depend on τὸ (εἶδος), and ἀνάξιος is used absolutely, as often.

434 C 16 **μάλιστα κακουργία.** μάλιστα is omitted in Ξ and one or two other MSS; but cf. VII 532 B ἔτι ἀδυναμία, VIII 564 A εἰς ἄγαν δουλείαν (with Stallbaum ad loc.), and other examples in Kühner *Gr. Gr.* II p. 526. That μάλιστα should be taken with κακουργία is clear from μεγίστη βλάβη and κακουργίαν τὴν μεγίστην.

19 **πάλιν**: not 'again,' but 'conversely,' "umgekehrt" (Schneider).

φυλακικοῦ γένους οἰκειοπραγία, ἑκάστου τούτων τὸ αὑτοῦ πράττοντος ἐν πόλει, τοὐναντίον ἐκείνου δικαιοσύνη τ' ἂν εἴη καὶ τὴν πόλιν δικαίαν παρέχοι. Οὐκ ἄλλῃ ἔμοιγε | δοκεῖ, ἦ δ' ὅς, ἔχειν ἢ ταύτῃ. D Μηδέν, ἦν δ' ἐγώ, πω πάνυ παγίως αὐτὸ λέγωμεν, ἀλλ' ἐὰν μὲν ἡμῖν καὶ εἰς ἕνα ἕκαστον τῶν ἀνθρώπων ἰὸν τὸ εἶδος τοῦτο ὁμολογῆται καὶ ἐκεῖ δικαιοσύνη εἶναι, συγχωρησόμεθα ἤδη· τί γὰρ καὶ ἐροῦμεν; εἰ δὲ μή, τότε ἄλλο τι σκεψόμεθα. νῦν δ' ἐκτελέσωμεν τὴν σκέψιν, ἣν ᾠήθημεν, εἰ ἐν μείζονί τινι τῶν ἐχόντων δικαιοσύνην πρότερον ἐκεῖ ἐπιχειρήσαιμεν θεάσασθαι, ῥᾷον ἂν ἐν

---

20 **ἑκάστου—πόλει** is cancelled by Herwerden as a marginal note on *οἰκειοπραγία*. The words add to the weight and impressiveness of the sentence, and have a decidedly Platonic sound.

21 **τοὐναντίον ἐκείνου.** *ἐκείνου* is 'the other,' i.e. *πολυπραγμοσύνης* (rather than *ἀδικίας*); and *τοὐναντίον* is probably nominative, and not adverbial accusative. So also Schneider. It is not necessary to add *ὄν* after *τοὐναντίον* as I formerly did. The style of argument is the familiar *τόπος ἐκ τῶν ἐναντίων* (see Arist. *Rhet.* II 23. 1397^a 7 ff.).

To sum up. Civic Justice is the fulfilment of the maxim *τὸ αὑτοῦ πράττειν* by the three classes in the City. There is nothing transcendental or metaphysical about it, as Krohn rightly observes (*Pl. St.* p. 48); it is simply the principle *εἷς ἓν κατὰ φύσιν* applied to the three component units or factors of the State. Cf. II 370 A *n.* It is moreover the soil out of which all the other virtues grow; its fruits are Wisdom, Courage, Temperance, of which the last appears in the Farmers and Artisans, the last two in the Auxiliaries, while the Rulers possess all three (432 A *n.*). Thus all the Virtues meet in Justice (*ἐν δὲ δικαιοσύνῃ συλλήβδην πᾶσ' ἀρετή 'νι* ap. Arist. *Eth. Nic.* V 3. 1129^b 25 ff.) and it is in Justice, not in *σοφία* (as the historical Socrates held *Mem.* III 9. 5), that the true unity of Virtue consists. Plato's Justice is in reality not so much a specific virtue, as Virtue or Righteousness in general: *καὶ οὔθ' ἕσπερος οὔθ' ἑῷος οὕτω θαυμαστός* (Arist. l.c.): cf. 442 E *n.* He desired to build a city, wherein Righteousness dwelleth (*καινοὺς δὲ οὐρανοὺς καὶ γῆν καινὴν—προσδοκῶμεν, ἐν οἷς δικαιοσύνη κατοικεῖ* 1 Pet. 3. 13), and interpreted Righteousness as the law of *εἷς ἓν κατὰ φύσιν*. In taking this view of political *δικαιοσύνη*, there is every reason to suppose (with Krohn l.c. p. 46) that Plato was not uninfluenced by the *πολυπραγμοσύνη* (as he conceived it) of Athenian democracy, although it is in reality a particular psychological interpretation of Nature's law of *ἁπλότης* that forms the true philosophical basis of the City described in Books II—IV. See also on II 370 A.

434 D—435 A *Adimantus agrees; but Socrates will wait until he has discovered Justice in Man before being sure that he is right. If the features of Justice are the same in Man and in the State, we shall be satisfied.*

434 D 23 **παγίως—λέγωμεν**: cf. V 479 C *παγίως νοῆσαι*, *Theaet.* 157 A *νοῆσαι —παγίως*, *Tim.* 49 D. *οὐκ ἔστι παγίως νοῆσαι* was probably a phrase in vogue among Heraclitus' followers: see Wohlrab on *Theaet.* l.c.

24 **ἰὸν τὸ εἶδος.** *εἶδος* is not yet the Idea (III 402 C) but refers to *οἰκειοπραγία*. For *ἰόν* Richards conjectures *ἰοῦσιν*; but surely *εἰς* would then be wrong. How can 'we' be said to pass *into* an individual? The *εἶδος* is half personified (cf. *ὅταν—ἐλθὸν ἐρώτημα ἔρηται* VII 538 D); it is said to 'pass into' the individual merely because we have discovered it first in the State. See also on *ἀπαμβλύνεται* 442 D. The passage in *Phaedr.* 249 B is different, whether we accept Badham's conjecture *ἰόντ'* or not.

27 **ἥν** is a loose internal accusative, exactly like *ὅ* in 443 B below. The reference is to II 368 D.

28 **ἐκεῖ.** The reading *ἐκεῖνο*, found in Ξ and other second-rate MSS, would probably have been discarded sooner, if it had been known that A as well as Π reads *ἐκεῖ*. Campbell first pointed this out. *ἐκεῖνο* is not quite suitable because,

E ἑνὶ ἀνθρώπῳ κατιδεῖν οἷόν ἐστιν. καὶ ǀ ἔδοξε δὴ ἡμῖν τοῦτο εἶναι πόλις, καὶ οὕτω ᾠκίζομεν ὡς ἐδυνάμεθα ἀρίστην, εὖ εἰδότες ὅτι ἔν γε τῇ ἀγαθῇ ἂν εἴη. ὃ οὖν ἡμῖν ἐκεῖ ἐφάνη, ἐπαναφέρωμεν εἰς τὸν ἕνα, κἂν μὲν ὁμολογῆται, καλῶς ἕξει· ἐὰν δέ τι ἄλλο ἐν τῷ ἑνὶ
435 ἐμφαίνηται, πάλιν ἐπανιόντες ἐπὶ τὴν πόλιν βασανιοῦμεν· | καὶ τάχ' ἂν παρ' ἄλληλα σκοποῦντες καὶ τρίβοντες ὥσπερ ἐκ πυρείων ἐκλάμψαι ποιήσαιμεν τὴν δικαιοσύνην, καὶ φανερὰν γενομένην βεβαιωσαίμεθ' ἂν αὐτὴν παρ' ἡμῖν αὐτοῖς. Ἀλλ', ἔφη, καθ' ὁδόν τε λέγεις καὶ ποιεῖν χρὴ οὕτως. Ἆρ' οὖν, ἦν δ' ἐγώ, ὅ γε

4. βεβαιωσαίμεθ' *q*: βεβαιωσώμεθ' A[1]Π: βεβαιωσόμεθ' A[2]Ξ.

although it must mean justice, it suggests something more remote. ἐκεῖ on the other hand helps out the antithesis between ἐν μείζονι—ἐχόντων and ἐν ἑνὶ ἀνθρώπῳ, and is in harmony with ἐκεῖ ἐφάνη below. δικαιοσύνην depends on θεάσασθαι, and τῶν ἐχόντων is 'its possessors': cf. II 367 B, D, E. In reciting the sentence, the voice pauses after ἐχόντων and pronounces ἐκεῖ with emphasis. ἐκεῖ (with which cf. ἐκείνου in *Parm.* 133 D) was rightly retained by Stallbaum, who did not know that it was the reading of A.

434 E 29 **τοῦτο**: i.e. τὸ μεῖζον τῶν ἐχόντων δικαιοσύνην.

435 A 4 **καθ' ὁδόν**. Cf. (with Schneider) infra VII 533 B and *Crat.* 425 B. μέθοδον for καθ' ὁδόν (Herwerden) is a sorry piece of criticism.

435 A—**435** D *The point to be determined is this: are there three psychological forms or kinds in the soul of the Individual, corresponding to the three orders in our City? And is the Individual temperate, brave, wise and just in virtue of the corresponding affections of these kinds? Our present methods of investigation are wanting in exactness; but they are sufficient for our immediate object.*

435 A ff. The passages in Plato dealing with psychology have been collected and carefully expounded by E. W. Simson *Der Begriff der Seele bei Plato* (Leipzig 1889). I have found Simson's treatise more serviceable than Chaignet *De la Psychologie de Platon* (Paris 1862). Dr Brandt's Program *Zur Entwickelung der Platonischen Lehre von den Seelentheilen* (Leipzig 1890) will also be found useful in studying the psychological theory here unfolded. For an attempt to shew that Plato always believed in the unity of soul see Archer-Hind in *J. Ph.* X pp. 120—131. The fundamental principle on which the theory of Book IV should be interpreted is that the just soul is an image of the just city. Now the just city is a ἕν with three πολλά: so therefore is the just soul. Plato states this quite clearly in 443 E ἕνα γενόμενον ἐκ πολλῶν. In this sense, therefore—and to Plato it was something real and no mere figure of speech—the soul has unity; but not, strictly speaking, in any other sense; otherwise we are in danger of obliterating the distinction between the three orders of the city, and so destroying the whole fabric. Of course nothing which Plato now says should be taken as prejudging the question about the nature of soul in its ἀληθεστάτη φύσις, i.e. when exempt from all the evils which are inseparable from matter (X 611 B ff.): if wholly separated from material accretions it is probably μονοειδές (612 A), λογιστικόν alone remaining. See on X 611 B. But for the present we are concerned with soul incarnate; and Plato certainly speaks of this as having three parts. Cf. Zeller[4] II 1, pp 845 ff. In what sense an immaterial thing like the soul even when present in body can be said to contain 'parts' or 'kinds' (μέρη, εἴδη, γένη) is a further question, which Plato does not here raise, although his followers have done so. It is doubtless true (as Archer-Hind holds l.c.) that 'parts' of soul can only be different modes of its operation; and a consciousness of this fact seems to betray itself in 439 B, D; but we shall best apprehend the meaning of Plato in this passage by treating the analogy as Plato does, i.e. as valid throughout, and speaking, in common with Plato and his commentators, of 'parts' of soul. See also on 435 B.

ταὐτὸν ἄν τις προσείποι μεῖζόν τε καὶ ἔλαττον, ἀνόμοιον τυγχάνει
ὂν ταύτῃ, ᾗ ταὐτὸν προσαγορεύεται, ἢ ὅμοιον; Ὅμοιον, ἔφη.
Καὶ δίκαιος ἄρα ἀνὴρ δικαίας πόλεως | κατ' αὐτὸ τὸ τῆς δικαιο- B
σύνης εἶδος οὐδὲν διοίσει, ἀλλ' ὅμοιος ἔσται. Ὅμοιος, ἔφη. Ἀλλὰ
μέντοι πόλις γε ἔδοξεν εἶναι δικαία, ὅτι ἐν αὑτῇ τριττὰ γένη
φύσεων ἐνόντα τὸ αὑτῶν ἕκαστον ἔπραττεν· σώφρων δὲ αὖ καὶ
ἀνδρεία καὶ σοφὴ διὰ τῶν αὐτῶν τούτων γενῶν ἄλλ' ἄττα πάθη
τε καὶ ἕξεις. Ἀληθῆ, ἔφη. Καὶ τὸν ἕνα ἄρα, ὦ φίλε, οὕτως
ἀξιώσομεν, τὰ αὐτὰ ταῦτα εἴδη ἐν τῇ αὑτοῦ | ψυχῇ ἔχοντα, διὰ C
τὰ αὐτὰ πάθη ἐκείνοις τῶν αὐτῶν ὀνομάτων ὀρθῶς ἀξιοῦσθαι τῇ
πόλει. Πᾶσα ἀνάγκη, ἔφη. Εἰς φαῦλόν γε αὖ, ἦν δ' ἐγώ, ὦ
θαυμάσιε, σκέμμα ἐμπεπτώκαμεν περὶ ψυχῆς, εἴτε ἔχει τὰ τρία
εἴδη ταῦτα ἐν αὑτῇ εἴτε μή. Οὐ πάνυ μοι δοκοῦμεν, ἔφη, εἰς
φαῦλον. ἴσως γάρ, ὦ Σώκρατες, τὸ λεγόμενον ἀληθές, ὅτι χαλεπὰ
τὰ καλά. Φαίνεται, ἦν δ' ἐγώ. καὶ εὖ γ' ἴσθι, ὦ Γλαύκων, | ὡς D
ἡ ἐμὴ δόξα, ἀκριβῶς μὲν τοῦτο ἐκ τοιούτων μεθόδων, οἵαις νῦν ἐν

10. ὅτι Π: ὅτε A. αὑτῇ Π: ἑαυτῇ A.

---

435 A 6 **μεῖζον—ἔλαττον**: 'whether greater or smaller.' The insertion of ὄν after ἔλαττον, suggested by Dobree, is unnecessary.

435 B 14 **τὰ αὐτὰ ταῦτα εἴδη**. εἴδη used in this sense is slightly confusing after εἶδος has just been applied to δικαιοσύνη; and τῶν αὐτῶν τούτων γενῶν would lead us to expect γένη. The psychological elements are called εἴδη, γένη, or μέρη: εἴδη in 435 B, C, E, 439 E, γένη in 441 C, 443 D, μέρη in 442 B, C and (by implication) 439 B, C, D and *passim*. Cf. Brandt l.c. p. 17 and Zeller[4] II 1, p. 845. εἴδη ψυχῆς does not, strictly speaking, mean '*varieties* of soul' but rather 'kinds' belonging to or present in soul (εἴδη ἐν ψυχῇ 439 E: see also on III 402 C), and much the same is true of γένη. There is some authority for holding that the Pythagoreans before the time of Plato recognised at least two 'parts' of soul—an ἄλογον and a λογικόν (see Diels *Dox. Gr.* pp. 389 f. and other evidence in Rohde *Psyche*[2] II p. 170 *n.*); but Zeller I[5] pp. 447, 448 may be right in regarding the Pythagorean form of this theory as post-Platonic.

435 C 16 **φαῦλον** is of course ironical, although Glauco pretends to take it seriously. Cf. (with J. and C.) 423 C—E, 426 A, B.

435 D 20 **καὶ εὖ γ'—ἐξαρκέσει.** The difficulties connected with this passage have led to much discussion: see for example Rettig *Proleg.* pp. 126 ff., Krohn *Pl. St.* pp. 128 ff., 144, Pfleiderer *Zur Lösung* etc. pp. 25, 73, Hirmer *Entst. u. Komp.* etc. p. 618. τοῦτο in ἀκριβῶς μὲν τοῦτο and in ἡ ἐπὶ τοῦτο ἄγουσα ought, so far as grammar goes, to mean the question whether the soul has τρία εἴδη or not. But the μακροτέρα περίοδος in VI 504 B ff., where Plato expressly refers back to this passage, eschews the psychological problem altogether. The μακροτέρα περίοδος of Books VI—VII is in harmony with the present enquiry in so far as it seeks to determine the nature of Justice and the other virtues (VI 504 D, 506 A), but it is nowhere in the Republic expressly used either to confirm or to overthrow the triple division of soul which is here propounded. (The analysis of mental faculties in VI 509 D—511 E is introductory to the μακροτέρα περίοδος, not a result obtained by it; nor has that analysis, strictly speaking, any bearing on the question whether soul has three εἴδη or not: cf. Pfleiderer *Zur Lösung* etc. p. 25.) Krohn accordingly

τοῖς λόγοις χρώμεθα, οὐ μή ποτε λάβωμεν· ἄλλη γὰρ μακροτέρα
καὶ πλείων ὁδὸς ἡ ἐπὶ τοῦτο ἄγουσα· ἴσως μέντοι τῶν γε προειρη-
μένων τε καὶ προεσκεμμένων ἀξίως. Οὐκοῦν ἀγαπητόν; ἔφη·
ἐμοὶ μὲν γὰρ ἔν γε τῷ παρόντι ἱκανῶς ἂν ἔχοι. Ἀλλὰ μέντοι,
εἶπον, ἔμοιγε καὶ πάνυ ἐξαρκέσει. Μὴ τοίνυν ἀποκάμῃς, ἔφη,
E ἀλλὰ σκόπει. Ἆρ' οὖν ἡμῖν, | ἦν δ' ἐγώ, πολλὴ ἀνάγκη ὁμολογεῖν,
ὅτι γε τὰ αὐτὰ ἐν ἑκάστῳ ἔνεστιν ἡμῶν εἴδη τε καὶ ἤθη, ἅπερ ἐν
τῇ πόλει; οὐ γάρ που ἄλλοθεν ἐκεῖσε ἀφῖκται. γελοῖον γὰρ ἂν

22. ἄλλη Flor. T cum Galeno (v p. 481 Kühn): ἀλλὰ ΑΠΞ *q*.

---

holds that the 'longer ways' of IV and VI are different and distinct (*Pl. St.* p. 128); and Schleiermacher supposes (*Einleitung* p. 71) that the πλείων ὁδός of IV is to be found in the psychology of the *Timaeus*; but that Plato meant the two ways to be identical is certain, for he explicitly says that they are (VI 504 B ff.). The only way out of these difficulties is to suppose that τοῦτο here was not intended by Plato to refer to the psychological, but to the ethical question, to which the psychological enquiry is introductory. τοῦτο must then be taken as δικαιοσύνης τε πέρι καὶ σωφροσύνης καὶ ἀνδρείας καὶ σοφίας ὃ ἕκαστόν ἐστι (VI 504 A). This view becomes easy if we suppose that the words καὶ εὖ γε—ἐξαρκέσει were not written by Plato immediately after he wrote 435 C, but at a later time, when VI 504 A—D was composed. It is in itself highly probable that the most important passages referring forward or backward to one another throughout the dialogue were either written together, or at all events revised by Plato side by side. Cf. Brandt l.c. p. 13 *n.* 3, where a kindred view is taken. In any case, we must adhere to our explanation of τοῦτο, if we would preserve the artistic unity of the *Republic*. See also on VI 504 A—D.

22 **ἄλλη**. See *cr. n.* ἄλλη is in itself much better, to say the least, than ἀλλά, and is confirmed by ἄλλη μακροτέρα—περίοδος in VI 504 B. The corruption was easy, owing to the frequency of ἀλλὰ γάρ.

435 E—**439** E *The presence of three kinds or characters in the city establishes the existence of the same characters in the individual; but the question is, do they exist in him as three separate elements, or not? Do we employ the whole soul in every psychical act, or do we learn with one part, feel angry with a second, desire with a third? In examining this question we begin by laying it down that the same thing cannot do or suffer opposites at the same time in the same part of itself, and with reference to the same thing. This rule is of universal application; apparent exceptions there may be, but never real. Desire and Aversion are opposites; and Hunger and Thirst are two specific varieties of Desire, relating to meat and drink, considered absolutely and without qualification. Now it sometimes happens that we are at one and the same moment both thirsty and unwilling to drink, in other words, experience both Desire and Aversion. But Desire and Aversion are opposites. They must therefore spring from different psychical elements. The truth is, in such cases it is one part of soul, the Rational part, which says 'Refrain!', another, the Appetitive, which bids us drink.*

435 E 28 **ὅτι γε—πόλει.** Broadly speaking, what Plato says is true, that the predominant character of a State depends on the predominant character of the individual citizens (cf. Bosanquet *Companion* pp. 147 f.): but it does not necessarily follow, because a city contains three psychologically different classes of citizens, that each of us (ἑκάστῳ ἡμῶν) has within his soul the three corresponding psychological elements. In making this assertion, Plato relies upon the fundamental hypothesis of the *Republic*, viz. that the individual is a commonwealth writ small. See on II 369 A. γε after ὅτι, though omitted in Ξ, is strictly appropriate, and warns us of a further point—τόδε δὲ ἤδη χαλεπόν 436 A—on which agreement is not so easy.

εἴη, εἴ τις οἰηθείη τὸ θυμοειδὲς μὴ ἐκ τῶν ἰδιωτῶν ἐν ταῖς πόλεσιν ἐγγεγονέναι, οἳ δὴ καὶ ἔχουσι ταύτην τὴν αἰτίαν, οἷον οἱ κατὰ τὴν Θρᾴκην τε καὶ Σκυθικὴν καὶ σχεδόν τι κατὰ τὸν ἄνω τόπον, ἢ τὸ φιλομαθές, ὃ δὴ περὶ τὸν παρ' ἡμῖν μάλιστ' ἄν τις αἰτιάσαιτο τόπον, ἢ τὸ | φιλοχρήματον, ὃ περὶ τούς τε Φοίνικας εἶναι καὶ 436
τοὺς κατὰ Αἴγυπτον φαίη τις ἂν οὐχ ἥκιστα. Καὶ μάλα, ἔφη. Τοῦτο μὲν δὴ οὕτως ἔχει, ἦν δ' ἐγώ, καὶ οὐδὲν χαλεπὸν γνῶναι. Οὐ δῆτα.

XII. Τόδε δὲ ἤδη χαλεπόν, εἰ τῷ αὐτῷ τούτων ἕκαστα πράττομεν ἢ τρισὶν οὖσιν ἄλλο ἄλλῳ· μανθάνομεν μὲν ἑτέρῳ, θυμούμεθα δὲ ἄλλῳ τῶν ἐν ἡμῖν, ἐπιθυμοῦμεν δ' αὖ τρίτῳ τινὶ τῶν περὶ τὴν τροφήν τε καὶ γέννησιν ἡδονῶν καὶ | ὅσα τούτων B
ἀδελφά, ἢ ὅλῃ τῇ ψυχῇ καθ' ἕκαστον αὐτῶν πράττομεν, ὅταν ὁρμήσωμεν. ταῦτ' ἔσται τὰ χαλεπὰ διορίσασθαι ἀξίως λόγου. Καὶ ἐμοὶ δοκεῖ, ἔφη. Ὧδε τοίνυν ἐπιχειρῶμεν αὐτὰ ὁρίζεσθαι, εἴτε τὰ αὐτὰ ἀλλήλοις εἴτε ἕτερά ἐστι. Πῶς; Δῆλον ὅτι ταὐτὸν τἀναντία ποιεῖν ἢ πάσχειν κατὰ ταὐτόν γε καὶ πρὸς ταὐτὸν οὐκ ἐθελήσει ἅμα, ὥστε ἄν που εὑρίσκωμεν ἐν αὐτοῖς ταῦτα γιγνόμενα,

1. ὃ Ξ et in mg. q^2: τὸ ΑΠ q^1. 5. τούτων Apelt (cum q^2): τούτῳ ΑΠΞ q^1.

---

31 **οἳ δὴ—αἰτίαν**: 'that is, among peoples who bear this reputation.' ταύτην is τοῦ θυμοειδεῖς εἶναι. The phrase αἰτίαν ἔχειν is used both in a good and in a bad sense as the passive of αἰτιῶμαι: for the good sense cf. (with Ast) *Gorg.* 503 B. What follows is (as Teichmüller observes *Lit. Fehd.* I p. 146) conceived in the vein of Hippocrates' enquiries as to the influence of climate on character: see his treatise *de aere aquis locis* 12 ff. ed. Kuehlewein, and cf. also Arist. *Physiog.* 2. 806^b 15, *Probl.* XIV 8, 15, 16, and especially *Pol.* H 7. 1327^b 23—33 with Susemihl's note. Aristotle for his part represents the Greek nature as the mean between the two extremes of oriental διανοητικόν and τεχνικόν and northern θυμός. There is no good reason for supposing (with Steinhart *Einleitung* p. 191) that Plato was thinking of the wild races of the North when he instituted his second order of citizens, and of Egyptians etc. when he established his third. On the Phoenician and Egyptian characters cf. *Laws* 747 C ff.

32 **τὸν ἄνω τόπον**: 'the Northern region,' not 'the *highland* country' (L. and S.): cf. Arist. *Meteor.* II 5. 362^a 33 τὸν ἄνω πόλον and Hdt. I 142 al.

33 **αἰτιάσαιτο.** εἶναι should be understood. For the construction cf. X 599 E.

436 A 1 **φιλοχρήματον** is another name for ἐπιθυμητικόν, ὅτι διὰ χρημάτων μάλιστα ἀποτελοῦνται αἱ τοιαῦται ἐπιθυμίαι (IX 580 E).

5 **τούτων ἕκαστα** refers to the actions described in μανθάνομεν μὲν ἑτέρῳ etc. τούτῳ (see *cr. n.*) can only be defended by referring it (with Schneider) "to the subject of the triple predicate τὸ θυμοειδές, τὸ φιλομαθές, and τὸ φιλοχρήματον." There is a certain obscurity in this construction, and τούτων ἕκαστα prepares us for μανθάνομεν μὲν ἑτέρῳ, θυμούμεθα δέ etc. better than ἕκαστα alone would do.

436 B 12 **ταὐτὸν—ἅμα** is the earliest explicit statement in Greek literature of the maxim of Contradiction; cf. *Theaet.* 188 A, *Phaed.* 102 E, 103 B, *Soph.* 230 B and infra X 602 E. Plato may have been led to formulate it in opposition to Heracliteanism, which was supposed by some to be the negation of the principle (see Arist. *Met.* Γ 3. 1005^b 24 and *Theaet.* 152 D ff.), or against the Megarian puzzles

C εἰσόμεθα ὅτι οὐ ταὐτὸν ἦν ἀλλὰ πλείω. Εἶεν. Σκόπει δὴ ὃ λέγω. Λέγε, ἔφη. Ἑστάναι, εἶπον, καὶ κινεῖσθαι τὸ αὐτὸ ἅμα κατὰ τὸ αὐτὸ ἆρα δυνατόν; Οὐδαμῶς. Ἔτι τοίνυν ἀκριβέστερον ὁμολογησώμεθα, μή πῃ προϊόντες ἀμφισβητήσωμεν. εἰ γάρ τις λέγοι ἄνθρωπον ἑστηκότα, κινοῦντα δὲ τὰς χεῖράς τε καὶ τὴν κεφαλήν, ὅτι ὁ αὐτὸς ἕστηκέ τε καὶ κινεῖται ἅμα, οὐκ ἄν, οἶμαι,
D ἀξιοῖμεν οὕτω λέγειν δεῖν, ἀλλ' ὅτι τὸ μέν τι αὐτοῦ ἕστηκε, τὸ δὲ κινεῖται. οὐχ οὕτω; Οὕτω. Οὐκοῦν καὶ εἰ ἔτι μᾶλλον χαριεντίζοιτο ὁ ταῦτα λέγων, κομψευόμενος ὡς οἵ γε στρόβιλοι ὅλοι ἑστᾶσί τε ἅμα καὶ κινοῦνται ὅταν ἐν τῷ αὐτῷ πήξαντες τὸ κέντρον περιφέρωνται, ἢ καὶ ἄλλο τι κύκλῳ περιιὸν ἐν τῇ αὐτῇ ἕδρᾳ τοῦτο δρᾷ, οὐκ ἂν ἀποδεχοίμεθα, ὡς οὐ κατὰ ταὐτὰ ἑαυτῶν
E τὰ τοιαῦτα τότε μενόντων τε καὶ φερομένων, ἀλλὰ φαῖμεν ἂν

26. ἀποδεχοίμεθα *q*: ἀποδεχώμεθα A^1Ξ: ἀποδεχόμεθα A^2Π.

(see RP.[7] § 226), or as a counterblast to both. Many of the sophistries of the *Euthydemus* turn on the violation of this law. In Aristotle's formula (*Met.* l.c. 1005^b 19) πρὸς ταὐτόν does not occur; and Hartman would cancel καὶ πρὸς ταὐτόν here and πρὸς τὸ αὐτό in 436 E, on the ground that it means the same as κατὰ ταὐτόν. But assuredly it does not. κατὰ ταὐτόν is 'in the same part of it' as the instances presently cited shew; while πρὸς ταὐτόν is 'relatively to the same thing,' viz. to something *other* than the subject of the proposition. πρὸς τὰ αὐτά and κατὰ ταὐτά are also both of them found in the parallel passage *Soph.* 230 B. πρὸς ταὐτόν covers such cases as are adduced in *Theaet.* 154 C—155 C: six dice are πλείους πρὸς τέτταρας, ἐλάττους πρὸς δώδεκα, but they are not ἐναντία πρὸς ταὐτόν. Cf. VII 524 A ff., and see also on ἢ καὶ εἴη in 437 A.

436 C 15 **ἦν** is not precisely ἐστὶν ὥσπερ ᾠόμεθα (Stallbaum); for the reference is actually to the past, and the past tense should be kept in translating it. See II 357 A *n.* and cf. X 609 B. The so-called 'philosophic imperfect' gets credit for more than it deserves, because we are apt to suppose that the past excludes the present, which is not always true: cf. VI 497 C *n.*

εἶεν by itself in replies is rare. It occurs (if the MSS are right) in *Symp.* 206 E, *Crat.* 410 C, *Men.* 75 C. In the last two passages, Heindorf (on *Crat.* l.c.) is inclined to rearrange the speakers; but it is safer, both there and here, to keep the traditional arrangement. See on I 332 D.

436 D 23 **χαριεντίζοιτο—κομψευόμενος** may refer to some Megarian quibbles on this subject. Zeno's argument to shew that ἡ οἰστὸς φερομένη ἕστηκεν proceeded on a different principle: see Arist. *Phys.* VI 9. 239^b 30 ff.

25 **ἢ καὶ—δρᾷ.** "Repetendum ὡς ex praegressis" (Stallbaum). Schneider connects δρᾷ with ὅταν: in that case we must understand after τοῦτο δρᾷ something like ὡς καὶ τοῦτο ὅλον ἕστηκέ τε ἅμα καὶ κινεῖται. Stallbaum's view is the simpler, and should, I think, be preferred. I have accordingly removed the comma usually printed after κινοῦνται.

26 **ὡς οὐ—φερομένων.** This clause has proved a source of great perplexity. Schneider suggests that μενόντων is a partitive genitive, ἐστί being omitted; Stallbaum, that τὰ τοιαῦτα is adverbial, like τοιουτοτρόπως; while, according to J. and C., τὰ τοιαῦτα "is to be taken as cognate accusative with the participles." Rather than accept any of these suggestions, it would, I think, be preferable to expunge τὰ τοιαῦτα altogether (with Ast), or to place it after ἀποδεχοίμεθα (as Gildersleeve suggests, *A. J. Ph.* VI p. 333 *n.* 2), or even perhaps to read τῶν τοιούτων with Richards, although little short of a miracle could have corrupted

ἔχειν αὐτὰ εὐθύ τε καὶ περιφερὲς ἐν αὐτοῖς, καὶ κατὰ μὲν τὸ εὐθὺ
ἑστάναι, οὐδαμῇ γὰρ ἀποκλίνειν, κατὰ δὲ τὸ περιφερὲς κύκλῳ
κινεῖσθαι· ὅταν δὲ τὴν εὐθυωρίαν ἢ εἰς δεξιὰν ἢ εἰς ἀριστερὰν
ἢ εἰς τὸ πρόσθεν ἢ εἰς τὸ ὄπισθεν ἐγκλίνῃ ἅμα περιφερόμενον,
τότε οὐδαμῇ ἔστιν ἑστάναι. Καὶ ὀρθῶς γε, ἔφη. Οὐδὲν ἄρα ἡμᾶς
τῶν τοιούτων λεγόμενον ἐκπλήξει, οὐδὲ μᾶλλόν τι πείσει, ὥς ποτέ
τι ἂν τὸ αὐτὸ ὂν ἅμα κατὰ τὸ αὐτὸ πρὸς τὸ αὐτὸ τἀναντία | πάθοι 437
ἢ καὶ εἴη ἢ καὶ ποιήσειεν. Οὔκουν ἐμέ γε, ἔφη. Ἀλλ᾽ ὅμως,
ἦν δ᾽ ἐγώ, ἵνα μὴ ἀναγκαζώμεθα πάσας τὰς τοιαύτας ἀμφισβητήσεις
ἐπεξιόντες καὶ βεβαιούμενοι ὡς οὐκ ἀληθεῖς οὔσας μηκύνειν,
ὑποθέμενοι ὡς τούτου οὕτως ἔχοντος εἰς τὸ πρόσθεν προΐωμεν,
ὁμολογήσαντες ἐάν ποτε ἄλλῃ φανῇ ταῦτα ἢ ταύτῃ, πάντα ἡμῖν

30. ἢ εἰς δεξιὰν Π: ἢ καὶ εἰς δεξιὰν A. 2. ἢ καὶ εἴη A¹Π: punctis notavit A².

τῶν τοιούτων to τὰ τοιαῦτα. The following interpretation, which appears to me right, has not, so far as I know, been hitherto suggested. ταὐτά goes closely with the partitive genitive ἑαυτῶν, and is a *predicate* to τὰ τοιαῦτα, which is also governed by κατά (cf. the familiar usage with ὥσπερ and a preposition in similes, e.g. *Theaet.* 170 A ὥσπερ πρὸς θεοὺς ἔχειν τοὺς ἐν ἑκάσταις ἄρχοντας etc.: see on VIII 553 B). μενόντων τε καὶ φερομένων is a genitive absolute. The sentence is in every respect an elegant and idiomatic piece of Greek, and means: 'because such parts, in respect of which they both stand still and move on these occasions, are *different* parts of them.' τὰ τοιαῦτα—the meaning of which is easy to catch after the examples given above—forms a welcome preparation for εὐθύ τε καὶ περιφερές in the following clause.

436 E 32 **ἔστιν**. I formerly rejected this word (with Galen *de Hipp. et Plat. decr.* IX Vol. V p. 799 ed. Kühn, Herwerden, and Flor. U). It is certainly more pointed to connect ἑστάναι with φαῖμεν ἄν, and Glauco's καὶ ὀρθῶς γε (sc. φαῖμεν ἄν) is easier without ἔστιν. But there is not sufficient ground for deserting the best MSS. For other examples of replies referring to the earlier part of the previous sentence see V 465 E *n.*

437 A 2 **ἢ καὶ εἴη**. I agree with Bekker, Schneider, and J. and C. in retaining these words, which Galen l.c. also read, and only a few inferior MSS (with the majority of editors) omit. If the words are spurious, no satisfactory theory has yet been advanced to account for their presence in the text; certainly no scribe is at all likely to have added them. A fuller and more emphatic statement of the maxim is natural enough after the emphasis with which the sentence opens (οὐδὲν—ἐκπλήξει), and Schneider truly observes: "obiter et quodam modo praeter exspectationem eius" (i.e. τοῦ εἶναι), "mentionem fieri adiectum καὶ indicat, quod semel positum mox sine offensione repetitur, omissis vero verbis ἢ καὶ εἴη ante ποιήσειεν non magis quam supra p. 436 B ante πάσχειν locum habiturum fuisset." πάθοι and ποιήσειεν have reference to actions, εἴη to a state, and εἴη naturally follows πάθοι because e.g. πλείους γίγνεσθαι (an example of πάσχειν) leads up to πλείους εἶναι. It should also be observed that the meaning of πρὸς τὸ αὐτό, which the discussion has not yet brought out, is best apprehended in examples not of πάσχειν or ποιεῖν, but of εἶναι τἀναντία: see 436 B *n.*

ἀλλ᾽ ὅμως κτλ. The usual Greek idiom, as shewn for example in ἀλγῶ τὴν κεφαλήν (cf. V 462 C ff.), rests on a psychological theory which is inconsistent with that now proposed by Plato. This may be one reason why Plato is at such pains to establish and emphasize his point.

τὰ ἀπὸ τούτου ξυμβαίνοντα λελυμένα ἔσεσθαι. Ἀλλὰ χρή, ἔφη, ταῦτα ποιεῖν.

B XIII. Ἆρ' οὖν, ἦν δ' ἐγώ, τὸ ἐπινεύειν τῷ ἀνανεύειν καὶ τὸ ἐφίεσθαί τινος λαβεῖν τῷ ἀπαρνεῖσθαι καὶ τὸ προσάγεσθαι τῷ ἀπωθεῖσθαι, πάντα τὰ τοιαῦτα τῶν ἐναντίων ἂν ἀλλήλοις θείης εἴτε ποιημάτων εἴτε παθημάτων; οὐδὲν γὰρ ταύτῃ διοίσει. Ἀλλ', ἦ δ' ὅς, τῶν ἐναντίων. Τί οὖν; ἦν δ' ἐγώ· διψῆν καὶ πεινῆν καὶ ὅλως τὰς ἐπιθυμίας, καὶ αὖ τὸ ἐθέλειν καὶ τὸ βούλεσθαι, οὐ πάντα C ταῦτα εἰς ἐκεῖνά ποι ἂν θείης τὰ εἴδη τὰ νῦν δὴ λεχθέντα; οἷον ἀεὶ τὴν τοῦ ἐπιθυμοῦντος ψυχὴν οὐχὶ ἤτοι ἐφίεσθαι φήσεις ἐκείνου οὗ ἂν ἐπιθυμῇ, ἢ προσάγεσθαι τοῦτο ὃ ἂν βούληταί οἱ γενέσθαι, ἢ αὖ καθ' ὅσον ἐθέλει τί οἱ πορισθῆναι, ἐπινεύειν τοῦτο πρὸς αὑτὴν ὥσπερ τινὸς ἐρωτῶντος, ἐπορεγομένην αὐτοῦ τῆς γενέσεως; Ἔγωγε. Τί δέ; τὸ ἀβουλεῖν καὶ μὴ ἐθέλειν μηδ' ἐπιθυμεῖν οὐκ εἰς τὸ ἀπωθεῖν καὶ ἀπελαύνειν ἀπ' αὑτῆς καὶ εἰς ἅπαντα τἀναντία D ἐκείνοις θήσομεν; Πῶς γὰρ οὔ; Τούτων δὴ οὕτως ἐχόντων ἐπιθυμιῶν τι φήσομεν εἶναι εἶδος, καὶ ἐναργεστάτας αὐτῶν τούτων ἥν τε δίψαν καλοῦμεν καὶ ἣν πεῖναν; Φήσομεν, ἦ δ' ὅς. Οὐκοῦν

11. ἂν Baiter: om. codd.   19. ἐρωτῶντος $A^1\Pi$: ἐρῶντος A^2.

---

437 B 10 **λαβεῖν** has been doubted: but see III 407 B *n.*

11 **ἂν** (see *cr. n.*) is better inserted after ἐναντίων than after θείης (Ast) or τοιαῦτα (Hartman). Stallbaum (who formerly read ἂν θείης) in his last edition acquiesces, like Schneider, in the omission of ἄν; but few will agree with him. I have noted the—certain or probable—omission of ἄν in all or the best MSS in *Phaed.* 62 C, 109 E, *Euthyd.* 291 E (?), *Rep.* V 457 D, VII 516 E, VIII 558 D, where the omission is lipographical; also in *Phaed.* 72 B, *Euthyd.* 281 C, *Crat.* 389 E, 409 A, *Alc.* I 132 B, 133 E, *Soph.* 266 A, *Phil.* 47 B, *H. Mai.* 295 A. Sometimes (as occasionally after πρίν) the omission is perhaps a poetical touch: see my note in *Cl. Rev.* IV p. 103.

14 **καὶ αὖ.** Krohn (*Pl. St.* p. 57) presses αὖ too much when he says that ἐθέλειν and βούλεσθαι are definitely represented as not belonging to the category of ἐπιθυμίαι. Plato expresses no opinion on this point; for αὖ, 'also,' merely marks the introduction of two new terms.

437 C 18 **ἐθέλει—ἐρωτῶντος.** The difference between ἐθέλει, 'is willing,' and βούλεται, 'wishes,' is well brought out by the contrast between the more active process described in προσάγεσθαι and the passive assent which ἐπινεύειν expresses. The point is missed by translating (with J. and C.) 'beckons this with a nod towards herself': it is merely 'nods assent to this in reply to herself.' One part of the soul asks, and the other answers, the psychological process being compared to a kind of dialectic or question and answer inside the soul: see III 400 D *n.* and cf. Isocr. *Antid.* 256. For the confusion of ἐρῶντος and ἐρωτῶντος—ἐρῶντος is found in several MSS—cf. [*Erast.*] 132 D, and *Euthyphr.* 14 C. With the analysis of desire in this passage cf. *Phil.* 34 E ff.

21 **ἀπ' αὐτῆς.** ἀφ' αὑτῆς Hartman (with Vind. E only), but ἀπελαύνειν is active, not middle. The actions are described as though by a spectator *ab externo*.

437 D 23 **ἐπιθυμιῶν**: a defining genitive. For εἶδος see III 402 C *n.*

τὴν μὲν ποτοῦ, τὴν δ' ἐδωδῆς; Ναί. Ἆρ' οὖν, καθ' ὅσον δίψα ἐστί, πλέονος ἄν τινος ἦ οὗ λέγομεν ἐπιθυμία ἐν τῇ ψυχῇ εἴη; οἷον δίψα ἐστὶ δίψα ἆρά γε θερμοῦ ποτοῦ ἢ ψυχροῦ, ἢ πολλοῦ ἢ ὀλίγου, ἢ καὶ ἑνὶ λόγῳ ποιοῦ τινὸς πώματος; ἢ ἐὰν μέν τις θερμότης τῷ δίψει προσῇ, τὴν | τοῦ ψυχροῦ ἐπιθυμίαν προσπαρέ- **E** χοιτ' ἄν, ἐὰν δὲ ψυχρότης, τὴν τοῦ θερμοῦ; ἐὰν δὲ διὰ πλήθους παρουσίαν πολλὴ ἡ δίψα ᾖ, τὴν τοῦ πολλοῦ παρέξεται, ἐὰν δὲ ὀλίγη, τὴν τοῦ ὀλίγου; αὐτὸ δὲ τὸ διψῆν οὐ μή ποτε ἄλλου γένηται

26. ἦ οὗ Ast: που A[1]ΠΞ: ἢ οὐ A[2]: ἢ ποτοῦ *q*. 28. ἑνὶ λόγῳ Cornarius: ἐν ὀλίγῳ codd.

---

25 **ἆρ' οὖν κτλ.** This discussion (down to 438 E) is apparently regarded by Susemihl (*Gen. Entw.* II pp. 163 f.) as unnecessary for the immediate purposes of the argument, but it is not so. Plato's object is to remove a difficulty which might be felt in holding that desire is restrained, and that by the λογιστικόν. Why should thirst be restrained? an objector might ask. You yourself, Socrates, hold that (1) desire is always of the good; consequently (2) thirst is always the desire of good drink, and (3) is therefore always good. See 438 A, where the gist of the objection is contained. Socrates would reply: The fallacy lurks in (2), for 'good' drink is ambiguous. If 'good' drink means drink which desire *thinks* good, then (2) is true; if it means drink which is in reality good, (2) is not true. Desire cannot know what is good. We must therefore amend (2) by omitting 'good,' for in reality it is sometimes good and sometimes bad to drink. To what then is the final appeal? To the λογιστικόν. It is this which decides on each occasion whether it is really good or bad to drink, and gives or refuses its assent accordingly (439 C). Bosanquet takes a somewhat similar view (*Companion* p. 154). See also notes on 438 A.

27 **οἷον δίψα—ψυχροῦ.** 'Thus thirst is thirst—of hot drink, is it, or of cold?' For the genitive with δίψα (which Richards doubts) cf. 439 A. The repetition of δίψα is like that of ἐπιστήμη in 438 C, and makes the statement formal and precise.

437 E 29 **ψυχροῦ—θερμοῦ.** Hermann transposes these words and is followed by Stallbaum, Baiter, and others. "Palmaria emendatio," cries Stallbaum; whereas J. and C. hold that it "makes nonsense of the passage." It is not at first sight quite easy to decide between these conflicting views. The words ἐὰν μέν τις—προσπαρέχοιτ' ἄν clearly mean that the desire of cold drink is due to thirst *plus* heat, i.e. thirst supplies the desire of drink, and the heat present in the thirst supplies in addition (προσπαρέχοιτ' ἄν) the desire of cold: see also on τοῦ δὲ—προσγιγνόμενα below. This is in harmony with common sense and also with the theory of *Lys.* 215 E ἐπιθυμεῖν γὰρ τοῦ τοιούτου (sc. ἐναντίου) ἕκαστον, ἀλλ' οὐ τοῦ ὁμοίου. τὸ μὲν γὰρ ξηρὸν ὑγροῦ, τὸ δὲ ψυχρὸν θερμοῦ κτλ.: cf. also *Symp.* 186 B. But ἐὰν δὲ—πολλὴ ἡ δίψα ᾖ seems to proceed on the opposite or homoeopathic principle. The presence of πλῆθος produces a desire not for its opposite but for itself. The solution of the difficulty is to be found in the different character of the notions θερμότης and πλῆθος. θερμότης is something distinct from δίψος, though superadded to it, for which reason Plato does not use the expression θερμὸν δίψος; whereas πλῆθος is in reality πλῆθος δίψης, and πολλὴ δίψα, as experience shews, desires much drink. The common sense point of view is taken by Plato throughout, and is expressly justified by him in 438 E οὔ τι λέγω ὡς οἵων ἂν ᾖ, τοιαῦτα καὶ ἔστιν. For these reasons I heartily agree with the Oxford editors. Hermann's proposal is a product of the inveterate tendency to suppose that wherever we turn in Plato we rub against the theory of Ideas; but the use of παρουσία here (in spite of Peiper's *Ontol. Pl.* pp. 602 ff., Zeller[4] II 1, p. 560 *n.*, and many other critics) is not metaphysical, but logical, and πλῆθος is certainly not an Idea in this passage. See on this point 438 B, 438 C *nn*.

ἐπιθυμία ἢ οὗπερ πέφυκεν, αὐτοῦ πώματος, καὶ αὖ τὸ πεινῆν βρώματος; Οὕτως, ἔφη, αὐτή γε ἡ ἐπιθυμία ἑκάστη αὐτοῦ μόνου ἑκάστου οὗ πέφυκεν, τοῦ δὲ τοίου ἢ τοίου τὰ προσγιγνόμενα.
438 | Μήτοι τις, ἦν δ' ἐγώ, ἀσκέπτους ἡμᾶς ὄντας θορυβήσῃ, ὡς οὐδεὶς ποτοῦ ἐπιθυμεῖ, ἀλλὰ χρηστοῦ ποτοῦ, καὶ οὐ σίτου, ἀλλὰ χρηστοῦ σίτου· πάντες γὰρ ἄρα τῶν ἀγαθῶν ἐπιθυμοῦσιν. εἰ οὖν ἡ δίψα ἐπιθυμία ἐστί, χρηστοῦ ἂν εἴη εἴτε πώματος εἴτε ἄλλου ὅτου ἐστὶν ἐπιθυμία, καὶ αἱ ἄλλαι οὕτω. Ἴσως γὰρ ἄν, ἔφη, δοκοῖ τι λέγειν
B ὁ ταῦτα λέγων. Ἀλλὰ μέντοι, ἦν δ' ἐγώ, ὅσα γ' ἐστὶ τοιαῦτα | οἷα εἶναί του, τὰ μὲν ποιὰ ἄττα ποιοῦ τινός ἐστιν, ὡς ἐμοὶ δοκεῖ, τὰ δ' αὐτὰ ἕκαστα αὐτοῦ ἑκάστου μόνου. Οὐκ ἔμαθον, ἔφη. Οὐκ ἔμαθες, ἔφην, ὅτι τὸ μεῖζον τοιοῦτόν ἐστιν οἷον τινὸς εἶναι μεῖζον; Πάνυ γε. Οὐκοῦν τοῦ ἐλάττονος; Ναί. Τὸ δέ γε πολὺ μεῖζον πολὺ ἐλάττονος. ἦ γάρ; Ναί. Ἆρ' οὖν καὶ τὸ ποτὲ μεῖζον ποτὲ

---

33 **αὐτοῦ πώματος**: 'merely of drink')(much drink, cold drink, etc. Cf. VIII 559 A αὐτοῦ σίτου τε καὶ ὄψου. For καὶ αὖ κτλ. Herwerden would expect καὶ αὐτὸ <τὸ> πεινῆν <αὐτοῦ> βρώματος. Further specification than Plato gives is unnecessary, for τὸ πεινῆν as well as αὐτὸ τὸ δίψος is subject to οὐ μή ποτε—οὗπερ πέφυκεν. The voice pauses slightly after πεινῆν.

35 **τοῦ δὲ—προσγιγνόμενα**: as e.g. θερμότης, where it προσγίγνεται τῷ δίψει (cf. E above), is the desire of ψυχροῦ, ψυχρότης of θερμοῦ. The type of desires illustrated by the desire of ψυχρὸν πῶμα appears to Plato composite and not simple.

438 A 1 **μήτοι** has been doubted, and is not, apparently, elsewhere so used in Plato (Kugler *de part.* τοι etc. p. 11), though often in Tragedy. Here too it strikes, I think, a lofty note 'Wherefore let not any' etc. θορυβήσῃ is also highly dramatic. All this parade is affected because it is a deduction from one of his own favourite commonplaces which Socrates is about to parry: see next note.

3 **πάντες γὰρ κτλ.** γὰρ ἄρα—a rare combination—occurs also in *Prot.* 315 D, *Symp.* 205 B (according to Ven. T, but the Bodleian reads γάρ), *Laws* 698 D. ἄρα indicates that the objector is quoting another man's view (II 358 C *n.*), and the doctrine that all men desire the good was in point of fact a commonplace in the Platonic school. See for example *Gorg.* 468 A, *Men.* 77 C ff., *Symp.* 204 E and *Rep.* III 413 A, VI 505 D. Here, as always, Socrates would of course concede that all men desire the good; but we need the λογιστικόν in each act of desire to specify what the good really is (437 D *n.*). Moreover, according to our present theory, the desire of good drink is the product of *two* desires, viz. (1) thirst or the desire of drink, and (2) the desire of good. That (2) is in a certain sense universal, does not alter the fact that the two desires are logically distinct. See on τοῦ δὲ—προσγιγνόμενα 437 E.

438 B 8 **αὐτὰ ἕκαστα.** αὐτά is *ipsa*, i.e. by themselves, alone, without qualification: cf. αὐτὰ—μόνα αὐτῶν μόνων in D and αὐτοῦ πώματος etc. 437 E. Plato now proceeds to establish the universality of his rule. It is obvious that the reasons for believing the rule true of ἐπιθυμία are confirmed if we can shew that it is true universally. The phraseology of this passage—πλήθους παρουσία, αὐτὰ ἕκαστα, αὐτὴ ἐπιστήμη—is no doubt interesting for the light which it throws on the origin of the terminology adopted in the Theory of Ideas (cf. VI 507 B *n.*): but we could make no greater mistake than to suppose that Plato is here speaking of hypostasized Ideas. Cf. Pfleiderer *Zur Lösung* etc. p. 19.

9 **τὸ μεῖζον—μεῖζον.** Cf. (with Stallbaum) *Charm.* 168 B ff., where the nature of relative notions is similarly defined: also *Gorg.* 476 B ff.

ἐλάττονος, καὶ τὸ ἐσόμενον μεῖζον ἐσομένου ἐλάττονος; Ἀλλὰ τί μήν; ἦ δ' ὅς. Καὶ τὰ πλείω δὴ πρὸς τὰ ἐλάττω | καὶ τὰ διπλάσια C πρὸς τὰ ἡμίσεα καὶ πάντα τὰ τοιαῦτα, καὶ αὖ βαρύτερα πρὸς κουφότερα καὶ θάττω πρὸς τὰ βραδύτερα, καὶ ἔτι γε τὰ θερμὰ πρὸς τὰ ψυχρὰ καὶ πάντα τὰ τούτοις ὅμοια ἆρ' οὐχ οὕτως ἔχει; Πάνυ μὲν οὖν. Τί δὲ τὰ περὶ τὰς ἐπιστήμας; οὐχ ὁ αὐτὸς τρόπος; ἐπιστήμη μὲν αὐτὴ μαθήματος αὐτοῦ ἐπιστήμη ἐστίν, ἢ ὅτου δὴ δεῖ θεῖναι τὴν ἐπιστήμην, ἐπιστήμη δέ τις καὶ ποιά τις ποιοῦ τινὸς καὶ τινός. λέγω δὲ τὸ τοιόνδε· | οὐκ, ἐπειδὴ οἰκίας ἐργασίας D ἐπιστήμη ἐγένετο, διήνεγκε τῶν ἄλλων ἐπιστημῶν, ὥστε οἰκοδομικὴ κληθῆναι; Τί μήν; Ἆρ' οὐ τῷ ποιά τις εἶναι, οἵα ἑτέρα οὐδεμία τῶν ἄλλων; Ναί. Οὐκοῦν ἐπειδὴ ποιοῦ τινός, καὶ αὐτὴ ποιά τις ἐγένετο; καὶ αἱ ἄλλαι οὕτω τέχναι τε καὶ ἐπιστῆμαι; Ἔστιν οὕτω.

XIV. Τοῦτο τοίνυν, ἦν δ' ἐγώ, φάθι με τότε βούλεσθαι λέγειν, εἰ ἄρα νῦν ἔμαθες, ὅτι ὅσα ἐστὶν οἷα εἶναί του, αὐτὰ μὲν μόνα αὐτῶν μόνων ἐστίν, τῶν δὲ ποιῶν τινῶν | ποιὰ ἄττα. καὶ οὔ τι E λέγω, ὡς, οἵων ἂν ᾖ, τοιαῦτα καὶ ἔστιν, ὡς ἄρα καὶ τῶν ὑγιεινῶν καὶ νοσωδῶν ἡ ἐπιστήμη ὑγιεινὴ καὶ νοσώδης καὶ τῶν κακῶν καὶ τῶν ἀγαθῶν κακὴ καὶ ἀγαθή· ἀλλ' ἐπειδὴ οὐκ αὐτοῦ οὗπερ ἐπιστήμη ἐστὶν ἐγένετο ἐπιστήμη, ἀλλὰ ποιοῦ τινός, τοῦτο δ' ἦν

20. *οἰκίας* Ξ *q*: *οἰκείας* ΑΠ.

---

438 C 15 **τὰ βραδύτερα.** Stallbaum and others read *βραδύτερα* without the article (on slight MS authority), but *praestat lectio difficilior*. Cf. *εἴτε ἐγγείων εἴτε τῶν ζῴων* VI 491 D. *τά* is certainly not wrong, and the variety of expression is pleasing: 'and heavier also to lighter, and swifter to that which is slower—do they not stand to one another in this relation?' i.e. such that if *βαρύτερα*, for example, is qualified, *κουφότερα* is qualified too.

18 **ἐπιστήμη μὲν αὐτή.** 'Knowledge and nothing more,' as opposed to knowledge plus some specification, e.g. astronomical knowledge, literary knowledge etc. It is interesting and instructive to study *Parm.* 134 A ff. side by side with this passage. There *αὐτὴ ἐπιστήμη* has for its object *τῆς ὃ ἔστιν ἀλήθεια*, i.e. the Ideas; here we do not soar so high, for *μαθήματος αὐτοῦ* is only 'learning and nothing more')(e.g. physical learning, classical learning, etc.

438 D 20 **ἐπειδὴ—κληθῆναι.** Plato's theory is very clearly conceived. *οἰκοδομικὴ ἐπιστήμη* is a combination of *αὐτὴ ἐπιστήμη* and *οἰκοδομία*: *ἐπιστήμη* correlates with *μάθημα*, *οἰκοδομία* with *οἰκίας ἐργασία*, so that *ἐπιστήμη οἰκοδομική* is *ἐπιστήμη οἰκίας ἐργασίας μαθήματος*: it is therefore *ποίου τινός* (i.e. in this case *οἰκοδομικοῦ*) *μαθήματος*. Cf. note on *τοῦ δὲ—προσγιγνόμενα* in 437 E.

438 E 29 **τῶν ὑγιεινῶν καὶ νοσωδῶν.** If we carry the analysis less far than Plato, we can still make the added determinants the same by saying that *ἰατρικὴ ἐπιστήμη* is of *ἰατρικὸν μάθημα*. But this will not suit with *κακή*, for 'bad knowledge' is not 'knowledge of bad things'; nor does it—in many cases—apply to desires. Cf. 437 E *n*.

31 **αὐτοῦ οὗπερ—ἐστίν**: i.e. *μαθήματος αὐτοῦ*. *αὐτοῦ* is emphatic and contrasted with *ποιοῦ τινός*.

ὑγιεινὸν καὶ νοσῶδες, ποιὰ δή τις συνέβη καὶ αὐτὴ γενέσθαι, καὶ τοῦτο αὐτὴν ἐποίησεν μηκέτι ἐπιστήμην ἁπλῶς καλεῖσθαι, ἀλλὰ τοῦ ποιοῦ τινὸς προσγενομένου ἰατρικήν. Ἔμαθον, ἔφη, καί μοι
439 δοκεῖ οὕτως ἔχειν. Τὸ δὲ δὴ δίψος, ἦν δ' ἐγώ, οὐ | τούτων θήσεις τῶν τινὸς εἶναι τοῦτο ὅπερ ἐστὶν—ἔστι δὲ δήπου δίψος—; Ἔγωγε, ἦ δ' ὅς· πώματός γε. Οὐκοῦν ποιοῦ μέν τινος πώματος ποιόν τι καὶ δίψος, δίψος δ' οὖν αὐτὸ οὔτε πολλοῦ οὔτε ὀλίγου, οὔτε ἀγαθοῦ οὔτε κακοῦ, οὐδ' ἑνὶ λόγῳ ποιοῦ τινός, ἀλλ' αὐτοῦ πώματος μόνον αὐτὸ δίψος πέφυκεν; Παντάπασι μὲν οὖν. Τοῦ διψῶντος ἄρα ἡ ψυχή, καθ' ὅσον διψῇ, οὐκ ἄλλο τι βούλεται ἢ πιεῖν, καὶ
B τούτου | ὀρέγεται καὶ ἐπὶ τοῦτο ὁρμᾷ. Δῆλον δή. Οὐκοῦν εἴ ποτέ τι αὐτὴν ἀνθέλκει διψῶσαν, ἕτερον ἄν τι ἐν αὐτῇ εἴη αὐτοῦ τοῦ διψῶντος καὶ ἄγοντος ὥσπερ θηρίον ἐπὶ τὸ πιεῖν; οὐ γὰρ δή, φαμέν, τό γε αὐτὸ τῷ αὐτῷ ἑαυτοῦ περὶ τὸ αὐτὸ ἅμα τἀναντία πράττει. Οὐ γὰρ οὖν. Ὥσπερ γε, οἶμαι, τοῦ τοξότου οὐ καλῶς ἔχει λέγειν, ὅτι αὐτοῦ ἅμα αἱ χεῖρες τὸ τόξον ἀπωθοῦνταί τε καὶ προσέλκονται, ἀλλ' ὅτι ἄλλη μὲν ἡ ἀπωθοῦσα χείρ, ἑτέρα δὲ ἡ

5. οὐδ' ἑνὶ vel οὐδὲ ἑνὶ Ξ *q*: οὐδενὶ ΑΠ. 9. αὐτῇ A^2Π: ἑαυτῇ A^1.
10. θηρίον Ξ: θηρίου ΑΠ *q*. 12. πράττει Ast: πράττοι ΑΠΞ *q*.

---

36 **τὸ δὲ δὴ δίψος κτλ.** Here begins the application of the argument on Relativity.

439 A 1 **οὐ τούτων κτλ.**: i.q. *οὐ θήσεις τὸ δίψος εἶναι τοῦτο, ὅπερ ἐστί, τούτων τῶν τινὸς sitim esse id, quod est, inter ea s. tanquam unum eorum, quae alicuius sunt* (Schneider). We must, I think, acquiesce in this interpretation, if the text is sound; but there is grave difficulty in taking *εἶναι* twice over, as Schneider virtually does ('is that which it is, and is one of,' etc.). I am strongly inclined to think that Plato wrote *οὐ τούτων θήσεις τῶν τινός, <καὶ τινὸς> εἶναι τοῦτο ὅπερ ἐστὶν κτλ.* With this emendation the meaning is: 'Well now, about thirst, will you not place it in this category of things relative, and hold that it is what it is—that is, of course, thirst—relatively to something? Yes, said he, relatively to drink.' *τὰ τινός* i.e. 'the things relative to something' for 'the category of things relative,' is further explained in *καὶ τινὸς—ὅπερ ἐστίν*. *ἔγωγε* answers the first part of Socrates' question, and *πώματός γε* the second. For other views on this passage see App. III.

4 **δίψος δ' οὖν κτλ.** *δ' οὖν* = 'however,' as in I 337 C. The reading *δ' αὖ* (*q* and some other inferior MSS) is unpleasantly cacophonous before *αὐτό*.

439 B 10 **οὐ γὰρ δὴ—πράττει.** See *cr. n.* Ast's emendation *πράττει* is preferable to inserting *ἄν* or changing *δή* to *ἄν* (with Schanz). The particle *δή* could ill be spared. The infinitive *πράττειν* is read by Galen (*de Hipp. et Plat. decr.* V p. 488 ed. Kühn) and two inferior MSS. Those who retain the MS reading suppose that *ἄν* is carried on from *ἕτερον ἂν εἴη*; but the instances cited in support (I 352 E, II 360 C, 382 D, III 398 A) are very much easier than this. *περὶ τὸ αὐτό* refers of course to the object of the action in question: *πῶμα* for instance in a case of thirst. Note that Plato betrays a sense of the unity of soul when he uses the expressions *αὐτὴν—διψῶσαν*, and *τό γε αὐτὸ—πράττει*. So also in D below *ᾧ λογίζεται* sc. *ἡ ψυχή*. See on 435 A ff.

13 **αὐτοῦ.** See 428 A *n.* The illustration, as Bosanquet conjectures, may have been suggested by Heraclitus' *παλίντροπος ἁρμονίη ὅκωσπερ τόξου καὶ λύρης* (*Fr.* 45 Byw.).

προσαγομένη. | Παντάπασι μὲν οὖν, ἔφη. Πότερον δὴ φῶμέν C
τινας ἔστιν ὅτε διψῶντας οὐκ ἐθέλειν πιεῖν; Καὶ μάλα γ', ἔφη,
πολλοὺς καὶ πολλάκις. Τί οὖν, ἔφην ἐγώ, φαίη τις ἂν τούτων
πέρι; οὐκ ἐνεῖναι μὲν ἐν τῇ ψυχῇ αὐτῶν τὸ κελεῦον, ἐνεῖναι δὲ
τὸ κωλῦον πιεῖν, ἄλλο ὂν καὶ κρατοῦν τοῦ κελεύοντος; Ἔμοιγε,
ἔφη, δοκεῖ. Ἆρ' οὖν οὐ τὸ μὲν κωλῦον τὰ τοιαῦτα ἐγγίγνεται,
ὅταν ἐγγίγνηται, ἐκ λογισμοῦ, | τὰ δὲ ἄγοντα καὶ ἕλκοντα διὰ D
παθημάτων τε καὶ νοσημάτων παραγίγνεται; Φαίνεται. Οὐ δὴ
ἀλόγως, ἦν δ' ἐγώ, ἀξιώσομεν αὐτὰ διττά τε καὶ ἕτερα ἀλλήλων
εἶναι, τὸ μὲν ᾧ λογίζεται λογιστικὸν προσαγορεύοντες τῆς ψυχῆς,
τὸ δὲ ᾧ ἐρᾷ τε καὶ πεινῇ καὶ διψῇ καὶ περὶ τὰς ἄλλας ἐπιθυμίας
ἐπτόηται ἀλόγιστόν τε καὶ ἐπιθυμητικόν, πληρώσεών τινων καὶ
ἡδονῶν ἑταῖρον. Οὔκ, ἀλλ' εἰκότως, | ἔφη, ἡγοίμεθ' ἂν οὕτως. E

21. ἐγγίγνηται coniecit Schneider: ἐγγένηται codd. 27. ἑταῖρον Π: ἕτερον A.

---

439 C 16 **οὐκ ἐθέλειν**: 'refuse': cf. infra τὸ κωλῦον—κρατοῦν τοῦ κελεύοντος. So also Bosanquet 'decline to drink.'

18 **ἐνεῖναι δέ.** The repetition of ἐνεῖναι with μέν and δέ has almost the force of a conjunction: cf. *Phaed.* 83 A ἀπάτης μὲν μεστὴ ἡ διὰ τῶν ὀμμάτων σκέψις, ἀπάτης δὲ ἡ διὰ τῶν ὤτων. It is quite unnecessary to insert καί after δέ (with Ast and Hartman). For the verbal play in κελεῦον—κωλῦον cf. III 406 B *n.*

21 **ὅταν ἐγγίγνηται—παραγίγνεται.** See *cr. n.* The present ἐγγίγνηται is, I think, necessary, and the corruption (through ἐγγίνηται) easy enough. ὅταν ἐγγένηται could scarcely mean ἑκάστοτε, which is the meaning here required. The subject to ἐγγίγνηται is τὸ κωλῦον. It is not hinted that 'all men have not right reason' (J. and C.), but only that there is not on every occasion a conflict between reason and desire. See 431 C and 437 D *n.* Reason readily acquiesces when it is good to gratify desire. τὰ—ἄγοντα καὶ ἕλκοντα is translated by Jowett 'that which bids and attracts': but ἄγοντα is said like ἄγοντος in 439 B and ἕλκοντα is 'dragging.' The plural should also be retained in the translation, otherwise τὰ ἄγοντα may be identified with the ἐπιθυμητικόν, which would be a mistake, for the appetitive part of soul is certainly not *produced* by παθήματα of any kind. τὰ ἄγοντα καὶ ἕλκοντα are in reality 'impulses leading and dragging' the soul, impulses engendered by 'particular conditions and diseases' (not 'passive states' or 'passion,' etc. with the English translators), i.e. in other words by abnormal bodily states favourable to desires, as for example fevers etc.: cf. *Phil.* 45 A, B. These impulses are no doubt special instances of the action of ἐπιθυμητικόν, but should be distinguished from the appetitive principle itself.

439 D 24 **λογιστικόν.** The φιλόσοφον of II and III shewed itself in moral rather than in intellectual relations: see II 376 B *n.* λογιστικόν, though as yet directed only to moral questions, is intellectual more than moral. Intellect gradually asserts its predominance over will until in Books VI and VII it achieves its final triumph. Cf. 439 E, 441 E *nn.*

439 E—**441** C *There is also a third element or part of soul, that which we call the element of Spirit. It is distinct from the Appetitive element, with which, indeed, it frequently contends. Its function is to support the Rational part of the soul. In a man of noble character the spirited element is quiescent or the reverse in accordance with the commands of Reason. It must not however be identified with Reason; for it is present in children and the lower animals, whereas Reason is not. Homer also recognises that the two elements are distinct.*

439 E ff. The analogy between the righteous city and the righteous soul is

Ταῦτα μὲν τοίνυν, ἦν δ' ἐγώ, δύο ἡμῖν ὡρίσθω εἴδη ἐν ψυχῇ ἐνόντα· τὸ δὲ δὴ τοῦ θυμοῦ καὶ ᾧ θυμούμεθα πότερον τρίτον, ἢ τούτων ποτέρῳ ἂν εἴη ὁμοφυές; Ἴσως, ἔφη, τῷ ἑτέρῳ, τῷ ἐπιθυμητικῷ. Ἀλλ', ἦν δ' ἐγώ, ποτὲ ἀκούσας τι πιστεύω τούτῳ, ὡς ἄρα Λεόντιος ὁ Ἀγλαΐωνος ἀνιὼν ἐκ Πειραιέως ὑπὸ τὸ βόρειον τεῖχος ἐκτός, αἰσθόμενος νεκροὺς παρὰ τῷ δημίῳ κειμένους, ἅμα

---

continued throughout this section. It should be noted however that the parallel is no longer quite exact. The difference between *θυμοειδές* and λογιστικόν in the soul is greater than that between auxiliaries and rulers in the State: for the λογιστικόν is not a select part of the *θυμοειδές*—as the rulers are of the soldiers—but something generically distinct from it. Otherwise the analogy holds (with the reservations mentioned on 435 A). Cf. Steinhart *Einleitung* p. 192 and Susemihl *Gen. Entw.* II p. 166.

439 E 29 **τὸ δὲ δὴ τοῦ θυμοῦ κτλ.** Hitherto *θυμοειδές* has been chiefly the source of courage and the natural antithesis of *φιλόσοφον* (II 375 A ff., III 410 D, 411 C). It now enters on a wider sphere as the ally of λογιστικόν, and becomes, thus far, more intellectual, as Krohn points out: note also the *ὀρθὴ δόξα* of 430 B. Its ethical connotation is also intensified; for it is not now simply spirit, but the sentiment of moral indignation at everything evil—"ein edler Unwille über alles Schlechte" (Krohn *Pl. St.* p. 55)—everything which tends to destroy the *πολιτεία ἐν ἡμῖν*. It becomes in short, as Brandt (*Zur Entwick. d. Pl. Lehr. v. d. Seelentheilen* p. 18) says truly enough though ponderously, "leidenschaftlicher Selbsterhaltungs- und Selbstvervollkommnungstrieb." Cf. Simson *der Begriff der Seele bei Plato* p. 110, and see also on II 375 A.

30 **ἴσως κτλ.** The *θνητὸν εἶδος ψυχῆς* of the *Timaeus* includes both the *θυμοειδές* and the *ἐπιθυμητικόν*: see 69 C ff. and cf. *Pol.* 309 C. Similarly in the *Phaedrus* the two lower faculties are figured as the two horses, and the highest as the charioteer of the soul's chariot (253 D): cf. Simson l.c. p. 109 *nn.*

31 **ποτὲ—τούτῳ.** The antecedent of *τούτῳ* is *τι*: 'having once heard something I trust to this,' i.e. 'I rely on an incident which I once heard.' *πιστεύω* means that he relies on it for a proof; and *ὡς ἄρα* goes with *ἀκούσας*. So Schneider correctly explains the Greek. The precise force of *πιστεύω τούτῳ* has, I think, been missed by most of those who have suspected corruption. For *τι* there have been various conjectures: *ἔτι* (Madvig), *ἄρτι* (Liebhold *Fl. Jahrb.* 1888 p. 110), *τινος* (Zeller *Archiv f. Gesch. d. Phil.* II p. 694)—all superfluous, and the first two very weak; while Campbell suggests that *οὐ* has dropped before *πιστεύω*, taking *τούτῳ* to refer to Glauco's suggestion. But in that case *τοῦτο* would be necessary.

32 **Λεόντιος.** "Ad hunc Leontium eiusque insanam cupiditatem spectat depravatissimus Theopompi comici Καπηλίδων locus" (Herwerden *Mn.* N.S. XI p. 346). The fragment is emended by Kock (*Com. Att. Frag.* I p. 739) into Λεωτροφίδης ὁ τρίμνεως (*trium librarum homo*, i.e. levissimus) Λεοντίῳ | εὔχρως τε φαίνεται χαρίεις θ' ὥσπερ νεκρός. Bergk was the first to connect the two passages.

ὑπὸ—ἐκτός: 'close to the outer side of the North wall.' Cf. (with Stallbaum) *Lys.* 203 A *τὴν ἔξω τείχους ὑπ' αὐτὸ τὸ τεῖχος*. The North wall was the outer of the two walls connecting Athens with the Piraeus; the other, or South wall, was called *τὸ διὰ μέσου τεῖχος*, because it lay between the *βόρειον* and the *Φαληρικόν*, which connected Athens and the Phalerum. See *Gorg.* 455 E and the other authorities cited by Milchhöfer *Schriftquellen zur Topographie von Athen* pp. CXIII ff., and Curtius u. Kaupert *Atlas von Athen* Bl. II.

33 **παρὰ—κειμένους**: 'lying by' or 'near the executioner'; not of course 'at the executioner's' as has been suggested. When seen by Leontius, the hangman was engaged in throwing the bodies into the pit (*ὄρυγμα* or *βάραθρον*, from which he was often called *ὁ ἐπὶ* s. *πρὸς τῷ ὀρύγματι*). The *βάραθρον* into which the bodies of executed criminals

μὲν ἰδεῖν ἐπιθυμοῖ, ἅμα δὲ αὖ δυσχεραίνοι καὶ ἀποτρέποι ἑαυτόν,
καὶ τέως μάχοιτό τε καὶ πα|ρακαλύπτοιτο, κρατούμενος δ' οὖν ὑπὸ **440**
τῆς ἐπιθυμίας διελκύσας τοὺς ὀφθαλμοὺς προσδραμὼν πρὸς τοὺς
νεκρούς, Ἰδοὺ ὑμῖν, ἔφη, ὦ κακοδαίμονες, ἐμπλήσθητε τοῦ καλοῦ
θεάματος. Ἤκουσα, ἔφη, καὶ αὐτός. Οὗτος μέντοι, ἔφην, ὁ λόγος
σημαίνει τὴν ὀργὴν πολεμεῖν ἐνίοτε ταῖς ἐπιθυμίαις ὡς ἄλλο ὂν
ἄλλῳ. Σημαίνει γάρ, ἔφη.

XV. *Οὐκοῦν καὶ ἄλλοθι, ἔφην, πολλαχοῦ αἰσθανόμεθα, ὅταν*
βιάζωνταί τινα παρὰ τὸν λογισμὸν ἐπιθυμίαι, | λοιδοροῦντά τε **B**
αὐτὸν καὶ θυμούμενον τῷ βιαζομένῳ ἐν αὑτῷ, καὶ ὥσπερ δυοῖν
στασιαζόντοιν ξύμμαχον τῷ λόγῳ γιγνόμενον τὸν θυμὸν τοῦ
τοιούτου; ταῖς δ' ἐπιθυμίαις αὐτὸν κοινωνήσαντα, αἱροῦντος λόγου
μὴ δεῖν ἀντιπράττειν, οἶμαί σε οὐκ ἂν φάναι γενομένου ποτὲ ἐν
σαυτῷ τοῦ τοιούτου αἰσθέσθαι, οἶμαι δ' οὐδ' ἐν ἄλλῳ. Οὐ μὰ
τὸν Δία, ἔφη. Τί δέ; ἦν δ' ἐγώ· | ὅταν τις οἴηται ἀδικεῖν, οὐχ **C**
ὅσῳ ἂν γενναιότερος ᾖ, τοσούτῳ ἧττον δύναται ὀργίζεσθαι καὶ
πεινῶν καὶ ῥιγῶν καὶ ἄλλο ὁτιοῦν τῶν τοιούτων πάσχων ὑπ'
ἐκείνου, ὃν ἂν οἴηται δικαίως ταῦτα δρᾶν, καί, ὃ λέγω, οὐκ ἐθέλει
πρὸς τοῦτον αὐτοῦ ἐγείρεσθαι ὁ θυμός; Ἀληθῆ, ἔφη. Τί δέ;

13. *σαυτῷ* (vel *σεαυτῷ*) A¹Ξ*q*: *ἑαυτῷ* A²Π.

---

were thrown, was a deep ravine outside the walls, in the deme Κειριάδαι. Leontius would pass near it, just before entering the city (probably by the Μελιτίδες πύλαι): see Curtius u. Kaupert l.c. Bl. II. The place is still pointed out to visitors to Athens on the western declivity of the Hill of the Nymphs. For the ancient authorities see Milchhöfer l.c. pp. I—II. Various suggestions have been made for *δημίῳ*. Valckenaer's *δημείῳ* is a coinage of his own, and otherwise objectionable; *Λυκείῳ* (also Valckenaer) is topographically impossible, and so is *Διομείῳ* (Hemsterhuis), if it has anything to do with the *Διομηΐς πύλη*. The explanation which I have given seems also to have been held by Milchhöfer, for he quotes the present passage among the authorities for the *βάραθρον*.

440 A 3 **ὦ κακοδαίμονες.** 'Confound you!'

5 **τὴν ὀργήν.** *q* reads *τὸν θυμόν*, which Ast and others have preferred. But, as Schneider observes, *ὀργή* is to *θυμός*, as *ἐπιθυμίαι* to *ἐπιθυμητικόν*. If anger fights with desire, the source of anger, *θυμοειδές*, must be different from that of desire, *ἐπιθυμητικόν*. This is the whole moral of the anecdote, which is intended to establish the difference between *θυμοειδές* and *ἐπιθυμητικόν* only, not also *λογιστικόν*.

440 B 11 **ταῖς δ' ἐπιθυμίαις κτλ.** *αὐτόν* is *τὸν θυμόν*. *ἀντιπράττειν* "ad singularem aliquam actionem referendum est, quam ratio suscipere eaque in re sibi repugnare prohibeat, quasi dictum sit: *μὴ δεῖν τι πράττειν καὶ τοῦτο δρῶντα ἀντιπράττειν*" (Schneider). The words *γενομένου τοῦ τοιούτου* refer to *ταῖς—κοινωνήσαντα*. The anacoluthon is an easy one. Plato means merely that *θυμός* does not unite with the desires against the reason. For *αἱροῦντος λόγου* cf. X 604 C *n*. On other views on this passage consult App. IV.

440 C 15 **ὅσῳ—ᾖ.** The restriction will be noted. It is not *οἱ γενναῖοι* who, as the saying is, hate those whom they have injured.

ὅταν ἀδικεῖσθαί τις ἡγῆται, οὐκ ἐν τούτῳ ζεῖ τε καὶ χαλεπαίνει,
καὶ ξυμμαχεῖ τῷ δοκοῦντι δικαίῳ, καὶ διὰ τὸ πεινῆν καὶ διὰ τὸ
D ῥιγῶν καὶ πάντα τὰ τοιαῦτα | πάσχειν, καὶ ὑπομένων νικᾷ, καὶ
οὐ λήγει τῶν γενναίων, πρὶν ἂν ἢ διαπράξηται ἢ τελευτήσῃ ἢ
ὥσπερ κύων ὑπὸ νομέως ὑπὸ τοῦ λόγου τοῦ παρ' αὐτῷ ἀνακληθεὶς
πραυνθῇ; Πάνυ μὲν οὖν, ἔφη, ἔοικε τούτῳ ᾧ λέγεις· καίτοι γ' ἐν
τῇ ἡμετέρᾳ πόλει τοὺς ἐπικούρους ὥσπερ κύνας ἐθέμεθα ὑπηκόους
τῶν ἀρχόντων ὥσπερ ποιμένων πόλεως. Καλῶς γάρ, ἦν δ' ἐγώ,
νοεῖς ὃ βούλομαι λέγειν. ἀλλ' ἦ πρὸς τούτῳ καὶ τόδε ἐνθυμεῖ;
E | Τὸ ποῖον; Ὅτι τοὐναντίον ἢ ἀρτίως ἡμῖν φαίνεται περὶ τοῦ
θυμοειδοῦς. τότε μὲν γὰρ ἐπιθυμητικόν τι αὐτὸ ᾠόμεθα εἶναι, νῦν
δὲ πολλοῦ δεῖν φαμέν, ἀλλὰ πολὺ μᾶλλον αὐτὸ ἐν τῇ τῆς ψυχῆς
στάσει τίθεσθαι τὰ ὅπλα πρὸς τὸ λογιστικόν. Παντάπασιν, ἔφη.
Ἆρ' οὖν ἕτερον ὂν καὶ τούτου, ἢ λογιστικοῦ τι εἶδος, ὥστε μὴ τρία,

19. *ζεῖ* Ξ *q*: *ζητεῖ* ΑΠ. 21. *καὶ ὑπομένων* Ξ: *ὑπομένων καὶ* ΑΠ: *καὶ* om. *q*. 27. *ἦ* Ast: *εἰ* codd. 29. *αὐτὸ* Ξ *q*: *αὐτῷ* ΑΠ. 32. *τούτου* Ξ: *τοῦτο* ΑΠ *q*. *τι* Π: om. Α.

---

19 **οὐκ ἐν τούτῳ κτλ.**: 'does not he then fume and chafe—and fight on the side of what he believes to be just—both at hunger and at cold and all such inflictions, and bide his ground and conquer, abating not his noble indignation, until he has either achieved his purpose, or perished, or has been called back and soothed by the reason within him, as a herdsman recalls his dog?' The words *καὶ διὰ τὸ πεινῆν—πάσχειν* must be taken with *ζεῖ τε καὶ χαλεπαίνει*, but possibly *καὶ ξυμμαχεῖ τῷ δοκοῦντι δικαίῳ* has been displaced, and we should read *ζεῖ τε καὶ χαλεπαίνει καὶ διὰ τὸ πεινῆν—πάσχειν, καὶ ξυμμαχεῖ τῷ δοκοῦντι δικαίῳ, καὶ ὑπομένων κτλ.* *νικᾷ* is not merely 'tries to conquer' or 'perseveres' (Schneider), but 'conquers,' in spite of the pardonable inconsistency of this translation with *τελευτήσῃ—πραυνθῇ*. *τῶν γενναίων* cannot mean "in the case of the noble' (P. Shorey *A. J. Ph.* XVI p. 237), unless *θυμός* is the subject of *λήγει*, which is not, I think, the case. The meaning is caught the more readily by reason of *οὐχ ὅσῳ ἂν γενναιότερος ᾖ* in C, and we ought not to substitute *ἀγανακτῶν* or the like with Richards. See on the whole passage App. V.

440 D 24 **καίτοι γε**='and surely' has no adversative force here. See Kugler *de part.* *τοι* etc. p. 18. Hartman emends, but see on I 331 E.

27 **ἦ**. See *cr. n.* *εἰ* in direct interrogation is unclassical, and *ἐρωτῶ* cannot be supplied. Nor can *εἰ* well be taken as conditional (with Stallbaum) and *τὸ ποῖον* as a sudden interruption. For the confusion of *ει* and *η* see *Introd.* § 5.

440 E 28 **ἀρτίως**. 439 E.

31 **τίθεσθαι κτλ.**: 'defends the rational element.' I have retained the accusative on the strength of CIA II 317. 9 *λαβόντος τοῦ δήμου τὰ ὅπλα ὑπὲρ τῆς ἐλευθ<ερί>ας καὶ παρακαλοῦ<ν>τος καὶ τοὺς στρατιώτας τίθεσθαι πρὸς τὴν πόλιν*. The inscription dates from about 280 B.C. Other editors read *τοῦ λογιστικοῦ* (with Ξ alone among the MSS), but do not cite any example of the phrase *τίθεσθαι τὰ ὅπλα πρός τινος*, although *πρός* with the genitive is common enough in similar expressions. Thucydides (II 2. 4) has *παρά* with the accusative like *πρός* here. The original meaning of the idiom was to take up a position in arms by the side of: see Schneider's Xen. *Anabasis* pp. 537—540 and the commentators on Thuc. l.c. For the metaphor cf. Arist. *Pol. Ath.* 8. 5. F. K. Hertlein (quoted in Hartman) also defends the accusative, citing Aen. Polior. 4. 3 *ἐτίθεντο τὰ ὅπλα παρὰ τοὺς πολεμίους ὡς παρὰ φιλίους*.

ἀλλὰ δύο εἴδη εἶναι ἐν ψυχῇ, λογιστικὸν καὶ ἐπιθυμητικόν; ἢ
καθάπερ ἐν τῇ πόλει ξυνεῖχεν αὐτὴν τρία ὄντα γένη, | χρηματι- 441
στικόν, ἐπικουρικόν, βουλευτικόν, οὕτως καὶ ἐν ψυχῇ τρίτον τοῦτό
ἐστι τὸ θυμοειδές, ἐπίκουρον ὂν τῷ λογιστικῷ φύσει, ἐὰν μὴ ὑπὸ
κακῆς τροφῆς διαφθαρῇ; Ἀνάγκη, ἔφη, τρίτον. Ναί, ἦν δ' ἐγώ,
ἄν γε τοῦ λογιστικοῦ ἄλλο τι φανῇ, ὥσπερ τοῦ ἐπιθυμητικοῦ
ἐφάνη ἕτερον ὄν. Ἀλλ' οὐ χαλεπόν, ἔφη, φανῆναι. καὶ γὰρ ἐν
τοῖς παιδίοις τοῦτό γ' ἄν τις ἴδοι, ὅτι θυμοῦ μὲν εὐθὺς γενόμενα
μεστά ἐστι, λογισμοῦ δ' ἔνιοι μὲν ἔμοιγε δοκοῦσιν | οὐδέποτε B
μεταλαμβάνειν, οἱ δὲ πολλοὶ ὀψέ ποτε. Ναὶ μὰ Δί', ἦν δ' ἐγώ,
καλῶς γε εἶπες. ἔτι δὲ ἐν τοῖς θηρίοις ἄν τις ἴδοι ὃ λέγεις, ὅτι
οὕτως ἔχει. πρὸς δὲ τούτοις καὶ ὃ ἄνω που ἐκεῖ εἴπομεν, τὸ τοῦ
Ὁμήρου μαρτυρήσει, τὸ

στῆθος δὲ πλήξας κραδίην ἠνίπαπε μύθῳ·

ἐνταῦθα γὰρ δὴ σαφῶς ὡς ἕτερον ἑτέρῳ ἐπιπλῆττον πεποίηκεν
Ὅμηρος τὸ ἀναλογισάμενον | περὶ τοῦ βελτίονός τε καὶ χείρονος C
τῷ ἀλογίστως θυμουμένῳ. Κομιδῇ, ἔφη, ὀρθῶς λέγεις.

XVI. Ταῦτα μὲν ἄρα, ἦν δ' ἐγώ, μόγις διανενεύκαμεν, καὶ
ἡμῖν ἐπιεικῶς ὁμολογεῖται, τὰ αὐτὰ μὲν ἐν πόλει, τὰ αὐτὰ δ' ἐν

2. ἐπικουρικὸν Π: ἐπικουρητικὸν A.

---

441 A 3 **ἐὰν μὴ κτλ.** See App. IV.

441 B 11 **ἐκεῖ**: 'in the other place,' viz. III 390 D. If Kühn is to be trusted, Galen (Vol. V p. 500) does not, as Hartman asserts, omit the word; and there is no good reason for suspecting corruption.

441 C—**443** B *Thus we see that the soul contains within itself the same kinds or elements as our city. It follows that the individual is wise, brave etc. in the same way and in virtue of the same internal elements. We are therefore just when each of our psychological factors does its own work. Reason should rule, with Spirit for its obedient ally; and both of them together, harmonised by music and gymnastic, will control Desire, and ward off foreign enemies from soul and body. The individual is brave in virtue of the element of Spirit, if in spite of pain and pleasure that element continues faithful to the commands of Reason touching what should and should not be feared; wise, by reason of the part of soul that rules and knows; temperate, through the harmony of ruled and ruler on the question which shall rule; and just, in virtue of our oft-repeated principle. We may examine our view of Justice by various tests derived from the popular connotation of the word, and we shall find that we are right.*

441 C ff. The parallel between the City and the Soul is maintained throughout this section. Like the City, the Soul is also wise and brave, in virtue of the wisdom and courage of its parts, and temperate and just for similar reasons (see on τί τὴν πόλιν προσαγορεύεις 428 D); the relation between λογιστικόν, θυμοειδές, and ἐπιθυμητικόν is the same as that between the three orders of the city (see however on 442 C); and the specific virtues are defined in the same way. Finally, as Justice in the State was at last identified with Righteousness or Moral Perfection, so likewise is Justice in the soul (442 E—443 B).

441 C 18 **ὁμολογεῖται.** ὡμολογεῖται (sic) q^1: ὡμολόγηται q^2 (with Stob. *Flor.* 9. 64). The present, 'we pretty well agree,' is satisfactory enough.

ἑνὸς ἑκάστου τῇ ψυχῇ γένη ἐνεῖναι καὶ ἴσα τὸν ἀριθμόν. Ἔστι
ταῦτα. Οὐκοῦν ἐκεῖνό γε ἤδη ἀναγκαῖον, ὡς πόλις ἦν σοφὴ καὶ ᾧ,
οὕτω καὶ τὸν ἰδιώτην καὶ τούτῳ σοφὸν εἶναι; Τί μήν; Καὶ ᾧ δὴ
D ἀνδρεῖος ἰδιώτης καὶ ὥς, τούτῳ | καὶ πόλιν ἀνδρείαν καὶ οὕτως, καὶ
τἆλλα πάντα πρὸς ἀρετὴν ὡσαύτως ἀμφότερα ἔχειν. Ἀνάγκη.
Καὶ δίκαιον δή, ὦ Γλαύκων, οἶμαι, φήσομεν ἄνδρα εἶναι τῷ αὐτῷ
τρόπῳ, ᾧπερ καὶ πόλις ἦν δικαία. Καὶ τοῦτο πᾶσα ἀνάγκη.
Ἀλλ' οὔ πῃ μὴν τοῦτο ἐπιλελήσμεθα, ὅτι ἐκείνη γε τῷ τὸ ἑαυτοῦ
ἕκαστον ἐν αὐτῇ πράττειν τριῶν ὄντων γενῶν δικαία ἦν. Οὔ μοι
δοκοῦμεν, ἔφη, ἐπιλελῆσθαι. Μνημονευτέον ἄρα ἡμῖν, ὅτι καὶ
E ἡμῶν ἕκαστος, ὅτου ἂν τὰ αὑτοῦ ἕκαστον τῶν ἐν αὐτῷ | πράττῃ,
οὗτος δίκαιός τε ἔσται καὶ τὰ αὑτοῦ πράττων. Καὶ μαλα, ἦ δ' ὅς,
μνημονευτέον. Οὐκοῦν τῷ μὲν λογιστικῷ ἄρχειν προσήκει, σοφῷ
ὄντι καὶ ἔχοντι τὴν ὑπὲρ ἁπάσης τῆς ψυχῆς προμήθειαν, τῷ δὲ
θυμοειδεῖ ὑπηκόῳ εἶναι καὶ ξυμμάχῳ τούτου; Πάνυ γε. Ἀρ' οὖν
οὐχ, ὥσπερ ἐλέγομεν, μουσικῆς καὶ γυμναστικῆς κρᾶσις σύμφωνα
442 αὐτὰ ποιήσει, τὸ μὲν ἐπιτείνουσα καὶ τρέφουσα λόγοις | τε καλοῖς
καὶ μαθήμασιν, τὸ δὲ ἀνιεῖσα παραμυθουμένη, ἡμεροῦσα ἁρμονίᾳ
τε καὶ ῥυθμῷ; Κομιδῇ γε, ἦ δ' ὅς. Καὶ τούτω δὴ οὕτω
τραφέντε καὶ ὡς ἀληθῶς τὰ αὑτῶν μαθόντε καὶ παιδευθέντε
προστατήσετον τοῦ ἐπιθυμητικοῦ, ὃ δὴ πλεῖστον τῆς ψυχῆς ἐν
ἑκάστῳ ἐστὶ καὶ χρημάτων φύσει ἀπληστότατον· ὃ τηρήσετον,
μὴ τῷ πίμπλασθαι τῶν περὶ τὸ σῶμα καλουμένων ἡδονῶν πολὺ

19. ἑνὸς Ξq: ἑνὶ ΑΠ. γένη Π[2]Ξq: γένει ΑΠ[1]. 22. ἀνδρείαν Ξq: καὶ ἀνδρείαν ΑΠ. 5. προστατήσετον coniecit Bekker: προστήσετον codd. 6. ὃ Ξq: ὦ Α[1]Π: ᾧ Α[2].

441 D 22 **ἀνδρείαν**. See *cr. n.*, and for the error in A cf. IX 573 B *n.*

23 **ἔχειν** is intransitive, and not transitive as D. and V. suppose.

441 E 34 **ὥσπερ ἐλέγομεν**. III 411 E—412 A. This passage enables us to identify the λογιστικόν with the φιλόσοφον of Books II—III. See on 439 D, and cf. Krohn *Pl. St.* p. 57.

35 **τὸ μέν**: i.e. τὸ λογιστικόν, as τὸ δέ is τὸ θυμοειδές. As the subject to the participles is κρᾶσις, we see again that Plato did not intend 'Music' and Gymnastic each to affect one part of Soul exclusively. It is curious however that the participles here describe the effect of music only: for it is music (*not* gymnastic) which ἐπιτείνει τὸ φιλόσοφον: see on ὅπως ἂν—προσήκοντος III 411 E. The partial ignoring of gymnastic in this passage is perhaps premonitory of the intellectualism of VI and VII: cf. on 439 D and E.

442 A 2 **ἀνιεῖσα κτλ.**: 'slackening the other by soothing address, taming it,' etc. The three participles are not coordinate, but παραμυθουμένη explains the action of ἀνιεῖσα. It is unnecessary to desert the best MSS (as I once did) and read ἀνιεῖσα, παραμυθουμένη καὶ ἡμεροῦσα with Ξ v and the older editors.

5 **προστατήσετον κτλ.** Bekker's emendation—see *cr. n.*—is now generally accepted. τούτω means λογιστικόν and θυμοειδές: so also in B below. On ὃ δὴ πλεῖστον etc. see II 379 C *n.*

7 **καλουμένων κτλ.** καλουμένων is said because such pleasures are no true

καὶ ἰσχυρὸν γενόμενον οὐκ αὖ τὰ αὑτοῦ πράττῃ, ἀλλὰ καταδουλώ-
σασθαι | *καὶ ἄρχειν ἐπιχειρήσῃ ὧν οὐ προσῆκον αὐτῷ γένει, καὶ* B
ξύμπαντα τὸν βίον πάντων ἀνατρέψῃ. Πάνυ μὲν οὖν, ἔφη. Ἆρ' οὖν, ἦν δ' ἐγώ, καὶ τοὺς ἔξωθεν πολεμίους τούτω ἂν κάλλιστα φυλαττοίτην ὑπὲρ ἁπάσης τῆς ψυχῆς τε καὶ τοῦ σώματος, τὸ μὲν βουλευόμενον, τὸ δὲ προπολεμοῦν, ἑπόμενον δὲ τῷ ἄρχοντι καὶ τῇ ἀνδρείᾳ ἐπιτελοῦν τὰ βουλευθέντα; Ἔστι ταῦτα. Καὶ ἀνδρεῖον
δή, οἶμαι, τούτῳ τῷ μέρει καλοῦμεν ἕνα ἕκαστον, | *ὅταν αὐτοῦ τὸ* C
θυμοειδὲς διασῴζῃ διά τε λυπῶν καὶ ἡδονῶν τὸ ὑπὸ τοῦ λόγου παραγγελθὲν δεινόν τε καὶ μή. Ὀρθῶς γ', ἔφη. Σοφὸν δέ γε ἐκείνῳ τῷ σμικρῷ μέρει, τῷ ὃ ἦρχέν τ' ἐν αὐτῷ καὶ ταῦτα παρήγγελλεν, ἔχον αὖ κἀκεῖνο ἐπιστήμην ἐν αὐτῷ τὴν τοῦ ξυμφέροντος

11. *τούτω* A²Π: *τούτῳ* A¹. 12. *φυλαττοίτην* *q*: *φυλάττοι· τὴν* A: *φυλάττοι* Π¹: *φυλάττοιτον τὴν* Π²: *φυλάττοι· τὼ* Ξ. 16. *τοῦ λόγου* Ξ *q*²: *τῶν λόγων* AΠ et fortasse *q*¹. 17. *δέ γε* (vel *δέ γ'*) A²Π: *δ'* A¹.

---

pleasures: cf. I 336 A *n.* and (for the implication itself) IX 583 B ff., *Phil.* 36 C ff. On *οὐκ αὖ* see 426 E *n.* The imagery of this passage suggests that the *ἐπιθυμητικόν* is a sort of *θηρίον*: cf. IX 588 E ff.

442 B 9 **ὧν—γένει**: sc. *ἄρχειν*. "Dativus causam indicat, cur tertiae parti non conveniat duabus reliquis praeesse et imperare, eamque in ipsius genere et indole positam demonstrat" (Schneider). If this is the meaning, we should expect *φύσει* rather than *γένει*. Perhaps Plato wrote *γενῶν* (so *q* Flor. U, Stallbaum etc.): cf. *γένη* in 441 C. To *προσῆκον* Campbell prefers *προσῆκεν*, but the present (*προσῆκον* sc. *ἐστίν*) is better here.

12 **φυλαττοίτην**. The two higher parts of soul are to be *φύλακες* both of the lower part and (in a different sense) 'also' (*καί*) 'of external enemies': cf. III 415 D, E. Dobree's *φυλαττοίσθην* fails to give its proper force to *καί* before *τοὺς ἔξωθεν*. For *φυλάττω* used in this way cf. II 367 A *οὐκ ἂν ἀλλήλους ἐφυλάττομεν μὴ ἀδικεῖν, ἀλλ' αὐτὸς αὑτοῦ ἦν ἕκαστος φύλαξ*.

442 C 16 **ὑπὸ τοῦ λόγου**. In this particular the analogy between the city and the soul is not quite exact, otherwise it would be the rulers in the city who prescribe *τὸ δεινόν τε καὶ μή*, whereas it is the legislator (see on *ὁ νομοθέτης* 429 C). This point is emphasized, perhaps unduly so, by Krohn (*Pl. St.* p. 43). Unless Plato made the Deity the *οἰκιστής* of the soul, as the original legislator is of the city, it was impossible for him to avoid placing the *λογιστικόν* in a position of even greater authority than the rulers. In Books VI and VII the inequality is redressed by making the power of the Rulers in the city commensurate with that of *λόγος* in the soul: see VI 497 C *n.*

18 **ἦρχέν τε κτλ.**: 'ruled within him and issued these instructions.' The imperfect is used because the instructions must be given *before* they can be obeyed by *θυμοειδές*, as described in the last sentence. J. and C. say that *ἦρχε* refers to 428 E; but Plato is not there speaking of the individual, only of the State. Although a reference to 439 C or 441 E is barely possible, it is much simpler to regard the imperfect as real, and not 'philosophic.' See above on III 406 E. Schneider, to judge from his translation, takes the same view. With *σμικρῷ μέρει* cf. Arist. *Eth. Nic.* X 7. 1177ᵇ 34 ff. *εἰ γὰρ καὶ τῷ ὄγκῳ μικρόν ἐστι* (sc. *τὸ κράτιστον τῶν ἐν αὐτῷ*) *κτλ.*

19 **αὖ κἀκεῖνο κτλ.** *αὖ καί* has been interpreted (1) as implying that the *θυμοειδές* also has a *sort* of knowledge: cf. 429 C and 439 E *n.*: (2) as 'like the rulers in the State': cf. 428 B ff. The first view is slightly more natural on linguistic grounds, but I think Plato would hardly have attributed *ἐπιστήμη* in any shape to the *θυμοειδές*. Probably (2) is right, for the analogy between the

ἑκάστῳ τε καὶ ὅλῳ τῷ κοινῷ σφῶν αὐτῶν τριῶν ὄντων. Πάνυ
μὲν οὖν. Τί δέ; σώφρονα οὐ τῇ φιλίᾳ καὶ ξυμφωνίᾳ τῇ αὐτῶν
D | τούτων, ὅταν τό τε ἄρχον καὶ τὼ ἀρχομένω τὸ λογιστικὸν
ὁμοδοξῶσι δεῖν ἄρχειν καὶ μὴ στασιάζωσιν αὐτῷ; Σωφροσύνη
γοῦν, ἦ δ' ὅς, οὐκ ἄλλο τί ἐστιν ἢ τοῦτο, πόλεώς τε καὶ ἰδιώτου.
Ἀλλὰ μὲν δὴ δίκαιός γε, ᾧ πολλάκις λέγομεν, τούτῳ καὶ οὕτως
ἔσται. Πολλὴ ἀνάγκη. Τί οὖν; εἶπον ἐγώ· μή πῃ ἡμῖν ἀπαμβλύνεται ἄλλο τι δικαιοσύνη δοκεῖν εἶναι ἢ ὅπερ ἐν τῇ πόλει
ἐφάνη; Οὐκ ἔμοιγε, ἔφη, δοκεῖ. Ὧδε γάρ, ἦν δ' ἐγώ, παντάπασιν
E | ἂν βεβαιωσαίμεθα, εἴ τι ἡμῶν ἔτι ἐν τῇ ψυχῇ ἀμφισβητεῖ, τὰ
φορτικὰ αὐτῷ προσφέροντες. Ποῖα δή; Οἷον εἰ δέοι ἡμᾶς ἀνο-
μολογεῖσθαι περί τε ἐκείνης τῆς πόλεως καὶ τοῦ ἐκείνῃ ὁμοίως
πεφυκότος τε καὶ τεθραμμένου ἀνδρός, εἰ δοκεῖ ἂν παρακαταθήκην
χρυσίου ἢ ἀργυρίου δεξάμενος ὁ τοιοῦτος ἀποστερῆσαι, τίν' ἂν
443 οἴει οἰηθῆναι τοῦτο αὐτὸν | δρᾶσαι μᾶλλον ἢ ὅσοι μὴ τοιοῦτοι;

22. *τὼ ἀρχομένω* v: *τῷ ἀρχομένῳ* ΑΠΞ: *τὸ ἀρχόμενον* q. 26. *ἀπαμβλύνεται* Α[1]Π: *ἀπαμβλύνηται* Α[2]. 34. *τοῦτο* Ξq: *τοῦτον* ΑΠ.

---

city and the soul is in Plato's mind all through this section: see 441 C, D, and 442 D.

442 D 25 **ᾧ πολλάκις κτλ.**: 'in virtue of our oft-repeated maxim and in that way': i.e. *τῷ τὰ αὑτοῦ πράττειν*. Ficinus seems to have read *καὶ ὡς* after *λέγομεν*. At first sight *καὶ οὕτως* appears to demand the insertion; but Plato is speaking with less formality and precision than in 441 C, D. The reading of Vind. E *καὶ οὗτος* (for *καὶ οὕτως*), i.e. 'the individual, as well as the city,' is attractive, but unnecessary. Hartman proposes *ᾧ* <*πόλιν*> *πολλάκις* <*ἐ*>*λέγομεν, τούτῳ καὶ οὗτος ἔσται*, a solution which will commend itself to few.

26 **μή πῃ—εἶναι.** 'Do we find Justice growing dimmer in any way? Does it appear something different from what it was discovered to be in the city?' lit. 'blunted, so as to appear' etc. In the language of 434 D (to which Socrates' question refers) Justice has now 'passed into' the Individual; and no feature has been blunted, or lost its clearness of outline. We are therefore confirmed in our view of Justice, both civic and individual. Hartman would read *ἀπήμβλυνται*, taking *ἡμῖν* as 'by us,' but the present is more expressive, and (with *ἡμῖν*) represents us as in a certain sense spectators of the self-evolution of Justice: cf. *ἐὰν μὲν ἡμῖν καὶ εἰς ἕνα ἰὸν τὸ εἶδος τοῦτο κτλ.* 434 D. *ἀπαμβλύνεται* = 'retunditur' (Schneider).

442 E 29 **τὰ φορτικά.** Plato tests his view of Justice by four criteria taken as it were *de foro* and turning on various popular associations of the word: cf. IX 573 B ff. Of these the first three are concerned with honesty and trustworthiness in public and private life; while the last (*μοιχεῖαι—ἀθεραπευσίαι*) refers to morality in general, including the service of the gods. Taken together, they sum up the leading features of the perfect character, and shew that Plato's conception of private, as of political, Justice is in reality Righteousness or Moral Perfection, whereof the other virtues are the fruit. Plato's innovation lay in interpreting Righteousness as *τὰ αὑτοῦ πράττειν*, or rather in the peculiar meaning which he attached to this phrase: see on 434 C and infra 443 B *n*.

32 **παρακαταθήκην χρυσίου κτλ.** Honesty and truthfulness were generally recognised as characteristic of the *δίκαιος ἀνήρ*: see the passages collected by Nägelsbach *Nachhom. Theol.* pp. 240—246.

34 **τοῦτο αὐτόν.** See *cr. n.* "Fortasse Plato *τοῦτον αὐτό* scripsit" (Schneider).

Οὐδέν' ἄν, ἔφη. Οὐκοῦν καὶ ἱεροσυλιῶν καὶ κλοπῶν καὶ προδοσιῶν ἢ ἰδίᾳ ἑταίρων ἢ δημοσίᾳ πόλεων ἐκτὸς ἂν οὗτος εἴη; Ἐκτός. Καὶ μὴν οὐδ' ὁπωστιοῦν ἄπιστος ἢ κατὰ ὅρκους ἢ κατὰ τὰς ἄλλας ὁμολογίας. Πῶς γὰρ ἄν; Μοιχεῖαι μὴν καὶ γονέων ἀμέλειαι καὶ θεῶν ἀθεραπευσίαι παντὶ ἄλλῳ μᾶλλον ἢ τῷ τοιούτῳ προσήκουσι. Παντὶ μέντοι, ἔφη. Οὐκοῦν τούτων | πάντων αἴτιον, ὅτι αὐτοῦ **B** τῶν ἐν αὐτῷ ἕκαστον τὰ αὑτοῦ πράττει ἀρχῆς τε πέρι καὶ τοῦ ἄρχεσθαι; Τοῦτο μὲν οὖν, καὶ οὐδὲν ἄλλο. Ἔτι τι οὖν ἕτερον ζητεῖς δικαιοσύνην εἶναι ἢ ταύτην τὴν δύναμιν, ἣ τοὺς τοιούτους ἄνδρας τε παρέχεται καὶ πόλεις; Μὰ Δία, ἦ δ' ὅς, οὐκ ἔγωγε.

XVII. Τέλεον ἄρα ἡμῖν τὸ ἐνύπνιον ἀποτετέλεσται, ὃ ἔφαμεν

2. οὐδέν' Π: οὐδὲν A. 4. ἢ κατὰ ὅρκους Ξ *q*: ἢ κατὰ ὅρκους ΑΠ. 5. μὴν Π: μὲν A. 12. τέλεον Π: τελευταῖον A, sed in mg. γρ τέλεον.

---

443 A 2 **ἱεροσυλιῶν—προδοσιῶν.** See Nägelsbach l.c. pp. 293 ff., 298 f.

4 **ἄπιστος—κατὰ ὅρκους.** εὐορκία was an indispensable element in Greek morality: see Nägelsbach l.c. p. 242, and the interesting monograph of Augustin *Der Eid im Gr. Volksglauben u. in d. Pl. Ethik* Elbing 1894.

5 **μοιχεῖαι—ἀθεραπευσίαι.** Nägelsbach l.c. pp. 264 ff., 275 ff., 191 ff. The virtue of εὐσέβεια was commonly regarded as δικαιοσύνη ἡ περὶ τοὺς θεούς (e.g. *Euthyph.* 12 E), and εὐσέβεια is concerned with θεῶν θεραπεία. See *Euthyph.* l.c. and cf. also the Stoic Zeno in D. L. VII 119 εἶναί τε τὴν εὐσέβειαν ἐπιστήμην θεῶν θεραπείας, and Sext. Emp. *adv. Math.* IX 123.

443 B—**444** A *We were right then in suspecting that Justice in a certain shape was with us from the first when we founded our city. But the principle that every one should do his professional work and no more, is in reality only an image or shadow of Justice. True Justice is concerned with the inner man and consists in the performance of its own peculiar office by each of the three elements within the soul. It is this which produces spiritual unity, and spiritual unity shews itself in outward acts. We may now claim to have discovered Justice both in the City and in the Individual.*

443 B ff. This section deals with the relation between Civic and Individual virtue. Although we discovered the latter by means of the former, it is the virtue of the soul which is alone original; the other, its outward expression, is but a copy. All true virtue therefore rests upon psychology; not yet, as in VI and VII, on the metaphysical knowledge of the Idea of Good. The full meaning of Plato's 'natural city' (κατὰ φύσιν οἰκισθεῖσα πόλις) now appears. It is a commonwealth whose institutions and political life are the outward expression or embodiment of the true and uncorrupted nature of the soul, regarded as in very truth a φυτὸν οὐκ ἔγγειον, ἀλλ' οὐράνιον (*Tim.* 90 A). Hence arise the three orders of the city; hence too, each order performs its own function; for it is part of soul's 'nature' τὰ ἑαυτῆς πράττειν, and πολυπραγμονεῖν is a consequence of unnatural degeneration (441 A). This optimistic view of 'nature' is noteworthy. It rests on the wide-spread Greek belief that good is natural, and evil unnatural; cf. infra 444 D and Aristotle's ὁ δὲ θεὸς καὶ ἡ φύσις οὐδὲν μάτην ποιοῦσι (*de Caelo* I 4. 271ᵃ 33), οὐδὲν τῶν παρὰ φύσιν καλόν (*Pol.* H 3. 1325ᵇ 10) and the like. For more on this subject I may be allowed to refer to my essay on *Classical Education*, Deighton, Bell and Co. 1895 pp. 12 ff. Although not itself expressly a deduction from the theory of Ideas, Plato's conception of 'nature' as good and not evil is altogether in harmony with the sovereignty of the Idea of Good in Book VI: see on 505 A ff.

12 **τέλεον κτλ.** The language is suggested by Homer's οὐκ ὄναρ, ἀλλ' ὕπαρ ἐσθλόν, ὅ τοι τετελεσμένον ἔσται (*Od.* XIX 547). ὅ is a vague internal accusative: see on ἣν ᾠήθημεν in 434 D.

ἔφαμεν κτλ. The reference is to 433 A.

ὑποπτεῦσαι, ὡς εὐθὺς ἀρχόμενοι τῆς πόλεως οἰκίζειν κατὰ θεόν
C τινα εἰς ἀρχήν τε | καὶ τύπον τινὰ τῆς δικαιοσύνης κινδυνεύομεν
ἐμβεβηκέναι. Παντάπασιν μὲν οὖν. Τὸ δέ γε ἦν ἄρα, ὦ Γλαύκων,
δι' ὃ καὶ ὠφέλει, εἴδωλόν τι τῆς δικαιοσύνης, τὸ τὸν μὲν σκυτοτο-
μικὸν φύσει ὀρθῶς ἔχειν σκυτοτομεῖν καὶ ἄλλο μηδὲν πράττειν,
τὸν δὲ τεκτονικὸν τεκταίνεσθαι, καὶ τἆλλα δὴ οὕτως. Φαίνεται.
Τὸ δέ γε ἀληθές, τοιοῦτο μέν τι ἦν, ὡς ἔοικεν, ἡ δικαιοσύνη, ἀλλ'
D οὐ περὶ τὴν | ἔξω πρᾶξιν τῶν αὑτοῦ, ἀλλὰ περὶ τὴν ἐντός, ὡς
ἀληθῶς περὶ ἑαυτὸν καὶ τὰ ἑαυτοῦ, μὴ ἐάσαντα τἀλλότρια πράττειν
ἕκαστον ἐν αὑτῷ μηδὲ πολυπραγμονεῖν πρὸς ἄλληλα τὰ ἐν τῇ
ψυχῇ γένη, ἀλλὰ τῷ ὄντι τὰ οἰκεῖα εὖ θέμενον καὶ ἄρξαντα αὐτὸν
αὑτοῦ καὶ κοσμήσαντα καὶ φίλον γενόμενον ἑαυτῷ καὶ ξυναρμόσαντα
τρία ὄντα ὥσπερ ὅρους τρεῖς ἁρμονίας ἀτεχνῶς, νεάτης τε καὶ

16. ὠφέλει Ast: ὠφελεῖ ΑΠΞ*q*. 21. ἑαυτὸν Π: ἑαυτῶν A. 23. αὐτὸν—ἑαυτῷ Π: om. A.

On *οἰκίζειν* see III 407 B *n*. For *κινδυνεύομεν* Hartman suggests *ἐκινδυνεύομεν*; but presents do not of course become imperfects in indirect.

443 C 15 **τὸ δέ γε**: 'yes, but in point of fact.' For *τὸ δέ* in this sense cf. I 340 D *n*. *τὸ δέ γε ἀληθές* below expresses the same meaning more fully and emphatically.

16 **δι' ὃ—οὕτως**. The imperfect *ὠφέλει* (see *cr. n.*), 'for which reason also it was of service to us,' viz. in discovering the real or original justice, seems to me better than the present. See II 368 D ff. Plato is justifying himself for having taken so much trouble about a mere *εἴδωλον*; it was in order to learn the original through the copy. So also Hartman. The present could only mean 'benefits the city' (so Schneider, Rettig and others). Madvig, strangely enough, suspects the whole phrase. Civic Justice is an *εἴδωλον* of Justice in the soul as being its reflection in outward conduct. See also on 443 B ff. above.

19 **τοιοῦτο** takes its meaning from *τὸ τὸν μὲν σκυτοτομικόν* etc. 'Justice was indeed something of this kind' (i.e. a sort of *τὰ αὑτοῦ πράττειν*), but *not περὶ τὴν ἔξω πρᾶξιν*. The warning conveyed by *εἶδος* and *τρόπον τινά* in 433 A (where see note), 433 B and 432 E is now justified: for Justice is said to be *περὶ τὴν ἐντὸς πρᾶξιν*, and is therefore not, strictly speaking, that which we have called 'Civic Justice.'

443 D 20 **ὡς ἀληθῶς** should be construed with *περὶ ἑαυτόν*. The soul is the true self, as Socrates continually maintained. It is better to regard *περί* before *ἑαυτόν* as coordinate with *περί* in *περὶ τὴν ἐντός*, than to translate "with internal actions which are in very truth concerned with himself" (J. and C.). *ὡς ἀληθῶς περὶ ἑαυτόν* etc. merely emphasizes and explains *περὶ τὴν ἐντός*.

22 **ἕκαστον**. Ast would read *ἕκαστον τῶν*; but the meaning is easily caught after *τὰ ἑαυτοῦ* just before.

23 **τῷ ὄντι κτλ.**: 'having set his house in order in the truest sense.' So Schneider, rightly. For *οἰκεῖα* cf. III 405 B *n*.

24 **ξυναρμόσαντα—ἡρμοσμένον**. Cf. 432 A, where a similar image is employed. The figure here is taken from the Octachord, the *λογιστικόν* being represented by the *ὑπάτη* or highest string (which gave out the lowest note), the *ἐπιθυμητικόν* by the *νεάτη* (an octave higher in pitch), and the *θυμοειδές* by the *μέση* or fourth. See *Dict. Ant.* II p. 195 or Gleditsch *Die Musik d. Gr.* p. 860. The single notes of a *ἁρμονία* could be called *ὅροι* because they were in reality terms in a proportion and depended on the relative length of the string: cf. *Tim.* 35 B, C. Hartman's correction of *νεάτης, ὑπάτης, μέσης* to *νεάτην, ὑπάτην, μέσην* is very attractive: for the genitives can only be explained as *ὅρον νεάτης* etc., and the effect is unpleasing, especially with

ὑπάτης καὶ μέσης, καὶ εἰ ἄλλα ἄττα μεταξὺ τυγχάνει ὄντα, E
πάντα ταῦτα ξυνδήσαντα καὶ παντάπασιν ἕνα γενόμενον ἐκ πολλῶν, σώφρονα καὶ ἡρμοσμένον, οὕτω δὴ πράττειν ἤδη, ἐάν τι πράττῃ, ἢ περὶ χρημάτων κτῆσιν ἢ περὶ σώματος θεραπείαν ἢ καὶ πολιτικόν τι ἢ περὶ τὰ ἴδια ξυμβόλαια, ἐν πᾶσι τούτοις ἡγούμενον καὶ ὀνομάζοντα δικαίαν μὲν καὶ καλὴν πρᾶξιν, ἣ ἂν ταύτην τὴν ἕξιν σῴζῃ τε καὶ συναπεργάζηται, σοφίαν δὲ τὴν ἐπιστατοῦσαν ταύτῃ
τῇ πράξει ἐπιστήμην, ἄδικον δὲ πρᾶξιν, | ἣ ἂν ἀεὶ ταύτην λύῃ, 444
ἀμαθίαν δὲ τὴν ταύτῃ αὖ ἐπιστατοῦσαν δόξαν. Παντάπασιν, ἦ δ' ὅς, ὦ Σώκρατες, ἀληθῆ λέγεις. Εἶεν, ἦν δ' ἐγώ· τὸν μὲν δίκαιον καὶ ἄνδρα καὶ πόλιν, καὶ δικαιοσύνην, ὃ τυγχάνει ἐν αὐτοῖς

26. καὶ εἰ Π: εἰ καὶ A.

ἁρμονίας coming between. Retaining the Greek nomenclature, we may translate: 'having harmoniously joined together three different elements, just like three terms in a musical proportion or scale, lowest and highest and intermediate,' etc. In ἄλλα ἄττα μεταξύ Plato indicates (as J. and C. observe) that his threefold division of soul may not be 'strictly exhaustive' (cf. VIII 548 D *n.*). The missing faculties would thus correspond to the notes intervening between the ὑπάτη and μέση, and the μέση and νεάτη. It will be noted that the unity resulting is not that of unison, but that of a scale or mode. Nevertheless it is clear from the language used that the ἁρμονία which Plato describes is, as before, σωφροσύνη: cf. ἄρξαντα αὐτὸν αὑτοῦ with 431 A, B, φίλον γενόμενον with 442 C; κοσμήσαντα too suggests κοσμιότης, and the word σώφρονα itself is finally employed. Cf. 434 C *n.* A different explanation is given by the Scholiast. Holding that Plato is referring to a system of two octaves (δὶς διὰ πασῶν) he explains νεάτη, μέση and ὑπάτη as e.g. A', A, and *b* (not *a*, which is the προσλαμβανόμενος). His note is as follows: νεάτη ἤγουν νήτη ὑπερβολαίων ἡ ἐσχάτη χορδὴ τοῦ δὶς διὰ πασῶν συστήματος, ὑπάτη δὲ ἡ μετὰ τὸν προλαμβανόμενον (leg. προσλαμβανόμενον) φθόγγον πρώτη χορδὴ τοῦ αὐτοῦ τοῦ δὶς διὰ πασῶν συστήματος. μέση δὲ καὶ αὐτὴ ἤτοι φθόγγος ἢ χορδὴ ἡ τελευταία μὲν τοῦ πρώτου διὰ πασῶν, ἀρχὴ δὲ τοῦ δευτέρου, ὡς εἶναι τούτων κοινήν, ὡς Πτολεμαῖός τέ φησι καὶ οἱ ἄλλοι μουσικοί. But in the δὶς διὰ πασῶν σύστημα, the ὑπάτη is not σύμφωνος with the νήτη ὑπερβολαίων, although the προσλαμβανόμενος of course is (see Gleditsch l.c. p. 861 and Euclid *Sect. Can.* 10 ed. von Jan): so that according to the Scholiast there is a serious breach of συμφωνία. It seems to me quite clear that in ὥσπερ ὅρους τρεῖς—μέσης Plato is thinking of three ξύμφωνοι φθόγγοι, and in the *single* octave or διὰ πασῶν, the ὑπάτη, μέση or fourth, and νεάτη were σύμφωνα ἀλλήλοις: see Cleonid. *Isag. Harm.* 5 ed. von Jan. In 432 A also, Plato contemplates only a single octave: see note ad loc.

443 E 27 **ἕνα—πολλῶν.** Cf. 423 D *n.* and [*Epin.*] 992 B ἐκ πολλῶν ἕνα γεγονότα. The phrase εἷς ἐκ πολλῶν is a sort of Platonic motto or text (like the φωναί of post-Aristotelian ethics).

28 **οὕτω δὴ—ἤδη**: emphatic, as Hirzel points out (*Hermes* VIII p. 393): for the just man will not take part in practical affairs until he has ordered his own soul aright. Cf. *Alc.* I 113 B ff., *Ap.* 36 C, and Xen. *Mem.* III 7. 9, IV 3. 1.

29 **ἢ καί.** Stallbaum and others add περί (with Ξ) before πολιτικόν, but τι πράττῃ περὶ πολιτικόν τι is very unpleasing. πολιτικόν depends directly on πράττῃ and is equivalent to περὶ πόλιν. The slight variety of expression is easy and elegant after ἢ καί 'aut etiam.'

33 **ἐπιστήμην—δόξαν.** This is, as Krohn points out (*Pl. St.* p. 68), the first precise and explicit separation of ἐπιστήμη and δόξα in the *Republic.* Each of them, however, is still concerned with conduct, and not, as in the end of V, with the theory of knowledge.

444 A 4 **τυγχάνει—ὄν** = 'really is': I 337 B *n.*

ὄν, εἰ φαῖμεν ηὑρηκέναι, οὐκ ἂν πάνυ τι, οἶμαι, δόξαιμεν ψεύδεσθαι. Μὰ Δία οὐ μέντοι, ἔφη. Φῶμεν ἄρα; Φῶμεν.

XVIII. Ἔστω δή, ἦν δ' ἐγώ· μετὰ γὰρ τοῦτο σκεπτέον, οἶμαι, ἀδικίαν. Δῆλον. Οὐκοῦν στάσιν τινὰ αὖ τριῶν ὄντων
B | τούτων δεῖ αὐτὴν εἶναι καὶ πολυπραγμοσύνην καὶ ἀλλοτριοπραγμοσύνην καὶ ἐπανάστασιν μέρους τινὸς τῷ ὅλῳ τῆς ψυχῆς, ἵν' ἄρχῃ ἐν αὐτῇ οὐ προσῆκον, ἀλλὰ τοιούτου ὄντος φύσει, οἵου πρέπειν αὐτῷ δουλεύειν τῷ τοῦ ἀρχικοῦ γένους ὄντι; τοιαῦτ' ἄττα, οἶμαι, φήσομεν καὶ τὴν τούτων ταραχὴν καὶ πλάνην εἶναι τήν τε ἀδικίαν καὶ ἀκολασίαν καὶ δειλίαν καὶ ἀμαθίαν καὶ συλ-
C λήβδην πᾶσαν κακίαν. Ταὐτὰ μὲν οὖν ταῦτα, | ἔφη. Οὐκοῦν,

11. ἀλλὰ—γένους ὄντι Ξ: pro τῷ τοῦ ΑΠ habent τοῦ δ' αὖ δουλεύειν, q τὼ δ' αὖ δουλεύειν.

---

444 A—444 E *Injustice, like every variety of Vice, implies sedition and confusion among the parts of the soul. It is spiritual disease, deformity and weakness; while Virtue is the reverse. Virtuous institutions promote virtue, vicious institutions vice.*

444 A 8 **ἀδικίαν.** Now that we have discovered Justice, it is necessary to look for Injustice, in order that we may compare the two and decide the question at issue, viz. πότερον δεῖ κεκτῆσθαι τὸν μέλλοντα εὐδαίμονα εἶναι, ἐάν τε λανθάνῃ ἐάν τε μὴ πάντας θεούς τε καὶ ἀνθρώπους (427 D: cf. II 368 E *nn.*). The full exposition of Injustice is reserved for Books VIII and IX, where Plato takes the subject in its proper order, considering civic injustice first, and afterwards that of the individual. At present he contents himself with a preliminary or exoteric sketch of Injustice in the soul, representing it as unrighteousness in general, just as Justice, both in the State and in the individual, has been identified with righteousness or moral perfection (434 C, 442 E *nn.*).

444 B 11 **ἀλλὰ τοιούτου—ὄντι.** See *cr. n.* The reading of Ξ and other inferior MSS, which (in common with all the editors) I have printed above, seems to be an attempt to emend the older and more difficult reading preserved in A and Π. Stallbaum supposes that A here represents a corruption of Ξ, αὖ δουλεύειν being presumably a correction (of αὐτῷ δουλεύειν) which has crept into the text; but this is unlikely in itself, and also leaves τοῦ δ' before αὖ δουλεύειν unexplained. The text of Ξ is not in itself quite satisfactory, as Richards has pointed out. οἵου πρέπειν αὐτῷ for ὥστε πρέπειν αὐτῷ seems unexampled, although οἵου δουλεύειν would of course be right. The expression τῷ τοῦ ἀρχικοῦ γένους ὄντι, 'that which is of the ruling class,' is also curious for the more direct and accurate τῷ ἀρχικῷ γένει. The reading of A and Π yields no tolerable sense, and certainly cannot come from Plato. Madvig (with Vind. E) proposes οἵου πρέπειν αὐτῷ δουλεύειν, τὸ δ' αὖ <μὴ> δουλεύειν ἀρχικοῦ γένους ὄντι, which is intelligible, if weak. I have thought of οἵου πρέπειν αὐτῷ δουλεύειν, τῷ δ' αὖ βουλεύειν (or δεσπόζειν, after Schneider) ἀρχικοῦ γένους ὄντι, but there are obvious objections. I should not be surprised if the whole clause ἀλλὰ—ὄντι, as it appears in A and Π, is only an attempt by some illiterate scribe to work out the antithesis of προσῆκον: lit. 'being by nature such as to be proper for it to be a slave, and the slavery again <being such as to be slavery> to that which is of the ruling class.' The clause, even as read in Ξ, adds nothing to the sense, and the references in τοιαῦτ' ἄττα and τούτων just below are caught more easily without the obnoxious words. See 442 B ἄρχειν ἐπιχειρήσῃ ὧν οὐ προσῆκον αὐτῷ γένει. Cf. III 413 C *n.*

13 **τούτων**: sc. τῶν γενῶν.

15 **ταὐτὰ—ταῦτα.** μὲν οὖν corrects τοιαῦτ' ἄττα: "immo haec eadem" (Schneider). For ταὐτά some prefer, with one MS of Stobaeus *Flor.* 9. 64, αὐτά ('immo

ἦν δ' ἐγώ, καὶ τὸ ἄδικα πράττειν καὶ τὸ ἀδικεῖν καὶ αὖ τὸ δίκαια ποιεῖν, ταῦτα πάντα τυγχάνει ὄντα κατάδηλα ἤδη σαφῶς, εἴπερ καὶ ἡ ἀδικία τε καὶ δικαιοσύνη; Πῶς δή; Ὅτι, ἦν δ' ἐγώ, τυγχάνει οὐδὲν διαφέροντα τῶν ὑγιεινῶν τε καὶ νοσωδῶν, ὡς ἐκεῖνα ἐν σώματι, ταῦτα ἐν ψυχῇ. Πῇ; ἔφη. Τὰ μέν που ὑγιεινὰ ὑγίειαν ἐμποιεῖ, τὰ δὲ νοσώδη νόσον. Ναί. Οὐκοῦν καὶ τὸ μὲν δίκαια πράττειν δικαιοσύνην ἐμποιεῖ, τὸ δ' ἄδικα | ἀδικίαν; D Ἀνάγκη. Ἔστι δὲ τὸ μὲν ὑγίειαν ποιεῖν τὰ ἐν τῷ σώματι κατὰ φύσιν καθιστάναι κρατεῖν τε καὶ κρατεῖσθαι ὑπ' ἀλλήλων, τὸ δὲ νόσον παρὰ φύσιν ἄρχειν τε καὶ ἄρχεσθαι ἄλλο ὑπ' ἄλλου. Ἔστι γάρ. Οὐκοῦν αὖ, ἔφην, τὸ δικαιοσύνην ἐμποιεῖν τὰ ἐν τῇ ψυχῇ κατὰ φύσιν καθιστάναι κρατεῖν τε καὶ κρατεῖσθαι ὑπ' ἀλλήλων, τὸ δὲ ἀδικίαν παρὰ φύσιν ἄρχειν τε καὶ ἄρχεσθαι ἄλλο ὑπ' ἄλλου; Κομιδῇ, ἔφη. Ἀρετὴ μὲν ἄρα, ὡς ἔοικεν, ὑγίειά τέ τις ἂν εἴη καὶ κάλλος καὶ εὐεξία | ψυχῆς, κακία δὲ νόσος τε καὶ E αἶσχος καὶ ἀσθένεια. Ἔστιν οὕτω. Ἆρ' οὖν οὐ καὶ τὰ μὲν καλὰ ἐπιτηδεύματα εἰς ἀρετῆς κτῆσιν φέρει, τὰ δ' αἰσχρὰ εἰς κακίας; Ἀνάγκη.

XIX. Τὸ δὴ λοιπὸν ἤδη, ὡς ἔοικεν, ἡμῖν ἐστὶ σκέψασθαι,

16. *αὖ τὸ q*: *αὖ τὰ* ΑΞ: *αὐτὰ* Π.

---

haec ipsa'), others *τοιαῦτα*, but there is not sufficient reason for deserting A.

444 C 22 **δίκαια—ἐμποιεῖ.** Krohn (*Pl. St.* p. 59) reminds us of Arist. *Eth. Nic.* II 1. 1103^{a} 34 ff. *τὰ μὲν δίκαια πράττοντες δίκαιοι γινόμεθα κτλ.* On the Socratic analogy between body and soul cf. II 380 B *n.*

444 D 23 **ὑγίειαν ποιεῖν.** Ξ (with a few other MSS) reads *ἐμποιεῖν*; and Stallbaum and others adopt this reading. *ποιεῖν*, 'to produce,' is however satisfactory: cf. 422 A.

24 **τὸ δὲ νόσον—ὑπ' ἄλλου.** Here and in *Tim.* 82 A ff. Plato adopts the Hippocratean theory of the origin of disease: see *de nat. hom.* VI p. 40 c. 4 Littré *ὑγιαίνει μὲν οὖν μάλιστα, ὁκόταν μετρίως ἔχῃ ταῦτα* (sc. *αἷμα καὶ φλέγμα καὶ χολὴ ξανθή τε καὶ μέλαινα*) *τῆς πρὸς ἄλληλα κρήσιός τε καὶ δυνάμιος καὶ τοῦ πλήθεος, καὶ μάλιστα μεμιγμένα ᾖ. ἀλγέει δὲ ὁκόταν τι τουτέων ἔλασσον ἢ πλέον ᾖ ἢ χωρισθῇ ἐν τῷ σώματι καὶ μὴ κεκρημένον ᾖ τοῖσι ξύμπασιν* (Poschenrieder *die pl. dial. in ihr. Verhältnisse zu d. Hippokr. Schr.* p. 37). Cf. also Pl. *Symp.* 186 D with Hug ad loc. On *κατὰ φύσιν* see 443 B *n.*

30 **κάλλος—εὐεξία**: with reference perhaps to Thrasymachus' statement in I 348 E f. that Injustice is *καλόν* and *ἰσχυρόν*.

444 E—**445** E *It remains to ask whether Justice is better than Injustice. Regarding Injustice as a disease of soul, Glauco is ready to declare for Justice; but Socrates would examine the question more carefully. There are four varieties of Vice which deserve investigation, alike in cities and in individuals. Let us take them in order. The perfect commonwealth, which we have described, may be called Kingship or Aristocracy, according as there are one or more rulers. Glauco assents.*

444 E 34 **τὸ δὴ λοιπὸν κτλ.** 'What remains for us now to enquire is whether,' etc. For the position of *ἡμῖν* cf. that of *πάντων* in 445 B. Herwerden suggests *τόδε* or *τόδε δή*, neither of which is necessary.

445 πότερον αὖ λυσιτελεῖ δίκαιά τε πράττειν καὶ | καλὰ ἐπιτηδεύειν καὶ εἶναι δίκαιον, ἐάν τε λανθάνῃ ἐάν τε μὴ τοιοῦτος ὤν, ἢ ἀδικεῖν τε καὶ ἄδικον εἶναι, ἐάνπερ μὴ διδῷ δίκην μηδὲ βελτίων γίγνηται κολαζόμενος. Ἀλλ', ἔφη, ὦ Σώκρατες, γελοῖον ἔμοιγε φαίνεται τὸ σκέμμα γίγνεσθαι ἤδη, εἰ τοῦ μὲν σώματος τῆς φύσεως διαφθειρομένης δοκεῖ οὐ βιωτὸν εἶναι οὐδὲ μετὰ πάντων σιτίων τε καὶ ποτῶν καὶ παντὸς πλούτου καὶ πάσης ἀρχῆς, τῆς δὲ αὐτοῦ
B τούτου ᾧ ζῶμεν φύσεως ταραττομένης καὶ | διαφθειρομένης βιωτὸν ἄρα ἔσται, ἐάνπερ τις ποιῇ ὃ ἂν βουληθῇ ἄλλο πλὴν τοῦτο, ὁπόθεν κακίας μὲν καὶ ἀδικίας ἀπαλλαγήσεται, δικαιοσύνην δὲ καὶ ἀρετὴν κτήσεται, ἐπειδήπερ ἐφάνη γε ὄντα ἑκάτερα οἷα ἡμεῖς διεληλύθαμεν. Γελοῖον γάρ, ἦν δ' ἐγώ. Ἀλλ' ὅμως ἐπείπερ ἐνταῦθα ἐληλύθαμεν, ὅσον οἷόν τε σαφέστατα κατιδεῖν ὅτι ταῦτα οὕτως ἔχει, οὐ χρὴ ἀποκάμνειν. Ἥκιστα νὴ τὸν Δία, ἔφη, πάντων
C ἀποκνητέον. Δεῦρο νῦν, | ἦν δ' ἐγώ, ἵνα καὶ ἴδῃς, ὅσα καὶ εἴδη ἔχει ἡ κακία, ὥς ἐμοὶ δοκεῖ, ἅ γε δὴ καὶ ἄξια θέας. Ἕπομαι, ἔφη· μόνον λέγε. Καὶ μήν, ἦν δ' ἐγώ, ὥσπερ ἀπὸ σκοπιᾶς μοι φαίνεται, ἐπειδὴ ἐνταῦθα ἀναβεβήκαμεν τοῦ λόγου, ἓν μὲν εἶναι εἶδος τῆς ἀρετῆς, ἄπειρα δὲ τῆς κακίας, τέτταρα δ' ἐν αὐτοῖς ἄττα, ὧν καὶ

---

35 **πότερον αὖ κτλ.** See I 354 B, C, and note on 444 A.

445 A 2 **ἐάν τε λανθάνῃ.** Cf. 427 D and II 367 E.

3 **βελτίων—κολαζόμενος.** II 380 B *n.*

8 **ᾧ ζῶμεν.** Cf. I 353 D *τί δ' αὖ τὸ ζῆν; ψυχῆς φήσομεν ἔργον εἶναι; μάλιστά γε* and note ad loc. *βιωτὸν ἄρα ἔσται* should not be made interrogative. The sentence means: 'if life, which men deem unbearable when the bodily constitution decays, even when they are surrounded by every variety of food and drink and wealth and power, shall be, forsooth, when tumult and decay affect the constitution of the very principle whereby we live, worth living, if so be we do what we desire, and take no steps to escape from wickedness and injustice, and acquire justice and virtue.' Life is *not* (says Plato) *βιωτός* to the guilty man who works his will; it may become so if he takes steps to rid himself of vice, i.e. *ἐὰν διδῷ δίκην καὶ βελτίων γίγνηται κολαζόμενος.* For the sentiment cf. *Crit.* 47 D, E, *Gorg.* 477 B—E, *Prot.* 313 A, B.

445 B 13 **ὅσον—σαφέστατα.** "Quam certissime fieri potest" is Ficinus' rendering, with which Schneider and later editors agree, taking *κατιδεῖν* as explanatory of *ἐνταῦθα*. But it is hard to find another instance of *ὅσον οἷόν τε*, although *καθ' ὅσον οἷόν τε* and *ὅσον δυνατόν* (Thuc. I 22. 2) occur. *ὡς οἷόν τε* is the almost invariable phrase. For *ὅσον* Stephanus proposed *ὅθεν*, Ast *ὅπου*. I think the meaning is 'now that we have come far enough to be able most clearly to descry that these things are so,' *ἐνταῦθα* being equivalent to *ἐπὶ τοσοῦτον*, and *ὅσον οἷόν τε* to *ὅσον ἐλθόντας οἷόν τέ ἐστιν*.

445 C 15 **ἀποκνητέον.** I have reverted to the MS reading. Bekker's emendation *ἀποκμητέον* is very attractive, but *ἀποκνητέον* gives excellent sense (cf. I 349 A), and there is no real reason why Glauco should repeat the word employed by Socrates (see on V 465 E); nor does there appear to be any instance in Greek literature of the verbal of *ἀποκάμνω*.

16 **ἄξια θέας.** Plato does not claim that his enumeration of degenerate commonwealths is complete. Cf. VIII 544 D.

18 **ἓν—κακίας.** An old Pythagorean principle, whence the parade with which

ἄξιον ἐπιμνησθῆναι. Πῶς λέγεις; ἔφη. Ὅσοι, ἦν δ' ἐγώ, πολιτειῶν τρόποι εἰσὶν εἴδη ἔχοντες, τοσοῦτοι κινδυνεύουσι καὶ ψυχῆς τρόποι εἶναι. Πόσοι | δή; Πέντε μέν, ἦν δ' ἐγώ, πολιτειῶν, **D** πέντε δὲ ψυχῆς. Λέγε, ἔφη, τίνες. Λέγω, εἶπον, ὅτι εἷς μὲν οὗτος ὃν ἡμεῖς διεληλύθαμεν πολιτείας εἴη ἂν τρόπος, ἐπονομασθείη δ' ἂν καὶ διχῇ· ἐγγενομένου μὲν γὰρ ἀνδρὸς ἑνὸς ἐν τοῖς ἄρχουσι διαφέροντος βασιλεία ἂν κληθείη, πλειόνων δὲ ἀριστοκρατία. Ἀληθῆ, ἔφη. Τοῦτο μὲν τοίνυν, ἦν δ' ἐγώ, ἓν εἶδος λέγω· οὔτε γὰρ ἂν πλείους οὔτε εἷς ἐγγενόμενος | κινήσειεν ἂν τῶν ἀξίων **E** λόγου νόμων τῆς πόλεως, τροφῇ τε καὶ παιδείᾳ χρησάμενος, ᾗ διήλθομεν. Οὐ γὰρ εἰκός, ἔφη.

ΤΕΛΟΣ ΠΟΛΙΤΕΙΑΣ Δ'.

28. ἐγγενόμενος Ξ *q*: ἐγγενόμενοι ΑΠ.

Plato announces it. See Arist. *Met.* I 5. 986ᵃ 22 ff. (RP.⁷ § 55) and *Eth. Nic.* I 4. 1096ᵇ 6 with Stewart's note.

21 **εἴδη ἔχοντες**: 'having' (i.e. as we should say 'forming') 'specific kinds': cf. VIII 544 D.

445 D 25 **ἐγγενομένου—ἀριστοκρατία.** Knowledge, not number, is the criterion of good government: cf. *Pol.* 292 C. Hitherto however the rulers have always been represented as a plurality, and we have heard nothing of a king. In the later books (from V 473 C onwards) we often hear of kingship; and in IX 576 D (as Newman points out *Politics of Aristotle* I p. 413 *n.*) the ideal city is called βασιλευομένην, οἵαν τὸ πρῶτον διήλθομεν. With the present passage cf. VII 540 D ἢ πλείους ἢ εἷς and IX 587 D, where the ἀριστοκρατικός and the βασιλικός are identified. The fact is, as Henkel has pointed out (*Stud. zur Gesch. d. gr. Lehr. v. St.* p. 57), that "Kingship is only a form of Aristocracy throughout the whole political theory of antiquity, and rests on no distinct and independent basis of its own." It must be regarded as exceptional when in the *Politicus* (302 C ff.), probably a later dialogue, Plato distinguishes between kingship and aristocracy and places aristocracy on a lower plane. See also Whibley *Gk. Olig.* pp. 15 ff.

445 E 28 **τῶν—νόμων.** For the genitive cf. (with Stallbaum) *Gorg.* 514 A δημοσίᾳ πράξοντας τῶν πολιτικῶν πραγμάτων, and infra VI 485 B.

APPENDICES TO BOOK IV.

I.

IV **421** A, B. *εἰ μὲν οὖν ἡμεῖς μὲν φύλακας ὡς ἀληθῶς ποιοῦμεν, ἥκιστα κακούργους τῆς πόλεως, ὁ δ' ἐκεῖνο λέγων* **γεωργούς** *τινας καὶ ὥσπερ ἐν πανηγύρει ἀλλ' οὐκ ἐν πόλει ἑστιάτορας εὐδαίμονας, ἄλλο ἄν τι ἢ πόλιν λέγοι.*

I hope my note has proved that this sentence is sound in the main; but Madvig's emendation has obtained such a wide currency, owing to its adoption by Baiter, that the text has fallen under grave suspicion, and it may be well to record the different conjectures.

They are as follows:

(1) εἶεν οὖν· ἡμεῖς κτλ. (Orelli, cited by Schneider): (2) ἡμεῖς μὲν οὖν φύλακας κτλ. (Ast in his third edition): (3) ἢ μὲν οὖν ἡμεῖς <λέγο>μεν, φύλακας κτλ. (Herwerden, with whom Hartman agrees so far, although Hartman goes further and expunges καί before ὥσπερ as well as the entire clause ἄλλο ἄν τι ἢ πόλιν λέγοι): (4) εἰ μὲν οὖν—ἑστιάτορας, εὔδαιμον ἄλλο ἄν τι ἢ πόλιν λέγοι (Madvig): (5) εἰ [μὲν] οὖν ἡμεῖς—λέγων ἀργούς (or κακούργους) τινας—εὐδαίμονας, ἄλλο δή τι ἢ πόλιν λέγει (Richards).

It should be mentioned also that Wyttenbach (quoted by Stallbaum) had conjectured ἑστιάτορας καὶ δαιτυμόνας instead of ἑστιάτορας εὐδαίμονας (ἑστιάτορας καὶ εὐδαίμονας in a few inferior MSS).

A glance at these proposals will shew that the difficulties felt have been chiefly in connexion with (*a*) εἰ μὲν οὖν ἡμεῖς μέν, (*b*) γεωργούς, (*c*) ἑστιάτορας εὐδαίμονας and (*d*) ἄλλο ἄν τι ἢ πόλιν λέγοι. I can see no reason for Richards' correction of (*d*): 'mixed' conditional sentences of this kind are surely common enough.

For ἑστιάτορας εὐδαίμονας cf. III 420 A οἱ εὐδαίμονες δοκοῦντες εἶναι and especially X 612 A τῶν εὐδαιμόνων λεγομένων ἑστιάσεων. The μέν after εἰ is omitted in one Florentine MS, but μέν without δέ occurs tolerably often in Plato (cf. V 475 E *n.*). Here it has the effect of italicising the preceding word by suggesting a possible antithesis. The only real difficulty is in γεωργούς, and in view of 419 A to which ὁ δ' ἐκεῖνο λέγων refers, some may doubt whether even γεωργούς is not also genuine. For my own part I am inclined to think that Plato wrote λεωργούς.

II.

IV **430** E. *Κόσμος πού τις, ἦν δ' ἐγώ, ἡ σωφροσύνη ἐστὶν καὶ ἡδονῶν τινῶν καὶ ἐπιθυμιῶν ἐγκράτεια, ὥς φασι, κρείττω δὴ αὑτοῦ* **λέγοντες** *οὐκ οἶδ' ὅντινα τρόπον. καὶ ἄλλα ἄττα τοιαῦτα ὥσπερ ἴχνη αὐτῆς λέγεται.*

The reading φαίνονται, which replaces λέγοντες in A[1], Π and a majority of MSS, is admittedly corrupt. One Florentine MS has λέγοντες φαίνονται, another φαίνονται λέγοντες: and it is possible that φαίνονται was originally only an adscript intended to be taken with λέγοντες. The emendations proceed for the most part on the assumption that λέγοντες and not φαίνονται is the gloss. This may be so, but unfortunately no satisfactory remedy has yet been suggested on these lines. The most important corrections are ἀποφαίνονται (Cornarius), φαίνοντα (Madvig, taking the participle in agreement with κόσμος and ἐγκράτεια, but φαίνοντα cannot be used for ἀπεργαζόμενα, as Hartman points out), φαίνεσθαι (Hartman, who connects the infinitive with φασί, and construes ὡς boldly as *quoniam*). Other corrections enumerated by Hartman are φασίν τινα (Dobree), φαμέν (Badham), ἀποφαίνοντες (Richards). Apelt has thought of cancelling the entire clause κρείττω δὴ—τρόπον as an "interpretatio etymologica ad praegressam vocem ἐγκράτεια pertinens" (*Obs. cr. in Pl. dialogos*, p. 11). It would be easy to multiply conjectures of this sort; but until something better is proposed, we should hold fast to λέγοντες. The λέγεται of the next sentence suits λέγοντες very well, for the phrase κρείττω αὑτοῦ is itself one of the ἴχνη. I have placed a full stop before καὶ ἄλλα. Ast suggested a colon, and wished to add ἃ after τοιαῦτα, but no change is necessary.

III.

IV **438** E—**439** A. *Τὸ δὲ δὴ δίψος, ἦν δ' ἐγώ, οὐ τούτων θήσεις τῶν* **τινὸς εἶναι τοῦτο ὅπερ ἐστὶν—ἔστι δὲ δήπου δίψος—; Ἔγωγε, ἦ δ' ὅς· πώματός γε.**

In this difficult passage Stallbaum, who is followed by the Oxford editors, construes εἶναι with τούτων ("is one of" etc.), and regards τοῦτο ὅπερ ἐστίν as no more than "ipsam per se" ("as far as its essence is concerned," J. and C.). This interpretation is grammatically awkward, and otherwise objectionable, inasmuch as it anticipates δίψος δ' οὖν αὐτό below. Plato evidently means to present his argument in two steps: (1) Thirst, as you will agree, is something relative to drink, (2) Thirst qualified is relative to drink qualified, and thirst by itself, without qualification, to drink by itself, without qualification.

A large number of emendations has been proposed. The late Mr W. A. Gill was inclined to omit τοῦτο ὅπερ ἐστίν (*Proceedings of the Cambridge Philol. Soc.* XVIII p. 35), and Hartman boldly expunges the words, leaving ἔστι δὲ δήπου δίψος, as it appears to me, in a lonely and unsheltered situation. The suggestion τῶν οἵων τινος (Madvig), i.e. 'which are such as to be that which they are relatively to something,' is very cumbrous, and renders ἔστι δὲ δήπου δίψος far from natural. Mr Cook Wilson's defence or explanation of Madvig's proposal in the *Academy* no. 824 (Feb. 18, 1888) does not carry conviction to my mind. Baiter combines the conjecture of Madvig with Morgenstern's δή του for δήπου, in which case Socrates repeats his question, if ἔστι δὲ δήπου δίψος is interrogative, or, if not, answers it himself. It seems to me clear that ἔστι δὲ δήπου δίψος is intended to explain τοῦτο ὅπερ ἐστίν and nothing more. J. and C. translate "Thirst is, I imagine— Yes, said he, thirst is of drink," remarking that "two questions are asked; before the second is completed Glauco breaks in with a reply to the first (ἔγωγε): and in πώματός γε he completes and answers the second." I can see no occasion for so much impatience on Glauco's part. The insertion of καὶ τινός after τῶν τινός appears to me to solve all the difficulties, and the error is of a kind that frequently occurs in our oldest MS. See *Introd.* § 5.

IV.

IV **440** B. ταῖς δ' ἐπιθυμίαις αὐτὸν κοινωνήσαντα, αἱροῦντος λόγου μὴ δεῖν ἀντιπράττειν, οἶμαί σε οὐκ ἂν φάναι γενομένου ποτὲ ἐν σαυτῷ τοῦ τοιούτου αἰσθέσθαι, οἶμαι δ' οὐδ' ἐν ἄλλῳ.

The difficulties of this passage have been much canvassed. The only important variant is ἐν ἑαυτῷ (Π and corr. A², with several other MSS) instead of ἐν σαυτῷ. Π does not, as Bekker asserted, give μηδέν, but μὴ δεῖν like A. The ἄν τι πράττειν for ἀντιπράττειν of *q*, although adopted by Bekker, is indefensible, as other editors have observed, for ἄν has no meaning or construction.

Against the ordinary interpretation, which I have given in the notes, it has been urged that θυμός does, in point of fact, sometimes join with the Desires against the Reason. Thus in the degenerate phases of character depicted in VIII 553 C ff. and elsewhere, θυμοειδές is the slave and minister of the ἐπιθυμητικόν, and in 441 A ἐπίκουρον ὂν τῷ λογιστικῷ φύσει ἐὰν μὴ ὑπὸ κακῆς τροφῆς διαφθαρῇ, the same implication appears to be involved. Cf. Krohn *Pl. St.* pp. 52 ff. But in such cases the λογιστικόν would seem also to be corrupted (τὸ δέ γε, οἶμαι, λογιστικόν τε καὶ θυμοειδὲς χαμαὶ ἔνθεν καὶ ἔνθεν παρακαθίσας ὑπ' ἐκείνῳ—sc. τῷ ἐπιθυμητικῷ—καὶ καταδουλωσάμενος VIII l.c.), so that there is no conflict between the allied forces of the θυμοειδές and ἐπιθυμητικόν on the one hand and the λογιστικόν on the other. It is true that the language of 441 A, taken in its full force, appears to imply that the θυμοειδές can be corrupted without the λογιστικόν, but Plato would hardly, I think, have held such a view, and the implication is not to be pressed. See *Phaedr.* 253 D—256 E. There is some difficulty about the construction of ἀντιπράττειν, and Hartman would expunge the word. Schneider's punctuation, which I have adopted, connects it with δεῖν. Others make its subject αὐτόν ('but that θυμός, having made common cause with the desires, when Reason forbids, should oppose Reason—this' etc.). The explanation of Hermann (adopted also by Schmelzer) avoids the anacoluthon, but is exceedingly tortuous and unpleasing: 'I think you would not say that you have perceived θυμός making common cause with the desires and opposing Reason when Reason forbade' etc. Richter also (*Fl. Jahrb.* 1867 p. 139) evades the anacoluthon by defending the more than dubious construction αἰσθέσθαι αὐτὸν κοινωνήσαντα.

Finally Nitzsch conjectures (*Rh. Mus.* 1857 p. 472) μὴ δεῖν <τι πράττειν>, ἀντιπράττειν, or μηδ' εἶν<αί τι πράττειν>, ἀντιπράττειν. None of these devices seems to me so probable as Schneider's view.

An entirely different view of this passage is suggested by a Scholiast's note, to which Warren has recently again called attention. The Scholium runs: ὁ δὲ νοῦς οὗτος. ταῖς δὲ ἐπιθυμίαις σε κοινωνήσαντα ταῖς εὐλογίστοις, καὶ γινώσκοντά σε τοῦτο ἐκ τῆς πείρας, οὐχ ὑπολαμβάνω σε εἰπεῖν ὅτι ᾔσθημαι ἐν ταῖς τοιαύταις ἀγαθαῖς ἡδοναῖς τὸν θυμὸν ἀντιπράττοντα ταῖς ἐπιθυμίαις, ὥσπερ ἐπὶ ταῖς τοῦ Λεοντίου ἀλόγοις ἡδοναῖς ἀντέπραττεν. It is obvious that the Scholiast connected σε with αὐτόν and took the sentence to mean, broadly speaking, that when Reason on the other hand *sanctions* indulgence (αἱροῦντος λόγου μὴ δεῖν ἀντιπράττειν sc. ταῖς ἐπιθυμίαις), we do not find any conflict between θυμός and the desires. The meaning is satisfactory, and furnishes a fair antithesis to the first half of the sentence ὅταν βιάζωνται—τοῦ τοιούτου, but it is difficult to reconcile this view with the Greek as we have it. Warren, who sympathises in general with the Scholiast, translates "but that dealing with desires it"—viz. θυμός—"should, when reason says it ought not, oppose them, this I imagine" etc. κοινωνήσαντα must however be more than 'dealing with,' and the aorist (which on the ordinary view means 'having joined,' 'made common cause with') presents a serious difficulty in this interpretation.

Reading ἐν ἑαυτῷ, for which there is good authority (see *cr. n.*), I formerly construed the passage as follows: 'but when he' (αὐτόν with reference not to τὸν θυμόν, but to τινά and τοῦ τοιούτου alone) 'has joined partnership with his desires, because reason decides that he ought not to oppose them, you will not, I imagine, say that he has observed anything of the sort' (i.e. such internal στάσις as has just been described) 'ever happen in his own soul, or in the soul of another? Assuredly not.' By this solution we get rid of the anacoluthon, while adopting generally the Scholiast's view; but it is an unnecessary and irrelevant elaboration to make Glauco speak of what the hypothetical person has observed in himself or in another: we wish to know what Glauco has himself observed.

On the whole I am now inclined to believe that the traditional interpretation is correct.

V.

IV **440** C. Τί δέ; ὅταν ἀδικεῖσθαί τις ἡγῆται, οὐκ ἐν τούτῳ ζεῖ τε καὶ χαλεπαίνει, καὶ ξυμμαχεῖ τῷ δοκοῦντι δικαίῳ, **καὶ διὰ τὸ πεινῆν καὶ διὰ τὸ ῥιγῶν** καὶ πάντα τὰ τοιαῦτα πάσχειν, **καὶ ὑπομένων** νικᾷ, καὶ οὐ λήγει τῶν γενναίων, πρὶν ἂν ἢ διαπράξηται ἢ τελευτήσῃ ἢ ὥσπερ κύων ὑπὸ νομέως ὑπὸ τοῦ λόγου τοῦ παρ' αὐτῷ ἀνακληθεὶς πραυνθῇ;

The interpretation of this sentence is very difficult, and has given rise to a vast amount of discussion. The only important variants are καὶ διὰ τοῦ πεινῆν καὶ διὰ τοῦ ῥιγοῦν in *q* and Flor. U, and ὑπομένων καί (A, Π etc.) instead of καὶ ὑπομένων.

On account of ὀργίζεσθαι καὶ πεινῶν καὶ ῥιγῶν καὶ ἄλλο ὁτιοῦν τῶν τοιούτων πάσχων in the previous sentence, it appears to me certain (1) that καὶ διὰ τὸ πεινῆν etc. is right as against καὶ διὰ τοῦ πεινῆν etc., and (2) that these words should be construed with ζεῖ τε καὶ χαλεπαίνει. That which in the first case was represented as the *cause* of anger should be so represented in the second case also. The same view was held by Schneider. It is more difficult to defend ὑπομένων καί, and Schneider is probably justified in preferring the less authoritative reading καὶ ὑπομένων. The expression πάσχειν ὑπομένων can hardly be a mere periphrasis for πάσχειν, nor is πάσχειν ὑπομένων altogether equivalent to ὑπομένειν πάσχων, as Jowett supposes. If the best MSS are right in placing καὶ after ὑπομένων, it is possible that ὑπομένων is corrupt, and conceals ὑπό with a genitive (cf. πάσχων ὑπ' ἐκείνου in the parallel passage just before), but until the right correction has been proposed, we must adhere to the text of Ξ.

The subject of ζεῖ and the other verbs is supposed by J. and C. to be not the man himself, but ὁ θυμός. This is unlikely, on account of πεινῆν etc., and still more of τελευτήσῃ. The parallel with 440 C τοσούτῳ ἧττον δύναται ὀργίζεσθαι κτλ. is also in favour of making the individual the subject.

That the text of A is in the main sound I have no doubt, although I should like to read καὶ ξυμμαχεῖ τῷ δοκοῦντι δικαίῳ after πάσχειν rather than after χαλεπαίνει.

There is an unusually large supply of emendations. That of Madvig is peculiarly unhappy, though adopted by Baiter in his text, and apparently approved by Apelt (*Berl. Philol. Wochenschr.* 1895 p. 968): καὶ δι' αὐτὸ πεινῆν καὶ δι' αὐτὸ ῥιγοῦν καὶ πάντα τὰ τοιαῦτα πάσχειν ὑπομένων, κἂν νικᾶται, οὐ λήγει κτλ. The other proposals are enumerated by Hartman. They are as follows: καὶ διὰ τὸ πεινῆν καὶ διὰ τὸ—πάσχειν καὶ ὑπομένει νικᾶν καὶ οὐ λήγει κτλ. (Ast): καὶ δι' αὐτὸ πεινῆν καὶ δι' αὐτὸ—πάσχειν ὑπομένων διανεκῆ οὐ λήγει κτλ. (H. Sauppe, quoted by Hartman): καὶ διὰ τοῦ πεινῆν καὶ διὰ τοῦ—πάσχων ὑπομένειν νικᾷ καὶ κτλ. (Liebhold): καὶ διὰ τοῦ πεινῆν καὶ διὰ τοῦ κτλ. (Campbell, who in other respects acquiesces in the text of A): καὶ διὰ τοῦ πεινῆν καὶ διὰ τοῦ—ὑπομένων [καὶ] νικᾶν [καὶ] οὐ λήγει κτλ. (Hartman). Richards apparently accepts the suggestion of Madvig as far as it goes, but thinks that τῶν γενναίων 'is most feeble. Plainly Plato wrote οὐ λήγει ἀγανακτῶν, possibly with some additional word before ἀγανακτῶν' (*Cl. Rev.* VII p. 254). The reading printed above is not only more authoritative but also in my judgment infinitely better than any of these rash and unjustifiable alterations.

E.

I. Ἀγαθὴν μὲν τοίνυν τὴν τοιαύτην πόλιν τε καὶ πολιτείαν 449 καὶ ὀρθὴν καλῶ, καὶ ἄνδρα τὸν τοιοῦτον· κακὰς δὲ τὰς ἄλλας καὶ ἡμαρτημένας, εἴπερ αὕτη ὀρθή, περί τε πόλεων διοικήσεις καὶ περὶ ἰδιωτῶν ψυχῆς τρόπου κατασκευήν, ἐν τέτταρσι πονηρίας εἴδεσιν

---

449 A—**451** C *Socrates is about to describe the different kinds of depraved polities, when Adimantus, prompted by Polemarchus, and supported by Glauco and Thrasymachus, demands from him a fuller explanation of the community of wives and children, and of the arrangements for begetting and rearing offspring. Socrates professes reluctance, both because it will be doubted whether his scheme is either practicable or expedient, and because he is himself uncertain of his ground and unwilling to involve his friends in possible discomfiture. At last, after propitiating Nemesis, and being exonerated by his friends, he proceeds to comply with their request.*

449 A ff. Considered in its merely formal aspect, the portion of the *Republic* contained in Books V—VII may be described as a digression (ἀναμνησθῶμεν πόθεν δεῦρο ἐξετραπόμεθα VIII 543 C). In reality, these books fulfil the hopes held out in sundry parts of III and IV (see III 414 A, 416 B, IV 423 E, 435 D, 439 E, 442 C *nn.*), and complete the picture of the perfect city and the perfect man by giving us Plato's third or crowning effort—the philosophic City and the Philosopher-King. See on II 372 D. As we often find in Plato (see e.g. *Phaed.* 84 C ff.), the new departure is occasioned by an objection, or rather a request for further information, on the part of one of the interlocutors. Adimantus invites Socrates to explain the remark made by him in IV 423 E f. and fully expound the principle of κοινὰ τὰ φίλων as it affects women and children. The challenge is accepted, and Socrates deals with the question under three main heads, which he figures as waves through which the argument must swim in safety. The first wave concerns Community of Education between the male and female Guardians (451 C—457 B); the second, Community in wives and children (457 B—466 D); the third and greatest, whose advent is long delayed, deals with the question whether Communism and therewithal the perfect city itself can be realised in the world (471 C ff.). The last of these three waves is not finally surmounted until the description of the Philosopher and his City reaches its conclusion at the end of VII: so that Books V—VII closely cohere together. In the first two divisions (V 451 C—466 D), the dominating principle is still φύσις or Nature (see on 451 C): but from 474 D onwards the psychological standpoint is gradually superseded by the metaphysical, until in Book VII the Idea of Good becomes the supreme inspiring force—at once the formal, the efficient, and the final cause—of Plato's City. See on VI 506 E, 509 B ff. On the alleged connexion between the earlier part of Book V (451 C—466 D) and the *Ecclesiazusae* of Aristophanes see App. I.

4 **ἰδιωτῶν—κατασκευήν**: 'the organization of the character of the individual soul.' ψυχῆς was doubted by Ast; but cf. IV 445 C τοσοῦτοι κινδυνεύουσι καὶ ψυχῆς τρόποι εἶναι, and for the collocation

οὔσας. Ποίας δὴ ταύτας; ἔφη. καὶ ἐγὼ μὲν ᾖα τὰς ἐφεξῆς
B ἐρῶν, ὥς μοι ἐφαίνοντο ἕκασται | ἐξ ἀλλήλων μεταβαίνειν· ὁ δὲ Πολέμαρχος—σμικρὸν γὰρ ἀπωτέρω τοῦ Ἀδειμάντου καθῆστο—ἐκτείνας τὴν χεῖρα καὶ λαβόμενος τοῦ ἱματίου ἄνωθεν αὐτοῦ παρὰ τὸν ὦμον ἐκεῖνόν τε προσηγάγετο καὶ προτείνας ἑαυτὸν ἔλεγεν ἄττα προσκεκυφώς, ὧν ἄλλο μὲν οὐδὲν κατηκούσαμεν, τόδε δέ· Ἀφήσομεν οὖν, ἔφη, ἢ τί δράσομεν; Ἥκιστά γε, ἔφη ὁ Ἀδείμαντος, μέγα ἤδη λέγων. καὶ ἐγώ, Τί μάλιστα, ἔφην, ὑμεῖς οὐκ
C ἀφίετε; Σέ, ἦ δ' ὅς. | Ὅτι ἐγὼ εἶπον τί μάλιστα; Ἀπορρᾳθυμεῖν ἡμῖν δοκεῖς, ἔφη, καὶ εἶδος ὅλον οὐ τὸ ἐλάχιστον ἐκκλέπτειν τοῦ λόγου, ἵνα μὴ διέλθῃς, καὶ λήσειν οἰηθῆναι εἰπὼν αὐτὸ φαύλως, ὡς ἄρα περὶ γυναικῶν τε καὶ παίδων παντὶ δῆλον, ὅτι κοινὰ τὰ φίλων ἔσται. Οὐκοῦν ὀρθῶς, ἔφην, ὦ Ἀδείμαντε; Ναί, ἦ δ' ὅς· ἀλλὰ τὸ ὀρθῶς τοῦτο, ὥσπερ τἆλλα, λόγου δεῖται, τίς ὁ τρόπος τῆς κοινωνίας. πολλοὶ γὰρ ἂν γένοιντο. μὴ οὖν παρῇς ὅντινα σὺ
D λέγεις. ὡς ἡμεῖς πάλαι | περιμένομεν οἰόμενοί σέ που μνησθήσεσθαι παιδοποιίας τε πέρι, πῶς παιδοποιήσονται, καὶ γενομένους πῶς θρέψουσιν, καὶ ὅλην ταύτην ἣν λέγεις κοινωνίαν γυναικῶν

5. ἔφη Π: om. A.　　13. ὅτι Ξ: ἔτι ΑΠΞq.

---

of genitives VII 525 C *αὐτῆς τῆς ψυχῆς ῥᾳστώνης μεταστροφῆς*, VIII 544 D, 559 E, 560 B, *Tim.* 24 B and other cases in Kühner *Gr. Gr.* II p. 289. *ψυχῆς τρόπου* is practically a single word like 'soul-character' ("Seelenbeschaffenheit" Schneider).

449 B 7 **σμικρὸν κτλ.** explains *ἐκτείνας τὴν χεῖρα*: 'paullo longius ab Adimanto, quam clandestinum colloquium requirebat' or 'paullo remotior, quam reliqui a suis vicinis,' not "a little further away from Socrates than Adimantus" (J. and C.): for "cur propterea manum protenderit et Adimantum attraxerit, non apparet" (Schneider).

449 B, C 12 **τί μάλιστα κτλ.** 'What particular thing is it that you decline to let off?' 'You,' said he. 'Because of what particular remark of *mine*?' (lit. 'because I said what in particular?') There is not, as J. and C. suppose, a play on the two senses of *τί μάλιστα*—*cur* potissimum and *quid* potissimum: for it must be observed that *ἀφήσομεν* has no expressed object, and Socrates could not have known that it was intended to refer to him. The removal of the commas usually printed after *ὅτι* and *εἶπον* restores sense, I think, to the remainder of this passage. *ἔτι* for *ὅτι* (see *cr. n.*) can scarcely stand, for *ἔτι ἐγὼ εἶπον* cannot mean 'I repeated' (Jowett), nor can we read *ἔτι, ἐγὼ εἶπον, τί μάλιστα* 'once more, said I' etc. In none of the parallels hitherto cited does *ἔτι* mean merely 'once more' or 'again.' Those who print *ὅτι, ἐγὼ εἶπον, τί μάλιστα* (Stallbaum) mostly take *ὅτι—τί μάλιστα* as in I 343 A *ὅτι δὴ τί μάλιστα; ἦν δ' ἐγώ.* *Ὅτι κτλ.* But in such cases (as Schneider points out) there must be a second *ὅτι* to introduce the answer, and here there is not.

14 **ἐκκλέπτειν** = 'to cheat out of' as in *μὴ—ἐκκλέψῃς λόγον* Soph. *Trach.* 436 f.: see Jebb ad loc.

16 **κοινὰ τὰ φίλων.** See IV 423 E, 424 A *nn.* *κοινὰ τὰ τῶν φίλων* is preferred by Ast and Stallbaum (with two late MSS), but the shorter form is far more racy of the soil, and occurs also in *Lys.* 207 C, *Laws* 739 C (Schneider on IV 424 A).

449 D 22 **καὶ ὅλην κτλ.**: i.e. *καὶ*

τε καὶ παίδων· μέγα γάρ τι οἰόμεθα φέρειν καὶ ὅλον εἰς πολιτείαν
ὀρθῶς ἢ μὴ ὀρθῶς γιγνόμενον. νῦν οὖν, ἐπειδὴ ἄλλης ἐπιλαμβάνει
πολιτείας πρὶν ταῦτα ἱκανῶς διελέσθαι, δέδοκται ἡμῖν τοῦτο, ὃ σὺ
ἤκουσας, τὸ σὲ | μὴ μεθιέναι, πρὶν ἂν ταῦτα πάντα ὥσπερ τἆλλα **450**
διέλθῃς. Καὶ ἐμὲ τοίνυν, ὁ Γλαύκων ἔφη, κοινωνὸν τῆς ψήφου
ταύτης τίθετε. Ἀμέλει, ἔφη ὁ Θρασύμαχος, πᾶσι ταῦτα δεδογ-
μένα ἡμῖν νόμιζε, ὦ Σώκρατες.

II. Οἷον, ἦν δ' ἐγώ, εἰργάσασθε ἐπιλαβόμενοί μου. ὅσον
λόγον πάλιν ὥσπερ ἐξ ἀρχῆς κινεῖτε περὶ τῆς πολιτείας· ἣν ὡς
ἤδη διεληλυθὼς ἔγωγε ἔχαιρον, ἀγαπῶν εἴ τις ἐάσοι ταῦτα ἀπο-
δεξάμενος ὡς τότε ἐρρήθη. ἃ νῦν ὑμεῖς | παρακαλοῦντες οὐκ ἴστε **B**
ὅσον ἐσμὸν λόγων ἐπεγείρετε· ὃν ὁρῶν ἐγὼ παρῆκα τότε, μὴ
παράσχοι πολὺν ὄχλον. Τί δέ; ἦ δ' ὃς ὁ Θρασύμαχος· χρυσοχοήσοντας οἴει τούσδε νῦν ἐνθάδε ἀφῖχθαι, ἀλλ' οὐ λόγων ἀκουσο-

3. ταῦτα Π: τἀυτὰ (sic, ut solet) A.

ἐξηγήσεσθαι or the like, supplied from *μνησθήσεσθαι*. The construction cannot (as J. and C. suggest) go back to *μὴ οὖν παρῇς*.

23 **μέγα κτλ.** *καί* after *φέρειν* = 'or rather' (atque) as in *ὀλίγου τινὸς—καὶ οὐδενός* (*Ap.* 23 A). For *γιγνόμενον* Liebhold proposes *γιγνομένην*, but see on IV 427 D. The feminine would be awkward after *πολιτείαν*, and *κοινωνίαν—παίδων*, though grammatically feminine, is logically neuter.

24 **ἄλλης—πολιτείας** is explained by *ᾖα τὰς ἐφεξῆς ἐρῶν* (449 A). Stallbaum makes a curious slip: "quoniam ad *alias πολιτείας partes* considerandas celeriter accedis."

450 A, B 3 **τίθετε.** Glauco addresses both Polemarchus and Adimantus. There is no occasion to write *τίθει* (with Hartman).

5 **οἷον—εἰργάσασθε κτλ.** Chiappelli (*Riv. di Filologia* etc. XI p. 195) finds in this and the following sentences a *vaticinium ex eventu* of Aristophanes' *Ecclesiazusae*. But the word *παρῆκα* shews that the *ἑσμὸς λόγων* does not refer to swarms of adverse criticism, but merely to the topics which Socrates must now discuss. See App. I, and (on the subject in general) *Laws* 779 E.

8 **τότε.** IV 423 E.

ἃ νῦν ὑμεῖς κτλ.: 'in appealing to these topics now you' etc. *παρακαλοῦντες* means literally 'calling to you': "das ruft ihr nun herbei" (Schneider). This interpretation is in harmony with *ἐπεγείρετε*, and gives the right antithesis to *ἐάσοι*. Neither "excitantes" (Ast), nor "in disputationem vocantes" (Stallbaum) is quite accurate. J. and C. give two alternative renderings (1) "and in now calling in this fresh argument," (2) "and in now urging me to this." But the antecedent can only be *ταῦτα*.

450 B 10 **χρυσοχοήσοντας κτλ.** Socrates shudders at the swarm of *λόγοι* to be encountered. 'Why,' says Thrasymachus, 'it was precisely to listen to *λόγοι*, and not to smelt ore for gold, that we came here.' *χρυσοχοεῖν* is a proverbial expression said of those who neglect their proper duty for some more fascinating—if less profitable—pursuit. Cf. Harpocr. s.v. *χρυσοχοεῖον*: *Δείναρχος ἐν τῷ κατὰ Πυθέου· πάλιν παρ' Αἰσχίνην ἀποφοιτήσας παρὰ τούτῳ δῆλον ὅτι χρυσοχοεῖν ἐμάνθανεν, ἀλλ' οὐ τὸ προκείμενον αὐτὸ ποιεῖν ἢ πάσχειν.* Here *τὸ προκείμενον* is *λόγων ἀκούειν*. The origin of the proverb is thus explained. A heap of gold-dust having been discovered on Hymettus, the Athenian populace deserted their usual avocations, and sallied out to seize it. But as it was guarded *ὑπὸ τῶν μαχίμων μυκτήρων* (cf. Hdt. III 102 ff. with the parallels cited by Stein), they failed. On returning *ἔσκωπτον ἀλλήλους λέγοντες 'σὺ δὲ ᾤου χρυσοχοήσειν.'* Cf. Suidas s.v. and Leutsch u. Schneidewin *Paroem.*

μένους; Ναί, εἶπον, μετρίων γε. Μέτρον δέ γ', ἔφη, ὦ Σώκρατες, ὁ Γλαύκων, τοιούτων λόγων ἀκούειν ὅλος ὁ βίος νοῦν ἔχουσιν. ἀλλὰ τὸ μὲν ἡμέτερον ἔα· σὺ δὲ περὶ ὧν ἐρωτῶμεν μηδαμῶς **C** ἀποκάμῃς ᾗ σοι δοκεῖ διεξιών, τίς ἡ κοινωνία τοῖς φύλαξιν ἡμῖν παίδων τε πέρι καὶ γυναικῶν ἔσται καὶ τροφῆς νέων ἔτι ὄντων, τῆς ἐν τῷ μεταξὺ χρόνῳ γιγνομένης γενέσεώς τε καὶ παιδείας, ἣ δὴ ἐπιπονωτάτη δοκεῖ εἶναι. πειρῶ οὖν εἰπεῖν τίνα τρόπον δεῖ γίγνεσθαι αὐτήν. Οὐ ῥᾴδιον, ὦ εὔδαιμον, ἦν δ' ἐγώ, διελθεῖν· πολλὰς γὰρ ἀπιστίας ἔχει ἔτι μᾶλλον τῶν ἔμπροσθεν ὧν διήλθομεν. καὶ γὰρ ὡς δυνατὰ λέγεται, ἀπιστοῖτ' ἄν, καὶ εἰ ὅ τι μάλιστα γένοιτο, **D** ὡς ἄριστ' ἂν εἴη ταῦτα, καὶ ταύτῃ ἀπιστήσεται. διὸ δὴ καὶ ὄκνος τις αὐτῶν ἅπτεσθαι, μὴ εὐχὴ δοκῇ εἶναι ὁ λόγος, ὦ φίλε ἑταῖρε. Μηδέν, ἦ δ' ὅς, ὄκνει· οὔτε γὰρ ἀγνώμονες οὔτε ἄπιστοι οὔτε δύσνοι οἱ ἀκουσόμενοι. καὶ ἐγὼ εἶπον Ὦ ἄριστε, ἦ που βουλόμενός με παραθαρρύνειν λέγεις; Ἔγωγ', ἔφη. Πᾶν τοίνυν, ἦν δ' ἐγώ, τοὐναντίον ποιεῖς. πιστεύοντος μὲν γὰρ ἐμοῦ ἐμοὶ

18. *οὖν* Π: *ἂν* A. 23. *δοκῇ* A^2q^2: *δοκεῖ* $A^1Πq^1$: *δοκοῖ* Ξ.

Gr. I p. 464, II pp. 91, 727. A gloss in Bekker's *Anec. Gr.* I p. 316 (cited by Schneider) explains *χρυσοχοεῖν* in Dinarchus as proverbial for *πορνεύειν*; but it cannot have so offensive a meaning here, for (among other reasons) Thrasymachus and Socrates are now reconciled. Ast's explanation "aurum fundere proverbialiter dicitur, quem magna, quam animo conceperat, spes frustratur" expresses only one side of the proverb: the other—neglecting the duty which lies nearest—is more important and relevant here. "To find an Eldorado" (Warren) may perhaps meet the case. Thomas Gray's explanation is not altogether right: "a proverbial expression used of such as are idly employed or sent (as we say) on a fool's errand."

12 **μέτρον δὲ κτλ.** An *argumentum ad hominem*, for the sentiment is Socratic: cf. VI 504 C. *δέ γε*='yes, but' helps to bring out this point. *ἀκούειν* is the common epexegetic infinitive: cf. III 407 B *n.* To insert *τοῦ* before *τοιούτων* (with Herwerden and Richards) is both unnecessary and inelegant.

14 **τὸ μὲν ἡμέτερον ἔα**: 'never mind us': *we* are equal to a long discourse (so also J. and C.).

450 C 17 **τῷ μεταξὺ χρόνῳ.** The interval between *γένεσις* and *παιδεία* is nowhere defined in the *Republic*: in *Laws* 794 C it is reckoned at six years. For the regulations applying to this period see infra 460 B—D, and cf. *Laws* 788 D ff.

18 **οὖν.** See *cr. n.* It is admitted that Π is independent of A, so that *οὖν* (which most MSS have) may well be right. The tendency to confuse *οὖν* and *ἄν* may help to explain A's variants *οὔκουν* and *οὐκ ἂν οὖν* in I 333 E. Baiter reads *δή*. The confusion of *ἄν* and *δή* occurs no doubt in MSS, but its frequency has been much exaggerated, as for instance in *Cl. Rev.* VI p. 338.

19 **ὦ εὔδαιμον.** Cf. IV 422 E *n.*

450 D 23 **μὴ εὐχὴ κτλ.** For *εὐχή*=an impossible aspiration, a Utopian or chimerical proposal, cf. 456 C, VII 540 D and see Susemihl and Hicks on Arist. *Pol.* B 1. 1260ᵇ 29.

24 **ἀγνώμονες**: i.q. *ἀνεπιστήμονες*, as explained (with reference to this passage) in Bekker's *Anec. Gr.* I p. 334: cf. *Phaedr.* 275 A. Hence *φρονίμοις* in E below. The more usual meaning, 'inconsiderate,' 'unkind,' is less suitable here on account of *δύσνοι*.

εἰδέναι ἃ λέγω, καλῶς εἶχεν ἡ παραμυθία· ἐν γὰρ | φρονίμοις τε E
καὶ φίλοις περὶ τῶν μεγίστων τε καὶ φίλων τἀληθῆ εἰδότα λέγειν ἀσφαλὲς καὶ θαρραλέον, ἀπιστοῦντα δὲ καὶ ζητοῦντα ἅμα τοὺς λόγους ποιεῖσθαι, ὃ δὴ ἐγὼ δρῶ, φοβερόν τε καὶ σφαλερόν, οὔ τι γέλωτα | ὀφλεῖν· παιδικὸν γὰρ τοῦτό γε· ἀλλὰ μὴ σφαλεὶς τῆς 451
ἀληθείας οὐ μόνον αὐτὸς ἀλλὰ καὶ τοὺς φίλους ξυνεπισπασάμενος κείσομαι περὶ ἃ ἥκιστα δεῖ σφάλλεσθαι. προσκυνῶ δὲ Ἀδράστειαν, ὦ Γλαύκων, χάριν οὗ μέλλω λέγειν· ἐλπίζω γὰρ οὖν ἔλαττον ἁμάρτημα ἀκουσίως τινὸς φονέα γενέσθαι, ἢ ἀπατεῶνα καλῶν τε καὶ ἀγαθῶν καὶ δικαίων νομίμων πέρι. τοῦτο οὖν τὸ κίνδυνευμα κινδυνεύειν ἐν ἐχθροῖς κρεῖττον ἢ φίλοις· ὥστε εὖ | με παραμυθεῖ. B

---

450 E 29 **φίλων κτλ.** *φίλων* though neuter is of course intended to balance *φίλοις*. The conjecture *φιλτάτων* (Richards, Hartman) destroys the balance and is in itself superfluous: see Kühner *Gr. Gr.* II p. 23. Note the characteristic chiasmus *ἀσφαλὲς καὶ θαρραλέον—φοβερόν τε καὶ σφαλερόν*.

451 A 1 **ὀφλεῖν κτλ.** The infinitive depends on *φοβερόν*, and is like the infinitive after *φοβοῦμαι*. In the antithetical clause Plato substitutes the more usual construction with *μή*. The future indicative (*κείσομαι*) is rare after words of fearing (Goodwin *MT.* p. 132), and represents the danger as imminent. To regard *οὔ τι γέλωτα ὀφλεῖν* as a reference to the *Ecclesiazusae* is rash and unjustifiable: see App. I.

3 **προσκυνῶ κτλ.** The apology looks forward, and not backward; whence *δέ* rather than *δή* (which Herwerden would read).

Ἀδράστειαν. Adrasteia was originally, perhaps, a personification of *ἀνάγκη* in its relation to humanity and the issues of human conduct. This meaning survived in the Orphic theology (Abel *Orph. Fr.* 36, 109—111) and appears in *Phaedr.* 248 C. Specifically, she was viewed as a variety of Nemesis, *θεά τις τοὺς ὑπερηφάνους τιμωροῦσα* (Schol. on Aesch. *Prom.* 936), and in this sense Aeschylus (l.c.) writes *οἱ προσκυνοῦντες τὴν Ἀδράστειαν σοφοί* (the first mention of Adrasteia in Greek literature). Adrasteia is in a still more special sense the punisher of proud words; so that *προσκυνῶ Ἀδράστειαν* becomes, as here, a sort of apologetic preface to a bold assertion or rash utterance: cf. Eur. *Rhes.* 342, 468 (*ξὺν δ' Ἀδραστείᾳ λέγω*). See Nägelsbach *Nachhom. Theol.* p. 47 and Seymour in the *Proceedings of the Amer. Philol. Assoc.* for July 1891 pp. XLVIII ff.

4 **ἐλπίζω κτλ.** *ἐλπίζω* is 'I fancy,' not 'I expect': cf. II 383 B *n.* The omission of *εἶναι* is curious: Madvig would restore it after *ἁμάρτημα*. I can find no parallel to its omission with *ἐλπίζω*, but *οἴομαι*, *ἡγοῦμαι* and other verbs of thinking often dispense with it. For examples see Schanz *Nov. Comm. Pl.* p. 34.

5 **καλῶν κτλ.**: "concerning noble and good and just institutions" (D. and V.), not "about the beautiful, the good, and the just, in the matter of laws" (J. and C.). The latter explanation gives a good sense, but it is harsh to separate *δικαίων* from *νομίμων*, and still harsher to take *καλῶν* as equivalent to *περὶ καλῶν*. Schneider was inclined to treat *δικαίων* as a gloss on *νομίμων*. But 'about things beautiful and good and institutions' is an anti-climax; and, besides, it is of institutions in conjunction with, not as distinct from, justice etc. that Plato is about to speak. In his translation Schneider takes the right view.

7 **εὖ.** *q* has *οὐκ εὖ*, an obvious but audacious correction, suggested, no doubt, by *καλῶς εἶχεν ἡ παραμυθία* in 450 D. *εὖ* is ironical. Glauco had comforted Socrates by saying *inter alia* that his hearers were friendly (*οὔτε δύσνοι οἱ ἀκουσόμενοι* 450 D). Excellent comfort! says Socrates: I had rather, in the circumstances, that they were enemies! Stallbaum and others read *οὐκ εὖ*, and Hermann *οὐ*, for *εὖ*, thinking the irony misplaced; but Glauco's smile (*γελάσας*)

καὶ ὁ Γλαύκων γελάσας Ἀλλ', ὦ Σώκρατες, ἔφη, ἐάν τι πάθωμεν πλημμελὲς ὑπὸ τοῦ λόγου, ἀφίεμέν σε ὥσπερ φόνου καθαρὸν εἶναι καὶ μὴ ἀπατεῶνα ἡμῶν. ἀλλὰ θαρρήσας λέγε. Ἀλλὰ μέντοι, εἶπον, καθαρός γε καὶ ἐκεῖ ὁ ἀφεθείς, ὡς ὁ νόμος λέγει· εἰκὸς δέ γε, εἴπερ ἐκεῖ, κἀνθάδε. Λέγε τοίνυν, ἔφη, τούτου γ' ἕνεκα. Λέγειν δή, ἔφην ἐγώ, χρὴ ἀνάπαλιν αὖ νῦν, ἃ τότε ἴσως ἔδει ἐφεξῆς λέγειν.
C τάχα δὲ οὕτως ἂν | ὀρθῶς ἔχοι, μετὰ ἀνδρεῖον δρᾶμα παντελῶς

9. καθαρὸν Π: καὶ καθαρὸν Α. 13. δὴ Π: δὲ Α. ἃ τότε *v*: ἅ ποτε ΑΠΞ*q*.

favours the ironical interpretation, and so does the 'Socratic irony' with which the whole sentence is overflowing. I agree with J. and C. in rejecting the pointless alternative rendering 'you do well to comfort me.'

451 B 9 **ὥσπερ φόνου κτλ.** See *cr. n.* καί before καθαρόν is absent from the great majority of MSS and can scarcely, I think, be sound: for the difference in meaning between καθαρόν and μὴ ἀπατεῶνα is hardly enough to carry off the double καί. ὥσπερ belongs to the whole expression φόνου καθαρόν, which is virtually one word. Hartman would expunge καὶ μὴ ἀπατεῶνα ἡμῶν, but it is quite in Plato's way to subjoin the interpretation of a metaphor or simile (cf. 470 C, VIII 553 D, 555 D, and my note on *Prot.* 314 A), nor have we any right to excise such expressions wholesale, as many Dutch critics would do (especially J. J. Hartman *de embl. in Pl. text. obviis* 1898).

11 **ἐκεῖ**: viz. in cases of φόνος ἀκούσιος (so Schneider, Stallbaum, etc.), not (with D. and V.) 'in the next world.' κἀνθάδε is relevant only if it means 'in this case too,' i.e. ἐν τῷ ἀπατεῶνα εἶναι καλῶν τε καὶ ἀγαθῶν κτλ.: and this fixes the meaning of ἐκεῖ.

ὡς ὁ νόμος λέγει is explained by Dem. πρὸς Παντaίνετον 58 καὶ γὰρ ἀκούσιοι φόνοι—καὶ πολλὰ ἄλλα τοιαῦτα γίγνεται· ἀλλ' ὅμως ἁπάντων τούτων ὅρος καὶ λύσις τοῖς παθοῦσι τέτακται τὸ πεισθέντας ἀφεῖναι, and ib. 59. See also *Laws* 869 E.

451 C 14 **ἀνδρεῖον δρᾶμα κτλ.** There is probably a playful allusion to the mimes of Sophron, as was first pointed out by R. Förster in *Rhein. Mus.* XXX (1875) p. 316. According to Suidas (s.v. Σώφρων) and others, Sophron's mimes were classified as ἀνδρεῖοι μῖμοι and γυναικεῖοι μῖμοι. In the former, as may be inferred from Choricius' *Defence of Mimes* (first published by Graux in *Revue de Philologie* I pp. 209 ff.) Sophron represented male characters, in the latter female (μιμεῖται μὲν ἄνδρας, μιμεῖται δὲ γύναια ib. p. 215). This is corroborated by many of the titles of his plays, such as ὁ ἀγροιώτας, ὁ θυννοθήρας, ὁ ἄγγελος contrasted with ταὶ ἀκέστριαι, ἁ νυμφόπονος, ἁ πενθερά etc. Sophron's mimes are called δράματα (cf. ἀνδρεῖον δρᾶμα) by Demetrius περὶ ἑρμηνείας § 156 σχεδόν τε πάσας ἐκ τῶν δραμάτων αὐτοῦ τὰς παροιμίας ἐκλέξαι ἐστίν. The point here is that just as custom required an ἀνδρεῖος μῖμος to precede a γυναικεῖος—this is not otherwise attested, so far as I can discover—, so it will be proper (ὀρθῶς ἂν ἔχοι) for Plato's women to come on the stage after his men have played their part. Plato's partiality for Sophron is frequently mentioned by ancient authors, as for example by D. L. III 18, Quintil. I 10. 17: see Schuster in *Rhein. Mus.* XXIX (1874) pp. 605 ff., where these and other authorities are cited. Susemihl (Bursian's *Jahresbericht* 1874—1875 III p. 343) doubted whether Plato has Sophron in view here; but the allusion, which was admitted by Graux (l.c. p. 215 *n.*), and successfully reaffirmed by Förster (*Rhein. Mus.* for 1880 p. 472), is highly probable. I can see no point in making δρᾶμα γυναικεῖον an ironical reference to the *Ecclesiazusae* of Aristophanes (with Munk *die nat. Ordnung d. Pl. Schr.* p. 296, and Chiappelli l.c. p. 196), nor is it likely that the words allude to a dramatic caricature of Plato's policy by some other comedian, as is supposed by Bergk *Gr. Literaturgesch.* IV p. 462 *n.* 134. On Sophron's prose-mimes as a preparation for the Socratic Dialogue see Hirzel *der Dialog* I pp. 20—26.

451 C—**452** E *We declared at the*

διαπερανθὲν τὸ γυναικεῖον αὖ περαίνειν, ἄλλως τε καὶ ἐπειδὴ σὺ οὕτω προκαλεῖ.

III. Ἀνθρώποις γὰρ φῦσι καὶ παιδευθεῖσιν ὡς ἡμεῖς διήλθομεν, κατ' ἐμὴν δόξαν οὐκ ἔστ' ἄλλη ὀρθὴ παίδων τε καὶ γυναικῶν κτῆσίς τε καὶ χρεία ἢ κατ' ἐκείνην τὴν ὁρμὴν ἰοῦσιν, ἥνπερ τὸ

---

outset that our men were to be as it were guardians of the flock. Now the principle of community requires that our female watch-dogs shall share the active duties of the males, allowance being made for their inferiority in strength. Their education must therefore be the same: they will have to learn music, gymnastic, and the art of war. No doubt the spectacle of women, especially old women, exercising themselves naked along with men, will seem ludicrous at first; but it is not long since the Greeks would have thought it ludicrous even for men to strip for athletic exercises. Nothing is truly ludicrous except what is mischievous.

451 C ff. Socrates now prepares to encounter the first 'wave' (451 C—457 B): see on 449 A ff. The outstanding feature in his argument throughout this part of the dialogue is the constant appeal which he makes to φύσις (452 E, 453 B, C, E, 454 B, C, D, 455 A, D, E, 456 A, B, C, D). He maintains that community of work and education between certain selected men and women is 'natural' in two senses. In the first place, it is, he maintains, in harmony with *human* nature, that is, with the nature of man and woman (455 E ff.), and in the second place, it is recommended by the analogy of Nature's other children, the lower animals (451 D). See also on II 370 A. Pöhlmann (*Gesch. d. antik. Kommunismus* etc. pp. 114—146) has shewn that the desire for a 'return to Nature' found frequent and manifold expression in the literature of Plato's times, and we can see that Plato was himself powerfully affected by the same impulse, although his interpretation of 'Nature' is coloured by an Idealism which is peculiarly his own (IV 443 B *n.*). The special regulations of Book V may be illustrated in some particulars from the practices of certain 'Natur-völker' before the time of Plato (see e.g. Hdt. IV 116 and infra 463 C *n.*), as well as by certain features of the Pythagorean and Spartan disciplines (see RP.[7] 48 A f. and *nn.* on 452 B al.), but it is more important and relevant to observe that Plato's assignment of common duties and common training to the two sexes is part of a well-reasoned and deliberate attempt by the Socratic school to improve the position of women in Greece. In this respect, as in many others, the teaching of Socrates inaugurated an era of protest against the old Hellenic view of things. See in particular, for the views of Socrates himself, Xen. *Mem.* II 2. 5, *Symp.* 2. 9 ἡ γυναικεία φύσις οὐδὲν χείρων τῆς τοῦ ἀνδρὸς οὖσα τυγχάνει, γνώμης δὲ καὶ ἰσχύος δεῖται, *Oecon.* 3. 12—15, 7. 11 ff.; for Plato, *Symp.* 201 D ff. and *Laws* 780 E ff.; and for the opinion of Antisthenes consult D. L. VI 12 ἀνδρὸς καὶ γυναικὸς ἡ αὐτὴ ἀρετή. It is possible that some of Euripides' pictures of noble and disinterested women were also inspired in some measure by the influence of the same movement. In later times the Stoics constituted themselves the champions of similar views, and Cleanthes wrote a treatise entitled περὶ τοῦ ὅτι ἡ αὐτὴ ἀρετὴ καὶ ἀνδρὸς καὶ γυναικός: see Dyroff *Ethik d. alten Stoa* pp. 311—314, where other evidence is cited. A learned and acute discussion on the attitude of the Socratic school in this matter will be found in Chiappelli *Riv. di Filologia* etc. XI pp. 229 ff. Finally it should be observed that, from Plato's point of view, the selection of suitable women as φύλακες is strictly in harmony with the fundamental principle of our city, viz. 'to each one work according to his or her nature' (II 370 B *n.*); that it removes a dangerous source of unrest, intrigue, and sedition, by providing an outlet for the energies of able and politically-minded women in legitimate channels and silencing them with the responsibilities of rule, while it at the same time secures for the service of the State all that is best in the other half of the population (*Laws* 781 A), and justifies the claim of the perfect city to be in literal truth an Aristocracy.

451 C 19 **κατ' ἐκείνην κτλ.**: "in following out that original impulse which we communicated to them" (D. and V.).

πρῶτον ὡρμήσαμεν· ἐπεχειρήσαμεν δέ που ὡς ἀγέλης φύλακας
D τοὺς ἄνδρας καθιστάναι τῷ λόγῳ. Ναί. Ἀκολουθῶμεν | τοίνυν
καὶ τὴν γένεσιν καὶ τροφὴν παραπλησίαν ἀποδιδόντες, καὶ σκοπῶμεν, εἰ ἡμῖν πρέπει ἢ οὔ. Πῶς; ἔφη. Ὧδε. τὰς θηλείας τῶν
φυλάκων κυνῶν πότερα ξυμφυλάττειν οἰόμεθα δεῖν, ἅπερ ἂν οἱ
ἄρρενες φυλάττωσι, καὶ ξυνθηρεύειν καὶ τἆλλα κοινῇ πράττειν,
ἢ τὰς μὲν οἰκουρεῖν ἔνδον ὡς ἀδυνάτους διὰ τὸν τῶν σκυλάκων
τόκον τε καὶ τροφήν, τοὺς δὲ πονεῖν τε καὶ πᾶσαν ἐπιμέλειαν
ἔχειν περὶ τὰ ποίμνια; Κοινῇ, ἔφη, πάντα· πλὴν ὡς ἀσθενε-
E στέραις | χρώμεθα, τοῖς δὲ ὡς ἰσχυροτέροις. Οἷόν τ' οὖν, ἔφην
ἐγώ, ἐπὶ τὰ αὐτὰ χρῆσθαί τινι ζῴῳ, ἂν μὴ τὴν αὐτὴν τροφήν τε
καὶ παιδείαν ἀποδιδῷς; Οὐχ οἷόν τε. Εἰ ἄρα ταῖς γυναιξὶν ἐπὶ
ταὐτὰ χρησόμεθα καὶ τοῖς ἀνδράσι, ταὐτὰ καὶ διδακτέον αὐτάς.
452 | Ναί. Μουσικὴ μὲν ἐκείνοις τε καὶ γυμναστικὴ ἐδόθη. Ναί.
Καὶ ταῖς γυναιξὶν ἄρα τούτω τὼ τέχνα καὶ τὰ περὶ τὸν πόλεμον
ἀποδοτέον καὶ χρηστέον κατὰ ταὐτά. Εἰκὸς ἐξ ὧν λέγεις, ἔφη.
Ἴσως δή, εἶπον, παρὰ τὸ ἔθος γελοῖα ἂν φαίνοιτο πολλὰ περὶ τὰ
νῦν λεγόμενα, εἰ πράξεται ᾗ λέγεται. Καὶ μάλα, ἔφη. Τί, ἦν δ'

32. καὶ διδακτέον A^2Π: διδακτέον A^1.

---

20 **ὡρμήσαμεν** (sc. αὐτούς) is causative, and not intransitive, as Jowett supposes.

ἀγέλης. Cf. II 375 D and infra 460 C, 466 D *nn.*

451 D 28 **πλὴν κτλ.** One MS inserts ταῖς μέν after πλήν; but, "ταῖς θηλείαις utpote ex ipsa sententia et ex adjectivo ἀσθενεστέραις facile intelligendum enuntiatum non est" (Schneider). Schneider's explanation is more accurate than to say (with Stallbaum) that ταῖς μέν is idiomatically suppressed, like τὸ μέν before ἄλλο in *Prot.* 330 A (ἄλλο, τὸ δὲ ἄλλο): cf. infra 455 E. This passage is thus criticised by Aristotle (*Pol.* B. 5. 1264^b 4) ἄτοπον δὲ καὶ τὸ ἐκ τῶν θηρίων ποιεῖσθαι τὴν παραβολήν, ὅτι δεῖ τὰ αὐτὰ ἐπιτηδεύειν τὰς γυναῖκας τοῖς ἀνδράσιν, οἷς οἰκονομίας οὐδὲν μέτεστιν. But, from Plato's point of view, the analogy holds; for he regards οἰκονομία as παρὰ φύσιν even for human beings, and aims at abolishing it.

452 A 1 **μουσικὴ μέν.** The particle μέν "Latino *atqui* non multo debilius" (Schneider, comparing I 339 B and III 412 C ὅτι μὲν πρεσβυτέρους τοὺς ἄρχοντας δεῖ εἶναι—δῆλον). Richards conjectures μήν, which would certainly be more usual (cf. 465 B): but no change is necessary. Although the position of τε (which a few inferior MSS omit) is irregular, we ought not to read γε: cf. infra 465 E *n.*, and (with Schneider) *Laws* 800 A, 966 A (ἢ καὶ ὅπως ἔν τε καὶ ὅπῃ). In these cases τε suffers hyperbaton, being attracted forward by καί. The reverse kind of hyperbaton is more usual with this word: see *Prot.* 316 D, with my note ad loc. Here it would be awkward to place τε after either μουσική or μέν. For ἐδόθη Richards proposes ἀπεδόθη, to correspond with ἀποδιδῷς above; but cf. δοτέον infra 457 A and see on I 336 E.

4 **παρὰ τὸ ἔθος**: 'contra consuetudinem,' not 'respectu consuetudinis' as Hartman thinks. The phrase specifies the particular variety of γελοῖα intended by Plato: 'many ludicrous breaches of etiquette.' It is not quite easy (with J. and C.) to understand πραττόμενα.

5 **πράξεται.** *q* has πεπράξεται, which is tempting, and may be right; but, as Schneider points out, 'si peragentur' is somewhat more appropriate than 'si peracta fuerint.' πράξεται as passive seems to occur only here in Attic.

ἐγώ, γελοιότατον αὐτῶν ὁρᾷς; ἢ δῆλα δή, ὅτι γυμνὰς τὰς γυναῖκας
ἐν ταῖς παλαίστραις γυμναζομένας μετὰ τῶν ἀνδρῶν, | οὐ μόνον τὰς B
νέας, ἀλλὰ καὶ ἤδη τὰς πρεσβυτέρας, ὥσπερ τοὺς γέροντας ἐν τοῖς
γυμνασίοις, ὅταν ῥυσοὶ καὶ μὴ ἡδεῖς τὴν ὄψιν ὅμως φιλογυμναστῶ-
σιν; Νὴ τὸν Δία, ἔφη· γελοῖον γὰρ ἄν, ὥς γε ἐν τῷ παρεστῶτι,
φανείη. Οὐκοῦν, ἦν δ' ἐγώ, ἐπείπερ ὡρμήσαμεν λέγειν, οὐ φοβητέον
τὰ τῶν χαριέντων σκώμματα, ὅσα καὶ οἷα ἂν εἴποιεν εἰς τὴν
τοιαύτην μεταβολὴν γενομένην καὶ περὶ τὰ γυμνάσια | καὶ περὶ C
μουσικὴν καὶ οὐκ ἐλάχιστα περὶ τὴν τῶν ὅπλων σχέσιν καὶ ἵππων
ὀχήσεις. Ὀρθῶς, ἔφη, λέγεις. Ἀλλ' ἐπείπερ λέγειν ἠρξάμεθα,
πορευτέον πρὸς τὸ τραχὺ τοῦ νόμου, δεηθεῖσίν τε τούτων μὴ τὰ
αὑτῶν πράττειν ἀλλὰ σπουδάζειν, καὶ ὑπομνήσασιν, ὅτι οὐ πολὺς
χρόνος ἐξ οὗ τοῖς Ἕλλησιν ἐδόκει αἰσχρὰ εἶναι καὶ γελοῖα, ἅπερ
νῦν τοῖς πολλοῖς τῶν βαρβάρων, γυμνοὺς ἄνδρας ὁρᾶσθαι, καὶ ὅτε
ἤρχοντο τῶν γυμνασίων πρῶτοι μὲν Κρῆτες, | ἔπειτα Λακεδαιμόνιοι, D
ἐξῆν τοῖς τότε ἀστείοις πάντα ταῦτα κωμῳδεῖν. ἢ οὐκ οἴει;

---

452 B 8 **ἤδη** = *demum* adds emphasis to ἀλλὰ καί. We may translate: 'but positively also the older women.' On this use of ἤδη ('now that we have reached this point') and kindred words see Cope *Aristotle's Rhetoric* Vol. I pp. 13 ff. J. and C. (with other editors) suppose a hyperbaton for τὰς ἤδη πρεσβυτέρας (which Herwerden would actually read): but the hyperbaton is harsh, and no parallel has yet been adduced. The rules laid down by Plato in this passage are an exaggeration of Spartan usage: cf. Plut. *Lyc.* 14 and the passages cited by Paley on Eur. *Androm.* 596 ff. Σπαρτιάδων —αἳ ξὺν νέοισιν ἐξερημοῦσαι δόμους | γυμνοῖσι μηροῖς καὶ πέπλοις ἀνειμένοις | δρόμους παλαίστρας τ' οὐκ ἀνασχέτους ἐμοὶ | κοινὰς ἔχουσι, and by Blaydes on Ar. *Lys.* 82: cf. also *Laws* 813 E ff., 833 C ff. and infra 457 A. The words ὅταν ῥυσοί—φιλογυμναστῶσιν are a characteristically Hellenic touch: cf. *Theaet.* 162 B.

12 **τῶν χαριέντων**. It is tempting to see in this an allusion to the author of the *Ecclesiazusae* (with Krohn *Pl. St.* p. 81 and Chiappelli *Riv. di Filol.* XI p. 198). If —with the majority of modern critics—we hold that the *Ecclesiazusae* is earlier than Book V, and if we consider the play as at least in some measure directed against theories on communism and the position of women with which the Socratic school sympathised, it is easy to interpret Plato here as addressing a rebuke to the comic stage in the form of a further challenge. In any case, however, the words οὐ φοβητέον—ὀχήσεις are not a *vaticinium ex eventu*, for the *Ecclesiazusae* does not touch on any of the points specifically mentioned here. See also on 452 D, 455 A, 457 B, 464 B, and 473 E f. In each of these passages there is some *prima facie* ground for suspecting a personal or polemical motive of some kind. See on the whole subject App. I.

452 C 16 **τὰ αὑτῶν πράττειν**: i.e. παίζειν. Herwerden's conjecture τὰ τοιαῦτα παίζειν is both needless and inelegant.

17 **οὐ πολὺς χρόνος κτλ.** Stallbaum cites Hdt. I 10 παρὰ γὰρ τοῖσι Λυδοῖσι, σχεδὸν δὲ καὶ παρὰ τοῖσι ἄλλοισι βαρβάροισι, καὶ ἄνδρα ὀφθῆναι γυμνὸν ἐς αἰσχύνην μεγάλην φέρει, and Thuc. I 6 ἐγυμνώθησάν τε πρῶτοι (Λακεδαιμόνιοι) κτλ.

20 **γυμνασίων** is used in its strict etymological sense of γυμνοὶ ἀγῶνες: we ought not to insert γυμνῶν (with Richards) or τοιούτων (with Herwerden) before γυμνασίων.

πρῶτοι—Κρῆτες. Plato contradicts Thucydides l.c. Cf. [*Minos*] 318 D, where Spartan institutions are derived from Crete, and see Hermann-Thumser *Gr. Staatsalt.* p. 141 *nn.*

Ἔγωγε. Ἀλλ' ἐπειδή, οἶμαι, χρωμένοις ἄμεινον τὸ ἀποδύεσθαι
τοῦ συγκαλύπτειν πάντα τὰ τοιαῦτα ἐφάνη, καὶ τὸ ἐν τοῖς
ὀφθαλμοῖς δὴ γελοῖον ἐξερρύη ὑπὸ τοῦ ἐν τοῖς λόγοις μηνυθέντος
ἀρίστου, καὶ τοῦτο ἐνεδείξατο, ὅτι μάταιος ὃς γελοῖον ἄλλο τι
ἡγεῖται ἢ τὸ κακόν, καὶ ὁ γελωτοποιεῖν ἐπιχειρῶν πρὸς ἄλλην
E τινὰ ὄψιν ἀποβλέπων ὡς γελοίου ἢ τὴν | τοῦ ἄφρονός τε καὶ κακοῦ
καὶ καλοῦ αὖ σπουδάζει πρὸς ἄλλον τινὰ σκοπὸν στησάμενος ἢ
τὸν τοῦ ἀγαθοῦ. Παντάπασι μὲν οὖν, ἔφη.

IV. Ἆρ' οὖν οὐ πρῶτον μὲν τοῦτο περὶ αὐτῶν ἀνομολογητέον,
εἰ δυνατὰ ἢ οὔ, καὶ δοτέον ἀμφισβήτησιν, εἴτε τις φιλοπαίσμων

30. αὐτῶν Ξ*q*: αὐτὸν ΑΠ.

---

452 D 23 **καὶ κτλ.** καί begins the apodosis: 'then too' etc. The general idea is that when experience proved that it was *better* to take exercise in a nude condition, nudity also ceased to be ludicrous. Plato thus prepares the way for the identification to be presently made (see next note). The particle δή ('forsooth') hints that the eye is less trustworthy than the reason; and the contrast is further accentuated by the somewhat artificial balance between ἐν τοῖς ὀφθαλμοῖς and ἐν τοῖς λόγοις. D. and V. wrongly make the apodosis begin with καὶ τοῦτο (where τοῦτο is of course nominative).

25 **μάταιος κτλ.** I have (with the Oxford editors) retained the text of A. It at least affords an intelligible sense, and none of the numerous variants or emendations is at all convincing. The general drift of the passage is clear enough. Nothing is γελοῖον except what is κακόν (μάταιος—κακόν), and, conversely, nothing is σπουδαῖον except what is ἀγαθόν (καὶ καλοῦ—ἀγαθοῦ. σπουδαῖον is involved in σπουδάζει). Both inferences are expressed in such a way as to suggest a personal reference: cf. χαριέντων in B, and see App. I. γελωτοποιεῖν, especially after κωμῳδεῖν just above, points to the comic stage: and Aristophanes is perhaps intended. See on 452 B. The whole sentence means: 'Foolish is the man who identifies the laughable with anything but the bad, and he who attempts to raise a laugh by looking at any spectacle as laughable except the spectacle of folly and evil aims in all seriousness also at another standard of beauty, which he has set up for himself, than the standard of the good.' The analysis of τὸ γελοῖον, so far as it goes, is in harmony with *Phil.* 48 A ff.: cf. especially 49 A. With στησάμενος we must supply αὐτόν, i.e. τὸν σκοπόν. On the difficulties of this passage see App. II.

452 E—**456** C *Let us first determine whether our proposal is possible—in other words, whether woman is naturally able to share the duties of man—all, or none, or some, and, if some, whether war is one of these. It may be argued: 'man's nature is different from that of woman: we should therefore assign them different duties.' A little analysis will shew the superficial and eristic character of such reasoning. The word 'different' is ambiguous. Natures may differ without differing at all in respect of the powers by which certain duties are performed. Consequently, if man and woman differ only in sex, they may each perform those duties in which sex plays no part. Among such duties are those which appertain to the administration of a city. Doubtless man is superior, as a whole, in capacity and strength, although many women excel many men; but the natural aptitudes of individual women are as various as those of men, and there is no administrative duty which is by Nature exclusively appropriated either to men, or to women. Thus Nature produces women who are fitted to guard our city. These we shall select as the wives and colleagues of the male guardians. Our proposal is possible, because it is natural: the term 'unnatural' may sooner be applied to the present condition of women.*

452 E ff. On the principle laid down in this part of Socrates' argument see 451 C ff. *nn.*

εἴτε σπουδαστικὸς ἐθέλει ἀμφισβητῆσαι, πότερον δυνατὴ φύσις
ἡ ἀν|θρωπίνη ἡ θήλεια τῇ τοῦ ἄρρενος γένους κοινωνῆσαι εἰς 453
ἅπαντα τὰ ἔργα, ἢ οὐδ' εἰς ἕν, ἢ εἰς τὰ μὲν οἵα τε, εἰς δὲ τὰ οὔ,
καὶ τοῦτο δὴ τὸ περὶ τὸν πόλεμον ποτέρων ἐστίν; ἆρ' οὐχ οὕτως
ἂν κάλλιστά τις ἀρχόμενος ὡς τὸ εἰκὸς καὶ κάλλιστα τελευτήσειεν;
Πολύ γε, ἔφη. Βούλει οὖν, ἦν δ' ἐγώ, ἡμεῖς πρὸς ἡμᾶς αὐτοὺς
ὑπὲρ τῶν ἄλλων ἀμφισβητήσωμεν, ἵνα μὴ ἔρημα τὰ τοῦ ἑτέρου
λόγου πολιορκῆται; | Οὐδέν, ἔφη, κωλύει. Λέγωμεν δὴ ὑπὲρ B
αὐτῶν ὅτι Ὦ Σώκρατες τε καὶ Γλαύκων, οὐδὲν δεῖ ὑμῖν ἄλλους
ἀμφισβητεῖν· αὐτοὶ γὰρ ἐν ἀρχῇ τῆς κατοικίσεως, ἣν ᾠκίζετε
πόλιν, ὡμολογεῖτε δεῖν κατὰ φύσιν ἕκαστον ἕνα ἓν τὸ αὑτοῦ
πράττειν. Ὡμολογήσαμεν, οἶμαι· πῶς γὰρ οὔ; Ἔστιν οὖν ὅπως
οὐ πάμπολυ διαφέρει γυνὴ ἀνδρὸς τὴν φύσιν; Πῶς δ' οὐ διαφέρει;
Οὐκοῦν ἄλλο καὶ ἔργον ἑκατέρῳ προσήκει προστάττειν τὸ κατὰ
τὴν αὑτοῦ | φύσιν; Τί μήν; Πῶς οὖν οὐχ ἁμαρτάνετε νῦν καὶ C
τἀναντία ὑμῖν αὐτοῖς λέγετε, φάσκοντες αὖ τοὺς ἄνδρας καὶ τὰς
γυναῖκας δεῖν τὰ αὐτὰ πράττειν, πλεῖστον κεχωρισμένην φύσιν
ἔχοντας; ἕξεις τι, ὦ θαυμάσιε, πρὸς ταῦτ' ἀπολογεῖσθαι; Ὡς
μὲν ἐξαίφνης, ἔφη, οὐ πάνυ ῥᾴδιον· ἀλλὰ σοῦ δεήσομαί τε καὶ
δέομαι καὶ τὸν ὑπὲρ ἡμῶν λόγον, ὅστις ποτ' ἐστίν, ἑρμηνεῦσαι.
Ταῦτ' ἔστιν, ἦν δ' ἐγώ, ὦ Γλαύκων, καὶ ἄλλα πολλὰ τοιαῦτα,
ἃ ἐγὼ πάλαι | προορῶν ἐφοβούμην τε καὶ ὤκνουν ἅπτεσθαι τοῦ D
νόμου τοῦ περὶ τὴν τῶν γυναικῶν καὶ παίδων κτῆσιν καὶ τροφήν.
Οὐ μὰ τὸν Δία, ἔφη, οὐ γὰρ εὐκόλῳ ἔοικεν. Οὐ γάρ, εἶπον· ἀλλὰ

---

33 **ἡ ἀνθρωπίνη** was objected to by Cobet; but ἡ θήλεια alone would be too general: we are dealing only with 'female *human* nature.'

453 A 4 **καὶ κάλλιστα.** Dobree conjectured κάλλιστα καί, neatly, but needlessly, for καλὴ τελευτή, like καλὴ ἀρχή, may be treated as a single notion. Cf. III 404 B *n.*

453 B 9 **κατοικίσεως**: sc. τῆς πόλεως, but the antecedent is attracted into the relative clause (ἣν ᾠκίζετε πόλιν), as often: cf. I 350 C *n.*

10 **ὡμολογεῖτε.** II 369 E ff.

12 **πῶς δ' οὐ διαφέρει;** Baiter follows Hirschig in bracketing διαφέρει. The formula πῶς δ' οὔ; is however so common, that no scribe is likely to have added διαφέρει. Cf. διαφέρει in VI 496 A. For the sentiment see Xen. *Oec.* 7. 22 τὴν φύσιν—εὐθὺς παρεσκεύασεν ὁ θεὸς—τὴν μὲν τῆς γυναικὸς ἐπὶ τὰ ἔνδον ἔργα καὶ ἐπιμελήματα, τὴν δὲ τοῦ ἀνδρὸς ἐπὶ τὰ ἔξω ἔργα καὶ ἐπιμελήματα—the orthodox Greek view.

453 D 23 **οὐ γὰρ εὐκόλῳ κτλ.** The MS reading has been defended in two ways. Schneider prints a colon after ἔφη, and explains οὐ μὰ τὸν Δία as "minime, per Jovem, <temere tu et sine causa hanc rem tractare dubitabas>"; but it is exceedingly difficult to supply the words in brackets. This difficulty induced Apelt (*Obs. Crit.* p. 12) to suggest οὐ <μάτην> μὰ τὸν Δία, ἔφη· οὐ γὰρ κτλ. Others explain the oath as emphasizing οὐ γὰρ εὐκόλῳ ἔοικεν, and compare X 605 E οὐ μὰ τὸν Δί', ἔφη, οὐκ εὐλόγῳ ἔοικεν and *Parm.* 131 E οὐ μὰ τὸν Δία, φάναι, οὔ μοι δοκεῖ εὔκολον εἶναι τὸ τοιοῦτον διορίσασθαι. But the whole difficulty centres round γάρ,

δὴ ὧδ' ἔχει· ἄν τέ τις εἰς κολυμβήθραν μικρὰν ἐμπέσῃ, ἄν τε εἰς
τὸ μέγιστον πέλαγος μέσον, ὅμως γε νεῖ οὐδὲν ἧττον. Πάνυ μὲν
οὖν. Οὐκοῦν καὶ ἡμῖν νευστέον καὶ πειρατέον σῴζεσθαι ἐκ τοῦ
λόγου, ἤτοι δελφῖνά τινα ἐλπίζοντας ἡμᾶς ὑπολαβεῖν ἄν, ἤ τινα
E ἄλλην ἄπορον σωτηρίαν. | Ἔοικεν, ἔφη. Φέρε δή, ἦν δ' ἐγώ, ἐάν
πῃ εὕρωμεν τὴν ἔξοδον. ὡμολογοῦμεν γὰρ δὴ ἄλλην φύσιν ἄλλο
δεῖν ἐπιτηδεύειν, γυναικὸς δὲ καὶ ἀνδρὸς ἄλλην εἶναι· τὰς δὲ ἄλλας
φύσεις τὰ αὐτά φαμεν νῦν δεῖν ἐπιτηδεῦσαι. ταῦτα ἡμῶν κατηγο-
454 ρεῖτε; Κομιδῇ γε. Ἦ γενναία, ἦν δ' ἐγώ, ὦ Γλαύκων, ἡ | δύναμις
τῆς ἀντιλογικῆς τέχνης. Τί δή; Ὅτι, εἶπον, δοκοῦσί μοι εἰς
αὐτὴν καὶ ἄκοντες πολλοὶ ἐμπίπτειν καὶ οἴεσθαι οὐκ ἐρίζειν,
ἀλλὰ διαλέγεσθαι, διὰ τὸ μὴ δύνασθαι κατ' εἴδη διαιρούμενοι τὸ

29. ὡμολογοῦμεν Ξ q: ὁμολογοῦμεν ΑΠ.

---

and γάρ is absent from each of these passages. Hartman strangely explains γάρ as 'profecto'; while Stallbaum inclines to cut it out. Groen van Prinsterer (*Prosop. Plat.* p. 209) proposed to read οὐ γὰρ εὐκόλῳ ἔοικεν. Οὐ μὰ τὸν Δία, ἔφη. Οὐ γάρ, εἶπον. It appears to me that the emphatic οὐ μὰ τὸν Δία is more appropriate in the mouth of Socrates, who is continually dwelling on the difficulty of his task, and I therefore think that Plato wrote Οὐ γὰρ εὐκόλῳ ἔοικεν, ἔφη. Οὐ γάρ, εἶπον, οὐ μὰ τὸν Δία, although I have not ventured to change the text. εὐκόλῳ is of course neuter, not masculine, as Richter supposed (*Fl. Jahrb.* 1867 p. 143).

24 **κολυμβήθραν**: a swimming tank. See Blümner *Privatalt.* p. 210 *n.* 2. In what follows we have the first suggestion of the wave metaphor, which dominates nearly the whole of Book V: see on 449 A.

28 **ἄπορον**. As ἄλλην here means 'other' and not 'else,' the epithet ἄπορον ('difficult to procure,' cf. II 378 A) must be applicable to the dolphin also. The Platonic *litotes* seems delicately to suggest that the miraculous story of Arion and the dolphin is not above suspicion. Herwerden conjectured ἄτοπον, but no change is necessary.

453 E 31 **κατηγορεῖτε**. Socrates identifies his audience with the imaginary opponents of 453 A—C, and Glauco replies in their name. As ἡμῶν means primarily Socrates and Glauco (453 B), the situation is somewhat confusing: and some may wish to read κατηγορεῖται, as I formerly printed (with Vind. F, Flor. R T, Ficinus and Hartman). The confusion of ε and αι is of course common (see *Introd.* § 5), but it is better to adhere to the best MSS. Cf. VI 489 B.

454 A 2 **ἀντιλογικῆς τέχνης**. ἀντιλογική is defined in *Soph.* 225 B as a variety of ἀμφισβητητικόν: viz. τὸ ἐν ἰδίοις—opposed to τὸ δικανικόν, which is δημοσίᾳ—αὖ καὶ κατακεκερματισμένον ἐρωτήσεσι πρὸς ἀποκρίσεις. It is described in *Phaedr.* 261 D ff., and practical illustrations are given in the sophisms of *Euthyd.* 275 C ff. The Ἀντιλογικοί are spoken of as almost a distinct sect in Plato's time: see *Lys.* 216 A and Isocr. περὶ ἀντιδόσεως 45 ἄλλοι δέ τινες περὶ τὰς ἐρωτήσεις καὶ τὰς ἀποκρίσεις—οὓς ἀντιλογικοὺς καλοῦσιν. Here Plato probably has in view some of the 'Sophists' (as in VI 499 A) as well as the Megarian school, whose well-known puzzles—ὁ ψευδόμενος, ὁ διαλανθάνων, Ἠλέκτρα, ὁ ἐγκεκαλυμμένος: see D. L. II 108—are excellent examples of verbal fallacies. The same class of people are also called ἐριστικοί and ἀγωνιστικοί: see *Men.* 75 C and cf. *Theaet.* 167 E, *Phil.* 17 A and Isocr. *in Soph.* 20 τῶν περὶ τὰς ἔριδας καλινδουμένων—τοιαῦτα λογίδια διεξιόντες οἷς εἴ τις ἐπὶ τῶν πράξεων ἐμμείνειεν, εὐθὺς ἂν ἐν πᾶσιν εἴη κακοῖς. On the history and place of Eristic in Greek philosophy see E. S. Thompson's elaborate excursus in his edition of the *Meno* pp. 272—285.

4 **κατ' εἴδη διαιρούμενοι**. εἴδη is not of course 'the Ideas': but 'species'

λεγόμενον ἐπισκοπεῖν, ἀλλὰ κατ' αὐτὸ τὸ ὄνομα διώκειν τοῦ
λεχθέντος τὴν ἐναντίωσιν, ἔριδι, οὐ διαλέκτῳ πρὸς ἀλλήλους
χρώμενοι. Ἔστι γὰρ δή, ἔφη, περὶ πολλοὺς τοῦτο τὸ πάθος·
ἀλλὰ μῶν καὶ πρὸς ἡμᾶς τοῦτο τείνει ἐν τῷ παρόντι; Παντάπασι
| μὲν οὖν, ἦν δ' ἐγώ· κινδυνεύομεν γοῦν ἄκοντες ἀντιλογίας ἅπτε- B
σθαι. Πῶς; Τὸ μὴ τὴν αὐτὴν φύσιν ὅτι οὐ τῶν αὐτῶν δεῖ
ἐπιτηδευμάτων τυγχάνειν πάνυ ἀνδρείως τε καὶ ἐριστικῶς κατὰ
τὸ ὄνομα διώκομεν, ἐπεσκεψάμεθα δὲ οὐδ' ὁπῃοῦν, τί εἶδος τὸ τῆς
ἑτέρας τε καὶ τῆς αὐτῆς φύσεως καὶ πρὸς τί τεῖνον ὡριζόμεθα
τότε, ὅτε τὰ ἐπιτηδεύματα ἄλλῃ φύσει ἄλλα, τῇ δὲ αὐτῇ τὰ αὐτὰ
ἀπεδίδομεν. Οὐ γὰρ οὖν, ἔφη, ἐπεσκεψάμεθα. | Τοιγάρτοι, εἶπον, C
ἔξεστιν ἡμῖν, ὡς ἔοικεν, ἀνερωτᾶν ἡμᾶς αὐτούς, εἰ ἡ αὐτὴ φύσις
φαλακρῶν καὶ κομητῶν καὶ οὐχ ἡ ἐναντία, καὶ ἐπειδὰν ὁμολογῶμεν
ἐναντίαν εἶναι, ἐὰν φαλακροὶ σκυτοτομῶσιν, μὴ ἐᾶν κομήτας, ἐὰν
δ' αὖ κομῆται, μὴ τοὺς ἑτέρους. Γελοῖον μέντ' ἂν εἴη, ἔφη. Ἆρα
κατ' ἄλλο τι, εἶπον ἐγώ, γελοῖον, ἢ ὅτι τότε οὐ πάντως τὴν αὐτὴν

10. μὴ Ξ: om. AΠ*q*.

'kinds': cf. *Pol.* 285 A κατ' εἴδη—διαιρουμένους and *Soph.* 253 D κατὰ γένη διαιρεῖσθαι. That κατὰ γένη (s. εἴδη) διαλέγειν is the peculiar province of dialectic was the view of Socrates as well as of Plato: see Xen. *Mem.* IV 5. 12 ἔφη δὲ καὶ τὸ διαλέγεσθαι ὀνομασθῆναι ἐκ τοῦ συνιόντας κοινῇ βουλεύεσθαι διαλέγοντας κατὰ γένη τὰ πράγματα. See also on III 402 C.

5 **κατ' αὐτὸ—ἐναντίωσιν**: lit. 'pursue the contradiction of what has been said according to the name and nothing more' i.e. 'aim at the merely verbal contradiction of what has been said.' We are told by Clement (*Strom.* II 7. 968 B ed. Migne) that Critolaus called such persons ὀνοματομάχοι. With διώκειν ἐναντίωσιν cf. III 410 B γυμναστικὴν διώκειν. The implied antithesis to κατ' αὐτὸ τὸ ὄνομα is κατ' αὐτὸ τὸ πρᾶγμα: cf. *Soph.* 218 C δεῖ δὲ ἀεὶ παντὸς πέρι τὸ πρᾶγμα αὐτὸ μᾶλλον διὰ λόγων ἢ τοὔνομα μόνον συνομολογήσασθαι χωρὶς λόγου.

6 **ἔριδι—διαλέκτῳ**: a common opposition: cf. *Men.* 75 C ff. and *Phil.* 17 A.

454 B 10 **τὸ μὴ τὴν αὐτὴν κτλ.** See *cr. n.* The omission of μή was perhaps due to the erroneous idea that διώκομεν below meant 'to attack.' In reality, it means 'we are pursuing' (the proposition that), i.e. 'we are insisting that.' The way for this somewhat strained use is prepared by διώκειν τὴν ἐναντίωσιν just above. Plato is in fact applying the expression τοῦ λεχθέντος τὴν ἐναντίωσιν to the special case before us. τὸ λεχθέν would in this case be that 'different natures are to follow the same pursuits' (453 E τὰς ἄλλας φύσεις τὰ αὐτά φαμεν νῦν δεῖν ἐπιτηδεῦσαι). Its ἐναντίωσις is that 'different natures are not to have the same pursuits.' For τὴν αὐτήν we must therefore read either <μὴ> τὴν αὐτήν or else τὴν ἄλλην (with Baiter). I prefer the former, both because it has some MS authority, and also because, if Plato had chosen to use ἄλλος, he would probably have written τὰς ἄλλας φύσεις as in 453 E. It is also true, as J. and C. observe, that "the opposition of μὴ τὴν αὐτήν, οὐ τῶν αὐτῶν is more like Plato than the conjectural reading τὴν ἄλλην." Translate 'we cling to the verbal point and insist that what is *not* the same nature ought *not* to have the same pursuits.'

454 C 16 **ὡς ἔοικεν** marks the irony. For ἡ ἐναντία in the next line a few MSS have ἐναντία, which Hartman approves. If ἡ αὐτή were predicative, Plato would have written ἐναντία, but, as it is, ἡ ἐναντία is correct, being, like ἡ αὐτὴ φύσις, the subject to an ἐστίν understood.

καὶ τὴν ἑτέραν φύσιν ἐτιθέμεθα, ἀλλ' ἐκεῖνο τὸ εἶδος τῆς ἀλλοιώ-
D σεώς τε καὶ ὁμοιώσεως μόνον | ἐφυλάττομεν, τὸ πρὸς αὐτὰ τεῖνον τὰ ἐπιτηδεύματα; οἷον ἰατρικὸν μὲν καὶ ἰατρικὸν τὴν αὐτὴν φύσιν ἔχειν ἐλέγομεν· ἢ οὐκ οἴει; Ἔγωγε. Ἰατρικὸν δὲ καὶ τεκτονικὸν ἄλλην; Πάντως που.

V. Οὐκοῦν, ἦν δ' ἐγώ, καὶ τὸ τῶν ἀνδρῶν καὶ τὸ τῶν γυναικῶν γένος, ἐὰν μὲν πρὸς τέχνην τινὰ ἢ ἄλλο ἐπιτήδευμα διαφέρον φαίνηται, τοῦτο δὴ φήσομεν ἑκατέρῳ δεῖν ἀποδιδόναι· ἐὰν δ' αὐτῷ τούτῳ φαίνηται διαφέρειν, τῷ τὸ μὲν θῆλυ τίκτειν, τὸ δὲ ἄρρεν
E ὀχεύειν, οὐδέν τί | πω φήσομεν μᾶλλον ἀποδεδεῖχθαι, ὡς πρὸς ὃ ἡμεῖς λέγομεν διαφέρει γυνὴ ἀνδρός, ἀλλ' ἔτι οἰησόμεθα δεῖν τὰ αὐτὰ ἐπιτηδεύειν τούς τε φύλακας ἡμῖν καὶ τὰς γυναῖκας αὐτῶν. Καὶ ὀρθῶς, ἔφη. Οὐκοῦν μετὰ τοῦτο κελεύομεν τὸν τὰ ἐναντία

21. *καὶ τὴν* Π et in mg. A²: om. A¹. 22. *τὸ—τεῖνον τὰ* *q* cum Galeno v p. 738 ed. Kühn: *τὰ—τείνοντα* ΑΠ et in mg. *γρ* Ξ²: *τὸ—τεῖνον* Ξ¹. 23. *ἰατρικὸν μὲν* A²Π: *ἰατρικῶν μὲν* A¹. *ἰατρικὸν* nos: *ἰατρικὴν τὴν ψυχὴν ὄντα* ΑΠ: *ἰατρικὸν τὴν ψυχὴν ὄντα* *q*: *τὴν ψυχὴν ὄντα* Ξ, omisso *καὶ ἰατρικόν*.

---

454 D 22 **πρὸς—τεῖνον** corresponds to *πρὸς τί τεῖνον* in B above. On the corruption in A see *Introd.* § 5.

23 **ἰατρικὸν κτλ.** Plato is illustrating that particular variety of *ὁμοίωσις* and *ἀλλοίωσις* which *πρὸς αὐτὰ τείνει τὰ ἐπιτηδεύματα*. As an instance of *ὁμοίωσις* he gives two *ἰατρικοί* (cf. I 350 A): these clearly have the same nature *πρὸς αὐτὰ τὰ ἐπιτηδεύματα*, i.e. in this case *πρὸς τὸ ἰατρεύεσθαι*. *ἀλλοίωσις* he illustrates by the difference between an *ἰατρικός* and a *τεκτονικός*: these have different natures *πρὸς τὰ ἐπιτηδεύματα*, for the one is qualified *ἰατρεύεσθαι*, the other *τεκταίνεσθαι*. Nothing could be more clear; but the text has been plunged into confusion by the introduction of the words *τὴν ψυχὴν ὄντα* after the second *ἰατρικόν*. The reading of A—see *cr. n.*—is indefensible; and the majority of recent editors print *ἰατρικὸν μὲν καὶ ἰατρικὸν τὴν ψυχὴν ὄντα* with *q*. But *τὴν ψυχὴν ὄντα* adds nothing to *ἰατρικόν*. It has indeed been thought that *ἰατρικόν* by itself suggests a doctor in actual practice, whereas an *ἰατρικὸς τὴν ψυχήν* need not practise. If so, we may fairly doubt whether the two have the same nature; and at all events the difference between them renders them inapt illustrations of Plato's argument. Jowett and Campbell attempt to escape these difficulties by taking *τὴν ψυχὴν ὄντα* with the first *ἰατρικόν* as well as with the second; but the Greek does not permit of this solution. Similar objections apply to the readings of Bekker (and apparently Ficinus) *ἰατρὸν μὲν καὶ ἰατρικὸν τὴν ψυχὴν ὄντα*, of Stephanus and other early editors *ἰατρικὸν μὲν καὶ ἰατρικὴν τὴν ψυχὴν ἔχοντα* (partly supported by Θ), and also, with some modifications, to Richards' otherwise unhappy proposal *ἰατρικὸν μὲν καὶ ἰατρικὸν* <*εὐφυᾶ*> *τὴν ψυχὴν ὄντα*. Hermann reads *ἰατρικὸν μὲν καὶ ἰατρικὴν τὴν ψυχὴν ὄντας*, but the introduction of women is of course premature. I regard *τὴν ψυχὴν ὄντα* as a relic of *ἰατρὸν τὴν ψυχὴν ὄντα*, a marginal annotation on *ἰατρικόν*. Cf. *Introd.* § 5.

24 **ἐλέγομεν**: 'we were saying,' i.e. 'we meant.' Nothing of the sort was actually said before.

27 **διαφέρον**: 'excelling' rather than 'differing' (D. and V.): hence *τοῦτο δὴ—ἀποδιδόναι*. Richards proposes *διαφέρειν*, to avoid the singular. But the subjects are distributed, as appears from *καὶ τό—καὶ τό*, as well as from *ἑκατέρῳ*; and the infinitive is somewhat less suitable here than it is below. Translate 'if either the male or the female sex plainly excels the other' etc.

454 E 33 **οὐκοῦν κτλ.** 'Is not our next step to invite?' &c. Ξ reads *κελεύωμεν*, which may be right, but the

λέγοντα τοῦτο αὐτὸ δι|δάσκειν ἡμᾶς, πρὸς τίνα τέχνην ἢ τί 455
ἐπιτήδευμα τῶν περὶ πόλεως κατασκευὴν οὐχ ἡ αὐτή, ἀλλὰ ἑτέρα φύσις γυναικός τε καὶ ἀνδρός; Δίκαιον γοῦν. Τάχα τοίνυν ἄν, ὅπερ σὺ ὀλίγον πρότερον ἔλεγες, εἴποι ἂν καὶ ἄλλος, ὅτι ἐν μὲν τῷ παραχρῆμα ἱκανῶς εἰπεῖν οὐ ῥᾴδιον, ἐπισκεψαμένῳ δὲ οὐδὲν χαλεπόν. Εἴποι γὰρ ἄν. Βούλει οὖν δεώμεθα τοῦ τὰ τοιαῦτα ἀντιλέγοντος ἀκολουθῆσαι ἡμῖν, ἐάν πως ἡμεῖς | ἐκείνῳ ἐνδειξώμεθα, B
ὅτι οὐδέν ἐστιν ἐπιτήδευμα ἴδιον γυναικὶ πρὸς διοίκησιν πόλεως; Πάνυ γε. Ἴθι δή, φήσομεν πρὸς αὐτόν, ἀποκρίνου· ἆρα οὕτως ἔλεγες τὸν μὲν εὐφυῆ πρός τι εἶναι, τὸν δὲ ἀφυῆ, ἐν ᾧ ὁ μὲν ῥᾳδίως τι μανθάνοι, ὁ δὲ χαλεπῶς, καὶ ὁ μὲν ἀπὸ βραχείας μαθήσεως ἐπὶ πολὺ εὑρετικὸς εἴη οὗ ἔμαθεν, ὁ δὲ πολλῆς μαθήσεως τυχὼν καὶ μελέτης μηδ᾽ ἃ ἔμαθε σῴζοιτο, καὶ τῷ μὲν τὰ τοῦ σώματος ἱκανῶς
| ὑπηρετοῖ τῇ διανοίᾳ, τῷ δὲ ἐναντιοῖτο; ἆρ᾽ ἄλλα ἄττα ἐστὶν ᾗ C
ταῦτα, οἷς τὸν εὐφυῆ πρὸς ἕκαστα καὶ τὸν μὴ ὡρίζου; Οὐδείς, ἦ δ᾽ ὅς, ἄλλα φήσει. Οἶσθά τι οὖν ὑπὸ ἀνθρώπων μελετώμενον, ἐν ᾧ οὐ πάντα ταῦτα τὸ τῶν ἀνδρῶν γένος διαφερόντως ἔχει ἢ τὸ τῶν γυναικῶν; ἢ μακρολογῶμεν τήν τε ὑφαντικὴν λέγοντες καὶ τὴν τῶν ποπάνων τε καὶ ἑψημάτων θεραπείαν, ἐν οἷς δή τι δοκεῖ
| τὸ γυναικεῖον γένος εἶναι, οὗ καὶ καταγελαστότατόν ἐστι πάντων D
ἡττώμενον; Ἀληθῆ, ἔφη, λέγεις, ὅτι πολὺ κρατεῖται ἐν ἅπασιν ὡς ἔπος εἰπεῖν τὸ γένος τοῦ γένους. γυναῖκες μέντοι πολλαὶ

---

indicative is quite defensible. With τὸν τὰ ἐναντία λέγοντα cf. infra 455 A. It is not likely that a specific allusion to Aristophanes is here intended (see Chiappelli *Riv. di Filolog.* XI p. 200), but there is some plausibility in the conjecture that the coming argument may be inspired in some measure by the *Ecclesiazusae*, where the essentially domestic qualities of women are contrasted with their incapacity for government. See App. I.

455 A 4 **ὀλίγον πρότερον.** 453 C.

6 **τοῦ—ἀντιλέγοντος.** 454 E *n.*

455 C 18 **ἢ μακρολογῶμεν κτλ.** Socrates is unwilling to bore us (μακρολογεῖν) by enumerating the exceptions, which are —he implies—quite trivial. Cf. Xen. *Mem.* III 9. 11 ἐν δὲ ταλασίᾳ καὶ τὰς γυναῖκας ἐπεδείκνυεν ἀρχούσας τῶν ἀνδρῶν, διὰ τὸ τὰς μὲν εἰδέναι ὅπως χρὴ ταλασιουργεῖν, τοὺς δὲ μὴ εἰδέναι. It is hinted in οὗ—ἡττώμενον that, even in these, women may sometimes be excelled by men; but the general rule was the other way, otherwise the ridicule would be pointless. Grote somewhat exaggerates the significance of the clause οὗ —ἡττώμενον, when he suggests that Plato may have seen finer webs in Egypt— where weaving was performed by men— than in Greece (Plato III p. 200 *n.*). Cf. Proclus *in remp.* I pp. 242, 253 ed. Kroll.

455 D 21 **κρατεῖται** is construed like ἡττᾶται, μειοῦται, νικᾶται and the like; but a parallel instance is hard to find. (In Aeschin. *F. L.* 152, cited by J. and C., the reading is ποίᾳ κρατηθεὶς ἡδονῇ;). Richards proposes κρατεῖ, in which case τὸ γένος would be the male sex—an awkward change of subject.

22 **ὡς ἔπος εἰπεῖν.** See I 341 B *n.* The sentiment is illustrated by J. and C. from *Crat.* 392 C πότερον οὖν αἱ γυναῖκες ἐν ταῖς πόλεσιν φρονιμώτεραί σοι δοκοῦσιν εἶναι ἢ οἱ ἄνδρες, ὡς τὸ ὅλον εἰπεῖν γένος; Οἱ ἄνδρες.

πολλῶν ἀνδρῶν βελτίους εἰς πολλά· τὸ δὲ ὅλον ἔχει ὡς σὺ λέγεις. Οὐδὲν ἄρα ἐστίν, ὦ φίλε, ἐπιτήδευμα τῶν πόλιν διοικούντων γυναικὸς διότι γυνή, οὐδ᾽ ἀνδρὸς διότι ἀνήρ, ἀλλ᾽ ὁμοίως διεσπαρμέναι αἱ φύσεις ἐν ἀμφοῖν τοῖν ζῴοιν, καὶ πάντων μὲν μετέχει
E γυνὴ ἐπιτηδευμάτων κατὰ φύσιν, πάντων δὲ ἀνήρ, ἐπὶ πᾶσι δὲ ἀσθενέστερον γυνὴ ἀνδρός. Πάνυ γε. Ἦ οὖν ἀνδράσι πάντα προστάξομεν, γυναικὶ δ᾽ οὐδέν; Καὶ πῶς; Ἀλλ᾽ ἔστι γάρ, οἶμαι, ὡς φήσομεν, καὶ γυνὴ ἰατρική, ἡ δ᾽ οὔ, καὶ μουσική, ἡ δ᾽ ἄμουσος
456 φύσει. Τί μήν; Γυμναστικὴ δ᾽ ἄρα οὔ, οὐδὲ πολεμική, ἡ δὲ ἀπόλεμος καὶ οὐ φιλογυμναστική; Οἶμαι ἔγωγε. Τί δέ; φιλόσοφός τε καὶ μισόσοφος; καὶ θυμοειδής, ἡ δ᾽ ἄθυμος; Ἔστι καὶ ταῦτα. Ἔστιν ἄρα καὶ φυλακικὴ γυνή, ἡ δ᾽ οὔ. ἢ οὐ τοιαύτην καὶ τῶν ἀνδρῶν τῶν φυλακικῶν φύσιν ἐξελεξάμεθα; Τοιαύτην μὲν οὖν. Καὶ γυναικὸς ἄρα καὶ ἀνδρὸς ἡ αὐτὴ φύσις εἰς φυλακὴν πόλεως, πλὴν ὅσα ἀσθενεστέρα ἢ ἰσχυροτέρα ἐστίν. Φαίνεται.

B VI. Καὶ γυναῖκες ἄρα αἱ τοιαῦται τοῖς τοιούτοις ἀνδράσιν ἐκλεκτέαι συνοικεῖν τε καὶ συμφυλάττειν, ἐπείπερ εἰσὶν ἱκαναὶ καὶ ξυγγενεῖς αὐτοῖς τὴν φύσιν. Πάνυ γε. Τὰ δ᾽ ἐπιτηδεύματα οὐ

29. προστάξομεν A²Ξ*q*: προστάξωμεν A¹Π. 7. ἢ ἰσχυροτέρα Π: ἰσχυροτέρα A¹: ἰσχυροτέρας A².

---

26 **πάντων μὲν κτλ.** Plato, in short, makes government a question of capacity, and not of sex. With what follows cf. the passages cited above on 451 C. For the relative weakness of woman cf. infra 457 A and *Laws* 781 A.

455 E 27 **ἐπὶ πᾶσι** is doubted by Herwerden, who proposes ἐν πᾶσι or ἐν ἅπασι. ἐπί may however mean 'with a view to,' 'for,' as in 471 A.

30 **ἡ δ᾽ οὔ.** ἡ μέν is idiomatically omitted: see 451 D *n.*

31 **ἄρα** is better, I think, than ἆρα, though somewhat more difficult: the interrogative ἆρα is moreover generally elided before οὐ. The sentence (as J. and C. remark) is "an ironical negation with an interrogative tone." The irony in this passage lies in ἄρα. As might be expected from the accumulation of negatives, late MSS shew a great variety of readings. Bekker follows *q* and reads καὶ γυμναστικὴ ἄρα καὶ πολεμική—an obvious but wholly superfluous attempt to simplify the authoritative text.

456 A 7 **πλὴν ὅσα κτλ.** For ὅσα Eusebius (*Praep. Ev.* XII 32. 5) read ὅσῳ followed by ἀσθενεστέρα, ἡ δὲ ἰσχυροτέρα ἐστί, and the dative was also preferred by Schneider (*Addit.* p. 38). The neuter plural of ὅσος is however used adverbially as well as the neuter singular; and the dative of 'amount of difference' is scarcely to the point. Instead of ἀσθενεστέρα ἢ ἰσχυροτέρα we might read (with A²) ἀσθενεστέρα ἰσχυροτέρας. But the reading in the text is preferable, because it lays more stress on the identity of the male and female nature. It is the same nature, only it is stronger in men, and weaker in women. ἤ = 'or' and not 'than.'

456 B 10 **ξυγγενεῖς—τὴν φύσιν.** J. and C. remark that "in the *Politicus* and *Laws*, on the other hand, the aim of the legislator is rather to unite in marriage opposite natures that they may supplement each other: *Pol.* 309, 310, *Laws* 773 ff." Such a marriage law is unnecessary in the *Republic*, where the opposite qualities of strength and sensibility are already united in the character of each of the parents. See on II 375 C.

τὰ αὐτὰ ἀποδοτέα ταῖς αὐταῖς φύσεσιν; Τὰ αὐτά. Ἥκομεν ἄρα εἰς τὰ πρότερα περιφερόμενοι, καὶ ὁμολογοῦμεν μὴ παρὰ φύσιν εἶναι ταῖς τῶν φυλάκων γυναιξὶ μουσικήν τε καὶ γυμναστικὴν ἀποδιδόναι. Παντάπασιν μὲν οὖν. Οὐκ ἄρα | ἀδύνατά γε οὐδὲ **C** εὐχαῖς ὅμοια ἐνομοθετοῦμεν, ἐπείπερ κατὰ φύσιν ἐτίθεμεν τὸν νόμον· ἀλλὰ τὰ νῦν παρὰ ταῦτα γιγνόμενα παρὰ φύσιν μᾶλλον, ὡς ἔοικε, γίγνεται. Ἔοικεν. Οὐκοῦν ἡ ἐπίσκεψις ἡμῖν ἦν, εἰ δυνατά τε καὶ βέλτιστα λέγοιμεν; Ἦν γάρ. Καὶ ὅτι μὲν δὴ δυνατά, διωμολόγηται; Ναί. Ὅτι δὲ δὴ βέλτιστα, τὸ μετὰ τοῦτο δεῖ διομολογηθῆναι; Δῆλον. Οὐκοῦν πρός γε τὸ φυλακικὴν γυναῖκα γενέσθαι οὐκ ἄλλη μὲν ἡμῖν ἄνδρας ποιήσει παιδεία, ἄλλη δὲ γυναῖκας, ἄλλως τε καὶ | τὴν αὐτὴν φύσιν παραλαβοῦσα; **D** Οὐκ ἄλλη. Πῶς οὖν ἔχεις δόξης τοῦ τοιοῦδε πέρι; Τίνος δή; Τοῦ ὑπολαμβάνειν παρὰ σεαυτῷ τὸν μὲν ἀμείνω ἄνδρα, τὸν δὲ χείρω· ἢ πάντας ὁμοίους ἡγεῖ; Οὐδαμῶς. Ἐν οὖν τῇ πόλει, ἣν ᾠκίζομεν, πότερον οἴει ἡμῖν ἀμείνους ἄνδρας ἐξειργάσθαι τοὺς φύλακας τυχόντας ἧς διήλθομεν παιδείας, ἢ τοὺς σκυτοτόμους τῇ σκυτικῇ παιδευθέντας; Γελοῖον, ἔφη, ἐρωτᾷς. Μανθάνω, ἔφην. τί δέ; τῶν ἄλλων πολιτῶν | οὐχ οὗτοι ἄριστοι; Πολύ γε. Τί δέ; **E** αἱ γυναῖκες τῶν γυναικῶν οὐχ αὗται ἔσονται βέλτισται; Καὶ τοῦτο, ἔφη, πολύ. Ἔστι δέ τι πόλει ἄμεινον ἢ γυναῖκάς τε καὶ ἄνδρας ὡς ἀρίστους ἐγγίγνεσθαι; Οὐκ ἔστιν. Τοῦτο δὲ μουσική τε καὶ γυμναστικὴ παραγιγνόμεναι, ὡς ἡμεῖς | διήλθομεν, ἀπεργά- **457** σονται; Πῶς δ' οὔ; Οὐ μόνον ἄρα δυνατόν, ἀλλὰ καὶ ἄριστον πόλει νόμιμον ἐτίθεμεν. Οὕτως. Ἀποδυτέον δὴ ταῖς τῶν φυλάκων

18. τε Flor. T: γε ΑΠΞ *q*.

---

456 C 15 **εὐχαῖς ὅμοια.** Cf. 450 D *n.* **κατὰ φύσιν.** 449 A *nn.* Plato's proposals—so he asserts—are 'natural,' because in harmony with the natural endowments of gifted women; and it is because they are natural that he calls them possible. The definition of *δυνατόν* is interesting and noteworthy: see 466 D and 471 C *n.* Grote (*Plato* III p. 201) has observed that Plato is here refuting a current objection to his theories: in the next sentence he turns his adversaries' weapon against themselves.

17 **ἦν.** 452 E.

456 C—**457** B *It remains to prove that our policy is the best for the State. We are agreed that the training which qualifies a man to be a guardian will qualify a woman also, if their natural capacities are the same to start with. Now our male guardians, owing to their education, are the best men in the city. Our female guardians will in like manner be the best women. And there is nothing better for a city than to be peopled by the best women and the best men. This end is secured by our system of education. Therefore our women must strip for athletic exercises, and share all the labours of guardianship, in spite of the foolish laughter of those who forget that utility is the true standard of good taste.*

γυναιξίν, ἐπείπερ ἀρετὴν ἀντὶ ἱματίων ἀμφιέσονται, καὶ κοινωνητέον πολέμου τε καὶ τῆς ἄλλης φυλακῆς τῆς περὶ τὴν πόλιν, καὶ οὐκ ἄλλα πρακτέον· τούτων δ' αὐτῶν τὰ ἐλαφρότερα ταῖς γυναιξὶν
B ἢ τοῖς ἀνδράσι δοτέον διὰ τὴν τοῦ γένους | ἀσθένειαν. ὁ δὲ γελῶν ἀνὴρ ἐπὶ γυμναῖς γυναιξί, τοῦ βελτίστου ἕνεκα γυμναζομέναις, ἀτελῆ τοῦ γελοίου δρέπων καρπόν, οὐδὲν οἶδεν, ὡς ἔοικεν, ἐφ' ᾧ γελᾷ οὐδ' ὅ τι πράττει. κάλλιστα γὰρ δὴ τοῦτο καὶ λέγεται

9. γελοίου J. G. S. Schneider: γελοίου σοφίας codd.

---

457 A 4 **ἀρετὴν—ἀμφιέσονται**: 'they will clothe themselves with excellence instead of garments,' viz. by thus stripping for exercise, because τοῦ βελτίστου ἕνεκα γυμνάζονται: see B below. Jowett's translation "for their virtue will be their robe" is incorrect, and would require the future perfect instead of ἀμφιέσονται. The correct explanation is given by Schneider on p. 300 of his translation. ἀμφιέσονται (for the usual Attic ἀμφιοῦνται, which Herwerden would write) has a certain archaic effect (cf. I 330 B *n.*), and the saying may be borrowed or adapted from some earlier author. The same metaphor is found in Plutarch *Praec. Coniug.* 10. 139 C τοὐναντίον γὰρ ἡ σώφρων ἀντενδύεται τὴν αἰδῶ (with reference to Hdt. I 8, a passage which is hardly likely—as Ast supposed—to have suggested Plato's phrase), but Plutarch's meaning is different from Plato's. So—except for the metaphor—is Tennyson's in the line quoted by Warren from *Godiva* "Then she rode forth, clothed on with chastity."

κοινωνητέον πολέμου κτλ. The wives of the Sauromatae are described by Herodotus (IV 116) as ἐπὶ θήρην ἐπ' ἵππων ἐκφοιτέουσαι ἅμα τοῖσι ἀνδράσι καὶ χωρὶς τῶν ἀνδρῶν, καὶ ἐς πόλεμον φοιτέουσαι καὶ στολὴν τὴν αὐτὴν τοῖσι ἀνδράσι φορέουσαι. Cf. also *Laws* 804 E—806 B. See also on 451 C ff.

7 **δοτέον.** There is no reason whatever for thinking (as some critics have thought) that Plato is not serious in making these regulations. Stobaeus (*Flor.* 43. 100) has ἀποδοτέον: but see 452 A *n.*

457 B 7 **γελῶν ἀνήρ.** ἀνήρ is said with a fine touch of scorn. It is difficult to read this passage without suspecting a personal reference, perhaps to some representative of the comic stage. J. and C. remark that jests of the kind objected to by Plato occur in Ar. *Lys.* 80—83. See also next note and App. I. Spartan precedents are cited by Hermann-Thumser *Gr. Staatsalt.* p. 180 *n.* 3.

9 **ἀτελῆ—καρπόν**: 'plucking unripe fruit of laughter.' Pindar (*Fr.* 209 Bergk) satirised physical speculation (τοὺς φυσιολογοῦντας) in the words ἀτελῆ σοφίας δρέπων καρπόν, where σοφίας is a defining genitive, denoting not the tree, but the fruit. Pindar means that their σοφία is ἀτελής or inconsummate—misses its mark—is no real σοφία at all. *More suo* Plato adapts the Pindaric fragment to his own purpose. The object of his attack is Comedy, and Comedy cultivates, not σοφία, but τὸ γελοῖον. Hence—according to the reading of the text—Plato replaces Pindar's σοφίας by the words τοῦ γελοίου. The humour of his adversary is ἀτελές or inconsummate—no real humour at all: for οὐδὲν οἶδεν—ἐφ' ᾧ γελᾷ οὐδ' ὅ τι πράττει. Cf. 452 D μάταιος ὃς γελοῖον ἄλλο τι ἡγεῖται ἢ τὸ κακόν. This interpretation assumes that σοφίας in Plato is a gloss interpolated to complete the quotation. See *cr. n.* and App. III.

10 **κάλλιστα κτλ.** The doctrine of this famous sentence, which sounds like a manifesto, and was characteristically selected by Grote as one of the mottoes to his *Plato*, is essentially Socratic: see especially Xen. *Mem.* IV 6. 8, 9 and other passages quoted by Zeller[4] II 1. pp. 149—153. Utilitarianism of this kind pervades the *Republic*, as Krohn has amply proved (*Pl. St.* p. 370), and asserts itself even in the highest flights of Plato's idealism (ἡ τοῦ ἀγαθοῦ ἰδέα—ᾗ δίκαια καὶ τἆλλα προσχρησάμενα χρήσιμα καὶ ὠφέλιμα γίγνεται VI 505 A). But even Socrates ennobles his utilitarianism by placing soul far above body in dignity and worth. In Plato utilitarianism becomes transfigured by Idealism and the doctrine of Immortality. Here it should be noted that καλόν

καὶ λελέξεται, ὅτι τὸ μὲν ὠφέλιμον καλόν, τὸ δὲ βλαβερὸν αἰσχρόν. Παντάπασι μὲν οὖν.

VII. Τοῦτο μὲν τοίνυν ἓν ὥσπερ κῦμα φῶμεν διαφεύγειν τοῦ

---

combines, as often, the ideas of artistic fitness or propriety, and propriety of conduct. The moral sense of the Greeks lay in their appreciation of the beautiful.

457 B—**458** B *Thus do we successfully evade one of the waves which threatened us, but a more formidable wave is now approaching. The women and children are to belong to all the guardians in common. No one shall know his father or his child. That such a state of society is both possible and beneficial, we shall have to prove; but for the present, we will assume its possibility, and try to shew that community of wives and children is the best of all policies for the city and its guardians.*

457 B ff. We now confront the second wave (see 449 A ff. *n.*). The Platonic doctrine of community in wives and children, as a certain critic drily remarks, has been more often censured than understood. The object of the present note is not to sit in judgment upon Plato, but to endeavour to explain his attitude on this subject. In its general aspect, the theory should be regarded as an extreme development of the Naturalism prevailing in Books II—IV: see on II 370 A f. and supra 451 C ff. Several precedents have been cited from the institutions of various primitive peoples who were sometimes regarded by the Greeks as types of 'natural' societies, as for example the Scythians (see on 463 C and other references in Pöhlmann *Gesch. d. antik. Kommunismus etc.* pp. 121 ff., with Newman's *Politics of Aristotle* Vol. II p. 282 and especially Riese's interesting tract on *Die Idealisirung der Naturvölker d. Nordens in d. gr. u. röm. Literatur* 1875), and even Sparta, a State which was constantly extolled by Greek political theorists as a model of the κατὰ φύσιν οἰκισθεῖσα πόλις (Pöhlmann l.c. pp. 125 ff., Grote *Plato* III p. 209 f.), furnished some parallels to the Platonic communism in this respect (Plut. *Lyc.* 15. 9—11, Xen. *Rep. Lac.* 1. 8, 9). But Plato's real motive in advocating his theory is simply and solely the good of the commonwealth (462 A). On the one hand, he dreaded the effect of domestic ties in encouraging selfishness and weakening the bonds of civic obligation; and, with his customary disregard of the limitations of ordinary human nature, he expected his citizens to transfer the domestic affections, without surrendering aught of their intensity, from the family to the State. We may therefore truly say that Plato's intention was not to abolish the family, but rather to enlarge its borders and make it coincident with the State. "Die Sonderfamilie," as Nohle remarks (*die Statslehre Platos* etc. p. 133), "wird nur aufgehoben, damit das Ganze eine grosse Familie sei." On the other hand, he was profoundly impressed with the necessity of restricting the population, and at the same time maintaining and improving the breed of guardians, and the measures which he here prescribes are to a large extent devised with a view to securing these ends (459 A—461 E). In this respect Plato might fairly hope that his proposals would not be abhorrent to a nation whose idea of marriage was primarily only a legalised union for the procreation of legitimate children. It may be argued that Plato sacrifices more than he gains, even if we judge him from the standpoint of his own political idealism, but it shews a complete misapprehension of the situation to charge him with deliberate encouragement of vice: the community of wives and children "hat mit 'freier Liebe' nichts zu thun" (Pöhlmann l.c. p. 280). Finally, we should remember that it is only the Guardians and Auxiliaries who are subject to these rules (see on III 417 A), and that in the second-best city depicted in the *Laws* Plato revives the institution of marriage, as we understand the word, without, however, surrendering in the smallest degree his earlier ideal (807 B). Perhaps the wisest and most temperate discussion on Plato's conception of marriage and the family is that of Grote (*Plato* III pp. 220—234). Some judicious remarks will also be found in Jowett *Introduction* pp. clxxxi—cxciv, and Nettleship *Lectures and Remains* II pp. 174—180: but Jowett goes beyond the province of the interpreter, and lays too much stress on the antagonism between the views of Plato and those of modern civilised communities. See also on 458 E and App. I ad fin.

13 **διαφεύγειν.** The present is less

γυναικείου πέρι νόμου λέγοντες, ὥστε μὴ παντάπασι κατακλυσθῆ- C ναι τιθέντας ὡς δεῖ κοινῇ πάντα ἐπιτηδεύειν τούς τε φύλακας ἡμῖν καὶ τὰς φυλακίδας, ἀλλά πῃ τὸν λόγον αὐτὸν αὑτῷ ὁμολογεῖσθαι, ὡς δυνατά τε καὶ ὠφέλιμα λέγει; Καὶ μάλα, ἔφη, οὐ σμικρὸν κῦμα διαφεύγεις. Φήσεις γε, ἦν δ' ἐγώ, οὐ μέγα αὐτὸ εἶναι, ὅταν τὸ μετὰ τοῦτο ἴδῃς. Λέγε δή, ἴδω, ἔφη. Τούτῳ, ἦν δ' ἐγώ, ἕπεται νόμος καὶ τοῖς ἔμπροσθεν τοῖς ἄλλοις, ὡς ἐγᾦμαι, ὅδε. Τίς; Τὰς γυναῖκας ταύτας τῶν ἀνδρῶν τούτων πάντων D πάσας εἶναι κοινάς, ἰδίᾳ δὲ μηδενὶ μηδεμίαν συνοικεῖν, καὶ τοὺς παῖδας αὖ κοινούς, καὶ μήτε γονέα ἔκγονον εἰδέναι τὸν αὑτοῦ μήτε παῖδα γονέα. Πολύ, ἔφη, τοῦτο ἐκείνου μεῖζον πρὸς ἀπιστίαν καὶ τοῦ δυνατοῦ πέρι καὶ τοῦ ὠφελίμου. Οὐκ οἶμαι, ἦν δ' ἐγώ, περί γε τοῦ ὠφελίμου ἀμφισβητεῖσθαι ἄν, ὡς οὐ μέγιστον ἀγαθὸν κοινὰς μὲν τὰς γυναῖκας εἶναι, κοινοὺς δὲ τοὺς παῖδας, εἴπερ οἷόν τε· ἀλλ' οἶμαι περὶ τοῦ εἰ δυνατὸν ἢ μὴ πλείστην ἂν ἀμφισβήτησιν E γενέσθαι. Περὶ ἀμφοτέρων, ἦ δ' ὅς, εὖ μάλ' ἂν ἀμφισβητηθείη. Λέγεις, ἦν δ' ἐγώ, λόγων σύστασιν· ἐγὼ δ' ᾤμην ἔκ γε τοῦ ἑτέρου ἀποδράσεσθαι, εἴ σοι δόξειεν ὠφέλιμον εἶναι, λοιπὸν δὲ δή μοι

16. ὁμολογεῖσθαι A^1Ξ: ὡμολογῆσθαι Π*q* et corr. A^2.
28. ἂν q^2 (cum *v*): om. ΑΠΞq^1.

presumptuous than διαφυγεῖν conjectured by Herwerden. It is proved to be right by διαφεύγεις below, which Herwerden *more suo* ejects.

14 **γυναικείου—νόμου.** If γυναικεῖος is equivalent only to περὶ γυναικῶν, it is strangely used. I suspect that Plato is playing on the musical sense of νόμος, as in VII 532 A: cf. IV 424 D, E *nn.* γυναικείου νόμου—a melody sung by women—is thus exactly parallel to the γυναικεῖον δρᾶμα (451 C *n.*), which it is clearly intended to recall.

457 C 19 **λέγε** is changed to φέρε by Cobet, to ἄγε by Richards. ἄγε *may* of course be right: the confusion occurs in the MSS of Plato *Theaet.* 162 D and 169 C (see Schanz's critical notes on these two passages), and doubtless elsewhere also. But in default of MS authority, it is safer to retain λέγε. Praestat lectio difficilior. 'Say on: let me see it' gives an excellent meaning, and could not have been otherwise expressed. The hortatory subjunctive of the first person is occasionally used after imperatives other than ἄγε and φέρε, as in Eur. *Hipp.* 567. See Kühner *Gr. Gr.* II p. 185.

21 **τὰς γυναῖκας κτλ.** Plato imitates the emphasis and precision of a legal enactment. The Aristophanic parallel is καὶ ταύτας γὰρ κοινὰς ποιῶ τοῖς ἀνδράσι συγκατακεῖσθαι (*Eccl.* 614, 615). See App. I.

457 D 25 **οὐκ οἶμαι κτλ.** Aristotle disappointed Plato's expectations: for he will not admit that such arrangements are even ὠφέλιμα (*Pol.* B 1. 1261^a 2 ff.).

28 **πλείστην ἂν κτλ.** On the omission of ἄν see IV 437 B *n.* and *Prot.* 316 C, with my note ad loc. Without ἄν, the reference must, I think, be to the past, in which case πλείστην—γενέσθαι will allude to some controversy which the doctrine of the community of wives may have occasioned before these words were written. But εὖ μάλ' ἂν ἀμφισβητηθείη makes it pretty clear that Plato is thinking of the future.

457 E 30 **λόγων σύστασιν**: "sermonum conspirationem" Ficinus, rightly. The passage which follows is an excellent example of Socratic εἰρωνεία.

ἔσεσθαι περὶ τοῦ δυνατοῦ καὶ μή. Ἀλλ' οὐκ ἔλαθες, ἦ δ' ὅς, ἀποδιδράσκων· ἀλλ' ἀμφοτέρων πέρι δίδου λόγον. Ὑφεκτέον, ἦν δ' ἐγώ, δίκην. τοσόνδε μέντοι χάρισαί μοι· ἔασόν με | ἑορτάσαι, 458
ὥσπερ οἱ ἀργοὶ τὴν διάνοιαν εἰώθασιν ἑστιᾶσθαι ὑφ' ἑαυτῶν, ὅταν μόνοι πορεύωνται. καὶ γὰρ οἱ τοιοῦτοί που, πρὶν ἐξευρεῖν, τίνα τρόπον ἔσται τι ὧν ἐπιθυμοῦσι, τοῦτο παρέντες, ἵνα μὴ κάμνωσι βουλευόμενοι περὶ τοῦ δυνατοῦ καὶ μή, θέντες ὡς ὑπάρχον εἶναι ὃ βούλονται, ἤδη τὰ λοιπὰ διατάττουσιν καὶ χαίρουσιν διεξιόντες οἷα δράσουσι γενομένου, ἀργὸν καὶ ἄλλως ψυχὴν ἔτι ἀργοτέραν ποιοῦντες. ἤδη οὖν | καὶ αὐτὸς μαλθακίζομαι, καὶ ἐκεῖνα μὲν B
ἐπιθυμῶ ἀναβαλέσθαι καὶ ὕστερον ἐπισκέψασθαι, ᾗ δυνατά, νῦν δὲ ὡς δυνατῶν ὄντων θεὶς σκέψομαι, ἄν μοι παριῇς, πῶς διατάξουσιν αὐτὰ οἱ ἄρχοντες γιγνόμενα, καὶ ὅτι πάντων ξυμφορώτατ'

---

33 **ὑφεκτέον—δίκην**: 'I must pay the penalty,' viz. for trying to run away. The natural penalty for running away is of course to have to stay and fight. Herwerden misses the point when he proposes to excise δίκην and understand λόγον.

34 **ἔασόν με κτλ.** For the metaphor in ἑορτάσαι and ἑστιᾶσθαι see I 354 A *n.* ἑστιᾶσθαι ὑφ' ἑαυτῶν is like our 'castles in the air.'

458 A 3 **πρὶν ἐξευρεῖν κτλ.** Cf. *Men.* 86 E.

5 **θέντες κτλ.** εἶναι goes with θέντες: "das Dasein des gewünschten als gegeben annehmend" (Schneider). A few inferior MSS omit εἶναι; but "apparet εἶναι facile supervacaneum, minime vero explicationis gratia addendum videri librariis potuisse" (id.). To write ἤδη for εἶναι (with Vind. E: cf. also Postgate in *J. Ph.* XV p. 113) is too great a change, and otherwise objectionable, in view of the ἤδη which follows.

458 B 9 **καὶ ὕστερον.** καί is 'and' (Jowett), not 'also' (Campbell).

ᾗ δυνατά. Stallbaum (with *q* and a few late MSS) reads εἰ δυνατά, which is more accurate, no doubt. But in saying 'how it is possible' instead of 'whether it is possible' Socrates hints that he will be able to prove the possibility of his scheme. We have here in fact a sort of prophecy of 473 B ff. Schneider (*Addit.* p. 39) cites a close parallel from *Tim.* 27 C ᾗ γέγονεν ἢ καὶ ἀγενές ἐστιν.

11 **ὅτι πάντων κτλ.** Cf. Ar. *Eccl.* 583 καὶ μὴν ὅτι μὲν χρηστὰ διδάξω πιστεύω. See App. I.

458 B—**461** E *The mutual association of male and female guardians will naturally lead them to form conjugal ties. But no irregular unions will be permitted. We too shall have our 'holy wedlocks,' but by 'holy' we shall mean 'profitable' or 'beneficial.' Now the most beneficial unions among lower animals are those by which the best offspring is produced from parents in the prime of life. If the same is true of the human race, how skilful must our rulers be! They must unite the best couples as frequently, the worst as rarely as possible; and only the children of the best couples shall be reared. No one except the archons is to know how this result is attained. Bridegrooms and brides will be brought together at certain marriage festivals, accompanied with sacrifice and song; and the number of marriages will be settled on each occasion by the rulers, so as to keep the population as far as possible the same. The rulers will effect their object by using lots with which they have already tampered. They will also reward excellence in fighting and otherwise by more liberal intercourse with women. The children who are to be reared will be taken to an establishment of nurses, where the mothers, and other women, will come to suckle them, but every precaution will be taken to prevent the mothers from recognising their offspring. Woman is in her prime from twenty to forty, man from twenty-five to fifty-five, and it is only during these periods that we shall permit them to bear and beget children for the State. Violations of this rule will be severely condemned. After the prescribed*

ἂν εἴη πραχθέντα τῇ πόλει καὶ τοῖς φύλαξιν. ταῦτα πειράσομαί σοι πρότερα συνδιασκοπεῖσθαι, ὕστερα δ' ἐκεῖνα, εἴπερ παρίῃς. Ἀλλὰ παρίημι, ἔφη, καὶ σκόπει.

Οἶμαι τοίνυν, ἦν δ' ἐγώ, εἴπερ ἔσονται οἱ ἄρχοντες ἄξιοι C τούτου | τοῦ ὀνόματος, οἵ τε τούτοις ἐπίκουροι κατὰ ταὐτά, τοὺς μὲν ἐθελήσειν ποιεῖν τὰ ἐπιταττόμενα, τοὺς δὲ ἐπιτάξειν τὰ μὲν αὐτοὺς πειθομένους τοῖς νόμοις, τὰ δὲ καὶ μιμουμένους, ὅσα ἂν ἐκείνοις ἐπιτρέψωμεν. Εἰκός, ἔφη. Σὺ μὲν τοίνυν, ἦν δ' ἐγώ, ὁ νομοθέτης αὐτοῖς ὥσπερ τοὺς ἄνδρας ἐξέλεξας οὕτω καὶ τὰς γυναῖκας ἐκλέξας παραδώσεις καθ' ὅσον οἷόν τε ὁμοφυεῖς· οἱ δὲ ἅτε οἰκίας τε καὶ ξυσσίτια κοινὰ ἔχοντες, ἰδίᾳ δὲ οὐδενὸς οὐδὲν D τοιοῦτο κεκτημένου, ὁμοῦ δὴ | ἔσονται, ὁμοῦ δὲ ἀναμεμιγμένων καὶ ἐν γυμνασίοις καὶ ἐν τῇ ἄλλῃ τροφῇ ὑπ' ἀνάγκης, οἶμαι, τῆς ἐμφύτου ἄξονται πρὸς τὴν ἀλλήλων μῖξιν. ἢ οὐκ ἀναγκαῖά σοι δοκῶ λέγειν; Οὐ γεωμετρικαῖς γε, ἦ δ' ὅς, ἀλλ' ἐρωτικαῖς ἀνάγ-

---

age has been passed, we shall remove the restrictions on sexual intercourse, observing only such regulations as are necessary to prevent incest; but, if possible, these unofficial unions shall be barren, and, in any case, their offspring must not be reared. Socrates lays down some further regulations about new meanings to be attached to names of family relationships, and adds that 'brothers' and 'sisters' may marry, with the sanction of the lot and the Pythian priestess's approval.

458 C 18 **αὐτοὺς—νόμοις.** In issuing their commands, the rulers will either themselves obey the laws (i.e. issue such orders as the laws direct) or act in accordance with the spirit of the laws: see next note. αὐτούς = ipsos sc. as well as τοὺς ἀρχομένους. The reading αὐτοῖς (K and Ficinus) is intrinsically good, and may be right: for it accentuates the contrast between cases prescribed for by actual law, and such as are left to the rulers' discretion. But there is hardly sufficient ground for deserting A.

μιμουμένους: sc. τοὺς νόμους. In matters not actually prescribed for by legislative enactment, the rulers will 'imitate,' i.e. will issue commands in harmony with the spirit of, such laws as do exist. The reading of q^2, μὴ πειθομένους, recommended by Herwerden, gives a poor, if not actually an erroneous, meaning.

21 **ὁμοφυεῖς.** See on 456 B.

458 D 23 **ἀναμεμιγμένων.** ἀναμεμιγμένοι would be more usual, but the genitive lays more stress on the participial clause: cf. Thuc. III 13. 6 βοηθησάντων δὲ ὑμῶν προθύμως πόλιν τε προσλήψεσθε κτλ., and other examples quoted in Kühner *Gr. Gr.* II p. 666. See also infra on 459 C. Here, too, it should be noted that the addition of a parenthetical οἶμαι helps to render ἀναμεμιγμένων independent of ἔσονται. The genitive absolute in ἰδίᾳ δὲ—κεκτημένου may also, as Jackson suggests, have influenced Plato's choice of construction in this clause. Plato perhaps thought of Sparta when he wrote the present sentence: cf. Plut. *Lyc.* 15. 1 ἦν μὲν οὖν καὶ ταῦτα παρορμητικὰ πρὸς γάμους· λέγω δὲ τὰς πομπὰς τῶν παρθένων καὶ τὰς ἀποδύσεις καὶ τοὺς ἀγῶνας ἐν ὄψει τῶν νέων, ἀγομένων οὐ γεωμετρικαῖς, ἀλλ' ἐρωτικαῖς, ὥς φησιν ὁ Πλάτων, ἀνάγκαις.

26 **γεωμετρικαῖς γε**: sc. ἀναγκαῖα, with which the dative goes, as in *Soph.* 252 D ταῖς μεγίσταις ἀνάγκαις ἀδύνατον (cited by J. and C.). We have here one of the earliest assertions of the famous doctrine which has played so large and important a part in the history of philosophy—the doctrine of the so-called 'necessity' of mathematical reasoning. See for instance Mill's *Logic* Book II c. 5. In the rest of this sentence Schneider suspects that Glauco is paraphrasing some passage of poetry. τὸν πολὺν λεών certainly sounds tragic.

καις, αἳ κινδυνεύουσιν ἐκείνων δριμύτεραι εἶναι πρὸς τὸ πείθειν τε καὶ ἕλκειν τὸν πολὺν λεών.

VIII. Καὶ μάλα, εἶπον. ἀλλὰ μετὰ δὴ ταῦτα, ὦ Γλαύκων, ἀτάκτως μὲν μίγνυσθαι ἀλλήλοις ἢ | ἄλλο ὁτιοῦν ποιεῖν οὔτε ὅσιον **E** ἐν εὐδαιμόνων πόλει οὔτ' ἐάσουσιν οἱ ἄρχοντες. Οὐ γὰρ δίκαιον, ἔφη. Δῆλον δὴ ὅτι γάμους τὸ μετὰ τοῦτο ποιήσομεν ἱεροὺς εἰς δύναμιν ὅ τι μάλιστα· εἶεν δ' ἂν ἱεροὶ οἱ ὠφελιμώτατοι. Παντάπασι μὲν οὖν. | Πῶς οὖν δὴ ὠφελιμώτατοι ἔσονται; τόδε μοι λέγε, **459** ὦ Γλαύκων· ὁρῶ γάρ σου ἐν τῇ οἰκίᾳ καὶ κύνας θηρευτικοὺς καὶ τῶν γενναίων ὀρνίθων μάλα συχνούς· ἆρ' οὖν, ὦ πρὸς Διός, προσέσχηκάς τι τοῖς τούτων γάμοις τε καὶ παιδοποιίαις; Τὸ ποῖον; ἔφη. Πρῶτον μὲν αὐτῶν τούτων, καίπερ ὄντων γενναίων, ἆρ' οὐκ εἰσί τινες καὶ γίγνονται ἄριστοι; Εἰσίν. Πότερον οὖν ἐξ ἁπάντων ὁμοίως γεννᾷς, ἢ προθυμεῖ ὅ τι μάλιστα ἐκ τῶν ἀρίστων; Ἐκ τῶν ἀρίστων. | Τί δ'; ἐκ τῶν νεωτάτων ἢ ἐκ τῶν γεραιτάτων **B** ἢ ἐξ ἀκμαζόντων ὅ τι μάλιστα; Ἐξ ἀκμαζόντων. Καὶ ἂν μὴ οὕτω γεννᾶται, πολύ σοι ἡγεῖ χεῖρον ἔσεσθαι τό τε τῶν ὀρνίθων

30. μίγνυσθαι Π: γυμνοῦσθαι A.
4. παιδοποιίαις Ξ: παιδοποιίᾳ A*q*: παιδοποίᾳ (sic) Π.

---

458 E 32 **γάμους—ἱερούς.** Cf. *Laws* 841 D ταῖς μετὰ θεῶν καὶ ἱερῶν γάμων ἐλθούσαις εἰς τὴν οἰκίαν. The nuptials of Zeus and Hera were known as the Θεογαμία, or ἱερὸς γάμος, and were celebrated by a special festival in Athens and elsewhere: see H. Graillot's article on ἱερὸς γάμος in Daremberg and Saglio's dictionary, where the authorities are cited, or Farnell's *Cults of the Greek States* I pp. 184—192. To Greek religious sentiment the marriage of Zeus and Hera was (as Graillot says) the ideal type of all human marriages, and for this reason Plato characteristically applies the expression ἱερὸς γάμος to his ideal of marriage in his ideal city. Cf. also Proclus *in Tim.* 16 B τῶν ἐν ἀπορρήτοις λεγομένων ἱερῶν γάμων, οἷς καὶ ὁ Πλάτων εἰς δύναμιν ἐξομοιῶν περὶ τοὺς πολίτας καὶ τοὺς τῶνδε γάμους ἱεροὺς γάμους προσηγόρευσε, and see Abel *Orphic.* p. 243. It is clear from Plato's words that he would have repudiated with scorn the charge of seeking to abolish marriage. We have already seen that he endeavours to make the State into one vast family (457 B *n.*); and it is in the same spirit that he now tries to raise marriage from a private into a public institution, without sacrificing any of the religious ceremonies and associations by which the union of the sexes was hallowed in the eyes of his contemporaries: cf. 459 E. If his vaulting idealism "o'erleaps itself and falls on the other," that is no reason why we should impugn his motives, or refuse our homage to his unquenchable faith in the possibilities of human nature.

459 A 2 **κύνας θηρευτικοὺς κτλ.** Cf. 451 D and Plut. *Lyc.* 15. 12 πολλὴν ἀβελτερίαν καὶ τῦφον ἐνεώρα τοῖς περὶ ταῦτα τῶν ἄλλων νομοθετήμασιν· οἱ κύνας μὲν καὶ ἵππους ὑπὸ τοῖς κρατίστοις τῶν ὀχείων βιβάζουσι—τὰς δὲ γυναῖκας ἐγκλεισάμενοι φρουροῦσιν κτλ. See also on 451 C, 460 C.

6 **γίγνονται**: 'prove themselves to be' (J. and C.), rather than 'grow to be' (D. and V.): cf. III 412 C οἱ δὲ γεωργῶν ἄριστοι ἆρ' οὐ γεωργικώτατοι γίγνονται;

459 B 10 **γεννᾶται**: viz. τό τε—γένος, not τὸ γεννώμενον (suggested as an alternative explanation by J. and C.). For the sense cf. Xen. *Mem.* IV 23 (Jackson).

καὶ τὸ τῶν κυνῶν γένος; Ἔγωγ', ἔφη. Τί δὲ ἵππων οἴει, ἦν δ' ἐγώ, καὶ τῶν ἄλλων ζῴων; ἦ ἄλλῃ πῃ ἔχειν; Ἄτοπον μέντ' ἄν, ἦ δ' ὅς, εἴη. Βαβαί, ἦν δ' ἐγώ, ὦ φίλε ἑταῖρε, ὡς ἄρα σφόδρα ἡμῖν δεῖ ἄκρων εἶναι τῶν ἀρχόντων, εἴπερ καὶ περὶ τὸ τῶν ἀνθρώπων

C γένος ὡσαύτως ἔχει. | Ἀλλὰ μὲν δὴ ἔχει, ἔφη· ἀλλὰ τί δή; Ὅτι ἀνάγκη αὐτοῖς, ἦν δ' ἐγώ, φαρμάκοις πολλοῖς χρῆσθαι. ἰατρὸν δέ που μὴ δεομένοις μὲν σώμασι φαρμάκων, ἀλλὰ διαίτῃ ἐθελόντων ὑπακούειν, καὶ φαυλότερον ἐξαρκεῖν ἡγούμεθα· ὅταν δὲ δὴ καὶ φαρμακεύειν δέῃ, ἴσμεν ὅτι ἀνδρειοτέρου δεῖ εἶναι τοῦ ἰατροῦ. Ἀληθῆ· ἀλλὰ πρὸς τί λέγεις; Πρὸς τόδε, ἦν δ' ἐγώ· συχνῷ τῷ ψεύδει καὶ τῇ ἀπάτῃ κινδυνεύει ἡμῖν δεήσειν χρῆσθαι

D τοὺς ἄρχοντας | ἐπ' ὠφελείᾳ τῶν ἀρχομένων. ἔφαμεν δέ που ἐν φαρμάκου εἴδει πάντα τὰ τοιαῦτα χρήσιμα εἶναι. Καὶ ὀρθῶς γε, ἔφη. Ἐν τοῖς γάμοις τοίνυν καὶ παιδοποιίαις ἔοικε τὸ ὀρθὸν τοῦτο

12. ἦ Π: ᾖ A. 19. εἶναι post δεῖ nos: post ἡγούμεθα codd.

---

14 **ἄκρων εἶναι.** *εἶναι* is omitted by *q* and Flor. U. Without it, however, as Schneider points out, *σφόδρα* might be taken with *δεῖ*; whereas the sense requires it to go with *ἄκρων*. We should expect *ἄκρους εἶναι—τοὺς ἄρχοντας*, but the accusatives are attracted into the genitive by *δεῖ*. For an analogous idiom see III 407 B *n.*

459 C 17 **ἰατρὸν δέ που κτλ.** *μέν* after *δεομένοις* balances *δέ* in *ὅταν δὲ δή*, and not *ἀλλὰ—ὑπακούειν*, which merely explains *φαρμάκων* by stating its antithesis. There is consequently no sufficient reason for changing *ἐθελόντων* into *ἐθέλουσιν* (with some inferior MSS, Stephanus, Madvig, and others), although *ἐθέλουσιν* would no doubt be more usual. For the genitive absolute cf. 458 D *n.* I agree with Schneider and Campbell in taking the participle as neuter and not masculine (so Stallbaum and Jowett). *ὑπακούειν* is not 'submit to' but 'respond to'—'are willing to respond to,' i.e. be cured by 'a course of treatment without drugs': cf. *Prot.* 325 A, and for *δίαιτα* contrasted with drugs III 406 D.

18 **ἡγούμεθα κτλ.** See *cr. n.* If *εἶναι* is retained after *ἡγούμεθα*, we must (with Ast in his second edition) understand Plato to mean *ἡγούμεθα ἐξαρκεῖν καὶ φαυλότερον εἶναι*, i.e. *καίπερ φαυλότερον ὄντα*, or else suppose that *ἰατρὸν καὶ φαυλότερον εἶναι* is an accusative and infinitive forming the subject to *ἐξαρκεῖν*. Neither explanation is simple or natural; and Stephanus, Madvig, and others have in my judgment some reason for expunging *εἶναι*, although its intrusion is not altogether easy to explain. It is possible enough that Plato wrote *ἀνδρειοτέρου δεῖ* <*εἶναι*> *τοῦ ἰατροῦ* in line 19 (cf. *δεῖ ἄκρων εἶναι τῶν ἀρχόντων* in B above); and the possibility is raised, I think, into a probability, when we thus obtain a natural explanation of the erroneous *εἶναι* after *ἡγούμεθα*. *εἶναι* following *δεῖ* appeared difficult, and was omitted, as it is in B above by *q*; a later scribe reinserted it in the wrong place. I have therefore ventured to transpose the word.

19 **ἀνδρειοτέρου.** It needs more courage to use drugs than to prescribe a regimen, because the risk is greater. Nothing could be more appropriate than Plato's use of the word, although it has been doubted by Richards, who proposed *αὖ δριμυτέρου* at first, and afterwards *ἀνδρικωτέρου*. With the general sentiment Poschenrieder (*die Plat. Dial. in ihrem Verhältnisse zu den Hippokr. Schr.* p. 57) compares [Hippocr.] *de victus ratione* VI p. 592 c. 67 Littré *προκαταλαμβάνειν τὴν ὑγίειαν, ὥστε τὰς νούσους μὴ προσπελάζειν, εἰ μή τις μεγάλα πάνυ ἐξαμαρτάνοι καὶ πολλάκις· ταῦτα δὲ φαρμάκων δέεται ἤδη.*

459 D 22 **ἔφαμεν.** III 389 B. Cf. also II 382 C, D.

24 **τὸ ὀρθὸν τοῦτο**: i.e. this which

γίγνεσθαι οὐκ ἐλάχιστον. Πῶς δή; Δεῖ μέν, εἶπον, ἐκ τῶν
ὡμολογημένων τοὺς ἀρίστους ταῖς ἀρίσταις συγγίγνεσθαι ὡς
πλειστάκις, τοὺς δὲ φαυλοτάτους ταῖς φαυλοτάταις τοὐναντίον,
καὶ τῶν μὲν τὰ ἔκγονα τρέφειν, | τῶν δὲ μή, εἰ μέλλει τὸ ποίμνιον E
ὅ τι ἀκρότατον εἶναι· καὶ ταῦτα πάντα γιγνόμενα λανθάνειν πλὴν
αὐτοὺς τοὺς ἄρχοντας, εἰ αὖ ἡ ἀγέλη τῶν φυλάκων ὅ τι μάλιστα
ἀστασίαστος ἔσται. Ὀρθότατα, ἔφη. Οὐκοῦν δὴ ἑορταί τινες
νομοθετητέαι, ἐν αἷς ξυνάξομεν τάς τε νύμφας καὶ τοὺς νυμφίους,
καὶ θυσίαι, καὶ ὕμνοι ποιητέοι τοῖς ἡμετέροις ποιηταῖς πρέποντες
| τοῖς γιγνομένοις γάμοις· τὸ δὲ πλῆθος τῶν γάμων ἐπὶ τοῖς 460
ἄρχουσι ποιήσομεν, ἵν' ὡς μάλιστα διασῴζωσι τὸν αὐτὸν ἀριθμὸν
τῶν ἀνδρῶν, πρὸς πολέμους τε καὶ νόσους καὶ πάντα τὰ τοιαῦτα
ἀποσκοποῦντες, καὶ μήτε μεγάλη ἡμῖν ἡ πόλις κατὰ τὸ δυνατὸν
μήτε σμικρὰ γίγνηται. Ὀρθῶς, ἔφη. Κλῆροι δή τινες, οἶμαι,
ποιητέοι κομψοί, ὥστε τὸν φαῦλον ἐκεῖνον αἰτιᾶσθαι ἐφ' ἑκάστης
συνέρξεως τύχην, ἀλλὰ μὴ τοὺς ἄρχοντας. Καὶ μάλα, ἔφη.

IX. Καὶ τοῖς | ἀγαθοῖς γέ που τῶν νέων ἐν πολέμῳ ἢ ἄλλοθί B
που γέρα δοτέον καὶ ἆθλα ἄλλα τε καὶ ἀφθονεστέρα ἡ ἐξουσία τῆς

---

you call right, viz. *τὸ ψεῦδος*. The medicinal lie frequently appears (*γίγνεται οὐκ ἐλάχιστον*) in connexion with the marriages of the guardians, as Plato proceeds to shew. *τοῖς γάμοις* should not be made general; the reference is specific.

25 **δεῖ μὲν κτλ.** "The case resembles that of a breeding stud of horses and mares, to which Plato compares it: nothing else is wanted but the finest progeny attainable" Grote *Plato* III p. 205. It is worth while to compare Plato's arrangements with those of Aristophanes in *Eccl.* 616—634, in spite of the comedian's lewdness and buffoonery.

459 E 28 **τῶν δὲ μή.** Cf. 460 C and 461 C. It seems to me certain from these passages that Plato in this book lends his sanction to infanticide. This has often been denied, but without sufficient reason. The subject is discussed in App. IV.

29 **ἀκρότατον.** Cf. (with Schneider) *σφόδρα ἄκρων* in B above and *ὡς ἀκρότατον* in *Laws* 730 E. Stephanus' *ἀκρατότατον* is neat, but unnecessary, in spite of *καθαρόν* in 460 C.

30 **ἀγέλη**, like *ποίμνιον*, is intended "to recall the analogy of the lower animals" (J. and C.). Cf. 451 C *n*. *αὖ* serves the same purpose, by suggesting that *ἀγέλη* has another and a more primitive signification.

31 **ἑορταὶ κτλ.** As the *ἱερὸς γάμος* was celebrated with a procession and sacrifices, ending with the *κλίνη τῆς Ἥρας*, so Plato's *ἱεροὶ γάμοι* are attended with religious rites and ceremonies: see 458 E *n*. Plato apparently does not intend these State-marriages to last beyond the duration of a single festival. At each successive festival fresh unions would be tried.

460 A 2 **τὸν αὐτὸν ἀριθμόν.** See IV 423 A *n*.

460 B 9 **γέρα κτλ.** Special privileges seem to have been awarded at Sparta for bravery in the field (cf. Tyrtaeus *Fr.* 12. 35—44): it is certain at all events that cowardice was visited with every mark of disgrace (Xen. *Rep. Lac.* 9. 4—6 and other references in Gilbert's *Gk. Const. Ant.* E. T. p. 77). *γέρα* must be nominative, and *δοτέον* passive, in spite of its singular number: cf. *Symp.* 188 B *πάχναι καὶ χάλαζαι καὶ ἐρυσῖβαι—γίγνεται*. Examples like *Crat.* 410 C *αἱ μὲν δὴ ὧραι Ἀττικιστὶ ὡς τὸ παλαιὸν ῥητέον* (cited by Schneider and others) are not to the point, because *αἱ—ὧραι*

τῶν γυναικῶν ξυγκοιμήσεως, ἵνα καὶ ἅμα μετὰ προφάσεως ὡς πλεῖστοι τῶν παίδων ἐκ τῶν τοιούτων σπείρωνται. Ὀρθῶς. Οὐκοῦν καὶ τὰ ἀεὶ γιγνόμενα ἔκγονα παραλαμβάνουσαι αἱ ἐπὶ τούτων ἐφεστηκυῖαι ἀρχαὶ εἴτε ἀνδρῶν εἴτε γυναικῶν εἴτε ἀμφότερα— κοιναὶ μὲν γάρ που καὶ ἀρχαὶ γυναιξί τε καὶ ἀνδράσιν. Ναί. C | Τὰ μὲν δὴ τῶν ἀγαθῶν, δοκῶ, λαβοῦσαι εἰς τὸν σηκὸν οἴσουσιν παρά τινας τροφοὺς χωρὶς οἰκούσας ἔν τινι μέρει τῆς πόλεως, τὰ δὲ τῶν χειρόνων, καὶ ἐάν τι τῶν ἑτέρων ἀνάπηρον γίγνηται, ἐν ἀπορρήτῳ τε καὶ ἀδήλῳ κατακρύψουσιν ὡς πρέπει. Εἴπερ μέλλει, ἔφη, καθαρὸν τὸ γένος τῶν φυλάκων ἔσεσθαι. Οὐκοῦν καὶ τροφῆς οὗτοι ἐπιμελήσονται τάς τε μητέρας ἐπὶ τὸν σηκὸν

19. μέλλει Ξ: μέλλοι ΑΠ *q*.

---

means τὸ ὄνομα 'αἱ ὧραι.' It is scarcely possible to take δοτέον as active, and understand from it a passive δοτέα with ἐξουσία, because the connexion between γέρα, ἆθλα, and ἐξουσία—note ἄλλα τε καὶ κτλ.—is too close to permit of γέρα being in the accusative case.

12 **ἐπὶ τούτων.** For the construction cf. Dem. *F. L.* 298 τοὺς ἐπὶ τῆς πολιτείας ἐφεστηκότας and *de Cor.* 247 τοὺς ἐπὶ τῶν πραγμάτων.

13 **ἀμφότερα.** *q* and some other MSS read ἀμφότεραι, which is quite wrong: cf. *Lach.* 187 A πείθωμεν ἢ δώροις ἢ χάρισιν ἢ ἀμφότερα.

14 **καὶ ἀρχαί**: sc. as well as the other duties of guardians. It has not yet been specifically said that magistracies are to be open to women as well as men. J. and C. observe that "Plato seems to betray a certain consciousness that the office immediately in question might be specially suitable for women." Kindred duties are actually assigned to a female vigilance committee in *Laws* 784 A, 794 A ff.

460 C 15 **τὸν σηκόν.** A σηκός is an enclosed pen or fold in which the young of animals may be reared. Hartman prefers τινα σηκόν (with *q* and a Florentine MS), because the σηκός has not been mentioned before. The way has, however, been prepared for it by 459 A, 459 B (τί δὲ ἵππων κτλ.), ποίμνιον (459 E), ἀγέλη (ib.), and σύνερξις (460 A). The comparison with a sort of 'breeding-stud'—see above on 459 D—runs through all this passage and supplies the metaphors. See also on 460 E. The whole discussion affords an excellent example of the uncompromising rationalism with which Plato carries out his theories to their logical conclusion.

17 **ἀνάπηρον.** Pollux (II 61) explains this word as ὁ πᾶν τὸ σῶμα πεπηρωμένος; but it is little more than πηρός: cf. ἀνάπλεως, ἀναπιμπλάναι etc. The present passage is not inconsistent with III 415 B, for ὑπόχαλκος and ὑποσίδηρος do not imply deformity.

18 **ἐν ἀπορρήτῳ κτλ.** is a euphemism for infanticide: see App. IV. Compare the Spartan usage: εἰ δ' ἀγεννὲς καὶ ἄμορφον, ἀπέπεμπον εἰς τὰς λεγομένας Ἀποθέτας, παρὰ Ταΰγετον βαραθρώδη τόπον (Plut. *Lyc.* 16. 1). (The word for the exposure of infants was ἀπόθεσις.) See also Whibley *Greek Oligarchies* p. 113 *nn*.

εἴπερ μέλλει. μέλλοι (see *cr. n.*) might possibly be defended, if it referred to a previous statement to the same effect ('if, as we saw,' etc.). But there has been no such statement, unless with Stephanus we write ἀκρατότατον for ἀκρότατον in 459 E. εἴπερ γε μέλλει, conjectured by Herwerden, would be in danger of meaning κατακρύψουσιν, εἴπερ μέλλει κτλ. As it is, εἴπερ μέλλει qualifies ὡς πρέπει 'as is proper.' *Gl.* 'If the class of guardians is to be kept pure.' Glauco, in fact, takes the words out of Socrates' mouth. On the meaning and usage of εἴπερ in Greek see E. S. Thompson's edition of the *Meno* pp. 258—264.

ἄγοντες, ὅταν σπαργῶσι, πᾶσαν μηχανὴν μηχανώμενοι, ὅπως
μηδεμία | τὸ αὑτῆς αἰσθήσεται, καὶ ἄλλας γάλα ἐχούσας ἐκπορί- D
ζοντες, ἐὰν μὴ αὐταὶ ἱκαναὶ ὦσι, καὶ αὐτῶν τούτων ἐπιμελήσονται,
ὅπως μέτριον χρόνον θηλάσονται, ἀγρυπνίας δὲ καὶ τὸν ἄλλον
πόνον τίτθαις τε καὶ τροφοῖς παραδώσουσιν; Πολλὴν ῥᾳστώνην,
ἔφη, λέγεις τῆς παιδοποιίας ταῖς τῶν φυλάκων γυναιξίν. Πρέπει
γάρ, ἦν δ' ἐγώ. τὸ δ' ἐφεξῆς διέλθωμεν ὃ προὐθέμεθα. ἔφαμεν
γὰρ δὴ ἐξ ἀκμαζόντων δεῖν τὰ ἔκγονα γίγνεσθαι. Ἀληθῆ. | Ἆρ' E
οὖν σοι ξυνδοκεῖ μέτριος χρόνος ἀκμῆς τὰ εἴκοσι ἔτη γυναικί,

24. θηλάσονται Ξ: θηλάσωνται ΑΠ *q*. 27. προὐθέμεθα *v* (cum Stobaeo *Flor.* 116. 50): προθυμούμεθα A et (antecedente non δ sed ὧ) Ξ[1]: προμηθούμεθα ΠΞ[2] *q*.

---

21 **πᾶσαν μηχανὴν κτλ.** Aristotle (*Pol.* B 3. 1262ª 14 ff.) argues that no precautions would prevent parents from occasionally recognising their children. In such cases Plato might reasonably hope that the general weakening of parental sentiment would secure his city against serious harm.

460 D 22 **ἄλλας.** The mothers of the children who have been exposed.

23 **αὐτῶν τούτων**: viz. the mothers. This provision is conceived in their interests, rather than in the interests of the children, as the next clause also shews.

24 **θηλάσονται.** θηλάσωνται has more MS authority than θηλάσονται; but the future indicative (and not the aorist subjunctive) is the regular construction after ὅπως in semi-final clauses: cf. IV 429 D, VII 519 E. The exceptions are—besides this passage—*Symp.* 198 E, *Phaed.* 91 A, *Gorg.* 480 A, B, 510 A. In most of these places there is inferior MS authority for the future, which editors now for the most part read. See Weber *Entwickelung d. Absichtssätze* in Schanz's *Beiträge* II 2. p. 66; and for the confusion in Paris A of ο and ω *Introd.* § 5.

27 **προὐθέμεθα.** See *cr. n.* προὐθέμεθα is intrinsically so much better than προθυμούμεθα that we can hardly refuse to regard this as one of the passages in which *v* has preserved the right reading. See *Introd.* § 5.

ἔφαμεν. Cf. 459 B.

28 **ἐξ ἀκμαζόντων.** The same principle was observed in Sparta (Xen. *Rep. Lac.* 1. 6 and Plut. *Lyc.* 15. 4). It is possible, though I believe incapable of proof, that Plato's limits of age were in agreement with Spartan usage.

460 E 29 **τὰ εἴκοσι ἔτη κτλ.** A woman's ἀκμή lasts 'the twenty,' a man's 'the thirty' years. Glauco asks 'which twenty and which thirty?' and Socrates then explains. τά before εἴκοσι is correctly explained by Stallbaum: "articulum ponit de certo quodam cogitans temporis spatio quod deinceps definit accuratius." The antecedent to αὐτῶν is not simply ἔτη (so J. and C., with the English translators), but the duplicate expression εἴκοσι ἔτη and τριάκοντα. In γυναικὶ μὲν κτλ. Socrates proceeds as if Glauco had not interrupted: the construction is μέτριος χρόνος ἀκμῆς—γυναικί, ἀνδρὶ δὲ τὰ τριάκοντα, γυναικὶ μὲν—τίκτειν, ἀνδρὶ δὲ—γεννᾶν. τὸ ποῖον, τὰ ποῖα and the like are idiomatically used in asking for further specification, and are sometimes only impatient interruptions, intended to draw attention to the important point and add liveliness to the style: see Kühner *Gr. Gr.* II p. 540. Schneider takes τὰ εἴκοσι ἔτη and τὰ τριάκοντα as twenty and thirty years of age respectively, comparing τῶν ἐνενήκοντα ἐτῶν in *Tim.* 21 A, but χρόνος in χρόνος ἀκμῆς means duration, as is clear from ἀμφοτέρων—φρονήσεως below. It should be observed that in the *Laws* Plato fixes the inferior limit for men sometimes at 25 (772 D), sometimes at 30 (721 A, 785 B). By thirty-five he expected them to be married (*ib.*). Girls are to marry between 16 (785 B) or 18 (833 D) and 20 (*ib.*). Cf. Hesiod *OD.* 696 ff., pseudo-Solon *Fr.* 27. 9 and Arist. *Pol.* H 16. 1335ª 28. The Greeks seem generally to have recommended men to marry a little under or a little over thirty. See on this subject Blümner *Privatalterthümer* p. 36 *n.* 1.

ἀνδρὶ δὲ τὰ τριάκοντα; Τὰ ποῖα αὐτῶν; ἔφη. Γυναικὶ μέν, ἦν δ' ἐγώ, ἀρξαμένῃ ἀπὸ εἰκοσιέτιδος μέχρι τετταρακονταέτιδος τίκτειν τῇ πόλει· ἀνδρὶ δέ, ἐπειδὰν τὴν ὀξυτάτην δρόμου ἀκμὴν παρῇ, τὸ ἀπὸ τούτου γεννᾶν τῇ πόλει μέχρι πεντεκαιπεντηκον-
461 ταέτους. Ἀμφοτέρων | γοῦν, ἔφη, αὕτη ἀκμὴ σώματός τε καὶ φρονήσεως. Οὐκοῦν ἐάν τε πρεσβύτερος τούτων ἐάν τε νεώτερος τῶν εἰς τὸ κοινὸν γεννήσεων ἅψηται, οὔτε ὅσιον οὔτε δίκαιον φήσομεν τὸ ἁμάρτημα, ὡς παῖδα φιτύοντος τῇ πόλει, ὅς, ἂν λάθῃ, γεννήσεται οὐχ ὑπὸ θυσιῶν οὐδ' ὑπὸ εὐχῶν φύς, ἃς ἐφ' ἑκάστοις τοῖς γάμοις εὔξονται καὶ ἱέρειαι καὶ ἱερεῖς καὶ ξύμπασα ἡ πόλις ἐξ ἀγαθῶν ἀμείνους καὶ ἐξ ὠφελίμων ὠφελιμωτέρους ἀεὶ τοὺς ἐκγόνους

4. φήσομεν A¹Π: θήσομεν corr. A². 5. φύς Ξ *q*: φύσας AΠ.

---

32 **τίκτειν τῇ πόλει—γεννᾶν τῇ πόλει.** These phrases express concisely the Platonic view of marriage. They are equally applicable to the Spartan ideal, and may have been borrowed from Sparta. Cf. Plut. *Pyrrh.* 28. 5 τῶν δὲ πρεσβυτέρων τινὲς ἐπηκολούθουν βοῶντες· Οἶχε, Ἀκρότατε, καὶ οἶφε τὰν Χιλωνίδα· μόνον παῖδας ἀγαθοὺς τᾷ Σπάρτᾳ ποίει. "What Lucan observes about Cato of Utica, is applicable to the Guardians of the Platonic Republic:—Venerisque huic maximus usus | progenies: Urbi pater est, Urbique maritus" (*Phars.* II 387 f.) Grote.

ἐπειδὰν—ἀκμήν: 'when he has outlived his swiftest prime of running.' The expression ὀξυτάτην δρόμου ἀκμήν is doubtless borrowed from some epinikian poet, perhaps Bacchylides or Pindar. The dactylic rhythm is not in itself enough to justify us in assigning the phrase (with Herwerden) to epic or elegy. The author of the quotation was probably speaking not of a man, but of a race-horse. By applying the phrase (of course in a metaphorical sense) to his bridegrooms, Plato contrives again to suggest the now familiar analogy of a 'breeding-stud of horses and mares': see on 460 C. The comparison gains in realism and point, if it was the custom of antiquity, as it is now, to bring a first-rate racer to the stud (ἱπποφόρβιον, ἱπποτροφεῖον) when he ceased to run. This is probable in itself, and supported to some extent by a comparison of Plut. *Lyc.* 15. 12 ἵππους ὑπὸ τοῖς κρατίστοις τῶν ὀχείων βιβάζουσι, χάριτι πείθοντες ἢ μισθῷ τοὺς κυρίους with Virg. *Georg.* 3. 209—211. Just so Plato will not allow his guardians to marry until the fever in the blood has somewhat cooled: cf. *Laws* 775 B—776 B and J. B. Mayor in *Cl. Rev.* X p. 111. Stallbaum was the first to detect the poetical quotation. J. and C., though translating by "his swiftest prime of running," follow Schleiermacher in understanding the phrase literally; but we may fairly doubt if Greek runners had passed their prime at 25, and, even if they had, "non hic erat tali designationi locus, nisi forte ob id ipsum, quod cursui minus idonei forent, ad nuptias idoneos visos credimus" (Schneider). παρῇ means 'let go by,' "hinter sich hat" (Schneider): cf. such expressions as παριέναι καιρόν (II 370 B al.), νύκτα μέσην παρέντες (Hdt. VIII 9), and especially Soph. *O. C.* 1230 εὖτ' ἂν τὸ νέον παρῇ 'when he hath seen youth go by' (Jebb), and Bacchylides 3. 88 ed. Kenyon ἀνδρὶ δ' [οὐ θ]έμις πολιὸν π[αρ]έντα | γῆρας θάλ[εια]ν αὖτις ἀγκομίσσαι | ἥβαν.

461 A 4 **ἂν λάθῃ.** "Si non latuerit foetus praeter legem susceptus, ne in lucem quidem edetur, sed antea opprimetur" (Schneider). Cf. C below.

5 **γεννήσεται** = 'will be produced' must, if right, refer to birth ("hervorkommen wird" Schneider), otherwise φύς is superfluous. Bekker and others are possibly right in reading γενήσεται with Ξ¹ *q*, and some other MSS: cf. Hdt. VI 69, where Stein prints γεγενημένος in place of γεγεννημένος. See *Introd.* § 5.

φὺς ἅς. See *cr. n.* and *Introd.* § 5.

7 **ἐξ ὠφελίμων κτλ.** Cf. IV 424 A *n.*

γίγνεσθαι, ἀλλ' ὑπὸ σκότου μετὰ δεινῆς ἀκρατείας γεγονώς. B
Ὀρθῶς, ἔφη. Ὁ αὐτὸς δέ γ', εἶπον, νόμος, ἐάν τις τῶν ἔτι
γεννώντων μὴ συνέρξαντος ἄρχοντος ἅπτηται τῶν ἐν ἡλικίᾳ
γυναικῶν· νόθον γὰρ καὶ ἀνέγγυον καὶ ἀνίερον φήσομεν αὐτὸν
παῖδα τῇ πόλει καθιστάναι. Ὀρθότατα, ἔφη. Ὅταν δὲ δή,
οἶμαι, αἵ τε γυναῖκες καὶ οἱ ἄνδρες τοῦ γεννᾶν ἐκβῶσι τὴν ἡλικίαν,
ἀφήσομέν που ἐλευθέρους αὐτοὺς συγγίγνεσθαι ᾧ ἂν ἐθέλωσι,
πλὴν θυγατρὶ καὶ μητρὶ καὶ ταῖς τῶν θυγατέρων παισὶ καὶ ταῖς C
ἄνω μητρός, καὶ γυναῖκας αὖ πλὴν ὑεῖ καὶ πατρὶ καὶ τοῖς τούτων
εἰς τὸ κάτω καὶ ἐπὶ τὸ ἄνω, καὶ ταῦτά γ' ἤδη πάντα διακελευσάμενοι προθυμεῖσθαι μάλιστα μὲν μηδ' εἰς φῶς ἐκφέρειν κύημα
μηδὲ ἕν, ἐὰν γένηται, ἐὰν δέ τι βιάσηται, οὕτω τιθέναι, ὡς οὐκ

14. ἀφήσομεν Eusebius (*Praep. Ev.* XIII 19. 18) et Theodoretus (*Therap.* IX p. 941): φήσομεν codd. 19. μηδὲ ἕν Cobet: μηδέ γ' ἕν A[1], sed ἑ et γ punctis notavit A[2]: μηδὲν ΠΞ *q*.

---

461 B 8 **ὑπὸ σκότου.** Cf. (with J. and C.) σκότιος = 'an unlawful child.'

γεγονώς = 'produced,' 'a product of,' is cancelled by Hartman; but φύς is too far away, and γίγνεσθαι ('to be produced') is sufficiently accurate: cf. γένηται in 461 C.

11 **ἀνέγγυον**: 'unauthorised,' because the child of an irregular union. An ἀνέγγυος γάμος is a marriage without an ἐγγύη or contract between the parents of the betrothing parties (Blümner *Privatalt.* p. 262 *n.* 2).

14 **ᾧ.** ᾗ is read by Ξ, Vind. E and Eusebius (*Praep. Ev.* XIII 19. 18); but αὐτούς includes both sexes, and in such cases the masculine is preferred to the feminine. Hartman strangely thinks ᾧ neuter.

15 **θυγατρὶ κτλ.** The cases enumerated are all in the direct line, and nothing is said forbidding unions between 'brothers' and 'sisters.' See however 461 E *n.* Greek law permitted the marriage of uncles with nieces, aunts with nephews, and even half-brothers and half-sisters, provided they were not ὁμομήτριοι (Becker's *Charicles* E. T. p. 478, with the passages there cited). Some of Plato's contemporaries, notably the Cynics, entertained peculiarly revolting views on this subject, and the question was frequently agitated in his time: see Dümmler *Proleg. zu Pl. St.* pp. 52 ff. The Stoics agreed with the Cynics: see the authorities cited in Henkel *Stud. zur Geschichte d. Gr. Lehre vom Staat* p. 30.

461 C 17 **καὶ ταῦτά γ' ἤδη κτλ.**: 'and all this only after we have exhorted them' etc. ἤδη goes with ἀφήσομεν (or the like) understood after πάντα. J. and C. wrongly connect πάντα with προθυμεῖσθαι ('to use all diligence'). The voice should pause a little before διακελευσάμενοι.

18 **μηδ' εἰς φῶς κτλ.**: *ne in lucem quidem efferre.* Much less shall we permit it to live if born: see App. IV. μηδέ prepares the way for ἐὰν δέ τι βιάσηται κτλ. Hartman strangely prefers μή, "cum post μάλιστα coniunctio μηδέ prorsus frigeat." But μάλιστα μέν is, of course, 'if possible.'

19 **μηδὲ ἕν.** See *cr. n.* μηδέ γ' ἕν occurs in a few inferior MSS besides A, and is read by Baiter and others, but we do not find γε thus interposed between οὐδέ (μηδέ) and εἷς.

γένηται κτλ. γένηται sc. κύημα. βιάσηται means 'force its way' sc. εἰς τὸ φῶς (J. and C.). The extreme emphasis shews what importance Plato attached to this provision. The procuring of abortion, though perhaps in certain cases punishable by law (Meier and Schömann *Att. Process* p. 381), was in practice common enough: see Blümner *Privatalt.* p. 76. Plato permits it also in the *Laws* (740 D). The general Greek sentiment on this matter is fairly represented by Aristotle when he says (*Pol.* H 16. 1335[b]

οὔσης τροφῆς τῷ τοιούτῳ. Καὶ ταῦτα μέν γ', ἔφη, μετρίως
D λέγεται· πατέρας δὲ καὶ θυγατέρας καὶ ἃ νῦν δὴ ἔλεγες, πῶς
διαγνώσονται ἀλλήλων; Οὐδαμῶς, ἦν δ' ἐγώ· ἀλλ' ἀφ' ἧς ἂν
ἡμέρας τις αὐτῶν νυμφίος γένηται, μετ' ἐκείνην δεκάτῳ μηνὶ καὶ
ἑβδόμῳ δὴ ἃ ἂν γένηται ἔκγονα, ταῦτα πάντα προσερεῖ τὰ μὲν
ἄρρενα ὑεῖς, τὰ δὲ θήλεα θυγατέρας, καὶ ἐκεῖνα ἐκεῖνον πατέρα, καὶ
οὕτω δὴ τὰ τούτων ἔκγονα παίδων παῖδας, καὶ ἐκεῖνα αὖ ἐκείνους
πάππους τε καὶ τηθάς, τὰ δ' ἐν ἐκείνῳ τῷ χρόνῳ γεγονότα, ἐν ᾧ αἱ
μητέρες καὶ οἱ πατέρες αὐτῶν ἐγέννων, ἀδελφάς τε καὶ ἀδελφούς,
E ὥστε, ὃ νῦν δὴ ἐλέγομεν, ἀλλήλων μὴ ἅπτεσθαι· ἀδελφοὺς δὲ καὶ

25. ἐκεῖνον A²Π: ἐκείνων A¹. 26. ἐκεῖνα Ξ q: ἐκείνου AΠ.

22 ff.) ὡρίσθαι γὰρ δεῖ τῆς τεκνοποιίας τὸ πλῆθος. ἐὰν δέ τισι γίνηται παρὰ ταῦτα συνδυασθέντων, πρὶν αἴσθησιν ἐγγενέσθαι καὶ ζωήν, ἐμποιεῖσθαι δεῖ τὴν ἄμβλωσιν· τὸ γὰρ ὅσιον καὶ τὸ μὴ διωρισμένον τῇ αἰσθήσει καὶ τῷ ζῆν ἔσται.

τιθέναι κτλ.: 'so deal with them.' *τιθέναι* is more delicate than *ἐκτιθέναι*, which was read before Bekker, although it has no MS authority. Herwerden suggests that *τιθέναι* means *θάπτειν* (as in 469 A), but Plato expresses himself with more refinement. *τροφῆς* does not mean, as some are fain to believe, merely the educational system reserved for the guardians: see on 459 E and App. IV.

21 **πατέρας κτλ.**: 'how will they distinguish one another's fathers' etc.? The Aristophanic parallel is here very close: Πῶς οὖν οὕτω ζώντων ἡμῶν τοὺς αὑτοῦ παῖδας ἕκαστος | ἔσται δυνατὸς διαγιγνώσκειν; Τί δὲ δεῖ; πατέρας γὰρ ἅπαντας | τοὺς πρεσβυτέρους αὑτῶν εἶναι τοῖσι χρόνοισιν νομιοῦσιν (*Eccl.* 635—637). The question touches an obvious difficulty in any system of the community of children; but, as a link in the chain of evidence connecting the *Ecclesiazusae* and the *Republic*, the parallel deserves to carry weight, although it has sometimes been pressed too far. See on the one hand Teichmüller *Lit. Fehd.* I pp. 18—19 and Chiappelli *Riv. di Filolog.* XI p. 213, and on the other Zeller⁴ II 1. p. 551 *n.* 2. Cf. also App. I.

461 D 23 **δεκάτῳ κτλ.**: 'in the tenth month and also in the seventh month.' *δή* (as J. and C. remark) draws attention to the more exceptional case: cf. II 367 C *n.* The Greek cannot, I think, be taken as an inexact way of saying "from seven to ten months after" (J. and C.). In point of fact the majority of ancient writers on the subject denied that children were ever born in the eighth month of pregnancy: see Gellius *Noct. Att.* III 16 and Censorinus *de die natali* 7. 2.

28 **ἐγέννων**: 'were engaged in begetting children': cf. 460 E, and 461 B (*τῶν ἔτι γεννώντων*). Richards has pointed out (*Cl. Rev.* IV p. 7) that the imperfect refers "to the whole time of life during which father and mother were allowed, if the lot fell upon them, to take part in the regular unions." Cf. *Tim.* 18 D νομιοῦσι δὲ πάντες πάντας αὑτοὺς ὁμογενεῖς, ἀδελφὰς μὲν καὶ ἀδελφοὺς ὅσοιπερ ἂν τῆς πρεπούσης ἐντὸς ἡλικίας γίγνωνται. Jowett's version—"all who were begotten at the time when their fathers and mothers came together"—mistakes both *ἐν* and *ἐγέννων*. Schneider translates the passage correctly.

29 **ὥστε—ἅπτεσθαι.** I agree with Richards in understanding this of the "irregular unions which were last mentioned" (461 C). But in spite of the explicit reference in *ὃ νῦν δὴ ἐλέγομεν*, Plato has not as yet forbidden such unions between 'brothers' and 'sisters': see 461 C *n.* The discrepancy is hard to explain, especially as the list in 461 C seems intended to be exhaustive. The effect of the prohibition (owing to the meaning now given to 'brother' and 'sister') would be greatly to restrict, but not to abolish, unauthorised liaisons.

461 E 29 **ἀδελφοὺς κτλ.** refers only to State-marriages, as *ὁ κλῆρος* shews. Without this exemption Plato's proposals would (according to Richards l.c.) "have rendered all unions whatever practically

ἀδελφὰς δώσει ὁ νόμος συνοικεῖν, ἐὰν ὁ κλῆρος ταύτῃ ξυμπίπτῃ
καὶ ἡ Πυθία προσαναιρῇ. Ὀρθότατα, ἦ δ' ὅς.
X. Ἡ μὲν δὴ κοινωνία, ὦ Γλαύκων, αὕτη τε καὶ τοιαύτη
γυναικῶν τε καὶ παίδων τοῖς φύλαξί σοι τῆς πόλεως· ὡς δὲ
ἑπομένη τε τῇ ἄλλῃ πολιτείᾳ καὶ μακρῷ βελτίστη, δεῖ δὴ τὸ μετὰ
τοῦτο βεβαιώσασθαι παρὰ τοῦ λόγου. ἢ πῶς ποιῶμεν; | Οὕτω 462
νὴ Δία, ἦ δ' ὅς. Ἆρ' οὖν οὐχ ἥδε ἀρχὴ τῆς ὁμολογίας, ἐρέσθαι
ἡμᾶς αὐτούς, τί ποτε τὸ μέγιστον ἀγαθὸν ἔχομεν εἰπεῖν εἰς πόλεως
κατασκευήν, οὗ δεῖ στοχαζόμενον τὸν νομοθέτην τιθέναι τοὺς
νόμους, καὶ τί μέγιστον κακόν, εἶτα ἐπισκέψασθαι, ἆρα ἃ νῦν δὴ
διήλθομεν εἰς μὲν τὸ τοῦ ἀγαθοῦ ἴχνος ἡμῖν ἁρμόττει, τῷ δὲ τοῦ
κακοῦ ἀναρμοστεῖ; Πάντων μάλιστα, ἔφη. Ἔχομεν οὖν τι

33. ὡς δὲ Ξ*q*: ὡδὲ (sic) A, eraso super ὡ accentu: ὧδε Π. 34. ἑπομένη—βελτίστη Π: ἑπομένη—βελτίστῃ A.

---

impossible." Surely not; although they would have unduly favoured the τηλύγετος παῖς. A son, for example, who is born when his mother is 21 and his father 26, cannot marry till he is 49, because he is 29 before his bride can possibly be born, and she cannot marry under 20; whereas a son, whose father is 54 and mother 39 when he is born, can marry a girl only one year younger than himself, because his father and mother retire at 55 and 40 respectively. Did Plato intend the sons of elderly couples to marry young, and those of young couples to marry late? Such an inference is unlikely, although it is the logical outcome of his theories. In any case Plato did well to introduce a saving clause. The κομψὸς κλῆρος, obedient to the archons, would couple 'brothers' and 'sisters,' whenever it seemed desirable in the interests of the State, so long as they were not really blood-relations. (This the archons of course would know.) Apollo's priestess would platonize. We must suppose that her assent is given in advance, and once for all (although προσαναιρῇ is present and follows ξυμπίπτῃ), unless she had an accredited representative on the spot, which there is nothing to indicate. On Plato's attitude to Apollo see IV 427 C *n.*

461 E—**464** B *Let us now endeavour to shew that community of wives and children is best, and in agreement with the general plan of our constitution. That it is the best policy Plato proves as follows. A legislator should above all things aim at maintaining unity within his city. The most effective instrument for this purpose is community of pleasure and pain. As in an individual man, the sufferings of a single member affect the whole, so also in a well-governed city, the joys and sorrows of every citizen are shared by all. It is easy to shew that our ideal city fulfils this condition in a unique degree, both by means of its other institutions, and more especially through the community of wives and children.*

461 E 34 **ἑπομένη—πολιτείᾳ**. This topic was not specified in the original distribution of the subject (458 B), but it is closely connected with ὡς μακρῷ βελτίστη. Plato does not deal with it till 464 B.

35 **βεβαιώσασθαι κτλ.** Hirschig cancelled παρὰ τοῦ λόγου: but cf. (with Stallbaum) *Gorg.* 489 A ἵνα—βεβαιώσωμαι ἤδη παρὰ σοῦ. 'The argument' is personified, as often.

462 A 5 **ἆρα.** <εἰ> ἄρα was suggested by Dobree; but cf. (with Stallbaum) *Gorg.* 475 B πρῶτον μὲν δὴ σκεψώμεθα, ἆρα—ὑπερβάλλει κτλ. The exact translation is 'to enquire, Do the institutions we have described' etc.

7 **ἔχομεν οὖν κτλ.** Cf. IV 422 E. στάσις was the greatest evil which a Greek city had to fear, and Athens had suffered from it grievously. Now individualism was the peculiar pride and glory of the Athenian State (Thuc. II 37), so that we need not wonder if Plato traced στάσις to individualism, and rushed to the

B μεῖζον κακὸν πόλει ἢ ἐκεῖνο, ὃ ἂν αὐτὴν διασπᾷ καὶ ποιῇ πολλὰς ἀντὶ μιᾶς; ἢ μεῖζον ἀγαθὸν τοῦ ὃ ἂν ξυνδῇ τε καὶ ποιῇ μίαν; Οὐκ ἔχομεν. Οὐκοῦν ἡ μὲν ἡδονῆς τε καὶ λύπης κοινωνία ξυνδεῖ, ὅταν ὅ τι μάλιστα πάντες οἱ πολῖται τῶν αὐτῶν γιγνομένων τε καὶ ἀπολλυμένων παραπλησίως χαίρωσι καὶ λυπῶνται; Παντάπασι μὲν οὖν, ἔφη. Ἡ δέ γε τῶν τοιούτων ἰδίωσις διαλύει, ὅταν οἱ μὲν περιαλγεῖς, οἱ δὲ περιχαρεῖς γίγνωνται ἐπὶ τοῖς αὐτοῖς παθήμασι
C τῆς πόλεώς τε καὶ τῶν ἐν τῇ πόλει; Τί δ' οὔ; Ἆρ' οὖν ἐκ τοῦδε τὸ τοιόνδε γίγνεται, ὅταν μὴ ἅμα φθέγγωνται ἐν τῇ πόλει τὰ τοιάδε ῥήματα, τό τε ἐμὸν καὶ τὸ οὐκ ἐμόν; καὶ περὶ τοῦ ἀλλοτρίου κατὰ ταὐτά; Κομιδῇ μὲν οὖν. Ἐν ᾗτινι δὴ πόλει πλεῖστοι ἐπὶ

9. ξυνδῇ Ξ*q*: ξυνδεῖ ΑΠ.

---

opposite extreme. Cf. Krohn *Pl. Fr.* p. 4, Pöhlmann *Gesch. d. ant. Kommunismus* etc. pp. 146—184, and see on II 369 A.

462 B 9 **ποιῇ μίαν**. J. and C. assert that Plato "has no idea of a unity of opposites or differences—τὸ ἀντίξουν συμφέρον," and Aristotle argues to the same effect in *Pol.* B 2. 1261ª 22 ff. But it is in fact on such a unity that the entire fabric of Plato's city rests: see IV 423 D *n.*, and cf. also 432 A, 443 D. The perfect city is a ἕν with three πολλά—rulers, auxiliaries, farmers and artisans, or, if rulers and auxiliaries are classed together as guardians, then with two. Plato's object throughout this episode is to keep the whole city 'one' by preventing *one* of its constituent factors, viz. the guardians, from becoming 'many.' If the guardians are united—so he holds—no danger to the city's unity need be apprehended from the others (465 B). With the sentiment generally cf. Ar. *Eccl.* 594 and 674 (μίαν οἴκησίν φημι ποιήσειν συρρήξασ' εἰς ἓν ἅπαντα | ὥστε βαδίζειν εἰς ἀλλήλους). See also on 463 E and App. I.

13 **οἱ μὲν—τῆς πόλεως**. As when a national disaster is made the occasion of a party victory. Plato may be thinking of scenes which he had witnessed in his native city. Bosanquet cites an excellent illustration from Dem. *de Cor.* 217.

462 C 17 **καὶ—ταὐτά**: i.e. ὅταν μὴ ἅμα φθέγγωνται—τό τε ἀλλότριον καὶ τὸ οὐκ ἀλλότριον. Hartman ejects καὶ περὶ τοῦ ἀλλοτρίου as a "futile interpretamentum" on τὸ οὐκ ἐμόν. There is nothing to prove that καὶ—ταὐτά was read by Aristotle (*Pol.* B 3. 1261ᵇ 18), Plutarch (140 D, 484 B, 767 D), Iamblichus (*de vita Pythag.* 167) or Proclus (*in remp.* ed. Kroll II pp. 78. 28, 365. 11), though Iamblichus uses the word ἀλλότριον instead of Plato's οὐκ ἐμόν. But as none of these authors pretends to be quoting Plato's *ipsissima verba*, the omission proves nothing. Although the words add nothing to the sense, they approach the matter from another point of view, and are in my judgment certainly genuine.

18 **ἐν ᾗτινι κτλ.** 'Thus in whatever city the largest number of men agree in applying these expressions, "mine" and "not mine," to the same thing,' etc. τοῦτο agrees with the nearest of the two objects, viz. τὸ ἐμόν. For the use of ἐπί cf. *Parm.* 147 D. The reading ἐπὶ τὸ αὐτό—see *cr. n.*—is as old as Iamblichus: see the passage referred to above, where Iamblichus has ἐπὶ τὸ αὐτὸ τὸ ἐμὸν φθέγγεσθαι καὶ τὸ ἀλλότριον. It is retained by the majority of editors; but no other instance of λέγειν ἐπί τι has yet been adduced, and the expression is certainly very strange. φέρειν ὄνομα ἐπί τι (*Soph.* 237 C, D: cf. also *Tim.* 37 E), of which Schneider reminds us, is a different thing from λέγειν ὄνομα ἐπί τι. Various emendations have been proposed. The choice seems to me to lie between ἐπὶ τῷ αὐτῷ and ἐπὶ τοῦ αὐτοῦ. The latter emendation—which I once adopted—was (as I learn from Schneider) proposed by Küster instead of ἐπὶ τὸ αὐτό in Iamblichus: cf. ὥσπερ ἐπὶ τοῦ

τῷ αὐτῷ κατὰ ταὐτὰ τοῦτο λέγουσι τὸ ἐμὸν καὶ τὸ οὐκ ἐμόν, αὕτη ἄριστα διοικεῖται; Πολύ γε. Καὶ ἥτις δὴ ἐγγύτατα ἑνὸς ἀνθρώπου ἔχει; οἷον ὅταν που ἡμῶν δάκτυλός του πληγῇ, πᾶσα ἡ κοινωνία ἡ κατὰ τὸ σῶμα πρὸς τὴν ψυχήν, τεταγμένη εἰς μίαν σύνταξιν τὴν τοῦ ἄρχοντος ἐν αὐτῇ, ᾔσθετό τε καὶ πᾶσα ἅμα D ξυνήλγησεν μέρους πονήσαντος ὅλη, καὶ οὕτω δὴ λέγομεν, ὅτι ὁ ἄνθρωπος τὸν δάκτυλον ἀλγεῖ· καὶ περὶ ἄλλου ὁτουοῦν τῶν τοῦ ἀνθρώπου ὁ αὐτὸς λόγος, περί τε λύπης πονοῦντος μέρους καὶ

19. τῷ αὐτῷ Wyttenbach: τὸ αὐτὸ ΑΞ: κομιδῇ—ταὐτὰ om. Π *q*.
22. τεταγμένη Ξ: τεταμένη ΑΠ *q*.

δακτύλου ἐλέγομεν VII 524 E ('in the case of the finger') al. Although the genitive may be right, the dative now seems to me slightly more natural and easy. Hartman ejects ἐπὶ τὸ αὐτό altogether, but there is no occasion for the knife. Cf. IV 436 B *n*. For the error see *Introd.* § 5.

20 **καὶ ἥτις δὴ κτλ.** δή is illative, and καί 'also.' καὶ—ἔχει (sc. ἄριστα διοικεῖται) is certainly interrogative, as Schneider pointed out: see in D below τοῦτο δ' ἐρωτᾷς. Plato recurs to his favourite analogy between man and the State: cf. II 368 E f. *nn*.

21 **οἷον ὅταν κτλ.** Poschenrieder (*Die Pl. Dial. in ihrem Verhältnisse zu d. Hippokratischen Schr.* p. 67) cites a remarkable parallel from the author of the treatise *de locis in homine* (Littré VI p. 278 c. 1) εἴ τις βούλεται τοῦ σώματος ἀπολαβὼν μέρος κακῶς ποιέειν τὸ σμικρότατον, πᾶν τὸ σῶμα αἰσθήσεται τὴν πεῖσιν, ὁκοίη ἄν τις ᾖ, διὰ τόδε, ὅτι τοῦ σώματος τὸ σμικρότατον πάντα ἔχει, ὅσαπερ καὶ τὸ μέγιστον· τοῦτο δ' ὁποῖον ἄν τις πάθῃ ἐπαναφέρει πρὸς τὴν ὁμοεθνίην ἕκαστον πρὸς τὴν ἑωυτοῦ, ἤν τε κακόν, ἤν τε ἀγαθὸν ᾖ· καὶ διὰ ταῦτα καὶ ἀλγέει καὶ ἥδεται ὑπὸ ἔθνεος τοῦ σμικροτάτου τὸ σῶμα, ὅτι ἐν τῷ σμικροτάτῳ πάντ' ἔνι τὰ μέρεα καὶ ταῦτα ἐπαναφέρουσι ἐς τὰ σφῶν αὐτῶν ἕκαστα καὶ διαγγέλλουσι πάντα. The 'sympathy' of the different parts of the human body was a Hippocratean tenet (ξυμπαθέα πάντα *de alimento* IX c. 23 Littré). Cf. Shakespeare *Othello* III 4. 146—148, "For let our finger ache, and it indues Our other healthful members ev'n to that sense Of pain." Plato goes farther, and represents the partnership as extending also to the soul: see next note.

πᾶσα ἡ κοινωνία κτλ.: 'the entire partnership pervading the body with the soul, organized into a single composite organization, viz. that of the ruling power in the partnership' etc. Plato's language is precise, but difficult. I take ἡ—ψυχήν as defining the κοινωνία. κατὰ τὸ σῶμα is written rather than τοῦ σώματος, because the partnership is not only a partnership of body with soul, but also a partnership of the different parts of body with one another. τεταγμένη—see *cr. n.* and App. V—appears to suit σύνταξις better than τεταμένη. A σύνταξις is the ordered combination of two or more elements: cf. *Tim.* 24 C and *Laws* 903 D ψυχὴ συντεταγμένη σώματι. The words τοῦ ἄρχοντος define the σύνταξις; although neuter in gender, they really refer, not to the soul, but to the whole σύνταξις or σύνολον, i.e. ὁ ἄνθρωπος. It is ὁ ἄνθρωπος who rules in the partnership, although he is himself a partner only in the sense in which the whole is partner with its parts. The expression ὁ ἄνθρωπος τὸν δάκτυλον ἀλγεῖ is thus seen to be as exact as possible. The confusion between τεταγμένος and τεταμένος is easy: συντεταμένως, for example, and συντεταγμένως are often confused in MSS: see Ast's *Lex. Plat.* s.v. ξυντεταμένως and my edition of the *Apology* p. 127. Cf. also infra 474 A *n*.

23 **ἐν αὐτῇ**: i.e. ἐν τῇ κοινωνίᾳ (so also Schneider), not (as Stallbaum) ἐν τῇ ψυχῇ. Plato means that every single man (ἑνὸς ἀνθρώπου above) is a single organized whole—a partnership in which the whole is partner with, and rules, the parts. See also App. V.

462 D 23 **ᾔσθετό—ξυνήλγησεν**: 'momentary' aorists: cf. *Theaet.* 156 E.

25 **ἄλλου ὁτουοῦν**: sc. besides the finger.

περὶ ἡδονῆς ῥαΐζοντος. Ὁ αὐτὸς γάρ, ἔφη· καὶ τοῦτο ὃ ἐρωτᾷς,
τοῦ τοιούτου ἐγγύτατα ἡ ἄριστα πολιτευομένη πόλις οἰκεῖ. Ἑνὸς
δή, οἶμαι, πάσχοντος τῶν πολιτῶν ὁτιοῦν ἢ ἀγαθὸν ἢ κακὸν ἡ
E τοιαύτη πόλις μάλιστά | τε φήσει ἑαυτῆς εἶναι τὸ πάσχον καὶ
ἢ συνησθήσεται ἅπασα ἢ ξυλλυπήσεται. Ἀνάγκη, ἔφη, τήν γε
εὔνομον.

XI. Ὥρα ἂν εἴη, ἦν δ' ἐγώ, ἐπανιέναι ἡμῖν ἐπὶ τὴν ἡμετέραν
πόλιν, καὶ τὰ τοῦ λόγου ὁμολογήματα σκοπεῖν ἐν αὐτῇ, εἰ αὕτη
μάλιστ' ἔχει, εἴτε καὶ ἄλλη τις μᾶλλον. Οὐκοῦν χρή, ἔφη.
463 Τί οὖν; ἔστι μέν | που καὶ ἐν ταῖς ἄλλαις πόλεσιν ἄρχοντές τε
καὶ δῆμος, ἔστι δὲ καὶ ἐν αὐτῇ; Ἔστι. Πολίτας μὲν δὴ πάντες
οὗτοι ἀλλήλους προσεροῦσι; Πῶς δ' οὔ; Ἀλλὰ πρὸς τῷ πολίτας
τί ὁ ἐν ταῖς ἄλλαις δῆμος τοὺς ἄρχοντας προσαγορεύει; Ἐν μὲν
ταῖς πολλαῖς δεσπότας, ἐν δὲ ταῖς δημοκρατουμέναις αὐτὸ τοὔνομα
τοῦτο, ἄρχοντας. Τί δ' ὁ ἐν τῇ ἡμετέρᾳ δῆμος; πρὸς τῷ πολίτας
B τί τοὺς ἄρχοντάς φησιν εἶναι; Σωτῆράς | τε καὶ ἐπικούρους, ἔφη.

34. αὕτη *q*: αὐτῇ ΑΠΞ.

---

28 **ἑνὸς δὴ κτλ.** We may compare the Stoic doctrine "incommoda autem et commoda (ita enim εὐχρηστήματα et δυσχρηστήματα appello) communia (sc. inter sapientes) esse voluerunt" (see Cicero *de Fin.* III 69, and Madvig's note). Not a few of Plato's regulations in Book V foreshadow the communistic theories of Stoicism: see Dyroff *Ethik d. alten Stoa* pp. 211 f., 226—231. Plato however contrives to make his communism live; whereas the Stoics seldom did.

462 E 34 **αὕτη**. See *cr. n.* Schneider says αὐτῇ is "ea potissimum," referring to VII 516 B, where however we should (I believe) read οὗτος. See note ad loc. Here αὕτη is required by the contrast with εἴτε καὶ ἄλλη τις μᾶλλον. For the error cf. VIII 552 A, where *q* and several MSS wrongly read αὐτῇ. See also *Introd.* § 5.

36 **ἔστι.** For the syntax see on II 363 A. ἔστι is a privileged verb in Attic prose: cf. Kühner *Gr. Gr.* II p. 61.

463 A 5 **δεσπότας.** Demosthenes remarks that the subjects in an oligarchy are 'cowards and slaves' (ἄνανδροι καὶ δοῦλοι). See *in Timocr.* 75 and Whibley *Gk. Oligarchies* p. 143.

6 **ἄρχοντας.** Plato is thinking of the Athenian Archons. The object of this chapter, which seems at first sight somewhat loosely constructed, is to prove that συμπάθεια prevails to a unique extent in the Platonic city. The appellations σωτῆρες and ἐπίκουροι, on the one hand, and μισθοδόται and τροφεῖς on the other, involve a greater degree of interdependence than is expressed by the corresponding names in other cities. The archons too are more than fellow-rulers: they are fellow-guardians, their official designation among one another serving continually to remind them of their duty to the lower classes. Among themselves they use the terms of family relationship, and with these their actions correspond. Thus the distinction between *meum* and *tuum* is more nearly obliterated than in any other city. Everything is *meum*.

463 B 7 **ἐπικούρους.** The official designation of the second order is applied by the people to the ruling class as a whole. They are expected to look upon the ἐπίκουροι as 'helpers of the people' rather than as the rulers' auxiliaries, although it is the latter function which gave them their name (III 414 B). This is clear from σωτῆράς τε καὶ ἐπικούρους, both of which epithets are suggestive of protecting deities. See also on 464 B.

Τί δ' οὗτοι τὸν δῆμον; Μισθοδότας τε καὶ τροφέας. Οἱ δ' ἐν ταῖς ἄλλαις ἄρχοντες τοὺς δήμους; Δούλους, ἔφη. Τί δ' οἱ ἄρχοντες ἀλλήλους; Ξυνάρχοντας, ἔφη. Τί δ' οἱ ἡμέτεροι; Ξυμφύλακας. Ἔχεις οὖν εἰπεῖν τῶν ἀρχόντων τῶν ἐν ταῖς ἄλλαις πόλεσιν εἴ τίς τινα ἔχει προσειπεῖν τῶν ξυναρχόντων τὸν μὲν ὡς οἰκεῖον, τὸν δ' ὡς ἀλλότριον; Καὶ πολλούς γε. Οὐκοῦν τὸν μὲν οἰκεῖον ὡς ἑαυτοῦ νομίζει τε καὶ λέγει, | τὸν δ' ἀλλότριον ὡς οὐχ C ἑαυτοῦ; Οὕτω. Τί δὲ οἱ παρὰ σοὶ φύλακες; ἔσθ' ὅστις αὐτῶν ἔχοι ἂν τῶν ξυμφυλάκων νομίσαι τινὰ ἢ προσειπεῖν ὡς ἀλλότριον; Οὐδαμῶς, ἔφη· παντὶ γάρ, ᾧ ἂν ἐντυγχάνῃ τις, ἢ ὡς ἀδελφῷ ἢ ὡς ἀδελφῇ ἢ ὡς πατρὶ ἢ ὡς μητρὶ ἢ ὑεῖ ἢ θυγατρὶ ἢ τούτων ἐκγόνοις ἢ προγόνοις νομιεῖ ἐντυγχάνειν. Κάλλιστα, ἦν δ' ἐγώ, λέγεις· ἀλλ' ἔτι καὶ τόδε εἰπέ· πότερον αὐτοῖς τὰ ὀνόματα μόνον οἰκεῖα νομοθετήσεις, ἢ καὶ τὰς πράξεις πάσας | κατὰ τὰ ὀνόματα πράττειν, D περί τε τοὺς πατέρας, ὅσα νόμος περὶ πατέρας αἰδοῦς τε πέρι καὶ κηδεμονίας καὶ τοῦ ὑπήκοον δεῖν εἶναι τῶν γονέων, ἢ μήτε πρὸς θεῶν μήτε πρὸς ἀνθρώπων αὐτῷ ἄμεινον ἔσεσθαι, ὡς οὔτε ὅσια οὔτε δίκαια πράττοντος ἄν, εἰ ἄλλα πράττοι ἢ ταῦτα; αὗταί σοι ἢ ἄλλαι φῆμαι ἐξ ἁπάντων τῶν πολιτῶν ὑμνήσουσιν εὐθὺς περὶ τὰ τῶν παίδων ὦτα καὶ περὶ πατέρων, οὓς ἂν αὐτοῖς τις ἀποφήνῃ, καὶ περὶ τῶν ἄλλων ξυγγενῶν; Αὗται, ἔφη· γελοῖον γὰρ ἂν εἴη, E εἰ ἄνευ ἔργων οἰκεῖα ὀνόματα διὰ τῶν στομάτων μόνον φθέγγοιντο. Πασῶν ἄρα πόλεων μάλιστα ἐν αὐτῇ ξυμφωνήσουσιν ἑνός τινος ἢ εὖ ἢ κακῶς πράττοντος ὃ νῦν δὴ ἐλέγομεν τὸ ῥῆμα, τὸ ὅτι τὸ ἐμὸν

11. τῶν ἐν *q*: ἐν ΑΠΞ.

---

463 C 17 **παντὶ γὰρ—ἐντυγχάνειν.** A slight exaggeration: see 461 D, E *nn.* Cf. Hdt. IV 104 *ἐπίκοινον δὲ τῶν γυναικῶν τὴν μῖξιν ποιεῦνται (οἱ Ἀγάθυρσοι), ἵνα κασίγνητοί τε ἀλλήλων ἔωσι καὶ οἰκήιοι ἐόντες πάντες μήτε φθόνῳ μήτε ἔχθεϊ χρέωνται ἐς ἀλλήλους* and ib. 180 *ad fin.* Similar motives for domestic communism are mentioned by Diod. Sic. II 58. See also, for other traces, whether real or legendary, of community of wives and children in antiquity Xanthus *Fr.* 28, Ephorus *Fr.* 76 and Theopompus *Fr.* 222 (in Müller *Frag. Hist. Gr.* Vol. I), together with Arist. *Pol.* B 3. 1262ª 19.

463 D 22 **περί τε κτλ.** *τε* is *ἀνακόλουθον*: we should expect *καὶ περὶ τοὺς ἄλλους ξυγγενεῖς* to follow. Instead, we have a change of construction, and *καὶ περὶ πατέρων—καὶ περὶ τῶν ἄλλων ξυγγενῶν* (line 27). Cf. II 373 B *n.* *ἢ*='alioquin,' as often after a verb of obligation (here *δεῖν*): cf. VI 489 E, 503 A.

νόμος: sc. *ἔστι πράττειν.*

24 **αὐτῷ**: though *αὐτοῖς* in C: cf. I 347 A *n.*

26 **φῆμαι.** See on III 415 D. *φήμη* is the half-personified *vox populi, vox Dei*: cf. Nägelsbach *Nachhom. Theol.* p. 165. It is the quasi-personification of *φῆμαι* which accounts for the active *ὑμνήσουσιν* ('will sing in the ears of' etc.): cf. IX 573 A *περὶ αὐτὸν βομβοῦσαι.*

463 E 31 **ὃ—ῥῆμα** is the object of *ξυμφωνήσουσιν* (Schneider), just as in IV 432 A *ταὐτόν* depends upon *ξυνᾴδοντας.*

εὖ πράττει, ἢ ὅτι τὸ ἐμὸν κακῶς. Ἀληθέστατα, ἦ δ' ὅς. Οὐκοῦν
464 μετὰ | τούτου τοῦ δόγματός τε καὶ ῥήματος ἔφαμεν ξυνακολουθεῖν τάς τε ἡδονὰς καὶ τὰς λύπας κοινῇ; Καὶ ὀρθῶς γε ἔφαμεν. Οὐκοῦν μάλιστα τοῦ αὐτοῦ κοινωνήσουσιν ἡμῖν οἱ πολῖται, ὃ δὴ ἐμὸν ὀνομάσουσιν, τούτου δὲ κοινωνοῦντες οὕτω δὴ λύπης τε καὶ ἡδονῆς μάλιστα κοινωνίαν ἕξουσιν; Πολύ γε. Ἆρ' οὖν τούτων αἰτία πρὸς τῇ ἄλλῃ καταστάσει ἡ τῶν γυναικῶν τε καὶ παίδων κοινωνία τοῖς φύλαξιν; Πολὺ μὲν οὖν μάλιστα, ἔφη.

B XII. Ἀλλὰ μὴν μέγιστόν γε | πόλει αὐτὸ ὡμολογήσαμεν ἀγαθόν, ἀπεικάζοντες εὖ οἰκουμένην πόλιν σώματι πρὸς μέρος αὐτοῦ λύπης τε πέρι καὶ ἡδονῆς ὡς ἔχει. Καὶ ὀρθῶς γ', ἔφη, ὡμολογήσαμεν. Τοῦ μεγίστου ἄρα ἀγαθοῦ τῇ πόλει αἰτία ἡμῖν πέφανται ἡ κοινωνία τοῖς ἐπικούροις τῶν τε παίδων καὶ τῶν

Aristotle's criticism deserves to be quoted (*Pol.* B 3. 1262[a] 1 ff.) οὕτως ἕκαστος 'ἐμὸς' λέγει τὸν εὖ πράττοντα τῶν πολιτῶν ἢ κακῶς, ὁπόστος τυγχάνει τὸν ἀριθμὸν ὤν, οἷον 'ἐμὸς ἢ τοῦ δεῖνος,' τοῦτον τὸν τρόπον λέγων καθ' ἕκαστον τῶν χιλίων, ἢ ὅσων ἡ πόλις ἐστί, καὶ τοῦτο διστάζων· ἄδηλον γὰρ ᾧ συνέβη γενέσθαι τέκνον ἢ σωθῆναι γενόμενον. There is a far deeper truth in Plato's saying than in Aristotle's animadversions thereupon, and "das schöne Wort, dass alle dasselbe mein nennen sollen, hat es nicht verdient, von Aristoteles mit logischen Regeln gehetzt zu werden. Die Geschichte hat überall wo eine erhabene Idee eine Gruppe von Menschen so durchdringen sollte, dass der Wille jedes Einzelnen nur auf dieses Gemeinsame gerichtet sei, dem platonischen Gedanken im Prinzipe Recht gegeben" (Nohle *Die Statslehre Platos* etc. p. 133). See also on 457 B ff.

464 A 1 **ἔφαμεν κτλ.** 462 B, C. οὐκοῦν—ἕξουσιν sums up. ὃ δὴ—ὀνομάσουσιν is parenthetical, 'to which, as we have seen, they will apply the name "mine."'

464 B 9 **ἀπεικάζοντες κτλ.** See on 462 C and App. V.

12 **ἐπικούροις.** Why not φύλαξι? The word φύλακες regularly includes both the ἄρχοντες and the ἐπίκουροι, but it is strange to find ἐπίκουροι including the τέλεοι φύλακες or rulers (see on II 374 D), as it appears to do here and in 466 A. The following explanations may be suggested. (1) Plato intends the community of wives and children to extend only to the Auxiliaries, and not also to the Guardians. This view is taken by Blaschke (*Familien- u. Gütergem. d. Pl. St.* p. 10), who asserts that the Rulers proper have already past the limits of age prescribed for matrimony. In point of fact, however, a man may become a τέλεος φύλαξ at 50 (VII 540 A, B), whereas he can marry till he is 55 (460 E). (2) As by far the largest number of husbands would be only Auxiliaries, Plato speaks somewhat loosely, as if matrimonial community were confined to them. This explanation is possible enough in itself, but fails to explain the usage in 466 A. (3) ἐπίκουροι is used with the new and deeper meaning given to it in 463 B (where see note), 'helpers of the people,' rather than in its original and technical sense of the rulers' auxiliaries. This suits all the passages, and is in my judgment what Plato intended. ἐπίκουρος is not the only term whose connotation deepens as the *Republic* proceeds: cf. II 376 B, III 392 C *nn.*

464 B—**465** D *Domestic communism is also in harmony with the general communistic character of the city. It will cement the union of the guardians and so consolidate the State. It will also deliver us from lawsuits arising out of disputes about the family and property. In cases of attempted violence to the person, we shall expect a man's fellows to defend him. The older citizens will exercise disciplinary powers over the younger; reverence and fear will keep the latter from retaliating. All these arrangements will tend to keep the rulers at peace with one another, and,*

γυναικῶν. Καὶ μάλ', ἔφη. Καὶ μὲν δὴ καὶ τοῖς πρόσθεν γε ὡμολογοῦμεν· ἔφαμεν γάρ που οὔτε οἰκίας τούτοις ἰδίας δεῖν εἶναι οὔτε γῆν οὔτε τι κτῆμα, ἀλλὰ παρὰ τῶν | C ἄλλων τροφὴν λαμβάνοντας μισθὸν τῆς φυλακῆς κοινῇ πάντας ἀναλίσκειν, εἰ μέλλοιεν ὄντως φύλακες εἶναι. Ὀρθῶς, ἔφη. Ἆρ' οὖν οὐχ, ὅπερ λέγω, τά τε πρόσθεν εἰρημένα καὶ τὰ νῦν λεγόμενα ἔτι μᾶλλον ἀπεργάζεται αὐτοὺς ἀληθινοὺς φύλακας καὶ ποιεῖ μὴ διασπᾶν τὴν πόλιν τὸ ἐμὸν ὀνομάζοντας μὴ τὸ αὐτό, ἀλλ' ἄλλον ἄλλο, τὸν μὲν εἰς τὴν ἑαυτοῦ οἰκίαν ἕλκοντα, ὅ τι ἂν δύνηται χωρὶς τῶν ἄλλων κτήσασθαι, τὸν δὲ εἰς τὴν ἑαυτοῦ ἑτέραν | D οὖσαν, καὶ γυναῖκά τε καὶ παῖδας ἑτέρους, ἡδονάς τε καὶ ἀλγηδόνας ἐμποιοῦντας ἰδίων ὄντων ἰδίας, ἀλλ' ἑνὶ δόγματι τοῦ οἰκείου πέρι ἐπὶ τὸ αὐτὸ τείνοντας πάντας εἰς τὸ δυνατὸν ὁμοπαθεῖς λύπης τε καὶ ἡδονῆς εἶναι; Κομιδῇ μὲν οὖν, ἔφη. Τί δέ; δίκαι τε καὶ ἐγκλήματα πρὸς ἀλλήλους οὐκ οἰχήσεται ἐξ αὐτῶν, ὡς ἔπος εἰπεῖν, διὰ τὸ μηδὲν ἴδιον ἐκτῆσθαι πλὴν τὸ σῶμα, τὰ δ' ἄλλα κοινά; ὅθεν δὴ ὑπάρχει τούτοις ἀστασιάστοις εἶναι ὅσα γε διὰ χρημάτων E ἢ παίδων καὶ ξυγγενῶν κτῆσιν ἄνθρωποι στασιάζουσιν; Πολλὴ ἀνάγκη, ἔφη, ἀπηλλάχθαι. Καὶ μὴν οὐδὲ βιαίων γε οὐδ' αἰκείας δίκαι δικαίως ἂν εἶεν ἐν αὐτοῖς. ἥλιξι μὲν γὰρ ἥλικας ἀμύνεσθαι

---

if they are united, we shall not expect sedition in the rest of the State. Other minor advantages there are, too trivial to specify.

464 B 14 **ὡμολογοῦμεν**. I formerly read ὁμολογοῦμεν with Ξ q^2, Stallbaum, and others; but Schneider, as I now think, is right in retaining the imperfect and referring it to the original mention of domestic communism in Book IV. The whole of this discussion may in fact be regarded as a defence in the form of an explanation of the sentence IV 423 E—424 A. See also App. I.

464 C 15 **τροφὴν λαμβάνοντας κτλ.** summarises III 416 D, E.

464 D 23 **ἑτέρους** = *μὴ τοὺς αὐτούς* depends on *ὀνομάζοντας* understood. D. and V. make *ἕλκοντα* govern *γυναῖκα—ἑτέρους*, as Stallbaum formerly did, but Plato could not have said anything so ludicrous.

25 **ὁμοπαθεῖς**: 'simultaneously affected by' D. and V. *ὁμοιοπαθής* (Ast) would mean 'of like passions with.'

27 **ὡς ἔπος εἰπεῖν** with *οἰχήσεται* = 'almost have disappeared,' "so gut wie verschwunden sein" (Schneider): see on I 341 B. The English translators either omit or misinterpret the phrase. Aristophanes furnishes several pretty close parallels to Plato's reasoning here: cf. *Eccl.* 560—610 and especially 657 (*ἀλλ' οὐδὲ δίκαι πρῶτον ἔσονται*)—672. See Chiappelli *Riv. di Filol.* XI pp. 212 ff. and on the whole subject App. I.

464 E 31 **οὐδὲ—αὐτοῖς.** The first *οὐδέ* is of course *ne—quidem*. Hoefer should not have conjectured *οὔτε—οὔτε* (*de part. Pl.* p. 41).

32 **δικαίως** is ejected by Cobet and Herwerden, but *δίκαιον* just below supports it. There cannot justly be any lawsuits for outrages on the person, if we declare it just and honourable for a man to take the law into his own hands. This explanation is perhaps better than to translate 'we may fairly suppose that there will not be' etc.

ἥλιξι κτλ. Cf. (with J. and C.) *Laws* 879 E *ἧλιξ δὲ ἥλικα—ἀμυνέσθω κατὰ φύσιν ἄνευ βέλους ψιλαῖς ταῖς χερσίν.* It should be remembered that in cases of *αἰκεία* the guilty party was the one *ὃς ἂν*

καλὸν καὶ δίκαιόν που φήσομεν, ἀνάγκην σωμάτων ἐπιμελείᾳ
465 τιθέντες. Ὀρθῶς, ἔφη. Καὶ γὰρ τόδε ὀρθὸν ἔχει, ἦν δ' ἐγώ, οὗτος ὁ νόμος· εἴ πού τίς τῳ θυμοῖτο, ἐν τῷ τοιούτῳ πληρῶν τὸν θυμὸν ἧττον ἐπὶ μείζους ἂν ἴοι στάσεις. Πάνυ μὲν οὖν. Πρεσβυτέρῳ μὴν νεωτέρων πάντων ἄρχειν τε καὶ κολάζειν προστετάξεται. Δῆλον. Καὶ μὴν ὅτι γε νεώτερος πρεσβύτερον, ἂν μὴ ἄρχοντες προστάττωσιν, οὔτε ἄλλο βιάζεσθαι ἐπιχειρήσει ποτὲ οὔτε τύπτειν, ὡς τὸ εἰκός· οἶμαι δ' οὐδὲ ἄλλως ἀτιμάσει· ἱκανὼ γὰρ τὼ φύλακε
B κωλύοντε, δέος τε καὶ αἰδώς, αἰδὼς μὲν ὡς γονέων μὴ ἅπτεσθαι εἴργουσα, δέος δὲ τὸ τῷ πάσχοντι τοὺς ἄλλους βοηθεῖν, τοὺς μὲν

33. ἐπιμελείᾳ A²Π: ἐπιμέλειαν A¹Ξ: ἐπιμελείας *q*. 4. πάντων A¹Π: πάντῃ corr. A². 7. ἄλλως Ξ*q*: ἄλλος AΠ.

ἄρξῃ χειρῶν ἀδίκων πρότερος (Meier u. Schömann *Att. Process* p. 648).

33 **ἀνάγκην—τιθέντες** = 'curae corporum necessitatem imponentes,' 'compelling them to keep themselves in condition.' Cf. Xen. *Rep. Lac.* 4. 6 ἀνάγκη δ' αὐτοῖς εὐεξίας ἐπιμελεῖσθαι· καὶ γὰρ πυκτεύουσι διὰ τὴν ἔριν, ὅπου ἂν ξυμβάλωσι. It is probably of Sparta that Plato is thinking. I have now reverted to the best supported reading, although the use of τιθέντες as virtually equivalent to ἐπιτιθέντες is not free from difficulty. There is considerable MS authority (including Π) for ἀνάγκῃ, and as ἐπιμέλειαν was read by A¹ (see *cr. n.*) and several other MSS, I once conjectured <ἐν> ἀνάγκῃ σωμάτων ἐπιμέλειαν τιθέντες, taking ἐν ἀνάγκῃ as meaning ἀναγκαίαν; but this idiom is very rare except with ἐστί, ἦν and the like. Stobaeus (*Flor.* 43. 102) and Stallbaum read ἀνάγκην σωμάτων ἐπιμελείας. In *q* and two other MSS the text runs ἀνάγκῃ (or ἀνάγκη) σωμάτων ἐπιμελείας τιθέντες. Does this mean 'requiring them to guard against violence to the person' (ἀνάγκῃ σωμάτων)? If Plato meant to convey this meaning, it would be preferable to read ἀνάγκῃ σωμάτων ἐπιμέλειαν τιθέντες (for which there is also better MS authority), or possibly ἀνάγκῃ σωμάτων ἐπιμέλειαν <ἀντι>τιθέντες, but ἀνάγκῃ σωμάτων would be a fantastic expression, though perhaps intelligible after βιαίων and αἰκείας. On the whole, I think the reading printed above has most in its favour.

465 A 2 **ἐν τῷ τοιούτῳ**: i.e. by a personal encounter.

3 **πρεσβυτέρῳ κτλ.** This too is probably Spartan: cf. Xen. *Rep. Lac.* 2. 10. Patriarchal discipline is in perfect harmony with Plato's conception of the State as a single family.

5 **καὶ μὴν ὅτι γε κτλ.** An anacoluthon, the construction being broken by οἶμαι δ' οὐδὲ κτλ.: see I 352 B *n.* and infra 471 C. Here the apodosis would have been δῆλον ἂν εἴη or the like: cf. Stallbaum on *Laws* 677 B. Schneider and others suppose that ὡς τὸ εἰκός is substituted ἀνακολούθως for εἰκός ἐστι—a tolerably common form of anacoluthon in Plato and elsewhere (I 347 A *n.*): but such an idiom is awkward here. It is difficult again to supply δῆλον from Glauco's answer, though the presence of δῆλον may render the anacoluthon a trifle easier; nor can a governing verb be elicited from προστετάξεται. Others propose to abolish the anacoluthon: Ast by reading ὅ γε νεώτερος, Hartman by emending to προστετάξεσθαι <δῆλον>. Δῆλον. Καὶ μὴν κτλ. Neither alternative is satisfactory: and Hartman's is not even Greek. It should be noted that Aristophanes deals with the same subject in *Eccl.* 638 ff. See App. I.

ἄρχοντες. Stallbaum reads οἱ ἄρχοντες with *q*. "At varii sunt in civitate magistratus, neque semper eorundem nedum omnium est, tale quid mandare iunioribus" (Schneider).

465 B 9 **τὸ—βοηθεῖν.** τό belongs to δέος, "ut sensus idem sit, ac si dictum esset δέος δὲ τὸ τῆς τῶν ἄλλων βοηθείας τῷ πάσχοντι. δέος ἐστὶ τοὺς ἄλλους βοηθεῖν quin recte dicatur, nemo ambigit: quidni etiam τὸ τοὺς ἄλλους βοηθεῖν δέος dicere liceat" (Schneider)? Cf. οὐ παρὰ φύσιν

ὡς ὑεῖς, τοὺς δὲ ὡς ἀδελφούς, τοὺς δὲ ὡς πατέρας. Ξυμβαίνει γὰρ οὕτως, ἔφη. Πανταχῇ δὴ ἐκ τῶν νόμων εἰρήνην πρὸς ἀλλήλους οἱ ἄνδρες ἄξουσι; Πολλήν γε. Τούτων μὴν ἐν ἑαυτοῖς μὴ στασιαζόντων οὐδὲν δεινὸν μή ποτε ἡ ἄλλη πόλις πρὸς τούτους ἢ πρὸς ἀλλήλους διχοστατήσῃ. Οὐ γὰρ οὖν. Τά γε μὴν σμικρότατα C
τῶν κακῶν δι' ἀπρέπειαν ὀκνῶ καὶ λέγειν, ὧν ἀπηλλαγμένοι ἂν εἶεν, κολακείας τε πλουσίων πένητες ἀπορίας τε καὶ ἀλγηδόνας ὅσας ἐν παιδοτροφίᾳ καὶ χρηματισμοῖς διὰ τροφὴν οἰκετῶν ἀναγκαίαν ἴσχουσι, τὰ μὲν δανειζόμενοι, τὰ δ' ἐξαρνούμενοι, τὰ δὲ πάντως πορισάμενοι, θέμενοι παρὰ γυναῖκάς τε καὶ οἰκέτας, ταμιεύειν παραδόντες, ὅσα τε, ὦ φίλε, περὶ αὐτὰ καὶ οἷα πάσχουσι, δῆλά τε δὴ καὶ ἀγεννῆ καὶ οὐκ ἄξια λέγειν. D

14. διχοστατήσῃ A^2Ξ *q*: διχοστατήσει A^1Π.

τὴν τοῦ θήλεος πρὸς τὸ ἄρρεν (466 D). Madvig's change of τό to τοῦ has met with much favour, and is accepted even by J. and C. To my mind it destroys the balance of the two clauses, by dropping the personification of δέος, while retaining that of αἰδώς. For the sense cf. Ar. *Eccl.* 641—643 ἀλλ' ὁ παρεστὼς οὐκ ἐπιτρέψει· τότε δ' αὐτοῖς οὐκ ἔμελ' οὐδὲν | τῶν ἀλλοτρίων (sc. πατέρων) ὅστις τύπτοι· νῦν δ' ἣν πληγέντος ἀκούσῃ, | μὴ αὐτὸν ἐκεῖνον (illum ipsum sc. suum ipsius parentem, as Blaydes explains) τύπτῃ δεδιὼς τοῖς δρῶσιν τοῦτο μαχεῖται. Aristophanes' verses illustrate τοὺς μὲν ὡς ὑεῖς exactly; the parallel could scarcely be closer. Cf. App. I.

13 **οὐδὲν δεινὸν μή.** This construction occurs only four times in the Platonic corpus: viz. in *Ap.* 28 A, *Phaed.* 84 B, *Gorg.* 520 D, and *Epp.* 7. 344 E (Weber in Schanz's *Beiträge* II 2, p. 50).

465 C 16 **κολακείας κτλ.** πένητες has been variously explained as (1) for <αἷς ἔνοχοι ἂν εἶεν> πένητες or the like (Schneider), (2) in partitive apposition with the subject of ἀπηλλαγμένοι ἂν εἶεν (one of J. and C.'s alternatives), (3) nominative to ἴσχουσι (Shorey in *A. J. Ph.* XVI p. 237). J. and C. also suggest that κολακείας is "genitive singular in the same case as ὧν." If so, we should read ἀλγηδόνος with *q*: but there is no room for doubt that κολακείας is the accusative plural. Of these interpretations (1) is too difficult, while (3) is hardly possible, unless πένητες is placed after ἴσχουσι, as was once proposed by Ast, who afterwards preferred to read ἀπηλλαγμένοι ἂν εἶεν <πένητες>, and finally wished to excise the word altogether. (2) is, I think, defensible, if we remember the Greek partiality for this kind of construction (IV 431 A *n.*), and the occasional irregularities of Platonic style. See also on VIII 556 C, D. Jackson conjectures πένητος ('the poor man's flatteries of the rich'), Stallbaum πενίας in the sense of πενήτων. I think πένητες is probably due to Plato: but if not, the word may be a gloss on κολακείας τε πλουσίων or on ἴσχουσι.

17 **οἰκετῶν**: not = οἰκείων as the Scholiast says, but *domestici*, 'those of the household' (οἱ κατὰ τὸν οἶκον πάντες Hesychius), including, of course, slaves. Where there is no οἰκία, as in Plato's city, there can be no οἰκέται. Plato's communism involves the abolition of domestic slavery as well as of family ties. See also on 469 B, C.

18 **τὰ μὲν—παραδόντες**: an interesting glimpse of the economic condition of the Athenian poor. Cf. Ar. *Clouds* 1172 ff. The agreement in tense makes it probable that πορισάμενοι, θέμενοι, and παραδόντες are grammatically coordinate; although the money must of course be procured before it is deposited. The asyndeton has a rhetorical effect: cf. II 362 B *n.* Hartman would omit παραδόντες; but παραδιδόναι takes an infinitive more easily than τίθεσθαι.

20 **ὅσα τε κτλ.**: 'and the various and

XIII. Δῆλα γάρ, ἔφη, καὶ τυφλῷ. Πάντων τε δὴ τούτων
ἀπαλλάξονται, ζήσουσί τε τοῦ μακαριστοῦ βίου, ὃν οἱ ὀλυμπιονῖκαι
ζῶσι, μακαριώτερον. Πῇ; Διὰ σμικρόν που μέρος εὐδαιμονίζονται
ἐκεῖνοι ὧν τούτοις ὑπάρχει. ἥ τε γὰρ τῶνδε νίκη καλλίων, ἥ τ'
ἐκ τοῦ δημοσίου τροφὴ τελεωτέρα. νίκην τε γὰρ νικῶσι ξυμπάσης
τῆς πόλεως σωτηρίαν, τροφῇ τε καὶ τοῖς ἄλλοις πᾶσιν, ὅσων βίος
E δεῖται, αὐτοί τε καὶ παῖδες ἀναδοῦνται, καὶ γέρα δέχονται παρὰ
τῆς αὑτῶν πόλεως ζῶντές τε καὶ τελευτήσαντες ταφῆς ἀξίας
μετέχουσιν. Καὶ μάλα, ἔφη, καλά. Μέμνησαι οὖν, ἦν δ' ἐγώ,
ὅτι ἐν τοῖς πρόσθεν οὐκ οἶδα ὅτου λόγος ἡμῖν ἐπέπληξεν, ὅτι τοὺς
466 φύλακας οὐκ εὐδαίμο|νας ποιοῖμεν, οἷς ἐξὸν πάντα ἔχειν τὰ τῶν

1. ποιοῖμεν Π: ποιοῦμεν A.

manifold troubles which men suffer in connexion with such matters, all of them obvious enough and ignoble, and not worth spending words upon.' δειλά τε for δῆλά τε δή has slight MS authority, but is only an absurd attempt to represent δι' ἀπρέπειαν in C above. Still worse is the conjecture δοῦλά, which Herwerden approves.

465 D—466 D *The life of our guardians will be more glorious than that of victors in the games. So far from being unhappy, they are the happiest of the citizens, and any attempt to aggrandise themselves at the expense of their country will only make them miserable. We conclude that the best policy for a city is to make women share with men in everything, and such community is in harmony with the natural relations between the sexes.*

465 D 23 **ἀπαλλάξονται.** I formerly adopted Cobet's conjecture ἀπηλλάξονται (*N. L.* p. 243), which is attractive in itself, and also because of its correspondence with ἀπηλλαγμένοι ἂν εἶεν in C. But even on the score of meaning the change can hardly be called a necessary one, and there is no MS authority for the form ἀπηλλάξονται either here or (so far as I can discover) elsewhere.

ὀλυμπιονῖκαι κτλ. 'To him that overcometh' etc. Plato frequently borrows similitudes and phrases from the national games. Cf. VI 503 A, 504 A, IX 583 B *n.*, X 613 B, C, 621 D, and *Phaedr.* 256 B. Here he sings a sort of paean in honour of his more than Olympic conquerors. νίκη, ἡ ἐκ τοῦ δημοσίου τροφή (cf. *Ap.* 36 D), ἀναδοῦνται, γέρα (such as προεδρία Xenophanes *Fr.* 2. 7) and ταφῆς ἀξίας μετέχουσιν are each of them significant points in the comparison.

25 **ὧν—ὑπάρχει.** The nominative of a relative pronoun is very rarely attracted into the genitive. Van Cleef (*de attract. in enunt. rel. usu Plat.* p. 42) cites only two other certain instances in Plato, viz. *Theaet.* 158 A and *Alc.* II 148 A. περὶ πάντων ὧν γέγονε is found in an Attic inscription about the end of the fourth century B.C. (Meisterhans[3] p. 238). In *Phaed.* 69 A the nominative passes into a dative: cf. also οἷς ἐξόν in 466 A and *Gorg.* 492 B.

465 E 29 **ζῶντές τε.** We should expect τε to follow γέρα, but cf. 452 A. Here, as there, one or two MSS (with Stobaeus *Flor.* 43. 102 ad fin.) omit τε. Hartman is suspicious of ταφῆς ἀξίας μετέχουσιν, especially as καὶ μάλα—καλά refers to γέρα. καλά might conceivably be the marginal comment of an approving reader; but this kind of looseness is not uncommon in replies (cf. II 372 A, III 405 D, IV 436 E, 468 A, VI 500 B, VII 535 C, VIII 558 A, B, *Gorg.* 467 E and elsewhere, with Riddell *Digest of Platonic Idioms* § 306), and the expression ταφῆς ἀξίας μετέχουσιν is much too quiet and refined for the ordinary scribe.

31 **οὐκ οἶδα ὅτου**: said with a glance at Adimantus, who had been the spokesman of these views (IV 419 A ff.). Cf. the use of τισίν in II 372 E.

466 A 1 **ποιοῖμεν — σκεψοίμεθα.** See *cr. nn.* I agree with most of the recent editors in writing the optative.

πολιτῶν οὐδὲν ἔχοιεν; ἡμεῖς δέ που εἴπομεν, ὅτι τοῦτο μέν, εἴ που παραπίπτοι, εἰσαῦθις σκεψοίμεθα, νῦν δὲ τοὺς μὲν φύλακας φύλακας ποιοῖμεν, τὴν δὲ πόλιν ὡς οἷοί τ' εἶμεν εὐδαιμονεστάτην, ἀλλ' οὐκ εἰς ἓν ἔθνος ἀποβλέποντες ἐν αὐτῇ τοῦτο εὔδαιμον πλάττοιμεν; Μέμνημαι, ἔφη. Τί οὖν; νῦν ἡμῖν ὁ τῶν ἐπικούρων βίος, εἴπερ τοῦ γε τῶν ὀλυμπιονικῶν πολύ τε καλλίων καὶ ἀμείνων φαίνεται, μή πῃ | κατὰ τὸν τῶν σκυτοτόμων φαίνεται βίον ἤ τινων B ἄλλων δημιουργῶν ἢ τὸν τῶν γεωργῶν; Οὔ μοι δοκεῖ, ἔφη. Ἀλλὰ μέντοι, ὅ γε καὶ ἐκεῖ ἔλεγον, δίκαιον καὶ ἐνταῦθα εἰπεῖν, ὅτι εἰ οὕτως ὁ φύλαξ ἐπιχειρήσει εὐδαίμων γίγνεσθαι, ὥστε μηδὲ φύλαξ εἶναι, μηδ' ἀρκέσει αὐτῷ βίος οὕτω μέτριος καὶ βέβαιος καὶ ὡς ἡμεῖς φαμὲν ἄριστος, ἀλλ' ἀνόητός τε καὶ μειρακιώδης δόξα ἐμπεσοῦσα εὐδαιμονίας πέρι ὁρμήσει αὐτὸν διὰ δύναμιν ἐπὶ τὸ ἅπαντα | τὰ ἐν τῇ πόλει οἰκειοῦσθαι, γνώσεται τὸν Ἡσίοδον ὅτι C τῷ ὄντι ἦν σοφὸς λέγων πλέον εἶναί πως ἥμισυ παντός. Ἐμοὶ μέν, ἔφη, ξυμβούλῳ χρώμενος μενεῖ ἐπὶ τούτῳ τῷ βίῳ. Συγχωρεῖς ἄρα, ἦν δ' ἐγώ, τὴν τῶν γυναικῶν κοινωνίαν τοῖς ἀνδράσιν, ἣν

3. σκεψοίμεθα v: σκεψόμεθα ΑΠΞ q. 4. ποιοῖμεν Π: ποιοῦμεν A.

σκεψόμεθα is perhaps defensible, for we may regard τοῦτο μὲν—σκεψόμεθα as *oratio recta*; but ποιοῦμεν would be very awkward, if not positively wrong, in view of the optative ὡς οἷοί τ' εἶμεν. It is noticeable that Plato did not expressly promise to examine this point; although the solution is already hinted at in IV 420 B.

οἷς ἐξόν. Hirschig would write οἵ for οἷς, but see 465 D *n.* The same attraction is found in other authors besides Plato: see Kühner *Gr. Gr.* II p. 925.

6 **ἐπικούρων** has now a more exalted sense than formerly (see 463 B, 464 B *nn.*), and includes the Rulers. Aristotle perversely misrepresents Plato's position in regard to the happiness of the guardians when he remarks ἔτι δὲ καὶ τὴν εὐδαιμονίαν ἀφαιρούμενος τῶν φυλάκων, ὅλην φησὶ δεῖν εὐδαίμονα ποιεῖν τὴν πόλιν τὸν νομοθέτην (*Pol.* B 5. 1264^b^ 15 ff.): see Susemihl ad loc.

466 B 10 **ἐκεῖ.** IV 420 ff.

14 **διὰ δύναμιν**: 'because he has the power,' "weil er kann" (Schneider). The possession of the power to do wrong is itself a temptation, according to Plato: cf. *Gorg.* 525 D οὗτοι (tyrants etc.) γὰρ διὰ τὴν ἐξουσίαν μέγιστα καὶ ἀνοσιώτατα ἁμαρτήματα ἁμαρτάνουσι, and ib. 526 A. Whibley points out that in the language of Greek politics and political science δύναμις was often used in a quasi-technical sense, denoting 'power due to wealth, connexions,' etc. (*Gk. Olig.* p. 125 *n.* 7), but it can hardly have such a meaning here. Madvig conjectures, absurdly enough, διαδῦναι.

466 C 15 **Ἡσίοδον.** *OD.* 40.

17 **μενεῖ ἐπί**: 'will remain true to,' as in VI 496 B.

συγχωρεῖς is followed first by the accusative κοινωνίαν and afterwards by the accusative with infinitive κατά τε πόλιν—ἄρρεν (J. and C.). Ast desired to cancel καί before παίδων, and is commended for this by Hartman, who remarks "quasi unquam παῖδες gigni possint sine mulieris et viri κοινωνίᾳ!" "Nodum in scirpo," as Schneider caustically observes. Plato is speaking of κοινωνία περὶ παίδων not between *one* woman and *one* man, but between several women and several men (τῶν γυναικῶν τοῖς ἀνδράσι). The children are common to all the guardians of either sex.

διεληλύθαμεν, παιδείας τε πέρι καὶ παίδων καὶ φυλακῆς τῶν
ἄλλων πολιτῶν, κατά τε πόλιν μενούσας εἰς πόλεμόν τε ἰούσας
D καὶ ξυμφυλάττειν δεῖν καὶ ξυνθηρεύειν ὥσπερ κύνας καὶ | πάντα
πάντῃ κατὰ τὸ δυνατὸν κοινωνεῖν, καὶ ταῦτα πραττούσας τά τε
βέλτιστα πράξειν καὶ οὐ παρὰ φύσιν τὴν τοῦ θήλεος πρὸς τὸ
ἄρρεν, ᾗ πεφύκατον πρὸς ἀλλήλω κοινωνεῖν; Συγχωρῶ, ἔφη.
XIV. Οὐκοῦν, ἦν δ' ἐγώ, ἐκεῖνο λοιπὸν διελέσθαι, εἰ ἄρα καὶ
ἐν ἀνθρώποις δυνατόν, ὥσπερ ἐν ἄλλοις ζῴοις, ταύτην τὴν κοινωνίαν
ἐγγενέσθαι, καὶ ὅπῃ δυνατόν; Ἔφθης, ἔφη, εἰπὼν ᾗ ἔμελλον
E ὑπολήψεσθαι. Περὶ μὲν γὰρ τῶν ἐν τῷ πολέμῳ οἶμαι, | ἔφην,
δῆλον ὃν τρόπον πολεμήσουσιν. Πῶς; ἦ δ' ὅς. Ὅτι κοινῇ
στρατεύσονται, καὶ πρός γε ἄξουσι τῶν παίδων εἰς τὸν πόλεμον
ὅσοι ἁδροί, ἵν' ὥσπερ οἱ τῶν ἄλλων δημιουργῶν θεῶνται ταῦτα,
ἃ τελεωθέντας δεήσει δημιουργεῖν· πρὸς δὲ τῇ θέᾳ διακονεῖν καὶ
467 | ὑπηρετεῖν πάντα τὰ περὶ τὸν πόλεμον καὶ θεραπεύειν πατέρας
τε καὶ μητέρας. ἢ οὐκ ᾔσθησαι τὰ περὶ τὰς τέχνας, οἷον τοὺς
τῶν κεραμέων παῖδας, ὡς πολὺν χρόνον διακονοῦντες θεωροῦσι
πρὶν ἅπτεσθαι τοῦ κεραμεύειν; Καὶ μάλα. Ἦ οὖν ἐκείνοις
ἐπιμελέστερον παιδευτέον ἢ τοῖς φύλαξι τοὺς αὑτῶν ἐμπειρίᾳ
τε καὶ θέᾳ τῶν προσηκόντων; Καταγέλαστον μέντ' ἄν, ἔφη,
B εἴη. Ἀλλὰ μὴν καὶ μαχεῖταί γε πᾶν ζῷον διαφερόντως | παρόντων

---

466 D 23 **οὐ παρὰ φύσιν.** Before taking leave of the subject, Plato reiterates the principle on which his communism rests. "Equal companionship in the work and interests of life is the natural relation of the sexes, whereas it is the existing relation which is unnatural" (Bosanquet). Cf. 456 C *n.*

466 D—**467** E *We have still to determine whether such a state of society is possible among men, as it is among the lower animals. But first let us provide for the management of war.*

Our men and our women will take the field in common, accompanied by such of their offspring as are not too young. The children will attend to their parents' wants and encourage them by their presence on the ground. They will thus have the advantage of witnessing the actual exercise of the profession which awaits them in later life. The risk is considerable, but the issues at stake require it to be run: and we shall take every precaution to ensure the children's safety.

466 D 26 **ὥσπερ—ζῴοις.** Cf. 451 D.

28 **περὶ μὲν γὰρ κτλ.** = 'for as to *war*' etc. is a dexterous way of making room for the episode on war, and at the same time postponing 'the great *peripeteia*, the on-rushing of the third wave,' which "is made more impressive by being delayed" (J. and C.). For μὲν γάρ cf. VIII 562 A *n.*

466 E 31 **ὥσπερ κτλ.** Handicrafts were usually hereditary among the Greeks: cf. *Prot.* 328 A and Blümner *Privatalt.* p. 395 *nn.* διακονεῖν should be taken with ἄξουσι. The change of construction is illustrated by Schneider (*Addit.* p. 41) from *Tim.* 74 B ἐμηχανᾶτο, ἵνα—παρέχοι, τὴν δὲ σάρκα—ἔσεσθαι κτλ. Herwerden inserts δεῖ, and Richards διδάσκωνται, after θέᾳ, but the text is probably sound.

467 A 7 **μαχεῖται—τέκη.** Cf. Xen. *Cyr.* IV 3. 2 and Tac. *Germ.* 7 quodque praecipuum fortitudinis incitamentum est —in proximo pignora, unde feminarum ululatus audiri, unde vagitus infantium.

ὧν ἂν τέκῃ. Ἔστιν οὕτω. κίνδυνος δέ, ὦ Σώκρατες, οὐ σμικρὸς σφαλεῖσιν, οἷα δὴ ἐν πολέμῳ φιλεῖ, πρὸς ἑαυτοῖς παῖδας ἀπολέσαντας ποιῆσαι καὶ τὴν ἄλλην πόλιν ἀδύνατον ἀναλαβεῖν. Ἀληθῆ, ἦν δ' ἐγώ, λέγεις. ἀλλὰ σὺ πρῶτον μὲν ἡγεῖ παρασκευαστέον τὸ μή ποτε κινδυνεῦσαι; Οὐδαμῶς. Τί δ'; εἴ που κινδυνευτέον, οὐκ ἐν ᾧ βελτίους ἔσονται κατορθοῦντες; Δῆλον δή. | Ἀλλὰ σμικρὸν οἴει διαφέρειν καὶ οὐκ ἄξιον κινδύνου θεωρεῖν **C** ἢ μὴ τὰ περὶ τὸν πόλεμον παῖδας τοὺς ἄνδρας πολεμικοὺς ἐσομένους; Οὔκ, ἀλλὰ διαφέρει πρὸς ὃ λέγεις. Τοῦτο μὲν ἄρα ὑπαρκτέον, θεωροὺς πολέμου τοὺς παῖδας ποιεῖν, προσμηχανᾶσθαι δ' αὐτοῖς ἀσφάλειαν, καὶ καλῶς ἕξει. ἦ γάρ; Ναί. Οὐκοῦν, ἦν δ' ἐγώ, πρῶτον μὲν αὐτῶν οἱ πατέρες, ὅσα ἄνθρωποι, οὐκ ἀμαθεῖς ἔσονται, ἀλλὰ γνωμονικοὶ τῶν στρατειῶν, ὅσαι τε καὶ **D** μὴ ἐπικίνδυνοι; Εἰκός, ἔφη. Εἰς μὲν ἄρα τὰς ἄξουσιν, εἰς δὲ τὰς εὐλαβήσονται. Ὀρθῶς. Καὶ ἄρχοντάς γέ που, ἦν δ' ἐγώ, οὐ τοὺς φαυλοτάτους αὐτοῖς ἐπιστήσουσιν, ἀλλὰ τοὺς ἐμπειρίᾳ τε καὶ ἡλικίᾳ ἱκανοὺς ἡγεμόνας τε καὶ παιδαγωγοὺς εἶναι. Πρέπει γάρ. Ἀλλὰ γάρ, φήσομεν, καὶ παρὰ δόξαν πολλὰ πολλοῖς δὴ ἐγένετο. Καὶ μάλα. Πρὸς τοίνυν τὰ τοιαῦτα, ὦ φίλε, πτεροῦν χρὴ παιδία ὄντα εὐθύς, ἵν' ἄν τι δέῃ πετόμενοι ἀποφεύγωσιν. | Πῶς λέγεις; ἔφη. Ἐπὶ τοὺς ἵππους, ἦν δ' ἐγώ, ἀναβιβαστέον **E**

---

467 B 10 **ἀναλαβεῖν** = 'to recover.' This intransitive use of *ἀναλαμβάνειν* is especially common in medical writers: see Stephanus-Hase *Lex.* s.v. It arises from the omission of the reflexive pronoun, which is a common way of making transitive verbs into intransitive: see on I 336 B.

467 C 15 **παῖδας τοὺς ἄνδρας**. Ξ with several other MSS reads *τοὺς παῖδας* instead of *παῖδας*. But *παῖδας* is predicative, and goes with *θεωρεῖν*. "Socrates plurimum referre dicit, ut qui *adulti* bellicosi futuri sint, iam pueri res bellicas spectent" (Schneider). Hartman seriously weakens the contrast between *παῖδας* and *ἄνδρας* by reading *ἄνδρας* <*τοὺς*> *πολεμικούς*.

16 **διαφέρει**. We should at first sight expect <*πολὺ*> *διαφέρει*, and so Richards suggests. But (as Hartman points out) the introduction of *οὐκ ἄξιον κινδύνου* breaks the continuity between the original question and the reply. Hence, too, the reply has *διαφέρει*, not *διαφέρειν* (the reading of Ξ and a few other MSS, wrongly preferred by Hartman).

τοῦτο μὲν κτλ. *ὑπαρκτέον* = *δεῖ ὑπάρχειν* (intransitive), not 'we must begin with,' as J. and C. suppose. Cf. *ἑκτέον* 468 A. *τοῦτο* (accusative: see on III 400 D) is explained by *θεωροὺς—ποιεῖν*. With *προσμηχανᾶσθαι*, *δεῖ* or the like is understood out of *ὑπαρκτέον*: cf. *Gorg.* 492 D *τὰς μὲν ἐπιθυμίας φῂς οὐ κολαστέον—ἐῶντα δὲ αὐτὰς ὡς μεγίστας πλήρωσιν—ἑτοιμάζειν* and *Crito* 51 C. Richards needlessly proposes to read *προσμηχανητέον* or to insert "something like *δεήσει*."

467 D 22 **εὐλαβήσονται**: sc. *ἄγειν*.

24 **παιδαγωγούς**. The tutorial office in Athens was assigned to slaves. In Plato it is exercised by the very best of the citizens. Bosanquet justly emphasizes the revolution which Plato's arrangement would involve in the education of the young.

25 **ἀλλὰ γάρ**. II 365 C *n.*

ὡς νεωτάτους, καὶ διδαξαμένους ἱππεύειν ἐφ' ἵππων ἀκτέον ἐπὶ
τὴν θέαν μὴ θυμοειδῶν μηδὲ μαχητικῶν, ἀλλ' ὅ τι ποδωκεστάτων
καὶ εὐηνιωτάτων. οὕτω γὰρ κάλλιστά τε θεάσονται τὸ αὑτῶν
ἔργον, καὶ ἀσφαλέστατα, ἄν τι δέῃ, σωθήσονται μετὰ πρεσβυτέρων
468 ἡγεμόνων ἑπόμενοι. Ὀρθῶς, ἔφη, μοι δοκεῖς | λέγειν.
Τί δὲ δή, εἶπον, τὰ περὶ τὸν πόλεμον; πῶς ἑκτέον σοι τοὺς
στρατιώτας πρὸς αὑτούς τε καὶ τοὺς πολεμίους; ἆρ' ὀρθῶς μοι
καταφαίνεται ἢ οὔ; Λέγ', ἔφη, ποῖα. Αὐτῶν μέν, εἶπον, τὸν
λιπόντα τάξιν ἢ ὅπλα ἀποβαλόντα ἤ τι τῶν τοιούτων ποιήσαντα
διὰ κάκην ἆρα οὐ δημιουργόν τινα δεῖ καθιστάναι ἢ γεωργόν;
Πάνυ μὲν οὖν. Τὸν δὲ ζῶντα εἰς τοὺς πολεμίους ἁλόντα ἆρ' οὐ
B δωρεὰν διδόναι τοῖς ἑλοῦσι χρῆσθαι τῇ ἄγρᾳ ὅ τι ἂν | βούλωνται;

29. διδαξαμένους q^2: διδαξομένους AΠ q^1: διδαχθέντας Ξ. 4. ποῖα Ξ: ποῖ ἂν A: ποίαν Π: ποῖον q. 8. ἑλοῦσι J. van Leeuwen: θέλουσι AΠΞ q.

---

467 E 29 **διδαξαμένους.** Schneider reads διδαχθέντας, while preferring his own conjecture δεδιδαξομένους. The future διδαξομένους cannot be right: for the children would certainly be taught to ride, before going on such expeditions (J. and C.). It would be too hazardous in such a case ἐν πίθῳ κεραμεύειν. Against Schneider's conjecture it may be urged that the future perfect participle should not be used where the aorist participle is enough. διδαχθέντας is an obvious 'correction.' With διδαξαμένους the meaning is simply 'when they have taught them to ride.' The middle expresses personal interest; and does not imply that the ἐπίκουροι get them taught by others. See on this point IV 421 E *n*. It may be noted that in Sparta great importance was attached to learning the accomplishment of riding (Müller *Dorians* II p. 316).

468 A—**469** B *Touching the citizens' duty to one another in the field, Socrates enumerates various means by which cowardice will be discouraged and bravery rewarded.*

468 A 2 **τί δὲ δὴ κτλ.** This punctuation is better than to place the mark of interrogation after δή, and take τὰ περὶ τὸν πόλεμον as an internal accusative with πῶς ἑκτέον κτλ., because τὰ περὶ τὸν πόλεμον is already practically involved in the word στρατιώτας. I agree with Hartman that Richards' proposal—τί δὲ δή; εἶπον· τὰ περὶ τὸν πόλεμον, πῶς—πολεμίους, ἆρα κτλ.;—is far from elegant.

4 **ποῖα.** See *cr. n.* ποῖ' ἄν, which is generally read, surely cannot be right. Schneider remarks "ποῖ' ἄν breviter dictum accipio pro ποῖα ἂν ὄντα τὰ περὶ τὸν πόλεμον ὀρθῶς ἔχειν λέγεις." J. and C. are content with supplying εἴη τὰ σοὶ καταφαινόμενα. But ellipses of this kind are too severe a strain upon the imagination. ποῖα δή is suggested by Richards, πῇ δή by Hartman: but is δή in place here? I think not. I take ποῖα sc. ἐστι to refer to τὰ περὶ τὸν πόλεμον. Glauco addresses himself to the first of Socrates' questions: cf. 465 E *n*. and Soph. *Trach.* 421—423. The corruption is common enough: see *Introd.* § 5.

αὐτῶν = 'ipsorum' contrasts Plato's soldiers with their enemies (cf. πρὸς αὑτούς τε καὶ τοὺς πολεμίους just before). μέν prepares us for the second part of this topic, beginning at 469 B. We certainly should not read μήν (with Hartman). Plato's treatment of cowardice in battle may be compared with the punishment of τρέσαντες in Sparta: see Gilbert *Gk. Constit. Ant.* E.T. p. 77. Cf. also *Laws* 943 D ff.

8 **ἑλοῦσι.** Van Leeuwen's emendation—see *cr. n.*—seems to me admirable. The contrast between ἁλόντα and ἑλοῦσι is precisely what is wanted: cf. Xen. *Cyr.* VII 5. 73 νόμος γὰρ ἐν πᾶσιν ἀνθρώποις ἀΐδιός ἐστιν, ὅταν πολεμούντων πόλις ἁλῷ, τῶν ἑλόντων εἶναι καὶ τὰ σώματα—καὶ τὰ χρήματα. With the infinitive van Leeuwen compares *Laws* 879 A παραδότω τὸν δοῦλον—χρῆσθαι ὅ τι ἂν

Κομιδῇ γε. Τὸν δὲ ἀριστεύσαντά τε καὶ εὐδοκιμήσαντα οὐ πρῶτον μὲν ἐπὶ στρατείας ὑπὸ τῶν συστρατευομένων μειρακίων τε καὶ παίδων ἐν μέρει ὑπὸ ἑκάστου δοκεῖ σοι χρῆναι στεφανωθῆναι; ἢ οὔ; Ἔμοιγε. Τί δέ; δεξιωθῆναι; Καὶ τοῦτο. Ἀλλὰ τόδ', οἶμαι, ἦν δ' ἐγώ, οὐκέτι σοι δοκεῖ. Τὸ ποῖον; Τὸ φιλῆσαί τε καὶ φιληθῆναι ὑπὸ ἑκάστου. Πάντων, ἔφη, μάλιστα· καὶ προστίθημί γε τῷ νόμῳ, ἕως ἂν ἐπὶ ταύτης | ὦσι τῆς στρατείας, μηδενὶ ἐξεῖναι C ἀπαρνηθῆναι, ὃν ἂν βούληται φιλεῖν, ἵνα καί, ἐάν τίς του τύχῃ ἐρῶν ἢ ἄρρενος ἢ θηλείας, προθυμότερος ᾖ πρὸς τὸ τἀριστεῖα φέρειν. Καλῶς, ἦν δ' ἐγώ. ὅτι μὲν γὰρ ἀγαθῷ ὄντι γάμοι τε ἕτοιμοι πλείους ἢ τοῖς ἄλλοις καὶ αἱρέσεις τῶν τοιούτων πολλάκις παρὰ τοὺς ἄλλους ἔσονται, ἵν' ὅ τι πλεῖστοι ἐκ τοῦ τοιούτου γίγνωνται, εἴρηται ἤδη. Εἴπομεν γάρ, ἔφη.

XV. Ἀλλὰ μὴν καὶ καθ' Ὅμηρον τοῖς τοιοῖσδε δίκαιον τιμᾶν τῶν νέων ὅσοι ἀγαθοί. καὶ | γὰρ Ὅμηρος τὸν εὐδοκιμήσαντα ἐν D

12. τί δέ; δεξιωθῆναι A^1Ξ*q*: τί δαὶ δ' ἐξιαθῆναι corr. A^2 et in mg. γρ τί δὲ ἐξιαθῆναι. Pro δεξιωθῆναι Π praebet δεξιαθῆναι (sic). 15. στρατείας q^2: στρατιᾶς AΞ: στρατίας (sic) Πq^1.

ἐθέλῃ. θέλουσι is not free from objection. Paris A generally has ἐθέλω, the usual Attic form; moreover, the word itself, if taken with χρῆσθαι, is too weak; nor can we (with J. and C.) readily understand ἔχειν. Plato's ordinances on this matter are far more drastic than anything known even in Sparta: see Müller *Dorians* II p. 238.

468 B 13 **οὐκέτι σοι δοκεῖ**: said with playful irony, for Glauco is an ἀνὴρ ἐρωτικός (474 D). A vein of irony runs through all this passage, as Dugas has pointed out (*L'Amitié Antique* p. 121); but it is not wholly ironical. Plato may have been willing to allow more latitude to soldiers on a campaign than he would permit to others, without sanctioning the usual abuses of camp life (see Dugas l.c. p. 87). There is nothing in this passage which is necessarily inconsistent with the self-restraint enjoined in III 403 B, although in practice abuses might have arisen. See also *Laws* 636 C ff.

14 **καὶ προστίθημί γε κτλ.** Glauco's enthusiasm is in keeping with his character: see last note.

468 C 16 **βούληται**: sc. ὁ ἀριστεύσας τε καὶ εὐδοκιμήσας.

ἐάν τις—φέρειν. See *Symp.* 178 E—179 B. The principle underlying Glauco's remark was widely accepted by Greek military authorities (see Hug on *Symp.* l.c. and Dugas l.c. pp. 90—104). The Theban Sacred Band, composed of ἐρασταί and ἐρώμενοι, is the best-known instance of its application in actual warfare (Athen. XIII 561 F).

19 **αἱρέσεις** means selections by the rulers (so also Schneider): cf. 460 B, to which εἴρηται ἤδη refers. J. and C.'s alternative rendering "success in winning such prizes" cannot stand: still less the translation of D. and V. "to exercise more than the usual liberty of choice in such matters."

τῶν τοιούτων: i.e. τῶν ἀγαθῶν.

468 D 23 **Ὅμηρος κτλ.** *Il.* 7. 321 f. νώτοισιν δ' Αἴαντα διηνεκέεσσι γέραιρεν | ἥρως Ἀτρείδης. In Plato, Αἴαντα is omitted by *q*, and three other MSS: one MS places it before νώτοισιν, and four after ἔφη. The word may be a gloss; but as it is present in AΠΞ, in the same position as in Homer, it is safer to retain it. Plato often makes his Homeric quotations complete, even at the cost of a little awkwardness: cf. II 363 B. Aristophanes, it may be noted, has the converse of Plato's proposal in *Eccl.* 680.

τῷ πολέμῳ νώτοισιν Αἴαντα ἔφη διηνεκέεσσι γεραίρεσθαι,
ὡς ταύτην οἰκείαν οὖσαν τιμὴν τῷ ἡβῶντί τε καὶ ἀνδρείῳ, ἐξ ἧς
ἅμα τῷ τιμᾶσθαι καὶ τὴν ἰσχὺν αὐξήσει. Ὀρθότατα, ἔφη.
Πεισόμεθα ἄρα, ἦν δ' ἐγώ, ταῦτά γε Ὁμήρῳ. καὶ γὰρ ἡμεῖς ἔν
τε θυσίαις καὶ τοῖς τοιούτοις πᾶσι τοὺς ἀγαθούς, καθ' ὅσον ἂν
ἀγαθοὶ φαίνωνται, καὶ ὕμνοις καὶ οἷς νῦν δὴ ἐλέγομεν τιμήσομεν,
E πρὸς δὲ τούτοις ἕδραις τε καὶ κρέασιν ἰδὲ πλείοις δεπάεσσιν, ἵνα ἅμα τῷ τιμᾶν ἀσκῶμεν τοὺς ἀγαθοὺς ἄνδρας τε καὶ
γυναῖκας. Κάλλιστα, ἔφη, λέγεις. Εἶεν· τῶν δὲ δὴ ἀποθανόντων
ἐπὶ στρατείας ὃς ἂν εὐδοκιμήσας τελευτήσῃ, ἆρ' οὐ πρῶτον μὲν
φήσομεν τοῦ χρυσοῦ γένους εἶναι; Πάντων γε μάλιστα. Ἀλλ'
οὐ πεισόμεθα Ἡσιόδῳ, ἐπειδάν τινες τοῦ τοιούτου γένους τελευτή-
σωσιν, ὡς ἄρα

469 οἱ μὲν δαίμονες ἁγνοὶ ἐπιχθόνιοι τελέθουσιν,
ἐσθλοί, ἀλεξίκακοι, φύλακες μερόπων ἀνθρώπων;

Πεισόμεθα μὲν οὖν. Διαπυθόμενοι ἄρα τοῦ θεοῦ, πῶς χρὴ τοὺς
δαιμονίους τε καὶ θείους τιθέναι καὶ τίνι διαφόρῳ, οὕτω καὶ ταύτῃ
θήσομεν ᾗ ἂν ἐξηγῆται; Τί δ' οὐ μέλλομεν; Καὶ τὸν λοιπὸν
δὴ χρόνον, ὡς δαιμόνων, οὕτω θεραπεύσομέν τε καὶ προσκυνήσομεν
B αὐτῶν τὰς θήκας; ταὐτὰ δὲ ταῦτα νομιοῦμεν, ὅταν τις γήρᾳ ἢ

33. *στρατείας* Π: *στρατιᾶς* A. 6. *θεραπεύσομεν* Π: *θεραπεύσωμεν* A. *προσκυνήσομεν* A¹Π: *προσκυνήσωμεν* A². 7. *ταὐτὰ* v: *ταῦτα* ΑΠΞ q.

---

27 **γε** reminds us that Homer is not in other respects a *persona grata* in our city.

468 E 30 **ἕδραις κτλ.** *ἕδρῃ τε κρέασίν τε ἰδὲ πλείοις δεπάεσσιν* in *Il.* VIII 162 al.

33 **στρατείας**: not of course *στρατιᾶς* (Herwerden), for *στρατιά* is 'army,' *στρατεία* 'campaign.'

34 **τοῦ χρυσοῦ γένους.** III 415 A. Cf. Heracl. *Fr.* 102 ed. Bywater *ἀρηιφάτους θεοὶ τιμῶσι καὶ ἄνθρωποι.*

35 **τοῦ τοιούτου γένους.** Plato compares his 'golden citizens' with the heroes of the Hesiodic golden age. He would fain surround them with some of the romantic and religious sentiment that clung around the golden age of Greek poetry and legend.

469 A 1 **οἱ μὲν—ἀνθρώπων.** Cf. *Crat.* 397 E. The nearest approach to these lines in our Hesiod is to be found in *OD.* 122 f. *τοὶ μὲν*—the departed children of the golden age—*δαίμονές εἰσι Διὸς μεγάλου διὰ βουλὰς | ἐσθλοί, ἐπιχθόνιοι, φύλακες θνητῶν ἀνθρώπων.*

3 **τοῦ θεοῦ.** Apollo, our *πάτριος ἐξηγητής*: see IV 427 B *n.*

4 **τιθέναι**: 'to bury.'

τίνι διαφόρῳ: 'with what distinction' ("mit welcher Auszeichnung" Schneider). The occurrence of *θήκας διαφόρους* in *Laws* 947 B is no ground for reading <*θήκῃ*> *τίνι διαφόρῳ* here, as Richards bids us read.

6 **ὡς δαιμόνων—θήκας** is another link with Greek religion. Cf. Eur. *Alc.* 1000 ff. *καί τις δοχμίαν κέλευθον | ἐμβαίνων τόδ' ἐρεῖ | "αὕτα ποτὲ προὔθαν' ἀνδρός, | νῦν δ' ἐστὶ μάκαιρα δαίμων. | χαῖρ' ὦ πότνι', εὖ δὲ δοίης." | τοῖαί νιν προσεροῦσι φᾶμαι*, and other passages cited by Nägelsbach *Nachhom. Theol.* pp. 108—110.

469 B—**471** C *We have also a duty to our enemies. No Greek city is to be*

τινι ἄλλῳ τρόπῳ τελευτήσῃ τῶν ὅσοι ἂν διαφερόντως ἐν τῷ βίῳ ἀγαθοὶ κριθῶσιν; Δίκαιον γοῦν, ἔφη.

Τί δέ; πρὸς τοὺς πολεμίους πῶς ποιήσουσιν ἡμῖν οἱ στρατιῶται; Τὸ ποῖον δή; Πρῶτον μὲν ἀνδραποδισμοῦ πέρι δοκεῖ δίκαιον Ἕλληνας Ἑλληνίδας πόλεις ἀνδραποδίζεσθαι, ἢ μηδ' ἄλλῃ ἐπιτρέπειν κατὰ τὸ δυνατὸν καὶ τοῦτο ἐθίζειν, τοῦ Ἑλληνικοῦ γένους φείδεσθαι, εὐλαβουμένους τὴν ὑπὸ τῶν βαρβάρων δουλείαν; C
Ὅλῳ καὶ παντί, ἔφη, διαφέρει τὸ φείδεσθαι. Μηδὲ Ἕλληνα ἄρα

---

enslaved, and there must be no unseemly plundering of the dead. Armour captured in the field shall not be dedicated in temples, least of all such armour as we take from Greeks, unless the God shall otherwise decree. We forbid Greek territory to be ravaged, or Greek houses to be burnt. The entire Hellenic race are children of one family, and conflicts between its members should not be called war, but civil strife. Our natural enemy is the Barbarian, and if we plunder Greece, we do but ravage our nurse and mother. Remember that our city is a Greek city. She may chastise, but will not enslave, other Greek States. Glauco agrees: he thinks our citizens should treat the Barbarian as Greeks now treat their fellow-countrymen.

469 B ff. In this episode Plato discusses the principles which are to regulate the international policy of his city in her dealings both with Greeks and Barbarians. The Greeks themselves recognised certain unwritten laws or usages (νόμοι κοινοὶ τῆς Ἑλλάδος, νόμιμα τῶν Ἑλλήνων) in matters of this kind, and to these Plato frequently makes allusion throughout his argument: see on 469 E, 470 C al. Cf. Nägelsbach *Nachhom. Theol.* pp. 300—307. The policy which Plato here prescribes for his ideal city was clearly intended by him to have a direct and immediate bearing on the circumstances of his own day; and this part of the *Republic* is in no small degree, as Jackson remarks, "a contribution to practical politics." See on 470 C.

12 **Ἕλληνας—ἄλλῃ.** Ἕλληνας is the object, not, as is sometimes held, the subject, of ἀνδραποδίζεσθαι. It rightly occupies the emphatic place, because the point is that Greek cities should not enslave *Greeks*—no one objects to their enslaving barbarians,—and not that *Greeks* (as opposed to barbarians) should not enslave Greek cities. Cf. the order in 471 A οὐδ' ἄρα τὴν Ἑλλάδα Ἕλληνες ὄντες κεροῦσιν. A further reason for taking this view is that Ἑλληνίδας πόλεις points the allusion to Plato's city, which is a Ἑλληνὶς πόλις (470 E), and therefore will not reduce Greeks to slavery. Finally, μηδ' ἄλλῃ (sc. Ἑλληνίδι πόλει) is easy and natural only if Ἑλληνίδας πόλεις is treated as the subject. The difficulty of μηδ' ἄλλῃ (on the usual interpretation) led to the correction μηδ' ἄλλοις (Stallbaum with *v* and Flor. RT), and has recently caused Hartman to propose μηδαμῇ, on the ground that ἄλλῃ after Ἕλληνας could only mean βαρβάρῳ. In so saying, he goes, I think, too far; but my explanation removes the difficulty.

13 **ἐθίζειν**: sc. τοὺς Ἕλληνας.

14 **εὐλαβουμένους** agrees with the subject of φείδεσθαι rather than with that of ἐθίζειν. The Spartan Callicratidas agreed with Plato here: οὐκ ἔφη ἑαυτοῦ γε ἄρχοντος οὐδένα Ἑλλήνων εἰς τοὐκείνου δυνατὸν ἀνδραποδισθῆναι (Xen. *Hell.* I 6. 14). To enslave barbarians, on the other hand, is just: for the barbarian is φύσει δοῦλος (Eur. *Iph. Aul.* 1401 and elsewhere: Arist. *Pol.* A 2. 1252b 9). See also on 470 C.

469 C 15 **ὅλῳ καὶ παντί.** So in *Phaed.* 79 E, *Crat.* 433 E. In VII 527 C we have τῷ ὅλῳ καὶ παντί, and even τῷ παντὶ καὶ ὅλῳ in *Laws* 734 E.

μηδέ: with ἐκτῆσθαι. They must neither enslave their countrymen (ἀνδραποδίζεσθαι above), nor hold a Greek in slavery: cf. I 351 B. J. and C. wrongly translate μηδέ as 'not even,' and Hartman needlessly proposes μηδέν'. Greek slaves were of foreign nationality, except such as had been sold into slavery on the destruction of their city by war (Blümner *Privatalt.* p. 87 *n.* 1). Plato disapproves of the exception: does he mean to approve the rule, so far as his own city is concerned? Steinhart (*Einleitung* p. 202)

δοῦλον ἐκτῆσθαι μήτε αὐτοὺς τοῖς τε ἄλλοις Ἕλλησιν οὕτω
ξυμβουλεύειν; Πάνυ μὲν οὖν, ἔφη· μᾶλλόν γ' ἂν οὖν οὕτω πρὸς
τοὺς βαρβάρους τρέποιντο, ἑαυτῶν δ' ἀπέχοιντο. Τί δέ; σκυλεύειν,
ἦν δ' ἐγώ, τοὺς τελευτήσαντας πλὴν ὅπλων, ἐπειδὰν νικήσωσιν,
ἦ καλῶς ἔχει; ἢ οὐ πρόφασιν μὲν τοῖς δειλοῖς ἔχει μὴ πρὸς τὸν
D μαχόμενον ἰέναι, ὥς τι τῶν δεόντων δρῶντας, ὅταν περὶ τὸν
τεθνεῶτα κυπτάζωσι, πολλὰ δὲ ἤδη στρατόπεδα διὰ τὴν τοιαύτην
ἁρπαγὴν ἀπώλετο; Καὶ μάλα. Ἀνελεύθερον δὲ οὐ δοκεῖ καὶ
φιλοχρήματον νεκρὸν συλᾶν, καὶ γυναικείας τε καὶ σμικρᾶς διανοίας
τὸ πολέμιον νομίζειν τὸ σῶμα τοῦ τεθνεῶτος ἀποπταμένου τοῦ
ἐχθροῦ, λελοιπότος δὲ ᾧ ἐπολέμει; ἢ οἴει τι διάφορον δρᾶν τοὺς
E τοῦτο ποιοῦντας τῶν κυνῶν, αἳ τοῖς λίθοις, οἷς ἂν βληθῶσι,
χαλεπαίνουσι, τοῦ βάλλοντος οὐχ ἁπτόμεναι; Οὐδὲ σμικρόν, ἔφη.
Ἐατέον ἄρα τὰς νεκροσυλίας καὶ τὰς τῶν ἀναιρέσεων διακωλύσεις;
Ἐατέον μέντοι, ἔφη, νὴ Δία.

XVI. Οὐδὲ μὴν που πρὸς τὰ ἱερὰ τὰ ὅπλα οἴσομεν ὡς ἀναθή-

28. *βάλλοντος* Π: *βαλόντος* unus A.

---

asserts that Plato expressly recognises slavery in his State. It is clear from the present section that Plato does not impugn the principle of slavery, so long as the slaves are of barbarian origin; but he nowhere says that his perfect city is actually to contain slaves, nor is it easy to see what there would be for them to do, unless they were employed to work under the farmers and artizans, or as personal attendants at the *συσσίτια* and the like. Slaves are present, of course, in the city of the *Laws* (776 C ff.).

18 **σκυλεύειν—καλῶς ἔχει.** Cf. Xen. *Hell.* II 4. 19 (quoted by J. and C.) *καὶ τὰ μὲν ὅπλα ἔλαβον, τοὺς δὲ χιτῶνας οὐδενὸς τῶν πολιτῶν ἐσκύλευσαν.* Such moderation was unusual.

469 D 25 **ἀποπταμένου** is (as Schulze pointed out in *Fl. Jahrb.* 1887 pp. 226 ff.) a reminiscence of Homer's *ἀπὸ δ' ἔπτατο θυμός* (*Il.* 16. 469 and elsewhere). Hence the poetic form, as in *οἴχεται ἀποπτάμενος* (*Symp.* 183 E from *Il.* II 71). The ordinary aorist in prose is *-επτόμην*, as in II 365 A. Compare *Phaed.* 115 C f. and Eur. *Fr.* 176. 3—6 *τίς γὰρ πετραῖον σκόπελον οὐτάζων δορὶ | ὀδύναισι δώσει; τίς δ' ἀτιμάζων νέκυς, | εἰ μηδὲν αἰσθάνοιτο τῶν παθημάτων;* and Plut. *Apophtheg. Lac.* 228 F.

469 E 27 **αἳ—ἁπτόμεναι.** Aristotle read *βάλλοντος*, and not *βαλόντος* (see *cr. n.*), as appears from *Rhet.* III 4. 1406ᵇ 33, where he refers to Plato's illustration as follows: *καὶ τὸ ἐν τῇ πολιτείᾳ τῇ Πλάτωνος, ὅτι οἱ τοὺς τεθνεῶτας σκυλεύοντες ἐοίκασι τοῖς κυνιδίοις, ἃ τοὺς λίθους δάκνει τοῦ βάλλοντος οὐχ ἁπτόμενα.* The present is more picturesque and true to nature: the dog worries the stones, while his tormentor amuses himself by throwing more. It is true that the simile is not quite accurate, because a 'flown antagonist' cannot continue to do mischief; but *βαλόντος*, which is generally read, though not by Schneider, is also inexact, because you cannot attack a vanished foe. In either case, the analogy is near enough. Moreover the consensus of all the other MSS, coupled with Aristotle, outweighs the authority of A where lipography is possible. See *Introd.* § 5.

29 **ἀναιρέσεων.** The laws of Greek warfare permitted *ἀναίρεσις* of the dead, unless the petitioning parties had forfeited their rights by robbing a temple or desecrating a shrine (Busolt *Gr. Alterth.* p. 55, where the authorities are cited).

31 **οὐδὲ μὴν—Ἑλλήνων**: as was usual in Greece: see for example Thuc. III

σοντες, ἄλλως τε καὶ τὰ τῶν Ἑλλήνων, ἐάν τι ἡμῖν μέλῃ τῆς πρὸς τοὺς | ἄλλους Ἕλληνας εὐνοίας· μᾶλλον δὲ καὶ φοβησόμεθα, μή 470
τι μίασμα ᾖ πρὸς ἱερὸν τὰ τοιαῦτα ἀπὸ τῶν οἰκείων φέρειν, ἐὰν μή τι δὴ ὁ θεὸς ἄλλο λέγῃ. Ὀρθότατα, ἔφη. Τί δέ; γῆς τε τμήσεως τῆς Ἑλληνικῆς καὶ οἰκιῶν ἐμπρήσεως ποῖόν τί σοι δράσουσιν οἱ στρατιῶται πρὸς τοὺς πολεμίους; Σοῦ, ἔφη, δόξαν ἀποφαινομένου ἡδέως ἂν ἀκούσαιμι. Ἐμοὶ μὲν τοίνυν, ἦν δ' ἐγώ, δοκεῖ τούτων | μηδέτερα ποιεῖν, ἀλλὰ τὸν ἐπέτειον καρπὸν ἀφαιρεῖσθαι, καὶ ὧν B
ἕνεκα, βούλει σοι λέγω; Πάνυ γε. Φαίνεταί μοι, ὥσπερ καὶ ὀνομάζεται δύο ταῦτα τὰ ὀνόματα, πόλεμός τε καὶ στάσις, οὕτω καὶ εἶναι δύο, ὄντα ἐπὶ δυοῖν τινοῖν διαφοραῖν. λέγω δὲ τὰ δύο, τὸ μὲν οἰκεῖον καὶ ξυγγενές, τὸ δὲ ἀλλότριον καὶ ὀθνεῖον. ἐπὶ μὲν οὖν τῇ τοῦ οἰκείου ἔχθρᾳ στάσις κέκληται, ἐπὶ δὲ τῇ τοῦ ἀλλοτρίου

9. τὰ A^2Ξ: om. A^1Π*q*.

---

114. 1. Plutarch however implies that the Spartans were an honourable exception to this rule (*Apophtheg. Lac.* 224 B). With Plato's sentiment cf. "aeternum inimicitiarum monumentum Graios de Graiis statuere non oportet" (Cic. *de Inv.* II 70. Cicero is referring to an incident arising out of a war between Sparta and Thebes).

470 A 2 **ἐὰν μή τι—λέγῃ.** Apollo might not wish to surrender his rights, and Plato would do no violence to the patron god of his city (IV 427 B). It was usual to dedicate a tithe of the spoil to the gods (Xen. *Hell.* III 3. 1).

3 **τί δέ; κτλ.** So Schneider punctuates. Stallbaum and others place the mark of interrogation after ἐμπρήσεως, comparing VII 515 B, IX 582 C (where however see my notes), and other examples: but the analogy of 469 B and 469 C, as well as the emphasis on γῆς, is in favour of Schneider's view. We may compare the use of the genitive instead of περί with the genitive after verbs of speaking, asking about etc.; cf. IX 576 D and Jebb on Soph. *Trach.* 169.

470 B 8 **ὥσπερ καὶ—δύο.** Literally 'as these names, war and civil discord, are *named* two, so also they *are* two.' ὀνομάζεται δύο is opposed to εἶναι δύο, which means δύο οὐσίας εἶναι 'are,' 'express two realities,' as is further explained in ὄντα—διαφοραῖν. Instead of ταῦτα τὰ ὀνόματα, ταῦτα ὀνόματα—see *cr. n.*—is now usually read. With this reading, the sense would be 'as these things' (viz. War and Discord) 'are called by two names, so also they are in reality two,' ὄντα ἐπὶ κτλ. That is to say, ὄντα ἐπί would be said of things; but it is clearly intended to be said of names: cf. κέκληται ἐπί just below. Schneider noticed the difficulty, but thought the confusion between names and things excusable. It is surely a grave blemish in a passage which is written expressly to distinguish between the two. Richards would transpose and read ὥσπερ καὶ—στάσις, ὄντα ἐπὶ δυοῖν τινοῖν διαφοραῖν, οὕτω καὶ εἶναι δύο, or make ὄντα—διαφοραῖν follow ὀνόματα. This solution effects, at great cost, what is only after all a partial cure.

10 **ὄντα ἐπὶ κτλ.** ἐπί governs διαφοραῖν, and δυοῖν τινοῖν, which is neuter, depends on διαφοραῖν. The literal meaning is 'being applied to two kinds of disagreements, arising in two things.' The two things—continues Plato—are τὸ οἰκεῖον (ξυγγενές), and τὸ ἀλλότριον (ὀθνεῖον). Disagreement—for διαφορά is substituted ἐχθρά—in τὸ οἰκεῖον is called στάσις, in τὸ ἀλλότριον, πόλεμος. ὄντα—διαφοραῖν is a marvellous example of Greek brevity, simplicity, and precision. Schneider, and J. and C., explain the words correctly; but D. and V. plunge everything into confusion by taking δυοῖν τινοῖν with διαφοραῖν.

πόλεμος. Καὶ οὐδέν γε, ἔφη, ἄπο τρόπου λέγεις. Ὅρα δὴ καὶ εἰ
C τόδε | πρὸς τρόπου λέγω. φημὶ γὰρ τὸ μὲν Ἑλληνικὸν γένος αὐτὸ
αὐτῷ οἰκεῖον εἶναι καὶ ξυγγενές, τῷ δὲ βαρβαρικῷ ὀθνεῖόν τε καὶ
ἀλλότριον. Καλῶς γε, ἔφη. Ἕλληνας μὲν ἄρα βαρβάροις καὶ
βαρβάρους Ἕλλησι πολεμεῖν μαχομένους τε φήσομεν καὶ πολεμίους
φύσει εἶναι, καὶ πόλεμον τὴν ἔχθραν ταύτην κλητέον· Ἕλληνας
δὲ Ἕλλησιν, ὅταν τι τοιοῦτο δρῶσιν, φύσει μὲν φίλους εἶναι,
D νοσεῖν δ' ἐν τῷ τοιούτῳ τὴν Ἑλλάδα καὶ στασιάζειν, | καὶ στάσιν
τὴν τοιαύτην ἔχθραν κλητέον. Ἐγὼ μέν, ἔφη, συγχωρῶ οὕτω
νομίζειν. Σκόπει δή, εἶπον, ὅτι ἐν τῇ νῦν ὁμολογουμένῃ στάσει,
ὅπου ἂν τι τοιοῦτον γένηται, καὶ διαστῇ πόλις, ἐὰν ἑκάτεροι
ἑκατέρων τέμνωσιν ἀγροὺς καὶ οἰκίας ἐμπιμπρῶσιν, ὡς ἀλιτηριώδης

---

470 C 14 **φημὶ γὰρ κτλ.**: a formal declaration of Plato's political faith in the Panhellenic ideal, which Cimon—Πανελλήνων πρόμος, as Cratinus calls him (*Archil.* 1 ed. Meineke)—and Callicratidas (see Grote VII pp. 406—415) had striven to realise in fact, and which Isocrates as well as Plato constantly proclaimed in theory. See on I 336 A, and cf. Spengel *Isokrates u. Plato* pp. 7 ff. and Isocrates *Panegyricus* passim. The rallying points of Plato's Panhellenism are two—internally, the Delphic oracle (IV 427 B, C *nn.*), and externally, hostility with Persia: cf. *Menex.* 245 C ff. See also on πολεμίους φύσει below.

17 **πολεμεῖν μαχομένους.** Hirschig and others transpose these words, on slight MS authority, including a marginal correction in A. But it is hard to see why they should have become displaced. By adopting the order in the text Plato restricts μαχομένους to πολεμεῖν: otherwise the participle would naturally go with πολεμίους φύσει too. The MS order also lays more stress on the emphatic πολεμεῖν than Hirschig's transposition would do. Cf. (with Stallbaum) *Ap.* 18 D.

πολεμίους φύσει. The universal Greek view: see e.g. Hdt. I 4 ad fin., Eur. *Hec.* 1199, Isocrates *Paneg.* 158 al., and Nägelsbach *Nachhom. Theol.* pp. 305—307. "We should bear in mind," says Bosanquet, "that Greek civilisation was to Plato much what white civilisation is to us." This is, in part at least, true; but sentiments of chivalry and romance were far more powerful factors in fostering the ancestral feud with Persia than any apprehensions for the safety of Greek civilisation. The idea of a war against Persia always stirred the pulse of Hellas with a sense of continuity with the heroic past; and it was more than a meaningless ceremony when Agesilaus sacrificed at Aulis, and Alexander visited Achilles' tomb. See Grote IX p. 81 and XI pp. 395—397. None the less, in spite of his emphatic expression of the old Greek policy of splendid isolation, it is difficult to overestimate the effect of Plato's writings, and especially of the *Republic*, in breaking down the barrier between Barbarian and Greek. See on 470 E.

20 **νοσεῖν κτλ.** Compare the melancholy picture of the state of contemporary Greece in Isocr. *Paneg.* 115—117. Hartman would cancel καὶ στασιάζειν; but see 451 B *n.*

470 D 21 **συγχωρῶ κτλ.** 'I agree to view the matter in this way.' οὕτως ὀνομάζειν would be more pointed, but is unnecessary. We are hardly justified in making νομίζειν = 'to hold this language' (with J. and C.): for φωνῇ νομίζειν, φωνὴν νομίζειν and the like have a somewhat different meaning. See Stephanus-Hase *Thes.* s.v. νομίζειν.

22 **ὅτι—ὡς.** ὡς can hardly be exclamatory, as J. and C. suppose. For the anacoluthon cf. Hdt. III 71 ad fin. ἴστε ὑμῖν ὅτι, ἢν ὑπερπέσῃ ἡ νῦν ἡμέρη, ὡς οὐκ ἄλλος φθὰς ἐμεῦ κατήγορος ἔσται and other examples cited in Kühner *Gr. Gr.* II p. 886. τῇ—στάσει is not 'that which we have acknowledged to be sedition' (Jowett), but 'that which, *as things now are*, is allowed to be sedition,'

τε δοκεῖ ἡ στάσις εἶναι καὶ οὐδέτεροι αὐτῶν φιλοπόλιδες· οὐ γὰρ
ἄν ποτε ἐτόλμων τὴν τροφόν τε καὶ μητέρα κείρειν· ἀλλὰ μέτριον
εἶναι τοὺς καρποὺς ἀφαιρεῖσθαι τοῖς | κρατοῦσι τῶν κρατουμένων, **E**
καὶ διανοεῖσθαι ὡς διαλλαγησομένων καὶ οὐκ ἀεὶ πολεμησόντων.
Πολὺ γάρ, ἔφη, ἡμερωτέρων αὕτη ἡ διάνοια ἐκείνης. Τί δὲ δή;
ἔφην· ἣν σὺ πόλιν οἰκίζεις, οὐχ Ἑλληνὶς ἔσται; Δεῖ γ' αὐτήν,
ἔφη. Οὐκοῦν καὶ ἀγαθοί τε καὶ ἥμεροι ἔσονται; Σφόδρα γε.
Ἀλλ' οὐ φιλέλληνες; οὐδὲ οἰκείαν τὴν Ἑλλάδα ἡγήσονται, οὐδὲ
κοινωνήσουσιν ὧνπερ οἱ ἄλλοι ἱερῶν; Καὶ σφόδρα γε. Οὐκοῦν
τὴν πρὸς τοὺς Ἕλληνας διαφορὰν | ὡς οἰκείους στάσιν ἡγήσονται **471**
καὶ οὐδὲ ὀνομάσουσιν πόλεμον; Οὐ γάρ. Καὶ ὡς διαλλαγησόμενοι
ἄρα διοίσονται; Πάνυ μὲν οὖν. Εὐμενῶς δὴ σωφρονιοῦσιν, οὐκ
ἐπὶ δουλείᾳ κολάζοντες οὐδ' ἐπ' ὀλέθρῳ, σωφρονισταὶ ὄντες, οὐ

33. *οἱ* A^2Ξ: om. A^1Π *q*.

---

viz. when *one* city is divided against itself (*διαστῇ πόλις*). Plato, it will be observed, does not deny that the abuses which he condemns occasionally happened in Greek civil strife: they certainly often did. He only asserts (and the admission is interesting and important) that the public conscience of Greece condemned them. The conduct of Athens in emergencies of this kind was sometimes honourable and patriotic: see for example Grote VII p. 318, VIII pp. 69, 70.

26 **τρόφον τε καὶ μητέρα.** Cf. III 414 E. Not patriotism only, but filial love, such as Virgil felt for Italy (*Georg.* II 136—176), inspires these words.

μέτριον εἶναι: sc. *δοκεῖ*. Plato is still describing Greek public opinion.

470 E 28 **διανοεῖσθαι κτλ.** The converse of Bias's maxim *φιλεῖν ὡς μισήσοντας* (D. L. I 87). *ἐκείνης* = 'than the other,' viz. the *γνώμη* which *διανοεῖται ὡς οὐ διαλλαγησομένων καὶ ἀεὶ πολεμησόντων*. In view of Arist. *Rhet.* II 21. 1395ᵃ 25, where an orator is recommended, if he wishes to seem amiable, to say *οὐ δεῖ ὥσπερ φασί, φιλεῖν ὡς μισήσοντας, ἀλλὰ μᾶλλον μισεῖν ὡς φιλήσοντας*, it is tempting on a first glance to regard *ἐκείνης* as the maxim of Bias itself: but the other interpretation is more natural and relevant. On Bias' saying see Jebb's Appendix on Soph. *Ajax* 679 ff.

30 **οὐχ Ἑλληνὶς ἔσται;** Plato speaks hopefully, as if his perfect city were but one Greek city among many—a living example to the brotherhood of Hellas. It may be admitted that the city of II—IV has not a few claims to be called Hellenic. But the 'third city'—that of the philosopher-king—is not Hellenic, nor even, in any proper sense, an earthly city at all: it is an ideal, an ensample in the heavens—*ἐν οὐρανῷ παράδειγμα τῷ βουλομένῳ ὁρᾶν καὶ ὁρῶντι ἑαυτὸν κατοικίζειν* (IX 592 B). The animating spirit of V 473 B—VII is assuredly not Hellenic exclusiveness, but the enthusiasm of humanity, if by 'humanity' we understand (with Plato) the divine element in man, in virtue of which we are most distinctively and truly human. See on VI 501 B, IX 589 D. In a certain sense it is even true that Platonism is the "strongest protest ever raised against pre-Christian hellenism" (Krohn *Pl. St.* p. 33). But Plato's is no barren protest; for his city foreshadows the future while it passes judgment on the past. Cf. VI 499 C *n.* and IX 592 B *nn.*, with Zeller[4] II 1. pp. 921—923 and the same author's article on *Der platonische Staat in seiner Bedeutung für die Folgezeit* in his *Vorträge u. Abhandlungen* I pp. 68—88.

471 A 2 **οὐδὲ ὀνομάσουσιν**: much less consider it so.

3 **σωφρονιοῦσιν.** The word *σωφρονίζω* ('make *σώφρων*,' i.e. 'chastise') implies the remedial view of punishment: see on II 380 B.

4 **οὐ πολέμιοι.** A few inferior MSS read *ὡς οὐ πολέμιοι*, and *ὡς* appears also

πολέμιοι. Οὕτως, ἔφη. Οὐδ' ἄρα τὴν Ἑλλάδα Ἕλληνες ὄντες κεροῦσιν, οὐδὲ οἰκήσεις ἐμπρήσουσιν, οὐδὲ ὁμολογήσουσιν ἐν ἑκάστῃ πόλει πάντας ἐχθροὺς αὐτοῖς εἶναι, καὶ ἄνδρας καὶ γυ- B ναῖκας καὶ παῖδας, ἀλλ' ὀλίγους ἀεὶ ἐχθροὺς τοὺς αἰτίους τῆς διαφορᾶς, καὶ διὰ ταῦτα πάντα οὔτε τὴν γῆν ἐθελήσουσιν κείρειν αὐτῶν, ὡς φίλων τῶν πολλῶν, οὔτε οἰκίας ἀνατρέπειν, ἀλλὰ μέχρι τούτου ποιήσονται τὴν διαφοράν, μέχρι οὗ ἂν οἱ αἴτιοι ἀναγκασθῶσιν ὑπὸ τῶν ἀναιτίων ἀλγούντων δοῦναι δίκην. Ἐγὼ μέν, ἔφη, ὁμολογῶ οὕτω δεῖν πρὸς τοὺς ἐναντίους τοὺς ἡμετέρους πολίτας προσφέρεσθαι, πρὸς δὲ τοὺς βαρβάρους ὡς νῦν οἱ Ἕλληνες πρὸς C ἀλλήλους. Τιθῶμεν δὴ καὶ τοῦτον τὸν νόμον τοῖς φύλαξι, μήτε γῆν τέμνειν μήτε οἰκίας ἐμπιμπράναι; Θῶμεν, ἔφη, καὶ ἔχειν γε καλῶς ταῦτά τε καὶ τὰ πρόσθεν.

XVII. Ἀλλὰ γάρ μοι δοκεῖς, ὦ Σώκρατες, ἐάν τίς σοι τὰ τοιαῦτα ἐπιτρέπῃ λέγειν, οὐδέποτε μνησθήσεσθαι ὃ ἐν τῷ πρόσθεν παρωσάμενος πάντα ταῦτα εἴρηκας, τὸ ὡς δυνατὴ αὕτη ἡ πολιτεία

20. αὕτη Π et in mg. A[2]: om. A[1].

---

in the margin of A. Campbell suggests <καὶ> οὐ πολέμιοι, Förster <ὡς> σωφρονισταί; but neither suggestion is nearly so expressive and good as the reading of the best MSS.

7 **αὑτοῖς**. The ambiguity in αὑτοῖς can mislead nobody, and αὐτοῖς (Hartman, with A etc.) would be very unpleasing. In such cases the authority of Plato's MSS is nought. The behaviour of Athens in connexion with the Mitylenean revolt is a conspicuous example of the inhumanity which Plato here condemns: see Thuc. III 36 ff.

471 B 12 **ἀλγούντων**. "Significatur necessitas innocentibus quoque damnum inferendi, quo nocentes punire et ad pacem adigere cogantur" Schneider.

13 **τοὺς ἐναντίους**. "Graecos adversarios vocat, non hostes" Stallbaum. *q* has Ἕλληνας for ἐναντίους—an obvious 'interpretamentum.'

14 **πρὸς δὲ—ἀλλήλους**. A bitter commentary on the foreign policy of Greek cities. The 'natural' relations between Greece and Barbary had been reversed: not only did Greeks treat Greeks as enemies, but they had begun to treat barbarians as friends. Christ (*Pl. Stud.* pp. 37—39) supposes that Plato wrote this passage in 374, when Plataea was destroyed by Thebes, and the surviving inhabitants fled to Athens (Xen. *Hell.* VI 3. 1, Isocr. *Plat.* 1 ff.). The same view is held by Hirmer *Entst. u. Komp.* etc. p. 662. Plato's rebuke would have been equally or even more telling in 386, when Greece was exhausted by the Corinthian war, and friendship with the 'natural enemy' had forced the peace of Antalcidas upon the Greeks, to the bitter grief and shame of patriots: cf. Isocr. *Paneg.* 120, 121. In any case νῦν should no doubt be referred to the time when Plato wrote these words, and not to the date of action of the dialogue. See also *Introd.* § 4.

471 C—**472** B *Glauco recalls Socrates to the task, already twice postponed, of demonstrating that such a State is possible.*

471 C Here begins the transition to the 'third' or philosophic city. See on 449 A.

20 **ὡς δυνατή**. In a certain sense, this has already been proved, for the city is κατὰ φύσιν: cf. 456 C, 466 D. We have, however, still to shew that the harmony with nature can be attained, and this is what Plato proceeds to do.

γενέσθαι καὶ τίνα τρόπον ποτὲ δυνατή· ἐπεὶ ὅτι γε, εἰ γένοιτο,
πάντ' ἂν εἴη ἀγαθὰ πόλει ᾗ γένοιτο, καὶ ἃ σὺ παραλείπεις ἐγὼ
λέγω, ὅτι καὶ τοῖς πολεμίοις ἄριστ' ἂν | μάχοιντο τῷ ἥκιστα D
ἀπολείπειν ἀλλήλους, γιγνώσκοντές τε καὶ ἀνακαλοῦντες ταῦτα
τὰ ὀνόματα ἑαυτούς, ἀδελφούς, πατέρας, ὑεῖς· εἰ δὲ καὶ τὸ θῆλυ
συστρατεύοιτο, εἴτε καὶ ἐν τῇ αὐτῇ τάξει εἴτε καὶ ὄπισθεν ἐπι-
τεταγμένον, φόβων τε ἕνεκα τοῖς ἐχθροῖς καὶ εἴ ποτέ τις ἀνάγκη
βοηθείας γένοιτο, οἶδ' ὅτι ταύτῃ πάντῃ ἄμαχοι ἂν εἶεν· καὶ οἴκοι
γε ἃ παραλείπεται ἀγαθά, ὅσα ἂν εἴη αὐτοῖς, ὁρῶ· ἀλλ' ὡς ἐμοῦ
| ὁμολογοῦντος πάντα ταῦτα ὅτι εἴη ἄν, καὶ ἄλλα γε μυρία, εἰ E
γένοιτο ἡ πολιτεία αὕτη, μηκέτι πλείω περὶ αὐτῆς λέγε, ἀλλὰ
τοῦτο αὐτὸ ἤδη πειρώμεθα ἡμᾶς αὐτοὺς πείθειν, ὡς δυνατὸν καὶ
ᾗ δυνατόν, τὰ δ' ἄλλα χαίρειν ἐῶμεν. | Ἐξαίφνης γε σύ, ἦν δ' ἐγώ, 472
ὥσπερ καταδρομὴν ἐποιήσω ἐπὶ τὸν λόγον μου, καὶ οὐ συγγι-
γνώσκεις στραγγευομένῳ. ἴσως γὰρ οὐκ οἶσθα, ὅτι μόγις μοι τὼ
δύο κύματε ἐκφυγόντι νῦν τὸ μέγιστον καὶ χαλεπώτατον τῆς
τρικυμίας ἐπάγεις, ὃ ἐπειδὰν ἴδῃς τε καὶ ἀκούσῃς, πάνυ συγγνώμην
ἕξεις, ὅτι εἰκότως ἄρα ὤκνουν τε καὶ ἐδεδοίκη οὕτω παράδοξον
λέγειν λόγον τε καὶ ἐπιχειρεῖν διασκοπεῖν. Ὅσῳ ἄν, ἔφη, τοιαῦτα
πλείω λέγῃς, ἧττον ἀφεθήσει ὑφ' ἡμῶν | πρὸς τὸ μὴ εἰπεῖν, πῇ B

29. γε Ξ et corr. A²: τε A¹Π q.
3. στραγγευομένῳ corr. Vind. F: στρατευομένῳ ΑΠΞ q.

---

21 **ἐπεὶ ὅτι γε κτλ.** We should expect ὁμολογῶ after ᾗ γένοιτο, but anacolutha after ὅτι are so frequent that something of the sort may be mentally supplied: cf. I 352 B, V 465 A *nn.* Richards would insert ὁμολογῶ in the text. I formerly proposed καὶ ἐγὼ λέγω, <καὶ> ἃ σὺ παραλείπεις ὅτι κτλ., 'I too assert' (sc. no less than you), 'and also what you omit, that' etc., but now acquiesce in the anacoluthon.

471 D 27 **φόβων—ἐχθροῖς.** Cf. *Laws* 806 B.

472 A 3 **στραγγευομένῳ.** See *cr. n.* στρατευομένῳ could only be understood (with Stallbaum, who retains it, and Huber *zu den Plat. Gleichnissen* p. 10) as half-jocular for 'de re militari disputanti.' Such a usage is possible in itself (see on ἀποτίνουσι II 363 C); but ὤκνουν τε καὶ ἐδεδοίκη and μὴ διάτριβε (in B) are strongly in favour of στραγγευομένῳ. The same corruption—due to confusion of γ and τ, combined with lipography—occurs in the MSS of Ar. *Ach.* 126, as well as in Hesychius (στρατεύομαι· διατρίβω) and elsewhere: see Blaydes on Ar. l.c.

τὼ δύο κύματε. See 457 B, C. The first was ὡς δεῖ κοινῇ πάντα ἐπιτηδεύειν τούς τε φύλακας καὶ τὰς φυλακίδας; the second community of wives and children.

7 **λέγειν λόγον τε.** J. and C. read λόγον λέγειν τε with Ξ and M; but the other reading has far more authority, and is perhaps *exquisitius.* Cf. 452 A.

472 B—**472** E *Socrates reminds Glauco that it is the investigation of Justice and Injustice which has brought us to this point. It was in order to reach a standard or model of Justice that we examined the nature of perfect justice and the perfectly just man. By comparing them with their opposites in respect of happiness and unhappiness, we intended to obtain a measure by which to estimate*

δυνατὴ γίγνεσθαι αὕτη ἡ πολιτεία. ἀλλὰ λέγε καὶ μὴ διάτριβε. Οὐκοῦν, ἦν δ' ἐγώ, πρῶτον μὲν τόδε χρὴ ἀναμνησθῆναι, ὅτι ἡμεῖς ζητοῦντες δικαιοσύνην οἷόν ἐστι καὶ ἀδικίαν δεῦρο ἥκομεν. Χρή· ἀλλὰ τί τοῦτο; ἔφη. Οὐδέν· ἀλλ' ἐὰν εὕρωμεν οἷόν ἐστι δικαιοσύνη, ἆρα καὶ ἄνδρα τὸν δίκαιον ἀξιώσομεν μηδὲν δεῖν αὐτῆς
C ἐκείνης διαφέρειν, ἀλλὰ πανταχῇ τοιοῦτον εἶναι, οἷον | δικαιοσύνη ἐστίν; ἢ ἀγαπήσομεν, ἐὰν ὅ τι ἐγγύτατα αὐτῆς ᾖ καὶ πλεῖστα τῶν ἄλλων ἐκείνης μετέχῃ; Οὕτως, ἔφη, ἀγαπήσομεν. Παραδείγματος ἄρα ἕνεκα, ἦν δ' ἐγώ, ἐζητοῦμεν αὐτό τε δικαιοσύνην οἷόν ἐστι, καὶ ἄνδρα τὸν τελέως δίκαιον, εἰ γένοιτο, καὶ οἷος ἂν εἴη γενόμενος, καὶ ἀδικίαν αὖ καὶ τὸν ἀδικώτατον, ἵνα εἰς ἐκείνους ἀποβλέποντες, οἷοι ἂν ἡμῖν φαίνωνται εὐδαιμονίας τε πέρι καὶ τοῦ ἐναντίου,
D ἀναγκαζώμεθα καὶ περὶ ἡμῶν αὐτῶν ὁμολογεῖν, ὃς ἂν | ἐκείνοις ὅ τι ὁμοιότατος ᾖ, τὴν ἐκείνοις μοῖραν ὁμοιοτάτην ἕξειν, ἀλλ' οὐ τούτου ἕνεκα, ἵν' ἀποδείξωμεν ὡς δυνατὰ ταῦτα γίγνεσθαι. Τοῦτο

12. τοῦτο A[1]Π: τοῦτό γ' A[2]. 22. ἐκείνοις Ξq: ἐκείνης AΠ.

---

the effect of Justice and Injustice upon happiness in human life. Our object was not to prove that perfect justice is attainable, and therefore we are not obliged to shew that our city can be realised.

472 B 12 **ἀλλὰ τί τοῦτο;** See *cr. n.* γε after τοῦτο is certainly wrong. It has no MS authority except that of A[2], and (as Stallbaum shews) ἀλλὰ τί τοῦτο is the regular form of this phrase in Plato: cf. *Gorg.* 497 E, *Charm.* 164 A. In both these cases the reply is Οὐδέν, followed by ἀλλά, as here.

472 C 16 **παραδείγματος κτλ.** παράδειγμα is not here an 'illustration,' but a 'model' or 'standard' ("Musterbild" Schneider) exactly as in IX 592 B and *Theaet.* 176 E.

17 **αὐτό—δικαιοσύνην**: 'justice by itself': see II 363 A *n.* Here however the expression means 'abstract justice' rather than merely 'justice apart from its consequences.' It is not yet a metaphysical 'Idea' in the sense of VI and VII: see on III 402 C, and cf. Pfleiderer *zur Lösung* etc. p. 19 with Susemihl *Gen. Entw.* II pp. 176 f.

καὶ ἄνδρα κτλ.: 'and the man who is perfectly just if he should come into existence, and what his character would be if he did.' εἰ γένοιτο must be understood as a kind of protasis to τὸν τελέως δίκαιον (i.q. τὸν τελέως ὄντα or ἂν ὄντα δίκαιον). Schneider's explanation is less simple: "virum perfecte iustum quaesituri *ea conditione* rem susceperant, *si* fieri et existere talis posset." We must beware of translating 'num existeret' (Stallbaum): for it is just in order to shew the irrelevancy of the question, 'Can such a man exist?' that Plato wrote this sentence. Madvig omits καί before οἷος. In that case εἰ γένοιτο goes with the following clause (cf. IV 419 A *n.*), and the meaning is: 'if he *should* come into existence, what his character would be when he did.' By this means we obtain an exact parallel between δικαιοσύνην οἷόν ἐστι and ἄνδρα—οἷος ἂν εἴη. It must be admitted, I think, that the emendation is an improvement: but the MS reading may stand. Campbell needlessly questions εἰ γένοιτο, thinking it a gloss on γενόμενος. The pleonasm is characteristic: cf. 471 C εἰ γένοιτο, πάντ' ἂν εἴη ἀγαθὰ ᾗ γένοιτο.

18 **καὶ ἀδικίαν αὖ κτλ.** See IV 420 C *n.*

19 **ἵνα—ἕξειν.** Cf. VIII 544 A.

22 **ἐκείνοις.** See *cr. n.* ἐκείνης, which Schneider alone retains, can hardly be defended. For the error see *Introd.* § 5.

472 D 23 **τοῦτο μέν.** On μέν without δέ see 475 E *n.*

μέν, ἔφη, ἀληθὲς λέγεις. Οἴει ἂν οὖν ἧττόν τι ἀγαθὸν ζῳγράφον
εἶναι, ὃς ἂν γράψας παράδειγμα, οἷος ἂν εἴη ὁ κάλλιστος ἄνθρωπος,
καὶ πάντα εἰς τὸ γράμμα ἱκανῶς ἀποδοὺς μὴ ἔχῃ ἀποδεῖξαι, ὡς
καὶ δυνατὸν γενέσθαι τοιοῦτον ἄνδρα; Μὰ Δί' οὐκ ἔγωγ', ἔφη.
Τί οὖν; οὐ καὶ ἡμεῖς, φαμέν, παράδειγμα | ἐποιοῦμεν λόγῳ ἀγαθῆς E
πόλεως; Πάνυ γε. Ἧττόν τι οὖν οἴει ἡμᾶς εὖ λέγειν τούτου
ἕνεκα, ἐὰν μὴ ἔχωμεν ἀποδεῖξαι, ὡς δυνατὸν οὕτω πόλιν οἰκῆσαι
ὡς ἐλέγετο; Οὐ δῆτα, ἔφη. Τὸ μὲν τοίνυν ἀληθές, ἦν δ' ἐγώ,
οὕτω· εἰ δὲ δὴ καὶ τοῦτο προθυμηθῆναι δεῖ σὴν χάριν, ἀποδεῖξαι,
πῇ μάλιστα καὶ κατὰ τί δυνατώτατ' ἂν εἴη, πάλιν μοι πρὸς τὴν
τοιαύτην ἀπόδειξιν τὰ αὐτὰ διομολόγησαι. Τὰ ποῖα; Ἆρ' οἷόν
τέ τι | πραχθῆναι ὡς λέγεται, ἢ φύσιν ἔχει πρᾶξιν λέξεως ἧττον 473
ἀληθείας ἐφάπτεσθαι, κἂν εἰ μή τῳ δοκεῖ; ἀλλὰ σὺ πότερον

25. οἷος *q*: οἷον ΑΠΞ.

---

24 **οἴει—ἄνδρα.** For οἴει ἄν Richards reads οἴει δή: but δή is unpleasing here. See also on 450 C. After ἄν—εἶναι we might expect ὃς ἄν—μὴ ἔχοι, 'who would not be able,' and so Ξ, *q* and several other MSS actually read. The irregularity is however no more than 'cannot' for 'would not be able to' in English. I have restored οἷος (which used to be read before Bekker) for οἷον (see *cr. n.*). The corruption is easy, and in such cases the relative regularly agrees with its subject: see *Phil.* 29 E with Stallbaum's note. It is also wrong in point of sense to refer the relative to παράδειγμα here. Art is credited with higher possibilities in this passage than in Book X, unless we suppose that the painter's κάλλιστος ἄνθρωπος is only an artificial combination of individual features imitated from human beings. But in that case the illustration is less apposite; for Plato's perfect city is more than imitation of the actual. See also on X 598 A, and cf. Xen. *Mem.* III 10. 2 and Arist. *Pol.* Γ. 11. 1281ᵇ 10—15.

28 **παράδειγμα κτλ.** Cf. *Laws* 713 B and 739 C—E.

472 E—**474** C *I am nevertheless willing, says Socrates, to shew you how our constitution may be realised most nearly. A perfect realisation we cannot expect, for action is everywhere less true than language or theory. One great, yet possible change, and only one, is needed, and it is this. 'Philosophers' must become kings or kings 'philosophers.' Till this shall come to pass, there will be no respite from trouble, either to cities or to mankind, nor will our hypothetical city ever become (so far as may be) a reality. A paradox, you say, and certain to arouse hostility and scorn; but let us explain what we mean by 'philosophers.'*

472 E With the breaking of the third and greatest wave (473 C *n.*) begins the transition to the third and final stage of Plato's ideal city. See on 449 A.

33 **δυνατώτατα κτλ.** "Superlativus facultatem, quam relativam dicunt, indicat" Schneider. It is important to observe that Plato does not expect a perfect realisation even when philosophers become kings: cf. 473 E. Why he does not, is explained in 473 A. πάλιν refers to 472 C.

473 A 2 **κἂν εἰ μή τῳ δοκεῖ** shews that Plato is contradicting a common view: cf. IX 577 D. Most men would of course admit that a perfect scheme must usually be modified if it is to be put in force. But they would not allow that λέξις has more *truth* than πρᾶξις; for the truth of a theory—they would say—is best tested by experience. Not so Plato, according to whom the world of Mind is not only more perfect, but truer than the world of Matter: cf. ἡ παντελῶς ἀληθής VI 502 D and note ad loc. The pointed ἀλλὰ σύ invites the assent of Glauco as a Platonist: cf. infra 475 E.

ὁμολογεῖς οὕτως ἢ οὔ; Ὁμολογῶ, ἔφη. Τοῦτο μὲν δὴ μὴ ἀνά-
γκαζέ με, οἷα τῷ λόγῳ διήλθομεν, τοιαῦτα παντάπασι καὶ τῷ ἔργῳ
δεῖν γιγνόμενα ἀποφαίνειν· ἀλλ', ἐὰν οἷοί τε γενώμεθα εὑρεῖν,
ὡς ἂν ἐγγύτατα τῶν εἰρημένων πόλις οἰκήσειεν, φάναι ἡμᾶς
B ἐξηυρηκέναι, ὡς δυνατὰ ταῦτα γίγνεσθαι, ἃ σὺ ἐπιτάττεις. ἢ οὐκ
ἀγαπήσεις τούτων τυγχάνων; ἐγὼ μὲν γὰρ ἂν ἀγαπῴην. Καὶ
γὰρ ἐγώ, ἔφη.

XVIII. Τὸ δὲ δὴ μετὰ τοῦτο, ὡς ἔοικε, πειρώμεθα ζητεῖν τε
καὶ ἀποδεικνύναι, τί ποτε νῦν κακῶς ἐν ταῖς πόλεσι πράττεται,
δι' ὃ οὐχ οὕτως οἰκοῦνται, καὶ τίνος ἂν σμικροτάτου μεταβαλόντος
ἔλθοι εἰς τοῦτον τὸν τρόπον τῆς πολιτείας πόλις, μάλιστα μὲν
ἑνός, εἰ δὲ μή, δυοῖν, εἰ δὲ μή, ὅ τι ὀλιγίστων τὸν ἀριθμὸν καὶ
C σμικροτάτων τὴν δύναμιν. Παντάπασι μὲν οὖν, ἔφη. Ἑνὸς μὲν
τοίνυν, ἦν δ' ἐγώ, μεταβαλόντος δοκοῦμέν μοι ἔχειν δεῖξαι ὅτι
μεταπέσοι ἄν, οὐ μέντοι σμικροῦ γε οὐδὲ ῥᾳδίου, δυνατοῦ δέ.
Τίνος; ἔφη. Ἐπ' αὐτὸ δή, ἦν δ' ἐγώ, εἶμι, ὃ τῷ μεγίστῳ προσῃκάζομεν κύματι· εἰρήσεται δ' οὖν, εἰ καὶ μέλλει γέλωτί τε ἀτεχνῶς

16. μεταβαλόντος A^1Π: μεταβάλλοντος corr. A^2. 18. προσῃκάζομεν *v*: προεικάζομεν AΠ*q*: παρεικάζομεν Ξ. 19. ἀτεχνῶς A^1Π: ἀτέχνῳ corr. A^2.

---

5 **δεῖν κτλ.** δεῖν is tautological after ἀνάγκαζε, but the addition of τοῦτο μέν makes it easier. Π has δεῖ, perhaps a mistake for δή, which was read by Stobaeus *Flor.* 43. 109. For γιγνόμενα Bywater (*J. Ph.* X p. 73) would write γιγνόμεν' ἂν or ἂν γιγνόμενα. The categoric statement is however more in harmony with ἆρ' οἷόν τέ τι—ἐφάπτεσθαι. 'Do not compel me to shew that what we described in words is in all respects reproduced by experience.' See also on ἐπιτάττεις below.

6 **φάναι**: infinitive for imperative as in VI 508 B, 509 B, all of them examples of φάναι, although Plato is not averse to φάθι (VI 508 E) and ξύμφαθι (VII 523 A). The imperatival infinitive is very common in Attic inscriptions (Meisterhans[3] p. 244).

7 **ἐπιτάττεις**: sc. γίγνεσθαι. It is hardly possible to understand ἐξευρεῖν ὡς δυνατὰ ταῦτα γίγνεσθαι (with J. and C.). As in γιγνόμενα above, so also here Socrates represents Glauco as requiring that the city should be made into a reality: cf. ἣν σὺ πόλιν οἰκίζεις in 470 E.

473 B 10 **πειρώμεθα**: subjunctive, i.q. δεῖ πειρᾶσθαι: cf. λέγωμεν δή, ὡς ἔοικεν (*Theaet.* 173 C, quoted by J. and C.).

473 C 18 **ἐπ' αὐτὸ—εἶμι**: 'well, said I, I will enter on the very topic which' etc. Cf. Thuc. II 36. 4 εἶμι καὶ ἐπὶ τὸν τῶνδε ἔπαινον. I have returned to the most authoritative reading, though previously I read (with Richards) ἐπ' αὐτῷ δὴ —εἰμί. In point of sense, εἶμι is only a sort of quasi-future, and should be compared with ἀλλ' εἶμι in the mouth of characters just about to leave the stage (e.g. Soph. *Trach.* 86). Cf. also *Phaed.* 100 B ἔρχομαι —ἐπιχειρῶν—καὶ εἶμι πάλιν ἐπ' ἐκεῖνα—καὶ ἄρχομαι κτλ. According to Kühner-Blass (*Gr. Gr.* I 2, p. 217) the present use of εἶμι is found only in poetry and late prose; but ἀνίασιν in VII 531 C is a certain case, and so also in my opinion are ἐπίασιν and ἀπίασι in Thuc. IV 61. 3, 8. It should also be remembered that Plato by no means abjures archaic and poetic forms and idioms: see I 330 B *n.* Vind. F reads ἐπ' αὐτῶ (i.q. αὐτῷ) δ' εἰμι, and εἰμί was the reading of q^1. ἐπ' αὐτῷ δὴ εἰμι is highly idiomatic and may be supported (with Richards) by VI 490 D, *Pol.* 274 B; but it is safer to follow the MSS, which are all but unanimous.

19 **εἰ καὶ—κατακλύσειν**: 'even al-

ὥσπερ κῦμα ἐκγελῶν καὶ ἀδοξίᾳ κατακλύσειν. σκόπει δὲ ὃ μέλλω
λέγειν. Λέγε, ἔφη. Ἐὰν μή, ἦν δ' ἐγώ, ἢ οἱ φιλόσοφοι βασιλεύσω-
σιν ἐν ταῖς πόλεσιν, ἢ οἱ βασιλῆς τε νῦν λεγόμενοι καὶ δυνάσται D
φιλοσοφήσωσι γνησίως τε καὶ ἱκανῶς, καὶ τοῦτο εἰς ταὐτὸν ξυμπέσῃ, δύναμίς τε πολιτικὴ καὶ φιλοσοφία, τῶν δὲ νῦν πορευομένων

---

though it is likely—just like a wave with its cachinnations—to swamp me with laughter and disgrace.' Hartman would insert <*με*> before *μέλλει*, but the object is easily supplied; and *με* before *μέλλει* is very cacophonous. For other views of this passage see App. VI.

21 **ἐὰν μὴ κτλ.** Cf. *Laws* 709 E ff. Plato's famous and often quoted paradox is not in its essence so paradoxical as it appears. The abiding truth of Plato's suggestion is "that somehow or other the best and deepest ideas about life and the world must be brought to bear on the conduct of social and political administration if any real progress is to take place in society" (Bosanquet). But it was a paradox in the Athenian democracy, or so at least Plato, like Socrates, thought: hence *πολὺ παρὰ δόξαν ῥηθήσεται* 473 E. See for example *Prot.* 319 A—323 A and *Gorg.* 514 A—519 D: and cf. Krohn *Pl. St.* p. 93. Political evil is in Plato's view the result of a divorce between political power and knowledge of the good; it can only be cured by effecting their reconciliation. In the *Politicus* Plato's remedy is to make the philosopher (who is the true king) act through the statesman (305 C ff.: cf. Nohle *Die Statslehre Platos* pp. 82, 88, whose interpretation is—wrongly, as I think—questioned by Zeller[4] II 1, p. 901 *n.* 5): but in the *Republic* the union between Thought and Action is complete, and the philosopher is himself a statesman. Whether even then he would be strong enough to found the perfect city of the *Republic*, depends upon the amount of resistance which he would be likely to encounter: see on VI 499 B and IX 577 A.

473 D 22 **λεγόμενοι.** Though called kings and potentates, they are so in nothing but the name: cf. I 336 A *n.* True kingship belongs only to the scientific ruler: *Euthyd.* 291 B ff. It is probable that Plato was already thinking throughout this passage of the hopes which he seems to have formed of the Syracusan dynasty: see *Epp.* VII and XIII with *n.* on VI 499 B.

23 **τοῦτο κτλ.**: 'unless this coalition of political power and philosophy come to pass,' lit. 'unless this coalesce,' i.e. unless there be this coalescence, viz. 'political power and philosophy.' For a somewhat similar idiom see VII 527 B *n.* *δύναμις—φιλοσοφία* is in explanatory apposition to the whole phrase *τοῦτο—ξυμπέσῃ*, rather than to *τοῦτο* alone. Otherwise we must suppose that *τοῦτο* is virtually for *ταῦτα*, the singular number emphasizing by anticipation the union of political power and philosophy (so J. and C.). But on this explanation the singular *τοῦτο* goes ill with *εἰς ταὐτὸν ξυμπέσῃ*, and with *ἑκάτερον*; nor are we justified in writing *ταῦτα* (with Richards). The dual *τούτω* might easily have been corrupted into *τοῦτο*, but *τούτω ξυμπέσῃ* is hardly defensible, in spite of *εἰ ἔστι τούτω διττὼ τὼ βίω* (*Gorg.* 500 D): cf. Kühner *Gr. Gr.* II p. 57.

24 **τῶν δὲ νῦν κτλ.**: 'while the numerous natures who at present pursue either to the exclusion of the other are forcibly debarred,' sc. from *exclusively* pursuing either. The genitive *τῶν—πορευομένων* is not partitive (Schneider, Stallbaum, and others), but rather possessive, and depends on *φύσεις*. Had Plato meant to say 'most of those who pursue' he would have written *οἱ πολλοί* instead of *αἱ πολλαὶ φύσεις*, as Hartman points out. There is moreover no reason to suppose that Plato wishes to allow any exceptions whatever to his rule. Nor is *πολλαί* 'volgares' (Baiter), or 'commoner' (Jowett), but simply 'numerous,' 'plentiful': cf. the usage of *ὁ πολύς* in II 376 E *τῆς ὑπὸ τοῦ πολλοῦ χρόνου ηὑρημένης* (*παιδείας*) and *τὸν πολὺν λεών* 458 D. Exclusive devotion either to politics or *φιλοσοφία* was common, but by no means universal, as the examples of Pythagoras, Solon, and many others sufficiently attest: see Arist. *Rhet.* II 23. 1398[b] 16—19. Various emendations have been proposed for *πολλαί*, such as *χωλαί* (Madvig), *πονηραί* (Liebhold), and *πολιτικαί* (Apelt), but the above explanation removes the difficulty. As regards the sentiment, it

χωρὶς ἐφ' ἑκάτερον αἱ πολλαὶ φύσεις ἐξ ἀνάγκης ἀποκλεισθῶσιν,
οὐκ ἔστι κακῶν παῦλα, ὦ φίλε Γλαύκων, ταῖς πόλεσι, δοκῶ δ'
οὐδὲ τῷ ἀνθρωπίνῳ γένει, οὐδὲ αὕτη ἡ πολιτεία μή ποτε πρότερον
E φυῇ τε εἰς τὸ δυνατὸν καὶ φῶς ἡλίου ἴδῃ, ἣν νῦν λόγῳ διεληλύθαμεν. ἀλλὰ τοῦτό ἐστιν, ὃ ἐμοὶ πάλαι ὄκνον ἐντίθησι λέγειν,
ὁρῶντι ὡς πολὺ παρὰ δόξαν ῥηθήσεται. χαλεπὸν γὰρ ἰδεῖν, ὅτι
οὐκ ἂν ἄλλῃ τις εὐδαιμονήσειεν οὔτε ἰδίᾳ οὔτε δημοσίᾳ. καὶ ὅς,
Ὦ Σώκρατες, ἔφη, τοιοῦτον ἐκβέβληκας ῥῆμά τε καὶ λόγον, ὃν
εἰπὼν ἡγοῦ ἐπὶ σὲ πάνυ πολλούς τε καὶ οὐ φαύλους νῦν οὕτως
474 οἷον ῥίψαντας τὰ ἱμάτια | γυμνοὺς λαβόντας ὅ τι ἑκάστῳ παρέτυχεν
ὅπλον, θεῖν διατεταμένους ὡς θαυμάσια ἐργασομένους· οὓς εἰ μὴ
ἀμυνεῖ τῷ λόγῳ καὶ ἐκφεύξει, τῷ ὄντι τωθαζόμενος δώσεις δίκην.
Οὐκοῦν σύ μοι, ἦν δ' ἐγώ, τούτων αἴτιος; Καλῶς γ', ἔφη, ἐγὼ
ποιῶν. ἀλλά τοί σε οὐ προδώσω, ἀλλ' ἀμυνῶ οἷς δύναμαι·
δύναμαι δὲ εὐνοίᾳ τε καὶ τῷ παρακελεύεσθαι, καὶ ἴσως ἂν ἄλλου
B του ἐμμελέστερόν σοι ἀποκριναίμην. ἀλλ' ὡς ἔχων τοιοῦτον
βοηθὸν πειρῶ τοῖς ἀπιστοῦσιν ἐνδείξασθαι, ὅτι ἔχει ᾗ σὺ λέγεις.

31. ἄλλῃ *q*: ἄλλη ΑΠΞ. 2. ἐργασομένους A^2Ξ*q*: ἐργασαμένους A^1Π.

should be noted that Plato refuses to sanction the exclusive pursuit of knowledge as well as of politics. He holds "that a specialised study of merely abstract questions unfits a man for the true grasp of life and character which is the centre of real philosophy" (Bosanquet), and on this ground he would probably have condemned the one-sided enthusiasm which many persons now profess for what is usually called by them 'research.' Cf. VI 497 A *n.* and 499 B.

473 E 28 **εἰς τὸ δυνατόν.** See 472 E *n.*

30 **πολὺ παρὰ δόξαν.** 473 C *n.*

32 **ἐκβέβληκας** = 'have let fall' is more appropriate here than *ἐμβέβληκας*, which Hartman (with Flor. T) prefers, on the strength of I 344 D and other passages. *ἐκβάλλειν* in this sense is half-poetic, and suits well with Glauco's excited mood.

33 **πάνυ πολλούς τε κτλ.** Chiappelli (l.c. p. 202) supposes that the allusion is to Aristophanes and the comic stage. Comedy would doubtless join in the outcry; but the loudest clamour would be raised by the 'practical politician' to whom philosophy is foolishness, and worse: see *Gorg.* 484 C—486 C and cf. *Theaet.* 172 D—175 B. The attitude of Isocrates and his adherents would also be hostile and contemptuous (Dümmler *Chron. Beiträge* pp. 43—45). Glauco clearly anticipates a combined assault from different quarters.

νῦν οὕτως: "jetzt ohne weiteres" (Schneider). *οὕτως* is used as in *ἐξαίφνης οὕτως* and the like: cf. II 377 B *n.*

34 **ῥίψαντας τὰ ἱμάτια** is illustrated by Blaydes on Ar. *Wasps* 408.

474 A 2 **διατεταμένους.** Here and in VI 501 C Ξ (with a few other MSS) reads *διατεταγμένους*, which is less appropriate: "nulla enim *τάξις* in turba tumultuantium" (Stallbaum). Cf. 462 C *n.*

ὡς—ἐργασομένους: "intending to do heaven knows what" (Jowett). The phrase is idiomatic in Plato for any excess of ill-regulated zeal: cf. *Ap.* 35 A with my note ad loc.

3 **τῷ ὄντι—δίκην**: 'you will learn to your cost what flouting means.' *τῷ ὄντι* indicates that *τωθαζόμενος* is to be taken in the fullest sense of the word: cf. IX 579 D, I 343 C, VI 511 B *nn.* *τωθάζω* always implies personal abuse, often of an indecent kind: see Cope's interesting account of the word in *Aristotle's Rhetoric* Vol. II pp. 49 f.

Πειρατέον, ἦν δ' ἐγώ, ἐπειδὴ καὶ σὺ οὕτω μεγάλην ξυμμαχίαν παρέχει. ἀναγκαῖον οὖν μοι δοκεῖ, εἰ μέλλομέν πῃ ἐκφεύξεσθαι οὓς λέγεις, διορίσασθαι πρὸς αὐτοὺς τοὺς φιλοσόφους τίνας λέγοντες τολμῶμεν φάναι δεῖν ἄρχειν, ἵνα διαδήλων γενομένων δύνηταί τις ἀμύνεσθαι, ἐνδεικνύμενος ὅτι τοῖς μὲν προσήκει φύσει ἅπτεσθαί τε φιλοσοφίας ἡγεμονεύειν τ' ἐν πόλει, τοῖς δ' ἄλλοις C
μήτε ἅπτεσθαι ἀκολουθεῖν τε τῷ ἡγουμένῳ. Ὥρα ἂν εἴη, ἔφη, ὁρίζεσθαι. Ἴθι δή, ἀκολούθησόν μοι τῇδε, ἐὰν αὐτὸ ἁμῇ γέ πῃ ἱκανῶς ἐξηγησώμεθα. Ἄγε, ἔφη. Ἀναμιμνῄσκειν οὖν σε, ἦν δ' ἐγώ, δεήσει, ἢ μέμνησαι ὅτι ὃν ἂν φῶμεν φιλεῖν τι, δεῖ φανῆναι αὐτόν, ἐὰν ὀρθῶς λέγηται, οὐ τὸ μὲν φιλοῦντα ἐκείνου, τὸ δὲ μή, ἀλλὰ πᾶν στέργοντα;

XIX. Ἀναμιμνῄσκειν, ἔφη, ὡς ἔοικεν, δεῖ· οὐ γὰρ πάνυ γε D
ἐννοῶ. Ἄλλῳ, εἶπον, ἔπρεπεν, ὦ Γλαύκων, λέγειν ἃ λέγεις·

---

474 B 13 **ἀμύνεσθαι.** The promise is fulfilled in VI 501—502 C.

474 C—**480** A *The philosopher, as analogy proves, is one who loves not a part of knowledge, but the whole. His passion is for Truth, and Truth means the Ideas. The Ideas are each of them One, but they appear many by union with particular things and one another. Lovers of sights and sounds and such like persons believe only in the many beautifuls; they cannot understand the One. Like dreamers, they mistake the copy for the original. Their condition of mind may be described as Opinion, that of the philosophers as Knowledge.*

Let us proceed to prove this statement. The object of Knowledge 'is'; that of Ignorance 'is not.' If therefore anything both 'is' and 'is not,' it must lie between Being and not-Being, and the faculty which cognizes it will be something between Knowledge and Ignorance.

'Powers' differ from one another according to the objects over which they preside, and the effects which they produce. The 'power' called Knowledge presides over Being, and produces the act of knowing. It is therefore different from the 'power' called Opinion, whose result is opining. What then is the object over which Opinion presides? We have seen that it is not Being; neither is it not-Being. Therefore Opinion is different both from Knowledge and from Ignorance. It is, in fact, something between Knowledge and Ignorance, less luminous than the one, more luminous than the other. Its object will therefore be that which both 'is' and 'is not.'

Now it is just the many beautifuls etc. which both are and are not. There is not one of them which 'is' more than it 'is not' that which we say it is. We are therefore justified in saying that the many beautifuls etc. lie between Being and not-Being. Thus we have discovered the object of Opinion.

We conclude that those who have eyes for the many beautifuls etc., opine; while those who see the Beautiful itself, know. The former are lovers of Opinion, the latter lovers of Knowledge or philosophers.

474 D ff. The δευτέρα πόλις of Books II—IV rested on a psychological basis and was the expression of a moral rather than of an intellectual ideal: see on II 370 A and IV 443 B. In harmony with this conception Plato formerly used the word φιλόσοφος primarily and for the most part in its ethical sense (II 376 B *n.*). Now that he is about to leave psychology for metaphysics, and describe the kingship of Knowledge, it becomes necessary to analyse again the meaning of φιλόσοφος. Henceforward, throughout Books VI and VII, the φιλόσοφος is one whose consuming passion is the love of Truth, that is, of the Ideas. See 480 A and VI 486 E *nn.*

22 **ἐννοῶ**: i.q. νῷ ἔχω, 'remember,' not 'understand' (as D. and V.). Cf. *Euthyphr.* 2 B, *Polit.* 296 A. The illus-

ἀνδρὶ δ' ἐρωτικῷ οὐ πρέπει ἀμνημονεῖν, ὅτι πάντες οἱ ἐν ὥρᾳ τὸν
φιλόπαιδα καὶ ἐρωτικὸν ἁμῇ γέ πῃ δάκνουσί τε καὶ κινοῦσι,
δοκοῦντες ἄξιοι εἶναι ἐπιμελείας τε καὶ τοῦ ἀσπάζεσθαι. ἢ οὐχ
οὕτω ποιεῖτε πρὸς τοὺς καλούς; ὁ μέν, ὅτι σιμός, ἐπίχαρις κληθεὶς
ἐπαινεθήσεται ὑφ' ὑμῶν, τοῦ δὲ τὸ γρυπὸν βασιλικόν φατε εἶναι,
E τὸν δὲ δὴ διὰ μέσου τούτων ἐμμετρώτατα ἔχειν, | μέλανας δὲ
ἀνδρικοὺς ἰδεῖν, λευκοὺς δὲ θεῶν παῖδας εἶναι· μελιχλώρους δὲ
καὶ τοὔνομα οἴει τινὸς ἄλλου ποίημα εἶναι ἢ ἐραστοῦ ὑποκοριζο-
μένου τε καὶ εὐχερῶς φέροντος τὴν ὠχρότητα, ἐὰν ἐπὶ ὥρᾳ ᾖ; καὶ
475 ἑνὶ λόγῳ πάσας προφάσεις προφασίζεσθέ τε | καὶ πάσας φωνὰς
ἀφίετε, ὥστε μηδένα ἀποβάλλειν τῶν ἀνθούντων ἐν ὥρᾳ. Εἰ
βούλει, ἔφη, ἐπ' ἐμοῦ λέγειν περὶ τῶν ἐρωτικῶν ὅτι οὕτω ποιοῦσι,
συγχωρῶ τοῦ λόγου χάριν. Τί δέ; ἦν δ' ἐγώ· τοὺς φιλοίνους οὐ

27. *ἐπαινεθήσεται* $A^1Π$: *ἐπαινεῖται* corr. A^2. 29. *μελιχλώρους γρ* A^2 in marg.: *μελαγχλώρους* $A^1ΠΞ$. In *q* refingitur *τὸ δὲ μελίχλωρον, τίνος ἄλλου τοὔνομα οἴει εἶναι ἢ ἐραστοῦ κτλ.*

---

tration which follows is all the more appropriate because the *φιλόσοφος* is himself an *ἐραστής*, in love with Truth: cf. VI 490 B.

23 **πάντες οἱ ἐν ὥρᾳ κτλ.** So in *Charm.* 154 B (cited by J. and C.) Socrates, an *ἀνὴρ ἐρωτικός* (*Symp.* 177 D), confesses *ἀτεχνῶς γὰρ λευκὴ στάθμη εἰμὶ πρὸς τοὺς καλούς· σχεδὸν γάρ τί μοι πάντες οἱ ἐν τῇ ἡλικίᾳ καλοὶ φαίνονται.*

26 **ὁ μέν, ὅτι σιμὸς κτλ.** The point is that the *ἀνὴρ ἐρωτικός*, loving *πάντας τοὺς ἐν ὥρᾳ*, finds beauty even where there is none. He 'sees Helen's beauty in a brow of Egypt.' The passage has often been imitated, and may have suggested the well-known satirical outburst of Lucretius (IV 1160—1170).

ἐπίχαρις: 'pleasing,' *χάριν ἔχουσα πρὸς τὴν ὄψιν* Arist. *Pol.* E 9. 1309[b] 24. With *τὸ γρυπὸν βασιλικόν* cf. *Phaedr.* 253 D and Arist. *Physiog.* 6. 811[a] 36 *οἱ δὲ γρυπὴν ἔχοντες (τὴν ῥῖνα) καὶ τοῦ μετώπου διηρθρωμένην μεγαλόψυχοι· ἀναφέρεται ἐπὶ τοὺς ἀετούς.* Neither *τὸ σιμόν* nor *τὸ γρυπόν* are marks of beauty; the straight nose is the fairest (Arist. *Pol.* l.c.).

474 E 29 **λευκοὺς δὲ θεῶν παῖδας** is in harmony with *Laws* 956 A *χρώματα δὲ λευκὰ πρέποντ' ἂν θεοῖς εἴη καὶ ἄλλοθι καὶ ἐν ὑφῇ.* See also Dieterich *Nekyia* pp. 39 ff.

μελιχλώρους κτλ.: 'and honey-pale darlings, with their name—do you suppose they are the creation of anybody but a fond and euphemistic lover, who readily excuses pallor, if appearing on the cheek of youth?' Plato is ridiculing the idea, as well as the name, *μελίχλωρος*: there never was a *μελίχλωρος* except in the lover's brain. The word is not, apparently, earlier than Plato, and does not occur again till Aristotle (*Physiog.* 6. 812[a] 19): Theocritus uses it hypocoristically of the silkworm (10. 27). It is difficult, if not impossible, to connect *τοὔνομα* with *μελιχλώρους*, as is usually done, translating. 'and the name honey-pale, too,' etc. Hartman proposes *μελίχλωρος*, which is ungrammatical, Richards *μελιχλώρου.* *μελιχλώρου* (which the poet Gray had already conjectured) is harmless enough: but emendation is unnecessary if *καί* is 'and.' *μελιχλώρους*—see *cr. n.*—has less MS authority than *μελαγχλώρους*, though supported by the Scholiast on VI 485 B, by *μελίχλωρος* in Aristotle and Theocritus (ll. cc.), and by the suitability of the word in the mouth of an *ἐραστὴς ὑποκοριζόμενος.* *μελίχρους* was apparently read by Plutarch (*de recta rat. audiendi* 45 A) and other ancient authorities: see Schneider's note.

475 A 3 **ἐπ' ἐμοῦ**: 'in my case,' 'taking me as your example': cf. VII 524 E *ὥσπερ ἐπὶ τοῦ δακτύλου ἐλέγομεν* and X 597 B.

τὰ αὐτὰ ταῦτα ποιοῦντας ὁρᾷς, πάντα οἶνον ἐπὶ πάσης προφάσεως ἀσπαζομένους; Καὶ μάλα. Καὶ μὴν φιλοτίμους γε, ὡς ἐγᾦμαι, καθορᾷς, ὅτι, ἂν μὴ στρατηγῆσαι δύνωνται, τριττυαρχοῦσιν, κἂν μὴ ὑπὸ μειζόνων καὶ σεμνοτέρων | τιμᾶσθαι, ὑπὸ σμικροτέρων καὶ B φαυλοτέρων τιμώμενοι ἀγαπῶσιν, ὡς ὅλως τιμῆς ἐπιθυμηταὶ ὄντες. Κομιδῇ μὲν οὖν. Τοῦτο δὴ φάθι ἢ μή· ἆρα ὃν ἄν τινος ἐπιθυμητικὸν λέγωμεν, παντὸς τοῦ εἴδους τούτου φήσομεν ἐπιθυμεῖν, ἢ τοῦ μέν, τοῦ δὲ οὔ; Παντός, ἔφη. Οὐκοῦν καὶ τὸν φιλόσοφον σοφίας φήσομεν ἐπιθυμητὴν εἶναι, οὐ τῆς μέν, τῆς δ' οὔ, ἀλλὰ πάσης; Ἀληθῆ. Τὸν ἄρα περὶ τὰ | μαθήματα δυσχεραίνοντα, ἄλλως τε C καὶ νέον ὄντα καὶ μήπω λόγον ἔχοντα τί τε χρηστὸν καὶ μή, οὐ φήσομεν φιλομαθῆ οὐδὲ φιλόσοφον εἶναι, ὥσπερ τὸν περὶ τὰ σιτία δυσχερῆ οὔτε πεινῆν φαμὲν οὔτ' ἐπιθυμεῖν σιτίων, οὐδὲ φιλόσιτον ἀλλὰ κακόσιτον εἶναι. Καὶ ὀρθῶς γε φήσομεν. Τὸν δὲ δὴ εὐχερῶς ἐθέλοντα παντὸς μαθήματος γεύεσθαι καὶ ἀσμένως ἐπὶ τὸ μανθάνειν ἰόντα καὶ ἀπλήστως ἔχοντα, τοῦτον δ' ἐν δίκῃ φήσομεν φιλόσοφον. ἢ γάρ; καὶ ὁ Γλαύκων ἔφη, Πολλοὶ ἄρα καὶ ἄτοποι | ἔσονταί σοι τοιοῦτοι. οἵ τε γὰρ φιλοθεάμονες πάντες D ἔμοιγε δοκοῦσι τῷ καταμανθάνειν χαίροντες τοιοῦτοι εἶναι, οἵ τε φιλήκοοι ἀτοπώτατοί τινές εἰσιν ὥς γ' ἐν φιλοσόφοις τιθέναι, οἳ πρὸς μὲν λόγους καὶ τοιαύτην διατριβὴν ἑκόντες οὐκ ἂν ἐθέλοιεν ἐλθεῖν, ὥσπερ δὲ ἀπομεμισθωκότες τὰ ὦτα ἐπακοῦσαι πάντων χορῶν περιθέουσι τοῖς Διονυσίοις, οὔτε τῶν κατὰ πόλεις οὔτε

---

7 **τριττυαρχοῦσιν.** If they cannot become (not 'be' as J. and C.) *στρατηγοί*, they are glad to be *τριττύαρχοι*. In time of war, a *στρατηγός* was commander in chief; next to him came the 10 *ταξίαρχοι*, or "commanders of the 10 *τάξεις* of hoplites corresponding to the 10 *φυλαί*"; under the *ταξίαρχοι* were the *τριττύαρχοι*, who each commanded the hoplites of a single *τριττύς*. There were in all 30 *τριττύες*, 3 in each tribe. See Gilbert's *Gk. Const. Ant.* pp. 209 f. and Sandys on Arist. *Pol. Ath.* 61 §§ 1—3.

475 B 14 **τὸν ἄρα κτλ.** Cf. *Lach.* 182 D ἀλλ' ἔστι μὲν—χαλεπὸν λέγειν περὶ ὁτουοῦν μαθήματος, ὡς οὐ χρὴ μανθάνειν· πάντα γὰρ ἐπίστασθαι ἀγαθὸν δοκεῖ εἶναι and Xen. *Mem.* IV 1. 2.

475 D 23 **καταμανθάνειν.** Apelt conjectures *καλὰ μανθάνειν*, but the text is free from objection.

τοιοῦτοι εἶναι: i.e. *φιλοθεάμονες εἶναι*, not *φιλόσοφοι εἶναι*, as the English translators appear to suppose. Glauco has clearly indicated that he does *not* consider such men philosophers. But as it is the love of learning which produces them, they will have to be included, unless Socrates narrows his definition, as Glauco is in fact inviting him to do. *σοφία* in *φιλο-σοφία* is presently defined so as to exclude sense-perception: hence 'lovers of sights and sounds' are not 'lovers of knowledge.' See also on *ὁμοίους μὲν φιλοσόφοις* in E.

25 **πρὸς μὲν λόγους κτλ.** Cf. *Prot.* 347 C, D with my note ad loc. *ἐπακοῦσαι* should be taken with *ἀπομεμισθωκότες*.

27 **οὔτε—κώμας.** Hartman would read *πόλιν* for *πόλεις*, "verum non Atticis solis urbana et ruralia erant Dionysia"

τῶν κατὰ κώμας ἀπολειπόμενοι. τούτους οὖν πάντας καὶ ἄλλους
E τοιούτων τινῶν | μαθητικοὺς καὶ τοὺς τῶν τεχνυδρίων φιλοσόφους
φήσομεν; Οὐδαμῶς, εἶπον, ἀλλ' ὁμοίους μὲν φιλοσόφοις.
XX. Τοὺς δὲ ἀληθινούς, ἔφη, τίνας λέγεις; Τοὺς τῆς ἀληθείας, ἦν δ' ἐγώ, φιλοθεάμονας. Καὶ τοῦτο μέν γ', ἔφη, ὀρθῶς·
ἀλλὰ πῶς αὐτὸ λέγεις; Οὐδαμῶς, ἦν δ' ἐγώ, ῥᾳδίως πρός γε
ἄλλον· σὲ δὲ οἶμαι ὁμολογήσειν μοι τὸ τοιόνδε. Τὸ ποῖον;
476 Ἐπειδή ἐστιν ἐναντίον καλὸν αἰσχρῷ, δύο αὐ|τὼ εἶναι. Πῶς δ'
οὔ; Οὐκοῦν ἐπειδὴ δύο, καὶ ἓν ἑκάτερον; Καὶ τοῦτο. Καὶ περὶ
δικαίου καὶ ἀδίκου καὶ ἀγαθοῦ καὶ κακοῦ καὶ πάντων τῶν εἰδῶν

29. μαθητικοὺς A[1]: μαθηματικοὺς ΑΠΞ *q* et corr. A[2].

(Schneider, quoting *Laws* 637 A, B). In Attica rural Dionysia were held during the month of Poseidon in many κῶμαι, e.g. Eleusis, Phlya, etc. "Prizes were offered by the different demes, and companies seem to have been formed in Athens for the purpose of travelling about the country and taking part in these provincial competitions" (Haigh *Att. Theatre* pp. 42 ff. Cf. Mommsen *Fest. d. Stadt Athen* pp. 349—359).

475 E 29 **τοὺς τῶν τεχνυδρίων**: sc. μαθητικούς, or rather perhaps φίλους or the like, supplied from the termination of μαθητικούς. Cf. φιλοτέχνους in 476 A. Athenaeus (X 452 C) wrongly connects τούς with φιλοσόφους.

30 **ὁμοίους μὲν φιλοσόφοις.** μέν without δέ is common enough after ἀλλά, the antithesis being contained in the preceding negative: cf. *Prot.* 344 A and *Crito* 43 D. It is also found in other cases where the antithesis is easy to supply: cf. IV 421 A, V 472 D, and Heindorf on *Theaet.* 161 E. Such men resemble φιλόσοφοι as the shadow resembles the substance; for the objects of sense, which they love, are shadows or copies of the objects of knowledge. The phrase receives its fullest interpretation from the simile of the Cave in Book VII.

33 **οὐδαμῶς—τοιόνδε.** Cf. 473 A *n.* Socrates again appeals to Glauco as one Platonist to another. We are to infer that the Theory of Ideas was already familiar in the school of Plato.

35 **δύο αὐτὼ εἶναι** should not be translated 'that they are two things' (D. and V.), but simply 'that they are two.'

476 A 2 **καὶ περὶ δικαίου κτλ.** This is the first appearance of the Theory of 'Ideas' properly so called in the *Republic.* It should be carefully noted that Plato is not attempting to prove the theory: Glauco, in fact, admits it from the first. The Theory was approached from two directions, from the side of Mind or Thought (οἱ λόγοι οἱ ἐκ τῶν ἐπιστημῶν Arist. *Met.* I 9. 990^{b} 12), and from the side of Existence (τὸ ἓν ἐπὶ πολλῶν l.c. Cf. Zeller[4] II 1, pp. 652 ff.). It is the first of these methods which is followed throughout the present investigation. The εἴδη provide objects for Knowledge, as opposed to Opinion, and they are capable of being known: see 476 C, E ff., 478 A, 479 E. Throughout a large part of the following discussion, we are not much concerned with the Ideas as strictly transcendent entities or χωριστά, existing apart not only from particulars but also from the knowing Mind, for it is only in so far as he knows the Ideas that the philosopher-king can make use of them (cf. VI 484 C, D): he cannot possibly frame political institutions on the model of Ideas which he does not know. We must admit that the philosopher's apprehension of the Ideas is the relevant consideration here (cf. VI 484 C ἐναργὲς ἐν τῇ ψυχῇ ἔχοντες παράδειγμα), but it is none the less true, and the fact cannot be too strongly insisted on, that the Ideas themselves are not mere concepts of the mind, but have a separate and independent existence of their own. See the Appendix to Book VII '*On Plato's Dialectic.*' The translation 'Class' for εἶδος (Jowett) is inappropriate on many grounds: 'Form' is better: but it will be most convenient to retain the usual

πέρι ὁ αὐτὸς λόγος, αὐτὸ μὲν ἓν ἕκαστον εἶναι, τῇ δὲ τῶν πράξεων καὶ σωμάτων καὶ ἀλλήλων κοινωνίᾳ πανταχοῦ φανταζόμενα πολλὰ φαίνεσθαι ἕκαστον. Ὀρθῶς, ἔφη, λέγεις. Ταύτῃ τοίνυν, ἦν δ' ἐγώ, διαιρῶ, χωρὶς μὲν οὓς νῦν δὴ ἔλεγες φιλοθεάμονάς τε καὶ φιλοτέχνους καὶ πρακτικούς, καὶ χωρὶς αὖ περὶ ὧν ὁ λόγος, **B** οὓς μόνους ἄν τις ὀρθῶς προσείποι φιλοσόφους. Πῶς, ἔφη, λέγεις; Οἱ μέν που, ἦν δ' ἐγώ, φιλήκοοι καὶ φιλοθεάμονες τάς τε καλὰς φωνὰς ἀσπάζονται καὶ χρόας καὶ σχήματα καὶ πάντα τὰ ἐκ τῶν τοιούτων δημιουργούμενα, αὐτοῦ δὲ τοῦ καλοῦ ἀδύνατος αὐτῶν ἡ διάνοια τὴν φύσιν ἰδεῖν τε καὶ ἀσπάσασθαι. Ἔχει γὰρ

10. *που* II: *ποι* A.

---

expression 'Idea,' although it is not a translation, but a transliteration, whose unfortunate identity with the English word 'idea' is responsible in no small measure for many imperfect and erroneous interpretations of Plato's Ideal Theory. The German translators mostly render by 'Begriff.' The further specifications of the Ideal Theory in this passage are as follows. Each Idea is, in and by itself, one (476 A), changeless (479 A, 479 E), and perfect (VI 484 C, D), contrasting, in each of these respects, with the phenomena which 'partake' of or 'imitate' it (476 D *n.*). Plato does not now touch on the question how it is that Mind has knowledge of a perfection above and beyond what can be derived from observation and experience. This faculty of Mind is elsewhere—in the *Meno* and the *Phaedo*—explained by the pre-existence of the Soul. See on 476 C.

Krohn has pointed out (*Pl. St.* p. 96) that the examples of *εἴδη* now cited by Plato are all of them attributes—*δίκαιον*, *ἄδικον*, *ἀγαθόν*, *κακόν*, etc. It does not however follow from this that the theory of Ideas is still in process of formation: on the contrary, the appeal to Glauco just above (475 E) implies that it was already a recognised dogma of the Platonic school. The simple explanation is that Plato prefers to cite relevant examples. The *εἴδη* of *δίκαιον*, *ἀγαθόν*, *καλόν* etc. are precisely those which it is the philosopher's duty to introduce into the practical administration of the State: cf. VI 484 C and X 596 A *n.*

4 **αὐτὸ μὲν κτλ.**: 'each is, in itself' (i.e. viewed apart from its association with *πράξεις* etc.), 'one, but by reason of their partnership with actions and bodies and one another, they each of them make their appearance everywhere and appear many.' The *εἶδος* of Beautiful, for example, *is*, in itself, one, but by *κοινωνία* with e.g. an act of heroism, a sunset, a river, etc., it *appears* many. Similarly the *εἶδος* of Beautiful *appears* many by *κοινωνία* with other *εἴδη*, as when we say 'the Good is beautiful,' the 'Useful is beautiful' etc. The expression *πανταχοῦ φανταζόμενα* is better suited to describe Ideas allied with sensible particulars, than Ideas allied with Ideas; but statements involving the *κοινωνία* of Ideas with Ideas 'make their appearance everywhere' as well as those which connect the objects of sense with Ideas. In all such cases the statements themselves are of course true or false according as the *κοινωνία* is real or imaginary; but whether they are false or true, the appearance of *plurality* which they give to the Idea is always fallacious. Cf. Zeller[4] II 1, p. 738 *n.* 3 and see on 479 D. The words *ἀλλήλων κοινωνία* are further discussed in App. VII.

8 **πρακτικούς**: 'men of action.' These were not mentioned in 475 D, but they clearly belong to the same category.

476 B 13 **τὴν φύσιν**. Krohn (*Pl. St.* p. 95) justly observes that the *φύσις τοῦ καλοῦ* of III 401 C is "the true beauty, which *has* an adequate external form, whereas that of Book V is the *essence* of Beauty, which is never fully expressed in any outward form." The contrast significantly marks the greater Idealism of Books V—VII. Cf. X 597 B *n.*

οὖν δή, ἔφη, οὕτως. Οἱ δὲ δὴ ἐπ' αὐτὸ τὸ καλὸν δυνατοὶ ἰέναι C τε καὶ ὁρᾶν καθ' αὑτὸ ἆρα οὐ σπάνιοι ἂν εἶεν; Καὶ μάλα. Ὁ οὖν καλὰ μὲν πράγματα νομίζων, αὐτὸ δὲ κάλλος μήτε νομίζων μήτε, ἄν τις ἡγῆται ἐπὶ τὴν γνῶσιν αὐτοῦ, δυνάμενος ἕπεσθαι, ὄναρ ἢ ὕπαρ δοκεῖ σοι ζῆν; σκόπει δέ. τὸ ὀνειρώττειν ἆρα οὐ τόδε ἐστίν, ἐάν τε ἐν ὕπνῳ τις ἐάν τ' ἐγρηγορὼς τὸ ὅμοιόν τῳ μὴ ὅμοιον ἀλλ' αὐτὸ ἡγῆται εἶναι ᾧ ἔοικεν; Ἐγὼ γοῦν ἄν, ἦ δ' ὅς, φαίην ὀνειρώττειν τὸν τοιοῦτον. Τί δέ; ὁ τἀναντία τούτων D ἡγούμενός τέ τι αὐτὸ καλὸν καὶ δυνάμενος καθορᾶν καὶ αὐτὸ καὶ τὰ ἐκείνου μετέχοντα, καὶ οὔτε τὰ μετέχοντα αὐτὸ οὔτε αὐτὸ τὰ μετέχοντα ἡγούμενος, ὕπαρ ἢ ὄναρ αὖ καὶ οὗτος δοκεῖ σοι ζῆν; Καὶ μάλα, ἔφη, ὕπαρ. Οὐκοῦν τούτου μὲν τὴν διάνοιαν ὡς γιγνώσκοντος γνώμην ἂν ὀρθῶς φαῖμεν εἶναι, τοῦ δὲ δόξαν ὡς δοξάζοντος; Πάνυ μὲν οὖν. Τί οὖν, ἐὰν ἡμῖν χαλεπαίνῃ οὗτος,

---

476 C 16 **καλὰ—πράγματα.** *πράγματα* is a sufficiently general term to include all the *φαινόμενα πολλά* which are specified in 476 A. The persons in question may be willing to assert that a *σῶμα*, a *πρᾶξις*, *τὸ δίκαιον*, *τὸ ἀγαθόν* etc. are *καλά*. But they refuse to go beyond isolated observations of this sort and admit that Beauty *itself* exists *αὐτὸ καθ' αὑτὸ μεθ' αὑτοῦ μονοειδὲς ἀεὶ ὄν* (*Symp.* 211 B); and hence their notions of beauty are uncoordinated, inconsistent, unstable.

17 **ἄν τις ἡγῆται κτλ.** Cf. *Symp.* 210 A.

19 **ἐάν τε ἐν ὕπνῳ κτλ.** It is the pre-existence of the soul which qualifies her by nature to distinguish between the Idea or Original, and the phenomenon or copy. But as we lost at birth our ante-natal knowledge of the Idea, we cannot distinguish between Ideas and phenomena until we recover that knowledge. To effect this recovery is the aim of education. The uneducated wander in a sort of dreamland, taking shadows for realities, the copy for the Original. Cf. *Phaed.* 74 A—76 D, *Men.* 81 A ff., *Symp.* 209 E—212 A.

476 D 23 **μετέχοντα.** Cf. *Phaed.* 100 D. The words by which Plato describes the relation of Ideas and particulars are of necessity figurative. *κοινωνία* is the vaguest, and least metaphorical; side by side with it comes *παρουσία* (of the Idea) and *μέθεξις* (of the particular). A somewhat different figure is involved when the Idea is regarded as the Original (Urbild), and the particular as its likeness. Plato does not scruple to use both figures side by side: here, for example, the Idea was a *παράδειγμα* just above (*αὐτὸ—ᾧ ἔοικεν* 476 C: cf. VI 500 E ff., X 596 B).

27 **οὗτος.** Dümmler (*Antisthenica* p. 42) supposes that Plato means Antisthenes. There was undoubtedly no love lost between the two philosophers: see the authorities cited in Urban *Ueber die Erwähnungen der Phil. d. Antisthenes in d. Pl. Schr.* (Königsberg 1882), and Zeller[4] II 1, p. 296 *n.* 2. Antisthenes was in particular a bitter opponent of the Theory of Ideas. The passage of arms between Plato and him is well known: *ὦ Πλάτων, ἵππον μὲν ὁρῶ, ἱππότητα δὲ οὐχ ὁρῶ, καὶ ὃς εἶπεν ἔχεις μὲν ᾧ ἵππος ὁρᾶται, τόδε τὸ ὄμμα, ᾧ δὲ ἱππότης θεωρεῖται, οὐδέπω κέκτησαι* (Simplicius in *Schol. Arist.* 66^b 44 ed. Brandis, and other authorities quoted by Urban l.c. p. 3). It is no doubt true, as Stein observes in his *Geschichte des Platonismus*, that Plato's "Kunst verallgemeinert nicht bloss das Historische, sondern individualisiert auch das Allgemeine"; but Antisthenes himself could scarcely deny that the cap fits. The deictic *οὗτος* is in favour of Dümmler's view, which certainly adds point to the whole passage; note in particular *χαλεπαίνῃ*, *παραμυθεῖσθαι*, *πείθειν ἠρέμα* (allusions perhaps to the ferocity of his opponent: Antisthenes had nicknamed Plato *Σάθων*! cf. Ath. V 220 D), *οὐχ*

ὃν φαμεν δοξάζειν ἀλλ' οὐ γιγνώσκειν, καὶ ἀμφισβητῇ ὡς οὐκ
ἀληθῆ λέγομεν; ἕξομέν τι παραμυθεῖσθαι | αὐτὸν καὶ πείθειν **E**
ἠρέμα, ἐπικρυπτόμενοι ὅτι οὐχ ὑγιαίνει; Δεῖ γέ τοι δή, ἔφη.
Ἴθι δή, σκόπει τί ἐροῦμεν πρὸς αὐτόν. ἢ βούλει ὧδε πυνθανώμεθα
παρ' αὐτοῦ, λέγοντες, ὡς εἴ τι οἶδεν, οὐδεὶς αὐτῷ φθόνος, ἀλλ'
ἄσμενοι ἂν ἴδοιμεν εἰδότα τι. ἀλλ' ἡμῖν εἰπὲ τόδε· ὁ γιγνώσκων
γιγνώσκει τὶ ἢ οὐδέν; σὺ οὖν μοι ὑπὲρ ἐκείνου ἀποκρίνου. Ἀπο-
κρινοῦμαι, ἔφη, ὅτι γιγνώσκει τί. Πότερον ὂν ἢ οὐκ ὄν; Ὄν·
πῶς γὰρ | ἂν μὴ ὄν γέ τι γνωσθείη; Ἱκανῶς οὖν τοῦτο ἔχομεν, **477**
κἂν εἰ πλεοναχῇ σκοποῖμεν, ὅτι τὸ μὲν παντελῶς ὂν παντελῶς
γνωστόν, μὴ ὂν δὲ μηδαμῇ πάντῃ ἄγνωστον; Ἱκανώτατα. Εἶεν·
εἰ δὲ δή τι οὕτως ἔχει ὡς εἶναί τε καὶ μὴ εἶναι, οὐ μεταξὺ ἂν κέοιτο
τοῦ εἰλικρινῶς ὄντος καὶ τοῦ αὖ μηδαμῇ ὄντος; Μεταξύ. Οὐκοῦν
εἰ ἐπὶ μὲν τῷ ὄντι γνῶσις ἦν, ἀγνωσία δ' ἐξ ἀνάγκης ἐπὶ μὴ ὄντι,

6. εἰ *q*: om. ΑΠΞ.

ὑγιαίνει ('is barely sane'), οὐδεὶς αὐτῷ φθόνος, and the delightful innuendo ἄσμενοι ἂν ἴδοιμεν εἰδότα τι. Antisthenes himself wrote a work περὶ δόξης καὶ ἐπιστήμης (D. L. VI 17), and Plato may well be thinking of it here: see next note. But we must be careful to note that Plato, even if we allow that Antisthenes is in his mind, does not refer to Antisthenes alone; he merely individualizes the type in him.

476 E 36 **πῶς γὰρ—γνωσθείη**; 'for how can something which is not, be known?' Cf. *Parm.* 132 B, C ἓν ἕκαστόν ἐστι τῶν νοημάτων, νόημα δὲ οὐδενός; Ἀλλ' ἀδύνατον, εἰπεῖν. Ἀλλὰ τινός; Ναί. Ὄντος ἢ οὐκ ὄντος; Ὄντος. Οὐχ ἑνός τινος, ὃ ἐπὶ πᾶσιν τὸ νόημα ἐπὸν νοεῖ, μίαν τινὰ οὖσαν ἰδέαν; Ναί. "Quod Parmenides simpliciter dicit ταὐτὸν δ' ἐστὶ νοεῖν τε καὶ οὕνεκέν ἐστι νόημα, id sibi prorsus probari Plato plus semel significat" Bonitz *Disput. Plato. duae* p. 11. That everything which is known exists in a certain sense, is of course a truism. But when Plato says that the objects of knowledge 'are,' the kind of οὐσία which he means is substantial, self-existent οὐσία. If it is really Antisthenes for whom Glauco is answering (ὑπὲρ ἐκείνου ἀποκρίνου), the words πῶς—γνωσθείη are exceedingly well chosen; for Antisthenes (perhaps in his περὶ δόξης ἢ ἐπιστήμης, perhaps in Σάθων, ἢ οὐκ ἔστιν ἀντιλέγειν) had argued in almost exactly the same way to prove the impossibility of contradiction. See Proclus *in Crat.* 37 (Zeller[4] II 1 p. 302 *n.* 1) Ἀντισθένης ἔλεγεν μὴ δεῖν ἀντιλέγειν· πᾶς γάρ, φησί, λόγος ἀληθεύει· ὁ γὰρ λέγων τὶ λέγει· ὁ δὲ τὶ λέγων τὸ ὂν λέγει· ὁ δὲ τὸ ὂν λέγων ἀληθεύει and cf. Plat. *Crat.* 429 D. It is by no means improbable that Plato has this or some similar argument of Antisthenes in view, and feathers his arrows from his victim's wing. Antisthenes and his friends would not of course admit the connotation which Plato gives to ὄν, but Plato is not attempting to prove the Ideal theory. The object of the whole investigation is to shew that his opponents possess only δόξα, on the assumption that the theory of Ideas is true: cf. 476 A *n.*

477 A 2 **κἂν εἰ—σκοποῖμεν.** Further investigation from other points of view cannot weaken the conviction which Socrates and Glauco have already formed. The phrase is another indication that we are not here proving the Ideal Theory: see last note. Hartman should not have revived Ast's conjecture ἔχομεν <ἢ> καὶ πλεοναχῇ σκοπῶμεν.

6 **εἰ ἐπὶ κτλ.** See *cr. n.* Hermann's conjecture, that ἐπεὶ has been lost before ἐπί, has met with most favour. But ἐπεὶ ἐπί has an unpleasing sound, and εἰ might just as easily have disappeared as ἐπεί. Schneider and Stallbaum (with Ξ and the older editors) read οὐκοῦν ἐπὶ μὲν—ἐπὶ τῷ

B ἐπὶ τῷ μεταξὺ τούτῳ | μεταξύ τι καὶ ζητητέον ἀγνοίας τε καὶ
ἐπιστήμης, εἴ τι τυγχάνει ὂν τοιοῦτον; Πάνυ μὲν οὖν. Ἆρ' οὖν
λέγομέν τι δόξαν εἶναι; Πῶς γὰρ οὔ; Πότερον ἄλλην δύναμιν
ἐπιστήμης ἢ τὴν αὐτήν; Ἄλλην. Ἐπ' ἄλλῳ ἄρα τέτακται δόξα
καὶ ἐπ' ἄλλῳ ἐπιστήμη, κατ' αὐτὴν τὴν δύναμιν ἑκατέρα τὴν αὑτῆς.
Οὕτω. Οὐκοῦν ἐπιστήμη μὲν ἐπὶ τῷ ὄντι πέφυκε, γνῶναι, ὡς
ἔστι τὸ ὄν; μᾶλλον δὲ ὧδέ μοι δοκεῖ πρότερον ἀναγκαῖον εἶναι
διελέσθαι. Πῶς;

C XXI. Φήσομεν δυνάμεις εἶναι γένος τι τῶν ὄντων, αἷς δὴ
καὶ ἡμεῖς δυνάμεθα ἃ δυνάμεθα, καὶ ἄλλο πᾶν ὅ τί περ ἂν
δύνηται; οἷον λέγω ὄψιν καὶ ἀκοὴν τῶν δυνάμεων εἶναι, εἰ ἄρα
μανθάνεις ὃ βούλομαι λέγειν τὸ εἶδος. Ἀλλὰ μανθάνω, ἔφη.
Ἄκουσον δὴ ὅ μοι φαίνεται περὶ αὐτῶν. δυνάμεως γὰρ ἐγὼ οὔτε
τινὰ χρόαν ὁρῶ οὔτε σχῆμα οὔτε τι τῶν τοιούτων, οἷον καὶ ἄλλων
πολλῶν, πρὸς ἃ ἀποβλέπων ἔνια διορίζομαι παρ' ἐμαυτῷ τὰ μὲν
D ἄλλα εἶναι, τὰ δὲ ἄλλα· δυνάμεως δ' | εἰς ἐκεῖνο μόνον βλέπω,
ἐφ' ᾧ τε ἔστι καὶ ὃ ἀπεργάζεται, καὶ ταύτῃ ἑκάστην αὐτῶν δύναμιν
ἐκάλεσα, καὶ τὴν μὲν ἐπὶ τῷ αὐτῷ τεταγμένην καὶ τὸ αὐτὸ
ἀπεργαζομένην τὴν αὐτὴν καλῶ, τὴν δὲ ἐπὶ ἑτέρῳ καὶ ἕτερον
ἀπεργαζομένην ἄλλην. τί δὲ σύ; πῶς ποιεῖς; Οὕτως, ἔφη.
Δεῦρο δὴ πάλιν, ἦν δ' ἐγώ, ὦ ἄριστε. ἐπιστήμην πότερον δύναμίν
E τινα φῂς εἶναι αὐτήν, ἢ εἰς τί γένος τίθης; Εἰς | τοῦτο, ἔφη,

11. αὐτὴν τὴν C. Schmidt: τὴν αὐτὴν AΠ *q*: κατ'—αὑτῆς om. Ξ.

μεταξὺ δὲ κτλ., but the reading of *q* is intrinsically better, and the error an easier one. The reference in ἦν ('is, as we saw') is to 476 E—477 A.

477 B 11 **κατ' αὐτὴν—αὑτῆς**: 'each of them in accordance just with its own peculiar power,' i.e. in accordance with this, and nothing else. αὐτήν is *ipsam* in the sense of *solam*. Cf. 477 D, where it is shewn that δυνάμεις should be classified on this same principle: also 478 A ἐφ' ἑτέρῳ ἄρα ἕτερόν τι δυναμένη ἑκατέρα αὐτῶν πέφυκεν. The reading κατὰ τὴν αὐτήν—see *cr. n.*—gives precisely the wrong sense. Schneider and others—perhaps rightly—omit αὐτήν (with Vind. F), while Baiter adopts Hermann's ἄλλην—a very improbable correction. It is best, I think, to follow Schmidt, supposing that αὐτήν was accidentally omitted, and afterwards wrongly replaced.

13 **μᾶλλον δὲ κτλ.** Socrates had somewhat awkwardly called δόξα a δύναμις, and at the same time spoken of it as possessing a δύναμις. The present sentence introduces a sort of πάρεργον in which the notion δύναμις is more accurately defined. We may infer that δυνάμεις in the sense of (the intellectual) 'powers' was unfamiliar at the time when this section was written. It was perhaps—like ποιότης for example—one of Plato's experiments in language. 'Faculties' is, I think, too concrete to be a right translation.

477 D 28 **αὐτήν** is difficult. It is not quite easy to understand the word as *ipsam*, especially as it is so far from ἐπιστήμην. Had Plato written αὐτὴν τὴν ἐπιστήμην, or ἐπιστήμην—καὶ αὐτήν there would have been little or no difficulty. As it is, if the text is right, we should probably (with Schneider and others) regard αὐτήν as tautological: cf. IV 428 A *n.*

πασῶν γε δυνάμεων ἐρρωμενεστάτην. Τί δέ; δόξαν εἰς δύναμιν
ἢ εἰς ἄλλο εἶδος οἴσομεν; Οὐδαμῶς, ἔφη· ᾧ γὰρ δοξάζειν δυνάμεθα, οὐκ ἄλλο τι ἢ δόξα ἐστίν. Ἀλλὰ μὲν δὴ ὀλίγον γε πρότερον
ὡμολόγεις μὴ τὸ αὐτὸ εἶναι ἐπιστήμην τε καὶ δόξαν. Πῶς γὰρ ἄν,
ἔφη, τό γε ἀναμάρτητον τῷ μὴ ἀναμαρτήτῳ ταὐτόν ποτέ τις νοῦν
ἔχων τιθείη; Καλῶς, ἦν δ' ἐγώ, καὶ δῆλον, ὅτι ἕτερον ἐπιστήμης
δό|ξα ὁμολογεῖται ἡμῖν. Ἕτερον. Ἐφ' ἑτέρῳ ἄρα ἕτερόν τι 478
δυναμένη ἑκατέρα αὐτῶν πέφυκεν. Ἀνάγκη. Ἐπιστήμη μέν γέ
που ἐπὶ τῷ ὄντι, τὸ ὂν γνῶναι ὡς ἔχει; Ναί. Δόξα δέ, φαμέν,
δοξάζει; Ναί. Ἦ ταὐτόν, ὅπερ ἐπιστήμη γιγνώσκει; καὶ ἔσται
γνωστόν τε καὶ δοξαστὸν τὸ αὐτό; ἢ ἀδύνατον; Ἀδύνατον, ἔφη,
ἐκ τῶν ὡμολογημένων, εἴπερ ἐπ' ἄλλῳ ἄλλη δύναμις πέφυκεν,
δυνάμεις δὲ ἀμφότεραί ἐστον, δόξα τε καὶ ἐπιστήμη, ἄλλη δὲ B
ἑκατέρα, ὥς φαμέν. ἐκ τούτων δὴ οὐκ ἐγχωρεῖ γνωστὸν καὶ
δοξαστὸν ταὐτὸν εἶναι. Οὐκοῦν εἰ τὸ ὂν γνωστόν, ἄλλο τι ἂν
δοξαστὸν ἢ τὸ ὂν εἴη; Ἄλλο. Ἆρ' οὖν τὸ μὴ ὂν δοξάζει;
ἢ ἀδύνατον καὶ δοξάσαι τὸ μὴ ὄν; ἐννόει δέ. οὐχ ὁ δοξάζων ἐπὶ

4. δοξάζει nos: δοξάζειν AΠ et (antecedente δόξαν) Ξ *q*. 11. τὸ A^1Π: τό γε corr. A^2.

Should we perhaps read Δεῦρο δὴ πάλιν, ἦν δ' ἐγώ, ὦ ἄριστε, <ἐπὶ> ἐπιστήμην. πότερον κτλ.? The conjecture is not convincing, although it was at ἐπιστήμη that the digression began in 477 B. "If I were to make any change" says Jackson "I would put αὐτήν before or after τίθης."

477 E 30 **οἴσομεν**. Θ with two Vienna MSS reads θήσομεν, which is also a correction in Cesenas M. θήσομεν was likewise conjectured by Cobet. A precise parallel is hard to find; but φέρειν is used elsewhere of the operations of the mind (cf. 478 B), and θήσομεν would not be likely to suffer corruption, especially as εἰς τί γένος τίθης occurs just before.

31 **δόξα**. Instead of δόξα O. Schneider (*Versuch ein. genet. Entw. d. Pl.* ἀγαθόν p. 13) would read δύναμις, but δυνάμεθα should of course be taken in its full etymological sense.

32 **πῶς γὰρ ἂν—τιθείη**. The infallibility of knowledge is a cardinal principle with Plato: cf. *Gorg.* 454 D and *Theaet.* 152 C, 186 C ff. See Zeller[4] II 1, p. 591.

478 A 4 **δοξάζει**. See *cr. n.* The same conjecture had occurred to Jackson. δοξάζειν is in itself defensible and seems at first sight required by the balance of clauses ἐπιστήμη μέν γέ που—δόξα δέ. But the introduction of φαμέν breaks the balance, and suggests a new departure. The real reason for writing δοξάζει is the occurrence of ἆρ' οὖν τὸ μὴ ὂν δοξάζει (sc. δόξα); in 478 B. Unless δοξάζει is read here, it is very difficult to supply the subject of δοξάζει there. Reading δοξάζει, again, we supply after ἢ ταὐτόν not δοξάζειν (as must be done if the infinitive is read), but δοξάζει. This too is an improvement, because it provides an exact balance to γιγνώσκει. If Plato had meant ἢ ταὐτὸν δοξάζειν, we should expect him to have written not γιγνώσκει, but γιγνώσκειν. On the corruption see *Introd.* § 5.

7 **ἀμφότεραί ἐστον**. The union of a plural subject with a dual verb is tolerably frequent in Plato: cf. *Euthyd.* 278 E, 303 C. These and other examples are quoted in Roeper *de dualis usu Plat.* p. 30.

478 B 10 **ἆρ' οὖν—δοξάζει**; J. and C. understand ὁ δοξάζων: but δόξα is more appropriate in itself, and much more easily supplied, especially if δοξάζει is read in 478 A: see note ad loc.

11 **ἢ ἀδύνατον κτλ.** Cf. *Theaet.* 189 B οὐκ ἄρα οἷόν τε τὸ μὴ ὂν δοξάζειν, οὔτε

τὶ φέρει τὴν δόξαν; ἢ οἷόν τε αὖ δοξάζειν μέν, δοξάζειν δὲ μηδέν;
Ἀδύνατον. Ἀλλ' ἕν γέ τι δοξάζει ὁ δοξάζων; Ναί. Ἀλλὰ μὴν
C μὴ ὄν γε οὐχ ἕν τι, ἀλλὰ μηδὲν ὀρθότατ' ἂν | προσαγορεύοιτο.
Πάνυ γε. Μὴ ὄντι μὴν ἄγνοιαν ἐξ ἀνάγκης ἀπέδομεν, ὄντι δὲ
γνῶσιν. Ὀρθῶς, ἔφη. Οὐκ ἄρα ὂν οὐδὲ μὴ ὂν δοξάζει. Οὐ γάρ.
Οὔτε ἄρα ἄγνοια οὔτε γνῶσις δόξα ἂν εἴη. Οὐκ ἔοικεν. Ἆρ' οὖν
ἐκτὸς τούτων ἐστίν, ὑπερβαίνουσα ἢ γνῶσιν σαφηνείᾳ ἢ ἄγνοιαν
ἀσαφείᾳ; Οὐδέτερα. Ἀλλ' ἆρα, ἦν δ' ἐγώ, γνώσεως μέν σοι
φαίνεται δόξα σκοτωδέστερον, ἀγνοίας δὲ φανότερον; Καὶ πολύ
D γε, ἔφη. Ἐντὸς δ' | ἀμφοῖν κεῖται; Ναί. Μεταξὺ ἄρα ἂν εἴη
τούτοιν δόξα. Κομιδῇ μὲν οὖν. Οὐκοῦν ἔφαμεν ἐν τοῖς πρόσθεν,
εἴ τι φανείη οἷον ἅμα ὄν τε καὶ μὴ ὄν, τὸ τοιοῦτον μεταξὺ κεῖσθαι
τοῦ εἰλικρινῶς ὄντος τε καὶ τοῦ πάντως μὴ ὄντος, καὶ οὔτε ἐπιστήμην οὔτε ἄγνοιαν ἐπ' αὐτῷ ἔσεσθαι, ἀλλὰ τὸ μεταξὺ αὖ φανὲν
ἀγνοίας καὶ ἐπιστήμης; Ὀρθῶς. Νῦν δέ γε πέφανται μεταξὺ
τούτοιν ὃ δὴ καλοῦμεν δόξαν. Πέφανται.
E XXII. Ἐκεῖνο | δὴ λείποιτ' ἂν ἡμῖν εὑρεῖν, ὡς ἔοικε, τὸ
ἀμφοτέρων μετέχον, τοῦ εἶναί τε καὶ μὴ εἶναι, καὶ οὐδέτερον
εἰλικρινὲς ὀρθῶς ἂν προσαγορευόμενον, ἵνα ἐὰν φανῇ, δοξαστὸν
αὐτὸ εἶναι ἐν δίκῃ προσαγορεύωμεν, τοῖς μὲν ἄκροις τὰ ἄκρα, τοῖς
δὲ μεταξὺ τὰ μεταξὺ ἀποδιδόντες. ἢ οὐχ οὕτως; Οὕτω. Τούτων
479 δὴ ὑποκειμένων λεγέτω μοι, φήσω, καὶ ἀποκρινέσθω | ὁ χρηστός,

---

περὶ τῶν ὄντων οὔτε αὐτὸ καθ' αὐτό. *μὴ ὄν* is here the bare negative—absolute not-being. Cf. Bosanquet *Companion* p. 212.

14 **μὴ ὄν γε**: i.q. *τὸ μὴ ὄν γε* (cf. *μὴ ὄντι* just below), not *εἰ μὴ εἴη γε* (as Stallbaum and Campbell suppose). Schneider and Jowett take the right view.

478 C 16 **δοξάζει**. The subject is *δόξα* rather than *ὁ δοξάζων*, in spite of *ὁ δοξάζων* above. *δόξα* was the subject of the verb where the two stages of the argument began (478 A *ἢ ταὐτόν* sc. *δόξα δοξάζει* and 478 B *ἆρ' οὖν τὸ μὴ ὂν δοξάζει*), and ought to be so in the conclusion also.

18 **σαφηνείᾳ—ἀσαφείᾳ**. The full significance of these words does not appear till VI 508 D ff., where the relation between Light and Truth is explained. See note ad loc. and VI 511 C *n*.

21 **ἐντὸς δ' ἀμφοῖν**. Hartman (with Ast) prefers *ἐντὸς δὴ ἀμφοῖν*. It is much better to regard the expression as a step in the argument, leading to the conclusion *μεταξὺ ἄρα κτλ*.

478 D 23 **οἷον—ὄν**. *οἷον* is adverbial; if it were an adjective the infinitive would follow. The qualification suggests that in the ultimate analysis it is inaccurate to say that phenomena 'both are and are not': the truth is that they lie somewhere *between* being and not being. Hence also *οὕτως ἔχει ὡς εἶναί τε καὶ μὴ εἶναι* in 477 A. See also on *καὶ γὰρ ταῦτα κτλ.* in 479 C. It should be noted that Plato now adds *ἅμα*: in 477 A it was absent. See on 479 A *τούτων γὰρ δὴ κτλ.*

479 A 1 **ὁ χρηστός**. Antisthenes is perhaps in Plato's mind (Dümmler *Antisth.* p. 42). Others have thought of Isocrates, but with less reason. *λεγέτω μοι, φήσω, καὶ ἀποκρινέσθω* certainly sounds like a personal challenge. See also on 476 D and 480 A.

ὃς αὐτὸ μὲν καλὸν καὶ ἰδέαν τινὰ αὐτοῦ κάλλους μηδεμίαν ἡγεῖται ἀεὶ κατὰ ταὐτὰ ὡσαύτως ἔχουσαν, πολλὰ δὲ τὰ καλὰ νομίζει, ἐκεῖνος ὁ φιλοθεάμων καὶ οὐδαμῇ ἀνεχόμενος, ἄν τις ἓν τὸ καλὸν φῇ εἶναι καὶ δίκαιον, καὶ τἆλλα οὕτω. τούτων γὰρ δή, ὦ ἄριστε, φήσομεν, τῶν πολλῶν καλῶν μῶν τι ἔστιν, ὃ οὐκ αἰσχρὸν φανήσεται; καὶ τῶν δικαίων ὃ οὐκ ἄδικον; καὶ τῶν ὁσίων, ὃ οὐκ ἀνόσιον; Οὔκ, ἀλλ' ἀνάγκη, ἔφη, καὶ καλά πως αὐτὰ | καὶ αἰσχρὰ B φανῆναι, καὶ ὅσα ἄλλα ἐρωτᾷς. Τί δέ; τὰ πολλὰ διπλάσια ἧττόν τι ἡμίσεα, ἢ διπλάσια φαίνεται; Οὐδέν. Καὶ μεγάλα δὴ καὶ σμικρὰ καὶ κοῦφα καὶ βαρέα μή τι μᾶλλον, ἃ ἂν φήσωμεν, ταῦτα προσρηθήσεται, ἢ τἀναντία; Οὔκ, ἀλλ' ἀεί, ἔφη, ἕκαστον ἀμφοτέρων ἕξεται. Πότερον οὖν ἔστι μᾶλλον ἢ οὐκ ἔστιν ἕκαστον τῶν πολλῶν τοῦτο, ὃ ἄν τις φῇ αὐτὸ εἶναι; Τοῖς ἐν ταῖς ἑστιά-

3. ἀεὶ Π: ἀεὶ μὲν A.

---

2 **ἰδέαν τινά.** ἰδέα has not yet been used in the *Republic* of the Idea; hence τινά. Krohn (*Pl. St.* pp. 64, 96) has pointed this out, but makes too much of it. In ἰδέα, as Cohen remarks (*Platons Ideenlehre u. d. Mathematik* p. 12), "das ἰδεῖν pulsirt": cf. 475 E τοὺς τῆς ἀληθείας—φιλοθεάμονας, VI 486 D and *Symp.* 211 D.

3 **ἀεὶ—νομίζει.** μέν after ἀεί—see *cr. n.*—is retained by Schneider and others. It is however much harsher than the ordinary cases of μέν without δέ (see on 475 E), and the majority of MSS agree with Π in omitting it. Madvig would delete the article before καλά; but its retention provides a better antithesis to ἄν τις ἓν τὸ καλὸν φῇ εἶναι. τὰ καλά is here the plural, not of καλόν τι, but of τὸ καλόν; and Plato means that the φιλοθεάμων has many *standards* of beauty: cf. 479 D *nn.*

4 **ἐκεῖνος—καί.** These words are certainly genuine, though omitted in Ξ, and supposed by Hartman to be a marginal note on ὁ χρηστός. οὐδαμῇ ἀνεχόμενος by itself would be comparatively tame.

5 **τούτων γὰρ δή κτλ.** The many καλά 'are' and 'are not,' because they are beautiful and not-beautiful. We may infer, on the other hand, that the αὐτὸ κάλλος always 'is,' because (among other reasons) it is always beautiful. In other words, the essence of an Idea consists in its eternal unity and identity with itself. Cf. *Symp.* 211 A, where the αὐτὸ καλόν is said to be οὐ τῇ μὲν καλόν, τῇ δ' αἰσχρόν, οὐδὲ τότε μέν, τότε δ' οὔ, οὐδὲ πρὸς μὲν τὸ καλόν, πρὸς δὲ τὸ αἰσχρόν, οὐδ' ἔνθα μὲν καλόν, ἔνθα δὲ αἰσχρόν, ὡς τισὶ μὲν ὂν καλόν, τισὶ δὲ αἰσχρόν. This passage will explain what Plato means by saying that there is not one of the πολλὰ καλά which is not also αἰσχρόν. Cf. also Bosanquet *Companion* pp. 213 f. Krohn (*Pl. Fr.* p. 73) argues that this passage is inconsistent with the Maxim of Contradiction as laid down in IV 436 B. But Plato does not mean that τὰ πολλὰ καλά are αἰσχρὰ κατὰ ταὐτὸν καὶ πρὸς ταὐτόν, nor should ἅμα in 478 D be interpreted in this sense. A particular καλόν is ἅμα καλὸν καὶ αἰσχρόν, ὡς τισὶ μὲν ὂν καλόν, τισὶ δὲ αἰσχρόν. Cf. Zeller[4] II 1, p. 627 *n.* 2.

479 B 9 **τὰ πολλὰ διπλάσια** are πρὸς μὲν τὸ διπλάσια, πρὸς δὲ τὸ ἡμίσεα, whereas the αὐτὸ διπλάσιον is always and in every relation διπλάσιον: see last note and VII 523 C ff., *Phaed.* 102 B, C. The examples of διπλάσια, μεγάλα, βαρέα are examples and nothing more; the others, καλά, δίκαια, ὅσια, are relevant in a wider sense, for the aim of the philosopher-king is to frame his καλλίπολις on the model of the αὐτὸ ἀγαθόν. See on 476 A.

13 **ἀμφοτέρων ἕξεται**: "utrisque adhaerescet" Stallbaum.

14 **τοῖς ἐν ταῖς κτλ.** ἐπαμφοτερίζουσιν is certainly neuter, as Schneider shews, and not masculine: cf. ταῦτα ἐπαμφοτερίζει below. The word is very frequently used in agreement with neuter or inanimate subjects: see Stephanus-

C σεσιν, ἔφη, ἐπαμφοτερίζουσιν ἔοικεν, καὶ τῷ τῶν παίδων αἰνίγματι,
τῷ περὶ τοῦ εὐνούχου, τῆς βολῆς πέρι τῆς νυκτερίδος, ᾧ καὶ ἐφ'
οὗ αὐτὸν αὐτὴν αἰνίττονται βαλεῖν· καὶ γὰρ ταῦτα ἐπαμφοτερίζει,
καὶ οὔτ' εἶναι οὔτε μὴ εἶναι οὐδὲν αὐτῶν δυνατὸν παγίως νοῆσαι
οὔτε ἀμφότερα οὔτε οὐδέτερον. Ἔχεις οὖν αὐτοῖς, ἦν δ' ἐγώ, ὅ τι
χρήσει, ἢ ὅποι θήσεις καλλίω θέσιν τῆς μεταξὺ οὐσίας τε καὶ τοῦ
μὴ εἶναι; οὔτε γάρ που σκοτωδέστερα μὴ ὄντος πρὸς τὸ μᾶλλον
D μὴ εἶναι φανήσεται, οὔτε φανότερα ὄντος πρὸς τὸ μᾶλλον εἶναι.
Ἀληθέστατα, ἔφη. Ηὑρήκαμεν ἄρα, ὡς ἔοικεν, ὅτι τὰ τῶν πολλῶν

17. ἐπαμφοτερίζει Vind. E et corr. q^2: ἐπαμφοτερίζειν ΑΠΞ *q*.

Hase *Thes.* s.v. The 'children's riddle' is (according to one of the two versions given by the Scholiast) αἶνός τίς ἐστιν ὡς ἀνήρ τε κοὐκ ἀνὴρ | ὄρνιθα κοὐκ ὄρνιθ' ἰδὼν τε κοὐκ ἰδών, | ἐπὶ ξύλου τε κοὐ ξύλου καθημένην | λίθῳ τε κοὐ λίθῳ βάλοι τε κοὐ βάλοι. Athenaeus (X 452 C) assigns it (on the authority of Clearchus) to Panarces. The interpretation is "a eunuch aimed at a bat which he saw imperfectly sitting upon a reed with a pumice-stone and missed him" (J. and C.). This riddle was used as an exercise in logic among the Stoics (Dümmler *Antisth.* p. 43), but that is not a sufficient reason for supposing (with Dümmler) that they took it from Antisthenes.

479 C 16 **τῆς βολῆς πέρι κτλ.** The MSS apparently read περί: πέρι is due to Benedictus. Stephanus wishes to delete the second, Richards the first preposition, but the whole sentence is loosely constructed, as if a mere child's riddle was not worth remembering or dwelling on: 'the children's riddle about the eunuch, don't you know, about hitting the bat, what it was the riddle says he struck it with, and on what it was sitting.' ᾧ and not ὡς (as Baiter supposed) is the reading of A.

17 **καὶ γὰρ ταῦτα κτλ.** ταῦτα is of course τὰ πολλά, as Jowett and others rightly explain. Campbell appears strangely to take it of the children's riddle. I agree with Ast that ἐπαμφοτερίζειν—see *cr. n.*—must be wrong. It is usual to supply ἔοικε, but this is very difficult, and the categoric affirmative is much more to the point. For the error see *Introd.* § 5. Hartman hastily pronounces οὔτ' ἀμφότερα οὔτε οὐδέτερον spurious on the ground that "illas res οὐδέτερον esse modo (οὔτε εἶναι—νοῆσαι) dictum est," and that "non verum est illas res non esse ἀμφότερα." The text is perfectly sound. Phenomena, says Glauco, cannot be 'fixedly conceived of' as either (*a*) being or (*b*) not being, nor yet as (*c*) neither of the two. The fourth alternative is to 'fix them in the mind' as (*d*) both being and not being. This too is impossible, although we may *say* that they 'both are and are not' (477 A, 478 D). The reason is that they are not, in the last analysis, 'both being and not-being,' but something between the two, as Socrates presently points out. (See also on οἷον in 478 D.) Phenomena cannot be fixedly conceived (παγίως νοῆσαι) in any kind of way, because they *have* no fixity themselves. They are in a constant state of Heraclitean flux: cf. κυλινδεῖται, πλανητόν in D and (for παγίως) IV 434 D *n.*

479 D 23 **τὰ τῶν πολλῶν κτλ.**: "the multitude's multitudinous formulae" Bosanquet. The words refer to general rules, standards, canons, believed in by the multitude (cf. τὰ τῶν πολλῶν δόγματα VI 493 A), who have on every single subject many such standards (πολλὰ νόμιμα), mutually inconsistent and uncoordinated, because they do not know that τὸ καλόν, τὸ ἀγαθόν etc. are each of them ἕν. They say, for example, 'τὸ ἡδύ is καλόν,' 'τὸ συμφέρον is καλόν,' 'τὸ ἀγαθόν is καλόν,' and so on. Such assertions give the appearance of plurality to τὸ καλόν, by connecting it, not indeed with the objects of sense, but with other εἴδη (cf. 476 A, 476 C *nn.*). The form in which Plato expresses his conclusion (τὰ τῶν πολλῶν πολλὰ νόμιμα καλοῦ πέρι and not simply τὰ πολλὰ καλά) prepares us for VI 484 C, where the whole purpose of this enquiry is disclosed. It is the business of the philosopher-king to bring order out of chaos by remodelling

πολλὰ νόμιμα καλοῦ τε πέρι καὶ τῶν ἄλλων μεταξύ που κυλινδεῖται τοῦ τε μὴ ὄντος καὶ τοῦ ὄντος εἰλικρινῶς. Ηὑρήκαμεν.
Προωμολογήσαμεν δέ γε, εἴ τι τοιοῦτον φανείη, δοξαστὸν αὐτὸ
ἀλλ' οὐ γνωστὸν δεῖν λέγεσθαι, τῇ μεταξὺ δυνάμει τὸ μεταξὺ
πλανητὸν ἁλισκόμενον. Ὡμολογήκαμεν. Τοὺς ἄρα πολλὰ καλὰ
θεωμένους, αὐτὸ δὲ τὸ καλὸν μὴ ὁρῶντας μηδ' ἄλλῳ ἐπ' αὐτὸ E
ἄγοντι δυναμένους ἕπεσθαι, καὶ πολλὰ δίκαια, αὐτὸ δὲ τὸ δίκαιον
μή, καὶ πάντα οὕτω, δοξάζειν φήσομεν ἅπαντα, γιγνώσκειν δὲ ὧν
δοξάζουσιν οὐδέν. Ἀνάγκη, ἔφη. Τί δὲ αὖ τοὺς αὐτὰ ἕκαστα
θεωμένους καὶ ἀεὶ κατὰ ταὐτὰ ὡσαύτως ὄντα; ἆρ' οὐ γιγνώσκειν
ἀλλ' οὐ δοξάζειν; Ἀνάγκη καὶ ταῦτα. Οὐκοῦν καὶ ἀσπάζεσθαί
τε καὶ φιλεῖν τούτους μὲν ταῦτα φήσομεν, ἐφ' οἷς γνῶσίς ἐστιν,
| ἐκείνους δὲ ἐφ' οἷς δόξα; ἢ οὐ μνημονεύομεν, ὅτι φωνάς τε καὶ 480
χρόας καλὰς καὶ τὰ τοιαῦτ' ἔφαμεν τούτους φιλεῖν τε καὶ θεᾶσθαι,
αὐτὸ δὲ τὸ καλὸν οὐδ' ἀνέχεσθαι ὥς τι ὄν; Μεμνήμεθα. Μὴ οὖν
τι πλημμελήσομεν φιλοδόξους καλοῦντες αὐτοὺς μᾶλλον ἢ φιλοσόφους; καὶ ἆρα ἡμῖν σφόδρα χαλεπανοῦσιν, ἂν οὕτω λέγωμεν;
Οὔκ, ἄν γ' ἐμοὶ πείθωνται, ἔφη· τῷ γὰρ ἀληθεῖ χαλεπαίνειν οὐ
θέμις. Τοὺς αὐτὸ ἄρα ἕκαστον τὸ ὂν ἀσπαζομένους φιλοσόφους
ἀλλ' οὐ φιλοδόξους κλητέον; Παντάπασι μὲν οὖν.

ΤΕΛΟΣ ΠΟΛΙΤΕΙΑΣ Ε.

the *νόμιμα* of the many in conformity with the Idea. He must not allow them to predicate *κοινωνία* of *εἴδη* unless the *εἴδη* really intercommunicate.

28 **πολλὰ καλά.** Is *καλά* the plural of '*the* beautiful,' or of '*a* beautiful'? This question is raised by Bosanquet, who answers it thus: "the sentence about formulae leads me to interpret it in the former sense = 'many standards,' or cases accepted as standards, 'of beauty.'" Cf. 479 A, where however we have *πολλὰ τὰ καλά*, and its antithesis *ἓν τὸ καλόν*. The expression *πολλὰ καλά* must, I think, be taken in its usual sense, as the plural of *καλόν τι*; but it includes not only the objects of sense, but also *νόμιμα περὶ καλοῦ*, which are themselves *πολλὰ καλά*, because they connect *αὐτὸ τὸ καλόν* with another *εἶδος*. See last note.

479 E 32 **αὐτὰ ἕκαστα**: the generalised expression including *αὐτὸ καλόν*, *αὐτὸ δίκαιον* and all the Ideas. Cf. VI 507 B *n.*

480 A 2 **ἔφαμεν.** 476 B.

5 **ἆρα—λέγωμεν;** See Isocrates *de Soph.* 8 *πλείω κατορθοῦντας τοὺς ταῖς δόξαις χρωμένους ἢ τοὺς τὴν ἐπιστήμην ἔχειν ἐπαγγελλομένους.* To this (according to Teichmüller *Lit. Fehd.* I p. 103) Plato here replies, and the retort is supposed to be the more telling, because Isocrates, in spite of the sentence just quoted, aspired to the name *φιλόσοφος*: see Spengel *Isokrates u. Platon* pp. 13, 22 ff. Dümmler, on the other hand, supposes that Antisthenes is meant, as before (see on 476 D). I can see no sufficient reason for holding that Plato is here thinking specially of either, although the cap fits both.

4 **φιλοσόφους.** The connotation of *φιλόσοφος* has greatly altered or developed since Book II: see II 376 B *n.*, and cf. Krohn *Pl. St.* pp. 9, 20, 102. Krohn is fully justified when he calls the concluding part of Book V "the turning-point" of the *Republic* (ib. p. 107). Plato's hitherto 'Hellenic city' is now well on the road to become an 'ensample in the Heavens.'

APPENDICES TO BOOK V.

I.

On the relation of the fifth book of the Republic to Aristophanes' Ecclesiazusae.

That there is some kind of connexion or interdependence between the Aristophanic and Platonic descriptions of a communistic ideal, is a theory which has been strenuously advocated by a succession of distinguished scholars from the middle of the 18th century to the present day. The author of the suggestion was apparently Bizet, who, as I learn from Tchorzewski (*de Politia, Timaeo, Critia* 1847 p. 150), appended to his argument of the *Ecclesiazusae* the note ὁ δ' Ἀριστοφάνης διὰ τούτων τοὺς φιλοσόφους, οἷς ἐχθρὸς ἦν, μάλιστα δὲ τὰ τοῦ Πλάτωνος περὶ πολιτείας βιβλία ψέγειν σκώπτειν καὶ κωμῳδεῖν δοκεῖ. An attempt to establish the connexion was made by Lebeau in 1760 (Tchorzewski l. c.), but the first to advance any serious arguments in its support was Morgenstern (*de Plat. Rep. comment. prima* 1794 pp. 74—78). In one form or another, the theory received the support of, among the older generation of scholars, Boeckh (*de simultate Xen. et Plat.* 1811 p. 26), Bergk (*Comment. de rel. com. Attic. antiq.* 1838 pp. 81, 404 *n.*), Meineke (*Hist. crit. com. Graec.* 1839 pp. 287 ff.), and Tchorzewski (l. c.): see Susemihl *Gen. Entwick.* II pp. 296 ff., where the author mentions the most important writings on the subject down to 1857. The original theory has undergone some new and remarkable developments since the efflorescence of the chorizontic school of criticism, in whose hands the apparent connexion between the *Ecclesiazusae* and the *Republic* has formed a useful weapon for attacking the unity of Plato's dialogue. Foremost of these critics is Krohn (*Pl. St.* 1876 pp. 72—83, and *Pl. Frage* 1878 pp. 36 f.); among the others, we may refer in particular to Stein (*de Ar. Eccles. arg. e quarto reip. Plat. lib. sumpto* 1880), Teichmüller (*Lit. Fehden* I 1881 pp. 15 ff. and II 1884 pp. 41 f.), Bergk (*Gr. Literaturgesch.* 1887 IV pp. 85, 462 ff.), Usener (in Brandt's *zur Entwick. d. Pl. Lehr. v. d. Seelentheilen* 1890 p. 6), and above all Chiappelli (in *Riv. di Filologia* etc. XI pp. 161—273 and XV pp. 343—352), to whom we owe what is in my opinion by far the most interesting and valuable discussion on the whole subject. A few distinguished writers still maintain that the philosopher and the comedian are probably independent of one another, notably Zeller (*Phil. d. Griechen*[4] II 1, p. 551 *n.* 2) and on the whole also Hirmer (*Entst. u. Komp. d. Plat. Pol.* pp. 655—660), but the balance of published opinion is in favour of recognising in some shape or other a historical connexion between the socialistic burlesque of Aristophanes and the serious communism of Plato.

In reviewing the available evidence, it will be convenient to consider, in the first place, any external indications which may be supposed to have a bearing on the theory; secondly, any alleged or possible references to Plato himself in the *Ecclesiazusae*, or to Aristophanes in the fifth book of the *Republic*; thirdly, the general similarity between the two writings; and finally, such particular resemblances of language and idea as have been adduced in support of the allegation that Plato has in view Aristophanes, or Aristophanes Plato.

I. *Alleged external evidence.*

According to Aristotle (*Pol.* B 7. 1266ª 34 ff.), οὐδεὶς—οὔτε τὴν περὶ τὰ τέκνα κοινότητα καὶ τὰς γυναῖκας ἄλλος (i.e. other than Plato) κεκαινοτόμηκεν οὔτε περὶ τὰ συσσίτια τῶν γυναικῶν, and Plato himself in the *Timaeus* 18 C remarks, with reference to the communism of the *Republic*, ἢ τοῦτο μὲν διὰ τὴν ἀήθειαν τῶν λεχθέντων εὐμνημόνευτον, ὅτι κοινὰ τὰ τῶν γάμων καὶ τὰ τῶν παίδων πᾶσιν ἁπάντων ἐτίθεμεν κτλ; On the strength of these passages Teichmüller (ll.cc.) has argued that the fifth book of the *Republic* must have preceded the *Ecclesiazusae.* The argument is, however, as Zeller points out (l.c.), altogether inconclusive; for Aristotle does not assert that Plato was the first, but that he was the only authority, who introduced this innovation. It is therefore clear that Aristotle, who must have known the *Ecclesiazusae*, is excluding the fantastic creations of comedy from his survey. This inference is further supported by another passage in the *Politics* (ib. 12. 1274ᵇ 9—11), where ἥ τε τῶν γυναικῶν καὶ παίδων καὶ τῆς οὐσίας κοινότης καὶ τὰ συσσίτια τῶν γυναικῶν are said to be ἴδια Πλάτωνος. See also Newman, *The Politics of Aristotle*, Vol. II p. 282. It has been maintained on the other hand that the *Ecclesiazusae* is earlier than the *Republic*, because Aristophanes declares his proposals to be μήτε δεδραμένα μήτ' εἰρημένα πω πρότερον (*Eccl.* 579), but, in point of fact, the educated Greeks of Aristophanes' time probably knew that communistic societies had already existed (see on V 451 C, 457 B), and Zeller takes the comedian much too seriously when he supposes this line to demonstrate the priority of Aristophanes' play even to the proposals of the philosopher. No ancient writer, so far as I am aware, has suggested either that Aristophanes refers to Plato, or that Plato refers to Aristophanes; and there is no other external evidence of any kind, if we except certain chorizontic conjectures which are in harmony, so far as they go, with the well-known statement of Gellius (*Noct. Att.* XIV 3) about the separate publication of part of the *Republic.* See *Introd.* § 4. The question must therefore be decided, if at all, on other grounds.

II. *Alleged or* primâ facie *possible allusions either* (*a*) *to Plato in the Ecclesiazusae, or* (*b*) *to Aristophanes in the fifth book of the Republic.*

(*a*) The name of Plato does not occur in the *Ecclesiazusae.* This fact has sometimes been used as an argument against the theories connecting the *Ecclesiazusae* and the *Republic*: see for example Zeller[4] II 1, p. 551 *n.* But, as Bergk (*Gr. Literaturgesch.* IV p. 86) and others have pointed out, the later comedies of Aristophanes comparatively seldom attack contemporaries by name[1], and in any case Aristophanes was quite at liberty, if he thought fit, to caricature the scheme of Plato without specifying its author. Cf. Krohn *Pl. St.* p. 76. Is Plato present in disguise in any portion of the play? Some critics have detected an allusion to the philosopher in the words with which the Aristophanic chorus introduces the communism of the *Ecclesiazusae*:

> νῦν δὴ δεῖ σε πυκνὴν φρένα καὶ **φιλόσοφον** ἐγείρειν
> φροντίδ' ἐπισταμένην
> ταῖσι φίλαισιν ἀμύνειν (vv. 571—573).

The reading of the MSS is φιλόσοφον, and there is no sufficient justification for the conjectures φιλόδημον or φιλόκοινον, for the dactylic measure may easily pass into the trochaic, as in *Frogs* 884 (quoted in Blaydes' note). It is of course possible, on the face of it, that Plato is in Aristophanes' mind, and the possibility becomes still more evident if we read φιλοσόφων, which Bergk declares—somewhat hastily, I think—to be necessary on metrical grounds (*Gr. Literaturgesch.* IV p. 463 *n.* 135). But φιλόσοφον gives the better construction and sense, and the words of Aristophanes as they stand in the MSS do not in themselves suggest a reference to the theories either of Plato or of any other philosopher. The adjective φιλόσοφον is merely an amplification of πυκνήν. Cf. Hirmer l.c. p. 659 *n.* 2. Others may be inclined to recognise Plato in the εὐπρεπὴς νεανίας who proposes the γυναικοκρατία of Aristophanes' play:

> μετὰ τοῦτο τοίνυν εὐπρεπὴς νεανίας
> λευκός τις ἀνεπήδησ' ὅμοιος Νικίᾳ
> δημηγορήσων, κἀπεχείρησεν λέγειν
> ὡς χρὴ παραδοῦναι ταῖς γυναιξὶ τὴν πόλιν κτλ.
> (vv. 427—454.)

But in this instance also the identification would be purely speculative, and much the same may be said of Bergk's conjecture (*Comm. de reliq. Com. Att. ant.* p. 404 *n.*) that τὸν τῶν γραφέων ἄριστον in verse 995 refers to Plato:

> Νεαν. ἀλλ' ὦ μέλ' ὀρρωδῶ τὸν ἐραστήν σου.
> Γρ. τίνα;
> Νεαν. τὸν τῶν γραφέων ἄριστον.
> Γρ. οὗτος δ' ἔστι τίς;
> Νεαν. ὃς τοῖς νεκροῖσι ζωγραφεῖ τὰς ληκύθους,
> ἀλλ' ἄπιθ', ὅπως μή σ' ἐπὶ θύραισιν ὄψεται.
> (vv. 994—997.)

[1] Plato and his school are however frequently mentioned by the poets of the New Comedy. The following references are due to Stein (l.c. p. 9 *n.*): Theopompus ap. Meineke *Frag. Comic. Gr.* II p. 797, Anaxandrides ib. III p. 170, Amphis pp. 302, 305, Ephippus p. 332, Epicrates p. 370, Cratinus Junior p. 378, Alexis pp. 382, 451, 453, 455, 468, Philippides IV p. 468. See D. L. III 26 ff.

There remains a single passage in which the fertile imagination of the same scholar discovered a precise and positive allusion to Plato. It is a tolerably well established tradition that Plato was originally called Aristocles (D. L. III 4, and other evidence in Zeller[4] II 1, p. 392 *n.* 1), and Aristyllus is a diminutive or hypocoristic form of that name. See Etym. M. p. 142. 55 ff. Ἀρίστυλλος· ὄνομα παρὰ Ἀριστοφάνει. εἴρηται δὲ ὑποκοριστικῶς ὁ Ἀριστοκλῆς, and Eustath. *ad Il.* p. 989. 45 ὑποκεκόρισται ὁ Ἥρυλλος ἐκ τοῦ Ἡρακλῆς ὡς ἐκ τοῦ Ἀριστοκλῆς ὁ Ἀρίστυλλος παρὰ τῷ κωμικῷ, with Fick *Griech. Personennam.* p. LII. Now in the *Ecclesiazusae* 646 ff., after Praxagora has described the advantages of domestic communism in language very like Plato's, we read:—

Πραξ. πολὺ μέντοι δεινότερον τούτου τοῦ πράγματός ἐστι,—
Βλεπ. τὸ ποῖον;
Πραξ. εἴ σε φιλήσειεν Ἀρίστυλλος, φάσκων αὑτοῦ πατέρ' εἶναι.
Βλεπ. οἰμώζοι τἂν καὶ κωκύοι.
Πραξ. σὺ δέ γ' ὄζοις ἂν καλαμίνθης,
ἀλλ' οὗτος μὲν πρότερον γέγονεν πρὶν τὸ ψήφισμα γενέσθαι,
ὥστ' οὐχὶ δέος μή σε φιλήσῃ.
Βλεπ. δεινὸν μέντἂν ἐπεπόνθη.

Why should not Aristyllus be Plato? Bergk had the boldness to suggest their identity (l.c. p. 403 *n.*), and in the following year Meineke upheld the same view by the citations which I have given. The conjecture deserves the praise of ingenuity, but is far from probable in itself, and has met with little favour at the hands of recent writers. If Plato is personated by Aristyllus, we can only say that his features are distorted beyond the possibility of recognition both here and in the *Plutus*

μινθώσομεν θ' ὥσπερ τράγου
τὴν ῥῖνα· σὺ δ' Ἀρίστυλλος ὑποχάσκων ἐρεῖς
ἕπεσθε μητρὶ χοῖροι (vv. 313—315):

nor is it at all likely that Aristophanes, even in a late comedy like the *Ecclesiazusae*, would have had recourse to so far-fetched a cryptogram. We meet with Aristyllus as a distinct and separate proper name before the archonship of Euclides (CIA I 299, CIA I 447 col. I, quoted by Hirmer l.c. p. 659), and we have no reason for disbelieving the Scholiasts when they remark that this particular Ἀρίστυλλος was only some αἰσχροποιός or other whom Aristophanes wished to deride. To judge from his posthumous history of Greek literature (IV pp. 86, 463), Bergk himself afterwards abandoned the idea that Aristyllus stands for Plato.

It will be seen that the available evidence under this head is quite insufficient to establish the probability of any kind of connexion between the *Ecclesiazusae* and the *Republic*.

(*b*) It has been maintained by Chiappelli (l.c.) and other writers that Plato makes frequent reference to Aristophanes in the course of Book V. The expressions in question have been separately dealt with as they occur: but it will be easier to estimate the cumulative value of their evidence if we bring them under the compass of a single survey.

The following passages claim consideration:

(1) οὐκ ἴστε ὅσον ἑσμὸν λόγων ἐπεγείρετε· ὃν ἐγὼ ὁρῶν παρῆκα τότε, μὴ παράσχοι πολὺν ὄχλον 450 B.

(2) ἀπιστοῦντα δὲ καὶ ζητοῦντα ἅμα τοὺς λόγους ποιεῖσθαι, ὃ δὴ ἐγὼ δρῶ, φοβερόν τε καὶ σφαλερόν, οὔ τι γέλωτα ὀφλεῖν κτλ. 450 E.

(3) τάχα δὲ οὕτως ἂν ὀρθῶς ἔχοι, μετὰ ἀνδρεῖον δρᾶμα παντελῶς διαπερανθὲν τὸ γυναικεῖον αὖ περαίνειν 451 B C.

(4) οὐ φοβητέον τὰ τῶν χαριέντων σκώμματα, ὅσα καὶ οἷα ἂν εἴποιεν εἰς τὴν τοιαύτην μεταβολὴν γενομένην καὶ περὶ τὰ γυμνάσια καὶ περὶ μουσικὴν καὶ οὐκ ἐλάχιστα περὶ τὴν τῶν ὅπλων σχέσιν καὶ ἵππων ὀχήσεις 452 B C.

(5) μάταιος ὃς γελοῖον ἄλλο τι ἡγεῖται ἢ τὸ κακόν, καὶ ὁ γελωτοποιεῖν ἐπιχειρῶν πρὸς ἄλλην τινὰ ὄψιν ἀποβλέπων ὡς γελοίου ἢ τὴν τοῦ ἄφρονός τε καὶ κακοῦ, καὶ καλοῦ αὖ σπουδάζει πρὸς ἄλλον τινὰ σκοπὸν στησάμενος ἢ τὸν τοῦ ἀγαθοῦ 452 D. Cf. also δεηθεῖσί τε τούτων μὴ τὰ αὑτῶν πράττειν, ἀλλὰ σπουδάζειν 452 C.

(6) τὸν τὰ ἐναντία λέγοντα 454 E and τοῦ τὰ τοιαῦτα ἀντιλέγοντος 455 A.

(7) ὁ δὲ γελῶν ἀνὴρ ἐπὶ γυμναῖς γυναιξίν, τοῦ βελτίστου ἕνεκα γυμναζομέναις, ἀτελῆ τοῦ γελοίου [σοφίας] δρέπων καρπόν, οὐδὲν οἶδεν, ὡς ἔοικεν, ἐφ' ᾧ γελᾷ οὐδ' ὅ τι πράττει 457 B.

(8) καὶ μὲν δὴ καὶ τοῖς πρόσθεν γε ὡμολογοῦμεν 464 B.

(9) ὦ Σώκρατες—τοιοῦτον ἐκβέβληκας ῥῆμά τε καὶ λόγον, ὃν εἰπὼν ἡγοῦ ἐπὶ σὲ πάνυ πολλούς τε καὶ οὐ φαύλους—θεῖν διατεταμένους ὡς θαυμάσια ἐργασομένους 473 E f.

In nearly all these places Chiappelli (l.c.) suspects that Plato has Aristophanes in view. As regards the first, it is tolerably clear from Plato's choice of the word παρῆκα that the ἑσμὸς λόγων means the swarm of subjects which Socrates will now have to discuss, and not the hostile criticism which he will encounter: see note ad loc. The notes on (2) and (3) will shew that neither of these passages warrants the conclusion that either Aristophanes or any other representative of Athenian comedy is intended. It would be almost equally rash to identify τὸν τὰ ἐναντία λέγοντα in (6) with Aristophanes, and in (9) Plato is manifestly thinking of a coalition of antagonists, not to mention the fact that the subject of the philosopher-king, which evokes this exclamation from Glauco, is nowhere hinted at in the *Ecclesiazusae*. If the imperfect ὡμολογοῦμεν is to be retained in (8), the sentence becomes more pointed on the supposition that Plato is replying to some criticism or caricature of his communistic theories; but even without such a hypothesis, the meaning is satisfactory enough. In the other three passages, viz. (4), (5) and (7), it is difficult to resist the impression that Plato's vigorous invective, though professedly general, has also a personal application. There are several places in the *Republic* where

Plato has with much probability been supposed to be thinking of an individual in describing the type, as, for example, when he pours contempt on the epideictic rhetorician in the person of Isocrates (VI 498 E *n.*); and it is quite possible that he thought of Aristophanes when he wrote these words. But there cannot be any reference to the *Ecclesiazusae* in particular, for the *Ecclesiazusae* does not touch upon any of the special topics which Plato here mentions, such as the athletic and military exercises of women. The most that we can reasonably affirm is that, if the *Ecclesiazusae* can be shewn on other grounds to be an attack either on Plato's own theories, or on views with which he sympathised, the personal tone of (4), and especially of (5) and (7), is most easily explicable on the hypothesis that they are a sort of counter attack on Aristophanes by Plato.

III. *The general resemblances between the two works in respect of subject-matter and content.*

The *Ecclesiazusae* falls into two well-marked divisions (1—876, and 877—1181), the second of which merely elaborates and illustrates the idea expressed in vv. 615—618, and contains nothing which can fairly be quoted in this connexion. It is otherwise with the first half of the play. There Aristophanes deals with a number of subjects which are treated also by Plato, viz. Community of Goods (590—594, 597—610, 673—692), Community of Women (611—634), Community of Children (635—650), the absence of every kind of δίκαι (657—672), and the establishment of ξυσσίτια (715 f.). The coincidence is remarkable and certainly requires explanation.

IV. *Specific parallels in idea, or in language, or in both idea and language.*

These are more numerous and sometimes, perhaps, more remarkable than is generally supposed. We may tabulate them as follows:

PLATO.	ARISTOPHANES.
(1) τὰς γυναῖκας ταύτας τῶν ἀνδρῶν τούτων πάντων πάσας εἶναι κοινάς, ἰδίᾳ δὲ μηδενὶ μηδεμίαν συνοικεῖν 457 C f.	καὶ ταύτας γὰρ κοινὰς ποιῶ τοῖς ἀνδράσι συγκατακεῖσθαι ¦ καὶ παιδοποιεῖν τῷ βουλομένῳ (614 f.)
(2) ὅτι πάντων ξυμφορώτατ' ἂν εἴη πραχθέντα τῇ πόλει καὶ τοῖς φύλαξιν 458 B.	καὶ μὴν ὅτι μὲν χρηστὰ διδάξω πιστεύω (583).
(3) πατέρας δὲ καὶ θυγατέρας καὶ ἃ νῦν δὴ ἔλεγες πῶς διαγνώσονται ἀλλήλων; 461 C f. παντὶ γάρ, ᾧ ἂν ἐντυγχάνῃ τις, ἢ ὡς ἀδελφῷ ἢ ὡς ἀδελφῇ ἢ ὡς πατρὶ ἢ ὡς μητρὶ ἢ ὑεῖ ἢ θυγατρὶ ἢ τούτων ἐκγόνοις ἢ προγόνοις νομιεῖ ἐντυγχάνειν 463 C: cf. 461 D.	πῶς οὖν οὕτω ζώντων ἡμῶν τοὺς αὑτοῦ παῖδας ἕκαστος ¦ ἔσται δυνατὸς διαγιγνώσκειν; Τί δὲ δεῖ; πατέρας γὰρ ἅπαντας ¦ τοὺς πρεσβυτέρους αὑτῶν εἶναι τοῖσι χρόνοισιν νομιοῦσιν (635—637).

(4) ἔχομεν οὖν—μεῖζον ἀγαθὸν τοῦ ὃ ἂν ξυνδῇ τε καὶ ποιῇ μίαν (sc. τὴν πόλιν); Οὐκ ἔχομεν 462 A f.	ἀλλ' ἕνα ποιῶ κοινὸν πᾶσιν βίοτον καὶ τοῦτον ὅμοιον (594: cf. 590—593). τὴν δὲ δίαιταν τίνα ποιήσεις; Κοινὴν πᾶσιν· τὸ γὰρ ἄστυ ¦ μίαν οἴκησίν φημι ποιήσειν συρρήξασ' εἰς ἓν ἅπαντα, ὥστε βαδίζειν εἰς ἀλλήλους (673—675: cf. 690 ff.)
(5) τί δέ; δίκαι τε καὶ ἐγκλήματα πρὸς ἀλλήλους οὐκ οἰχήσεται ἐξ αὐτῶν, ὡς ἔπος εἰπεῖν κτλ.; 464 D.	ἀλλ' οὐδὲ δίκαι πρῶτον ἔσονται κτλ. (657—672: cf. also 560—567).
(6) καὶ μὴν ὅτι γε νεώτερος πρεσβύτερον—οὔτε ἄλλο βιάζεσθαι ἐπιχειρήσει ποτέ, οὔτε τύπτειν ὡς τὸ εἰκός· οἶμαι δ' οὐδὲ ἄλλως ἀτιμάσει· ἱκανὼ γὰρ τὼ φύλακε κωλύοντε, δέος τε καὶ αἰδώς, αἰδὼς μὲν ὡς γονέων μὴ ἅπτεσθαι εἴργουσα, δέος δὲ τὸ τῷ πάσχοντι τοὺς ἄλλους βοηθεῖν, τοὺς μὲν ὡς υἱεῖς, τοὺς δὲ ὡς ἀδελφούς, τοὺς δὲ ὡς πατέρας 465 A f.	ἀλλ' ὁ παρεστὼς οὐκ ἐπιτρέψει· τότε δ' αὐτοῖς οὐκ ἔμελ' οὐδὲν ¦ τῶν ἀλλοτρίων ὅστις τύπτοι· νῦν δ' ἢν πληγέντος ἀκούσῃ ¦ μὴ αὐτὸν ἐκεῖνον τύπτῃ δεδιὼς τοῖς δρῶσιν τοῦτο μαχεῖται (641—643).
(7) ἀλλὰ μὴν καὶ καθ' Ὅμηρον τοῖς τοιοῖσδε δίκαιον τιμᾶν τῶν νέων ὅσοι ἀγαθοί· καὶ γὰρ Ὅμηρος τὸν εὐδοκιμήσαντα ἐν τῷ πολέμῳ νωτοῖσιν Αἴαντα ἔφη διηνεκέεσσι γεραίρεσθαι, ὡς ταύτην οἰκείαν οὖσαν τιμὴν τῷ ἡβῶντί τε καὶ ἀνδρείῳ, ἐξ ἧς ἅμα τῷ τιμᾶσθαι καὶ τὴν ἰσχὺν αὐξήσει. Ὀρθότατα, ἔφη. Πεισόμεθα ἄρα, ἦν δ' ἐγώ, ταῦτά γε Ὁμήρῳ 468 C f.	καὶ ῥαψῳδεῖν ἔσται τοῖς παιδαρίοισιν ¦ τοὺς ἀνδρείους ἐν τῷ πολέμῳ, κεἴ τις δειλὸς γεγένηται, ¦ ἵνα μὴ δειπνῶσ' αἰσχυνόμενοι (679—681).

I have drawn attention to the Aristophanic parallels in commenting on each of these passages of Plato individually. The impression which they produce as a whole will vary according to the observer's bent and attitude of mind. To Zeller and Hirmer they appear for the most part only accidental coincidences natural enough in the independent exposition and development of the same fundamental idea. By way of illustration Hirmer reminds us that one of the reasons which Plato assigns for domestic communism finds an echo in the motive to which Herodotus had already attributed the community of wives among the Agathyrsi: see note on 463 C. Susemihl on the other hand seems to think that the resemblances are too striking to be merely accidental (*Gen. Entwick.* II p. 297). Experience has shewn that it would be rash to limit the possible degrees of approximation between two writers of ability discussing the same or similar subjects; but for my own part I am disposed to think that we should give the preference to an ex-

planation which, while it is probable on other grounds, leaves room for the possibility that some at least of these coincidences are not altogether fortuitous.

On a retrospect of the foregoing discussion, we see that the residue of solid fact awaiting explanation is first, the general resemblance of subject and treatment between the fifth book of the *Republic* and the *Ecclesiazusae*, and secondly, certain particular coincidences of idea and phraseology. No very great stress should be laid on the personal and polemical tone which seems to make itself felt in some of the passages cited under heading II (*b*); but it may be found that a solution which explains the other phenomena will provide a reasonable account of this matter also.

What explanations may be, or have been, offered?

It may be suggested, in the first place, that Aristophanes and Plato are borrowing from the same literary source. According to Aristoxenus ap. D. L. III 37 and Favorinus ib. 57 the *Republic* of Plato was found almost entire ἐν τοῖς Πρωταγόρου Ἀντιλογικοῖς, but the fable is unworthy of serious discussion, and has not been accepted by any responsible critic (cf. Frei, *Quaestiones Protagoreae* p. 187). Apart from this testimony, there is no evidence to support the view that the resemblances between Aristophanes and Plato are due to imitations of the same original.

Secondly, it has been held that Aristophanes copies from Plato. According to this theory, the *Ecclesiazusae* caricatures the Platonic community of goods, wives and children, referred to or expounded in the end of Book III, in IV 423 E f., and especially in Book V of the *Republic.* Zeller and others have endeavoured to refute this view by urging that communism in the *Ecclesiazusae* is represented rather as an extreme development of democracy and the democratical spirit than as "das Hirngespenst eines aristokratischen Doctrinärs" (Zeller l.c. p. 552 *n.*); that Aristophanes depicts a γυναικοκρατία, and exhibits in fact "a bill in Parliament for the putting down of men" (*Merry Wives of Windsor* II 1), whereas in Plato we have an ἀριστοκρατία in which the best women and the best men are on an equality; and that there are many proposals in the fifth book of the *Republic* to which there is no analogy in the *Ecclesiazusae*, although they would have formed an admirable subject for Aristophanes' peculiar kind of wit, such as the κλῆροί τινες κομψοί (460 A), the gymnastic exercises of the female guardians (452 B C al.), and their presence on the field of battle (471 D al.). These observations are certainly true, and conclusive against the theory that the *Ecclesiazusae* was intended by Aristophanes as an exhaustive polemic against Plato's communism, and nothing more; but such a theory is quite indefensible and betrays a complete misapprehension of the genius of Comedy. The primary object of Aristophanic Comedy, when all is said and done, was to amuse (452 B C, 457 B), and the accurate and complete recapitulation of Plato's theories would not only be slavish and pedantic, but also much less amusing than a partial and distorted view. "Dass Aristophanes nicht naturgetreue Farben liebt, wenn er seine Opfer der Bühne überantwortet, braucht

nicht besonders gesagt zu werden; er hat am Sokrates eine wahrhaft thersiteische Rolle gespielt. Also soll Niemand behaupten, er habe den Wortlaut der Politie vor Augen seine Komödie gedichtet, bedacht dem Verfasser kein Unrecht zu thun. Er nahm, was seinem Zwecke diente; für seine Extravaganzen muss man zunächst das Wesen der Komik verantwortlich machen" (Krohn *Pl. St.* p. 79). The real question is whether the actual points of contact between the *Republic* and the *Ecclesiazusae* are sufficiently numerous and of such a kind as to shew that Aristophanes had the *Republic* in view in any *part* of his play. If we confine ourselves to the internal evidence, the possibility of such a direct and immediate reference to Plato's dialogue cannot be denied; but it is impossible for many reasons to believe that the whole of the *Republic* is earlier than 393—390 B.C., between which dates the *Ecclesiazusae* falls.

It is at this point that the separatist critics step in. In discussing the relationship between Aristophanes and Plato, Morgenstern (l.c. p. 83) had already made the suggestion that the *Republic* as we have it now is an *editio aucta et emendata* of an earlier *Republic*, and that Aristophanes had before him this preliminary treatise; and Teichmüller for his part places the first five books of the *Republic* in 392 or 391, and the *Ecclesiazusae* in 390 B.C. (l.c. I pp. 15 ff.). But the resemblances between the two works can be explained without having recourse to the hypotheses of the separatists, and the question whether the different books of the *Republic* were published together or not should be kept distinct from the present enquiry. See *Introd.* § 4, where I have tried to shew that the χωρίζοντες have hitherto failed to prove their case.

Thirdly, Plato may have had the *Ecclesiazusae* in view when he wrote the fifth book of the *Republic*. This opinion was first, I think, expressed by Boeckh, who remarks "Plato quinto Reipublicae lepidorum hominum facetiis perstricta haec placita significans Aristophanis comoediam videtur respicere" (l. c. p. 26). Boeckh's view seems to be regarded as possible both by Zeller (l. c.) and Hirmer (l. c.), the latter of whom reminds us that Plato alludes to Aristophanes also in other parts of the *Republic* (see on VII 529 B, C, and cf. VI 508 B *n.*): and, among the separatists, Krohn, Stein, Usener and Chiappelli, in one form or another, hold what is fundamentally the same belief. According to Krohn (*Pl. St.* l. c.), the order of publication was *Republic* I—IV, *Ecclesiazusae*, *Republic* V. In the *Ecclesiazusae* Aristophanes ridicules the Platonic community of wives and children alluded to in IV 423 E f., and doubtless familiar enough as a topic of conversation in the more cultivated circles of Athenian society; while the first half of *Republic* V reiterates, in view of Aristophanes' travesty, the principle of κοινὰ τὰ φίλων, adding new and well-considered arguments in its support. Stein and Chiappelli (ll. cc.) agree pretty closely with Krohn, except that Stein thinks the remark of Socrates in IV 423 E f. was enough by itself to inspire the author of the *Ecclesiazusae*, without any assistance from the oral diffusion of Plato's paradoxical innovations. The hypothesis proposed by Usener (ap. Brandt l.c.), regarded merely as a work of art, is singularly perfect and complete. Starting from the thesis that the recapitulation of the *Republic* in the *Timaeus* (17 C ff.) refers to a preliminary draft of a portion of the dialogue published before the production of the *Ecclesiazusae*, Usener maintains that in *Republic* II c. 15—IV c. 5 inclusive we have the substance of that earlier treatise, which included also a sketch of the community of wives and children, afterwards compressed into the single sentence IV 423 E f. Aristophanes' travesty of this forerunner of the *Republic* is contained in the *Ecclesiazusae*, which was put on the stage, according to Usener, in 393 B.C., and in Book V of the *Republic* Plato treats the whole subject afresh in view of Aristophanes' attack.

So much for the most important and representative theories which have been advanced on the question. In an enquiry of this kind, we cannot hope to attain the certainty of absolute demonstration; but I am strongly inclined to admit the probability that Plato had the *Ecclesiazusae* and its author in his mind when he wrote that part of the fifth book which deals with the subject of women and children. Granted that the *Ecclesiazusae* is earlier than Book V of the *Republic*, Plato must have known the play, and the subjects treated of in the two writings are so closely allied that it would have been difficult to ignore the comedian altogether in traversing what is nearly the same ground. The positive coincidences, again, both general and particular, though they do not perhaps compel us to assume any connexion between the two works, are, at all events in some cases, most readily explicable on that hypothesis. A similar remark will apply to the instances already cited of personal or apparently personal references to some representative of the comic stage in more than one passage of Book V. But there is nothing in this admission which lends support to any of the chorizontic hypotheses, and the separatists, with few exceptions, take much too narrow a view of the question at issue. No doubt Aristotle asserts that the community of wives and children and the συσσίτια γυναικῶν were novelties peculiar to Plato among all the authors both of theoretical and of practical polities (*Pol.* B 7. 1266ᵃ 34 ff.). As far as concerns actually existing States, Aristotle's remark is demonstrably incorrect, if the word 'polity' is held to include barbarian as well as Hellenic constitutions[1]; and though what he says may be true of the πολιτεῖαι τῶν φιλοσόφων, there is a considerable body of evidence to shew that the community of wives and children as well as of property was an idea freely mooted in Athenian speculative circles, even when it was not embodied in a formal πολιτεία like that of Plato, or that of Diogenes[2] after him. The attitude of Euripides is highly significant in a question of this kind; and Dümmler (*Proleg. zu Platons Staat* p. 55) has drawn attention to a fragment of the *Protesilaus* where Euripides forestalls the Platonic conception in the words κοινὸν γὰρ εἶναι χρῆν γυναικεῖον γένος (*Fr.* 655 Dindorf. Cf. also *Fr.* 406, *Med.* 573 ff. and *Hipp.* 616 ff.). The wide-spread desire in Plato's age to break

[1] See on V 457 B, 463 C.
[2] See Zeller⁴ II 1, pp. 321—326.

with 'convention' and reorganize society on a 'natural' basis, with the frequent appeal to the analogy of the dumb creation (see on 451 C), in which the 'vox Naturae' was supposed to be most plainly audible, points towards the same conclusion; and I do not think that Dümmler overshoots the mark when, in reviewing the available evidence, he affirms "Es ist kein Zweifel, Weiber- und Gütergemeinschaft liegen auf dem Wege der Weltbeglückungspläne des fünften Jahrhunderts" (l. c.). See also *Archiv für Geschichte der Philosophie* III p. 458 f., where Diels remarks "berühmte Gedanken, deren schulmässige Fassung uns erst aus dem Anfang des vierten Jahrhunderts vorliegt (z. B. Sclavenemancipation und Weibergemeinschaft), bereits im Jahrhundert der Aufklärung geboren sind." That such aspirations commanded a large measure of sympathy and support among some of Socrates' followers, including of course Plato, may be easily believed, both on account of the views which were afterwards promulgated by Plato and the Cynics, and also because there are signs that such an innovation would not have been altogether repugnant to the historical Socrates, whose attitude on sexual questions is almost repulsively utilitarian: see Xen. *Mem.* I 3. 14, II 1. 5, 2. 4. It is from political and social ideas of this kind that Aristophanes, who everywhere shews himself familiar with the intellectual movements of his day, derived the materials of his comedy. Everything else had been tried in Athens; why not have recourse to the remedy offered by the so-called 'natural' state of society? ἐδόκει γὰρ τοῦτο μόνον ἐν τῇ πόλει | οὔπω γεγενῆσθαι (*Eccl.* 456 f.). Aristophanes' *Ecclesiazusae* is thus a satire both on Athenian democracy and on the socialistic theories of his age. The philosopher may well have been dissatisfied with the comedian's unscrupulous travesty of views with which he had himself no little sympathy. In the fifth book of the *Republic* Plato touches with serious purpose on nearly all the proposals which Aristophanes had tried to make ridiculous, sometimes expressing himself as if he were the self-nominated champion of the ideal so licentiously burlesqued upon the stage, and even appears to carry the war into the enemy's camp by a vigorous onslaught upon the principles and practice of Athenian comedy (452 C f.).

II.

V 452 D, E. μάταιος ὃς γελοῖον ἄλλο τι ἡγεῖται ἢ τὸ κακόν, καὶ ὁ γελωτοποιεῖν ἐπιχειρῶν πρὸς ἄλλην τινὰ ὄψιν ἀποβλέπων ὡς γελοίου ἢ τὴν τοῦ ἄφρονός τε καὶ κακοῦ, καὶ καλοῦ αὖ σπουδάζει πρὸς ἄλλον τινὰ σκοπὸν στησάμενος ἢ τὸν τοῦ ἀγαθοῦ.

With this text (that of Paris A) Π agrees, except for the trifling error τινὰν ὄψιν for τινὰ ὄψιν. The words καὶ καλοῦ αὖ are omitted in Ξ and a few late MSS: in *q* they are replaced by καὶ οὐ καλοῦ αὖ. There is no other variant of any consequence in the MSS.

The explanation which I have given agrees with that of the Oxford editors except that they do not make ὁ γελωτοποιεῖν ἐπιχειρῶν subject to σπουδάζει, but to μάταιος, which will therefore have a threefold subject, viz. (1) ὃς—κακόν, (2) ὁ—κακοῦ, (3) ὃς (understood) καλοῦ αὖ σπουδάζει κτλ. I think the view taken in the notes is both grammatically easier and better in point of sense. In any case, however, the sentence must be allowed to be ill-constructed and awkward, although that in itself is not enough to justify us in accepting emendations which are far from probable or satisfactory.

The difficulties connect themselves (1) with ὡς γελοίου, (2) with καὶ καλοῦ αὖ, (3) with πρὸς ἄλλον τινὰ σκοπὸν στησάμενος. ὡς γελοίου is cancelled by Cobet and Herwerden, and may of course be a gloss on ἄφρονός τε καὶ κακοῦ. The omission of these two words improves the style, but, as they are in all the MSS, it is safer to retain them as a Platonic pleonasm.

As regards καὶ καλοῦ αὖ, the introduction of καλόν ('beauty' or 'taste') as apparently a sort of duplicate of ἀγαθόν seems at first sight unnecessary and irrelevant. But καλόν appears in the sister passage below (457 B), and I think that καλοῦ here makes Plato's allusion to the Old Comedy somewhat more pointed and telling, for Comedy, like every form of Greek art, might be supposed to aim at τὸ καλόν. It cannot however be denied that καὶ καλοῦ *may* be an erroneous duplication of καὶ κακοῦ, and in that case the meaning will be 'and he who attempts to raise a laugh etc. aims seriously also at another goal' etc., ὁ γελωτοποιεῖν ἐπιχειρῶν being the nominative to σπουδάζει. I formerly felt disposed to take this view.

The expression πρὸς ἄλλον τινὰ σκοπὸν στησάμενος has been taken by Jebb to mean 'having set himself to some other aim': cf. Soph. *Ant.* 299 πρὸς αἰσχρὰ πράγμαθ' ἵστασθαι. The Sophoclean line might justify στάς, but surely not στησάμενος, which is always I think—except of course where it means 'having stopped' (*desisto*, *desino*, *quiesco*: see Stephanus-Hase s.v.)—transitive in good Greek. My explanation of στησάμενος is due to J. and C.: it receives some support from the parallel idiom in 450 B (μέτρον—τοιούτων λόγων ἀκούειν), where see note: but at best we must allow that the participle is somewhat awkward. W. H. Thompson and others expunge the preposition πρός.

The other proposed solutions are as follows: (1) μάταιος ὃς γελοῖον ἄλλο τι ἡγεῖται—κακοῦ, ἢ σπουδάζει κτλ. (Bekker, Schneider. There is however no MS authority for ἤ. Schneider also favours Stephanus' conjecture σπουδάζειν for σπουδάζει). (2) μάταιος—κακοῦ, καὶ αὖ σπουδάζει (Stallbaum). (3) Hermann bracketed ὁ γελωτοποιεῖν—κακοῦ, καί, and (4) Cobet desired to cancel ὃς γελοῖον—κακόν, καί, as well as ὡς γελοίου and καὶ καλοῦ αὖ, reading, after κακοῦ, ἢ σπουδάζειν [πρὸς] ἄλλον τινὰ σκοπὸν <προ>στησάμενος κτλ. (5) μάταιος—κακόν, καὶ γελωτοποιεῖν —ἀποβλέπει [ὡς γελοίου]—κακοῦ, καὶ [καλοῦ] αὖ σπουδάζει [πρὸς] ἄλλον κτλ. (Herwerden).

There is, it will be observed, a general tendency to omit καὶ καλοῦ αὖ, or at least καλοῦ. The presence of these words both in A and in Π carries great weight. I have thought of suggesting μάταιος—κακοῦ καὶ καλὸν αὖ σπουδάζει πρὸς <ἄλλο>, ἄλλον τινὰ σκοπὸν κτλ. ('aims seriously also at another standard of taste, having set himself another goal' etc.), or καὶ καλοῦ αὖ σπουδάζει πρὸς ἄλλον τινὰ σκοπόν, <ἄλλον τινὰ σκοπὸν> στησάμενος κτλ.

III.

V **457** B ἀτελῆ τοῦ γελοίου [**σοφίας**] δρέπων καρπόν.

The word σοφίας is in all the MSS, but there is no consensus of opinion as to how it should be explained. Schneider translates "die Weisheitsfrucht des lächerlichen," explaining this to mean "fructum sapientiae, quem risor iste quasi de arbore sapientiae suae decerpere, h.e. sapientia sua invenisse sibi videtur." "Plucks from his laughter an unripe fruit of wisdom" is Campbell's translation. Each of these editors therefore understands one of the two genitives as representing the tree—Schneider σοφίας, Campbell τοῦ γελοίου; but neither alternative is satisfactory, although Schneider's gives the better sense. A third possibility would be to make τοῦ γελοίου depend on the negative idea contained in ἀτελῆ (cf. ἀτελεῖς τῆς τοῦ ὄντος θέας *Phaedr.* 248 B), the sense being that their wisdom or art falls short of τὸ γελοῖον, and so does not attain the end at which Comedy should aim. If the MS reading is to be retained, this explanation seems to me the best, but the relation of the two genitives still remains difficult and obscure. Jackson suggests that the expression may mean "a witcrop of ridicule." To me it appears most probable that σοφίας has been added by some scribe desirous of completing the quotation. See *Introd.* § 5. Others (Ast, Stallbaum, Herwerden, Hartman) retain σοφίας and omit τοῦ γελοίου, but the interpolation of these words is less easy to explain, and μάταιος ὃς γελοῖον ἄλλο τι ἡγεῖται ἢ τὸ κακόν in 452 D is strongly in favour of keeping τοῦ γελοίου here. The object of Plato's strictures in both passages is a particular view of τὸ γελοῖον with which he has no sympathy : see on 452 D.

IV.

On Infanticide in the Republic.

The disputed passages are as follows :—

(1) V **459** D, E δεῖ μέν, εἶπον, ἐκ τῶν ὡμολογημένων τοὺς ἀρίστους ταῖς ἀρίσταις συγγίγνεσθαι ὡς πλειστάκις, τοὺς δὲ φαυλοτάτους ταῖς φαυλοτάταις τοὐναντίον, καὶ τῶν μὲν τὰ ἔκγονα τρέφειν, τῶν δὲ μή, εἰ μέλλει τὸ ποίμνιον ὅ τι ἀκρότατον εἶναι, καὶ ταῦτα πάντα γιγνόμενα λανθάνειν πλὴν αὐτοὺς τοὺς ἄρχοντας, εἰ αὖ ἡ ἀγέλη τῶν φυλάκων ὅ τι μάλιστα ἀστασίαστος ἔσται.

(2) V **460** C τὰ δὲ τῶν χειρόνων, καὶ ἐάν τι τῶν ἑτέρων ἀνάπηρον γίγνηται, ἐν ἀπορρήτῳ τε καὶ ἀδήλῳ κατακρύψουσιν, ὡς πρέπει.

(3) V **461** B, C ὅταν δὲ δή, οἶμαι, αἵ τε γυναῖκες καὶ οἱ ἄνδρες τοῦ γεννᾶν ἐκβῶσι τὴν ἡλικίαν, ἀφήσομέν που ἐλευθέρους αὐτοὺς συγγίγνεσθαι

ᾧ ἂν ἐθέλωσι—, καὶ ταῦτά γ' ἤδη πάντα διακελευσάμενοι προθυμεῖσθαι, μάλιστα μὲν μηδ' εἰς φῶς ἐκφέρειν κύημα μηδὲ ἕν, ἐὰν γένηται, ἐὰν δέ τι βιάσηται, οὕτω τιθέναι, ὡς οὐκ οὔσης τροφῆς τῷ τοιούτῳ.

From these passages it would seem undeniable that Plato contemplates in Book v the exposure of (A) the offspring of inferior guardians, (B) any deformed offspring produced by guardians of the better sort, (C) the offspring of guardians who have passed the limits of age laid down for those who are to produce children for the State[1]. We have no right on linguistic grounds to suggest that *τρέφειν* in (1) and *τροφή* in (3) are "used in the emphatic sense of educating as Guardians and Auxiliaries" (Nettleship *Lect. and Rem.* II p. 174 *n.* 3. The same explanation has been advanced by others).

Nevertheless, a number of critics, from Morgenstern (*de Pl. Rep.* p. 228 *n.* 141) onwards, have taken a different view, and that for two reasons. It is desired, on the one hand, to acquit Plato of sanctioning "a practice so repugnant to modern Christian notions." The argument is irrelevant; and it is a sufficient reply that the practice was widely prevalent in ancient Greece (see Blümner, *Privatalterthümer* p. 77 *n.* 1), and expressly enjoined in Sparta on precisely the same grounds on which Plato prescribes it in the *Republic* (Plut. *Lyc.* 16. 1). Aristotle also permits infanticide in the case of deformed offspring (*Pol.* H 16. 1335[b] 19 ff.). In point of fact, Plato's abolition of marriage would strike the Greeks as far more revolutionary and offensive than his toleration of infanticide; nor would a legislator who is bold enough to overthrow the institution of marriage, as it is commonly understood, be likely to prohibit the exposure of weaklings, if it seemed to him conducive to the welfare of the State.

The second objection is at first sight more serious. When he is recapitulating the leading features of the *Republic* in the opening of the *Timaeus* (19 A), Plato writes: *καὶ μὴν ὅτι γε τὰ μὲν τῶν ἀγαθῶν θρεπτέον ἔφαμεν εἶναι, τὰ δὲ τῶν κακῶν εἰς τὴν ἄλλην λάθρᾳ διαδοτέον πόλιν· ἐπαυξανομένων δὲ σκοποῦντας ἀεὶ τοὺς ἀξίους πάλιν ἀνάγειν δεῖν, τοὺς δὲ παρὰ σφίσιν ἀναξίους εἰς τὴν τῶν ἐπανιόντων χώραν μεταλλάττειν; Οὕτως.* This sentence, taken strictly, asserts that the offspring of inferior guardians in the *Republic* were to be distributed among the lower classes, but says nothing about the other two classes enumerated above, viz. (B) and (C). The apparent contradiction has been variously explained. Zeller (*Phil. d. Gr.*[4] II 1, p. 909 *n.* 2) and others suppose that Plato had changed his view when the *Timaeus* was written, and this is doubtless possible, especially as nothing is said about the exposure of children in the *Laws*. The suggestion made by Jowett, that Plato "may have forgotten," surely lacks every element of probability.

A recent chorizontic theory on the subject is deserving of mention. According to Usener and Brandt, the earlier books of the *Republic*, as

[1] Aristotle also understood infanticide to be intended, when, in criticising Plato's community of children, he wrote *ἄδηλον γὰρ ᾧ συνέβη γενέσθαι τέκνον καὶ σωθῆναι γενόμενον* (*Pol.* B 3. 1262[a] 5).

we know it now, contain material which was originally published separately, and it is to this earlier edition that Aristophanes alludes in the *Ecclesiazusae*. It is further supposed that Plato's recapitulation in the *Timaeus* refers, not to the existing *Republic*, but to the original publication[1], in which, therefore, Plato did not countenance infanticide, but was content merely to degrade the offspring of the inferior guardians. The bulk of the present Book III, according to Usener, formed part of the first edition. Now, in III 415 B, C Plato does actually propose to deal with unsatisfactory offspring by the method described in the *Timaeus*. His words are ἐάν τε σφέτερος ἔκγονος ὑπόχαλκος ἢ ὑποσίδηρος γένηται, μηδενὶ τρόπῳ κατελεήσουσιν, ἀλλὰ τὴν τῇ φύσει προσήκουσαν τιμὴν ἀποδόντες ὤσουσιν εἰς δημιουργοὺς ἢ εἰς γεωργούς, καὶ ἂν αὖ ἐκ τούτων τις ὑπόχρυσος ἢ ὑπάργυρος φυῇ, τιμήσαντες ἀνάξουσι τοὺς μὲν εἰς φυλακήν, τοὺς δὲ εἰς ἐπικουρίαν. The cases of deterioration referred to in ἐάν τε σφέτερος—γένηται do not exactly coincide with any of the three cases for which Plato prescribes infanticide in the *Republic*; but he may have originally applied the milder remedy in dealing also with the offspring of inferior parents (A), as he tells us in the *Timaeus* that he did (ἔφαμεν). The difficulty of keeping down the population may have afterwards induced him to recommend the more drastic course. In the *Laws*, colonization provides an outlet for the surplus inhabitants (740 E); but this expedient is unknown in the *Republic*.

So much for Usener's theory. This is not the place in which to discuss it at length, but we may admit that it provides, though at tremendous and quite unjustifiable cost, an ingenious explanation of the particular difficulty with which we are here concerned. For my own part, I do not think sufficient stress has been laid upon the fact that the reference in the *Timaeus* is not to Book V of the *Republic*, but to III 415 B, C. That this is so, appears clearly from the words ἐπαυξανομένων—μεταλλάττειν, which correspond to ἀλλὰ τὴν τῇ φύσει προσήκουσαν τιμὴν—ἀνάξουσι in *Rep.* III 415 C, but are not echoed anywhere in Book V. It is true that the reference is inaccurate, for 'the offspring of inferior parents' (τὰ τῶν κακῶν) is not quite synonymous with the ἔκγονος ὑπόχαλκος ἢ ὑποσίδηρος of Book III; but it is not more inaccurate than Plato's cross-references often are, even within the limits of a single dialogue. The difficulty which calls for explanation is therefore Plato's silence on the subject of the exposure of children in the summary of the *Republic* which he prefixes to the *Timaeus*, rather than any positive contradiction—if we make allowance for the inaccuracy which I have spoken of—between the two dialogues. How is that silence to be accounted for? Plato *may* no doubt have altered his views; but his recapitulation in the *Timaeus* is by no means complete even in other respects (see Archer-Hind on 17 B), and I think it much more likely that he omitted this point because it seemed to him, as in point of fact it would have seemed to many, if not most, of his contemporaries, by no means one of the most peculiar and distinctive features of his common-

[1] See App. I and Brandt *Zur Entwickelung der Platonischen Lehren von den Seelentheilen*, Leipzig 1890, pp. 1—9.

wealth. Although Plato says nothing about the exposure of children in the constitution of the *Laws*, that is only a second-best polity, and he nowhere surrenders his earlier ideal (see *Laws* 739 C ff.). In any case, we must interpret the *Republic* by itself: and none of Plato's own contemporaries could possibly have read the sentences printed above without supposing that he meant Infanticide.

V.

V **462** C, D ὅταν που ἡμῶν δάκτυλός του πληγῇ, πᾶσα ἡ κοινωνία ἡ κατὰ τὸ σῶμα πρὸς τὴν ψυχὴν τεταγμένη εἰς μίαν σύνταξιν τὴν τοῦ ἄρχοντος ἐν αὐτῇ ᾔσθετό τε καὶ πᾶσα ἅμα ξυνήλγησεν μέρους πονήσαντος ὅλη, καὶ οὕτω δὴ λέγομεν ὅτι ὁ ἄνθρωπος τὸν δάκτυλον ἀλγεῖ.

The difficulties of this passage have not received sufficient attention at the hands of editors.

The only textual question is whether we should read τεταμένη or τεταγμένη. τεταγμένη occurs in one MS of Stobaeus (*Flor.* 43. 102), and also in Θ and Vind. E, as well as in Ξ. τεταμένη is much better supported, and has been preferred by former editors.

Schneider, Davies and Vaughan, and Jowett respectively translate as follows: "die ganze durch den Leib nach der Seele zur Einheit der Zusammenordnung unter das regierende in ihr" (i.e. der Gemeinschaft) "sich erstreckende Gemeinschaft," "the whole fellowship that spreads through the body up to the soul, and then forms an organized unit under the governing principle"; "the whole frame, drawn towards the soul as a centre and forming one kingdom under the ruling power therein." They apparently agree in taking τεταμένη both with πρὸς τὴν ψυχήν and with εἰς μίαν σύνταξιν, although the English translators evade the difficulty by a paraphrase which can hardly be elicited from the Greek. It is, I think, difficult, if not impossible, to connect τεταμένη with both πρός and εἰς, and as it cannot be separated from εἰς μίαν σύνταξιν, I take πρός with κοινωνία as in *Symp.* 188 C. If τεταμένη is right, it should probably be separated from πρὸς τὴν ψυχήν and understood as 'strung into a single organization,' an expression which suggests the Stoic theory of τόνος (see Stein, *Psych. d. Stoa* I pp. 73, 74 *nn.*). Jowett's "forming one kingdom" shews an instinctive sense of what the meaning ought to be. The ambiguity in τεταμένη is however perplexing, especially in view of IX 584 C αἵ γε διὰ τοῦ σώματος ἐπὶ τὴν ψυχὴν τείνουσαι—ἡδοναί and *Theaet.* 186 C ὅσα διὰ τοῦ σώματος παθήματα ἐπὶ τὴν ψυχὴν τείνει, although the general sense of these passages is somewhat different. Partly for this reason, but more for that mentioned in the notes, I now prefer τεταγμένη. The translators agree also in their view of τοῦ ἄρχοντος, which they apparently take as a sort of possessive genitive, the σύνταξις belonging to the ἄρχον as a kingdom belongs to its ruler. It is grammatically easier and more natural to regard τοῦ ἄρχοντος as a genitive of definition; and the sense also—see note ad loc.—favours this view. If Stallbaum is right in understanding ἐν αὐτῇ as ἐν τῇ ψυχῇ, the Stoic parallel is remarkably close. τοῦ ἄρχοντος would then correspond to the ἡγεμονικόν, or ruling part of soul, from which the various psychical activities radiate 'like the arms of a cuttle-fish': see Zeller[3] III 1, p. 199 *n.* 1. But it is more natural to refer αὐτῇ to κοινωνία. In view of 464 B, where Plato speaks as if he had merely compared the *body* with its parts, and not the whole man, consisting of body and soul, I have sometimes suspected that πρὸς τὴν ψυχήν and τὴν τοῦ ἄρχοντος ἐν αὐτῇ are from the pen of some Stoic, who may also have altered τεταγμένη into τεταμένη: but the reference is precise enough for Plato's purpose, and ὁ ἄνθρωπος τὸν δάκτυλον ἀλγεῖ makes it probable that room was made for the ψυχή in working out the illustration.

VI.

V **473** C εἰρήσεται δ' οὖν, εἰ καὶ μέλλει γέλωτί τε ἀτεχνῶς ὥσπερ κῦμα ἐκγελῶν καὶ ἀδοξίᾳ κατακλύσειν.

These words have given rise to much discussion. The literal translation is: 'said, however, it shall be, even although it is likely to drown me in laughter—just like a wave that laughs outright—and disgrace.' ἐκγελᾶν should be compared with "leviterque sonant plangore cachinni" (Cat. 64. 273), and not with Aeschylus's ποντίων τε κυμάτων ἀνήριθμον γέλασμα and similar expressions, which refer rather to the rippling of the sea's surface than to the sound of its waves: cf. Arist. *Probl.* XXIII 1. 931[a] 35 ff. Thus understood, κῦμα ἐκγελῶν is, I think, *taken by itself*, an intelligible expression, although no exact parallel to it has yet been found in Greek. (In Euripides *Troad.* 1176 f. ἐκγελᾷ refers, as Paley has pointed out, 'to the open lips of a wound' through which the mangled flesh is seen. So also E. S. Thompson in *Proceedings of the Camb. Philol. Soc.* 1889 p. 13.) The simile of the wave runs riot throughout the fifth Book, and when the last and greatest wave is about to break, and deluge him with ridicule, Socrates may be pardoned for a little extravagance of language. The sound of the wave was also hinted at in 472 A (ἀκούσῃς).

Whether the simile is applicable in all its details may be doubted. The wave is the proposal which Socrates is about to make; the laughter is that of derisive opponents. On a strict interpretation, Plato personifies the wave, and makes it laugh at itself. But a simile should not be hounded to death in this fashion; and the same difficulty is already implicitly involved in γέλωτι κατακλύσειν. The general idea is merely that the proposal dissolves in laughter as a wave in spray. For these reasons, I am inclined, on the whole, to believe that the text is sound. Numerous corrections have been proposed. The reading of *q*—εἰ καὶ μέλλει γέλως τέ τις ἀτεχνῶς ὥσπερ κῦμα καὶ ἀδοξία κατακλύσειν—is doubtless one; it is comparatively tame, but unobjectionable, and was formerly adopted by Stallbaum. Herwerden's proposal is on the same lines: εἰ καὶ μέλλει ἔκγελώς γέ τις καὶ ἀδοξία ἀτεχνῶς ὥσπερ κῦμα κατακλύσειν. (The word ἔκγελως is mentioned by Pollux VI 199, but it is not clear that he meant to attribute it to

Plato.) Few will feel themselves able to assent to this; nor is Richards' ἐκπηδῶν for ἐκγελῶν probable or satisfactory in point of meaning. Excision has also been freely resorted to. In his second edition Ast was disposed to bracket ὥσπερ κῦμα ἐκγελῶν, and Hartman applauds the proposal. E. S. Thompson (l. c.) would eject ἐκγελῶν; but it is difficult to see why such a word should have been added by itself. If excision is necessary, it would be better to cancel the whole phrase ἀτεχνῶς—ἐκγελῶν as a marginal explanation of γέλωτι κατακλύσειν. This suggestion was made in my edition of the Text, and I still hanker after it at intervals. Another solution has recently occurred to me. If we transpose and write εἰ καὶ μέλλει ἀτεχνῶς ὥσπερ κῦμα γέλωτί τε ἐκγελῶν καὶ ἀδοξίᾳ κατακλύσειν, the whole sentence might be translated 'Spoken, however, it shall be, even although it is likely to swamp us beneath a wave of roaring laughter'—lit. 'roaring with laughter'—'and disgrace.' On this view κῦμα is the object of κατακλύσειν, as Ast in his third edition wished it to be, although his emendation γελῶν τις ἀτεχνῶς ὥσπερ κῦμα ἀδοξίᾳ κατακλύσειν can hardly be right. (Benedictus' change of μέλλει into μέλλεις gives the same construction to κῦμα.) But it is not possible, I think, to extract this meaning from the Greek without transposition, and such a double transposition is very improbable. On the whole I believe the text is sound.

VII.

V **476** A καὶ περὶ δικαίου καὶ ἀδίκου καὶ ἀγαθοῦ καὶ κακοῦ καὶ πάντων τῶν εἰδῶν πέρι ὁ αὐτὸς λόγος, αὐτὸ μὲν ἓν ἕκαστον εἶναι, τῇ δὲ τῶν πράξεων καὶ σωμάτων **καὶ ἀλλήλων** κοινωνίᾳ πανταχοῦ φανταζόμενα πολλὰ φαίνεσθαι ἕκαστον.

The words καὶ ἀλλήλων are in all the MSS. They present no difficulty in point of construction; for it is an error to suppose, as Hartman does, that the subject of φαίνεσθαι is ἕκαστον. The subject is πάντα τὰ εἴδη, with which ἕκαστον is in 'distributive apposition,' as usual with this word: see Kühner *Gr. Gr.* II p. 245.

If καὶ ἀλλήλων is genuine, there can be no doubt that Plato is speaking of the κοινωνία of εἴδη with one another. It is impossible to take ἀλλήλων in the sense of ἑαυτῶν, and interpret 'by the partnership of actions and bodies and' i.e. 'with' 'themselves' viz. εἴδη. Nor can the words be explained by 479 A, B, for there it is not the εἶδος Beautiful which becomes ugly, but τὰ πολλὰ καλά. It is thought by Stumpf (*Verhältniss d. Pl. Gottes zur Idee des Guten* p. 49) that Plato means the παρουσία of two εἴδη in one object, as when a man is both beautiful and just. In such a case there is, no doubt, a sort of κοινωνία between the two εἴδη, but the juxtaposition of ἀλλήλων with πράξεων and σωμάτων shews that the kind of κοινωνία between εἴδη which Plato has here in view is analogous to the κοινωνία between an εἶδος and a πρᾶξις, an εἶδος and a σῶμα, etc. He is thinking, for example, of sentences like 'The Beautiful is good,' in which there is κοινωνία between the two Ideas, Good and Beautiful, just as 'Simmias is tall' is an instance of κοινωνία between a particular body and the Idea of Tallness.

The κοινωνία of εἴδη in Plato's philosophy has been discussed by Bonitz, *Plat. Stud.* pp. 200 ff., by Jackson in the *Journal of Philology* XIV pp. 212—218, by Zeller[4] II 1, pp. 673 ff., and by many other critics. The doctrine in question is sometimes supposed to be a later development, or at all events a 'Weiterbildung,' of the Theory of Ideas. It is explicitly laid down in the *Sophist* (251 A ff.), a large section of which dialogue is an attempt to prove the intercommunion of certain εἴδη. (Of course all εἴδη do not communicate with one another, otherwise every general statement would be true: it is the business of the philosopher to discover which do and which do not unite: *Soph.* 253 C ff. We should therefore distinguish between real or ontological κοινωνία εἰδῶν and the κοινωνία which *we* attribute to εἴδη when we predicate one general notion of another: see on 479 D. The former is true κοινωνία εἰδῶν: the latter may be either true or false.) Unless καὶ ἀλλήλων is corrupt or spurious, the κοινωνία of εἴδη must be attributed also to the *Republic*.

In point of fact, according to the Platonic theory of predication, the real and ontological κοινωνία of one εἶδος with others is inevitable, if any true proposition of any kind is to be predicated of the Ideas. And Plato constantly throughout the *Republic* describes the Ideas by a variety of predicates, such as ὄν, αὐτὸ καθ' αὐτό, ἀεὶ κατὰ ταὐτὰ ὡσαύτως ἔχον etc. Moreover, the κοινωνία of the Idea of Good with the other Ideas is surely implied in the description of the Good as the cause of Truth and Being in VI 508 E ff., although Plato does not himself express the relationship in this way. Such a statement as that 'the εἶδος of δίκαιον is good' is not merely admissible, but necessary, in the metaphysical theory of Books V—VII. And no such statement can be made, unless there is κοινωνία of the Ideas of Justice and Goodness. If it be urged that such a communion of Ideas is open to the objection known as τρίτος ἄνθρωπος, it may be replied 'So is the communion of Ideas and particulars, which Plato certainly maintains in the *Republic*.' If he was not aware of this objection in the one case, or deliberately ignored or overruled it, why not also in the other? Similarly with the unity of the Idea. The communion of Ideas with Ideas affects their unity just as much or as little as the community of Ideas with particulars. Compare Fouillée *La Phil. de Platon* I pp. 202—211, and Chiappelli *Della Interpetrazione panteistica di Platone* p. 119. There is accordingly, I think, no reason whatever for holding that Plato in the *Republic* denied the possibility of κοινωνία between εἴδη, although the full exposition of this difficult and important subject is reserved for the *Sophist*. We should therefore hesitate before regarding the words ἀλλήλων κοινωνία in our dialogue as either spurious or corrupt. Nor can it be said that any of the attempts at emendation is in the least degree convincing. The most elegant, I think, is Badham's ἄλλῃ ἄλλων (accepted by Schmitt *Die Verschiedenheit d. Ideenlehre in Pl. Rep. und Philebus* p. 3), though ἄλλῃ is somewhat unpleasing. Hartman proposes ἄλλων, Bywater (*J. Ph.* v p. 123) ἄλλ' ἄλλων (surely a doubtful piece of grammar), Voegelin the excision of καί, Liebhold ἄλλων πολλῶν. Others will no doubt think of cancelling καὶ ἀλλήλων altogether, regarding it as a confused attempt to indicate that the κοινωνία in question is a κοινωνία between 'one another,' i.e. between Ideas on the one hand, and πράξεις or σώματα on the other. I have myself no doubt that the text is sound. Jackson writes as follows: "I believe the text to be right. Plato realizes that Ideas *must* carry predicates: e.g. μεγάλη σωφροσύνη is a possible phrase. But it has not yet occurred to him that there is any difficulty in thus making one idea 'contain' other ideas. That there is a difficulty in *this* immanence is not perceived before the *Parmenides*." I do not feel sure that Plato was unaware of the difficulties involved in this conception even when he wrote the *Republic*: he may have known but passed them by: nor do I think that the *Parmenides* is certainly later than the *Republic*: but I am glad to find that Jackson also holds emphatically that ἀλλήλων κοινωνίᾳ was written by Plato in this passage.

END OF VOL. I.